THE
Collins Who's Who
OF
ENGLISH
FIRST-CLASS
CRICKET
1945-1984

THE
Collins Who's Who
OF
ENGLISH
FIRST-CLASS
CRICKET

1945-1984

Compiled and edited by
ROBERT BROOKE

Research Assistant
BRIAN HUNT

Willow Books
Collins
8 Grafton Street, London W1
1985

Dedicated to the memory of
Gordon Tratalos
an outstanding cricket researcher, a fine human
being and a dear friend, who died while this
book was being prepared for publication.

Willow Books
William Collins Sons & Co Ltd
London · Glasgow · Sydney · Auckland
Toronto · Johannesburg

First published 1985
© Robert Brooke 1985

British Library Cataloguing in Publication Data
Brooke, Robert
  The Collins Who's Who of English First-Class
  Cricket 1945–1984
  1. Cricket – England – Biography
  I. Title
  796 · 358 ′ 0922 ′2   GV919

ISBN 0–00–218096–0

Typeset in Plantin by
Filmtype Services Ltd, Scarborough, North Yorkshire

Printed and bound in Great Britain by
Wm Collins Sons & Co Ltd, Glasgow

CONTENTS

FOREWORD

This is a remarkable book, the result of many years of absorption in the minutiae of cricket and eventually in the game as a whole. I know about that absorption, because Robert Brooke has looked after Births and Deaths for me since I became editor of *Wisden* in 1980. A familiar figure at St Catherine's House and formerly at Somerset House, he knows better than many cricketers do themselves when and where they first saw the light of day. I sometimes think he probably has a shrewd idea, as well, where and when the 'great scorer' will come for each of us. Robert is perhaps the leading authority in his field.

He manages to be particular yet not pedantic. Although the founder of the Association of Cricket Statisticians, he is no longer to be counted among those of their number whose obsession has as much to do with dogmatism as accuracy. There are some who convey the impression that given half a chance they would re-write the Table of Kindred and Affinity. Standardization of cricket records is obviously desirable; but it is, I think, best based, so far as the status of a match is concerned, on contemporary rather than latter-day opinion.

As someone who describes himself as a 'youthful revolutionary' turned 'middle-aged reactionary', Robert would agree with this. He has trod the road to Damascus. He no longer found himself wanting to include in Herbert Sutcliffe's record in this book the runs Sutcliffe scored in the odd three-day match in Ceylon in the English winter of 1930-31, when he was there with the Maharaj Kumar of Vizianagram's side. To the general confusion some of Robert's colleagues have recently done so, in defiance even of what Jack Hobbs, who also played in the games, is known to have felt about them. Robert's 'conversion' will be further put to the test when, in future volumes of this *magnum opus*, he is tempted by fancy.

Eight years ago, when he was a wages clerk, he was spotted by one of his superiors watching Warwickshire play cricket during office hours. The bug had got a firm hold of him by then, and when called upon to account for the presence of someone who had looked uncommonly like him at Edgbaston he decided there and then to spend the rest of his days working for pleasure. So here we have the first consummation of innumerable happy hours spent burning the midnight oil. It is a book to stand alongside the great works of sporting reference, precise and unopinionated, informative, definitive, evocative and timeless. I am honoured and delighted to have this chance to acclaim it.

John Woodcock
Longparish   July 1985

ACKNOWLEDGEMENTS

Whatever value this work may have, much is due to the very many researchers who have beavered away down the years, often without either encouragement or acknowledgement. In recent years members of the Association of Cricket Statisticians have also, by their industry, brought to light a vast amount of unknown or forgotten information.

For this book specifically, my thanks are due to:

Tim Jollands, of Collins Willow, who has kept me going along a none too easy path, geeing me up when I became depressed, and allaying my fears when self-doubt was gaining the upper hand.

Brian Hunt, my research assistant; a good friend and remarkable seeker-out of 'unconsidered trifles', whose ability to get 'something from nothing', especially when this involved unknown Northern professionals, sometimes verged upon the miraculous. Without Brian's help, and willingness to put himself out, which must have involved him in astronomical telephone bills, this volume would be far less accurate, and far less comprehensive than it is. There were times when he, not I, seemed to be the compiler!

Simon Wilde, who came on the scene later, but without whose knowledge, alertness, and eye for detail, very many of my errors may have slipped through. His listing of every query, from a possible error of fact to the most obvious slip of the typing finger, caused many hours of extra work and, frankly, some most un-Christian thoughts towards him, but I really was grateful even if I sometimes did not show my gratitude.

Grateful thanks are due to many more people, but especially the following: Geoffrey Saulez, who rescued me when I was floundering in a sea of unresolved career records; Richard Miller (Scotland), Derek Scott and Edward Liddle (Ireland), Bob Harragan and Phil Clift (Glamorgan), Leslie Newnham (Essex), Ossie Osborne (Sussex), Bob Normandale, Reg Partridge, David Walden (Northants), Bill Frindall, Alan Oakman, the late Esmond Lewis, the late Gordon Tratalos, Jack Burrell, John Reeves, Anthony Woodhouse, Darren Senior, Roger Page and Ken Williams (Australia), Trevor Beling and Les Payn (South Africa), John Ward (Zimbabwe), Gul Hameed Bhatti (Pakistan), Adeeb Khalid (Canada), Sudhir Vaidya and Bapu Mama (India), Francis Payne (New Zealand), S. S. Perera (Sri Lanka); all those players who supplied their own details; various Births and Deaths Registrars; various Librarians; and all the cricketers who by their doings made the whole thing possible.

ROBERT BROOKE
Solihull   April 1985

INTRODUCTION

The idea of compiling a comprehensive cricketers' 'Who's Who' is not a new one: Arthur Haygarth, himself a noted nineteenth-century cricketer, devoted his life to compiling the monumental *Scores & Biographies*; fourteen volumes were published in his lifetime, while F. S. Ashley-Cooper compiled a further volume from Haygarth's notes in 1925. Subsequently much work has been involved with updating the Haygarth details, seeking out information on those players who eluded him, and recording the minutiae of the huge number of post-Haygarth cricketers.

The task I set myself involved collecting and collating all published information on every player to appear in first-class or 'Great' cricket matches played in the British Isles since 1744, pinpointing players for whom detail is lacking, endeavouring to fill some of the many gaps through my own research, and finally getting all the detail published in short biographies which, though hardly approaching Haygarth in wealth of information and trivia, bring together more information on the leading cricketers in the British Isles than any previous work. This first volume covers the period from the shortened 1945 season until the end of the 1984 season in Britain; projected future volumes will cover cricket in the British Isles back to 1744, when the first 'Great' match of which more or less full details are known, was played.

The cricketers in this volume have all appeared in at least one first-class match in the British Isles since 1945, which brings one to the question, What is a first-class match? First-class matches have in fact been officially defined since 1947; rulings are the responsibility of the various governing bodies and although there have been a few 'weird' decisions, and also some changes of mind *after* matches have been played, the system now seems to work reasonably well. The Association of Cricket Statisticians has produced lists of suggested first-class matches covering most cricketing countries and, during the period covered by this volume, ACS listings can be accepted without demur.

This does not always apply to earlier matches however. I have been forced to make my own decisions with regard to the career details of a small number of players who appear in this volume, as to whether their figures should include performances in certain pre-war overseas matches which were ignored at the time, but which have in recent years been used by some very dedicated statisticians to revise accepted records. The only such matches which affect this volume were played by a team organised by the Princely Patron of Indian cricket, the Maharaj of Vizianagram, which toured India and Ceylon in 1930–31. A number of leading contemporary Indian players were included in the party; so too were J. B. Hobbs and H. Sutcliffe. There is no doubt whatsoever that a number of three-day matches on this tour involved teams of first-class players and on the face of it these should have been designated as first-class. However, few record-keepers have included the performances in these matches and their inclusion now would mean major amendments to accepted cricket records.

Were this work to be compiled purely for statistical consumption I may have taken a different view, but I am now writing for the wider cricket world: the majority of cricket followers *know* that Hobbs scored 197 centuries and I do not feel I have the authority or the moral justification to use, after more than fifty years, performances which would suddenly change old, accepted records, and also alter the figures of someone like H. Sutcliffe who, unlike Hobbs, appears in this volume. Therefore the accepted figures will remain inviolate, and I, the youthful revolutionary who started the ACS in 1973, and stated in press interviews that one of our express purposes was the 'correction' of long accepted figures and records, seem to have become the middle-aged reactionary. My apparent metamorphosis may well be seen in this light, but the knowledge that both Hobbs and Sutcliffe rejected the Vizianagram matches as 'exhibitions', in which they were 'given' runs, is a balm to my conscience.

Cricket was once, to me, the ideal vehicle in which to exercise a lifetime's fascination with figures, but though statistics are still vitally important, perhaps years of watching and being connected with the game, it's players, and it's writers, have bred within me a greater appreciation of cricket's ethereal qualities, and it's traditions. One ignores those traditions at one's peril.

KEY TO ENTRIES

A statistical appendix, including full first-class and Test career records, complete to the end of the 1984 English season, for all who qualify for entry, is given at the end of the book.

Entries are in strict alphabetical order.

NAME
Full name. If known by name other than first, name in question italicised. If known by an adopted name (not a nickname) this is given in parentheses. Changes of name listed at foot of entry.

TYPE
Type of batsman, bowler; wicketkeeper.

BIRTH, DEATH
Date and place of birth and, where applicable, death.

EDUCATION
Schools, colleges and universities (with colleges if Oxford or Cambridge) attended.

DEBUT
Year of first-class debut.

WISDEN
Year chosen as one of the almanack's Five Cricketers of the Year.

STATUS
P indicates professional cricketer before November 1962, when the distinction between amateur and professional was abolished in the first-class game. Non-county players are regarded throughout as amateurs.

BRITISH TEAMS
Regular first-class teams (the 17 counties, Cambridge University, Oxford University, Ireland, Scotland and Wales) in Britain played for, with years and number of appearances. Given for each, where appropriate, are 1st XI county caps, Blues, Benefits and Testimonials, and years of captaincy. Other first-class sides played for, with years and

number of appearances, are sometimes also given.

OVERSEAS TEAMS
Listed under country. Regular first-class teams outside Britain played for, with years and, in the case of Australian states and New Zealand associations, the number of appearances. Given for each, where appropriate, the years of captaincy. Other overseas first-class teams are sometimes also listed.

TEST APPEARANCES
Listed by series, home series first. Number of Tests in which captain.

OTHER TOURS
Includes all tours, in which played a first-class match, not already listed under away Test appearances. Takes account of occasional first-class appearances overseas for non-domestic teams not making an organised tour.

HIGHEST SCORE
Highest innings in Test cricket (where appropriate) and highest innings in first-class cricket, both with match details.

BEST BOWLING
Best bowling return (most wickets for fewest runs) in Test cricket (where appropriate) and best bowling return in first-class cricket, both with match details. One-wicket returns are usually ignored.

1000 RUNS
Number of seasons in which reached 1000 runs and best aggregate (with average and year).

100 WICKETS
Number of seasons in which reached 100 wickets and best aggregate (with average and year).

| DOUBLES | Number of seasons in which scored 1000 runs and took 100 wickets, or scored 1000 runs and made 100 dismissals (wicketkeepers). Any outstanding aggregates noted. |

| RECORDS | Major (or unusual) first-class records to credit. |

| NOTABILIA | Any other outstanding or unusual achievements in first-class cricket. |

| OTHER MATTER | *First-class cricket*: Appearances in Gentlemen-Players matches; World Series Cricket (Kerry Packer); unofficial tours to South Africa; selection for tours which were cancelled; umpiring in first-class cricket; administrative posts held in the first-class game. *Non first-class cricket*: Minor Counties, league sides and clubs, etc. played for; non first-class tours; umpiring in Minor Counties cricket; non first-class administrative post held. |
| | Other major sports played to first-class level; achievements in non-sporting fields; titles or ranks held; autobiographies; other first-class cricketers or notable personages related to. |

ABBREVIATIONS

| GENERAL | * – not out or unbroken partnership; fc – first-class; wkt – wicket; @ – average; inns – innings; HS – highest innings; HST – highest innings in Tests; BB – best bowling; BBT – best bowling in Tests; occ – occasional. |

| BATTING AND BOWLING TYPES | RHB – right-hand batsman; LHB – left-hand batsman; RF – right-arm fast; RFM – right-arm fast-medium; RMF – right-arm medium-fast; RM – right-arm medium; LF – left-arm fast; LFM – left-arm fast-medium; LMF – left-arm medium-fast; LM – left-arm medium; OB – off-break; LB – leg-break; LBG – leg-break and googly; RAS – right-arm slow; SLA – slow left-arm orthodox; SLC – slow left-arm 'chinaman'; WK – wicketkeeper. |

| EDUCATION | S – School; HS – High School; CS – Comprehensive School; Sec S – Secondary School; Sec M – Secondary Modern; Coll S – College School; KCS – King's College School; GS – Grammar School; RGS – Royal Grammar School; RCS – Roman Catholic School; Univ S – University School; C – College; C of PE – College of Physical Education; C of Educ – College of Education; C of H Educ – College of Higher Education; C of H and F Educ – College of Higher and Further Education; RC – Royal College; Poly – Polytechnic; U – University. |

| TEAMS | A – Australia; E – England; I – India; NZ – New Zealand; P – Pakistan; SA – South Africa; SL – Sri Lanka; WI – West Indies. Derbys – Derbyshire; Glam – Glamorgan; Glos – Gloucestershire; Hants – Hampshire; Lancs – Lancashire; Leics – Leicestershire; M'sex – Middlesex; Northants – Northamptonshire; Notts – Nottinghamshire; Som – Somerset; Warwicks – Warwickshire; Worcs – Worcestershire; Yorks – Yorkshire; NSW – New South Wales; OFS – Orange Free State; ACC – Associated Cement Company; MCB – Muslim Commercial Bank; NWFP – North-West Frontier Province; PAF – Pakistan Air Force; PIA – Pakistan International Airlines; PWD – Public Works Department. |

| CRICKET BODIES | ACB – Australian Cricket Board; BCCI – Board of Control for Cricket in India; BCCP – Board of Control for Cricket in Pakistan; CA – Cricket Association; CU – Cricket Union; |

CWC—Cricket Writer's Club; ICU – Irish Cricket Union; MCC – Marylebone Cricket Club; NICC – Northern Ireland Cricket Club; SCU – Scottish Cricket Union; TCCB – Test and County Cricket Board; UAU – Universities Athletic Union; WICB – West Indies Cricket Board.

A

AAMER HAMEED
─────RHB, RMF─────

Born Lahore, Pakistan, 18 Oct 1954. Educ Lahore Central Model HS; Government C, Lahore; Punjab U; University C, Oxford. Debut 1972/73.
PAKISTAN DOMESTIC Universities, Lahore, Punjab, Servis Industries, National Bank, United Bank, 1972/73–77/78.
OXFORD UNIVERSITY (9) 1979 (Blue).
TOUR Pakistan to England 1978.
HS 103 Lahore A v Customs, Lyallpur, 1976/77.
BB 7–36 Lahore A v Sargodha, Lahore, 1975/76.

ABBERLEY, Robert *Neal*
─────RHB, RM─────

Born Birmingham, 22 Apr 1944. Educ Saltley GS, Birmingham. Debut 1964.
WARWICKSHIRE (258) 1964–79. Cap 1966. Benefit (£39,752) 1979.
TOUR MCC Under-25 to Pakistan 1966/67.
HS 117* Warwicks v Essex, Edgbaston, 1966.
BB 2–19 Warwicks v Oxford U, The Parks, 1972.
1000 RUNS (3) 1315 @ 28.58 in 1966.
Warwickshire chief coach since 1981.
Club: Moseley.

ABBEY, David Robert
─────LHB, SLA─────

Born Edmonton, London, 11 Dec 1941. Debut 1967.
MIDDLESEX (2) 1967.
HS 12 M'sex v Som, Lord's, 1967.

ABBOTT, Alan Wesley
─────RHB─────

Born Sutton-in-the-Elms, Leics, 15 Nov 1926. Educ Hinckley GS. Debut 1946.
LEICESTERSHIRE (1) 1946. *P.*
HS 5 Leics v Kent, Tunbridge Wells, 1946.

ABDUL QADIR Khan
─────RHB, LBG─────

Born Lahore, Pakistan, 15 Sept 1955. Educ Arif HS, Lahore. Debut 1975/76.
PAKISTAN DOMESTIC Punjab, Lahore, Habib Bank, 1975/76–.
PAKISTAN (27) 1977/78–83/84. E 1977/78 (3), 1983/84 (3); WI 1980/81 (2); A 1982/83 (3); I 1982/83 (5). *E 1982 (3); A 1983/84 (5); I 1979–80 (3).*
OTHER TOUR Pakistan to England 1978.
HST 50 P v E, Faisalabad, 1983/84. HS 112 Lahore C v Bahawalpur, Bahawalpur, 1975/76.
BBT 7–142 P v A, Faisalabad, 1982/83.
BB 9–49 Habib Bank v Rawalpindi, Rawalpindi, 1982/83.
100 WKTS (1) 103 @ 22.98 in 1982/83 – first bowler to do so in Pakistan season.

ABELL, John Norman
─────RHB, WK─────

Born Chelsfield, Kent, 18 Sept 1931. Educ Marlborough; Oxford U. Debut 1952.
OXFORD UNIVERSITY (3) 1952–53.
HS 25 Oxford U v Sussex, The Parks, 1952.
Father G. E. B. Abell (Worcs and Oxford U); brother T. G. Abell (Free Foresters).

ABELL, Roy Beverley
─────RHB, LB─────

Born Birmingham, 21 Jan 1931. Educ Waverley GS, Birmingham. Debut 1967.
WARWICKSHIRE (1) 1967.
BB 3–64 Warwicks v Cambridge U, Edgbaston, 1967.
Club: Moseley. Professional artist; commissioned for Silver Jubilee commemorative picture by HM Queen Elizabeth II.

ABELL, Timothy George
─────RHB, OB─────

Born Lahore, India, 29 Apr 1930. Educ Marlborough; Corpus Christi C, Oxford. Debut 1954.
FREE FORESTERS (1) 1954.

HS 4* Free Foresters v Cambridge U, Fenner's, 1954.
Clubs: Free Foresters, I Zingari, Southgate. Father G. E. B. Abell (Worcs and Oxford U); brother J. N. Abell (Oxford U).

ABID ALI, Syed
─────RHB, RM─────

Born Hyderabad, India, 9 Sept 1941. Educ St George's GS; All Saints HS, Hyderabad, India. Debut 1959/60.
INDIA DOMESTIC Hyderabad 1959/60–78/79. Capt 1977/78–78/79.
INDIA (29) 1967/68–74/75. E 1972/73 (4); A 1969/70 (1); WI 1974/75 (2); NZ 1969/70 (3). *E 1971 (3), 1974 (3); A 1967/68 (4); WI 1970/71 (5); NZ 1967/68 (4).*
OTHER TOUR Rest of World XI to Pakistan 1970/71 (relief match).
HST 81 I v A, Sydney, 1967/68. HS 173* Hyderabad v Kerala, Hyderabad, 1968/69.
BBT 6–55 I v A, Adelaide, 1967/68. BB 6–23 Indians v Surrey, Oval, 1974.

ABLACK, Robert Kenneth
─────SLA─────

Born Port of Spain, Trinidad, 5 Jan 1919. Debut 1946.
NORTHAMPTONSHIRE (3) 1946–49.
HS 16 Northants v Combined Services, Kettering, 1946.
BB 3–32 Northants v Glam, Rushden, 1946.
Club: BBC (London). Broadcaster and public relations officer at West Indian High Commission in London.

ABRAHAMS, John
─────LHB, ROB─────

Born Salt River, Cape Town, S Africa, 21 July 1952. Educ Heywood GS. Debut 1973.
LANCASHIRE (190) 1973–. Cap 1982. Capt 1984.
HS 201* Lancs v Warwicks, Nuneaton, 1984.
BB 3–27 Lancs v Worcs, Old Trafford, 1981.

1000 RUNS (3) 1261 @ 39.40 in 1983.
Club: Egerton. Father C. J. Abrahams
(league professional).

ACFIELD, David Laurence
—RHB, OB—

Born Chelmsford, Essex, 24 July 1947.
Educ Brentwood S; Christ's C, Cambridge. Debut 1966.
CAMBRIDGE UNIVERSITY (37) 1966–68
(Blue 1967, 1968).
ESSEX (335) 1966–. Cap 1970. Benefit
(£42,788) 1981.
TOUR MCC to E Africa 1973/74.
HS 42 Cambridge U v Leics, Leicester,
1967.
BB 8–55 Essex v Kent, Canterbury,
1981.
International and Olympic fencer
(sabre).

ACKERMAN, Hylton Michael
—LHB, RM—

Born Springs, S Africa, 28 Apr 1947.
Educ Dale C, East London, S Africa.
Debut 1963/64.
S AFRICA DOMESTIC Border, North-
Eastern Transvaal, Natal, Western
Province (capt 1977/78–81/82) 1963/
64–81/82.
NORTHAMPTONSHIRE (98) 1967–71. Cap
1969.
TOUR World XI to Australia 1971/72.
HS 208 Northants v Leics, Leicester,
1970.
BB 4–61 W Province B v Natal B, Pieter-
maritzburg, 1981/82.
1000 RUNS (3) 1565 @ 33.29 in 1970.
Selected for S Africa to Australia 1971/
72 (tour cancelled).

A'COURT, Dennis George
—RHB, RFM—

Born Tredegar, Monmouthshire, 27
July 1937. Debut 1960. P.
GLOUCESTERSHIRE (49) 1960–63. Cap
1961.
HS 47* Glos v Hants, Portsmouth, 1961.
BB 6–25 Glos v S Africans, Bristol, 1960.
Club: Bohemians.

ADAMS, Keith
—RHB—

Born Pudsey, Yorks, 6 June 1932. Educ
St Peter's, York; Emmanuel C, Cam-
bridge. Debut 1954.
CAMBRIDGE UNIVERSITY (1) 1954.
HS 34 Cambridge U v M'sex, Fenner's,
1954.

ADCOCK, Neil Amwin Treharne
—RHB, RF—

Born Cape Town, S Africa, 8 Mar 1931.
Educ St George's, Pietermaritzburg;
Grey HS, Port Elizabeth; Jeppe HS,
J'burg. Debut 1952/53. Wisden 1961.
S AFRICA DOMESTIC Transvaal, Natal,
1952/53–62/63.
S AFRICA (26) 1953/54–61/62. E 1956/57
(5); A 1957/58 (5); NZ 1953/54 (5);
1961/62 (2). E 1955 (4), 1960 (5).
OTHER TOUR Commonwealth XI to New
Zealand 1961/62.
HST 24 SA v NZ, Port Elizabeth, 1961/
62. HS 41 Transvaal v Natal, Durban,
1959/60.
BBT 6–43 SA v A, Durban, 1957/58. BB
8–39 (13–65 match) Transvaal v OFS,
J'burg, 1953/54.
100 WKTS (1) 108 @ 14.02 in 1960.

ADDERLEY, Charles Henry
—RHB, RM—

Born Kings Heath, Birmingham, 16
Sept 1912. Died Moseley, Birmingham,
28 Feb 1985. Debut 1946.
WARWICKSHIRE (5) 1946.
HS 12 Warwicks v Notts, Trent Bridge,
1946.
Club: Kings Heath.

ADDISON, James Paul
—RHB, SLA—

Born Leek, Staffordshire, 14 May 1965.
Debut 1983.
LEICESTERSHIRE (1) 1983.
HS 51 Leics v N Zealanders, Leicester,
1983.

ADHIKARI,
Hemchandra Ramchandra (Hemu)
—RHB, OB—

Born Poona, India, 31 July 1919. Debut
1936/37.
INDIA DOMESTIC Gujerat, Baroda, Ser-
vices (capt), Hindus, 1936/37–59/60.
INDIA (21) 1947/48–58/59. E 1951/52
(3); A 1956/57 (2); WI 1948/49 (5),
1958/59 (1); P 1952/53 (2). E 1952 (3);
A 1947/48 (5). Capt 1.
HST 114* I v WI, Delhi, 1948/49. HS 230*
Services v Rajasthan, Ajmer, 1951/52.
BBT 3–68 I v WI, Delhi, 1958/59. BB 3–2
Baroda v Gujerat, Baroda, 1939/40.
RECORD Added 109 for 10th wkt with
Ghulam Ahmed, I v P, Delhi, 1952/53,
India Test record.
Manager India to England 1971, 1974.
MCC Hon. member. Colonel in Indian
Army (ret).

AERS, David Roland
—RHB, SLA—

Born Lahore, India, 3 Oct 1946. Educ
Tonbridge; Queen's C, Cambridge.
Debut 1966.
CAMBRIDGE UNIVERSITY (15) 1966–68
(Blue 1967).
HS 48 Cambridge U v Warwicks, Edg-
baston, 1967.
BB 5–116 Cambridge U v Yorks, Scar-
borough, 1967.
Club: Crusaders.

AFAQ HUSSAIN
—RHB, OB—

Born Lucknow, India, 3 Dec 1939. Educ
Karachi U. Debut 1957/58.
PAKISTAN DOMESTIC Karachi, Univer-
sities, Karachi U, Pakistan International
Airlines, Public Works Department,
1957/58–74/75.
PAKISTAN (2) 1961/62–64/65. E 1961/62
(1). A 1964/65 (1).
OTHER TOURS Pakistan to England 1962.
Pakistan Eaglets to England 1963.
HST 35* P v E, Lahore, 1961/62. HS 122*
PIA v Lahore Blues, Lahore, 1969/70.
BBT 1–40 P v E, Lahore, 1961/62. BB
8–108 Karachi U v Railways-Quetta,
Karachi, 1960/61.

AFFORD, John Andrew
—RHB, SLA—

Born Crowland, Lincs, 12 May 1964.
Educ Spalding GS. Debut 1984.
NOTTINGHAMSHIRE (3) 1984.
Has not batted.
BB 2–49 Notts v Lancs, Old Trafford,
1984.

AFTAB BALOCH
—RHB, OB—

Born Karachi, Pakistan, 1 Apr 1953.
Educ London Academy, Karachi; Na-
tional C, Karachi. Debut 1969/70.
PAKISTAN DOMESTIC Public Works
Department, Pakistan International
Airlines, Karachi, Sind, National Bank,
1969/70–.
PAKISTAN (2) 1969/70–74/75. WI 1974/
75 (1); NZ 1969/70 (1).
TOURS Pakistan Under-25 to Sri Lanka
1973/74. Pakistan to England 1974. PIA
to Zimbabwe 1981/82.
HST 60* P v WI, Lahore, 1974/75. HS 428
Sind v Baluchistan, Karachi, 1973/74.
BB 8–171 Sind v Railways, Karachi,
1972/73.
RECORDS Inns of 428 is 6th-highest fc
score. At age 20 yrs 326 days is
youngest-ever to make fc score of 400.

Clubs: Rishton, Todmorden. Father M. S. Baloch (Karachi).

AFTAB GUL
————RHB, LB————

Born Gujjar Khan, Rawalpindi, India, 31 Mar 1946. Educ Punjab U. Debut 1964/65.
PAKISTAN DOMESTIC Punjab U, Lahore, Universities, Punjab, Servis Industries, 1964/65–79/80.
PAKISTAN (6) 1968/69–71. E 1968/69 (2); NZ 1969/70 (1). *E 1971 (3)*.
OTHER TOUR Pakistan to England 1974.
HST 33 P v E, Lord's, 1971. HS 140 Punjab v Universities, Lahore, 1973/74.
1000 RUNS (1) 1154 @ 46.16 in 1971.
Former student leader and political activist. Applied for political asylum in England in 1983.

AGNEW, Jonathan Philip
————RHB, RF————

Born Macclesfield, Cheshire, 4 Apr 1960. Educ Uppingham. Debut 1978.
LEICESTERSHIRE (75) 1978–. Cap 1984.
ENGLAND (2) 1984. WI 1984 (1); SL 1984 (1).
TOUR Leics XI to Zimbabwe 1980/81.
HST 5 E v WI, Oval, 1984. HS 56 Leics v Worcs, Worcester, 1982.
BBT 2–51 E v WI, Oval, 1984. BB 8–47 Leics v Cambridge U, Fenner's, 1984.
Cousin late Mary Duggan (England Women's cricket captain).

AINSWORTH,
Michael Lionel Yeoward
————RHB————

Born Hooton, Cheshire, 13 May 1922. Died during a match at Hillingdon, London, 28 Aug 1978. Educ Shrewsbury. Debut 1946.
COMBINED SERVICES (23) 1946–58.
WORCESTERSHIRE (17) 1948–50.
MCC (1) 1950.
FREE FORESTERS (8) 1953–64.
HS 137 Free Foresters v Cambridge U, Fenner's, 1959.
Lt-Commander RN.

AITCHISON, James
————RHB, RM————

Born Kilmarnock, Scotland, 26 May 1920. Educ Kilmarnock Academy; Glasgow U. Debut 1946.
SCOTLAND (50) 1946–63.
HS 190* Scotland v Ireland, Dublin, 1959.

RECORD 2786 runs for Scotland in fc cricket.
Church of Scotland minister.

AITCHISON, John Edward
————RHB, OB————

Born Gillingham, Kent, 27 Dec 1928. Debut 1949. *P.*
KENT (3) 1949–50.
HS 4 Kent v Worcs, Tunbridge Wells, 1950.
BB 3–33 Kent v Glam, Gravesend, 1949.
Clubs: Bexleyheath, Ramsgate.

AIZAZUDDIN, Fakir Syed
————RHB, LBG————

Born Lahore, India, 17 Aug 1935. Educ Cambridge U. Debut 1957.
CAMBRIDGE UNIVERSITY (5) 1957.
PAKISTAN DOMESTIC Khairpur, Karachi, 1959/60–71/72.
TOURS Pakistan Eaglets to England 1963. Pakistan to Ceylon 1964/65. Pakistan to England 1967.
HS 187 Pakistan Eaglets v Cambridge U, Fenner's, 1963.
BB 4–36 South Zone v Pakistan Board, Hyderabad, 1961/62.

ALABASTER, John Chaloner
————RHB, LBG————

Born Invercargill, N Zealand, 11 July 1930. Debut 1955/56.
N ZEALAND DOMESTIC Otago (65) 1956/57–71/72.
NEW ZEALAND (21) 1955/56–71/72. E 1962/63 (2); WI 1955/56 (1); I 1967/68 (4). *E 1958 (2); SA 1961/62 (5); WI 1971/72 (2); I 1955/56 (4); P 1955/56 (1)*.
OTHER TOUR N Zealand to Australia 1967/68.
HST 34 NZ v I, Dunedin, 1967/68. HS 82 N Zealand XI v Auckland XI, Auckland, 1957/58.
BBT 4–46 NZ v E, Edgbaston, 1958. BB 7–41 N Zealanders v S African Colts, East London, 1961/62.
Made fc debut on tour of India and Pakistan 1955/56. Brother G. D. Alabaster (Otago, Canterbury and Northern Districts).

ALDERMAN, Albert Edward
————RHB, occ WK————

Born Alvaston, Derbys, 30 Oct 1907. Debut 1928. *P.*
DERBYSHIRE (318) 1928–48. Cap. Testimonial (£1659) 1948.

HS 175 Derbys v Leics, Chesterfield, 1937.
BB 3–37 Derbys v Essex, Derby, 1929.
1000 RUNS (6) 1509 @ 33.53 in 1937.
Fc umpire 1966–67. Berkshire 1950. Minor Counties umpire 1949. Cricket coach at Repton and OTC, Camberley. Soccer: Derby County, Burnley.

ALDERMAN, Terence Michael
————RHB, RFM————

Born Subiaco, Perth, W Australia, 12 June 1956. Debut 1974/75.
AUSTRALIA DOMESTIC Western Australia (58) 1974/75–.
KENT (20) 1984.
AUSTRALIA (19) 1981–83/84. E 1982/83 (1); WI 1981/82 (2); P 1981/82 (3). *E 1981 (6); WI 1983/84 (3); NZ 1981/82 (3); P 1982/83 (1)*.
HST 21* A v WI, Port of Spain, 1983/84.
HS 52* Kent v Sussex, Hastings, 1984.
BBT 6–135 A v E, Headingley, 1981. BB 7–28 W Australia v NSW, Perth, 1981/82.
RECORD 42 wkts @21.26 in 6 Tests in 1981, record for Australian in Test series in England.

ALDERSON, Ralph
————RHB————

Born Newton-le-Willows, Lancs, 7 June 1920. Debut 1948. *P.*
LANCASHIRE (2) 1948–49.
HS 55 Lancs v Kent, Old Trafford, 1949.
Minor Counties umpire 1964–68.

ALDRIDGE, Keith *John*
————RHB, RFM————

Born Evesham, Worcs, 13 Mar 1935. Debut 1956. *P.*
WORCESTERSHIRE (73) 1956–60. Cap 1959.
AUSTRALIA DOMESTIC Tasmania (6) 1961/62–63/64.
HS 24* Worcs v Glam, Pontypridd, 1960.
BB 6–26 Worcs v Sussex, Hove, 1958.
Called for 'throwing' in 1959 and 1960. 6 ft 6 in tall. Club: Kidderminster and Walsall (Birmingham League).

ALEXANDER,
Franz Copeland Murray (Gerry)
————RHB, WK————

Born Kingston, Jamaica, 2 Nov 1928. Educ Wolmer's S, Jamaica; Caius & Gonville C, Cambridge. Debut 1952.

CAMBRIDGE UNIVERSITY (27) 1952–53 (Blue 1952–53).
W INDIES DOMESTIC Jamaica 1956/57–59/60.
N Zealand Governor-General's XI v MCC, Auckland, 1960/61.
WEST INDIES (25) 1957–60/61. E 1959/60 (5); P 1957/58 (5). *E 1957 (2); A 1960/61 (5); I 1958/59 (5); P 1958/59 (3).* Capt 18.
HST 108 WI v A, Sydney, 1960/61. HS as above.
Made 23 dismissals WI v E in 1959/60 — former record for Test series.
Cambridgeshire 1954. Soccer: Cambridge Blue and England (amateur).

ALEXANDER, Frederick Russell
————————RHB, RM————————

Born Acton, London, 4 June 1924. Died Harrow, 17 May 1984. Debut 1951. *P.*
MIDDLESEX (2) 1951.
HS 8 M'sex v Surrey, Lord's, 1951.

ALIM-UD-DIN
————————RHB, occ LB————————

Born Ajmer, India, probably 15 Dec 1930. Debut 1942/43.
INDIA DOMESTIC Rajasthan, Gujerat, 1942/43–1946/47.
PAKISTAN DOMESTIC Sind, Bahawalpur, Karachi, Public Works Department, 1948/49–67/68.
PAKISTAN (25) 1954–62. E 1961/62 (2); A 1956/57 (1), 1959/60 (1); WI 1958/59 (1); NZ 1955/56 (3); I 1954/55 (5). *E 1954 (3), 1962 (3); WI 1957/58 (5); I 1960/61 (1).*
HST 109 P v E, Karachi, 1961/62. HS 142 Pakistanis v Worcs, Worcester, 1954.
BB 4–36 Karachi v PWD, Karachi, 1964/65.
Later Pakistan national coach. Age uncertain: other versions include date of birth as 15 Apr 1928. Brother Salim-ud-Din (Karachi).

ALLAN, David Walter
————————RHB, WK————————

Born Bridgetown, Barbados, 11 May 1937. Debut 1955/56.
W INDIES DOMESTIC Barbados 1955/56–65/66.
WEST INDIES (5) 1961/62–66. A 1964/65 (1); I 1961/62 (2). *E 1966 (2).*
OTHER TOUR W Indies to England 1963.
HST 40* WI v I, Bridgetown, 1961/62.
HS 56 W Indians v Warwicks, Edgbaston, 1966.

ALLAN, James Moffat
————————RHB, SLA————————

Born Leeds, Yorks, 2 Apr 1932. Educ Edinburgh Academy; Worcester C, Oxford. Debut 1953.
OXFORD UNIVERSITY (49) 1953–56 (Blue 1953–56).
SCOTLAND (39) 1954–72.
KENT (40) 1954–57. Cap 1955.
WARWICKSHIRE (48) 1966–68.
HS 153 Oxford U v Sussex, The Parks, 1953.
BB 7–54 Scotland v Pakistanis, Selkirk, 1971.
1000 RUNS (2) 1369 @ 27.93 in 1955.
Five wkts short of the double in 1955. 1765 runs @ 25.21 and 151 wkts @ 26.06 for Oxford U.
Gentlemen v Players (1) 1956.

ALLAN, John
————————RHB, RM————————

Born Hamilton, Scotland, 20 Jan 1911. Educ Uddingston GS. Debut 1951.
SCOTLAND (1) 1951.
HS 2 Scotland v Worcs, Dundee, 1951.
BB 3–78 Scotland v Worcs, Dundee, 1951.

ALLAN, Walter Ramsay
————————RHB————————

Born Riccarton, Ayrshire, Scotland, 26 Oct 1927. Educ Edinburgh Academy; Edinburgh U. Debut 1950.
SCOTLAND (3) 1950.
HS 30 Scotland v Ireland, Perth, 1950.

ALLBROOK, Mark Edward
————————RHB, OB————————

Born Frimley, Surrey, 15 Nov 1954. Educ Tonbridge; Trinity Hall, Cambridge. Debut 1975.
CAMBRIDGE UNIVERSITY (35) 1975–78 (Blue 1975–78).
NOTTINGHAMSHIRE (12) 1976–80.
HS 39 Cambridge U v Yorks, Fenner's, 1976.
BB 7–79 Cambridge U v Notts, Fenner's, 1978.
Club: Tunbridge Wells.

ALLDIS, James Stephen
————————LHB, SLA————————

Born Paddington, London, 27 Dec 1949. Debut 1970.
MIDDLESEX (2) 1970.
HS 4* M'sex v Hants, Basingstoke, 1970.
MCC staff at Lord's for two yrs prior to M'sex debut.

ALLEN, Antony William
————————RHB————————

Born Brackley, Northants, 22 Dec 1912. Educ Eton; Magdalene C, Cambridge. Debut 1932.
CAMBRIDGE UNIVERSITY (23) 1932–34 (Blue 1933, 1934).
NORTHAMPTONSHIRE (8) 1932–36.
FREE FORESTERS (3) 1946–47.
HS 144 Cambridge U v Sussex, Hove, 1933.

ALLEN, Basil Oliver
————————LHB————————

Born Clifton, Bristol, 13 Oct 1911. Died Wells, Somerset, 1 May 1981. Educ Clifton; Caius C, Cambridge. Debut 1932.
CAMBRIDGE UNIVERSITY (15) 1932–33 (Blue 1933).
GLOUCESTERSHIRE (285) 1932–51. Cap 1932. Capt 1937–38, 1947–50.
HS 220 Glos v Hants, Bournemouth, 1947.
1000 RUNS (7) 1785 @ 34.32 in 1938.
Gentlemen v Players (2) 1938. President Gloucestershire 1978–79.

ALLEN, David Arthur
————————RHB, OB————————

Born Bristol, 29 Oct 1935. Educ Cotham GS. Debut 1953. *P.*
GLOUCESTERSHIRE (349) 1953–72. Cap 1959. Benefit 1972.
ENGLAND (39) 1959/60–66. A 1961 (4), 1964 (1); SA 1960 (2); WI 1963 (2), 1966 (1); P 1962 (4). *A 1962/63 (1), 1965/66 (4); SA 1964/65 (4); WI 1959/60 (5); NZ 1965/66 (3); I 1961/62 (5); P 1961/62 (3).*
OTHER TOURS MCC to N Zealand 1960/61. Commonwealth XI to Pakistan 1967/68.
HST 88 E v NZ, Christchurch, 1965/66.
HS 121* Glos v Notts, Trent Bridge, 1961.
BBT 5–30 E v P, Dacca, 1961/62. BB 8–34 Glos v Sussex, Lydney, 1969.
1000 RUNS (2) 1165 @ 24.78 in 1964.
100 WKTS (1) 124 @ 19.44 in 1961.
DOUBLE (1) 1961.
Players v Gentlemen (2) 1960. CWC Young Cricketer of 1960. Club: Almondsbury.

ALLEN, George Oswald Browning (Gubby)
————————RHB, RF————————

Born Belle View Hill, Sydney, NSW, Australia, 31 July 1902. Educ Eton; Trinity C, Cambridge. Debut 1921.

CAMBRIDGE UNIVERSITY (19) 1922–23 (Blue 1922, 1923).
MIDDLESEX (146) 1921–50. Cap.
FREE FORESTERS (13) 1947–54.
ENGLAND (25) 1930–47/48. A 1930 (1), 1934 (2); WI 1933 (1); NZ 1931 (3); I 1936 (3). *A 1932/33 (5), 1936/37 (5); WI 1947/48 (3); NZ 1932/33 (2)*. Capt 11.
OTHER TOUR MCC to S America 1926/27.
HST 122 E v NZ, Lord's, 1931. HS 180 Free Foresters v Cambridge U, Fenner's, 1948.
BBT 7–80 E v I, Oval, 1936. BB 10–40 M'sex v Lancs, Lord's, 1929.
RECORDS During HST (above) added 246 for 8th wkt with L. E. G. Ames, world Test record and record for all cricket at Lord's. BB (above) best-ever inns return for M'sex.
Gentlemen v Players (11) 1923–38. Test selector 1955–61 (chairman). MCC committee 1947–63; treasurer 1964–76; president 1963–64. Awarded CBE. Uncle R. C. Allen (Australia).

ALLEN, John Wallace
RHB

Born Cullion, Co Londonderry, Ireland, 17 Feb 1921. Educ Foyle C, Londonderry. Debut 1948.
IRELAND (1) 1948.
Did not score.
Club: City of Derry.

ALLEN, Michael Henry John
RHB, SLA

Born Bedford, 7 Jan 1933. Educ Bedford S. Debut 1956. *P.*
NORTHAMPTONSHIRE (155) 1956–63. Cap 1957.
DERBYSHIRE (31) 1964–66.
HS 59 Northants v Warwicks, Northampton, 1959.
BB 8–48 Northants v Derbys, Northampton, 1961.
Scored 51 on fc debut, but did not bowl. In second fc match took 8–88 inns.
Players v Gentlemen (1) 1961. Bedfordshire 1950.

ALLERTON, Jeremy William Orde
LHB, RM

Born Windsor, Berks, 2 Feb 1944. Educ Stowe; Hertford C, Oxford. Debut 1967.
OXFORD UNIVERSITY (15) 1967–69 (Blue 1969).
HS 67 Oxford U v Worcs, The Parks, 1969.
Club: I Zingari.

ALLEY, William Edward
LHB, RM

Born Brooklyn, Sydney, NSW, Australia, 3 Feb 1919. Debut 1945/46. *Wisden* 1961. *P.*
AUSTRALIA DOMESTIC New South Wales (12) 1945/46–47/48.
SOMERSET (350) 1957–68. Cap 1957. Testimonial (£2700) 1961.
TOURS Commonwealth XI to India, Pakistan and Ceylon 1949/50. Commonwealth XI to Rhodesia 1962/63. Commonwealth XI to Pakistan 1963/64. International Cavaliers to S Africa 1962/63.
HS 221* Som v Warwicks, Nuneaton, 1961.
BB 8–65 Som v Surrey, Oval, 1962.
1000 RUNS (10+1) 3019 @ 56.96 in 1961.
DOUBLE (1) 1962 (1915 @ 36.82, 112 @ 20.74).
RECORDS 2761 runs and 10 centuries for Som in 1961 — both county records. Added 265 for 6th wkt with K. E. Palmer, Som v Northants, Northampton, 1961, county record.
Players v Gentlemen (1) 1961. Fc umpire 1969–84 (10 Tests, 1974–81). League professional Colne, Blackpool 1947–56. Clubs: Brooklands, North District (Sydney), Petersham. Successful boxer in youth. Autobiography *My Incredible Innings* (1969).

ALLEYNE, Hartley Leroy
RHB, RF

Born St James, Bridgetown, Barbados, 28 Feb 1957. Debut 1978/79.
W INDIES DOMESTIC Barbados 1978/79–82/83.
WORCESTERSHIRE (38) 1980–82.
TOUR Young W Indies to Zimbabwe 1981/82.
HS 72 Worcs v Lancs, Stourport, 1980.
BB 8–43 Worcs v M'sex, Lord's, 1981.
No-balled for throwing three times in W Indies in 1982/83.
Barred from W Indian cricket for touring S Africa 1983/84 (W Indies XI). Lincolnshire 1979. Professional: Rochdale 1979.

ALLIN, Anthony William
RHB, SLA

Born Bideford, Devon, 20 Apr 1954. Educ Belmont C, Barnstaple. Debut 1976.
GLAMORGAN (13) 1976.
HS 32 Glam v Som, Weston-super-Mare, 1976.
BB 8–63 Glam v Sussex, Cardiff, 1976.
Devon 1975, 1977–.

ALLISON, David Farquhar
RHB, WK

Born London, 26 June 1948. Educ Greenmore C; Brasenose C, Oxford. Debut 1970.
OXFORD UNIVERSITY (6) 1970 (Blue).
HS 21 Oxford U v Glam, The Parks, 1970.

ALLOM, Anthony Thomas Carrick
RHB, RFM

Born Bletchingley, Surrey, 21 Oct 1938. Educ Charterhouse. Debut 1959.
FREE FORESTERS (3) 1959–61.
SURREY (1) 1960.
MCC (1) 1960.
HS 34* Free Foresters v Oxford U, The Parks, 1959.
BB 5–79 same match.
6 ft 9 in tall. Father M. J. C. Allom (Surrey and England).

ALLOTT, Paul John Walter
RHB, RFM

Born Altrincham, Cheshire, 14 Sept 1956. Educ Altrincham County GS; Durham U. Debut 1978.
LANCASHIRE (93) 1978–. Cap 1981.
ENGLAND (9) 1981–84. A 1981 (1); WI 1984 (3); I 1982 (2); SL 1984 (1). *I 1981/82 (1); SL 1981/82 (1)*.
OTHER TOUR International XI to Jamaica 1982/83.
HST 52* E v A, Old Trafford, 1981. HS as above.
BBT 6–61 E v WI, Headingley, 1984. BB 8–48 Lancs v Northants, Northampton, 1981.
Cheshire 1976. Club: Bowdon.

ALTHAM, Richard James Livingstone
RHB, RM

Born Winchester, 21 Jan 1924. Educ Marlborough; Trinity C, Oxford. Debut 1947.
OXFORD UNIVERSITY (1) 1947.
FREE FORESTERS (1) 1948.
HS 14 Oxford U v Free Foresters, The Parks, 1947.
Hertfordshire 1952. Father H. S. Altham (player, selector and writer).

ALWYN, Nicholas
RHB

Born Finchley, London, 13 June 1938. Educ King Alfred's S, Finchley; Caius C, Cambridge. Debut 1961.

CAMBRIDGE UNIVERSITY (5) 1961.
HS 41 Cambridge U v Essex, Fenner's, 1961.
Clubs: Hornsey, Hampstead.

AMARNATH Bhardwaj, Mohinder (Jimmie)
──────RHB, RM──────

Born Patiala, India, 24 Sept 1950. Debut 1966/67.
INDIA DOMESTIC Punjab, Delhi (capt 1981/82), 1966/67–.
INDIA (42) 1969/70–83/84. E 1976/77 (2); A 1969/70 (1), 1979/80 (1); WI 1978/79 (2), 1983/84 (3); NZ 1976/77 (3); P 1983/84 (2). *E 1979 (2); WI 1975/76 (4), 1982/83 (5); A 1977/78 (5); NZ 1975/76 (3); P 1978/79 (3), 1982/83 (6).*
HST 120 I v P, Lahore, 1982/83. HS 207 North Zone v South Zone, Bombay, 1982/83.
BBT 4–63 I v NZ, Christchurch, 1975/76. BB 7–27 Punjab v Jammu and Kashmir, Patiala, 1969/70.
1000 RUNS (2) 2234 @ 79.78 in 1982/83 — record total for any overseas season. Scored only one run in six completed Test inns v WI in 1983/84.
Father N. (Lala) Amarnath (India); brothers R. Amarnath (Delhi and Punjab) and S. Amarnath (India).

AMARNATH Bhardwaj, Nanik (Lala)
──────RHB, RM, originally WK──────

Born Lahore, India, 11 Sept 1911. Debut 1931/32. Educ Aligarh U.
INDIA DOMESTIC South Punjab (capt 1944/45, 1950/51), Gujerat (capt 1952/53), Patiala (capt 1953/54, 1956/57, 1957/58), Uttar Pradesh (capt 1954/55), Railways (capt 1958/59, 1959/60), 1931/32–63/64.
India and Ceylon XI v MCC, Colombo, 1933/34.
INDIA (24) 1933/34–52/53. E 1933/34 (3), 1951/52 (3); WI 1948/49 (5); P 1952/53 (5). *E 1946 (3); A 1947/48 (5).* Capt 15.
OTHER TOURS India to England 1936 (sent home early after dispute). India to Ceylon 1944/45. India to Pakistan 1954/55 (manager). Indian Starlets to Pakistan 1959/60.
HST 118 I v E, Bombay, 1933/34 (Test debut). HS 262 India in England v The Rest, Calcutta, 1946/47 (added 410 for 3rd wkt with R. S. Modi, Indian fc record).
BBT 5–96 I v E, Old Trafford, 1946. BB 7–30 Pepsu v Services, Delhi, 1956/57.

Indian selector, sometime chairman. League professional Nelson, Burnley, Ratcliffe. MCC Hon. member. Sons M. Amarnath, S. Amarnath (both India) and R. Amarnath (Delhi and Punjab).

AMES, Leslie Ethelbert George
──────RHB, WK, LB──────

Born Elham, Kent, 3 Dec 1905. Educ F. D. Harvey GS, Folkestone. Debut 1926. *Wisden* 1929.
KENT (430) 1926–51. Cap 1927. Benefits 1937 (£1265), 1948 (£4336).
ENGLAND (47) 1929–38/39. A 1934 (5), 1938 (2); SA 1929 (1), 1935 (4); WI 1933 (3); NZ 1931 (3), 1937 (3); I 1932 (1). *A 1932/33 (5), 1936/37 (5); SA 1938/39 (5); WI 1929/30 (4), 1934/35 (4); NZ 1932/33 (2).*
OTHER TOURS MCC to Australia 1928/29. Commonwealth XI to India and Ceylon 1950/51 (capt).
HST 149 E v WI, Kingston, 1929/30. HS 295 Kent v Glos, Folkestone, 1933.
BB 3–23 Kent v Surrey, Oval, 1946.
1000 RUNS (17) 3058 @ 58.80 in 1933.
RECORDS Most wicketkeeping dismissals in season, 127 in 1929. Three times 100 dismissals or more in season (1928, 1929, 1932), a record; in each year, in addition, scored 1000 runs — only other wicketkeeper to perform double J. T. Murray in 1957. 64 stumpings in 1932, a record. One of 20 batsmen to score 100 fc centuries. Went from 25* to 148* before lunch, E v SA, Oval, 1935: most runs before lunch in a Test. Added 246 for 8th wkt with G. O. B. Allen (E v NZ, Lord's, 1931), world Test record and record for all cricket at Lord's. Added 277 for 5th wkt with F. E. Woolley, Kent v New Zealanders, Canterbury, 1931, county record. Won Lawrence Trophy for fastest century of the season twice — only player to do so more than once.
Scored centuries against every fc county except his own.
Players v Gentlemen (12) 1928–47. England selector 1950–58. Kent secretary-manager 1957–73. Kent president 1976. Managed three MCC teams abroad. MCC Hon. member. MCC committee. Soccer: Gillingham. Awarded CBE.

AMISS, Dennis Leslie
──────RHB, LM/SLA──────

Born Harborne, Birmingham, 7 Apr 1943. Educ Oldknow S, Birmingham. Debut 1960. *Wisden* 1975. *P.*
WARWICKSHIRE (470) 1960–. Cap 1965. Benefit (£34,947) 1975.

ENGLAND (50) 1966–77. A 1968 (1), 1975 (2), 1977 (2); WI 1966 (1), 1973 (3), 1976 (1); NZ 1973 (3); I 1967 (2), 1971 (1), 1974 (3); P 1967 (1), 1971 (3), 1974 (3). *A 1974/75 (5), 1976/77 (1); WI 1973/74 (5); NZ 1974/75 (2); I 1972/73 (3), 1976/77 (5); P 1972/73 (3).*
OTHER TOURS MCC Under-25 to Pakistan 1966/67. International XI to India, Pakistan and Ceylon 1967/68. Rest of World XI to Pakistan 1970/71 (relief match).
HST 262* E v WI, Kingston, 1973/74. HS as above.
BB 3–21 Warwicks v M'sex, Lord's, 1970.
1000 RUNS (20 + 1) 2239 @ 55.97 in 1984.
RECORD 1379 Test runs @ 68.95 in 1974 — most runs by England batsman in calendar year.
Scored centuries against every fc county except his own. 374 catches in career.
World Series Cricket (Kerry Packer) 1977/78–78/79. Barred from Test cricket for three years for touring S Africa 1981/82 (SAB England XI).

ANDERSON, Ewan William
──────RHB, RFM──────

Born Bromley, Kent, 28 Mar 1938. Educ Dulwich; Edmund Hall, Oxford. Debut 1961.
OXFORD UNIVERSITY (12) 1961–62.
HS 13* Oxford U v Leics, The Parks, 1961.
BB 3–69 Oxford U v Glam, The Parks, 1961.

ANDERSON, Iain Stuart
──────RHB, OB──────

Born Derby, 24 Apr 1960. Educ Dovecliff GS; Wulfric S, Burton-on-Trent. Debut 1978.
DERBYSHIRE (87) 1978–.
S AFRICA DOMESTIC Boland 1983/84.
HS 112 Derbys v Kent, Chesterfield, 1983.
BB 4–35 Derbys v Australians, Derby, 1981.
1000 RUNS (1) 1233 @ 37.36 in 1983.

ANDERSON, Ian Mair
──────RHB, RFM──────

Born Calcutta, India, 11 May 1931. Educ Dollar Academy; Glasgow U. Debut 1951.
SCOTLAND (5) 1951–53.
HS 40 Scotland v Worcs, Dundee, 1951.
Toronto 1957. Canada to Bermuda 1958.

ANDERSON, Ivan John
RHB, OB

Born Armagh, Ireland, 13 Aug 1944.
Educ Royal S, Armagh. Debut 1966.
IRELAND (19) 1966–82.
HS 147 Ireland v Scotland, Glasgow,
1976 (103* in 2nd inns — only instance
of two centuries in match in
Ireland–Scotland fixture).
BB 5–21 Ireland v Scotland, Ayr, 1974.

ANDERSON, James Duncan
RHB, OB

Born Melbourne, Australia, 17 Dec
1931. Educ Melbourne GS; Melbourne
U; Oxford U. Debut 1955.
OXFORD UNIVERSITY (2) 1955.
HS 4* Oxford U v Warwicks, The Parks,
1955.
BB 4–68 Oxford U v Yorks, The Parks,
1955.
Australian Rules Football for Australia.

ANDERSON, Reginald Mervyn Bulford
RHB, RMF

Born Brynhyfryd, Swansea, 25 Apr
1914. Died Uplands, Swansea, 12 Aug
1972. Educ Manseltown Central S,
Swansea. Debut 1946.
GLAMORGAN (1) 1946.
No runs, no wkts.
Clubs: Llanelli, Morewoods, Swansea.

ANDERSON, Robert Wickham
RHB, LB

Born Christchurch, N Zealand, 2 Oct
1948. Debut 1967/68.
N ZEALAND DOMESTIC Canterbury (4)
1967/68, Northern Districts (6) 1969/
70, Otago (33) 1971/72–76/77, Central
Districts (30) 1977/78–81/82.
NEW ZEALAND (9) 1976/77–78. E. 1977/
78 (3). E 1978 (3); P 1976/77 (3).
OTHER TOURS N Zealand B to Australia
1971/72. N Zealand to England 1973.
HST 92 NZ v P, Lahore, 1976/77. HS 155
N Zealanders v Scotland, Dundee,
1978.
BB 4–49 Otago v Wellington, Dunedin,
1976/77.
RECORD During HST (above) added 183
for 5th wkt with M. G. Burgess, N
Zealand Test record.
Father W. McD. Anderson (New
Zealand).

ANDERSON, William Alexander
LHB, RM

Born Eastry, Kent, 27 July 1909. Died
Much Hadham, Herts, 21 Apr 1975.
Educ Charterhouse. Debut 1946.
FREE FORESTERS (1) 1946.
HS 14 Free Foresters v Cambridge U,
Fenner's, 1946.
Club: West Kent. Brother-in-law J. H.
Pawle (Essex and Cambridge U).

ANDERTON, Frederic Michael
RHB, OB

Born Agra, India, 8 Dec 1931. Educ
Sherborne; Cambridge U. Debut 1953.
CAMBRIDGE UNIVERSITY (3) 1953.
HS 38 Cambridge U v M'sex, Fenner's,
1953.

ANDREW, Christopher Robert
LHB, ROB

Born Richmond, Yorks, 18 Feb 1963.
Educ Barnard Castle S; St John's C,
Cambridge. Debut 1984.
CAMBRIDGE UNIVERSITY (9) 1984 (Blue).
HS 101* Cambridge U v Notts, Trent
Bridge, 1984.
BB 3–77 Cambridge U v Leics,
Fenner's, 1984.
Rugby: Blue and England (5 in 1984/
85).

ANDREW, Frederick James
RHB, RM

Born Southmead, Bristol, 29 May 1937.
Educ St David's C, Bristol. Debut 1959.
P.
GLOUCESTERSHIRE (21) 1959–63.
HS 6 Glos v Hants, Portsmouth, 1961
and v Warwicks, Edgbaston, 1962.
BB 5–8 (10–91 match) Glos v Kent,
Dartford, 1962.
Club: Shirehampton. Coach at Clifton
C.

ANDREW, Keith Vincent
RHB, WK

Born Oldham, Lancs, 15 Dec 1929.
Debut 1952. P.
COMBINED SERVICES (2) 1952.
NORTHAMPTONSHIRE (351) 1953–66.
Cap 1954. Capt 1962–66. Benefit
(£3762) 1963.
ENGLAND (2) 1954/55–63. WI 1963 (1).
A 1954/55 (1).
OTHER TOURS MCC to W Indies 1959/60.
Commonwealth XIs to Pakistan 1963/
64 and India 1964/65.

HST 15 E v WI, Old Trafford, 1963. HS
76 Northants v Yorks, Harrogate, 1957.
BB 2–9 Northants v Yorks, Sheffield,
1962.
RECORDS 7 dismissals in inns, Northants
v Lancs, Old Trafford, 1962, equals
record for county cricket. Record dismissals (810) for Northants.
Players v Gentlemen (1) 1962. Former
NCA Director of Coaching. MCC Hon.
member.

ANDREW, Stephen Jon Walter
RHB, RM

Born London, 27 Jan 1966. Educ Port-
chester Sec S. Debut 1984.
HAMPSHIRE (7) 1984.
HS 6* Hants v M'sex, Bournemouth,
1984.
BB 4–30 Hants v Sussex, Hove, 1984.

ANDREWS, Clifford Jack
RHB, WK

Born Swindon, Wilts, 6 Aug 1912. Died
Eastleigh, Hants, 11 Dec 1973. Debut
1938. P.
HAMPSHIRE (7) 1938–48.
HS 29 Hants v Glos, Gloucester, 1948.
Wiltshire 1953. Brother W. H. R. And-
rews (Somerset).

ANDREWS, William Harry Russell
RHB, RFM

Born Swindon, Wilts, 14 Apr 1908.
Debut 1930. P.
SOMERSET (226) 1930–47. Cap.
Testimonial 1948.
HS 80 Som v Lancs, Old Trafford, 1937.
BB 8–12 Som v Surrey, Oval, 1937.
1000 RUNS (2) 1141 @ 20.74 in 1937.
100 WKTS (4) 143 @ 20.53 in 1937.
DOUBLE (2) 1937, 1938.
Somerset coach 1955–57, 1963–70.
Devon 1950. Forfarshire 1933–34.
Clubs: Stourbridge (Birmingham
League), Ebbw Vale, Weston. Journal-
ist. Autobiography *The Hand That
Bowled Bradman* (1973). Brother C. J.
Andrews (Hants).

ANGELL, Frederick *Leslie*
RHB

Born Norton St Philip, Somerset, 29
June 1922. Debut 1947. *P from 1949*.
SOMERSET (132) 1947–56. Cap 1950.
HS 114 Som v Pakistanis, Taunton,
1954.

1000 RUNS (1) 1125 @ 22.95 in 1954.
Club: Lansdown. Coach at Monkton
Combe S.

ANGUS, Thomas
————LHB, RFM————

Born Gateshead, Co Durham, 23 Nov
1934. Debut 1956. *P.*
MIDDLESEX (7) 1956–57.
HS 18* M'sex v Kent, Dover, 1957.
BB 4–81 M'sex v Oxford U, The Parks,
1957.
Professional at Hordern, Philadelphia,
Eppleton.

ANSON, Geoffrey Frank
————RHB————

Born Sevenoaks, Kent, 8 Oct 1922. Died
Birchington, Sussex, 4 Dec 1977. Educ
Harrow; Caius C, Cambridge. Debut
1947.
CAMBRIDGE UNIVERSITY (3) 1947.
KENT (7) 1947.
HS 106 Cambridge U v M'sex, Fenner's,
1947.
Left Cambridge before University
match in 1947 to take up position in
Colonial Service. Nigeria 1949.

ANTON, John *Hamish* Hugh
————RHB, RM————

Born Kidderminster, Worcs, 19 Sept
1926. Educ Rugby; Caius C, Cambridge. Debut 1949.
CAMBRIDGE UNIVERSITY (10) 1949–50.
WORCESTERSHIRE (4) 1950.
HS 45 Cambridge U v Sussex, Fenner's,
1949.

ANTROBUS, Edward Philip
————RHB, LB————

Born Long Acre, Cradock, Cape
Province, S Africa, 28 Sept 1938. Educ
St Andrews, Grahamstown; Magdalene
C, Cambridge. Debut 1963.
CAMBRIDGE UNIVERSITY (2) 1963.
HS 31 Cambridge U v Leics, Fenner's,
1963.
Heir to Sir Philip Antrobus, 7th
Baronet.

ANURASIRI, Sangarange Don
————RHB, SLA————

Born Panadura, Sri Lanka, 25 Feb 1966.
Debut 1984.
SRI LANKA to England (4) 1984.
HS 5 Sri Lankans v Sussex, Hove, 1984.

APPLEYARD, Francis
————RHB, RFM————

Born Clifton, Yorks, 26 Sept 1905. Died
Stevenage, Herts, 11 Oct 1971. Debut
1939.
MINOR COUNTIES (2) 1939.
ESSEX (14) 1946–47.
MCC (1) 1950.
HS 15* Essex v Sussex, Hove, 1946.
BB 5–14 Essex v Glam, Chelmsford,
1946.
Hertfordshire 1932–50. Farmer and
noted agriculturist.

APPLEYARD, Robert
————RHB, RMF/OB————

Born Wibsey, Bradford, Yorks, 27 June
1924. Educ Priestman County S, Bradford. Debut 1950. *Wisden* 1952. *P.*
YORKSHIRE (133) 1950–58. Cap 1951.
Testimonial (£2000) 1959.
ENGLAND (9) 1954–56. A 1956 (1); SA
1955 (1); P 1954 (1). *A 1954/55 (4); NZ
1954/55 (2).*
HST 19* E v A, Sydney, 1954/55. HS 63
Yorks v Kent, Tunbridge Wells, 1957.
BBT 5–51 E v P, Trent Bridge, 1954. BB
8–76 Yorks v MCC, Scarborough,
1951.
100 WKTS (3) 200 @ 14.14 in 1951 —
record tally for first full season.
Missed most of 1952 and all of 1953
through illness. Players v Gentlemen (2)
1954. Yorkshire committee 1984–.
Clubs: Manningham Mills, Bowling
Old Lane, Undercliffe. Collector of
cricketana.

APTE, Arvind Laxman Rao
————RHB————

Born Bombay, India, 24 Oct 1934. Educ
Bombay U. Debut 1955/56.
INDIA DOMESTIC Universities, Bombay,
Rajasthan, 1955/56–70/71.
INDIA (1) *E 1959.*
HST 8 I v E, Headingley, 1959. HS 165
Indians v Derbys, Chesterfield, 1959.
Brother M. L. Apte (India).

ARCHER, Kenneth Alan
————RHB, OB————

Born Yeerongpilly, Queensland,
Australia, 17 Jan 1928. Educ U of
Queensland. Debut 1946/47.
AUSTRALIA DOMESTIC Queensland (58)
1946/47–56/57.
COMMONWEALTH XI (1) 1954.
AUSTRALIA (5) 1950/51–51/52. E 1950/
51 (3); WI 1951/52 (2).
TOUR Australia to S Africa 1949/50.

HST 48 A v E, Sydney, 1950/51. HS 134
Australians v Griqualand West, Kim-
berley, 1949/50.
BB 2–16 Queensland v Victoria, Mel-
bourne, 1951/52.
League professional Accrington 1954.
Brother R. G. Archer (Australia).

ARCHER, Ronald Graham
————RHB, RFM————

Born Brisbane, Queensland, Australia,
25 Oct 1933. Debut 1951/52.
AUSTRALIA DOMESTIC Queensland (35)
1951/52–58/59.
AUSTRALIA (19) 1952/53–56/57. E 1954/
55 (4); SA 1952/53 (1). *E 1953 (3), 1956
(5); WI 1954/55 (5); P 1956/57 (1).*
HST 128 A v WI, Kingston, 1954/55. HS
148 Australians v Glam, Swansea, 1956.
BBT 5–53 A v E, Oval, 1956. BB 7–56
Australians v Northants, Northampton,
1953.
Career curtailed through injury.
Brother K. A. Archer (Australia).

ARDINGTON, Anthony John
————RHB————

Born N Zealand, 26 Mar 1940. Educ
Corpus Christi C, Oxford. Debut 1965.
OXFORD UNIVERSITY (3) 1965.
HS 11 Oxford U v Derbys, The Parks,
1965.

ARENHOLD, John Adolf
————RHB, RFM————

Born Cape Town, S Africa, 9 May 1931.
Educ Diocesan C, S Africa; Western
Province U; UC, Oxford. Debut 1953.
OXFORD UNIVERSITY (24) 1953–55 (Blue
1954).
CEYLON DOMESTIC Ceylon 1956/57.
S AFRICA DOMESTIC Orange Free State
1959/60.
HS 45 OFS v Griqualand West, Bloem-
fontein, 1959/60.
BB 7–97 D. R. Jardine's XI v Oxford U,
Eastbourne, 1955.
Rugby: Ceylon.

ARIF BUTT
————RHB, RFM————

Born Lahore, India, 17 May 1944.
Debut 1960/61.
PAKISTAN DOMESTIC Lahore, Railways,
1960/61–76/77.
PAKISTAN (3) 1964/65. *A 1964/65 (1);
NZ 1964/65 (2).*
OTHER TOURS Pakistan to Ceylon 1964/
65. Pakistan to England 1967.

HST 20 P v NZ, Auckland, 1964/65. HS 180 Railways v Punjab, Lahore, 1973/74.
BBT 6–89 P v A, Melbourne, 1964/65. BB 8–45 Railways v Sargodha, Lahore, 1972/73.

ARKELL, Richard Henry Myles
—RHB, SLA—

Born Northampton, 16 June 1932. Educ Aldenham; King's C, Cambridge. Debut 1953.
CAMBRIDGE UNIVERSITY (3) 1953–55.
HS 10 Cambridge U v Free Foresters, Fenner's, 1953.
BB 3–39 same match.
Hockey: Northants. Father H. J. D. Arkell (Northants).

ARMITAGE, Alan Kenneth
—RHB, WK—

Born Nottingham, 25 Jan 1930. Educ Nottingham HS; Wadham C, Oxford. Debut 1950.
NOTTINGHAMSHIRE (5) 1950–51.
OXFORD UNIVERSITY (2) 1951.
HS 115 Oxford U v Free Foresters, The Parks, 1951.

ARMSTRONG, Gregory De Lisle
—RHB, RFM—

Born St Michael, Barbados, 11 May 1950. Debut 1973/74.
W INDIES DOMESTIC Barbados 1973/74–77/78.
GLAMORGAN (30) 1974–76.
HS 93 Barbados v Combined Islands, Castries, 1977/78.
BB 6–91 Glam v Warwicks, Swansea, 1975.
Barred from W Indian cricket for touring S Africa 1982/83 (asst-manager W Indies XI).

ARMSTRONG, Philip Alexander Nikolas
—RHB, RM—

Born Lambeth, London, 23 Jan 1962. Educ Eastbourne C; Manchester C, Oxford. Debut 1982.
OXFORD UNIVERSITY (1) 1982.
HS 34 Oxford U v Glam, Swansea, 1982.

ARMSTRONG, Robert Lloyd George
—RHB, RM—

Born Donaghloney, Co Armagh, Ireland, 22 May 1914. Died Downpatrick, Co Down, Ireland, 9 Apr 1959. Educ Portadown C. Debut 1948.
IRELAND (5) 1948–53.
HS 29* Ireland v MCC, Dublin, 1948.
BB 4–16 Ireland v Glam, Port Talbot, 1953.

ARMSTRONG, Thomas Riley
—LHB, SLA—

Born Clay Cross, Derbys, 13 Oct 1909. Debut 1929. P.
DERBYSHIRE (58) 1929–50.
HS 28* Derbys v Worcs, Chesterfield, 1934.
BB 7–36 Derbys v Glos, Buxton, 1937. Hit for five successive sixes by A. W. Wellard, Derbys v Som, Wells, 1936. Smethwick (Birmingham League).

ARNOLD, Geoffrey Graham
—RHB, RMF—

Born Balham, London, 3 Sept 1944. Educ Elliott CS, Putney Heath. Debut 1963. Wisden 1972. P.
SURREY (218) 1963–77. Cap 1967. Benefit (£15,000) 1976.
SUSSEX (77) 1978–82. Cap 1979.
ORANGE FREE STATE 1976/77.
ENGLAND (34) 1967–75. A 1972 (3), 1975 (1); WI 1973 (3); NZ 1969 (1), 1973 (3); I 1974 (2); P 1967 (2), 1974 (3). A 1974/75 (4); WI 1973/74 (3); NZ 1974/75 (2); I 1972/73 (4); P 1972/73 (3).
OTHER TOURS MCC Under-25 to Pakistan 1966/67. International XI to India and Pakistan 1967/68. MCC to Ceylon 1969/70.
HST 59 E v P, Oval, 1967. HS 73 MCC Under-25 v Central Zone, Sahiwal, 1966/67.
BBT 6–45 E v I, Delhi, 1972/73. BB 8–41 Surrey v Glos, Oval, 1967.
100 WKTS (1) 109 @ 18.22 in 1967.
Surrey coaching staff 1984.

ARNOLD, John
—RHB, SRA—

Born Cowley, Oxford, 30 Nov 1907. Died Southampton, Hants, 4 Apr 1984. Debut 1929. P.
HAMPSHIRE (396) 1929–50. Cap 1930. Joint Benefit (£1470) 1948–50.
ENGLAND (1) NZ 1931.
HST 34 E v NZ, Lord's, 1931. HS 227 Hants v Glam, Cardiff, 1932.
BB 3–34 Hants v Kent, Southampton, 1930.
1000 RUNS (14) 2261 @ 48.10 in 1934. Players v Gentlemen (5) 1931–35. Fc umpire 1961–72. Minor Counties umpire 1951. Soccer: Southampton, Fulham and England (double international).

ARNOLD, Peter
—RHB, RM—

Born Wellington, N Zealand, 16 Oct 1926. Debut 1951. P.
NORTHAMPTONSHIRE (167) 1951–60. Cap 1955.
N ZEALAND DOMESTIC Canterbury (5) 1953/54.
HS 122 Northants v Som, Taunton, 1955.
1000 RUNS (3) 1699 @ 30.89 in 1955.
Northamptonshire committee.

ARROWSMITH, Robert
—RHB, SLA—

Born Denton, Manchester, 21 May 1953. Educ Two Trees S, Denton. Debut 1976.
LANCASHIRE (43) 1976–79.
HS 39 Lancs v Derbys, Chesterfield, 1979.
BB 6–29 Lancs v Oxford U, The Parks, 1977.
Northumberland 1983–. Clubs: Milnrow, Delph.

ARSHAD PERVEZ
—RHB, RM—

Born Sargodha, Pakistan, 1 Oct 1952. Educ Government S, Sargodha; Government C, Lahore; Punjab, U. Debut 1969/70.
PAKISTAN DOMESTIC Sargodha, Lahore, Universities, Punjab U, Servis Industries, Habib Bank, Punjab, 1969/70–81/82.
TOUR Pakistan to England 1978.
HS 251* Habib Bank v Karachi Whites, Karachi, 1976/77.
BB 3–37 Sargodha v PAF, Sargodha, 1970/71.
RECORD Added 426 for 2nd wkt with Mohsin Khan, Habib Bank v Income Tax Department, Lahore, 1977/78, Pakistan fc record.
Professional: Stockport 1977.

ASGARALI, Nyron Sultan
—RHB, RAS—

Born St James, Trinidad, 28 Dec 1920. Debut 1940/41.
W INDIES DOMESTIC Trinidad 1940/41–62/63.
COMMONWEALTH XI (1) 1956.
WEST INDIES (2) E 1957.
HST 29 WI v E, Oval, 1957. HS 141* Trinidad v British Guiana, Georgetown, 1953/54.
BB 4–72 W Indians v T. N. Pearce's XI, Scarborough, 1957.
1000 RUNS (1) 1011 @ 29.73 in 1957.
Professional Enfield 1955–56. Son G. Asgarali (Trinidad).

ASH, David Leslie
—RHB, SLA—

Born Bingley, Yorks, 18 Feb 1944. Educ Fulneck S, Pudsey. Debut 1965.
YORKSHIRE (3) 1965.
HS 12 Yorks v M'sex, Scarborough, 1965.
Cumberland 1968–. Professional Keighley, Rochdale, Penrith, Lancaster.

ASHDOWN, William Henry
—RHB, RM—

Born Bromley, Kent, 27 Dec 1898. Died Rugby, Warwicks, 15 Sept 1979. Debut 1914 (G. J. V. Weigall's XII v Oxford U). P.
KENT (482) 1920–37. Cap. Benefit 1935.
HS 332 Kent v Essex, Brentwood, 1934.
BB 6–23 Kent v Glos, Maidstone, 1923.
1000 RUNS (11) 2247 @ 43.21 in 1928.
RECORDS Only player to appear in fc cricket in England before First World War and after Second (M. Leyland's XI v The Rest, Harrogate, 1947). HS (above) the highest-ever inns for Kent (included 307* on 1st day of match) and during it added 352 for 2nd wkt with F. E. Woolley, county record.
Triple centuries for Kent in consecutive seasons (332 in 1934, 305* in 1935).
Players v Gentlemen (1) 1933. Fc umpire 1947–50. Leics coach and scorer. Coach at Rugby S 1938–47.

ASHENDEN, Martin
—RHB, RMF—

Born Bexhill-on-Sea, Sussex, 4 Aug 1937. Debut 1959. P.
NORTHAMPTONSHIRE (19) 1959–61.
GLOUCESTERSHIRE (15) 1962–65.
HS 15 Northants v Glam, Northampton, 1961.
BB 4–50 Northants v Essex, Ilford, 1959.
Bedfordshire 1957–58, 1966. 10–15 inns Beds v Shropshire, 1958.

ASHMAN, John Robert
—LHB, SLA—

Born Rotherham, Yorks, 20 May 1926. Debut 1951. P.
YORKSHIRE (1) 1951.
WORCESTERSHIRE (33) 1953–54.
HS 24 Worcs v Derbys, Derby, 1953.
BB 7–111 Worcs v Oxford U, The Parks, 1954.
Clubs: Bowling Old Lane, Sheffield. Brother Allan Ashman (soccer manager).

ASHMORE, William Scott
—LHB, LMF—

Born St John's Wood, London, 29 Oct 1929. Debut 1946. P.
MIDDLESEX (2) 1946–47.
COMBINED SERVICES (1) 1948.
HS 15* M'sex v Cambridge U, Fenner's, 1947.
BB 2–37 same match.
Wife employed at Lord's library and museum and first female scorer at Lord's.

ASHWORTH, David Anthony
—RHB—

Born Ranikhet, India, 18 July 1944. Educ Uppingham; Oxford U. Debut 1966.
OXFORD UNIVERSITY (7) 1966–67.
HS 67 Oxford U v Surrey, Oval, 1967.
Clubs: I Zingari, Free Foresters, Uppingham Rovers.

ASIF AHMAD
—RHB, WK—

Born Karachi, India, 1 Apr 1942. Educ Pembroke C, Oxford. Debut 1959/60.
PAKISTAN DOMESTIC Universities, Karachi U, Karachi, Public Works Department, 1959/60–71/72.
OXFORD UNIVERSITY (18) 1963–64.
TOUR Pakistan to England 1962.
HS 148 Universities v E Pakistan, Karachi, 1959/60.
Hon. PRO for BCCP.

ASIF DIN, Mohamed (Gunga)
—RHB, LB—

Born Kampala, Uganda, 21 Sept 1960. Educ Ladywood S, Birmingham. Debut 1981.
WARWICKSHIRE (65) 1981–.
HS 102 Warwicks v M'sex, Coventry, 1982.
BB 5–100 Warwicks v Glam, Edgbaston, 1982.

ASIF IQBAL Razvi, Syed
—RHB, RM—

Born Hyderabad, Deccan, India, 6 June 1943. Educ Alyia S, Hyderabad; Osmania U, Hyderabad; SM C, Karachi. Debut 1959/60.
INDIA DOMESTIC Hyderabad 1959/60.
PAKISTAN DOMESTIC Karachi, Pakistan International Airlines, National Bank, 1961/62–79/80.
KENT (243) 1968–82. Cap 1968. Capt 1977, 1981–82. Benefit (£63,494) 1981.

PAKISTAN (58) 1964/65–79/80. E 1968/69 (3), 1972/73 (3); A 1964/65 (1); WI 1974/75 (2); NZ 1964/65 (3), 1969/70 (3), 1976/77 (3); I 1978/79 (3). *E 1967 (3), 1971 (3), 1974 (3); A 1964/65 (1), 1972/73 (3), 1976/77 (3), 1978/79 (2); WI 1976/77 (5); NZ 1964/65 (3), 1972/73 (3), 1978/79 (2); I 1979/80 (6).* Capt 6.
OTHER TOURS Pakistan Eaglets to England 1963. PIA to E Africa 1964. Pakistan A to Ceylon (Sri Lanka) 1964/65 and 1972/73.
HST 175 P v NZ, Dunedin, 1972/73. HS 196 National Bank v PIA, Lahore, 1976/77.
BBT 5–48 P v NZ, Wellington, 1964/65.
BB 6–45 Pakistan Eaglets v Cambridge U, Fenner's, 1963.
1000 RUNS (7 + 2) 1379 @ 39.40 in 1970.
RECORDS Added 190 for 9th wkt with Intikhab Alam, P v E, Oval, 1967 — world Test and Pakistan fc record. During HST (above) added 350 for 4th wkt with Mushtaq Mohammed; added 281 for 5th wkt with Javed Miandad, P v NZ, Lahore, 1976/77; added 130 for 8th wkt with Hanif Mohammed, P v E, Lord's, 1967; the first a Pakistan fc record, the others Pakistan Test records. World Series Cricket (Kerry Packer) 1977/78–78/79. Uncle Ghulam Ahmed (India).

ASIF MASOOD, Syed
—RHB, RFM—

Born Lahore, India, 23 Jan 1946. Educ Punjab U. Debut 1963/64.
PAKISTAN DOMESTIC Lahore, Punjab U, Pakistan International Airlines, 1963/64–76/77.
PAKISTAN (16) 1968/69–76/77. E 1968/69 (2), 1972/73 (1); WI 1974/75 (2); NZ 1969/70 (1). *E 1971 (3), 1974 (3); A 1972/73 (3), 1976/77 (1).*
OTHER TOURS World XI to Australia 1971/72. Pakistan to Sri Lanka 1975/76.
HST 30* P v WI, Lahore, 1974/75. HS 34 Z. A. Bhutto's XI v N Zealanders, Rawalpindi, 1976/77.
BBT 5–111 P v E, Edgbaston, 1971. BB 8–97 Punjab U v Lahore Greens, Lahore, 1967/68.
Northumberland 1975–76.

ASLETT, David George
—RHB, LB—

Born Dover, Kent, 12 Feb 1958. Educ Dover GS; Leicester U. Debut 1981.
KENT (64) 1981–. Cap 1983.
HS 221* Kent v Sri Lankans, Canterbury, 1984.
BB 4–119 Kent v Sussex, Hove, 1982.

1000 RUNS (2) 1491 @ 35.50 in 1984.
Scored 146* Kent v Hants, Bournemouth, 1981 on fc debut.

ASPINALL, Ronald
————RHB, RFM————

Born Almondbury, Yorks, 26 Oct 1918.
Debut 1946. *P.*
YORKSHIRE (37) 1946–50. Cap 1948.
HS 75* Yorks v Notts, Trent Bridge,
1948.
BB 8–47 Yorks v Northants, Rushden,
1949.
Retired through injury 1950. Fc umpire
1960–81. Durham 1951–57. Clubs:
Yeadon, Almondbury, Durham City,
Gateshead Fell. Coach at St Peter's
York 1958–59.

ASQUITH, John Patrick Kenyon
————RHB, WK————

Born Carshalton, Surrey, 1 Mar 1932.
Educ Purley GS; Pembroke C, Cambridge. Debut 1953.
CAMBRIDGE UNIVERSITY (5) 1953–54.
HS 12 Cambridge U v Worcs, Fenner's,
1953 and v Pakistanis, Fenner's, 1954.
Rugby: Blue.

ATHEY, Charles William Jeffrey
————RHB, RM————

Born Middlesbrough, Yorks, 27 Sept
1957. Educ Acklam Hall S, Middlesbrough. Debut 1976.
YORKSHIRE (151) 1976–83. Cap 1980.
GLOUCESTERSHIRE (26) 1984–.
ENGLAND (3) 1980–80/81. A 1980 (1).
WI 1980/81 (2).
OTHER TOUR D. H. Robins' XI to N
Zealand 1979/80.
HST 9 E v A, Lord's, 1980. HS 134 Yorks
v Derbys, Derby, 1982.
BB 3–38 Yorks v Surrey, Oval, 1978.
1000 RUNS (3) 1812 @ 37.75 in 1984.
Clubs: Saltburn, Bowling Old Lane.
Brother-in-law C.R. Cook (M'sex).

ATKINS, Gerald
————LHB, RLB————

Born Great Missenden, Bucks, 14 May
1938. Educ Challenors S, Amersham;
Emmanuel C, Cambridge. Debut 1958.
COMBINED SERVICES (2) 1958–59.
CAMBRIDGE UNIVERSITY (18) 1960–61
(Blue 1960).
HS 49 Cambridge U v Notts, Fenner's,
1960.
BB 2–25 Cambridge U v L.C. Steven's
XI, Eastbourne, 1960.
Buckinghamshire 1957–70. Club:
Amersham.

ATKINSON,
Colin Richard Michael
————RHB, LBG/RM————

Born Thornaby-on-Tees, Yorks, 23
July 1931. Debut 1959.
MINOR COUNTIES (1) 1959.
SOMERSET (163) 1960–67. Cap 1961.
Capt 1965–67.
HS 97 Som v Warwicks, Edgbaston,
1967.
BB 7–54 Som v Glos, Taunton, 1962.
1000 RUNS (1) 1120 @ 26.04 in 1966.
Somerset president 1976–. Northumberland 1956–58. Durham 1959. Headmaster Millfield S.

ATKINSON, Denis St Eval
————RHB, RMF/OB————

Born Christchurch, Barbados, 9 Aug
1926. Debut 1946/47.
W INDIES DOMESTIC Barbados, Trinidad,
1946/47–60/61.
WEST INDIES (22) 1948/49–57/58. E
1953/54 (4); A 1954/55 (4); P 1957/58
(1). E 1957 (2); A 1951/52 (2); NZ
1951/52 (1), 1955/56 (4); I 1948/49
(4). Capt 7.
HST 219 WI v A, Bridgetown, 1954/55.
HS as above.
BBT 7–53 WI v NZ, Auckland, 1955/56.
BB 8–58 W Indians v Essex, Ilford,
1957.
RECORD Added 347 for 7th wkt with C.
C. De Peiaza, WI v A, Bridgetown,
1954/55 — world record.
Brother E. StE. Atkinson (W Indies).

ATKINSON, Graham
————RHB, OB————

Born Lofthouse, Yorks, 29 Mar 1938.
Debut 1954. *P.*
SOMERSET (271) 1954–66. Cap 1958.
LANCASHIRE (62) 1967–69. Cap 1967.
HS 190 Som v Glam, Bath, 1960.
BB 4–63 Som v Hants, Taunton, 1960.
1000 RUNS (9) 2078 @ 37.10 in 1961.
Players v Gentlemen (1) 1961. Professional Crompton 1970–73. Rugby
League administrator on retirement
from cricket.

ATKINSON, Thomas
————RHB, RFM————

Born Millom, Cumberland, 27 Sept
1930. Debut 1957. *P.*
NOTTINGHAMSHIRE (64) 1957–60.
HS 48 Notts v Hants, Bournemouth,
1958.

BB 6–61 Notts v Derbys, Ilkeston, 1960.
Cumberland 1955, 1961–64.

AUGUST, George Lawrence
Bagley
————RHB————

Born Mymensingh, Bangalore, India,
16 Sept 1917. Educ Bedford S. Debut
1953.
MINOR COUNTIES (2) 1950–53.
HS 27 Minor Counties v MCC, Lord's,
1950.
Bedfordshire 1936–60. Hon. secretary
Beds 1969–.

AVERY, Alfred Victor
————RHB, occ SLA————

Born Beckton, Essex, 19 Dec 1914.
Educ Windsor Intermediate S. Debut
1935. *P.*
ESSEX (268) 1935–54. Cap 1937. Benefit
(£2800) 1950.
HS 224 Essex v Northants, Northampton, 1952.
1000 RUNS (7) 1890 @ 46.09 in
1948.
RECORDS Added 270 for 1st wkt with T.
C. Dodds, Essex v Surrey, Oval, 1946;
added 298 for 4th wkt with R. Horsfall,
Essex v Worcs, Clacton, 1948; both
county records.
With Toc H in India 1945.

AWORTH, Christopher John
————LHB, SLA————

Born Wimbledon, London, 19 Feb
1953. Educ Tiffin S, Kingston-upon-Thames; St Catharine's C, Cambridge.
Debut 1973.
CAMBRIDGE UNIVERSITY (29) 1973–75
(Blue 1973–75). Capt 1975.
SURREY (26) 1974–76.
HS 135 Cambridge U v Essex, Fenner's,
1975.
BB 2–23 Surrey v Worcs, Worcester,
1975.
1000 RUNS (1) 1057 @ 31.08 in
1975.

AXFORD, William Ian
————RHB, RM————

Born N Zealand, 2 Jan 1933.
Educ Christ's C, Cambridge. Debut
1960.
CAMBRIDGE UNIVERSITY (2) 1960.
HS 7 Cambridge U v Hants, Fenner's,
1960.

AZAD, Kirti Vardhan Bhagwat Jha
————RHB, OB————

Born Purnea, Bihar, India, 2 Jan 1959.
Educ Stephen C, Delhi. Debut 1976/77.
INDIA DOMESTIC Universities, Delhi,
1976/77–.
D. B. CLOSE'S XI (1) 1983.
INDIA (7) 1980/81–83/84. E 1981/82 (3);
WI 1983/84 (2); P 1983/84 (1). *NZ 1980/
81 (1)*.
HST 24 I v E, Bangalore, 1981/82. HS 186
Delhi v Tamil Nadu, Delhi, 1982/83.
BBT 2–84 I v WI, Delhi, 1983/84. BB
7–63 Board President's XI v England
XI, Nagpur, 1981/82.
Club: Lowerhouse.

AZMAT RANA
————LHB, ROB————

Born Lahore, Pakistan, 3 Nov 1951.
Debut 1969/70.
PAKISTAN DOMESTIC Bahawalpur, Pakis-
tan International Airlines, Punjab,
Lahore, Muslim Commercial Bank,
1969/70–82/83.
PAKISTAN (1) A 1979/80.
TOURS Pakistan to England 1971. Pakis-
tan to N Zealand 1972/73.
HST 49 P v A, Lahore, 1979/80. HS 206*
Punjab Greens v NWFP, Peshawar,
1977/78.
Brother Shafqat Rana (Pakistan).

B

BACCHUS, Sheik Faoud Ahumul Fasiel
──────RHB, RM──────

Born Georgetown, British Guiana, 31 Jan 1954. Educ St Theresa's Anglican S, Demerara. Debut 1971/72 (Demerara).
W INDIES DOMESTIC Guyana 1972/73–82/83. Capt 1982/83.
WEST INDIES (19) 1977/78–81/82. A 1977/78 (2). E 1980 (5); A 1981/82 (2); I 1978/79 (6); P 1980/81 (4).
OTHER TOUR Young W Indies to Zimbabwe 1981/82 (capt).
HST 250 WI v I, Kanpur, 1979/80. HS as above.
Barred from W Indian cricket for touring S Africa 1983/84 (W Indian XI).

BACHER, Aron (Ali)
──────RHB──────

Born Roodepoort, J'burg, S Africa, 24 May 1942. Educ King Edward VII HS, Transvaal; Witwatersrand U. Debut 1959/60.
S AFRICA DOMESTIC Transvaal 1959/60–73/74 (capt 1963/64–73/74).
SOUTH AFRICA (12) 1965–69/70. A 1966/67 (5), 1969/70 (4). E 1965 (3). Capt 4.
HST 73 SA v A, Port Elizabeth, 1969/70.
HS 235 Transvaal v Australians, J'burg, 1966/67.
1000 RUNS (1) 1008 @ 40.32 in 1965.
Selected as S Africa capt for cancelled tours of England 1970 and Australia 1971/72. Managing director of Transvaal cricket council. Medical practitioner.

BADCOCK, Frederick Theodore
──────RHB, RM──────

Born Abbottabad, India, 9 Aug 1897. Died Perth, W Australia, 19 Sept 1982. Educ Wellington C, N Zealand. Debut 1924/25.
N ZEALAND DOMESTIC Wellington (19), Otago (21), 1924/25–36/37.
L. PARKINSON'S XI (1) 1935.
NEW ZEALAND (7) 1929/30–32/33. E 1929/30 (3), 1932/33 (2); SA 1931/32 (2).
TOUR N Zealand Services to England 1945.

HST 64 NZ v SA, Christchurch, 1931/32.
HS 155 Wellington v Canterbury, Christchurch, 1926/27.
BBT 4–80 NZ v E, Wellington, 1929/30.
BB 7–50 Wellington v Canterbury, Christchurch, 1924/25.

BAIG, Abbas Ali
──────RHB, occ LB──────

Born Hyderabad, Deccan, India, 19 Mar 1939. Educ Aliya C, Osmania U; University C, Oxford. Debut 1954/55.
INDIA DOMESTIC Hyderabad (68) 1954/55–75/76.
OXFORD UNIVERSITY (52) 1959–62 (Blue 1959–62).
SOMERSET (23) 1960–62. Cap 1961.
INDIA (10) 1959–66/67. A 1959/60 (3); WI 1966/67 (2); P 1960/61 (3). E 1959 (2).
OTHER TOURS E. W. Swanton's XI to W Indies 1960/61. Hyderabad Blues to Ceylon 1966/67. India to England 1971.
HST 112 I v E, Old Trafford, 1959 (Test debut). HS 224* South Zone v North Zone, Delhi, 1966/67.
BB 2–26 Hyderabad v Bombay, Hyderabad, 1964/65.
1000 RUNS (3). 1821 @ 39.58 in 1959.
Scored 105 Hyderabad v Mysore, Hyderabad, 1954/55, aged 15. Gentlemen v Players (1) 1961. Brother M. A. Baig (Oxford U and Hyderabad).

BAIG, Murtuza Ali
──────RHB, occ OB──────

Born Hyderabad, Deccan, India, 8 Nov 1941. Educ Osmania U; New C, Oxford. Debut 1958/59.
INDIA DOMESTIC Hyderabad 1958/59–70/71.
OXFORD UNIVERSITY (28) 1961–64 (Blue 1962–64).
HS 103 Oxford U v Derbys, The Parks, 1962.
BB 4–44 Oxford U v Essex, The Parks, 1962.
Brother A. A. Baig (Oxford U and India).

BAILEY, David
──────RHB, OB──────

Born West Hartlepool, Co Durham, 9 Sept 1944. Educ Malvern. Debut 1968.
LANCASHIRE (27) 1968–69.
MINOR COUNTIES (5) 1973–81. Capt 1981.
HS 136 Lancs v Kent, Old Trafford, 1969.
BB 3–67 Minor Counties v Sri Lankans, Reading, 1981.
Durham 1961–68. Cheshire 1973–83. Clubs: Accrington, Northwich, Bowdon, Alderley Edge, Didsbury. Brother H. J. Bailey (Minor Counties).

BAILEY,
Sir Derrick Thomas Louis
──────RHB, RM──────

Born London, 15 Aug 1918. Educ Winchester; Christchurch C, Cambridge. Debut 1949.
GLOUCESTERSHIRE (60) 1949–52. Cap 1949. Capt 1951–52.
HS 111 Glos v Sussex, Hove, 1951.
BB 2–19 Glos v Som, Bristol, 1951.
1000 RUNS (1) 1003 @ 30.39 in 1951.
Baronet. Father Sir Abe Bailey (Transvaal; S African cricket pioneer).

BAILEY, Frederick Raymond
──────LHB──────

Born Newcastle-under-Lyme, 2 Nov 1919. Debut 1950.
MINOR COUNTIES (3) 1950–60.
HS 79 Minor Counties v Indians, Longton, Stoke-on-Trent, 1959.
Staffordshire 1939–63. Professional Porthill, Kidsgrove, Michelin, Audley.

BAILEY, Harry John
──────RHB, LM──────

Born West Hartlepool, Co Durham, 23 Apr 1940. Educ Malvern. Debut 1967.
MINOR COUNTIES (3) 1967–69.
HS 25 Minor Counties v Pakistanis, Swindon, 1967.
BB 2–20 same match.
Durham 1961–71. Club: West Hartlepool. Brother D. Bailey (Lancs).

BAILEY, Jack Arthur
————RHB, RFM————

Born Brixton, London, 22 June 1930.
Educ Christ's Hospital; UC, Oxford.
Debut 1953.
ESSEX (71) 1953–58. Cap 1954.
OXFORD UNIVERSITY (31) 1956–58 (Blue
1956–58). Capt 1958.
HS 29* Oxford U v N Zealanders, The
Parks, 1958.
BB 8–24 MCC v Ireland, Dublin, 1966.
Took 7–32 on fc debut, Essex v Notts,
Southend, 1953.
Gentlemen v Players (1) 1958. MCC
secretary 1974–. Clubs: MCC, Buck-
hurst Hill.

BAILEY, James
————LHB, SLA————

Born Shawford, Winchester, Hants, 6
Apr 1908. Debut 1927. *P.*
HAMPSHIRE (242) 1927–52. Cap. Joint
benefit (£1470) 1948–50.
HS 133 Hants v Worcs, Southampton,
1946.
BB 7–7 Hants v Notts, Southampton,
1932.
1000 RUNS (4) 1410 @ 30.00 in 1946.
100 WKTS (1) 121 @ 18.13 in 1948.
DOUBLE (1) 1948.
Players v Gentlemen (1) 1932. League
cricket 1934–38.

BAILEY, Michael John
————LHB, ROB————

Born Cheltenham, Glos, 1 Aug 1954.
Educ Cheltenham GS. Debut 1979.
HAMPSHIRE (20) 1979–82.
HS 24 Hants v Surrey, Portsmouth, 1979
and v Northants, Wellingborough,
1980.
BB 5–89 Hants v Northants, Welling-
borough, 1980.
Club: Cheltenham.

BAILEY, Raymond Reginald
————RHB, RFM————

Born St Neots, Hunts, 16 May 1944.
Debut 1964.
NORTHAMPTONSHIRE (49) 1964–72.
HS 25 Northants v M'sex, Lord's, 1971.
BB 5–25 Northants v Hants, Northamp-
ton, 1964.
Bowled unchanged in match with B. S.
Crump, Northants v Glam, Cardiff,
1967 — last instance in fc cricket.
Bedfordshire 1963, Buckinghamshire
1975–80. Clubs: Bedford Town, Milton
Keynes. Soccer: Gillingham, North-
ampton Town.

BAILEY, Robert John
————RHB, OB————

Born Biddulph, Staffs, 28 Oct 1963.
Educ Biddulph HS. Debut 1982.
NORTHAMPTONSHIRE (30) 1982–.
HS 114 Northants v Som, Northampton,
1984.
BB 3–33 Northants v Cambridge U,
Fenner's, 1983.
1000 RUNS (1) 1405 @ 37.97 in 1984.
Staffordshire 1980. Club: Knypersley.

BAILEY, Ronald Anthony
————RHB, RFM————

Born Camberwell, London, 30 July
1923. Debut 1948.
KENT (3) 1948.
Did not score.
Royal Navy 1950.

BAILEY, Trevor Edward
————RHB, RFM————

Born Westcliff, Essex, 3 Dec 1923. Educ
Dulwich; St John's C, Cambridge.
Debut 1945 (England Under-33). *Wis-
den* 1949.
ESSEX (482) 1946–67. Cap 1947. Capt
1961–66. Testimonial 1968.
CAMBRIDGE UNIVERSITY (22) 1947–48
(Blue 1947, 1948).
ENGLAND (61) 1949–58/59. A 1953 (5),
1956 (4); SA 1951 (2), 1955 (5); WI 1950
(2), 1957 (4); NZ 1949 (4), 1958 (4); P
1954 (3). *A 1950/51 (4), 1954/55 (5),
1958/59 (5); SA 1956/57 (5); WI
1953/54 (5); NZ 1950/51 (2), 1954/55
(2).*
OTHER TOURS Cavaliers to Jamaica 1963/
64. Cavaliers to W Indies 1964/65.
Prime Minister's XI v President's XI,
Bombay, 1963/64.
HST 134* E v NZ, Christchurch, 1950/
51. HS 205 Essex v Sussex, Eastbourne,
1947.
BBT 7–34 E v WI, Kingston, 1953/54. BB
10–90 Essex v Lancs, Clacton, 1949.
1000 RUNS (17) 2011 @ 46.76 in 1959.
100 WKTS (9) 133 @ 21.01 in 1961.
DOUBLES (8) 1949, 1952, 1954, 1957,
1959–62. 2011 runs @ 46.76 and 100
wkts @ 24.69 in 1959, only such performance since 1937.
Gentlemen v Players (21) 1947–62.
Essex secretary 1954–65. MCC Hon.
member. Cricket writer and broadcaster. Soccer: Blue.

BAINBRIDGE, Alfred *Brian*
————RHB, OB————

Born Middlesbrough, Yorks, 15 Oct
1932. Debut 1961. *P.*

YORKSHIRE (5) 1961–63.
HS 24 Yorks v Worcs, Worcester, 1961.
BB 6–53 (12–111 match) Yorks v Essex,
Harrogate, 1961.
Clubs: Saltburn, Middlesbrough.

BAINBRIDGE, Philip
————RHB, RM————

Born Sneyd Green, Stoke-on-Trent,
Staffs, 16 Apr 1958. Educ Hanley HS;
Borough Road C of Educ. Debut 1977.
GLOUCESTERSHIRE (122) 1977–. Cap
1981.
HS 146 Glos v N Zealanders, Bristol,
1983.
BB 6–59 Glos v Glam, Swansea, 1982.
1000 RUNS (4) 1217 @ 29.68 in 1983.
Cousin S. G. Wilkinson (Somerset).

BAIRAMIAN, Robert
————RHB————

Born Nicosia, Cyprus, 18 Mar 1935.
Educ Dover C; St Catharine's C, Cam-
bridge. Debut 1957.
CAMBRIDGE UNIVERSITY (2) 1957.
HS 24 Cambridge U v M'sex, Fenner's,
1957.
Headmaster Dover C.

BAIRSTOW, David Leslie
————RHB, WK, RM————

Born Bradford, 1 Sept 1951. Educ Han-
son GS, Bradford. Debut 1970 (while
still at school).
YORKSHIRE (330) 1970–. Cap 1973.
Benefit (£56,913) 1982. Capt 1984–.
S AFRICA DOMESTIC Griqualand West
1976/77–77/78 (capt).
ENGLAND (4) 1979–80/81. A 1980 (1);
WI 1980 (1); I 1979 (1). *WI 1980/81
(1).*
OTHER TOURS England to Australia 1978/
79 (late replacement), 1979/80.
HST 59 E v I, Oval, 1979. HS 145 Yorks
v M'sex, Scarborough, 1980.
BB 3–82 Griqualand West v Transvaal
B, J'burg, 1976/77.
1000 RUNS (2) 1102 @ 38.00 in 1983.
RECORDS 11 catches in match, Yorks v
Derbys, Scarborough, 1982, equalling
world record held by A. Long and R. W.
Marsh.
886 dismissals (770 ct, 116 st) in fc
cricket. Soccer: Bradford City.

BAKER, David William
————RHB, LBG————

Born Hull, Yorks, 26 July 1935. Debut
1961. *P.*

KENT (27) 1961–63.
NOTTINGHAMSHIRE (7) 1964–65.
HS 15 Kent v Glos, Canterbury, 1961.
BB 5–47 Kent v Essex, Colchester, 1961.
Lincolnshire 1956.

BAKER, John
—RHB, RM—

Born Weston-super-Mare, 18 May 1933. Educ Taunton S; Bristol U; Jesus C, Oxford. Debut 1953.
SOMERSET (9) 1952–54.
OXFORD UNIVERSITY (5) 1955.
COMBINED SERVICES (1) 1956.
HS 91* Oxford U v Free Foresters, The Parks, 1955.
BB 2–26 Oxford U v Free Foresters, The Parks, 1955.
Dorset 1960–70.

BAKER, Raymond Paul
—RHB, RM—

Born Carshalton, Surrey, 9 Apr 1954. Educ Wallington HS. Debut 1973.
SURREY (54) 1973–78.
HS 91 Surrey v Hants, Portsmouth, 1978.
BB 6–29 Surrey v Essex, Ilford, 1974.

BAKER, Richard Kenneth
—RHB, WK—

Born Gidea Park, Essex, 28 Apr 1952. Educ Brentwood S; Fitzwilliam C, Cambridge. Debut 1972.
ESSEX (1) 1972.
CAMBRIDGE UNIVERSITY (19) 1973–74 (Blue 1973, 1974).
HS 59* Cambridge U v Glam, Fenner's, 1973.

BALDERSTONE, John Christopher
—RHB, SLA—

Born Longwood, Huddersfield, Yorks, 16 Nov 1940. Educ Paddock County S, Huddersfield. Debut 1961. P.
YORKSHIRE (68) 1961–69.
LEICESTERSHIRE (277) 1971–. Cap 1973.
ENGLAND (2) WI 1976.
TOUR Leics XI to Zimbabwe 1980/81.
HST 35 E v WI, Headingley, 1976. HS 181* Leics v Glos, Leicester, 1984.
BBT 1–80 E v WI, Oval, 1976. BB 6–25 Leics v Hants, Southampton, 1978.
1000 RUNS (10) 1482 @ 39.00 in 1982.
RECORD Added 239* for 2nd wkt with D. I. Gower, Leics v Essex, Leicester, 1981, county record.
Past chairman of Cricketers' Association. Soccer: Huddersfield Town, Car-

lisle United, Doncaster Rovers, Queen of the South. On 15 Sept 1975 played cricket (Leics v Derbys, Chesterfield, 11.30 a.m. to 6.30 p.m.) and soccer (Doncaster Rovers v Brentford, Doncaster, 7.30 p.m. to 9.10 p.m.).

BALDRY, Dennis Oliver
—RHB, OB/RM—

Born Acton, London, 26 Dec 1931. Debut 1953. P.
MIDDLESEX (49) 1953–58.
HAMPSHIRE (85) 1959–62. Cap 1959.
HS 151 Hants v Glam, Portsmouth, 1959 (Hants debut).
BB 7–76 Hants v Lancs, Old Trafford, 1959.
1000 RUNS (1) 1715 @ 29.06 in 1959.

BAMBER, Martin John
—RHB, RM—

Born Cheam, Surrey, 7 Jan 1961. Educ Carshalton HS, Millfield. Debut 1982.
NORTHAMPTONSHIRE (13) 1982–.
HS 77 Northants v Cambridge U, Fenner's, 1983.

BANERJEE, Sarbindu Surendrakumar (Shute)
—RHB, RFM—

Born Calcutta, India, 3 Oct 1911 (other versions state 1913). Died Calcutta, India, 14 Oct 1980. Educ Scotch C, Calcutta; City C, Calcutta; Calcutta U. Debut 1931/32.
INDIA DOMESTIC Hindus, Bengal, Nawanagar, Bihar (capt 1942/43–52/53), Madhya Pradesh, 1935/36–59/60.
INDIA (1) WI 1948/49.
TOURS India to England 1936, 1946. India to Ceylon 1944/45.
HST 8 I v WI, Bombay, 1948/49. HS 138 Bihar v Bengal, Calcutta, 1952/53.
BBT 4–54 I v WI, Bombay, 1948/49. BB 8–25 Nawanagar v Maharashtra, Jamnagar, 1941/42.
RECORDS Added 249 for 10th wkt with C. T. Sarwate, Indians v Surrey, Oval, 1946 — Indian fc record and second-largest ever last-wkt stand, and only instance of numbers 10 (Sarwate 124*) and 11 (Banerjee 121) scoring centuries in same inns.
Cricket commentator 1974–77.

BANKS, David Andrew
—RHB, RM—

Born Pensnett, Staffs, 11 Jan 1961. Educ Pensnett Secondary S; Dudley Technical C. Debut 1983.

WORCESTERSHIRE (13) 1983–.
HS 100 Worcs v Oxford U, The Parks, 1983 (fc debut).

BANNISTER, Charles Stuart
—RHB, RM—

Born Redhill, Surrey, 22 May 1956. Educ Caterham S; Downing C, Cambridge. Debut 1975.
CAMBRIDGE UNIVERSITY (17) 1975–77 (Blue 1976).
HS 50 Cambridge U v Essex, Fenner's, 1976.
BB 5–50 Cambridge U v Derbys, Burton-upon-Trent, 1976.
Hertfordshire 1982–. Club: Bishop's Stortford.

BANNISTER, John David
—RHB, RFM—

Born Wolverhampton, Staffs, 23 Aug 1930. Educ King Edward's GS, Five Ways, Birmingham. Debut 1950. P.
WARWICKSHIRE (368) 1950–68. Cap 1950. Benefit (£8846) 1964.
HS 71 Warwicks v Derbys, Nuneaton, 1960.
BB 10–41 Warwicks v Combined Services, Portland Rd, Birmingham, 1959.
100 WKTS (4) 137 @ 20.83 in 1961.
Cricket journalist. Cricketers' Association treasurer 1968; chairman 1968–69; secretary 1970–.

BAPTISTE, Eldine Ashworth Elderfield
—RHB, RFM—

Born Liberta, Antigua, 12 Mar 1960. Educ All Saints, Liberta. Debut 1981.
KENT (41) 1981–.
W INDIES DOMESTIC Leeward Islands 1981/82–.
W INDIES (9) 1983/84–84. A 1983/84 (3). E 1984 (5); I 1983/84 (1).
HST 87* WI v E, Edgbaston, 1984. HS 136* Kent v Yorks, Dore, Sheffield, 1983.
BBT 3–31 WI v E, Old Trafford, 1984.
BB 5–37 Kent v Lancs, Maidstone, 1981.

BARBER, Robert William
—LHB, RALBG—

Born Withington, Manchester, 26 Sept 1935. Educ Ruthin C; Magdalene C, Cambridge. Debut 1954. Wisden 1967.
LANCASHIRE (156) 1954–62. Cap 1958. Capt 1960–61.
CAMBRIDGE UNIVERSITY (26) 1955–57 (Blue 1956, 1957).

WARWICKSHIRE (124) 1963–69. Cap 1963.
ENGLAND (28) 1960–68. A 1964 (1), 1968 (1); SA 1960 (1), 1965 (3); WI 1966 (2); NZ 1965 (3). A 1965/66 (5); SA 1964/65 (4); I 1961/62 (5); P 1961/62 (3).
OTHER TOURS MCC A to N Zealand 1960/61. E. W. Swanton's XI to W Indies 1960/61. Rest v Barbados, Bridgetown, 1966/67.
HST 185 E v A, Sydney, 1965/66. HS as above.
BBT 4–132 E v NZ, Edgbaston, 1965. BB 7–35 Lancs v Derbys, Chesterfield, 1960.
1000 RUNS (7 + 1) 1573 @ 31.46 in 1964. Gentlemen v Players (4) 1959–62. Cheshire 1952. MCC Hon. member.

BARBER, Thomas David
RHB, WK

Born Carlton-in-Lindrick, Notts, 18 Nov 1937. Educ Eton; Trinity C, Cambridge. Debut 1960.
NOTTINGHAMSHIRE (1) 1960.
FREE FORESTERS (1) 1960.
HS 3 Notts v Cambridge U, Fenner's, 1960.
Member XL Club. Great-uncle W. D. Barber (Notts).

BARBER, Wilfred
RHB, occ RAB

Born Cleckheaton, Yorks, 18 Apr 1901. Died Bradford, Yorks, 10 Sept 1968. Debut 1926. P.
YORKSHIRE (352) 1926–47. Cap 1932. Testimonial (£2958) 1946.
ENGLAND (2) SA 1935.
TOUR MCC to Australasia 1935/36.
HST 44 E v SA, Old Trafford, 1935. HS 255 Yorks v Surrey, Bramall Lane, Sheffield, 1935.
BBT 1–0 E v SA, Headingley, 1935. BB 2–1 Yorks v Worcs, Bradford, 1934.
1000 RUNS (8) 2147 @ 42.09 in 1935.
RECORDS Added 346 for 2nd wkt with M. Leyland, Yorks v M'sex, Sheffield, 1932, county record.
Players v Gentlemen (1) 1935. Coach to North Riding Education Dept. Coach/groundsman, Ashville S, Harrogate.

BARBER, William
WK

Born Dalston, London, 25 Oct 1920. Debut 1946.
COMBINED SERVICES (1) 1946.
HS 4 Combined Services v Surrey, Oval, 1946.

BARCLAY, John Robert Troutbeck
RHB, OB

Born Bonn, West Germany, 22 Jan 1954. Educ Eton. Debut 1970.
SUSSEX (241) 1970–. Cap 1976. Capt 1981–.
S AFRICA DOMESTIC Orange Free State 1978/79.
HS 119 Sussex v Leics, Hove, 1980.
BB 6–61 Sussex v Sri Lankans, Hove, 1979.
1000 RUNS (4) 1093 @ 32.14 in 1979.
Great-uncle F. G. J. Ford (M'sex and England).

BARCROFT, Peter
RHB

Born Sharneyford, nr Bacup, Lancs, 14 Aug 1929. Died Bacup, Lancs, 26 Aug 1977. Debut 1956. P.
LANCASHIRE (3) 1956.
HS 29 Lancs v Essex, Old Trafford, 1956.
Club: Bacup.

BARFORD, Michael Thomas
RHB, RM

Born Eastbourne, Sussex, 7 June 1950. Educ Eastbourne; St Catharine's C, Cambridge. Debut 1970.
CAMBRIDGE UNIVERSITY (15) 1970–71 (Blue 1970, 1971).
HS 95 Cambridge U v Sussex, Horsham, 1971.

BARING, Amyas Evelyn Giles
RHB, RF

Born Roehampton, London, 21 Jan 1910. Educ Gresham's Holt; Magdalene C, Cambridge. Debut 1930.
CAMBRIDGE UNIVERSITY (2) 1930–31.
HAMPSHIRE (62) 1930–39.
MCC (3) 1935–46.
HS 46 Hants v Som, Bournemouth, 1939.
BB 9–26 Hants v Essex, Colchester, 1931.
Gentlemen v Players (2) 1931–34.

BARKER, Andrew Hunter
LHB, SLA

Born Salisbury, Wiltshire, 7 Aug 1945. Educ Charterhouse; Keble C, Oxford. Debut 1964.
OXFORD UNIVERSITY (44) 1964–67 (Blue 1964, 1965, 1967).
HS 94 Oxford U v Glam, The Parks, 1967.

BB 5–42 Oxford U v Som, The Parks, 1967.
Wiltshire 1966–73. Club: Arabs.

BARKER, Anthony Royston Paul
RHB, ROB

Born Maybank, Newcastle-under-Lyme, Staffs, 30 May 1947. Debut 1967.
WORCESTERSHIRE (27) 1967–69.
HS 67 Worcs v Lancs, Southport, 1969. Staffordshire 1970. Birmingham League for Dudley, Walsall, Kidderminster, Duport. Professional: Burslem.

BARKER, Gordon
RHB, occ RM

Born Bramley, Leeds, Yorks, 6 July 1931. Debut 1954. P.
ESSEX (444) 1954–71. Cap 1955. Benefit (£2400) 1965. Testimonial 1971.
HS 181* Essex v Kent, Colchester, 1961.
BB 2–34 Essex v Northants, Northampton, 1969.
1000 RUNS (15) 1741 @ 36.27 in 1960.
107* on fc debut, Essex v Canadians, Clacton, 1954. Players v Gentlemen (1) 1956. Soccer: Southend United.

BARKER, Maurice Percy
RHB, RFM

Born Leamington Spa, Warwicks, 4 Feb 1917. Debut 1946.
WARWICKSHIRE (5) 1946.
HS 17 Warwicks v Sussex, Hove, 1946.
BB 7–68 Warwicks v Yorks, Edgbaston, 1946.

BARKER, Philip David
RHB, LM/SLA

Born Edmonton, London, 22 Sept 1951. Educ Latymer GS, Edmonton; Northgate GS, Ipswich; Mansfield C, Oxford. Debut 1974.
OXFORD UNIVERSITY (1) 1974.
HS 14 Oxford U v Notts, The Parks, 1974.
Suffolk 1972–76. Hockey: Blue and Suffolk.

BARKHAM, Frederick
RHB, RM

Born Scarborough, Yorks, 26 Oct 1905. Debut 1948.
SCOTLAND (2) 1948–49.
HS 3* Scotland v Yorks, Hull, 1949.

BARLING, Henry Thomas
—RHB—

Born Kensington, London, 1 Sept 1906.
Debut 1927. *P.*
SURREY (389) 1927–48. Cap 1928. Joint
benefit 1946.
HS 269 Surrey v Hants, Southampton,
1933.
BB 3–46 Surrey v Oxford U, Oval, 1933.
1000 RUNS (9) 2014 @ 43.78 in 1946.
Coach at Harrow 1949–66. Known as T.
H. Barling.

BARLOW, Alfred
—RHB, WK—

Born Little Lever, Lancs, 31 Aug 1915.
Died Middleton, Lancs, 9 May 1983.
Debut 1947. *P.*
LANCASHIRE (74) 1947–51. Cap 1950.
TOUR Commonwealth XI to India and
Ceylon 1950/51.
HS 44 Lancs v Derbys, Old Trafford,
1949.
Club: Middleton (Central Lancs
League).

BARLOW, Edgar John
—RHB, RMF, former WK—

Born Pretoria, S Africa, 12 Aug 1940.
Educ Pretoria HS; Witwatersrand U.
Debut 1959/60.
S AFRICA DOMESTIC Transvaal, Eastern
Province, Western Province (capt 79
times, a record for Currie Cup), Boland
(capt), 1959/60–82/83.
DERBYSHIRE (60) 1976–78. Cap 1976.
Capt 1976–78.
SOUTH AFRICA (30) 1961/62–69/70. E
1964/65 (5); A 1966/67 (5), 1969/70 (4);
NZ 1961/62 (5). *E 1965 (3); A 1963/64
(5); NZ 1963/64 (3).*
OTHER TOURS Rest of World to England
1970 (replaced cancelled S Africa tour).
International XI to S Africa 1974/75.
HST 201 SA v A, Adelaide, 1963/64. HS
217 Derbys v Surrey, Ilkeston, 1976.
BBT 5–85 SA v A, Cape Town, 1966/67.
BB 7–24 W Province v Natal, Durban,
1972/73.
1000 RUNS (2 + 1) 1900 @ 63.33 in
Australasia 1963/64.
RECORDS During HST (above) added 341
for 3rd wkt with R. G. Pollock, S
African fc record.
Hat-trick (4 wkts in 5 balls) Rest of
World v England, Headingley, 1970.
Professional: Accrington 1964. World
Series Cricket (Kerry Packer 1977/
78–78/79).

BARLOW, Graham Derek
—LHB, RM—

Born Folkestone, Kent, 26 Mar 1950.
Educ Ealing GS; Loughborough, C.
Debut 1969.
MIDDLESEX (214) 1969–. Cap 1976.
ENGLAND (3) 1976/77–77. A 1977 (1). *I
1976/77 (2).*
HST 7* E v I, Calcutta, 1976/77. HS 177
M'sex v Lancs, Southport, 1981.
1000 RUNS (6) 1545 @ 48.28 in 1983.
RECORD Added 367* for 1st wkt with W.
N. Slack, M'sex v Kent, Lord's, 1981,
county record.
Club: Brentham. Rugby: Rosslyn Park.

BARNARD, Henry *Michael*
—RHB, RM—

Born Portsmouth, Hants, 18 July 1933.
Educ Portsmouth GS. Debut 1952. *P.*
HAMPSHIRE (276) 1952–66. Cap 1955.
HS 128* Hants v MCC, Lord's, 1956 and
128 v Indians, Bournemouth, 1959.
BB 3–35 Hants v Oxford U, The Parks,
1954.
1000 RUNS (1) 1114 @ 27.17 in 1962.
Soccer: Portsmouth.

BARNES, Frederic Barrie
—LHB, WK—

Born Kingwilliamstown, S Africa, 4
May 1923. Educ Michaelhouse; Christ's
C, Cambridge. Debut 1948.
CAMBRIDGE UNIVERSITY (2) 1948.
HS 39 Cambridge U v Sussex, Fenner's,
1948.

BARNES, Robert James
—LHB, SLA—

Born Armagh, Co Armagh, Ireland, 25
Apr 1911. Educ RS, Armagh; Dublin U.
Debut 1930.
IRELAND (8) 1930–47.
HS 48 Ireland v Scotland, Greenock,
1946.
BB 4–18 same match.
Club: Waringstown, Armagh. Rugby:
Ireland (1). Clerk in Holy Orders.
Brother J. H. Barnes (Ireland).

BARNES, Sidney George
—RHB, LB, occ WK—

Born Charters Towers, Queensland,
Australia, 5 June 1916. Died, by own
hand, Collaroy, Sydney, NSW,
Australia, 16 Dec 1973. Debut 1936/37.
AUSTRALIA DOMESTIC New South Wales
(56) 1936/37–52/53.

AUSTRALIA (13) 1938–48. E 1946/47 (4);
I 1947/48 (3). *E 1938 (1), 1948 (4); NZ
1945/46 (1).*
HST 234 A v E, Sydney, 1946/47. HS as
above.
BBT 2–25 A v I, Melbourne, 1947/48. BB
3–0 Australians v Canterbury, Canterbury, 1945/46.
1000 RUNS (1) 1354 @ 56.41 in 1948.
RECORD During HS (above) added 405 for
5th wkt with D. G. Bradman, world fc
record.
Professional: Burnley 1947 (resigned in
July). Cricket writer; *Eyes on The Ashes*
(1953), *It Isn't Cricket* (1953), *The Ashes
Ablaze* (1955). Recognized as one of
cricket's 'eccentrics'.

BARNES, Terry Peter
—RHB, WK—

Born Coventry, Warwicks, 13 Nov
1933. Educ King Henry VIII S,
Coventry. Debut 1956. *P.*
WARWICKSHIRE (1) 1956.
HS 7 Warwicks v Scotland, Edgbaston,
1956.

BARNETT, Benjamin Arthur
—LHB, WK—

Born Auburn, East Melbourne,
Australia, 23 Mar 1908. Died New-
castle, NSW, Australia, 27 June 1979.
Educ Scotch C, Melbourne. Debut
1929/30.
AUSTRALIA DOMESTIC Victoria (73) 1929/
30–46/47.
COMMONWEALTH XI (1) 1961.
AUSTRALIA (4) *E 1938.*
OTHER TOURS Australia to England 1934.
Australia to S Africa 1935/36. Com-
monwealth XI to India 1953/54 (capt).
HST 57 A v E, Headingley, 1938. HS 131
Victoria v Tasmania, Launceston, 1929/
30.
Gentlemen v Players (2) 1954–55.
Buckinghamshire 1951–64 (capt).
Australian delegate to ICC for 20 years;
also delegate to International Lawn
Tennis Federation and to Imperial Ser-
vicemen's Legion. Awarded Australian
Medal 1977.

BARNETT, Charles John
—RHB, RM—

Born Cheltenham, Glos, 3 July 1910.
Educ Wycliffe C. Debut 1927. *Wisden
1937. P from 1929.*
GLOUCESTERSHIRE (424) 1927–48. Cap.
Benefit (£4164) 1947.
ENGLAND (20) 1933–48. A 1938 (3), 1948
(1); SA 1947 (3); WI 1933 (1); NZ 1937
(3); I 1936 (1). *A 1936/37 (5); I 1933/34
(3).*

OTHER TOUR Commonwealth XI to India 1953/54.
HST 129 E v A, Adelaide, 1936/37. HS 259 MCC v Queensland, Brisbane, 1936/37.
BB 6–17 Glos v Essex, Clacton, 1936.
1000 RUNS (12 + 1) 2489 @ 40.14 in 1937.
Hit 11 sixes in inns of 194, Glos v Som, Bath, 1934. During inns of 126, E v A, Trent Bridge, 1938, 98* at lunch, reaching century first ball afterwards.
Players v Gentlemen (9) 1933–47. Professional: Rochdale, Longton, Mitchells and Butlers. Coach at Wycliffe C. MCC Hon. member. Father C. S. Barnett, uncles E. P. and P. P. Barnett (all Glos).

BARNETT, Kim John
——————RHB, LB/RM——————

Born Stoke-on-Trent, Staffs, 17 July 1960. Educ Leek HS. Debut 1979.
DERBYSHIRE (122) 1979–. Cap 1982. Capt 1983–.
S AFRICA DOMESTIC Boland 1982/83.
TOUR D. H. Robins' XI to N Zealand 1979/80.
HS 144 Derbys v M'sex, Derby, 1984.
BB 4–76 Derbys v Warwicks, Edgbaston, 1980.
1000 RUNS (2) 1734 @ 45.63 in 1984.
Club: Leek.

BARNWELL, Charles John Patrick
——————RHB——————

Born Stoke-on-Trent, Staffs, 23 June 1914. Educ Repton. Debut 1935.
SOMERSET (69) 1935–48. Cap.
HS 83 Som v Hants, Taunton, 1939.
Club: Neston. Nephew L. M. L. Barnwell (Somerset).

BARNWELL, Lionel *Michael* Lowry
——————RHB, RM——————

Born Crewkerne, Som, 12 Aug 1943. Educ Repton; Christ's C, Cambridge. Debut 1965.
CAMBRIDGE UNIVERSITY (4) 1965–66.
SOMERSET (6) 1967–68.
S AFRICA DOMESTIC Eastern Province 1969/70–70/71.
HS 74 E Province v Transvaal, J'burg, 1969/70.
Soccer: Blue (capt). Uncle C. J. P. Barnwell (Somerset).

BARR, Douglas
——————RHB, RFM——————

Born Edinburgh, Scotland, 1 Feb 1935. Educ Melville C. Debut 1954.
SCOTLAND (41) 1954–70.
HS 86 Scotland v MCC, Glasgow, 1967.
BB 6–89 Scotland v Warwicks, Edgbaston, 1967.

BARRACLOUGH, Eric Scott
——————RHB, RFM——————

Born Bradford, Yorks, 30 Mar 1923. Educ Priestman S, Bradford. Debut 1949. P.
YORKSHIRE (2) 1949–50.
HS 24* Yorks v MCC, Lord's, 1949.
BB 2–39 Yorks v Northants, Northampton, 1950.
Clubs: Bradford, Undercliffe. RAF.

BARRATT, Roy James
——————LHB, SLA——————

Born Leicester, 3 May 1942. Debut 1961. P.
LEICESTERSHIRE (70) 1961–70.
HS 39 Leics v Yorks, Leicester, 1961.
BB 7–35 Leics v Glos, Leicester, 1969.

BARRETT, Arthur George
——————RHB, LBG——————

Born Kingston, Jamaica, 4 Apr 1944 (not 1945). Debut 1966/67.
W INDIES DOMESTIC Jamaica 1966/67–80/81.
WEST INDIES (6) 1970/71–74/75. E 1973/74 (2); I 1970/71 (2). I 1974/75 (2).
OTHER TOUR Jamaica to England 1970.
HST 19 WI v I, Port of Spain, 1970/71.
HS 102* Jamaica v Combined Islands, Castries, 1969/70 (also took 10–82 in match).
BBT 3–43 WI v I, Port of Spain, 1971/72.
BB 7–90 Jamaica v Cavaliers, Kingston, 1969/70.

BARRETT, Peter
——————LHB——————

Born Winchester, Hants, 3 June 1955. Died, in road traffic accident, Everton, Hants, 28 Oct 1983.
HAMPSHIRE (6) 1975–76.
HS 26 Hants v Som, Bournemouth, 1976.

BARRICK, Desmond William
——————RHB, LBG——————

Born Fitzwilliam, Yorks, 28 Apr 1926. Debut 1949. P.

NORTHAMPTONSHIRE (267) 1949–60. Cap 1952. Benefit (£3051) 1960.
TOURS Commonwealth XI to India 1953/54. Duke of Norfolk's XI to Jamaica 1957.
HS 211 Northants v Essex, Northampton, 1952.
BB 5–71 Northants v Essex, Chelmsford, 1951.
1000 RUNS (7) 1570 @ 37.38 in 1952.
RECORD During HS (above) added 347 for 5th wkt with D. Brookes, county record.
Players v Gentlemen (1) 1953. Clubs: Hemsworth Colliery, Spen Victoria, Todmorden, Knottingley.

BARRINGTON, Kenneth Frank
——————RHB, LBG——————

Born Reading, Berks, 24 Nov 1930. Died Needham's Point, Bridgetown, Barbados, 14 Mar 1981. Debut 1953. *Wisden 1959. P.*
SURREY (362) 1953–68. Cap 1955. Benefit (£10,656) 1964.
ENGLAND (82) 1955–68. A 1961 (5), 1964 (5), 1968 (3); SA 1955 (2), 1960 (4), 1965 (3); WI 1963 (5), 1966 (2); NZ 1965 (2); I 1959 (5), 1967 (3); P 1962 (4), 1967 (3). *A 1962/63 (5), 1965/66 (5); SA 1964/65 (5); WI 1959/60 (5), 1967/68 (5); NZ 1962/63 (3); I 1961/62 (5), 1963/64 (1); P 1961/62 (2).*
OTHER TOURS MCC A to Pakistan 1955/56. Surrey to Rhodesia 1959/60. Commonwealth XI to S Africa and Rhodesia 1960/61.
HST 256 E v A, Old Trafford, 1964 (batted 683 mins, second-longest fc inns by Englishman). HS as above.
BBT 3–4 E v SA, Cape Town, 1964/65. BB 7–40 MCC v Griqualand West, Kimberley, 1964/65.
1000 RUNS (12 + 3) 2499 @ 54.32 in 1959.
RECORDS Added 369 for 2nd wkt with J. H. Edrich, E v NZ, Headingley, 1965 — record for any wkt in E–NZ Tests. First player to score Test centuries on all six current England Test grounds (he scored only six Test centuries in England).
Players v Gentlemen (7) 1955–62. Retired from fc cricket in 1968 after heart attack. Died of heart attack while assistant-manager England in West Indies 1980/81. Test selector 1975–80. MCC Hon. member. CWC Best Young Cricketer of 1955.

BARRINGTON, William Edward *James*
——————RHB——————

Born Carshalton, Surrey, 4 Jan 1960. Educ Lancing C; St Catharine's C, Cambridge. Debut 1982.

CAMBRIDGE UNIVERSITY (4) 1982 (Blue).
HS 59 Cambridge U v Essex, Fenner's,
1982.
Squash: Blue.

BARRON, William
—————LHB, occ WK—————

Born Herrington, Co Durham, 26 Oct
1917. Debut 1945. *P.*
LANCASHIRE (1) 1945.
NORTHAMPTONSHIRE (118) 1946–51.
Cap 1946.
HS 161* Northants v Cambridge U,
Fenner's, 1948.
1000 RUNS (2) 1123 @ 26.11 in 1946.
Durham 1937–45. Clubs: Philadelphia,
British Timken. Soccer: Bishop Auck-
land, Northampton Town, Wolver-
hampton Wanderers.

BARTELS, Clarence Wilfred (Bob)
—————RHB, RFM—————

Born Colombo, Ceylon, 24 June 1922.
CEYLON DOMESTIC Ceylon 1952/53–53/
54.
COMMONWEALTH XI (2) 1957–58.
TOUR Ceylon to India 1952/53.
HS 88 Ceylon v Madras, Colombo, 1953/
54.
BB 3–24 same match.
Professional: Werneth, Ashton, Lower-
house, Mill Hill Park, Walsden,
Newcastle and Hartshill, Great Chell,
Marsden.

BARTLETT, Hugh Tryon
—————LHB—————

Born Balaghat, India, 7 Oct 1914. Educ
Dulwich; Pembroke C, Cambridge.
Debut 1933. *Wisden* 1939.
SURREY (3) 1933–35.
CAMBRIDGE UNIVERSITY (35) 1934–36
(Blue 1934–36). Capt 1936.
SUSSEX (152) 1937–49. Cap 1938. Capt
1947–49.
TOUR MCC to S Africa 1938/39.
HS 183 Cambridge U v Notts, Fenner's,
1935.
1000 RUNS (4) 1548 @ 57.33 in 1938.
Gentlemen v Players (3) 1935–39.
Selected MCC to India 1939/40 (can-
celled due to war). President Sussex
1977–79.

BARTLETT, John Norton
—————RHB, SLA—————

Born Mickleover, Derbys, 16 June
1928. Educ Chichester; Lincoln C, Oxford. Debut 1946.

OXFORD UNIVERSITY (32) 1946–51 (Blue
1946, 1951).
SUSSEX (7) 1946–50.
COMBINED SERVICES (4) 1947–48.
TOUR MCC to Canada 1951.
HS 28 Oxford U v Yorks, The Parks,
1949.
BB 5–77 Oxford U v Hants, The Parks,
1949.
Gentlemen v Players (1) 1946. Clubs:
Free Foresters, I Zingari.

BARTON, Michael Richard
—————RHB—————

Born Dereham, Norfolk, 14 Oct 1914.
Educ Winchester; Oriel C, Oxford.
Debut 1935.
OXFORD UNIVERSITY (28) 1935–37 (Blue
1936, 1937).
COMBINED SERVICES (1) 1946.
SURREY (110) 1948–54. Cap 1948. Capt
1949–51.
HS 192 Oxford U v Glos, The Parks,
1937.
1000 RUNS (3) 1187 @ 22.82 in 1948.
Norfolk 1935–47. Clubs: The Mote,
Free Foresters.

BARWELL, Terence Ian
—————RHB, occ WK—————

Born Bloemhof, Transvaal, S Africa, 29
Apr 1937. Educ Rondesbosch HS; St
Luke's C, Exeter. Debut 1959. *P.*
SOMERSET (43) 1959–68.
MINOR COUNTIES (1) 1973.
HS 84* Som v Glam, Weston-super-
Mare, 1965.
Wiltshire 1971–75. Clubs: Alme, Fish
Hook (both Cape Town), Milterton,
Taunton, Street, Morlands, St Thomas's
Exeter, Sidmouth, Savernake Forest,
Malmesbury, Heathcote. Rugby: Taun-
ton (capt), S African Schools 1956.

BARWICK, Stephen Royston
—————RHB, RM—————

Born Neath, Glamorgan, 6 Sept 1960.
Educ Dwr-y-Felin CS. Debut 1981.
GLAMORGAN (47) 1981–.
HS 25 Glam v Derbys, Derby, 1984.
BB 8–42 Glam v Worcs, Worcester, 1983.

BASKERVYLE-GLEGG, John
—————RHB, WK—————

Born Windsor, Berkshire, 10 Nov 1940.
Educ Eton. Debut 1962.
COMBINED SERVICES (1) 1962.
HS 35 Combined Services v Ireland, Bel-
fast, 1962.
Club: I Zingari.

BATES, Donald Lawson
—————RHB, RMF—————

Born Hove, Sussex, 10 May 1933. Educ
Hove GS. Debut 1950. *P.*
SUSSEX (315) 1950–71. Cap 1957. Benefit
(£8000) 1968.
HS 37* Sussex v Kent, Tunbridge Wells,
1960.
BB 8–51 Sussex v Essex, Hove, 1966.
100 WKTS (3) 113 @ 22.65 in 1961.
Soccer: Brighton and Hove Albion.

BAXTER, Austin Godfrey
—————RHB, RM—————

Born West Bridgford, Nottingham, 21
Sept 1931. Educ Ratcliffe C; Notting-
ham U. Debut 1952.
NOTTINGHAMSHIRE (13) 1952–53.
HS 98 Notts v Essex, Southend, 1953.
UAU 1954. Hockey: Nottinghamshire.

BAYLEY, Martin George
—————RHB, SLA—————

Born Leamington Spa, Warwicks, 10
July 1952. Debut 1969.
WARWICKSHIRE (2) 1969.
HS 1* Warwicks v Scotland, Edgbaston,
1969.
BB 2–54 same match.

BAYLIS, Keith Rodney
—————RHB, LB—————

Born Redditch, Worcs, 5 Nov 1947.
Educ Ellesmere C. Debut 1966.
WORCESTERSHIRE (6) 1966–67.
HS 26 Worcs v Cambridge U, Fenner's,
1966.
BB 4–112 Worcs v Essex, Worcester,
1967.
Club: Mitchells and Butlers.

BEAR, Michael John
—————LHB, RLB—————

Born Brentwood, Essex, 23 Feb 1934.
Educ Brentwood Sec M. Debut 1954. *P.*
ESSEX (322) 1954–68. Cap 1958. Benefit
1968.
HS 137 Essex v Glam, Cardiff, 1967.
1000 RUNS (4) 1833 @ 32.15 in 1966.
Canterbury (N Zealand) coach 1960/61.
Coached in Argentina 1958.

BEARD, Graeme Robert
—————RHB, RM/OB—————

Born Auburn, New South Wales,
Australia, 19 Aug 1950. Debut 1975/76.

AUSTRALIA DOMESTIC New South Wales (39) 1975/76–82/83.
AUSTRALIA (3) *P 1979/80.*
OTHER TOURS Australia to Sri Lanka 1980/81. Australia to England 1981.
HST 49 A v P, Lahore, 1979/80. HS 75 NSW v Victoria, Melbourne, 1975/76 and v W Australia, Perth, 1981/82.
BBT 1–26 A v P, Lahore, 1979/80. BB 5–33 NSW v Queensland, Lismore, 1979/80.

BEAUMONT, David John
RHB

Born West Bridgford, Nottingham, 17 Sept 1944. Educ West Bridgford GS; Bramshill C; Wolfson C, Cambridge. Debut 1977.
CAMBRIDGE UNIVERSITY (11) 1977–78 (Blue 1978).
HS 44 Cambridge U v Yorks, Fenner's, 1977.
Police inspector at Cambridge on Home Office scholarship. Club: Notts Police.

BEAUMONT, Harold
RHB, RM

Born Huddersfield, Yorks, 14 Oct 1916. Debut 1946. *P.*
YORKSHIRE (28) 1946–47.
HS 60 Yorks v Sussex, Bradford, 1947.
BB 4–31 Yorks v Kent, Canterbury, 1946.
Clubs: Thongsbridge, Spen Victoria, Crompton.

BECK, Geoffrey Edward
RHB, OB

Born Wisbech, Cambridgeshire, 16 June 1918. Educ Whitgift; Mansfield C, Oxford. Debut 1946.
OXFORD UNIVERSITY (3) 1946.
HS 50 Oxford U v Surrey, Guildford, 1946.
Oxfordshire 1951. War-time Blue 1945. Non-conformist minister.

BEDDOW, Alan Michael
RHB, RM

Born St Helens, Lancs, 12 Oct 1941. Educ Cowley GS, St Helens. Debut 1962. *P.*
LANCASHIRE (32) 1962–66.
HS 112* Lancs v Oxford U, The Parks, 1965.
BB 3–10 Lancs v Derbys, Southport, 1965.
Club: Blackhall (professional). Rugby League: St Helens.

BEDFORD, Philip *Ian*
RHB, LBG

Born Friern Barnet, M'sex, 11 Feb 1930. Died, after collapsing at the wicket, Wanstead, 18 Sept 1966. Educ Woodhouse GS, Finchley, London. Debut 1947.
MIDDLESEX (65) 1947–62. Cap 1948. Capt 1961–62.
HS 75* M'sex v Glos, Gloucester, 1961.
BB 6–52 M'sex v Yorks, Bradford, 1948.
Club: Finchley.

BEDI, Bishansingh Giansingh
RHB, SLA

Born Amritsar, India, 25 Sept 1946. Educ St Francis C, Amritsar; Punjab U. Debut 1961/62.
INDIA DOMESTIC Northern Punjab, Delhi (capt 1969/70–80/81), 1961/62–80/81.
NORTHAMPTONSHIRE (110) 1972–77. Cap 1972.
INDIA (67) 1966/67–79. E 1972/73 (5), 1976/77 (5); A 1969/70 (5); WI 1966/67 (2), 1974/75 (4), 1978/79 (3); NZ 1969/70 (3), 1976/77 (3). *E 1967 (3), 1971 (3), 1974 (3), 1979 (3); A 1967/68 (2), 1977/78 (5); WI 1970/71 (5), 1975/76 (4); NZ 1967/68 (4), 1975/76 (2); P 1978/79 (3).* Capt 22.
OTHER TOURS India to E Africa 1967. World XI to Australia 1971/72. International XI to Pakistan 1981/82.
HST 50* I v NZ, Kanpur, 1976/77. HS 61 Delhi v Jammu and Kashmir, Srinigar, 1970/71 and Northants v Glos, Northampton, 1974.
BBT 7–98 I v A, Calcutta, 1969/70. BB 7–5 (13–34 match) Delhi v Jammu and Kashmir, Delhi, 1974/75.
100 WKTS (2) 112 @ 24.64 in 1974.
RECORD First Indian to take 200 Test wkts.

BEDSER, Alec Victor
RHB, RFM

Born Reading, Berkshire, 4 July 1918. Debut 1939. *Wisden 1947. P.*
SURREY (371) 1939–60. Cap 1946. Acting capt 1960 (P. B. H. May ill). Benefit (£12,866) 1953.
ENGLAND (51) 1946–55. A 1948 (5), 1953 (5); SA 1947 (2), 1951 (5), 1955 (1); WI 1950 (3); NZ 1949 (2); I 1946 (3), 1952 (4); P 1954 (2). *A 1946/47 (5), 1950/51 (5), 1954/55 (1); SA 1948/49 (5); NZ 1946/47 (1), 1950/51 (2).*
OTHER TOURS C. G. Howard's XI to India 1956/57. Surrey to Rhodesia 1959/60.
HST 79 E v A, Headingley, 1948. HS 126 Surrey v Som, Taunton, 1947.

BBT 7–44 E v A, Trent Bridge, 1953. BB 8–18 Surrey v Notts, Oval, 1952 and v Warwicks, Oval, 1953.
100 WKTS (11) 162 @ 16.67 in 1953.
RECORDS First bowler to take 200 Test wkts for England.
Players v Gentlemen (12) 1947–55. Assistant manager MCC to Australasia 1962/63; manager MCC to Australasia 1974/75; manager England to Australia 1979/80. England Test selector 1962–82; chairman 1969–81 — both record runs. OBE and CBE for services to cricket. Twin brother E. A. Bedser (Surrey).

BEDSER, Eric Arthur
RHB, OB

Born Reading, Berkshire, 4 July 1918. Debut 1939. *P.*
SURREY (444) 1939–61. Cap 1947. Benefit (£7700) 1958.
TOURS MCC to Australia 1950/51 (companion for brother, but played one match). Surrey to Rhodesia 1959/60.
HS 163 Surrey v Notts, Oval, 1949.
BB 7–33 Surrey v Leics, Oval, 1955.
1000 RUNS (6) 1740 @ 34.11 in 1949.
Players v Gentlemen (2) 1954–55. Match double (71, 30 and 7–142, 3–89) Surrey v Glos, Oval, 1951. Twin brother A. V. Bedser (Surrey and England).

BEET, Gordon Albert
RHB, OB

Born Heanor, Derbys, 5 May 1939. Debut 1956. *P.*
DERBYSHIRE (6) 1956–61.
HS 17 Derbys v Essex, Chelmsford, 1961.
Grandfather George Beet and uncle G. H. C. Beet (both Derbys).

BEGBIE, Denis Warburton
RHB, LB

Born Middelburg, Transvaal, S Africa, 12 Dec 1914. Debut 1933/34.
S AFRICA DOMESTIC Transvaal 1933/34–49/50.
SOUTH AFRICA (5) 1948/49–49/50. E 1948/49 (3); A 1949/50 (2).
TOUR S Africa to England 1947.
HST 48 SA v E, Durban, 1948/49. HS 207* Transvaal v OFS, J'burg, 1937/38.
BBT 1–38 SA v A, Port Elizabeth, 1949/50. BB 7–96 (13–174 match) Transvaal v E Province, J'burg, 1936/37.

BELL, David Lauder
RHB

Born Edinburgh, Scotland, 28 Apr 1949. Educ George Watson's; Oxford U. Debut 1971.
OXFORD UNIVERSITY (3) 1971.
SCOTLAND (4) 1979–81.
HS 60 Scotland v Ireland, Dublin, 1981.

BELL, Ronald Victor
LHB, SLA

Born Chelsea, London, 7 Jan 1931. Debut 1952. *P.*
MIDDLESEX (5) 1952–54.
SUSSEX (183) 1957–64. Cap 1961.
HS 53* Sussex v Kent, Hastings, 1962.
BB 8–54 Sussex v Notts, Trent Bridge, 1963.
Norfolk 1967–69. Club: Arbroath 1956. Professional coach at City of London S 1966. Soccer: Chelsea.

BELLE, Brian Henry
RHB, RM

Born Woodford Green, Essex, 7 Apr 1914. Educ Forest S; Keble C, Oxford. Debut 1934.
MCC (1) 1934.
OXFORD UNIVERSITY (12) 1935–36 (Blue 1936).
ESSEX (26) 1935–37.
MINOR COUNTIES (2) 1949–50.
TOUR Oxford and Cambridge Universities to Jamaica 1938/39.
HS 70 Oxford U v Surrey, Oval, 1936.
Suffolk 1946–57, now president. Club: Southgate.

BENAUD, Richard (Richie)
RHB, LBG

Born Penrith, NSW, Australia, 6 Oct 1930. Educ Paramatta HS. Debut 1948/49. *Wisden 1962.*
AUSTRALIA DOMESTIC New South Wales (86) 1948/49–63/64. Capt 32.
AUSTRALIA (63) 1951/52–63/64. E 1954/55 (5), 1958/59 (5), 1962/63 (5); SA 1952/53 (4), 1963/64 (4); WI 1951/52 (1), 1960/61 (5). *E 1953 (3), 1956 (5), 1961 (4); SA 1957/58 (5); WI 1954/55 (5); I 1956/57 (3), 1959/60 (5); P 1956/57 (1), 1959/60 (3).* Capt 28.
OTHER TOURS Australia to N Zealand 1956/57. Commonwealth XI to S Africa 1960/61 (capt). Cavaliers to India, Pakistan and Ceylon 1961/62 (capt). Cavaliers to India and S Africa 1962/63 (capt). E. W. Swanton's XI to India 1963/64. Commonwealth XI to Pakistan 1967/68 (capt).
HST 122 A v SA, J'burg, 1957/58. HS 187 Australians v Natal, Pietermaritzburg, 1957/58.
BBT 7–72 A v I, Madras, 1956/57. BB 7–18 (10–79 match) NSW v MCC, Sydney, 1962/63.
100 WKTS (1) 106 @ 19.40 for Australians in S Africa 1957/58 — record for S African season.
RECORDS 82 wkts @ 19.25 in Australia 1958/59 — best since 1930. Reached 100* in 78 mins in scoring 121, A v WI, Kingston, 1954/55 — third-fastest Test century and fastest in a post-war Test. Hit 11 sixes in inns of 135, Australians v T. N. Pearce's XI, Scarborough, 1953 — most by an Australian.
Broadcaster and journalist with several books to his credit. OBE for services to Australian cricket. PRO to Kerry Packer. Brother J. Benaud (Australia).

BENHAM, Frederick Charles
RHB

Born Bexley, Kent, 18 Dec 1905. Debut 1949. *P.*
SCOTLAND (1) 1949.
HS 9 Scotland v Yorks, Hull, 1949.
Father C. E. Benham (Essex and Scotland).

BENKE, Andrew Frederick
RHB, OB

Born Southampton, 3 Sept 1938. Educ Cheltenham; Sidney Sussex C, Cambridge. Debut 1962.
CAMBRIDGE UNIVERSITY (19) 1962 (Blue).
HS 26 Cambridge U v Northants, Northampton, 1962.
BB 5–75 Cambridge U v Combined Services, Fenner's, 1962.

BENNETT, Alfred Charles Leopold
RHB

Born West Norwood, London, 31 Dec 1914. Died Thames Ditton, 24 Sept 1971. Educ Dulwich. Debut 1947.
NORTHAMPTONSHIRE (16) 1947–49.
HS 68 Northants v Notts, Northampton, 1947.
Club: BBC. Capt Club Cricket Conference in representative matches.

BENNETT, Barry William Prosser
LHB

Born RAF Abyad, Ismailia, Egypt, 6 Feb 1955. Educ Welbeck C, Sandhurst; Queen's C, Cambridge. Debut 1979.

CAMBRIDGE UNIVERSITY (2) 1979 (Blue).
HS 4 Cambridge U v Notts, Fenner's, 1979.
Army and Combined Services.

BENNETT, Donald
RHB, RFM

Born Wakefield, Yorks, 18 Dec 1933. Debut 1950. *P.*
MIDDLESEX (392) 1950–68. Cap 1952.
Benefit (£5464) 1964.
HS 117* M'sex v Kent, Maidstone, 1961.
BB 7–47 M'sex v Sussex, Hove, 1956.
1000 RUNS (2) 1144 @ 22.00 in 1955.
M'sex coach. Soccer: Coventry City.

BENNETT, M.

Debut 1946.
WORCESTERSHIRE (1) 1946.
HS 8 Worcs v Combined Services, Worcester, 1946.

BENNETT, Nigel Harvie
RHB

Born Walton-on-Thames, Surrey, 23 Sept 1912. Educ Stowe. Debut 1946.
SURREY (31) 1946. Cap 1946. Capt 1946.
HS 79 Surrey v Kent, Oval, 1946.
Clubs: Brondesbury, Maories.

BENNETT, Robert
RHB

Born Bacup, Lancs, 16 June 1940. Educ Rossall. Debut 1962.
LANCASHIRE (49) 1962–66. Cap 1963.
HS 112 Lancs v Notts, Trent Bridge, 1962.
Club: Bacup.

BENSON, Gwynfor Leonard
RHB, OB

Born Birmingham, 7 Jan 1941. Educ King Edward's, Birmingham. Debut 1959.
WARWICKSHIRE (3) 1959–61.
HS 46 Warwicks v Cambridge U, Portland Road, Birmingham, 1961.
BB 2–25 same match.
Club: Smethwick. Hockey: Warwickshire.

BENSON, Mark Richard
LHB

Born Shoreham, Sussex, 6 July 1958. Educ Sutton Valence S. Debut 1980.

KENT (83) 1980–. Cap 1981.
HS 152* Kent v Warwicks, Edgbaston, 1983.
1000 RUNS (3) 1515 @ 44.55 in 1983.

BENTLEY, Michael
————————LHB————————

Born Rotherham, Yorks, 14 Feb 1934. Debut 1957. *P.*
DERBYSHIRE (1) 1957.
HS 10 Derbys v Cambridge U, Fenner's, 1957.
Member XL Club.

BERGIN, Stanley Francis
————————LHB————————

Born Dublin, Ireland, 18 Dec 1926. Died Dublin, Ireland, 4 Aug 1969. Educ Christian Brothers S, Dublin. Debut 1949.
IRELAND (27) 1949–65.
HS 137 Ireland v Scotland, Dublin, 1959.
RECORDS 1610 runs for Ireland in fc cricket.
Journalist who wrote on Irish cricket. Brother B. F. Bergin (Ireland).

BERNARD, John *Richard*
————————RHB, RM————————

Born Clifton, Bristol, 7 Dec 1938. Educ Clifton C; St John's C, Cambridge. Debut 1956.
GLOUCESTERSHIRE (11) 1956–61.
CAMBRIDGE UNIVERSITY (36) 1958–60 (Blue 1958–60).
HS 119* Cambridge U v Free Foresters, Fenner's, 1959.
BB 4–44 Cambridge U v Oxford U, Lord's, 1959.
Medical practitioner. Guy's Hospital CC 1961. Club: Optimists. Distant relative of W. G. Grace.

BERNSTEIN, Rodney Elliott
————————RHB, RFM————————

Born Dublin, Ireland, 15 Dec 1937. Educ Stratford C, Dublin. Debut 1960.
IRELAND (6) 1960–62.
HS 18 Ireland v Scotland, Greenock, 1962.
BB 4–23 Ireland v MCC, Dublin, 1960.

BERRY, George *Leslie*
————————RHB————————

Born Dorking, Surrey, 28 Apr 1906. Died Leicester, 2 Feb 1985. Debut 1924. *P.*

LEICESTERSHIRE (606) 1924–51. Cap. Benefit 1938. Testimonial (£1440) 1951. Capt 1946–48.
HS 232 Leics v Sussex, Leicester, 1930.
1000 RUNS (18) 2446 @ 52.04 in 1937.
LEICS RECORDS Most runs in a season (2446 in 1937); most runs in a career (30,143 @ 30.32); most hundreds in a season (7), equal with W. Watson and B. F. Davison; most hundreds in a career (45).
Former coach at Uppingham. Soccer: Sheffield Wednesday, Bristol Rovers, Swindon Town. Other sources usually state L. G. not G. L. Berry.

BERRY, Robert
————————LHB, SLA————————

Born Manchester, 29 Jan 1926. Debut 1948. *P.*
LANCASHIRE (93) 1948–54. Cap 1950.
WORCESTERSHIRE (94) 1955–58. Cap 1957.
DERBYSHIRE (54) 1959–62. Cap 1961 (first player to be capped for three counties).
ENGLAND (2) WI 1950.
TOURS MCC to Australia 1950/51. Commonwealth XI to India 1953/54.
HST 4* E v WI, Old Trafford, 1950. HS 40 Derbys v Notts, Ilkeston, 1960.
BBT 5–63 E v WI, Old Trafford, 1950 (Test debut). BB 10–102 (14–125 match) Lancs v Worcs, Blackpool, 1953. 14–125 match Lancs v Som, Old Trafford, 1953.
Well-known pigeon breeder.

BETHELL, Joseph Arthur L
————————LHB, LM————————

Born St Thomas, Barbados, 18 Dec 1940. Debut 1963/64.
W INDIES DOMESTIC Barbados (16) 1963/64–70/70. Capt 8.
TOUR Barbados to England 1969 (capt).
HS 84* Barbados v Notts, Trent Bridge, 1969.
BB 2–16 Barbados v Trinidad, Port of Spain, 1968/69.
Club: Pickwick.

BETTS, Gilbert Frederick
————————RHB, RFM————————

Born Fulbrook, Oxfordshire, 21 Dec 1916. Died Abingdon, Oxfordshire, 5 Jan 1982. Debut 1951.
MINOR COUNTIES (1) 1951.
HS 1 Minor Counties v Kent, Canterbury, 1951.
BB 5–95 same match.
Oxfordshire 1950–56. Clubs: Oxford City, Combe, Abingdon.

BEVAN, David Gordon
————————RHB, occ LB————————

Born Gloucester, 11 June 1943. Educ Ipswich; Leeds U. Debut 1964.
GLOUCESTERSHIRE (33) 1964–70.
S AFRICA DOMESTIC Eastern Province 1973/74.
HS 80 E Province v S African Universities, Grahamstown, 1973/74.
BB 3–30 same match.
Lecturer Cape Town University 1967–70.

BHATIA, Anand Naraian
————————RHB, OB————————

Born Lucknow, India, 23 Jan 1947. Educ Doon S, India; Emmanuel C, Cambridge. Debut 1966/67.
INDIA DOMESTIC Delhi 1966/67.
CAMBRIDGE UNIVERSITY (10) 1969 (Blue).
HS 43 Cambridge U v Oxford U, Lord's, 1969.
BB 4–36 Cambridge U v Notts, Fenner's, 1969.

BICK, Donald Albert
————————RHB, OB————————

Born Hampstead, London, 22 Feb 1936. Debut 1954. *P.*
MIDDLESEX (145) 1954–67. Cap 1965.
HS 85 L. C. Steven's XI v Cambridge U, Eastbourne, 1960.
BB 5–22 M'sex v Yorks, Scarborough, 1959 and v Cambridge U, Fenner's, 1965.
Hertfordshire 1968–74. Clubs: Brondesbury, Hertford. Professional coach at City of London S from 1969.

BIDDULPH, Kenneth David
————————RHB, RM————————

Born Chingford, Essex, 29 May 1932. Debut 1955. *P.*
SOMERSET (91) 1955–61. Cap 1959.
HS 41 Som v Essex, Southend, 1960.
BB 6–30 Som v Combined Services, Taunton, 1959.
Durham 1962–72 (300 wkts). Clubs: Hartlepool, Sunderland, Whitburn, Boldon.

BIELBY, Stephen Richard
————————RHB, OB————————

Born Windsor, Berks, 9 Mar 1947. Educ Radley. Debut 1967.
NOTTINGHAMSHIRE (43) 1967–71.
HS 62 Notts v Som, Taunton, 1969.
Buckinghamshire 1965.

BIGGS, Anthony Llewellyn
————————RHB, OB————————

Born Graaf-Reinet, S Africa, 26 Apr 1946. Educ Union HS, Graaf-Reinet; Natal U. Debut 1964/65.
S AFRICA DOMESTIC Eastern Province 1964/65–80/81.
TOURS S African Universities to England 1967.
HS 156 S African Universities v W Province, Cape Town, 1967/68.
BB 7–62 (10–73 match) E Province v Border, East London, 1970/71.
Selected for S Africa to Australia 1971/72 (tour cancelled). Capt S African Schools 1964/65.

BILBIE, Anthony *Robin*
————————RHB————————

Born Nottingham, 29 Apr 1942. Debut 1960. *P.*
NOTTINGHAMSHIRE (14) 1960–63.
HS 39 Notts v Hants, Trent Bridge, 1960.

BINKS, James Graham
————————RHB, WK————————

Born Hull, Yorks, 5 Oct 1935. Educ Hull Technical C. Debut 1955. *Wisden* 1969. *P.*
YORKSHIRE (491) 1955–69. Cap 1957. Benefit (£5351) 1967.
ENGLAND (2) *I 1963/64.*
OTHER TOUR MCC to India, Pakistan and Ceylon 1961/62 (late replacement).
HS 95 Yorks v M'sex, Lord's, 1964.
RECORDS 96 catches in 1960 — fc record. Played in first 303 Yorks fc matches after debut, and 491 of 492 played during career. 412 consecutive championship matches 1955–69 — second only to K. G. Suttle (Sussex); played in every championship match during career — unique for a career of such length. 1071 dismissals in career (895 ct, 176 st).
Lincolnshire 1971–73.

BIRCH, John Dennis
————————RHB, RM————————

Born Nottingham, 18 June 1955. Educ William Crane Bilateral S. Debut 1973.
NOTTINGHAMSHIRE (168) 1973–. Cap 1981.
HS 125 Notts v Leics, Trent Bridge, 1982.
BB 6–64 Notts v Hants, Bournemouth, 1975.
1000 RUNS (2) 1086 @ 30.16 in 1983.
Clubs: Steetley, Thongsbridge.

BIRD, Harold Denis
————————RHB————————

Born Barnsley, Yorks, 19 Apr 1933. Debut 1956. *P.*
YORKSHIRE (14) 1956–59.
LEICESTERSHIRE (79) 1960–64. Cap 1960.
HS 181* Yorks v Glam, Bradford, 1959.
1000 RUNS (1) 1028 @ 21.41 in 1960.
Fc umpire (27 Tests, 1973–84) since 1970. Clubs: Barnsley, Paignton.

BIRD, Ronald Ernest
————————RHB, RMF————————

Born Quarry Bank, Staffs, 4 Apr 1915. Died Feckenham, Worcs, 20 Feb 1985. Debut 1946.
WORCESTERSHIRE (190) 1946–54. Cap 1946. Capt 1952–54.
HS 158* Worcs v Som, Taunton, 1952.
BB 3–39 Worcs v Cambridge U, Worcester, 1949.
1000 RUNS (3) 1591 @ 37.00 in 1952.
Clubs: Moseley, Stourbridge, Old Hill, XL Club.

BIRKENSHAW, Jack
————————LHB, ROB————————

Born Rothwell, Leeds, Yorks, 13 Nov 1940. Educ Rothwell GS. Debut 1958. *P.*
YORKSHIRE (30) 1958–60.
LEICESTERSHIRE (420) 1961–80. Cap 1965. Benefit (£13,100) 1974.
WORCESTERSHIRE (10) 1981.
ENGLAND (5) 1972/73–73/74. *WI 1973/74 (2); I 1972/73 (2); P 1972/73 (1).*
OTHER TOURS International XI to India and Pakistan 1967/68. Duke of Norfolk's XI to W Indies 1969/70.
HST 64 E v I, Kanpur, 1972/73. HS 131 Leics v Surrey, Guildford, 1969.
BBT 5–57 E v P, Karachi, 1972/73. BB 8–94 Leics v Somerset, Taunton, 1972.
100 WKTS (2) 111 @ 21.41 in 1967.
RECORD Added 206 for 7th wkt with B. Dudleston, Leics v Kent, Canterbury, 1969, county record.
Fc umpire 1982–.

BIRKS,
Douglas Thomas Montague
————————RHB, RMF————————

Born Roche, Cornwall, 4 July 1919. Educ Radley. Debut 1949.
FREE FORESTERS (1) 1949.
HS 3 Free Foresters v Cambridge U, Fenner's, 1949.
Suffolk 1947–48. Clubs: Maidenhead and Bray, Felixstowe.

BIRRELL, Henry Berson
————————RHB, OB————————

Born Pietermaritzburg, S Africa, 12 Dec 1927. Educ St Andrew's, Grahamstown; Rhodes U; Lincoln C, Oxford. Debut 1947/48.
S AFRICA DOMESTIC Eastern Province 1947/48–56/57, Rhodesia 1957/58–59/60.
OXFORD UNIVERSITY (19) 1953–54 (Blue 1953, 1954).
HS 134 Oxford U v Worcs, Worcester, 1953.
BB 5–20 Oxford U v Cambridge U, Lord's, 1954.
Rugby: Blue.

BIRTLE, Thomas William
————————RHB, RFM————————

Born Stockton-on-Tees, Durham, 28 Mar 1926. Debut 1952. *P.*
NOTTINGHAMSHIRE (7) 1952.
HS 4* Notts v Kent, Gillingham, 1952.
BB 2–68 same match.
Durham 1946–55. Clubs: Norton, Mainsworth. Professional coach Gresham's S, Holt 1952.

BISHOP, Michael Mark
————————RHB, RM————————

Born Marlborough, Wiltshire, 20 Oct 1952. Educ Cranbrook S, Sydney; Sydney U; Christ's C, Cambridge. Debut 1976.
CAMBRIDGE UNIVERSITY (3) 1976–78.
HS 3 Cambridge U v Warwicks, Fenner's, 1976.

BISSEX, Michael
————————RHB, SLA————————

Born Bath, Somerset, 28 Sept 1944. Debut 1961.
GLOUCESTERSHIRE (204) 1961–72. Cap 1970.
TOUR MCC Under-25 to Pakistan 1966/67.
HS 104* Glos v Oxford U, Bristol, 1964 and 104 v Kent, Cheltenham, 1970.
BB 7–50 Glos v Worcs, Cheltenham, 1971.
1000 RUNS (1) 1316 @ 37.60 in 1970.
Cheshire 1977–78, Cornwall 1984. Clubs: Bath, Denton, Walkden, Littleborough, Looe.

BLACK,
Christopher James Robert (Sam)
——RHB, RM——

Born J'burg, S Africa, 15 Dec 1947. Educ Michaelhouse S, Natal; Stowe S. Debut 1970.
MIDDLESEX (17) 1970–73.
HS 71 M'sex v Hants, Lord's, 1971.
BB 3–51 M'sex v Cambridge U, Fenner's, 1971.

BLACK, Thomas MacMillan
——RHB, RM——

Born Greenock, Scotland, 7 Feb 1956. Educ Greenock Academy; Jordanhill C. Debut 1979.
SCOTLAND (1) 1979.
HS 57 Scotland v Ireland, Dublin, 1979.

BLACKBURN, John Derek
Hepburn
——RHB, RM——

Born Leeds, Yorks, 27 Oct 1924. Educ West Leeds HS. Debut 1956.
YORKSHIRE (1) 1956.
HS 15 Yorks v Cambridge U, Fenner's, 1956.
Clubs: Undercliffe, Bradford, Leeds. President Bradford.

BLACKBURN, Paul Hamer
——RHB, RM——

Born Stockport, Cheshire, 29 Mar 1934. Educ Cheltenham C; Emmanuel C, Cambridge. Debut 1954.
CAMBRIDGE UNIVERSITY (1) 1954.
HS 5 Cambridge U v Sussex, Fenner's, 1954.

BLACKLEDGE, Joseph
Frederick
——RHB——

Born Chorley, Lancs, 15 Apr 1928. Educ Repton. Debut 1962.
LANCASHIRE (26) 1962. Cap 1962. Capt 1962.
HS 68 Lancs v Glam, Cardiff, 1962.

BLACKMORE,
George *Patrick* Maxwell
——RHB, RFM——

Born Gillingham, Kent, 8 Oct 1908. Died Isleworth, London, 29 Jan 1984. Educ Windlesham House, Hove; Blundell's, Tiverton. Debut 1944/45.

INDIA DOMESTIC Europeans in Bombay 1944/45.
KENT (2) 1948.
HS 8 Europeans v Parsees, Bombay, 1944/45.
Clubs: Band of Brothers, West Kent, Slough, XL Club.

BLADES, Colin Francis
——RHB, RM——

Born Barbados, 10 Aug 1944. Debut 1963/64.
W INDIES DOMESTIC Barbados 1963/64–69/70.
TOUR Barbados to England 1969.
HS 75 Barbados v Jamaica, Bridgetown, 1968/69.
Bermuda ICC Trophy 1979.

BLAGG, Edward Arthur
——RHB, RF——

Born Shireoaks, Notts, 9 Feb 1918. Died Shireoaks, Notts, 28 Oct 1976. Debut 1948. *P.*
NOTTINGHAMSHIRE (1) 1948.
No runs or wkts.
Soccer: Nottingham Forest, Southport.

BLAIR, Philbert Duncan
——RHB, RFM——

Born Georgetown, Demerara, British Guiana, 30 Oct 1943. Debut 1967/68.
W INDIES DOMESTIC Guyana 1967/68–70/71.
TOUR W Indies to England 1969.
HS 20* Guyana v Trinidad, Georgetown, 1968/69.
BB 5–60 Guyana v Jamaica, Kingston, 1968/69.

BLAIR, Robert William
——RHB, RFM——

Born Petone, N Zealand, 23 June 1932. Debut 1951/52.
N ZEALAND DOMESTIC Wellington (59), Central Districts (5), 1951/52–64/65.
NEW ZEALAND (19) 1952/53–63/64. E 1954/55 (1), 1958/59 (2), 1962/63 (2); SA 1952/53 (2), 1963/64 (3); WI 1955/56 (2). *E 1958 (3); SA 1953/54 (4)*.
HST 64* NZ v E, Wellington, 1962/63.
HS 79 N Zealanders v Griqualand West, Kimberley, 1953/54.
BBT 4–85 NZ v SA, Auckland, 1963/64.
BB 9–72 Wellington v Auckland, Wellington, 1956/57.
Leading N Zealand domestic wkt-taker in fc cricket until overtaken by H. J. Howarth.
Professional: Crompton.

BLAKE, David Eustace
——LHB, WK——

Born Havant, Hants, 27 Apr 1925. Educ Aldenham. Debut 1949.
HAMPSHIRE (50) 1949–58. Cap 1953.
TOURS E. W. Swanton's XI to W Indies 1955/56. Duke of Norfolk's XI to Jamaica 1956/57.
HS 100 Hants v Som, Bournemouth, 1954.
Guy's Hospital CC 1950–51. Brother J. P. Blake (Hants).

BLAKE, Peter Douglas Stuart
——RHB——

Born Calcutta, India, 23 May 1927. Educ Eton; Brasenose C, Oxford. Debut 1946.
SUSSEX (24) 1946–51. Cap 1948.
OXFORD UNIVERSITY (34) 1950–52 (Blue 1950–52). Capt 1952.
HS 130 Oxford U v Worcs, The Parks, 1952.
Ordained priest (Church of England).

BLAND, Kenneth *Colin*
——RHB, RM——

Born Bulawayo, Rhodesia, 5 Apr 1938. Educ Milton S, Bulawayo. Debut 1956/57. *Wisden* 1966.
S AFRICA DOMESTIC Rhodesia, Eastern Province, Orange Free State, 1956/57–73/74. Official coach to each.
SOUTH AFRICA (21) 1961/62–66/67. E 1964/65 (5); A 1966/67 (1); NZ 1961/62 (5). *E 1965 (3); A 1963/64 (4); NZ 1963/64 (3)*.
OTHER TOURS S African Fezelas to England 1961. International XI to Pakistan 1961/62. Rest of World XI in England 1966, 1967.
HST 144* SA v E, J'burg, 1964/65. HS 197 Rhodesia v Border, East London, 1967/68.
BBT 2–16 SA v NZ, Wellington, 1963/64. BB 4–40 Rhodesia v Transvaal B, Salisbury, 1967/68.
1000 RUNS (1) 1048 @ 69.86 in S Africa in 1964/65.
One of best fieldsman away from bat of all time.

BLATCHER, Richard Brian
——RHB, RMF——

Born Barnes, London, 2 Apr 1934. Educ Kingston GS; St John's C, Cambridge. Debut 1955.
CAMBRIDGE UNIVERSITY (2) 1955–56.
HS 15 Cambridge U v M'sex, Fenner's, 1955.
BB 2–42 Cambridge U v M'sex, Fenner's, 1956.

BLAXLAND, Lionel Bruce
————————RHB, RFM————————

Born Lilleshall, Shropshire, 25 Mar 1898. Died Temple Ewell, Kent, 29 Apr 1976. Educ Shrewsbury; Oriel C, Oxford. Debut 1925.
DERBYSHIRE (19) 1925–47.
HS 64 Derbys v Warwicks, Derby, 1933. Soccer: Blue and Corinthians. Master Repton 1922–58. Afterwards ordained into Church of England. Nephew J. M. H. Graham-Brown (Kent and Derbyshire).

BLENKIRON, William
————————RHB, RFM————————

Born Newfield Estate, Bishop Auckland, Co Durham, 21 July 1942. Debut 1964. *P.*
WARWICKSHIRE(117)1964–74.Cap 1969.
HS 62 Warwicks v Worcs, Dudley, 1969.
BB 5–37 Warwicks v Leics, Leicester, 1968.
Durham 1975–76. Club: Bishop Auckland.

BLOCK, Spencer Allen
————————RHB————————

Born Esher, Surrey, 15 July 1908. Died Meadle, Buckinghamshire, 15 Oct 1979. Educ Marlborough; Pembroke C, Cambridge. Debut 1928.
CAMBRIDGE UNIVERSITY (14) 1928–29 (Blue 1929).
SURREY (30) 1928–33.
FREE FORESTERS (7) 1935–48.
HS 117 Surrey v Leics, Oval, 1931. Scored 91 in 50 mins, Surrey v M'sex, Oval, 1933. Rugby: Harlequins.

BLOFELD, Henry Calthorpe
————————RHB, WK————————

Born Hoveton, Norfolk, 23 Sept 1939. Educ Eton; King's C, Cambridge. Debut 1958.
CAMBRIDGE UNIVERSITY (16) 1958–59 (Blue 1959).
FREE FORESTERS (1) 1960.
HS 138 Cambridge U v MCC, Lord's, 1959.
Norfolk 1956–65. Uncle F. S. Gough-Calthorpe (Sussex, Warwicks and England). Well-known cricket writer and broadcaster. Club: Arabs.

BLOOM, George Raymond
————————LHB————————

Born Aston, Sheffield, 13 Sept 1941. Debut 1964.

YORKSHIRE (1) 1964.
HS 2 Yorks v Kent, Dover, 1964.
Clubs: Scarborough, Farsley.

BLOY, Nigel Clement Francis
————————LHB, RLB————————

Born Plymouth, Devon, 2 Jan 1923. Educ Dover C; Brasenose C, Oxford. Debut 1946.
OXFORD UNIVERSITY (28) 1946–48 (Blue 1946, 1947).
FREE FORESTERS (2) 1951–54.
MCC (1) 1958.
HS 77 Oxford U v Yorks, The Parks, 1946.
BB 3–80 Oxford U v Combined Services, The Parks, 1946.
Devon 1951–58, Dorset 1961. Incorrectly obituarized in *Wisden* 1946.

BLUETT, John Douglas Jeremy
————————RHB————————

Born Kensington, London, 29 May 1930. Educ Cranbrook. Debut 1950.
KENT (2) 1950.
HS 10 Kent v Leics, Loughborough, 1950.
Clubs: Bromley, Streatham, Incogniti.

BLUNT, Leonard
————————RHB, RMF————————

Born Worcester, 29 Mar 1921. Debut 1942/43. *P.*
INDIA DOMESTIC Madras Europeans 1942/43.
WORCESTERSHIRE (14) 1946–48.
HS 18 Worcs v Combined Services, Worcester, 1946.
BB 5–60 Worcs v Hants, Southampton, 1946.
Cheshire 1950–53. Club: Nantwich.

BODDINGTON, Myles Alan
————————LHB, RMF————————

Born Hale, Cheshire, 30 Nov 1924. Educ Rugby. Debut 1946.
ROYAL AIR FORCE (1) 1946.
HS 23 RAF v Worcs, Worcester, 1946. Retired from cricket through injury 1947. Father R. A. Boddington (Lancs).

BODELL, Ernest Herbert
————————RHB, RFM————————

Born Dublin, Ireland, 17 Aug 1928. Educ HS, Dublin. Debut 1954.
IRELAND (5) 1954–59.
HS 11* Ireland v Scotland, Dublin, 1955.
BB 4–27 Ireland v Scotland, Dublin, 1957.

BODKIN, Peter Ernest
————————LHB, LM————————

Born Barnet, Herts, 15 Sept 1924. Educ Bradfield; Caius C, Cambridge. Debut 1946.
CAMBRIDGE UNIVERSITY (9) 1946 (Blue).
Capt 1946.
HS 52 Cambridge U v Yorks, Fenner's, 1946.
BB 2–27 Cambridge U v Glos, Gloucester, 1946.
War-time Blue 1944, 1945. Hertfordshire 1946–47. Clubs: Southgate, Esher. Soccer: Blue. Medical practitioner.

BOLTON, Alan
————————RHB, OB————————

Born Darwen, Lancs, 1 July 1939. Debut 1957. *P.*
LANCASHIRE (40) 1957–61.
HS 96 Lancs v Leics, Leicester, 1959.
Club: Darwen.

BOLUS, John *Brian*
————————RHB, LM————————

Born Whitkirk, Leeds, Yorks, 31 Jan 1934. Educ St Michael's C, Leeds. Debut 1956. *P.*
YORKSHIRE (107) 1956–62. Cap 1960.
NOTTINGHAMSHIRE (269) 1963–72. Cap 1963. Capt 1972. Benefit (£7820) 1971.
DERBYSHIRE (64) 1973–75. Cap 1973. Capt 1973–75.
ENGLAND (7) 1963–63/64. *WI 1963 (2); I 1963/64 (5).*
HST 88 E v I, Madras, 1963/64. HS 202* Notts v Glam, Trent Bridge, 1963.
BB 4–40 Yorks v Pakistanis, Bradford, 1962.
1000 RUNS (14) 2190 @ 41.32 in 1963.
Clubs: Bradford, Leeds, York, Brighouse.

BOND, John David
————————RHB, occ LB————————

Born Kearsley, Lancs, 6 May 1932. Educ Bolton S. Debut 1955. *Wisden* 1971. *P.*
LANCASHIRE (344) 1955–72. Cap 1961. Capt 1968–72. Benefit (£7230) 1970.
NOTTINGHAMSHIRE (17) 1974. Capt 1974.
HS 157 Lancs v Hants, Old Trafford, 1962.
1000 RUNS (2) 2125 @ 36.01 in 1963.
Notts player-coach 1974. Lancs coach 1973; manager 1980–. Test selector 1974.

BOND, Raymond Ernest
————————LHB, RMF————————

Born Slough, Bucks, 7 Sept 1944. Debut 1973.
MINOR COUNTIES (1) 1973.
Did not bat.
Bucks 1965–79. Club: Beaconsfield.

BOOBBYER, Brian
————————RHB————————

Born Ealing, London, 25 Feb 1928. Educ Uppingham; Brasenose C, Oxford. Debut 1949.
OXFORD UNIVERSITY (40) 1949–52 (Blue 1949–52).
HS 126 Oxford U v Sussex, Chichester, 1950.
Rugby: Oxford Blue, Rosslyn Park and England (9 caps).

BOOCK, Stephen Lewis
————————RHB, SLA————————

Born Dunedin, N Zealand, 20 Sept 1951. Debut 1973/74.
N ZEALAND DOMESTIC Otago (50) 1973/74–74/75 and 1978/79–, Canterbury (23) 1975/76–77/78.
NEW ZEALAND (12) 1977/78–79/80. E 1977/78 (3); WI 1979/80 (3); P 1978/79 (3). E 1978 (3).
OTHER TOUR N Zealand to Australia 1980/81.
HST 8 NZ v E, Trent Bridge, 1978. HS 35* Otago v Canterbury, Dunedin, 1973/74.
BBT 5–67 NZ v E, Auckland, 1977/78. BB 8–59 Otago v Wellington, Invercargill, 1978/79.
RECORDS 66 wkts @ 16.48 in 1977/78 — a N Zealand record.

BOODEN, Christopher Derek
————————RHB, RFM————————

Born Newport Pagnell, Buckinghamshire, 22 June 1961. Educ Radcliffe CS, Wolverton. Debut 1980.
NORTHAMPTONSHIRE (4) 1980–81.
HS 6* Northants v Derbys, Derby, 1980.
BB 2–30 Northants v Glos, Bristol, 1981.
Bucks 1983–. Club: Wolverton.

BOON, Timothy James
————————RHB, RM————————

Born Doncaster, Yorks, 1 Nov 1961. Educ Edlington CS, Doncaster. Debut 1980.
LEICESTERSHIRE (57) 1980–.
TOUR Leics XI to Zimbabwe 1980/81.
HS 144 Leics v Glos, Leicester, 1984.

1000 RUNS (1) 1233 @ 39.77 in 1984.
RECORD Added 290* for 4th wkt with P. Willey, Leics v Warwicks, Leicester, 1984, county record.
Captained Young England 1980–81.

BOOTH, Arthur
————————RHB, SLA————————

Born Featherstone, Yorks, 3 Nov 1902. Died Rochdale, Lancs, 17 Aug 1974. Debut 1931. P.
YORKSHIRE (36) 1931–47. Cap 1946.
HS 29 Yorks v M'sex, Bramall Lane, Sheffield, 1947.
BB 6–21 Yorks v Warwicks, Edgbaston, 1946.
100 WKTS (1) 111 @ 11.61 in 1946.
Northumberland 1936–39. Professional: Keighley, Milnrow, Walsall, Smethwick, Blythe Works. Coach Manchester GS from 1965.

BOOTH, Arthur
————————RHB————————

Born Droylsden, Lancs, 8 Jan 1926. Debut 1950. P.
LANCASHIRE (4) 1950–51.
HS 49 Lancs v Hants, Liverpool, 1951.
Scored 253 Lancs 2nd XI v Lincs, Grimsby, 1950. Clubs: Haslingden, Ashton, Werneth.

BOOTH, Brian Charles
————————RHB, RM/OB————————

Born Perthville, nr Bathurst, NSW, Australia, 19 Oct 1933. Debut 1954/55.
AUSTRALIAN DOMESTIC New South Wales (93) 1954/55–68/69.
AUSTRALIA (29) 1961–65/66. E 1962/63 (5), 1965/66 (3); SA 1963/64 (4); P 1964/65 (1). E 1961 (2), 1964 (5); WI 1964/65 (5); I 1964/65 (3); P 1964/65 (1).
OTHER TOURS Australia to N Zealand 1959/60, 1966/67.
HST 169 A v SA, Brisbane, 1963/64. HS 214* Australians v Central Districts, Palmerston North, 1966/67.
BBT 2–33 A v I, Calcutta, 1964/65. BB 2–29 Australians v N Zealand, Wellington, 1959/60.
1000 RUNS (2 + 2) 1551 @ 55.39 in 1964.
Autobiography Booth to Bat (1983).

BOOTH, Brian Joseph
————————RHB, LBG————————

Born Blackburn, Lancs, 3 Oct 1935. Debut 1956. P.
LANCASHIRE (117) 1956–63. Cap 1961.
LEICESTERSHIRE (232) 1964–73. Cap 1964. Testimonial 1973.

BOOTH, Paul Anthony
————————LHB, SLA————————

Born Huddersfield, Yorks, 5 Sept 1965. Educ Honley HS, Huddersfield. Debut 1982.
YORKSHIRE (12) 1982–.
HS 26 Yorks v Worcs, Scarborough, 1984.
BB 3–22 Yorks v Northants, Northampton, 1984.

BOOTH, Peter
————————RHB, RMF————————

Born Shipley, Yorks, 2 Nov 1952. Educ Whitcliffe Mount GS, Cleckheaton; Loughborough C. Debut 1972.
LEICESTERSHIRE (83) 1972–81.
TOUR Leics XI to Zimbabwe 1980/81.
HS 58* Leics v Lancs, Leicester, 1976.
BB 6–93 Leics v Glam, Swansea, 1978.

BOOTH, Roy
————————RHB, WK————————

Born Marsden, Yorks, 1 Oct 1926. Debut 1951. P.
YORKSHIRE (65) 1951–55.
WORCESTERSHIRE (402) 1956–70. Cap 1956. Benefit (£6240) 1966.
TOURS Worcs to Rhodesia 1964/65. Worcs to Jamaica 1965/66.
HS 113* Worcs v Sussex, Hove, 1959.
1000 RUNS (1) 1042 @ 27.42 in 1959.
RECORD 1015 dismissals in career for Worcs, county record.
1122 dismissals in career (946 ct, 176 st).
101 dismissals in 1960, 100 in 1964.
Worcs committee.

BOOTH, Stephen Charles
————————RHB, SLA————————

Born Leeds, Yorkshire, 30 Oct 1963. Educ Boston CS. Debut 1983.
SOMERSET (22) 1983–.
HS 42 Som v Derbys, Taunton, 1984.
BB 4–26 Som v M'sex, Lord's, 1983.

BOOTH-JONES, Timothy Douglas
————————RHB————————

Born Dover, Kent, 6 Aug 1952. Educ Hastings GS; St Luke's C, Exeter. Debut 1980.
SUSSEX (26) 1980–81.
HS 95 Sussex v Som, Hove, 1981.
Club: Hastings.

HS 183* Lancs v Oxford U, Old Trafford, 1961.
BB 7–143 Lancs v Worcs, Southport, 1959
1000 RUNS (8) 1752 @ 31.85 in 1961.

BOOTON, Walter Thomas
──────RHB, RFM──────

Born Kidderminster, Worcs, 13 Jan 1941. Debut 1970.
IRELAND (1) 1970.
HS 12 Ireland v Scotland, Perth, 1970.
BB 2–72 same match.
Clubs: Kidderminster (Birmingham League), Cork Wanderers.

BORDE,
Chandrakant Gulabrao (Chandu)
──────RHB, LBG──────

Born Poona, India, 21 July 1934. Debut 1952/53.
INDIA DOMESTIC Baroda, Maharashtra (capt 1963/64–72/73), 1952/53–73/74.
INDIA (55) 1958/59–69/70. E 1961/62 (5), 1963/64 (5); A 1959/60 (5), 1964/65 (3), 1969/70 (1); WI 1958/59 (4), 1966/67 (3); NZ 1964/65 (4); P 1961/62 (5). *E 1959 (4), 1967 (3); A 1967/68 (4); WI 1961/62 (5); NZ 1967/68 (4)*. Capt 1.
OTHER TOURS India to Pakistan 1954/55. Commonwealth XI to Rhodesia 1962/63.
HST 177* I v P, Madras, 1960/61. HS 207* Maharashtra v Bengal, Poona, 1972/73.
BBT 5–88 I v E, Madras, 1963/64. BB 7–44 Baroda v Maharashtra, Baroda, 1958/59.
1000 RUNS (1 + 3) 1604 @ 64.16 in India 1964/65.
4338 runs @ 52.90 and 14 centuries in Ranji Trophy. Professional: Werneth, Rawtenstall. Son R. G. Borde (Maharashtra).

BORDER, Allan Robert
──────LHB, LM/SLA──────

Born Cremorne, Sydney, NSW, Australia, 27 July 1955. Educ North Sydney Boys' HS. Debut 1976/77. *Wisden 1982*.
AUSTRALIA DOMESTIC New South Wales (25) 1976/77–79/80, Queensland (21) 1980/81–.
GLOUCESTERSHIRE (1) 1977.
AUSTRALIA (61) 1978/79–83/84. E 1978/79 (3), 1979/80 (3), 1982/83 (5); WI 1979/80 (3), 1981/82 (3); I 1980/81 (3); NZ 1980/81 (3); P 1978/79 (2), 1981/82 (3), 1983/84 (5). *E 1980 (1), 1981 (6); WI 1983/84 (5); NZ 1981/82 (3); I 1979/80 (6); P 1979/80 (3), 1982/83 (3); SL 1982/83 (1)*.
OTHER TOUR Australia to Sri Lanka 1980/81.
HST 162 A v I, Madras, 1979/80. HS 200 NSW v Queensland, Brisbane, 1979/80.
BBT 3–20 A v NZ, Christchurch, 1981/82. BB 4–61 Queensland v NSW,

Sydney, 1980/81.
1000 RUNS (2) 1220 @ 55.45 in Australia 1978/79.
RECORD First player to score 150 in each inns of a Test, 150* and 153, A v P, Lahore, 1979/80.
Club: Downend (Bristol).

BORE, Michael Kenneth
──────RHB, LM/SLA──────

Born Hull, Yorks, 2 June 1947. Educ Maybury HS, Hull. Debut 1969.
YORKSHIRE (74) 1969–78.
NOTTINGHAMSHIRE (78) 1979–. Cap 1980.
HS 37* Yorks v Notts, Bradford, 1973.
BB 8–89 Notts v Kent, Folkestone, 1979.
Professional: Redcar. Clubs: Leeds, Bradford, Lightcliffe, Hull.

BORRETT, Norman Francis
──────RHB, SLA──────

Born Wanstead, Essex, 1 Oct 1917. Educ Framlingham; Pembroke C, Cambridge. Debut 1937.
ESSEX (3) 1937–46.
HS 15* Essex v Cambridge U, Fenner's, 1938.
Devon 1949–59. Club: Seaton. Hockey: England.

BORRILL, Peter David
──────RHB, RFM──────

Born Leeds, Yorks, 4 July 1951. Educ Leeds Modern S. Debut 1971.
YORKSHIRE (2) 1971.
Did not bat.
BB 2–6 Yorks v Oxford U, The Parks, 1971.
Professional: Darlington. Club: Leeds.

BORRINGTON, Anthony John
──────RHB, occ WK──────

Born Spondon, Derbys, 8 Dec 1948. Educ Spondon Park GS; Loughborough U. Debut 1971.
DERBYSHIRE (122) 1971–80. Cap 1977.
HS 137 Derbys v Yorks, Dore, Sheffield, 1978.
Club: Spondon.

BOSE, Gopal
──────RHB, OB──────

Born Calcutta, India, 20 May 1947. Debut 1968/69.
INDIA DOMESTIC Bengal 1968/69–78/79 (capt 1974/75–75/76).

TOURS India to Sri Lanka 1973/74. India to England 1974.
HS 170 Rest of India v Bombay, Bangalore, 1973/74.
BB 5–66 Bengal v Haryana, Rai, 1976/77.

BOSHIER, Brian Stanley
──────RHB, RMF──────

Born Leicester, 6 Mar 1932. Debut 1953. *P*.
LEICESTERSHIRE (169) 1953–64. Cap 1958.
HS 30 Leics v Glos, Leicester, 1957.
BB 8–45 Leics v Essex, Brentwood, 1957.
100 WKTS (2) 108 @ 18.77 in 1958 and 108 @ 17.87 in 1961.
Club: Harrogate.

BOSTON, Granger Farwell
──────RHB──────

Born West Derby, Liverpool, 24 May 1921. Died Marylebone, London, 4 Feb 1958. Educ Wellington C; Clare C, Cambridge. Debut 1946.
CAMBRIDGE UNIVERSITY (3) 1946.
HS 19 Cambridge U v Lancs, Fenner's, 1946.

BOTHAM, Ian Terence
──────RHB, RMF──────

Born Heswall, Cheshire, 24 Nov 1955. Educ Buckler's Mead Sec S, Yeovil. Debut 1974. *Wisden 1978*.
SOMERSET (147) 1974–. Cap 1976. Capt 1984–.
ENGLAND (73) 1977–84. A 1977 (2), 1980 (1), 1981 (6); WI 1980 (5), 1984 (5); NZ 1978 (3), 1983 (4); I 1979 (4), 1982 (3); P 1978 (3), 1982 (3); SL 1984 (1). *A 1978/79 (6), 1979/80 (3), 1982/83 (5); WI 1980/81 (4); NZ 1977/78 (3), 1983/84 (3); I 1979/80 (1), 1981/82 (6); P 1983/84 (1). SL 1981/82 (1)*. Capt 12.
OTHER TOUR England to Pakistan 1977/78.
HST 208 E v I, Oval, 1982. HS 228 Som v Glos, Taunton, 1980 (10 sixes; scored 182 between lunch and tea).
BBT 8–34 E v P, Lord's, 1978. BB as above.
1000 RUNS (3) 1241 @ 44.32 in 1982.
100 WKTS (1) 100 @ 16.40 in 1978.
TEST RECORDS First player to score century and take 8 wkts in inns, E v P, Lord's, 1978. First to score century and take 10 wkts in match, E v I, Bombay, 1979/80. Took 100th and 200th wkts in record time: 2 yrs 9 days (1979, now beaten by Kapil Dev) and 4 yrs 34 days (1981). Achieved Test doubles of 1000

runs/100 wkts in 21st Test in 1979 (a record) and 2000 runs/200 wkts in 42 Tests in 1981/82 - fewest Tests and shortest time (4 yrs 126 days). Achieved 1000 runs/100 wkts double in A v E Tests in record 22 matches. In 1984, first to 4000 runs/300 wkts in Tests.

FAST SCORING Centuries off Australia from 87 balls (149*, Headingley, 1981) and 86 balls (118, Old Trafford, 1981) — only J. M. Gregory (67), R. C. Fredericks (71), G. L. Jessop (76), Kapil Dev (83) and C. H. Lloyd (85) have scored Test centuries off fewer balls. Scored 122 in 58 mins off 55 balls (7 sixes, 16 fours), England XI v Central Zone, Indore, 1981/82, reaching century in 50 mins off 48 balls. Scored 131* in 65 mins (10 sixes, 12 fours), Som v Warwicks, Taunton, 1982, reaching century in 52 mins from 56 balls. Scored 32 runs off one over from I. R. Snook (466466), England XI v Central Districts, Palmerston North, 1983/84, and 30 runs off one over from P. A. Smith (4466460 including no-ball), Som v Warwicks, Taunton, 1982.

PARTNERSHIPS During HS (above) added 310 for 4th wkt with P. W. Denning; added 172 for 8th wkt with I. V. A. Richards, Som v Leics, Leicester, 1983, both county records.

Soccer: Scunthorpe United.

BOTTEN, James Thomas (Jackie)
RHB, RFM

Born Pretoria, S Africa, 21 June 1938. Educ Pretoria Boys' HS. Debut 1957/58.

S AFRICA DOMESTIC North-East Transvaal (Northern Transvaal) 1957/58–71/72.

SOUTH AFRICA (3) E 1965.

OTHER TOUR S African Fezelas to England 1961.

HST 33 SA v E, Lord's, 1965. HS 90 S Africans v Leics, Leicester, 1965.

BBT 2–56 SA v E, Oval, 1965. BB 9–23 NE Transvaal v Griqualand West, Pretoria, 1958/59.

RECORDS Added 181 for 9th wkt with A. Bacher in HS above — record for any S African touring team. 55 wkts @ 10.09 in Currie Cup in 1958/59 — record until beaten by M. J. Procter in 1976/77.

BOTTON, Norman Dennis
LHB, LM

Born Hammersmith, London, 21 Jan 1954. Educ King Edwards', Bath; Hertford C, Oxford. Debut 1974.

OXFORD UNIVERSITY (15) 1974–75 (Blue 1974).

HS 38* Oxford U v Warwicks, The Parks, 1974.

BB 2–53 Oxford U v Derbys, The Parks, 1975.

BOUCHER, James Chrysostum
RHB, OB

Born Dublin, Ireland, 22 Dec 1910. Educ Belvedere C, Dublin. Debut 1930.

IRELAND (28) 1930–54.

HS 85 Ireland v MCC, Rathmines, 1936.

BB 7–13 Ireland v N Zealanders, Dublin, 1937 (finished on losing side). Hon. secretary Irish Cricket Union 1954–73. Irish cricket commentator.

BOURNE, William Anderson
RHB, RFM

Born Clapham St Michael, Barbados, 15 Nov 1952. Educ Harrison C, Barbados. Debut 1970/71.

W INDIES DOMESTIC Barbados 1970/71.

WARWICKSHIRE (59) 1973–77.

HS 107 Warwicks v Sussex, Edgbaston, 1976.

BB 6–47 Warwicks v Cambridge U, Fenner's, 1976.

Appeared in Moin-ud-Dowlah Gold Cup Tournament in India and for Zambia. Currently player-coach and writer in Zimbabwe. Club: Redcar.

BOWDEN, Jack
RHB, SLA

Born Lisburn, Co Antrim, Ireland, 17 Oct 1916. Educ Lisburn Technical C. Debut 1946.

IRELAND (6) 1946–55.

HS 34 Ireland v MCC, Dublin, 1950.

BB 6–23 Ireland v Scotland, Belfast, 1948.

Hockey: Ireland.

BOWES, John Barton
RHB, RMF

Born Stretford, Manchester, 2 Jan 1918. Died Manchester, 22 May 1969. Debut 1938. P.

LANCASHIRE (10) 1938–48.

HS 39 Lancs v Northants, Northampton, 1938.

BB 4–103 Lancs v S Africans, Old Trafford, 1947.

Professional: Colne. Minor Counties umpire 1955–57, 1960–63. Fc umpire 1958–59. 6 ft 4½ in tall.

BOWES, William Eric
RHB, RFM

Born Elland, Yorks, 25 July 1908. Debut 1928 (MCC). Wisden 1932. P.

YORKSHIRE (301) 1929–47. Cap 1930. Benefit (£8083) 1947.

ENGLAND (15) 1932–46. A 1934 (3), 1938 (2); SA 1935 (4); WI 1939 (2); I 1932 (1), 1946 (1). A 1932/33 (1); NZ 1932/33 (1).

OTHER TOUR Yorks to Jamaica 1935/36.

HST 10* E v A, Lord's, 1934. HS 43* Yorks v Glos, Scarborough, 1938.

BBT 6–33 E v WI, Old Trafford, 1939. BB 9–121 Yorks v Essex, Scarborough, 1932.

100 WKTS (9) 193 @ 15.44 in 1935.

Players v Gentlemen (6) 1931–39. Cricket journalist since retirement. Autobiography Express Deliveries (1949). 6 ft 4 in tall.

BOWLES, Roger Andrew
RHB, LBG

Born Carshalton, Surrey, 11 Feb 1936. Educ Wallington GS; Brasenose C, Oxford. Debut 1957.

OXFORD UNIVERSITY (3) 1957.

HS 43 Oxford U v Worcs, The Parks, 1957.

Clubs: Beddington, Horsham.

BOWLING, Kenneth
RHB

Born Leyland, Lancs, 10 Nov 1931. Debut 1954. P.

LANCASHIRE (1) 1954.

HS 4* Lancs v Derbys, Old Trafford, 1954.

Clubs: Leyland Motors, Honley.

BOWMAN, Richard
RHB, RF

Born Cleveleys, Lancs, 26 Jan 1934. Educ Fettes; UC, Oxford. Debut 1955.

OXFORD UNIVERSITY (14) 1955–57 (Blue 1957).

LANCASHIRE (9) 1957–59.

HS 75 Oxford U v Essex, Westcliff, 1957.

BB 7–60 same match.

Clubs: Free Foresters, Whalley.

BOXILL, Darnley Da Costa
RHB, WK

Born Christchurch, Barbados, 2 Oct 1944. Debut 1964/65.

W INDIES DOMESTIC Barbados 1964/65–71/72.

TOUR Barbados to England 1969.
HS 38 Barbados v Leeward Islands, Bridgetown, 1968/69.
Club: Empire.

BOYCE, Keith David
RHB, RFM

Born St Peter, Barbados, 11 Oct 1943. Educ Coleridge Parry S, St Peter. Debut 1964/65. *Wisden 1974.*
W INDIES DOMESTIC Barbados 1964/65–74/75.
ESSEX (211) 1966–77. Cap 1967. Benefit 1977.
WEST INDIES (21) 1970/71–75/76. E 1973/74 (4); A 1972/73 (4); I 1970/71 (1). *E 1973 (3); A 1975/76 (4); I 1974/75 (3); P 1974/75 (2).*
OTHER TOURS Commonwealth XI to Pakistan 1967/68. Rest of World XI to Pakistan 1973/74 (relief matches).
HST 95* WI v A, Adelaide, 1975/76. HS 147* Essex v Hants, Ilford, 1969.
BBT 6–77 WI v E, Oval, 1973. BB 9–61 Essex v Cambridge U, Brentwood, 1966 (county debut).
1000 RUNS (1) 1023 @ 30.08 in 1972.
RECORD Added 124 for 8th wkt with I. V. A. Richards, WI v I, Delhi, W Indies Test record.
Match double of 113 (century in 58 mins) and 12–73, Essex v Leics, Chelmsford, 1975. Retired 1977 through injury.

BOYCOTT, Geoffrey
RHB, RM

Born Fitzwilliam, Yorks, 21 Oct 1940. Educ Hemsworth GS. Debut 1962. *Wisden 1965. P.*
YORKSHIRE (381) 1962–. Cap 1963. Capt 1971–78. Benefit (£20,639) 1974. Testimonial 1984.
S AFRICA DOMESTIC Northern Transvaal 1971/72.
ENGLAND (108) 1964–81/82. A 1964 (4), 1968 (3), 1972 (2), 1977 (3), 1980 (1), 1981 (6); SA 1965 (2); WI 1966 (4), 1969 (3), 1973 (3), 1980 (5); NZ 1965 (2), 1969 (3), 1973 (3), 1978 (2); I 1967 (2), 1971 (1), 1974 (1), 1979 (4); P 1967 (1), 1971 (2). *A 1965/66 (5), 1970/71 (5), 1978/79 (6), 1979/80 (3); SA 1964/65 (5); WI 1967/68 (5), 1973/74 (5), 1980/81 (4); NZ 1965/66 (2), 1977/78 (3); I 1979/80 (1), 1981/82 (4); P 1977/78 (3).* Capt 4.
OTHER TOUR MCC to Ceylon 1969/70.
HST 246* E v I, Headingley, 1967. HS 261* MCC v WICB President's XI, Bridgetown, 1973/74.
BBT 3–47 E v SA, Cape Town, 1964/65. BB 4–14 Yorks v Lancs, Headingley, 1979.

1000 RUNS (22 + 3) 2503 @ 100.12 in 1971.
RECORDS 8114 runs @ 47.72 in 108 matches, England Test record; 22 Test centuries, equals England record. Only English batsman to average 100 in a season (100.12 in 1971 and 102.53 in 1979). Scored 100th century in 1977 — first batsman to do so in Test match (E v A, Headingley). In 1979 joined K. F. Barrington in having scored Test centuries on all six current England Test grounds. Added 149 for 10th wkt with G. B. Stevenson, Yorks v Warwicks, Edgbaston, 1982, county record. Carried bat for 99* in total of 215, E v A, Perth, 1979/80. Scored centuries against all fc counties except his own.
CWC Young Cricketer of 1964. OBE in 1980. Barred from Test cricket for three yrs for touring S Africa 1981/82 (SAB England XI). Yorkshire committee 1984–.

BOYD-MOSS, Robin James
RHB, SLA

Born Hattoh, Ceylon, 16 Dec 1959. Educ Bedford S; Magdalene C, Cambridge. Debut 1980.
CAMBRIDGE UNIVERSITY (36) 1980–83 (Blue 1980–83).
NORTHAMPTONSHIRE (60) 1980–.
HS 139 Cambridge U v Oxford U, Lord's, 1983.
BB 5–27 same match.
1000 RUNS (2) 1602 @ 44.50 in 1982.
RECORDS First batsman to score a century in each inns of the University match and to score centuries in three consecutive inns of that fixture. His aggregate of 489 runs is also a record for the University match.
Rugby: Blue.

BOYERS, Michael John Herbert
RHB, RMF

Born Plaistow, London, 16 Apr 1948. Educ George Monoux S, Walthamstow; Loughborough U. Debut 1969.
ESSEX (1) 1969.
HS 2 Essex v M'sex, Westcliff, 1969.

BOYNS, Cedric Nigel
RHB, RM

Born Harrogate, Yorks, 14 Aug 1954. Educ Adams GS, Newport, Salop; London U; Hughes Hall, Cambridge. Debut 1976.
CAMBRIDGE UNIVERSITY (4) 1976.
WORCESTERSHIRE (33) 1976–79.
HS 95 Worcs v Yorks, Scarborough, 1976.

BB 3–24 Worcs v Oxford U, The Parks, 1977.
Shropshire 1973, 1980–. Club: Old Hill.

BOYS, Frank Cecil
RHB

Born Kensington, London, 21 June 1918. Educ RNC Dartmouth. Debut 1947.
COMBINED SERVICES (7) 1947–51.
HS 84 Combined Services v Essex, Chelmsford, 1950.
Lt-Commander RN (retired). Member I Zingari.

BRACEWELL, Brendon Paul
RHB, RFM

Born Auckland, N Zealand, 14 Sept 1959. Educ Tauranga Boys' C. Debut 1977/78.
N ZEALAND DOMESTIC Central Districts (9) 1977/78–79/80, Otago (15) 1981/82–82/83, Northern Districts (9) 1983/84.
NEW ZEALAND (5) 1978–80/81. P 1978/79 (1). *E 1978 (3); A 1980/81 (1).*
HST 8 NZ v A, Brisbane, 1980/81. HS 36* Otago v Wellington, Alexandra, 1982/83.
BBT 3–110 NZ v E, Trent Bridge, 1978. BB 4–23 N Districts v Canterbury, Christchurch, 1983/84.
Professional: Ayr. Brothers J. G. Bracewell (N Zealand), D. W. Bracewell (Canterbury) and M. A. Bracewell (Otago).

BRACEWELL, John Garry
RHB, OB

Born Auckland, N Zealand, 15 Apr 1958. Educ Tauranga Boys' C. Debut 1978/79.
N ZEALAND DOMESTIC Otago (15) 1978/79–81/82, Auckland (16) 1982/83–.
NEW ZEALAND (8) 1980/81–83. I 1980/81 (1). *E 1983 (4); A 1980/81 (3).*
HST 28 NZ v E, Trent Bridge, 1983. HS 62 President's XI v Australians, Christchurch, 1981/82.
BBT 5–75 NZ v A, Auckland, 1980/81. BB 7–9 Otago v Canterbury, Dunedin, 1981/82.
Professional: Bishop Auckland. Brothers B. P. Bracewell (N Zealand), D. W. Bracewell (Canterbury) and M. A. Bracewell (Otago).

BRADBURY, Leslie
RHB, RMF

Born Matlock, Derbys, 19 Apr 1938. Debut 1971.

DERBYSHIRE (1) 1971.
Did not bat, 1 wkt.
Club: Undercliffe, Holmfirth.

BRADFIELD, Geoffrey Winston
———————RHB———————

Born Grahamstown, S Africa, 28 Feb
1948.
NORTHAMPTONSHIRE (1) 1970.
HS 50 Northants v Cambridge U, North-
ampton, 1970.
Club: Walsall. Represented S African
Country Districts v Transvaal, 1969.

BRADLEY, Peter
———————LHB, RM———————

Born Gee Cross, Hyde, Cheshire, 3 Mar
1937. Debut 1974.
MINOR COUNTIES (2) 1973–74.
HS 9* Minor Counties v Pakistanis, Jes-
mond, 1974.
BB 4–57 Minor Counties v W Indians,
Torquay, 1973.
Shropshire 1957–75. Clubs: St
Georges, West Bromwich Dartmouth.

BRADLEY, Michael Ewart
———————RHB, SLA———————

Born Halesowen, Worcs, 29 Mar 1934.
Educ Halesowen Technical C. Debut
1951.
WORCESTERSHIRE (9) 1951–52.
HS 6* Worcs v Scotland, Dundee, 1951.
BB 6–162 Worcs v Notts, Dudley, 1952.
Clubs: Old Hill, Halesowen.

BRADMAN, Donald George
———————RHB, LB———————

Born Cootamundra, NSW, Australia,
27 Aug 1908. Educ Bowral HS. Debut
1927/28. *Wisden* 1931.
AUSTRALIA DOMESTIC New South Wales
(41) 1927/28–33/34, South Australia
(44) 1935/36–48/49 (capt 1935/36–47/
48). Testimonial match ($A 9,342) 1948.
AUSTRALIA (52) 1928/29–48. E 1928/29
(4), 1932/33 (4), 1936/37 (5), 1946/47
(5); SA 1931/32 (5); WI 1930/31 (5); I
1947/48 (5). *E 1930 (5), 1934 (5), 1938
(4), 1948 (5)*. Capt 24.
HST 334 A v E, Headingley, 1930. HS
452* NSW v Queensland, Sydney,
1929/30.
BBT 1–8 A v WI, Adelaide, 1930/31. BB
3–35 Australians v Cambridge U,
Fenner's, 1930.
1000 RUNS (4+12) 2960 @ 98.66 in
1930.
RECORDS Bradman's Test average of
99.94 (for 6996 runs) and fc average of

95.14 (for 28,067 runs) are highest
career averages for any batsman of sig-
nificance. C. S. Dempster (723 @ 65.72)
and V. M. Merchant (12,876 @ 72.74)
respectively lie second. Of the 8 instances of a player scoring over 800 runs
in a Test series, Bradman provides 974
@ 139.14 v E, 1930 (record total – W. R.
Hammond lies second with 905 @
113.12 v A, 1928/29); 810 @ 90.00 v E,
1936/37; 806 @ 201.50 v SA, 1931/32
(record average). Bradman's 6996 runs
in 52 Tests most for A until G. S. Chappell passed him with 7110 in 87 Tests.
His 5028 runs v E is most by any player
against one country. Average of 115.66
in 1938 was first of more than 100 in
England and remains the highest.
Multiple centuries HS (above) was highest
score in fc cricket until 1958/59 when
beaten by Hanif Mohammed's 499 — it
remains highest not-out inns and
highest in second inns of match. Match
aggregate of 455 exceeded only by
Hanif's 499. HST (above) remains Test
record for A. Record 3 Test double-
centuries v E in 1930 and one of only six
players to have scored 2 double-
centuries in a series. Six double-
centuries in E in 1930 remains a record,
while career total of 37 — one more than
W. R. Hammond — is likely to remain
record for all time. During HST (above)
scored 309* on 1st day of match (including century — 105* — before lunch),
record for one day's Test cricket.
Centuries 29 Test centuries (including 2
treble- and 10 double-centuries, both
records), in 80 inns, record until passed
by S. M. Gavaskar with 30 in 174 inns.
His 4 centuries in 1930 series equals
record for Test rubber in England. Six
consecutive centuries (118, 143, 225,
107, 186, 135*) in 1938/39 joint world
record with C. B. Fry (1901) and M. J.
Procter (1970/71); also scored centuries
in 4 successive fc inns twice, in 1931/32
and 1948–48/49. Reached 100 fc centuries in 1947 in 295th inns — D. C. S.
Compton is second-fastest in 552 inns.
1000 runs Reached 1000 runs in England
in 1938 on 27 May — earliest date ever
(also reached 1000 runs before June in
1930, only batsman to do so twice).
Scored 1000 runs in A in 12 separate
seasons — I. M. Chappell lies second
with 6 such instances.
Test partnerships World Test record and
Australian fc record for 2nd wkt, 451
with W. H. Ponsford, A v E, Oval, 1934
(equals record for any wkt in Tests);
Australia Test record for 4th wkt, 388
with W. H. Ponsford, A v E, Headingley, 1934; world fc record for 5th wkt,
405 with S. G. Barnes, A v E, Sydney,
1946/47; world Test record for 6th wkt,
346 with J. H. W. Fingleton, A v E, Melbourne, 1936/37.
Took 30 runs off one over from A. P.

Freeman (466464), Australians v England XI, Folkestone, 1934.
Bradman was knighted in 1949 for his
services to cricket. After retirement he
served as an Australian Test selector.

BRAILSFORD, Frank Collis
———————RHB, RM———————

Born Chesterfield, Derbys, 26 Aug
1933. Debut 1958. *P.*
DERBYSHIRE (3) 1958.
HS 14 Derbys v Hants, Buxton, 1958.
Clubs: Undercliffe, Chesterfield.

BRAIN, Brian Maurice
———————RHB, RFM———————

Born Worcester, 13 Sept 1940. Educ
King's S, Worcester. Debut 1959. *P.*
WORCESTERSHIRE (149) 1959–75. Cap
1966.
GLOUCESTERSHIRE (110) 1976–81. Cap
1977.
TOURS Worcs to Rhodesia 1964/65.
Worcs to Jamaica 1965/66.
HS 57 Glos v Essex, Cheltenham, 1976.
BB 8–55 Worcs v Essex, Worcester,
1975.
Clubs: Stourbridge, West Bromwich
Dartmouth, Old Hill. Occasional cricket
writer; author of *Another Day, Another
Match* (1981).

BRANCKER, Rawle Cecil
———————LHB, SLA———————

Born Barbados, 19 Nov 1937. Debut
1955/56.
W INDIES DOMESTIC Barbados 1955/
56–69/70.
TOURS W Indies to England 1966. Barbados to England 1969.
HS 135* Barbados v Jamaica, Bridgetown, 1966/67.
BB 7–78 W Indians v Kent, Canterbury,
1966.

BRANSTON, John Richard
Martin
———————RHB, RM———————

Born Nuneaton, Warwicks, 20 Apr
1932. Educ Oxford U. Debut 1955.
FREE FORESTERS (1) 1955.
OXFORD UNIVERSITY (4) 1956.
HS 19 Oxford U v Surrey, Oval, 1956.
BB 3–50 same match.

BRASSINGTON, Andrew James
———————RHB, WK———————

Born Bagnall, Staffs, 9 Aug 1954. Educ
Endon Sec S, Stoke on Trent. Debut
1974.
GLOUCESTERSHIRE (124) 1974–. Cap
1978.
HS 35 Glos v Sussex, Hastings, 1982.

BRAYSHAY, Peter Beldon
————RHB, RMF————

Born Leeds, Yorks, 14 Oct 1916. Educ
Bootham S. Debut 1945/46.
INDIA DOMESTIC Europeans 1945/46.
YORKSHIRE (2) 1952.
HS 13 Yorks v Derbys, Chesterfield,
1952.
BB 2–48 same match.

BRAZIER, Alan Frederick
————RHB, RM————

Born Paddington, London, 7 Dec 1924.
Educ Southall Technical S. Debut
1948. *P*.
SURREY (36) 1948–54.
KENT (20) 1955–56.
HS 92 Surrey v Northants, Northampton, 1953.
BB 2–45 Kent v Cambridge U, Fenner's,
1956.
1212 runs for Surrey 2nd XI in 1949
remains Minor Counties record. Club:
Ealing Dean. Former professional coach
at St George's, Weybridge (from 1965).

BREAKWELL, Dennis
————LHB, SLA————

Born Brierley Hill, Staffs, 2 July 1948.
Educ Ounsdale CS, Wombourne,
Staffs. Debut 1969.
NORTHAMPTONSHIRE (64) 1969–72.
SOMERSET (165) 1973–83. Cap 1976.
HS 100* Som v N Zealanders, Taunton,
1978.
BB 8–39 Northants v Kent, Dover, 1970.
Clubs: Dudley, Walsall.

BREARLEY, Horace
————RHB————

Born Heckmondwike, Yorks, 26 June
1913. Debut 1937.
YORKSHIRE (1) 1937.
MINOR COUNTIES (2) 1937.
MIDDLESEX (2) 1949.
HS 37 Minor Counties v Oxford U, The
Parks, 1937.
Club: Brentham. Son J. M. Brearley
(Cambridge U, M'sex and England).

BREARLEY, John *Michael*
————RHB, occ WK————

Born Harrow, Middlesex, 28 Apr 1942.
Educ City of London S; St John's C,
Cambridge. Debut 1961. *Wisden 1977*.
CAMBRIDGE UNIVERSITY (64) 1961–66
(Blue 1961–64). Capt 1963–64.
MIDDLESEX (291) 1961–83. Cap 1964.
Capt 1971–82. Benefit (£31,000) 1978.

ENGLAND (39) 1976–81. A 1977 (5), 1981
(4); WI 1976 (2); NZ 1978 (3); I 1979 (4);
P 1978 (3). *A 1976/77 (1), 1978/79 (6),
1979/80 (3); I 1976/77 (5), 1979/80
(1); P 1977/78 (2)*. Capt 31.
OTHER TOURS MCC to S Africa 1964/65.
MCC Under-25 to Pakistan 1966/67
(capt). Rest of World XI to Pakistan
1973/74 (relief matches). M'sex to Zimbabwe 1980/81 (capt). Overseas XI to
India 1980/81.
HST 91 E v I, Bombay, 1976/77. HS 312*
MCC Under-25 v North Zone,
Peshawar, 1966/67 (made on 1st day of
match).
1000 RUNS (11) 2178 @ 44.44 in 1964.
RECORDS Most runs (4310 @ 38.48) for
Cambridge U.
Gentlemen v Players (2) 1961. CWC
Young Cricketer of 1964. Awarded
OBE. MCC Hon. member. Father H.
Brearley (Yorks and M'sex).

BREDDY, Martin Nicholas
————RHB————

Born Torquay, Devon, 23 Sept 1961.
Educ Cheltenham GS; Fitzwilliam C,
Cambridge. Debut 1984.
CAMBRIDGE UNIVERSITY (10) 1984 (Blue).
HS 61 Cambridge U v Oxford U, Lord's,
1984.
Club: Cheltenham.

BREMNER, Colin David
————RHB, WK————

Born Hawthorn, Melbourne, Victoria,
Australia, 29 Jan 1920. Debut 1945.
AUSTRALIA DOMESTIC Australian Services (3) 1945/46.
DOMINIONS (1) 1945.
TOUR Australian Services in India 1945/
46.
HS 4* Australian Services v Tasmania,
Hobart, 1945/46.
Stumped W. R. Hammond twice on fc
debut. Club: East Melbourne.

BRENNAN, Donald Vincent
————RHB, WK————

Born Eccleshill, Yorks, 10 Feb 1920.
Died Ilkley, Yorks, 9 Jan 1985. Educ
Downside. Debut 1947.
YORKSHIRE (204) 1947–53. Cap 1947.
MCC (1) 1964.
ENGLAND (2) SA 1951.
TOUR MCC to India, Pakistan and Ceylon 1951/52.
HST 16 E v SA, Headingley, 1951. HS 67*
MCC v Maharashtra, Poona, 1951/52.
Gentlemen v Players (6) 1950–53. Club:
Eccleshill. Yorkshire committee to
1984.

BRETTELL, David Norman
————LHB, SLA————

Born Woking, Surrey, 10 Mar 1956.
Educ Cheltenham C; Trinity C, Oxford.
Debut 1975.
OXFORD UNIVERSITY (13) 1975–78 (Blue
1977).
HS 39 Oxford U v Notts, The Parks,
1977.
BB 3–22 Oxford U v Som, The Parks,
1978.

BRETTELL, James Gordon
————RHB, SLA————

Born Woking, Surrey, 19 Dec 1962.
Educ Cheltenham C; Lincoln C, Oxford. Debut 1984.
OXFORD UNIVERSITY (1) 1984.
No runs.
Brother D. N. Brettell (Oxford U).

BREWSTER, Vincent Crescedo
————LHB, SLA————

Born Bridgetown, Barbados, 2 Jan 1940.
Debut 1965.
WARWICKSHIRE (2) 1965.
HS 35* Warwicks v Oxford U, Edgbaston, 1965.
BB 7–58 same match (fc debut).
Professional: Norton 1966.

BRICE, Gordon Harry Joseph
————RHB, RFM————

Born Bedford, 4 May 1924. Educ Bedford Modern S. Debut 1949. *P*.
NORTHAMPTONSHIRE (25) 1949–52.
HS 82* Northants v Hants, Bournemouth, 1950.
BB 4–20 Northants v Surrey, Kettering, 1951.
Bedfordshire 1953–55. Soccer: Luton
Town, Wolverhampton Wanderers,
Reading, Fulham.

BRIDGE, Derek James Wilson
————RHB, OB————

Born Manchester, 30 Oct 1921. Educ
King's S, Peterborough; Hertford C,
Oxford. Debut 1947.
OXFORD UNIVERSITY (1) 1947.
NORTHAMPTONSHIRE (3) 1947.
HS 25* Northants v S Africans, Northampton, 1947.
BB 2–14 Northants v Warwicks, Edgbaston, 1947.
Dorset 1949–69. Rugby: Blue. Captain
in, and represented, Territorial Army.

BRIDGE, Walter *Basil*
—RHB, OB—

Born Birmingham, 29 May 1938. Debut 1955. *P.*
WARWICKSHIRE (98) 1955–68. Cap 1961.
HS 56* Warwicks v Indians, Edgbaston, 1959.
BB 8–56 Warwicks v Cambridge U, Edgbaston, 1959.
100 WKTS (1) 123 @ 22.99 in 1961.
Clubs: Pickwick, Studley.

BRIDGER, John Richard
—RHB—

Born Dulwich, London, 8 Apr 1920. Educ Rugby; Clare C, Cambridge. Debut 1945 (Under-33).
HAMPSHIRE (38) 1946–54. Cap 1954.
HS 142 Hants v M'sex, Bournemouth, 1946.
War-time Blue. Ordained (Church of England) 1945.

BRIERLEY, Thomas Leslie
—RHB, WK—

Born Southampton, 15 June 1910. Debut 1931. *P.*
GLAMORGAN (181) 1931–39.
LANCASHIRE (46) 1946–48. Cap 1946.
CANADA (5) 1951–54.
TOUR Canada to England 1954.
HS 116 Glam v Lancs, Old Trafford, 1938 and 116* Lancs v Glam, Liverpool, 1947.
1000 RUNS (1) 1183 @ 23.66 in 1938.
Lancs assistant coach 1948. Coach Vancouver 1949–51. British Colombia 1952. Groundsman Shawnigan Lake in 1960s.

BRIERS, Nigel Edwin
—RHB, occ RM—

Born Leicester, 15 Jan 1955. Educ Lutterworth GS; Borough Road C. Debut 1971.
LEICESTERSHIRE (163) 1971–. Cap 1981.
HS 201* Leics v Warwicks, Edgbaston, 1983.
BB 3–48 Leics v Lancs, Leicester, 1984.
1000 RUNS (3) 1289 @ 40.28 in 1983.
TOUR Leics XI to Zimbabwe 1980/81.
RECORDS Added 233 for 5th wkt with R. W. Tolchard, Leics v Som, Leicester, 1979, county record. Debut aged 16 yrs 103 days, youngest-ever Leics player. Cousin N. Briers (Leics).

BRIERS, Norman
—RHB, RFM—

Born Leicester, 10 Feb 1947. Debut 1967.
LEICESTERSHIRE (1) 1967.
HS 1 Leics v Cambridge U, Fenner's, 1967.
Cousin N. E. Briers (Leics).

BRIGGS, Kenneth Robert
—RHB, OB—

Born Guildford, Surrey, 17 July 1933. Educ KCS, Wimbledon. Debut 1961.
COMBINED SERVICES (1) 1961.
HS 17* Combined Services v Notts, Trent Bridge, 1961.
Regular RAF officer.

BRIGGS, Patrick David
—RHB—

Born Timperley, Cheshire, 24 Aug 1940. Educ Pocklington S; Cambridge U. Debut 1963.
CAMBRIDGE UNIVERSITY (21) 1963–64.
HS 91 Cambridge U v Essex, Fenner's, 1963.
Cheshire 1960–67. Bedfordshire 1969–73. Club: Bedford Town. Rugby: Blue.

BRIGHT, Raymond James
—RHB, SLA—

Born Footscray, Victoria, Australia, 13 July 1954. Debut 1972/73.
AUSTRALIAN DOMESTIC Victoria (69) 1972/73–82/83.
AUSTRALIA (16) 1977–82/83. E 1979/80 (1); WI 1979/80 (1). *E 1977 (3), 1980 (1), 1981 (5); P 1979/80 (3), 1982/83 (2).*
OTHER TOURS Australia to N Zealand 1973/74, 1976/77, 1981/82. Australia to Sri Lanka 1980/81.
HST 33 A v E, Lord's, 1981. HS 108 Victoria v Tasmania, Hobart, 1980/81.
BBT 7–87 A v P, Karachi, 1979/80. BB as above.
World Series Cricket (Kerry Packer) 1977/78–78/79.

BRINDLE, Reginald Gordon
—RHB—

Born Warrington, Lancs, 3 Oct 1925. Debut 1949. *P.*
WARWICKSHIRE (1) 1949.
HS 42 Warwicks v Combined Services, Edgbaston, 1949.

BRISTOWE, William Robert
—RHB, OB—

Born Woking, Surrey, 17 Nov 1963. Educ Charterhouse; St Edmund Hall, Oxford. Debut 1984.
OXFORD UNIVERSITY (5) 1984 (Blue).
HS 30* Oxford U v Glos, The Parks, 1984.

BROAD, Brian *Christopher*
—LHB, RM—

Born Bristol 29 Sept 1957. Educ Colstons S, Bristol; St Paul's C, Cheltenham. Debut 1979.
GLOUCESTERSHIRE (89) 1979–83. Cap 1981.
NOTTINGHAMSHIRE (18) 1984–.
ENGLAND (5) 1984. WI 1984 (4); SL 1984 (1).
HST 86 E v SL, Lord's, 1984. HS 145 Glos v Notts, Bristol, 1983.
BB 2–14 Glos v W Indians, Bristol, 1980.
1000 RUNS (4) 1549 @ 44.25 in 1984.

BROADBENT, Robert Gillespie
—RHB, RMF—

Born Beckenham, Kent, 21 June 1924. Educ Caterham S. Debut 1950. *P from 1951.*
WORCESTERSHIRE (307) 1950–63. Cap 1951. Benefit (£5402) 1961.
HS 155 Worcs v M'sex, Worcester, 1951.
1000 RUNS (7) 1556 @ 33.10 in 1952.
Hertfordshire 1964.

BROCKLEBANK, John Montague
—RHB, LB—

Born London, 3 Sept 1915. Died Rabat, Malta, 13 Sept 1974. Educ Eton; Magdalene C, Cambridge. Debut 1936.
CAMBRIDGE UNIVERSITY (7) 1936 (Blue).
MCC (4) 1938–48.
LANCASHIRE (4) 1939.
FREE FORESTERS (4) 1947–49.
INDIA DOMESTIC Bengal 1947/48.
HS 23 Cambridge U v Som, Taunton, 1936.
BB 6–92 (10–139 match) Cambridge U v Oxford U, Lord's, 1936.
Selected for cancelled MCC tour of India 1939/40. Gentlemen v Players (1) 1939. Clubs: The Arabs, I Zingari, Northern Nomads. Chairman of Cunard 1959–65. Knighted. Uncle Sir F. S. Jackson (Yorkshire and England); brother T. A. L. Brocklebank (Cambridge U).

BROCKLEHURST, Benjamin Gilbert
———RHB———

Born Knapton, Norfolk, 18 Feb 1922.
Educ Bradfield C. Debut 1952.
SOMERSET (64) 1952–54. Cap 1953. Capt
1953–54.
HS 89 Som v Pakistanis, Taunton, 1954.
Berkshire 1955. Managing director *The
Cricketer International*. Outstanding
schoolboy athlete. Son-in-law R. A.
Hutton (Cambridge U and Yorkshire).

BRODERICK, Vincent
———LHB, SLA———

Born Bacup, Lancs, 17 Aug 1920. Debut
1939. *P.*
NORTHAMPTONSHIRE (245) 1939–57.
Cap 1947. Testimonial (£1367) 1954.
HS 190 Northants v Scotland, Peterborough, 1953 (added 361 for 1st wkt
with N. Oldfield, Northants record).
BB 9–35 Northants v Sussex, Horsham,
1948.
1000 RUNS (2) 1066 @ 26.65 in 1948.
100 WKTS (1) 100 @ 22.77 in 1948.
DOUBLE (1) 1948.
Professional coach at Winchester C
1960–.

BRODHURST, Arthur Hugh
———RHB, LB———

Born Buenos Aires, Argentina, 21 July
1916. Educ Malvern; Pembroke C,
Cambridge. Debut 1937.
CAMBRIDGE UNIVERSITY (10) 1937–39
(Blue 1939).
GLOUCESTERSHIRE (6) 1939–46.
TOURS Oxford and Cambridge Univer-
sities to Jamaica 1938/39. MCC to
Canada 1951.
HS 111 Cambridge U v Leics, Fenner's,
1939.
BB 4–83 Cambridge U v Army,
Fenner's, 1939.
Father-in-law H. S. Altham (Surrey and
Hants; cricket writer).

BRODIE, James Bruce
———RHB, RFM———

Born Graaff-Reinet, S Africa, 19 Mar
1937. Educ Union HS, Graaff-Reinet;
Natal U; Fitzwilliam C, Cambridge.
Debut 1959.
CAMBRIDGE UNIVERSITY (17) 1959–60
(Blue 1960).
COMMONWEALTH XI (1) 1960.
S AFRICA DOMESTIC Eastern Province
1961/62–63/64.
HS 37 Cambridge U v MCC, Lord's,
1960.

BB 5–47 Cambridge U v S Africans,
Fenner's, 1960.
Berkshire 1960.

BRODRICK, Peter Dawson
———RHB, SLA———

Born North Shields, Northumberland,
11 May 1937. Educ Newcastle GS;
Caius C, Cambridge. Debut 1959.
CAMBRIDGE UNIVERSITY (22) 1959–61
(Blue 1961).
HS 49 Cambridge U v Essex, Fenner's,
1961.
BB 4–74 Cambridge U v Essex,
Fenner's, 1961.
Northumberland 1956–68.

BROMFIELD, Harry Dudley
———RHB, OB———

Born Mossel Bay, S Africa, 26 June
1932. Educ Observatory Boys' HS.
Debut 1956/57.
S AFRICA DOMESTIC Western Province
1956/57–68/69.
SOUTH AFRICA (9) 1961/62–65. E 1964/65
(3); NZ 1961/62 (5). *E 1965 (1).*
HS 44 W Province v E Province, Port
Elizabeth, 1962/63. HST 21 SA v NZ,
Port Elizabeth, 1961/62.
BBT 5–88 SA v E, Cape Town, 1964/65.
BB 7–60 W Province v Transvaal, Cape
Town, 1960/61.

BROMLEY, Philip Harry
———RHB, OB———

Born Stratford-upon-Avon, 30 July
1930. Educ Warwick S. Debut 1947. *P.*
WARWICKSHIRE (49) 1947–56.
HS 121* Warwicks v Essex, Edgbaston,
1952.
BB 5–61 Warwicks v Worcs, Worcester,
1953.
Shropshire 1958–70. Club: Leamington
Spa.

BROMLEY, Richard Charles
———LHB, WK———

Born Oxted, Surrey, 23 June 1946. Educ
Christ's C, Brecon; St Catharine's C,
Cambridge. Debut 1970.
CAMBRIDGE UNIVERSITY (5) 1970 (Blue).
HS 18 Cambridge U v Warwicks,
Fenner's, 1970.

BROOKE, Bernard
———RHB, RMF———

Born Newsome, Huddersfield, 3 Mar
1930. Debut 1950. *P.*

YORKSHIRE (2) 1950.
HS 14 Yorks v MCC, Lord's, 1950.
Clubs: Armitage Bridge, Lightcliffe,
Honley, Bingley, Thongsbridge, Pud-
sey St Laurence, Broad Oak.

BROOKER, Mervyn Edward William
———RHB, RMF———

Born Burton-on-Trent, 24 Mar 1954.
Educ Lancaster RGS; Burnley GS;
Jesus C, Cambridge. Debut 1974.
CAMBRIDGE UNIVERSITY (15) 1974–76
(Blue 1976).
HS 9 Cambridge U v Surrey, Fenner's,
1976.
BB 4–58 Cambridge U v Leics,
Fenner's, 1976.
Cambridgeshire 1976–80. Clubs:
Colne, Granta, Kidderminster.

BROOKES, Dennis
———RHB———

Born Kippax, Yorks, 29 Oct 1915.
Debut 1934. *P.*
NORTHAMPTONSHIRE (492) 1934–59.
Cap 1937. Benefit (£3280) 1958. Capt
1954–57.
ENGLAND (1) *WI 1947/48.*
HST 10 E v WI, Bridgetown, 1947/48. HS
257 Northants v Glos, Bristol, 1949.
1000 RUNS (17) 2229 @ 47.42 in 1952.
NORTHANTS RECORDS Most appearances
(492); runs (28,980 — J. E. Timms
second with 20,384); centuries (67 —
Mushtaq Mohammed second with 32);
runs in a season (2198 in 1952); 1000
runs in a season (17 — J. E. Timms
second with 11). Added 347 for 5th wkt
with D. W. Barrick, Northants v Essex,
Northampton, 1952, county record.
Scored centuries against all fc counties
except his own.
Players v Gentlemen (2) 1947–59. Northants president 1982. Justice of the Peace.

BROOKE-TAYLOR, David Kirby
———RHB———

Born Bakewell, Derbys, 15 June 1920.
Educ Cheltenham C. Debut 1947.
DERBYSHIRE (15) 1947–49.
HS 61* Derbys v Northants, Rushden,
1947.
Lives in Queensland. Father G. P.
Brooke-Taylor (Derbys); cousin Tim
Brooke-Taylor (comedian).

BROOKS, Kevin Graham
————RHB, RM————

Born Reading, Berkshire, 15 Oct 1959. Educ Clarkes GS, Bristol; Monkseaton GS, Whitley Bay. Debut 1980.
DERBYSHIRE (1) 1980.
HS 8 Derbys v Warwicks, Edgbaston, 1980.
Lincolnshire 1983.

BROOKS, Richard Alan
————RHB, WK————

Born Edgware, M'sex, 14 June 1943. Educ Quintin S; Bristol U; St Edmund Hall, Oxford. Debut 1967.
OXFORD UNIVERSITY (9) 1967 (Blue).
SOMERSET (26) 1968.
HS 44 Oxford U v Cambridge U, Lord's, 1967.
Berkshire 1977.

BROOKS, Victor Charles George
————LHB, occ WK————

Born East Ham, London, 29 June 1948. Educ East Ham GS; Manchester U. Debut 1970.
ESSEX (3) 1970–71.
HS 22 Essex v Warwicks, Edgbaston, 1971.

BROOME, Ian
————RHB, RFM————

Born Bradenstoke-cum-Clack, Wilts, 6 May 1960. Educ Mitcham Technical C, Melbourne, Australia; Box Hill Technical C, Melbourne, Australia. Debut 1984.
DERBYSHIRE (2) 1984.
HS 26* Derbys v Kent, Derby, 1984.
Played for Glos in John Player League in 1980.

BROUGHTON, Peter Norman
————RHB, RFM————

Born Castleford, Yorks, 22 Oct 1935. Debut 1956. P.
YORKSHIRE (6) 1956.
LEICESTERSHIRE (24) 1960–62.
HS 17* Leics v Surrey, Leicester, 1960 and 17 v Warwicks, Hinckley, 1962.
BB 6–38 Yorks v Som, Taunton, 1956.
Cumberland 1963–69. Clubs: Idle, Leeds.

BROWN, Alan
————RHB, RFM————

Born Rainworth, Notts, 17 Oct 1935. Educ High Oakham GS. Debut 1957. P.

KENT (237) 1957–70. Cap 1961. Joint benefit (with D. M. Sayer) 1971.
ENGLAND (2) 1961/62. I 1961/62 (1); P 1961/62 (1).
HST 3* E v P, Lahore, 1961/62. HS 81 Kent v Glam, Folkestone, 1968.
BBT 3–27 E v P, Lahore, 1961/62. BB 8–47 Kent v Warwicks, Nuneaton, 1963.
100 WKTS (1) 116 @ 19.04 in 1965.
Club: Tunbridge Wells.

BROWN, Alan
————RHB, WK————

Born Darwen, Lancs, 23 Dec 1957. Educ Darwen GS; St John's C, York U. Debut 1979.
WORCESTERSHIRE (1) 1979.
Did not bat.

BROWN, Alexander
————RHB, RM————

Born Coatbridge, Lanarkshire, Scotland, 7 Oct 1950. Educ St Patrick's. Debut 1977.
SCOTLAND (5) 1977–82.
HS 25 Scotland v Ireland, Dublin, 1977.

BROWN, Andrew John Trevor
————LHB, ROB————

Born Edinburgh, Scotland, 27 June 1935. Educ Sherborne S. Debut 1960.
COMBINED SERVICES (2) 1960.
HS 40* Combined Services v Cambridge U, Fenner's, 1960.

BROWN, Anthony Stephen
————RHB, RM————

Born Bristol, Glos, 24 June 1936. Educ Fairfield GS, Bristol. Debut 1953. P.
GLOUCESTERSHIRE (489) 1953–76. Cap 1957. Capt 1969–76. Benefit 1969.
TOUR D. H. Robins' XI to S Africa 1972/73. International XI to S Africa 1974/75.
HS 116 Glos v Som, Bristol, 1971.
BB 8–80 Glos v Essex, Leyton, 1963.
1000 RUNS (1) 1149 @ 20.15 in 1964.
100 WKTS (2) 110 @ 23.08 in 1959 and 110 @ 26.40 in 1962.
RECORD 7 catches in inns, Glos v Notts, Trent Bridge, 1966, equals world record for fielder.
12,684 runs and 1223 wkts for Glos. 495 catches in fc career.
Glos secretary 1977–82. Som secretary 1983–. Manager England to India and Sri Lanka 1984/85.

BROWN, David Basil Stuart
————LHB————

Born Insch, Scotland, 14 June 1941. Educ Aberdeen GS. Debut 1973.
SCOTLAND (3) 1973–76.
HS 58 Scotland v Ireland, Cork, 1973.

BROWN, David John
————RHB, RFM————

Born Walsall, Staffs, 30 Jan 1942. Educ Queen Mary GS, Walsall. Debut 1961. P.
WARWICKSHIRE (325) 1961–82. Cap 1964. Capt 1975–77. Benefit (£21,109) 1973.
ENGLAND (26) 1965–69. A 1968 (4); SA 1965 (2); WI 1966 (1), 1969 (3); NZ 1969 (1); I 1967 (2). A 1965/66 (4); WI 1967/68 (4); NZ 1965/66 (2); P 1968/69 (3).
OTHER TOURS MCC to S Africa 1964/65. MCC Under-25 to Pakistan 1966/67. Rest of World XI to Pakistan 1970/71. D. H. Robins' XI to S Africa 1972/73.
HST 44 E v NZ, Christchurch, 1965/66. HS 79 Warwicks v Derbys, Edgbaston, 1972.
BBT 5–42 E v A, Lord's, 1968. BB 8–60 Warwicks v M'sex, Lord's, 1975.
Warwicks manager 1980–. MCC Hon. member. Club: Walsall.

BROWN, David Wyndham James
————RHB, OB————

Born Cheltenham, Glos, 26 Feb 1942. Educ Cheltenham GS. Debut 1964.
GLOUCESTERSHIRE (88) 1964–67.
HS 142 Glos v Glam, Bristol, 1965.
BB 3–84 A. E. R. Gilligan's XI v W Indians, Hastings, 1966.
Club: Cheltenham.

BROWN, Frederick Richard
————RHB, LBG/RM————

Born Lima, Peru, 16 Dec 1910. Educ The Leys; St John's C, Cambridge. Debut 1930. Wisden 1933.
CAMBRIDGE UNIVERSITY (25) 1930–31 (Blue 1930–31).
SURREY (106) 1931–48. Cap 1932.
NORTHAMPTONSHIRE (102) 1949–53. Cap 1949. Capt 1949–53.
FREE FORESTERS (11) 1935–61.
ENGLAND (22) 1931–53. A 1953 (1); SA 1951 (5); WI 1950 (1); NZ 1931 (2), 1937 (1), 1949 (2); I 1932 (1). A 1950/51 (5); NZ 1932/33 (2), 1950/51 (2). Capt 15.
OTHER TOURS MCC to Australia 1932/33. F.R. Brown's XI to E Africa 1961/62 (not fc).
HST 79 E v A, Sydney, 1950/51. HS 212 Surrey v M'sex, Oval, 1932.

BBT 5–49 E v A, Melbourne, 1950/51. BB 8–34 Surrey v Som, Weston-super-Mare, 1939.
1000 RUNS (4) 1135 @ 32.42 in 1932.
100 WKTS (3) 120 @ 20.46 in 1932.
DOUBLE (2) 1932, 1949.
RECORD Added 155 for 8th wkt with A. E. Nutter, Northants v Glam, Northampton, 1952, county record.
Gentlemen v Players (16) 1931–53. England Test selector 1951–53 (chairman 1953). Manager MCC to S Africa 1956/57. MCC president 1971/72. MCC committee 1951–81. Chairman Cricket Council 1974–79. NCA President. MBE for services to cricket.

BROWN, James
—RHB, WK—

Born Perth, Scotland, 24 Sept 1931. Educ Perth Academy. Debut 1953.
SCOTLAND (57) 1953–73.
HS 90 Scotland v Yorks, Paisley, 1957. Dismissed seven batsmen in an inns (4 ct, 3 st) Scotland v Ireland, Dublin, 1957.
Gentlemen v Players (2) 1959–60. MBE for services to Scottish cricket.

BROWN, Keith Robert
—RHB, WK—

Born Edmonton, M'sex, 18 Mar 1963. Educ Chace S, Enfield. Debut 1984.
MIDDLESEX (1) 1984.
HS 6 M'sex v Hants, Bournemouth, 1984.

BROWN, Robin David
—RHB, WK—

Born Gatooma, Southern Rhodesia, 11 Mar 1951. Debut 1976/77.
S AFRICA DOMESTIC Rhodesia B, Rhodesia, 1976/77–79/80.
ZIMBABWE 1980/81–.
TOURS Zimbabwe to England 1982. Zimbabwe to Sri Lanka 1983/84.
HS 200* (maiden century) Rhodesia B v E Province B, Salisbury, 1978/79.

BROWN, Sydney Maurice
—RHB—

Born Eltham, Kent, 8 Dec 1917. Debut 1937. P.
MIDDLESEX (313) 1937–55. Cap 1938. Benefit (£5695) 1953.
HS 232* M'sex v Som, Lord's, 1951.
BB 2–19 M'sex v Sussex, Hove, 1951.
1000 RUNS (9) 2078 @ 37.78 in 1947.

BROWN, William Alfred
—RHB—

Born Toowoomba, Queensland, Australia, 31 July 1912. Debut 1932/33. *Wisden* 1939.
AUSTRALIA DOMESTIC New South Wales (22) 1932/33–34/35, Queensland (50) 1936/37–49/50.
AUSTRALIA (22) 1934–48. E 1936/37 (2); I 1947/48 (3). *E 1934 (5), 1938 (4), 1948 (2); SA 1935/36 (5); NZ 1945/46 (1)*. Capt 1.
OTHER TOUR Australia to N Zealand 1949/50.
HST 206* A v E, Lord's, 1938 (carried bat through inns of 422). HS 265* Australians v Derbys, Chesterfield, 1938.
BB 4–16 Australians v South of England, Hastings, 1948.
1000 RUNS (3 + 2) 1854 @ 57.93 in 1938.

BRUYNS, André
—RHB, occ WK—

Born Pietermaritzburg, S Africa, 19 Sept 1946. Educ Stellenbosch U. Debut 1965/66.
S AFRICA DOMESTIC S African Universities 1965/66–67, Western Province 1965/66–71/72, 1973/74–76/77, Natal 1972/73.
TOURS S African Universities to England 1967.
HS 197 W Province v Natal B, Cape Town, 1966/67.

BRYANT, David John
—RHB, RFM—

Born London, 29 Oct 1950. Educ Pembroke C, Oxford. Debut 1970.
OXFORD UNIVERSITY (6) 1970–71.
HS 6* Oxford U v Hants, The Parks, 1971.
BB 3–40 Oxford U v Leics, Leicester, 1971.

BRYANT, Leonard Eric
—LHB, SLA—

Born Weston-super-Mare, Som, 2 June 1936. Debut 1958. P.
SOMERSET (22) 1958–60.
HS 17 Som v Glos, Bath, 1960.
BB 5–64 Som v Worcs, Stourbridge, 1958.
No-balled five times for throwing, Som v Glos, Bath, 1960. Retired same season.

BRYANT, Michael
—RHB, RFM—

Born Camborne, Cornwall, 5 Apr 1959. Debut 1982.
SOMERSET (2) 1982.
HS 6 Som v Essex, Chelmsford, 1982. Cornwall 1978–81. Club: Redruth.

BUCK, William Dalton
—RHB, RM—

Born Southampton, 30 Sept 1946. Educ Claysmore S. Debut 1969.
HAMPSHIRE (1) 1969.
SOMERSET (1) 1969.
HS 6 Som v W Indians, Taunton, 1969.
BB 2–54 same match.
Non-championship games for two counties in same season.

BUCKINGHAM, Amyand David
—RHB, OB—

Born Sydney, Australia, 28 Jan 1930. Educ Barker C, Hornsby, NSW; Sydney U; Cambridge U. Debut 1955.
CAMBRIDGE UNIVERSITY (4) 1955.
FREE FORESTERS (6) 1957–60.
HS 61 Free Foresters v Cambridge U, Fenner's, 1957.

BUCKLAND, Joseph Edwin
—LHB, LF—

Born Lingfield, Surrey, 24 Sept 1916. Debut 1948.
SOMERSET (1) 1948.
HS 17* Som v Glam, Newport, 1948.
BB 2–35 same match.

BUDD, William *Lloyd*
—RHB, RFM—

Born Hawkley, Hants, 25 Oct 1913. Debut 1934. P.
HAMPSHIRE (60) 1934–46.
HS 77* Hants v Surrey, Oval, 1937.
BB 4–22 Hants v Essex, Southend, 1937.
Fc umpire 1969–82 (4 Tests, 1976–78). Minor Counties umpire until 1968.

BUGGÉ, David Anthony Bowdell
—RHB, RMF—

Born Aden, 12 Dec 1956. Educ Cranleigh; Oriel C, Oxford. Debut 1977.
OXFORD UNIVERSITY (1) 1977.
No runs, no wkts.
Club: Blackheath (Surrey).

BULCOCK, Leslie
—RHB, RM/OB—

Born Colne, Lancs, 5 Jan 1913. Educ Park S, Colne. Debut 1946. *P.*
LANCASHIRE (1) 1946.
HS 1 Lancs v Sussex, Old Trafford, 1946.
BB 2–41 same match.
Professional: Heywood, Colne, Bingley, Windhill, Baildon, Kearsley, Walkden, Egerton.

BULLEN, Christopher Keith
—RHB, OB—

Born Clapham, London, 5 Nov 1962. Educ Chaucer Middle S; Rutlish S. Debut 1982.
SURREY (1) 1982.
Did not bat, no wkts.

BULLER, John Sydney
—RHB, WK—

Born Wortley, Bramley, Yorks, 23 Aug 1909. Died, while umpiring a match at Edgbaston, 7 Aug 1970. Debut 1930. *P.*
YORKSHIRE (1) 1930.
WORCESTERSHIRE (110) 1935–46.
HS 64 Worcs v Northants, Kettering, 1938.
Fc umpire 1951–70 (33 Tests, 1956–69). MBE 1965 for services to cricket umpiring.

BUNYARD, Graham Stuart
—RHB, RF—

Born Port Elizabeth, S Africa, 17 Mar 1939. Educ Witwatersrand U. Debut 1959/60.
S AFRICA DOMESTIC Transvaal 1959/60–60/61, Rhodesia 1962/63.
TOUR S African Fezelas to England 1961.
HS 35 Transvaal v Natal, J'burg, 1959/60.
BB 5–35 Transvaal v Rhodesia, Bulawayo, 1959/60.

BURCH, Geoffrey Worth
—RHB, WK—

Born Leicester, 12 Apr 1937. Debut 1958. *P.*
LEICESTERSHIRE (46) 1958–64.
HS 64* Leics v Notts, Coalville, 1959.
Professional artist.

BURCHNALL, Richard Langley
—RHB—

Born Oxford, 8 Aug 1948. Educ Winchester; Lincoln C, Oxford. Debut 1968.

OXFORD UNIVERSITY (32) 1968–71 (Blue 1970–71).
HS 85 Oxford U v Notts, Trent Bridge, 1968.

BURDEN, Mervyn Derek
—RHB, OB—

Born Southampton, 4 Oct 1930. Educ King Edward VI S, Southampton. Debut 1953. *P.*
HAMPSHIRE (174) 1953–63. Cap 1955.
HS 51 Hants v Warwicks, Portsmouth, 1960.
BB 8–38 Hants v Som, Frome, 1961.

BURGE, Peter John Parnell
—RHB—

Born Buranda, Queensland, Australia, 17 May 1932. Educ Brisbane GS. Debut 1952/53.
AUSTRALIA DOMESTIC Queensland (91) 1952/53–67/68 (capt 30).
AUSTRALIA (42) 1954/55–65/66. E 1954/55 (1), 1958/59 (1), 1962/63 (3), 1965/66 (4); SA 1963/64 (5); WI 1960/61 (2). *E 1956 (3), 1961 (5), 1964 (5); SA 1957/58 (1); WI 1954/55 (1); I 1956/57 (3), 1959/60 (2), 1964/65 (3); P 1959/60 (2), 1964/65 (1).*
OTHER TOURS Australia to N Zealand 1956/57, 1966/67.
HST 181 A v E, Oval, 1961. HS 283 Queensland v NSW, Brisbane, 1963/64.
1000 RUNS (2 + 5) 1376 @ 55.04 in 1961.
RECORDS 283 (above) best-ever score for Queensland in fc cricket.
MCC Hon. member.

BURGER,
Christopher George de Villiers
—RHB—

Born Randfontein, S Africa, 12 July 1935. Educ Michaelhouse. Debut 1955.
FREE FORESTERS (1) 1955.
S AFRICA DOMESTIC Natal 1955/56–65/66.
SOUTH AFRICA (2) A 1957/58.
TOUR S African Fezelas to England 1961.
HST 37* SA v A, Port Elizabeth, 1957/58. HS 131 Natal v E Province, Port Elizabeth, 1962/63.
Executive committee Natal CA 1982/83–.

BURGESS, Alan Thomas
—RHB, SLA—

Born Christchurch, N Zealand, 1 May 1920. Educ Christchurch Technical C. Debut 1940/41.

N ZEALAND DOMESTIC Canterbury (11) 1940/41–51/52.
TOUR N Zealand Services to England 1945.
HS 61* N Zealand Services v H. D. G. Leveson Gower's XI, Scarborough, 1945 and 61* Canterbury v Wellington, Wellington, 1940/41.
BB 6–52 Canterbury v Otago, Christchurch, 1940/41.
Club: Sydenham.

BURGESS, Graham Iefvion
—RHB, RM—

Born Glastonbury, Som, 5 May 1943. Educ Millfield. Debut 1966.
SOMERSET (252) 1966–79. Cap 1968. Testimonial (£24,800) 1977.
HS 129 Som v Glos, Taunton, 1973.
BB 7–43 (13–75 match) Som v Oxford U, The Parks, 1975.
Wiltshire 1981–82, Cambridgeshire 1983–84. Professional coach at Monmouth S.

BURGESS, Mark Gordon
—RHB, OB—

Born Auckland, N Zealand, 17 July 1944. Educ Auckland GS. Debut 1963/64 (N Zealand Under-23 XI).
N ZEALAND DOMESTIC Auckland (68) 1966/67–79/80.
NEW ZEALAND (50) 1967/68–80/81. E 1970/71 (1), 1977/78 (3); A 1973/74 (1), 1976/77 (2); WI 1968/69 (2); I 1967/68 (4), 1975/76 (3); P 1972/73 (3), 1978/79 (3). *E 1969 (2), 1973 (3), 1978 (3); A 1980/81 (3); WI 1971/72 (5); I 1969/70 (3), 1976/77 (3); P 1969/70 (3), 1976/77 (3).* Capt 9.
OTHER TOURS N Zealand to Australia 1967/68, 1969/70, 1970/71, 1973/74. Prime Minister's XI v President's XI, Bombay, 1967/68 (relief match).
HST 119* NZ v P, Dacca, 1969/70. HS 146 Auckland v Central Districts, Auckland, 1971/72.
BBT 3–23 NZ v I, Nagpur, 1969/70. BB as above.
RECORD Added 183 for 5th wkt with R. W. Anderson, NZ v P, Lahore, 1976/77, N Zealand Test record.
Father G. C. Burgess (Auckland).

BURGIN, Eric
—RHB, RMF—

Born Pitsmoor, Sheffield, 4 Jan 1924. Debut 1952. *P.*
YORKSHIRE (12) 1952–53.
HS 32 Yorks v M'sex, Bramall Lane, Sheffield, 1952.

BB 6–43 Yorks v Surrey, Headingley, 1952.
Clubs: Sheffield Utd (CC), Atlas and Norfolk (Yorks Council). Soccer: York City. Brother Ted Burgin (soccer for Sheffield United).

BURKE, Cecil
RHB, LB

Born Auckland, N Zealand, 22 Mar 1914. Debut 1937/38.
N ZEALAND DOMESTIC Auckland (37) 1937/38–53/54.
NEW ZEALAND (I) A 1945/46.
TOUR N Zealand to England 1949.
HST 3 NZ v A, Wellington, 1945/46. HS 51* Auckland v Wellington, Auckland, 1945/46.
BBT 2–30 NZ v A, Wellington, 1945/46.
BB 6–23 N Zealanders v Derbys, Derby, 1949.

BURKE, James Wallace
RHB, OB

Born Mosman, NSW, Australia, 12 June 1930. Died, by his own hand, Manly, Sydney, NSW, Australia, 2 Feb 1979. Educ Sydney GS. Debut 1948/49. *Wisden* 1957.
AUSTRALIA DOMESTIC New South Wales (67) 1948/49–58/59.
AUSTRALIA (24) 1950/51–58/59. E 1950/51 (2), 1954/55 (2), 1958/59 (5); WI 1951/52 (1). *E 1956 (5); SA 1957/58 (5); I 1956/57 (3); P 1956/57 (1).*
OTHER TOUR Australia to N Zealand 1949/50.
HST 189 A v SA, Cape Town, 1957/58.
HS 220 NSW v S Australia, Adelaide, 1956/57.
BBT 4–37 A v I, Calcutta, 1956/57. BB 6–40 Australians v S African Universities, Cape Town, 1956/57.
1000 RUNS (I + I) 1339 @ 47.82 in 1956. Century in second inns of Test debut, A v E, Adelaide, 1950/51. Cricket broadcaster.

BURKE, Joseph Patrick
RHB, RFM

Born Dublin, Ireland, 31 Jan 1923. Educ Blackrock C, Dublin. Debut 1953.
IRELAND (3) 1953–58.
HS 19* Ireland v Scotland, Paisley, 1954.
BB 2–32 Ireland v MCC, Dublin, 1958.

BURN, Edmund Holcroft Miller
RHB, RM

Born Brigg, Lincolnshire, 6 Oct 1922. Died, in road accident, Grimsby Beach,

Ontario, Canada, 22 Oct 1969. Debut 1954.
CANADA to England (2) 1954.
HS 12 Canadians v Essex, Clacton, 1954.
Clubs: Manitoba, Ontario. Editor *The Canadian Cricketer* 1952–65. Teacher/cricket coach Ridley C and St Catherine's C 1951–69.

BURNELL, Philip John
RHB, RM, WK

Born Woodford Green, Essex, 12 June 1945. Educ Chigwell S; Oriel C, Oxford. Debut 1967.
OXFORD UNIVERSITY (6) 1967.
HS 28 Oxford U v Som, The Parks, 1967.
Club: Buckhurst Hill.

BURNET, John Ronald
RHB

Born Saltaire, Yorks, 11 Oct 1918. Educ Ottershaw C. Debut 1958.
YORKSHIRE (55) 1958–59. Cap 1958. Capt 1958–59.
HS 54 Yorks v Sussex, Bradford, 1958 and v Hants, Bournemouth, 1958.
Gentlemen v Players (I) 1959. Member Yorks executive committee to 1984. Capt Yorks 2nd XI 1952–57.

BURNETT, Anthony Compton
RHB, occ WK

Born Chipstead, Surrey, 26 Oct 1923. Educ Lancing; Pembroke C, Cambridge. Debut 1949.
CAMBRIDGE UNIVERSITY (18) 1949–50 (Blue 1949).
GLAMORGAN (8) 1958.
HS 79* Cambridge U v M'sex, Fenner's, 1949.
Club: Yellowhammers. Later A. Compton-Burnett. Son R. J. Compton-Burnett (Cambridge U).

BURNLEY, Ian David
RHB

Born Darlington, Co Durham, 11 Mar 1963. Educ Hummersknott S; Queen Elizabeth C, Darlington; Churchill C, Cambridge. Debut 1984.
CAMBRIDGE UNIVERSITY (3) 1984 (Blue).
HS 86 Cambridge U v Oxford U, Lord's, 1984.

BURRIDGE, Alan James
LHB

Born Sunderland, Co Durham, 8 Oct 1936. Debut 1973.

MINOR COUNTIES (I) 1973.
HS 37 Minor Counties v W Indians, Torquay, 1973.
Secretary Middlesex 1980–81. Durham 1961–72, Lincolnshire 1973–74, Hertfordshire 1975–78. Clubs: Wearmouth, Horden, Enfield, Penrith, Sunderland, Newick, Walsden.

BURROUGH, Herbert Dickinson
RHB

Born Wedmore, Som, 6 Feb 1909. Educ King's S, Bruton; St Catharine's C, Cambridge. Debut 1927.
SOMERSET (171) 1927–47.
HS 135 Som v Northants, Kettering, 1932.
1000 RUNS (I) 1007 @ 25.17 in 1933.
Father W. G. Burrough (Som); uncle J. Burrough (Cambridge U); cousin J. W. Burrough (Glos).

BURROWS, Dean Andrew
RHB, RMF

Born Peterlee, Co Durham, 20 June 1966. Educ Shotton Hall County S. Debut 1984.
GLOUCESTERSHIRE (I) 1984.
No runs, no wkts.
Durham 1984. Club: Hartlepool.

BURTON, Clifford
RHB, RFM

Born Moston, nr Manchester, 15 June 1931. Died Oldham, Lancs, 20 May 1978. Debut 1956.
LANCASHIRE (2) 1956.
No runs, no wkts.
Clubs: Werneth, Royton. Professional: Kendal.

BURTON,
Michael St John Whitehead
RHB, OB

Born Bulawayo, Rhodesia, 14 Feb 1944. Educ Umtali HS; Rhodes U; Mansfield C, Oxford. Debut 1964/65.
S AFRICA DOMESTIC Eastern Province 1964/65–67/68.
OXFORD UNIVERSITY (32) 1969–71 (Blue 1969–71). Capt 1970.
HS 84 Oxford U v Surrey, Guildford, 1970.
BB 5–96 Oxford U v Notts, The Parks, 1970.

BURTT, Thomas Browning
————LHB, SLA————

Born Christchurch, N Zealand, 22 Jan 1915. Educ West Christchurch HS. Debut 1943/44.
N ZEALAND DOMESTIC Canterbury (46) 1943/44–54/55.
NEW ZEALAND (10) 1946/47–52/53. E 1946/47 (1), 1950/51 (2); SA 1952/53 (1); WI 1951/52 (2). E 1949 (4).
HST 42 NZ v E, Christchurch, 1950/51.
HS 68* N Zealanders v Derbys, Derby, 1949.
BBT 6–162 NZ v E, Old Trafford, 1949.
BB 8–35 Canterbury v Otago, Dunedin, 1953/54.
100 WKTS (1) 128 @ 22.88 in 1949.
Hockey: N Zealand. Brother N. Burtt (Canterbury).

BURY, Thomas Edward Oswell
————RHB, WK————

Born Chelmsford, Essex, 14 May 1958. Educ Charterhouse; St Edmund Hall, Oxford. Debut 1979.
OXFORD UNIVERSITY (4) 1979–80 (Blue 1980).
HS 22 Oxford U v Worcs, The Parks, 1980.

BUSE, Herbert Francis Thomas
————RHB, RM————

Born Ashley Down, Bristol, 5 Aug 1910. Debut 1929. P.
SOMERSET (304) 1929–53. Cap 1934. Benefit (£2814) 1953.
HS 132 Som v Northants, Kettering, 1938.
BB 8–41 Som v Derby, Taunton, 1939.
1000 RUNS (5) 1279 @ 26.10 in 1948.
Benefit, Som v Lancs, Bath, 1953, over in one day. Rugby: Bath and Somerset.

BUSH, John Edgar
————RHB————

Born Oxford, 28 Aug 1928. Educ Magdalen College S; Magdalen C, Oxford. Debut 1950.
OXFORD UNIVERSITY (8) 1950–52 (Blue 1952).
HS 67 Oxford U v M'sex, The Parks, 1952.
Oxfordshire 1949–70.

BUSHBY, Michael Howard
————RHB————

Born Macclesfield, Cheshire, 29 July 1931. Educ Dulwich; Queen's C, Cambridge. Debut 1952.
CAMBRIDGE UNIVERSITY (43) 1952–54 (Blue 1952–54). Capt 1954.
HS 113 Cambridge U v Lancs, Fenner's, 1954.
Club: Yellowhammers. Cricket master Tonbridge S from 1956.

BUSHE, Edwin Alexander
————RHB, WK————

Born Lurgan, Co Armagh, Ireland, 11 Apr 1951. Educ Lurgan C. Debut 1979.
IRELAND (2) 1979–80.
HS 14 Ireland v Scotland, Dublin, 1979.
Club: Waringstown.

BUSS, Anthony
————RHB, RMF————

Born Brightling, Sussex, 1 Sept 1939. Educ Bexhill GS. Debut 1958. P.
SUSSEX (305) 1958–74. Cap 1963. Benefit (£8000) 1971.
HS 83 Sussex v Northants, Hove, 1969.
BB 8–23 Sussex v Notts, Hove, 1966.
100 WKTS (3) 120 @ 20.30 in 1965 and 120 @ 22.55 in 1966.
Sussex manager 1976–80. Brother M. A. Buss (Sussex).

BUSS, Michael Alan
————LHB, SLA/LM————

Born Brightling, Sussex, 24 Jan 1944. Educ Heathfield Sec S. Debut 1961. P.
SUSSEX (296) 1961–78. Cap 1967. Benefit (£12,000) 1976.
S AFRICA DOMESTIC Orange Free State 1972/73–77/78.
TOUR MCC Under-25 to Pakistan 1966/67.
HS 159 Sussex v Glam, Swansea, 1967.
BB 7–58 Sussex v Hants, Bournemouth, 1970.
1000 RUNS (5) 1379 @ 37.27 in 1970.
Brother A. Buss (Sussex).

BUTCHART, Iain Peter
————RHB, RM————

Born Bulawayo, Rhodesia, 9 May 1960. Debut 1980/81.
ZIMBABWE 1980/81–83/84.
TOUR Zimbabwe to England 1982. Zimbabwe to Sri Lanka 1983/84.
HS 54 Zimbabwe v Leics, Leicester, 1982.
BB 2–22 same match.

BUTCHER, Alan Raymond
————LHB, LM————

Born Croydon, Surrey, 7 Jan 1954. Educ Heath Clark GS. Debut 1972.
SURREY (241) 1972–. Cap 1975.
ENGLAND (1) I 1979.
HST 20 E v I, Oval, 1979. HS 216* Surrey v Cambridge U, Fenner's, 1980.
BB 6–48 Surrey v Hants, Guildford, 1972.
TOURS Overseas XI to India 1980/81. International XI to Jamaica 1982/83.
1000 RUNS (6) 1713 @ 46.29 in 1980.
Brothers I. P. Butcher (Leics) and M. S. Butcher (Surrey).

BUTCHER, Basil Fitzherbert
————RHB, LBG————

Born Port Mourant, Berbice, British Guiana, 3 Sept 1933.
W INDIES DOMESTIC Guyana 1954/55–70/71, Berbice 1971/72.
WEST INDIES (44) 1958/59–69. E 1959/60 (2), 1967/68 (5); A 1964/65 (5). E 1963 (5), 1966 (5), 1969 (3); A 1968/69 (5); NZ 1968/69 (3); I 1958/59 (5), 1966/67 (3); P 1958/59 (3).
OTHER TOURS Commonwealth XI to Pakistan 1963/64. Commonwealth XI to India 1964/65. Rest of World XI in England 1968.
HST 209* WI v E, Trent Bridge, 1966. HS as above.
BBT 5–34 WI v E, Port of Spain, 1967/68. BB as above.
1000 RUNS (2+3) 1294 @ 44.62 in 1963.
RECORD Added 335 for 5th wkt with C. H. Lloyd, W Indians v Glam, Swansea, 1969, W Indian fc record.
MCC Hon. member. Cousin R. O. Butcher (M'sex and England).

BUTCHER, Ian Paul
————RHB————

Born Farnborough, Kent, 1 July 1962. Educ John Ruskin HS. Debut 1980.
LEICESTERSHIRE (49) 1980–.
HS 139 Leics v Notts, Leicester, 1983.
1000 RUNS (1) 1349 @ 32.90 in 1984.
Brothers A. R. and M. S. Butcher (both Surrey).

BUTCHER, Martin Simon
————RHB————

Born Thornton Heath, Surrey, 17 May 1958. Debut 1982.
SURREY (1) 1982.
No runs or wkts.
Brothers A. R. Butcher (Surrey) and I. P. Butcher (Leics).

BUTCHER, Roland Orlando
------RHB, RM------

Born East Point, St Philip, Barbados, 14 Oct 1953. Debut 1974.
MIDDLESEX (148) 1974–. Cap 1979.
W INDIES DOMESTIC Barbados 1974/75.
AUSTRALIA DOMESTIC Tasmania (12) 1982/83.
ENGLAND (3) *WI 1980/81*.
OTHER TOURS M'sex to Zimbabwe 1980/81. International XI to Pakistan 1981/82. International XI to Jamaica 1982/83.
HST 32 E v WI, Kingston, 1980/81. HS 197 M'sex v Yorks, Lord's, 1982.
1000 RUNS (2) 1326 @ 40.18 in 1984.
Cousin B. F. Butcher (W Indies).

BUTLER, Harold James
------RHB, RFM------

Born Clifton, Notts, 12 Mar 1913. Debut 1933. *P*.
NOTTINGHAMSHIRE (306) 1933–54. Cap 1937. Benefit (£2679) 1950.

INDIA DOMESTIC Services 1943/44–44/45.
ENGLAND (2) 1947–47/48. SA 1947 (1). *WI 1947/48 (1)*.
HST 15* E v WI, Port of Spain, 1947/48.
HS 62 Notts v Glam, Swansea, 1939.
BBT 4–34 E v SA, Headingley, 1947. BB 8–15 Notts v Surrey, Trent Bridge, 1937.
100 WKTS (2) 106 @ 22.55 in 1947.
Players v Gentlemen (2) 1947.

BUXTON, Ian Ray
------RHB, RM------

Born Cromford, Derbys, 17 Apr 1938. Educ Wirksworth GS. Debut 1959. *P*.
DERBYSHIRE (350) 1959–73. Cap 1962. Capt 1970–72. Testimonial (£5603) 1972.
HS 118* Derbys v Lancs, Derby, 1964.
BB 7–33 Derbys v Oxford U, Derby, 1969.
1000 RUNS (5) 1219 @ 28.34 in 1964.

RECORD Added 203 for 5th wkt with C. P. Wilkins, Derbys v Lancs, Old Trafford, 1971, county record.
Soccer: Derby County, Luton Town, Notts County, Port Vale.

BYNOE, Michael *Robin*
------RHB, SLA------

Born Christchurch, Barbados, 23 Feb 1941. Debut 1957/58.
W INDIES DOMESTIC Barbados 1957/58–71/72.
WEST INDIES (4) 1958/59–66/67. *I 1966/67 (3); P 1958/59 (1)*.
OTHER TOUR Barbados to England 1969.
HST 48 WI v I, Madras, 1966/67. HS 190 Barbados v Trinidad, Bridgetown, 1971/72.
BBT 1–5 WI v I, Madras, 1966/67. BB 2–7 Barbados v Guyana, Georgetown, 1971/72.
Club: Wanderers (Bridgetown, Barbados).

C

CAESAR, William Cecil
RHB, RF

Born Clapham, London, 25 Nov 1899.
Debut 1922.
SURREY (1) 1922.
SOMERSET (3) 1946.
HS 7 Som v Leics, Melton Mowbray, 1946.
BB 4–59 same match.
Soccer: England (amateur); Darlington, Fulham, Walsall.

CAIRNS, Bernard *Lance*
RHB, RMF

Born Picton, N Zealand, 10 Oct 1949.
Educ Marlborough Boys' C. Debut 1971/72 (N Zealand Under-23s).
N ZEALAND DOMESTIC Central Districts (17) 1972/73–75/76, Otago (33) 1976/77–79/80, Northern Districts (20) 1981/82–.
NEW ZEALAND (37) 1973/74–83/84. E 1974/75 (1), 1977/78 (1), 1983/84 (3); A 1976/77 (1), 1981/82 (3); WI 1979/80 (3); I 1975/76 (1), 1980/81 (3); P 1978/79 (3); SL 1982/83 (2). *E 1978 (2), 1983 (4); A 1973/74 (1), 1980/81 (3); I 1976/77 (2); P 1976/77 (2); SL 1983/84 (2)*.
HST 64 NZ v E, Wellington, 1983/84. HS 110 Otago v Wellington, Hutt, 1979/80.
BBT 7–74 NZ v E, Headingley, 1983. BB 8–46 Otago v Wellington, Invercargill, 1978/79.
RECORDS In HS (above) reached 50 off 22 balls in 31 mins, and 100 off 45 balls in 52 mins, fastest-ever fc century in N Zealand. Added 118 for 9th wkt with J. V. Coney, NZ v E, Wellington, 1983/84, N Zealand Test record.
Durham 1979–81. Clubs: Whitburn, Bishop Auckland (as professional).

CAIRNS, John David
RHB

Born Gibraltar, 10 Feb 1925. Educ Highgate S; Balliol C, Oxford. Debut 1946.
OXFORD UNIVERSITY (6) 1946.
FREE FORESTERS (1) 1949.

HS 36 Oxford U v Indians, The Parks, 1946.
Club: Hornsey. Toronto 1966.

CAMACHO, George *Stephen*
RHB, LBG

Born British Guiana, 15 Oct 1945.
Debut 1964/65.
W INDIES DOMESTIC Guyana 1964/65–78/79.
WEST INDIES (11) 1967/68–70/71. E 1967/68 (5); I 1970/71 (2). *E 1969 (2); A 1968/69 (2)*.
OTHER TOUR W Indies to England 1973.
HST 87 WI v E, Port of Spain, 1967/68.
HS 166 Demerera v Berbice, Rose Hall, 1974/75.
BB 3–10 Guyana v Trinidad, Georgetown, 1970/71.
West Indies Test selector. Secretary WIBC. Grandfather G. C. Learmond (Barbados and Trinidad).

CAME, Kenneth Charles
LHB, RM

Born Reading, Berkshire, 29 Oct 1925.
Educ Bournemouth S. Debut 1957.
FREE FORESTERS (1) 1957.
HS 6 Free Foresters v Oxford U, The Parks, 1957.
Berkshire 1955–57. Brigadier and retired Hon. Colonel Territorial Army. OBE for services to TA.

CAMERON, Francis James
RHB, OB

Born Kingston, Jamaica, 22 June 1923.
Educ Wolmer's S, Jamaica. Debut 1945/46.
W INDIES DOMESTIC Jamaica 1945/46–58/59.
WEST INDIES (5) *I 1948/49*.
OTHER TOUR Canada to England 1954.
HST 75* WI v I, Bombay, 1948/9. HS as above.
BBT 2–74 WI v I, Delhi, 1948/9. BB 4–52 W Indians v Sind, Karachi, 1948/9.

Father J. J. Cameron (W Indians to England 1906); brother J. H. Cameron (Oxford U, Somerset and W Indies).

CAMERON, Francis James
RHB, RMF

Born Dunedin, N Zealand, 1 June 1932.
Debut 1952/53.
N ZEALAND DOMESTIC Otago (68) 1952/53–66/67.
NEW ZEALAND (19) 1961/62–65. E 1962/63 (3); SA 1963/64 (3); P 1964/65 (3). *E 1965 (2); SA 1961/62 (5); I 1964/65 (1); P 1964/65 (2)*.
HST 27* NZ v I, Delhi, 1964/65. HS 43 Otago v Wellington, Wellington, 1953/54.
BBT 5–34 NZ v P, Auckland, 1964/65. BB 7–27 N Zealanders v W Australia, Perth, 1961/62.
Former chairman N Zealand selection committee.

CAMERON, John Hensley
RHB, OB/LB

Born Kingston, Jamaica, 8 Apr 1914.
Educ Taunton S; St Catharine's C, Cambridge. Debut 1932.
SOMERSET (48) 1932–47.
CAMBRIDGE UNIVERSITY (36) 1934–37 (Blue 1935–37).
W INDIES DOMESTIC Jamaica 1946/47.
WEST INDIES (2) *E 1939*.
OTHER TOUR Oxford and Cambridge Universities to Jamaica 1938/39.
HST 5 WI v E, Old Trafford, 1939. HS 113 Som v Sussex, Eastbourne, 1937.
BBT 3–66 WI v E, Lord's, 1939. BB 7–73 Cambridge U v Oxford U, Lord's, 1935. Gentlemen v Players (1) 1935. Master Chigwell S from 1948. Brother F. J. Cameron (W Indies and Canada); father J. J. Cameron (W Indians to England 1906).

CAMMISH, James William
RHB, LBG

Born Scarborough, Yorks, 21 May 1921. Educ Central S, Scarborough. Debut 1950/51. *P*.

N ZEALAND DOMESTIC Auckland (5) 1950/51.
YORKSHIRE (2) 1954.
HS 7* Auckland v Wellington, Wellington, 1950/51.
BB 6–93 Auckland v Canterbury, Auckland, 1950/51.
Clubs: North Shore (N Zealand), Scarborough (England). Emigrated to Australia.

CAMPBELL, Andrew Neville
————————LHB————————

Born Amersham, Buckinghamshire, 17 June 1949. Educ Berkhamsted S; New C, Oxford. Debut 1968.
OXFORD UNIVERSITY (15) 1968–70 (Blue 1970).
HS 73 Oxford U v Surrey, Guildford, 1970.
Buckinghamshire 1970–72.

CAMPBELL, Anthony U.
————————RHB, WK————————

Born Kingston, Jamaica, 25 Sept 1950. Debut 1969/70.
W INDIES DOMESTIC Jamaica 1969/70–79/80.
TOUR Jamaica to England 1970.
HS 48* Jamaica v Trinidad, Port of Spain, 1979/80.
Club: Kingston.

CAMPBELL, Ian Parry
————————RHB, WK————————

Born Purley, Surrey, 5 Feb 1928. Educ Canford; Trinity C, Oxford. Debut 1946.
KENT (1) 1946.
COMBINED SERVICES (1) 1947.
OXFORD UNIVERSITY (18) 1949–51 (Blue 1949–50).
MCC (1) 1954.
TOUR MCC to Canada 1951.
HS 60* Oxford U v Leics, The Parks, 1951.
Rugby: Kent, London Counties. Hockey: Blue.

CANDLER, David Cecil
————————RHB, LB————————

Born Bulawayo, Rhodesia, 18 Oct 1924. Educ Bulawayo Technical S; Cape Town U; Keble C, Oxford. Debut 1950.
OXFORD UNIVERSITY (5) 1950–51.
HS 54 Oxford U v Yorks, The Parks, 1950.

CANGLEY, Barron George Merriman
————————RHB————————

Born Blakesley, Towcester, Northants, 12 Sept 1922. Educ Felsted; Trinity Hall, Cambridge. Debut 1947.
CAMBRIDGE UNIVERSITY (8) 1947 (Blue).
HS 76 Cambridge U v Som, Bath, 1947.
Cambridgeshire 1946. Secretary Western Province Cricket Union 1971–74. War-time Blue 1942.

CANNINGS, Victor Henry Douglas
————————RHB, RM————————

Born Bighton, Hants, 3 Apr 1919. Debut 1947. P.
WARWICKSHIRE (53) 1947–49. Cap 1947.
HAMPSHIRE (230) 1950–59. Cap 1950.
Benefit (£3188) 1959.
HS 61 Warwicks v Notts, Edgbaston, 1947.
BB 7–52 Hants v Oxford U, The Parks, 1950.
100 WKTS (4) 112 @ 21.56 in 1952.
Bowled unchanged with D. Shackleton, Hants v Kent, Southampton, 1952.
Buckinghamshire 1960–62. Coach at Eton from 1960.

CANTLAY, Charles Peter Thrale
————————RHB, RMF————————

Born Victoria, London, 4 Feb 1954. Educ Radley; Oriel C, Oxford. Debut 1975.
OXFORD UNIVERSITY (6) 1975.
HS 9 Oxford U v Warwicks, The Parks, 1975.
BB 4–85 Oxford U v Sussex, The Parks, 1975.

CANTWELL, Noel Euchuria Cornelius
————————LHB, RM————————

Born Cork, Ireland, 28 Dec 1932. Educ Presentation Brothers' C, Cork. Debut 1956.
IRELAND (1) 1956.
HS 31 Ireland v Scotland, Edinburgh, 1956.
Club: Cork Bohemians. Soccer: Ireland, West Ham United, Manchester United; manager Coventry City, Peterborough United.

CAPEL, David John
————————RHB, RM————————

Born Northampton, 6 Feb 1963. Educ Roade CS. Debut 1981.

NORTHAMPTONSHIRE (49) 1981–.
HS 109* Northants v Som, Northampton, 1983.
BB 5–28 Northants v Surrey, Oval, 1984.

CAPLAN, Jeremy John Notley
————————RHB, OB————————

Born Colar Goldfields, Mysore, India, 9 Oct 1941. Educ Cheltenham C; Magdalene C, Cambridge. Debut 1962.
CAMBRIDGE UNIVERSITY (2) 1962.
HS 26 Cambridge U v M'sex, Fenner's, 1962.
Clubs: Frogs, Middleton.

CAPLE, Robert Graham
————————LHB, RM————————

Born Chiswick, London, 8 Dec 1939. Debut 1958. P.
MCC (1) 1958.
MIDDLESEX (2) 1959.
HAMPSHIRE (65) 1961–67.
HS 64* Hants v Surrey, Oval, 1964.
BB 5–54 Hants v Oxford U, Bournemouth, 1967.

CAPON, Stephen
————————RHB, RFM————————

Born Snodland, Kent, 25 Apr 1927. Educ Rochester Mathematical S. Debut 1950.
KENT (1) 1950.
HS 4 Kent v Notts, Trent Bridge, 1950.

CAPRANI, Joseph Desmond
————————RHB————————

Born Clontarf, Co Dublin, Ireland, 27 May 1920. Educ Honth Road S, Clontarf. Debut 1948.
IRELAND (5) 1948–60.
HS 44 Ireland v Scotland, Dublin, 1955.
Clubs: Clontarf, Leinster, Malahide.

CARD, Anthony James
————————SLA————————

Born Doncaster, Yorks, 13 Sept 1929. Debut 1955. P.
MCC (2) 1955–58.
HS 19* MCC v Cambridge U, Lord's, 1958.
BB 4–26 MCC v Glos, Lord's, 1955.
Yorkshire 2nd XI 1953–54; Middlesex 2nd XI 1956–58.

CAREW, Michael Conrad (Joey)
———LHB, ROB———

Born Port of Spain, Trinidad, 15 Sept 1937. Educ Fatima C, Port of Spain. Debut 1955/56.
W INDIES DOMESTIC Trinidad 1955/56–73/74 (capt 1967/68–72/73).
WEST INDIES (19) 1963–71/72. E 1967/68 (1); NZ 1971/72 (3); I 1970/71 (3). *E 1963 (2), 1966 (1), 1969 (1); A 1968/69 (5); NZ 1968/69 (3).*
HST 109 WI v NZ, Auckland, 1968/69. HS 182 North Trinidad v Central Trinidad, California, 1970/71.
BB 5–28 Trinidad v Jamaica, Port of Spain, 1969/70.
1000 RUNS (1 + 1) 1222 @ 45.25 in Australasia in 1968/69.
Test selector 1975–. Club: Queen's Park.

CARLESS, Ernest Francis
———RHB, OB, WK———

Born Barry, Glam, 9 Sept 1912. Educ Cadoxton S, Barry. Debut 1934. *P* in 1934.
GLAMORGAN (3) 1934–46.
HS 25 Glam v Surrey, Cardiff, 1934.
Devon 1947–49. Professional Briton Ferry. Clubs: Cardiff, Plymouth, Barry (still playing for Barry 1982 in 70th year). Soccer: Cardiff City, Plymouth Argyle.

CARLING, Philip George
———LHB, WK———

Born Carshalton, Surrey, 25 Nov 1946. Educ Kingston GS; St Catharine's C, Cambridge. Debut 1967.
CAMBRIDGE UNIVERSITY (30) 1967–70 (Blue 1968, 1970).
HS 104 Cambridge U v Glam, Fenner's, 1970.
Chief executive Notts 1978–82; Glam 1983–.

CARLSTEIN, Peter Rudolph
———RHB, RM———

Born Klerksdorp, S Africa, 28 Oct 1938. Educ St Andrew's Bloemfontein, S Africa. Debut 1954/55.
S AFRICA DOMESTIC Orange Free State 1954/55–57/58, Transvaal 1958/59–63/64, 1969/70–71/72, Natal 1964/65–66/67, Rhodesia 1967/68–68/69, 1972/73–79/80.
SOUTH AFRICA (8) 1957/58–63/64. A 1957/58 (1). *E 1960 (5); A 1963/64 (2).*
OTHER TOUR International XI to S Africa 1974/75.

HST 42 SA v E, Oval, 1960. HS 229 Transvaal v International Cavaliers, J'burg 1962/63.
BB 3–37 S Africans v T. N. Pearce's XI, Scarborough, 1960.
Club: Old Hill (barred from playing for a period mid-season 1977 for not having work permit; later allowed to play on condition earned no money).

CARMICHAEL, Ian Robert
———LBH, LFM———

Born Hull, Yorks, 17 Dec 1960. Debut 1983/84.
AUSTRALIA DOMESTIC South Australia (11) 1983/84.
LEICESTERSHIRE (6) 1984.
HS 4* Leics v Lancs, Leicester, 1984.
BB 6–112 S Australia v Tasmania, Devonport, 1983/84.

CARMODY, Douglas *Keith*
———RHB———

Born Mosman, NSW, Australia, 16 Feb 1919. Died Concord, NSW, Australia, 21 Oct 1977. Debut 1939/40.
AUSTRALIA DOMESTIC New South Wales (13) 1939/40–46/47, Western Australia (35) 1947/48–55/56 (capt).
TOUR Australian Services to England 1945 and India 1945/46 (capt in England).
HS 198 W Australia v S Australia, Perth, 1947/48.
Originator of the 'Carmody (Umbrella) field'.

CARNILL, Denys John
———LHB, RLB———

Born Hampstead, London, 11 Mar 1926. Educ Hitchin GS; Worcester C, Oxford. Debut 1950.
OXFORD UNIVERSITY (1) 1950.
HS 8 Oxford U v Free Foresters, The Parks, 1950.
Hertfordshire 1949–56. Hockey: captained England and Oxford U.

CARPENTER, David
———RHB, occ OB———

Born Stroud, Glos, 12 Sept 1935. Educ Tetbury GS. Debut 1954. *P*.
GLOUCESTERSHIRE (117) 1954–63. Cap 1961.
HS 95 Glos v Derbys, Derby, 1962.
1000 RUNS (1) 1353 @ 23.32 in 1961.
Club: Chipping Sodbury.

CARR, Donald Brice
———RHB, SLA———

Born Wiesbaden, West Germany, 28 Dec 1926. Educ Repton; Worcester C, Oxford. Debut 1945, for England XI v Australia XI, Lord's (Victory match).
DERBYSHIRE (336) 1946–63. Cap 1951. Capt 1955–62.
OXFORD UNIVERSITY (36) 1948–51 (Blue 1949–51). Capt 1950.
ENGLAND (2) *I 1951/52.* Capt 1.
OTHER TOURS MCC A to Pakistan 1955/56 (capt).
HST 76 E v I, Delhi, 1951/52. HS 170 Oxford U v Leics, The Parks, 1949.
BBT 2–84 E v I, Madras, 1951/52. BB 7–53 Derbys v Lancs, Chesterfield 1955.
1000 RUNS (11) 2292 @ 44.07 in 1959.
RECORD 2165 runs @ 48.10 for Derbys in 1959, county record.
Gentlemen v Players (4) 1950–61. Secretary Derbys 1959–62. Assistant-Secretary MCC 1962–74. Secretary TCCB 1974–. Managed three MCC tours. Soccer: Oxford U, Pegasus. Father J. L. Carr (Army); son J. D. Carr (Oxford U and M'sex).

CARR, John Donald
———RHB, OB———

Born St John's Wood, London, 15 June 1963. Educ Repton; Worcester C, Oxford. Debut 1983.
OXFORD UNIVERSITY (13) 1983–84 (Blue 1983–84).
MIDDLESEX (5) 1983–84.
HS 123 Oxford U v Lancs, The Parks, 1984.
BB 5–57 Oxford U v Glos, The Parks, 1984.
Hertfordshire 1982–. Father D. B. Carr (Oxford U, Derbys and England); grandfather J. L. Carr (Army).

CARR, Michael Lewis
———RHB, WK———

Born Alexandria, Egypt, 24 June 1933. Educ Malvern; Peterhouse C, Cambridge. Debut 1953.
CAMBRIDGE UNIVERSITY (1) 1953.
HS 1* Cambridge U v Warwicks, Fenner's, 1953.
Changed his name from Kerner-Cohen to Carr.

CARR, Ronald Bernard
———RHB, LBG———

Born J'burg, S Africa, 12 Jan 1938. Educ Marist Brothers C, J'burg. Debut 1960. *P*.

ESSEX (1) 1960.
S AFRICA DOMESTIC Transvaal 1964/65.
HS 28* Transvaal v MCC, J'burg, 1964/65.

CARRICK, Phillip
────────RHB, SLA────────

Born Armley, Leeds, Yorks, 16 July 1952. Educ Bramley CS; Intake CS; Park Lane C of PE. Debut 1970.
YORKSHIRE (244) 1970–. Cap 1976.
S AFRICA DOMESTIC Eastern Province 1976/77, Northern Transvaal 1982/83.
TOURS D. H. Robins' XI to S Africa 1975/76. D. H. Robins' XI to Sri Lanka 1977/78.
HS 131* Yorks v Northants, Northampton, 1980.
BB 8–33 Yorks v Cambridge U, Fenner's, 1973.
Club: Farsley.

CARROLL, Peter Robert
────────RHB, RM────────

Born Sydney, NSW, Australia, 7 Nov 1941. Educ Newington C; Sydney U; Mansfield C, Oxford. Debut 1969.
OXFORD UNIVERSITY (14) 1969–71 (Blue 1971).
HS 60* Oxford U v Notts, The Parks, 1971.
Clubs: I Zingari, Arabs, Free Foresters, Stragglers.

CARSE, James Alexander
────────RHB, RF────────

Born Salisbury, Rhodesia, 13 Dec 1958. Educ Churchill HS. Debut 1977/78.
S AFRICA DOMESTIC Rhodesia 1977/78–79/80, Western Province 1980/81, Eastern Province 1981/82–.
NORTHAMPTONSHIRE (11) 1983.
HS 44 Rhodesia v N Transvaal, Pretoria, 1979/80.
BB 6–50 E Province v N Transvaal, Port Elizabeth, 1981/82.

CARTER, Charles Edward Peers
────────RHB, WK────────

Born Richmond, Surrey, 7 Aug 1947. Educ Radley. Debut 1968.
SOMERSET (26) 1968–69.
HS 16 Som v M'sex, Lord's, 1969.
Retired from county cricket to enter the army. Club: Hurlingham.

CARTER, Horatio Stratton (Raich)
────────RHB, SLA────────

Born Hendon, Sunderland, 21 Dec 1913. Debut 1946. P.
DERBYSHIRE (3) 1946.
HS 7 Derbys v Surrey, Oval, 1946.
BB 2–39 Derbys v Worcs, Stourbridge, 1946.
Durham 1933–34. Clubs: Chaddesden (1946), Hendon. Soccer: England (13), Sunderland, Derby County, Hull City; manager Hull City, Middlesbrough.

CARTER, John William
────────RHB────────

Born Oxford, 23 June 1935. Educ Magdalen Coll S, Oxford. Debut 1959. P.
LEICESTERSHIRE (7) 1959.
HS 41 Leics v Hants, Leicester, 1959.
Oxfordshire 1954–57, 1961.

CARTER, Raymond George
────────RHB, RFM/OB────────

Born Billesley, Birmingham, 14 Apr 1933. Debut 1951. P.
WARWICKSHIRE (88) 1951–61. Cap 1958.
COMBINED SERVICES (1) 1952.
HS 37 Warwicks v Cambridge U, Portland Road, Birmingham, 1961.
BB 8–82 (14–136 match) Warwicks v Som, Edgbaston, 1958.
Clubs: Sparkhill, Mitchells and Butlers.

CARTER, Reginald
────────RHB, SLA────────

Born Whitwell, Derbys, 7 Nov 1933. Debut 1953. P.
DERBYSHIRE (17) 1953–55.
HS 25 Derbys v Pakistanis, Derby, 1954.
BB 7–46 Derbys v Som, Chesterfield, 1953 (in second match).

CARTER, Robert George Mallaby
────────LHB, RFM────────

Born Horden, Co Durham, 11 July 1937. Educ Nunthorpe GS, York. Debut 1961. P.
WORCESTERSHIRE (177) 1961–72. Cap 1965.
MCC (1) 1973.
HS 23 Worcs v Leics, Leicester, 1967.
BB 7–61 Worcs v Yorks, Dudley, 1971.
A leading national coach. Clubs: Dudley, Stourbridge.

CARTER, Robert Michael (Cooch)
────────RHB, RM────────

Born King's Lynn, Norfolk, 25 May 1960. Educ Gaywood Park Sec S; Norfolk C of Arts and Technology, King's Lynn. Debut 1978.
NORTHAMPTONSHIRE (51) 1978–82.
N ZEALAND DOMESTIC Canterbury (7) 1982/83.
HS 79 Northants v Indians, Northampton, 1982.
BB 4–27 Northants v Glos, Bristol, 1980.
Club: Walsall.

CARTER-SHAW, Robert
────────RHB, SLA────────

Born Berkhamsted, Herts, 21 Nov 1941. Educ Radley; Sydney Sussex C, Cambridge. Debut 1962.
CAMBRIDGE UNIVERSITY (1) 1962.
HS 2 Cambridge U v Glam, Fenner's, 1962.

CARTRIDGE, Donald Colin
────────RHB, OB────────

Born Southampton, Hants, 31 Dec 1933. Educ Itchen GS, Southampton. Debut 1953. P.
HAMPSHIRE (3) 1953.
HS 4 Hants v Oxford U, The Parks, 1953.
Clubs: XL Club, The Deanery, Southampton Touring, Trojans, The Rams.

CARTWRIGHT, Harold
────────RHB────────

Born Halfway, Derbys, 12 May 1951. Debut 1973.
DERBYSHIRE (82) 1973–79. Cap 1978.
HS 141* Derbys v Warwicks, Chesterfield, 1977.

CARTWRIGHT, Thomas William
────────RHB, RM────────

Born Coventry, Warwicks, 22 July 1935. Educ Foxford S, Coventry. Debut 1952. P.
WARWICKSHIRE (353) 1952–69. Cap 1958. Benefit (£9592) 1968.
SOMERSET (101) 1970–76. Cap 1970. Testimonial 1975.
GLAMORGAN (7) 1977.
ENGLAND (5) 1964–65. A 1964 (2); SA 1965 (1); NZ 1965 (1). SA 1964/65 (1).
OTHER TOURS MCC to E Africa 1963/64, 1973/74.

HST 9 E v SA, J'burg, 1964/65. HS 210 Warwicks v M'sex, Nuneaton, 1962. BBT 6–94 E v SA, Trent Bridge, 1965. BB 8–39 Warwicks v Som, Weston-super-Mare, 1962. Match analysis of 15–89 Warwicks v Glam, Swansea, 1967. 1000 RUNS (3) 1668 @ 30.88 in 1961. 100 WKTS (8) 147 @ 15.52 in 1967. DOUBLE (1) 1962. Bowled 77 and 62 overs in two completed innings of his first two Tests, v A in 1964. Players v Gentlemen (1) 1954. Chief coach Glam 1980. Coach Millfield S 1970–76.

CARTY, Richard Arthur
RHB, RFM

Born Southampton, Hants, 28 July 1922. Debut 1949. *P.*
HAMPSHIRE (55) 1949–54.
HS 53 Hants v Oxford U, Bournemouth, 1949.
BB 7–29 Hants v Oxford U, Basingstoke, 1951.

CASS, George *Rodney*
LHB, WK

Born Overton, Yorks, 23 Apr 1940. Educ Dewsbury Technical C. Debut 1964.
ESSEX (45) 1964–67.
WORCESTERSHIRE (104) 1969–75. Cap 1970.
AUSTRALIA DOMESTIC Tasmania (6) 1970/71–72/73.
HS 172* Worcs v Leics, Leicester, 1975. Shropshire 1976–. Coached in Tasmania 1970–73. Clubs: Pudsey St Laurence, Bradford, Great Chell, South Hobart (Tasmania).

CASSIDY, John Joseph
RHB, RM

Born Leeds, Yorks, 31 Jan 1963. Educ Cardinal Heenan HS, Leeds; UC, Oxford. Debut 1982.
OXFORD UNIVERSITY (1) 1982.
No runs, no wkts.

CASTELL, Alan Terry
RHB, LBG/RM

Born Oxford, 6 Aug 1943. Debut 1961. *P.*
HAMPSHIRE (110) 1961–71.
TOUR Cavaliers to Jamaica 1963/64.
HS 76 Hants v Surrey, Southampton, 1962.
BB 6–22 Hants v Som, Bath, 1969.

RECORD During HS (above) added 230 for 9th wkt with D. A. Livingstone, county record.
Berkshire 1972–73.

CASTLE, Frederick
RHB

Born Elham, Kent, 9 Apr 1909. Debut 1946.
SOMERSET (23) 1946–49. Cap 1946.
HS 60* Som v Surrey, Weston-super-Mare, 1946.

CATT, Anthony William
RHB, WK

Born Edenbridge, Kent, 2 Oct 1933. Educ Tower Ramparts Sec M, Ipswich. Debut 1954. *P.*
KENT (126) 1954–64. Cap 1962.
S AFRICA DOMESTIC Western Province 1965/66–67/68.
HS 162 Kent v Leics, Maidstone, 1962 (scoring 121 before lunch).
Conceded 48 byes in inns, Kent v Northants, Northampton, 1955 (suffering from effects of the sun).

CAVE, Henry Butler
RHB, RMF

Born Wanganui, N Zealand, 10 Oct 1922. Debut 1945/46.
N ZEALAND DOMESTIC Wellington (11) 1945/46–49/50, Central Districts (36) 1950/51–58/59.
NEW ZEALAND (19) 1949–58. E 1954/55 (2); WI 1955/56 (3). *E 1949 (4), 1958 (2); I 1955/56 (5); P 1955/56 (3).* Capt 9.
HST 22* NZ v I, Madras, 1955/56. HS 118 Central Districts v Otago, Dunedin, 1952/53.
BBT 4–21 NZ v WI, Auckland, 1955/56. BB 7–31 Central Districts v Auckland, Palmerston North, 1952/53 (match analysis of 13–64 returned in one day).
RECORD In HS (above) added 239 for 9th wkt with I. B. Leggat, N Zealand record.
MCC Hon. member. One of large family of Wanganui cricketers.

CAWTHRAY, George
LHB, RMF

Born Brayton, nr Selby, Yorks, 28 Sept 1913. Debut 1939. *P.*
YORKSHIRE (4) 1939–52.
HS 30 Yorks v Glam, Swansea, 1952.
BB 2–64 Yorks v Derbys, Chesterfield, 1952.
Groundsman: Hull to 1963; Headingley 1964–78. Club: Hull.

CHADD, John Etheridge
RHB, OB

Born Whitestone, Hereford, 27 Oct 1933. Educ Hereford Cathedral S. Debut 1955. *P.*
WORCESTERSHIRE (2) 1955–56.
HS 4 Worcs v Oxford U, Worcester, 1956.
BB 2–84 same match.
Worcestershire committee.

CHADWICK, John Peter Granville
RHB, RM

Born Pateley Bridge, Yorks, 8 Nov 1934. Debut 1960. *P.*
YORKSHIRE (6) 1960–65.
HS 59 Yorks v M'sex, Scarborough, 1965.
BB 2–58 Yorks v Derbys, Chesterfield, 1963.
Club: Harrogate.

CHADWICK, Mark Robert
RHB, RM

Born Rochdale, Lancs, 9 Feb 1963. Educ Roch Valley HS, Milnrow. Debut 1983.
LANCASHIRE (8) 1983–.
HS 61 Lancs v Notts, Blackpool, 1984.

CHAMBERLAIN, William Richard Frank
RHB, LB

Born Elton, Huntingdonshire, 13 Apr 1925. Educ Uppingham. Debut 1946.
NORTHAMPTONSHIRE (6) 1946.
HS 14 Northants v Combined Services, Kettering, 1946.
Bedfordshire 1956–66. Clubs: Incogniti, Kettering, Free Foresters, MCC.

CHAMBERS, Robert Edwin Jeffrey
RHB

Born Battle, Sussex, 19 Nov 1943. Educ Forest S; Queen's C, Cambridge. Debut 1966.
CAMBRIDGE UNIVERSITY (12) 1966 (Blue).
HS 58 Cambridge U v Glam, Cardiff, 1966.
Staffordshire 1969; Hertfordshire 1972–74.

CHANDRASEKHAR, Bhagwat Subramanya
RHB, LBG

Born Mysore City, India, 17 May 1945. Educ Bangalore HS. Debut 1963/64. *Wisden* 1972.

INDIA DOMESTIC Mysore (Karnataka) 1963/64–79/80. Capt 1971/72.
INDIA (58) 1963/64–79. E 1963/64 (4), 1972/73 (5), 1976/77 (5); A 1964/65 (2); WI 1966/67 (3), 1974/75 (4), 1978/79 (4); NZ 1964/65 (2), 1976/77 (3). *E 1967 (3), 1971 (3), 1974 (2), 1979 (1); A 1967/68 (2), 1977/78 (5); WI 1975/76 (4); NZ 1975/76 (3); P 1978/79 (3).*
OTHER TOUR India to E Africa 1967.
HST 22 I v E, Edgbaston, 1967. HS 25 W Bengal Chief Minister's XI v Commonwealth XI, Calcutta, 1964/65.
BBT 8–79 I v E, Delhi, 1972/73. BB 9–72 Mysore v Kerala, Bijapur, 1969/70. Match analysis 13–148 Karnataka v Andhra Pradesh, Guntur, 1973/74.
RECORDS 35 wkts @ 18.91 in series, I v E, 1972/73 – Indian record. 436 wkts @ 19.15 in Ranji Trophy, third behind R. Goel and S. Venkataraghavan.

CHANMUGAM, Dennis Ravindran
——RHB, RMF——

Born Colombo, Ceylon, 13 Aug 1948. Debut 1972/73.
SRI LANKA DOMESTIC Sri Lanka 1973/74–75/76.
TOURS Sri Lanka to Pakistan 1973/74. Sri Lanka to India 1974/75, 1975/76. Sri Lanka to England 1975.
HS 35 Sri Lankans v Universities, Bangalore, 1975/76.
BB 4–60 Sri Lankans v Universities, Rawalpindi, 1973/74.
Club: Sinhalese Sports.

CHAPMAN, Thomas Alan
——RHB——

Born Barwell, Leics, 14 May 1919. Died Marandellas, Rhodesia, 19 Feb 1979. Debut 1946. *P.*
LEICESTERSHIRE (53) 1946–50.
S AFRICA DOMESTIC Rhodesia 1952/53.
HS 124* Rhodesia v Griqualand West, Salisbury, 1952/53 (debut for Rhodesia – went from 5* to 124* on third morning).

CHAPPELL, Gregory Stephen
——RHB, LB/RM——

Born Unley, Adelaide, S Australia, 7 Aug 1948. Educ Prince Alfred C, Adelaide. Debut 1966/67. *Wisden 1973.*
AUSTRALIA DOMESTIC South Australia (57) 1966/67–72/73, Queensland (61) 1973/74–83/84.
SOMERSET (52) 1968–69. Cap 1968.
AUSTRALIA (87) 1970/71–83/84. E 1970/71 (5), 1974/75 (6), 1976/77 (1), 1979/80 (3), 1982/83 (5); WI 1975/76 (6), 1979/

80 (3), 1981/82 (3); NZ 1973/74 (3), 1980/81 (3); I 1980/81 (3); P 1972/73 (3), 1976/77 (3), 1981/82 (3), 1983/84 (5). *E 1972 (5), 1975 (4), 1977 (5), 1980 (1); WI 1972/73 (5); NZ 1973/74 (3), 1976/77 (2), 1981/82 (3); P 1979/80 (3); SL 1982/83 (1).* Capt 48.
OTHER TOURS Australia to N Zealand 1969/70. International Wanderers to S Africa 1975/76.
HST 247* A v NZ, Wellington, 1973/74. HS as above.
BBT 5–61 A v P, Sydney, 1972/73. BB 7–40 Som v Yorks, Headingley, 1969.
1000 RUNS (4+8) 1547 @ 85.94 in Australia in 1975/76.
RECORDS Scored 247* and 133 A v NZ, Wellington, 1973/74, match aggregate of 380 highest in Test cricket. Most Test runs for Australia, 7110 @ 53.86. Only batsman to score century in each inns of debut match as Test capt (123 and 109* A v WI, Brisbane, 1975/76). Only batsman to score century in first and last Test inns (R. A. Duff and W. H. Ponsford, both A, scored century in first and last Test matches): 108 A v E, Perth, 1970/71 and 182 A v P, Sydney, 1983/84. Took 7 catches in match, A v E, Perth, 1974/75, equals Test record for non-wicketkeeper. Total of 122 catches in Test cricket, world record for non-wicketkeeper.
World Series Cricket (Kerry Packer) 1977/78–78/79. Grandfather V. Y. Richardson (Australia); brothers I. M. and T. M. Chappell (both Australia). MBE for services to Australian cricket.

CHAPPELL, Ian Michael
——RHB, LB——

Born Unley, Adelaide, S Australia, 26 Sept 1943. Educ Prince Alfred C, Adelaide. Debut 1961/62. *Wisden 1976.*
AUSTRALIA DOMESTIC South Australia (109) 1961/62–79/80 (capt 1970/71–79/80).
LANCASHIRE (1) 1963.
AUSTRALIA (75) 1964/65–79/80. E 1965/66 (2), 1970/71 (6), 1974/75 (6), 1979/80 (2); WI 1968/69 (5), 1975/76 (6), 1979/80 (1); NZ 1973/74 (3); I 1967/68 (4); P 1964/65 (1), 1972/73 (3). *E 1968 (5), 1972 (5), 1975 (4); SA 1966/67 (5), 1969/70 (4); WI 1972/73 (5); NZ 1973/74 (3); I 1969/70 (5).* Capt 30.
OTHER TOURS International Wanderers to S Africa 1974/75, 1975/76.
HST 196 A v P, Adelaide, 1972/73. HS 209 Australians v Barbados, Bridgetown, 1972/73.
BBT 2–21 A v WI, Brisbane, 1968/69. BB 5–29 S Australia v NSW, Adelaide, 1972/73.
1000 RUNS (3+8) 1476 @ 82.00 in Australia in 1968/69.
World Series Cricket (Kerry Packer)

1977/78–78/79. Grandfather V. Y. Richardson (Australia); brothers G. S. and T. M. Chappell (both Australia).

CHAPPELL, Trevor Martin
——RHB, RM——

Born Glenelg, Adelaide, S Australia, 21 Oct 1952. Educ Prince Alfred C, Adelaide. Debut 1972/73.
AUSTRALIA DOMESTIC South Australia (17) 1972/73–75/76, Western Australia (4) 1976/77, New South Wales (48) 1979/80–.
AUSTRALIA (3) *E 1981.*
OTHER TOUR D. H. Robins' XI to S Africa 1975/76.
HST 27 A v E, Headingley, 1981. HS 150 NSW v W Australia, Sydney, 1979/80.
BBT 3–31 A v E, Headingley, 1981. BB 4–12 NSW v Victoria, St Kilda, 1981/82.
World Series Cricket (Kerry Packer) 1977/78–78/79. Clubs: Walsden, East Lancs (both as professional). Grandfather V. Y. Richardson (Australia); brothers G. S. and I. M. Chappell (both Australia).

CHATFIELD, Ewen John
——RHB, RMF——

Born Dannevirke, N Zealand, 3 July 1950. Educ Dannevirke District HS. Debut 1973/74.
N ZEALAND DOMESTIC Wellington (61) 1973/74–.
NEW ZEALAND (15) 1974/75–83/84. E 1974/75 (1), 1977/78 (1), 1983/84 (3); A 1976/77 (2), 1981/82 (1); SL 1982/83 (2). *E 1983 (3); SL 1983/84 (2).*
HST 13* NZ v E, Auckland, 1976/77. HS 24* Wellington v N Districts, Gisborne, 1981/82.
BBT 5–63 NZ v SL, Colombo, 1983/84. BB 8–24 (12–39 match) Wellington v N Districts, Lower Hutt, 1979/80. Match analysis 13–86, Wellington v W Indians, Lower Hutt, 1979/80.

CHAUHAN, Chetandra Pratap Singh Navratasingh
——RHB, OB——

Born Bareilly, Uttar Pradesh, India, 21 July 1947. Debut 1967/68.
INDIA DOMESTIC Maharashtra 1967/68–74/75, Delhi 1975/76–.
INDIA (40) 1969/70–80/81. E 1972/73 (2); A 1969/70 (1), 1979/80 (6); WI 1978/79 (6); NZ 1969/70 (2); P 1979/80 (6). *E 1979 (4); A 1977/78 (4), 1980/81 (3); NZ 1980/81 (3); P 1978/79 (3).*
HST 97 I v A, Adelaide, 1980/81. HS 207 Maharashtra v Vidarbha, Poona, 1972/73.

BB 6–26 Maharashtra v Gujerat, Bulsar, 1971/72.
1000 RUNS (0 + 2) 1138 @ 75.86 in India in 1972/73.
Career total of Test runs (2084) highest not to include a century.

CHEATLE, Robert *Giles* Lenthall
——————LHB, SLA——————

Born Paddington, London, 31 July 1953. Educ Stowe S. Debut 1974.
SUSSEX (40) 1974–79.
SURREY (20) 1980–83.
HS 49 Sussex v Kent, Tunbridge Wells, 1978.
BB 6–32 Sussex v Yorks, Hove, 1979.

CHECKSFIELD, Martin Frederic James
——————RHB——————

Born London, 29 Apr 1939. Educ Bryanston S; Christ Church C, Oxford. Debut 1960.
FREE FORESTERS (1) 1960.
OXFORD UNIVERSITY (1) 1961.
HS 42 Free Foresters v Oxford, The Parks, 1960.
Club: Banstead.

CHEETHAM, Albert George
——————RHB, RFM——————

Born Ryde, Sydney, NSW, Australia, 7 Dec 1915. Debut 1936/37.
AUSTRALIA DOMESTIC New South Wales (20) 1936/37–39/40, Australian Services (1) 1945/46.
TOUR Australian Services to England 1945.
HS 85 NSW v Queensland, Brisbane, 1939/40.
BB 4–75 same match.
Club: Balmain.

CHEETHAM, John Erskine
——————RHB——————

Born Mowbray, Cape Province, S Africa, 26 May 1920. Died J'burg, S Africa, 21 Aug 1980. Educ S African C, Cape Town; Cape Town U. Debut 1939/40.
S AFRICA DOMESTIC Western Province 1939/40–54/55.
SOUTH AFRICA (24) 1948/49–55. E 1948/49 (1); A 1949/50 (3); NZ 1953/54 (5). *E 1951 (5), 1955 (3); A 1952/53 (5); NZ 1952/53 (2)*. Capt 15.
HST 89 SA v NZ, Cape Town, 1953/54.
HS 271* W Province v OFS, Bloemfontein, 1950/51.

BB 2–38 W Province v Griqualand West, Cape Town, 1939/40.
1000 RUNS (1) 1196 @ 42.71 in 1951.
Author of *Caught by the Springboks* (1954) and *I Declare* (1956). President S African CA 1968–72. MCC Hon. member. Sons J. R. and R. S. Cheetham (both Transvaal).

CHEETHAM, John *Leslie*
——————RHB, WK——————

Born Hull, Yorks, 17 Mar 1918. Educ Bridlington Commercial S. Debut 1947.
GENTLEMEN V PLAYERS (1) 1947. Played one fc match as 'emergency' stand-in at Scarborough. Highest score 6.
Clubs: Bridlington, Harrogate, Bradford, Burnley, Otley.

CHESSHER, John Robert
——————RHB, RM——————

Born Banstead, Surrey, 21 Aug 1962. Educ Ipswich S; Lincoln C, Oxford. Debut 1982.
OXFORD UNIVERSITY (4) 1982–83.
HS 47 Oxford U v Northants, The Parks, 1982.

CHESTERTON, George Herbert
——————RHB, RM——————

Born Chirbury, Shropshire, 15 July 1922. Educ Malvern; Brasenose C, Oxford. Debut 1948 (Free Foresters).
OXFORD UNIVERSITY (12) 1949 (Blue).
WORCESTERSHIRE (47) 1950–57. Cap 1950.
TOUR MCC to Canada 1951.
HS 43 Oxford U v Free Foresters, The Parks, 1949.
BB 7–14 MCC v Ireland, Dublin, 1956.
Cornwall 1948–49.

CHIDGEY, Graham James
——————RHB——————

Born London, 1 Jan 1937. Educ City of London S. Debut 1962.
FREE FORESTERS (3) 1962–64.
HS 113 Free Foresters v Cambridge U, Fenner's, 1962 (on fc debut).
Surrey 2nd XI 1955–58. Army 1956–57. Clubs: Old Citizens, Free Foresters, I Zingari, Frogs, Hampshire Hogs. MCC committee 1972–74.

CHILDS, John Henry
——————LHB, SLA——————

Born Plymouth, Devon, 15 Aug 1951. Educ Audley Park Sec M, Torquay. Debut 1975.

GLOUCESTERSHIRE (164) 1975–. Cap 1977.
HS 34* Glos v Notts, Cheltenham, 1982.
BB 9–56 Glos v Som, Bristol, 1981.
Devon 1973–74.

CHILDS-CLARK, Arthur William
——————RHB, RM——————

Born Exeter, Devon, 13 May 1905. Died Mevagissey, Cornwall, 19 Feb 1980. Educ Christ's Hospital. Debut 1923.
MIDDLESEX (10) 1923–34.
MINOR COUNTIES (2) 1936–37.
NORTHAMPTONSHIRE (53) 1947–48. Cap 1947. Capt 1947–48.
HS 68 Northants v Leics, Leicester, 1948.
BB 3–72 H. D. G. Leveson Gower's XI v Oxford U, Reigate, 1934.

CHISHOLM, Jack Richardson
——————RHB, RF——————

Born Enfield, M'sex, 9 Oct 1924. Died Leytonstone, London, 24 Aug 1977. Debut 1947. *P.*
MIDDLESEX (1) 1947.
HS 12 M'sex v Oxford U, The Parks, 1947.
Bedfordshire 1949–51. Devon 1956. Club: St Just 1954. Soccer: Tottenham Hotspur, Brentford, Sheffield United, Plymouth Argyle.

CHISHOLM, Ronald Harry Eddie
——————RHB, LBG——————

Born Aberdeen, Scotland, 22 May 1927. Educ Robert Gordon's C; Aberdeen U. Debut 1948.
SCOTLAND (61) 1948–71.
HS 105 Scotland v Ireland, Perth, 1970.
BB 4–9 Scotland v Ireland, Dublin, 1969.
Club: Aberdeen.

CHOWDHURY, Nirode Ranjan (Putu)
——————RHB, RM/OB——————

Born Jamshedpur, India, 20 Oct 1926 (other sources state 23 May 1923). Died Durgapur, Pakistan, 14 Dec 1979. Debut 1941/42.
INDIA DOMESTIC Bihar 1941/42–43/44, 1955/56–57/58, Bengal 1944/45–54/55.
INDIA (2) 1948/49–51/52. E 1951/52 (1); WI 1948/49 (1).
TOUR India to England 1952.

HST 3★ I v WI, Madras, 1948/49. HS 30★ Bengal Governor's XI v Services, Calcutta, 1944/45.
BBT 1–130 I v WI, Madras, 1948/49. BB 7–79 (11–165 match) Bihar v Bengal, Jamshedpur, 1941/42 (on fc debut). Took 11, 9 and 10 wkts in first three fc matches respectively for Bengal in Ranji Trophy. Coach at Durgapur Steel Plant at death.

CHRISTEN, Brian
—LHB, LFM—

Born Bradford, Yorks, 27 Nov 1926. Debut 1951.
CANADA (5) 1951–54.
TOUR Canada to England 1954.
HS 9★ Canada v MCC, Toronto, 1951 and 9 Canadians v Yorks, Scarborough, 1954.
BB 7–80 Canada v MCC, Toronto, 1951 (fc debut).
Club: Dovercourt (Toronto).

CHRISTIANI, Robert Julian
—RHB, OB, WK—

Born Georgetown, British Guiana, 19 July 1920. Debut 1938/39.
W INDIES DOMESTIC British Guiana 1938/39–53/54.
WEST INDIES (22) 1947/48–53/54. E 1947/48 (4), 1953/54 (1); I 1952/53 (2). E 1950 (4); A 1951/52 (5); NZ 1951/52 (1); I 1948/49 (5).
HST 107 WI v I, Delhi, 1948/49. HS 181 British Guiana v Jamaica, Georgetown, 1947/48.
BBT 3–52 WI v I, Delhi, 1948/49. BB 3–31 British Guiana v Jamaica, Georgetown, 1947/48.
1000 RUNS (1) 1094 @ 45.58 in England in 1950.
Brothers C. M. and E. S. Christiani (both British Guiana).

CHRISTIE, Robert Douglas
—RHB, RM—

Born Delhi, India, 7 Mar 1942. Educ Eton; New C, Oxford. Debut 1964.
OXFORD UNIVERSITY (4) 1964.
HS 21 Oxford U v Glos, The Parks, 1964.
BB 4–44 same match.

CHUBB, Geoffrey Walter Ashton
—RHB, RMF—

Born East London, S Africa, 12 Apr 1911. Died East London, S Africa, 28 Aug 1982. Educ Selborn C, S Africa. Debut 1931/32.

S AFRICA DOMESTIC Border 1931/32, Transvaal 1936/37–50/51.
SOUTH AFRICA (5) E 1951.
HST 15★ E v SA, Old Trafford, 1951. HS 71★ Transvaal v E Province, J'burg, 1939/40.
BBT 6–51 SA v E, Old Trafford, 1951. BB 7–54 Transvaal v Natal, Cape Town, 1950/51.
RECORDS Test debut aged 40 yrs 56 days – oldest S African Test debutant and oldest S African to play Test cricket. National selector and S African CA board member. President S African CA 1955–57, 1959–60.

CHURCH, Lewis Girling
—RHB, LB—

Born Peterborough, Northants, 17 Oct 1928. Educ King's S, Peterborough. Debut 1957.
D. R. JARDINE'S XI (1) 1957.
HS 1 D. R. Jardine's XI v Oxford U, Eastbourne, 1957.
Clubs: Peterborough Town, Royal Navy, Arbroath, Helston, Littlehampton.

CLAPP, Robert John
—RHB, RM—

Born Weston-super-Mare, Somerset, 12 Dec 1948. Debut 1972.
SOMERSET (15) 1972–77.
HS 32 Som v Lancs, Old Trafford, 1975.
BB 3–15 Som v Northants, Northampton, 1975.

CLARK, Antony Roy
—RHB—

Born Grahamstown, S Africa, 7 Nov 1956. Educ St Andrew's C, Grahamstown; Rhodes U; Downing C, Cambridge. Debut 1981.
CAMBRIDGE UNIVERSITY (1) 1981.
HS 12 Cambridge U v Notts, Fenner's, 1981.

CLARK, David Graham
—RHB—

Born Barming, nr Maidstone, Kent, 27 Jan 1919. Educ Rugby. Debut 1946.
KENT (75) 1946–51. Cap 1949. Capt 1949–51.
HS 78 Kent v Surrey, Oval, 1951.
Manager MCC to Australasia 1970/71. Chairman of 1966 committee which produced report on condition and future of county cricket ('The Clark Report'). MCC committee 1960–81. MCC president 1977/78. Club: The Mote (Maidstone).

CLARK, Edward Austen
—RHB, LM—

Born Balham, S London, 15 Apr 1937. Debut 1959. P.
MIDDLESEX (196) 1959–76. Cap 1961.
TOUR MCC to E Africa 1973/74.
HS 149 M'sex v Kent, Gravesend, 1966.
BB 5–61 M'sex v Surrey, Oval, 1964.
1000 RUNS (5) 1454 @ 32.31 in 1964.
Scored 100★ M'sex v Cambridge U, Fenner's, 1959 on fc debut. Clubs: Spencer, Teddington. MCC committee 1981.

CLARK, Edward Winchester
—LHB, LF—

Born Elton, Huntingdonshire, 9 Aug 1902. Died King's Lynn, Norfolk, 28 Apr 1982. Debut 1922. P.
NORTHAMPTONSHIRE (307) 1922–47. Cap.
ENGLAND (8) 1929–34. A 1934 (2); SA 1929 (1); WI 1933 (2). I 1933/34 (3).
OTHER TOUR L. H. Tennyson's XI to Jamaica 1927/28.
HST 10 E v I, Calcutta, 1933/34. HS 30 Northants v Worcs, Northampton, 1929.
BBT 5–98 E v A, Oval, 1934. BB 8–59 Northants v Worcs, Worcester, 1927.
100 WKTS (2) 149 @ 19.10 in 1929.
Players v Gentlemen (2) 1926–33. Cambridgeshire 1948. Clubs: Bradford, Todmorden.

CLARK, John
—RHB, RFM—

Born Greenock, Scotland, 9 Dec 1943. Educ Greenock Academy. Debut 1969.
SCOTLAND (13) 1969–82.
HS 29 Scotland v Ireland, Dublin, 1975.
BB 4–10 Scotland v Ireland, Dublin, 1978.

CLARK, Leonard Stanley
—RHB, RM—

Born Manor Park, East London, 6 Mar 1914. Educ Leigh Hall C. Debut 1946.
ESSEX (24) 1946–47. Cap 1947.
HS 64 Essex v Northants, Ilford, 1947.

CLARK, Thomas Henry
—RHB, OB—

Born Luton, Beds, 5 Oct 1924. Died Luton, Beds, 14 June 1981. Debut 1947. P.
SURREY (260) 1947–59/60. Cap 1952. Benefit 1961.
TOUR Surrey to Rhodesia 1959/60.
HS 191 Surrey v Kent, Blackheath, 1956.
BB 5–23 Surrey v M'sex, Lord's, 1952.
1000 RUNS (6) 1570 @ 32.70 in 1957.

Players v Gentlemen (1) 1957. Bedfordshire 1946. Clubs: Vauxhall Motors, Luton. Career curtailed by chronic arthritis. Soccer: Walsall.

CLARK, William
RHB, WK

Born Crieff, Scotland, 8 Sept 1905. Educ Grove Academy. Debut 1946 (aged 40).
SCOTLAND (1) 1946.
HS 9 Scotland v Ireland, Greenock, 1946.
Club: Stirling County.

CLARKE, Carlos Bertram
RHB, LBG

Born Bridgetown, Barbados, 7 Apr 1918. Educ Harrison C, Barbados; Guy's Hospital, London. Debut 1937/38.
W INDIES DOMESTIC Barbados 1937/38–38/39.
NORTHAMPTONSHIRE (49) 1946–49. Cap 1947.
ESSEX (18) 1959–60.
MCC (4) 1955–61.
WEST INDIES (3) E 1939.
HST 2 WI v E, Oval, 1939. HS 86 Northants v Worcs, Worcester, 1947.
BBT 3–59 WI v E, Old Trafford, 1939. BB 7–75 (13–107 match) W Indies v Hants, Bournemouth, 1939.
Clubs: BBC, Cross Arrows.

CLARKE, Charles Cyril
RHB

Born Burton upon Trent, Staffordshire, 22 Dec 1910. Educ Repton. Debut 1929.
DERBYSHIRE (25) 1929–33.
SUSSEX (3) 1947.
HS 35★ Derbys v Kent, Ilkeston, 1930.
Staffordshire 1935–39.

CLARKE, Donald Hugh
RHB

Born Bromborough, Cheshire, 15 May 1926. Educ Oundle; St John's C, Cambridge. Debut 1946.
CAMBRIDGE UNIVERSITY (2) 1946.
HS 24 Cambridge U v Lancs, Fenner's, 1946.

CLARKE, Frank
RHB, RFM

Born St Fagans, Cardiff, 8 Oct 1936. Debut 1956. P.
GLAMORGAN (31) 1956–60.

HS 31 Glam v Indians, Swansea, 1959.
BB 5–66 Glam v M'sex, Lord's, 1959.
Clubs: Neath, Maesteg.

CLARKE, John Michael
LHB, RMF

Born Barcombe, Sussex, 25 Dec 1948. Debut 1969.
SUSSEX (1) 1969.
No runs, no wkts.

CLARKE, Robert Wakefield
LHB, LFM

Born Finedon, Northants, 22 Apr 1924. Died Sherborne, Dorset, 3 Aug 1981. Debut 1947. P.
NORTHAMPTONSHIRE (208) 1947–57. Cap 1949. Testimonial (£1903) 1957.
HS 56 Northants v Notts, Trent Bridge, 1948.
BB 8–26 Northants v Hants, Peterborough, 1951.
Devon 1960. Coached at RNC Dartmouth, Christ's Hospital and Sherborne.

CLARKE, Simon John Scott
RHB

Born Westcliff, Essex, 2 Apr 1938. Educ Wellington C; Christ's C, Cambridge. Debut 1958.
COMBINED SERVICES (1) 1958.
CAMBRIDGE UNIVERSITY (7) 1961–62.
HS 19 Cambridge U v Essex, Fenner's, 1961.
Rugby: England (13), Cambridge U, Bath, Blackheath.

CLARKE, Sylvester Theophilus
RHB, RF

Born Lead Vale, Christchurch, Barbados, 11 Dec 1954. Educ St Bartholomew's, Barbados. Debut 1977/78.
W INDIES DOMESTIC Barbados 1977/78–1981/82.
SURREY (121) 1979–. Cap 1980.
S AFRICA DOMESTIC Transvaal 1983/84.
WEST INDIES (11) 1977/78–81/82. A 1977/78 (1). A 1981/82 (1); I 1978/79 (5); P 1980/81 (4).
HST 35★ WI v P, Faisalabad, 1980/81. HS 100★ Surrey v Glam, Swansea, 1981.
BBT 5–126 WI v I, Bangalore, 1978/79.
BB 7–34 (12–100 match) W Indies XI v S Africa, J'burg, 1982/83.
Barred from W Indian cricket for touring S Africa in 1982/83 and 1983/84 (W Indies XI).

CLARKSON, Anthony
RHB, OB

Born Killinghall, Harrogate, Yorks, 5 Sept 1939. Educ Harrogate GS. Debut 1963. P.
YORKSHIRE (6) 1963.
SOMERSET (104) 1966–71. Cap 1968.
HS 131 Som v Northants, Northampton, 1969.
BB 3–51 Som v Essex, Yeovil, 1967.
1000 RUNS (2) 1246 @ 27.68 in 1970.
Clubs: Keighley, Harrogate.

CLAUGHTON, John Alan
RHB

Born Leeds, Yorks, 17 Sept 1956. Educ King Edward's S, Birmingham; Merton C, Oxford. Debut 1976.
OXFORD UNIVERSITY (37) 1976–79 (Blue 1976–79). Capt 1978.
WARWICKSHIRE (18) 1979–80.
HS 130 Oxford U v Sussex, The Parks, 1978.
Scored 51 and 112 on debut, Oxford U v Glos, The Parks, 1976.
Berkshire 1982. Gave up full-time cricket 1980 owing to knee injury. Great-uncle H. M. Claughton (Yorks).

CLAY, John Charles
RHB, OB

Born Bonvilston, Glam, 18 Mar 1898. Died Cardiff, Wales, 11 Aug 1973. Educ Winchester C. Debut 1921.
GLAMORGAN (358) 1921–49. Cap. Capt 1924–27, 1929 (with N. V. H. Riches), 1946.
WALES (4) 1923–26.
ENGLAND (1) SA 1935 (no runs, no wkts).
HS 115★ Glam v N Zealanders, Cardiff, 1927.
BB 9–54 Glam v Northants, Llanelli, 1935. Match analysis 17–212 Glam v Worcs, Swansea, 1937.
100 WKTS (3) 176 @ 17.34 in 1937. Took 130 wickets @ 13.40 in 1946 aged 48.
RECORD Added 203★ for 9th wkt with J. J. Hills, Glam v Worcs, Swansea, 1929, county record.
Gentlemen v Players (3) 1923–35. England Test selector 1947–48. Glamorgan secretary 1946–55; president 1960–73.

CLAY, John Desmond
RHB

Born West Bridgford, Notts, 15 Oct 1924. Debut 1948. P.
NOTTINGHAMSHIRE (236) 1948–61. Cap 1952. Capt 1961.

HS 192 Notts v Hants, Trent Bridge, 1952.
1000 RUNS (6) 1497 @ 25.81 in 1961.
Club: Lightcliffe.

CLAYTON, Geoffrey
RHB, WK

Born Mossley, Lancs, 3 Feb 1938. Debut 1957. *P.*
COMBINED SERVICES (1) 1957.
LANCASHIRE (183) 1959–64. Cap 1960.
SOMERSET (89) 1965–67. Cap 1965.
HS 106 Som v M'sex, Taunton, 1965.
669 dismissals (605 ct, 64 st) in career.

CLEATON, Howard
RHB, OB

Born Merthyr Tydfil, Wales, 15 Nov 1949. Educ Bristol GS; St Luke's C, Exeter. Debut 1971.
GLOUCESTERSHIRE (1) 1971.
HS 1 Glos v Notts, Gloucester, 1971.

CLEMENTS, Simon Mark
LHB, RM

Born Felixstowe, Suffolk, 29 Apr 1956. Educ Ipswich S; Trinity C, Oxford. Debut 1976.
OXFORD UNIVERSITY (29) 1976–79 (Blue 1976, 1979). Capt 1979.
HS 91 Oxford U v Glos, The Parks, 1976 (fc debut).
Suffolk 1974–.

CLEVELEY, Alan Barnard
RHB, RFM

Born Chaddesden, Derbys, 5 Jan 1932. Debut 1955. *P.*
NOTTINGHAMSHIRE (1) 1955.
HS 4* Notts v Essex, Trent Bridge, 1955.
BB 3–63 same match.

CLIFFORD, Christopher Craven
RHB, OB

Born Hovingham, Yorks, 5 July 1942. Educ Malton GS; Carnegie Hall, Leeds C of Educ. Debut 1972.
YORKSHIRE (11) 1972.
WARWICKSHIRE (36) 1978–80.
HS 26 Warwicks v Surrey, Oval, 1979.
BB 6–89 Warwicks v Som, Weston-super-Mare, 1978.

CLIFT, Patrick Bernard
RHB, RM

Born Salisbury, Rhodesia, 14 July 1953. Educ St George's C, Salisbury. Debut 1971/72.
S AFRICA DOMESTIC Rhodesia 1971/72–79/80, Natal 1981/82–.
ZIMBABWE 1980/81.
LEICESTERSHIRE (165) 1975–. Cap 1976.
HS 100* Leics v Sussex, Hove, 1983 (fastest-ever fc century for Leics).
BB 8–17 Leics v MCC, Lord's, 1976.
Returned 8–26 inns Leics v Warwicks, Edgbaston, 1984.
Club: West Bromwich Dartmouth (professional 1975).

CLIFT, Phil Brittain
RHB

Born Usk, Monmouthshire, Wales, 3 Sept 1918. Debut 1937. *P.*
GLAMORGAN (183) 1937–55. Cap 1947.
Testimonial (£3000) 1959.
HS 125* Glam v Derbys, Cardiff, 1949.
BB 3–6 Glam v Sussex, Llanelli, 1951.
1000 RUNS (3) 1226 @ 26.08 in 1949.
Glamorgan coach 1959–77; secretary 1978–83. Clubs: Maesteg Celtic, Neath, Usk.

CLIFTON, Ernest George
RHB, WK

Born Lambeth, South London, 15 June 1939. Debut 1962.
MIDDLESEX (25) 1962–66.
HS 25 M'sex v Hants, Lord's, 1962.
Director of coaching S Australia 1970–84. Club: Beddington.

CLINTON, Grahame Selvey
LHB, RM

Born Sidcup, Kent, 5 May 1953. Educ Chislehurst and Sidcup GS. Debut 1974.
KENT (32) 1974–78.
SURREY (114) 1979–. Cap 1980.
S AFRICA DOMESTIC Rhodesia 1979/80.
HS 192 Surrey v Yorks, Oval, 1984.
BB 2–8 Kent v Pakistanis, Canterbury, 1978.
1000 RUNS (3) 1240 @ 37.57 in 1980.

CLOSE, Dennis *Brian*
LHB, ROB/RM

Born Rawdon, Leeds, Yorks, 24 Feb 1931. Educ Aireborough GS. Debut 1949. *Wisden 1964. P.*
YORKSHIRE (536) 1949–70. Cap 1949.
Benefit (£8154) 1961. Capt 1963–70.

SOMERSET (142) 1971–77. Cap 1971.
Testimonial 1976. Capt 1972–77.
D. B. CLOSE'S XI (3) 1982–84.
ENGLAND (22) 1949–76. A 1961 (1); SA 1955 (1); WI 1957 (2), 1963 (5), 1966 (1), 1976 (3); NZ 1949 (1); I 1959 (1), 1967 (3); P 1967 (3). *A 1950/51 (1).* Capt 7.
OTHER TOURS MCC A to Pakistan 1955/56. Commonwealth XI to S Africa 1959/60. Commonwealth XI to India 1964/65. International Wanderers to Rhodesia 1972/73 (capt). D. H. Robins' XI to S Africa 1973/74 (capt). International Wanderers to S Africa 1974/75 (capt). D. H. Robins' XI to S Africa 1974/75 (capt).
HST 70 E v WI, Lord's, 1963. HS 198 Yorks v Surrey, Oval, 1960.
BBT 4–35 E v I, Headingley, 1959. BB 8–41 Yorks v Kent, Headingley, 1959.
1000 RUNS (20) 1985 @ 35.44 in 1961.
100 WKTS (2) 114 @ 24.08 in 1952.
DOUBLES (2) 1949 (debut season), 1952 (next full season after National Service).
RECORDS Double in first season (1949) unique achievement; youngest-ever to perform double. Test debut in 1949 (E v NZ, Old Trafford) aged 18 yrs 149 days – youngest-ever England player. 811 catches in career – fifth-highest of all time.
Players v Gentlemen (6) 1949–62. Test selector 1979–80. CBE for services to cricket. Clubs: Yeadon, Todmorden. Yorkshire chairman cricket committee 1984. Soccer: Bradford City, England Youth international.

CLOSE, Peter Alwen
RHB, OB

Born Murree, India, 1 June 1943. Educ Haileybury and ICS; Caius C, Cambridge. Debut 1964.
CAMBRIDGE UNIVERSITY (15) 1964–65 (Blue 1965).
HS 54 Cambridge U v Glam, Pontypridd, 1965.
Dorset 1963–66. Clubs: Free Foresters, Privateers, Quidnuncs.

CLUBE, Stace *Victor* Murray
RHB, OB

Born Merton, Surrey, 22 Oct 1934. Educ St John's S, Leatherhead; Christchurch C, Oxford. Debut 1956.
OXFORD UNIVERSITY (16) 1956–57 (Blue 1956).
FREE FORESTERS (1) 1959.
HS 25 Oxford U v M'sex, The Parks, 1956.
BB 5–49 Oxford U v Free Foresters, The Parks, 1957.
Well-known space scientist.

CLUGSTON, David *Lindsey*
—————LHB, SLA—————

Born Belfast, Ireland, 5 Feb 1908.
Debut 1928.
WARWICKSHIRE (6) 1928–46.
HS 17 Warwicks v Notts, Coventry, 1928.
BB 2–75 Warwicks v M'sex, Edgbaston, 1928.
18 yrs between third (1928) and fourth (1946) matches for Warwicks. Public-address announcer at Edgbaston.

COBB, Russell Alan
—————RHB, SLA—————

Born Leicester, 18 May 1961. Educ Trent C, Nottingham. Debut 1980.
LEICESTERSHIRE (42) 1980–.
TOURS D. H. Robins' XI to N Zealand 1979/80. Leics XI to Zimbabwe 1980/81.
HS 64 Leics v Zimbabweans, Leicester, 1982.

COBHAM, Michael *David*
—————RHB, RMF—————

Born Boynton, Yorks, 11 May 1930. Educ Stowe S. Debut 1953.
FREE FORESTERS (1) 1953.
No runs.
BB 2–21 Free Foresters v Cambridge U, Fenner's, 1953.
Berkshire 1948. Clubs: I Zingari, Crusaders, Frogs, Hampstead.

COCK, David Frederick
—————RHB—————

Born Great Dunmow, Essex, 22 Oct 1914. Educ Bishop's Stortford C. Debut 1939.
ESSEX (14) 1939–46.
HS 98 Essex v Som, Westcliff, 1939.
Cambridgeshire 1951. Club: Bishop's Stortford.

COCKBAIN, Ian
—————RHB, SLA—————

Born Bootle, Lancs, 19 Apr 1958. Educ Bootle GS. Debut 1979.
LANCASHIRE (46) 1979–83.
HS 98 Lancs v Warwicks, Southport, 1982.
Cheshire 1984–.

COCKETT, John Ashley
—————RHB—————

Born Broadstairs, Kent, 23 Dec 1927. Educ Aldenham; Trinity Hall, Cambridge. Debut 1951.

CAMBRIDGE UNIVERSITY (7) 1951 (Blue).
MINOR COUNTIES (1) 1953.
HS 121 Cambridge U v Sussex, Worthing, 1951.
Made a pair in last two fc matches.
Buckinghamshire 1949–62. Hockey: England.

COE, Geoffrey
—————LHB, LM—————

Born Earl Shilton, Leics, 29 Mar 1943. Debut 1963.
LEICESTERSHIRE (1) 1963.
Did not bat.

COGGER, Gerald Lindley
—————RHB, RMF—————

Born Uckfield, Sussex, 7 Sept 1933. Debut 1954. *P.*
SUSSEX (8) 1954–57.
HS 5 Sussex v Hants, Hove, 1957.
BB 3–20 same match.
Sussex 12th man aged 15, v Northants, Worthing, 1949. Assistant groundsman on retirement. Clubs: Sydenhurst Ramblers, Three Bridges.

COGHLAN, Timothy Boyle Lake
—————RHB, RFM—————

Born Chelsea, London, 29 Mar 1939. Educ Rugby; Pembroke C, Cambridge. Debut 1958.
CAMBRIDGE UNIVERSITY (19) 1958–60 (Blue 1960).
L. C. STEVENS' XI (1) 1961.
HS 24 Cambridge U v Kent, Fenner's, 1958.
BB 3–70 Cambridge U v Kent, Gillingham, 1959.

COHEN, Mark Francis
—————RHB—————

Born Cork, Ireland, 27 Mar 1961. Educ Stratford C, Dublin. Debut 1980.
IRELAND (1) 1980.
No runs, no wkts.
Middlesex staff 1981; did not play and not retained. Club: Carlisle.

COHEN, Rudolph A.
—————RHB, RFM—————

Born Kingston, Jamaica, 4 Aug 1942. Educ Excelsior S, Kingston. Debut 1963/64.
W INDIES DOMESTIC Jamaica 1963/64–66/67.
TOUR W Indies to England 1966.

HS 32* W Indians v Kent, Canterbury, 1966.
BB 6–71 W Indians v Sussex, Hove, 1966.
Club: Smethwick.

COLDWELL, Leonard John
—————RHB, RFM—————

Born Newton Abbot, Devon, 10 Jan 1933. Debut 1955. *P.*
WORCESTERSHIRE (296) 1955–69. Cap 1959. Benefit (£7502) 1968.
ENGLAND (7) 1962–64. A 1964 (2); P 1962 (2). *A 1962/63 (2); NZ 1962/63 (1).*
OTHER TOURS Worcs to Rhodesia 1964/65. Commonwealth XI to India 1964/65. Worcs to Jamaica 1965/66.
HST 6* E v A, Lord's, 1964. HS 37 Worcs v Notts, Worcester, 1962.
BBT 6–85 E v P, Lord's, 1962 (Test debut). BB 8–38 Surrey v Worcs, Worcester, 1965.
100 WKTS (2) 152 @ 17.90 in 1962.
Devon 1953–54.

COLDWELL, William Rodney
—————RHB, occ OB—————

Born Petersfield, Hants, 4 June 1932. Debut 1954. *P.*
MCC (2) 1954–55.
HS 8 MCC v Cambridge U, Lord's, 1955.
PRO Surrey 1970. Professional: Greenock. Coach at St George's, Weybridge in 1968. Non-league soccer manager for Guildford, Dunstable.

COLE, Derek Henry
—————RHB, RMF/OB—————

Born Dawlish, Devon, 9 Mar 1925. Debut 1956.
SOUTH OF ENGLAND (1) 1956.
MINOR COUNTIES (2) 1959–67.
HS 36 Minor Counties v Indians, Longton, Stoke on Trent, 1959.
Devon 1947–70 (capt 1963–69). Club: Torquay.

COLES, Walter Neill
—————RHB—————

Born Northwood, M'sex, 11 Feb 1928. Educ Eton; Jesus C, Cambridge. Debut 1949.
CAMBRIDGE UNIVERSITY (2) 1949.
HS 14 Cambridge U v Lancs, Fenner's, 1949.
Club: I Zingari.

COLHOUN, Osmund David
―――――RHB, WK―――――

Born Sion Mills, Northern Ireland, 6 June 1939. Educ Sion Mills PES. Debut 1959.
IRELAND (28) 1959–79.
HS 9* Ireland v Scotland, Londonderry, 1963.
RECORD 46 wicketkeeping dismissals for Ireland.
Clubs: Sion Mills, Royal Ulster Constabulary.

COLLEDGE, Fred
―――――RHB, RFM―――――

Born Renfrew, Scotland, 7 May 1915. Educ Camphill Sec S. Debut 1949.
SCOTLAND (4) 1949–52.
HS 12* Scotland v Yorks, Hull, 1949.
BB 2–50 Scotland v Northants, Edinburgh, 1951.

COLLEY, David John
―――――RHB, RFM―――――

Born Mosman, Sydney, NSW, Australia, 15 Mar 1947. Debut 1969/70.
AUSTRALIA DOMESTIC New South Wales (71) 1969/70–77/78.
AUSTRALIA (3) E 1972.
HST 54 A v E, Trent Bridge, 1972. HS 101 NSW v S Australia, Adelaide, 1970/71.
BBT 3–83 A v E, Old Trafford, 1972. BB 6–30 NSW v S Australia, Sydney, 1976/77.
Club: Mosman-Mid Harbour.

COLLINGE, John Gregory
―――――RHB, OB―――――

Born N Zealand, 10 May 1939. Educ Auckland U; University C, Oxford. Debut 1964.
OXFORD UNIVERSITY (2) 1964.
HS 9 Oxford U v Glos, Bristol, 1964.

COLLINGE, Rex Alan
―――――RHB, RM―――――

Born Nottingham, 23 Apr 1935. Educ Bedford S. Debut 1962.
COMBINED SERVICES (2) 1962.
HS 41 Combined Services v Cambridge U, Fenner's, 1962.
BB 6–52 same match.
Suffolk 1955–62. RAF.

COLLINGE, Richard Owen
―――――RHB, LFM―――――

Born Wellington, N Zealand, 2 Apr 1946. Educ Wairarapa C. Debut 1963/64.

N ZEALAND DOMESTIC Central Districts (21) 1963/64–66/67, 1969/70, Wellington (28) 1967/68–68/69, 1970/71–74/75, Northern Districts (19) 1975/76–77/78.
NEW ZEALAND (35) 1964/65–78. E 1970/71 (2), 1974/75 (2), 1977/78 (3); A 1973/74 (3); I 1967/68 (2), 1975/76 (3); P 1964/65 (3), 1972/73 (2). E 1965 (3), 1969 (1), 1973 (3), 1978 (1); I 1964/65 (2), 1976/77 (1); P 1964/65 (2), 1976/77 (2).
OTHER TOURS N Zealand to Australia 1967/68, 1969/70, 1970/71.
HST 68* NZ v P, Auckland, 1972/73. HS as above.
BBT 6–63 NZ v I, Christchurch, 1975/76.
BB 8–64 Wellington v Auckland, Auckland, 1967/68.
RECORDS Added 151 for 10th wkt with B. F. Hastings during HST (above), world Test record. His 68* also highest score by number 11 batsman in Test cricket.

COLLINGWOOD, Boris Esmond
―――――RHB―――――

Born Lewisham, London, 8 Jan 1920. Died Storrington, Sussex, 18 Nov 1968. Educ Dulwich C; Clare C, Cambridge. Debut 1948.
CAMBRIDGE UNIVERSITY (1) 1948.
SOMERSET (1) 1953.
HS 15 Som v Notts, Weston-super-Mare, 1953.
Club: Beckenham.

COLLINS, Brian George
―――――RHB, RFM―――――

Born Enfield, M'sex, 11 Aug 1941. Debut 1979.
MINOR COUNTIES (1) 1979.
Did not bat.
BB 3–83 Minor Counties v Indians, Wellington, 1979.
Hertfordshire 1965–. Club: Berkhamsted.

COLLINS, Ross Philip
―――――RHB, RM―――――

Born Paddington, NSW, Australia, 9 Dec 1945. Debut 1967/68.
AUSTRALIA DOMESTIC New South Wales (22) 1967/68–75/76.
International Cavaliers v Barbados, Scarborough, 1969.
HS 88* NSW v S Australia, Adelaide, 1968/69.
BB 5–54 NSW v N Zealanders, Sydney, 1969/70.
Clubs: North Sydney, Lowerhouse.

COLLINS, Roy
―――――RHB, OB―――――

Born Clayton, Manchester, 10 Mar 1934. Debut 1954. P.
LANCASHIRE (120) 1954–62. Cap 1961.
HS 107* Lancs v Som, Bath, 1961.
BB 6–63 Lancs v Sussex, Old Trafford, 1961.
Cheshire 1963–70. Clubs: Leek, Longsight, Lowerhouse, Rochdale. Brother-in-law J. Cumbes (Lancs, Surrey, Worcs and Warwicks).

COLLINSON, John
―――――RHB, OB―――――

Born Sotterley, Suffolk, 2 Oct 1911. Died Hove, Sussex, 29 Aug 1979. Educ St John's S, Leatherhead. Debut 1939.
MIDDLESEX (2) 1939.
WORCESTERSHIRE (1) 1946.
HS 34 M'sex v Glos, Cheltenham, 1939.

COLLYER, Francis Edward
―――――RHB, WK―――――

Born Brentford, M'sex, 4 Feb 1947. Educ Cambridge U. Debut 1967.
CAMBRIDGE UNIVERSITY (2) 1967–69.
MINOR COUNTIES (3) 1973–79.
HS 46 Minor Counties v Indians, Wellington, 1979.
Hertfordshire 1967–. Club: Westcliff.

COMBER, Joseph Thomas Henry
―――――RHB, WK―――――

Born 26 Feb 1911. Died Paddington, London, 3 May 1976. Educ Marlborough C; Pembroke C, Cambridge. Debut 1931.
CAMBRIDGE UNIVERSITY (36) 1931–33 (Blue 1931–33).
FREE FORESTERS (6) 1934–46.
MCC (5) 1935–48.
HS 62 Free Foresters v Cambridge U, Fenner's, 1936.

COMPTON, Denis Charles Scott
―――――RHB, SLA―――――

Born Hendon, M'sex, 23 May 1918. Educ Bell Lane S, Hendon. Debut 1936. Wisden 1939. P to 1957.
MIDDLESEX (78) 1936–58. Cap 1936.
Benefit (£12,200) 1949. Joint capt 1951–52.
INDIA DOMESTIC Holkar 1944/45, Europeans 1945/46.
ENGLAND (78) 1937–56/57. A 1938 (4), 1948 (5), 1953 (5), 1956 (1); SA 1947 (5), 1951 (4), 1955 (5); WI 1939 (3), 1950 (1); NZ 1937 (1), 1949 (4); I 1946 (3), 1952 (2);

P 1954 (4). *A 1946/47 (5), 1950/51 (4), 1954/55 (4)*; *SA 1948/49 (5), 1956/57 (5)*; *WI 1953/54 (5)*; *NZ 1946/47 (1), 1950/51 (2)*.
OTHER TOUR Cavaliers to Jamaica 1963/64 (capt).
HST 278 E v P, Trent Bridge, 1954. HS 300 MCC v North-Eastern Transvaal, Benoni, 1948/49.
BBT 5–70 E v SA, Cape Town, 1948/49. BB 7–36 (11–49 match) MCC v Auckland, Auckland, 1946/47.
1000 RUNS (14 + 3) 3816 @ 90.86 in 1947.
RECORDS 3816 runs @ 90.86 and 18 centuries in 1947 both records for one season. Scored 1004 runs @ 34.62 in debut season, youngest to score 1000 runs in first season. Reached 100 centuries in 552 innings, second fastest after D. G. Bradman (295). HS (above) made in 181 mins, fastest-ever triple-century. Added 370 for 3rd wkt with W. J. Edrich, E v SA, Lord's, 1947 – 3rd wkt record for England. Added 424* with W. J. Edrich, M'sex v Som, Lord's, 1948 – English fc record and highest for any wkt at Lord's. 4 centuries in Test series v SA in 1947 equals record for series in England.
Scored centuries in 4 consecutive fc inns in 1946/47.
CBE for services to cricket. Cricket writer; author of several books. Soccer: Arsenal. Brother L. H. Compton (M'sex).

COMPTON, Leslie Harry
————RHB, WK, RM————

Born Woodford, Essex, 12 Sept 1912. Died Essex, 27 Dec 1984. Debut 1938. *P*.
MIDDLESEX (272) 1938–56. Cap 1947. Benefit (£6817) 1954.
HS 107 M'sex v Derbys, Derby, 1947.
BB 2–21 M'sex v Essex, Westcliff, 1946.
Brother D. C. S. Compton (M'sex and England). Soccer: England (2), Arsenal.

COMPTON-BURNETT, Richard James
————RHB————

Born Windsor, Berks, 1 July 1961. Educ Eton; Pembroke C, Cambridge. Debut 1981.
CAMBRIDGE UNIVERSITY (1) 1981.
HS 18 Cambridge U v Notts, Fenner's, 1981.
Father A. C. Burnett (Cambridge U and Glam).

CONEY, Jeremy Vernon
————RHB, RM————

Born Wellington, N Zealand, 21 July 1952. Debut 1970/71.
N ZEALAND DOMESTIC N Zealand Under-23 XI 1970/71, Wellington (64) 1971/72–.
NEW ZEALAND (30) 1973/74–1983/84. E 1983/84 (3); A 1973/74 (2), 1981/82 (3); WI 1979/80 (3); I 1980/81 (3); P 1978/79 (3); SL 1982/83 (2). *E 1983 (4)*; *A 1973/74 (2), 1980/81 (2)*; *SL 1983/84 (3)*.
HST 174* NZ v E, Wellington 1983/84. HS as above.
BBT 3–28 NZ v A, Melbourne, 1980/81.
BB 6–17 Wellington v Central Districts, Upper Hutt, 1979/80.
RECORD During HST (above) added 118 for 9th wkt with B. L. Cairns, N Zealand Test record.

CONGDON, Bevan Ernest
————RHB, RM————

Born Motueka, N Zealand, 11 Feb 1938. Educ Motueka District HS. Debut 1960/61. *Wisden 1974*.
N ZEALAND DOMESTIC Central Districts (55) 1960/61–70/71, Wellington (7) 1971/72, Otago (6) 1972/73–73/74, Canterbury (26) 1974/75–77/78.
NEW ZEALAND (61) 1964/65–78. E 1965/66 (3), 1970/71 (2), 1974/75 (2), 1977/78 (3); A 1973/74 (3), 1976/77 (2); WI 1968/69 (3); I 1967/68 (4), 1975/76 (3); P 1964/65 (3), 1972/73 (3). *E 1965 (3), 1969 (3), 1973 (3), 1978 (3); A 1973/74 (3); WI 1971/72 (5); I 1964/65 (3), 1969/70 (3); P 1964/65 (1), 1969/70 (3)*. Capt 17.
OTHER TOURS N Zealand to Australia 1967/68, 1969/70, 1970/71, 1972/73.
HST 176 NZ v E, Trent Bridge, 1973. HS 202* Central Districts v Otago, Nelson, 1968/69.
BBT 5–65 NZ v I, Auckland, 1975/76. BB 6–42 Canterbury v Central Districts, Palmerston North, 1976/77.
1000 RUNS (1 + 1) 1081 @ 60.06 in 1973.
RECORDS 61 Test appearances, most for N Zealand; 3448 Test runs @ 32.22 and 7 Test centuries, a record and joint-record respectively for N Zealand. Added 229 for 4th wkt with B. F. Hastings, NZ v A, Wellington, 1973/74 and 136 for 8th wkt with R. S. Cunis, NZ v WI, Port of Spain, 1971/72, both N Zealand Test records.
OBE for services to cricket.

CONIBERE, William Jack
————RHB, LMF————

Born Wiveliscombe, Som, 11 Aug 1923. Died Torbay, Devon, 19 Aug 1982. Debut 1950.

SOMERSET (4) 1950.
HS 8 Som v Hants, Bournemouth, 1950.
BB 4–66 Som v Warwicks, Edgbaston, 1950.

CONNOLLY, Alan Norman
————RHB, RFM————

Born Skipton, Victoria, Australia, 29 June 1939. Educ Geelong HS. Debut 1959/60.
AUSTRALIA DOMESTIC Victoria (83) 1959/60–70/71.
MIDDLESEX (44) 1969–70. Cap 1969.
AUSTRALIA (29) 1963/64–70/71. E 1965/66 (1), 1970/71 (1); SA 1963/64 (3); WI 1968/69 (5); I 1967/68 (3). *E 1968 (5); SA 1969/70 (4); I 1964/65 (2), 1969/70 (5)*.
OTHER TOURS Australia to England 1964. Australia to N Zealand 1966/67.
HST 37 A v I, Sydney, 1968/69. HS 40 Victoria v Queensland, Brisbane, 1964/65.
BBT 6–47 A v SA, Port Elizabeth, 1969/70. BB 9–67 Victoria v Queensland, Brisbane, 1964/65.
RECORD 330 wkts for Victoria, state record.

CONNOR, Cardigan Adolphus
————RHB, RFM————

Born The Valley, Anguilla, 24 Mar 1961. Educ Langley C. Debut 1984.
HAMPSHIRE (21) 1984.
HS 13* Hants v Kent, Bournemouth, 1984.
BB 7–37 Hants v Kent, Bournemouth, 1984.
Bucks 1979–83. Club: Slough.

CONRADI, Eric Ralph
————LHB————

Born Kensington, London, 25 July 1920. Died Droitwich, 22 Aug 1972. Educ Oundle; Caius C, Cambridge. Debut 1946.
CAMBRIDGE UNIVERSITY (7) 1946 (Blue).
HS 50* Cambridge U v Som, Bath, 1946.
Clubs: Bury, Heywood, Horsham. Represented England at world Jewish sports festival 1957.

CONSTABLE, Bernard
————RHB, LB————

Born East Molesey, Surrey, 19 Feb 1921. Debut 1939. *P*.
SURREY (434) 1939–64. Cap 1950. Benefit (£6515) 1959.
TOUR Surrey to Rhodesia 1959/60.
HS 205* Surrey v Som, Oval, 1952.

BB 5–131 RAF v Worcs, Worcester, 1946.
1000 RUNS (12) 1799 @ 39.97 in 1961.
Club: East Molesey. Brother D. Constable (Northants).

CONSTABLE, Dennis
————RHB, WK————

Born East Molesey, Surrey, 14 Aug 1925. Debut 1949. *P.*
NORTHAMPTONSHIRE (2) 1949.
HS 12 Northants v N Zealanders, Northampton, 1949.
Clubs: East Molesey, Band of Brothers. Brother B. Constable (Surrey).

CONSTANT, David John
————LHB, SLA————

Born Bradford-on-Avon, Wiltshire, 9 Nov 1941. Debut 1961. *P.*
KENT (8) 1961–63.
LEICESTERSHIRE (53) 1965–68.
HS 80 Leics v Glos, Bristol, 1966.
Fc umpire 1969– (28 Tests, 1971–84).
Club: Catford Wanderers.

CONSTANTINE, Learie Nicholas
————RHB, RF————

Born Diego Martin, Trinidad, 21 Sept 1902. Died Hampstead, London, 1 July 1971. Educ St Anne's RC S. Debut 1921/22. *Wisden* 1940.
W INDIES DOMESTIC Trinidad 1921/22–34/35, Barbados 1938/39.
DOMINIONS (1) 1945.
WEST INDIES (18) 1928–39. E 1929/30 (3), 1934/35 (3). *E 1928 (3), 1933 (1), 1939 (3); A 1930/31 (5).*
OTHER TOUR W Indies to England 1923.
HST 90 WI v E, Port of Spain, 1934/35.
HS 133 Trinidad v Barbados, Port of Spain, 1928/29.
BBT 5–75 WI v E, Oval, 1939. BB 8–38 Trinidad v Barbados, Bridgetown, 1923/24.
1000 RUNS (1) 1381 @ 34.52 in 1928.
100 WKTS (2) 107 @ 22.95 in 1928.
DOUBLE (1) 1928.
RECORD Scored 100 in 52 mins, W Indians v Tasmania, Launceston, 1930/31 – fastest fc century by a W Indian.
High Commissioner for Trinidad and Tobago in London 1962–64. MBE 1945; knighted 1962; created 'Baron Constantine of Maraval in Trinidad and Tobago, and of Nelson in the County Palatine of Lancaster' in 1969. Author of several cricket books. Club: Nelson. Father L. S. Constantine (Trinidad); uncle V. Pascall (Trinidad).

CONTRACTOR, Nariman Jamshedji
————LHB, occ RM————

Born Godhra, Gujerat, India, 7 Mar 1934. Debut 1952/53.
INDIA DOMESTIC Gujerat 1952/53–57/58, 1960/61–70/71 (capt 1960/61–65/66, 1967/68–70/71), Railways 1958/59–59/60 (capt 1959/60).
INDIA (31) 1955/56–61/62. E 1961/62 (5); A 1956/57 (1), 1959/60 (5); WI 1958/59 (5); NZ 1955/56 (4); P 1960/61 (5). *E 1959 (4); WI 1961/62 (2).* Capt 12.
OTHER TOURS India to Ceylon 1956/57.
HST 108 I v A, Bombay, 1959/60. HS 176 Gujerat v Bombay, Bombay, 1956/57.
BB 4–85 Gujerat v Bombay, Bombay, 1950/51.
1000 RUNS (1) 1183 @ 31.13 in 1959.
RECORD Scored 152 and 102* on fc debut, Gujerat v Baroda, Baroda, 1952/53 – only A. R. Morris (NSW, 1940/41) and Aamer Malik (Lahore, 1979/80) have equalled this feat.
Scored centuries in 4 consecutive fc inns in 1957/58.
Suffered serious injury when struck on head by C. C. Griffith, Indians v Barbados, Bridgetown, 1961/62. MCC Hon. member. Son H. N. Contractor (Bombay).

COOK, Cecil
————RHB, SLA————

Born Tetbury, Glos, 23 Aug 1921. Debut 1946. *P.*
GLOUCESTERSHIRE (498) 1946–64. Cap 1946. Benefit (£3067) 1957. Testimonial 1964.
ENGLAND (1) SA 1947.
HST 4 E v SA, Trent Bridge, 1947. HS 35* Glos v Sussex, Hove, 1957.
BB 9–42 Glos v Yorks, Bristol, 1947.
100 WKTS (9) 149 @ 14.16 in 1956.
Took wkt with first ball in fc cricket, Glos v Oxford U, The Parks, 1946. Fc umpire since 1971.

COOK, Charles *John*
————RHB, OB————

Born Retford, Notts, 5 June 1946. Debut 1974.
NOTTINGHAMSHIRE (2) 1974–75.
HS 1 Notts v Indians, Trent Bridge, 1974.

COOK, Colin Roy
————RHB————

Born Edgware, M'sex, 11 Jan 1960. Educ Merchant Taylors' S, Northwood. Debut 1981.

MIDDLESEX (11) 1981–84.
HS 79 M'sex v Lancs, Southport, 1981.
Brother-in-law C. W. J. Athey (Yorks, Glos and England). Club: Southgate.

COOK, David Roland
————RHB, LFM————

Born Birmingham, 2 Sept 1936. Educ Warwick S. Debut 1962.
WARWICKSHIRE (9) 1962–68.
HS 28* Warwicks v Som, Taunton, 1968.
BB 4–66 Warwicks v Yorks, Edgbaston, 1967.
Clubs: Walsall (professional), Moseley. Rugby: Warwicks and Coventry. Brother M. S. Cook (Warwicks).

COOK, Geoffrey
————RHB, SLA————

Born Middlesbrough, Yorks, 9 Oct 1951. Educ Middlesbrough HS. Debut 1971.
NORTHAMPTONSHIRE (297) 1971–. Cap 1975. Capt 1981–.
S AFRICA DOMESTIC Eastern Province 1978/79–80/81.
ENGLAND (7) 1981/82–82/83. I 1982 (3). *A 1982/83 (3); SL 1981/82 (1).*
HST 66 E v I, Old Trafford, 1982. HS 172 E Province v Northern Transvaal, Port Elizabeth, 1979/80.
BB 3–47 England XI v South Australia, Adelaide, 1983/84.
1000 RUNS (9) 1759 @ 43.97 in 1981.

COOK, Geoffrey William
————RHB, OB————

Born Beckenham, Kent, 9 Feb 1936. Educ Dulwich; Queen's C, Cambridge. Debut 1956.
CAMBRIDGE UNIVERSITY (37) 1956–58 (Blue 1957–58).
KENT (4) 1957.
HS 140 Free Foresters v Cambridge U, Fenner's, 1961.
BB 4–45 Cambridge U v Som, Fenner's, 1957.
RECORD Added 289 for 7th wkt with G. Goonesena, Cambridge U v Oxford U, Lord's, 1957 – highest stand for any wkt in University match. Berkshire 1967–68.

COOK, Jeremy
————RHB, RFM————

Born Leicester, 20 July 1941. Debut 1961. *P.*
MCC (2) 1961–63.

HS 35 MCC v Oxford U, The Parks, 1963.
BB 5–48 MCC v Ireland, Dublin, 1961.
MCC staff 1961–63.

COOK, Michael Stephen
————LHB, WK————

Born Birmingham, 19 Feb 1939. Educ Warwick S. Debut 1961.
WARWICKSHIRE (2) 1961–62.
HS 52 Warwicks v Cambridge U, Portland Road, Birmingham, 1961.
Club: Aston Unity. Brother D. R. Cook (Warwicks).

COOK, Nicholas Grant Billson
————RHB, SLA————

Born Broughton Astley, Leics, 17 June 1956. Educ Lutterworth S. Debut 1978.
LEICESTERSHIRE (132) 1978–. Cap 1982.
ENGLAND (9) 1983–84. WI 1984 (3); NZ 1983 (2). *NZ 1983/84 (1); P 1983/84 (3).*
TOURS D. H. Robins' XI to N Zealand 1979/80. Leics XI to Zimbabwe 1980/81.
HST 26 E v NZ, Trent Bridge, 1983. HS 75 Leics v Som, Taunton, 1980.
BBT 6–65 (11–83 match) E v P, Karachi, 1983/84. BB 7–63 Leics v Som, Taunton, 1982.
RECORD Took 34 wkts in first four Tests, England record.

COOKE, Noel Henry
————RHB, OB————

Born West Derby, Liverpool, 5 Jan 1935. Educ Liverpool C. Debut 1958. *P.*
LANCASHIRE (12) 1958–59.
HS 33 Lancs v Combined Services, Old Trafford, 1958.
BB 2–10 Lancs v Glos, Blackpool, 1958.
Cheshire 1962–63. Clubs: Sefton, Eagley, Neston, Hightown. Hockey: Lancs.

COOKE, Robert Michael Oliver
————LHB, LBG————

Born Adlington, Cheshire, 30 Sept 1943. Educ Rossall. Debut 1972.
MINOR COUNTIES (2) 1972–76.
ESSEX (40) 1973–75.
HS 139 Essex v Sussex, Ilford, 1973.
BB 2–55 Essex v Cambridge U, Fenner's, 1975.
Cheshire 1969–72, 1976–. Professional: Stockport, Fleetwood, Knypersley, Bramhall.

COOMARASWAMY, Inderajit
————RHB, SLA————

Born Colombo, Ceylon, 16 Mar 1950. Educ Harrow; Emmanuel C, Cambridge. Debut 1971.
CAMBRIDGE UNIVERSITY (2) 1971–72.
HS 4 Cambridge U v Warwicks, Fenner's, 1971.

COOMB, Arthur Grenfell
————RHB, RMF————

Born Kempston, Bedfordshire, 3 Mar 1929. Educ Bedford Modern. Debut 1948.
COMBINED SERVICES (3) 1948–49.
MINOR COUNTIES (2) 1951–53.
HS 16 Combined Services v Hants, Portsmouth, 1949.
BB 3–61 same match.
Bedfordshire 1948–62, Norfolk 1963. Royal Navy.

COOPE, Miles
————RHB, occ LB————

Born Gildersome, Yorks, 28 Nov 1916 (not 1917). Died Gildersome, Yorks, 5 July 1974. Debut 1947. *P.*
SOMERSET (70) 1947–49. Cap 1947.
HS 113 Som v M'sex, Taunton, 1947.
BB 3–29 Som v Yorks, Taunton, 1948.
1000 RUNS (1) 1172 @ 22.11 in 1948.
Clubs: Salts, Bath. Former professional coach at Queen Elizabeth GS, Wakefield.

COOPER, Alfred William Madison
————RHB, RFM————

Born Dublin, Ireland, 12 June 1932. Educ Dublin HS; Dublin U. Debut 1954.
IRELAND (1) 1954.
HS 31 Ireland v MCC, Dublin, 1954.
BB 2–35 same match.
Clubs: Dublin U, Clontarf.

COOPER, Edwin
————RHB————

Born Bacup, Lancs, 30 Nov 1915. Died Birmingham, 29 Oct 1968. Debut 1936. *P.*
WORCESTERSHIRE (249) 1936–51. Cap 1937. Benefit (£3000) 1951.
HS 216* Worcs v Warwicks, Dudley, 1938.
1000 RUNS (9) 1916 @ 43.54 in 1949.
Devon 1953–54. Professional coach at RNC Dartmouth 1953, Bedford S 1958–68. Club: Aston Unity. Brother F. Cooper (Worcs and Lancs).

COOPER, Fred
————RHB————

Born Bacup, Lancs, 18 Apr 1921. Debut 1946. *P.*
LANCASHIRE (4) 1946.
WORCESTERSHIRE (40) 1947–50.
HS 113* Worcs v Notts, Trent Bridge, 1948.
Clubs: Old Hill, Kidderminster, Scarborough. Brother E. Cooper (Worcs) – opened inns together on occasions.

COOPER, Graham Charles
————RHB, OB————

Born East Grinstead, Sussex, 2 Sept 1936. Debut 1955. *P.*
SUSSEX (252) 1955–69. Cap 1961. Joint benefit (with L. J. Lenham) 1969.
HS 142 Sussex v Essex, Hove, 1963.
BB 5–13 Sussex v Oxford U, Hove, 1963.
1000 RUNS (3) 1095 @ 28.81 in 1961.

COOPER, Howard Pennett
————LHB, RM————

Born Great Horton, Yorks, 17 Apr 1949. Educ Buttershaw CS; St Peter's C, Birmingham. Debut 1971.
YORKSHIRE (98) 1971–80.
S AFRICA DOMESTIC Northern Transvaal 1973/74.
HS 56 Yorks v Notts, Worksop, 1976.
BB 8–62 Yorks v Glam, Cardiff, 1975.
Club: Bankfoot, Redcar.

COOPER, Kevin Edwin
————LHB, RFM————

Born Sutton-in-Ashfield, Notts, 27 Dec 1957. Debut 1976.
NOTTINGHAMSHIRE (158) 1976–. Cap 1980.
TOUR D. H. Robins' XI to N Zealand 1979/80 (no fc matches).
HS 38* Notts v Cambridge U, Fenner's, 1982.
BB 7–33 Notts v Worcs, Worcester, 1983.

COOPER, Nicholas Henry Charles
————LHB————

Born Bristol, 14 Oct 1953. Educ St Brendan's C, Bristol; U of East Anglia; Fitzwilliam C, Cambridge. Debut 1975.
GLOUCESTERSHIRE (17) 1975–78.
CAMBRIDGE UNIVERSITY (7) 1979 (Blue).
HS 106 Glos v Oxford U, The Parks, 1976.
BB 2–11 Cambridge U v Som, Bath, 1979.

COOPER, Richard Claude
——RHB, RM——

Born Malmesbury, Wiltshire, 9 Dec 1945. Debut 1972.
SOMERSET (1) 1972.
HS 4 Som v Notts, Trent Bridge, 1972. Wiltshire 1967–71, 1975–. Club: Malmesbury. Shot and discus: Wiltshire.

COOPER, Ruston Sorabji (Rusi)
——RHB——

Born Bombay, India, 14 Dec 1922. Educ Bombay U. Debut 1941/42.
INDIA DOMESTIC Parsis (Bombay) 1941/ 42–44/45, Bombay 1943/44–44/45.
MIDDLESEX (8) 1949–51.
HS 127* Cricket Club of India v C. K. Nayudu's XI, Bombay, 1944/45.
Clubs: Hornsey from 1946, Indian Gymkhana 1949–50.

COOTE, David Edward
——LHB——

Born Winkburn, Notts, 8 Apr 1955. Debut 1977.
NOTTINGHAMSHIRE (1) 1977.
HS 20 Notts v Yorks, Trent Bridge, 1977.

COPE, Geoffrey Alan
——RHB, OB——

Born Leeds, Yorks, 23 Feb 1947. Educ Temple Moor S, Leeds. Debut 1966.
YORKSHIRE (230) 1966–80. Cap 1970. Joint benefit (with B. Leadbeater) (£16,923 each) 1980.
ENGLAND (3) P 1977/78.
OTHER TOURS D. H. Robins' XI to S Africa 1975/76. MCC to India 1976/77.
HST 22 E v P, Hyderabad, 1977/78. HS 78 Yorks v Essex, Middlesbrough, 1977.
BBT 3–102 E v P, Lahore, 1977/78. BB 8–73 Yorks v Glos, Bristol, 1975.
Suspended 1972 and 1978 owing to suspect bowling action; subsequently cleared each time. Lincolnshire 1981–. Club: Leeds.

COPSON, William Henry
——RHB, RF——

Born Stonebroom, nr Alfreton, Derbys, 27 Apr 1908. Died Clay Cross, Derbys, 13 Sept 1971. Debut 1932. *Wisden* 1937. *P.*
DERBYSHIRE (261) 1932–50. Cap 1933. Testimonial (£2500) 1949.
ENGLAND (3) 1939–47. SA 1947 (1); WI 1939 (2).
TOUR MCC to Australia 1936/37.

HST 6 E v SA, Oval, 1947. HS 43 Derbys v Lancs, Blackpool, 1933.
BBT 5–85 E v WI, Lord's, 1939. BB 8–11 Derbys v Warwicks, Derby, 1937.
100 WKTS (3) 160 @ 13.34 in 1936.
RECORD During BB (above) took 5 wkts in 6 balls – only other fc instance in England by P. I. Pocock in 1972.
Took wkt of A. Sandham with first ball in fc cricket, v Surrey in 1932. Performed hat-trick for Derbys three times, twice in 1937. Fc umpire 1958–67.
Clubs: Saltaire, Lidget Green.

CORDAROY, Terence Michael
——RHB, RM——

Born Hampstead, London, 26 May 1944. Debut 1968.
MIDDLESEX (2) 1968.
HS 81 M'sex v Leics, Leicester, 1968. Bucks 1977–79. Club: South Hampstead.

CORDLE, Anthony Elton
——RHB, RFM——

Born St Michael, Barbados, 12 Sept 1940. Debut 1963.
GLAMORGAN (312) 1963–80. Cap 1967. Benefit (£8000) 1977.
TOUR Glamorgan to W Indies 1969/70.
HS 81 Glam v Cambridge U, Swansea, 1972.
BB 9–49 (13–110 match) Glam v Leics, Colwyn Bay, 1969.

CORDNER, John Pruen
——RHB, LFM——

Born Diamond Creek, Victoria, Australia, 20 Mar 1929. Educ Melbourne GS. Debut 1951/52.
AUSTRALIA DOMESTIC Victoria (3) 1951/ 52.
WARWICKSHIRE (1) 1952.
HS 8* Victoria v Queensland, Brisbane, 1951/52.
BB 2–37 same match.
Played for Warwicks while on course in England. Clubs: University (Melbourne), West Bromwich Dartmouth (Birmingham League). Cousin L. O. Cordner (Victoria).

CORKE, Martin Dewe
——RHB——

Born Murree, India, 8 June 1923. Educ Radley. Debut 1953.
FREE FORESTERS (5) 1953–58.
HS 53 Free Foresters v Oxford U, The Parks, 1956.
Suffolk 1946–64 (Capt 1954–64). Clubs: Gents of Suffolk, Stragglers.

CORLETT, Simon Charles
——RHB, RFM——

Born Blantyre, Nyasaland, 18 Jan 1950. Educ Worksop; Exeter C, Oxford. Debut 1970.
OXFORD UNIVERSITY (18) 1970–72 (Blue 1971–72).
IRELAND (12) 1974–84.
HS 60 Ireland v Scotland, Dublin, 1977.
BB 7–82 Ireland v Scotland, Edinburgh, 1982.
Club: Northern Ireland CC.

CORLING, Grahame Edward
——RHB, RFM——

Born Newcastle, NSW, Australia, 13 July 1941. Debut 1963/64.
AUSTRALIA DOMESTIC New South Wales (46) 1963/64–68/69.
AUSTRALIA (5) E 1964.
HST 3 A v E, Trent Bridge, 1964. HS 42* NSW v W Australia, Sydney, 1965/66.
BBT 4–60 A v E, Lord's, 1964. BB 5–44 NSW v S Australia, Adelaide, 1966/67.
Clubs: Newcastle, West Suburbs (Australia), Accrington (England).

CORNELIUS, Bernard William
——RHB——

Born Northampton, 16 Mar 1919. Educ Kettering Road S, Northampton. Debut 1947.
NORTHAMPTONSHIRE (1) 1947.
HS 9* Northants v Leics, Leicester, 1947.
Club: Northampton Vallence.

CORNFORD, James Henry
——RHB, RFM——

Born Crowborough, Sussex, 9 Dec 1911. Debut 1931. *P.*
SUSSEX (333) 1931–52. Cap 1932. Benefit (£2905) 1950.
HS 34 Sussex v Leics, Ashby-de-la-Zouch, 1949.
BB 9–53 Sussex v Northants, Rushden, 1949.
Coach St George's C, Salisbury, Rhodesia, 1952.

CORNFORD, Walter Latter
——RHB, WK——

Born Hurst Green, Sussex, 25 Dec 1900. Died Brighton, Sussex, 6 Feb 1964. Debut 1921. *P.*
SUSSEX (484) 1921–47. Cap 1924. Benefit (£1200) 1934.
ENGLAND (4) NZ 1929/30.
HST 18 E v NZ, Auckland, 1929/30. HS 82 Sussex v Yorks, Eastbourne, 1928.
1000 dismissals (656 ct, 344 st) in fc career. Professional coach at Brighton C 1945–62.

CORNOCK, Walter Brearley
RHB, LM

Born Bondi, NSW, Australia, 1 Jan 1921. Debut 1948. *P.*
LEICESTERSHIRE (26) 1948.
HS 60 Leics v M'sex, Lord's, 1948.
BB 3–46 Leics v Glos, Bristol, 1948.
Club: Rochdale. Soccer: Rochdale.

CORNWALL, Anthony Ewart Frank
RHB, RMF

Born Parkstone, Dorset, 19 Aug 1929. Educ Radley. Debut 1949.
FREE FORESTERS (1) 1949.
No runs.
BB 3–60 Free Foresters v Oxford U, The Parks, 1949.
Dorset 1947–50. Clubs: Chalfont St Peter, RAF.

CORRALL, Percy (Paddy)
RHB, WK

Born Aylestone Park, Leicester, 16 July 1906. Debut 1930. *P.*
LEICESTERSHIRE (285) 1930–51. Cap 1932. Benefit (£2333) 1949.
INDIA DOMESTIC Services 1944/45.
HS 64 Leics v Sussex, Hove, 1934.
10 dismissals in match, Leics v Sussex, Hove, 1936. Fc umpire 1952–58.

CORRAN, Andrew John
RHB, RMF

Born Norwich, Norfolk, 25 Nov 1936. Educ Gresham's S, Holt; Trinity C, Oxford. Debut 1958.
OXFORD UNIVERSITY (29) 1958–60 (Blue 1958–60).
NOTTINGHAMSHIRE (101) 1961–65. Cap 1962. Capt 1962.
HS 75 Notts v West Indians, Trent Bridge, 1963.
BB 7–45 Oxford U v Lancs, The Parks, 1960.
100 WKTS (1) 111 @ 20.31 in 1965.
Appointed assistant-secretary Notts 1960; left county 1965. Norfolk 1958–60. Hockey: Blue and Norfolk.

CORRY, Charles Victor
RHB

Born Belfast, Northern Ireland, 26 Nov 1940. Educ Grosvenor HS, Belfast. Debut 1959.
IRELAND (4) 1959–66.
HS 17 Ireland v Scotland, Greenock, 1962.
Club: Cregagh.

COSH, Nicholas John
RHB, OB

Born Camberwell, London, 6 Aug 1946. Educ Dulwich C; Queen's C, Cambridge. Debut 1966.
CAMBRIDGE UNIVERSITY (30) 1966–68 (Blue 1966–68).
SURREY (6) 1969.
HS 138 Cambridge U v Warwicks, Edgbaston, 1967.
Rugby: Blue and Blackheath.

COSH, Stephen *Hunter*
RHB, WK

Born Ayr, Scotland, 31 Jan 1920. Educ Edinburgh Academy. Debut 1950.
SCOTLAND (36) 1950–59.
HS 99 Scotland v Derbys, Buxton, 1954.

COSIER, Gary John
RHB, RM

Born Richmond, Victoria, Australia, 25 Apr 1953. Debut 1971/72.
AUSTRALIA DOMESTIC Victoria (4) 1971/72–80/81, South Australia (24) 1974/75–76/77, Queensland (26) 1977/78–79/80.
AUSTRALIA (18) 1975/76–78/79. E 1976/77 (1), 1978/79 (2); WI 1975/76 (3); I 1977/78 (4); P 1976/77 (3). *WI 1977/78 (3); NZ 1976/77 (2).*
OTHER TOUR Australia to England 1977.
HST 168 A v P, Melbourne, 1976/77. HS as above.
BBT 2–26 A v I, Sydney, 1977/78. BB 3–20 S Australia v W Australia, Adelaide, 1975/76.
Clubs: Balmoral Wynnum, Western Suburbs, Northcote.

COTTAM, Robert Michael Henry
RHB, RFM

Born Cleethorpes, Lincolnshire, 16 Oct 1944. Debut 1963.
HAMPSHIRE (188) 1963–71. Cap 1965.
NORTHAMPTONSHIRE (76) 1972–76. Cap 1972.
ENGLAND (4) 1968/69–72/73. *I 1972/73 (2); P 1968/69 (2).*
OTHER TOUR Commonwealth XI to Pakistan 1970/71.
HST 13 E v I, Calcutta, 1972/73. HS 62* Northants v Glos, Northampton, 1974.
BBT 4–50 E v P, Lahore, 1968/69. BB 9–25 Hants v Lancs, Old Trafford, 1965 (best-ever inns analysis by Hants bowler).
100 WKTS (3) 130 @ 17.56 in 1968.

CWC Best Young Cricketer of 1968. Devon 1977–78. Professional coach at All-Hallows S.

COTTERELL, Thomas Archbold
RHB, SLA

Born Marylebone, London, 12 May 1963. Educ Downside; Peterhouse C, Cambridge. Debut 1983.
CAMBRIDGE UNIVERSITY (20) 1983–84 (Blue 1983–84).
HS 52 Cambridge U v Notts, Trent Bridge, 1984.
BB 5–89 Cambridge U v Essex, Fenner's, 1983.

COTTON, John
RHB, RFM

Born Newstead, Notts, 7 Nov 1940. Debut 1958. *P.*
NOTTINGHAMSHIRE (138) 1958–64. Cap 1960.
LEICESTERSHIRE (94) 1965–69. Cap 1965.
HS 58 Notts v Hants, Trent Bridge, 1960.
BB 9–29 Leics v Indians, Leicester, 1967.

COTTON, Robert Henry
RHB, RFM

Born Birmingham, 5 Nov 1909. Died Warley, West Midlands, 17 Jan 1979. Educ Abbey Road S, Smethwick. Debut 1947.
WARWICKSHIRE (2) 1947.
No runs.
BB 2–42 Warwicks v Sussex, Hove, 1947.
Club: Mitchells and Butlers.

COTTRELL, Grahame Allan
RHB, RM

Born Datchet, Slough, Buckinghamshire, 23 Mar 1945. Educ Kingston GS; St Catharine's C, Cambridge. Debut 1966.
CAMBRIDGE UNIVERSITY (39) 1966–68 (Blue 1966–68). Capt 1968.
HS 81 Cambridge U v Notts, Fenner's, 1967.
BB 4–31 Cambridge U v Oxford U, Lord's, 1968.
Cambridgeshire 1976.

COTTRELL, Peter Richard
——————RHB, WK——————

Born Welling, Kent, 22 May 1957. Educ Chislehurst and Sidcup GS; Trinity C, Cambridge. Debut 1979.
CAMBRIDGE UNIVERSITY (10) 1979 (Blue).
HS 34 Cambridge U v Glos, Fenner's, 1979.
Club: Blackheath.

COURTENAY, Geofrey William List
——————RHB——————

Born Castle Carey, Som, 16 Dec 1921. Died Edinburgh, Scotland, 17 Oct 1980. Educ Sherborne. Debut 1947.
SOMERSET (4) 1947.
MINOR COUNTIES (1) 1953.
SCOTLAND (3) 1955–57.
HS 69 Scotland v Derbys, Edinburgh, 1955.
Dorset 1952–57.

COUSENS, Peter
——————RHB, SLA——————

Born Durban, S Africa, 15 May 1932. Debut 1950. P.
ESSEX (39) 1950–55.
HS 13 Essex v Worcs, Worcester, 1954.
BB 4–63 Essex v Yorks, Romford, 1954.
Club: Epping.

COUTTS, Ian Douglas Freeman
——————RHB, RMF——————

Born Herne Hill, London, 27 Apr 1928. Educ Dulwich C; Lincoln C, Oxford. Debut 1951.
OXFORD UNIVERSITY (15) 1951–52 (Blue 1952).
HS 16* Oxford U v Yorks, The Parks, 1951.
BB 5–64 Oxford U v Kent, The Parks, 1952.
Rugby: Blue, Scotland.

COVERDALE, Stephen Peter
——————RHB, WK——————

Born York, 20 Nov 1954. Educ St Peter's York; Emmanuel C, Cambridge. Debut 1973.
YORKSHIRE (6) 1973–80.
CAMBRIDGE UNIVERSITY (38) 1974–77 (Blue 1974–77).
HS 85 Cambridge U v Som, Fenner's, 1976.

COWAN, James Ferguson
——————LHB——————

Born Milton Bridge, Scotland, 17 May 1929. Educ Watson's C; Edinburgh U. Debut 1960.
SCOTLAND (3) 1960–62.
HS 18 Scotland v Warwicks, Edgbaston, 1961.

COWAN, Michael Joseph
——————LHB, LFM——————

Born Doncaster, Yorks, 10 June 1933. Educ St Michael's C, Leeds. Debut 1953. P.
YORKSHIRE (91) 1953–62. Cap 1960.
TOUR MCC A to Pakistan 1955/56.
HS 22 Yorks v Warwicks, Edgbaston, 1955.
BB 9–43 Yorks v Warwicks, Edgbaston, 1960.
Fc career curtailed by back trouble. Northumberland 1964. Clubs: British Ropes, Bingley, Doncaster, Rochdale, Littleborough, Wakefield.

COWAN, Ralph Stewart
——————RHB, RM——————

Born Hamlin, West Germany, 30 Mar 1960. Educ Lewes Priory; Magdalen C, Oxford. Debut 1980.
OXFORD UNIVERSITY (22) 1980–82 (Blue 1980–82).
SUSSEX (6) 1982–83.
HS 143* Oxford U v Northants, The Parks, 1982.
BB 2–75 Oxford U v Warwicks, The Parks, 1982.
Soccer: Blue.

COWANS, Norman George
——————RHB, RFM——————

Born Enfield St Mary, Jamaica, 17 Apr 1961. Educ Park High Sec S, Stanmore, M'sex. Debut 1980.
MIDDLESEX (46) 1980–. Cap 1984.
ENGLAND (13) 1982/83–84. WI 1984 (1); NZ 1983 (4). A 1982/83 (4); NZ 1983/84 (2); P 1983/84 (2).
OTHER TOUR M'sex to Zimbabwe 1980/81.
HST 36 E v A, Perth, 1982/83. HS 66 M'sex v Surrey, Lord's, 1984.
BBT 6–77 E v A, Melbourne, 1982/83. BB 6–64 M'sex v Warwicks, Lord's, 1984.

COWDREY, Christopher Stuart
——————RHB, RM——————

Born Farnborough, Kent, 20 Oct 1957. Educ Tonbridge S. Debut 1977.

KENT (155) 1977–. Cap 1979. Appointed capt for 1985.
TOURS D. H. Robins' XI to Sri Lanka 1977/78. D. H. Robins' XI to N Zealand 1979/80 (capt).
HS 125* Kent v Essex, Colchester, 1984.
BB 3–17 Kent v Hants, Bournemouth, 1980.
1000 RUNS (2) 1364 @ 56.83 in 1983.
Father M. C. Cowdrey (Kent and England); brother G. R. Cowdrey (Kent); grandfather E. A. Cowdrey (Europeans).

COWDREY, Graham Robert
——————RHB, RM——————

Born Farnborough, Kent, 27 June 1964. Educ Tonbridge S; Durham U. Debut 1984.
KENT (1) 1984.
HS 7 Kent v Sri Lankans, Canterbury, 1984.
Father M. C. Cowdrey (Kent and England); brother C. S. Cowdrey (Kent); grandfather E. A. Cowdrey (Europeans).

COWDREY, Michael *Colin*
——————RHB, LBG——————

Born Ootacamund, Malabar, India, 24 Dec 1932. Educ Tonbridge S; Brasenose C, Oxford. Debut 1950. *Wisden 1956.*
KENT (402) 1950–76. Cap 1951 (youngest-capped Kent player). Capt 1957–71.
OXFORD UNIVERSITY (40) 1952–54 (Blue 1952–54). Capt 1954.
ENGLAND (114) 1954/55–74/75. A 1956 (5), 1961 (4), 1964 (3), 1968 (4); SA 1955 (1), 1960 (5), 1965 (3); WI 1957 (5), 1963 (2), 1966 (4); NZ 1958 (4), 1965 (3); I 1959 (5); P 1962 (4), 1967 (2), 1971 (1). *A 1954/55 (5), 1958/59 (5), 1962/63 (5), 1965/66 (4), 1970/71 (3), 1974/75 (5); SA 1956/57 (5); WI 1959/60 (5), 1967/68 (5); NZ 1954/55 (2), 1958/59 (2), 1962/63 (3), 1965/66 (3), 1970/71 (1); I 1963/64 (3); P 1968/69 (3).* Capt 27.
OTHER TOURS E. W. Swanton's XI to W Indies 1955/56 (capt). International XI to India and Pakistan 1961/62. Cavaliers to W Indies 1964/65. Commonwealth XI to India 1964/65. Duke of Norfolk's XI to W Indies 1969/70 (capt).
HST 182 E v P, Oval, 1962. HS 307 MCC v S Australia, Adelaide, 1962/63.
BB 4–22 Kent v Surrey, Blackheath, 1951.
1000 RUNS (21 + 6) 2093 @ 63.42 in 1965.
RECORDS 114 Test appearances – world record. 22 Test centuries – England

record with G. Boycott and W. R. Hammond. Added 411 with P. B. H. May, E v WI, Edgbaston, 1957 – world Test 4th wkt record. Added 163* for 9th wkt with A. C. Smith, E v NZ, Wellington, 1962/63, England Test record. 120 catches in Tests – England record for non-wicketkeeper. HS (above) highest score by any tourist in Australia. 1000 runs in six overseas seasons – record for Englishman. First batsman to score hundreds against every Test-playing country other than his own. 638 catches in fc career. CBE for services to cricket. MCC committee 1970–72, 1979–. Father E. A. Cowdrey (Europeans); sons C. S. and G. R. Cowdrey (both Kent).

COWIE, John
RHB, RF

Born Auckland, N Zealand, 30 Mar 1912. Debut 1932/33.
N ZEALAND DOMESTIC Auckland (34) 1932/33–49/50.
NEW ZEALAND (9) 1937–49. E 1946/47 (1); A 1945/46 (1). E 1937 (3), 1949 (4).
OTHER TOUR N Zealand to Australia 1937/38.
HST 45 NZ v E, Christchurch, 1946/47.
HS 54 Auckland v Otago, Auckland, 1937/38.
BBT 6–40 NZ v A, Wellington, 1945/46.
BB 6–3 N Zealanders v Ireland, Dublin, 1937.
100 WKTS (1) 114 @ 19.95 in 1937.

COWLEY, Nigel Geoffrey
RHB, OB

Born Shaftesbury, Dorset, 1 Mar 1953. Educ Mere Dutchy Manor, Mere, Wiltshire. Debut 1974.
HAMPSHIRE (208) 1974–. Cap 1978.
HS 109* Hants v Som, Taunton, 1977.
BB 6–48 Hants v Leics, Southampton, 1982.
1000 RUNS (1) 1042 @ 30.65 in 1984.
Dorset 1972.

COWNLEY, John Michael
LHB, LBG

Born Wales, Yorks, 24 Feb 1929. Educ Woodhouse GS, Sheffield; Sheffield U. Debut 1952.
YORKSHIRE (2) 1952.
LANCASHIRE (2) 1962.
HS 25 Lancs v Warwicks, Southport, 1962.
BB 2–36 Lancs v Pakistanis, Old Trafford, 1962.
Cheshire 1961. UAU 1950. Clubs: Sheffield United CC, British Rope.

COWPER, Robert Maskew
LHB, ROB

Born Kew, Melbourne, Australia, 5 Oct 1940. Educ Melbourne U. Debut 1959/60.
AUSTRALIA DOMESTIC Victoria (66) 1959/60–69/70, Western Australia (3) 1968/69.
MCC (1) 1966.
AUSTRALIA (27) 1964–68. E 1965/66 (4); I 1967/68 (4); P 1964/65 (1). E 1964 (1), 1968 (4); SA 1966/67 (5); WI 1964/65 (5); I 1964/65 (2); P 1964/65 (1).
HST 307 A v E, Melbourne, 1965/66. HS as above.
BBT 4–48 A v E, Old Trafford, 1968. BB 7–42 Australians v Essex, Southend, 1968.
1000 RUNS (1 + 2) 1287 @ 51.48 in 1964.
RECORDS HST (above) longest inns (727 mins) ever played in Australia.
Clubs: East Lancs, Hawthorne-East Melbourne. MCC Hon. member.
Brother D. R. Cowper (Victoria).

COX, Arthur Leonard
RHB, LB

Born Northampton, 22 July 1907. Debut 1927. P.
NORTHAMPTONSHIRE (229) 1927–47.
HS 104 Northants v Notts, Trent Bridge, 1930.
BB 7–91 Northants v Derbys, Chesterfield, 1932.
Club: Aston Unity. Father M. Cox (Northants); brother M. H. D. Cox (Northants).

COX, David William
RHB, RFM

Born Oakhill, Som, 19 May 1946. Debut 1969.
SOMERSET (1) 1969.
HS 8 Som v Hants, Portsmouth, 1969.

COX, Dennis Frank
RHB, RFM

Born Bermondsey, London, 21 Dec 1925. Debut 1949. P.
SURREY (42) 1949–57.
HS 57 Surrey v Glos, Cheltenham, 1955.
BB 7–22 Surrey v Cambridge U, Oval, 1952.
Cheshire 1961–67. Clubs: Peek Frean, Walham Green, Crewe LMR, Walsall.

COX, George
RHB, RM

Born Warnham, nr Horsham, Sussex, 23 Aug 1911. Died Burgess Hill, Sussex, 30 Mar 1985. Debut 1931. P.
SUSSEX (448) 1931–60. Cap 1935. Benefit (£6620) 1951.
L. C. STEVENS' XI (1) 1961.
HS 234* Sussex v Indians, Hove, 1946.
BB 6–125 Sussex v MCC, Hastings, 1946.
1000 RUNS (13) 2369 @ 49.35 in 1950.
RECORD Added 326* for 4th wkt with James Langridge, Sussex v Yorks, Headingley, 1949, county record.
Coach Winchester C from 1955. Club: Horsham. Soccer: Arsenal, Fulham, Luton Town. Father G. R. Cox (Sussex).

COX, Henry Ramsey
RHB, RM

Born Radcliffe-on-Trent, Notts, 19 May 1911. Educ Uppingham; Magdalene C, Cambridge. Debut 1930.
NOTTINGHAMSHIRE (23) 1930–54.
CAMBRIDGE UNIVERSITY (7) 1934.
HS 64 Notts v Worcs, Worcester, 1951.
BB 6–30 Notts v Derbys, Trent Bridge, 1951.
Club: XL Club.

COX, Roger
RHB, RM

Born Luton, Beds, 27 Apr 1947. Educ Stopsley Sec S, Luton. Debut 1971.
MINOR COUNTIES (1) 1971.
HS 24 Minor Counties v Indians, Lakenham, 1971.
Bedfordshire 1967–75. Club: Luton Town.

COXON, Alan John
LHB, LM/SLA

Born London, 18 Mar 1930. Educ Harrow GS; Lincoln C, Oxford. Debut 1951.
OXFORD UNIVERSITY (17) 1951–54 (Blue 1952).
MCC (1) 1958.
HS 43* Oxford U v Cambridge U, Lord's, 1952.
BB 3–55 Oxford U v Kent, The Parks, 1952.
Buckinghamshire 1978. Clubs: Chesham, Ealing.

COXON, Alexander
------RHB, RMF------

Born Huddersfield, Yorks, 18 Jan 1916. Debut 1945. *P.*
YORKSHIRE (142) 1945–50. Cap 1947.
ENGLAND (1) A 1948.
HST 19 E v A, Lord's, 1948. HS 83 Yorks v Notts, Headingley, 1948.
BBT 2–90 E v A, Lord's, 1948. BB 8–31 Yorks v Worcs, Headingley, 1946.
100 WKTS (2) 131 @ 18.60 in 1950.
Durham 1951–54. Clubs: Sunderland, Boldon.

CRABTREE, Harry Pollard
------RHB, RM------

Born Barnoldswick, Yorks, 30 Apr 1906. Died Great Baddow, Essex, 28 May 1982. Educ Ermysteds GS, Skipton; International C of PE, Silkeborg, Denmark. Debut 1931.
ESSEX (24) 1931–47. Cap 1946.
HS 146 Essex v Notts, Clacton, 1946.
MCC Youth coaching adviser from 1951. MBE for services to cricket 1957. Club: Westcliffe.

CRAGG, James Richard Allen
------RHB------

Born Stockport, Cheshire, 28 Oct 1946. Educ King's S, Macclesfield; Leeds U; Queen's C, Cambridge. Debut 1970.
CAMBRIDGE UNIVERSITY (7) 1970.
HS 55 Cambridge U v M'sex, Fenner's, 1970.
Cheshire 1966–79. UAU 1969. Club: Bramall.

CRAIG, Edward John
------RHB------

Born Formby, Lancs, 26 Mar 1942. Educ Charterhouse; Trinity C, Cambridge. Debut 1961.
CAMBRIDGE UNIVERSITY (42) 1961–63 (Blue 1961–63).
LANCASHIRE (6) 1961–62.
HS 208* Cambridge U v L. C. Stevens' XI, Eastbourne, 1961.
1000 RUNS (2) 1528 @ 42.44 in 1961 (debut season).

CRAIG, Hartley Samuel
------LHB------

Born Prospect, Adelaide, Australia, 17 Sept 1917. Debut 1945.
DOMINIONS (1) 1945.
HS 56 Dominions v England XI, Lord's, 1945.
Club: Cumberland (Sydney Grade).

CRAIG, Ian David
------RHB------

Born Yass, NSW, Australia, 12 June 1935. Debut 1951/52.
AUSTRALIA DOMESTIC New South Wales (55) 1951/52–61/62.
FREE FORESTERS (1) 1957.
AUSTRALIA (11) 1952/53–57/58. SA 1952/53 (1). *E 1956 (2); SA 1957/58 (5); I 1956/57 (2); P 1956/57 (1).* Capt 5.
OTHER TOURS Australia to England 1953. Australia to N Zealand 1956/57, 1959/60. Commonwealth XI to S Africa 1959/60. Commonwealth XI to N Zealand and India 1961/62.
HST 53 A v SA, Melbourne, 1952/53. HS 213* NSW v S Africans, Sydney, 1952/53.
RECORDS, Debut NSW v S Australia, Sydney, 1951/52, aged 16 yrs 249 days – youngest player to appear in Sheffield Shield. Youngest player to score double-century (HS above) and youngest Australian tourist (1953).

CRAIG, Ian Thornton
------RHB, RFM------

Born Maidstone, Kent, 26 Jan 1931. Educ The Leys S. Debut 1959.
MINOR COUNTIES (1) 1959.
HS 1 Minor Counties v Indians, Longton, Stoke-on-Trent, 1959.
BB 2–46 same match.
Cambridgeshire 1955–59. Clubs: St Giles, Ilford, Harpenden, Dolphins.

CRAIG, Victor Alexander
------LHB, WK------

Born Strabane, N Ireland, 27 July 1917. Educ Foyle C, Londonderry. Debut 1948.
IRELAND (1) 1948.
HS 12 Ireland v MCC, Dublin, 1948.
Clubs: Strabane, St Johnstone, Limavady.

CRANFIELD, Lionel *Montague*
------RHB, OB/LB------

Born Bristol, 29 Aug 1909. Debut 1934. *P.*
GLOUCESTERSHIRE (162) 1934–51. Cap. Testimonial 1950.
HS 90 Glos v Essex, Bristol, 1947.
BB 8–45 (13–54 match) Glos v Cambridge U, Gloucester, 1946.
Club: Castleton Moor. Father L. L. Cranfield (Glos and Som).

CRANMER, Peter
------RHB, RMF------

Born Acocks Green, Birmingham, 10 Sept 1914. Educ St Edward's, Oxford; Christ Church C, Oxford. Debut 1934.
WARWICKSHIRE (166) 1934–54. Cap 1934. Capt 1938–47.
INDIA DOMESTIC Bombay Europeans 1944/45, Services 1944/45.
MCC (4) 1955–59.
HS 113 Warwicks v Northants, Edgbaston, 1934.
BB 7–52 Services v Governor's XI, Calcutta, 1944/45.
1000 RUNS (3) 1192 @ 22.49 in 1947.
Cheshire 1948. Club: Harborne. Rugby: Oxford U, England (16, two as capt), Moseley, Blackheath. Journalist.

CRANSTON, Kenneth
------RHB, RMF------

Born Liverpool, 20 Oct 1917. Debut 1947.
LANCASHIRE (50) 1947–48. Capt 1947–48.
MCC (3) 1947–49.
NORTH (3) 1947–50.
H. D. G. LEVESON GOWER'S XI (2) 1948–50.
ENGLAND (8) 1947–48. A 1948 (1); SA 1947 (3). *WI 1947/48 (4).* Capt 1.
HST 45 E v SA, Oval, 1947. HS 156* MCC v Yorks, Scarborough, 1949.
BBT 4–12 E v SA, Headingley, 1947 (all 4 wkts in one over). BB 7–43 (10–82 match) Lancs v Surrey, Oval, 1948.
1000 RUNS (2) 1228 @ 33.18 in 1947.
Club: Neston.

CRAPP, John Frederick
------LHB------

Born St Columb Major, Cornwall, 14 Oct 1912. Died Bristol, 13 Feb 1981. Debut 1936. *P.*
GLOUCESTERSHIRE (422) 1936–56. Cap 1936. Benefit (£3611) 1951. Capt 1953–54.
ENGLAND (7) 1948–48/49. A 1948 (3). *SA 1948/49 (4).*
OTHER TOUR Commonwealth XI to India 1953/54.
HST 56 E v SA, J'burg, 1948/49. HS 175 Glos v Cambridge U, Fenner's, 1947.
BB 3–24 Glos v Leics, Leicester, 1937.
1000 RUNS (14) 2014 @ 45.77 in 1949. 1052 runs in debut season.
383 catches in fc career. Fc umpire 1957–78 (4 Tests 1964–65).

CRAWFORD, Ian Cunningham
——————RHB, OB——————

Born Bristol, 13 Sept 1954. Educ Colston's S, Bristol; University C, Swansea. Debut 1975.
GLOUCESTERSHIRE (5) 1975–78.
HS 73 Glos v Oxford U, The Parks, 1978.

CRAWFORD, Michael Grove
——————RHB——————

Born Leeds, Yorks, 30 July 1920. Educ Shrewsbury; Magdalene C, Cambridge. Debut 1951.
YORKSHIRE (1) 1951 (capt).
HS 13 Yorks v Worcs, Scarborough, 1951.
Yorks chairman 1982–84. Club: Leeds. Soccer: Blue. Son N. C. Crawford (Cambridge U).

CRAWFORD, Neil Cameron
——————RHB, RM——————

Born Leeds, Yorks, 26 Nov 1958. Educ Shrewsbury; Magdalene C, Cambridge. Debut 1978.
CAMBRIDGE UNIVERSITY (22) 1978–80 (Blue 1979–80).
HS 46 Cambridge U v Sussex, Fenner's, 1979.
BB 6–80 Cambridge U v Notts, Fenner's, 1979.
Father M. G. Crawford (Yorks).

CRAWFORD, Thomas Alan
——————RHB——————

Born Hoo, Kent, 18 Feb 1910. Died Whitechapel, London, 6 Dec 1979. Educ Tonbridge. Debut 1930.
KENT (13) 1930–51.
HS 32 Kent v Derbys, Derby, 1937.
Kent president 1968. Capt Kent 2nd XI 1950–55.

CRAWFORD, William *Patrick* Anthony
——————RHB, RF——————

Born Sydney, NSW, Australia, 3 Aug 1933. Debut 1954/55.
AUSTRALIA DOMESTIC New South Wales (14) 1954/55–57/58.
AUSTRALIA (4) 1956–56/57. *E 1956 (1); I 1956/57 (3)*.
HST 34 A v I, Madras, 1956/57. HS 86 NSW v Queensland, Brisbane, 1955/56.
BBT 3–28 A v I, Bombay, 1956/57. BB 6–55 (12–114 match) NSW v Queensland, Brisbane, 1955/56.

Clubs: Petersham-Marrickville (Australia); East Lancs (England). Early retirement owing to injury.

CRAWLEY, Aidan Merivale
——————RHB, RM——————

Born Benenden, Kent, 10 Apr 1908. Educ Harrow; Trinity C, Oxford. Debut 1927.
OXFORD UNIVERSITY (39) 1927–30 (Blue 1927–30).
KENT (33) 1927–47. Cap.
FREE FORESTERS (2) 1948–49.
HS 204 Oxford U v Northants, Wellingborough, 1929 (10 sixes).
BB 2–45 Oxford U v Surrey, Oval, 1928.
1000 RUNS (1) 1316 @ 48.74 in 1928.
Buckinghamshire 1948. MCC committee 1965–76. Member of Parliament: Labour 1945–51 (Buckingham), Conservative 1962–67 (W Derbys). Father A. S. Crawley (MCC); brother C. S. Crawley (Hants and M'sex); nephews E. and H. E. (both Cambridge U); cousin L. G. Crawley (Essex).

CRAY, Stanley James (Chick)
——————RHB——————

Born Stratford, East London, 29 May 1921. Debut 1938. *P*.
ESSEX (99) 1938–50. Cap 1947.
INDIA DOMESTIC Services 1943/44–44/45.
HS 163 Essex v Notts, Ilford, 1950.
1000 RUNS (2) 1339 @ 26.78 in 1947.
Devon 1957. Professional Paignton. Former professional coach Wrekin S (from 1960).

CREESE, William Leonard Charles
——————LHB, LM——————

Born Parktown, Johannesburg, S Africa, 28 Dec 1907. Died Dover, Kent, 9 Mar 1974. Debut 1928. *P*.
HAMPSHIRE (278) 1928–39. Cap.
COMBINED SERVICES (1) 1946.
HS 241 Hants v Northants, Northampton, 1939.
BB 8–37 Hants v Lancs, Southampton, 1936.
1000 RUNS (5) 1421 @ 28.42 in 1938.
1331 runs and 95 wkts in 1936.
Dorset 1949–51. Minor Counties umpire 1947–48. Professional coach Sherborne S 1946–54. Groundsman at Hastings, then Hove. Youth cricket organiser in Argentina during 1939–45 war. Father W. H. Creese (Transvaal; curator of Newlands).

CRERAR, George Graham
——————RHB, SLA——————

Born Glasgow, Scotland, 1 Oct 1914. Educ Glasgow Academy; Glasgow U. Debut 1947.
SCOTLAND (2) 1947–48.
HS 36 Scotland v Ireland, Cork, 1947.

CRESSWELL, George Fenwick
——————LHB, RM——————

Born Wanganui, N Zealand, 22 Mar 1915. Died, by own hand, Blenheim, N Zealand, 10 Jan 1966. Debut 1948/49.
N ZEALAND DOMESTIC Rest of N Zealand (2) 1948/49 (trials), Wellington (3) 1949/50, Central Districts (7) 1950/51–54/55.
NEW ZEALAND (3) 1949–50/51. *E 1950/51 (2)*.
HST 12* NZ v E, Oval, 1949. HS as above.
BBT 6–168 same match. BB 8–100 N Zealand XI v Australia XI, Dunedin, 1949/50.
Scored fewer fc runs (89) than he took wkts (124). Marlborough (Hawke Cup) 1933/34–48/49. Brother A. E. Cresswell (Central Districts).

CRICHTON, Ian Gordon
——————LHB, LFM——————

Born St Anne's, Lancs, 7 Jan 1943. Educ St Paul's S; Hertford C, Oxford. Debut 1963.
OXFORD UNIVERSITY (1) 1963.
HS 4 Oxford U v Notts, The Parks, 1963.

CRICK, Harry
——————RHB, WK——————

Born Eccleshall, Yorks, 29 Jan 1911. Died in road accident, Lower Wyke, Bradford, Yorks, 10 Feb 1960. Debut 1937. *P*.
YORKSHIRE (10) 1937–47.
COMBINED SERVICES (1) 1949.
HS 22 South v North, Harrogate, 1947.
RAF Flight-Lt.

CRISP, James George
——————RHB, RFM——————

Born Newtown, Montgomeryshire, Wales, 15 Nov 1927. Educ Alleyn's S; Worcester C, Oxford. Debut 1951.
OXFORD UNIVERSITY (1) 1951.
HS 12 Oxford U v Leics, The Parks, 1951.
Suffolk 1957–58. Club: Beckenham.

CRISTOFANI, Desmond *Robert*
————RHB, RM/LBG————

Born Waverley, Sydney, NSW, Australia, 14 Nov 1920. Debut 1941/42.
AUSTRALIA DOMESTIC New South Wales (3) 1941/42–46/47.
DOMINIONS (1) 1945.
TOUR Australian Services to England 1945 and India 1945/46.
HS 110* Australia XI v England XI, Old Trafford, 1945 (Victory match).
BB 5–49 Australia XI v England XI, Lord's, 1945 (Victory match).
Clubs: St George (Sydney), Accrington (England). Appointed Australian Trade Commissioner, Accra, Ghana, 1959.

CROFT, Colin Everton Hunte
————RHB, RF————

Born Mahaica, British Guiana, 15 Mar 1953. Debut 1971/72.
W INDIES DOMESTIC Guyana 1971/72–81/82.
LANCASHIRE (49) 1977–82.
WEST INDIES (27) 1976/77–81/82. E 1980/81 (4); A 1977/78 (2); P 1976/77 (5). E 1980 (3); A 1979/80 (3), 1981/82 (3); P 1979/80 (3); P 1980/81 (4).
HST 33 WI v E, Bridgetown, 1980/81. HS 46* Lancs v Worcs, Worcester, 1977.
BBT 8–29 WI v P, Port of Spain, 1976/77. BB as above.
World Series Cricket (Kerry Packer) 1977/78–78/79. Barred from Test cricket for touring S Africa 1982/83 and 1983/84 (W Indies XI). Clubs: Smethwick, Royton.

CROFT, Peter Downton
————RHB, OB————

Born Purley, Surrey, 7 July 1933. Educ Gresham's S, Holt; Jesus C, Cambridge. Debut 1955.
CAMBRIDGE UNIVERSITY (18) 1955–57 (Blue 1955).
HS 47* Cambridge U v MCC, Lord's, 1955.
Clubs: Esher, XL Club. Fc hockey.

CROMACK, Bernard
————RHB, SLA————

Born Rothwell, Leeds, Yorks, 5 June 1937. Debut 1959. *P.*
LEICESTERSHIRE (34) 1959–68.
HS 55 Leics v Hants, Bournemouth, 1960.
BB 6–48 Leics v M'sex, Lord's, 1960.
Club: Pudsey St Lawrence.

CROOKES, Dennis Victor
————RHB, LB————

Born Durban, S Africa, 18 June 1931. Educ Michaelhouse, Natal; Jesus C, Cambridge. Debut 1953.
CAMBRIDGE UNIVERSITY (11) 1953–54 (Blue 1953).
HS 33 Cambridge U v M'sex, Fenner's, 1954.

CROOKES, Norman Samuel
————RHB, OB————

Born Renishaw, Natal, S Africa, 15 Nov 1935. Educ Hilton C, Natal. Debut 1962/63.
S AFRICA DOMESTIC Natal 1962/63–69/70.
TOUR S Africa to England 1965.
HS 68 Natal v Rhodesia, Salisbury, 1964/65.
BB 8–47 S Africans v M'sex, Lord's, 1965.

CROOM, Leslie Charles Bryan
————RHB————

Born Wybunbury, Cheshire, 20 Apr 1920. Debut 1949. *P.*
WARWICKSHIRE (4) 1949.
HS 26 Warwicks v Essex, Brentwood, 1949.
Club: West Bromwich Dartmouth. Father A. J. W. Croom (Warwicks).

CROSS, Anthony John
————RHB————

Born Fulmer, Buckinghamshire, 5 Aug 1945. Educ George Dixon GS, Birmingham; Fitzwilliam C, Cambridge. Debut 1966.
CAMBRIDGE UNIVERSITY (5) 1966–67.
WARWICKSHIRE (1) 1969.
HS 39* Cambridge U v Essex, Fenner's, 1969.

CROSS, Graham Frederick
————RHB, RM————

Born Leicester, 15 Nov 1943. Debut 1961. *P.*
LEICESTERSHIRE (83) 1961–76.
HS 78 Leics v Hants, Portsmouth, 1964.
BB 4–28 Leics v Lancs, Old Trafford, 1970.
Soccer: England Under-23, Leicester City, Chesterfield, Brighton and Hove Albion, Preston North End and Lincoln City.

CROSSKEY, Thomas Roland
————RHB, RFM————

Born Hastings, Sussex, 4 July 1905. Died Totnes, Devon, 25 Mar 1971. Debut 1949. *P.*
SCOTLAND (4) 1949–50.
HS 81 Scotland v N Zealanders, Glasgow, 1949.
Coach Edinburgh Royal HS from 1928. Appointed coach Edinburgh Education Authority 1947. Clubs: Grange, Carlton. Soccer: Crystal Palace, Heart of Midlothian, Albion Rovers.

CROTHERS, George Marcus
————RHB, WK————

Born Belfast, Ireland, 30 Jan 1909. Educ Royal Belfast Academical Institute. Debut 1931.
IRELAND (10) 1931–47.
HS 41 Ireland v Scotland, Greenock, 1932.
Club: Lisburn.

CROTHERS, John *Graham*
————RHB————

Born Belfast, N Ireland, 8 Apr 1949. Educ Belfast Royal Academical Institute; Queen's U, Belfast. Debut 1972.
IRELAND (1) 1972.
HS 10 Ireland v Scotland, Greenock, 1972.

CROUCH, Henry Russell
————RHB————

Born Calcutta, India, 10 Dec 1914. Educ Tonbridge. Debut 1935.
MINOR COUNTIES (2) 1935.
SURREY (1) 1946.
HS 7 Minor Counties v S Africans, Skegness, 1935.
Clubs: Esher, XL Club.

CROUCH, Maurice Alfred
————RHB————

Born Wisbech, Cambridgeshire, 9 Aug 1917. Educ Oundle. Debut 1950.
MCC (3) 1950–52.
MINOR COUNTIES (1) 1951.
HS 81 MCC v Oxford U, The Parks, 1952.
Cambridgeshire 1946–65 (capt from 1952). Clubs: March, Wisbech, Camden, St Giles, XL Club.

CROWE, Jeffrey John
——— RHB ———

Born Auckland, N Zealand, 14 Sept 1958. Educ Auckland GS. Debut 1977/78.
AUSTRALIA DOMESTIC South Australia (34) 1977/78–81/82.
N ZEALAND DOMESTIC Auckland (8) 1982/83–.
NEW ZEALAND (10) 1982/83–83. E 1983/84 (3); SL 1982/83 (2). E 1983 (2); SL 1983/84 (3).
HST 128 NZ v E, Auckland, 1983/84. HS 157 S Australia v NSW, Adelaide, 1981/82.
Father D. W. Crowe (Wellington and Canterbury); brother M. D. Crowe (N Zealand).

CROWE, Martin David
——— RHB, RM ———

Born Auckland, N Zealand, 22 Sept 1962. Educ Auckland GS. Debut 1979/80. Wisden 1985.
N ZEALAND DOMESTIC Auckland (25) 1979/80–82/83, Central Districts (6) 1983/84. Young New Zealand 1979/80.
D. B. CLOSE'S XI (1) 1982.
SOMERSET (25) 1984.
NEW ZEALAND (13) 1981/82–83/84. A 1981/82 (3); E 1983/84 (3). E 1983 (4); SL 1983/84 (3).
HST 100 NZ v E, Wellington, 1983/84.
HS 190 Som v Leics, Taunton, 1984.
BBT 2–35 NZ v E, Lord's, 1983. BB 5–66 Som v Leics, Leicester, 1984.
1000 RUNS (1) 1870 @ 53.42 in 1984.
RECORD During HS (above) added 319 for 3rd wkt with P. M. Roebuck, county record.
Scored 104 on fc debut in England, D. B. Close's XI v Pakistanis, Scarborough, 1982. Father D. W. Crowe (Wellington and Canterbury); brother J. J. Crowe (N Zealand).

CROWE, Philip John
——— LHB, LM ———

Born London, 27 Oct 1955. Educ Scotch C, Sydney, Australia; University C, Oxford. Debut 1982.
OXFORD UNIVERSITY (1) 1982.
HS 11 Oxford v Glos, The Parks, 1982.
Rugby: Blue (capt), Australia (6).

CROWTHER, Peter Gwynne
——— RHB, OB ———

Born Neath, S Wales, 26 Apr 1952. Educ University C, Aberystwyth. Debut 1977.

GLAMORGAN (9) 1977–78.
HS 99 Glam v Cambridge U, Fenner's, 1977 (on debut).

CRUMP, Brian Stanley
——— RHB, RM ———

Born Stoke-on-Trent, Staffordshire, 25 Apr 1938. Educ Chell Sec MS, Stoke. Debut 1960. P.
NORTHAMPTONSHIRE (317) 1960–72. Cap 1962. Benefit 1972. Vice-capt 1971.
HS 133* Northants v Warwicks, Edgbaston, 1971.
BB 7–29 Northants v Glam, Cardiff, 1967.
1000 RUNS (2) 1396 @ 29.08 in 1961. Other instance in debut season, 1960 (1000 @34.48).
100 WKTS (2) 112 @ 18.88 in 1965.
Staffordshire 1955–58 (with father S. Crump). Club: Todmorden. Cousins D. S. Steele (Northants and Derbys) and J. F. Steele (Leics and Glam).

CRUSH, Edmund
——— RHB, RM ———

Born Dover, Kent, 25 Apr 1917. Educ Dover GS. Debut 1946.
KENT (45) 1946–49. Cap 1948.
HS 78 Kent v Hants, Canterbury, 1948.
BB 6–50 same match.
Clubs: Highland Court, Dover. Former professional coach at Dover C (from 1959).

CRUTCHLEY, Edward
——— RHB ———

Born Paddington, London, 2 Apr 1922. Died Guildford, Surrey, 18 Oct 1982. Educ Harrow; Christ Church C, Cambridge. Debut 1947.
MIDDLESEX (2) 1947.
HS 14 M'sex v Cambridge U, Fenner's, 1947.
War-time Blue 1941. Father G. E. V Crutchley (Oxford U and M'sex).

CULLINAN, Mark Ronald
——— RHB, WK ———

Born Johannesburg, S Africa, 3 Apr 1957. Educ Hilton C, Natal; Cape Town U; Worcester C, Oxford. Debut 1979/80.
S AFRICA DOMESTIC South African Universities 1979/80.
OXFORD UNIVERSITY (15) 1983– (Blue 1983–84).
HS 59 Oxford U v Som, The Parks, 1984.

CUMBES, James
——— RHB, RFM ———

Born East Didsbury, Manchester, 4 May 1944. Educ Didsbury Technical HS, Manchester. Debut 1963.
LANCASHIRE (9) 1963–67, 1971.
SURREY (29) 1968–69.
WORCESTERSHIRE (109) 1972–81. Cap 1978.
WARWICKSHIRE (14) 1982.
HS 43 Worcs v Sussex, Hove, 1980.
BB 6–24 Worcs v Yorks, Worcester, 1977.
Joined Warwicks 1982 as player and commercial manager; retired same yr after illness. Clubs: Longsight, West Bromwich Dartmouth. Soccer: Tranmere Rovers, West Bromwich Albion, Aston Villa. Broadcaster for local radio. Brother-in-law R. Collins (Lancs).

CUNIS, Robert Smith
——— RHB, RFM ———

Born Whangarei, N Zealand, 5 Jan 1941. Educ Whangarei Boys HS. Debut 1960/61.
N ZEALAND DOMESTIC Auckland (62) 1960/61–73/74, Northern Districts (7) 1975/76.
NEW ZEALAND (20) 1963/64–71/72. E 1965/66 (3), 1970/71 (2); SA 1963/64 (1); WI 1968/69 (3). E 1969 (1); WI 1971/72 (5); I 1969/70 (3); P 1969/70 (2).
OTHER TOURS N Zealand to Australia 1969/70, 1970/71. World XI to Australia 1971/72.
HST 51 NZ v WI, Port of Spain, 1971/72.
HS 111 Auckland v Otago, Auckland, 1966/67.
BBT 6–76 NZ v E, Auckland, 1970/71. BB 7–29 Auckland v Central Districts, Auckland, 1961/62.
RECORD During HST (above) added 136 for 8th wkt with B. E. Congdon, N Zealand Test record.

CUNNINGHAM, Edward James
——— LHB, OB ———

Born Oxford, 16 May 1962. Educ Marlborough C. Debut 1982.
GLOUCESTERSHIRE (14) 1982–.
HS 61* Glos v Sri Lankans, Cheltenham, 1984.
BB 2–55 Glos v Worcs, Worcester, 1983.
Uncle F. G. Mann, great uncle F. T. Mann (both M'sex and England).

CURLEY, Simon Andrew
----------LHB----------

Born Dublin, Ireland, 21 July 1917. Educ Catholic Univ S, Dublin. Debut 1948.
IRELAND (5) 1948–51.
HS 43 Ireland v Scotland, Glasgow, 1948.
Clubs: Merion, Cork Bohemians.

CURRAN, Kevin Malcolm
----------RHB, RFM----------

Born Rusape, Rhodesia, 7 Sept 1959. Debut 1980/81.
ZIMBABWE 1980/81–.
TOURS Zimbabwe to England 1982. Zimbabwe to Sri Lanka 1983/84.
HS 96 Zimbabwe v Sri Lanka, Bulawayo, 1982/83.
BB 4–24 Zimbabwe v Sri Lanka, Harare, 1982/83.
Father K. P. Curran (Rhodesia).

CURRIE, John David
----------RHB----------

Born Clifton, Bristol, 3 May 1932. Educ Bristol GS; Wadham C, Oxford. Debut 1953.
SOMERSET (1) 1953.
OXFORD UNIVERSITY (9) 1956–57.
HS 38 Oxford U v Yorks, The Parks, 1957.
Clubs: Keynsham, Bristol Imperial. Rugby: Oxford U, Harlequins, Glos, England (25 caps, 1956–62).

CURTIS, Andrew David
----------RHB----------

Born Bedford, 12 Jan 1943. Educ Bedford Modern S; Sheffield U; St Edmund Hall, Oxford. Debut 1966.

OXFORD UNIVERSITY (1) 1966.
HS 15 Oxford U v Northants, The Parks, 1966.
Bedfordshire 1963–65. UAU 1963.

CURTIS, Ian James
----------LHB, SLA----------

Born Purley, Surrey, 13 May 1959. Educ Whitgift S; Lincoln C, Oxford. Debut 1980.
OXFORD UNIVERSITY (17) 1980–82 (Blue 1980, 1982).
SURREY (14) 1983–.
HS 20* Oxford U v Warwicks, The Parks, 1982.
BB 6–28 Surrey v Oxford U, Oval, 1983.

CURTIS, Timothy Stephen
----------RHB, LB----------

Born Chislehurst, Kent, 15 Jan 1960. Educ RGS Worcester; Durham U; Cambridge U. Debut 1979.
WORCESTERSHIRE (49) 1979–. Cap 1984.
CAMBRIDGE UNIVERSITY (10) 1983 (Blue).
HS 129 Worcs v Cambridge U, Worcester, 1984.
1000 RUNS (1) 1405 @ 42.57 in 1984.

CURZON, Christopher Colin
----------RHB, WK----------

Born Lenton, Nottingham, 22 Dec 1958. Educ Peverill Sec S. Debut 1978.
NOTTINGHAMSHIRE (17) 1978–80.
HAMPSHIRE (1) 1981.
HS 45 Notts v Glam, Swansea, 1980.
Brother J. T. Curzon (Notts).

CURZON, John Timothy
----------RHB, RM----------

Born Apsley, Nottingham, 4 June 1954.

Educ Bilborough GS, Nottingham. Debut 1978.
NOTTINGHAMSHIRE (1) 1978.
HS 1 Notts v Cambridge U, Fenner's, 1978.
Brother C. C. Curzon (Notts and Hants).

CUSHING, Vincent Gordon Burke
----------RHB----------

Born Chichester, Sussex, 17 Jan 1950. Educ KCS Wimbledon; Oriel C, Oxford. Debut 1971.
OXFORD UNIVERSITY (14) 1971–73 (Blue 1973).
HS 77* Oxford U v Cambridge U, Lord's, 1973.

CUTHBERTSON, John Layton
----------RHB, RM----------

Born Bombay, India, 24 Feb 1942. Educ Rugby; Worcester C, Oxford. Debut 1962.
OXFORD UNIVERSITY (21) 1962–63 (Blue 1962–63).
SURREY (7) 1963.
HS 94 Oxford U v W Indians, The Parks, 1963.
BB 5–32 Oxford U v Sussex, Hove, 1963.
Clubs: Purley, Barclays Bank. Hockey: Blue.

CUTLER, Roy William
----------RHB, RMF----------

Born West Hartlepool, Co Durham, 28 Mar 1945. Educ Jesus C, Cambridge. Debut 1965.
CAMBRIDGE UNIVERSITY (6) 1965–66.
HS 18 Cambridge U v Glam, Pontypridd, 1965.
BB 5–39 same match.

D

DALE, Christopher Stephen
————RHB, OB————

Born Canterbury, Kent, 15 Dec 1961.
Debut 1984.
GLOUCESTERSHIRE (8) 1984.
HS 49 Glos v Yorks, Bradford, 1984.
BB 3–10 Glos v Oxford U, The Parks,
1984.

DALE, John Ronald
————RHB, SLA————

Born Cleethorpes, Lincs, 24 Oct 1930.
Debut 1958. P.
KENT (1) 1958.
No runs, one wkt.
Lincolnshire 1949–52; 1973–79. Clubs:
Canterbury St Lawrence, Middleton.

DALRYMPLE, John James
Hamilton
————RHB, RMF————

Born St John's Wood, London, 14 Oct
1957. Educ Ampleforth C; Queen's C,
Oxford. Debut 1978.
OXFORD UNIVERSITY (3) 1978.
HS 15 Oxford U v Glos, The Parks, 1978.
BB 3–34 Oxford U v Sussex, The Parks,
1978.
Rugby: Oxford U, Harlequins, Had-
dington.

DALTON, Andrew John
————RHB————

Born Horsforth, Yorks, 14 Mar 1947.
Educ Leeds GS; Newcastle U. Debut
1969.
YORKSHIRE (21) 1969–72.
HS 128 Yorks v M'sex, Headingley,
1972.

DANIEL, Adrian Richard Huw
————RHB, RM————

Born Ealing, London, 17 Jan 1955.
Educ Bishop Gore S, Swansea;
Emmanuel C, Cambridge. Debut 1975.

CAMBRIDGE UNIVERSITY (4) 1975–77.
HS 75 Cambridge U v Glam, Fenner's,
1977.

DANIEL, Wayne Wendell
————RHB, RF————

Born St Philip, Barbados, 16 Jan 1956.
Debut 1975/76.
W INDIES DOMESTIC Barbados 1975/76–.
MIDDLESEX (158) 1977–. Cap 1977.
AUSTRALIA DOMESTIC Western Australia
(2) 1981/82.
WEST INDIES (11) 1975/76–83/84. A
1983/84 (3); I 1975/76 (1). E 1976 (4);
I 1983/84 (3).
OTHER TOUR Young W Indies to Zim-
babwe 1981/82.
HST 11 WI v I, Kingston, 1975/76. HS
53* Barbados v Jamaica, 1979/80 and
M'sex v Yorks, Lord's, 1981.
BBT 5–39 WI v I, Ahmedabad, 1983/84.
BB 9–61 M'sex v Glam, Swansea, 1982.

DANIELS, David Michael
————RHB————

Born Bexleyheath, Kent, 29 Mar 1942.
Educ Rutlish S; Caius C, Cambridge.
Debut 1964.
CAMBRIDGE UNIVERSITY (18) 1964–65
(Blue 1964–65).
HS 82 Cambridge U v Worcs,
Halesowen, 1964.
Dorset 1966–75; Bedfordshire 1976–.

DANIELS, John Giles Upton
————RHB, OB————

Born Birmingham, 25 Jan 1942. Educ
Winchester C. Debut 1964.
GLOUCESTERSHIRE (1) 1964.
COMBINED SERVICES (1) 1964.
HS 22 Combined Services v Oxford U,
Aldershot, 1964.
Brother R. C. Daniels (Oxford U).

DANIELS, Rupert Chandos
————RHB, OB————

Born Birmingham, 28 June 1945. Educ
Eton; Oxford U. Debut 1965.

OXFORD UNIVERSITY (7) 1965–66.
HS 26 Oxford U v Hants, The Parks,
1966.
Brother J. G. U. Daniels (Glos and
Combined Services).

DANIELS, Simon Anthony
Brewis
————RHB, RFM————

Born Darlington, Co Durham, 23 Aug
1958. Educ Sedbergh S; Newcastle
Poly. Debut 1981.
GLAMORGAN (16) 1981–82.
HS 73 Glam v Glos, Swansea, 1982.
BB 3–33 Glam v Essex, Colchester,
1981.
RECORD During HS (above) added 143 for
10th wkt with T. Davies, county record.
Durham 1979–80. Club: Darlington.

D'ARCY, John William
————RHB————

Born Christchurch, N Zealand, 23 Apr
1936. Debut 1955/56.
N ZEALAND DOMESTIC Canterbury (20)
1955/56–58/59, Wellington (1) 1959/60,
Otago (8) 1960/61–61/62.
NEW ZEALAND (5) E 1958.
HST 33 NZ v E, Lord's, 1958. HS 89 N
Zealanders v Glam, Cardiff, 1958.

DARE, Reginald
————RHB, SLA————

Born Blandford Forum, Dorset, 26 Nov
1921. Debut 1949. P.
HAMPSHIRE (109) 1949–54. Cap 1954.
HS 109* Hants v Worcs, Bournemouth,
1952.
BB 6–28 Hants v Oxford U, The Parks,
1950.
Buckinghamshire 1958. Clubs: Tor-
quay, High Wycombe. Soccer:
Southampton, Exeter City.

DARGAN, Michael James
——————RHB——————

Born Dublin, Ireland, 9 Oct 1928. Educ Belvedere C, Dublin; Clongowes Wood C, Kildare. Debut 1954.
IRELAND (1) 1954.
HS 7 Ireland v MCC, Dublin, 1954.
Club: Phoenix. Rugby: Old Belvedere, Ireland (2).

DARKS, Geoffrey Charlton
——————RHB, RMF——————

Born Bewdley, Worcs, 28 June 1926. Educ New Meeting S, Kidderminster. Debut 1946. *P.*
WORCESTERSHIRE (7) 1946–50.
HS 39 Worcs v Cambridge U, Worcester, 1950.
BB 5–49 Worcs v Combined Services, Worcester, 1950.
Clubs: Kidderminster, Whitehaven, Carpet Trades, Smethwick Drop Forgings.

DARVELL, Bruce Stanley
——————RHB, OB——————

Born Chipperfield, Herts, 29 Apr 1931. Educ Dartington Hall, Devon. Debut 1952. *P.*
KENT (1) 1952.
HS 5 Kent v Oxford U, The Parks, 1952.
Hertfordshire 1957–58. Clubs: Chorleywood, Broxbourne.

DARWALL-SMITH, Randle Frederick Hicks Darwall
——————RHB, RFM——————

Born London, 11 July 1914. Educ Charterhouse; Brasenose C, Oxford. Debut 1935.
OXFORD UNIVERSITY (41) 1935–38 (Blue 1935–38).
SUSSEX (5) 1946.
HS 54 Oxford U v Glos, The Parks, 1936.
BB 7–44 Oxford U v Glos, The Parks, 1937.
Brother J. A. D. Darwall-Smith (Oxford U).

DATTA, Punya Brata
——————RHB, SLA——————

Born Calcutta, India, 21 June 1924. Educ Asutoch C, Calcutta; Trinity Hall, Cambridge. Debut 1942/43.
INDIA DOMESTIC Bengal 1942/43–55/56 (capt 1954/55).
CAMBRIDGE UNIVERSITY (13) 1947 (Blue).
HS 143 Bengal v Bihar, Calcutta, 1952/53.

BB 5–52 Cambridge U v Essex, Fenner's, 1947.
Cambridgeshire 1947.

DAUNCEY, John *Gilbert*
——————RHB——————

Born Ystalyfera, S Wales, 9 Apr 1936. Debut 1957. *P.*
GLAMORGAN (2) 1957.
HS 34 Glam v Glos, Swansea, 1957.
Clubs: Metal Box, Swansea, Pontardawe, Clydach.

DAVEY, Clive Frederick
——————RHB, LB——————

Born North Petherton, Som, 2 June 1932. Debut 1953.
SOMERSET (13) 1953–55.
HS 46 Som v Leics, Bath, 1955.

DAVEY, Jack
——————LHB, LFM——————

Born Tavistock, Devon, 4 Sept 1944. Educ Tavistock GS. Debut 1966.
GLOUCESTERSHIRE (175) 1966–78. Cap 1971. Joint benefit (with D. R. Shepherd) 1978.
HS 53* Glos v Glam, Bristol, 1977.
BB 6–95 Glos v Notts, Gloucester, 1967.
Devon 1964–65, 1981.

DAVIDSON, Alan Keith
——————LHB, LF——————

Born Lisarow, nr Gosford, NSW, Australia, 14 June 1929. Educ Gosford HS. Debut 1949/50. *Wisden* 1962.
AUSTRALIA DOMESTIC New South Wales (72) 1949/50–62/63.
AUSTRALIA (44) 1953–62/63. E 1954/55 (3), 1958/59 (5), 1962/63 (5); WI 1960/61 (4). E 1953 (5), 1956 (2), 1961 (5); SA 1957/58 (5); I 1956/57 (1), 1959/60 (5); P 1956/57 (1), 1959/60 (3).
OTHER TOURS Australia to N Zealand 1949/50. Australia to W Indies 1954/55.
HST 80 A v WI, Brisbane, 1960/61. HS 129 Australians v W Province, Cape Town, 1957/58.
BBT 7–93 A v I, Kanpur, 1959/60. BB 7–31 NSW v W Australia, Perth, 1961/62.
President NSW CA. OBE for services to cricket.

DAVIDSON, James *Norman* Grieve
——————RHB——————

Born Hawick, Scotland, 28 Jan 1931. Educ Hawick HS; Edinburgh U. Debut 1951.

SCOTLAND (4) 1951.
HS 40 Scotland v Northants, Edinburgh, 1951.
Clubs: Southport, Edinburgh U. Rugby: Edinburgh U, Scotland (7).

DAVIDSON, William Watkins
——————RHB, WK——————

Born Poplar, London, 20 Mar 1920. Educ Brighton C; King's C, London; Wadham C, Oxford. Debut 1947.
OXFORD UNIVERSITY (16) 1947–48 (Blue 1947–48).
SUSSEX (5) 1948–51.
MCC (1) 1956.
HS 31 MCC v Oxford U, Lord's, 1956.
Ordained into Church of England 1949.

DAVIES, Andrew George
——————RHB, WK——————

Born Altrincham, Cheshire, 15 May 1962. Educ Birkenhead S; Robinson C, Cambridge. Debut 1982.
CAMBRIDGE UNIVERSITY (12) 1982–84 (Blue 1984).
HS 69 Cambridge U v Surrey, Banstead, 1984.
Uncle H. G. Davies (Glam).

DAVIES, David *Emrys*
——————LHB, SLA——————

Born Llanelli, S Wales, 27 June 1904. Died Llanelli, S Wales, 10 Nov 1975. Debut 1924. *P.*
GLAMORGAN (612) 1924–54. Cap 1928. Benefit (£688) 1938. Glam senior professional 1939–54.
WALES (3) 1926–29.
HS 287* Glam v Glos, Newport, 1939.
BB 6–24 Glam v Leics, Newport, 1935.
1000 RUNS (16) 2012 @ 40.24 in 1937.
100 WKTS (2) 103 @ 23.03 in 1937.
DOUBLE (2) 1935, 1937 (2,012 runs, 103 wkts).
RECORDS HS (above) highest inns for Glam. Added 313 for 3rd wkt with W. E. Jones, Glam v Essex, Brentwood, 1948, county record.
Century and hat-trick, Glam v Leics, Leicester, 1937.
Selected for MCC to India 1939/40 (cancelled owing to war). Fc umpire 1955–60 (9 Tests, 1956–59). Coached Llandovery C. Brother Gwynfor Davies (Glam 1932).

DAVIES, Gwynfor
——————RHB——————

Born Cardiff, Wales, 10 June 1919. Educ Cathays HS, Cardiff. Debut 1947.

GLAMORGAN (2) 1947–48.
HS 7 Glam v Lancs, Newport, 1948.
Club: Cardiff.

DAVIES, Haydn George
——————RHB, WK——————

Born Llanelli, S Wales, 23 Apr 1912.
Debut 1935. *P.*
GLAMORGAN (423) 1935–58. Cap 1938.
Benefit (£4500) 1951.
HS 80 Glam v S Africans, Cardiff, 1951.
788 dismissals (584 ct, 204 st) in fc
career.
Squash professional; appointed secretary Edinburgh squash and tennis club
1964. Brother R. D. Davies (Glam);
nephew A. G. Davies (Cambridge U).

DAVIES, Hugh Daniel
——————RHB, RMF——————

Born Pembrey, Llanelli, S Wales, 23
July 1932. Debut 1955. *P.*
GLAMORGAN (52) 1955–60.
HS 28 Glam v Essex, Westcliff, 1958.
BB 6–85 Glam v Yorks, Bramall Lane,
Sheffield, 1957.
Clubs: Llanelli, Neath, Barry, Steel Co
of Wales.

DAVIES, Jack Gale Wilmot
——————RHB, OB——————

Born Broadclyst, Devon, 10 Sept 1911.
Educ Tonbridge; St John's C, Cam-
bridge. Debut 1931.
CAMBRIDGE UNIVERSITY (38) 1931–34
(Blue 1933–34).
KENT (99) 1934–51. Cap.
ENGLAND XI (1) 1945.
OVER-33S (1) 1945.
MCC (9) 1953–61.
HS 168 Kent v Worcs, Worcester, 1946.
BB 7–20 Kent v Essex, Tunbridge
Wells, 1936.
1000 RUNS (1) 1246 @ 32.78 in 1946.
Gentlemen v Players (1) 1946. Club:
Bishop's Stortford. MCC committee
1971–81; treasurer 1977–81. Rugby:
Kent and Blackheath.

DAVIES, John Antony
——————RHB——————

Born Pontypridd, S Wales, 3 Feb 1926.
Educ Pontypridd County S. Debut
1952.
GLAMORGAN (1) 1952.
HS 11 Glam v Worcs, Cardiff, 1952.
Clubs: Pontypridd, Cowbridge.

DAVIES, John Trevor
——————RHB——————

Born Shrewsbury, Shropshire, 26 Dec
1932. Educ Priory S, Shrewsbury;
Christ's C, Cambridge. Debut 1956.
CAMBRIDGE UNIVERSITY (8) 1956–58.
HS 29 Cambridge U v Worcs, Fenner's,
1957.
Dorset 1959–64. Club: Wimborne.

DAVIES, Mark Nicholas
——————LHB, ROB——————

Born Bridgend, S Wales, 28 Dec 1959.
Educ Archbishop McGrath CS; Brid-
gend C of Technology. Debut 1982.
GLAMORGAN (2) 1982.
No runs, no wkts.

DAVIES, Morean Kimsley
——————LHB, WK——————

Born Clydach, Glam, 13 Oct 1954. Educ
Cwmtawe CS, Pontardawe. Debut
1975.
GLAMORGAN (2) 1975–76.
HS 12 Glam v Cambridge U, Swansea,
1975.
Rugby: Aberavon.

DAVIES, Roy *David*
——————RHB——————

Born Llanelli, S Wales, 12 Aug 1928.
Debut 1950. *P.*
GLAMORGAN (1) 1950.
HS 7 Glam v Som, Weston-super-Mare,
1950.
Brother H. G. Davies (Glam).

DAVIES, Richard John
——————RHB, RM——————

Born Selly Oak, Birmingham, 11 Feb
1954. Educ Westlake HS, Auckland, N
Zealand; Marple Hall GS. Debut 1976.
WARWICKSHIRE (1) 1976.
HS 18 Warwicks v Oxford U, Edgbaston,
1976.
Berkshire 1979. Combined Services and
Army.

DAVIES, Terry
——————RHB, WK——————

Born St Albans, Hertfordshire, 25 Oct
1960. Educ Townsend S, St Albans.
Debut 1979.
GLAMORGAN (50) 1979–.
HS 66* Glam v Glos, Swansea, 1982.

RECORD During HS (above) added 143 for
10th wkt with S. A. B. Daniels, county
record.

DAVIES, Thomas *Clive*
——————RHB, SLA——————

Born Pontrhydyfen, Glam, 7 Nov 1951.
Debut 1971.
GLAMORGAN (7) 1971–72.
HS 5 Glam v Yorks, Swansea, 1971.
BB 3–22 Glam v Leics, Cardiff, 1971.
MCC groundstaff 1969–70.

DAVIES, Trefor Elliott
——————RHB, LB——————

Born Stourbridge, Worcs, 14 Mar 1938.
Debut 1955. *P.*
WORCESTERSHIRE (20) 1955–61.
HS 76 Worcs v Glam, Cardiff, 1961.
BB 2–22 Worcs v Cambridge U, Wor-
cester, 1955.
Club: Stourbridge.

DAVIES, William George
——————RHB, RMF——————

Born Barry, S Wales, 3 July 1936. Debut
1954. *P.*
GLAMORGAN (32) 1954–60.
HS 64 Glam v Som, Bath, 1960.
BB 2–23 Glam v Warwicks, Edgbaston,
1960.
Clubs: Gorseinon, Maesteg, Celtic,
Clydach, Pontardawe, Hills
(Plymouth).

DAVIS, Anthony Tilton
——————RHB, SLA——————

Born Reading, Berkshire, 14 Aug 1931.
Died, by own hand, Reading School,
Berkshire, 20 Nov 1978. Debut 1967.
MCC (1) 1967.
MINOR COUNTIES (1) 1967.
HS 37 Minor Counties v Pakistanis,
Swindon, 1967.
Berkshire 1950–70 (capt 1960–70).
Royal Navy 1957–60. Club: Reading.
Headmaster Reading S to 1978.

DAVIS, Bryan Allan
——————RHB, OB——————

Born Port of Spain, Trinidad, 2 May
1940. Educ St Mary's C, Port of Spain.
Debut 1959/60.
W INDIES DOMESTIC Trinidad 1959/
60–70/71.
GLAMORGAN (60) 1968–70. Cap 1969.
WEST INDIES (4). A 1964/65.

OTHER TOURS W Indies to India and Ceylon 1966/67. Glamorgan to W Indies 1969/70.
HST 68 WI v A, Bridgetown, 1964/65. HS 188* N Trinidad v S Trinidad, Port of Spain, 1966/67.
BB 4–79 W Indians v Indian Board President's XI, Nagpur, 1966/67.
1000 RUNS (2) 1532 @ 31.26 in 1970.
Member WICB. Brother C. A. Davis (Trinidad and W Indies).

DAVIS, Charles Allan
—RHB, RM—

Born Port of Spain, Trinidad, 1 Jan 1944. Educ St Mary's C, Port of Spain. Debut 1960/61 (aged 16).
W INDIES DOMESTIC Trinidad 1960/61–74/75, North Trinidad 1975/76.
WEST INDIES (15) 1968/69–72/73. A 1972/73 (2); NZ 1971/72 (5); I 1970/71 (4). E 1969 (3); A 1968/69 (1).
HST 183 WI v NZ, Bridgetown, 1971/72. HS as above.
BB 7–106 W Indians v S Australia, Adelaide, 1968/69.
Scored 115, N Trinidad v S Trinidad, 1960/61, aged 16 yrs 4 months. Club: Queen's Park. Brother B. A. Davis (Glam and W Indies).

DAVIS, Charles Percy (Sparrow)
—RHB, occ WK—

Born Brackley, Northants, 24 May 1915. Debut 1935. P.
NORTHAMPTONSHIRE (170) 1935–52. Cap 1939. Testimonial (£1600) 1950.
HS 237 Northants v Som, Northampton, 1947.
BB 2–13 Northants v Hants, Northampton, 1947.
1000 RUNS (3) 1435 @ 32.61 in 1946.
Northants coach to 1980. Professional coach Harrow. Brother E. Davis (Northants).

DAVIS, Edward
—RHB—

Born Brackley, Northants, 8 Mar 1922. Debut 1947. P.
NORTHAMPTONSHIRE (104) 1947–56. Cap 1953.
HS 171 Northants v Leics, Northampton, 1949.
Cambridgeshire 1958–63. Brother C. P. Davis (Northants).

DAVIS, Francis John
—RHB, SLA—

Born Cardiff, 23 Mar 1939. Educ Blundell's S; St John's C, Oxford. Debut 1959.

GLAMORGAN (14) 1959–67.
OXFORD UNIVERSITY (14) 1963 (Blue).
HS 63 Oxford U v Northants, The Parks, 1963.
BB 5–67 Oxford U v Cambridge U, Lord's, 1963.
Brother R. C. Davis (Glam).

DAVIS, Ian Charles
—RHB—

Born North Sydney, NSW, Australia, 25 June 1953. Debut 1973/74.
AUSTRALIA DOMESTIC New South Wales (46) 1973/74–74/75, 1976/77–82/83, Queensland (9) 1975/76.
AUSTRALIA (15) 1973/74–77. E 1976/77 (1); NZ 1973/74 (3); P 1976/77 (3). E 1977 (3); NZ 1973/74 (3), 1976/77 (2).
HST 105 A v P, Adelaide, 1976/77. HS 156 NSW v S Australia, Sydney, 1976/77.
World Series Cricket (Kerry Packer) 1977/78–78/79.

DAVIS, Mark Richard
—LHB, LFM—

Born Kilve, Som, 26 Feb 1962. Educ West Somerset S; Bridgewater C. Debut 1982.
SOMERSET (42) 1982–.
HS 60* Som v Glam, Taunton, 1984.
BB 7–55 Som v Northants, Northampton, 1984.

DAVIS, Michael John
—RHB, RF—

Born Bolton, Lancs, 18 Aug 1943. Educ King's S, Macclesfield. Debut 1963.
NORTHAMPTONSHIRE (1) 1963.
Did not bat.
Cheshire 1961, 1965–69.

DAVIS, Percy Vere
—RHB—

Born Forest Hill, London, 4 Apr 1912. Debut 1946. P.
COMBINED SERVICES (4) 1946.
KENT (6) 1946.
HS 136 Combined Services v Oxford U, The Parks, 1946.

DAVIS, Roger Clive
—RHB, OB—

Born Cardiff, S Wales, 15 Jan 1946. Educ Blundell's S. Debut 1964.
GLAMORGAN (213) 1964–76. Cap 1969.
TOUR Glamorgan to W Indies 1969/70.
HS 134 Glam v Worcs, Cardiff, 1971.

BB 6–82 Glam v Glos, Cheltenham, 1970.
1000 RUNS (1) 1243 @ 31.07 in 1975.
Seriously injured in 1971 when hit on head fielding at square-leg. Brother F. J. Davis (Glam).

DAVIS, Winston Walter
—RHB, RFM—

Born Sion Hill, St Vincent, W Indies, 18 Sept 1958. Educ Emmanuel HS, St Vincent. Debut 1979/80.
W INDIES DOMESTIC Windward Islands 1979/80–, Combined Islands 1979/80–80/81.
GLAMORGAN (45) 1982–.
WEST INDIES (9) 1982/83–84. A 1983/84 (1); I 1982/83 (1). E 1984 (1); I 1983/84 (6).
OTHER TOUR Young W Indies to Zimbabwe 1981/82.
HST 77 WI v E, Old Trafford, 1984. HS as above.
BBT 3–21 WI v I, Ahmedabad, 1983/84.
BB 7–70 Glam v Notts, Ebbw Vale, 1983.
Club: Sunderland. Durham v Scotland, 1980.

DAVISON, Brian Fettes
—RHB, RM—

Born Bulawayo, Rhodesia, 21 Dec 1946. Educ Gifford HS, Rhodesia. Debut 1967/68.
S AFRICA DOMESTIC Rhodesia (90) 1967/68–78/79. Capt 25.
LEICESTERSHIRE (303) 1970–83. Cap 1971. Capt 1980. Benefit 1982.
AUSTRALIA DOMESTIC Tasmania (32) 1979/80–83/84.
HS 189 Leics v Australians, Leicester, 1975.
BB 5–52 Rhodesia v Griqualand West, Bulawayo, 1967/68.
1000 RUNS (13 + 1) 1818 @ 56.81 in 1976.
Centuries in five successive matches for Tasmania, 1979/80–80/81.
Hockey: Rhodesia.

DAVISON, Ian Joseph
—RHB, RFM—

Born Hemel Hempstead, Hertfordshire, 4 Oct 1937. Educ Berkhamsted S. Debut 1959. P.
NOTTINGHAMSHIRE (177) 1959–66. Cap 1962.
HS 60* Notts v Sussex, Trent Bridge, 1962.
BB 7–28 Notts v Derbys, Trent Bridge, 1962.
100 WKTS (1) 111 @ 21.92 in 1963.

Bedfordshire 1955–58, 1967–69. Clubs: Luton Town, Milnrow. Professional coach Trent C from 1969.

DAWKES, George Owen
RHB, WK

Born Aylestone Park, Leicester, 19 July 1920. Debut 1937. *P*.
LEICESTERSHIRE (63) 1937–39. Cap 1938.
DERBYSHIRE (392) 1947–61. Cap 1947.
Testimonial (£2629) 1956.
TOUR Commonwealth XI to India, Pakistan and Ceylon 1949/50.
HS 143 Derbys v Hants, Burton upon Trent, 1954.
1043 dismissals (895 ct, 148 st) in fc career. Club: Windhill. Soccer: Leicester City.

DAWSON, Gilbert Wilkinson
RHB

Born Bradford, Yorks, 9 Dec 1916. Died Glasgow, Scotland, 23 May 1969. Debut 1947. *P*.
HAMPSHIRE (60) 1947–49. Cap 1948.
HS 158★ Hants v Notts, Trent Bridge, 1949.
1000 RUNS (2) 1229 @ 23.63 in 1948.
Clubs: Yeadon, Ferguslie, Poloc, Golfhill.

DAWSON, Harold
RHB, RM

Born Todmorden, Yorks, 10 Aug 1914. Debut 1947. *P*.
HAMPSHIRE (10) 1947–48.
HS 37 Hants v Cambridge U, Aldershot, 1948.
Club: Todmorden. Lancashire League president 1985.

DAWSON, Oswald Charles
RHB, RMF

Born Durban, S Africa, 1 Sept 1919. Debut 1938/39.
S AFRICA DOMESTIC Natal 1938/39–49/50, Border 1951/52–61/62.
SOUTH AFRICA (9) 1947–48/49. E 1948/49 (4). *E 1947 (5)*.
HST 55 SA v E, Oval, 1947. HS 182 Border v Transvaal, East London, 1951/52.
BBT 2–57 E v SA, Trent Bridge, 1947.
BB 5–42 S Africans v Warwicks, Edgbaston, 1947.
1000 RUNS (1) 1002 @ 32.32 in 1947.

DAY, Alan Richard
RHB

Born Muswell Hill, London, 12 Nov 1938. Educ Aldenham. Debut 1968.
MCC (1) 1968.
HS 5 MCC v Ireland, Dublin, 1968.
Hertfordshire 1962–75. Berkshire 1977–80. Clubs: Hornsey, North Oxfordshire, Free Foresters, XL Club.

DAY, Anthony Samuel
RHB

Born Ascot, Berkshire, 20 June 1930. Educ Harrow; Magdalene C, Cambridge. Debut 1953.
CAMBRIDGE UNIVERSITY (1) 1953.
HS 2 Cambridge U v Worcs, Fenner's, 1953.
Club: I Zingari. Father S. H. Day (Cambridge U and Kent).

DAY, Frederick Gordon Kenneth
RHB, WK

Born Yatton, Som, 25 June 1919. Debut 1950.
SOMERSET (7) 1950–56.
HS 56★ Som v Lancs, Old Trafford, 1956.
Club: Knowle (Bristol).

DAY, Kenneth Brian
RHB, WK

Born Hendon, M'sex, 19 May 1935. Died, when fell off ladder window-cleaning, Fulham, London, 19 Jan 1971. Debut 1958. *P*.
MCC (1) 1958.
MIDDLESEX (2) 1959.
Did not bat.

DEAKIN, Michael John
RHB, WK

Born Bury, Lancs, 6 May 1957. Educ Priest Thorpe S, Pudsey, Yorks. Debut 1981.
DERBYSHIRE (4) 1981.
HS 15 Derbys v Som, Taunton, 1981.

DEAN, Philip James
LHB

Born Skipton, Yorks, 4 June 1955. Educ Mill Hill S; Sandhurst; Mansfield C, Oxford. Debut 1978.
OXFORD UNIVERSITY (2) 1978.
HS 39 Oxford U v Sussex, The Parks, 1978.

DEAN, Thomas Arthur
RHB, LBG

Born Gosport, Hants, 21 Nov 1920. Educ St Charles C, Pietermaritzburg, S Africa. Debut 1939. *P*.
HAMPSHIRE (28) 1939–49.
S AFRICA DOMESTIC Eastern Province 1956/57.
HS 26 Hants v Essex, Bournemouth, 1947.
BB 7–51 (10–129 match) Hants v Derbys, Ilkeston, 1946.
Four wkts in five balls, including hattrick, Hants v Worcs, Bournemouth, 1939.
Devon 1954. Hon. secretary Eastern Province CU.

DEAN, William Henry
RHB, RFM

Born Leeds, Yorks, 25 Nov 1928. Debut 1952. *P*.
SOMERSET (1) 1952.
HS 21 Som v Indians, Taunton, 1952, adding 133 for 9th wkt with J. Lawrence.
Clubs: Keighley, Stockport.

DEARLOVE, John Alban
RHB, RM

Born London, 30 Apr 1931. Educ Downside; Jesus C, Cambridge. Debut 1954.
CAMBRIDGE UNIVERSITY (1) 1954.
HS 6 Cambridge U v M'sex, Fenner's, 1954.

DEAS, Kenneth Robin
RHB, SLA

Born Papatoetoe, N Zealand, 10 July 1927. Debut 1947/48.
N ZEALAND DOMESTIC Auckland (16) 1947/48–60/61.
SCOTLAND (2) 1955–56.
HS 73 Auckland v Canterbury, Auckland, 1950/51.
BB 4–81 Auckland v Wellington, Wellington, 1960/61.

DEBNAM, Alexander Frederick Henry
RHB, LBG

Born Belvedere, Kent, 12 Oct 1922. Debut 1948.
KENT (11) 1948–49.
HAMPSHIRE (10) 1950–51.
HS 64 Hants v Cambridge U, Bournemouth, 1951.
BB 5–87 Kent v Glos, Bristol, 1949.

DE COURCY, James Harry
—————RHB—————

Born Newcastle, NSW, Australia, 18 Apr 1927. Debut 1947/48.
AUSTRALIA DOMESTIC New South Wales (50) 1947/48–57/58.
AUSTRALIA (3) *E 1953*.
HST 41 A v E, Old Trafford, 1953. HS 204 Australians v Combined Services, Kingston, 1953 (adding 377 for 4th wkt with K. R. Miller).
1000 RUNS (1) 1214 @ 41.86 in England 1953.
Club: Newcastle.

DEIGHTON, John Harold Greenway
—————RHB, RFM—————

Born Prestwich, Manchester, 5 Apr 1920. Educ Denstone. Debut 1947.
COMBINED SERVICES (20) 1947–62.
LANCASHIRE (7) 1948–50.
MCC (6) 1948–54.
FREE FORESTERS (2) 1953–61.
HS 79 Lancs v Leics, Blackpool, 1949.
BB 6–50 (10–91 match) MCC v Ireland, Dublin, 1954.
Northumberland 1947. Major in Northumberland Fusiliers. Instructor Sandhurst 1948. Served with UNO in Korea 1950–52.

DELISLE, Gustave Peter Saprine
—————RHB—————

Born St Kitts, W Indies, 25 Dec 1924. Educ Stonyhurst; Lincoln C, Oxford. Debut 1954.
OXFORD UNIVERSITY (32) 1954–56 (Blue 1955–56).
MIDDLESEX (55) 1954–57. Cap 1955.
COMBINED SERVICES (1) 1958.
HS 130 M'sex v Cambridge U, Fenner's, 1957.
1000 RUNS (1) 1185 @ 22.78 in 1955.
Club: Hornsey.

DELLER, Reginald Patrick
—————RHB, RFM—————

Born Paddington, London, 27 Mar 1933. Debut 1951. *P*.
MIDDLESEX (3) 1951–53.
HS 3* M'sex v Oxford U, The Parks, 1953.
Club: Barnet.

DE MEL, Asantha Lakdasa Francis
—————RHB, RMF—————

Born Colombo, Ceylon, 9 May 1959. Educ RC, Colombo. Debut 1980/81.
SRI LANKAN DOMESTIC Sri Lanka 1980/81.
SRI LANKA (7) 1981/82–84. E 1981/82 (1); A 1982/83 (1). *E 1984 (1); I 1982/83 (1); P 1981/82 (3)*.
OTHER TOURS Sri Lanka to India 1980/81. Sri Lanka to Australasia 1982/83. Sri Lanka to Zimbabwe 1982/83.
HST 34 SL v P, Lahore, 1981/82. HS 100* President's XI v Tamil Nadu, Colombo, 1982/83.
BBT 5–68 SL v I, Madras, 1982/83. BB as above.
Club: Sinhalese Sports.

DEMPSTER, Charles *Stewart*
—————RHB, occ WK, SRA—————

Born Wellington, N Zealand, 15 Nov 1903. Died Wellington, N Zealand, 14 Feb 1974. Debut 1921/22.
N ZEALAND DOMESTIC Wellington (40) 1921/22–47/48.
SCOTLAND (1) 1934.
LEICESTERSHIRE (69) 1935–39. Cap 1936. Capt 1936–38.
WARWICKSHIRE (3) 1946.
NEW ZEALAND (10) 1929/30–32/33. E 1929/30 (4), 1932/33 (2); SA 1931/32 (2). *E 1931 (2)*.
OTHER TOURS N Zealand to England 1927. N Zealand to Australia 1927/28. Sir J. Cahn's XI to Ceylon 1936/37. Sir J. Cahn's XI to N Zealand 1938/39.
HST 136 NZ v E, Wellington, 1929/30.
HS 212 N Zealanders v Essex, Leyton, 1931.
BB 2–4 N Zealanders v Glam, Cardiff, 1927.
1000 RUNS (5) 1778 @ 59.26 in 1931.

DENMAN, Henry Wynne
—————RHB, WK—————

Born Liverpool, 5 July 1929. Educ Oundle; Magdalene C, Cambridge. Debut 1949.
CAMBRIDGE UNIVERSITY (7) 1950–52.
HS 3 Cambridge U v Indians, Fenner's, 1952.

DENMAN, John
—————RHB, RM—————

Born Crawley, Sussex, 13 June 1947. Educ Ifield S, Crawley; Leicester U. Debut 1970.
SUSSEX (49) 1970–73.
HS 50* Sussex v Surrey, Oval, 1973.
BB 5–45 Sussex v Cambridge U, Fenner's, 1972.

DENNESS, Michael Henry
—————RHB—————

Born Bellshill, Scotland, 1 Dec 1940. Educ Ayr Academy. Debut 1959. *Wisden 1975*.
SCOTLAND (14) 1959–67.
KENT (333) 1962–76. Cap 1964. Capt 1972–76. Benefit (£19,219) 1974.
ESSEX (83) 1977–80. Cap 1977.
ENGLAND (28) 1969–75. A 1975 (1); NZ 1969 (1); I 1974 (3); P 1974 (3). *A 1974/75 (5); WI 1973/74 (5); NZ 1974/75 (2); I 1972/73 (5); P 1972/73 (3)*. Capt 19.
OTHER TOURS International XI to Pakistan, India and Ceylon 1967/68. Duke of Norfolk's XI to W Indies 1969/70. International Wanderers to S Africa 1975/76. D. H. Robins' XI to Sri Lanka 1977/78 (capt).
HST 188 E v A, Melbourne, 1974/75. HS 195 Essex v Leics, Leicester, 1977.
1000 RUNS (14 + 1) 1606 @ 31.49 in 1966.
411 catches in career.
World Series Cricket (Kerry Packer) official. MCC Hon. member. Essex Youth manager to 1983.

DENNING, Peter William
—————LHB, occ ROB—————

Born Wells, Som, 16 Dec 1949. Educ Millfield; St Luke's C, Exeter. Debut 1969.
SOMERSET (269) 1969–84. Cap 1973. Benefit 1981.
HS 184 Som v Notts, Trent Bridge, 1980.
1000 RUNS (6) 1222 @ 42.13 in 1979.
RECORD Added 310 for 4th wkt with I. T. Botham, Som v Glos, Taunton, 1980, county record.

DENNIS, Simon John
—————RHB, LFM—————

Born Scarborough, Yorks, 18 Oct 1960. Educ Scarborough C. Debut 1980.
YORKSHIRE (42) 1980–.
S AFRICA DOMESTIC Orange Free State 1982/83.
HS 53* Yorks v Notts, Trent Bridge, 1984.
BB 5–35 Yorks v Som, Dore, Sheffield, 1981.
Uncles Sir L. Hutton (Yorks and England) and F. Dennis (Yorks); cousin R. A. Hutton (Yorks and England).

DENNISON, David George
—————RHB—————

Born Banbridge, Co Down, Ireland, 22 Dec 1961. Debut 1983.
IRELAND (1) 1983.

HS 16 Ireland v Scotland, Downpatrick, 1983.
Club: Waringstown.

DERMONT, Roger Wayne Archie
RHB, RMF

Born Whitwell, Hertfordshire, 1 Apr 1945. Educ Hitchin S. Debut 1967.
MCC (1) 1967.
No runs.
BB 2–23 MCC v Cambridge U, Fenner's, 1967.
Lord's staff for six yrs. Hertfordshire 1967–74. Clubs: Hitchin Town, Letchworth, Hertfordshire Police.

DERRICK, John
RHB, RM

Born Aberdare, Glam, 15 Jan 1963. Educ Blaengwawr S, Aberdare. Debut 1983.
GLAMORGAN (15) 1983–.
HS 69* Glam v Surrey, Swansea, 1984.
BB 3–42 Glam v Derbys, Swansea, 1984.

DESAI, Avinash Harkant
RHB, LBG

Born Surat, Gujerat, India, 7 Aug 1932. Educ Bombay U. Debut 1947/48.
INDIA DOMESTIC Rajputana 1947/48, Bombay 1952/53–57/58, Railways 1958/59–63/64.
COMMONWEALTH XI (1) 1957.
HS 147* Railways v N Punjab, Delhi, 1961/62.
BB 6–108 Bombay v Gujerat, Bombay, 1956/57.
Professional: Whitehaven 1956–57.
Father H. Desai (Baroda and Gujerat).

DESAI, Ramakant Bhakaji
RHB, RFM

Born Bombay, India, 20 June 1939. Educ Bombay U. Debut 1958/59.
INDIA DOMESTIC Bombay 1958/59–68/69.
INDIA (28) 1958/59–67/68. E 1961/62 (4), 1963/64 (2); A 1959/60 (3); WI 1958/59 (1); NZ 1964/65 (3); P 1960/61 (5). E 1959 (5); A 1967/68 (1); WI 1961/62 (3); NZ 1967/68 (1).
OTHER TOUR A. L. Wadekar's XI to Sri Lanka 1975/76.
HST 85 I v P, Bombay, 1960/61. HS 107 Bombay v Rajasthan, Jaipur, 1962/63.
BBT 6–56 I v NZ, Bombay, 1964/65. BB 7–46 Bombay v Rajasthan, Udaipur, 1960/61.
RECORDS In HST (above) added 149 for

9th wkt with P. G. Joshi, India Test record. 50 wkts @ 11.10 for Bombay in debut Ranji Trophy season 1958/59 – record total for first season.

DESHON, David Peter Tower
RHB

Born London, 19 June 1923. Educ Sherborne. Debut 1947.
SOMERSET (4) 1947–53.
HS 21 Som v M'sex, Taunton, 1947.

DE SILVA, Dandeniyage *Somachandra*
RHB, LBG

Born Galle, Ceylon, 11 June 1942. Educ Prince of Wales C, Moratuwa. Debut 1966/67.
SRI LANKA DOMESTIC Ceylon (Sri Lanka) 1966/67–80/81.
SRI LANKA (12) 1981/82–1984. E 1981/82 (1); A 1982/83 (1); NZ 1983/84 (3). E 1984 (1); NZ 1982/83 (2); I 1982/83 (1); P 1981/82 (3). Capt 2.
OTHER TOURS Sri Lanka to India 1972/73, 1975/76. Sri Lanka to Pakistan 1973/74. Sri Lanka to England 1975, 1979, 1981. Sri Lanka to Zimbabwe 1982/83.
HST 61 SL v NZ, Wellington, 1982/83.
HS 97 Sri Lankans v Glos, Bristol, 1981.
BBT 5–59 SL v P, Faisalabad, 1982/83.
BB 8–46 (12–59 match) Sri Lankans v Oxford U, The Parks, 1979.
Lincolnshire 1976–78, Shropshire 1980–. Clubs: Bloomfield, Middleton.
Brother D. P. De Silva (Ceylon).

DE SILVA, Deva Lokesh *Stanley*
RHB, RFM

Born Ambalangoda, Ceylon, 17 Nov 1956. Died, in road accident, Colombo, Sri Lanka, 12 Apr 1980. Debut 1979.
TOURS Sri Lanka Under-19 to Pakistan 1975/76. Sri Lanka to England 1979.
HS 7 Sri Lankans v Derbys, Derby, 1979.
BB 2–28 Sri Lankans v Ireland, Eglinton, 1979.

DE SILVA, Ginigalgodage Ramba *Ajit*
LHB, SLA

Born Ambalagoda, Ceylon, 12 Dec 1952. Educ Ananda C, Ceylon. Debut 1973/74.
SRI LANKA DOMESTIC Sri Lanka 1973/74–80/81.
SRI LANKA (4) 1981/82–82/83. E 1981/82 (1). I 1982/83 (1); P 1981/82 (2).

OTHER TOURS Sri Lanka to Pakistan 1973/74. Sri Lanka to India 1974/75, 1975/76, 1976/77. Sri Lanka to England 1975, 1979, 1981.
HST 14 SL v I, Madras, 1982/83. HS 75 Board President's XI v Tamil Nadu, Madras, 1976/77.
BBT 2–38 SL v P, Faisalabad, 1981/82.
BB 6–30 Board President's XI v Tamil Nadu, Colombo, 1975/76 and Sri Lankans v Oxford U, The Parks, 1979.
Barred from Sinhalese cricket for 25 yrs for touring S Africa 1982/83 (Arosa Sri Lanka). Club: Denton.

DE SILVA, Pinnaduwage *Aravinda*
RHB, RM

Born Colombo, Ceylon, 17 Nov 1965. Debut 1983/84.
SRI LANKA DOMESTIC Sri Lanka Board President's XI 1983/84.
SRI LANKA (1) E 1984.
HST 16 SL v E, Lord's, 1984. HS 75 Sri Lankans v Hants, Southampton, 1984.

DEVAPRIYA, Hemanthe Hettiwatte
RHB, WK

Born Galle, Ceylon, 12 Apr 1958. Educ Nalanda C, Ceylon. Debut 1980/81.
TOURS Sri Lanka to India 1980/81. Sri Lanka to England 1981.
HS 95 Sri Lanka Under-25 v Tamil Nadu Under-25, Salem, 1980/81.
Barred from Sinhalese cricket for 25 yrs for touring S Africa 1982/83 (Arosa Sri Lanka). Club: Colombo.

DEVEREUX, Louis Norman
RHB, OB

Born Heavitree, Exeter, Devon, 20 Oct 1931. Debut 1949. *P*.
MIDDLESEX (2) 1949.
WORCESTERSHIRE (79) 1950–55.
COMBINED SERVICES (5) 1950–51.
GLAMORGAN (106) 1956–60. Cap 1956.
HS 108* Glam v Lancs, Old Trafford, 1957.
BB 6–29 Glam v Yorks, 1956.
1000 RUNS (1) 1039 @ 22.58 in 1957.
Club: Gorseinon. Table tennis: England 1949.

DEVEREUX, Richard Jeynes
RHB, LM

Born Castle Bromwich, Warwicks, 26 Dec 1938. Educ Malvern. Debut 1963.
WORCESTERSHIRE (11) 1963.

HS 55* Worcs v Cambridge U, Worcester, 1963.
BB 3–44 same match.
Club: Walsall.

DE VILLE, Roger Thomas
———————RHB, LB———————

Born Uttoxeter, Staffordshire, 21 Jan 1935. Educ Denstone C. Debut 1963.
DERBYSHIRE (3) 1963–64.
HS 17 Derbys v Yorks, Chesterfield, 1963.
BB 2–47 Derbys v Northants, Derby, 1963.
Staffordshire 1959–60, 1966–70. Club: Longton.

DE VILLIERS, John Oliver
———————RHB———————

Born Cape Town, S Africa, 28 Feb 1930. Educ Diocesan C; Stellenbosch U; University C, Oxford. Debut 1951.
OXFORD UNIVERSITY (8) 1951–52.
S AFRICA DOMESTIC Orange Free State 1953/54.
HS 81 Oxford U v Free Foresters, The Parks, 1951.
Hockey: Blue.

DEW, David Gerveys du Breul
———————RHB, WK———————

Born London, 16 Sept 1935. Educ Stowe; Corpus Christi C, Cambridge. Debut 1959.
CAMBRIDGE UNIVERSITY (2) 1959.
HS 4 Cambridge U v M'sex, Fenner's, 1959.

DEW, John Alexander
———————RHB, WK———————

Born Horsham, Sussex, 12 May 1920. Educ Tonbridge; St Catharine's C, Cambridge. Debut 1947.
SUSSEX (2) 1947.
L. C. STEVENS' XI (1) 1961.
HS 29 Sussex v Warwicks, Edgbaston, 1947.
Club: Horsham (president 1969). Medical practitioner.

DEWAR, Arthur
———————RHB, RFM———————

Born Perth, Scotland, 15 Mar 1934. Educ Perth Academy. Debut 1960.
SCOTLAND (5) 1960–62.
HS 4* Scotland v Ireland, Paisley, 1960 and Scotland v MCC, Greenock, 1961.
BB 7–71 Scotland v Warwicks, Edgbaston, 1961.

DEWDNEY, David Thom
———————RHB, RFM———————

Born Kingston, Jamaica, 23 Oct 1933. Debut 1954/55.
W INDIES DOMESTIC Jamaica 1954/55–57/58.
COMMONWEALTH XI (1) 1961.
WEST INDIES (9) 1954/55–57/58. A 1954/55 (2); P 1957/58 (3). E 1957 (1); NZ 1955/56 (3).
OTHER TOURS W Indies to Australia 1960/61.
HST 5* WI v NZ, Auckland, 1955/56. HS 37* W Indians v Queensland, Brisbane, 1960/61.
BBT 5–21 WI v NZ, Auckland, 1955/56.
BB 7–55 Jamaica v Duke of Norfolk's XI, Kingston, 1956/57.
Club: Burslem.

DEWES, Anthony Roy
———————RHB, occ LB———————

Born Rugby, Warwicks, 2 June 1957. Educ Dulwich C; St John's C, Cambridge. Debut 1978.
CAMBRIDGE UNIVERSITY (14) 1978–79 (Blue 1978).
HS 84 Cambridge U v Glos, Fenner's, 1979.
Father J. G. Dewes (Cambridge U, M'sex and England).

DEWES, John Gordon
———————LHB———————

Born North Latchford, Cheshire, 11 Oct 1926. Educ Aldenham; St John's C, Cambridge. Debut 1945.
ENGLAND XI (1) (Victory match) 1945.
COMBINED SERVICES (11) 1946–47.
CAMBRIDGE UNIVERSITY (38) 1948–50 (Blue 1948–50).
MIDDLESEX (62) 1948–56. Cap 1948.
ENGLAND (5) 1948–50/51. A 1948 (1); WI 1950 (2). A 1950/51 (2).
HST 67 E v WI, Trent Bridge, 1950. HS 212 Cambridge U v Sussex, Hove, 1950.
1000 RUNS (3) 2432 @ 59.32 in 1950.
RECORD Added 429* for 2nd wkt with G. H. G. Doggart, Cambridge U v Essex, Fenner's, 1949, Cambridge U record for any wkt.
War-time Blue 1945. Schoolmaster Tonbridge, Rugby, Barker College NSW (headmaster). Son A. R. Dewes (Cambridge U.).

DEWS, George
———————RHB———————

Born Ossett, Yorks, 5 June 1921. Debut 1946. P.
WORCESTERSHIRE (374) 1946–61. Cap 1950. Benefit 1960 (£2795).
HS 145 Worcs v Combined Services, Worcester, 1951.
1000 RUNS (11) 1752 @ 41.71 in 1959. 1521 runs in last season (1961). 352 catches in fc career.
Club: Dudley. Soccer: Middlesbrough, Plymouth Argyle, Walsall.

DEXTER, Edward Ralph
———————RHB, RMF———————

Born Milan, Italy, 15 May 1935. Educ Radley; Jesus C, Cambridge. Debut 1956. Wisden 1961.
CAMBRIDGE UNIVERSITY (49) 1956–58 (Blue 1956–58). Capt 1958.
SUSSEX (137) 1957–68. Cap 1959. Capt 1960–65.
ENGLAND (62) 1958–68. A 1961 (5), 1964 (5), 1968 (2); SA 1960 (5); WI 1963 (5); NZ 1958 (1), 1965 (2); I 1959 (2); P 1962 (5). A 1958/59 (2), 1962/63 (5); SA 1964/65 (5); WI 1959/60 (5); NZ 1958/59 (2), 1962/63 (3); I 1961/62 (5); P 1961/62 (3). Capt 30.
OTHER TOURS Commonwealth XI to S Africa 1962/63. Cavaliers to Jamaica 1963/64, 1969/70.
HST 205 E v P, Karachi, 1961/62. HS as above.
BBT 4–10 E v P, Headingley, 1962. BB 7–24 Sussex v M'sex, Hove, 1960.
1000 RUNS (8 + 2) 2217 @ 43.47 in 1960.
MCC Hon. member. Fc golfer. Stood for Parliament as Conservative in Cardiff South-East in 1964 against future Prime Minister James Callaghan. Autobiography Ted Dexter Declares (1966).

DEXTER, Roy Evatt
———————RHB———————

Born Nottingham, 13 Apr 1955. Educ Nottingham HS; Lanchester Polytechnic. Debut 1975.
NOTTINGHAMSHIRE (22) 1975–81.
HS 57 Notts v Cambridge U, Fenner's, 1981.

DIAS, Roy Luke
———————RHB———————

Born Colombo, Ceylon, 18 Oct 1952. Educ St Peter's C, Colombo. Debut 1974/75.
SRI LANKA DOMESTIC Sri Lanka 1974/75–80/81.
SRI LANKA (9) 1981/82–84. E 1981/82 (1); A 1982/83 (1); NZ 1983/84 (2). E 1984 (1); A 1982/83 (1); I 1982/83 (1); P 1981/82 (3).
OTHER TOURS Sri Lanka to India 1974/75, 1975/76, 1976/77. Sri Lanka to England 1979, 1981. Sri Lanka to Zimbabwe

1982/83. Sri Lanka to Australasia 1982/83.
HST 109 SL v P, Lahore, 1981/82. HS 127 Sri Lankans v Leics, Leicester, 1981. Club: Droylesden.

DICK, Arthur Edward
——RHB, WK——

Born Middlemarch, Otago, N Zealand, 10 Oct 1936. Debut 1956/57.
N ZEALAND DOMESTIC Otago (16) 1956/57–60/61, Wellington (20) 1962/63–68/69.
NEW ZEALAND (17) 1961/62–65. E 1962/63 (3); SA 1963/64 (2); P 1964/65 (2). *E 1965 (2); SA 1961/62 (5); P 1964/65 (3).*
HST 50* NZ v SA, Cape Town, 1961/62.
HS 127 N Zealand XI v NSW, Sydney, 1961/62.

DICKINSON, David Christopher
——RHB, RM——

Born Blackheath, Kent, 11 Dec 1929. Educ Clifton; Trinity C, Cambridge. Debut 1953.
CAMBRIDGE UNIVERSITY (11) 1953 (Blue).
FREE FORESTERS (2) 1955–57.
HS 36* Cambridge U v Free Foresters, Fenner's, 1953.
BB 4–22 Cambridge U v Worcs, Fenner's, 1953.

DICKINSON, Thomas Eastwood
——LHB, RFM——

Born Parramatta, NSW, Australia, 11 Jan 1931. Educ Blackburn GS; Manchester U; Loughborough C. Debut 1950.
LANCASHIRE (4) 1950–51.
SOMERSET (5) 1957.
HS 9 Lancs v Surrey, Oval, 1950.
BB 5–36 Som v Glam, Weston-super-Mare, 1957.
Clubs: East Lancs, Keynsham.

DILLEY, Graham Roy
——LHB, RF——

Born Dartford, Kent, 18 May 1959. Educ Dartford West Sec S. Debut 1977.
KENT (78) 1977–. Cap 1980.
ENGLAND (18) 1979/80–83/84. A 1981 (3); WI 1980 (3); NZ 1983 (1). *A 1979/80 (2); WI 1980/81 (4); I 1981/82 (4); P 1983/84 (1).*
HST 56 E v A, Headingley, 1981. HS 81 Kent v Northants, Northampton, 1979.
BBT 4–24 E v A, Trent Bridge, 1981. BB 6–66 Kent v M'sex, Lord's, 1979.
Brother-in-law G. W. Johnson (Kent). CWC Young Cricketer of Year 1980.

DILLEY, Michael Reginald
——RHB, RMF——

Born Rushden, Northants, 28 Mar 1939. Educ Wellingborough GS. Debut 1957. *P.*
NORTHAMPTONSHIRE (33) 1957–63.
HS 31* Northants v Sussex, Worthing, 1959.
BB 6–74 Northants v Sussex, Hove, 1961.
Two hat-tricks in 1961, v Notts, Trent Bridge and v Sussex, Hove. Club: Rushden.

DIMENT, Robert *Anthony*
——RHB——

Born Tortworth, Glos, 9 Feb 1927. Debut 1952.
GLOUCESTERSHIRE (1) 1952.
LEICESTERSHIRE (59) 1955–58.
HS 71 Leics v Derbys, Ashby-de-la-Zouch, 1955.
Leics secretary 1957–59.

DINDAR, Andrew
——RHB, RM——

Born Johannesburg, S Africa, 26 June 1942. Debut 1962. *P.*
GLOUCESTERSHIRE (7) 1962–63.
HS 55 Glos v Oxford U, Bristol, 1962.
BB 3–32 same match.
Hertfordshire 1976–80, Berkshire 1981–. Sussex staff 1967. Clubs: Coombe Dingle, Berkhamsted, Brighton and Hove, Reading.

DINEEN, Patrick Joseph
——LHB——

Born Cork, Ireland, 13 May 1937. Educ Presentation Brothers' C, Cork. Debut 1962.
IRELAND (7) 1962–71.
HS 84 Ireland v Scotland, Glasgow, 1968.
Club: Cork Wanderers.

DINES, William James
——RHB, RM/OB——

Born Colchester, Essex, 14 Sept 1916. Educ Victoria S, Chelmsford. Debut 1947. *P.*
ESSEX (20) 1947–49.
HS 69* Essex v Sussex, Brentwood, 1947.
BB 3–35 Essex v Northants, Ilford, 1947.
Club: Crompton-Parkinson, Chelmsford.

DINSDALE, Stephen Charles
——LHB, LM——

Born Buckhurst Hill, Essex, 30 Dec 1948. Educ George Monoux S, Walthamstow. Debut 1969/70.
S AFRICA DOMESTIC Rhodesia 1969/70, Transvaal/Transvaal B 1974/75–75/76.
ESSEX (5) 1970.
HS 88 Transvaal B v OFS, Bloemfontein, 1974/75.
BB 4–24 Transvaal B v Natal B, J'burg, 1974/75.

DISBURY, Brian Elvin
——RHB, RM——

Born Bedford, 30 Sept 1929. Educ Bedford S; London U. Debut 1954. *P.*
KENT (14) 1954–57.
HS 74* Kent v Leics, Tunbridge Wells, 1956.
BB 2–76 Kent v S Africans, Canterbury, 1955.
Bedfordshire 1946–53. Clubs: Bedford Town, Canterbury St Lawrence. Lives in Zambia.

DIVECHA, Ramesh Vithaldao
——RHB, RMF/OB——

Born Bombay, India, 18 Oct 1927. Educ Podar HS; Bombay U; Worcester C, Oxford. Debut 1946/47 (A. A. Jasdenwala's XI).
OXFORD UNIVERSITY (30) 1948–51 (Blue 1950–51).
NORTHAMPTONSHIRE (1) 1948.
INDIA DOMESTIC Bombay 1951/52, Madhya Pradesh 1954/55 (capt), Saurashtra 1962/63.
INDIA (5) 1951/52–52/53. E 1951/52 (2); P 1952/53 (1). *E 1952 (2).*
HST 26 I v E, Calcutta, 1951/52. HS 92 Oxford U v Surrey, Guildford, 1950.
BBT 3–102 I v E, Old Trafford, 1952. BB 8–74 Indians v Glam, Swansea, 1952.
Oxfordshire 1949. Brother A. V. Divecha (Maharashtra).

DIXON, Alan Leonard
——RHB, RM/OB——

Born Dartford, Kent, 27 Nov 1933. Educ Dartford Technical C. Debut 1950. *P.*
KENT (378) 1950–70. Cap 1960. Benefit 1969.
TOUR MCC to E Africa 1973/74.
HS 125* Kent v Worcs, Worcester, 1960.
BB 8–61 Kent v Northants, Dover, 1964.
1000 RUNS (3) 1170 @ 24.37 in 1961.
100 WKTS (3) 122 @ 23.89 in 1964.

DIXON, Anthony Sumner
RHB

Born Bristol, 17 Nov 1948. Educ Clifton C; Trinity C, Cambridge. Debut 1971.
CAMBRIDGE UNIVERSITY (1) 1971.
HS 12 Cambridge U v Surrey, Fenner's, 1971.

DIXON, John Henry
RHB, RMF

Born Bournemouth, Hants, 3 Mar 1954. Educ Monkton Combe; Keble C, Oxford. Debut 1973.
GLOUCESTERSHIRE (16) 1973–81.
HS 13* Glos v Northants, Bristol, 1975.
BB 5–44 Glos v Glam, Cardiff, 1975.
Club: Lansdown.

DOBREE-CAREY, Paul Alexander Huntly
LHB, RFM

Born Horsham, Sussex, 21 May 1920. Debut 1942/43. P.
INDIA DOMESTIC Baroda 1942/43, Services 1943/44–44/45, Europeans 1944/45–45/46, Stuart's XI 1944/45, Bengal 1944/45.
SUSSEX (42) 1946–48.
HS 96 Sussex v Worcs, Worcester, 1947.
BB 6–80 Sussex v Surrey, Guildford, 1947.
Durham 1950. Clubs: Darlington, Shildon BR, Henfield.

DOCWRA, Edward David
RHB, LB

Born Paddington, London, 24 Apr 1953. Educ Canford; Worcester C, Oxford. Debut 1974.
OXFORD UNIVERSITY (1) 1974.
HS 20 Oxford U v Worcs, The Parks, 1974.
Grandfather H. S. Evans (NSW).

DODDS, Thomas Carter (Dickie)
RHB, RM/LB

Born Bedford, 19 May 1919. Educ Wellingborough S, Warwick S. Debut 1943/44. P from 1947.
INDIA DOMESTIC Services 1943/44.
ESSEX (380) 1946–59. Cap 1946. Benefit (£2325) 1957.
HS 157 Essex v Leics, Leicester, 1947.
BB 4–34 Essex v Kent, Clacton, 1955.
1000 RUNS (13) 2147 @ 38.33 in 1947.
RECORD Added 270 for 1st wkt with A. V. Avery, Essex v Surrey, Oval, 1946, county record.

Benefit money donated to Moral Rearmament. Autobiography *Hit Hard and Enjoy It* (1976).

DOGGART, Arthur *Peter*
RHB, LB

Born Earls Court, London, 3 Dec 1927. Died Epsom, Surrey, 17 Mar 1965. Educ Winchester. Debut 1947.
SUSSEX (9) 1947–51.
HS 43 Sussex v Cambridge U, Worthing, 1951.
BB 2–8 Sussex v Worcs, Horsham, 1947.
Staff of *The Cricketer* 1950–55. Squash: England. Father A. G. Doggart (Cambridge U and M'sex); brother G. H. G. Doggart (Sussex and England).

DOGGART, George *Hubert* Graham
RHB, OB

Born Earls Court, London, 18 July 1925. Educ Winchester; King's C, Cambridge. Debut 1948.
CAMBRIDGE UNIVERSITY (35) 1948–50 (Blue 1948–50). Capt 1950.
SUSSEX (155) 1948–61. Cap 1949. Capt 1954.
ENGLAND (2) WI 1950.
TOUR E. W. Swanton's XI to W Indies 1955/56.
HST 29 E v WI, Old Trafford, 1950. HS 219* Cambridge U v Essex, Fenner's, 1949.
BB 4–50 Free Foresters v Cambridge U, Fenner's, 1951.
1000 RUNS (4) 2063 @ 45.84 in 1949.
RECORDS Scored 215* Cambridge U v Lancs, Fenner's, 1948 on debut – highest debut-score in Britain. During HS (above) added 429* for 2nd wkt with J. G. Dewes, Cambridge U record for any wkt.
President Cricket Council 1981/82. MCC committee 1976–81; MCC president 1981/82. Club: Middleton (Bognor). Headmaster King's S, Bruton. Father A. G. Doggart (Cambridge U and M'sex); brother A. P. Doggart (Sussex); son S. J. G. Doggart (Cambridge U).

DOGGART, Simon Jonathan Graham
LHB, ROB

Born Winchester, Hants, 8 Feb 1961. Educ Winchester; Magdalene C, Cambridge. Debut 1980.
CAMBRIDGE UNIVERSITY (35) 1980–83 (Blue 1980–83).
HS 70 Cambridge U v Notts, Fenner's, 1983.

BB 3–3 same match.
Father G. H. G. Doggart (Sussex and England); grandfather A. G. Doggart (Cambridge U and M'sex).

DOLDING, Desmond *Leonard*
RHB, LB

Born Ooregaum, 13 Dec 1922. Died Wembley, London, 23 Nov 1954. Debut 1950. P.
MCC (2) 1950–51.
MIDDLESEX (1) 1950.
HS 8 MCC v Cambridge U, Lord's, 1951.
BB 3–43 same match.
Soccer: Chelsea, Norwich City.

D'OLIVEIRA, Basil Lewis
RHB, RM/OB

Born Signal Hill, Cape Town, S Africa, 4 Oct 1931. Educ Zonnebloem C. Debut 1961/62. *Wisden* 1967.
WORCESTERSHIRE (275) 1964–80. Cap 1965. Benefit (£27,000) 1975.
ENGLAND (44) 1966–72. A 1968 (2), 1972 (5); WI 1966 (4), 1969 (3); NZ 1969 (3); I 1967 (2), 1971 (3); P 1967 (3), 1971 (3). *A 1970/71 (6); WI 1967/68 (5); NZ 1970/71 (2); P 1968/69 (3).*
OTHER TOURS Commonwealth XI to Rhodesia 1961/62, 1962/63. Commonwealth XI to Pakistan 1963/64. Worcs to Rhodesia 1964/65. Worcs to Jamaica 1965/66. Rest of World to W Indies 1966/67. International Wanderers to Rhodesia 1972/73.
HST 158 E v A, Oval, 1968. HS 227 Worcs v Yorks, Hull, 1974.
BBT 3–46 E v P, Headingley, 1971. BB 6–29 Worcs v Hants, Portsmouth, 1968.
1000 RUNS (9) 1691 @ 43.35 in 1965.
As Cape-coloured unable to play fc cricket in S Africa. Selection for MCC to S Africa 1968/69 led to tour being cancelled and was factor in ultimate cessation of Test matches with S Africa. Worcs coach 1980–. Awarded OBE 1969. Son D. B. D'Oliveira (Worcs); brother I. D'Oliveira (Leics).

D'OLIVEIRA, Damian Basil
RHB, RM/OB

Born Cape Town, S Africa, 19 Oct 1960. Educ Blessed Edward Oldcorne Sec S. Debut 1982.
WORCESTERSHIRE (49) 1982–.
HS 102 Worcs v M'sex, Worcester, 1983.
Father B. L. D'Oliveira (Worcs and England); uncle I. D'Oliveira (Leics).

D'OLIVEIRA, Ivan
————RHB, RM————

Born Cape Town, S Africa, 19 Mar 1941. Debut 1967.
LEICESTERSHIRE (1) 1967.
No runs, no wkts.
Brother B. L. D'Oliveira (Worcs and England); nephew D. B. D'Oliveira (Worcs).

DOLLERY, Horace Edgar (Tom)
————RHB, occ WK————

Born Reading, Berkshire, 14 Oct 1914. Educ Reading S. Debut 1933. *Wisden* 1952. *P from 1934.*
MINOR COUNTIES (2) 1933.
WARWICKSHIRE (413) 1934–55. Cap 1935. Benefit (£6362) 1949. Joint capt (with R. H. Maudsley) 1948; capt 1949–55.
N ZEALAND DOMESTIC Wellington (4) 1950/51.
ENGLAND (4) 1947–50. A 1948 (2); SA 1947 (1); WI 1950 (1).
HST 37 E v A, Lord's, 1948. HS 212 Warwicks v Leics, Edgbaston, 1952.
1000 RUNS (15) 2084 @ 47.36 in 1949.
RECORDS Added 220 for 6th wkt with J. Buckingham, Warwicks v Derbys, Derby, 1938 and 250 for 7th wkt with J. S. Ord, Warwicks v Kent, Maidstone, 1953, both county records.
Selected for MCC to India 1939/40 (cancelled owing to war). England selector 1957–58. Warwicks coach 1956–69. Berkshire 1931–33. Club: Moseley.

DOLLERY, Keith Robert
————RHB, RFM————

Born Cooroy, Queensland, Australia, 9 Dec 1924. Debut 1947/48. *P.*
AUSTRALIA DOMESTIC Queensland (2) 1947/48, Tasmania (3) 1950/51.
N ZEALAND DOMESTIC Auckland (2) 1949/50.
WARWICKSHIRE (73) 1951–56. Cap 1954.
HS 41 Warwicks v Som, Edgbaston, 1954.
BB 8–42 Warwicks v Sussex, Edgbaston, 1954.
Club: Stockport.

DONALD, Peter Colligan Graham
————LHB, RM/OB————

Born Bristol, 8 Aug 1957. Educ Sherborne; St John's C, Oxford. Debut 1978.
OXFORD UNIVERSITY (1) 1978.
HS 1 Oxford U v Yorks, The Parks, 1978.

DONALD, William Alexander
————RHB, RM————

Born Huntly, Aberdeenshire, Scotland, 29 July 1953. Debut 1978.
SCOTLAND (5) 1978–83.
HS 45 Scotland v Ireland, Downpatrick, 1983.
Aberdeenshire.

DONNELLAN, Rory Owen
————RHB————

Born Durban, S Africa, 20 June 1941. Died The Drakensberg, S Africa, 15 Jan 1977. Educ Durban HS; University of Natal; Magdalen C, Oxford (Rhodes Scholar). Debut 1963.
OXFORD UNIVERSITY (5) 1963.
HS 47 Oxford U v Lancs, The Parks, 1963.

DONNELLY, Martin Paterson
————LHB, occ SLA————

Born Ngaruawahia, N Zealand, 17 Oct 1917. Educ New Plymouth HS; Canterbury U; Worcester C, Oxford. Debut 1936/37. *Wisden* 1948.
N ZEALAND DOMESTIC Wellington (5) 1936/37–37/38, 1940/41, Canterbury (6) 1938/39–39/40, Governor-General's XI (1) 1960/61.
MIDDLESEX (1) 1946.
OXFORD UNIVERSITY (23) 1946–47 (Blue 1946–47). Capt 1947.
WARWICKSHIRE (20) 1948–50. Cap 1948.
NEW ZEALAND (7) 1937–49. *E 1937 (3); 1949 (4).*
OTHER TOUR N Zealand to Australia 1937/38.
HST 206 NZ v E, Lord's, 1949. HS 208* MCC v Yorks, Scarborough, 1948.
BB 4–32 N Zealanders v Sussex, Hove, 1937.
1000 RUNS (5) 2287 @ 61.81 in England 1949.
Clubs: Taranaki, Smethwick, Castleton Moor. Rugby: Oxford U, Blackheath, England (1).

DOOLAND, Bruce
————RHB, LBG————

Born Adelaide, S Australia, 1 Nov 1923. Died Adelaide, S Australia, 8 Sept 1980. Educ Adelaide HS. Debut 1945/46. *Wisden* 1955. *P.*
AUSTRALIA DOMESTIC South Australia (29) 1945/46–57/58.
NOTTINGHAMSHIRE (140) 1953–57. Cap 1953. Benefit (£2991) 1957.
AUSTRALIA (3) 1946/47–47/48. E 1946/47 (2); I 1947/48 (1).
TOURS Australia to N Zealand 1945/46.

Commonwealth XI to India and Ceylon 1950/51. C. G. Howard's XI to India 1956/57.
HST 29 A v E, Adelaide, 1946/47. HS 115* Notts v Sussex, Worthing, 1957.
BBT 4–69 A v E, Melbourne, 1946/47. BB 8–20 Notts v Worcs, Trent Bridge, 1956.
1000 RUNS (2) 1604 @ 28.64 in 1957.
100 WKTS (5) 196 @ 15.48 in 1954.
DOUBLE (2) 1954 (1012 runs, 196 wkts), 1957 (1604 runs, 141 wkts).
Returned 16–83 match (8–39, 8–44) Notts v Essex, Trent Bridge, 1954; 15–193 match (7–83, 8–110) Notts v Kent, Gravesend, 1956. Match double, Notts v Sussex, Worthing, 1957: 115* and 4–54, 6–48.
Club: East Lancs. Baseball: Australia.

DORRELL, Philip George
————RHB————

Born Worcester, 6 Dec 1914. Educ Bromsgrove S. Debut 1946.
WORCESTERSHIRE (1) 1946.
HS 1 Worcs v Northants, Northampton, 1946.

DOSHI, Dilip Rasiklal
————LHB, SLA————

Born Rajkot, India, 22 Dec 1947. Educ J. J. Ajmera HS, Calcutta; St Xavier's C; Calcutta U. Debut 1968/69.
INDIA DOMESTIC Bengal 1968/69–. Capt 1978/79, 1981/82.
NOTTINGHAMSHIRE (44) 1973–78. Cap 1977.
WARWICKSHIRE (43) 1980–81. Cap 1980.
INDIA (33) 1979/80–83/84. E 1979/80 (1), 1981/82 (6); A 1979/80 (6); P 1979/80 (6), 1983/84 (1); SL 1982/83 (1). *E 1982 (3); A 1980/81 (3); NZ 1980/81 (2); P 1982/83 (4).*
OTHER TOUR Indian Universities to Ceylon 1970/71.
HST 20 I v P, Kanpur, 1979/80. HS 44 Bengal v Delhi, Calcutta, 1979/80.
BBT 6–103 I v A, Madras, 1979/80. BB 7–29 (11–59 match) Bengal v Assam, Nowgong, 1970/71.
100 WKTS (1) 101 @ 26.73 in 1980 (debut season for Warwicks).
Hertfordshire 1976, Northumberland 1979.

DOUGHTY, David George
————LHB, SLA————

Born Chiswick, London, 9 Nov 1937. Debut 1963.
SOMERSET (17) 1963–64.
HS 22 Som v Australians, Taunton, 1964.

BB 6–58 Som v Derbys, Weston-super-Mare, 1963.
Clubs: Beddington, Werneth.

DOUGHTY, Richard James
—RHB, RFM—

Born Bridlington, Yorks, 17 Nov 1960. Educ Scarborough C. Debut 1981.
GLOUCESTERSHIRE (14) 1981–.
HS 32* Glos v Worcs, Bristol, 1983.
BB 6–43 Glos v Glam, Bristol, 1982.

DOUGLAS-HOME, Andrew
—LHB, RM—

Born Galashiels, Berwickshire, Scotland, 14 May 1950. Educ Eton; Christ Church C, Oxford. Debut 1970.
OXFORD UNIVERSITY (4) 1970.
HS 23 Oxford U v Notts, The Parks, 1970.
BB 3–71 Oxford U v Warwicks, The Parks, 1970.
Clubs: Butterflies, St Boswell's, Coldstream, Borderers, Arabs. Uncle former Prime Minister Rt Hon. Sir Alexander Douglas-Home (M'sex, as Lord Dunglass).

DOUGLAS-PENNANT, Simon
—RHB, LFM—

Born Glasgow, Scotland, 28 June 1938. Educ Eton; Clare C, Cambridge. Debut 1959.
CAMBRIDGE UNIVERSITY (35) 1959–61 (Blue 1959).
HS 14* Cambridge U v M'sex, Fenner's, 1960.
BB 7–56 Cambridge U v Free Foresters, Fenner's, 1959.

DOVEY, Raymond Randall
—LHB, OB/RM—

Born Chislehurst, Kent, 18 July 1920. Died Tunbridge Wells, Kent, 27 Dec 1974. Educ Eltham C. Debut 1938. *P.*
KENT (249) 1938–54. Cap 1946. Benefit (£3536) 1954.
TOUR Commonwealth XI to India and Ceylon 1950/51.
HS 65* Kent v Northants, Dover, 1951.
BB 8–23 Kent v Surrey, Oval, 1950.
100 WKTS (1) 102 @ 25.48 in 1950. Dorset 1955–59. Professional coach Sherborne S 1955–65. Professional coach and school-shop proprietor Tonbridge 1965–74.

DOW, William David Fraser
—RHB, RFM—

Born Glasgow, Scotland, 27 Nov 1933. Educ St Aloysius Academy, Glasgow. Debut 1956. *P.*
SCOTLAND (11) 1956–67.
ESSEX (2) 1958–59.
HS 18 Scotland v Warwicks, Edgbaston, 1956.
BB 6–56 Scotland v Ireland, Dublin, 1964.
Cumberland 1956–58. Club: Clydesdale (Scotland). Rugby: West of Scotland.

DOWDING, Alan Lorimer
—RHB—

Born Adelaide, S Australia, 4 Apr 1929. Educ St Peter's C, Adelaide; Adelaide U; Balliol C, Oxford. Debut 1951.
OXFORD UNIVERSITY (33) 1951–53 (Blue 1952–53). Capt 1953.
HS 105 Oxford U v Notts, The Parks, 1951.
Club: I Zingari. Soccer: Blue.

DOWELL, Alistair McQueen
—RHB, RFM—

Born Kinross, Ayrshire, Scotland, 17 May 1920. Educ Kinross Sec S. Debut 1951.
SCOTLAND (3) 1951–55.
HS 5 Scotland v Lancs, Old Trafford, 1955.
BB 2–51 Scotland v Worcs, Dundee, 1951.
Club: Clackmannan County.

DOWLING, Graham Thorne
—RHB—

Born Christchurch, N Zealand, 4 Mar 1937. Educ St Andrews C, Christchurch. Debut 1958/59.
N ZEALAND DOMESTIC Canterbury (58) 1958/59–71/72.
NEW ZEALAND (39) 1962/63–71/72. E 1962/63 (3), 1970/71 (2); I 1967/68 (4); SA 1963/64 (1); WI 1968/69 (3); P 1964/65 (2). *E 1965 (3), 1969 (3); SA 1961/62 (4); WI 1971/72 (2); I 1964/65 (4), 1969/70 (3); P 1964/65 (2), 1969/70 (3).* Capt 19.
OTHER TOURS N Zealand to Australia 1961/62, 1969/70, 1970/71. Prime Minister's XI v President's XI, Bombay, 1967/68 (relief match).
HST 239 NZ v I, Christchurch, 1967/68.
HS as above.
BB 3–100 N Zealanders v Natal, Pietermaritzburg, 1961/62.
MCC Hon. member.

DOWNEND, Richard Hugh
—RHB, RM—

Born Manchester, 19 Jan 1945. Debut 1972.
MINOR COUNTIES (1) 1972.
HS 5 Minor Counties v Australians, Stoke on Trent, 1972.
Staffordshire 1964–77. Clubs: Audley, Bignall End, Norton, Longton.

DOWNER, Harry Rodney
—RHB—

Born Southampton, 19 Oct 1915. Educ King Edward VI S, Southampton. Debut 1946.
HAMPSHIRE (2) 1946.
HS 4 Hants v M'sex, Lord's, 1946.
Club: Old Edwardians. Lives in Canada.

DOWNTON, George Charles
—RHB, WK—

Born Sidcup, Kent, 1 Nov 1928. Debut 1948. *P.*
KENT (8) 1948.
MCC (2) 1957–59.
HS 20 MCC v Cambridge U, Lord's, 1957.
Clubs: Orpington, Sevenoaks Vine. Son P. R. Downton (Kent, M'sex and England).

DOWNTON, Paul Rupert
—RHB, WK—

Born Farnborough, Kent, 4 Apr 1957. Educ Sevenoaks S; Exeter U. Debut 1977.
KENT (45) 1977–79. Cap 1979.
MIDDLESEX (94) 1980–. Cap 1981.
ENGLAND (10) 1980/81–84. A 1981 (1); WI 1984 (5); SL 1984 (1). *WI 1980/81 (3).*
OTHER TOURS England to Pakistan and N Zealand 1977/78. Middlesex to Zimbabwe 1980/81.
HST 56 E v WI, Edgbaston, 1984.
HS 90* M'sex v Derbys, Uxbridge, 1980.
Father G.C. Downton (Kent).

DRAFFAN, Nigel Gordon Helm
—RHB—

Born Nakuru, Kenya, 1 Sept 1950. Educ Malvern; Emmanuel C, Cambridge. Debut 1971.
CAMBRIDGE UNIVERSITY (4) 1971–72.
HS 29 Cambridge U v Glam, Pontypridd, 1971.
Clubs: The Grannies, Old Malvernians, Rickling Green.

DREDGE, Colin Herbert
——————LHB, RMF——————

Born Frome, Som, 4 Aug 1954. Educ Oakfield S, Frome. Debut 1976.
SOMERSET (160) 1976–. Cap 1978.
HS 56★ Som v Yorks, Harrogate, 1977.
BB 6–37 Som v Glos, Bristol, 1981.
Club: Frome.

DRING, Clive Frederick
——————RHB——————

Born Shooters Hill, Kent, 30 June 1934. Debut 1955. P.
KENT (1) 1955.
HS 8 Kent v Lancs, Old Trafford, 1955.

DRUMMOND, Duncan Weir
——————RHB, RM——————

Born Greenock, Scotland, 12 May 1923. Died Greenock, Scotland, 17 May 1985. Educ Merchiston C. Debut 1951.
SCOTLAND (17) 1951–61.
HS 33 Scotland v MCC, Greenock, 1961.
BB 4–73 Scotland v Worcs, Worcester, 1952.
Club: Greenock.

DRYBROUGH, Colin David
——————RHB, SLA——————

Born Melbourne, Australia, 31 Aug 1938. Educ Highgate; Worcester C, Oxford. Debut 1958.
MIDDLESEX (92) 1958–64. Cap 1962. Capt 1963–64.
OXFORD UNIVERSITY (38) 1960–62 (Blue 1960–62). Capt 1961–62.
MCC (1) 1967.
HS 88 Oxford U v Australians, The Parks, 1961.
BB 7–35 Oxford U v Leics, The Parks, 1961.
Club: Hornsey.

D'SOUZA, Antao
——————RHB, RM/OB——————

Born Goa, India, 1 Jan 1938. Educ St Patrick's. Debut 1956/57.
PAKISTAN DOMESTIC Karachi, Peshawar, Pakistan International Airlines, 1956/57–66/67.
PAKISTAN (6) 1958/59–62. E 1961/62 (2); WI 1958/59 (1). *E 1962 (3).*
OTHER TOURS Pakistan Eaglets to England 1963. PIA to E Africa 1964.
HST 23★ P v E, Edgbaston, 1962. HS 45 PIA v Commissioner's XI, Peshawar, 1960/61.

BBT 5–112 P v E, Karachi, 1961/62. BB 7–38 Governor's XI v MCC, Lyallpur, 1961/62.
Brother M. D'Souza (Karachi).

DUCKWORTH, Christopher Anthony Russell
——————RHB, WK——————

Born Que Que, Rhodesia, 22 Mar 1933. Educ Chaplin HS, Gwelo; Natal U. Debut 1952/53.
S AFRICA DOMESTIC Natal 1952/53–53/54, Rhodesia 1954/55–62/63.
SOUTH AFRICA (2) E 1956/57.
TOURS S Africa to England 1955, 1960.
HST 13 SA v E, Johannesburg, 1956/57.
HS 158 S Africans v Northants, Northampton, 1955.
Club: Salisbury.

DUCKWORTH, George
——————RHB, WK——————

Born Warrington, Lancs, 9 May 1901. Died Warrington, Lancs, 6 Jan 1966. Educ Warrington GS. Debut 1923. *Wisden* 1929. P.
LANCASHIRE (424) 1923–38. Cap 1924. Benefit (£1257) 1934.
NORTH V SOUTH (1) 1947.
ENGLAND (24) 1924–36. A 1930 (5); SA 1924 (1), 1929 (4), 1935 (1); WI 1928 (1); I 1936 (3). *A 1928/29 (5); SA 1930/31 (3); NZ 1932/33 (1).*
OTHER TOUR MCC to Australasia 1936/37.
HST 39★ E v A, Sydney, 1928/29. HS 75 Lancs v Leics, Liverpool, 1929.
RECORD 921 dismissals for Lancs, county record.
107 Dismissals (77 ct, 30 st) 1928. 1090 dismissals (751 ct, 339 st) in fc career.
Manager Commonwealth XI to India 1949/50, 1950/51, 1953/54. Scorer/baggage-master MCC to Australia 1954/55, 1958/59; MCC to S Africa 1956/57. Cheshire 1939. MCC Hon. member.

DUDHIA, Magbul Hussein Ebrahim Mahomed (Mac)
——————RHB, RM——————

Born Lusaka, Zambia, 24 Aug 1954. Debut 1980/81.
ZIMBABWE 1980/81–82.
TOUR Zimbabwe to England 1982.
No runs.
BB 2–13 Zimbabwe v Worcs, Worcester, 1982.

DUDLESTON, Barry
——————RHB, SLA——————

Born Bebington, Cheshire, 16 July 1945. Educ Stockport S. Debut 1966.
LEICESTERSHIRE (262) 1966–80. Cap 1969. Benefit (£25,000) 1980.
GLOUCESTERSHIRE (9) 1981–83.
S AFRICA DOMESTIC Rhodesia 1976/77–1979/80.
HS 202 Leics v Derbys, Leicester, 1979.
BB 4–6 Leics v Surrey, Leicester, 1972.
1000 RUNS (8) 1374 @ 31.22 in 1970.
RECORDS During HS (above) put on 390 for 1st wkt with J. F. Steele, and added 206 for 7th wkt with J. Birkenshaw, Leics v Kent, Canterbury, 1969; both county records.
Scored 99 v Oxford U on Glos debut, 1981. Glos coach 1981–83. Fc umpire 1983–.

DUDLEY-JONES, Robert David Lewis
——————RHB, RM——————

Born Bridgend, Glam, 25 May 1952. Educ Millfield; Cardiff C of Education. Debut 1972.
GLAMORGAN (5) 1972–73.
HS 5 Glam v Worcs, Cardiff, 1973.
BB 4–31 Glam v Hants, Portsmouth, 1972.

DUDMAN, Leonard Charles
——————RHB——————

Born Dundee, Scotland, 4 Aug 1933. Educ Perth Academy. Debut 1955.
SCOTLAND (35) 1955–68.
HS 161 Scotland v Warwicks, Edgbaston, 1956.
Perthshire.

DUFF, Alan Robert
——————RHB, LBG——————

Born Kinver, Staffordshire, 12 Jan 1938. Educ Radley; Lincoln C, Oxford. Debut 1959.
OXFORD UNIVERSITY (24) 1959–61 (Blue 1960–61).
WORCESTERSHIRE (6) 1960–61.
FREE FORESTERS (1) 1964.
MCC (3) 1964–68.
HS 55★ Oxford U v Warwicks, The Parks, 1959.
BB 4–27 MCC v Ireland, Dublin, 1966.
Assistant manager England Youth to W Indies 1972/73.

DUFFIELD, John
————RHB, RFM————

Born Worthing, Sussex, 12 Aug 1917.
Died Worthing, Sussex, 7 Sept 1956.
Debut 1938. *P.*
SUSSEX (16) 1938–47.
HS 60* Sussex v Oxford U, Eastbourne,
1939.
BB 5–38 Sussex v Derbys, Derby, 1939.
Club: Worthing.

DUFFY, Gerard Andrew
Anthony
————RHB, LB————

Born Dublin, Ireland, 4 Nov 1930. Educ
St Mary's C, Rathmines. Debut 1953.
IRELAND (16) 1953–73.
HS 55* Ireland v Scotland, Paisley, 1960.
BB 3–8 Ireland v Scotland, Cork, 1961.
Club: Leinster.

DUMBRILL, Richard
————RHB, RM————

Born London, 19 Nov 1938. Educ
Durban HS; Natal U. Debut
1960/61.
S AFRICA DOMESTIC Natal 1960/61–1966/
67, Transvaal 1967/68.
SOUTH AFRICA (5) 1965–66/67. A 1966/
67 (2). *E 1965 (3).*
HST 36 SA v E, Oval, 1965. HS 94
Natal v E Province, Port Elizabeth,
1963/64.
BBT 4–30, SA v E, Lord's, 1965. BB 5–34
(10–75 match) Transvaal v NE Transvaal, Johannesburg, 1967/68.

DUNHAM, Norman Leonard
————RHB, RM————

Born Quorn, Leics, 9 Dec 1925. Debut
1949. *P.*
LEICESTERSHIRE (1) 1949.
HS 12* Leics v Hants, Leicester, 1949.

DUNKELS, Paul Renton
————LHB, RM————

Born Marylebone, London, 26 Nov
1947. Educ Harrow. Debut 1971.
WARWICKSHIRE (1) 1971.
MINOR COUNTIES (1) 1971.
SUSSEX (1) 1972.
HS 3* Sussex v Cambridge U, Fenner's,
1972.
BB 2–60 same match.
Devon 1969–75. Club: Torquay. 6 ft 9
in tall.

DUNNING, Michael Lindsay
————RHB————

Born Windsor, Berkshire, 11 Mar 1941.
Educ Eton. Debut 1962.
COMBINED SERVICES (2) 1962–64.
HS 85 Combined Services v Cambridge
U, Fenner's, 1962.
Dorset 1964. Member I Zingari.

DUNSTAN, Malcolm Stephen
Thomas
————RHB, RM————

Born Redruth, Cornwall, 14 Oct 1950.
Debut 1971.
GLOUCESTERSHIRE (12) 1971–74.
HS 52 Glos v Warwicks, Edgbaston,
1974.
Scored 201* Glos 2nd XI v Glam 2nd
XI, Bristol, 1974. Cornwall 1969–70,
1975– (capt 1978–81). Club: Helston.

DURACK, John Philip
————RHB, LB————

Born Perth, W Australia, 18 May 1956.
Educ Christ Church GS, Perth; U of W
Australia; Magdalen C, Oxford. Debut
1980.
OXFORD UNIVERSITY (7) 1980.
HS 45 Oxford U v Som, The Parks, 1980.

DURDEN-SMITH, Neil
————RHB, OB————

Born Richmond, Surrey, 18 Aug 1933.
Educ Aldenham. Debut 1961.
COMBINED SERVICES (3) 1961.
MCC (1) 1967.
HS 50 Combined Services v Notts, Trent
Bridge, 1961.
Clubs: Free Foresters, XL Club,
I Zingari, Incogniti, Lords and
Commons. Chairman Lord's Taverners
1980–82. Formerly Regular Naval Off-
icer. Currently broadcaster and
chairman Sports Sponsorship Interna-
tional Ltd. Wife Judith Chalmers
(broadcaster).

DURLEY, Anthony William
————RHB, WK————

Born Ilford, Essex, 30 Sept 1933. Educ
SW Essex Technical S. Debut 1957. *P.*
ESSEX (5) 1957.
HS 16 Essex v Derbys, Burton upon
Trent, 1957.
Bedfordshire 1960–76. Clubs: Buck-
hurst Hill, Luton Town.

DUROSE, Anthony Jack
————RHB, RFM————

Born Dukinfield, Cheshire, 5 Oct 1944.
Educ Hyde GS. Debut 1964.
NORTHAMPTONSHIRE (70) 1964–69.
HS 30 Northants v W Indians,
Northhampton, 1966 and v Leics,
Northampton, 1967 and v Lancs, Black-
pool, 1968.
BB 7–23 Northants v Leics, Peter-
borough, 1968.
Cheshire 1963–64, Bedfordshire 1980–.
Professional: Walsall.

DUTHIE, Peter Gordon
————RHB, RM————

Born Greenock, Scotland, 16 Apr 1959.
Debut 1984.
SCOTLAND (1) 1984.
HS 34 Scotland v Ireland, Glasgow,
1984.
Club: Greenock.

DUTTON, Richard Stuart
————RHB, RM————

Born Liverpool, 24 Nov 1959. Educ
Wrekin C; Fitzwilliam C, Cambridge.
Debut 1981.
CAMBRIDGE UNIVERSITY (6) 1981–82.
HS 7* Cambridge U v Northants,
Fenner's, 1981.

DYE, John Cooper James
————RHB, LFM————

Born Gillingham, Kent, 24 July 1942.
Educ Highfield GS. Debut 1962. *P.*
KENT (149) 1962–71. Cap 1966.
NORTHAMPTONSHIRE (112) 1972–77.
Cap 1972.
S AFRICA DOMESTIC Eastern Province
1972/73.
HS 29* Northants v Worcs, Northamp-
ton, 1972 and v Kent, Maidstone,
1976.
BB 7–45 Northants v Essex, Westcliff,
1973.
Bedfordshire 1978–79. Club: Dudley.

DYER, Alan Willoughby
————RHB, WK————

Born Winchester, Hants, 8 July 1945.
Educ Mill Hill; St Catherine's C, Oxford. Debut 1965.
OXFORD UNIVERSITY (25) 1965–66 (Blue
1965–66).
HS 67 Oxford U v Lancs, The Parks,
1966.

DYER, David Dennis
—RHB, WK—

Born Durban, S Africa, 3 Dec 1946.
Educ Michaelhouse; Natal U. Debut
1965/66.
S AFRICA DOMESTIC South African
Universities 1965/66–66/67, Natal B
1967/68–68/69 (capt 7), Natal 1969/
70–74/75, Transvaal 1975/76–81/82
(capt 1976/77–81/82).
TOUR S African Universities to England
1967.
HS 196* Natal B v Griqualand West,
Kimberley, 1969/70.
Father D. V. Dyer (Natal and S Africa);
brother G. D. Dyer (W Province and
Natal).

DYER, Dennis Victor
—RHB—

Born Durban, S Africa, 2 May 1914.
Debut 1939/40.
S AFRICA DOMESTIC Natal 1939/40–48/
49.
SOUTH AFRICA (3) *E 1947.*
HST 62 SA v E, Old Trafford, 1947. HS
185 Natal v W Province, Durban, 1939/
40 (on fc debut).
Life president Natal CA. Sons D. D.
Dyer (Natal and Transvaal) and G. D.
Dyer (W Province and Natal).

DYER, Robin Ian Henry Benbow
—RHB—

Born Hertford, 22 Dec 1958. Educ
Wellington C; Durham U. Debut 1981.
WARWICKSHIRE (34) 1981–.
HS 106* Warwicks v Glam, Cardiff,
1984.
1000 RUNS (1) 1187 @ 34.91 in 1984.

DYMOCK, Geoffrey
—RHB, LFM—

Born Maryborough, Queensland,
Australia, 21 July 1945. Debut 1971/72.
AUSTRALIA DOMESTIC Queensland (87)
1971/72–81/82.
AUSTRALIA (21) 1973/74–79/80. E 1974/
75 (1), 1978/79 (3), 1979/80 (3); WI
1979/80 (2); NZ 1973/74 (1); P 1978/79
(1). *NZ 1973/74 (2); I 1979/80 (5); P
1979/80 (3).*
OTHER TOURS Australia to England 1977,
1980.
HST 31* A v I, Delhi, 1979/80. HS 101*
Queensland v S Australia, Brisbane,
1981/82.
BBT 7–67 A v I, Kanpur, 1979/80
(12–166 match). BB as above.
Professional: Milnrow. Club: North
Suburbs (Brisbane).

DYSON, Arnold Herbert
—RHB—

Born Halifax, Yorks, 10 July 1905. Died
Goldsborough, Yorks, 7 June 1978.
Debut 1926. *P.*
GLAMORGAN (412) 1926–48. Cap 1929.
Benefit 1939. Testimonial 1948.
Sir J. Cahn's XI v N Zealand XI,
Wellington, 1938/39, while coaching in
N Zealand.
HS 208 Glam v Surrey, Oval, 1932.
1000 RUNS (10) 1885 @ 40.98 in 1938.
305 consecutive championship app-
earances 1930–47.
Clubs: Neath, Lidget Green.
Professional coach Oundle, 1948 until
retirement.

DYSON, Edward *Martin*
—RHB—

Born Wakefield, Yorks, 21 Oct 1935.
Educ Queen Elizabeth GS, Wakefield;
Keble C, Oxford. Debut 1958.

OXFORD UNIVERSITY (26) 1958–60 (Blue
1958).
MCC (1) 1968.
HS 68* Oxford U v Free Foresters, The
Parks, 1960.

DYSON, Jack
—RHB, OB—

Born Oldham, Lancs, 8 July 1934.
Debut 1954. *P.*
LANCASHIRE (150) 1954–64. Cap 1956.
HS 118* Lancs v Scotland, Paisley, 1956.
BB 7–83 Lancs v Som, Taunton, 1960.
1000 RUNS (1) 1087 @ 27.17 in 1956.
RECORD When Lancs beat Leics by 10
wkts, Old Trafford, 1956, Dyson (75*
and 31*) and A. Wharton only Lancs
batsmen to go to wkt (166–0 dec and 66
for 0); only such instance in English fc
cricket.
Clubs: Werneth, Newcastle and Hartshill. Soccer: Manchester City and Oldham Athletic.

DYSON, John
—RHB—

Born Kogarah, NSW, Australia, 11
June 1954. Debut 1975/76.
AUSTRALIA DOMESTIC New South Wales
(68) 1975/76–.
AUSTRALIA (27) 1977/78–82/83. E 1982/
83 (5); WI 1981/82 (2); NZ 1980/81 (3);
I 1977/78 (5), 1980/81 (3). *E 1981 (5);
NZ 1981/82 (3); P 1982/83 (3).*
OTHER TOURS Australia to England 1980.
HST 127* A v WI, Sydney, 1981/82. HS
241 NSW v S Australia, Adelaide, 1983/
84.
Professional: Haslingden. Clubs:
Sutherland, Randwick (Sydney).

E

EAGAR, Edward *Desmond* Russell
RHB, occ SLA

Born Cheltenham, Glos, 8 Dec 1917. Died Kingsbridge, Devon, 13 Sept 1977. Educ Cheltenham C; Brasenose C, Oxford. Debut 1935 (while still at school).
GLOUCESTERSHIRE (21) 1935–39.
OXFORD UNIVERSITY (23) 1938–39 (Blue 1939).
HAMPSHIRE (311) 1946–57. Cap 1946. Capt-secretary 1946–57; secretary 1958–77.
MCC (1) 1958.
TOUR Duke of Norfolk's XI to Jamaica 1956/57.
HS 158* Hants v Oxford U, The Parks, 1954.
BB 6–66 Oxford U v Sussex, Eastbourne, 1939.
1000 RUNS (6) 1200 @ 26.66 in 1949.
366 catches in fc career.
Assistant manager MCC to Australasia 1958/59. Journalist. Joint author *Hampshire County Cricket* (1957). Son Patrick Eagar (cricket photographer); nephew M. A. Eagar (Oxford U and Glos).

EAGAR, Michael Anthony
RHB

Born Kensington, London, 20 Mar 1934. Educ Rugby; Worcester C, Oxford. Debut 1956.
OXFORD UNIVERSITY (51) 1956–59 (Blue 1956–59).
GLOUCESTERSHIRE (6) 1957–61.
MCC (1) 1966.
HS 125 Oxford U v Free Foresters, The Parks, 1956.
Ireland (non-fc match). Hockey: Oxford U and Ireland. Teacher Eton to 1964; subsequently Shrewsbury. Uncle E. D. R. Eagar (Glos, Oxford U and Hants); cousin Patrick Eagar (cricket photographer).

EAGLESTONE, James Thomas
LHB

Born Paddington, London, 24 July 1923. Debut 1947. *P.*
MIDDLESEX (9) 1947.
GLAMORGAN (50) 1948–49. Cap 1948.
HS 77 MCC v Surrey, Lord's, 1947.

EALHAM, Alan George Ernest
RHB, OB

Born Willesborough, Ashford, Kent, 30 Aug 1944. Educ Folkestone Technical S. Debut 1966.
KENT (305) 1966–82. Cap 1970. Capt 1978–80. Benefit 1982.
HS 153 Kent v Worcs, Canterbury, 1979.
1000 RUNS (3) 1363 @ 34.94 in 1971.
Took five catches in field in one inns, Kent v Glos, Folkestone, 1966, all at either long-off or long-on and all off bowling of D. L. Underwood.

EAMES, David George Roniel
RHB, RM

Born London Colney, Hertfordshire, 15 Apr 1937. Educ London Colney Sec Modern S. Debut 1958. *P.*
MCC (1) 1958.
HS 14 MCC v Oxford U, Lord's, 1958.
Clubs: St Albans, Wheathampstead, Ballito.

EARL, Kenneth John
RHB, RFM

Born Low Fell, Gateshead, 10 Nov 1925. Educ Hemsworth GS. Debut 1950.
MINOR COUNTIES (2) 1950.
HS 4 Minor Counties v MCC, Lord's, 1950.
BB 5–75 same match.
Northumberland 1948–65. Clubs: County Club (Northumberland), Morpeth. Professional: Gateshead Fell.

EARLS-DAVIES, Michael Richard Gratwycke
LHB, RM

Born Hampstead, London, 21 Feb 1921. Educ Sherborne; Corpus Christi C, Cambridge. Debut 1947.
CAMBRIDGE UNIVERSITY (5) 1947.
SOMERSET (1) 1950.
HS 4 Cambridge U v Som, Bath, 1947 and Som v Worcs, Worcester, 1950.
BB 4–87 Cambridge U v Glos, Fenner's, 1947.
Club: Arabs. Grandfather Dr W. G. Heasman (Sussex and friend of W. G. Grace).

EARNSHAW, Richard Oliver
RHB, RFM

Born Huddersfield, Yorks, 8 Jan 1939. Died Westminster, London, 28 July 1963. Debut 1960.
COMBINED SERVICES (2) 1960–61.
HS 9 Combined Services v S Africans, Portsmouth, 1960.
Regular Serviceman REME.

EAST, David Edward
RHB, WK

Born Hackney, London, 27 July 1959. Educ Hackney Downs S; U of E Anglia. Debut 1981.
ESSEX (90) 1981–. Cap 1982.
HS 91 Essex v Sussex, Hove, 1983.

EAST, Raymond Eric
RHB, SLA

Born Manningtree, Essex, 20 June 1947. Educ East Bergholt S, Suffolk. Debut 1965.
ESSEX (405) 1965–84. Cap 1967. Benefit (£29,000) 1978.
TOURS D. H. Robins' XI to S Africa 1973/74. Overseas XI to India 1980/81.
HS 113 Essex v Hants, Chelmsford, 1976.
BB 8–30 Essex v Notts, Ilford, 1977.
Took 15–115 match Essex v Warwicks, Leyton, 1968.
Author *A Funny Turn* (1983).

EASTER, John Nicholas Cave
————RHB, RM————

Born Shawford, Hants, 17 Dec 1945. Educ St Edward's, Oxford; Christ Church C, Oxford. Debut 1966.
OXFORD UNIVERSITY (28) 1966–68 (Blue 1967–68).
HS 14 Oxford U v Glos, The Parks, 1967.
BB 5–62 Oxford U v Northants, The Parks, 1967.
Club: Sutton (Surrey).

EATO, Alwyn
————RHB, RFM————

Born Duckmanton, nr Bolsover, Derbys, 15 Feb 1929. Debut 1950. P.
DERBYSHIRE (25) 1950–55.
HS 44 Derbys v Scotland, Buxton, 1954.
BB 5–14 Derbys v Leics, Burton upon Trent, 1951.
Clubs: Thongsbridge, Camborne.

EATON, Vivian *John*
————RHB, WK————

Born Steyning, Sussex, 19 June 1902. Died Brighton, 31 Dec 1972. Debut 1926. P.
SUSSEX (36) 1926–46. Cap.
HS 44 Sussex v Oxford U, Eastbourne, 1939.
Club: Worthing.

ECKERSLEY, Ronald
————RHB, LFM————

Born Bingley, Yorks, 4 Sept 1925. Educ Bingley GS; Emmanuel C, Cambridge. Debut 1945.
YORKSHIRE (1) 1945.
HS 9* Yorks v RAF, Scarborough, 1945. War-time Blue 1945. Army. Clubs: Keighley, Accrington.

EDBROOKE, Roger Michael
————RHB————

Born Bristol, 30 Dec 1960. Educ Queen Elizabeth's Hospital, Bristol; Hertford C, Oxford. Debut 1982.
OXFORD UNIVERSITY (11) 1982–84 (Blue 1984).
HS 84* Oxford U v Glam, Swansea, 1982 (1st inns of debut match).
Soccer: Blue.

EDDINGTON, Roderick Ian
————LHB, SLA————

Born Perth, W Australia, 2 Jan 1950. Educ Christ Church GS, Perth; U of W

Australia; Lincoln C, Oxford. Debut 1975.
OXFORD UNIVERSITY (8) 1975–76.
HS 24 Oxford U v M'sex, The Parks, 1976.
BB 3–48 Oxford U v Northants, The Parks, 1976.
Australian Rules: All-Australian Universities.

EDGAR, Bruce Adrian
————LHB, occ WK————

Born Wellington, N Zealand, 23 Nov 1956. Debut 1975/76.
N ZEALAND DOMESTIC Wellington (46) 1975/76–.
NEW ZEALAND (27) 1978–83/84. E 1983/84 (3); A 1981/82 (3); WI 1979/80 (3); I 1980/81 (3); P 1978/79 (3); SL 1982/83 (2). *E 1978 (3), 1983 (4); A 1980/81 (3).*
HST 161 NZ v A, Auckland, 1981/82. HS as above.
Father A. J. Edgar (Wellington).

EDGE, Geoffrey Donald
————RHB, OB————

Born Eccles, Lancs, 12 Aug 1936. Educ Manchester GS; Caius C, Cambridge. Debut 1957.
CAMBRIDGE UNIVERSITY (2) 1957.
HS 33 Cambridge U v M'sex, Fenner's, 1957.

EDMEADES, Brian Ernest Arthur
————RHB, RM————

Born Matlock, Derbys, 17 Sept 1941. Educ Mark House S, Walthamstow. Debut 1961. P.
ESSEX (335) 1961–76. Cap 1965. Benefit (£12,000) 1975.
HS 163 Essex v Leics, Leyton, 1972.
BB 7–37 Essex v Glam, Leyton, 1966.
1000 RUNS (5) 1620 @ 35.21 in 1970.
100 WKTS (1) 106 @ 18.59 in 1966.

EDMONDS, James William
————RHB, LFM————

Born Smethwick, W Midlands, 4 June 1951. Educ Holly Lodge S, Warley. Debut 1975.
LANCASHIRE (1) 1975.
Did not bat.
BB 3–52 Lancs v Cambridge U, Fenner's, 1975.
Club: Mitchells and Butlers.

EDMONDS, Phillippe Henri
————RHB, SLA————

Born Lusaka, N Rhodesia, 8 Mar 1951. Educ Skinner's S, Tunbridge Wells; Cranbrook S; Fitzwilliam C, Cambridge. Debut 1971.
CAMBRIDGE UNIVERSITY (27) 1971–73 (Blue 1971–73). Capt 1973.
MIDDLESEX (217) 1971–. Cap 1974.
S AFRICA DOMESTIC Eastern Province 1975/76.
ENGLAND (23) 1975–83. A 1975 (2); NZ 1978 (3); 1983 (2); I 1979 (4), 1982 (3); *P 1978 (3). A 1978/79 (1); NZ 1977/78 (3); P 1977/78 (2).*
OTHER TOUR International Wanderers to S Africa 1975/76.
HST 64 E v I, Lord's, 1982. HS 142 M'sex v Glam, Swansea, 1984.
BBT 7–66 E v P, Karachi, 1977/78. BB 8–53 M'sex v Hants, Bournemouth, 1984.

EDMONDS, Roger Bertram
————RHB, RM/OB————

Born Birmingham, 2 Mar 1941. Educ Saltley GS; Loughborough C. Debut 1962. P.
WARWICKSHIRE (78) 1962–67.
HS 102* Warwicks v Scotland, Edgbaston, 1966.
BB 5–40 Warwicks v Derbys, Derby, 1963.
Clubs: Aston Unity, Moseley.

EDRICH, Brian Robert
————LHB, ROB————

Born Cantley, Norfolk, 18 Aug 1922. Debut 1947. P.
KENT (128) 1947–53. Cap 1949.
GLAMORGAN (52) 1954–56.
MINOR COUNTIES (1) 1967.
HS 193* Kent v Sussex, Tunbridge Wells, 1949.
BB 7–41 Kent v Hants, Southampton, 1949.
1000 RUNS (1) 1267 @ 26.39 in 1951.
RECORD During HS (above) added 161 for 9th wkt with F. Ridgway, county record. Oxfordshire 1966–70. Clubs: Maesteg, Merthyr, Hills Plymouth, Maesteg Celtic. Professional coach St Edward's, Oxford, 1964–65. Brothers E. H. Edrich (Lancs), G. A. Edrich (Lancs); W. J. Edrich (M'sex and England); cousin J. H. Edrich (Surrey and England).

EDRICH, Eric Harry
————RHB, WK————

Born Lingwood, Norfolk, 27 Mar 1914. Educ Brackendale S. Debut 1938

(Minor Counties). *P from 1946.*
LANCASHIRE (33) 1946–48. Cap 1948.
HS 121 Lancs v Yorks, Headingley, 1948.
Norfolk 1935–39, 1949–51. Brothers B. R. Edrich (Kent and Glam), G. A. Edrich (Lancs) and W. J. Edrich (M'sex and Lancs); cousin J. H. Edrich (Surrey and England).

EDRICH, Geoffrey Arthur
————————RHB————————

Born Lingwood, Norfolk, 13 July 1918.
Debut 1946. *P.*
LANCASHIRE (322) 1946–58. Cap 1946.
Benefit (£3500) 1955.
TOUR Commonwealth XI to India 1953/54.
HS 167* Lancs v Notts, Trent Bridge, 1954.
1000 RUNS (8) 2067 @ 41.34 in 1952.
Norfolk 1937–39, Cumberland 1960–62. Professional coach: Cheltenham 1962–65. Brothers B. R. Edrich (Kent and Glam), E. H. Edrich (Lancs) and W. J. Edrich (M'sex and England); cousin J. H. Edrich (Surrey and England).

EDRICH, John Hugh
————————LHB————————

Born Blofield, Norfolk, 21 June 1937.
Educ Brackendale S, Norwich. Debut 1956. *Wisden 1966. P.*
COMBINED SERVICES (4) 1956–57.
SURREY (410) 1958–78. Cap 1959.
Benefit (£10,551) 1968. Testimonial (£20,000) 1975. Capt 1973–77.
ENGLAND (77) 1963–76. A 1964 (3), 1968 (5), 1972 (5), 1975 (4); SA 1965 (1); WI 1963 (3), 1966 (1), 1969 (3), 1976 (2); NZ 1965 (1), 1969 (3), I 1967 (2), 1971 (3), 1974 (3); P 1971 (3), 1974 (3); *A 1965/66 (5), 1970/71 (6), 1974/75 (4); WI 1967/68 (5); NZ 1965/66 (3), 1970/71 (2), 1974/75 (2); I 1963/64 (2); P 1968/69 (3).* Capt 1.
OTHER TOURS Surrey to Rhodesia 1959/60. Commonwealth XI to S Africa 1962/63. D. H. Robins' XI to S Africa 1972/73, 1973/74.
HST 310* E v NZ, Headingley, 1965. HS as above.
1000 RUNS (19 + 2) 2482 @ 51.70 in 1962.
RECORDS Hit 57 boundaries in HS (above), most in Test inns. Inns of 310* highest against N Zealand, highest for England in post-war Tests and highest for England by left-hander. Scored nine consecutive fifties in 1965, best in England since G. E. Tyldesley's 10 in 1926. 5138 Test runs most by an English left-hander. 17th batsman to reach 100

centuries, when scored 101* Surrey v Derbys, Oval, 1977.
Scored centuries against every fc county except his own.
Norfolk 1954, 1979–80. Cousins B. R. Edrich (Kent and Glam), E. H. Edrich (Lancs), G. A. Edrich (Lancs) and W. J. Edrich (M'sex and England). MBE for services to cricket.

EDRICH, William John
————————RHB, RFM/OB————————

Born Lingwood, Norfolk, 26 Mar 1916.
Educ Brackendale S, Norwich. Debut 1934. *Wisden 1940. P until 1947.*
MINOR COUNTIES (3) 1934–36.
MCC (5) 1934–36.
MIDDLESEX (389) 1937–58. Cap 1937. Joint capt 1951–52; capt 1953–57.
ENGLAND (39) 1938–1954/55. A 1938 (4), 1948 (5), 1953 (3); SA 1947 (4), WI 1950 (2); NZ 1949 (4); I 1946 (1); P 1954 (1). *A 1946/47 (5), 1954/55 (4); SA 1938/39 (5); NZ 1946/47 (1).*
OTHER TOURS L. H. Tennyson's XI to India 1937/38. C. G. Howard's XI to India 1956/57.
HST 219 E v SA, Durban, 1938/39. HS 267* M'sex v Northants, Northampton, 1947.
BBT 4–68 E v I, Oval, 1946. BB 7–48 M'sex v Worcs, Worcester, 1946.
1000 RUNS (15) 3539 @ 80.43 in 1947.
RECORDS Added 370 for 3rd wkt with D. C. S. Compton, E v SA, Lord's, 1947, England Test record. 3539 runs in 1947, second to D. C. S. Compton's aggregate of runs (3816) for a season. 1000 runs by end of May 1938 (all scored at Lord's). Added 424* for 3rd wkt with D. C. S. Compton, M'sex v Som, Lord's, 1948, English fc record and highest at Lord's for any wkt.
Scored centuries against every fc county except his own. 526 catches in fc career.
Norfolk 1932–36, 1959–70. MCC Hon. member. Soccer: Tottenham Hotspur.
Brothers B. R. Edrich (Kent and Glam), E. H. Edrich (Lancs) and G. A. Edrich (Lancs); cousin J. H. Edrich (Surrey and England).

EDWARD, William Alfred
————————RHB, RM————————

Born Glasgow, Scotland, 19 June 1916.
Educ Hutcheson's GS. Debut 1947.
SCOTLAND (28) 1947–55.
HS 99 Scotland v Ireland, Perth, 1950.
BB 4–51 Scotland v Ireland, Dublin, 1955.
Club: Clydesdale.

EDWARDS, Aubrey Mansel Edward
————————RHB, RMF————————

Born Penycraig, Glam, 4 July 1918.
Debut 1947.
GLAMORGAN (1) 1947.
BB 2–34 Glam v Sussex, Hove, 1947.
No runs.
Club: Cowbridge. Lives in Canada.

EDWARDS, Gordon
————————LHB, ROB————————

Born Glapthorn, Northants, 17 Sept 1947. Educ Oundle; Nottingham U. Debut 1973.
NOTTINGHAMSHIRE (9) 1973.
HS 46* Notts v Worcs, Worcester, 1973.
BB 5–44 Notts v Derbys, Trent Bridge, 1973.

EDWARDS, Graham Neil
————————RHB, WK————————

Born Nelson, N Zealand, 27 May 1955.
Debut 1973/74.
N ZEALAND DOMESTIC Central Districts (66) 1973/74–81/82.
NEW ZEALAND (8) 1976/77–80/81. E 1977/78 (1); A 1976/77 (2); I 1980/81 (3). *E 1978 (2).*
OTHER TOURS N Zealand to Australia 1974/75.
HST 55 NZ v E, Auckland, 1977/78. HS 177* Central Districts v Wellington, Palmerston North, 1980/81.

EDWARDS, Herbert Charles
————————RHB, LB————————

Born Colley Gate, nr Halesowen, Staffs, 3 Dec 1913. Debut 1946.
WORCESTERSHIRE (1) 1946.
HS 10 Worcs v Lancs, Old Trafford, 1946.
Club: Old Hill.

EDWARDS, Michael John
————————RHB, OB————————

Born Balham, London, 1 Mar 1940.
Educ Alleyn's S; Christ's C, Cambridge. Debut 1960.
CAMBRIDGE UNIVERSITY (8) 1960–62.
SURREY (236) 1961–74. Cap 1966.
Benefit 1974.
TOURS Commonwealth XI to Pakistan 1967/68. Duke of Norfolk's XI to W Indies 1969/70.
HS 137 Surrey v MCC, Oval, 1969.
BB 2–53 Cambridge U v Pakistanis, Fenner's, 1962.
1000 RUNS (5) 1428 @ 36.61 in 1969.

EDWARDS, Richard Martin
——RHB, RFM——

Born Christchurch, Barbados, 3 June 1940. Debut 1961/62.
W INDIES DOMESTIC Barbados 1961/62–69/70.
WEST INDIES (5) 1968/69. *A 1968/69 (2); NZ 1968/69 (3).*
OTHER TOUR Barbados to England 1969.
HST 22 WI v NZ, Wellington, 1968/69.
HS 34 Governor-General's XI v W Indians, Auckland, 1968/69 (hit M. C. Carew for 34 runs in one over, record for eight-ball over).
BBT 5–84 WI v NZ, Wellington, 1968/69. BB 6–45 Barbados v Leeward Islands, St Kitts, 1966/67.

EDWARDS, Ross
——RHB, occ WK——

Born Cottesloe, Perth, W Australia, 1 Dec 1942. Debut 1964/65.
AUSTRALIA DOMESTIC Western Australia (71) 1964/65–74/75, New South Wales (5) 1979/80.
AUSTRALIA (20) 1972–75. *E 1974/75 (5); P 1972/73 (2). E 1972 (4), 1975 (4); WI 1972/73 (5).*
HST 170* A v E, Trent Bridge, 1972. HS as above.
World Series Cricket (Kerry Packer) 1977/78–78/79. Father E. K. Edwards (W. Australia).

EDWARDS, Timothy David Warneford
——LHB——

Born Merton, Surrey, 6 Dec 1958. Educ Sherborne; St John's C, Cambridge. Debut 1979.
CAMBRIDGE UNIVERSITY (12) 1979–81 (Blue 1981).
HS 57 Cambridge U v Notts, Fenner's, 1981.

EELE, Peter James
——LHB, WK——

Born Taunton, Som, 27 Jan 1935. Educ Taunton S. Debut 1958. *P.*
SOMERSET (54) 1958–65. Cap 1964.
HS 103* Som v Pakistan Eaglets, Taunton, 1963.
Fc umpire 1981–84. Devon 1966–70. Minor Counties umpire 1976–80. Club: Sidmouth.

EGGAR, John Drennan
——RHB——

Born Nowshera, NWFP, India, 1 Dec 1916. Died Hinton St George, Som, 3 May 1983. Educ Winchester; Brasenose C, Oxford. Debut 1938.
OXFORD UNIVERSITY (8) 1938 (Blue).
HAMPSHIRE (2) 1938.
DERBYSHIRE (31) 1946–54. Cap 1946.
HS 219 Derbys v Yorks, Bradford, 1949.
RECORD Added 349 for 2nd wkt with C. S. Elliot, Derbys v Notts, Trent Bridge, 1947, county record.

EHTESHAM-UD-DIN
——RHB, RFM——

Born Lahore, Pakistan, 4 Sept 1950. Educ Punjab U. Debut 1969/70.
PAKISTAN DOMESTIC Punjab University, Lahore, Pakistan International Airlines, Punjab, National Bank, United Bank, 1969/70–.
PAKISTAN (5) 1979/80–82. *A 1979/80 (1). E 1982 (1); I 1979/80 (3).*
OTHER TOUR Pakistan Under-25 XI to Sri Lanka 1973/74.
HST 2 P v I, Kanpur, 1979/80. HS 83 National Bank v PIA, Lyallpur, 1975/76.
BBT 5–47 P v I, Kanpur, 1979/80. BB 8–45 National Bank v PIA, Lahore, 1979/80.
Club: Daisy Hill.

ELDER, John Watson George
——RHB, RFM——

Born Bangor, Co Down, N Ireland, 16 Aug 1949. Educ Foyle C, Londonderry. Debut 1973.
IRELAND (8) 1973–80.
HS 7 Ireland v Scotland, Dublin, 1979.
BB 3–56 Ireland v Scotland, Glasgow, 1976.

ELGIE, Michael Kelsey (Kim)
——RHB, SLA——

Born Durban, S Africa, 6 Mar 1933. Educ Michaelhouse, Natal; St Andrew's U; London U. Debut 1957/58.
S AFRICA DOMESTIC Natal 1957/58–61/62.
SOUTH AFRICA (3) NZ 1961/62.
TOUR S African Fezelas to England 1961.
HST 56 SA v NZ, Johannesburg, 1961/62. HS 162* Natal v Border, East London, 1959/60.
BB 3–16 Natal v W Province, Cape Town, 1958/59.
Rugby: Middlesex, London Counties and Scotland (8).

ELGOOD, Bernard Cyril
——RHB——

Born Hampstead, London, 10 Mar 1922. Educ Bradfield; Pembroke C, Cambridge. Debut 1948.
CAMBRIDGE UNIVERSITY (12) 1948 (Blue).
COMBINED SERVICES (2) 1948.
HS 127* Cambridge U v Sussex, Fenner's, 1948.
Berkshire 1949. BAOR 1952. Major in Royal Engineers.

ELIOT, Robin Francis
——LHB, LM——

Born Gloucester, 7 Mar 1942. Educ Radley; Lincoln C, Oxford. Debut 1961.
OXFORD UNIVERSITY (2) 1961.
HS 30 Oxford U v Leics, The Parks, 1961.
Clubs: Free Foresters, Yellowhammers, Sussex Martlets, Grannies, Cuckfield, Withyham, Lloyds CC, I Zingari.

ELLCOCK, Ricardo McDonald
——RHB, RFM——

Born Bridgetown, Barbados, 17 June 1965. Educ Malvern C. Debut 1982.
WORCESTERSHIRE (22) 1982–.
W INDIES DOMESTIC Barbados 1983/84.
HS 45* Worcs v Essex, Worcester, 1984.
BB 4–34 Worcs v Glam, Worcester, 1984.

ELLIOTT, Charles Standish
——RHB, OB——

Born Bolsover, Derbys, 24 Apr 1912. Debut 1932. *P.*
DERBYSHIRE (275) 1932–53. Cap 1936. Testimonial (£1667) 1950.
HS 215 Derbys v Notts, Trent Bridge, 1947.
BB 2–25 Derbys v Leics, Derby, 1946.
1000 RUNS (6) 1599 @ 34.76 in 1952.
RECORD During HS (above) added 349 for 2nd wkt with J. D. Eggar, county record.
Fc umpire 1956–74. Stood in 42 Tests (1957–74), a record beaten only by F. Chester (48). England Test selector 1975–80. Soccer: Coventry City. Uncle H. Elliott (Derbys).

ELLIOTT, Harry
——RHB, WK——

Born Scarcliffe, Derbys, 2 Nov 1891. Died Derby, 2 Feb 1976. Debut 1920. *P.*
DERBYSHIRE (520) 1920–47. Cap.

ENGLAND (4) 1927/28–33/34. WI 1928 (1). *SA 1927/28 (1); I 1933/34 (2).*
HST 37* E v I, Bombay, 1933/34. HS 94 Derbys v Leics, Loughborough, 1933.
10 dismissals match, Derbys v Lancs, Old Trafford, 1935. 1206 dismissals (904 ct, 302 st) in fc career.
Fc umpire 1946, 1952–60. Derbys coach 1947–51. Played for Derbys in 426 out of 427 matches, 1920–37. Sports Outfitters partnership with Sammy Crookes (England footballer). Nephew C. S. Elliott (Derbys).

ELLIOTT, John William
——LHB, WK——

Born Worcester, 12 Feb 1942. Educ Worcester RGS. Debut 1959.
WORCESTERSHIRE (10) 1959–65.
HS 18* Worcs v Oxford U, The Parks, 1961.
Worcs committee. Club: Kidderminster.

ELLIS, Geoffrey Philip
——RHB, RM——

Born Llandudno, Caernarvonshire, Wales, 24 May 1950. Educ John Bright GS, Llandudno; Cardiff C of Educ. Debut 1970.
GLAMORGAN (75) 1970–76.
HS 116 Glam v M'sex, Cardiff, 1974.
BB 2–20 Glam v Lancs, Swansea, 1975.

ELLIS, Peter Michael
——RHB, RM——

Born Lewisham, London, 25 Sept 1932. Educ Marylebone GS. Debut 1953. *P.*
MCC (1) 1953.
No runs, no wkts.
Clubs: Stanmore, Clackmannan, Drumpelier, Ferguslie. Professional coach cricket and squash at Haileybury and ISC since 1963. Son R. G. P. Ellis (Oxford U and M'sex).

ELLIS, Reginald Sidney
——LHB, SLA——

Born Angaston, S Australia, 6 Nov 1917. Debut 1945.
AUSTRALIA DOMESTIC South Australia (1) 1945/46.
TOUR Australian Services to England 1945 and India and Ceylon 1945/46.
HS 10* Australian Services v Indian XI, Bombay, 1945/46.
BB 6–144 Australian Services v NSW, Sydney, 1945/46.

ELLIS, Richard Gary Peter
——RHB, OB——

Born Paddington, London, 20 Dec 1960. Educ Haileybury and ISC; St Edmond Hall, Oxford. Debut 1981.
OXFORD UNIVERSITY (27) 1981–83 (Blue 1981–83). Capt 1982.
MIDDLESEX (11) 1982–.
HS 105* Oxford U v Surrey, The Parks, 1982.
BB 2–40 same match.
Father P. M. Ellis (MCC).

ELLIS, Robert
——LHB, RM——

Born Kilmarnock, Scotland, 19 May 1940. Educ Kilmarnock Academy; Glasgow U. Debut 1963.
SCOTLAND (10) 1963–74.
HS 35 Scotland v Pakistan, Selkirk, 1971 and v Ireland, Greenock, 1972.
Club: Kilmarnock.

ELLIS, William
——RHB, RFM——

Born Rolleston, Notts, 15 Aug 1919. Debut 1948. *P.*
NOTTINGHAMSHIRE (2) 1948.
HS 29 Notts v Worcs, Trent Bridge, 1948.
Clubs: Cleckheaton, Spen Victoria, Baildon Green, Wath. Professional coach Liverpool C 1959.

ELLIS, William Arnot
——RHB——

Born Carriden, Scotland, 16 Sept 1923. Educ Linlithgow Academy. Debut 1954.
SCOTLAND (1) 1954.
HS 6 Scotland v Ireland, Paisley, 1954.
Clubs: West Lothian, Linlithgow.

ELLISON, Charles Christopher
——RHB, RM——

Born Pembury, Kent, 11 Feb 1962. Educ Tonbridge S; Homerton C, Cambridge. Debut 1982.
CAMBRIDGE UNIVERSITY (11) 1982–83 (Blue 1982–83).
HS 27 Cambridge U v Notts, Fenner's, 1983.
BB 4–36 Cambridge U v Notts, Fenner's, 1983.
Brother R. M. Ellison (Kent and England).

ELLISON, Richard Mark
——LHB, RM——

Born Ashford, Kent, 21 Sept 1959. Educ Tonbridge S; St Luke's C, Exeter. Debut 1981.
KENT (55) 1981–.
ENGLAND (2) 1984. WI 1984 (1); SL 1984 (1).
HST 41 E v SL, Lord's, 1984. HS 108 Kent v Oxford U, The Parks, 1984.
BBT 3–60 E v WI, Oval, 1984. BB 5–27 Kent v Essex, Canterbury, 1984.
Brother C. C. Ellison (Cambridge U).

ELMS, Richard Burtenshaw
——RHB, LFM——

Born Sutton, Surrey, 5 Apr 1949. Educ Bexley/Erith Technical HS. Debut 1970.
KENT (55) 1970–76.
HAMPSHIRE (17) 1977–78.
HS 48 Hants v Derbys, Derby, 1978.
BB 5–38 Kent v M'sex, Lord's, 1973.

ELSDON, Harold
——RHB, RFM——

Born Lemington, Newcastle upon Tyne, 19 Feb 1921. Debut 1949. *P.*
MINOR COUNTIES (1) 1949.
HS 12* Minor Counties v Yorks, Lord's, 1949.
BB 3–51 same match.
Northumberland 1938–56. Professional: Benwell, Swalwell, Blyth, Eppleton, Darlington.

ELSON, Geoffrey (Gus)
——LHB, SLA——

Born Coventry, Warwicks, 19 Mar 1913. Educ Rydal S. Debut 1947.
WARWICKSHIRE (1) 1947.
HS 4 Warwicks v Essex, Coventry, 1947.
Club: Coventry and North Warwicks.
Son Philip (Pip) Elson (professional golfer).

ELVISS, Richard William
——RHB, OB——

Born Sheffield, Yorks, 19 July 1945. Educ Leeds GS; Trinity C, Oxford. Debut 1966.
OXFORD UNIVERSITY (19) 1966–67 (Blue 1966–67).
HS 16 Oxford U v S African Universities, Roehampton, 1967.
BB 5–83 Oxford U v Lancs, The Parks, 1966.
Yorks 2nd XI.

EMBUREY, John Ernest
————RHB, OB————

Born Peckham, London, 20 Aug 1952.
Educ Peckham Manor Sec S. Debut
1973.
MIDDLESEX (178) 1973–. Cap 1977.
S AFRICA DOMESTIC Western Province
1982/83–83/84.
ENGLAND (22) 1978–81/82. A 1980 (1),
1981 (4); WI 1980 (3); NZ 1978 (1). *A
1978/79 (4); WI 1980/81 (4); I 1979/
80 (1), 1981/82 (3); SL 1981/82 (1)*.
OTHER TOURS D. H. Robins' XI to Sri
Lanka 1977/78. England to Australia
1979/80. M'sex to Zimbabwe 1980/81.
HST 57 E v A, Old Trafford, 1981. HS 133
M'sex v Essex, Chelmsford, 1982.
BBT 6–33 E v SL, Colombo, 1981/82. BB
7–36 M'sex v Cambridge U, Fenner's,
1977.
100 WKTS (1) 103 @ 17.88 in 1983.
Barred from Test cricket for three years
for touring S Africa in 1981/82 (SAB
England XI).

EMERY, Kevin St John Dennis
————RHB, RFM————

Born Swindon, Wiltshire, 28 Feb 1960.
Educ St Joseph's CS, Swindon; Bristol
U. Debut 1982.
HAMPSHIRE (29) 1982–83.
HS 18* Hants v Derbys, Derby, 1982.
BB 6–51 Hants v Glam, Portsmouth,
1982.
Took 83 wkts @ 23.72 in debut season
1982.
Wiltshire 1978–80. Club: Swindon.

EMMETT, George Malcolm
————RHB, LM————

Born Agra, India, 2 Dec 1912. Died
Knowle, Bristol, 18 Dec 1976. Educ St
Paul's S, Darjeeling, India. Debut 1936.
P.
GLOUCESTERSHIRE (454) 1936–59. Cap
1938. Capt 1955–58. Benefit (£2500)
1952.
ENGLAND (1) A 1948.
TOURS Commonwealth XI to India and
Ceylon 1950/51. Commonwealth XI to
India 1953/54.
HST 10 E v A, Old Trafford, 1948. HS 188
Glos v Kent, Bristol, 1950.
BB 6–137 Glos v Surrey, Bristol, 1938.
1000 RUNS (13 + 1) 2115 @ 35.25 in
1953.
Devon 1932–35. Club: Bristol Imperial.
Glos coach after retirement. Profession-
al coach Cheltenham 1961. Latterly
general secretary Imperial Athletic
Club, Bristol.

ENDEAN, William *Russell*
————RHB, WK————

Born Johannesburg, S Africa, 31 May
1924. Educ St John's C, Johannesburg.
Debut 1945/46.
S AFRICA DOMESTIC Transvaal 1945/
46–60/61.
MCC (2) 1963–64.
SOUTH AFRICA (28) 1951–57/58. E 1956/
57 (5); A 1957/58 (5); NZ 1953/54 (5). *E
1951 (1), 1955 (5); A 1952/53 (5); NZ
1952/53 (2)*.
HST 162* SA v A, Melbourne, 1952/53.
HS 247 Transvaal v E Province, Johan-
nesburg, 1955/56.
1000 RUNS (1 + 1) 1496 @ 55.40 in
Australasia 1952/53.
RECORDS Scored 197* before lunch on
first day, Transvaal v OFS, Johannes-
burg, 1954/55, world record (out for
235).
Dismissed 'handled the ball', SA v E,
Cape Town, 1956/57, first instance in
Test cricket.
Club: Malden Wands (England).
Hockey: South Africa.

ENGINEER, Farokh Maneksha
————RHB, WK————

Born Bombay, India, 25 Feb 1938. Educ
Don Bosco HS, Bombay U. Debut
1958/59.
INDIA DOMESTIC Combined Universities
1958/59, Bombay 1959/60–74/75.
LANCASHIRE (175) 1968–76. Cap 1968.
Benefit (£26,519) 1976.
INDIA (46) 1961/62–74/75. E 1961/62
(4), 1972/73 (5); A 1969/70 (5); WI
1966/67 (1), 1974/75 (5); NZ 1964/65
(4), 1969/70 (2). *E 1967 (3), 1971 (3),
1974 (3); A 1967/68 (4); WI 1961/62
(3); NZ 1967/68 (4)*.
OTHER TOURS Indian Starlets to Pakistan
1959/60. India to E Africa 1967. Rest of
World in England 1970. Rest of World
to Pakistan 1970/71 (relief match).
World XI to Australia 1971/72.
HST 121 I v E, Bombay, 1972/73. HS 192
World XI v Combined XI, Hobart,
1971/72.
1000 RUNS (0 + 1) 1050 @ 47.72 in 1964/
65.
RECORD Added 143 for 8th wkt with
R. G. Nadkarni, I v NZ, Madras, 1964/
65, India Test record.
824 dismissals (703 ct 121 st) in fc career.
Brother D. M. Engineer (Mysore).

ENGLISH, Winston
————LHB, LFM————

Born British Guiana, *circa* 1943. Debut
1966/67.

W INDIES DOMESTIC Guyana 1966/
67–69/70.
D. H. ROBINS' XI (1) 1969.
HS 112 Guyana v Trinidad, Geor-
getown, 1968/69.
BB 4–111 Guyana v Barbados, Geor-
getown, 1966/67.
Club: Haslingden 1969–70.

ENTHOVEN, Henry John
————RHB, RM————

Born Cartagena, Spain, 4 June 1903.
Died Kensington, London, 29 June
1975. Educ Harrow; Pembroke C, Cam-
bridge. Debut 1923.
CAMBRIDGE UNIVERSITY (42) 1923–26
(Blue 1923–26). Capt 1926.
MIDDLESEX (123) 1925–36. Cap. Joint
capt (with N. E. Haig) 1933–34.
FREE FORESTERS (8) 1927–39.
MCC (1) 1948.
HS 139 M'sex v Lancs, Lord's, 1927.
BB 6–64 (11–115 match) Cambridge U v
Army, Fenner's, 1925.
1000 RUNS (1) 1129 @ 31.36 in
1926.
Scored 104 in 1924 Varsity match and
129 in 1925 (second player to score two
centuries in this series). Took first hat-
trick for Gentlemen against the Players,
Lord's, 1926.
Gentlemen v Players (6) 1925–34.

ENTWISTLE, Robert
————RHB————

Born Burnley, Lancs, 20 Oct 1941.
Debut 1962. P.
LANCASHIRE (48) 1962–66.
MINOR COUNTIES (1) 1976.
HS 85 Lancs v MCC, Old Trafford,
1964.
1000 RUNS (1) 1030 @ 28.61 in 1964.
Cumberland 1967–. Clubs: Burnley,
Netherfield, Fleetwood, Darwen.

ESTCOURT, Noël Sidney
Dudley
————RHB, OB————

Born Ralolia, Rhodesia, 7 Jan 1929.
Educ Plumtree S, Rhodesia; Rhodes U;
Corpus Christi C, Cambridge. Debut
1953.
CAMBRIDGE UNIVERSITY (21) 1953–54
(Blue 1954).
HS 56* Cambridge U v Essex, Fenner's,
1954.
BB 4–79 same match.
S African Universities 1951/52. Rugby:
Cambridge U, Blackheath, England (1).

ETHERIDGE, Robert James
————RHB, WK————

Born Gloucester, 25 Mar 1934. Debut 1955. *P.*
GLOUCESTERSHIRE (39) 1955–66.
HS 48 Glos v Essex, Bristol, 1964.
Clubs: Gloucester City, Gloucester Nondescripts, Shirehampton. Soccer: Bristol City.

ETHERINGTON, Maurice William
————RHB, RFM————

Born Hammersmith, London, 24 Aug 1916. Debut 1946. *P.*
MIDDLESEX (2) 1946.
LEICESTERSHIRE (3) 1948.
HS 27 Leics v Essex, Loughborough, 1948.
BB 3–23 M'sex v Hants, Lord's, 1946.
Professional coach Repton S from 1949.

EVANS, David Gwillim Lloyd
————RHB, WK————

Born Lambeth, London, 27 July 1933. Debut 1956. *P.*
GLAMORGAN (270) 1956–69. Cap 1959. Benefit (£3500) 1969.
HS 46* Glam v Oxford U, The Parks, 1961.
Fc umpire 1971– (8 Tests, 1981–84).
Clubs: Briton Ferry Steel, Ammanford. Coach The Hague 1970. Awarded Churchill Scholarship 1967 to travel world studying coaching methods.

EVANS, Gwynn
————RHB, RM————

Born Bala, Merioneth, Wales, 13 Aug 1915. Educ St Asaph C; Brasenose C, Oxford. Debut 1938.
OXFORD UNIVERSITY (16) 1938–39 (Blue 1939).
GLAMORGAN (7) 1939.
LEICESTERSHIRE (10) 1949. Cap 1949. Capt in some matches.
HS 65* Leics v Glos, Leicester, 1949.
BB 6–80 Oxford U v Leics, The Parks, 1939.

EVANS, George Herbert David
————RHB, RM————

Born Bristol, 22 Aug 1928. Debut 1953.
SOMERSET (8) 1953.
HS 42 Som v Essex, Weston-super-Mare, 1953.
Club: Worcester City.

EVANS, John Brian
————RHB, RFM————

Born Clydach, Glam, 9 Nov 1936. Debut 1958. *P.*
GLAMORGAN (87) 1958–63. Cap 1960.
MINOR COUNTIES (1) 1969.
HS 62* Glam v Som, Weston-super-Mare, 1961, and 62 v Worcs, Pontypridd, 1960.
BB 8–42 Glam v Som, Cardiff, 1961.
Lincolnshire 1965–71. Clubs: Clydach, Briton Ferry, Swansea, Dafen, Pontarddulais.

EVANS, Kevin Paul
————RHB, RMF————

Born Calverton, Notts, 10 Sept 1963. Educ Frank Seely S, Calverton. Debut 1984.
NOTTINGHAMSHIRE (3) 1984.
HS 42 Notts v Cambridge U, Fenner's, 1984.

EVANS, Michael
————RHB, RFM————

Born Leicester, 3 May 1908. Died Leicester, 14 Nov 1974. Debut 1946.
LEICESTERSHIRE (2) 1946.
HS 14* Leics v Glam, Leicester, 1946.
BB 3–30 Leics v Surrey, Leicester, 1946.

EVANS, Nicholas John
————RHB, RM————

Born Weston-super-Mare, Som, 9 Sept 1954. Educ Uphill Sec S, Weston-super-Mare. Debut 1976.
SOMERSET (1) 1976.
No runs, no wkts.

EVANS, Ronald Ernest
————RHB————

Born East Ham, London, 22 July 1922. Educ Highfield C, Leigh-on-Sea, Essex. Debut 1950.
ESSEX (17) 1950–57.
HS 79 Essex v Kent, Clacton, 1950.
Club: Ilford (Capt 1960–66), XL Club.

EVANS, Thomas *Godfrey*
————RHB, WK————

Born Finchley, London, 18 Aug 1920. Educ Kent C, Canterbury. Debut 1939. *Wisden* 1949. *P.*
KENT (258) 1939–67. Cap 1946. Benefit (£5259) 1953.
International Cavaliers v Barbados, Scarborough, 1969.

ENGLAND (91) 1946–59. A 1948 (5), 1953 (5), 1956 (5); SA 1947 (5), 1951 (3), 1955 (3); WI 1950 (5), 1957 (5); NZ 1949 (4), 1958 (5); I 1946 (1), 1952 (4), 1959 (2); P 1954 (4). *A 1946/47 (4), 1950/51 (5), 1954/55 (4), 1958/59 (3); SA 1948/49 (3), 1956/57 (5); WI 1947/48 (4), 1953/54 (4); NZ 1946/47 (1), 1950/51 (2), 1954/55 (2).*
OTHER TOURS Commonwealth XI to S Africa 1959/60. Cavaliers to Jamaica 1963/64. Cavaliers to W Indies 1964/65. Indian Prime Minister's XI v BCCI Board XI, Bombay 1963/64.
HST 104 E v WI, Old Trafford, 1950 and v I, Lord's, 1952. HS 144 Kent v Som, Taunton, 1952.
BB 2–50 Kent v Notts, Trent Bridge, 1951.
1000 RUNS (4) 1613 @ 28.80 in 1952.
RECORDS Kept wkt throughout total of 659 for 8 dec, and 1384 balls, without conceding a bye, E v A, Sydney, 1946/47, a world record. 95 mins at wkt without scoring, E v A, Adelaide, 1946/47. Second player, first Englishman, to complete 1000 runs/100 dismissals double in Tests (in 1952); first to 2000 runs/200 dismissals double (in 1957).
1066 dismissals (816 ct, 250 st) in fc career.
CBE for services to cricket. MCC Hon. member.

EVE, Stanley Charles
————RHB————

Born Stepney, London, 18 Dec 1925. Educ Upminster S. Debut 1949.
ESSEX (32) 1949–57.
HS 120 Essex v Warwicks, Brentwood, 1949.
Clubs: Cranham, Upminster.

EXTON, Rodney Noel
————RHB, OB————

Born Bournemouth, Hants, 28 Dec 1927. Educ Clifton C.
HAMPSHIRE (4) 1946.
HS 24* Hants v Yorks, Bournemouth, 1946.
Gave up cricket owing to polio.

EYRE, John Richard
————RHB, RM————

Born Glossop, Derbys, 13 June 1944. Debut 1963.
DERBYSHIRE (48) 1963–67.
HS 106 Derbys v Lancs, Old Trafford, 1967.

EYRE, Thomas John *Peter* (Curly)
————————LHB, RFM————————

Born Brough, Derbys, 17 Oct 1939.
Educ New Mills GS. Debut 1959. *P.*
DERBYSHIRE (197) 1959–72. Cap 1967.
HS 102 Derbys v Leics, Chesterfield, 1969.
BB 8–65 Derbys v Som, Chesterfield, 1969.
Reported to MCC for unsatisfactory bowling action 1965.

EZEKOWITZ, Raymond *Alan* Brian
————————RHB————————

Born Durban, S Africa, 19 Jan 1954.
Educ Westhill HS, Durban; Cape Town U; Wolfson C, Oxford. Debut 1980.
OXFORD UNIVERSITY (18) 1980–81 (Blue 1980–81).
HS 93 Oxford U v Cambridge U, Lord's, 1981.

F

FABER, Mark James Julian
RHB, RM

Born Horsted Keynes, Sussex, 15 Aug 1950. Educ Eton; Balliol C, Oxford. Debut 1970.
OXFORD UNIVERSITY (21) 1970–72 (Blue 1972).
SUSSEX (57) 1973–76.
HS 176 Sussex v Hants, Hove, 1975.
1000 RUNS (1) 1060 @ 30.28 in 1975.
Grandfather Rt Hon. Harold Macmillan (former Conservative MP and British Prime Minister; now Earl of Stockton).

FAGG, Arthur Edward
RHB, occ WK

Born Chartham, Kent, 18 June 1915. Died Tunbridge Wells, Kent, 13 Sept 1977. Debut 1932. P.
KENT (414) 1932–57. Cap 1934. Benefit (£3456) 1951.
ENGLAND (5) 1936–39. WI 1939 (1); I 1936 (2). A 1936/37 (2).
HST 39 E v I, Old Trafford, 1936. HS 269* Kent v Notts, Trent Bridge, 1953.
1000 RUNS (13) 2456 @ 52.25 in 1938.
RECORDS Scored 244 and 202*, Kent v Essex, Colchester, 1938, only instance in fc cricket of a player scoring double-century in each inns; 446 runs in match, highest by a player in England; during 2nd inns put on 283 for 1st wkt with P. R. Sunnucks, county record.
Returned home early from MCC tour of Australia in 1936/37 with rheumatic fever (missed 1937 season). Fc umpire 1959–77 (18 Tests, 1967–75). Coach Cheltenham C 1946.

FAIRBAIRN, Alan
LHB

Born Winchmore Hill, M'sex, 25 Jan 1923. Educ Haileybury and ISC. Debut 1947.
MIDDLESEX (20) 1947–51.
HS 110* M'sex v Notts, Trent Bridge, 1947.
Scored 108 in second inns of fc debut, M'sex v Som, Taunton, 1947, and 110*

(above) in second inns of second match. Club: Southgate.

FAIRBROTHER, Neil Harvey
LHB, LM

Born Warrington, Lancs, 9 Sept 1963. Educ Lymm GS. Debut 1982.
LANCASHIRE (40) 1982–. Cap 1984.
HS 102 Lancs v Derbys, Buxton, 1984.
1000 RUNS (1) 1201 @ 31.61 in 1984.

FAIRWEATHER, James Henry Whitton
RHB

Born Edinburgh, Scotland, 16 July 1946. Educ Edinburgh Academy; St Andrew's U. Debut 1971.
SCOTLAND (2) 1971.
HS 9 Scotland v Ireland, Belfast, 1971.
Club: Edinburgh Academicals.

FALKNER, Nicholas James
RHB, RM

Born Redhill, Surrey, 30 Sept 1962. Educ Reigate GS. Debut 1984.
SURREY (1) 1984.
HS 101* Surrey v Cambridge U, Banstead, 1984 (only inns).
RECORD During HS (above) added 189* for 8th wkt with K. T. Medlycott (117*); first instance in Britain of two first-class debutants scoring hundreds in same inns.

FALLOWS, John Armstrong
RHB

Born Stockport, Cheshire, 25 July 1907. Died Macclesfield, Cheshire, 20 Jan 1974. Debut 1946.
LANCASHIRE (25) 1946. Cap 1946. Capt 1946.
HS 35 Lancs v Yorks, Old Trafford, 1946.
Cheshire 1932. Chairman Lancs selection committee to 1971.

FANTHAM, William Edward
RHB, OB

Born Birmingham, 14 May 1918. Debut 1935. P.
WARWICKSHIRE (63) 1935–48. Cap 1946.
HS 51 Warwicks v Notts, Edgbaston, 1946.
BB 5–55 (9–65 match) Warwicks v Som, Edgbaston, 1946.
Clubs: Mitchells and Butlers; league cricket in Coventry.

FARAGHER, Harold Alker
RHB, RM/LBG

Born Reddish, Lancs, 20 July 1917. Educ Ilford Central HS. Debut 1949.
ESSEX (6) 1949–50.
HS 85* Essex v Kent, Maidstone, 1950.
Clubs: XL Club, Ilford.

FARMER, John James Stewart
RHB

Born Leatherhead, Surrey, 5 Aug 1934. Educ Eton; Christ Church C, Oxford. Debut 1958.
OXFORD UNIVERSITY (2) 1958.
HS 6 Oxford U v Glos, The Parks, 1958.
Clubs: Nomads, Esher, Ifield.

FAROOQ HAMEED
RHB, RFM

Born Lahore, India, 3 Mar 1945. Debut 1961/62.
PAKISTAN DOMESTIC Lahore, Combined Education Boards, Pakistan International Airlines, 1961/62–68/69.
PAKISTAN (1) A 1964/65.
OTHER TOURS Pakistan Eaglets to England 1963. Pakistan to Ceylon 1964/65. PIA to E Africa 1964/65.
HST 3 P v A, Melbourne, 1964/65. HS 38 Lahore v Sargodha, Lahore, 1968/69.
BBT 1–82 P v A, Melbourne, 1964/65. BB 7–16 Pakistanis v Wellington, Wellington, 1964/65.

FARR, Bryan Henry
────────RHB, RM────────

Born Nottingham, 16 Mar 1924. Educ
Harrow; Trinity C, Cambridge. Debut
1949.
NOTTINGHAMSHIRE (6) 1949–51.
FREE FORESTERS (1) 1952.
HS 37 Notts v Worcs, Worcester, 1951.
BB 5–96 same match.
War-time Blue 1943. Club: Richmond
(Surrey).

FARRAR, Harry
────────LHB, LFM────────

Born Radcliffe, Lancs, 14 Mar 1930.
Educ Stand GS, Manchester. Debut
1955.
LANCASHIRE (1) 1955.
No runs, no wkts.
Clubs: Stand, Little Lever,
Westhoughton.

FARRIMOND, William
────────RHB, WK────────

Born Westhoughton, Lancs, 23 May
1903. Died Westhoughton, Lancs, 15
Nov 1979. Debut 1924. P.
LANCASHIRE (134) 1924–45. Cap 1929.
Benefit (£1000) 1939.
ENGLAND (4) 1930/31–35. SA 1935 (1).
SA 1930/31 (2); WI 1934/35 (1).
HST 35 E v SA, Durban, 1930/31. HS 174
Minor Counties v Oxford U, The Parks,
1934.
RECORD Made 7 dismissals in inns (6 ct,
1 st), Lancs v Kent, Old Trafford, 1930,
joint record for all county cricket.
Club: Heywood.

FASIHUDDIN, Rashid
────────RHB, WK────────

Born Quetta, India, 28 Dec 1939. Educ
Karachi U. Debut 1957/58.
PAKISTAN DOMESTIC Karachi, Karachi
University, Quetta, Baluchistan, 1957/
58–74/75.
TOURS Pakistan Eaglets to England 1961.
Pakistan to England 1967.
HS 237 Quetta v E Pakistan, Karachi,
1962/63.

FASKEN, David Kenneth
────────RHB, RMF────────

Born Batu Gajah, Ipoh, Malaya, 23 Mar
1932. Educ Wellington C; Trinity C,
Oxford. Debut 1953.
OXFORD UNIVERSITY (27) 1953–55 (Blue
1953–55).
MCC (2) 1956–59.

FREE FORESTERS (4) 1959–62.
HS 61 Oxford U v Pakistanis, The Parks,
1954.
BB 5–108 Oxford U v Australians, The
Parks, 1953.
Oxfordshire 1950–55.

FAULKNER, William George
────────RHB, RM────────

Born Poplar, East London, 5 May 1923.
Debut 1946.
ROYAL AIR FORCE (1) 1946.
HS 18 RAF v Worcs, Worcester, 1946.

FAWCETT, George Walter
────────RHB, WK────────

Born Ardglass, Co Down, Ireland, 6
Aug 1929. Educ Regent House GS;
Newtownards, Co Down. Debut 1956.
IRELAND (6) 1956–59.
HS 21 Ireland v Scotland, Edinburgh,
1956.
Clubs: Woodvale, Waringstown, North
Down.

FAWKES, John
────────LHB, WK────────

Born Brompton, Chesterfield, Derbys, 9
Oct 1933. Educ Retford GS. Debut
1959.
COMBINED SERVICES (4) 1959–60.
HS 41 Combined Services v Cambridge
U, Fenner's, 1960.
Army. Clubs: Retford Town, Firbeck
Colliery, Aldershot Services. East
Africa. Kenya.

FAZAL MAHMOOD
────────RHB, RFM────────

Born Lahore, India 18 Feb 1927. Educ
Islamia C, Lahore; Punjab U. Debut
1943/44. Wisden 1955.
INDIA DOMESTIC Northern India 1943/
44–46/47.
PAKISTAN DOMESTIC Punjab, Lahore,
1951/52–58/59.
PAKISTAN (34) 1952/53–62. E 1961/62
(1); A 1956/57 (1), 1959/60 (2); WI
1958/59 (3); NZ 1955/56 (2); I 1954/55
(4). E 1954 (4), 1962 (2); WI 1957/58
(5); I 1952/53 (5), 1960/61 (5). Capt
10.
OTHER TOUR Pakistan to Ceylon 1948/49.
HST 60 P v WI, Port of Spain, 1957/58.
HS 100* N Zone v S Zone, Bombay,
1946/47.
BBT 7–42 (12–94 match) P v I, Lucknow,
1952/53. BB 9–43 Punjab v Services,

Lahore, 1956/57.
Returned 13–114 match, P v A,
Karachi, 1956/57.
Clubs: East Lancs, Werneth. Deputy
inspector-general Lahore police.
Father-in-law Mohammed Mian Saeed
(Pakistan XI).

FEARNLEY, Charles Duncan
────────LHB, occ ROB────────

Born Pudsey, Yorks, 12 Apr 1940.
Debut 1962. P.
WORCESTERSHIRE (97) 1962–68.
HS 112 Worcs v Derbys, Kidderminster,
1966.
Lincolnshire 1969–71. Clubs: Farsley,
West Bromwich Dartmouth. Well-
known bat manufacturer. Brother M. C.
Fearnley (Yorks).

FEARNLEY, Michael Carruthers
────────RHB, RM────────

Born Horsforth, Leeds, 21 Aug 1936.
Died, during match, East Bierley,
Yorks, 7 July 1979. Debut 1962. P.
YORKSHIRE (3) 1962–64.
HS 11* Yorks v Essex, Bramall Lane,
Sheffield, 1962.
BB 3–56 same match.
Clubs: Farsley, Heywood, Bradford,
Bingley. Outstanding coach Yorks and
Leeds. Brother C. D. Fearnley (Worcs).

FEATHERSTONE, Norman George (Smokey)
────────RHB, OB────────

Born Que Que, Rhodesia, 20 Aug 1949.
Educ King Edward VII HS, Johannes-
burg, S Africa. Debut 1967/68.
S AFRICA DOMESTIC Transvaal B 1967/
68–76/77, Transvaal 1969/70–77/78,
Northern Transvaal 1981/82.
MIDDLESEX (216) 1968–79. Cap 1971.
Benefit (£30,000) 1979.
GLAMORGAN (45) 1980–81. Cap 1980.
HS 147 M'sex v Yorks, Scarborough,
1975.
BB 5–32 M'sex v Notts, Trent Bridge,
1978.
1000 RUNS (4) 1156 @ 35.03 in 1975.

FEE, Francis
────────RHB, RM/OB────────

Born Belfast, N Ireland, 14 May 1934.
Educ Methodist C, Belfast; Queen's U,
Belfast. Debut 1956.
IRELAND (5) 1956–59.
HS 15* Ireland v MCC, Dublin, 1958.
BB 9–26 (12–60 match) Ireland v Scot-
land, Dublin, 1957.

Took 14–100 Ireland v MCC, Dublin, 1956 on fc debut and 12–60 in second match (above).
Club: Cregagh.

FELL, Desmond Robert
LHB

Born Easton, Natal, S Africa, 16 Dec 1912. Educ Maritzburg C; U of Natal. Debut 1931/32.
S AFRICA DOMESTIC Natal 1931/32–49/50.
Dominions v England XI, Lord's, 1945.
HS 161 Natal v Rhodesia, Bulawayo, 1946/47.
Umpire SA v NZ, Durban, 1961/62.
Clubs: Old Collegians, Maritzburg.

FELL, Mark Andrew
RHB, SLA

Born Newark, Notts, 17 Nov 1960. Educ Grove CS. Debut 1982.
NOTTINGHAMSHIRE (15) 1982–83.
HS 108 Notts v Essex, Trent Bridge, 1982.

FELLOWS-SMITH, Jonathan Payn (Pom-Pom)
RHB, RM

Born Durban, S Africa, 3 Feb 1932. Educ Durban HS; Brasenose C, Oxford. Debut 1953.
OXFORD UNIVERSITY (35) 1953–55 (Blue 1953–55).
NORTHAMPTONSHIRE (13) 1957.
FREE FORESTERS (4) 1957–64.
S AFRICA DOMESTIC Transvaal 1958/59–59/60.
SOUTH AFRICA (4) E 1960.
HST 35 SA v E, Oval, 1960. HS 109* S Africans v Essex, Ilford, 1960 and 109 Northants v Sussex, Hove, 1957.
BB 7–26 Oxford U v D. R. Jardine's XI, Eastbourne, 1955.
Gentlemen v Players (1) 1955. Clubs: Dulwich, West Bromwich Dartmouth. Rugby: Northants. Father H. Fellows-Smith (Natal).

FELTHAM, Mark Andrew
RHB, RMF

Born St John's Wood, London, 26 June 1963. Educ Tiffin S. Debut 1983.
SURREY (13) 1983–.
HS 44 Surrey v Derbys, Oval, 1984.
BB 5–62 Surrey v Warwicks, Edgbaston, 1984.

FELTON, Nigel Alfred
LHB

Born Guildford, Surrey, 24 Oct 1960. Educ Millfield S; Loughborough U. Debut 1982.
SOMERSET (29) 1982–.
HS 173* Som v Kent, Taunton, 1983.

FELTON, Robert
RHB

Born Streatham, London, 27 Dec 1909. Died Ealing, London, 5 Oct 1982. Educ St Paul's S. Debut 1935.
MIDDLESEX (11) 1935–48.
HS 171 M'sex v Cambridge U, Fenner's, 1937.
Club: Brentham.

FENNER, Derek Alfred
RHB, SLA

Born Walthamstow, London, 17 Sept 1933. Educ Epsom; Cambridge U. Debut 1954.
CAMBRIDGE UNIVERSITY (1) 1954.
HS 21 Cambridge U v M'sex, Fenner's, 1954.
BB 2–33 same match.
Club: Banstead.

FENNER, Maurice David
LHB, WK

Born Linton, Kent, 16 Feb 1929. Educ Maidstone GS. Debut 1949.
COMBINED SERVICES (19) 1949–64.
KENT (14) 1951–54.
HS 77 Combined Services v Notts, Trent Bridge, 1961.
Kent secretary 1977–82. Father G. D. Fenner (Kent, MCC).

FERGUSON, William Henry Noel
LHB, RM

Born Downpatrick, Ireland, 6 Dec 1927. Educ Southwell S, Downpatrick. Debut 1951.
IRELAND (5) 1951–64.
HS 37 Ireland v Scotland, Londonderry, 1963.
BB 6–37 Ireland v Scotland, Greenock, 1962.
Club: Downpatrick.

FERNANDO, Edward Ranjith
RHB, WK

Born Colombo, Ceylon, 22 Feb 1944. Educ St Benedicts C. Debut 1964/65.

SRI LANKA DOMESTIC Ceylon (Sri Lanka) 1964/65–78/79.
TOURS Ceylon (Sri Lanka) to India 1964/65, 1966/67, 1968/69, 1970/71, 1975/76. Sri Lanka to Pakistan 1973/74. Sri Lanka to England 1975.
HS 81 Sri Lanka v E Africa, Taunton, 1975.
Club: Nondescripts.

FERNANDO, Lantra Jayantha
RHB, RMF

Born Colombo, Ceylon, 20 Aug 1956. Educ Prince of Wales C, Colombo. Debut 1980/81.
SRI LANKA DOMESTIC Sri Lanka 1980/81–82/83.
TOURS Sri Lanka to India 1980/81. Sri Lanka to England 1981.
HS 21 Arosa Sri Lanka v S Africa, J'burg, 1982/83.
BB 2–61 Arosa Sri Lankans v E Province, Port Elizabeth, 1982/83.
Barred from Sinhalese cricket for 25 yrs for touring S Africa 1982/83 (Arosa Sri Lanka).

FERREIRA, Anthonie Michal
RHB, RM

Born Pretoria, S Africa, 13 Apr 1955. Educ Hill View HS, Pretoria; Pretoria U. Debut 1974/75.
S AFRICA DOMESTIC Northern Transvaal 1974/75–.
WARWICKSHIRE (101) 1979–. Cap 1983.
HS 112* Warwicks v Indians, Edgbaston, 1982.
BB 8–38 N Transvaal v Transvaal B, Pretoria, 1977/78.
Former top-class boxer.

FERRIS, George John Fitzgerald
RHB, RF

Born Urlings Village, Antigua, 18 Oct 1964. Educ Jennings S, Antigua. Debut 1982/83.
W INDIES DOMESTIC Leeward Islands 1982/83–.
LEICESTERSHIRE (14) 1983–.
TOUR Young W Indies to Zimbabwe 1983/84.
HS 26 Leeward Islands v Guyana, Nevis, 1982/83.
BB 7–42 Leics v Glam, Leicester, 1983.

FERRIS, Stuart Wesley
RHB, RM

Born Lurgan, Co Armagh, Ireland, 2 May 1927. Educ Lurgan HS. Debut 1956.

IRELAND (2) 1956.
HS 4* Ireland v MCC, Dublin, 1956.
BB 4–106 Ireland v Scotland, Edinburgh, 1956.
Clubs: Eglinton, Waringstown, Malahide.

FETHERSTONHAUGH, Charles Bateman *Robert*
—RHB, WK—

Born Tavistock, Devon, 17 Nov 1932.
Educ Bradfield; Sandhurst. Debut 1956.
MCC (1) 1956.
FREE FORESTERS (3) 1962–64.
HS 20* Free Foresters v Oxford U, The Parks, 1962.
Devon 1953–63. Clubs: Tavistock, Army, I Zingari.

FIDDLING, Kenneth
—RHB, WK—

Born Hebden Bridge, Yorks, 13 Oct 1917. Debut 1938. *P.*
YORKSHIRE (18) 1938–46.
NORTHAMPTONSHIRE (142) 1947–53.
Cap 1947. Testimonial (£2028) 1952.
HS 68 Northants v Surrey, Oval, 1947.
Clubs: Bowling Old Lane, Lightcliffe.

FIELD, Maxwell Nicholas
—RHB, RM—

Born Coventry, Warwicks, 23 Mar 1950. Educ Bablake S, Coventry; London U; Emmanuel C, Cambridge. Debut 1974.
CAMBRIDGE UNIVERSITY (8) 1974 (Blue).
WARWICKSHIRE (3) 1974–75.
HS 39* Cambridge U v Warwicks, Fenner's, 1974.
BB 4–76 Cambridge U v Oxford U, Lord's, 1974.
Club: West Bromwich Dartmouth.

FILGAS, Frank Miroslav
—RHB, WK—

Born Carlow, Ireland, 3 Nov 1926. Educ Kings Hospital S, Dublin; Dublin U. Debut 1948.
IRELAND (1) 1948.
HS 3 Ireland v Scotland, Glasgow, 1948.
Clubs: Clontarf, Leinster.

FILLERY, Edward William Joseph
—RHB, LBG—

Born Heathfield, Sussex, 14 Apr 1944.
Educ St Lawrence C, Ramsgate; Oriel

C, Oxford. Debut 1963.
OXFORD UNIVERSITY (32) 1963–65 (Blue 1963–65).
KENT (13) 1963–66.
HS 75 Oxford U v Pakistanis, The Parks, 1963.
BB 6–77 Oxford U v Cambridge U, Lord's, 1963.

FINAN, Nicholas Hugh
—RHB, RM—

Born Knowle, Bristol, 3 July 1954. Educ St Brendan's C, Bristol. Debut 1975.
GLOUCESTERSHIRE (8) 1975–79.
HS 18 Glos v Worcs, Worcester, 1977.
BB 2–57 Glos v Sussex, Eastbourne, 1975.

FINCHAM, Anthony Leonard Rupert
—RHB, RM—

Born Lambeth, London, 19 Mar 1955. Educ Tonbridge S; Oriel C, Oxford. Debut 1976.
OXFORD UNIVERSITY (1) 1976.
HS 3* Oxford U v Glam, The Parks, 1976.
BB 4–42 same match.

FINDLAY, Francis
—RHB—

Born Aberdeen, Scotland, 4 Feb 1920. Died Kilmarnock, Scotland, 16 June 1963. Educ Robert Gordon's C, Aberdeen; Aberdeen U. Debut 1948.
SCOTLAND (2) 1948.
HS 6 Scotland v Ireland, Glasgow, 1948.
Aberdeenshire, Kowloon (Malaya), Hong Kong. Brother T. A. Findlay (Scotland).

FINDLAY, Thaddeus *Michael*
—RHB, WK—

Born Troumaka, St Vincent, 19 Oct 1943. Educ St Vincent GS. Debut 1964/65.
W INDIES DOMESTIC Windward Islands 1964/65–77/78, Combined Islands 1966/67–78/79.
W INDIES (10) 1969–72/73. A 1972/73 (1); NZ 1971/72 (5); I 1970/71 (2). *E 1969 (2).*
OTHER TOURS W Indians to Australasia 1968/69. W Indians to England 1976.
HST 44* WI v NZ, Bridgetown, 1971/72.
HS 90 Windward Islands v Leeward Islands, Antigua, 1974/75.

FINDLAY, Thomas Alexander
—RHB—

Born Aberdeen, Scotland, 22 Mar 1918. Educ Robert Gordon's C, Aberdeen. Debut 1947.
SCOTLAND (1) 1947.
HS 19 Scotland v Ireland, Cork, 1947.
Aberdeenshire. Brother F. Findlay (Scotland).

FINLAY, Aubrey James
—RHB—

Born Sion Mills, Co Tyrone, Ireland, 2 Mar 1938. Educ Strabane Technical C. Debut 1957.
IRELAND (9) 1957–65.
HS 30 Ireland v Scotland, Ayr, 1958.

FINLAY, Ian William
—LHB, LM—

Born Woking, Surrey, 14 May 1946. Educ Fullbrook S, Sussex; Witwatersrand U, S Africa. Debut 1965.
SURREY (23) 1965–67.
S AFRICA DOMESTIC Transvaal B 1967/68, North-Eastern Transvaal/Northern Transvaal 1968/69–75/76.
HS 150 NE Transvaal v OFS, Pretoria, 1969/70.
BB 3–17 NE Transvaal v Transvaal B, Pretoria, 1969/70.

FINNEY, Roger John
—RHB, LM—

Born Darley Dale, Derbys, 2 Aug 1960. Educ Lady Manners S, Bakewell. Debut 1982.
DERBYSHIRE (45) 1982–.
HS 78 Derbys v Lancs, Buxton, 1984.
BB 5–58 Derbys v Warwicks, Edgbaston, 1983 and v Glos, Gloucester, 1984.

FIRTH, Jack
—RHB, WK—

Born Cottingley, Yorks, 26 June 1917. Died Cottingley, Yorks, 7 Sept 1981. Debut 1949. *P.*
YORKSHIRE (8) 1949–50.
LEICESTERSHIRE (223) 1951–58. Cap 1951. Benefit 1958.
HS 90* Leics v Essex, Coalville, 1958.
Clubs: Salts, Farsley. Soccer: York City.

FISHER, Paul Bernard
—RHB, WK—

Born Edmonton, London, 19 Dec 1954. Educ St Ignatius C, Enfield; Christ

Church C, Oxford. Debut 1974.
OXFORD UNIVERSITY (41) 1974–78 (Blue 1975–78).
MIDDLESEX (2) 1979.
WORCESTERSHIRE (14) 1980–81.
HS 42 Oxford U v Warwicks, The Parks, 1975.
Club: Dudley.

FISHLOCK, Laurence Barnard
LHB, LM

Born Battersea, London, 2 Jan 1907. Debut 1931. *P. Wisden 1947.*
SURREY (347) 1931–52. Cap 1935. Benefit (£5250) 1950.
ENGLAND (4) 1936–46/47. I 1936 (2), 1946 (1). *A 1946/47 (1).*
OTHER TOURS MCC to Australia 1936/37. Commonwealth XI to India and Ceylon 1950/51.
HST 19* E v I, Oval, 1936. HS 253 Surrey v Leics, Leicester, 1948.
BB 4–62 Surrey v Derbys, Ilkeston, 1934.
1000 RUNS (12 + 1) 2426 @ 45.77 in 1949.
Players v Gentlemen (4) 1936–47. Professional coach St Dunstan's S. Soccer: Crystal Palace, Millwall, Southampton, Aldershot, Gillingham, England (amateur).

FISK, Eric
LHB, SLA

Born East Ardsley, Yorks, 27 Mar 1931. Educ Morley GS. Debut 1950.
COMBINED SERVICES (3) 1950–51.
HS 16 Combined Services v Warwicks, Edgbaston, 1951.
Yorks 2nd XI, RAF. Clubs: King's Cross, East Ardsley, Castleford, Undercliffe, Bowling Old Lane, Spen Victoria, Brighouse, Holmfirth.

FITZGERALD, James Francis
RHB, SLA

Born Sutton Coldfield, 28 Nov 1946. Educ St Brendan's, Bristol; Churchill C, Cambridge. Debut 1967.
CAMBRIDGE UNIVERSITY (12) 1966–68 (Blue 1968).
HS 27* Cambridge U v Derbys, Fenner's, 1968.
BB 6–70 Cambridge U v Essex, Fenner's, 1966.

FITZMAURICE, Desmond Michael John
RHB, RFM

Born Carlton, Victoria, Australia, 16

Oct 1917. Died Prahran, Victoria, Australia, 19 Jan 1981. Debut 1947/48.
AUSTRALIA DOMESTIC Victoria (2) 1947/48.
COMMONWEALTH XI (1) 1950.
TOUR Commonwealth XI to India, Pakistan and Ceylon 1949/50.
HS 45 Victoria v Queensland, Brisbane, 1947/48.
BB 3–29 Commonwealth XI v Indian Universities, Bombay, 1949/50.
Clubs: South Melbourne (Australia), Ashton (England). Brother D. J. A Fitzmaurice (Victoria).

FLAHERTY, Kevin Frederick
RHB, OB

Born Birmingham, 17 Sept 1939. Debut 1969.
WARWICKSHIRE (1) 1969.
Did not bat.
BB 3–38 Warwicks v Cambridge U, Edgbaston, 1969.

FLANAGAN, John *Patrick* Douglas
RHB, RM

Born Johannesburg, S Africa, 20 Sept 1947. Educ King Edward VII S, Johannesburg; Witwatersrand U. Debut 1965/66.
S AFRICA DOMESTIC Transvaal 1965/66–77/78.
TOUR S African Universities to England 1967.
HS 98 Transvaal B v Natal B, J'burg, 1968/69.
BB 8–113 (10–199 match) same match (match double of 100 runs – 98 and 17 – and 10 wkts).
Father F. F. Flanagan (Griqualand West and Transvaal).

FLAVELL, John Alfred
LHB, RFM

Born Brierley Hill, Staffordshire, 14 May 1929. Educ Kingswinford Sec S. Debut 1949. *P. Wisden 1965.*
WORCESTERSHIRE (392) 1949–67. Cap 1955. Benefit (£6840) 1963.
ENGLAND (4) 1961–64. A 1961 (2), 1964 (2).
TOURS Worcs to Rhodesia 1964/65. Worcs to Jamaica 1965/66.
HST 14 E v A, Oval, 1961. HS 54 Worcs v Warwicks, Dudley, 1959.
BBT 2–65 E v A, Old Trafford, 1961. BB 9–30 Worcs v Kent, Dover, 1955.
Three hat-tricks, including one all lbw, Worcs v Lancs, Old Trafford, 1963.

100 WKTS (8) 171 @ 17.79 in 1961.
Players v Gentlemen (1) 1961. Clubs: Stourbridge, Walsall. Soccer: Walsall.

FLEMING, Robert Christopher John
RHB, OB

Born Woking, Surrey, 20 July 1953. Educ KCS Wimbledon; Jesus C, Cambridge. Debut 1974.
CAMBRIDGE UNIVERSITY (9) 1974.
HS 13* Cambridge U v Glos, Fenner's, 1974.
BB 3–91 Cambridge U v Kent, Fenner's, 1974.

FLETCHER, Barry Elystan
LHB, occ WK

Born Birmingham, 7 Mar 1935. Educ Bishop Vesey's GS, Sutton Coldfield; Colwyn Bay GS. Debut 1956. *P.*
WARWICKSHIRE (49) 1956–61.
HS 102* Warwicks v Oxford U, Edgbaston, 1960.
Clubs: Colwyn Bay, Mitchells and Butlers, Moseley. Badminton: Wales.

FLETCHER, Christopher David Bryan
RHB, RFM

Born Harrogate, Yorks, 10 Dec 1957. Educ Torquay GS; Exeter U. Debut 1979.
SUSSEX (1) 1979.
Did not bat.
Devon 1976.

FLETCHER, David George William
RHB, occ RM

Born Sutton, Surrey, 6 July 1924. Debut 1946. *P.*
SURREY (300) 1946–61. Cap 1947. Benefit (£7600) 1957.
TOURS Commonwealth XI to India 1953/54. Surrey to Rhodesia 1959/60.
HS 194 Surrey v Notts, Trent Bridge, 1947.
1000 RUNS (4) 1960 @ 37.69 in 1952.
Players v Gentlemen (4) 1947–52. Club: Epsom. Professional coach Caterham S from 1963.

FLETCHER, Duncan Andrew Gwynne
LHB, RFM

Born Salisbury, Rhodesia, 27 Sept 1948. Educ Prince Edward HS, Salisbury.

Debut 1969/70.
S AFRICA DOMESTIC Rhodesia 1969/
70–78/79.
ZIMBABWE 1979/80–. Capt 1979/80–.
TOUR Zimbabwe to England 1982 (capt).
HS 89 Rhodesia v E Province, Port
Elizabeth, 1969/70.
BB 6–31 (11–92 match) Rhodesia v E
Province, Bulawayo, 1974/75.
Cambridgeshire 1977. Club: Rishton
(England). Brother A. W. R. Fletcher
(Rhodesia).

FLETCHER, Keith William Robert
—RHB, LB—

Born Worcester, 20 May 1944. Educ
Comberton Village C. Debut 1962. P.
Wisden 1974.
ESSEX (495) 1962–. Cap 1963. Capt
1974–. Benefit (£13,000) 1973.
Testimonial (£83,250) 1982.
ENGLAND (59) 1968–81/82. A 1968 (1),
1972 (1), 1975 (2); WI 1973 (3); NZ 1969
(2), 1973 (3); I 1971 (2), 1974 (3); P 1974
(3). A 1970/71 (5), 1974/75 (5), 1976/
77 (1); WI 1973/74 (4); NZ 1970/71
(1), 1974/75 (2); I 1972/73 (5), 1976/
77 (3), 1981/82 (6); P 1968/69 (3),
1972/73 (3); SL 1981/82 (1). Capt 7.
OTHER TOURS Cavaliers to W Indies
1964/65. MCC Under-25 XI to Pakistan
1966/67. International XI to Pakistan,
India and Ceylon 1967/68. MCC to
Ceylon 1969/70.
HS T 216 E v NZ, Auckland, 1974/75. HS
228* Essex v Sussex, Hastings, 1968.
BB 5–41 Essex v M'sex, Colchester,
1979.
1000 RUNS (20) 1890 @ 41.08 in 1968.
RECORDS During 122 E v P, Oval, 1974,
reached century in 458 mins, slowest fc
century in England. Added 254 for 5th
wkt with A. W. Greig, E v I, Bombay,
1972/73, England Test record.
588 catches in career. OBE for services
to cricket. Autobiography (with Alan
Lee) Captain's Innings (1983).

FLETCHER, Stuart David
—RHB, RFM—

Born Keighley, Yorks, 8 June 1964.
Educ Reins Wood Sec S. Debut 1983.
YORKSHIRE (11) 1983–.
HS 28* Yorks v Kent, Tunbridge Wells,
1984.
BB 4–24 Yorks v Som, Middlesbrough,
1984.

FLICK, Barry John
—RHB, WK—

Born Coventry, Warwicks, 5 Mar 1952.
Educ Caludon Castle S, Coventry.

Debut 1969.
WARWICKSHIRE (16) 1969–73.
HS 18 Warwicks v Glos, Cheltenham,
1973.
Clubs: Aston Unity, Coventry, North
Warwicks.

FLINT, Derrick
—RHB, LBG—

Born Creswell, Derbys, 14 June 1924.
Debut 1948. P.
WARWICKSHIRE (10) 1948–49.
HS 11 Warwicks v Derbys, Edgbaston,
1948.
BB 4–67 Warwicks v Cambridge U,
Edgbaston, 1948.
Clubs: Coventry and North Warwicks,
Harborne, Walsall. Professional coach
Dean Close S 1951. Father B. Flint
(Notts); uncle W. A. Flint (Notts); wife
Rachael Heyhoe-Flint (England
Women).

FLOCKTON, Raymond George
—RHB, RM—

Born Paddington, Sydney, NSW,
Australia, 14 Mar 1930. Debut 1951/52.
AUSTRALIA DOMESTIC New South Wales
(34) 1951/52–62/63.
COMMONWEALTH XI (1) 1950.
HS 264* NSW v S Australia, Sydney,
1959/60 (highest maiden century in
Sheffield Shield).
BB 4–33 NSW v W Australia, Sydney,
1960/61.
Clubs: Paddington, St George
(Australia), Colne (England).

FLOOD, Raymond David
—RHB, OB—

Born Southampton, Hants, 20 Nov
1935. Debut 1956. P.
HAMPSHIRE (24) 1956–60.
HS 138* Hants v Sussex, Hove, 1959.

FLOWER, Russell William
—LHB, SLA—

Born Stone, Staffordshire, 6 Nov 1942.
Educ Granville S, Stone. Debut 1978.
WARWICKSHIRE (9) 1978.
HS 10* Warwicks v Yorks, Bradford,
1978.
BB 3–45 Warwicks v Northants, North-
ampton, 1978.
Staffordshire 1964–77, 1979–. Club:
Stone.

FLYNN, Vincent Anthony Patrick
—RHB, WK—

Born Aylesbury, Buckinghamshire, 3
Oct 1955. Educ Aylesbury GS; Leeds
U. Debut 1976.
NORTHAMPTONSHIRE (3) 1976–78.
HS 15 Northants v Yorks, Northampton,
1978.
Buckinghamshire 1980–. Clubs: Ayles-
bury, Buckingham.

FOAT, James Clive
—RHB, occ RM—

Born Salford Priors, Warwicks, 21 Nov
1952. Educ Millfield S. Debut 1972.
GLOUCESTERSHIRE (91) 1972–79. Cap
1979.
HS 126 Glos v Hants, Gloucester, 1979.

FOLKES, Castell
—RHB, RFM—

Born Kingston, Jamaica, 29 July 1944.
Debut 1967/68.
W INDIES DOMESTIC Jamaica 1967/68–70/
71.
TOUR Jamaica to England 1970.
HS 9 Jamaica v Guyana, Kingston, 1968/
69.
BB 5–22 Jamaica v Sussex, Hove, 1970.

FOLLEY, Ian
—RHB, LMF—

Born Burnley, Lancs, 9 Jan 1963. Educ
Mansfield HS; Nelson and Colne C.
Debut 1982.
LANCASHIRE (46) 1982–.
HS 36 Lancs v Derbys, Old Trafford,
1982.
BB 5–101 Lancs v M'sex, Liverpool,
1984.

FOORD, Charles William
—RHB, RFM—

Born Scarborough, Yorks, 11 June
1924. Debut 1947. P.
YORKSHIRE (51) 1947–53.
HS 35 Yorks v Sussex, Hastings, 1953.
BB 6–63 Yorks v Hants, Bournemouth,
1953.
Club: Scarborough.

FORBES, Carlton
—LHB, LM—

Born Kingston, Jamaica, 9 Aug 1936.
Debut 1959. P.

NOTTINGHAMSHIRE (244) 1959–73. Cap 1965. Benefit 1969.
HS 86 Notts v Lancs, Southport, 1961.
BB 7–19 Notts v Kent, Trent Bridge, 1966.
1000 RUNS (1) 1020 @ 20.40 in 1961.
100 WKTS (3) 117 @ 19.64 in 1965.
Clubs: Middlesbrough, Church.

FORD, James *Malcolm* Clark
————LHB————

Born Edinburgh, Scotland, 29 Dec 1936. Debut 1960.
SCOTLAND (10) 1960–66.
HS 50 Scotland v Ireland, Cork, 1961.
West Lothian. Father A. C. Ford (Scotland).

FORD, John Kenneth
————RHB, RFM————

Born Bristol, 5 Mar 1934. Educ Gotham GS. Debut 1951. *P.*
GLOUCESTERSHIRE (1) 1951.
No runs, one wkt.

FORD, Walter Ronald
————LHB, WK————

Born Kingston-upon-Thames, Surrey, 19 Oct 1913. Educ Hampton GS. Debut 1946.
COMBINED SERVICES (4) 1946–49.
HS 36 Combined Services v Hants, Portsmouth, 1949.
Played for RAF. Assistant-secretary (administration) at Lord's, 1974. Wing-commander RAF.

FOREMAN, Dennis Joseph
————RHB, OB————

Born Cape Town, S Africa, 1 Feb 1933. Educ St Agnes C, Cape Town. Debut 1951/52. *P.*
S AFRICA DOMESTIC Western Province 1951/52.
SUSSEX (125) 1952–67. Cap 1966.
HS 104 Sussex v Notts, Hove, 1967.
BB 4–64 Sussex v Oxford U, Worthing, 1952.
Club: Brighton and Hove. Soccer: Brighton and Hove Albion.

FORMAN, Peter Ralph
————LHB, SLA————

Born Nottingham, 9 Mar 1934. Educ Oakham S. Debut 1959.
NOTTINGHAMSHIRE (16) 1959–62.
HS 26 Notts v Pakistanis, Trent Bridge, 1962.
BB 5–73 Notts v Glam, Swansea, 1962.

FORSTER, Grant
————LHB, ROB————

Born Seaham, Co Durham, 27 May 1961. Educ Seaham Northlea GS; Wearside Technical C. Debut 1980.
NORTHAMPTONSHIRE (1) 1980.
LEICESTERSHIRE (3) 1982.
TOUR Leics XI to Zimbabwe 1980/81.
HS 22* Leics v Zimbabweans, Leicester, 1982.
BB 2–30 Northants v Cambridge U, Fenner's, 1980.
Durham 1983–. Club: Boldon.

FORTIN, Richard Chalmers Gordon
————RHB, WK————

Born Singapore, 12 Apr 1940. Educ Wellington C; Corpus Christi C, Oxford. Debut 1963.
OXFORD UNIVERSITY (2) 1963.
HS 25 Oxford U v Lancs, The Parks, 1963.
Berkshire 1965–70.

FOSH, Matthew Kailey
————LHB, RM————

Born Epping, Essex, 26 Sept 1957. Educ Harrow; Magdalene C, Cambridge. Debut 1976.
ESSEX (14) 1976–78.
CAMBRIDGE UNIVERSITY (16) 1977–78 (Blue 1977–78).
HS 109 Cambridge U v Derbys, Fenner's, 1978.
Scored 161* in 145 mins, Harrow v Eton, Lord's, 1975. Rugby: Blue.

FOSTER, David Charles Geoffrey
————LHB, SLA————

Born Holbeach, Lincolnshire, 19 Sept 1959. Educ Sutton Valance S; Christ Church C, Oxford. Debut 1980.
OXFORD UNIVERSITY (4) 1980.
HS 67 Oxford U v Lancs, The Parks, 1980.

FOSTER, Maurice Linton Churchill
————RHB, OB————

Born St Mary, Jamaica, 9 May 1943. Educ Wolmer's S, Kingston. Debut 1963/64.
W INDIES DOMESTIC Jamaica 1963/64–77/78.
WEST INDIES (14) 1969–77/78. E 1973/74 (1); A 1972/73 (4), 1977/78 (1); NZ 1971/72 (3); I 1970/71 (2); P 1976/77 (1).

E 1969 (1), 1973 (1).
TOUR Jamaica to England 1970.
HST 125 WI v A, Kingston, 1972/73. HS 234 Jamaica v Trinidad, Montego Bay, 1976/77.
BBT 2–41 WI v P, Bridgetown, 1976/77.
BB 5–65 Jamaica v Guyana, Kingston, 1972/73.
Club: Kingston (W Indies). Former Jamaica table-tennis champion.

FOSTER, Neil Alan
————RHB, RFM————

Born Colchester, Essex, 6 May 1962. Educ Philip Morant CS, Colchester. Debut 1980.
ESSEX (40) 1982–. Cap 1983.
ENGLAND (6) 1983–84. WI 1984 (1); NZ 1983 (1). *NZ 1983/84 (2); P 1983/84 (2).*
HST 18* E v NZ, Auckland, 1983/84. HS 54* Essex v Sussex, Eastbourne, 1984.
BBT 5–67 E v P, Lahore, 1983/84. BB 6–30 England XI v N Districts, Hamilton, 1983/84.

FOSTER, Peter Geoffrey
————RHB, SLA————

Born Beckenham, Kent, 9 Oct 1916. Educ Winchester; Christ Church C, Oxford. Debut 1936.
OXFORD UNIVERSITY (5) 1936–38.
KENT (25) 1939–46.
HS 107 Kent v Leics, Leicester, 1939.
Clubs: I Zingari, Free Foresters, MCC, Butterflies, Band of Brothers, Stock Exchange, XL Club. Father G. N. Foster (Worcs and Kent); uncles B. S., H. K., M. K., N. J. A., R. E. and W. L. Foster (all Worcs); cousin C. K. Foster (Worcs).

FOSTER, William John
————RHB, SLA————

Born Glasgow, Scotland, 3 Feb 1934. Educ Harrow. Debut 1964.
COMBINED SERVICES (2) 1964. Capt.
HS 36 Combined Services v Oxford U, Aldershot, 1964.
Royal Navy. Clubs: Free Foresters, The Mount, Oatlands Park. Member I Zingari.

FOULDS, Frederick George
————RHB————

Born Leicester, 23 Apr 1935. Debut 1952. *P.*
LEICESTERSHIRE (2) 1952–56.
HS 1 Leics v Cambridge U, Fenner's, 1952.
Member XL Club.

FOWLER, Graeme
RHB, occ WK

Born Accrington, Lancs, 20 Apr 1957. Educ Accrington GS; Durham U. Debut 1979.
LANCASHIRE (81) 1979–. Cap 1981.
TOUR International XI to Jamaica 1982/83.
ENGLAND (16) 1982–84. WI 1984 (5); NZ 1983 (2); P 1982 (1); SL 1984 (1). *A 1982/83 (3); NZ 1983/84 (2); P 1983/84 (2).*
HST 106 E v WI, Lord's, 1984. HS 226 Lancs v Kent, Maidstone, 1984.
1000 RUNS (4) 1560 @ 39.00 in 1981.
RECORDS Added 201 in 43 mins for 1st wkt with S. J. O'Shaughnessy, Lancs v Leics, Old Trafford, 1983, fastest double-century stand in fc cricket; Fowler (100) hit 10 consecutive scoring-strokes for six, a fc record, and reached his century in 46 mins. Leics were concerned only with increasing their season's over rate and used non-regular bowlers.
Clubs: Accrington, Rawtenstall.

FOWLER, William Peter
RHB, SLA

Born St Helens, Lancs, 13 Mar 1959. Educ Kamo HS; Otago U; Auckland U. Debut 1979/80.
N ZEALAND DOMESTIC Northern Districts (9) 1979/80–80/81, Auckland (1) 1981/82–.
DERBYSHIRE (39) 1983–.
HS 116 Derbys v Glam, Derby, 1984.
BB 2–44 N Districts v C Districts, Gisborne, 1979/80.

FOX, John George
RHB, WK

Born Norton-on-Tees, Co Durham, 22 July 1929. Debut 1959. *P.*
WARWICKSHIRE (43) 1959–61.
HS 52 Warwicks v Indians, Edgbaston, 1959.
Durham 1950–64, Devon 1968–69.
Club: Norton-on-Tees.

FRANCIS, Bruce Colin
RHB, RM

Born Sydney, NSW, Australia, 18 Feb 1948. Educ Vaucluse HS, Sydney; Sydney U. Debut 1968/69.
AUSTRALIA DOMESTIC New South Wales (32) 1968/69–72/73.
ESSEX (47) 1971–73. Cap 1971.
AUSTRALIA (3) *E 1972.*
OTHER TOURS International XI to Rhodesia 1972/73. D. H. Robins' XI to

S Africa 1973/74, 1974/75.
HST 27 A v E, Old Trafford, 1972. HS 210 Australians v Oxford and Cambridge Universities, The Parks, 1972.
1000 RUNS (2) 1578 @ 38.48 in 1971.
Clubs: Waverley (Sydney), Accrington (England).

FRANCIS, David *Arthur*
RHB, OB

Born Clydach, Glam, 29 Nov 1953. Educ Cwmtawe CS, Pontardawe. Debut 1973.
GLAMORGAN (138) 1973–. Cap 1982.
HS 142* Glam v Kent, Canterbury, 1982.
1000 RUNS (1) 1076 @ 38.42 in 1982.
Club: Gowerton.

FRANKLIN, Trevor John
RHB, RM

Born Auckland, N Zealand, 15 Mar 1962. Debut 1980/81.
N ZEALAND DOMESTIC New Zealand Under-23 (1) 1980/81, Auckland (30) 1980/81–.
NEW ZEALAND (1) *E 1983.*
HST 7 NZ v E, Trent Bridge, 1983. HS 136 Auckland v N Districts, Gisborne, 1982/83.

FRANKS, Jonathan Guy
RHB

Born Stamford, Lincolnshire, 23 Sept 1962. Educ Stamford; St Edmund Hall, Oxford. Debut 1983.
OXFORD UNIVERSITY (13) 1983–84 (Blue 1984).
HS 42* Oxford U v M'sex, The Parks, 1984.
Lincolnshire 1980–. Club: Burghley Park.

FRASAT ALI
RHB, RMF

Born Kenya, 1950. Debut 1975.
E AFRICA to England (1) 1975.
HS 30 E Africa v Sri Lanka, Taunton, 1975.
BB 2–37 same match.

FRASER, Angus Robert Charles
RHB, RMF

Born Billinge, Lancs, 8 Aug 1965. Educ Gayton HS, Harrow. Debut 1984.
MIDDLESEX (1) 1984.
Did not bat, and 1 wkt.
Club: Stanmore.

FRASER, David Dempster
RHB, RFM

Born Edinburgh, Scotland, 9 Apr 1943. Educ RHS, Edinburgh; Edinburgh U. Debut 1967.
SCOTLAND (4) 1967–69.
No runs.
BB 3–29 Scotland v MCC, Glasgow, 1967.

FRASER, Thomas William
RHB, SLA

Born Johannesburg, S Africa, 26 June 1912. Educ Jeppe, S Africa; Pembroke C, Cambridge. Debut 1936.
CAMBRIDGE UNIVERSITY (13) 1936–37 (Blue 1937).
FREE FORESTERS (1) 1948.
S AFRICA DOMESTIC Orange Free State 1936/37–46/47.
HS 61* Cambridge U v Army, Fenner's, 1937.
BB 8–71 OFS v E Province, Port Elizabeth, 1939/40.

FRASER-DARLING, Callum *David*
RHB, RMF

Born Sheffield, 30 Sept 1963. Educ Edinburgh Academy. Debut 1984.
NOTTINGHAMSHIRE (1) 1984.
Did not bat.
BB 2–14 Notts v Cambridge U, Trent Bridge, 1984.

FREDERICK, Michael Campbell
RHB

Born St Peter, Barbados, 6 May 1927. Educ Lodge S, Barbados. Debut 1944/45.
W INDIES DOMESTIC Barbados 1944/45, Jamaica 1953/54.
DERBYSHIRE (2) 1949.
WEST INDIES (1) *E 1953/54.*
HST 30 WI v E, Kingston, 1953/54. HS 84 Derbys v Essex, Burton upon Trent, 1949.
Clubs: Windhill, Undercliffe.

FREDERICKS, Roy Clifton
LHB, SLC

Born Blairmont, Berbice, British Guiana, 11 Nov 1942. Educ New Amsterdam Technical S, British Guiana. Debut 1963/64.
W INDIES DOMESTIC British Guiana (Guyana) 1963/64–82/83.
GLAMORGAN (45) 1971–73. Cap 1971.

WEST INDIES (59) 1968/69–76/77. E
1973/74 (5); A 1972/73 (5); NZ 1971/72
(5); I 1970/71 (4), 1975/76 (4); P 1976/77
(5). *E 1969 (3), 1973 (3), 1976 (5); A
1968/69 (4), 1975/76 (6); NZ 1968/69
(3); I 1974/75 (5); P 1974/75 (2).*
HST 169 WI v A, Perth, 1975/76. HS 250
Guyana v Barbados, Bridgetown, 1974/
75.
BB 4–36 Guyana v Trinidad, Port of
Spain, 1971/72.
1000 RUNS (4 + 2) 1506 @ 43.02 in 1973.
RECORDS HS (above) highest-ever inns in
Shell Shield. Put on 330 for 1st wkt with
A. Jones, Glam v Northants, Swansea,
1972, county record.
Scored second-fastest Test century in
terms of balls received (71), during HST
(above). Scored 217 and 103 in last two
fc inns, in 1982/83 for Guyana.
World Series Cricket (Kerry Packer)
1977/78. Comrade Fredericks, Guyana
government minister.

FREEMAN, Eric Walter
—RHB, RFM—

Born Largs Bay, S Australia, 13 July
1944. Debut 1964/65.
AUSTRALIA DOMESTIC South Australia
(44) 1964/65–73/74.
AUSTRALIA (11) 1967/68–69/70. WI
1968/69 (4); I 1967/68 (2). E 1968 (2);
SA 1969/70 (2); I 1969/70 (1).
OTHER TOUR Australia to N Zealand
1966/67.
HST 76 A v WI, Sydney, 1968/69. HS 116
Australians v Northants, Northampton,
1968.
BBT 4–52 A v WI, Adelaide, 1968/69. BB
8–47 S Australia v N Zealanders,
Adelaide, 1967/68.
Club: Port Adelaide. Australian Rules
Football: South Australia.

FREEMAN, Terence
—RHB, RFM—

Born Wellingborough, 21 Oct 1931.
Debut 1954.
NORTHAMPTONSHIRE (1) 1954.
HS 4 Northants v Hants, Portsmouth,
1954.

FRENCH, Bruce Nicholas
—RHB, WK—

Born Warsop, Notts, 13 Aug 1959. Educ
Meden S, Warsop. Debut 1976.
NOTTINGHAMSHIRE (169) 1976–. Cap
1980.
HS 91 Notts v Lancs, Trent Bridge,
1984.
RECORD 86 dismissals for Notts in 1984,
county record.

FROST, Graham
—RHB, RM—

Born Old Basford, Notts, 15 Jan 1947.
Debut 1967.
NOTTINGHAMSHIRE (102) 1967–73.
HS 107 Notts v Surrey, Trent Bridge,
1970.
BB 3–33 Notts v W Indians, Trent
Bridge, 1969.

FROST, Patrick Douglas
—RHB—

Born Antigua, 3 Oct 1940. Educ Lodge
S, Barbados; Oxford U. Debut 1961.
OXFORD UNIVERSITY (1) 1961.
Did not bat or bowl.

FRY, Charles Anthony
—RHB—

Born Henley-in-Arden, Warwicks, 14
Jan 1940. Educ Repton; Trinity C, Oxford. Debut 1959.
OXFORD UNIVERSITY (41) 1959–61 (Blue
1959–61).
HAMPSHIRE (5) 1960.
NORTHAMPTONSHIRE (2) 1962.
FREE FORESTERS (2) 1964–68.
HS 103* Oxford U v Free Foresters, The
Parks, 1959.
Father S. Fry (Hants); grandfather C. B.
Fry (Oxford U, Sussex, Hants and England).

FULLER, Edward Russell Henry
—RHB, RFM—

Born Worcester, Cape Province, S
Africa, 2 Aug 1931. Educ Observatory
HS, Cape Town. Debut 1950/51.
S AFRICA DOMESTIC Western Province
1950/51–57/58.
COMMONWEALTH XI (1) 1958.
SOUTH AFRICA (7) 1952/53–57/58. A
1957/58 (1). *E 1955 (2); A 1952/53 (2);
NZ 1952/53 (2).*
HST 17 SA v NZ, Auckland, 1952/53. HS
69 W Province v Natal, Cape Town,
1954/55.
BBT 5–66 SA v A, Melbourne, 1952/53.
BB 7–40 W Province v Transvaal,
J'burg, 1955/56.
Took field for Yorkshire as substitute, v
W Indians, Middlesbrough, 1963.
Clubs: Claremont (Cape Town),
Middlesbrough, GKN (Bilston).

FULLERTON, George Murray
—RHB, occ WK, LM—

Born Johannesburg, S Africa, 8 Dec
1922. Debut 1942/43.
S AFRICA DOMESTIC Rest of South Africa

1942/43, Transvaal 1945/46–50/51.
SOUTH AFRICA (7) 1947–51. A 1949/50
(2). *E 1947 (2), 1951 (3).*
HST 88 SA v A, J'burg, 1949/50. HS 167
S Africans v Essex, Ilford, 1951.
BB 2–41 S Africans v Combined Services, Portsmouth, 1951.
1000 RUNS (1) 1129 @ 31.36 in 1951.

FULLERTON, Ian Ramsay
—RHB—

Born Johannesburg, S Africa, 24 Sept
1935. Educ Jeppe HS, Witwatersrand
U. Debut 1958/59.
S AFRICA DOMESTIC Transvaal/Transvaal
B 1958/59–65/66.
TOUR S African Fezelas to England 1961.
HS 145 Transvaal v W Province, J'burg,
1962/63.

FULLWOOD, Walter
—RHB, WK—

Born Holmewood, Derbys, 8 Feb 1907.
Debut 1946. *P.*
DERBYSHIRE (6) 1946.
HS 13 Derbys v Surrey, Oval, 1946.
Professional: Highgate. Clubs: Metropolitan Police, Hornsey, XL Club.

FURNISS, John *Brian*
—RHB, RFM—

Born Baslow, Derbys, 16 Nov 1934.
Debut 1955. *P.*
DERBYSHIRE (4) 1955–56.
HS 6 Derbys v Kent, Gravesend, 1956.
BB 3–52 same match.
Club: Leek.

FURSDON, Edward *David*
—RHB, RMF—

Born Sevenoaks, Kent, 20 Dec 1952.
Educ Sherborne; St John's C, Oxford.
Debut 1973.
OXFORD UNIVERSITY (17) 1973–75 (Blue
1974–75).
HS 112* Oxford U v Cambridge U,
Lord's, 1975.
BB 6–60 Oxford and Cambridge Universities v Indians, The Parks, 1974.
Devon 1981.

FUSSELL, Philip Hillier
—RHB, RM—

Born Rode, Bath, 12 Feb 1931. Educ
Monkton Combe S. Debut 1953.
SOMERSET (2) 1953–56.
HS 5 Som v Notts, Weston-super-Mare,
1953.
Club: Frome.

G

GAEKWAD, Anshuman Dattajirao
—————RHB, OB—————

Born Bombay, India, 23 Sept 1952.
Debut 1969/70.
INDIA DOMESTIC Baroda 1969/70–. Capt
1975/76–.
INDIA (35) 1974/75–83/84. E 1976/77
(4); WI 1974/75 (3), 1978/79 (5), 1983/
84 (6); NZ 1976/77 (3); P 1983/84 (3). E
1979 (2); A 1977/78 (1); WI 1975/76
(3), 1982/83 (5).
OTHER TOURS India to England 1975.
India to N Zealand 1975/76. A. L.
Wadekar's XI to Sri Lanka 1975/76.
India to Pakistan 1978/79.
HST 201 I v P, Jullundur, 1983/84 (in 689
mins, including slowest-ever fc double-
century, in 652 mins). HS 225 Baroda v
Gujerat, Baroda, 1982/83.
BB 6–49 Baroda v Saurashtra, Rajkot,
1971/72.
1000 RUNS (0 + 1) 1047 @ 43.62 in 1978/
79.
Father D. K. Gaekwad (India).

GAEKWAD, Dattajirao Krishnarao
—————RHB, LB—————

Born Baroda, India, 27 Oct 1928. Educ
Maharaja Sayajirao U. Debut 1943/44.
INDIA DOMESTIC Baroda 1947/48–63/64.
Capt 1957/58–60/61.
INDIA (11) 1952–60/61. WI 1958/59 (1);
P 1952/53 (2), 1960/61 (1). E 1952 (1),
1959 (4); WI 1952/53 (2). Capt 4.
HST 52 I v WI, Delhi, 1958/59. HS 249*
Baroda v Maharashtra, Poona, 1959/60.
BB 4–117 Board President's XI v
Holkar, Indore, 1957/58.
1000 RUNS (1) 1174 @ 34.52 in 1959.
Son A. D. Gaekwad (India).

GAEKWAD, Hiralal Ghasulal
—————LHB, LM/SLA—————

Born Nagpur, India, 29 Aug 1923. Educ
Sule HS, Nagpur. Debut 1941/42.
INDIA DOMESTIC Central Provinces and
Berar 1941/42, Holkar 1943/44–54/55,
Madhya Bharat 1955/56–56/57,

Madhya Pradesh 1957/58–63/64.
INDIA (1) P 1952/53.
TOURS Holkar to Ceylon 1947/48. India
to England 1952.
HST 14 I v P, Lucknow, 1952/53. HS 164
Holkar v Bihar, Jamshedpur, 1951/52.
BB 7–67 Holkar v Baroda, Indore, 1948/
49.
Club: Colne.

GALE, Robert Alec
—————LHB, RLB—————

Born Old Warden, Bedfordshire, 10
Dec 1933. Educ Bedford Modern S.
Debut 1955. P.
COMBINED SERVICES (1) 1955.
MIDDLESEX (219) 1956–65. Cap 1957.
FREE FORESTERS (1) 1968.
TOUR E. W. Swanton's XI to W Indies
1960/61.
HS 200 M'sex v Glam, Newport, 1962.
BB 4–57 M'sex v Cambridge U,
Fenner's, 1959.
1000 RUNS (6) 2211 @ 38.78 in 1962.
Players v Gentlemen (3) 1957–62. Bed-
fordshire 1950.

GALLACHER, Thomas Nesbitt
—————RHB—————

Born Kilmarnock, Scotland, 3 Apr
1936. Educ Kilmarnock Academy.
Debut 1965.
SCOTLAND (4) 1965–66.
HS 73 Scotland v N Zealanders, Glas-
gow, 1965.
Club: Kilmarnock.

GALLAUGHER, Robert George
—————RHB, SLA—————

Born Epsom, Auckland, N Zealand, 8
Jan 1923. Educ Auckland GS. Debut
1945.
NEW ZEALAND SERVICES XI to England (1)
1945.
HS 2 N Zealand Services XI v H. D. G.
Leveson Gower's XI, Scarborough,
1945.
Clubs: YMCA, Hamilton, Howick, N
Zealand Navy.

GALLEY, James
—————RHB—————

Born Brislington, Bristol, 4 Oct 1945.
Debut 1969.
SOMERSET (3) 1969.
HS 17 Som v Kent, Dover, 1969.
Wiltshire 1980. Club: Lansdown.
Rugby: Bath.

GAMBLE, Neil Walton
—————RHB, RM—————

Born Macclesfield, Cheshire, 17 Jan
1943. Educ Stockport GS; Manchester
U; St Edmund Hall, Oxford. Debut
1967.
OXFORD UNIVERSITY (13) 1967 (Blue).
HS 24 Oxford U v Surrey, The Parks,
1967.
BB 4–57 Oxford U v S African Univer-
sities, Roehampton, 1967.
Cheshire 1965–68. Club: Harlequins.

GAMSY, Dennis
—————RHB, WK—————

Born Durban, S Africa, 17 Feb 1940.
Educ Durban HS; Natal U. Debut
1958/59.
S AFRICA DOMESTIC Natal 1958/59–72/
73.
SOUTH AFRICA (2) A 1969/70.
TOUR S Africans to England 1965.
HST 30* SA v A, Cape Town, 1969/70.
HS 137 Natal v Transvaal, Durban,
1963/64.

GANDON, Nicholas John Charles
—————RHB, OB—————

Born Leicester, 7 July 1956. Educ
Haileybury and ISC; Durham U; St Ed-
mund Hall, Oxford. Debut 1979.
OXFORD UNIVERSITY (8) 1979.
HS 38 Oxford U v Som, The Parks, 1979.
Hertfordshire 1975–79. Club: Hoddes-
don.

GANTEAUME, Andrew Gordon
————RHB, OCC WK————

Born Port of Spain, Trinidad, 22 Jan 1921. Debut 1940/41.
W INDIES DOMESTIC Trinidad 1940/41–62/63.
WEST INDIES (1) E 1947/48.
TOUR W Indies to England 1957.
HST 112 WI v E, Port of Spain, 1947/48.
HS 159 Trinidad v Jamaica, Kingston, 1946/47.
RECORDS First player to score century in only Test and *only* player to score century in only Test inns.

GARD, Trevor
————RHB, WK————

Born West Lambrook, Som, 2 June 1957. Educ Huish Episcopi S, Langport. Debut 1976.
SOMERSET (64) 1976–.
HS 51* Som v Indians, Taunton, 1979 and 51 v Glam, Swansea, 1983.

GARDINER, Stuart James
————LHB, LM————

Born Bloemfontein, S Africa, 19 Mar 1947. Educ St Andrews S, Bloemfontein, S Africa; St John's C, Cambridge. Debut 1967/68.
S AFRICA DOMESTIC Orange Free State 1967/68–73/74.
CAMBRIDGE UNIVERSITY (8) 1978 (Blue).
HS 40* OFS v N Transvaal, Bloemfontein, 1971/72.
BB 6–49 OFS v N Transvaal, Pretoria, 1972/73.

GARDINER-HILL, Peter Farquhar
————RHB————

Born London, 22 Oct 1926. Educ Eton; Christ Church C, Oxford. Debut 1949.
OXFORD UNIVERSITY (2) 1949.
HS 50 Oxford U v M'sex, The Parks, 1949.

GARDNER, Fred Charles
————RHB————

Born Bell Green, Coventry, 4 June 1922. Died Coventry, 13 Jan 1979. Educ Windmill Road S, Coventry. Debut 1947. *P from 1948.*
WARWICKSHIRE (338) 1947–61. Cap 1949. Benefit (£3750) 1958.
HS 215* Warwicks v Som, Taunton, 1950.
1000 RUNS (10) 1911 @ 45.50 in 1950.
Players v Gentlemen (1) 1957. Clubs:

Courtaulds, Dunlop. Fc umpire 1962–65. Soccer: Newport County, Coventry City.

GARDNER, Leslie *Robin*
————RHB, OB————

Born Ledbury, Herefordshire, 23 Feb 1924. Debut 1954. *P.*
LEICESTERSHIRE (126) 1954–62. Cap 1961.
HS 102* Leics v Australians, Leicester, 1961.
BB 3–54 Leics v N Zealanders, Leicester, 1958.
1000 RUNS (1) 1000 @ 27.77 in 1959.
Hertfordshire 1964–65. Professional coach Hurstpierpoint C 1964–65.

GARDOM, Barrie *Keith*
————RHB, LB————

Born Birmingham, 31 Dec 1952. Educ Bishop Vesey's GS, Sutton Coldfield. Debut 1973.
WARWICKSHIRE (17) 1973–74.
HS 79* Warwicks v Surrey, Edgbaston, 1974.
BB 6–139 Warwicks v Essex, Chelmsford, 1974.

GARLICK, Paul Lawrence
————RHB, RFM————

Born Chiswick, London, 2 Aug 1964. Educ Sherborne S; Jesus C, Cambridge. Debut 1984.
CAMBRIDGE UNIVERSITY (10) 1984 (Blue).
HS 6* Cambridge U v Notts, Trent Bridge, 1984.
BB 2–69 Cambridge U v Sussex, Fenner's, 1984.
Failed to score in 9 successive fc inns in 1984 (one short of B. J. Griffiths' record).
Dorset 1984.

GARLICK, Richard *Gordon*
————RHB, OB————

Born Kirkby Lonsdale, Westmorland, 11 Apr 1917. Debut 1938. *P.*
LANCASHIRE (44) 1938–47.
NORTHAMPTONSHIRE (77) 1948–50. Cap 1949.
HS 62* Northants v Worcs, Worcester, 1950.
BB 6–27 (10–46 match) Lancs v Derbys, Buxton, 1946.
Clubs: Fleetwood, St Anne's.

GARNER, Joel
————RHB, RFM————

Born Barbados, 16 Dec 1952. Educ Foundation S, Christ Church, Barbados. Debut 1975/76.
W INDIES DOMESTIC Barbados 1975/76–.
SOMERSET (61) 1977–. Cap 1979.
AUSTRALIA DOMESTIC S Australia (8) 1982/83.
WEST INDIES (42) 1976/77–84. E 1980/81 (4); A 1977/78 (2), 1983/84 (5); I 1982/83 (4); P 1976/77 (5). E 1980 (5), 1984 (5); A 1979/80 (3), 1981/82 (3); NZ 1979/80 (3); P 1980/81 (3).
HST 60 WI v A, Brisbane, 1979/80. HS 104 WI v Glos, Bristol, 1980.
BBT 6–56 WI v NZ, Auckland, 1979/80.
BB 8–31 Som v Glam, Cardiff, 1977.
Professional Littleborough 1976–78.
MBE for services to cricket.

GARNHAM, Michael Anthony
————RHB, WK————

Born Johannesburg, S Africa, 20 Aug 1960. Educ Park S, Barnstaple; N Devon C, U of East Anglia. Debut 1979.
GLOUCESTERSHIRE (3) 1979.
LEICESTERSHIRE (49) 1980–.
HS 84 Leics v Surrey, Oval, 1984.
Club: North Devon.

GAROFALL, Alan Robert
————RHB, RM————

Born Kingston, Surrey, 1 June 1946. Educ Latymer Upper S; St Edmund Hall, Oxford. Debut 1966.
OXFORD UNIVERSITY (27) 1966–68 (Blue 1967–68).
HS 99 Oxford U v Warwicks, The Parks, 1967.
Hertfordshire 1970–. Professional Ockbrook and Borrowash. Clubs: St Albans, Dunstable Town.

GATEHOUSE, Peter Warlow
————RHB, LFM————

Born Caerphilly, S Wales, 3 May 1936. Educ Caerphilly GS. Debut 1957. *P.*
GLAMORGAN (19) 1957–62.
HS 20 Glam v Derbys, Llanelli, 1960.
BB 7–94 Glam v M'sex, Lord's, 1958.
Club: Cardiff. Rugby: Caerphilly.

GATTING, Michael William
————RHB, RM————

Born Kingsbury, M'sex, 6 June 1957. Educ John Kelly HS. Debut 1975.
MIDDLESEX (163) 1975–. Cap 1977. Capt 1983–.

ENGLAND (30) 1977/78–84. A 1980 (1), 1981 (6); WI 1980 (4), 1984 (1); NZ 1983 (2); P 1982 (3). *WI 1980/81 (1); NZ 1977/78 (1), 1983/84 (2); I 1981/82 (5); P 1977/78 (1), 1983/84 (3).*
OTHER TOURS M'sex to Zimbabwe 1980/81.
HST 81 E v NZ, Lord's, 1983. HS 258 M'sex v Som, Bath, 1984.
BB 5–34 M'sex v Glam, Swansea, 1982.
1000 RUNS (6) 2257 @ 68.39 in 1984.
Club: Brondesbury. CWC Young Cricketer of 1981.

GAUNT, Ronald Arthur
—LHB, RF—

Born Yarlu, W Australia, 26 Feb 1934. Debut 1955/56.
AUSTRALIA DOMESTIC Western Australia (29) 1955/56–59/60, Victoria (18) 1960/61–63/64.
AUSTRALIA (3) 1957/58–63/64. SA 1963/64 (1). *E 1961 (1); SA 1957/58 (1).*
OTHER TOURS Australia to New Zealand 1956/57, 1959/60.
HST 3 A v E, Oval, 1961. HS 32* Victoria v Tasmania, Hobart, 1961/62.
BBT 3–53 A v E, Oval, 1961. BB 7–104 W Australia v NSW, Sydney, 1956/57.
Club: Footscray.

GAUNTLETT, Gilbert Bernard
—RHB, WK—

Born Dolgellau, N Wales, 19 Sept 1936. Educ Charterhouse; Oriel C, Oxford. Debut 1957.
OXFORD UNIVERSITY (1) 1957.
Did not bat or bowl.
Church of England minister.

GAVASKAR, Sunil Manohar
—RHB, RM—

Born Bombay, India, 10 July 1949. Educ St Xavier's HS and C; Bombay U. Debut 1966/67.
INDIA DOMESTIC Bombay 1967/68–. Capt 1975/76–.
SOMERSET (15) 1980. Cap 1980.
INDIA (99) 1970/71–83/84. E 1972/73 (5), 1976/77 (5), 1979/80 (1), 1981/82 (6); A 1979/80 (6); WI 1974/75 (2), 1978/79 (6), 1983/84 (6); NZ 1976/77 (3); P 1979/80 (6), 1983/84 (3); SL 1982/83 (1). *E 1971 (3), 1974 (3), 1979 (4), 1982 (3); A 1977/78 (5), 1980/81 (3); WI 1970/71 (4), 1975/76 (4), 1982/83 (5); NZ 1975/76 (3), 1980/81 (3); P 1978/79 (3), 1982/83 (6).* Capt 45.
OTHER TOURS World XI to Australia 1971/72. India to Sri Lanka 1973/74.
HST 236* I v WI, Madras, 1983/84. HS 340 Bombay v Bengal, Bombay, 1981/82.

BB 3–43 President's XI v Ranji XI, Jamnagar, 1972/73.
1000 RUNS (2 + 10) 2121 @ 84.84 in India and Pakistan in 1978/79.
RECORDS In Test cricket, scorer of most runs (8394 @ 52.46), most centuries (30), most half-centuries (66), and shared in most century stands (49). Scored over 1000 Test runs in a calendar yr four times (1976, 1978, 1979 and 1983), only batsman to do so more than once. Most Test appearances for India (99) and HST (above) highest Test inns for India. Aggregate of runs in fc cricket (22,853) highest by an Indian. Carried bat for 127* in total of 286, I v P, Faisalabad, 1982/83; scored century and double-century (124 and 220) in same match, I v WI, Port of Spain, 1970/71; only Indian to do either in Test cricket. Batted 708 mins for 172 I v E, Bangalore, 1981/82 and 644 mins for 236* I v WI, Madras, 1983/84, longest and third-longest mins for India. Added 344* for 2nd wkt with D. B. Vengsarkar, I v WI, Calcutta, 1978/79 and 204 for 5th wkt with B. P. Patel, I v WI, Port of Spain, 1975/76, both India Test records.
Brother-in-law G. R. Visvanath (India); uncle M. K. Mantri (India). Autobiography *Sunny Days* (1976); author *Idols* (1984).

GAVIN, Norman Leslie
—LHB, SLA—

Born Camberwell, London, 5 Jan 1922. Educ Catford Commercial S. Debut 1946.
ROYAL AIR FORCE (1) 1946.
HS 29 RAF v Worcs, Worcester, 1946.
BB 3–76 same match.
Kent 2nd XI. Clubs: Catford Wanderers, Sevenoaks Vine.

GAY, David William Maurice
—RHB, RM—

Born London, 2 Apr 1920. Educ Shrewsbury. Debut 1949.
COMBINED SERVICES (2) 1949.
SUSSEX (2) 1949.
HS 11 Combined Services v Hants, Portsmouth, 1949.
BB 4–57 same match.
BAOR (capt). Regular Army officer, the Queen's Bays.

GENDERS, William *Roy*
—RHB—

Born Dore, Derbys, 21 Jan 1913. Educ King's S, Ely; St John's C, Cambridge. Debut 1946.

DERBYSHIRE (3) 1946.
WORCESTERSHIRE (5) 1947–48.
SOMERSET (2) 1949.
HS 55* Worcs v Derbys, Chesterfield, 1947.
BB 2–43 Worcs v Glos, Worcester, 1947.
Journalist.

GHAVRI, Karson Devji (Kit)
—LHB, LMF/SLA—

Born Rajkot, India, 28 Feb 1951. Debut 1969/70.
INDIA DOMESTIC Saurashtra 1969/70–72/73, 1982/83–, Bombay 1973/74–81/82.
INDIA (39) 1974/75–80/81. E 1976/77 (3), 1979/80 (1); A 1979/80 (6); WI 1974/75 (3), 1978/79 (6); NZ 1976/77 (2); P 1979/80 (6). *E 1979 (4); A 1977/78 (3), 1980/81 (3); NZ 1980/81 (1); P 1978/79 (1).*
OTHER TOURS Cricket Club of India to Sri Lanka 1972/73. India to Sri Lanka 1973/74. A. L. Wadekar's XI to Sri Lanka 1975/76. International XI to Jamaica 1982/83.
HST 86 I v A, Bombay, 1979/80. HS 102 Bombay v Uttar Pradesh, Bombay, 1978/79.
BBT 5–33 I v E, Bombay, 1976/77. BB 7–34 (10–78 match) Bombay v Haryana, Bombay, 1976/77.
Clubs: Ramsbottom, Blackpool, South Shields.

GHAZALI, Mohammed Ebrahim Zainuddin
—RHB, OB—

Born Gujerat, India, 15 June 1924. Debut 1942/43.
INDIA DOMESTIC Maharashtra 1942/43–46/47.
PAKISTAN DOMESTIC Combined Services 1953/54–54/55.
PAKISTAN (2) *E 1954.*
HST 18 P v E, Trent Bridge, 1954. HS 160 Services v Karachi, Karachi, 1953/54.
BB 5–28 Services v Punjab, Lahore, 1954/55.
Manager Pakistan to Australia 1972/73.
Pakistan Air Force officer (retired).

GHORPADE, Jayasinghrao Mansinghrao
—RHB, LBG—

Born Panchgani, Maharashtra, India, 2 Oct 1930. Died Baroda, India, 29 Mar 1978. Educ Baroda U. Debut 1948/49.
INDIA DOMESTIC Baroda 1948/49–65/66.
INDIA (8) 1952/53–59. A 1956/57 (1); WI 1958/59 (1); NZ 1955/56 (1). *E 1959 (3); WI 1952/53 (2).*

HST 41 I v E, Lord's, 1959. HS 123 Baroda v Rajasthan, Udaipur, 1957/58. BB 6–19 Indian Universities v Pakistanis, Bangalore, 1952/53.
Chairman Indian selection committee at death. Club: Rawtenstall.

GHULAM ABBAS
────────LHB, SLA────────

Born Delhi, India, 1 May 1947. Debut 1962/63.
PAKISTAN DOMESTIC Karachi, National Bank, Pakistan International Airlines, 1962/63–81/82.
PAKISTAN (1) E 1967.
OTHER TOURS Pakistan to Ceylon 1964/65. Pakistan to Australasia 1964/65. PIA to Zimbabwe 1981/82.
HST 12 P v E, Oval, 1967. HS 276 PIA v Punjab B, Karachi, 1975/76.
BB 2–39 Pakistan XI v The Rest, Sahiwal, 1967/68.
Club: Church.

GHULAM AHMED
────────RHB, OB────────

Born Hyderabad, Sind, India, 27 June 1922. Educ Madrasa-i-Aliya S; Nizam's C; Madras U. Debut 1939/40.
INDIA DOMESTIC Hyderabad 1939/40–58/59, Muslims 1945/46.
INDIA (22) 1948/49–58/59. E 1951/52 (2); A 1956/57 (2); WI 1948/49 (3), 1958/59 (2); NZ 1955/56 (1); P 1952/53 (4). E 1952 (4); P 1954/55 (4). Capt 3.
OTHER TOUR India to Ceylon 1956/57.
HST 50 I v P, Delhi, 1952/53 (adding 109 for 10th wkt with H. R. Adhikari, India Test record). HS 90 Hyderabad v Mysore, Secunderabad, 1946/47.
BBT 7–49 I v A, Calcutta, 1956/57. BB 9–53 (14–81 match) Hyderabad v Madras, Secunderabad, 1947/48.
RECORDS Bowled 555 balls in inns, Hyderabad v Holkar, Indore, 1950/51, record for any inns outside Test cricket. Nephew Asif Iqbal (Kent, Pakistan).

GIBAUT, Russel Philip
────────RHB, RMF────────

Born St Saviour, Jersey, Channel Islands, 5 Mar 1963. Educ De la Salle C, Jersey; Hertford C, Oxford. Debut 1983.
OXFORD UNIVERSITY (2) 1983.
HS 7 Oxford U v Lancs, The Parks, 1983.

GIBB, Paul Anthony
────────RHB, WK────────

Born Brandsby, Yorks, 11 July 1913. Died Guildford, Surrey, 7 Dec 1977. Educ St Edward's, Oxford; Emmanuel C, Cambridge. Debut 1934. P from 1951.
SCOTLAND (4) 1934–38.
CAMBRIDGE UNIVERSITY (40) 1935–38 (Blue 1935–38).
YORKSHIRE (36) 1935–46.
ESSEX (145) 1951–56. Cap 1951.
ENGLAND (8) 1938/39–46/47. I 1946 (2). A 1946/47 (1); SA 1938/39 (5).
OTHER TOURS Yorks to Jamaica 1935/36. L. H. Tennyson's XI to India 1937/38. Commonwealth XI to India 1953/54.
HST 120 E v SA, Durban, 1938/39. HS 204 Cambridge U v Free Foresters, Fenner's, 1938.
1000 RUNS (5) 1658 @ 48.76 in 1938.
RECORD Added 343 for 3rd wkt with R. Horsfall, Essex v Kent, Blackheath, 1951, county record.
Scored 93 and 106 on Test debut, E v SA, J'burg, 1938/39. Scored 157* on Yorks debut, v Notts, Sheffield, 1935. Gentlemen v Players (2) 1938. Fc umpire 1957–66. Coached in S Africa.

GIBBONS, Harold Harry Ian Haywood (Doc)
────────RHB────────

Born Devonport, Devon, 8 Oct 1904. Died Worcester, 16 Feb 1973. Debut 1927. P until 1939.
WORCESTERSHIRE (380) 1927–46. Cap 1928. Benefit 1938.
HS 212* Worcs v Northants, Dudley, 1939.
BB 2–27 Worcs v N Zealanders, Worcester, 1927.
1000 RUNS (12) 2654 @ 52.03 in 1934 (Worcs record).
RECORDS First two centuries of career, in 1928, were both scored before lunch, a unique feat. Added 274 for 2nd wkt with Nawab of Pataudi snr twice (Worcs v Kent, Worcester, 1933 and Worcs v Glam, Worcester, 1934) and 197 for 7th wkt with R. Howorth, Worcs v Surrey, Oval, 1938, all county records.
Players v Gentlemen (1) 1928. Club: Hampstead.

GIBBS, Lancelot Richard
────────RHB, OB────────

Born Georgetown, British Guiana, 29 Sept 1934. Educ Standard HS, Georgetown. Debut 1953/54.
W INDIES DOMESTIC British Guiana (Guyana) 1953/54–74/75.

WARWICKSHIRE (109) 1967–72. Cap 1968.
AUSTRALIA DOMESTIC South Australia (8) 1969/70.
WEST INDIES (79) 1957/58–75/76. E 1967/68 (5), 1973/74 (5); A 1964/65 (5), 1972/73 (5); NZ 1971/72 (2); I 1961/62 (5), 1970/71 (1); P 1957/58 (5). E 1963 (5), 1966 (5), 1969 (3), 1973 (3); A 1960/61 (3), 1968/69 (5); 1975/76 (6); NZ 1968/69 (3); I 1958/59 (1), 1966/67 (3), 1974/75 (5); P 1958/59 (3), 1974/75 (2).
OTHER TOURS Commonwealth XI to India 1964/65.
HST 25 WI v I, Georgetown, 1970/71. HS 43 W Indians v Combined XI, Hobart, 1960/61.
BBT 8–38 WI v I, Bridgetown, 1961/62. BB 8–37 Warwicks v Glam, Edgbaston, 1970.
100 WKTS (1) 131 @ 18.89 in 1971.
RECORDS In 1975/76 became the second bowler, after F. S. Trueman, to take 300 Test wkts; went on to take 309, which remained world record until beaten by D. K. Lillee (Australia) in 1981/82. 27,115 balls bowled in Tests remains record.
Rest of World v England 1970 (4). Clubs: Whitburn, Burnley. Sports administrator in Guyana. Cousin C. H. Lloyd (W Indies).

GIBBS, Peter John Keith
────────RHB, occ OB────────

Born Buglawton, Cheshire, 17 Aug 1944. Educ Hanley GS; UC, Oxford. Debut 1964.
OXFORD UNIVERSITY (33) 1964–66 (Blue 1964–66).
DERBYSHIRE (145) 1966–72. Cap 1968.
HS 138* Derbys v Som, Chesterfield, 1969.
BB 2–54 Derbys v Northants, Derby, 1968.
1000 RUNS (5) 1441 @ 41.17 in 1970.
Staffordshire 1961–64. Club: Norton. Playwright.

GIBSON, Alfred Leonard
────────RHB────────

Born Devon, Jamaica, 13 Feb 1912. Debut 1946. P.
LEICESTERSHIRE (2) 1946.
HS 11 Leics v Oxford U, The Parks, 1946.

GIBSON, David
────────RHB, RMF────────

Born Mitcham, Surrey, 1 May 1936. Educ Wallington GS. Debut 1957. P.

SURREY (183) 1957–69. Cap 1960. Testimonial 1969.
HS 98 Surrey v Leics, Oval, 1965.
BB 7–26 Surrey v Derbys, Oval, 1960.
Scored 996 runs and took 86 wkts in 1965.
Clubs: Beddington, Streatham. Professional coach Emmanuel S 1968–71.

GIBSON, Ian
RHB, LBG

Born Glossop, Derbys, 15 Aug 1936. Died Bowdon, Cheshire, 3 May 1963. Educ Manchester GS; Brasenose C, Oxford. Debut 1955.
OXFORD UNIVERSITY (40) 1955–58 (Blue 1955–58).
DERBYSHIRE (7) 1957–61.
HS 100* Oxford U v Glos, The Parks, 1957.
BB 5–29 Oxford U v D. R. Jardine's XI, Eastbourne, 1957.
Lancs 2nd XI 1953–56. Medical practitioner.

GIDNEY, Brian Bruce
RHB

Born Kingston, Surrey, 6 Apr 1938. Educ Kingston GS; Queen's C, Cambridge. Debut 1963.
CAMBRIDGE UNIVERSITY (1) 1963.
HS 9 Cambridge U v Pakistan Eaglets, Fenner's, 1963.
Surrey 2nd XI.

GIFFORD, Norman
LHB, SLA

Born Ulverston, Lancs, 30 Mar 1940. Debut 1960. P.
WORCESTERSHIRE (521) 1960–82. Cap 1961. Capt 1971–80. Benefit (£11,047) 1974. Testimonial 1981.
WARWICKSHIRE (47) 1983–. Capt for 1985.
ENGLAND (15) 1964–73. A 1964 (2), 1972 (3); NZ 1973 (2); I 1971 (2); P 1971 (2). I 1972/73 (2); P 1972/73 (2).
OTHER TOURS International XI to S Africa and Pakistan 1961/62. Worcs to Rhodesia 1964/65. Worcs to Jamaica 1965/66. Commonwealth XI to Pakistan 1970/71. World XI to Australia 1971/72. International Wanderers to S Africa 1972/73.
HST 25* E v NZ, Trent Bridge, 1973. HS 89 Worcs v Oxford U, The Parks, 1963.
BBT 5–55 E v P, Karachi, 1972/73. BB 8–28 Worcs v Yorks, Sheffield, 1968.
100 WKTS (4) 133 @ 19.66 in 1961.
Players v Gentlemen (1) 1962. Club: Dudley. Test selector 1982. Assistant

manager England to Australia 1982/83; England to Pakistan and N Zealand 1983/84; England to India and Sri Lanka 1984/85. MBE for services to cricket. Uncle H. Gifford (England rugby international).

GILCHRIST, Roy
RHB, RF

Born Jamaica, 18 June 1934. Debut 1956/57.
W INDIES DOMESTIC Jamaica 1956/57–57/58, 1961/62.
INDIA DOMESTIC Hyderabad (1) 1962/63, South Zone (2) 1962/63.
WEST INDIES (13) 1957–58/59. P 1957/58 (5). E 1957 (4); I 1958/59 (4).
HST 12 WI v P, Georgetown, 1957/58. HS 43* W Indies v Bihar Governor's XI, Jamshedpur, 1958/59.
BBT 6–55 WI v I, Calcutta, 1958/59. BB 6–16 W Indians v Combined Universities, Nagpur, 1958/59.
Clubs: Middleton, Bacup, Great Chell, Lowerhouse, Crompton, East Bierley. Autobiography Hit Me For Six (1963).

GILES, Ronald James
RHB, SLA

Born Chilwell, Notts, 17 Oct 1919. Debut 1937. P.
NOTTINGHAMSHIRE (195) 1937–59. Cap 1951. Benefit (£1250) 1959.
HS 142 Notts v Yorks, Trent Bridge, 1955.
BB 3–1 Notts v Hants, Bournemouth, 1938.
1000 RUNS (3) 1293 @ 34.94 in 1955.
Club: Salts.

GILFILLAN, Andrew Douglas
RHB, LB

Born Johannesburg, S Africa, 21 Aug 1959. Educ Hilton C, Natal; Natal U; Worcester C, Oxford. Debut 1982.
OXFORD UNIVERSITY (3) 1982.
HS 31 Oxford U v Glos, The Parks, 1982.
BB 2–177 Oxford U v Kent, The Parks, 1982.

GILL, Alan
RHB, LB

Born Underwood, Notts, 5 Aug 1940. Debut 1960. P.
NOTTINGHAMSHIRE (53) 1960–65.
HS 67 Notts v Cambridge U, Trent Bridge, 1962.
BB 2–28 Notts v Lancs, Trent Bridge, 1964.

GILL, James Rupert
RHB

Born Dublin, Ireland, 24 Sept 1911. Educ Masonic Boys' S, Dublin. Debut 1948.
IRELAND (1) 1948.
HS 106 Ireland v MCC, Dublin, 1948.
RECORDS Century and 'duck' on only fc appearance, unique feat.
President Irish CU 1961. Clubs: Leinster, Civil Service.

GILL, Peter Nigel
RHB, OB

Born Stoke on Trent, Staffordshire, 12 Nov 1947. Educ Repton. Debut 1976.
MINOR COUNTIES (2) 1976–79.
HS 20 Minor Counties v Indians, Wellington (Shropshire), 1979.
Staffordshire 1966– (capt 1982–). Club: Stone.

GILL, Roderick Ian
RHB, RM

Born Dublin, Ireland, 21 July 1919. Died Dublin, Ireland, 28 Oct 1983. Educ Mountjoy S, Dublin. Debut 1947.
IRELAND (3) 1947–50.
HS 37 Ireland v Scotland, Perth, 1950.
BB 2–19 Ireland v MCC, Dublin, 1950.
Club: YMCA Dublin.

GILLHOULEY, Keith
LHB, SLA

Born Huddersfield, Yorks, 8 Aug 1934. Debut 1961. P.
YORKSHIRE (24) 1961.
NOTTINGHAMSHIRE (83) 1963–66.
HS 75* Notts v Worcs, Trent Bridge, 1963.
BB 7–82 Yorks v M'sex, Bradford, 1961. His bowling action was often under scrutiny as to its legality.
Clubs: Dalton, Halifax, Ashton. Rothes amateurs.

GILLIAT, Richard Michael Charles
LHB, RLB

Born Ware, Hertfordshire, 20 May 1944. Educ Charterhouse; Christ Church C, Oxford. Debut 1964.
OXFORD UNIVERSITY (42) 1964–67 (Blue 1964–67). Capt 1966.
HAMPSHIRE (220) 1966–78. Cap 1969. Capt 1971–78. Benefit 1978.
TOUR MCC to Far East 1969/70 (no fc matches).

HS 223* Hants v Warwicks, Southampton, 1969.
1000 RUNS (4) 1386 @ 39.60 in 1969.
Hants assistant-secretary 1967–78. Devon 1965. Soccer: Blue (capt). Uncle I. A. W. Gilliat (Oxford U).

GILLOTT, Eric Kenneth
RHB, SLA

Born Waiuku, N Zealand, 15 Apr 1951. Debut 1971/72.
N ZEALAND DOMESTIC Northern Districts (31) 1971/72–78/79.
TOUR N Zealand to England 1973.
HS 22 Northern Districts v Wellington, Wellington, 1972/73.
BB 6–79 Northern Districts v Otago, Dunedin, 1971/72.
Buckinghamshire 1976. Clubs: Hampstead (England), Pukekohe, Franklin (N Zealand).

GILMOUR, Gary John
LHB, LFM

Born Waratah, NSW, Australia, 26 June 1951. Debut 1971/72.
AUSTRALIA DOMESTIC New South Wales (42) 1971/72–79/80.
AUSTRALIA (15) 1973/74–76/77. E 1976/77 (1); WI 1975/76 (5); NZ 1973/74 (2); P 1976/77 (3). *E 1975 (1); NZ 1973/74 (1), 1976/77 (2).*
OTHER TOUR International Wanderers to S Africa 1975/76.
HST 101 A v NZ, Christchurch, 1976/77 (adding 217 for 7th wkt with K. D. Walters, Australia Test record). HS 122 NSW v S Australia, Sydney, 1971/72 (second inns of debut match).
BBT 6–85 A v E, Headingley, 1975. BB as above.
World Series Cricket (Kerry Packer) 1977/78–78/79. Career curtailed by recurrent gout. Clubs: Western Suburbs (Sydney), Newcastle.

GIMBLETT, Harold
RHB, OB

Born Bicknoller, Som, 19 Oct 1914. Died, by own hand, Verwood, Dorset, 31 Mar 1978. Educ West Buckland S. Debut 1935. *P. Wisden* 1953.
SOMERSET (329) 1935–54. Cap 1935.
Benefit (£3367) 1952.
ENGLAND (3) 1936–39. WI 1939 (1); I 1936 (2).
TOUR Commonwealth XI to India and Ceylon 1950/51.
HST 67* E v I, Lord's, 1936. HS 310 Som v Sussex, Eastbourne, 1948.

BB 4–10 Som v Glos, Bath, 1935.
1000 RUNS (12 + 1) 2134 @ 39.51 in 1952.
RECORDS Scored 123 Som v Essex, Frome, 1935, on fc debut, reaching century in 63 mins, winning Lawrence Trophy for fastest century of season. HS (above) highest inns for Somerset; also most runs (21,142) and centuries (49) for the county.
Players v Gentlemen (3) 1936–50. Dorset 1959. Clubs: Watchet, Ebbw Vale. Professional coach Millfield 1957–58. Co-operated with biography *Harold Gimblett – Tortured Genius Of Cricket* by David Foot (published posthumously in 1982).

GLADWIN, Christopher
LHB, RM

Born East Ham, London, 10 May 1962. Educ Langdon CS, Newham. Debut 1981.
ESSEX (36) 1981–84. Cap 1984.
HS 162 Essex v Cambridge U, Fenner's, 1984.
1000 RUNS (1) 1396 @ 33.24 in 1984.
Young England to Young India 1981. Club: Wanstead.

GLADWIN, Clifford
RHB, RMF/OB

Born Doe Lea, Derbys, 3 Apr 1916. Debut 1939. *P.*
DERBYSHIRE (332) 1939–58. Cap 1946.
Testimonial (£3297) 1953.
ENGLAND (8) 1947–49. SA 1947 (2); NZ 1949 (1). *SA 1948/49 (5).*
HST 51* E v SA, Oval, 1947. HS 124* Derbys v Notts, Trent Bridge, 1949.
BBT 3–21 E v SA, Durban, 1948/49. BB 9–41 (16–84 match) Derbys v Worcs, Stourbridge, 1952.
100 WKTS (12) 152 @ 19.19 in 1952.
On strike when winning run made with leg-bye off last scheduled ball, E v SA, Durban, 1948/49, for victory by two wkts.
Players v Gentlemen (1) 1947. Clubs: Glapwell Colliery, Saltaire, Lidget Green, Longton. Father J. Gladwin (Derbys).

GLASSFORD, John
RHB, RFM

Born Sunderland, Co Durham, 20 July 1946. Educ Haswell Sec S. Debut 1969.
WARWICKSHIRE (2) 1969.
No runs.
BB 2–9 Warwicks v Cambridge U, Edgbaston, 1969.

Durham County 1968–74. Clubs: Eppleton, South Hetton CW, Blackhall CW, Darlington, Burnmoor, Peterlee, Ushaw Moor.

GLEESON, John William
RHB, LBG

Born Wiangaree, NSW, Australia, 14 Mar 1938. Debut 1966/67.
AUSTRALIA DOMESTIC New South Wales (35) 1966/67–72/73.
S AFRICA DOMESTIC Eastern Province (8) 1974/75.
AUSTRALIA (29) 1967/68–72. E 1970/71 (5); WI 1968/69 (5); I 1967/68 (4). *E 1968 (5), 1972 (3); SA 1969/70 (4); I 1969/70 (3).*
OTHER TOURS Australia to N Zealand 1966/67. D. H. Robins' XI to S Africa 1973/74.
HST 45 A v WI, Sydney, 1968/69. HS 59 Australians v Canterbury, Canterbury, 1966/67.
BBT 5–61 A v WI, Melbourne, 1968/69. BB 7–52 (10–86 match) NSW v Queensland, Sydney, 1971/72.
Clubs: Balmain, Newcastle.

GLENN, Michael
RHB, RM

Born Belper, Derbys, 14 June 1956. Educ Belper HS. Debut 1975.
DERBYSHIRE (7) 1975–76.
HS 11* Derbys v Cambridge U, Burton (Bass-Worthington), 1976.
BB 3–36 Derbys v Worcs, Worcester, 1976.

GLENNIE, Mervin Stephen
RHB, WK

Born Tours, France, 23 Oct 1918. Educ Sherborne; Trinity Hall, Cambridge. Debut 1939.
CAMBRIDGE UNIVERSITY (2) 1939.
MCC (1) 1947.
HS 11 Cambridge U v Northants, Fenner's, 1939.
Life vice-president of M'sex. Clubs: Southgate, Sherborne Pilgrims.

GLERUM, Herman Wilhelm (Bill)
RHB, RM

Born Amsterdam, Netherlands, 28 Aug 1911. Educ Lyceum, Amsterdam. Debut 1957.
FREE FORESTERS (1) 1957.
HS 1 Free Foresters v Oxford U, The Parks, 1957.
BB 2–16 same match.

South America to Argentina 1956 (capt). Clubs: VRA Amsterdam, Flamingos, 'Still Going Strong' Dutch Forty Club, MCC, Free Foresters, Wolverhampton, Hornsey, British Empire XI, RAF, Brazil CA, Rio de Janeiro, Sao Paulo, Santos, Curacao, Buenos Aires.

GLOVER, Trevor Richardson
————————RHB, OB————————

Born Lancaster, 26 Nov 1951. Educ Lancaster RGS; Lincoln C, Oxford.
OXFORD UNIVERSITY (22) 1973–75 (Blue 1973–75). Capt 1975.
HS 117 Oxford U v Worcs, Worcester, 1975.

GLYNN, Brian Thomas
————————RHB, OB————————

Born Birmingham, 27 Apr 1940. Debut 1959. P.
WARWICKSHIRE (2) 1959–61.
HS 7 Warwicks v Scotland, Edgbaston, 1961.
Club: West Bromwich Dartmouth.

GOBEY, Stanley Clarke
————————LHB, RM————————

Born Stafford, 18 June 1916. Debut 1946.
WARWICKSHIRE (2) 1946.
HS 2 Warwicks v Derbys, Derby, 1946.
Club: Bournville.

GODDARD, George Fergusson
————————RHB, OB————————

Born Edinburgh, Scotland, 19 May 1938. Educ Heriot's. Debut 1960.
SCOTLAND (22) 1960–80.
HS 39 Scotland v Ireland, Paisley, 1960.
BB 8–34 Scotland v Ireland, Greenock, 1972.
Club: Heriot's FP.

GODDARD, John Douglas Claude
————————LHB, RM/OB————————

Born St Michael, Barbados, 21 Apr 1919. Educ Harrison C, Barbados; Lodge S, Barbados. Debut 1936/37.
W INDIES DOMESTIC Barbados 1936/37–57/58.
WEST INDIES (27) 1947/48–57. E 1947/48 (4). *E 1950 (4), 1957 (5); A 1951/52 (4); NZ 1951/52 (2), 1955/56 (3); I 1948/49 (5).* Capt 22.

HST 83* WI v NZ, Christchurch, 1955/56. HS 218* Barbados v Trinidad, Bridgetown, 1943/44.
BBT 5–31 WI v E, Georgetown, 1947/48. BB as above.
During HS (above) added 502* for 4th wkt with F. M. M. Worrell, sixth-highest partnership in fc cricket. OBE for services to cricket.

GODDARD, Thomas William John
————————RHB, RFM/OB————————

Born Gloucester, 1 Oct 1900. Died Gloucester, 22 May 1966. Debut 1922. P.
GLOUCESTERSHIRE (558) 1922–52. Cap 1926. Benefit (£2097) 1936 and (£3355) 1948.
ENGLAND (8) 1930–39. A 1930 (1); WI 1939 (2); NZ 1937 (2). *SA 1938/39 (3).*
OTHER TOUR MCC to S Africa 1930/31.
HST 8 E v SA, J'burg, 1938/39. HS 71 Glos v Essex, Southend, 1932.
BBT 6–29 E v NZ, Old Trafford, 1937. BB 10–113 (16–181 match) Glos v Worcs, Cheltenham, 1937.
100 WKTS (16) 248 @16.76 in 1937. Took 200 wkts also in 1935, 1939, 1947.
RECORDS 222 wkts for Glos in 1937 and 1947, county record. Took 17 wkts in one day (17–106 match), Glos v Kent, Bristol, 1939, equals world record. Took 16–99 match Glos v Worcs, Bristol, 1939. Took 24 wkts in 3 consecutive inns, and 30 in 4, in 1939. Six hat-tricks in fc cricket, joint second after D. V. P. Wright (seven).
Players v Gentlemen (4) 1929–38.

GODDARD, Trevor Leslie
————————LHB, LMF————————

Born Durban, S Africa, 1 Aug 1931. Educ Durban HS. Debut 1952/53.
S AFRICA DOMESTIC Natal 1952/53–65/66, 1968/69–69/70, North-Eastern Transvaal 1966/67–67/68.
SOUTH AFRICA (41) 1955–69/70. E 1956/57 (5), 1964/65 (5); A 1957/58 (5), 1966/67 (5), 1969/70 (3). *E 1955 (5), 1960 (5); A 1963/64 (5); NZ 1963/64 (3).* Capt 13.
HST 112 SA v E, Johannesburg, 1964/65. HS 222 NE Transvaal v W Province, Cape Town, 1966/67.
BBT 6–53 SA v A, Johannesburg, 1966/67. BB 6–3 Natal v Border, East London, 1959/60.
1000 RUNS (2) 1377 @ 37.21 in 1960.
RECORDS First S African to score 10,000 runs and take 500 wkts. Only S African to score 2000 runs and take 100 wkts in Tests.
Carried bat for 56* in total of 99, SA v A, Cape Town, 1957/58.

GODFREY, John Frederick
————————RHB, RFM————————

Born Garsington, Oxfordshire, 18 Aug 1917. Debut 1939. P.
HAMPSHIRE (12) 1939–47.
HS 25* Hants v M'sex, Lord's, 1947.
BB 4–116 Hants v Derbys, Portsmouth, 1947.
Oxfordshire 1949, Cambridgeshire 1950–54.

GOLDIE, Christopher Frederick Evelyn
————————RHB, WK————————

Born Johannesburg, S Africa, 2 Nov 1960. Educ St Paul's S; Pembroke C, Cambridge. Debut 1981.
CAMBRIDGE UNIVERSITY (20) 1981–82 (Blue 1981–82).
HAMPSHIRE (2) 1983–.
HS 77 Cambridge U v Oxford U, Lord's, 1981.
Father T. H. E. Goldie (Oxfordshire).

GOLDING, Andrew Kenneth
————————RHB, SLA————————

Born Colchester, Essex, 5 Oct 1963. Educ Colchester RGS; St Catherine's C, Cambridge. Debut 1983.
ESSEX (1) 1983.
CAMBRIDGE UNIVERSITY (8) 1984.
HS 44 Cambridge U v Worcs, Worcester, 1984.
BB 2–100 Cambridge U v Warwicks, Fenner's, 1984.

GOLDRING, Stephen
————————RHB, RMF————————

Born Portsmouth, Hants, 18 Nov 1932. Educ St John's C, Southsea. Debut 1964.
COMBINED SERVICES (1) 1964.
HS 14* Combined Services v Oxford U, Aldershot, 1964.
Clubs: Fareham Town, Bath, Army. RAOC major.

GOLDSTEIN, Frederick Stephen
————————RHB, OB————————

Born Bulawayo, Rhodesia, 14 Oct 1944. Educ Falcon C, Essexvale, Rhodesia; St Edmund Hall, Oxford. Debut 1966.
OXFORD UNIVERSITY (48) 1966–69 (Blue 1966–69). Capt 1968–69.
NORTHAMPTONSHIRE (10) 1969.
S AFRICA DOMESTIC Transvaal B 1969/70. Transvaal 1970/71, Western Province 1971/72–77/78.

HS 155 Oxford U v Cambridge U, Lord's, 1968.
1000 RUNS (1) 1384 @ 32.18 in 1969.

GOMES, Hilary Angelo (Larry)
————LHB, RM————

Born Arima, Trinidad, 13 July 1953. Educ Holy Cross C, Trinidad. Debut 1971/72. *Wisden* 1985.
W INDIES DOMESTIC Trinidad 1971/72–. Capt 1978/79, 1981/82–.
MIDDLESEX (42) 1973–76.
WEST INDIES (40) 1976–84. E 1980/81 (4); A 1977/78 (3), 1983/84 (2); I 1982/83 (5). *E 1976 (2), 1984 (5); A 1981/82 (3); I 1978/79 (6), 1983/84 (6); P 1980/81 (4).*
OTHER TOUR W Indies to Australasia 1979/80.
HST 143 WI v E, Edgbaston, 1984. HS 200* W Indians v Queensland, Brisbane, 1981/82.
BBT 2–20 WI v A, Sydney, 1981/82. BB 4–22 M'sex v Yorks, Bradford, 1973.
1000 RUNS (1 + 2) 1435 @ 47.83 in 1976 and 1435 @ 53.15 in 1978/79.
Clubs: Queen's Park (Trinidad), Nelson, Oldham (England). Brother Sheldon Gomes (Trinidad).

GOMEZ, Gerald Ethridge
————RHB, RM————

Born Port of Spain, Trinidad, 10 Oct 1919. Educ Queen's Royal C, Trinidad. Debut 1937/38.
W INDIES DOMESTIC Trinidad 1937/38–55/56.
WEST INDIES (29) 1939–53/54. E 1947/48 (4), 1953/54 (4); I 1952/53 (4). *E 1939 (2), 1950 (4); A 1951/52 (5); NZ 1951/52 (1); I 1948/49 (5).* Capt 1.
HST 101 WI v I, Delhi, 1948/49. HS 216* Trinidad v Barbados, Port of Spain, 1942/43.
BBT 7–55 (10–113 match) WI v A, Sydney, 1951/52. BB 9–24 W Indians v South Zone, Madras, 1948/49.
1000 RUNS (1) 1116 @ 42.92 in 1950.
RECORD Added 434 for 3rd wkt with J. B. Stollmeyer, Trinidad v British Guiana, Port of Spain, 1946/47, W Indian fc record.
Manager W Indies to Australia 1960/61. Umpire WI v A, Georgetown, 1964/65, after C. F. Kippins withdrew on eve of Test. Radio commentator on cricket.

GOOCH, Graham Alan
————RHB, RM, occ WK————

Born Leytonstone, East London, 23 July 1953. Educ Norlington HS, Leytonstone. Debut 1973.

ESSEX (205) 1973–. Cap 1975.
S AFRICA DOMESTIC Western Province (16) 1982/83–83/84.
ENGLAND (42) 1975–81/82. A 1975 (2), 1980 (1), 1981 (5); WI 1980 (5); NZ 1978 (3); I 1979 (4); P 1978 (2). *A 1978/79 (6), 1979/80 (2); WI 1980/81 (4); I 1979/80 (1), 1981/82 (6); SL 1981/82 (1).*
HST 153 E v WI, Kingston, 1980/81. HS 227 Essex v Derbys, Chesterfield, 1984.
BBT 2–12 E v I, Delhi, 1981/82. BB 7–14 Essex v Worcs, Ilford, 1982.
1000 RUNS (8 + 1) 2559 @ 67.34 in 1984.
RECORD Added 321 for 2nd wkt with K. S. McEwan, Essex v Northants, Ilford, 1978, county record.
Banned from Test cricket for three yrs for touring S Africa 1981/82 (SAB England XI; capt). Cousin G. J. Saville (Essex). Semi-autobiography *Out of the Wilderness* (with Pat Murphy) (1985).

GOOCH, Peter Alan
————LHB, RFM————

Born Timperley, Cheshire, 2 May 1949. Debut 1970.
LANCASHIRE (4) 1970.
No runs.
BB 4–52 Lancs v Kent, Old Trafford, 1970.
Cheshire 1971, Buckinghamshire 1976–79. Clubs: Bedford Town, Tring Park, Ashton.

GOOD, Anthony John
————RHB, RFM————

Born Kumasi, Gold Coast, 10 Nov 1952. Educ Worksop C. Debut 1973.
LANCASHIRE (8) 1973–76.
HS 6 Lancs v Glos, Old Trafford, 1973.
BB 5–62 Lancs v Northants, Old Trafford, 1976.
Cheshire 1977–79. Club: Alderley Edge.

GOOD, Dennis Cunliffe
————RHB, RFM————

Born Leeds, Yorks, 29 Aug 1926. Educ Denstone; Sheffield U. Debut 1946. *P.*
WORCESTERSHIRE (1) 1946.
GLAMORGAN (3) 1947.
HS 21 Glam v Derbys, Derby, 1947.
BB 2–34 same match.
Clubs: RAF, Rawdon.

GOODFELLOW, Anthony
————LHB————

Born Seale, Surrey, 8 Jan 1940. Educ Marlborough C; Magdalene C, Cambridge. Debut 1960.

CAMBRIDGE UNIVERSITY (21) 1960–62 (Blue 1961–62).
HS 81 Cambridge U v Leics, Loughborough, 1961.
Club: Hampstead.

GOODREDS, William Arthur
————RHB, RFM————

Born Pensnett, nr Dudley, Worcs, 3 Nov 1920. Debut 1952.
WORCESTERSHIRE (1) 1952.
HS 4* Worcs v Cambridge U, Worcester, 1952.
Club: Dudley.

GOODSON, Donald
————RHB, RM————

Born Eastwell, Leics, 15 Oct 1932. Educ Melton Mowbray GS; Leicester U. Debut 1950. *P.*
LEICESTERSHIRE (9) 1950–53.
HS 22* Leics v Worcs, Hinckley, 1953.
BB 3–43 Leics v Glos, Leicester, 1953.

GOODWAY, Cyril Clement
————RHB, WK————

Born Smethwick, Staffordshire, 10 July 1909. Educ Bourne C, Quinton, Birmingham. Debut 1937.
WARWICKSHIRE (40) 1937–47.
HS 37* Warwicks v Glam, Edgbaston, 1946.
Chairman Warwicks 1972–83. Staffordshire 1933–36. Club: Smethwick.

GOODWIN, Douglas Edwin
————RHB, RFM————

Born Dublin, Ireland, 2 May 1938. Educ King's Hospital S, Dublin. Debut 1965.
IRELAND (11) 1965–73.
HS 39 Ireland v Scotland, Greenock, 1972.
BB 5–46 Ireland v MCC, Dublin, 1968.
Club: Malahide.

GOODWIN, Frederick
————RHB, RFM————

Born Heywood, Lancs, 28 June 1933. Debut 1955. *P.*
LANCASHIRE (11) 1955–56.
HS 21* Lancs v Derbys, Old Trafford, 1955.
BB 5–35 Lancs v M'sex, Lord's, 1955.
Club: Radcliffe. Soccer: Manchester United, Leeds United, Scunthorpe United; manager: Scunthorpe United, Birmingham City.

GOODWIN, Keith
———RHB, WK———

Born Oldham, Lancs, 21 June 1938.
Debut 1960. *P.*
LANCASHIRE (122) 1960–74. Cap 1965.
Benefit (£6700) 1973.
TOUR World XI to Pakistan 1973/74
(relief matches).
HS 23 Lancs v Glam, Swansea, 1965.

GOODWIN, Thomas Jeffery
———LHB, LFM———

Born Bignall End, Staffordshire, 22 Jan
1929. Debut 1952. *P.*
LEICESTERSHIRE (136) 1950–59. Cap
1953.
HS 23* Leics v Hants, Portsmouth,
1953.
BB 8–81 Leics v Sussex, Hove, 1956.
Club: Bignall End. Uncle A. Lockett
(Minor Counties).

GOONATILLEKE,
Hettiarachige *Mahes*
———RHB, WK———

Born Kandy, Ceylon, 16 Aug 1952.
Educ St Anthony's C, Kandy. Debut
1975/76.
SRI LANKA DOMESTIC Sri Lanka 1975/
76–82/83.
SRI LANKA (5) 1981/82–82/83. E 1981/82
(1). *I 1982/83 (1); P 1981/82 (3).*
OTHER TOURS Sri Lanka to India 1976/
77. Sri Lanka to England 1981. Sri
Lanka to India 1975/76.
HST 56 SL v P, Faisalabad, 1981/82. HS
as above.
Barred from Sinhalese cricket for 25 yrs
for touring S Africa 1982/83 (Arosa Sri
Lanka).

GOONESENA, Gamini
———RHB, LBG———

Born Colombo, Ceylon, 16 Feb 1931.
Educ Royal C, Colombo; Queen's C,
Cambridge. Debut 1947/48. *P until
1954.*
CEYLON 1947/48–61/62.
NOTTINGHAMSHIRE (94) 1952–64. Cap
1955.
CAMBRIDGE UNIVERSITY (50) 1954–57
(Blue 1954–57). Capt 1957.
AUSTRALIA DOMESTIC New South Wales
(7) 1960/61–63/64.
TOURS Ceylon to Pakistan 1949/50. E.
W. Swanton's XI to W Indies 1955/56.
Cavaliers to W Indies 1964/65. Interna-
tional XI to India, Pakistan and Ceylon
1967/68.
HS 211 Cambridge U v Oxford U,
Lord's, 1957.

BB 8–39 Cambridge U v Free Foresters,
Fenner's, 1954.
1000 RUNS (2) 1380 @ 28.75 in 1955.
100 WKTS (2) 134 @ 21.05 in 1955.
DOUBLES (2) 1955, 1957.
RECORDS HS above highest-ever inns for
Cambridge in varsity match. Added 289
for 7th wkt with G. Cook, record for
either side in this fixture.
Scored 2309 runs @ 29.22 and took 208
wkts @ 21.82 for Cambridge U.
Gentlemen v Players (8) 1954–58.
Clubs: Waverley (Sydney), Hampstead.

GOONETILLEKE, Frederick
Ranjan Manilal de Silva
———RHB, RMF———

Born Colombo, Ceylon, 15 Aug 1951.
Debut 1973/74.
SRI LANKA DOMESTIC Sri Lanka 1973/
74–1979.
TOUR Sri Lanka to England 1979.
HS 60* Sri Lanka v Tamil Nadu,
Madras, 1976/77.
BB 5–79 same match.
Club: Colombo.

GOPINATH, Coimbatore
Doraikannu
———RHB, RM———

Born Madras, India, 1 Mar 1930. Educ
Madras U. Debut 1949/50.
INDIA DOMESTIC Madras 1949/50–62/63.
INDIA (8) 1951/52–59/60. E 1951/52 (3);
A 1959/60 (1); P 1952/53 (1). *E 1952 (1)
P 1954/55 (2).*
HST 50* I v E, Bombay, 1951/52. HS 234
Madras v Mysore, Coimbatore, 1958/
59.
BB 3–15 Madras v Andhra Pradesh,
Madras, 1959/60.
Chairman Indian selection committee
1972–77. Manager India to England
1979.

GORDON, Alan
———RHB———

Born Coventry, Warwicks, 29 Mar
1944. Educ King Henry VII S,
Coventry. Debut 1966.
WARWICKSHIRE (34) 1966–71.
HS 65 Warwicks v Surrey, Oval, 1970.
Club: Coventry and N Warwicks.

GORDON-WALKER, Rupert
Adam
———LHB, WK———

Born Moniaive, Dumfrieshire, Scotland,
10 Aug 1961. Educ King Alfred's S,
Wantage; Keble C, Oxford. Debut 1981.

OXFORD UNIVERSITY (3) 1981.
HS 12 Oxford U v Leics, The Parks,
1981.

GORE, Hugh Edmund Ivor
———RHB, LFM———

Born St John's, Antigua, 18 June 1953.
Debut 1972/73.
W INDIES DOMESTIC Leeward Islands,
Combined Islands, 1972/73–78/79.
SOMERSET (11) 1980.
HS 67 Combined Islands v Jamaica,
Kingstown, St Vincent, 1976/77.
BB 5–66 Som v Surrey, Oval, 1980.
Father Leo Gore (Leeward Islands).

GOTHARD, Edward James
———RHB, RM———

Born Burton upon Trent, Staffordshire,
1 Oct 1904. Died Birmingham, 17 Jan
1979. Debut 1947.
DERBYSHIRE (45) 1947–48. Cap 1947.
Capt 1947–48.
HS 50 Derbys v Kent, Gillingham, 1948.
BB 3–84 Derbys v M'sex, Derby, 1947
(including hat-trick).
Derbys committee 1945–75. Stafford-
shire 1927. Clubs: Burton, The Friars.
Hockey: Staffordshire. MBE.

GOULD, Anthony Victor
Endersby
———RHB———

Born Windsor, Berkshire, 22 Feb 1944.
Educ Ardingley C; Fitzwilliam C, Cam-
bridge. Debut 1964.
CAMBRIDGE UNIVERSITY (13) 1964–66.
HS 38 Cambridge U v Lancs, Fenner's,
1966.
Sussex 2nd XI. Club: Old Ardinians.

GOULD, Ian James
———LHB, WK———

Born Taplow, Buckinghamshire, 19
Aug 1957. Educ Westgate S. Debut
1975.
MIDDLESEX (88) 1975–80. Cap 1977.
SUSSEX (81) 1981–. Cap 1981.
N ZEALAND DOMESTIC Auckland (3) 1979/
80.
TOURS M'sex to Zimbabwe 1980/81.
International XI to Pakistan 1980/81.
England to Australia 1982/83.
HS 128 M'sex v Worcs, Worcester, 1979.

GOVER, Alfred Richard
———RHB, RF———

Born Epsom, Surrey, 29 Feb 1908.
Debut 1928. *P.*

SURREY (336) 1928–47. Cap 1930. Joint benefit (with H. T. Barling) 1946 and 1947.
ALL ENGLAND XI (1) 1948.
ENGLAND (4) 1936–46. NZ 1937 (2); I 1936 (1), 1946 (1).
TOUR Lord Tennyson's XI to India 1937/38.
HST 2* E v NZ, Lord's, 1937. HS 41* Surrey v Som, Weston-super-Mare, 1939.
BBT 3–85 E v NZ, Oval, 1937. BB 8–34 (including four wkts in four balls) Surrey v Worcs, Worcester, 1935.
100 WKTS (8) 201 @ 18.98 in 1937.
RECORDS Took 200 wkts in 1936 and 1937, only fast bowler to reach this figure since T. Richardson in 1897.
Players v Gentlemen (3) 1934–36. Ran well-known cricket school in Clapham, London.

GOVINDARAJ, Devraj
—— RHB, RFM ——

Born Hyderabad, Deccan, India, 2 Jan 1947. Debut 1964/65.
INDIA DOMESTIC Hyderabad 1964/65–74/75.
TOURS Hyderabad Blues to Ceylon 1966/67. State Bank of India to Ceylon 1968/69. India to W Indies 1970/71. India to England 1971.
HS 72 State Bank of India v Dungarpur, Hyderabad, 1967/68.
BB 6–38 (11–70 match) All-India State Bank v Ceylon Board of Control Under-27 XI, Colombo, 1968/69.
Uncle C. K. Nayudu (India).

GOWER, David Ivon
—— LHB, SRA ——

Born Tunbridge Wells, Kent, 1 Apr 1957. Educ King's S, Canterbury; UC, London. Debut 1975. *Wisden* 1979.
LEICESTERSHIRE (130) 1975–. Cap 1977. Capt 1984.
ENGLAND (65) 1978–84. A 1980 (1), 1981 (5); WI 1980 (1), 1984 (5); NZ 1978 (3), 1983 (4), 1982 (3); I 1979 (4), 1982 (3); P 1978 (3), 1982 (3); SL 1984 (1). *A 1978/79 (6), 1979/80 (3), 1982/83 (5); WI 1980/81 (4); NZ 1983/84 (3); I 1979/80 (1), 1981/82 (6); P 1983/84 (3); SL 1981/82 (1).* Capt 8.
OTHER TOUR D. H. Robins' XI to Sri Lanka 1977/78.
HST 200* E v I, Edgbaston, 1979. HS as above.
BB 3–47 Leics v Essex, Leicester, 1977.
1000 RUNS (5) 1530 @ 46.36 in 1982.
RECORDS Added 289* for 2nd wkt with J. C. Balderstone, Leics v Essex, Leicester, 1981, county record.
CWC Young Cricketer of 1978.

GRACEY, Peter Bosworth Kirkwood
—— RHB, OB ——

Born Bannu, India, 12 Dec 1921. Educ Wellington C; Brasenose C, Oxford. Debut 1945/46.
INDIA DOMESTIC Madras Europeans 1945/46.
OXFORD UNIVERSITY (4) 1947–48.
HS 61 Madras Europeans v Madras Indians, Madras, 1945/46.
BB 2–21 same match.
War-time Blue 1941.

GRAF, Shaun Francis
—— LHB, RFM ——

Born Melbourne, Australia, 19 May 1957. Educ St Bede's C, Melbourne. Debut 1979/80.
AUSTRALIA DOMESTIC Victoria (28) 1979/80–82/83, Western Australia (11) 1983/84.
HAMPSHIRE (15) 1980.
HS 100* Victoria v W Australia, Melbourne, 1980/81.
BB 5–95 Victoria v W Australia, Perth, 1982/83.
Wiltshire 1979. Club: Knowle.

GRAHAM, David
—— RHB, RFM ——

Born Belfast, N Ireland, 13 Mar 1922. Debut 1948.
IRELAND (1) 1948.
HS 7 Ireland v Scotland, Glasgow, 1948.
Clubs: Northern Ireland, YMCA Belfast.

GRAHAM, Godfrey Richard
—— RHB, LBG ——

Born Dublin, Ireland, 23 Aug 1936. Educ Blackrock C, Dublin. Debut 1954.
IRELAND (1) 1954.
HS 1* Ireland v Scotland, Paisley, 1954.
BB 2–100 same match.
Clubs: Pembroke, Phoenix.

GRAHAM, John *Norman*
—— RHB, RM ——

Born Hexham, Northumberland, 8 May 1943. Educ Queen Elizabeth GS, Hexham; Birmingham U. Debut 1964.
KENT (186) 1964–77. Cap 1967. Benefit 1977.
HS 23 Kent v Cambridge U, Fenner's, 1968.
BB 8–20 Kent v Essex, Brentwood, 1969.
100 WKTS (1) 104 @ 13.90 in 1967.
Northumberland 1980–. Professional: Philadelphia. Club: Holmesdale.

GRAHAM, Peter Arthur Onslow
—— RHB, RF ——

Born Kurseong, India, 27 Dec 1920. Educ Tonbridge. Debut 1948. *P.*
SOMERSET (6) 1948.
HS 33 Som v Glam, Newport, 1948.
BB 3–47 same match.

GRAHAM-BROWN, James Martin Hilary
—— RHB, RM ——

Born Thetford, Norfolk, 11 July 1951. Educ Sevenoaks S; U of Kent. Debut 1974.
KENT (13) 1974–76.
DERBYSHIRE (17) 1977–78.
HS 43 Derbys v Cambridge U, Fenner's, 1978.
BB 2–23 Derbys v Worcs, Worcester, 1978.
Cornwall 1981–. Club: Camborne.
Great-uncle L. B. Blaxland (Derbys).

GRAINGE, Clifford Marshall
—— RHB, RMF ——

Born Heckmondwike, Yorks, 21 July 1927. Educ Heckmondwike GS; Keble C, Oxford. Debut 1950.
OXFORD UNIVERSITY (14) 1950–52.
HS 14* Oxford U v Lancs, The Parks, 1951.
BB 5–127 Oxford U v Surrey, Oval, 1951.
Yorks 2nd XI 1950.

GRANT, Christopher Robert Wellesley
—— LHB ——

Born Lincoln, 19 Dec 1935. Educ Magnus GS, Newark. Debut 1968.
NOTTINGHAMSHIRE (3) 1968.
HS 48 Notts v Derbys, Trent Bridge, 1968.
Club: Newark.

GRANT, Trevor John Duncan
—— RHB ——

Born Reigate, Surrey, 24 May 1926. Died, by own hand, HMS Ganges, Shotley, Suffolk, 10 or 11 Oct 1957 (Last seen alive on 10 Oct; body found on 11 Oct). Debut 1946.
SUSSEX (1) 1946.
HS 6 Sussex v Hants, Bournemouth, 1946.
Lt-Commander Royal Navy.

GRAVENEY, David Anthony
RHB, SLA

Born Bristol, 2 Jan 1953. Educ Millfield. Debut 1972.
GLOUCESTERSHIRE (263) 1972–. Cap 1976. Capt 1981–.
HS 119 Glos v Oxford U, The Parks, 1980.
BB 8–85 Glos v Notts, Cheltenham, 1974. Treasurer Cricketers' Association. Father J. K. R. Graveney (Glos); uncle T. W. Graveney (Glos, Worcs, England).

GRAVENEY, John *Kenneth* Richard
LHB, RMF

Born Hexham, Northumberland, 16 Dec 1924. Educ Bristol GS. Debut 1947. *P.*
GLOUCESTERSHIRE (110) 1947–64. Cap 1949. Capt 1963–64.
HS 62 Glos v Leics, Leicester, 1949.
BB 10–66 Glos v Derbys, Chesterfield, 1949.
Missed seasons 1952–62 after back injury. Club: Southville Wayfarers. Glos chairman 1978–79. Son D. A. Graveney (Glos); brother T. W. Graveney (Glos, Worcs, England).

GRAVENEY, Thomas William
RHB, LB

Born Riding Mill, Northumberland, 16 June 1927. Educ Bristol GS. Debut 1948. *P. Wisden* 1953.
GLOUCESTERSHIRE (296) 1948–60. Cap 1948. Capt 1959–60. Benefit (£5400) 1959.
WORCESTERSHIRE (208) 1961–70. Cap 1962. Capt 1968–70. Benefit (£7886) 1969.
AUSTRALIA DOMESTIC Queensland (7) 1969/70–71/72.
ENGLAND (79) 1951–69. A 1953 (5), 1956 (2), 1968 (5); SA 1951 (1), 1955 (5); WI 1957 (4), 1966 (4), 1969 (1); NZ 1958 (4); I 1952 (4), 1967 (3); P 1954 (3), 1962 (4), 1967 (3). *A 1954/55 (2), 1958/59 (5), 1962/63 (3); WI 1953/54 (5), 1967/68 (5); NZ 1954/55 (2), 1958/59 (2); I 1951/52 (4); P 1968/69 (3).* Capt 1.
OTHER TOURS E. W. Swanton's XI to W Indies 1955/56. Duke of Norfolk's XI to Jamaica 1956/57. C. G. Howard's XI to India 1956/57. Commonwealth XI to S Africa 1959/60. Cavaliers to S Africa 1960/61. International XI to Pakistan, N Zealand, India and Rhodesia 1961/62. Cavaliers to Jamaica 1963/64. Commonwealth XI to Pakistan 1963/64. Worcs to Rhodesia 1964/65. Rest of World XI v Barbados 1966/67.
HST 258 E v WI, Trent Bridge, 1957. HS as above.
BB 5–28 Glos v Derbys, Bristol, 1953.
1000 RUNS (20 + 2) 2397 @ 49.93 in 1956. 2000 runs (7).
RECORDS Scored 200 in inns of 298, Glos v Glam, Newport, 1956, lowest completed total to include double century. Scored more than 10,000 runs for two counties (Glos and Worcs), unique feat. Added 402 for 4th wkt with W. Watson, MCC v British Guiana, Georgetown, 1953/54, record for an English touring team. Added 256 for 2nd wkt with C. T. M. Pugh, Glos v Derbys, Chesterfield, 1960 and 314 for 3rd wkt with M. J. Horton, Worcs v Som, Worcester, 1962, both records for respective counties. First player to score 30,000 runs and 100 centuries in purely post-war cricket. Scored more than half teams' total in both inns (100 out of 153, 67 out of 107) Glos v Essex, Romford, 1956. 15th player to score 100 fc centuries, in 1964. 550 catches in career.
Players v Gentlemen (17) 1949–62. Banned for three Tests in 1969 after playing in a benefit match on the Sunday of a Test in which he was taking part. Author *Cricket through the Covers* (1958); *Cricket Over Forty* (1970). Cricket summariser on television. Brother J. K. R. Graveney (Glos); nephew D. A. Graveney (Glos). OBE for services to cricket.

GRAVES, Peter John
LHB, SLA

Born Hove, Sussex, 19 May 1946. Educ Hove Manor S. Debut 1965.
SUSSEX (270) 1965–80. Cap 1969. Benefit (£35,000) 1978.
S AFRICA DOMESTIC Orange Free State 1969/70–76/77.
HS 145* Sussex v Glos, Gloucester, 1974.
BB 3–69 OFS v Australians, Bloemfontein, 1969/70.
1000 RUNS (5), 1282 @ 38.84 in 1974. Retired due to hand injuries 1980. Assistant manager S African Country Districts, Rhodesia 1974.

GRAY, David Anthony Athelstan
RHB, SLA

Born London, 19 June 1922. Educ Winchester; Caius C, Cambridge. Debut 1947.
CAMBRIDGE UNIVERSITY (2) 1947.
ESSEX (1) 1947.
HS 8 Cambridge U v Sussex, Fenner's, 1947.
BB 2–67 same match.

GRAY, Evan John
RHB, SLA

Born Wellington, N Zealand, 18 Nov 1954. Debut 1975/76.
N ZEALAND DOMESTIC Wellington (61) 1975/76–, Young New Zealand 1977/78–78/79.
NEW ZEALAND (2) *E 1983.*
HST 17 NZ v E, Lord's, 1983. HS 126 Wellington v C Districts, Wellington, 1981/82 (added 226 for 6th wkt with R. W. Ormiston, N Zealand fc record).
BBT 3–73 NZ v E, Lord's, 1983. BB 6–53 Wellington v Otago, Dunedin, 1977/78.

GRAY, James Roy
RHB, RM

Born Southampton, Hants, 19 May 1926. Educ King Edward VI S, Southampton. Debut 1948. *P.*
HAMPSHIRE (453) 1948–66. Cap 1951. Benefit (£4350) 1960.
HS 213* Hants v Derbys, Portsmouth, 1962.
BB 7–52 Hants v Glam, Swansea, 1955.
1000 RUNS (13) 2224 @ 40.43 in 1962.
RECORD Added 249 for 1st wkt with R. E. Marshall, Hants v M'sex, Portsmouth, 1960, county record.
352 catches in career.
Soccer: Arsenal.

GRAY, John Denis
LHB, LMF

Born Coventry, Warwicks, 9 Oct 1948. Educ Woodlands CS, Coventry; Loughborough C. Debut 1968.
WARWICKSHIRE (7) 1968–69.
HS 18 Warwicks v Surrey, Edgbaston, 1969.
BB 5–2 Warwicks v Scotland, Edgbaston, 1968 (fc debut).
Rugby: Coventry. Rugby League in England and Australia.

GRAY, Laurence Herbert
RHB, RFM

Born Tottenham, London, 16 Dec 1915. Died Langdon Hills, Essex, 3 Jan 1983. Debut 1934. *P.*
MIDDLESEX (204) 1934–51. Cap 1937. Benefit (£6000) 1948.
HS 35* MCC v Kent, Folkestone, 1936.
BB 8–59 M'sex v Kent, Maidstone, 1938.
100 WKTS (1) 102 @ 18.43 in 1946.
Players v Gentlemen (1) 1946. Fc umpire 1953–70 (2 Tests, 1955–63). Clubs: Norwood, Wanstead.

GRAY, Roger Ibbotson
———RHB, RM———

Born Leeds, Yorks, 16 June 1921. Educ Wycliffe S; Queen's C, Oxford. Debut 1947.
OXFORD UNIVERSITY (1) 1947.
HS 11 Oxford U v Free Foresters, The Parks, 1947.

GREASLEY, Douglas George
———RHB, SLA———

Born Hull, Yorks, 20 Jan 1926. Debut 1950. *P*.
NORTHAMPTONSHIRE (58) 1950–55.
HS 104* Northants v Leics, Northampton, 1951.
BB 4–36 Northants v Yorks, Northampton, 1950.
Club: Brechin.

GREEN, Allan Michael
———RHB, RM———

Born Pulborough, Sussex, 28 May 1960. Educ Knoll S, Hove; Hove and Brighton Sixth Form C. Debut 1980.
SUSSEX (58) 1980–.
HS 99 Sussex v M'sex, Hove, 1982.
BB 2–30 Sussex v Worcs, Hove, 1983.
1000 RUNS (1) 1006 @ 26.47 in 1984.

GREEN, David John
———RHB———

Born Burton upon Trent, Staffordshire, 18 Dec 1935. Educ Burton GS; Christ's C, Cambridge. Debut 1953.
DERBYSHIRE (37) 1953–60.
CAMBRIDGE UNIVERSITY (47) 1957–59 (Blue 1957–59). Capt 1959.
HS 134 Free Foresters v Cambridge U, Fenner's, 1960.
Wiltshire 1963–67. Club: Devizes.

GREEN, David Michael
———RHB, OB———

Born Llanengan, Caernarfon, N Wales, 10 Nov 1939. Educ Manchester GS; Brasenose C, Oxford. Debut 1959. *Wisden* 1969.
OXFORD UNIVERSITY (39) 1959–61 (Blue 1959–61).
LANCASHIRE (135) 1959–67. Cap 1962.
GLOUCESTERSHIRE (81) 1968–71. Cap 1968.
TOUR International Wanderers to Rhodesia 1972/73.
HS 233 Glos v Sussex, Hove, 1968.
BB 5–61 Oxford U v Sussex, Hove, 1959.
1000 RUNS (7) 2137 @ 40.32 in 1968.

RECORDS 2037 @ 32.85 in 1965 highest season's aggregate by a batsman not to include a century.
1049 runs @ 24.97 in debut season, 1959.
Cricket writer.

GREEN, Russell Christopher
———RHB, RFM———

Born St Albans, Herts, 30 July 1959. Debut 1984.
GLAMORGAN (2) 1984.
HS 3* Glam v Worcs, Swansea, 1984.
BB 2–65 same match.
Suffolk 1982–83. Club: Bury St Edmunds.

GREENE, Robin Morton
———RHB, RFM———

Born Durban, Natal, S Africa, 1 Nov 1930. Educ Michaelhouse S, S Africa. Debut 1949/50.
S AFRICA DOMESTIC South African XI v Australians, J'burg, 1949/50.
GLOUCESTERSHIRE (1) 1951.
HS 26* Glos v Oxford U, Bristol, 1951.
Polo: Natal. President Sussex Cattle Breeders Society of S Africa.

GREENHOUGH, Thomas
———RHB, LBG———

Born Rochdale, Lancs, 9 Nov 1931. Debut 1951. *P*.
LANCASHIRE (241) 1951–66. Cap 1956. Benefit (£4504) 1964.
ENGLAND (4) 1959–60. SA 1960 (1); I 1959 (3).
TOURS Duke of Norfolk's XI to Jamaica 1956/57. MCC to W Indies 1959/60.
HST 2 E v I, Oval, 1959. HS 76* Lancs v Glos, Old Trafford, 1962.
BBT 5–35 E v I, Lord's, 1959. BB 7–56 Lancs v Worcs, Worcester, 1964.
100 WKTS (2) 122 @ 22.37 in 1959.
Club: Werneth.

GREENIDGE, Cuthbert *Gordon*
———RHB, RM———

Born St Peter, Barbados, 1 May 1951. Educ Sutton Sec S, Reading. Debut 1970. *Wisden* 1977.
HAMPSHIRE (225) 1970–. Cap 1972. Benefit 1983.
W INDIES DOMESTIC Barbados 1972/73–.
WEST INDIES (57) 1974/75–84. E 1980/81 (4); A 1977/78 (2), 1983/84 (5); I 1982/83 (5); P 1976/77 (5). *E 1976 (5), 1980 (5), 1984 (5); A 1975/76 (2), 1979/80 (3), 1981/82 (2); NZ 1979/80 (3); I 1974/75 (5), 1983/84 (6).*

OTHER TOUR W Indies to Pakistan 1980/81.
HST 223 WI v E, Old Trafford, 1984. HS 273* D. H. Robins' XI v Pakistanis, Eastbourne, 1974 (with 13 sixes).
BB 5–49 Hants v Surrey, Southampton, 1971.
1000 RUNS (12 + 1) 1952 @ 55.77 in 1976.
RECORD Added 296 for 1st wkt with D. L. Haynes, WI v I, Antigua, 1982/83, W Indies Test record. Twice hit 13 sixes in inns, during 259 Hants v Sussex, Southampton, 1975 and during HS (above).
Scored 93 and 107 on Test debut, WI v I, Bangalore, 1974/75.
World Series Cricket (Kerry Packer) 1977/78–78/79. MBE for services to cricket. Autobiography *The Man in the Middle* (1980).

GREENIDGE, Geoffrey Alan
———RHB, LBG———

Born Bridgetown, Barbados, 26 May 1948. Debut 1966/67.
W INDIES DOMESTIC Barbados 1966/67–75/76.
SUSSEX (152) 1968–75. Cap 1970.
WEST INDIES (5) 1971/72–72/73. A 1972/73 (3); NZ 1971/72 (2).
TOURS D. H. Robins' XI to S Africa 1974/75. International XI to Rhodesia 1975/76.
HST 50 WI v NZ, Georgetown, 1971/72. HS 205 Barbados v Jamaica, Bridgetown, 1966/67 (aged 18).
BB 7–124 same match.
1000 RUNS (5) 1334 @ 26.68 in 1971.
Club: Pickwick.

GREENSMITH, William Thomas
———RHB, LBG———

Born Middlesbrough, Yorks, 16 Aug 1930. Debut 1947. *P*.
ESSEX (371) 1947–63. Cap 1952. Benefit 1963.
COMBINED SERVICES (5) 1949–50.
HS 138* Essex v Kent, Blackheath, 1953.
BB 8–59 Essex v Glos, Bristol, 1956.
Club: Buckhurst Hill.

GREENSWORD, Stephen
———RHB, RM———

Born Gateshead, Co Durham, 6 Sept 1943. Educ Glebe Road Sec S, Gateshead. Debut 1963.
LEICESTERSHIRE (39) 1963–66.
MINOR COUNTIES (2) 1973–81.
HS 84* Minor Counties v W Indians, Torquay, 1973.

BB 3–22 Leics v Northants, Northampton, 1964.
Northumberland 1967–69, Durham 1970–. Clubs: Philadelphia, Gateshead, Fell, South Shields, Hartlepool, Whitburn, Sunderland.

GREENWOOD, Henry *William*
————RHB, WK————

Born East Preston, Sussex, 4 Sept 1909.
Died Bromley, Kent, 24 Mar 1979.
Debut 1933. *P.*
SUSSEX (19) 1933–36.
NORTHAMPTONSHIRE (60) 1938–46.
HS 115 Sussex v Essex, Hove, 1935.
Durham 1949. Club: South Shields.

GREENWOOD, Peter
————RHB, RM/OB————

Born Todmorden, Yorks, 11 Sept 1924.
Debut 1948. *P.*
LANCASHIRE (75) 1948–52. Cap 1949.
HS 113 Lancs v Kent, Old Trafford, 1951.
BB 6–35 Lancs v Northants, Old Trafford, 1949.
Clubs: Kendall, West Bromwich Dartmouth, Bradshaw. Soccer: Chester.

GREETHAM, Christopher Herbert Millington
————RHB, RM————

Born Wargrave, Berkshire, 28 Aug 1936. Educ Maidenhead S. Debut 1957. *P.*
SOMERSET (205) 1957–66. Cap 1962.
HS 151★ Som v Combined Services, Taunton, 1959.
BB 7–56 Som v Glam, Swansea, 1962.
1000 RUNS (2) 1186 @ 28.23 in 1963.
RECORDS Added 183 for 9th wkt with H. W. Stephenson, Som v Leics, Weston-super-Mare, 1963, county record.
Devon 1968–69.

GREGORY, Henry Vernon
————RHB, LB————

Born Manchester, Lancashire, 18 Jan 1936. Debut 1960. *P.*
SUSSEX (1) 1960.
HS 14 Sussex v Cambridge U, Fenner's, 1960.

GREGORY, Robert James
————RHB, LB————

Born Selsdon, Surrey, 26 Aug 1902.
Died Wandsworth, London, 6 Oct 1973.
Debut 1925. *P.*

SURREY (415) 1925–47. Cap 1928.
Benefit 1939.
TOUR MCC to India and Ceylon 1933/34.
HS 243 Surrey v Som, Oval, 1938.
BB 6–21 Surrey v Worcs, Oval, 1932.
1000 RUNS (9) 2379 @ 51.71 in 1934.
Soccer: Fulham, Norwich City. Secretary Watney-Mann Sports Club until death.

GREIG, Anthony William
————RHB, RM/OB————

Born Queenstown, S Africa, 6 Oct 1946.
Educ Queen's C, Queenstown. Debut 1965/66. *Wisden* 1975.
S AFRICA DOMESTIC Border 1965/66–69/70, Eastern Province 1970/71–71/72.
SUSSEX (209) 1966–78. Cap 1967. Capt 1973–77.
ENGLAND (58) 1972–77. A 1972 (5), 1975 (4), 1977 (5); WI 1973 (3), 1976 (5); NZ 1973 (3); I 1974 (3); P 1974 (3). *A 1974/ 75 (6), 1976/77 (1); WI 1973/74 (5); NZ 1974/75 (2); I 1972/73 (5); 1976/ 77 (5); P 1972/73 (3).* Capt 14.
OTHER TOURS International XI to India, Pakistan and Ceylon 1967/68. Duke of Norfolk's XI to W Indies 1969/70. Rest of World XI to Australia 1971/72. D. H. Robins' XI to S Africa 1974/75.
HST 148 E v I, Bombay, 1972/73 (adding 254 for 5th wkt with K. W. R. Fletcher, England Test record) and E v WI, Bridgetown, 1973/74. HS 226 Sussex v Warwicks, Hastings, 1975.
BBT 8–86 (13–156 match) E v WI, Port of Spain, 1973/74. BB 8–25 Sussex v Glos, Hove, 1967.
1000 RUNS (7 + 1) 1699 @ 47.19 in 1975.
World Series Cricket (Kerry Packer) 1977/78–78/79; cricket executive. CWC Young Cricketer of 1967. Brother I. A. Greig (Sussex, England).

GREIG, Ian Alexander
————RHB, RM————

Born Queenstown, S Africa, 8 Dec 1955.
Educ Queen's C, Queenstown; Downing C, Cambridge. Debut 1974/75.
S AFRICA DOMESTIC Border 1974/75, 1979/80, Griqualand West 1975/76.
CAMBRIDGE UNIVERSITY (22) 1977–79 (Blue 1977–79) Capt 1979.
SUSSEX (84) 1980–. Cap 1981.
ENGLAND (2) P 1982.
HST 14 E v P, Edgbaston, 1982. HS 147★ Sussex v Oxford U, The Parks, 1983.
BBT 4–53 E v P, Edgbaston, 1982. BB 7–43 Sussex v Cambridge U, Fenner's, 1981.
Rugby: Blue. Brother A. W. Greig (Sussex, England).

GRIEVES, Kenneth John
————RHB, LBG————

Born Sydney, NSW, Australia, 27 Aug 1925. Debut 1945/46. *P.*
AUSTRALIA DOMESTIC New South Wales (10) 1945/46–46/47.
LANCASHIRE (452) 1949–64. Cap 1949.
Capt 1963–64. Benefit (£5756) 1956.
HS 224 Lancs v Cambridge U, Fenner's, 1957.
BB 6–60 Lancs v Kent, Old Trafford, 1949.
1000 RUNS (13 + 1) 2253 @ 41.72 in 1959.
TOUR Commonwealth XI to India and Ceylon 1950/51.
RECORDS Six catches inns and eight catches match, Lancs v Sussex, Old Trafford, 1951, both county records for a fielder.
610 catches in career.
Clubs: Petersham (NSW), Rawtenstall, Accrington, Stockport, Milnrow. Soccer: Bury, Bolton Wanderers, Stockport County.

GRIFFIN, Geoffrey Merton
————RHB, RF————

Born Greytown, S Africa, 12 June 1939.
Educ Durban HS. Debut 1957/58.
S AFRICA DOMESTIC 1957/58–60/61, Rhodesia 1961/62–62/63.
SOUTH AFRICA (2) E 1960.
HST 14 SA v E, Edgbaston, 1960. HS 73 Natal v Transvaal, J'burg, 1959/60.
BBT 4–87 SA v E, Lord's, 1960. BB 7–11 Natal v Border, East London, 1959/60.
RECORDS Hat-trick SA v E, Lord's, 1960, only hat-trick for S Africa in Tests.
First overseas bowler called for throwing in Tests in England, at Edgbaston and Lord's in 1960; subsequently withdrawn from remainder of tour as a bowler.

GRIFFIN, Neville Fetherstone
————RHB, RM————

Born Croydon, Surrey, 17 Dec 1933.
Debut 1963.
SURREY (1) 1963.
HS 83★ Surrey v Oxford U, Oval, 1963.
Clubs: Wallington, Beddington.

GRIFFITH, Charles Christopher
————RHB, RF————

Born St Lucy, Barbados, 14 Dec 1938.
Debut 1959/60.
W INDIES DOMESTIC Barbados 1959/60–66/67.

WEST INDIES (28) 1959/60–68/69. E 1959/60 (1), 1967/68 (4); A 1964/65 (5). *E 1963 (5), 1966 (5); A 1968/69 (3); NZ 1968/69 (2); I 1966/67 (3).*
OTHER TOUR Commonwealth XI to Pakistan 1963/64.
HST 54 WI v A, Bridgetown, 1964/65. HS 98 Commonwealth XI v Pakistan XI, Karachi, 1963/64.
BBT 6–36 WI v E, Headingley, 1963. BB 8–23 W Indians v Glos, Bristol, 1963.
100 WKTS (1) 119 @ 12.83 in 1963.
No-balled for throwing, Barbados v Indians, Bridgetown, 1961/62 (during which match he severely injured N. J. Contractor, who was struck on the head by a ball); W Indians v Lancs, Old Trafford, 1966.
Club: Burnley 1964, 1967.

GRIFFITH, George Hugh Clarence
————RHB, LB————

Born Bridgetown, Barbados, 21 Aug 1929. Educ Harrison C, Barbados; St John's C, Cambridge. Debut 1949.
CAMBRIDGE UNIVERSITY (5) 1949–51.
HS 33 Cambridge U v Leics, Fenner's, 1950.
Father H. C. Griffith (W Indies); brothers E. H. C. and H. L. V. Griffith (both Barbados).

GRIFFITH, Kevin
————RHB, OB————

Born Warrington, Lancs, 17 Jan 1950. Educ Worcester RGS. Debut 1967.
WORCESTERSHIRE (44) 1967–72.
HS 59 Worcs v Yorks, Sheffield, 1971.
BB 7–41 Worcs v Oxford U, The Parks, 1969.
Club: Kidderminster.

GRIFFITH, Mike Grenville
————RHB, WK————

Born Beaconsfield, Buckinghamshire, 25 Nov 1943. Educ Marlborough C; Magdalene C, Cambridge. Debut 1962.
SUSSEX (232) 1962–74. Cap 1967. Capt 1968–72.
CAMBRIDGE UNIVERSITY (33) 1963–65 (Blue 1963–65).
TOURS E. W. Swanton's XI to India 1963/64. Duke of Norfolk's XI to W Indies 1969/70. MCC to E Africa 1973/74.
HS 158 Sussex v Cambridge U, Hove, 1969.
1000 RUNS (1) 1144 @ 30.10 in 1964.
Father S. C. Griffith (Surrey, Sussex, England). Hockey: Blue, England and Great Britain.

GRIFFITH, Stewart Cathie (Billy)
————RHB, WK————

Born Wandsworth, London, 16 June 1914. Educ Dulwich; Pembroke C, Cambridge. Debut 1934.
CAMBRIDGE UNIVERSITY (20) 1934–36 (Blue 1935).
SURREY (1) 1934.
SUSSEX (122) 1937–54. Cap. Capt 1946.
ENGLAND (3) 1947/48–48/49. *SA 1948/49 (2); WI 1947/48 (1).*
OTHER TOUR MCC to Australasia 1935/36.
HST 140 E v WI, Port of Spain, 1947/48.
HS as above.
Scored maiden fc century on Test debut (HST above).
Gentlemen v Players (7) 1938–51. England v Australia (5) 1945 (Victory matches). Sussex secretary 1946–50; MCC assistant-secretary 1952–62; MCC secretary 1962–74; Sussex president 1976; MCC president 1979/80. Prepared new code of The Laws of Cricket in 1980. *Sunday Times* cricket correspondent 1950–52. Son M. G. Griffith (Sussex).
MBE for Services to cricket.

GRIFFITHS, Alan
————RHB, WK————

Born Newcastle under Lyme, Staffordshire, 18 Sept 1957. Debut 1981.
MINOR COUNTIES (1) 1981.
HS 26 Minor Counties v Sri Lankans, Reading, 1981.
Staffordshire 1979–. Club: Burslem.

GRIFFITHS, Brian *James*
————RHB, RMF————

Born Wellingborough, Northants, 13 June 1949. Educ Irthlingborough Sec S. Debut 1974.
NORTHAMPTONSHIRE (154) 1974–. Cap 1978.
HS 16 Northants v Glos, Bristol, 1982.
BB 8–50 Northants v Glam, Northampton, 1981.
RECORD Fc record of 10 consecutive scoreless inns, 1974–77.

GRIFFITHS, Colin
————RHB, RM————

Born Upminster, Essex, 9 Dec 1930. Educ Brentwood S. Debut 1951.
ESSEX (27) 1951–53.
HS 105 Essex v Kent, Tunbridge Wells, 1952 (scored in 90 mins).
Club: Wimbledon.

GRIFFITHS, John Vesey Claude
————LHB, SLA————

Born Blackheath, Kent, 19 Jan 1931. Died Wedmore, Som, 18 Feb 1982. Educ Cheltenham GS. Debut 1952. *P.*
GLOUCESTERSHIRE (34) 1952–57.
HS 32 Glos v Combined Services, Bristol, 1953.
BB 4–74 Glos v Cambridge U, Bristol, 1955.
Fc umpire 1979. Club: Chipping Sodbury.

GRIFFITHS, Peter David
————RHB, SLA————

Born Bulawayo, Rhodesia, 13 July 1961. Educ Charterhouse; Magdalene C, Cambridge. Debut 1982.
CAMBRIDGE UNIVERSITY (1) 1982.
HS 1 Cambridge U v Northants, Fenner's, 1982.

GRIFFITHS, Shirley
————RHB, RF————

Born Barbados, 11 July 1930. Educ St Mark's C, Barbados. Debut 1956. *P.*
WARWICKSHIRE (27) 1956–58.
HS 17* Warwicks v Surrey, Edgbaston, 1957.
BB 7–62 Warwicks v Kent, Edgbaston, 1958.
Clubs: Middlesbrough, Lancaster.

GRIFFITHS, William Hugh
————RHB, RFM————

Born London, 26 Sept 1923. Educ Charterhouse; St John's C, Cambridge. Debut 1946.
CAMBRIDGE UNIVERSITY (29) 1946–48 (Blue 1946–48).
GLAMORGAN (8) 1946–48.
FREE FORESTERS (1) 1949.
HS 19 Cambridge U v Oxford U, Lord's, 1948.
BB 6–129 Cambridge U v Lancs, Fenner's, 1946.
Knighted.

GRIMES, Alexander David Hugh
————RHB, RM————

Born Beirut, Lebanon, 8 Jan 1965. Educ Tonbridge S; Pembroke C, Cambridge. Debut 1984.
CAMBRIDGE UNIVERSITY (7) 1984 (Blue).
HS 13 Cambridge U v Surrey, Banstead, 1984.
BB 1–24 Cambridge U v Warwicks, Fenner's, 1984.

GRIPPER, Raymond Arthur
————————RHB————————

Born Salisbury, Rhodesia, 7 July 1938.
Educ St George's C, Salisbury. Debut
1957/58.
RHODESIA (79) 1957/58–71/72.
TOUR S African Fezelas to England 1961.
HS 279* Rhodesia v OFS, Bloemfontein,
1967/68 (highest-ever individual score
in Currie Cup).
Chairman Mashonaland CA.

GROOME, Jeremy Jonathan
————————RHB, RM————————

Born Bognor Regis, Sussex, 7 Apr 1955.
Educ Seaford C. Debut 1974.
SUSSEX (40) 1974–78.
HS 86 Sussex v M'sex, Lord's, 1975.

GROUT, Arthur Theodore
Wallace
————————RHB, WK————————

Born Mackay, Queensland, Australia,
30 Mar 1927. Died Brisbane, Queensland, Australia, 9 Nov 1968. Debut
1946/47.
AUSTRALIA DOMESTIC Queensland (94)
1946/47–65/66.
AUSTRALIA (51) 1957/58–65/66. E 1958/
59 (5), 1962/63 (2), 1965/66 (5); SA
1963/64 (5); WI 1960/61 (5). E 1961 (5),
1964 (5); SA 1957/58 (5); WI 1964/65
(5); I 1959/60 (4), 1964/65 (1); P
1959/60 (3); 1964/65 (1).
Rest of World XI v England XI, Scarborough, 1965.
HST 74 A v E, Melbourne, 1958/59. HS
119* Queensland v NSW, Sydney,
1956/57.
RECORDS First wicket-keeper to take six
catches in Test inns, A v SA, J'burg,
1957/58 (Test debut). Only wicketkeeper to make eight dismissals (all c) in
a fc inns, Queensland v W Australia,
Brisbane, 1959/60.
Autobiography *My Country's Keeper*
(1965). Daughter J. Grout (qualified
umpire).

GROVE, Charles William
————————RHB, RMF————————

Born Birmingham, 16 Dec 1912. Died
Solihull, W Midlands, 15 Feb 1982.
Educ Yardley S. Debut 1938. *P.*
WARWICKSHIRE (201) 1938–53. Cap
1947. Benefit (£4469) 1951.
WORCESTERSHIRE (15) 1954.
HS 104* Warwicks v Leics, Leicester,
1948.

BB 9–39 Warwicks v Sussex, Edgbaston,
1952 (eight wkts before lunch).
100 WKTS (2) 118 @ 17.13 in 1952.
Warwicks scorer 1974–81. Clubs:
Mitchells and Butlers, Old Hill, Smethwick.

GROVES, Michael Godfrey
Melvin
————————RHB, RM————————

Born Taihape, N Zealand, 14 Jan 1943.
Educ Diocesan C, Rondebosch, S
Africa; St Edmund Hall, Oxford. Debut
1960/61.
S AFRICA DOMESTIC Western Province
1960/61.
FREE FORESTERS (3) 1962–68.
OXFORD UNIVERSITY (43) 1963–66 (Blue
1964–66).
SOMERSET (7) 1965.
MCC (1) 1967.
HS 86 Som v Derbys, Glastonbury,
1965.
BB 3–33 Oxford U v Free Foresters, The
Parks, 1964.
1000 RUNS (1) 1048 @ 29.11 in 1965.

GUARD, David Radclyffe
————————RHB————————

Born Romsey, Hants, 19 May 1928.
Died Hartfield, Sussex, 12 Dec 1978.
Educ Winchester. Debut 1946.
HAMPSHIRE (15) 1946–49.
COMBINED SERVICES (1) 1947.
HS 89 Hants v Glam, Cardiff, 1949.
Club: Lindfield.

GUEST, Melville Richard John
————————RHB, RM————————

Born Rhodesia, 18 Nov 1943. Educ
Rugby; Magdalen C, Oxford. Debut
1964.
OXFORD UNIVERSITY (23) 1964–66 (Blue
1964–66).
HS 77 Oxford U v Combined Services,
Aldershot, 1964.
BB 2–25 Oxford U v N Zealanders, The
Parks, 1965.
Wiltshire 1962–66.

GUHA, Subroto
————————RHB, RM————————

Born Calcutta, India, 31 Jan 1946. Educ
Calcutta U. Debut 1965/66.
INDIA DOMESTIC Bengal 1965/66–76/77.
INDIA (4) 1967–69/70. A 1969/70 (3). E
1967.
OTHER TOUR All-India State Bank to
Ceylon 1968/69.

HST 6 I v A, Kanpur, 1969/70. HS 75
Bengal v Mysore, Bangalore, 1968/69.
BBT 2–55 I v A, Kanpur, 1969/70. BB
7–18 Bengal v Assam, Gauhati, 1972/73.

GULZAR (Gul) MAHOMED
————————LHB, LM/SLA————————

Born Lahore, India, 15 Oct 1921. Debut
1938/39.
INDIA DOMESTIC Northern India, Mus-
lims, Baroda, Hyderabad, 1938/39–54/
55.
PAKISTAN DOMESTIC Punjab 1956/57,
Lahore 1957/58–58/59.
INDIA (8) 1946–52/53. P 1952/53 (2). E
1946 (1); A 1947/48 (5).
PAKISTAN (1) A 1956/57.
HST 34 I v A, Adelaide, 1947/48; (for
Pakistan) 27* P v A, Karachi, 1956/57.
HS 319 Baroda v Holkar, Baroda, 1946/
47.
BBT 2–21 I v P, Lucknow, 1952/53. BB
6–60 Baroda v Kathiawar, Baroda,
1949/50.
RECORDS During HS (above) added 577
for 4th wkt with V. S. Hazare, world
record for any wkt in fc cricket.
One of only 12 players to appear for two
countries in Test cricket, three of whom
played for India and Pakistan. Clubs:
Ramsbottom, Crompton.

GUNASEKERA, Yohan
————————LHB, LM/SLA————————

Born Colombo, Ceylon, 8 Nov 1957.
Educ Nalanda C. Debut 1980/81.
SRI LANKA DOMESTIC Sri Lanka 1980/
81–82/83.
SRI LANKA (2) NZ 1982/83.
OTHER TOURS Sri Lanka to India 1980/
81. Sri Lanka to England 1981.
HST 23 SL v NZ, Wellington, 1982/83.
HS 79* Sri Lankan Under-25 v Tamil
Nadu Under-25, Salem, 1980/81.

GUNN, Brian George Herbert
————————RHB————————

Born Gravesend, Kent, 19 Sept 1921.
Educ Gravesend GS. Debut 1946. *P.*
KENT (4) 1946.
HS 39 Kent v Notts, Gillingham, 1946.

GUNN, George Vernon
————————RHB, LB————————

Born West Bridgford, Notts, 21 July
1905. Died, in road accident, Shrewsbury, 15 Oct 1957. Educ Nottingham
HS. Debut 1928. *P.*
NOTTINGHAMSHIRE (264) 1928–50. Cap
1931.

HS 184 Notts v Leics, Trent Bridge, 1938.
BB 7–44 Notts v Essex, Trent Bridge, 1932.
1000 RUNS (5) 1763 @ 44.07 in 1937.
RECORDS Scored century (his maiden fc) in same inns as his father, Notts v Warwicks, Edgbaston, 1931, a unique feat. Worcs coach 1955. Clubs: Keighley, Pudsey St Laurence, King's Cross. Professional coach Wrekin S 1950; Wellington S 1952. Father G. Gunn (Notts, England); uncle J. R. Gunn (Notts, England); great-uncle W. Gunn (Notts, England).

GUNN, Lewis James Hamilton
—RHB, RM—

Born Corstorphine, Edinburgh, Scotland, 14 May 1918. Debut 1951.
CANADA (2) 1951–54.
TOUR Canada to England 1954.
HS 46 Canada v MCC, Toronto, 1951.
Club: Toronto. President Canadian CA.

GUNN, Terry
—RHB, WK—

Born Barnsley, Yorks, 27 Sept 1935. Educ Highfield Sec S, Bradford. Debut 1961. P.
SUSSEX (41) 1961–67. Cap 1965.
HS 19* Sussex v Worcs, Hove, 1965.
Clubs: East Bierley, Worthing.

GUPTE, Subhas Chandra Pandharinath (Fergie)
—RHB, LBG—

Born Bombay, India, 11 Dec 1929. Educ Elphinstone C; Bombay U. Debut 1948/49.

INDIA DOMESTIC Bombay 1948/49–58/59, Bengal 1953/54–57/58, Rajasthan 1960/61–62/63.
W INDIES DOMESTIC South Trinidad 1962/63–63/64, Trinidad 1963/64.
COMMONWEALTH XI (1) 1957.
INDIA (36) 1951/52–61/62. E 1951/52 (1), 1961/62 (2); A 1956/57 (3); WI 1958/59 (5); NZ 1955/56 (5); P 1952/53 (2), 1960/61 (3). *E 1959 (5); WI 1952/53 (5); P 1954/55 (5).*
OTHER TOURS India to Ceylon 1956/57. International XI to Rhodesia and Pakistan 1961/62.
HST 21 I v E, Headingley, 1959. HS 47 Bombay v Commonwealth XI, Bombay, 1950/51.
BBT 9–102 I v WI, Kanpur, 1958/59. BB 10–78 Bombay v Pakistan Services, Bahalwalpur, 1954/55.
Returned 15–104 match Rajasthan v Vidarbha, Nagpur, 1962/63.
RECORDS First Indian to take all ten wkts in a fc inns (BB above).
MCC Hon. member. Clubs: Rishton, Heywood. Brother B. P. Gupte (India).

GURR, David Roberts
—RHB, RFM—

Born Whitchurch, Buckinghamshire, 27 Mar 1956. Educ Aylesbury GS; Regents Park C, Oxford. Debut 1976.
OXFORD UNIVERSITY (17) 1976–77 (Blue 1976–77).
SOMERSET (24) 1976–79.
HS 46* Oxford U v Cambridge U, Lord's, 1977.
BB 6–82 Oxford U v Warwicks, Edgbaston, 1976.

GUTHRIE, James Shields
—RHB, OB—

Born Kandy, Ceylon, 14 Dec 1931. Educ Eton; Queen's C, Cambridge. Debut 1953.

CAMBRIDGE UNIVERSITY (1) 1953.
HS 1 Cambridge U v Surrey, Fenner's, 1953.

GUY, John Bernard
—RHB, LM—

Born Ramsgate, Kent, 16 May 1916. Educ Chatham House, Ramsgate; Brasenose C, Oxford. Debut 1938.
OXFORD UNIVERSITY (6) 1938–39.
KENT (1) 1938.
WARWICKSHIRE (2) 1950.
HS 45 Oxford U v Glam, The Parks, 1938.
Clubs: St George's Ramsgate, St Lawrence Canterbury, Harborne.

GUY, John Williams
—LHB—

Born Nelson, N Zealand, 29 Aug 1934. Educ Gisborne HS. Debut 1953/54. P.
N ZEALAND DOMESTIC Central Districts (18) 1953/54–56/57, 1962/63, Canterbury (10) 1957/58–58/59, Otago (4) 1959/60, Wellington (5) 1960/61, Northern Districts (11) 1964/65–72/73.
NORTHAMPTONSHIRE (2) 1958.
NEW ZEALAND (12) 1955/56–61/62. E 1958/59 (2); WI 1955/56 (2). *SA 1961/62 (2); I 1955/56 (5); P 1955/56 (1).*
OTHER TOUR N Zealand to Australia 1961/62.
HST 102 NZ v I, Hyderabad, 1955/56. HS 115 Central Districts v Otago, New Plymouth, 1953/54.
RECORDS During HST (above) scored slowest-ever century for N Zealand (435 mins).

H

HACKER, Peter John
————RHB, LFM————

Born Lenton Abbey, Notts, 16 July 1952. Educ People's C, Fernwood. Debut 1974.
NOTTINGHAMSHIRE (61) 1974–81. Cap 1980.
S AFRICA DOMESTIC Orange Free State 1979/80.
DERBYSHIRE (8) 1982.
HS 35 Notts v Kent, Canterbury, 1977.
BB 6–35 Notts v Hants, Trent Bridge, 1980.
Lincolnshire 1983. Club: Retford.

HACKING, John Kenneth
————RHB, RM————

Born Kenilworth, Warwicks, 21 Mar 1909. Educ Warwick S. Debut 1946.
WARWICKSHIRE (1) 1946.
HS 14 Warwicks v Lancs, Old Trafford, 1946.
Club: Moseley Ashfield.

HADLEE, Dayle Robert
————RHB, RFM————

Born Christchurch, N Zealand, 6 Jan 1948. Educ Christchurch HS. Debut 1966/67.
N ZEALAND DOMESTIC N Zealand Under-23 1966/67, South Island 1968/69, Canterbury (49) 1969/70–.
NEW ZEALAND (26) 1969–77/78. E 1974/75 (2), 1977/78 (1); A 1973/74 (3), 1976/77 (1); I 1975/76 (3); P 1972/73 (2). *E 1969 (2), 1973 (3); A 1973/74 (3); I 1969/70 (3); P 1969/70 (3).*
OTHER TOURS N Zealand to Australia 1969/70. N Zealand to England 1978.
HST 56 NZ v P, Karachi, 1969/70. HS 109* Canterbury v Sri Lankans, Christchurch, 1982/83.
BBT 4–30 NZ v I, Hyderabad, 1969/70.
BB 7–55 Canterbury v Wellington, Wellington, 1977/78.
Father W. A. Hadlee (N Zealand); brothers R. J. Hadlee (N Zealand) and B. G. Hadlee (Canterbury).

HADLEE, Richard John
————LHB, RF————

Born Christchurch, N Zealand, 3 July 1951. Educ Christchurch HS. Debut 1971/72. *Wisden 1982.*
N ZEALAND DOMESTIC Canterbury (48) 1971/72–.
NOTTINGHAMSHIRE (95) 1978–. Cap 1978.
AUSTRALIA DOMESTIC Tasmania (6) 1979/80.
NEW ZEALAND (50) 1972/73–83/84. E 1977/78 (3), 1983/84 (3); A 1973/74 (2), 1976/77 (2), 1981/82 (3); WI 1979/80 (3); I 1975/76 (2), 1980/81 (3); P 1972/73 (1), 1978/79 (3); SL 1982/83 (2). *E 1973 (1), 1978 (3), 1983 (4); A 1973/74 (3), 1980/81 (3); I 1976/77 (3); P 1976/77 (3); SL 1983/84 (3).*
OTHER TOUR N Zealand to Australia 1972/73.
HST 103 NZ v WI, Christchurch, 1979/80. HS 210* Notts v M'sex, Lord's, 1984.
BBT 7–23 NZ v I, Wellington, 1975/76.
BB as above, and 7–23 Notts v Sussex, Trent Bridge, 1979.
1000 RUNS (1) 1179 @ 51.26 in 1984.
100 WKTS (2) 117 @ 14.05 in 1984.
DOUBLE (1) 1984 (first player to perform feat since 1967).
RECORDS Only N Zealand Test cricketer to take 200 Test wkts. Added 186 for 7th wkt with W. K. Lees, NZ v P, Karachi, 1976/77, N Zealand Test record.
World Series Cricket (Kerry Packer) 1978/79. MBE for services to cricket. Wife Karen Hadlee (N Zealand Women); father W. A. Hadlee (N Zealand); brothers D. R. Hadlee (N Zealand) and B. G. Hadlee (Canterbury).

HADLEE, Walter Arnold
————RHB————

Born Lincoln, Canterbury, N Zealand, 4 June 1915. Educ Christchurch HS. Debut 1933/34.
N ZEALAND DOMESTIC Canterbury (43) 1933/34–51/52, Otago (7) 1945/46–46/47.
NEW ZEALAND (11) 1937–50/51. E 1946/47 (1), 1950/51 (2); A 1945/46 (1). *E 1937 (3), 1949 (4).* Capt 8.

OTHER TOUR N Zealand to Australia 1937/38.
HST 116 NZ v E, Christchurch, 1946/47.
HS 198 Otago v Australians, Dunedin, 1945/46.
BB 3–14 Otago v Canterbury, Dunedin, 1945/46.
1000 RUNS (2) 1439 @ 35.97 in 1949.
President N Zealand Cricket Council. Manager N Zealand to England 1965. Awarded OBE for services to cricket. Sons D. R. Hadlee, R. J. Hadlee (both N Zealand) and B. G. Hadlee (Canterbury).

HADLEY, Robert John
————RHB, LFM————

Born Neath, Glam, 22 Oct 1951. Educ Sandfields CS, Port Talbot; St John's C, Cambridge. Debut 1971.
CAMBRIDGE UNIVERSITY (24) 1971–73 (Blue 1971–73).
GLAMORGAN (2) 1971.
HS 17 Cambridge U v Northants, Fenner's, 1973.
BB 5–31 Cambridge U v Sussex, Fenner's, 1972.

HAGGETT, Norman Louis
————RHB, OB/LB————

Born Lee, Lewisham, London, 8 July 1926. Educ Roan S, Blackheath; St Paul's C, Cheltenham. Debut 1962.
COMBINED SERVICES (4) 1962–64.
HS 71 Combined Services v Cambridge U, Fenner's, 1962.
Clubs: Catford Wanderers, Oxford City. CRO RAF Brize-Norton.

HAGGO, David John
————RHB, WK————

Born Ayr, Scotland, 13 April 1964. Debut 1983.
SCOTLAND (1) 1983.
HS 9 Scotland v Ireland, Downpatrick, 1983.
Club: Ayr.

HAKE, George *John* Gordon
————————RHB, RFM————————

Born Sutton, Surrey, 24 Aug 1918.
Educ Bromsgrove S. Debut 1948.
MIDDLESEX (1) 1948.
HS 2 M'sex v Cambridge U, Fenner's,
1948.
Club: Hampstead.

HALE, Ivor Edward
————————RHB, OB————————

Born Worcester, 6 Oct 1922. Educ Wor-
cester RGS. Debut 1946. *P 1947–48.*
SUSSEX (3) 1946.
GLOUCESTERSHIRE (13) 1947–48.
HS 61 Glos v Cambridge U, Bristol,
1948.

HALE, Terrance Saville
————————LHB————————

Born Waterbeach, Cambridgeshire, 8
Oct 1936. Debut 1965.
MINOR COUNTIES (1) 1965.
HS 8 Minor Counties v S Africans, Jes-
mond, 1965.
Cambridgeshire 1960–78. Club: St
Giles.

HALES, Lloyd Archibald
————————RHB, RM————————

Born Leicester, 27 June 1921. Died
Leicester, 12 Sept 1984. Educ Wygges-
ton GS; Bristol GS. Debut 1947.
LEICESTERSHIRE (2) 1947.
HS 62 Leics v Warwicks, Leicester,
1947.

HALFYARD, David John
————————RHB, RFM/RM/LBG————————

Born Winchmore Hill, London, 3 Apr
1931. Educ Purley GS. Debut 1956. *P.*
KENT (185) 1956–64. Cap 1957.
Testimonial (£3216) 1965.
NOTTINGHAMSHIRE (77) 1968–70. Cap
1968.
HS 79 Kent v M'sex, Lord's, 1960.
BB 9–39 Kent v Glam, Neath, 1957.
100 WKTS (5) 135 @ 20.39 in 1958.
Retired as Kent player 1964 after injury
in car accident. Fc umpire 1967,
1977–81. Durham 1971–72, Northum-
berland 1973, Cornwall 1974–82,
Minor Counties umpire 1974, 1983–.
Clubs: Beddington, Mitcham, Bans-
tead, Marske, St Gluvius, Greenock,
Holman's, Veryan, Redruth.

HALL, Brian
————————RHB, RMF————————

Born Morley, Yorks, 16 Sept 1929.
Debut 1952. *P.*
YORKSHIRE (1) 1952.
HS 10 Yorks v MCC, Lord's, 1952.
Clubs: East Bierley, British Ropes.

HALL, Brian Charles
————————RHB, RM————————

Born Edgware, London, 2 Mar 1934.
Educ Gregg's Commercial C,
Marylebone. Debut 1956. *P.*
WORCESTERSHIRE (3) 1956–57.
HS 21 Worcs v Oxford U, Worcester,
1956.
BB 2–11 same match.
Clubs: MCC, Stanmore.

HALL, Derek
————————RHB, RFM————————

Born Bolsover, Derbys, 21 Feb 1932.
Died, in road accident, San Jose,
California, 13 Mar 1983. Debut 1955. *P.*
DERBYSHIRE (20) 1955–58.
HS 10* Derbys v Oxford U, The Parks,
1958.
BB 4–57 Derbys v Sussex, Derby, 1955.
Club: David Brown Tractors.

HALL, Geoffrey Harold
————————RHB, RF————————

Born Colne, Lancs, 1 June 1941. Debut
1961. *P.*
SOMERSET (48) 1961–65.
HS 12* Som v Yorks, Taunton, 1962.
BB 6–60 Som v Notts, Worksop, 1965.
Clubs: Colne, Broad Oak.

HALL, Ian William
————————RHB, occ RM————————

Born Sutton Scarsdale, Derbys, 27 Dec
1939. Educ The Brunts GS, Mansfield;
Tupton Hall GS, Clay Cross. Debut
1959. *P.*
DERBYSHIRE (270) 1959–72. Cap 1961.
Testimonial (£2840) 1971.
HS 136 Derbys v Northants, Derby,
1963 and 136* v Oxford U, The Parks,
1972.
1000 RUNS (5) 1449 @ 33.39 in 1971.
Soccer: Derby County, Mansfield
Town.

HALL, John Bernard
————————RHB, RM————————

Born Worksop, Notts, 17 June 1903.
Died Retford, Notts, 27 May 1979.
Educ Bloxham. Debut 1935.

NOTTINGHAMSHIRE (5) 1935–46.
SIR J. CAHN'S XI (2) 1935–36/37.
HS 24 Notts v M'sex, Trent Bridge, 1946
and Sir J. Cahn's XI v Lancs, West
Bridgford, 1935.
BB 6–75 Sir J. Cahn's XI v Lancs, West
Bridgford, 1935.
TOUR Sir J. Cahn's XI to Ceylon 1936/
37.
Clubs: Worksop, Saltaire, Retford.
Professional coach Worksop C. Son M.
J. Hall (Notts).

HALL, John Edwin
————————RHB————————

Born Basutoland, 5 Jan 1950. Educ
Ardingley S; Sidney Sussex C, Cam-
bridge. Debut 1969.
CAMBRIDGE UNIVERSITY (14) 1969–70
(Blue 1969).
HS 69 Cambridge U v Glam, Fenner's,
1969.
Suffolk 1968–70.

HALL, John Keith
————————RHB, RFM————————

Born West Wickham, Kent, 29 July
1934. Educ Lancing C. Debut 1958.
SURREY (13) 1958–59, 1962.
MCC (3) 1959–61.
FREE FORESTERS (4) 1959–61.
SUSSEX (1) 1960.
HS 22 Free Foresters v Cambridge U,
Fenner's, 1961.
BB 5–30 Surrey v Oxford U, The Parks,
1958.
Club: Beddington.

HALL, Michael John
————————RHB————————

Born Worksop, Notts, 29 May 1935.
Debut 1958. *P.*
NOTTINGHAMSHIRE (17) 1958–59.
HS 72 Notts v Cambridge U, Trent
Bridge, 1959.
Club: Retford. Father J. B. Hall (Notts).

HALL, Peter James
————————RHB, RM————————

Born Hong Kong, 4 Dec 1927. Educ
Geelong GS, Victoria; Cambridge U.
Debut 1948.
CAMBRIDGE UNIVERSITY (11) 1948–49
(Blue 1949).
N ZEALAND DOMESTIC Otago (1) 1955/56.
HS 49 Cambridge U v Sussex, Horsham,
1949.
BB 5–51 Cambridge U v Som, Bath,
1949.
Club: Carisbrook.

HALL, Thomas Auckland
————RHB, RFM————

Born Darlington, Co Durham, 19 Aug 1930. Died Rockland St Mary, Norfolk, 21 Apr 1984. Educ Uppingham. Debut 1949.
DERBYSHIRE (28) 1949–52.
SOMERSET (23) 1953–54. Cap 1953.
COMBINED SERVICES (2) 1954.
FREE FORESTERS (5) 1954–58.
HS 69* Som v Northants, Taunton, 1953.
BB 5–50 MCC v Yorks, Scarborough, 1955.
Gentlemen v Players (1) 1951. Norfolk 1956–57.

HALL, Wesley Winfield
————RHB, RF————

Born Bridgetown, Barbados, 12 Sept 1937. Debut 1955/56.
W INDIES DOMESTIC Barbados 1955/56–70/71, Trinidad 1966/67–69/70.
AUSTRALIA DOMESTIC Queensland (17) 1961/62–62/63.
WEST INDIES (48) 1958/59–68/69. E 1959/60 (5), 1967/68 (4); A 1964/65 (5); I 1961/62 (5). *E 1963 (5), 1966 (5); A 1960/61 (5), 1968/69 (2); NZ 1968/69 (1); I 1958/59 (5), 1966/67 (3); P 1958/59 (3).*
OTHER TOURS W Indies to England 1957. Commonwealth XI to Rhodesia 1962/63. Rest of World XI to England 1965, 1968.
HST 50* WI v I, Port of Spain, 1961/62 (added 98* for 10th wkt with F. M. M. Worrell, W Indies Test record) and 50 WI v A, Brisbane, 1960/61. HS 102* W Indians v Cambridge U, Fenner's, 1963.
BBT 7–69 WI v E, Kingston, 1959/60. BB 7–51 W Indians v Glam, Swansea, 1963.
RECORDS 43 wkts @ 20.25 for Queensland in Sheffield Shield 1961/62, State record.
Clubs: Great Chell, Accrington. Senator in Barbados Parliament.

HALLAM, Maurice Raymond
————RHB, occ WK————

Born Leicester, 10 Sept 1931. Debut 1950. *P.*
LEICESTERSHIRE (493) 1950–70. Cap 1954. Benefit (£5000) 1962. Capt 1963–65, 1968.
HS 210* Leics v Glam, Leicester, 1959.
1000 RUNS (13) 2262 @ 39.68 in 1961.
RECORDS Shares with Zaheer Abbas record of scoring double-century and single century in a match more than once (210* and 157 Leics v Glam, Leicester, 1959; 203* and 143* Leics v Sussex, Worthing, 1961). First batsman to score

two unbeaten centuries in a match on two occasions (203* and 143* as above and 107* and 149* Leics v Worcs, Leicester, 1965).
Players v Gentlemen (2) 1959–61. Leics coach after retirement.

HALLIDAY, Harry
————RHB, OB————

Born Pudsey, Yorks, 9 Feb 1920. Died Wakefield, Yorks, 27 Aug 1967. Debut 1938. *P.*
YORKSHIRE (182) 1938–53. Cap 1948. Testimonial (£2500) 1954.
HS 144 Yorks v Derbys, Chesterfield, 1950.
BB 6–79 Yorks v Derbys, Bramall Lane, Sheffield, 1952.
1000 RUNS (4) 1484 @ 38.05 in 1950.
Cumberland 1957–59. Clubs: Bingley, Lidget Green, Pudsey St Laurence, Church.
Appointed coach North Riding education committee 1954. Coach Scarborough 1960–61.

HALLIDAY, Michael
————RHB, OB————

Born Dublin, Ireland, 20 Aug 1948. Educ Wesley C, Dublin. Debut 1970.
IRELAND (10) 1970–83.
HS 30 Ireland v Scotland, Edinburgh, 1982.
BB 5–39 Ireland v Scotland, Dublin, 1979.
Clubs: Dublin University, Phoenix.

HALLIDAY, Simon John
————RHB, RM————

Born Haverfordwest, Pembroke, 13 July 1960. Educ Downside; St Benets Hall, Oxford. Debut 1980.
OXFORD UNIVERSITY (9) 1980–82 (Blue 1980).
HS 113* Oxford U v Kent, The Parks, 1982.
Dorset 1979–. Club: Sherborne. Rugby: Blue.

HAMBLIN, Christopher Bryan
————RHB, RM————

Born Kenley, Surrey, 14 Apr 1952. Educ King's S, Canterbury; Keble C, Oxford. Debut 1971.
OXFORD UNIVERSITY (28) 1971–73 (Blue 1971–73).
HS 123* Oxford U v Leics, The Parks, 1972.
BB 4–32 Oxford U v Cambridge U, Lord's, 1971.
Hockey: Blue.

HAMENCE, Ronald Arthur
————RHB, LB————

Born Hindmarsh, S Australia, 25 Nov 1915. Debut 1935/36.
AUSTRALIA DOMESTIC South Australia (69) 1935/36–50/51.
AUSTRALIA (3) 1946/47–47/48. E 1946/47 (1); I 1947/48 (2).
TOURS Australia to N Zealand 1945/46. Australia to England 1948.
HST 30* A v E, Sydney, 1946/47. HS 173 S Australia v NSW, Adelaide, 1948/49.
BB 2–13 Australians v Sussex, Hove, 1948.

HAMER, Arnold
————RHB, OB————

Born Huddersfield, Yorks, 8 Dec 1916. Debut 1938. *P.*
YORKSHIRE (2) 1938.
DERBYSHIRE (290) 1950–60. Cap 1950. Benefit (£2750) 1958.
HS 227 Derbys v Notts, Trent Bridge, 1955.
BB 4–27 Derbys v Leics, Chesterfield, 1950.
1000 RUNS (10) 1850 @ 36.27 in 1959.
Players v Gentlemen (1) 1954. Clubs: Pudsey St Laurence, Windhill, Spen Victoria, Great Horton.
1106 runs for Pudsey St Laurence in 1949, Bradford League record. Soccer: York City.

HAMILTON, Andrew Caradoc
————LHB, SLA————

Born Ardingly, Sussex, 23 Sept 1953. Educ Charterhouse; St Peter's C, Oxford. Debut 1975.
OXFORD UNIVERSITY (12) 1975–76 (Blue 1975).
HS 45 Oxford U v M'sex, The Parks, 1976.

HAMMOND, Herbert Edward
————RHB, RMF————

Born Brighton, Sussex, 7 Nov 1907. Died Brighton, June 1985.
Educ Stanford Road S, Brighton. Debut 1928. *P.*
SUSSEX (196) 1928–46. Cap 1934.
HS 103* Sussex v Warwicks, Edgbaston, 1936.
BB 8–76 Sussex v Surrey, Oval, 1934.
Fc umpire 1961–63. Clubs: St Peters, Hove. Professional coach Cheltenham C; Brighton C. Soccer: Fulham, England (amateur).

HAMMOND, Jeffrey Roy
RHB, RFM/RM

Born East Torrens, S Australia, 19 Apr 1950. Debut 1969/70.
AUSTRALIA DOMESTIC South Australia (46) 1969/70–80/81.
AUSTRALIA (5) *WI 1972/73*.
OTHER TOUR Australia to England 1972.
HST 19 A v WI, Port of Spain, 1972/73.
HS 53 S Australia v NSW, Sydney, 1971/72.
BBT 4–38 A v WI, Georgetown, 1972/73.
BB 6–15 Australians v Minor Counties, Longton, 1972.
Reduced pace to medium after back injury 1973/74. Club: Prospect.

HAMMOND, Reginald Joseph Leslie
RHB, WK

Born Wandsworth, London, 16 Dec 1909. Educ RHC, Dartmouth. Debut 1948.
COMBINED SERVICES (6) 1948–51.
HS 46 Combined Services v Essex, Chelmsford, 1950.
Commander RN (retired).

HAMMOND, Walter Reginald
RHB, RMF

Born Dover, Kent, 19 June 1903. Died Durban, S Africa, 1 July 1965. Educ Portsmouth GS; Cirencester GS. Debut 1920. *P to 1937. Wisden 1928.*
GLOUCESTERSHIRE (405) 1920–51. Cap 1923. Benefit 1934. Capt 1939–46.
S AFRICA DOMESTIC S African Air Force XI 1942/43.
ENGLAND (85) 1927/28–46/47. A 1930 (5), 1934 (5), 1938 (4); SA 1929 (4), 1935 (5); WI 1928 (3), 1933 (3), 1939 (3); NZ 1931 (3), 1937 (3); I 1932 (1), 1936 (2), 1946 (3). *A 1928/29 (5), 1932/33 (5), 1936/37 (5), 1946/47 (4); SA 1927/28 (5), 1930/31 (5), 1938/39 (5); WI 1934/35 (4); NZ 1932/33 (2), 1946/47 (1).* Capt 20.
OTHER TOUR MCC to W Indies 1925/26.
HST 336* E v NZ, Auckland, 1932/33. HS as above.
BBT 5–36 E v SA, J'burg, 1927/28. BB 9–23 Glos v Worcs, Cheltenham, 1928.
1000 RUNS (17+5) 3323 @ 67.81 in 1933. Also scored 3252 @ 65.04 in 1937 and 3011 @ 75.27 in 1938. 2000 runs 9 other times.
RECORDS *Fc cricket* Scored three other triple-centuries apart from HST: 317 Glos v Notts, Gloucester, 1936 (Glos Championship record), 302* Glos v Glam, Bristol, 1934, 302 Glos v Glam, Newport, 1939; only Englishman to make four fc scores of over 300. 36 double-centuries in fc cricket, second only to D. G. Bradman's 37, including four in 1933 and in 1934. Century in each inns seven times, record until beaten by Zaheer Abbas in 1982/83. During 1945 and 1946 scored six centuries in seven consecutive inns (including four in a row), a performance equalled by three other batsmen. Also scored four centuries in successive inns in 1936/37.
1042 runs in May, 1927, and 1281 runs in Aug, 1936, both records for respective months. Reached 3000 runs in 1937 by 20 Aug, equalling T. W. Hayward's record of 1906. 2860 runs @ 69.75 for Glos in 1933, county record; 1553 runs @ 91.35 MCC to Australia 1928/29, record for any tourist in Australia. Holds Glos career records for runs (33,664 @ 57.05) and centuries (113). 31,165 runs during 1930s, most for one decade. 78 catches in 1928, record for season by non-wicket keeper. 10 catches in match, Glos v Surrey, Cheltenham, 1928 also record for non-wicketkeeper.
Glos record partnerships 336 for 3rd wkt with B. H. Lyon, v Leics, Leicester, 1933; 321 for 4th wkt with W. L. Neale, v Leics, Gloucester, 1937; and 239 for 8th wkt with A. E. Wilson, v Lancs, Bristol, 1938.
Test cricket HST (above) record score for Test cricket at time. 905 runs @ 113.12 in series E v A 1928/29, England record. First batsman to pass totals of 6000 runs (1938) and 7000 runs (1946) in Tests. Final total of 7249, record until beaten by M. C. Cowdrey in 1970. 22 Test centuries, England record jointly with M. C. Cowdrey and G. Boycott. Fastest triple-century in Tests, 300* in 287 mins, during 336* E v NZ, Auckland, 1932/33. 10 sixes in this inns most for Test cricket.
Career total of 167 centuries third-highest ever. Scored centuries against all fc counties except his own. Headed fc batting averages in England five times in nine seasons (1933, 1935, 1936, 1937, 1946). Career total of 819 catches, fourth-highest ever.
Players v Gentlemen (19) 1923–37; Gentlemen v Players (3) 1938–46. Club: Esher. Coach groundsman Natal U at death. Author of several cricket books. Soccer: Bristol Rovers.

HAMPSHIRE, Alan Wesley
RHB, RM

Born Rotherham, Yorks, 18 Oct 1950. Educ Headlands GS, Bridlington; Loughborough C. Debut 1975.
YORKSHIRE (1) 1975.
HS 17 Yorks v Derbys, Chesterfield, 1975.
Club: Synthonia. Brother J. H. Hampshire (Yorks, Derbys, England); father J. Hampshire (Yorks).

HAMPSHIRE, John Harry
RHB, LBG

Born Thurnscoe, Yorks, 10 Feb 1941. Educ Oakwood Technical HS, Rotherham. Debut 1961. *P.*
YORKSHIRE (456) 1961–81. Cap 1963. Benefit (£28,425) 1976. Capt 1979–80.
DERBYSHIRE (57) 1982–. Cap 1982.
AUSTRALIA DOMESTIC Tasmania (15) 1967/68–78/79.
ENGLAND (8) 1969–75. A 1972 (1), 1975 (1); WI 1969 (2). *A 1970/71 (2); NZ 1970/71 (2).*
OTHER TOURS Cavaliers to W Indies 1964/65. Commonwealth XI to Pakistan 1967/68. MCC to Ceylon 1969/70. D. H. Robins' XI to S Africa 1972/73, 1974/75. Leicestershire XI to Zimbabwe 1980/81.
HST 107 E v WI, Lord's, 1969 (only player to score a century on Test debut, that match being at Lord's). HS 183* Yorks v Sussex, Hove, 1971.
BB 7–52 Yorks v Glam, Cardiff, 1963.
1000 RUNS (15) 1596 @ 53.20 in 1978. 444 catches in career.
Autobiography *Family Argument* (1983). Father J. Hampshire (Yorks); brother A. W. Hampshire (Yorks).

HANDS, Barry Onslow
LHB, ROB

Born Birmingham, 26 Sept 1916. Died Birmingham, 1 July 1984. Educ Woodroughs S. Debut 1946.
WARWICKSHIRE (3) 1946–47.
HS 9 Warwicks v Leics, Barwell, 1946.
BB 3–76 Warwicks v Glam, Swansea, 1947.
Club: Moseley Ashfield. Uncle W. C. Hands (Warwicks).

HANIF MOHAMMED
RHB, occ WK, occ OB

Born Junagadh, India, 21 Dec 1934. Educ Suid Madarasa S, Karachi. Debut 1951/52. *Wisden 1968.*
PAKISTAN DOMESTIC Karachi/Bahawalpur, Bahawalpur, Karachi, Pakistan International Airlines, 1951/52–75/76.
PAKISTAN (55) 1952/53–69/70. E 1961/62 (3), 1968/69 (3); A 1956/57 (1), 1959/60 (3), 1964/65 (1); WI 1958/59 (1); NZ 1955/56 (3), 1964/65 (3), 1969/70 (1); I 1954/55 (5). *E 1954 (4), 1962 (5), 1967 (3); A 1964/65 (1); WI 1957/58 (5); NZ 1964/65 (3); I 1952/53 (5), 1960/61 (5).* Capt 11.
OTHER TOUR International XI to Rhodesia 1961/62.
HST 337 P v WI, Bridgetown, 1957/58.
HS 499 Karachi v Bahawalpur, Karachi, 1958/59.

BB 3–4 Commissioner's XI v Fazal Mahmood's XI, Hyderabad, 1959/60.
1000 RUNS (2 + 3) 1623 @ 36.88 in 1954.
RECORDS HST (above) lasted 970 mins, longest inns in fc cricket and HS for Pakistan in Tests. HS (above) highest inns in fc cricket; run out going for 500th run from last ball of day. First Pakistan batsman to score 1000, 2000 and 3000 Test runs. Scored 12 Test centuries, Pakistan record. Added 217 for 6th wkt with Majid Khan, P v NZ, Lahore, 1964/65 and 130 for 8th wkt with Asif Iqbal, P v E, Lord's, 1967, both Pakistan Test records.
Chief editor *The Cricketer (Pakistan)* magazine. Brothers Wazir Mohammed, Mushtaq Mohammed, Sadiq Mohammed (all Pakistan) and Raees Mohammed (Karachi); nephews Asif Mohammed and Shahid Mohammed (both PIA).

HANLEY, Rupert William (Spook)
—RHB, RF—

Born Port Elizabeth, S Africa, 29 Jan 1952. Educ Grey HS; St Andrew's C, Grahamstown. Debut 1970/71.
S AFRICA DOMESTIC Eastern Province 1970/71–74/75, Orange Free State 1975/76, Transvaal 1976/77–.
D. H. ROBINS' XI (1) 1974.
NORTHAMPTONSHIRE (17) 1984.
HS 33* Northants v Warwicks, Northampton, 1984.
BB 7–31 Transvaal v E Province, J'burg, 1983/84.
Professional artist.

HANNA, Michael
—RHB, WK—

Born London, 6 June 1926. Debut 1951.
SOMERSET (2) 1951–54.
HS 4* Som v Northants, Northampton, 1954.
Wiltshire 1957–68. Clubs: Bath, Trowbridge, Chippenham. Rugby: Bath.

HANSELL, Thomas Michael Geoffrey
—LHB, SLA—

Born Sutton Coldfield, Warwicks, 24 Aug 1954. Educ Millfield. Debut 1975.
SURREY (14) 1975–77.
HS 54 Surrey v Notts, Oval, 1976.

HANSON, Raymond Leslie
—RHB, WK—

Born Chesterfield, Derbys, 12 Apr 1951. Debut 1973.
DERBYSHIRE (1) 1973.
HS 1* (only inns) Derbys v Sussex, Eastbourne, 1973.

HANUMANT SINGH (Maharaj Kumar Hanumant Pratap Singh of Banswara)
—RHB, LBG—

Born Banswara, Rajasthan, India, 29 Mar 1939. Educ Vikram U; Delhi U. Debut 1956/57.
INDIA DOMESTIC Madhya Bharat 1956/57, Rajasthan 1957/58–78/79.
INDIA (14) 1963/64–69/70. E 1963/64 (2); A 1964/65 (3); WI 1966/67 (2); NZ 1964/65 (4), 1969/70 (1). *E 1967 (2).*
OTHER TOURS State Bank to Ceylon 1966/67, 1968/69. India to E Africa 1967.
HST 105 I v E, Delhi, 1963/64 (Test debut). HS 213* Rajasthan v Bombay, Bombay, 1966/67.
BB 5–48 Rajasthan v Madhya Pradesh, Udaipur, 1959/60.
1000 RUNS (0 + 3) 1586 @ 68.95 in 1966/67.
RECORD Added 193* for 6th wkt with D. N. Sardesai, I v NZ, Bombay, 1964/65, India Test record.

HARBIN, Leonard
—RHB, OB—

Born Trinidad, 30 Apr 1915. Debut 1935/36.
W INDIES DOMESTIC Trinidad 1935/36–40/41.
GLOUCESTERSHIRE (4) 1949–51.
HS 89 Trinidad v Jamaica, Port of Spain, 1938/39.
BB 5–80 Glos v Combined Services, Bristol, 1949.
UAU 1945. Club: Westminster.

HARCOURT, Arthur Bryan
—RHB, WK—

Born S Africa, 14 Nov 1917. Educ Brasenose C, Oxford. Debut 1947.
OXFORD UNIVERSITY (4) 1947.
HS 25* Oxford U v MCC, Lord's, 1947.

HARDIE, Brian Ross
—RHB, RM—

Born Stenhousemuir, Scotland, 14 Jan 1950. Educ Larbert HS. Debut 1970.
SCOTLAND (4) 1970–72.
ESSEX (257) 1973–. Cap 1974. Benefit 1983.

HS 162 Essex v Warwicks, Edgbaston, 1975.
BB 2–39 Essex v Glam, Ilford, 1979.
1000 RUNS (9) 1522 @ 43.48 in 1975.
Club: Stenhousemuir. Brother K. M. Hardie (Scotland); father J. M. Hardie (Scotland).

HARDIE, Keith Millar
—RHB, SLA—

Born Larbert, Scotland, 13 May 1947. Educ Larbert HS. Debut 1966.
SCOTLAND (10) 1966–76.
HS 65* Scotland v Ireland, Glasgow, 1976.
BB 4–23 Scotland v Ireland, Edinburgh, 1966.
Clubs: Stenhousemuir, Clydesdale, South Hampstead. Brother B. R. Hardie (Essex); father J. M. Hardie (Scotland).

HARDING, Norman Walter
—RHB, RFM—

Born Woolston, Hants, 19 Mar 1916. Died Abingdon, Berkshire, 25 Sept 1947. Educ Reading S. Debut 1937. *P.*
KENT (83) 1937–47. Cap.
HS 71 Kent v Glam, Tonbridge, 1939.
BB 5–31 Kent v Leics, Tunbridge Wells, 1939.
Berkshire 1934–36. 18–100 match, Kent 2nd XI v Wiltshire, Swindon, 1936, best-ever bowling in Minor Counties cricket.

HARDSTAFF, Joseph
—RHB, occ RM—

Born Nuncargate, Notts, 3 July 1911. Educ Annesley Woodhouse S. Debut 1930. *P. Wisden* 1938.
NOTTINGHAMSHIRE (408) 1930–55. Cap 1931. Benefit (£3077) 1948. Testimonial (£1361) 1955.
INDIA DOMESTIC 1943/44–44/45, Europeans 1944/45.
N ZEALAND DOMESTIC Auckland (5) 1948/49–49/50.
ENGLAND (23) 1935–48. A 1938 (2), 1948 (1); SA 1935 (1); WI 1939 (3); NZ 1937 (3); I 1936 (2), 1946 (2). *A 1936/37 (5), 1946/47 (1); WI 1947/48 (3).*
OTHER TOURS MCC to Australasia 1935/36. Lord Tennyson's XI to India 1937/38. Sir J. Cahn's XI to N Zealand 1938/39.
HST 205* E v I, Lord's, 1946. HS 266 Notts v Leics, Leicester, 1937.
BB 4–43 Notts v Lancs, Old Trafford, 1947.
1000 RUNS (13 + 1) 2540 @ 57.72 in 1937.
Scored 126 in 70 mins Notts v Kent, Canterbury, 1937, reaching century in

51 mins and winning Lawrence Trophy for fastest century of season. Scored centuries against all fc counties except his own.
Players v Gentlemen (9) 1935–47. Clubs: Nuncargate, Annesley Colliery. MCC Hon. member. Father J. Hardstaff senior (Notts, England); son Group-captain J. Hardstaff (Free Foresters).

HARDSTAFF, Joseph
————RHB, RM————

Born Kirkby-in-Ashfield, Notts, 28 Feb 1935. Educ The Brunts S, Mansfield. Debut 1961.
FREE FORESTERS (I) 1961.
COMBINED SERVICES (I) 1962.
HS 36 Free Foresters v Cambridge U, Fenner's, 1961.
Clubs: Adastrians, Stragglers, MCC, RAF. Group-captain RAF. Awarded MBE. Father J. Hardstaff junior (Notts, England); grandfather J. Hardstaff senior (Notts, England).

HARDY, Donald Wrightson
————RHB, RM————

Born East Boldon, Co Durham, 24 Mar 1926. Educ Worksop C. Debut 1965.
MINOR COUNTIES (I) 1965.
HS 29 Minor Counties v S Africans, Jesmond, 1965.
Durham 1948–67. Club: Boldon.

HARDY, Evan *Michael* Pearce
————RHB, WK————

Born Bareilly, India, 3 Nov 1927. Educ Ampleforth C. Debut 1959.
COMBINED SERVICES (I) 1959.
HS 15 Combined Services v Warwicks, Portland Road, Birmingham, 1959.
Rugby: Services, Army, Blackheath, Headingley, England (3). Colonel (retired).

HARDY, Jonathan James Ean
————LHB————

Born Nakuru, Kenya, 2 Oct 1960. Educ Canford. Debut 1984.
HAMPSHIRE (13) 1984.
HS 94* Hants v Som, Taunton, 1984 (Championship debut).

HARDY, Michael John
————RHB, SLA————

Born Hendon, London, 30 July 1929. Educ Oundle. Debut 1958.
D. R. JARDINE'S XI (I) 1958.

HS 15 D. R. Jardine's XI v Oxford U, Eastbourne, 1958.
Buckinghamshire 1959–61. Clubs: Hampstead, Beaconsfield.

HARE, Peter Macduff Christian
————RHB, WK————

Born Wokingham, Berkshire, 12 Mar 1920. Educ Canford; Worcester C, Oxford. Debut 1947.
OXFORD UNIVERSITY (I) 1947.
HS 39 Oxford U v Leics, The Parks, 1947.

HARE, Thomas
————RHB, RFM————

Born London, 27 July 1930. Educ Eton; Cambridge U. Debut 1953.
CAMBRIDGE UNIVERSITY (9) 1953.
FREE FORESTERS (I) 1954.
HS 47 Cambridge U v Sussex, Fenner's, 1953.
BB 5–35 Cambridge U v Worcs, Fenner's, 1953.
Norfolk 1947–54. Baronet.

HARE, William Henry (Dusty)
————RHB————

Born Newark, Notts, 29 Nov 1952. Educ Magnus GS, Newark. Debut 1971.
NOTTINGHAMSHIRE (10) 1971–77.
HS 36 Notts v Warwicks, Coventry, 1974.
Rugby: East Midlands, Leicester, Newark, England (16).

HARFORD, Noel Sherwin
————RHB, RM————

Born Winton, N Zealand, 30 Aug 1930. Died, by own hand, Auckland, N Zealand, 30 Mar 1981. Debut 1953/54.
N ZEALAND DOMESTIC Central Districts (19) 1953/54–58/59, Auckland (13) 1963/64–66/67.
NEW ZEALAND (8) 1955/56–58. *E 1958 (4); I 1955/56 (2); P 1955/56 (2).*
HST 93 NZ v P, Lahore, 1955/56 (on Test debut; scored 64 in 2nd inns). HS 158 N Zealanders v Oxford U, The Parks, 1958.
BB 3–19 Central Districts v Wellington, Wanganui, 1956/57.
1000 RUNS (I) 1067 @ 26.02 in 1958.
Club: Manawatu.

HARILAL RAISHI SHAH
————RHB, RM————

Born Kenya, 1943. Debut 1975.
EAST AFRICA to England (I) 1975.

HS 59 E Africa v Sri Lanka, Taunton, 1975.
Club: Nairobi Gymkhana.

HARKNESS, Donald
————LHB, ROB————

Born Sydney, Australia, 13 Feb 1931. Debut 1954. *P.*
WORCESTERSHIRE (13) 1954.
HS 163 Worcs v Cambridge U, Worcester, 1954.
BB 3–29 Worcs v Notts, Trent Bridge, 1954.
Club: Kidderminster.

HARMAN, Roger
————RHB, SLA————

Born Hersham, Surrey, 28 Dec 1941. Debut 1961. *P.*
SURREY (141) 1961–68. Cap 1964.
HS 34 Surrey v Warwicks, Coventry, 1963.
BB 8–12 Surrey v Notts, Trent Bridge, 1964.
100 WKTS (I) 136 @ 21.01 in 1964.
Four wkts in five balls, including hat-trick, Surrey v Kent, Blackheath, 1963.
Club: Olinda.

HAROON RASHID Dar
————RHB, RM————

Born Karachi, Pakistan, 25 Mar 1953. Educ Church Missionary Society S; Sind Muslim C, Karachi. Debut 1971/72.
PAKISTAN DOMESTIC Karachi, Sind, National Bank, Pakistan International Airlines, United Bank, 1971/72–.
PAKISTAN (23) 1976/77–82/83. E 1977/78 (3); A 1979/80 (2), 1982/83 (3); I 1982/83 (1); SL 1981/82 (2). *E 1978 (3), 1982 (1); A 1976/77 (1), 1978/79 (1); WI 1976/77 (5); NZ 1978/79 (1).*
OTHER TOUR Pakistan to Sri Lanka 1975/76.
HST 153 P v SL, Karachi, 1981/82. HS as above.
BB 3–34 United Bank v Muslim Commercial Bank, Lahore, 1981/82.
Brother Mahmood Rashid (United Bank, Karachi).

HARPER, Nicholas John
————LHB, LM————

Born Forest Hill, London, 11 Apr 1939. Educ Caterham S; Downing C, Cambridge. Debut 1961.
CAMBRIDGE UNIVERSITY (I) 1961.
HS 1 Cambridge U v Free Foresters, Fenner's, 1961.

HARPER, Roger Andrew
——————RHB, OB——————

Born Georgetown, British Guiana, 17 Mar 1963. Debut 1979/80.
W INDIES DOMESTIC Demerara 1979/80–, Guyana 1979/80–.
D. B. CLOSE'S XI (1) 1983.
WEST INDIES (11) 1983/84–84. A 1983/84 (4). *E 1984 (5); I 1983/84 (2).*
HST 39* WI v E, Old Trafford, 1984. HS 86 Guyana v Australians, Georgetown, 1983/84.
BBT 6–57 WI v E, Old Trafford, 1984. BB as above.
Has joined Northamptonshire for 1985. Clubs: Demerara, Blackhall Colliery Welfare. Brother M. A. Harper (Guyana).

HARPUR, Thomas
——————RHB——————

Born Omagh, Co Tyrone, Ireland, 16 May 1944. Educ Sion Mills PE S. Debut 1980.
IRELAND (2) 1980–81.
HS 6 Ireland v Scotland, Clontarf, 1981.
Club: Sion Mills.

HARRINGTON, William John Roy
——————RHB, RFM——————

Born St John's Wood, London, 30 Jan 1915. Debut 1946. *P.*
MIDDLESEX (9) 1946–48.
MCC (3) 1946–51.
HS 45 M'sex v Oxford U, The Parks, 1946.
BB 6–57 M'sex v Yorks, Bramall Lane, Sheffield, 1946.
Club: Caterpillars. Professional coach Beaumont S 1958–65.

HARRIS, Alwyn
——————LHB——————

Born Aberdulais, S Wales, 31 Jan 1936. Debut 1960. *P.*
GLAMORGAN (49) 1960–64.
HS 110 Glam v Warwicks, Swansea, 1962.
1000 RUNS (1) 1048 @ 23.81 in 1962.
Clubs: Briton Ferry Steel, Ammanford, Gorseinon, Metal Box.

HARRIS, Charles Bowmar
——————RHB, RM——————

Born Underwood, Notts, 6 Dec 1907. Died Nottingham, 8 Aug 1954. Debut 1928. *P.*
NOTTINGHAMSHIRE (362) 1928–51. Cap 1931. Benefit (£3500) 1949.
HS 239* Notts v Hants, Trent Bridge, 1950.
BB 8–80 Notts v Lancs, Old Trafford, 1931.
1000 RUNS (11) 1891 @ 38.59 in 1934.
Fc umpire 1954 (resigned through ill-health after four matches). Clubs: Gainsborough Britannia, Yeadon, West of Scotland. Brother G. J. Harris (Glam).

HARRIS, Christopher Robin
——————RHB, RFM——————

Born Buckingham, 16 Oct 1942. Educ Buckingham RL S; Keble C, Oxford. Debut 1964.
OXFORD UNIVERSITY (12) 1964–65 (Blue 1964).
HS 14 Oxford U v Combined Services, Aldershot, 1964.
BB 6–83 (10–135 match) Oxford U v Free Foresters, The Parks, 1964.
Buckinghamshire 1965–75. Club: Maidenhead and Bray.

HARRIS, Dennis Frank
——————RHB——————

Born Birmingham, 18 Apr 1911. Died Birmingham, 17 Dec 1959. Educ King Edwards, Camp Hill, Birmingham. Debut 1946.
WARWICKSHIRE (1) 1946.
HS 2 Warwicks v Glos, Bristol, 1946.
Club: Moseley.

HARRIS, Earlsdon Joseph
——————RHB, RMF——————

Born St Kitts, W Indies, 3 Nov 1952. Educ Queensbridge Sec Modern S, Birmingham. Debut 1975.
WARWICKSHIRE (4) 1975.
HS 16 Warwicks v Lancs, Old Trafford, 1975.
BB 3–66 Warwicks v Kent, Edgbaston, 1975.
Clubs: Mitchells and Butlers, Smethwick, Moseley.

HARRIS, John Humphrey
——————LHB, RFM——————

Born Taunton, Som, 13 Feb 1936. Debut 1952. *P.*
SOMERSET (15) 1952–59.
HS 41 Som v Worcs, Taunton, 1957.
BB 3–29 Som v Worcs, Bristol Imperial, 1959.
Fc umpire 1983–. Suffolk 1960–62, Devon 1975. Minor Counties umpire 1980. Professional coach Framlingham C 1960–63. Groundsman/player Sidmouth and Exeter.

HARRIS, Leslie John
——————RHB, RMF——————

Born Cardiff, S Wales, 20 July 1915. Educ Ely S, Cardiff. Debut 1947.
GLAMORGAN (3) 1947.
HS 5 Glam v Derbys, Derby, 1947.
BB 3–39 same match.
Clubs: St Fagans, Beckenham. Took 44 wkts in the Beckenham Week, aged over 50. Secretary Primary Club.

HARRIS, Michael John
——————RHB, LBG, occ WK——————

Born St Just-in-Roseland, Cornwall, 25 May 1944. Educ Gerrans S. Debut 1964. *P.*
MIDDLESEX (72) 1964–68. Cap 1967.
NOTTINGHAMSHIRE (261) 1969–82. Cap 1970. Benefit 1977.
S AFRICA DOMESTIC Eastern Province 1971/72.
N ZEALAND DOMESTIC Wellington (7) 1975/76.
HS 201* Notts v Glam, Trent Bridge, 1973.
BB 4–16 Notts v Warwicks, Trent Bridge, 1969.
1000 RUNS (11) 2238 @ 50.86 in 1971.
RECORDS Nine centuries for Notts in 1971, equalling county record.
Squash: coach and club proprietor.

HARRIS, Terence Anthony
——————RHB——————

Born Kimberley, S Africa, 27 Aug 1916. Debut 1933/34.
S AFRICA DOMESTIC Griqualand West 1933/34–34/35, Transvaal 1936/37–48/49.
SOUTH AFRICA (3) 1947–48/49. E 1948/49 (1). *E 1947 (2).*
HST 60 SA v E, Trent Bridge, 1947. HS 191* Transvaal v NE Transvaal, Benoni, 1947/48.
RECORDS 114* on fc debut, aged 17 yrs 4 months, Griqualand West v OFS, Kimberley, 1933/34, youngest debut century in fc cricket.
Rugby: S Africa (5 caps, 1937–38). Five times Griqualand West junior lawn tennis champion.

HARRIS, Wilfred Ernest
——————RHB, RM——————

Born Cardiff, S Wales, 24 Apr 1919. Educ Canton HS, Cardiff. Debut 1938 (while still at school).
GLAMORGAN (5) 1938–47.
HS 25 Glam v Kent, Tonbridge, 1939.
Club: St Fagan's.

HARRISON, Bernard Reginald Stanhope
—————RHB, RM—————

Born Worcester, 28 Sept 1934. Debut 1957.
HAMPSHIRE (14) 1957–62.
HS 110 Hants v Oxford U, Portsmouth, 1961.
Club: Basingstoke and North Hants. Part-time cricket statistician. Soccer: Crystal Palace, Southampton, Exeter City.

HARRISON, Deryck William
—————RHB—————

Born Lurgan, Co Armagh, Ireland, 3 Nov 1943. Educ Lurgan C. Debut 1978.
IRELAND (2) 1978–79.
No runs, did not bowl.
Club: Waringstown. Brothers G. D., J. and R. Harrison (all Ireland).

HARRISON, Dominic Stephen
—————RHB, WK—————

Born Tittensor, Staffordshire, 15 Jan 1963. Educ Ampleforth; UC, Oxford. Debut 1983.
OXFORD UNIVERSITY (1) 1983.
HS 8 Oxford U v Surrey, Oval, 1983.

HARRISON, Edward Ernest
—————RHB, RFM—————

Born Chichester, Sussex, 25 May 1910. Educ Harrow. Debut 1946.
SUSSEX (10) 1946–47.
HS 23 Sussex v Oxford U, Chichester, 1947.
BB 2–28 Sussex v Glam, Newport, 1946.
Currently Sussex committee member.

HARRISON, Garfield David
—————LHB, RFM—————

Born Lurgan, Co Armagh, Ireland, 8 May 1962. Educ Lurgan C. Debut 1983.
IRELAND (2) 1983–.
HS 86 Ireland v Scotland, Downpatrick, 1983 (fc debut).
BB 2–30 same match.
Club: Waringstown. Brothers D. W., J. and R. Harrison (all Ireland); brother-in-law E. A. Bushe (Ireland).

HARRISON, James
—————RHB—————

Born Lurgan, Co Armagh, Ireland, 3 May 1941. Educ Lurgan C. Debut 1969.
IRELAND (8) 1969–77.

HS 100* Ireland v Scotland, Dublin, 1978.
Club: Waringstown. Brothers D. W., G. D. and R. Harrison (all Ireland).

HARRISON, Leo
—————RHB, WK—————

Born Mudeford, Hants, 5 June 1922. Debut 1939. P.
HAMPSHIRE (387) 1939–66. Cap 1951. Benefit (£3188) 1957.
HS 153 Hants v Notts, Bournemouth, 1952.
1000 RUNS (2) 1191 @ 27.06 in 1952.
RECORDS 83 dismissals for Hants in 1959, county record.
Players v Gentlemen (1) 1955.

HARRISON, Roy
—————LHB—————

Born Lurgan, Co Armagh, Ireland, 30 Aug 1939. Educ Lurgan C. Debut 1968.
IRELAND (1) 1968.
HS 12 Ireland v MCC, Dublin, 1968.
Club: Waringstown. Brothers D. W., G. D. and J. Harrison (all Ireland).

HARRISON, Stuart Charles
—————RHB, RM—————

Born Cwmbran, Monmouthshire, 21 Sept 1951. Educ Abersychen Grammar/Technical S; Caerleon C of Educ. Debut 1971.
GLAMORGAN (5) 1971–77.
HS 15 Glam v Derbys, Derby, 1971.
BB 3–47 Glam v Derbys, Buxton, 1973.

HARRON, Dawson Gascoigne
—————RHB—————

Born Langley Park, Co Durham, 12 Sept 1921. Debut 1951. P.
LEICESTERSHIRE (10) 1951.
HS 53 Leics v Surrey, Oval, 1951.
Durham 1947–48. Clubs: West of Scotland, Langley Park, Durham City.

HARROP, Douglas John
—————LHB, WK—————

Born Cosby, Leics, 16 Apr 1947. Educ Lutterworth GS. Debut 1972.
LEICESTERSHIRE (1) 1972.
HS 11* Leics v Oxford U, The Parks, 1972.
Club: Leicester Nomads.

HART, Martin de Lisle
—————RHB, RFM—————

Born Ealing, London, 17 Nov 1927. Educ Sherborne; St Edmund Hall, Oxford. Debut 1951.
OXFORD UNIVERSITY (4) 1951.
HS 4 Oxford U v Glos, The Parks, 1951.
BB 2–77 Oxford U v M'sex, The Parks, 1951.

HART, Philip Richard
—————RHB, SLA—————

Born Seamer, Yorks, 12 Jan 1951. Educ Pindar S, Scarborough. Debut 1981.
YORKSHIRE (3) 1981.
HS 11 Yorks v Glam, Cardiff, 1981.
Bowled seven consecutive maidens before conceding a run on debut, Yorks v Surrey, Harrogate, 1981.
Club: Scarborough, Normanby Hall.

HARTE, Christopher Charles John
—————RHB—————

Born Belfast, Ireland, 23 Feb 1949. Educ Belfast Royal Academy; Dublin U. Debut 1973.
IRELAND (2) 1973–81.
HS 40 Ireland v Scotland, Cork, 1973.
Clubs: NICC, Downpatrick, Bangor.

HARTLEY, Fred
—————RHB, SLA—————

Born Waterfoot, nr Bacup, 24 Apr 1906. Died Stacksteads, Bacup, 24 Dec 1976. Debut 1924.
LANCASHIRE (2) 1924–45 (21 yrs between two appearances).
HS 2 Lancs v Yorks, Bradford, 1945.
Clubs: Bacup, Tonge, Bradshaw, Church.

HARTLEY, George Edward
—————RHB, SRA—————

Born New Hebden Bridge, Yorks, 23 July 1909. Educ Rydal; St Catharine's C, Cambridge. Debut 1946.
MCC (1) 1946.
HS 3 MCC v Cambridge U, Lord's, 1946.
Denbighshire. Clubs: Jesters, Esher, Surbiton, Hampton Wick, Thames Ditton, Buccaneers.

HARTLEY, Peter John
—————RHB, RM—————

Born Keighley, Yorks, 18 Apr 1960. Debut 1982.

WARWICKSHIRE (3) 1982.
HS 16 Warwicks v Lancs, Southport, 1982.
BB 2–45 Warwicks v Yorks, Headingley, 1982.

HARTLEY, Stuart *Neil*
——————RHB, RM——————

Born Shipley, Yorks, 18 Mar 1956. Educ Beckfoot GS, Bingley; Cannington HS, Perth, W Australia. Debut 1978.
YORKSHIRE (83) 1978–. Cap 1981.
S AFRICA DOMESTIC Orange Free State 1981/82–82/83.
HS 114 Yorks v Glos, Bradford, 1982.
BB 3–40 Yorks v Glos, Dore, 1980.

HARVEY, John Frank
——————RHB, OB——————

Born Cambridge, 27 Sept 1939. Educ Cambridge Central Technical S. Debut 1961. *P.*
MCC (1) 1961.
DERBYSHIRE (204) 1963–72. Cap 1968.
HS 168 Derbys v Northants, Ilkeston, 1969.
1000 RUNS (3) 1226 @ 32.26 in 1971.
Cambridgeshire 1958–59, 1973–76, Berkshire 1978–. Clubs: Sonning, Undercliffe. Former groundsman Bradfield C.

HARVEY, Jonathan Robert William
——————RHB, RFM——————

Born Yeovil, Som, 3 Feb 1944. Educ Marlborough C; Christ's C, Cambridge. Debut 1963.
CAMBRIDGE UNIVERSITY (6) 1963–65.
HS 3 Cambridge U v Surrey, Fenner's, 1965.
BB 5–28 Cambridge U v Som, Taunton, 1965.
Rugby: Blue. Oxford and Cambridge Universities tour to Argentina 1965/66.

HARVEY, Peter Fairfield
——————RHB, LBG——————

Born Linby, Notts, 15 Jan 1923. Debut 1947. *P.*
NOTTINGHAMSHIRE (173) 1947–58. Cap 1949.
HS 150 Notts v Leics, Leicester, 1951.
BB 8–122 Notts v Som, Trent Bridge, 1949.
RECORD Added 303* for 6th wkt with F. H. Winrow, Notts v Derbys, Trent Bridge, 1947, county record.

HARVEY, Peter Vernon
——————LHB——————

Born Wallington, Surrey, 6 Jan 1926. Educ Epsom; UC, Oxford. Debut 1949.
OXFORD UNIVERSITY (1) 1949.
HS 9 Oxford U v Free Foresters, The Parks, 1949.
War-time Blue 1944.

HARVEY, Robert *Neil*
——————LHB, ROB——————

Born Fitzroy, Victoria, Australia, 8 Oct 1928. Educ North Fitzroy Central; Collingwood Technical S. Debut 1946/47. *Wisden* 1954.
AUSTRALIA DOMESTIC Victoria (64) 1946/47–56/57, New South Wales (30) 1958/59–62/63.
AUSTRALIA (79) 1947/48–62/63. E 1950/51 (5), 1954/55 (5), 1958/59 (5), 1962/63 (5); SA 1952/53 (5); WI 1951/52 (5), 1960/61 (4); I 1947/48 (2). *E 1948 (2), 1953 (5), 1956 (5), 1961 (5); SA 1949/50 (5), 1957/58 (4); WI 1954/55 (5); I 1956/57 (3), 1959/60 (5); P 1956/57 (1), 1959/60 (3).* Cap 1.
OTHER TOURS Commonwealth XI to Ceylon 1951/52. Australians to N Zealand 1956/57.
HST 205 A v SA, Melbourne, 1952/53. HS 231* NSW v S Australia, Sydney, 1962/63.
BB 4–8 Australians v M'sex, Lord's, 1961.
1000 RUNS (3 + 6) 2040 @ 65.80 in 1953.
RECORDS First Test century aged 19 yrs 121 days, youngest Australian Test century-maker. Added 295 for 3rd wkt with C. C. McDonald, A v WI, Kingston, 1954/55, Australia Test record. 834 runs @ 92.66 A v SA, 1952/53, third-highest aggregate for Test series. 6149 Test runs, third-highest career aggregate for Australia, after D. G. Bradman and G. S. Chappell. Australian selector. MBE for services to cricket. Autobiography *My World Of Cricket* (1963). Brothers C. E. Harvey (Victoria, Queensland), M. R. Harvey (Victoria) and R. Harvey (Victoria).

HARVEY, Ronald Charles
——————LHB, RFM——————

Born Chelmsford, Essex, 7 May 1934. Educ Rainsford Sec S. Debut 1952. *P.*
ESSEX (1) 1952.
HS 12* Essex v T. N. Pearce's XI, Chelmsford, 1952.
BB 3–88 same match.
Club: Chelmsford.

HARVEY-WALKER, Ashley John
——————RHB, OB——————

Born East Ham, London, 21 July 1944. Educ Strathallan S. Debut 1971.
DERBYSHIRE (81) 1971–78.
HS 117 Derbys v Warwicks, Edgbaston, 1974.
BB 7–35 (10–82 match) Derbys v Surrey, Ilkeston, 1978.
RECORD Scored 110* (in second inns) of debut match, Derbys v Oxford U, Burton upon Trent, 1971, first instance for county.
Clubs: Undercliffe, Stourbridge, Holmfirth, Chesterfield.

HASAN JAMIL Alvi
——————LHB, LMF——————

Born Karachi, Pakistan, 25 July 1952. Educ U of Technology and Engineering, Lahore. Debut 1969/70.
PAKISTAN DOMESTIC Kalat, Karachi, Universities, Pakistan International Airlines, 1969/70–.
TOURS Pakistan Under-25 to Sri Lanka 1973/74. Pakistan to Sri Lanka 1975/76. Pakistan to England (in emergency) 1978. PIA to Zimbabwe 1981/82.
HS 172 PIA v Dawood Industries, Lahore, 1975/76.
BB 5–38 Universities v Railways, Lahore, 1973/74.
Club: Kelburn.

HASLOP, Peter
——————RHB, RM——————

Born Midhurst, Sussex, 17 Sept 1941. Debut 1962.
HAMPSHIRE (1) 1962.
HS 2* Hants v Pakistanis, Bournemouth, 1962.
BB 2–82 same match.
Club: Deanery.

HASEEB AHSAN
——————RHB, OB——————

Born Peshawar, India, 15 July 1939. Educ Peshawar U. Debut 1956/57.
PAKISTAN DOMESTIC Peshawar, Combined Universities, Pakistan International Airlines, Karachi, 1956/57–62/63.
PAKISTAN (12) 1957/58–61/62. E 1961/62 (2); A 1959/60 (1); WI 1958/59 (1). *WI 1957/58 (3); I 1960/61 (5).*
OTHER TOURS Pakistan to England 1962. Pakistan Eaglets to England 1963.
HST 14 P v E, Lahore, 1961/62. HS 36 PIA v Commissioner's XI, Peshawar, 1960/61.

BBT 6–202 P v I, Madras, 1960/61. BB 8–23 (13–47 match) Peshawar v Punjab B, Peshawar, 1957/58.

HASSAN, Sheikh *Basharat*
————RHB, RM, occ WK————

Born Nairobi, Kenya, 24 Mar 1944. Educ City HS, Nairobi. Debut 1963/64.
EAST AFRICA (1) 1963/64.
NOTTINGHAMSHIRE (326) 1966–. Cap 1970. Benefit (£20,000) 1978.
HS 182* Notts v Glos, Trent Bridge, 1977.
BB 3–33 Notts v Lancs, Old Trafford, 1976.
1000 RUNS (5) 1395 @ 32.44 in 1970. Kenya.

HASSAN, Syed Farooq Azim
————RHB, RMF————

Born Lahore, India, 17 Oct 1941. Educ Punjab U; Jesus C, Oxford. Debut 1959/60.
PAKISTAN DOMESTIC President's XI, Punjab University, Universities, 1959/60.
OXFORD UNIVERSITY (7) 1962–63.
HS 17 Oxford U v Warwicks, The Parks, 1963.
BB 2–15 same match.

HASSETT, Arthur *Lindsay*
————RHB, RM————

Born Geelong, Victoria, Australia, 28 Aug 1913. Educ Geelong C. Debut 1932/33. *Wisden* 1949.
AUSTRALIA DOMESTIC Victoria (73) 1932/33–52/53.
AUSTRALIA (43) 1938–53. E 1946/47 (5), 1950/51 (5); SA 1952/53 (5); WI 1951/52 (4); I 1947/48 (4). *E 1938 (4), 1948 (5), 1953 (5); SA 1949/50 (5); NZ 1945/46 (1).* Capt 24.
OTHER TOURS Australian Services to England 1945 and India and Ceylon 1945/46.
HST 198* A v I, Adelaide, 1947/48. HS 232 Victoria v MCC, Melbourne, 1950/51.
BB 2–10 Australian Services v All Ceylon, Colombo, 1945/46.
1000 RUNS (3 + 2) 1589 @ 54.79 in 1938. MBE for services to cricket. Cricket commentator after retirement. Brother R. J. Hassett (Victoria).

HASTIE, James Henderson
————LHB, SLA————

Born Glasgow, Scotland, 20 June 1920. Debut 1951.

MINOR COUNTIES (1) 1951.
HS 22 Minor Counties v Kent, Canterbury, 1951.
Buckinghamshire 1948–53. Clubs: Slough, Formby, Burnham.

HASTINGS, Brian Frederick
————RHB————

Born Wellington, N Zealand, 23 Mar 1940. Educ Wellington C, N Zealand. Debut 1957/58.
N ZEALAND DOMESTIC Wellington (1) 1957/58, Central Districts (5) 1960/61, Canterbury (72) 1961/62–76/77.
NEW ZEALAND (31) 1968/69–75/76. E 1974/75 (2); A 1973/74 (3); WI 1968/69 (3); I 1975/76 (1); P 1972/73 (3). *E 1969 (3), 1973 (3); A 1973/74 (3); WI 1971/72 (5); I 1969/70 (2); P 1969/70 (3).*
OTHER TOUR N Zealand to Australia 1969/70.
HST 117* NZ v WI, Christchurch, 1968/69. HS 226 Canterbury v N Zealand Under-23 XI, Christchurch, 1964/65.
RECORDS Added 151 for 10th wkt with R. O. Collinge, NZ v P, Auckland, 1972/73, world Test record; and added 229 for 4th wkt with B. E. Congdon, NZ v A, Wellington, 1973/74, N Zealand Test record.

HATCH, Peter George
————RHB————

Born Kirkee, India, 3 July 1938. Educ Malvern C; Queen's C, Cambridge. Debut 1960.
COMBINED SERVICES (3) 1960–61.
FREE FORESTERS (2) 1961.
HS 15 Free Foresters v Oxford U, The Parks, 1961.

HATTEA, Saeed Ahmed
————RHB, RFM————

Born Bombay, India, 2 Feb 1950. Educ City of London S. Debut 1969/70.
INDIA DOMESTIC Bombay 1969/70–70/71, West Zone 1970/71.
REST OF WORLD XI (1) 1970.
HS 1 Bombay v Saurashtra, Bombay, 1969/70.
BB 5–33 Bombay v Gujerat, Surat, 1969/70.
Oxfordshire. Clubs: Old Citizens, Jack Frost, MCC, Marks and Spencer.

HATTON, Anthony George
————LHB, RFM————

Born Whitkirk, Leeds, Yorks, 25 Mar 1937. Educ Roundhay S, Leeds. Debut 1960. *P.*

YORKSHIRE (3) 1960–61.
HS 4* Yorks v Northants, Bramall Lane, Sheffield, 1960.
BB 2–21 same match.
Clubs: Castleford, Halifax, Idle.

HAUGHTON, William Edward
————RHB————

Born Bray, County Wicklow, Ireland, 31 Oct 1923. Educ Friend's S, Lisburn; Dublin U. Debut 1953.
IRELAND (1) 1953.
No runs, no wkts.
Clubs: Dublin U, Clontarf, Pembroke.
Hockey: Ireland.

HAWKE, Christopher Richard John
————RHB, WK————

Born Portsmouth, Hants, 12 Apr 1934. Educ Harrow; Oxford U. Debut 1953.
OXFORD UNIVERSITY (1) 1953.
HS 23* Oxford U v Leics, The Parks, 1953.

HAWKE, Neil James Napier
————RHB, RFM————

Born Cheltenham, S Australia, 27 Jan 1939. Debut 1959/60.
AUSTRALIA DOMESTIC Western Australia (7) 1959/60, South Australia (60) 1960/61–67/68, Tasmania (2) 1968/69.
AUSTRALIA (27) 1962/63–68. E 1962/63 (1), 1965/66 (4); SA 1963/64 (4); I 1967/68 (1); P 1964/65 (1). *E 1964 (5), 1968 (2); SA 1966/67 (2); WI 1964/65 (5); I 1964/65 (1); P 1964/65 (1).*
OTHER TOURS Rest of World to W Indies 1966/67 (one match). International Cavaliers v Barbados, Scarborough, 1969. Commonwealth XI to Pakistan 1970/71.
HST 45* A v WI, Kingston, 1964/65. HS 141* S Australia v Queensland, Adelaide, 1964/65.
BBT 7–105 A v E, Sydney, 1965/66. BB 8–61 S Australia v NSW, Sydney, 1967/68.
Clubs: Nelson, East Lancs (England); Launceston, North Perth, Port Adelaide (Australia). Fc Australia Rules football.

HAWKEY, Richard Blodworth
————RHB, RM————

Born Teddington, M'sex, 7 Aug 1923. Educ Merchant Taylor's, Northwood; Magdalene C, Cambridge. Debut 1948.
FREE FORESTERS (1) 1948.
CAMBRIDGE UNIVERSITY (2) 1949.

HS 13 Free Foresters v Cambridge U, Fenner's, 1948 and 13 Cambridge U v N Zealanders, Fenner's, 1949.
Clubs: Old Merchant Taylor's, Romanians.

HAWKINS, Christopher George
————————RHB, WK————————

Born Slough, Buckinghamshire, 31 Aug 1938. Debut 1957. *P.*
WARWICKSHIRE (4) 1957.
HS 11* Warwicks v Northants, Northampton, 1957.
Groundsman Old Trafford to 1983. Buckinghamshire 1956, 1965. Clubs: Pickwick, Old Hill, Mitchells and Butlers.

HAWKINS, Derek Graham
————————RHB, OB————————

Born Alveston, Glos, 18 May 1935. Debut 1952. *P.*
GLOUCESTERSHIRE (134) 1952–62. Cap 1957.
HS 106 Glos v Sussex, Hove, 1957.
BB 6–81 Glos v Kent, Cheltenham, 1961.
1000 RUNS (1) 1021 @ 21.72 in 1961.
Clubs: Thornbury, Westbury-on-Tryme.

HAYE, William
————————RHB, RM————————

Born Jamaica, 15 Sept 1948. Debut 1970.
W INDIES DOMESTIC Jamaica 1970–71/72.
TOUR Jamaica to England 1970.
HS 60 Jamaica v Indians, Kingston, 1970/71.
Club: Clarendon.

HAYES, Frank Charles
————————RHB————————

Born Preston, Lancs, 6 Dec 1946. Educ De la Salle C, Salford; Sheffield U. Debut 1970.
LANCASHIRE (228) 1970–84. Cap 1972. Capt 1978–80. Benefit 1983.
ENGLAND (9) 1973–76. WI 1973 (3), 1976 (2). *WI 1973/74 (4).*
OTHER TOURS D. H. Robins' XI to S Africa 1972/73, 1974/75, 1975/76. International XI to Rhodesia 1975/76. International XI to Pakistan 1981/82. Overseas XI v President's XI, Calcutta, 1980/81.
HST 106* E v WI, Oval, 1973 (2nd inns of Test debut). HS 187 Lancs v Indians, Old Trafford, 1974.
1000 RUNS (6) 1311 @ 35.43 in 1974.

Hit M. A. Nash for 34 runs in one over (646666) Lancs v Glam, Swansea, 1977, second-highest total from a six-ball over (no no-balls).

HAYES, John Arthur
————————RHB, RF————————

Born Auckland, N Zealand, 11 Jan 1927. Debut 1946/47.
N ZEALAND DOMESTIC Auckland (11) 1946/47–48/49, 1956/57–58/59, Canterbury (20) 1950/51–54/55, Governor-General's XI (1) 1960/61.
NEW ZEALAND (15) 1950/51–58. E 1950/51 (2), 1954/55 (1); WI 1951/52 (2). *E 1958 (4); I 1955/56 (5); P 1955/56 (1).*
OTHER TOUR N Zealand to England 1949.
HST 19 NZ v E, Christchurch, 1950/51.
HS 36 Canterbury v Auckland, Auckland, 1952/53.
BBT 4–36 NZ v E, Lord's, 1958. BB 7–28 (14–65 match) Auckland v Wellington, Auckland, 1957/58.

HAYES, Kevin Anthony
————————RHB, RM————————

Born Mexborough, Yorks, 26 Sept 1962. Educ Queen Elizabeth S, Blackburn; Merton C, Oxford. Debut 1980.
LANCASHIRE (12) 1980–.
OXFORD UNIVERSITY (27) 1981–84 (Blue 1981–84).
HS 152 Oxford U v Warwicks, The Parks, 1982.
BB 6–58 Oxford U v Warwicks, Edgbaston, 1983.

HAYES, Peter James
————————RHB, RM————————

Born Crowborough, Sussex, 20 May 1954. Educ Brighton C; Downing C, Cambridge. Debut 1974.
CAMBRIDGE UNIVERSITY (27) 1974–77 (Blue 1974–75, 1977).
HS 56* Cambridge U v Glam, Fenner's, 1977.
BB 5–48 Cambridge U v Notts, Fenner's, 1975.
Suffolk 1981–.

HAYLES, Basil Ratcliffe Marshal
————————RHB, WK————————

Born Andover, Hants, 29 Oct 1916. Educ Haileybury and ISC. Debut 1938.
ARMY (3) 1938–39.
COMBINED SERVICES (4) 1947–49.
HS 40 Army v Cambridge U, Fenner's, 1939.
Norfolk 1947. Major (retired).

HAYNES, Denis Marshall
————————RHB————————

Born Stoke-on-Trent, Staffordshire, 29 Dec 1923. Educ Denstone; St Catharine's C, Cambridge. Debut 1956.
MCC (1) 1956.
HS 8 MCC v Oxford U, Lord's, 1956.
War-time Blue 1944–45 (capt 1945). Staffordshire 1946–57 (capt 1952–57). President North Staffordshire and District League 1983–. Club: Stone.

HAYNES, Desmond Leo
————————RHB————————

Born St James, Barbados, 15 Feb 1956. Educ Federal HS, Barbados. Debut 1976/77.
W INDIES DOMESTIC Barbados 1976/77–.
WEST INDIES (45) 1977/78–84. E 1980/81 (4); A 1977/78 (2), 1983/84 (5); I 1982/83 (5). *E 1980 (5), 1984 (5); A 1979/80 (3), 1981/82 (3); NZ 1979/80 (3); I 1983/84 (6); P 1980/81 (4).*
OTHER TOUR Young West Indies to Zimbabwe 1981/82.
HST 184 WI v E, Lord's, 1980. HS as above.
World Series Cricket (Kerry Packer) 1978/79. Clubs: Carlton (W Indies), Melbourne (Australia).

HAYNES, John Perigoe
————————RHB, RMF————————

Born Canterbury, N Zealand, 27 Nov 1926. Educ Dauntseys S; St Catharine's C, Cambridge. Debut 1946.
CAMBRIDGE UNIVERSITY (1) 1946.
No runs, no wkts.

HAYNES, Michael William
————————RHB————————

Born Nottingham, 19 May 1936. Debut 1959. *P.*
NOTTINGHAMSHIRE (9) 1959–61.
HS 23 Notts v Yorks, Hull, 1961.

HAYS, David Leslie
————————RHB, WK————————

Born London, 5 Nov 1944. Educ Highgate; Selwyn C, Cambridge. Debut 1965.
CAMBRIDGE UNIVERSITY (24) 1965–68 (Blue 1966, 1968).
SCOTLAND (1) 1980.
HS 72 Cambridge U v Worcs, Fenner's, 1966.
Aberdeenshire.

HAYSMAN, Michael Donald
——RHB, OB——

Born Adelaide, S Australia, 22 Apr 1961. Educ Brighton HS, Adelaide. Debut 1982/83.
AUSTRALIA DOMESTIC South Australia (18) 1982/83–.
LEICESTERSHIRE (5) 1984.
TOUR Young Australia to Zimbabwe 1982/83.
HS 153 S Australia v Victoria, St Kilda, 1982/83.
Scored 126 on fc debut, S Australia v Queensland, Adelaide, 1982/83; and 102* in 2nd inns of Leics debut, v Cambridge U, Fenner's, 1984.

HAYWARD, James Gordon Rotherham
——LHB, RFM——

Born Bridlington, Yorks, 31 Dec 1926. Debut 1951. P.
NOTTINGHAMSHIRE (1) 1951.
No runs.
BB 2–78 Notts v Oxford U, The Parks, 1951.

HAYWARD, Richard Edward
——LHB, LM——

Born Hillingdon, M'sex, 15 Feb 1954. Educ Latymer Upper S, Hammersmith. Debut 1979.
MINOR COUNTIES (1) 1979.
HAMPSHIRE (13) 1981–82.
N ZEALAND DOMESTIC Central Districts (12) 1982/83–.
HS 102 C Districts v Wellington, Palmerston North, 1983/84.
Scored 101* and 53 on Hants debut, v Sri Lankans, Bournemouth, 1981.
Buckinghamshire 1978–80, 1983–84. Club: Ickenham. Uncle Sir Richard Hayward (president Civil Service Cricket Club).

HAYWARD, William Imrie Dudley
——RHB, RMF——

Born Adelaide, S Australia, 15 Apr 1930. Educ St Peter's Adelaide; Jesus C, Cambridge. Debut 1950.
CAMBRIDGE UNIVERSITY (26) 1950–53 (Blue 1950–51, 1953).
MCC (1) 1954.
HS 57 Cambridge U v Sussex, Worthing, 1951.
BB 6–89 Cambridge U v Surrey, Guildford, 1953.

HAYWOOD, David Charles
——LHB, RM——

Born Hucknall, Notts, 20 Mar 1945. Educ Nottingham GS; Jesus C, Cambridge. Debut 1968.
CAMBRIDGE UNIVERSITY (9) 1968 (Blue).
HS 62 Cambridge U v Oxford U, Lord's, 1968.

HAYWOOD, Paul Raymond
——RHB, RM——

Born Leicester, 30 Mar 1947. Educ Wyggeston GS, Leicester. Debut 1969.
LEICESTERSHIRE (54) 1969–73.
HS 100* Leics v M'sex, Lord's, 1972.
BB 4–60 Leics v Surrey, Leicester, 1972.
Hockey: Leicestershire and East Midlands Under-23 XI.

HAYWOOD, Robert Oliver
——RHB——

Born Northampton, 22 Apr 1917. Died Edinburgh, Scotland, 21 Dec 1963. Educ Stewart's, Edinburgh. Debut 1949.
SCOTLAND (1) 1949.
HS 12 Scotland v Ireland, Belfast, 1949.
Club: Stewart's FP. Father R. A. Haywood (Northants); grandfather R. J. Haywood (Kent).

HAZARE, Vijay Samuel
——RHB, RM——

Born Sangli, India, 11 Mar 1915. Educ Sangli HS, Maharashtra. Debut 1934/35.
INDIA DOMESTIC Maharashtra 1934/35, 1940/41, Central India 1935/36–38/39, Baroda 1941/42–60/61 (capt 1950/51–55/56), The Rest (Bombay) 1938/39–44/45. Board President's XI v West Indians, Nagpur, 1966/67 (Benefit; last fc match).
COMMONWEALTH XI (2) 1950–51.
INDIA (30) 1947–52/53. E 1951/52 (5); WI 1948/49 (5); P 1952/53 (3). E 1946 (3), 1952 (4); A 1947/48 (5); WI 1952/ 53 (5). Capt 14.
OTHER TOUR India to Ceylon 1944/45.
HST 164* I v E, Delhi, 1951/52. HS 316* Maharashtra v Baroda, Poona, 1939/40.
BBT 4–29 I v A, Sydney, 1947/48. BB 8–90 Baroda v Maharashtra, Baroda, 1946/47.
1000 RUNS (2 + 5) 1480 @ 87.05 in 1949/ 50.
RECORDS Added 577 for 4th wkt with Gul Mahomed, Baroda v Holkar, Baroda, 1946/47, world record for any wkt in fc cricket and added 245 for 9th wkt with N. D. Nagarwalla, Maharashtra v Baroda, Poona, 1939/40, India fc record and third-highest 9th-wkt stand. Added 222 for 4th wkt with V. L. Manjrekar, I v E, Headingley, 1952, India Test record. Scored 309 out of inns total of 387, Rest v Hindus, Bombay, 1943/44, a record proportion of a completed inns total (79.8 per cent) until beaten by G. M. Turner (83.4 per cent) in 1977. In same inns scored 266 (88.6 per cent) out of 6th-wkt stand of 300 with brother Vivekanand S. Hazare. Record 6312 runs @ 69.36 in Ranji Trophy.
Chairman Indian selectors after retirement. MCC Hon. member. Clubs: Rawtenstall, Royton. Brother Vivekanand S. Hazare (Baroda, Mysore); son R. Hazare (Baroda); nephews S. Hazare and W. Hazare (both Baroda).

HAZELL, Horace Leslie
——LHB, SLA——

Born Brislington, Som, 30 Sept 1909. Debut 1929. P.
SOMERSET (350) 1929–52. Cap 1932. Benefit (£2324) 1949.
HS 43 Som v Glos, Bristol, 1946.
BB 8–27 (12–63 match) Som v Glos, Taunton, 1949.
100 WKTS (2) 106 @ 19.48 in 1949.
RECORDS Bowled 17 consecutive overs – and 105 balls – without conceding a run, Som v Glos, Taunton, 1949, a record for English fc cricket and second-best ever. Bowled 61 consecutive overs in inns, Som v Warwicks, Griff and Coton, 1933.
Clubs: Mitchells and Butlers, Keynsham.

HEAD, Timothy John
——RHB, WK——

Born Hammersmith, London, 22 Sept 1957. Educ Lancing C. Debut 1976.
SUSSEX (22) 1976–81.
HS 52* Sussex v Australians, Hove, 1981.
Took seven catches in debut match, Sussex v Oxford U, Pagham, 1976.

HEADLEY, George Alphonso
——RHB, LB——

Born Panama, 30 May 1909. Died Kingston, Jamaica, 30 Nov 1983. Debut 1927/28. Wisden 1934.
W INDIES DOMESTIC Jamaica 1927/ 28–53/54.
WEST INDIES (22) 1929/30–53/54. E 1929/30 (4), 1934/35 (4), 1947/48 (1), 1953/54 (1). E 1933 (3), 1939 (3); A 1930/31 (5); I 1948/49 (1). Capt 1.
COMMONWEALTH XI (3) 1951–54.

HST 270* WI v E, Kingston, 1934/35. HS 344* Jamaica v L. H. Tennyson's XI, Kingston, 1931/32.
BB 5–33 Jamaica v Trinidad, Kingston, 1945/46.
1000 RUNS (2 + 1) 2320 @ 66.28 in 1933.
RECORDS Added 487 unbroken for 6th wkt with C. C. Passailaigue, Jamaica v L. H. Tennyson's XI, Kingston, 1931/32, world record. Test career average (60.83) best for completed career by West Indian.
MCC Hon. member. Clubs: Bacup, Dudley, Old Hill. Professional coach Bromcesgrove S 1951–54. Awarded MBE for services to cricket. Sons R. G. A. Headley (Worcs, W Indies) and L. Headley (Jamaican Olympic athlete).

HEADLEY, Ronald George Alphonso
——————LHB, RLB——————

Born Kingston, Jamaica, 29 June 1939. Debut 1958. *P.*
WORCESTERSHIRE (403) 1958–74. Cap 1961. Benefit (£10,014) 1972.
W INDIES DOMESTIC Jamaica 1965/66–73/74.
WEST INDIES (2) *E 1973*.
TOURS Cavaliers to W Indies 1964/65. Worcs to Rhodesia 1964/65. Worcs to Jamaica 1965/66.
HST 42 WI v E, Oval, 1973. HS 187 Worcs v Northants, Worcester, 1971.
BB 4–40 Worcs v Glam, Worcester, 1963.
1000 RUNS (13) 2040 @ 31.87 in 1961.
Shared in century 1st-wkt stands twice in a match in first two matches in which opened with P. J. Stimpson, for Worcs in 1971.
Clubs: Dudley, Old Hill. Father G. A. Headley (W Indies).

HEAL, Michael George
——————RHB, RM——————

Born Bristol, 7 Sept 1948. Educ St Brendan's C, Bristol; St Edmund Hall, Oxford. Debut 1969.
OXFORD UNIVERSITY (22) 1969–72 (Blue 1970, 1972).
HS 124* Oxford U v Warwicks, The Parks, 1972.
Rugby: Blue.

HEALEY, Robert Dennis
——————RHB, RMF——————

Born Plymouth, Devon, 10 Feb 1934. Educ Falmouth GS. Debut 1964.
COMBINED SERVICES (2) 1964.
HS 7 Combined Services v Oxford U, Aldershot, 1964.

Devon 1954–65. Clubs: Plymouth, United Services, Royal Navy. Naval officer.

HEANE, George Frank Henry
——————LHB, RM——————

Born Worksop, Notts, 2 Jan 1904. Died Skendleby, Lincs, 24 Oct 1969. Educ King Edward VI GS, Retford. Debut 1927.
NOTTINGHAMSHIRE (172) 1927–51. Cap 1935. Joint capt (with S. D. Rhodes) 1935. Capt 1936–46.
SIR J. CAHN'S XI (6) 1929–38/39.
TOURS Sir J. Cahn's XI to Argentina 1929/30. Sir J. Cahn's XI to N Zealand 1938/39.
HS 138 Notts v Hants, Portsmouth, 1939.
BB 6–52 Notts v Hants, Trent Bridge, 1939.
1000 RUNS (3) 1627 @ 37.83 in 1939.
RECORD Added 220 for 8th wkt with R. Winrow, Notts v Som, Trent Bridge, 1935, county record.
Gentlemen v Players (3) 1935–47. Lincolnshire 1947–50. Clubs: Worksop, Sir J. Cahn's XI.

HEARD, Hartley
——————RHB, RM——————

Born Bristol, 29 Oct 1947. Educ Queen Elizabeth's Hospital S, Bristol; Exeter C, Oxford. Debut 1967.
OXFORD UNIVERSITY (30) 1967–70 (Blue 1969–70).
HS 31 Oxford U v Glam, The Parks, 1970.
BB 6–78 Oxford U v M'sex, The Parks, 1969.

HEARN, Peter
——————LHB, SLA——————

Born Tunbridge Wells, Kent, 18 Nov 1925. Educ Skinners S, Tunbridge Wells. Debut 1947. *P.*
KENT (196) 1947–56. Cap 1947.
HS 172 Kent v Worcs, Dudley, 1954.
BB 3–34 Kent v Som, Gravesend, 1950.
1000 RUNS (3) 1413 @ 30.06 in 1954.
Scored 124 Kent v Warwicks, Gillingham, 1947 on fc debut.
Clubs: Tunbridge Wells, Tonbridge. Uncle S. G. Hearn (Kent).

HEATH, David Michael William
——————RHB——————

Born Birmingham, 14 Dec 1931. Educ Moseley GS. Debut 1949.
WARWICKSHIRE (16) 1949–53.

COMBINED SERVICES (3) 1951–52.
HS 149 Combined Services v Worcs, Worcester, 1952.
Club: Moseley.

HEATH, George Edward Mansell
——————RHB, RFM——————

Born Hong Kong, 20 Feb 1913. Debut 1937. *P.*
HAMPSHIRE (132) 1937–49. Cap 1937. Testimonial 1951.
HS 34* Hants v Lancs, Southampton, 1939.
BB 7–49 Hants v Derbys, Portsmouth, 1947.
Took 97 wkts @ 23.77 in 1938.

HEATH, Jeremy Richard Percy
——————LHB——————

Born Turners Hill, Sussex, 26 Apr 1959. Educ Imberhorne CS, East Grinstead. Debut 1980.
SUSSEX (17) 1980–83.
HS 101* Sussex v Sri Lankans, Hastings, 1981.

HEATH, Malcolm
——————LHB, RFM——————

Born Bournemouth, Hants, 9 Mar 1934. Debut 1954. *P.*
HAMPSHIRE (143) 1954–62. Cap 1957.
HS 33 Hants v Sussex, Portsmouth, 1955.
BB 8–43 (13–86 match) Hants v Sussex, Portsmouth, 1958.
100 WKTS (1) 126 @ 16.42 in 1958.
Club: Scarborough. Executive Guinness Superlatives.

HEBDEN, Geoffrey George Lockwood
——————RHB, RMF——————

Born London, 14 July 1918. Educ King's S, Bruton. Debut 1937.
HAMPSHIRE (6) 1937–51.
HS 22* Hants v Cambridge U, Bournemouth, 1951.
Dorset 1952–60. Club: Bournemouth. Father G. L. Hebden (M'sex).

HECTOR, Patrick Anthony
——————RHB, RM——————

Born Islington, London, 29 July 1958. Educ Warren CS, Chadwell Heath. Debut 1977.
ESSEX (3) 1977.
HS 40 Essex v Cambridge U, Fenner's, 1977.

BB 3–56 Essex v Leics, Leicester, 1977.
Club: Ilford.

HEDGES, Bernard
————RHB————

Born Pontypridd, S Wales, 20 July
1927. Debut 1950. *P*.
GLAMORGAN (421) 1950–67. Cap 1954.
Benefit (£4402) 1963.
HS 182 Glam v Oxford U, The Parks,
1967.
1000 RUNS (9) 2026 @ 32.15 in 1961.
Club: Pontardulais. Rugby: Swansea,
Pontypridd.

HEGGIE, William Robert
————RHB————

Born Cupar, Fife, Scotland, 10 Aug
1914. Educ Bell Baxter HS. Debut 1937.
SCOTLAND (5) 1937–47.
HS 44 Scotland v Ireland, Belfast, 1937.
Clubs: Dunfermline, Greenock.

HEIGHES, Bernard Roy
————RHB, SLA————

Born Chiswick, London, 16 Jan 1947.
Educ Chiswick Sec S. Debut 1967.
MCC (1) 1967.
HS 6* MCC v Scotland, Glasgow, 1967.
Professional MCC. Clubs: Hounslow,
Paddington.

HEINE, Peter Samuel
————RHB, RF————

Born Winterton, Natal, S Africa, 28
June 1928. Educ Winterton HS. Debut
1951/52.
S AFRICA DOMESTIC North-Eastern
Transvaal 1951/52–52/53, Orange Free
State 1953/54–54/55, Transvaal 1955/
56–64/65.
SOUTH AFRICA (14) 1955–61/62. E 1956/
57 (5); A 1957/58 (4); NZ 1961/62 (1). *E
1955 (4)*.
HST 31 SA v NZ, J'burg, 1961/62. HS 67
OFS v Natal, Bloemfontein, 1954/55.
BBT 6–58 SA v A, J'burg, 1957/58. BB
8–92 OFS v Transvaal, Welkom, 1954/
55.
Sister Bobbie Heine (top-class lawn ten-
nis player).

HELLAWELL, Michael Stephen
————RHB, RM————

Born Keighley, Yorks, 30 June 1938.
Debut 1962.
WARWICKSHIRE (1) 1962.
HS 30* Warwicks v Oxford U, Edgbas-
ton, 1962.

BB 4–54 same match.
Clubs: Keighley, Walsall, Crossflatts.
Soccer: Queen's Park Rangers, Birmingham City, Sunderland, Huddersfield Town, Peterborough, England (2).

HELLMUTH, Leon
————LHB, SLA————

Born Blackheath, Kent, 14 Aug 1934.
Educ Haberdashers' Aske's S. Debut
1951. *P*.
KENT (7) 1951–52.
HS 11 Kent v Leics, Loughborough,
1952.
BB 2–11 Kent v Hants, Southampton,
1952.

HEMMING, Leonard Ernest
Gerald
————RHB, OB————

Born Edmonton, 30 Sept 1916. Debut
1951.
MINOR COUNTIES (1) 1951.
HS 14 Minor Counties v Kent, Canter-
bury, 1951.
Oxfordshire 1946–54. Clubs: Witney
Mills, Oxford City.

HEMMINGS, Edward Ernest
————RHB, OB (originally RM)————

Born Leamington Spa, Warwicks, 20
Feb 1949. Educ Campion S,
Leamington Spa. Debut 1966.
WARWICKSHIRE (177) 1966–78. Cap
1974.
NOTTINGHAMSHIRE (132) 1979–. Cap
1980.
ENGLAND (5) 1982–82/83. *P 1982 (2). A
1982/83 (3)*.
OTHER TOURS D. H. Robins' XI to S
Africa 1974/75. International XI to
Pakistan 1981/82. International XI to
Jamaica 1982/83.
HST 95 E v A, Sydney, 1982/83. HS 127*
Notts v Yorks, Worksop, 1982.
BBT 3–68 E v A, Sydney, 1982/83. BB
10–175 International XI v W Indian XI,
Kingston, 1982/83.
RECORDS BB (above) first all-ten return in
fc cricket in W Indies.

HEMSLEY, Edward John Orton
————RHB, RM————

Born Norton, Stoke on Trent, Staffordshire, 1 Sept 1943. Educ Bridgnorth
GS. Debut 1963.
WORCESTERSHIRE (243) 1963–82. Cap
1969. Benefit 1982.
HS 176* Worcs v Lancs, Worcester,
1977.

BB 3–5 Worcs v Warwicks, Worcester,
1971.
1000 RUNS (1) 1168 @ 38.93 in 1978.
RECORDS Added 227 for 6th wkt with D.
N. Patel, Worcs v Oxford U, The Parks,
1976, county record.
Shropshire 1961. Club: Stourbridge.
Soccer: Shrewsbury Town, Sheffield
United, Doncaster Rovers.

HEMSLEY, Philip David
————RHB, RM————

Born Buxted, Sussex, 23 Nov 1959.
Educ Lewes Priory, Clare C, Cam-
bridge. Debut 1980.
CAMBRIDGE UNIVERSITY (3) 1980–81.
HS 12* Cambridge U v Surrey,
Fenner's, 1980.

HENDERSON, Andrew Arthur
————RHB, RM————

Born Chadwell Heath, Essex, 14 July
1941. Educ Rutherford GS, Newcastle
upon Tyne. Debut 1972.
SUSSEX (1) 1972.
HS 9 Sussex v Glos, Gloucester, 1972.
BB 3–65 same match.

HENDERSON, Andrew William
————RHB, RM————

Born Selkirk, Scotland, 23 Jan 1922.
Educ Selkirk HS; Edinburgh U. Debut
1953.
SCOTLAND (1) 1953.
HS 2 Scotland v Ireland, Belfast, 1953.
Club: Selkirk.

HENDERSON, Derek
————RHB, RM————

Born Battle, nr Hastings, Sussex, 9 Mar
1926. Educ St Edward's Oxford; Trinity C, Oxford. Debut 1949.
OXFORD UNIVERSITY (11) 1949–50 (Blue
1950).
FREE FORESTERS (5) 1950–54.
HS 21* Oxford U v Derbys, The Parks,
1950.
BB 4–39 Oxford U v Surrey, Guildford,
1950.
Son S. P. Henderson (Worcs, Glam).

HENDERSON, James Douglas
————LHB, LM————

Born Kelso, Scotland, 13 Oct 1918.
Educ Forfar Academy; St Andrew's U.
Debut 1946.
SCOTLAND (14) 1946–56.
HS 121 Scotland v Ireland, Paisley, 1954.

BB 5–27 Scotland v Ireland, Paisley, 1952.
Club: Forfarshire.

HENDERSON, Stephen Peter
————————LHB, RM————————

Born Oxford, 24 Sept 1958. Educ Downside; Durham U; Magdalene C, Cambridge. Debut 1977.
WORCESTERSHIRE (24) 1977–81.
CAMBRIDGE UNIVERSITY (19) 1982–83 (Blue 1982–83).
GLAMORGAN (20) 1983–.
HS 209* Cambridge U v M'sex, Fenner's, 1982 (maiden century).
BB 2–48 Glam v Surrey, Swansea, 1983.
Club: Dudley. Father D. Henderson (Oxford U).

HENDRICK, Michael
————————RHB, RFM————————

Born Darley Dale, Derbys, 22 Oct 1948. Debut 1969. *Wisden* 1978.
DERBYSHIRE (167) 1969–81. Cap 1972. Benefit (£36,050) 1980.
NOTTINGHAMSHIRE (34) 1982–84.
ENGLAND (30) 1974–81. A 1977 (3), 1980 (1), 1981 (2), 1980 (2); WI 1976 (2), NZ 1978 (2); I 1974 (3), 1979 (4); P 1974 (2).
A 1974/75 (2), 1978/79 (5); NZ 1974/ 75 (1), 1977/78 (1).
OTHER TOURS MCC to W Indies 1973/74. D. H. Robins' XI to S Africa 1975/76. England to Pakistan 1977/78. England to Australia 1979/80.
HST 15 E v A, Oval, 1977. HS 46 Derbys v Essex, Chelmsford, 1973.
BBT 4–28 E v I, Edgbaston, 1974. BB 8–45 Derbys v Warwicks, Chesterfield, 1973.
Barred from Test cricket for three years for touring S Africa in 1981/82 (SAB England XI). CWC Young Cricketer of 1973.

HENDRIKS, John Leslie
————————RHB, WK————————

Born Kingston, Jamaica, 21 Dec 1933. Educ Wolmer's S, Kingston. Debut 1953/54.
W INDIES DOMESTIC Jamaica 1953/ 54–68/69.
WEST INDIES (20) 1961/62–69. A 1964/65 (4); I 1961/62 (1). E 1966 (3), 1969 (1); A 1968/69 (5); NZ 1968/69 (3); I 1966/67 (3).
OTHER TOURS W Indies to India and Pakistan 1958/59. W Indies to Australia 1960/61.
HST 64 WI v I, Port of Spain, 1961/62. HS 82 W Indians v Combined XI, Hobart, 1960/61.

Did not concede a bye during total of 619, WI v A, Sydney, 1968/69.
Manager W Indies to England 1984.

HENDY, A. S. (Bill)
————————LHB, SLA————————

Born circa 1913. Died circa 1965. Debut 1951.
CANADA (4) 1951–54.
TOUR Canada to England 1954.
HS 22 Canadians v Yorks, Scarborough, 1954.
BB 4–73 Canada v MCC, Toronto, 1951.
Club: Burrard, Vancouver. British Columbia 1954 (capt).

HENLEY-WELCH, David Francis
————————RHB, RFM————————

Born Melton, Suffolk, 21 July 1923. Educ Harrow; Trinity C, Oxford. Debut 1946.
OXFORD UNIVERSITY (16) 1946–48 (Blue 1947).
MINOR COUNTIES (1) 1949.
HS 58 Oxford U v Sussex, Chichester, 1947.
BB 3–28 Oxford U v Free Foresters, The Parks, 1947.
Suffolk 1946–57. War-time Blue 1942. Changed name from Henley in 1948.

HENRY, Denis Philip
————————RHB, OB————————

Born Stamford Hill, London, 7 July 1907. Educ Colchester RGS. Debut 1948.
FREE FORESTERS (1) 1948.
HS 1 Free Foresters v Oxford U, The Parks, 1948.
Clubs: Bank of England, Incognito, Royal Navy, XL Club. Free Foresters to BAOR 1952.

HENWOOD, Pelham Peter
————————RHB, SLA————————

Born Durban, S Africa, 22 May 1946. Educ Maritzburg C; Natal U. Debut 1965/66.
S AFRICA DOMESTIC Orange Free State 1965/66, South African Universities 1966/67, Natal 1966/67–79/80.
TOUR S African Universities to England 1967.
HS 46 Natal B v Rhodesia, Bulawayo, 1970/71.
BB 7–34 Natal v Transvaal, Durban, 1973/74.

HERBERT, Reuben
————————RHB, OB————————

Born Cape Town, S Africa, 1 Dec 1957. Educ Barnstaple CS, Basildon. Debut 1976.
ESSEX (6) 1976–80.
HS 14* Essex v Lancs, Blackpool, 1980.
BB 3–64 same match.

HERKES, Robert
————————RHB, RFM————————

Born Lincoln, 30 June 1957. Educ Lincoln Christ's Hospital GS. Debut 1978.
MIDDLESEX (3) 1978–79.
No runs.
BB 6–60 M'sex v Worcs, Lord's, 1979.
Lincolnshire 1977. Club: Hartsholme.

HERMAN, Oswald William
————————RHB, RMF————————

Born Cowley, Oxford, 18 Sept 1907. Debut 1929. *P.*
HAMPSHIRE (321) 1929–48. Cap. Joint benefit (with four other players) (£1470) 1948–50.
HS 92 Hants v Leics, Leicester, 1948.
BB 8–49 Hants v Yorks, Bournemouth, 1930.
100 WKTS (5) 142 @ 22.07 in 1937.
Players v Gentlemen (1) 1932. Fc umpire 1963–71. Wiltshire 1950–51. Club: Rochdale. Son R. S. Herman (M'sex, Hants).

HERMAN, Robert Stephen
————————RHB, RFM————————

Born Southampton, 30 Nov 1946. Debut 1965.
MIDDLESEX (92) 1965–71. Cap 1969.
HAMPSHIRE (89) 1972–77. Cap 1972.
S AFRICA DOMESTIC Border 1972/73, Griqualand West 1974/75.
HS 56 Hants v Worcs, Portsmouth, 1972.
BB 8–42 Hants v Warwicks, Portsmouth, 1972.
Fc umpire 1980–82. Dorset 1978–79. Father O. W. Herman (Hants).

HERMISTON, William
————————RHB, RFM————————

Born Makerston, Scotland, 4 Feb 1913. Educ Leith Academy. Debut 1949.
SCOTLAND (2) 1949.
HS 21 Scotland v N Zealanders, Glasgow, 1949.
BB 2–21 Scotland v Ireland, Belfast, 1949.
Club: Leith Franklin.

HERON, Jack Gunner
RHB

Born Salisbury, Rhodesia, 8 Nov 1948. Educ Churchill HS, Bulawayo; Bulawayo Teachers' Training C. Debut 1967/68.
S AFRICA DOMESTIC Rhodesia 1967/68–79/80.
ZIMBABWE 1980/81–. Capt 1978/79.
TOUR Zimbabwe to England 1982.
HS 175 Rhodesia v Transvaal, Salisbury, 1975/76.
Hockey: Rhodesia.

HEROYS, Nicholas
RHB, RMF

Born London, 1 Apr 1937. Educ Tonbridge; Sidney Sussex C, Cambridge. Debut 1960.
CAMBRIDGE UNIVERSITY (1) 1960.
HS 10 Cambridge U v Hants, Fenner's, 1960.
Clubs: Old Tonbridgians, Band of Brothers.

HERTING, Frederick John
RHB, LMF

Born South Ruislip, 25 Feb 1940. Educ Millfield. Debut 1960. P.
SOMERSET (5) 1960.
HS 16* Som v Lancs, Taunton, 1960.
BB 4–85 Som v Glos, Bath, 1960.

HESELTINE, Philip John
RHB, RM/OB

Born Skipton, Yorks, 21 June 1960. Educ Barnsley & District GS; Keble C, Oxford. Debut 1983.
OXFORD UNIVERSITY (6) 1983 (Blue).
HS 40 Oxford U v Worcs, The Parks, 1983.

HETTIARATCHY, Nirmal Dilhan Peter
RHB, WK

Born Colombo, Ceylon, 30 Sept 1951. Educ Royal C, Colombo. Debut 1970/71.
SRI LANKA DOMESTIC Ceylon (Sri Lanka) 1970/71–81/82.
TOUR Sri Lanka to England 1981.
HS 80 Sri Lankans v Northants, Northampton, 1981.
Banned from Sinhalese cricket for 25 yrs for touring S Africa 1982/83 (Arosa Sri Lanka).

HEVER, Norman George
RHB, RFM

Born Marylebone, London, 17 Dec 1924. Debut 1947. P.
MIDDLESEX (9) 1947.
GLAMORGAN (135) 1948–53. Cap 1948.
HS 40 Glam v Leics, Leicester, 1950.
BB 7–55 Glam v Hants, Swansea, 1952.
Clubs: Ferndale, Clydach, Maesteg.
Father H. L. Hever (Kent).

HEWITT, Eric Joseph
RHB, LBG

Born Erdington, Birmingham, 19 Dec 1935. Educ Coleshill GS. Debut 1954.
WARWICKSHIRE (1) 1954.
COMBINED SERVICES (1) 1957.
HS 40 Warwicks v Oxford U, Edgbaston, 1954.
Clubs: Aston Unity, Kings Heath, Solihull. Former professional motor-racing driver.

HEWITT, Francis Stanley Arnot
RHB, RFM/OB

Born Belfast, Ireland, 13 Mar 1936. Educ Royal Belfast Academy Institute. Debut 1966.
IRELAND (1) 1966.
HS 36 Ireland v Scotland, Edinburgh, 1966.
Club: NICC.

HEWITT, Simon Mark
RHB, RM

Born Radcliffe, Lancs, 30 July 1961. Educ Bradford GS; Wadham C, Oxford. Debut 1984.
OXFORD UNIVERSITY (4) 1984.
HS 22 Oxford U v Som, The Parks, 1984.
Brother S. G. P. Hewitt (Cambridge U).

HEWITT, Steven Guy Paul
RHB, WK

Born Radcliffe, Lancs, 6 Apr 1963. Educ Bradford GS; Peterhouse C, Cambridge. Debut 1983.
CAMBRIDGE UNIVERSITY (9) 1983–84 (Blue 1983).
HS 14* Cambridge U v Hants, Fenner's, 1984.
Brother S. M. Hewitt (Oxford U).

HEYS, William
RHB, WK

Born Oswaldtwistle, Lancs, 19 Feb 1931. Debut 1957. P.

LANCASHIRE (5) 1957.
HS 46 Lancs v W Indians, Old Trafford, 1957.

HICHENS, Andrew Lionel
RHB, RFM

Born Westminster, London, 24 Aug 1936. Educ Winchester; Trinity C, Oxford. Debut 1957.
OXFORD UNIVERSITY (3) 1957–59.
HS 4 Oxford U v Essex, The Parks, 1959.
BB 4–97 same match.
Oxfordshire 1957–64. Member I Zingari.

HICK, Graeme Ashley
RHB, OB

Born Salisbury, Rhodesia, 23 May 1966. Educ Prince Edward HS, Salisbury. Debut 1983/84.
ZIMBABWE 1983/84.
WORCESTERSHIRE (1) 1984.
TOUR Zimbabwe to Sri Lanka 1983/84.
HS 82* Worcs v Surrey, Oval, 1984 (county debut).
BB 3–39 Zimbabweans v Board President's XI, Moratuwa, 1983/84.
Club: Kidderminster.

HICKINBOTTOM, Geoffrey Alfred
RHB, WK

Born Leicester, 15 Nov 1932. Debut 1959. P.
LEICESTERSHIRE (5) 1959.
HS 4* Leics v Hants, Southampton, 1959.

HICKMAN, Malcolm Francis
RHB

Born Market Harborough, 30 June 1936. Debut 1954. P.
LEICESTERSHIRE (12) 1954–57.
HS 40 Leics v Kent, Leicester, 1954.
Club: Market Harborough.

HIGGINSON, Thomas William
RHB, RM

Born Esher, Surrey, 6 Nov 1936. Educ Acton County GS. Debut 1960. P.
MIDDLESEX (3) 1960.
L. C. STEVENS' XI (1) 1960.
HS 20 L. C. Stevens' XI v Cambridge U, Eastbourne, 1960.
Surrey 2nd XI capt 1972–73. Minor counties umpire 1970–71, 1977–78. XL Club. Former coach Dulwich C (to 1971).

HIGGS, James Donald
———RHB, LBG———

Born Kyabram, Victoria, Australia, 11 July 1950. Debut 1970/71.
AUSTRALIA DOMESTIC Victoria (83) 1970/71–82/83.
AUSTRALIA (22) 1977/78–80/81. E 1978/79 (5), 1979/80 (1); WI 1979/80 (1); NZ 1980/81 (3); I 1980/81 (3). *WI 1977/78 (4); I 1979/80 (6)*.
OTHER TOUR Australians to England 1975.
HST 16 A v E, Adelaide, 1978/79. HS 21 Victoria v W Australia, Perth, 1974/75.
BBT 7-143 A v I, Madras, 1979/80. BB 8-66 Victoria v W Australia, Melbourne, 1974/75.
Failed to score a run in eight fc matches during tour of England in 1975. Has taken more wkts than he has scored runs.
Victoria State selector 1983/84–. Clubs: University, Richmond.

HIGGS, Kenneth
———LHB, RFM/RM———

Born Kidsgrove, Staffordshire, 14 Jan 1937. Educ Tunstall Sec Modern S. Debut 1958. *P. Wisden 1968.*
LANCASHIRE (306) 1958–69. Cap 1959. Benefit (£8390) 1968.
LEICESTERSHIRE (165) 1972–82. Cap 1972. Capt 1979.
ENGLAND (15) 1965–68. A 1968 (1); WI 1966 (5); SA 1965 (1); I 1967 (1); P 1967 (3). *A 1965/66 (1); NZ 1965/66 (3)*.
OTHER TOUR MCC to W Indies 1967/68.
HST 63 E v WI, Oval, 1966. HS 98 Leics v Northants, Leicester, 1977.
BBT 6-91 E v WI, Lord's, 1966. BB 7-19 Lancs v Leics, Old Trafford, 1965.
100 WKTS (5) 132 @ 19.42 in 1960.
RECORDS In HST (above) added 128 for 10th wkt with J. A. Snow, England Test record in England. In HS above added 228 for 10th wkt with R. Illingworth, county record.
Leics coach. Staffordshire 1957. Clubs: Meakins, Rishton.

HIGHTON, Edward Frederick William
———RHB, RFM———

Born Formby, Lancs, 29 Aug 1924. Educ King Edward VI S, Southport. Debut 1950. *P.*
MINOR COUNTIES (1) 1950.
LANCASHIRE (1) 1951.
HS 26 Minor Counties v MCC, Lord's, 1950.
BB 4-87 same match.
Lancs 2nd XI 1949–52. Clubs: Meakins, Formby.

HIGNELL, Alastair James
———RHB, LB———

Born Cambridge, 4 Sept 1955. Educ Denstone C; Fitzwilliam C, Cambridge. Debut 1974.
GLOUCESTERSHIRE (137) 1974–83. Cap 1977.
CAMBRIDGE UNIVERSITY (33) 1975–78 (Blue 1975–78). Capt 1977–78.
HS 149* Glos v Northants, Bristol, 1979.
BB 2-13 Glos v Sri Lankans, Bristol, 1981.
Rugby: Bristol, Cambridge U, England (14 caps). Father A. F. Hignell (Glos).

HIGNELL, Antony Francis
———RHB, RM———

Born Kroonstad, Orange Free State, S Africa, 6 July 1928. Educ Denstone; Caius C, Cambridge. Debut 1947.
GLOUCESTERSHIRE (1) 1947.
HS 7 Glos v Cambridge U, Fenner's, 1947.
Son A. J. Hignell (Cambridge U, Glos).

HIGSON, Thomas Atkinson (Junior)
———LHB, RM———

Born Whaley Bridge, Derbys, 25 Mar 1911. Educ Cheltenham C; Jesus C, Cambridge. Debut 1932.
DERBYSHIRE (6) 1932–35.
LANCASHIRE (20) 1936–46.
HS 51 Derbys v Essex, Leyton, 1933.
Lancs president 1977–78. XL Club. Father T. A. Higson senior (Lancs, Derbys); brother P. Higson (Lancs).

HILL, Alan
———RHB, OB———

Born Buxworth, Derbys, 29 June 1950. Educ New Mills GS; Chester C of Educ. Debut 1972.
DERBYSHIRE (219) 1972–. Cap 1976.
S AFRICA DOMESTIC Orange Free State 1976/77.
HS 160* Derbys v Warwicks, Coventry, 1976.
BB 3-5 OFS v N Transvaal, Pretoria, 1976/77.
1000 RUNS (4) 1352 @ 32.98 in 1984.

HILL, Eric
———RHB———

Born Taunton, Som, 9 July 1923. Educ Taunton S. Debut 1947. *P.*
SOMERSET (72) 1947–51. Cap 1949.
HS 85 Som v Northants, Kettering, 1948.
Journalist in West Country.

HILL, Geoffrey Harry
———LHB, SLA———

Born Halesowen, Worcs, 17 Sept 1934. Educ Handsworth Technical C. Debut 1957. *P.*
COMBINED SERVICES (1) 1957.
WARWICKSHIRE (41) 1958–60.
HS 23 Warwicks v Worcs, Edgbaston, 1958.
BB 8-70 Warwicks v Glos, Cheltenham, 1958.
Clubs: King's Heath, Stourbridge, Dudley. Rugby: Birmingham.

HILL, Gerald
———RHB, OB———

Born Brook, Hants, 15 Apr 1913. Debut 1932. *P.*
HAMPSHIRE (371) 1932–54. Cap 1935. Joint benefit (with four others) (£1470) 1948–50.
HS 161 Hants v Sussex, Portsmouth, 1937 (added 235 for 5th wkt with D. F. Walker, county record).
BB 8-62 (14-146 match) Hants v Kent, Tonbridge, 1935.
1000 RUNS (2) 1051 @ 22.36 in 1946.

HILL, John Charles
———RHB, LBG———

Born Murrumbeena, Victoria, Australia, 25 June 1923. Died Caulfield, Victoria, Australia, 11 Aug 1974. Debut 1945/46.
AUSTRALIA DOMESTIC Victoria (38) 1945/46–55/56.
AUSTRALIA (3) 1953–54/55. *E 1953 (2); WI 1954/55 (1)*.
HST 8* A v E, Old Trafford, 1953. HS 51* Australians v Kent, Canterbury, 1953.
BBT 3-35 A v E, Trent Bridge, 1953. BB 7-51 Victoria v S Australia, Adelaide, 1952/53.
Club: St Kilda.

HILL, John William
———RHB, OB———

Born Coleraine, Co Londonderry, Ireland, 10 June 1912. Died Dublin, Ireland, 17 Jan 1984. Debut 1946.
IRELAND (7) 1946–51.
HS 18* Ireland v MCC, Dublin, 1948.
BB 3-16 Ireland v Yorks, Harrogate, 1947.
Clubs: Clontarf, NICC.

HILL, Leonard Winston
———RHB, occ WK———

Born Caerleon-on-Usk, Monmouthshire, Wales, 14 Apr 1942. Debut 1964.

GLAMORGAN (76) 1964–76. Cap 1974.
HS 96* Glam v Glos, Swansea, 1974.
Soccer: Newport County, Swansea.

HILL, Maurice
————RHB, LB————

Born Scunthorpe, Lincolnshire, 14 Sept
1935. Debut 1953. *P*.
NOTTINGHAMSHIRE (237) 1953–65. Cap
1961.
DERBYSHIRE (32) 1966–67.
SOMERSET (22) 1970–71.
HS 137* Notts v Lancs, Worksop, 1961.
BB 2–60 Notts v W Indians, Trent
Bridge, 1957.
1000 RUNS (6) 1416 @ 27.76 in 1964.
Groundsman after retirement. Club:
Marske.

HILL, Michael John
————LHB, WK————

Born Harwell, Berkshire, 1 July 1951.
Educ Abingdon S. Debut 1973.
HAMPSHIRE (6) 1973–76.
HS 27* Hants v Sussex, Basingstoke,
1976.

HILL, Norman Wilfred
————LHB————

Born Holbeck, Notts, 22 Aug 1935.
Debut 1953. *P*.
NOTTINGHAMSHIRE (280) 1953–68. Cap
1959. Capt 1966–67. Testimonial 1968.
HS 201* Notts v Sussex, Shireoaks,
Worksop, 1961.
1000 RUNS (8) 2239 @ 39.98 in 1961.
Conceded 50 runs in two overs (18 and
32), Notts v Leics, Trent Bridge, 1965,
bowling for a declaration; C. C. Inman's
32 in the second over been bettered by
only two other batsmen in six-ball overs
that included no no-balls.
Players v Gentlemen (1) 1961.

HILL, Robert Gribben
————LHB————

Born Kilmarnock, Scotland, 15 July
1938. Educ Kilmarnock Academy.
Debut 1963.
SCOTLAND (6) 1963–69.
HS 50 Scotland v Warwicks, Edgbaston,
1964.
Club: Kilmarnock.

HILL, Rupert Knight
————RHB, RM————

Born Kingston, Jamaica, 14 Aug 1954.
Debut 1975.

GLAMORGAN (1) 1975.
Did not bat.

HILL, William *Aubrey*
————RHB————

Born Carmarthen, Wales, 27 Apr 1910.
Educ Edgewick S, Coventry. Debut
1929. *P from 1931*.
WARWICKSHIRE (169) 1929–48. Cap
1933.
HS 147* Warwicks v Northants, Edgbas-
ton, 1936.
1000 RUNS (2) 1197 @ 24.42 in 1947.
Oxford U coach in 1960s. Club:
Foleshill Albion.

HILLARY, Anthony Aylmer
————RHB, OB————

Born Shenfield, Essex, 28 Aug 1926.
Educ Brentwood S; Jesus C, Cam-
bridge. Debut 1951.
CAMBRIDGE UNIVERSITY (1) 1951.
HS 49 Cambridge U v Sussex, Fenner's,
1951.
Berkshire 1955–62.

HILLER, Robert
————LHB, RFM————

Born Woking, Surrey, 14 Oct 1942.
Educ Bec S; St Edmund Hall, Oxford.
Debut 1966.
OXFORD UNIVERSITY (8) 1966 (Blue).
HS 64 Oxford U v Essex, The Parks,
1966.
BB 4–53 Oxford U v Leics, The Parks,
1966.
Rugby: Oxford U, Harlequins, England
(19; seven as capt).

HILLS, Richard William
————RHB, RM————

Born Borough Green, Kent, 8 Jan 1951.
Educ Holmdale Sec Modern. Debut
1973.
KENT (85) 1973–80. Cap 1977.
HS 45 Kent v Hants, Canterbury, 1975.
BB 6–64 Kent v Glos, Folkestone, 1978.

HILL-WOOD, Peter Denis
————RHB, RM————

Born Kensington, London, 25 Feb
1936. Educ Eton. Debut 1960.
FREE FORESTERS (1) 1960.
HS 30 Free Foresters v Cambridge U,
Fenner's, 1960.
Clubs: Free Foresters, MCC committee
1970–71. Soccer: current Arsenal chair-
man. Father D. J. C. H. Hill-Wood;

uncles Sir B. S. H. Hill-Wood, C. K. H.
Hill-Wood, Sir W. W. H. Hill-Wood;
grandfather Sir S. H. Wood (all
Derbys).

HILTON, Colin
————RHB, RF————

Born Atherton, Lancs, 26 Sept 1937.
Debut 1957. *P*.
LANCASHIRE (91) 1957–63. Cap 1962.
ESSEX (24) 1964.
HS 36 Lancs v Som, Glastonbury, 1962.
BB 6–38 Lancs v Notts, Liverpool, 1962.
Took 94 wkts @ 26.62 in 1962.
Clubs: Ribblesdale Wanderers, Old-
ham, Daisy Hill.

HILTON, Jim
————RHB, OB————

Born Chadderton, Lancs, 29 Dec 1930.
Debut 1952. *P*.
LANCASHIRE (8) 1952–53.
SOMERSET (71) 1954–57.
HS 61* Som v Notts, Taunton, 1955.
BB 7–98 Som v Warwicks, Bath, 1954.
Clubs: Werneth, Kelbourne. Brother
M. J. Hilton (Lancs, England).

HILTON, Malcolm Jameson
————RHB, SLA————

Born Chadderton, Lancs, 2 Aug 1928.
Debut 1946. *P*.
LANCASHIRE (241) 1946–61. Cap 1950.
Joint benefit (with R. Tattersall)
(£11,655) 1960.
ENGLAND (4) 1950–51/52. SA 1951 (1);
WI 1950 (1). *I 1951/52 (2)*.
HST 15 E v I, Madras, 1951/52. HS 100*
Lancs v Northants, Northampton,
1955.
BBT 5–61 (9–93 match) E v I, Kanpur,
1951/52. BB 8–19 Lancs v N Zealanders,
Old Trafford, 1958. 14–88 match Lancs
v Som, Weston-super-Mare, 1956.
100 WKTS (4) 158 @ 13.96 in 1956.
Players v Gentlemen (1) 1951. Took 103
wkts for Lancs 2nd XI in 1949. Clubs:
Werneth, Burnley, Radcliffe, Marsden.
Brother J. Hilton (Lancs, Som).

HINDLEKAR, Dattaram Dharmaji
————RHB, WK————

Born Bombay, India, 1 Jan 1909. Died
Bombay, 31 Mar 1949. Debut 1934/35.
INDIA DOMESTIC Bombay 1934/35–46/
47, Hindus (Bombay) 1935/36–45/46.
INDIA (4) 1936–46. *E 1936 (1)*, *1946
(3)*.
HST 26 I v E, Lord's, 1936. HS 135 Hindus
v Mohammedans, Bombay, 1936/37.
Nephew V.L. Manjrekar (India).

HINKS, Simon Graham
—————LHB, RM—————

Born Northfleet, Kent, 12 Oct 1960.
Educ St George's S, Gravesend. Debut
1982.
KENT (16) 1982–.
HS 87 Kent v Glam, Cardiff, 1983.
Scored 1165 runs @ 52.95 for Kent in
2nd XI championship in 1982, county
record.

HIRST, Christopher Halliwell
—————RHB, OB—————

Born Bradford, Yorks, 27 May 1947.
Educ Merchant Taylors', Northwood;
Trinity Hall, Cambridge. Debut 1967.
CAMBRIDGE UNIVERSITY (1) 1967.
HS 6★ Cambridge U v M'sex, Fenner's,
1967.
Chile v N Zealand 1970. Buckingham-
shire 1967–68. Clubs: Lightcliffe,
Chorleywood, Free Foresters. Master-
in-charge of cricket Radley S.

HITCHCOCK, Raymond Edward
—————LHB, LB—————

Born Christchurch, N Zealand, 28 Nov
1929. Educ West Christchurch HS.
Debut 1947/48. P except 1957–59.
N ZEALAND DOMESTIC Canterbury (1)
1947/48.
WARWICKSHIRE (319) 1949–64. Cap
1951. Benefit (£6410) 1963.
HS 153★ Warwicks v Derbys, Chesterfield, 1962.
BB 7–76 Warwicks v Scotland, Edgbaston, 1959.
1000 RUNS (5) 1840 @ 34.07 in 1961.
Chairman Warwicks cricket committee
1980–84. Club: Knowle and Dorridge.
Rugby: North Midlands, Nuneaton.

HOADLEY, Simon Peter
—————RHB, OB—————

Born Eridge, Sussex, 16 Aug 1956.
Educ Uckfield S. Debut 1978.
SUSSEX (12) 1978–79.
HS 112 Sussex v Glam, Swansea, 1978.
Brother S. J. Hoadley (Sussex).

HOADLEY, Stephen John
—————RHB, OB—————

Born Pembury, Kent, 7 July 1955. Educ
Uckfield S. Debut 1975.
SUSSEX (7) 1975–76.
HS 58 Sussex v Hants, Southampton,
1975.
Brother S. P. Hoadley (Sussex).

HOBBS, John Anthony David
—————RHB—————

Born Liverpool, 30 Nov 1935. Educ
Liverpool C; St Peters Hall, Oxford.
Debut 1956.
OXFORD UNIVERSITY (18) 1956–58 (Blue
1957).
HS 95 Oxford U v M'sex, The Parks,
1957.
Club: Northern (Liverpool). Hockey:
Lancashire.

HOBBS, Robin Nicholas Stuart
—————RHB, LBG—————

Born Chippenham, Wiltshire, 8 May
1942. Educ Raines Foundation S, Step-
ney, London. Debut 1961. P.
ESSEX (325) 1961–75. Cap 1964. Benefit
(£13,500) 1974.
GLAMORGAN (41) 1979–81. Cap 1979.
Capt 1979.
ENGLAND (7) 1967–71. I 1967 (3); P 1967
(1), 1971 (1). WI 1967/68 (1); P 1968/
69 (1).
OTHER TOURS Cavaliers to Jamaica 1963/
64. MCC to E Africa 1963/64. MCC to
S Africa 1964/65. MCC Under-25 XI to
Pakistan 1966/67. Duke of Norfolk's XI
to W Indies 1969/70. Commonwealth
XI to Pakistan 1970/71. D. H. Robins'
XI to S Africa 1972/73. World XI to
Pakistan 1973/74.
HST 15★ E v I, Edgbaston, 1967. HS 100
Essex v Glam, Ilford, 1968 and 100
Essex v Australians, Chelmsford, 1975.
BBT 3–25 E v I, Edgbaston, 1967. BB
8–63 (13–164 match) Essex v Glam,
Swansea, 1966.
100 WKTS (2) 102 @ 21.40 in 1970.
RECORDS In HS in 1975 above reached
century in 44 mins, fastest-ever century
for Essex and fastest-ever against any
touring team.
Suffolk 1976–78, 1982. Club: Duport.

HOBSON, Barry Sinton
—————RHB, RM—————

Born Dunmurry, Co Antrim, N Ireland,
22 Nov 1925. Educ Taunton; St
Catharine's C, Cambridge. Debut 1946.
CAMBRIDGE UNIVERSITY (7) 1946 (Blue).
HS 16★ Cambridge U v Som, Bath, 1946.
BB 3–60 Cambridge U v Lancs,
Fenner's, 1946.
Wiltshire 1950–53.

HODGE, Robert Stevenson
—————RHB, RFM—————

Born Greenock, Scotland, 5 Nov 1914.
Educ Greenock Academy. Debut 1938.
SCOTLAND (9) 1938–51.

UNDER-33 (1) 1945.
HS 38 Scotland v Ireland, Greenock,
1946.
BB 5–82 Under-33 v Over-33, Lord's,
1945.
Clubs: Greenock, Dunfermline, Ealing.

HODGKINS, John Seymour
—————RHB, RFM—————

Born West Bridgford, Notts, 2 Jan 1916.
Educ Nottingham HS. Debut 1938.
NOTTINGHAMSHIRE (3) 1938–51.
HS 44 Notts v Surrey, Trent Bridge,
1946.
Club: Notts Forest.

HODGKINSON, Gilbert Frank
—————RHB—————

Born Derby, 19 Feb 1913. Educ Derby
S. Debut 1935.
DERBYSHIRE (19) 1935–46. Capt 1946.
HS 44 Derbys v S Africans, Ilkeston,
1935.
Erroneously reported dead during
1939–45 war.

HODGSON, Alan
—————LHB, RFM—————

Born Moorside, Co Durham, 27 Oct
1951. Educ Annfield Plain GS. Debut
1970.
NORTHAMPTONSHIRE (99) 1970–79. Cap
1976. Benefit 1980.
HS 41 Northants v N Zealanders, Northampton, 1973 and 41★ v Glos, Northampton, 1976.
BB 5–30 Northants v Oxford U, The
Parks, 1976.
Clubs: Dudley, Walsall.

HODGSON, Craig Andrew Thornton
—————RHB—————

Born East London, S Africa, 13 July
1955. Debut 1979/80.
S AFRICA DOMESTIC Rhodesia B 1979/80.
ZIMBABWE 1980/81–82/83.
TOUR Zimbabwe to England 1982.
HS 87 Zimbabwe v PIA, Harare, 1981/82.

HODGSON, Geoffrey
—————RHB, WK—————

Born Huddersfield, Yorks, 24 July 1938.
Debut 1964.
YORKSHIRE (1) 1964.
LANCASHIRE (1) 1965.
HS 4 Yorks v Oxford U, The Parks,
1964.
Club: Spen Victoria.

HODGSON, Kenneth Ian
————RHB, RM————

Born Port Elizabeth, S Africa, 24 Feb 1960. Educ Oundle; Downing C, Cambridge. Debut 1981.
CAMBRIDGE UNIVERSITY (17) 1981–82 (Blue 1981–82).
HS 50 Cambridge U v Lancs, Fenner's, 1982.
BB 8–68 Cambridge U v Glam, Fenner's, 1982.
Buckinghamshire 1980–. Club: Gerrards Cross. Squash: half-Blue.

HODGSON, Philip
————RHB, RFM————

Born Todmorden, Yorks, 21 Sept 1935. Educ Woodhouse GS. Debut 1954. P.
YORKSHIRE (13) 1954–56.
COMBINED SERVICES (4) 1956–57.
HS 26 Yorks v Glam, Cardiff, 1956.
BB 5–41 Yorks v Sussex, Hove, 1954.
Clubs: Sheffield United, Salts, Pudsey St Laurence, XL Club.

HODSON, Richard *Philip*
————RHB, RM/OB————

Born Wakefield, Yorks, 26 Apr 1951. Educ Queen Elizabeth GS, Wakefield; Downing C, Cambridge. Debut 1971.
CAMBRIDGE UNIVERSITY (18) 1971–73 (Blue 1972–73).
HS 111 Cambridge U v Kent, Fenner's, 1973.
BB 4–54 Cambridge U v Glam, Fenner's, 1973.

HOFMEYR, Murray Bernard
————RHB————

Born Pretoria, S Africa, 9 Dec 1925. Educ Pretoria HS; Rhodes U, Grahamstown; Worcester C, Oxford. Debut 1949.
OXFORD UNIVERSITY (35) 1949–51 (Blue 1949–51). Capt 1951.
S AFRICA DOMESTIC North-East Transvaal (9) 1951/52–53/54.
HS 161 Oxford U v Glos, The Parks, 1950.
1000 RUNS (1) 1063 @ 55.94 in 1950.
Carried bat through inns in Varsity match, in 1949, only second such instance in the series.
Rugby: Blue, England (3).

HOGAN, Charles *Ronald*
————RHB, RFM————

Born Paisley, Scotland, 10 Jan 1939. Educ St Minus Academy. Debut 1962.
SCOTLAND (6) 1962–64.
HS 7 Scotland v Warwicks, Edgbaston, 1964.
BB 6–36 Scotland v Ireland, Londonderry, 1963.
Club: Ferguslie.

HOGAN, Raymond P.
————RHB, RFM————

Born Temora, NSW, Australia, 8 May 1932. Debut 1954. P.
NORTHAMPTONSHIRE (3) 1954–55.
HS 8 Northants v Yorks, Northampton, 1955.
BB 2–16 Northants v Cambridge U, Northampton, 1954.
Clubs: Heywood, Primrose Hill, Oldham. Rugby: Northampton.

HOGG, Rodney Malcolm
————RHB, RF————

Born Thornbury, Victoria, Australia, 5 Mar 1951. Debut 1975/76.
AUSTRALIA DOMESTIC South Australia (39) 1975/76–.
AUSTRALIA (34) 1978/79–83/84. E 1978/79 (6), 1982/83 (3); WI 1979/80 (2); NZ 1980/81 (2); I 1980/81 (2); P 1978/79 (2), 1983/84 (4). E 1981 (2); WI 1983/84 (4); I 1979/80 (6); SL 1982/83 (1).
OTHER TOUR Australia to Sri Lanka 1980/81.
HST 52 A v WI, Georgetown, 1983/84.
HS as above.
BBT 6–74 A v E, Brisbane, 1978/79. BB 7–53 (12–104 match) S Australia v Queensland, Adelaide, 1982/83.
RECORDS 41 wkts @ 12.85 in 6 Tests of debut series, A v E, 1978/79, record for Australia in Australia and at time most wkts in a debut series.
Club: Woodville (S Australia).

HOGG, Vincent Richard
————RHB, RFM————

Born Salisbury, Rhodesia, 3 July 1952. Educ Allan Wilson HS, Salisbury. Debut 1971/72.
S AFRICA DOMESTIC Rhodesia B/Rhodesia 1971/72–79/80.
ZIMBABWE 1980/81–.
TOUR Zimbabwe to England 1982.
HS 30 Rhodesia B v Griqualand West, Bulawayo, 1979/80.
BB 6–26 Zimbabwe v Sri Lanka, Harare, 1982/83.
RECORDS Batted 87 mins without scoring, Rhodesia B v Natal B, Pietermaritzburg, 1979/80: longest scoreless inns in fc cricket.

HOGG, William
————RHB, RFM————

Born Ulverston, Cumbria, 12 July 1955. Educ Ulverston CS. Debut 1976.
LANCASHIRE (44) 1976–80.
WARWICKSHIRE (50) 1981–83.
HS 31 Warwicks v Hants, Edgbaston, 1981.
BB 7–84 Lancs v Warwicks, Old Trafford, 1978.
Clubs: Milnrow, Preston. Father-in-law S. Ramadhin (W Indies).

HOLDER, John Wakefield
————RHB, RFM————

Born St George, Barbados, 19 Mar 1945. Educ Combermere S, Barbados. Debut 1968.
HAMPSHIRE (47) 1968–72.
HS 33 Hants v Sussex, Hove, 1971.
BB 7–79 Hants v Glos, Gloucester, 1972.
Fc umpire 1983–. Clubs: Rawtenstall, Royton.

HOLDER, Vanburn Alonzo
————RHB, RFM————

Born St Michael, Barbados, 8 Oct 1945. Debut 1966/67.
W INDIES DOMESTIC Barbados 1966/67–77/78.
WORCESTERSHIRE (181) 1968–80. Cap 1970. Benefit 1979.
WEST INDIES (40) 1969–78/79. E 1973/74 (1); A 1972/73 (3), 1977/78 (3); NZ 1971/72 (4); I 1970/71 (3), 1975/76 (1); P 1976/77 (1). E 1969 (3), 1973 (2), 1976 (4); A 1975/76 (3); I 1974/75 (4), 1978/79 (6); P 1974/75 (2).
OTHER TOUR World XI to Pakistan 1973/74 (relief matches).
HST 42 WI v NZ, Port of Spain, 1971/72.
HS 122 Barbados v Trinidad, Bridgetown, 1973/74.
BBT 6–28 WI v A, Port of Spain, 1977/78. BB 7–40 Worcs v Glam, Cardiff, 1974.
Shropshire 1981. Clubs: Melbourne (W Indies), West Bromwich Dartmouth (England).

HOLDING, Michael Anthony
————RHB, RF————

Born Kingston, Jamaica, 16 Feb 1954. Educ Kingston C. Debut 1972/73. *Wisden* 1977.
W INDIES DOMESTIC Jamaica 1972/73–.
LANCASHIRE (7) 1981.
DERBYSHIRE (6) 1983.
AUSTRALIA DOMESTIC Tasmania (7) 1982/83.
WEST INDIES (49) 1975/76–84. E 1980/81

(4); A 1983/84 (3); I 1975/76 (4), 1982/83 (5). *E 1976 (4), 1980 (5), 1984 (4); A 1975/76 (5), 1979/80 (3), 1981/82 (3); NZ 1979/80 (3); I 1983/84 (6).*
OTHER TOURS W Indies to Pakistan 1980/81. International XI to Pakistan 1981/82.
HST 69 WI v E, Edgbaston, 1984. HS as above.
BBT 8–92 (14–149 match) WI v E, Oval, 1976. BB as above.
RECORD BBT match (above) best for W Indies in Test cricket.
World Series Cricket (Kerry Packer) 1977/78–78/79. Clubs: Melbourne (W Indies), Rishton (England).

HOLDSWORTH, William Edgar Newman
RHB, RFM

Born Armley, Leeds, Yorks, 17 Sept 1928. Debut 1952. *P.*
YORKSHIRE (27) 1952–53.
HS 22* Yorks v Glam, Cardiff, 1953.
BB 6–58 Yorks v Derbys, Scarborough, 1953.
Clubs: Farsley, Bradford, XL Club.

HOLE, Graeme Blake
RHB, OB

Born Concord West, NSW, Australia, 6 Jan 1931. Debut 1949/50.
AUSTRALIA DOMESTIC New South Wales (1) 1949/50, South Australia (51) 1950/51–57/58.
AUSTRALIA (18) 1950/51–54/55. E 1950/51 (1), 1954/55 (3); SA 1952/53 (4); WI 1951/52 (5). *E 1953 (5).*
OTHER TOUR Commonwealth XI to Ceylon 1951/52.
HST 66 A v E, Old Trafford, 1953. HS 226 S Australia v Queensland, Adelaide, 1953/54.
BB 5–109 A. R. Morris's XI v A. L. Hassett's XI, Melbourne, 1953/54.
1000 RUNS (1) 1118 @ 33.87 in 1953.
Club: St George.

HOLFORD, David Anthony Jerome
RHB, LBG

Born St Michael, Barbados, 16 Apr 1940. Educ Harrison C, Barbados; UC of W Indies; McDonald C, Quebec, Canada. Debut 1960/61.
W INDIES DOMESTIC Barbados 1960/61–78/79 (capt 1969/70–78/79), Trinidad 1962/63.
WEST INDIES (24) 1966–76/77. E 1967/68 (4); NZ 1971/72 (5); I 1970/71 (1), 1975/76 (2); P 1976/77 (1). *E 1966 (5); A 1968/69 (2); NZ 1968/69 (3); I 1966/67 (1).*

OTHER TOUR Barbados to England 1969.
HST 105* WI v E, Lord's, 1966. HS 111 Barbados v Indians, Bridgetown, 1970/71.
BBT 5–23 WI v I, Bridgetown, 1975/76.
BB 8–52 W Indians v Cambridge U, Fenner's, 1966.
RECORDS Added 274* for 6th wkt with G. S. Sobers, WI v E, Lord's, 1966, W Indies Test record.
World Series Cricket (Kerry Packer) 1977/78–78/79. Cousin G. S. Sobers (W Indies).

HOLLICK, Alexander Francis George *Philip*
RHB

Born Cairo, Egypt, 13 Feb 1936. Educ Royal Belfast Academy Institute; RS, Armagh. Debut 1957.
IRELAND (1) 1957.
No runs, no wkts.
USA to England 1968. Club: Istonians.

HOLLIDAY, David Charles
RHB, LB

Born Cambridge, 20 Dec 1958. Educ Oundle; Christ's C, Cambridge. Debut 1979.
CAMBRIDGE UNIVERSITY (29) 1979–81 (Blue 1979–81).
HS 76* Cambridge U v Notts, Fenner's, 1980.
BB 2–23 Cambridge U v Sussex, Fenner's, 1979.
Cambridgeshire 1979–. Club: Grasshoppers.

HOLLIES, William *Eric*
RHB, LBG

Born Old Hill, Staffordshire, 5 June 1912. Died Chinley, Derbys, 16 Apr 1981. Debut 1932. *P. Wisden* 1956.
WARWICKSHIRE (476) 1932–57. Cap 1933. Capt 1956. Benefit (£4896) 1948. Testimonial (£1796) 1954.
ENGLAND (13) 1934/35–50. A 1948 (1); SA 1947 (3); WI 1950 (2); NZ 1949 (4). *WI 1934/35 (3).*
OTHER TOUR MCC to Australia 1950/51.
HST 18* E v SA, Trent Bridge, 1947. HS 47 Warwicks v Sussex, Edgbaston, 1954.
BBT 7–50 E v WI, Georgetown, 1934/35.
BB 10–49 Warwicks v Notts, Edgbaston, 1946 (with no assistance from the field; 7 bowled, 3 lbw).
100 WKTS (14) 184 @ 15.60 in 1946.
RECORDS 2201 wkts @ 20.45 for Warwicks, county record, next best S. Santall with 1207.

Players v Gentlemen (4) 1946–57. Staffordshire 1958. Clubs: Old Hill, West Bromwich Dartmouth, Mitchells and Butlers. Autobiography *I'll Spin You A Tale* (1955).

HOLLINGTON, Hugh Basil
LHB

Born Harpenden, Herts, 14 Aug 1949. Educ Haileybury and ISC. Debut 1972.
MINOR COUNTIES (1) 1972.
HS 15 Minor Counties v Australians, Longton, 1972.
Hertfordshire 1966–72. Clubs: Southgate, Darlington.

HOLLINSHEAD, Cyril
LHB, LFM

Born Timberland, Lincolnshire, 26 May 1902. Debut 1946.
GLOUCESTERSHIRE (1) 1946.
No runs, no wkts.
Lincolnshire 1931. Clubs: Cheltenham Town, XL Club.

HOLMAN, John Charles
RHB, WK

Born Calcutta, India, 5 Apr 1938. Educ Tonbridge; RMA Sandhurst. Debut 1962.
COMBINED SERVICES (2) 1962–64.
HS 17 Combined Services v Cambridge U, Fenner's, 1962.
Army 1963 (capt). Clubs: Free Foresters, Stragglers of Asia. Colonel Queen's Regiment. In Uganda with Commonwealth training team.

HOLMES, Errol Reginald Thorold
RHB, RMF

Born Calcutta, India, 21 Aug 1905. Died Marylebone, London, 16 Aug 1960. Educ Malvern; Trinity C, Oxford. Debut 1924.
SURREY (198) 1924–55. Cap 1926. Capt 1934–38, 1947–48.
OXFORD UNIVERSITY (31) 1925–27 (Blue 1925–27). Capt 1927.
ENGLAND (5) 1934/35–35. SA 1935 (1). *WI 1934/35 (4).*
OTHER TOURS L. H. Tennyson's XI to Jamaica 1926/27. MCC to N Zealand 1935/36 (capt).
HST 85* E v WI, Port of Spain, 1934/35. HS 236 Oxford U v Free Foresters, The Parks, 1927.
BB 6–16 Surrey v MCC, Lord's, 1934.
1000 RUNS (6) 1925 @ 41.84 in 1935.
RECORD Added 168 for 9th wkt with

E. W. J. Brooks, Surrey v Hants, Oval,
1936, county record.
Gentlemen v Players (9) 1927–36. MCC
committee 1946–60. Surrey committee.
Author *Flannelled Foolishness* (1957).
Soccer: Blue.

HOLMES, Geoffrey Clark
——————RHB, RM——————

Born Newcastle upon Tyne, 16 Sept
1958. Educ West Denton HS. Debut
1978.
GLAMORGAN (75) 1978–.
HS 100★ Glam v Glos, Bristol, 1979.
BB 5–86 Glam v Surrey, Oval, 1980.
1000 RUNS (1) 1039 @ 29.69 in 1984.

HOLMES, John Rodney Reay
——————RHB, WK——————

Born Hastings, Sussex, 24 Apr 1924.
Died, of heart attack, Cervinia, Italy, 3
Feb 1980. Educ Repton. Debut 1949.
FREE FORESTERS (2) 1949–50.
SUSSEX (1) 1951.
HS 24 Free Foresters v Oxford U, The
Parks, 1949.
Father A. J. Holmes (Sussex).

HOLMES, John Trevor
——————RHB, WK——————

Born Holmfirth, Yorks, 16 Nov 1939.
Debut 1969.
SOMERSET (1) 1969.
HS 8 Som v W Indians, Taunton, 1969.

HOLT, Arthur George
——————RHB, OB——————

Born Southampton, Hants, 8 Apr 1911.
Educ Bitterne Park S, Southampton.
Debut 1935. *P.*
HAMPSHIRE (79) 1935–48. Cap 1946.
Testimonial (£1641) 1954.
HS 116 Hants v Leics, Leicester, 1938.
Hants coach after retirement. Clubs:
Deanery, Southampton Wednesday.
Soccer: Southampton.

HOLT, Richard Anthony Appleby
——————RHB——————

Born Kensington, London, 11 Mar
1920. Educ Harrow; King's C, Cambridge. Debut 1938.
SUSSEX (5) 1938–39.
FREE FORESTERS (1) 1947.
HS 30 Sussex v Hants, Portsmouth,
1938.
Club: Guildford.

HONE, David Jeremy
——————RHB, RM——————

Born Melbourne, Australia, 30 June
1946. Educ Worcester C, Oxford.
Debut 1970.
OXFORD UNIVERSITY (3) 1970.
HS 13 Oxford U v Notts, The Parks,
1970.
Father Sir Brian Hone (S Australia, Oxford U).

HOOD, John Antony
——————RHB, OB——————

Born Napier, N Zealand, 2 Jan 1952.
Educ Westlake HS, Auckland; U of
Auckland; Worcester C, Oxford. Debut
1977.
OXFORD UNIVERSITY (2) 1977.
HS 7 Oxford U v Warwicks, The Parks,
1977.

HOOK, John Stanley
——————RHB, OB——————

Born Weston-super-Mare, Som, 27
May 1954. Educ Weston-super-Mare
GS; Southampton U. Debut 1975.
SOMERSET (1) 1975.
HS 4★ Som v Oxford U, The Parks, 1975.

HOOKER, Ronald William
——————RHB, RM——————

Born Shoreditch, London, 22 Feb 1935.
Debut 1956. *P.*
MIDDLESEX (300) 1956–69. Cap 1959.
Benefit (£5500) 1968.
HS 137 M'sex v Kent, Gravesend, 1959.
BB 7–18 M'sex v Worcs, Worcester,
1965.
1000 RUNS (2) 1449 @ 30.18 in 1959.
Took 90 wkts @ 24.86 in 1965.
Buckinghamshire 1970–75. Clubs:
Hampstead, South Hampstead.

HOOKES, David William
——————LHB, occ SLA——————

Born Mile End, S Australia, 3 May
1955. Debut 1975/76.
AUSTRALIA DOMESTIC South Australia
(52) 1975/76–. Capt 1981/82–.
AUSTRALIA (19) 1976/77–83/84. E 1976/
77 (1), 1982/83 (5); WI 1979/80 (1). *E
1977 (5), WI 1983/84 (5); P 1979/80
(1); SL 1982/83 (1).*
HST 143★ A v SL, Kandy, 1982/83. HS
193 S Australia v Victoria, St Kilda,
Melbourne, 1982/83.
BB 3–114 Australians v Windward Islands, Castries, St Lucia, 1983/84.
1000 RUNS (2) 1424 @ 64.73 in 1982/83.

RECORDS Scored century in each inns of
consecutive matches in 1976/77: 185 and
105 S Australia v Queensland, Adelaide:
135 and 156 S Australia v NSW,
Adelaide – only T. W. Hayward, in
1906, has also performed this feat.
Reached century in 43 mins, from 34
balls, during inns of 107 S Australia v
Victoria, Adelaide, 1982/83: fastest-ever
century in Australia; in terms of balls
received almost certainly fastest-ever fc
century. Reached 1000 runs in 1982/83
on 19 Dec, earliest date for such an
aggregate in Australia; scored 1163 runs
in season by end of the calendar year,
also a record.
Club: West Torrens.

HOOL, Nathan Bernard
——————RHB, SLA——————

Born Dublin, Ireland, 28 Jan 1924.
Educ Wesley C, Dublin; Dublin U.
Debut 1947.
IRELAND (9) 1947–61.
HS 27 Ireland v Scotland, Paisley, 1954.
BB 5–73 Ireland v Scotland, Cork, 1947.
Clubs: NICC, Clontarf. England World
Jewish Sports Festival 1957.

HOOPER, Andrew James Mendez
——————RHB, SLA——————

Born Denmark Hill, London, 17 Sept
1945. Educ Shooter's Hill GS. Debut
1966.
KENT (13) 1966–69.
HS 35 Kent v Som, Weston-super-Mare,
1968.
BB 6–92 Kent v Oxford U, The Parks,
1969.

HOOPER, John Michael Mackenzie
——————RHB, RM——————

Born Milford, Surrey, 23 Apr 1947.
Educ Charterhouse. Debut 1967.
SURREY (21) 1967–71.
HS 41★ Surrey v Oxford U, Guildford,
1970.
Club: Guildford.

HOPE, Kenneth William
——————RHB, OB——————

Born Portarlington, Co Leix, Ireland, 3
May 1939. Educ Wesley C, Dublin.
Debut 1958.
IRELAND (9) 1958–66.
HS 21 Ireland v MCC, Dublin, 1960.
BB 6–59 Ireland v Scotland, Paisley,
1960.
Club: Pembroke.

HOPKINS, David Charles
—RHB, RM—

Born Birmingham, 11 Feb 1957. Educ Moseley GS. Debut 1977.
WARWICKSHIRE (36) 1977–81.
HS 34* Warwicks v Essex, Edgbaston, 1979.
BB 6–67 Warwicks v Som, Taunton, 1979.
Buckinghamshire 1982. Club: West Bromwich Dartmouth.

HOPKINS, Jeffris David
—RHB, WK—

Born Bridgend, S Wales, 23 Aug 1950. Educ Maesteg CS. Debut 1969.
MIDDLESEX (4) 1969–72.
HS 4 M'sex v Cambridge U, Fenner's, 1970 and 4 v Northants, Lord's, 1972.
Brother J. A. Hopkins (Glam).

HOPKINS, John Anthony
—RHB, occ WK—

Born Maesteg, S Wales, 16 June 1953. Educ Trinity C of Educ, Carmarthen. Debut 1970.
GLAMORGAN (233) 1970–. Cap 1977.
S AFRICA DOMESTIC Eastern Province 1981/82.
HS 230 Glam v Worcs, Worcester, 1977.
1000 RUNS (7) 1500 @ 33.33 in 1984.
Brother J. D. Hopkins (M'sex).

HOPKINS, Victor
—RHB, WK—

Born Dumbleton, Glos, 21 Jan 1911. Died Dumbleton, 6 Aug 1984. Debut 1934. P.
GLOUCESTERSHIRE (139) 1934–48. Cap.
HS 83* Glos v Sussex, Worthing, 1939.

HOPWOOD, John Anthony
—RHB—

Born Herne Bay, Kent, 23 Oct 1926. Educ Dulwich C. Debut 1951.
FREE FORESTERS (1) 1951.
HS 8 Free Foresters v Cambridge U, Fenner's, 1951.
Clubs: Bank of England, United Banks, Royal Navy, Hong Kong.

HORNER, Norman Frederick
—RHB—

Born Queensbury, Bradford, Yorks, 10 May 1926. Debut 1950. P.
YORKSHIRE (2) 1950.
WARWICKSHIRE (357) 1951–65. Cap 1953. Benefit (£6465) 1962.

HS 203* Warwicks v Surrey, Oval, 1960.
1000 RUNS (12) 1902 @ 33.36 in 1960.
RECORDS In HS (above) added 377* for 1st wkt with Khalid Ibadulla, county record and highest unbroken 1st-wkt stand in English fc cricket.
Players v Gentlemen (1) 1962. Club: Shirley. Groundsman.

HORREX, Graham Wade
—RHB—

Born Goodmayes, Ilford, Essex, 27 Dec 1932. Educ Brentwood S. Debut 1956.
ESSEX (7) 1956–57.
HS 41 Essex v Australians, Southend, 1956.
Clubs: Brentwood, Preston. Squash: Essex.

HORSFALL, Richard
—RHB—

Born Todmorden, Yorks, 26 June 1920. Died Halifax, Yorks, 25 Aug 1981. Debut 1947. P.
ESSEX (207) 1947–55. Cap 1948.
GLAMORGAN (5) 1956.
HS 206 Essex v Kent, Blackheath, 1951.
1000 RUNS (4) 1731 @ 37.63 in 1953.
RECORDS During HS (above) added 343 for 3rd wkt with P. A. Gibb and added 298 for 4th wkt with A. V. Avery, Essex v Worcs, Clacton, 1948, both county records.
Gave up county cricket through nervous trouble.

HORSLEY, Norman
—RHB, RFM—

Born Leicester, 20 Aug 1922. Debut 1947. P.
NOTTINGHAMSHIRE (3) 1947.
No runs.
BB 2–27 Notts v Yorks, Bramall Lane, Sheffield, 1947.

HORTON, Henry
—RHB—

Born Colwall Green, Herefordshire, 18 Apr 1923. Debut 1946. P.
WORCESTERSHIRE (11) 1946–49.
HAMPSHIRE (405) 1953–67. Cap 1955. Benefit (£5900) 1964.
HS 160* Hants v Yorks, Scarborough, 1961.
BB 2–0 Hants v Essex, Bournemouth, 1960.
1000 RUNS (12) 2428 @ 47.60 in 1959.
Players v Gentlemen (1) 1960. Fc umpire 1973–75. Soccer: Blackburn Rovers, Southampton, Bradford. Brother J. Horton (Worcs).

HORTON, Martin John
—RHB, OB—

Born Worcester, 21 Apr 1934. Debut 1952. P.
WORCESTERSHIRE (376) 1952–66. Cap 1955. Benefit (£5860) 1965.
N ZEALAND DOMESTIC Northern Districts (19) 1967/68–70/71.
ENGLAND (2) I 1959.
TOURS Worcs to Rhodesia 1964/65. Worcs to Jamaica 1965/66.
HST 58 E v I, Trent Bridge, 1959. HS 233 Worcs v Som, Worcester, 1962.
BBT 2–24 E v I, Lord's, 1959. BB 9–56 Worcs v S Africans, Worcester, 1955.
1000 RUNS (11) 2468 @ 44.87 in 1959.
100 WKTS (2) 103 @ 27.38 in 1955.
DOUBLES (2) 1955, 1961.
RECORDS In HS (above) added 314 for 3rd wkt with T. W. Graveney, county record.
Players v Gentlemen (1) 1959. N Zealand national coach 1966–84. Club: Stourbridge.

HOSEN, Roger Wills
—RHB, RMF—

Born Falmouth, Cornwall, 12 June 1933. Educ Falmouth HS; Loughborough C. Debut 1965.
MINOR COUNTIES (1) 1965.
HS 2 Minor Counties v S Africans, Jesmond, 1965.
Cornwall 1955–69. Clubs: Falmouth, Leamington Spa. Rugby: Loughborough C, Plymouth Albion, Wasps, Cheltenham, Bristol, Northampton, Penryn, England (10 caps).

HOSKYNS, John Chevallier
—LHB—

Born Cambridge, 28 May 1926. Died Pewick, Worcs, 12 Apr 1956. Educ Marlborough C; King's C, Cambridge. Debut 1949.
CAMBRIDGE UNIVERSITY (2) 1949.
HS 42* Cambridge U v Warwicks, Fenner's, 1949.
15th Baronet Hoskyns.

HOSSELL, John Johnson
—LHB, SLA—

Born Birmingham, 25 May 1914. Educ Wylde Green C, Sutton Coldfield. Debut 1939.
WARWICKSHIRE (35) 1939–47. Cap 1946.
HS 83 Warwicks v Leics, Edgbaston, 1946.
BB 3–24 Warwicks v Cambridge U, Edgbaston, 1947.
Clubs: Aston Unity, Stratford on Avon.

HOTCHKIN, Neil Stafford
———RHB———

Born Horncastle, Lincolnshire, 4 Feb 1914. Educ Eton; Trinity C, Cambridge. Debut 1934.
CAMBRIDGE UNIVERSITY (14) 1934–35 (Blue 1935).
MIDDLESEX (6) 1939–48.
INDIA DOMESTIC Combined Services 1944/45–45/46, Europeans 1944/45.
HS 74 Combined Services v Bengal Governor's XI, Calcutta, 1944/45.
Lincolnshire 1934–37.

HOUGH, Edwin John
———RHB, RFM———

Born Rusape, Rhodesia, 29 July 1957. Debut 1981/82.
ZIMBABWE 1981/82–82/83.
TOUR Zimbabwe to England 1982.
HS 9 Zimbabwe v Sri Lanka, Bulawayo, 1982/83.
BB 4–48 Zimbabwe v PIA, Harare, 1981/82.

HOUGHTON, David Laud
———RHB, WK———

Born Salisbury, Rhodesia, 23 June 1957. Debut 1978/79.
ZIMBABWE 1978/79–83/84.
TOUR Zimbabwe to England 1982.
HS 87 Zimbabwe v Young W Indians, Harare, 1981/82.
Hockey: Rhodesia (Zimbabwe). Brother W. J. Houghton (Rhodesia).

HOUGHTON, William *Eric*
———RHB———

Born Billingborough, Lincolnshire, 29 June 1910. Educ Donington GS. Debut 1946.
WARWICKSHIRE (7) 1946–47.
HS 41 Warwicks v Northants, Edgbaston 1947.
Lincolnshire 1932–39. Clubs: Sleaford, Aston Unity, Olton. Soccer: Aston Villa, Notts County, England (7 caps); manager: Notts County, Aston Villa.

HOULTON, Gerard
———RHB, LFM———

Born St Helens, Lancs, 21 Apr 1939. Debut 1961.
LANCASHIRE (20) 1961–63.
HS 86 Lancs v Kent, Folkestone, 1961.
Clubs: Middleton, St Helens Recs, Pilkington's.

HOWARD, Arthur Stanley
———RHB, OB———

Born Grahamstown, S Africa, 14 Nov 1936. Educ Rhodes U, S Africa; Pembroke C, Cambridge. Debut 1961.
CAMBRIDGE UNIVERSITY (3) 1961.
No runs.
BB 3–100 Cambridge U v Free Foresters, Fenner's, 1961.

HOWARD, Barry John
———RHB———

Born Preston, Lancs, 21 May 1926. Educ Rossall; Manchester U. Debut 1947.
LANCASHIRE (33) 1947–51. Cap 1947.
HS 114 MCC v Essex, Lord's, 1949.
Clubs: Stockport, Sale, Brooklands, Manchester University. Brother N. D. Howard (Lancs and England); father R. Howard (Lancs).

HOWARD, Jack
———LHB, WK———

Born Leicester, 24 Nov 1917. Debut 1946. *P*.
LEICESTERSHIRE (41) 1946–48.
HS 38* Leics v M'sex, Lord's, 1946.
Career curtailed through illness. Father A. Howard (Leics); brother A. R. Howard (Glam).

HOWARD, Kenneth
———LHB, ROB———

Born Manchester, 2 June 1941. Debut 1960. *P*.
LANCASHIRE (61) 1960–66.
HS 23 Lancs v Sussex, Liverpool, 1965.
BB 7–53 Lancs v Warwicks, Old Trafford, 1963.

HOWARD, Nigel David
———RHB———

Born Preston, Lancs, 18 May 1925. Died Isle of Man, 31 May 1979. Educ Rossall; Manchester U. Debut 1946.
LANCASHIRE (170) 1946–53. Cap 1948. Capt 1949–53.
MCC (1) 1954.
FREE FORESTERS (1) 1954.
ENGLAND (4) *I 1951/52.* Capt 4.
HST 23 E v I, Calcutta, 1951/52. HS 145 Lancs v Derbys, Old Trafford, 1948.
1000 RUNS (1) 1174 @ 36.68 in 1950.
Gentlemen v Players (1) 1951. Clubs: Stockport, Manchester Club and Ground. Father R. Howard (Lancs); brother B. J. Howard (Lancs).

HOWARTH, Geoffrey Philip
———RHB, OB———

Born Auckland, N Zealand, 29 Mar 1951. Educ Auckland GS. Debut 1968/69.
N ZEALAND DOMESTIC N Zealand Under-23 XI 1968/69, Auckland (11) 1972/73–73/74, Northern Districts (47) 1974/75– (capt 1979/80–).
SURREY (186) 1971–. Cap 1974. Benefit 1983. Capt 1984.
NEW ZEALAND (40) 1974/75–83/84. E 1974/75 (2), 1977/78 (3), 1983/84 (3); A 1976/77 (2), 1981/82 (3); WI 1979/80 (3); I 1980/81 (3); P 1978/79 (3); SL 1982/83 (2). *E 1978 (3), 1983 (4); A 1980/81 (2); I 1976/77 (2); P 1976/77 (2); SL 1983/84 (3).* Capt 23.
OTHER TOUR D. H. Robins' XI to S Africa 1975/76.
HST 147 NZ v WI, Christchurch, 1979/80. HS 183 Surrey v Hants, Oval, 1979.
BB 5–32 Auckland v Central Districts, Auckland, 1973/74.
1000 RUNS (4) 1554 @ 37.90 in 1976.
RECORD Added 195 for 2nd wkt with J. G. Wright, NZ v P, Napier, 1978/79, N Zealand Test record.
MBE 1981 for services to N Zealand cricket. Brother H. J. Howarth (N Zealand).

HOWARTH, Hedley John
———LHB, SLA———

Born Auckland, N Zealand, 25 Dec 1943. Educ Auckland GS. Debut 1962/63.
N ZEALAND DOMESTIC N Zealand Under-23 XI 1962/63, Auckland (80) 1963/64–78/79.
NEW ZEALAND (30) 1969–76/77. E 1970/71 (2), 1974/75 (2); A 1973/74 (3), 1976/77 (2); I 1975/76 (2); P 1972/73 (3). *E 1969 (3), 1973 (2); WI 1971/72 (5); I 1969/70 (3); P 1969/70 (3).*
OTHER TOURS N Zealand to Australia 1969/70, 1970/71.
HST 61 NZ v A, Christchurch, 1976/77. HS as above.
BBT 5–34 NZ v I, Nagpur, 1969/70. BB 8–75 (11–98 match) Auckland v N Zealand Under-23 XI, Auckland, 1976/77.
RECORD Took 332 wkts for Auckland @ 22.17, record for that association. Brother G. P. Howarth (N Zealand).

HOWARTH, John Stirling
———RHB, RFM———

Born Stockport, Cheshire, 26 Mar 1945. Debut 1966.
NOTTINGHAMSHIRE (13) 1966–67.
No runs in 13 matches (seven inns).
BB 3–30 Notts v Glos, Trent Bridge, 1967.

Cheshire 1976–78. Clubs: Cheadle Hulme, Castleton Moor.

HOWAT, Michael Gerald
—RHB, RM—

Born Tavistock, Devon, 2 Mar 1958. Educ Abingdon S; Magdalene C, Cambridge. Debut 1977.
CAMBRIDGE UNIVERSITY (26) 1977–80 (Blue 1977, 1980).
HS 32 Cambridge U v M'sex, Fenner's, 1980.
BB 3–39 Cambridge U v Essex, Fenner's, 1977.
Club: Abingdon. Father Gerald Howat (cricket writer).

HOWGEGO, James Alan
—RHB, LB—

Born Folkestone, Kent, 3 Aug 1948. Debut 1977.
KENT (1) 1977.
HS 52 Kent v Cambridge U, Canterbury, 1977.

HOWICK, Nicholas *Keith*
—RHB, RM—

Born St Peter Port, Guernsey, Channel Islands. Educ Elizabeth C, Guernsey; Pembroke C, Oxford. Debut 1974.
OXFORD UNIVERSITY (5) 1974.
HS 14 Oxford U v Som, The Parks, 1974.
Hockey: Blue.

HOWLAND, Christopher Burfield
—RHB, WK—

Born Whitstable, Kent, 6 Feb 1936. Educ Dulwich; Clare C, Cambridge. Debut 1956.
COMBINED SERVICES (1) 1956.
CAMBRIDGE UNIVERSITY (48) 1958–60 (Blue 1958–60). Capt 1960.
SUSSEX (4) 1960.
FREE FORESTERS (2) 1961.
MCC (6) 1961–68.
KENT (2) 1965.
HS 124 Free Foresters v Cambridge U, Fenner's, 1961.
Gentlemen v Players (1) 1959. MCC committee from 1971. Brother P. C. Howland (Cambridge U).

HOWLAND, Peter Charles
—RHB, OB—

Born Orpington, Kent, 9 Mar 1947. Educ Dulwich; Clare C, Cambridge. Debut 1969.
CAMBRIDGE UNIVERSITY (6) 1969.

HS 21 Cambridge U v Leics, Fenner's, 1969.
Brother C. B. Howland (Cambridge U, Sussex, Kent).

HOWORTH, Richard
—LHB, SLA—

Born Bacup, Lancs, 26 Apr 1909. Died Worcester, 2 Apr 1980. Debut 1933. *P.*
WORCESTERSHIRE (348) 1933–51. Cap 1934. Benefit (£3000) 1949.
INDIA DOMESTIC Europeans 1944/45.
ENGLAND (5) 1947–47/48. SA 1947 (1). *WI 1947/48 (4).*
HST 45* E v SA, Oval, 1947. HS 114 Worcs v Kent, Dover, 1936 and 114 H. D. G. Leveson Gower's XI v Indians, Scarborough, 1946.
BBT 6–124 E v WI, Bridgetown, 1947/48. BB 7–18 (10–57 match) Worcs v Northants, Kettering, 1949.
1000 RUNS (4) 1510 @ 26.03 in 1947.
100 WKTS (9) 164 @ 17.85 in 1947.
DOUBLES (3) 1939, 1946, 1947. Three runs short of double in 1938.
RECORD Added 197 for 7th wkt with H. H. I. H. Gibbons, Worcs v Surrey, Oval, 1938, county record.
Players v Gentlemen (1) 1947. Worcs committee after retirement. Clubs: Stourbridge, Walsall, Old Hill.

HOYER-MILLAR, Gurth Christian
—RHB, WK—

Born Chelsea, London, 13 Dec 1929. Educ Harrow; Lincoln C, Oxford. Debut 1952.
OXFORD UNIVERSITY (2) 1952.
HS 10 Oxford U v Warwicks, The Parks, 1952.
Clubs: MCC, Free Foresters, I Zingari, Gents of Leicester. Rugby: Blue, Richmond, Scotland (1). Boxing: Blue.

HUDSON, Gideon Dacre
—RHB, WK—

Born Salisbury, Wiltshire, 8 Nov 1944. Educ St Edward's, Oxford; Exeter C, Oxford. Debut 1964.
OXFORD UNIVERSITY (1) 1964.
HS 6 Oxford U v Worcs, Worcester, 1964.
Buckinghamshire 1964–75. Clubs: Amersham, Cryptics, MCC, Free Foresters.

HUEY, Samuel *Scott* Johnston
—RHB, SLA—

Born Ture, Co Donegal, N Ireland, 21 Dec 1923. Educ Masonic Boys' S. Debut 1951.

IRELAND (20) 1951–66.
HS 23* Ireland v MCC, Dublin, 1954.
BB 8–48 (14–97 match) Ireland v MCC, Dublin, 1954.
Last bowler to dismiss Sir L. Hutton in fc cricket, Ireland v MCC, Dublin, 1960.
Clubs: Eglinton's, City of Derry. Badminton: Ireland.

HUGHES, David Garfield
—RHB, WK—

Born Taunton, Som, 21 May 1934. Educ Taunton S. Debut 1955.
SOMERSET (1) 1955.
HS 2 Som v Notts, Taunton, 1955.
Wiltshire 1965–68. XL Club.

HUGHES, David Paul
—RHB, SLA—

Born Newton-le-Willows, Lancs, 13 May 1947. Educ Newton-le-Willows GS. Debut 1967.
LANCASHIRE (333) 1967–. Cap 1970. Testimonial 1981.
AUSTRALIA DOMESTIC Tasmania (2) 1975/76–76/77.
TOUR D. H. Robins' XI to S Africa 1972/73.
HS 153 Lancs v Glam, Old Trafford, 1983.
BB 7–24 Lancs v Oxford U, The Parks, 1970.
1000 RUNS (2) 1303 @ 48.25 in 1982.
Club: Newton-le-Willows.

HUGHES, Gwyn
—RHB, SLA—

Born Cardiff, 26 Mar 1941. Educ Cardiff HS; Queen's C, Cambridge. Debut 1962.
GLAMORGAN (17) 1962–64.
CAMBRIDGE UNIVERSITY (10) 1965 (Blue).
HS 92 Glam v Australians, Cardiff, 1964.
BB 4–31 Cambridge U v N Zealanders, Fenner's, 1965.
Clubs: Briton Ferry Town, Buccaneers.

HUGHES, Kimberley John
—RHB—

Born Margaret River, W Australia, 26 Jan 1954. Debut 1975/76.
AUSTRALIA DOMESTIC Western Australia (52) 1975/76–. Capt 1980/81–.
AUSTRALIA (66) 1977–83/84. E 1978/79 (6), 1979/80 (3), 1982/83 (5); WI 1979/80 (3), 1981/82 (3); NZ 1980/81 (3); I 1977/78 (2), 1980/81 (3); P 1978/79 (2), 1981/82 (3); 1983/84 (5). *E 1977 (1), 1980 (1), 1981 (6); WI 1983/84 (5);*

NZ 1981/82 (3); I 1979/80 (6); P 1979/ 80 (3), 1982/83 (3). Capt 26.
OTHER TOURS Australia to N Zealand 1976/77. Australia to W Indies 1977/78.
HST 213 A v I, Adelaide, 1980/81. HS as above.
1000 RUNS (0 + 2) 1513 @ 43.22 in 1979/ 80.
Dismissed S. Shivnarine with first ball in fc cricket, Australians v Guyana, Georgetown, 1977/78.
Club: South Fremantle. Brother G. A. Hughes (W Australia).

HUGHES, Lewis *Patrick*
──────RHB, RFM──────

Born Blackrock, Co Dublin, Ireland, 10 Apr 1943. Educ Mountjoy S, Dublin. Debut 1965.
IRELAND (5) 1965–72.
HS 35 Ireland v Scotland, Dublin, 1969.
BB 3–77 same match.
Clubs: Malahide, Clontarf.

HUGHES, Mervyn Gregory
──────RHB, RFM──────

Born Euroa, Victoria, Australia, 23 Nov 1961. Educ Werribee HS. Debut 1981/ 82.
AUSTRALIA DOMESTIC Victoria (13) 1981/ 82–.
ESSEX (1) 1983.
HS 17 Victoria v NSW, St Kilda Oval, 1981/82.
BB 4–69 Victoria v Queensland, Geelong, 1981/82.

HUGHES, Noel
──────RHB, OB, occ WK──────

Born Sydney, NSW, Australia, 6 Apr 1929. Debut 1953. *P.*
WORCESTERSHIRE (21) 1953–54.
HS 95 Worcs v Essex, Worcester, 1954.
BB 4–19 Worcs v Hants, Portsmouth, 1954.

HUGHES, Richard Clive
──────LHB, LFM──────

Born Watford, Hertfordshire, 30 Sept 1926. Educ Watford GS. Debut 1950. *P.*
WORCESTERSHIRE (11) 1950–51.
HS 21 Worcs v Surrey, Oval, 1951.
BB 3–38 Worcs v Combined Services, Worcester, 1950.
Hertfordshire 1953–59.

HUGHES, Simon Peter
──────RHB, RFM──────

Born Kingston-upon-Thames, Surrey, 20 Dec 1959. Educ Latymer Upper S; Durham U. Debut 1980.
MIDDLESEX (57) 1980–. Cap 1981.
S AFRICA DOMESTIC Northern Transvaal 1982/83.
TOURS M'sex to Zimbabwe 1980/81. Overseas XI to India 1980/81.
HS 41* M'sex v Glos, Uxbridge, 1984.
BB 6–32 M'sex v Glos, Bristol, 1983.

HUGHES, Walter Laurence
──────Spin bowler──────

Born 9 Sept 1917. Educ New C, Oxford. Debut 1947.
OXFORD UNIVERSITY (1) 1947.
HS 3 Oxford U v Glos, The Parks, 1947.

HUGO, Stephanus Gideon
──────RHB, RFM──────

Born Caledon, S Africa, 20 July 1945. Educ Sea Point HS; Stellenbosch U. Debut 1966/67.
S AFRICA DOMESTIC South African Universities 1966/67, Western Province 1967/68–77/78.
TOUR S African Universities to England 1967.
HS 68* W Province v OFS, Bloemfontein, 1968/69.
BB 4–31 W Province v OFS, Cape Town, 1967/68.

HUMPAGE, Geoffrey William
──────RHB, WK, RM──────

Born Sparkhill, Birmingham, 24 Apr 1954. Educ Golden Hillock CS, Birmingham. Debut 1974. *Wisden 1985.*
WARWICKSHIRE (217) 1974–. Cap 1976.
S AFRICA DOMESTIC Orange Free State 1981/82.
HS 254 Warwicks v Lancs, Southport, 1982.
BB 2–13 Warwicks v Glos, Edgbaston, 1980.
1000 RUNS (7) 1891 @ 48.49 in 1984.
RECORDS During HS (above) added 470 for 4th wkt with A. I. Kallicharran, English record and record for any wkt other than 1st in English fc cricket; also highest stand for any wkt for a side losing the match. Hit 13 sixes during this inns, most in fc inns by an Englishman.
Scored four centuries in five inns during 1981.
Barred from Test cricket for three years for touring S Africa 1981/82 (SAB England XI).

HUMPHREY, Richard Geoffrey
──────RHB, WK──────

Born Hampstead, London, 17 Sept 1936. Debut 1964.
SURREY (2) 1964–70.
HS 58 Surrey v Cambridge U, Oval, 1964.
Buckinghamshire 1980–. Clubs: Guildford, Slough.

HUMPHRIES, David John
──────LHB, WK──────

Born Aveley, Shropshire, 6 Aug 1953. Educ Bridgnorth Sec S; Wulfrun C, Wolverhampton. Debut 1974.
LEICESTERSHIRE (5) 1974–76.
WORCESTERSHIRE (169) 1977–. Cap 1978.
HS 133 Worcs v Derbys, Worcester, 1984.
Shropshire 1971–73. Club: West Bromwich Dartmouth.

HUMPHRIES, Norman Hampton
──────RHB, LB──────

Born Kidderminster, Worcs, 19 May 1917. Debut 1946.
WORCESTERSHIRE (7) 1946.
HS 22 Worcs v Glam, Dudley, 1946.
Devon 1947–55. Clubs: Kidderminster, XL Club.
Brothers C. A. and G. H. Humphries (both Worcs).

HUNT, Robert Geoffrey
──────RHB, OB──────

Born Horsham, Sussex, 13 Apr 1915. Educ Aldenham; Pembroke C, Cambridge. Debut 1935.
CAMBRIDGE UNIVERSITY (14) 1935–37 (Blue 1937).
SUSSEX (11) 1936–47.
INDIA DOMESTIC Services 1943/44.
HS 117 Cambridge U v Army, Fenner's, 1937.
BB 5–51 Cambridge U v MCC, Lord's, 1937.
Appointed joint capt with G. H. G. Doggart for 1950 but withdrew after county committee voted out at extraordinary meeting.

HUNTE, Conrad Cleophas
──────RHB, occ RM──────

Born St Andrew, Barbados, 9 May 1932. Educ Alleyne S, Barbados. Debut 1950/ 51. *Wisden 1964.*
W INDIES DOMESTIC Barbados 1950/ 51–66/67.
COMMONWEALTH XI (1) 1956.

WEST INDIES (44) 1957/58–66/67. E 1959/60 (5); A 1964/65 (5); I 1961/62 (5); P 1957/58 (5). *E 1963 (5), 1966 (5); A 1960/61 (5); I 1958/59 (5), 1966/67 (3); P 1958/59 (1).*
OTHER TOURS Rest of World XI in England 1965, 1967.
HST 260 WI v P, Kingston, 1957/58. HS 263 Barbados v Jamaica, Georgetown, 1961/62.
BB 3–5 W Indians v President's XI, Nagpur, 1966/67.
1000 RUNS (1 + 1) 1367 @ 44.09 in 1963.
RECORDS During HST (above) added 446 for 2nd wkt with G. S. Sobers, W Indian Test record for any wkt and W Indian fc record for 2nd wkt.
Scored 142 in 1st inns of Test debut, WI v P, Bridgetown, 1957/58. Carried bat for 60* in total of 131, WI v A, Port of Spain, 1964/65.
After retirement full-time worker for Moral Rearmament (see T. C. Dodds).
Autobiography *Playing to Win* (1971).

HUNTER, Charles Michael Geoffrey
————RHB, RM————

Born St Helens, Lancs, 11 Sept 1937. Educ Malvern. Debut 1971.
MINOR COUNTIES (1) 1971.
HS 41 Minor Counties v Indians, Lakenham, 1971.
Dorset 1965–70. Club: Sherborne, Huyton.

HUNTER, William *Raymond*
————RHB, RM————

Born Belfast, N Ireland, 3 Apr 1938. Educ Wallace HS, Lisburn. Debut 1958.
IRELAND (11) 1958–65.
HS 39 Ireland v Hants, Dublin, 1965.
BB 5–22 Ireland v MCC, Dublin, 1961.
Clubs: Lisburn, Dunmurry. Rugby: Ireland (10 caps), British Lions.

HURD, Alan
————LHB, ROB————

Born Ilford, Essex, 7 Sept 1937. Educ Chigwell S; Clare C, Cambridge. Debut 1958.
CAMBRIDGE UNIVERSITY (52) 1958–60 (Blue 1958–60).
ESSEX (35) 1958–60.
HS 21 Cambridge U v Hants, Fenner's, 1960.
BB 6–15 Essex v Kent, Clacton, 1958.
Gentlemen v Players (3) 1959–60. Club: Sevenoaks Vine.

HURST, Alan George
————RHB, RF————

Born Altona, Victoria, Australia, 15 July 1950. Debut 1972/73.
AUSTRALIA DOMESTIC Victoria (50) 1972/73–80/81.
AUSTRALIA (12) 1973/74–79/80. E 1978/79 (6); NZ 1973/74 (1); I 1977/78 (1); P 1978/79 (2). *I 1979/80 (2).*
OTHER TOURS Australia to England 1975. International XI to S Africa 1975/76. Australia to N Zealand 1976/77.
HST 26 A v I, Brisbane, 1977/78. HS 27* Victoria v NSW, Sydney, 1975/76.
BBT 5–28 A v E, Sydney, 1978/79. BB 8–84 Victoria v Queensland, Melbourne, 1977/78.
Clubs: Footscray, North Melbourne.

HURST, Geoffrey Charles
————RHB, WK————

Born Ashton-under-Lyne, Lancs, 8 Dec 1941. Educ Rainsford Sec S, Chelmsford. Debut 1962. *P.*
ESSEX (1) 1962.
No runs.
Soccer: West Ham United, Stoke City, West Bromwich Albion, England (49 caps).

HURST, Gordon Thomas
————RHB, RM/LB————

Born Kenley, Surrey, 26 Aug 1920. Debut 1947. *P.*
SUSSEX (9) 1947–49.
HS 9 Sussex v Lancs, Old Trafford, 1949.
BB 6–80 Sussex v Warwicks, Hove, 1947.

HURST, Robert Jack
————RHB, SLA————

Born Hampton Hill, M'sex, 29 Dec 1933. Debut 1954. *P.*
MIDDLESEX (100) 1954–61. Cap 1957.
HS 62 M'sex v Sussex, Hove, 1956.
BB 8–65 M'sex v Oxford U, The Parks, 1956.
Club: Teddington.

HUSKINSON, Geoffrey Mark Clement
————RHB, LB————

Born Nottingham, 25 Mar 1935. Educ Ampleforth. Debut 1959.
FREE FORESTERS (1) 1959.
HS 7 Free Foresters v Oxford U, The Parks, 1959.
Father G. N. B. Huskinson (Notts).

HUTSON, Andrew Massey
————RHB, RM————

Born Tamworth, Staffordshire, 18 Mar 1952. Educ Kimbolton S; Corpus Christi C, Cambridge. Debut 1972.
CAMBRIDGE UNIVERSITY (1) 1972.
No runs, no wkts.

HUTTON, George
————RHB, RFM————

Born Paisley, Scotland, 20 Aug 1942. Educ John Neilson S, Paisley. Debut 1966.
SCOTLAND (2) 1966–67.
No runs.
BB 2–16 Scotland v Cambridge U, Fenner's, 1966.
Club: Kelburne.

HUTTON, Leonard
————RHB, LB————

Born Fulneck, Pudsey, Yorks, 23 June 1916. Educ Pudsey S. Debut 1934. *P. Wisden 1938.*
YORKSHIRE (341) 1934–55. Cap 1936. Benefit (£9713) 1950.
MCC (3) 1948–60.
L. C. STEVEN'S XI (1) 1960.
ENGLAND (79) 1937–54/55. A 1938 (3), 1948 (4), 1953 (5); SA 1947 (5), 1951 (5); WI 1939 (3), 1950 (3); NZ 1937 (3), 1949 (4); I 1946 (3), 1952 (4); P 1954 (2). *A 1946/47 (5), 1950/51 (5), 1954/55 (5); SA 1938/39 (4), 1948/49 (5); WI 1947/48 (2), 1953/54 (5); NZ 1950/51 (2), 1954/55 (2).* Capt 23.
OTHER TOUR Yorks to Jamaica 1935/36.
HST 364 E v A, Oval, 1938. HS as above.
BB 6–76 (10–101 match) Yorks v Leics, Leicester, 1937.
1000 RUNS (12 + 5) 3429 @ 68.58 in 1949 (fourth-highest ever seasonal aggregate). 2000 runs eight other times.
RECORDS *Tests* HS (above) highest Test score for and in England and in any Test involving either England or Australia. Inns lasted 797 mins, longest in Test or fc cricket until beaten by Hanif Mohammed (970 mins) in 1957/58. It is the highest score at the Oval and by a Test No. 1 batsman. During 364, added 382 for 2nd wkt with M. Leyland (England Test record) and 215 for 6th wkt with J. Hardstaff, only instance of batsman sharing in two stands of over 200 in one Test inns, 770 runs were added while at the wkt, another Test record. Added 359 for 1st wkt with C. Washbrook, E v SA, J'burg, 1948/49, England Test record and record for 1st wkt in all Tests until beaten by M. H. Mankad and P. Roy (413), I v NZ, Madras, 1955/56. Carried bat for 202* in total of

344, E v WI, Oval, 1950 and for 156* in total of 272, E v A, Adelaide, 1950/51, only batsman to do so twice for England. *Fc cricket* Scored 1294 runs @ 92.42 in June 1949, a record for one batsman in one month; also scored 1050 runs in Aug 1949. Reached 100 centuries in 619 inns, third-fastest ever and at time (1951) fastest by an Englishman.
Scored centuries against all fc counties except his own.
Players v Gentlemen (12) 1937–53. Test selector 1975–76. Club: Pudsey St Laurence. MCC Hon. member. Knighted for services to cricket 1956. Autobiographies *Cricket is My Life* (1949) and *Just My Story* (1956). Son R. A. Hutton (Yorks, England); nephew S. J. Dennis (Yorks); brother-in-law F. Dennis (Yorks).

HUTTON, Richard Anthony
————————RHB, RFM————————

Born Pudsey, Yorks, 6 Sept 1942. Educ Repton; Christ's C, Cambridge.

Debut 1962.
YORKSHIRE (208) 1962–74. Cap 1964.
CAMBRIDGE UNIVERSITY (46) 1962–64 (Blue 1962–64).
S AFRICA DOMESTIC Transvaal 1975/76.
ENGLAND (5) 1971. I 1971 (3); P 1971 (2).
TOURS E. W. Swanton's XI to India 1963/64. MCC Under-25 XI to Pakistan 1966/67. World XI to Australia 1971/72.
HST 81 E v I, Oval, 1971. HS 189 Yorks v Pakistanis, Bradford, 1971.
BBT 3–72 E v P, Headingley, 1971. BB 8–50 Cambridge U v Derbys, Burton upon Trent, 1963.
1000 RUNS (2) 1122 @ 27.36 in 1963.
Gentlemen v Players (1) 1962. Father Sir L. Hutton (Yorks, England); uncle F. Dennis (Yorks); cousin S. J. Dennis (Yorks); father-in-law B. G. Brocklehurst (Som).

HUXFORD, Peter Nigel
————————LHB, WK————————

Born Enfield, M'sex, 17 Feb 1960.

Educ Richard Hale S, Hertford; Christ Church C, Oxford. Debut 1980.
OXFORD UNIVERSITY (7) 1980–81 (Blue 1981).
HS 10 Oxford U v Kent, The Parks, 1981.

HUXTER, Rupert James Alexander
————————RHB, RM————————

Born Abingdon, Berkshire, 29 Oct 1959. Educ Magdalen College S, Oxford; St Catharine's C, Cambridge. Debut 1981.
CAMBRIDGE UNIVERSITY (4) 1981 (Blue 1981).
HS 20 Cambridge U v Sussex, Fenner's, 1981.
BB 2–49 Cambridge U v Sussex, Fenner's, 1981.

I/J

IDDON, John
RHB, SLA

Born Mawdesley, Ormskirk, Lancs, 8 Jan 1902. Died, in road accident, Madeley, Staffordshire, 17 Apr 1946. Debut 1924. *P.*
LANCASHIRE (483) 1924–45. Cap 1926. Benefit (£1266) 1936.
ENGLAND (5) 1934/35–35. SA 1935 (1); *WI 1934/35 (4)*.
OTHER TOURS Sir J. Cahn's XI to Jamaica 1928/29.
HST 73 E v WI, Port of Spain, 1934/35.
HS 222 Lancs v Leics, Liverpool, 1929.
BB 9–42 Lancs v Yorks, Bramall Lane, Sheffield, 1937.
1000 RUNS (13). 2381 @ 52.91 in 1934.
RECORD Added 278 for 6th wkt with H. R. W. Butterworth, Lancs v Sussex, Old Trafford, 1932, county record.
Scored centuries against all fc counties except his own.
Players v Gentlemen (1) 1931.

IFTIQAR ALI BOKHARI
RHB, RM

Born Lahore, India, 6 July 1935. Educ King's S, Ely; Caius C, Cambridge. Debut 1957.
CAMBRIDGE UNIVERSITY (1) 1957.
PAKISTAN DOMESTIC Sargodha, Punjab, Lahore, 1957/58–65/66.
HS 203 Lahore v Punjab, Lahore, 1960/61.
Cambridgeshire 1956 (Rhodes Trophy).

IJAZ BUTT
RHB, WK

Born Sialkot, India, 10 Mar 1938. Educ Punjab U. Debut 1955/56.
PAKISTAN DOMESTIC Punjab, Combined Universities, Lahore, Rawalpindi, Multan, 1955/56–67/68.
PAKISTAN (8) 1958/59–62. A 1959/60 (2); WI 1958/59 (3). *E 1962 (3)*.
OTHER TOURS Pakistan to W Indies 1957/58. Pakistan Eaglets to India 1959/60. PIA Eaglets to India 1960/61. Pakistan to India 1960/61.

HST 58 P v A, Karachi, 1959/60. HS 161 Pakistan Eaglets v Indian Starlets, Lahore, 1959/60.
1000 RUNS (1) 1016 @ 28.22 in 1962.
Pakistan selector from 1975. Manager Pakistan to Australia 1981/82.

IJAZ HUSSAIN
RHB, occ RM/LB, WK

Born Bahawalpur, India, 7 Apr 1942. Debut 1956/57.
PAKISTAN DOMESTIC Bahawalpur, Multan, Railways, Karachi, Public Works Department, National Bank, Sind, 1956/57–73/74.
TOURS Pakistan Eaglets to England 1963. Commonwealth XI to Pakistan 1967/68.
HS 173 Railway Reds v Lahore Reds, Rawalpindi, 1965/66.
BB 5–37 Bahawalpur–Multan v Railways–Quetta, Bahawalpur, 1960/61.

IKIN, John Thomas
LHB, RLBG

Born Bignall End, Staffordshire, 7 Mar 1918. Died Bignall End, Staffordshire, 15 Sept 1984. Debut 1938. *P.*
MINOR COUNTIES (3) 1938, 1959, 1960.
LANCASHIRE (288) 1939–57. Cap 1946. Benefit (£7175) 1953.
NORTH (4) 1949–61.
MCC (3) 1951–64.
ENGLAND (18) 1946–55. SA 1951 (3), 1955 (1); I 1946 (2), 1952 (2). *A 1946/47 (5); NZ 1946/47 (1); WI 1947/48 (4)*.
OTHER TOUR Commonwealth XI to India and Ceylon 1950/51.
HST 60 E v A, Sydney, 1946/47. HS 192 Lancs v Oxford U, The Parks, 1951.
BB 6–21 (11–119 match) Lancs v Notts, Old Trafford, 1947.
1000 RUNS (10 + 1) 1912 @ 45.52 in 1952.
In BB match above also scored 67 and 85* for match double.
Players v Gentlemen (2) 1946–51. Staffordshire 1933–38, 1958–68 (capt 1958–68). Club: Bignall End. MCC Hon. member. Professional coach Denstone C 1958–63. Coach and organiser of Schools cricket

after retirement. Son M. J. Ikin (Minor Counties).

IKIN, Michael John
LHB, ROB

Born Bignall End, Staffordshire, 31 Dec 1946. Debut 1972.
MINOR COUNTIES (2) 1972–79.
HS 31 Minor Counties v Indians, Wellington, 1979.
Staffordshire 1967–79. Clubs: Bignall End, Newcastle and Hartshill. Father J. T. Ikin (Lancs, England).

IKRAM ELAHI
RHB, RFM

Born Quetta, India, 3 Mar 1933. Debut 1952/53.
PAKISTAN DOMESTIC Rest of Pakistan, Sind, East Pakistan, Karachi, Public Works Department, 1952/53–69/70.
TOURS Pakistan to England 1954. Pakistan to West Indies 1957/58.
HS 73 Karachi v Bahawalpur, Bahawalpur, 1959/60.
BB 6–25 Karachi A v Sind A, Karachi, 1957/58.
Clubs: Haslingden, Bacup, Oldham, Daisy Hill.

ILLINGWORTH, Nigel John Bartle
RHB, RFM

Born Chesterfield, Derbys, 23 Nov 1960. Educ Denstone C. Debut 1981.
NOTTINGHAMSHIRE (15) 1981–83.
HS 49 Notts v Cambridge U, Fenner's, 1982.
BB 5–89 Notts v M'sex, Lord's, 1982.

ILLINGWORTH, Raymond
RHB, OB

Born Pudsey, Yorks, 8 June 1932. Educ Wesley Street S, Farsley, Yorks. Debut 1951. *P. Wisden* 1960.
YORKSHIRE (496) 1951–68, 1982–83.

Cap 1955. Capt 1982–83. Benefit (£6604) 1965.
LEICESTERSHIRE (176) 1969–78. Cap 1969. Capt 1969–78. Benefit 1977.
ENGLAND (61) 1958–73. A 1961 (2), 1968 (3), 1972 (5); SA 1960 (4); WI 1966 (2), 1969 (3), 1973 (3); NZ 1958 (1), 1965 (1), 1969 (3), 1973 (3); I 1959 (2), 1967 (3), 1971 (3); P 1962 (1), 1967 (1), 1971 (3). *A 1962/63 (2), 1970/71 (6); WI 1959/ 60 (5); NZ 1962/63 (3), 1970/71 (2).* Capt 31.
OTHER TOUR Commonwealth XI to S Africa and Rhodesia 1960/61.
HST 113 E v WI, Lord's, 1969. HS 162 Yorks v Indians, Bramall Lane, Sheffield, 1959.
BBT 6–29 E v I, Lord's, 1967. BB 9–42 Yorks v Worcs, Worcester, 1957.
1000 RUNS (8) 1726 @ 46.64 in 1959.
100 WKTS (10) 131 @ 14.36 in 1968.
DOUBLE (6) 1957, 1959–62, 1964.
RECORDS Added 228 for 10th wkt with K. Higgs, Leics v Northants, Leicester, 1977, county record. Took over Yorks captaincy during 1982 season, aged 50: oldest-ever player appointed Yorks capt and second-oldest player appointed to any county captaincy.
Match double of 135 and 14–101 Yorks v Kent, Dover, 1964.
Players v Gentlemen (3) 1955–59. England v Rest of World (5) 1970 (capt). Yorks cricket manager 1979–84. Club: Farsley. MCC Hon. member. CBE for services to cricket. Autobiography *Yorkshire and Back* (1980). Son-in-law A. A. Metcalfe (Yorks).

ILLINGWORTH, Richard Keith
——————RHB, SLA——————

Born Greengates, Bradford, Yorks, 23 Aug 1963. Educ Wroze Brow Middle Salts GS. Debut 1982.
WORCESTERSHIRE (57) 1982–.
HS 55 Worcs v Leics, Worcester, 1983.
BB 5–26 Worcs v Glos, Worcester, 1983.

ILSLEY, Stanley Thomas
——————LHB, SLA——————

Born Marylebone, London, 18 June 1938. Educ Priory S, Acton, London. Debut 1956. *P.*
MCC (2) 1956.
HS 8 MCC v Cambridge U, Lord's, 1956.
BB 3–39 same match.
M'sex staff 1954–58. Clubs: Chiswick, West Herts.

IMRAN AHMED KHAN NIAZI (Imran Khan)
——————RHB, RF——————

Born Lahore, Pakistan, 25 Nov 1952. Educ Aitchison C, Lahore; Cathedral S, Lahore; Worcester RGS; Keble C, Oxford. Debut 1969/70. *Wisden 1983.*
PAKISTAN DOMESTIC Lahore, Dawood Industries, Pakistan International Airlines, 1969/70–80/81.
WORCESTERSHIRE (42) 1971–76. Cap 1976.
OXFORD UNIVERSITY (24) 1973–75 (Blue 1973–75). Capt 1975.
SUSSEX (102) 1977–83. Cap 1978.
PAKISTAN (51) 1971–83/84. A 1979/80 (2), 1982/83 (3); WI 1980/81 (4); NZ 1976/77 (3); I 1978/79 (3), 1982/83 (6); SL 1981/82 (1). *E 1971 (1), 1974 (3), 1982 (3); A 1976/77 (3), 1978/79 (2), 1981/82 (3), 1983/84 (2); WI 1976/77 (5); NZ 1978/79 (2); I 1979/80 (5).* Capt 14.
OTHER TOUR Pakistan to Sri Lanka 1975/ 76.
HST 123 P v WI, Lahore, 1980/81. HS 170 Oxford U v Northants, The Parks, 1974.
BBT 8–58 P v SL, Faisalabad, 1981/82. BB as above.
1000 RUNS (4) 1339 @ 41.84 in 1978.
MATCH DOUBLES 111* and 13–99 Worcs v Lancs, Worcester, 1976. 117 and 11–180 P v I, Faisalabad, 1982/83 (only second player, after I. T. Botham, to perform the feat in a Test).
RECORDS 40 wkts @ 13.95 in series, P v I, 1982/83, and 232 Test wkts @ 22.91, both records for Pakistan.
World Series Cricket (Kerry Packer) 1977/78–78/79. Cousins (distaff) Majid Khan and Javed Burki (both Pakistan); uncle Mohammad Baqa Jilani (India). Clubs: Stourbridge, Worthing.

IMTIAZ AHMED
——————RHB, WK——————

Born Lahore, India, 5 Jan 1928. Educ Punjab U. Debut 1944/45.
INDIA DOMESTIC Northern India 1944/ 45–46/47.
PAKISTAN DOMESTIC Punjab University, Combined Universities, North-West Frontier Province, Pakistan Services, Peshawar, Pakistan Air Force, 1947/ 48–73/74.
PAKISTAN (41) 1952/53–62. E 1961/62 (3); A 1956/57 (1), 1959/60 (3); WI 1958/59 (3); NZ 1955/56 (3); I 1954/55 (5). *E 1954 (4), 1962 (4); WI 1957/58 (5); I 1952/53 (5), 1960/61 (5).* Capt 4.
OTHER TOURS Pakistan to Ceylon 1948/ 49, 1964/65. Pakistan Services to India and Ceylon 1954/55.
HST 209 P v NZ, Lahore, 1955/56. HS

300* Prime Minister's XI v Commonwealth XI, Bombay, 1950/51.
1000 RUNS (2 + 1) 1142 @ 49.65 in 1961/ 62.
RECORDS During HST (above) added 308 for 7th wkt with Waqar Hasan, Pakistan fc record. 80 dismissals in England in 1954, record for a tourist.
Did not concede a bye during inns of 544 for 5 dec, P v E, Edgbaston, 1962.
Former chairman Pakistan selectors.

INCHMORE, John Darling
——————RHB, RFM——————

Born Ashington, Northumberland, 22 Feb 1949. Educ Ashington GS. Debut 1973.
WORCESTERSHIRE (190) 1973–. Cap 1976.
S AFRICA DOMESTIC Northern Transvaal 1976/77.
HS 113 Worcs v Essex, Worcester, 1974.
BB 8–58 Worcs v Yorks, Worcester, 1977.
Club: Stourbridge.

Kumar Shri INDRAJITSINHJI
——————RHB, WK——————

Born Jamnagar, India, 15 June 1937. Educ Delhi U. Debut 1954/55.
INDIA DOMESTIC Saurashtra 1954/55–57/ 58, 1961/62–71/72, Delhi 1958/59–60/ 61.
L. C. STEVENS' XI (1) 1960.
INDIA (4) 1964/65–69/70. A 1964/65 (3); NZ 1969/70 (1).
TOUR India to Australia 1967/68.
HST 23 I v A, Bombay, 1964/65. HS 123 Saurashtra v Baroda, Baroda, 1962/63.

INGHAM, Peter Geoffrey
——————RHB, RM——————

Born Sheffield, Yorks, 28 Sept 1956. Educ Ashville C, Harrogate. Debut 1979.
YORKSHIRE (8) 1979–81.
HS 64 Yorks v Northants, Headingley, 1980.
Clubs: Birstall, Harrogate.

INGLEBY-MACKENZIE, Alexander *Colin* David
——————LHB, occ WK——————

Born Totnes, Devon, 15 Sept 1933. Educ Eton. Debut 1951.
HAMPSHIRE (309) 1951–65. Cap 1957. Capt 1958–65.
TOURS E. W. Swanton's XI to W Indies 1955/56, 1960/61 (capt). Duke of Norfolk's XI to Jamaica 1956/57. Commonwealth XI to S Africa 1959/60. F. R.

Brown's XI to E Africa 1961/62. Commonwealth XI to Rhodesia 1962/63. Cavaliers to Jamaica 1963/64. E. W. Swanton's XI to India 1963/64 (capt). Cavaliers to W Indies 1964/65.
HS 132* Hants v Essex, Cowes, 1961.
1000 RUNS (5) 1613 @ 25.68 in 1959.
Gentlemen v Players (3) 1958–60. MCC committee since 1980. Autobiography *Many a Slip* (1962).

INGLIS, Russell
———————RHB, RM———————

Born Crookhall, nr Blackhill, Co Durham, 13 June 1936. Died Gosforth, Newcastle upon Tyne, 28 Apr 1982. Debut 1965.
MINOR COUNTIES (3) 1965–69.
HS 43 Minor Counties v S Africans, Jesmond, 1965.
BB 2–2 Minor Counties v Pakistanis, Swindon, 1967.
Durham (140 matches) 1956–73. 6626 runs for Durham, county record. Clubs: Durham City, Chester-le-Street.

INGRAM, Edward
———————RHB, LB/RM———————

Born Dublin, Ireland, 14 Aug 1910. Died Basingstoke, Hants, 13 Mar 1973. Educ Belvedere C, Dublin. Debut 1928.
IRELAND (19) 1928–53. Capt 8.
MIDDLESEX (12) 1938–49. Cap 1948.
HS 64 Ireland v Scotland, Belfast, 1937.
BB 5–48 Ireland v Scotland, Edinburgh, 1936.
Clubs: Leinster, Ealing.

INMAN, Clive Clay
———————LHB, ROB———————

Born Colombo, Ceylon, 29 Jan 1936. Educ St Peter's C, Colombo. Debut 1956/57. *P.*
CEYLON 1956/57–66/67.
LEICESTERSHIRE (242) 1961–71. Cap 1963. Benefit 1970.
TOURS Ceylon to India 1957/58. Ceylon to Pakistan 1966/67.
HS 178 Leics v Essex, Leicester, 1965.
1000 RUNS (8) 1735 @ 36.91 in 1968.
RECORDS Reached fifty in 8 mins during inns of 57, Leics v Notts, Trent Bridge, 1965, fastest fifty in fc cricket, and hit an over of full tosses from N. W. Hill for 32 (466664) (Notts were bowling to expedite a declaration). Club: Penzance.

INSHAN ALI
———————LHB, SLC———————

Born San Fernando, Trinidad, 25 Sept 1949. Debut 1965/66.

W INDIES DOMESTIC South Trinidad, Trinidad, 1965/66–79/80.
WEST INDIES (12) 1970/71–76/77. E 1973/74 (2); A 1972/73 (3); I 1970/71 (1); P 1976/77 (1); NZ 1971/72 (3). *E 1973 (1); A 1975/76 (1).*
HST 25 WI v NZ, Port of Spain, 1971/72.
HS 63 W Indians v Minor Counties, Torquay, 1973.
BBT 5–59 WI v NZ, Port of Spain, 1971/72. BB 8–58 Trinidad v Duke of Norfolk's XI, Port of Spain, 1969/70.
Club: Preysel.

INSOLE, Douglas John
———————RHB, occ RM, occ WK———————

Born Clapton, London, 18 Apr 1926. Educ Monoux S, Walthamstow; St Catharine's C, Cambridge. Debut 1947. *Wisden* 1956.
CAMBRIDGE UNIVERSITY (36) 1947–49 (Blue 1947–49). Capt 1949.
ESSEX (345) 1947–63. Cap 1949. Capt 1950–60.
ENGLAND (9) 1950–57. A 1956 (1); SA 1955 (1); WI 1950 (1), 1957 (1). *SA 1956/57 (5).*
HST 110* E v SA, Durban, 1956/57. HS 219* Essex v Yorks, Colchester, 1949.
BB 5–22 Essex v Surrey, Ilford, 1955.
1000 RUNS (13) 2427 @ 42.57 in 1955.
RECORD Nine centuries for Essex in 1955, equalling county record.
Scored centuries against all fc counties except his own.
Gentlemen v Players (18) 1951–60. MCC committee 1956–80. England selector 1959–68. TCCB chairman 1975–78. Manager England to Australia 1978/79. CBE for services to cricket. Author *Cricket From The Middle* (1960). Soccer: Blue.

INTIKHAB ALAM Khan
———————RHB, LBG———————

Born Hoshiarpur, India, 28 Dec 1941. Educ Church Mission S, Karachi. Debut 1957/58.
PAKISTAN DOMESTIC Karachi, Pakistan International Airlines, Public Works Department, Sind, Punjab, 1957/58–75/76.
SURREY (232) 1969–81. Cap 1969. Benefit (£20,000) 1978.
PAKISTAN (47) 1959/60–76/77. E 1961/62 (3), 1968/69 (3), 1972/73 (3); A 1959/60 (1), 1964/65 (1); WI 1974/75 (2); NZ 1964/65 (3), 1969/70 (3), 1976/77 (3). *E 1962 (3), 1967 (3), 1971 (3), 1974 (3); A 1964/65 (1), 1972/73 (3); WI 1976/77 (1); NZ 1964/65 (3), 1972/73 (3); I 1960/61 (3).* Capt 17.
OTHER TOURS Pakistan Eaglets to England 1963. PIA to E Africa 1964.

Pakistan to Ceylon 1964/65. World XI to Australia 1971/72.
HST 138 P v E, Hyderabad, 1972/73. HS 182 Karachi Blues v PIA B, Karachi, 1970/71.
BBT 7–52 P v NZ, Dunedin, 1972/73. BB 8–54 Pakistanis v Tasmania, Hobart, 1972/73.
100 WKTS (1) 104 @ 28.36 in 1971.
RECORDS Added 190 for 9th wkt with Asif Iqbal, P v E, Oval, 1967, world Test and Pakistan fc record. Took wkt (C. C. McDonald) with first ball in Test cricket, P v A, Karachi, 1959/60, only Pakistani to do so.
Rest of World v England (5) 1970. Manager Pakistan to England 1982. Club: Western Scotland.

INVERARITY, Robert *John*
———————RHB, SLA———————

Born Subiaco, W Australia, 31 Jan 1944. Debut 1962/63.
AUSTRALIA DOMESTIC Western Australia (119) 1962/63–78/79, South Australia (43) 1979/80–.
AUSTRALIA (6) 1968–72. WI 1968/69 (1). *E 1968 (2), 1972 (3).*
OTHER TOUR Australia to N Zealand 1969/70.
HST 56 A v E, Oval, 1968. HS 187 W Australia v NSW, Sydney, 1978/79.
BBT 3–26 A v E, Headingley, 1972. BB 5–28 Australians v Otago, Dunedin, 1969/70.
RECORDS 9033 runs @ 39.27 and 150 appearances in Sheffield Shield, both records.
Clubs: University (Perth), Kensington (Adelaide). Father M. Inverarity (W Australia).

Mohammed IQBAL QASIM
———————LHB, SLA———————

Born Karachi, Pakistan, 6 Aug 1953. Educ Hussain S; Jinnah C, Karachi; Premier C, Karachi. Debut 1971/72.
PAKISTAN DOMESTIC Karachi, Sind, National Bank, 1971/72–.
PAKISTAN (37) 1976/77–83/84. E 1977/78 (3); A 1979/80 (3), 1982/83 (2); WI 1980/81 (4); I 1978/79 (3), 1982/83 (2); SL 1981/82 (3). *E 1978 (3); A 1976/77 (3), 1981/82 (2); WI 1976/77 (2); I 1979/80 (6), 1983/84 (1).*
OTHER TOURS Pakistan to Australasia 1978/79. Pakistan to England 1982.
HST 56 P v SL, Karachi, 1981/82. HS 61 National Bank v Universities, Lahore, 1978/79.
BBT 7–49 (11–118 match) P v A, Karachi, 1979/80. BB 9–80 Pakistan XI v International XI, Lahore, 1981/82.

IRISH, Arthur Frank
————RHB, RMF————

Born Dudley, Worcs, 23 Nov 1918.
Debut 1950. *P*.
SOMERSET (16) 1950.
HS 76 Som v Glam, Cardiff, 1950.
BB 2–5 Som v Leics, Bath, 1950.
Devon 1946–53. Clubs: Sidmouth, XL
Club.

IRVINE, Brian *Lee*
————LHB, occ RM, WK————

Born Durban, S Africa, 9 Mar 1944.
Educ Durban HS. Debut 1962/63.
S AFRICA DOMESTIC Western Province In-
vitation XI 1962/63, Natal 1965/66–68/
69, Transvaal 1969/70–76/77 (capt
1974/75–75/76).
ESSEX (54) 1968–69. Cap 1968.
SOUTH AFRICA (4) A 1969/70.
HST 102 SA v A, Port Elizabeth, 1969/
70. HS 193 Transvaal v E Province,
J'burg, 1972/73.
1000 RUNS (2) 1439 @ 32.70 in 1968.
RECORD Made nine dismissals in match,
Transvaal v Rhodesia, J'burg, 1974/75,
equalling S African record.

ISLES, Derek
————RHB, WK————

Born Bradford, Yorks, 14 Oct 1943.
Debut 1967.
WORCESTERSHIRE (1) 1967.
HS 17* Worcs v Pakistanis, Worcester,
1967.
Clubs: Undercliffe, Bingley.

IVEY, Alfred *Michael*
————RHB, RM————

Born Leeds, Yorks, 11 July 1928. Educ
Leeds GS; Brasenose C, Oxford. Debut
1949.
OXFORD UNIVERSITY (7) 1949–51.
HS 40 (both inns) Oxford U v Free
Foresters, The Parks, 1950.

JACKMAN, Robin David
————RHB, RMF————

Born Simla, India, 13 Aug 1945. Educ
St Edmund's, Canterbury. Debut 1966.
Wisden 1981.
SURREY (338) 1966–82. Cap 1970.
Benefit 1981.
S AFRICA DOMESTIC Western Province
1971/72, Rhodesia 1972/73–79/80.
ENGLAND (4) 1980/81–82. P 1982 (2). WI
1980/81 (2).

OTHER TOURS D. H. Robins' XI to S
Africa 1972/73. England to Australia
1982/83.
HST 17 E v P, Lord's, 1982. HS 92* Sur-
rey v Kent, Oval, 1974.
BBT 4–110 E v P, Lord's, 1982. BB 8–40
Rhodesia v Natal, Durban, 1972/73.
100 WKTS (1) 121 @ 15.40 in 1980.
England team to W Indies 1980/81 ex-
pelled from Guyana owing to Jackman's
S African connections.
Club: Byfleet.

JACKSON, Albert *Brian*
————RHB, RFM————

Born Kettleshulme, Cheshire, 21 Aug
1933. Debut 1963. *P*.
DERBYSHIRE (148) 1963–68. Cap 1963.
HS 27 Derbys v M'sex, Lord's, 1964 and
v Leics, Derby, 1965.
BB 8–18 Derbys v Warwicks, Coventry,
1966.
100 WKTS (1) 120 @ 12.42 in 1965.
Cheshire 1956–62. Club: Knypersley.

JACKSON, Edward John
Wycliffe
————RHB, LMF————

Born Singapore, 26 Mar 1955. Educ
Winchester C; Pembroke C, Cam-
bridge. Debut 1974.
CAMBRIDGE UNIVERSITY (27) 1974–76
(Blue 1974–76).
OXFORD AND CAMBRIDGE UNIVERSITIES (1)
1976.
HS 63 Cambridge U v Surrey, Fenner's,
1976.
BB 7–98 Cambridge U v Oxford U,
Lord's, 1975.
Club: I Zingari.

JACKSON, Herbert *Leslie*
————RHB, RFM————

Born Whitwell, Derbys, 5 Apr 1921.
Debut 1947. *P. Wisden* 1959.
DERBYSHIRE (394) 1947–63. Cap 1949.
Benefit (£2944) 1957. Joint testimonial
(with G. O. Dawkes) (£2902) 1962.
ENGLAND (2) 1949–61. A 1961 (1); NZ
1949 (1).
TOUR Commonwealth XI to India 1950/
51.
HST 8 E v A, Headingley, 1961. HS 39*
Derbys v Yorks, Harrogate, 1951.
BBT 2–26 E v A, Headingley, 1961. BB
9–17 Derbys v Cambridge U, Fenner's,
1959. Also 9–60 Derbys v Lancs, Old
Trafford, 1952.
100 WKTS (10) 160 @ 13.61 in 1960.
RECORDS Took 143 wkts @ 10.99 in
1958, lowest average for 100 wkts or
more since 1894. Aggregate of 1670 wkts

@ 17.11 for Derbys, county record.
Players v Gentlemen (3) 1949–60.
Clubs: Whitwell, Enfield, Undercliffe.

JACKSON, Paul Brian
————RHB, WK————

Born Belfast, N Ireland, 9 Dec 1959.
Debut 1981.
IRELAND (4) 1981–.
HS 46 Ireland v Scotland, Myreside,
Edinburgh, 1982.
Clubs: NICC, Ulster.

JACKSON, Percy Frederick
————RHB, OB————

Born Aberfeldy, Perthshire, Scotland,
11 May 1911. Debut 1929. *P*.
WORCESTERSHIRE (383) 1929–50. Cap
1931. Benefit (£2150) 1948.
HS 40 Worcs v Glos, Worcester, 1933.
BB 9–45 Worcs v Som, Dudley, 1935.
100 WKTS (4) 125 @ 23.70 in 1947.
Club: Old Hill.

JACKSON, Roger Frank
————RHB, RFM————

Born Woolwich, London, 5 Jan 1939.
Educ Hertford C, Oxford. Debut 1962.
OXFORD UNIVERSITY (2) 1962.
HS 5* Oxford U v Yorks, The Parks,
1962.

JACKSON, Victor Edward
————RHB, OB————

Born Sydney, NSW, Australia, 25 Oct
1916. Died, in level-crossing accident,
Manildra, Central NSW, Australia, 30
Jan 1965. Debut 1936/37. *P*.
AUSTRALIA DOMESTIC New South Wales
(20) 1936/37–40/41.
LEICESTERSHIRE (322) 1938–56. Cap
1946. Benefit (£2863) 1956.
COMMONWEALTH XI (2) 1957–1958.
TOUR Sir Julien Cahn's XI to N Zealand
1938/39.
HS 170 Leics v Northants, Leicester,
1948.
BB 8–43 Leics v Glam, Llanelli, 1956.
1000 RUNS (11) 1582 @ 29.29 in 1955.
100 WKTS (1) 112 @ 21.71 in 1955.
DOUBLE (1) 1955.
Clubs: Waverley (Sydney), Rawtenstall
(England).

JACOBS, Jack
————RHB, WK————

Born Dunedin, N Zealand, 16 Apr 1909.
Educ Dunedin HS. Debut 1927/28.

N ZEALAND DOMESTIC Canterbury (11) 1927/28–37/38.
TOUR N Zealand Services XI to England 1945.
HS 69 Canterbury v Otago, Christchurch, 1927/28.
Club: Riccarton.

JACOBSON, Louis Collins
————RHB————

Born Dublin, Ireland, 26 Jan 1918. Educ Wesley C, Dublin; Dublin U. Debut 1948.
IRELAND (4) 1948–52.
HS 101* Ireland v Scotland, Perth, 1950. Clubs: Clontarf, Carlisle. Represented England at world Jewish sports festival 1957.

JAFFEY, Isaac *Mervyn*
————RHB, WK————

Born Dublin, Ireland, 9 Sept 1929. Educ Wesley C, Dublin; Dublin U. Debut 1953.
IRELAND (1) 1953.
Did not bat or bowl.
Dublin University. Now known as Mervyn Jeffries.

JAISIMHA, Motganhalli Lakshminarasu
————RHB, RM————

Born Secunderabad, India, 3 Mar 1939. Educ Osmania U. Debut 1954/55.
INDIA DOMESTIC Hyderabad 1954/ 55–76/77 (capt 1959/60–76/77).
INDIA (39) 1959–70/71. E 1961/62 (5), 1963/64 (5); A 1959/60 (1), 1964/65 (3); WI 1966/67 (2); NZ 1964/65 (4), 1969/ 70 (1); P 1960/61 (4). *E 1959 (1); A 1967/68 (2); WI 1961/62 (4), 1970/71 (3); NZ 1967/68 (4)*.
OTHER TOURS Indian Starlets to Pakistan 1959/60. Hyderabad Blues to Ceylon 1966/67.
HST 129 I v E, Calcutta, 1963/64. HS 259 Hyderabad v Bengal, Secunderabad, 1964/65.
BBT 2–54 I v E, Kanpur, 1963/64. BB 7–45 Hyderabad v Madras, Hyderabad, 1959/60.
1000 RUNS (0 + 3) 1293 @ 41.70 in 1964/ 65.
Scored 99 in 505 mins, I v P, Kanpur, 1960/61, one of slowest of all fc inns.
Son V. Jaisimha (Hyderabad).

JAKEMAN, Frederick
————LHB————

Born Holmfirth, Yorks, 10 Jan 1920. Debut 1946. *P.*

YORKSHIRE (10) 1946–47.
NORTHAMPTONSHIRE (119) 1949–54. Cap 1951.
HS 258* Northants v Essex, Northampton, 1951.
BB 2–8 Northants v Essex, Northampton, 1951.
1000 RUNS (2) 1989 @ 56.82 in 1951.
RECORD Added 320 for 3rd wkt with L. Livingston, Northants v S Africans, Northampton, 1951, county record.
HS (above) part of sequence of 4 inns in which scored 558 runs before being dismissed.
Fc umpire 1961–72. Clubs: Lightcliffe, Salts, David Brown Tractors, Holmfirth. Son R. S. Jakeman (Northants).

JAKEMAN, Ronald Stuart
————LHB, occ WK————

Born Holmfirth, Yorks, 20 Sept 1943. Debut 1962. *P.*
NORTHAMPTONSHIRE (3) 1962–63.
HS 20 Northants v Leics, Wellingborough, 1962.
Cumberland 1965–66. Club: Bradley Mills. Father F. Jakeman (Yorks, Northants).

JAKOBSON, Tonu Robert
————RHB, RFM————

Born London, 17 Dec 1937. Educ Charterhouse; UC, Oxford. Debut 1960.
OXFORD UNIVERSITY (14) 1960–61 (Blue 1961).
HS 20 Oxford U v Yorks, The Parks, 1961.
BB 5–61 Oxford U v Hants, Portsmouth, 1961.

JALAL-UD-DIN
————RHB, RFM————

Born Karachi, Pakistan, 12 June 1959. Debut 1975/76.
PAKISTAN DOMESTIC Railways, Public Works Department, Karachi, Industrial Development Bank of Pakistan, Allied Bank, 1975/76–.
PAKISTAN (3) 1982/83. A 1982/83 (1); I 1982/83 (2).
TOURS Pakistan to England 1982.
HST 1* P v I, Lahore, 1982/83. HS 60* IDBP v Quetta, Bahawalpur, 1979/80.
BBT 3–77 P v A, Lahore, 1982/83. BB 7–43 IDBP v Railways, Lahore, 1981/ 82.
Club: Ashington.

JAMES, Albert *Edward*
————RHB, RM————

Born Newton Longville, Buckinghamshire, 7 Aug 1924. Debut 1948. *P.*

SUSSEX (299) 1948–60. Cap 1950. Benefit 1961.
HS 63* Sussex v Notts, Trent Bridge, 1950.
BB 9–60 Sussex v Yorks, Hove, 1955.
100 WKTS (2) 111 @ 21.31 in 1955.
Buckinghamshire 1947. Professional coach Eastbourne C from 1961.

JAMES, Brian
————LHB, LFM————

Born Darfield, Yorks, 23 Apr 1934. Debut 1954. *P.*
YORKSHIRE (4) 1954.
HS 11* Yorks v Cambridge U, Fenner's, 1954.
BB 4–74 same match.
Clubs: Honley, Brighouse, Bankfoot.

JAMES, David Harry
————RHB, RMF————

Born Briton Ferry, S Wales, 3 Mar 1921. Educ Cwrt Sart S, Briton Ferry. Debut 1948.
GLAMORGAN (1) 1948.
HS 17 Glam v Notts, Trent Bridge, 1948.
Clubs: Briton Ferry Town, Briton Ferry Steelworks. Father E. H. James (Glam).

JAMES, David John Gwynne
————RHB, RM————

Born Pembroke Dock, S Wales, 12 June 1937. Educ Cheltenham C; RMA Sandhurst. Debut 1961.
FREE FORESTERS (1) 1961.
HS 29 Free Foresters v Oxford U, The Parks, 1961.
Clubs: Army, Light Infantry, I Zingari, MCC. Captain in Regular Army. Now D. J. G. Gwynne-James.

JAMES, Evan Llewellyn
————RHB, RM————

Born Barry, Glam, 10 May 1918. Educ Gladstone Road S, Barry. Debut 1946.
GLAMORGAN (9) 1946–47.
HS 62* Glam v Indians, Swansea, 1946.
Clubs: Cardiff, Maesteg.

JAMES, Kenneth Cecil
————RHB, WK————

Born Wellington, N Zealand, 12 Mar 1904. Died Palmerston North, N Zealand, 21 Aug 1976. Educ Wellington C. Debut 1923/24. *P from 1935.*
N ZEALAND DOMESTIC Wellington (38) 1923/24–46/47.

NORTHAMPTONSHIRE (101) 1935–39. Cap 1936.
NEW ZEALAND (11) 1929/30–32/33. E 1929/30 (4), 1932/33 (2); SA 1931/32 (2). *E 1931 (3)*.
OTHER TOURS N Zealand to Australia 1925/26. N Zealand to England 1927. N Zealand Services XI to England 1945 (capt).
HST 14 NZ v E, Auckland, 1929/30. HS 109* Wellington v Canterbury, Christchurch, 1928/29.
1000 RUNS (1) 1032 @ 23.45 in 1938.
Clubs: Institute Old Boys, Wellington C Old Boys, Hutt Valley (Minor Association).

JAMES, Kevan David
———————LHB, LFM———————

Born Lambeth, London, 18 Mar 1961. Educ Edmonton County HS. Debut 1980.
MIDDLESEX (13) 1980–.
N ZEALAND DOMESTIC Wellington (2) 1982/83.
HS 34 M'sex v Northants, Northampton, 1983.
BB 5–28 M'sex v Cambridge U, Fenner's, 1983.

JAMES, Robert *Michael*
———————RHB, RM———————

Born Wokingham, Berkshire, 2 Oct 1934. Educ St John's, Leatherhead; Trinity C, Cambridge. Debut 1956.
CAMBRIDGE UNIVERSITY (45) 1956–58 (Blue 1956–58).
MINOR COUNTIES (1) 1959.
FREE FORESTERS (1) 1960.
MCC (1) 1961.
N ZEALAND DOMESTIC Wellington (3) 1964/65.
HS 168 Cambridge U v Glos, Bristol, 1957.
BB 4–5 Cambridge U v Warwicks, Edgbaston, 1957.
Berkshire 1954–70 (Rhodes Trophy 1962). Club: Mitcham.

JAMESON, John Alexander
————RHB, RM/OB, occ WK————

Born Bombay, India, 30 June 1941. Educ Taunton S. Debut 1960. P.
WARWICKSHIRE (345) 1960–76. Cap 1964. Benefit (£13,500) 1974.
ENGLAND (4) 1971–73/74. I 1971 (2). *WI 1973/74 (2)*.
OTHER TOUR International Wanderers to Rhodesia 1972/73.
HST 82 E v I, Oval, 1971. HS 240* Warwicks v Glos, Edgbaston, 1974.
BB 4–22 Warwicks v Oxford U, The Parks, 1971.

1000 RUNS (11) 1948 @ 48.70 in 1973.
RECORD During HS (above) added 465* for 2nd wkt with R. B. Kanhai, world record and highest-ever unbroken stand in England.
Run out in three of first four Test inns. Scored 103 before lunch, on 1st morning of match, in last fc inns, Warwicks v Glam, Edgbaston, 1976.
Fc umpire 1984. Clubs: Smethwick, Knowle and Dorridge. Brother T. E. N. Jameson (Cambridge U, Warwicks).

JAMESON, Thomas Edward Neville
———————LHB, RMF———————

Born Bombay, India, 23 July 1946. Educ Taunton S; Durham U; Emmanuel C, Cambridge. Debut 1970.
CAMBRIDGE UNIVERSITY (9) 1970 (Blue).
WARWICKSHIRE (1) 1970.
HS 32 Warwicks v Cambridge U, Edgbaston, 1970.
BB 2–21 Cambridge U v Derbys, Fenner's, 1970.
Club: Knowle and Dorridge. Brother J. A. Jameson (Warwicks, England).

JAQUES, Peter Heath
———————RHB———————

Born Leicester, 20 Nov 1919. Educ Wyggeston GS. Debut 1949.
LEICESTERSHIRE (1) 1949.
HS 55 Leics v Northants, Northampton, 1949.

JARDINE, Douglas Robert
———————RHB, SRA———————

Born Malabar Hill, Bombay, India, 23 Oct 1900. Died Montreux, Switzerland, 18 June 1958. Educ Winchester C; New C, Oxford. Debut 1920.
OXFORD UNIVERSITY (30) 1920–23 (Blue 1920–21, 1923).
SURREY (141) 1921–33. Cap. Capt 1932–33.
ALL ENGLAND XI (1) 1948.
INDIA DOMESTIC Services 1943/44.
ENGLAND (22) 1928–33/34. WI 1928 (2), 1933 (2); NZ 1931 (3); I 1932 (1). *A 1928/29 (5), 1932/33 (5); NZ 1932/33 (1); I 1933/34 (3)*. Capt 15.
HST 127 E v WI, Old Trafford, 1933. HS 214 MCC v Tasmania, Launceston, 1928/29.
BB 6–28 Oxford U v Essex, The Parks, 1920.
1000 RUNS (8 + 1) 1473 @ 46.03 in 1926. Scored 1002 runs @ 91.09 in 1927 and 1133 runs @ 87.15 in 1928.
Gentlemen v Players (12) 1924–33.
Capt England to Australia 1932/33 on

'Bodyline' tour. Author of four cricket books. Father M. R. Jardine (Oxford U, M'sex).

JARMAN, Barrington Noel
———————RHB, WK———————

Born Hindmarsh, S Australia, 17 Feb 1936. Debut 1955/56.
AUSTRALIA DOMESTIC South Australia (94) 1955/56–68/69.
AUSTRALIA (19) 1959/60–68/69. E 1962/63 (3); WI 1968/69 (4); I 1967/68 (4); P 1964/65 (1). *E 1968 (4); I 1959/60 (1), 1964/65 (2)*. Capt 1.
OTHER TOURS Australia to New Zealand 1956/57, 1966/67. Australia to S Africa 1957/58. Australia to England 1961, 1964. Australia to W Indies 1964/65.
HST 78 A v I, Bombay, 1964/65. HS 196 S Australia v NSW, Adelaide, 1965/66.
Made ten dismissals in match, S Australia v NSW, Adelaide, 1961/62.

JARMAN, Harold James
———————RHB———————

Born Bristol, 4 May 1939. Debut 1961. P.
GLOUCESTERSHIRE (45) 1961–71.
HS 67* Glos v Essex, Bristol, 1968.
Clubs: Bristol Optimists, Downend. Soccer: Bristol Rovers, Newport County.

JARRETT, David William
———————RHB, RM———————

Born Bromsgrove, Worcs, 19 Apr 1952. Educ Wellington C; Worcester C, Oxford; St Catharine's C, Cambridge. Debut 1974.
OXFORD UNIVERSITY (13) 1974–75 (Blue 1975).
CAMBRIDGE UNIVERSITY (8) 1976 (Blue).
HS 62 Cambridge U v Essex, Fenner's, 1976.
RECORDS First player to gain cricket Blues for both Oxford and Cambridge Universities.
Bedfordshire 1978–81. Club: Bedford Town.

JARRETT, Gordon Maurice
———————RHB, LBG———————

Born Bedford, 9 Feb 1937. Educ Bedford Modern. Debut 1971.
MINOR COUNTIES (3) 1971–74.
HS 24* Minor Counties v West Indians, Torquay, 1973.
BB 2–83 same match.
Bedfordshire 1961–77. Club: Forest Hill.

JARRETT, Keith Stanley
————————RHB, RM————————

Born Newport, Monmouthshire, 18 May 1948. Educ Monmouth S. Debut 1967.
GLAMORGAN (2) 1967.
HS 18* Glam v Pakistanis, Swansea, 1967.
Rugby Union: British Lions, Newport, Wales (10). Rugby League: Great Britain. Retired from Rugby League owing to ill-health. Father H. H. Jarrett (Warwicks, Glam).

JARVIS, Kevin Bertram Sidney
————————RHB, RFM————————

Born Dartford, Kent, 23 Apr 1953. Educ Springhead S, Northfleet; Thames Polytechnic. Debut 1975.
KENT (200) 1975–. Cap 1977.
TOUR D. H. Robins' XI to Sri Lanka 1977/78. International XI to Jamaica 1982/83.
HS 19 Kent v Derbys, Maidstone, 1984.
BB 8–97 Kent v Worcs, Worcester, 1978.

JARVIS, Paul William
————————RHB, RFM————————

Born Redcar, Yorks, 29 June 1965. Educ Bydales CS, Marske. Debut 1981.
YORKSHIRE (21) 1981–.
HS 11* Yorks v Surrey, Oval, 1984.
BB 6–61 Yorks v Lancs, Old Trafford, 1984.
RECORD Yorks debut at 16 yrs 75 days, youngest-ever player for the county.

JARVIS, Terrence Wayne
————————RHB————————

Born Auckland, N Zealand, 29 July 1944. Debut 1964/65.
N ZEALAND DOMESTIC Auckland (46) 1964/65–68/69, 1971/72–76/77, Canterbury (10) 1969/70–70/71.
NEW ZEALAND (13) 1964/65–1972/73. E 1965/66 (1); P 1972/73 (3). WI 1971/72 (4); I 1964/65 (2); P 1964/65 (3).
OTHER TOURS N Zealand to England 1965. N Zealand to Australia 1967/68.
HST 182 NZ v WI, Georgetown, 1971/72. HS as above.
RECORDS During HS (above) added 387 for 1st wkt with G. M. Turner, N Zealand Test record for any wkt.
Club: Parnell.

JAVED AKHTAR
————————RHB, OB————————

Born Delhi, India, 21 Nov 1940. Debut 1959/60.

PAKISTAN DOMESTIC Rawalpindi, Services, 1959/60–75/76.
PAKISTAN (1) E 1962.
HST 2* P v E, Headingley, 1962. HS 88 Rawalpindi Greens v Services, Peshawar, 1964/65.
BB 7–61 (12–117 match) Rawalpindi v Services, Rawalpindi, 1961/62.
Test umpire.

JAVED BURKI
————————RHB, RM————————

Born Meerut, India, 8 May 1938. Educ St Mart's, Rawalpindi; Punjab U; Christ's C, Oxford. Debut 1955/56.
PAKISTAN DOMESTIC Universities, Punjab, Lahore, Karachi, Rawalpindi, North-West Frontier Province, 1955/56–72/73.
OXFORD UNIVERSITY (44) 1958–60 (Blue 1958–60).
PAKISTAN (25) 1960/61–69/70. E 1961/62 (3); A 1964/65 (1); NZ 1964/65 (3), 1969/70 (1). E 1962 (5), 1967 (3); A 1964/65 (1); NZ 1964/65 (3); I 1960/61 (5). Capt 5.
OTHER TOUR Pakistan to Ceylon 1964/65.
HST 140 P v E, Dacca, 1961/62. HS 227 Karachi Whites v Khairpur, Karachi, 1963/64.
BB 4–12 Lahore Greens v Rawalpindi B, Rawalpindi, 1970/71.
1000 RUNS (1) 1257 @ 33.07 in 1962.
MCC Hon. member. Cousins (distaff) Majid Khan and Imran Khan (both Pakistan); uncle Mohammed Baqa Jilani (India).

Mohammed JAVED MIANDAD Khan
————————RHB, LBG————————

Born Karachi, Pakistan, 12 June 1957. Educ CMS Sec S, Karachi. Debut 1973/74. Wisden 1982.
PAKISTAN DOMESTIC Karachi, Sind, Habib Bank, 1973/74–.
SUSSEX (40) 1976–79. Cap 1977.
GLAMORGAN (62) 1980–. Cap 1980. Capt 1982.
PAKISTAN (60) 1976/77–83/84. E 1977/78 (3); A 1979/80 (3), 1982/83 (3); WI 1980/81 (4); NZ 1976/77 (3); I 1978/79 (3), 1982/83 (6); SL 1981/82 (3). E 1978 (3), 1982 (3); A 1976/77 (3), 1978/79 (2), 1981/82 (3), 1983/84 (5); WI 1976/77 (1); NZ 1978/79 (3); I 1979/80 (6), 1983/84 (3). Capt 13.
OTHER TOURS Pakistan to Sri Lanka 1975/76.
HST 280* P v I, Hyderabad, 1982/83. HS 311 Karachi Whites v National Bank, Karachi, 1974/75.
BBT 3–74 P v NZ, Hyderabad, 1976/77.

BB 7–39 Habib Bank v IDBP, Lahore, 1980/81.
1000 RUNS (4 + 8) 2083 @ 69.43 in 1981.
RECORDS During HST (above) added 451 for 3rd wkt with Mudassar Nazar, world Test record and equalling Test record for any wkt; added 281 for 5th wkt with Asif Iqbal, P v NZ, Lahore, 1976/77 (scoring 163 on Test debut), Pakistan Test record. HST (above) highest Test inns in Asian sub-continent. Scored 2083 runs and 8 centuries for Glam in 1981, both county records.
Brothers Anwar Miandad and Bashir Miandad (both Karachi).

JAWAHIR SHAH
————————RHB————————

Born Kenya, 1942.
EAST AFRICA (3) 1967/68–75.
TOUR East Africa to England 1975.
HS 50 E Africa v Sri Lanka, Taunton, 1975.

JAYANTILAL, Hirjee Kenia
————————RHB————————

Born Hyderabad, Deccan, India, 13 Jan 1948. Educ Osmania U, Hyderabad. Debut 1967/68.
INDIA DOMESTIC Hyderabad Blues 1967/68, Hyderabad 1968/69–78/79.
INDIA (1) WI 1970/71.
OTHER TOURS Indian Universities to Ceylon 1970/71. Indians to England 1971.
HST 5 I v WI, Kingston, 1970/71.
HS 197 Hyderabad v Kerala, Hyderabad, 1978/79.
BB 3–47 Hyderabad v Tamil Nadu, Hyderabad, 1978/79.
Scored 153 on Ranji Trophy debut, Hyderabad v Andhra, Guntur, 1968/69.

JAYASEKERA, Rohan Stanley Amarasiriwardena
————————RHB, WK————————

Born Colombo, Ceylon, 7 Dec 1957. Educ RC, Colombo. Debut 1979.
SRI LANKA 1979–81/82.
SRI LANKA (1) P 1981/82.
OTHER TOURS Sri Lanka to England 1979. Sri Lanka to India 1980/81.
HST 2 SL v P, Lahore, 1981/82. HS 79 Sri Lankans v Worcs, Worcester, 1979.
Club: Tamil Union.

JAYASINGHE, Sunil Asoka
————————RHB, WK————————

Born Matugama, Ceylon, 15 July 1955. Debut 1979.

SRI LANKA to England 1979.
HS 64 Sri Lankans v Derbys, Derby, 1979.
Club: Bloomfield.

JAYESINGHE, Stanley
————RHB, OB————

Born Badulla, Ceylon, 19 Jan 1931.
Debut 1949/50. *P.*
CEYLON 1949/50–55/56, 1961/62–66/67.
LEICESTERSHIRE (112) 1961–65. Cap 1963.
TOURS Ceylon to Pakistan 1949/50, 1966/67. Ceylon to India 1964/65.
HS 135 Ceylon v India, Hyderabad, 1964/65.
BB 6–38 Ceylon v India, Ahmedabad, 1964/65.
1000 RUNS (4) 1499 @ 29.39 in 1962.
Club: Colne.

JEFFERIES, Stephen Thomas
————LHB, LFM————

Born Cape Town, S Africa, 8 Dec 1959.
Educ Plumstead HS. Debut 1978/79.
S AFRICA DOMESTIC Western Province 1978/79–.
DERBYSHIRE (1) 1982.
LANCASHIRE (28) 1983–.
HS 75* Lancs v Essex, Old Trafford, 1983.
BB 8–46 Lancs v Notts, Trent Bridge, 1983.
S Africa (10) 1981/82–83/84.

JEFFERSON, Richard Ingleby
————RHB, RFM————

Born Frimley Green, Surrey, 15 Aug 1941. Educ Winchester C; Corpus Christi C, Cambridge. Debut 1961. *P 1962.*
CAMBRIDGE UNIVERSITY (14) 1961 (Blue).
SURREY (76) 1961–66. Cap 1964.
MINOR COUNTIES (1) 1969.
HS 136 Surrey v Northants, Northampton, 1963 (adding 138 for 10th wkt with D. A. D. Sydenham).
BB 6–25 Surrey v Worcs, Worcester, 1961.
Gentlemen v Players (1) 1962. Norfolk 1968–69.

JEFFERY, Howard William James
————RHB, RF————

Born Cockermouth, Cumberland, 5 May 1944. Educ Workington GS. Debut 1964.
LEICESTERSHIRE (2) 1964.
HS 6 Leics v Australians, Leicester, 1964.

BB 2–77 Leics v Worcs, Leicester, 1964.
Cumberland 1963–69. Club: Workington.

JEGANATHAN, Sridharan
————RHB, SLA————

Born Colombo, Ceylon, 11 July 1951.
Educ Wesley C, Colombo. Debut 1973/74.
SRI LANKA 1973/74–82/83.
SRI LANKA (2) *NZ 1982/83.*
OTHER TOURS Sri Lanka to Pakistan 1973/74. Sri Lanka to England 1979. Sri Lanka to Zimbabwe 1982/83.
HST 8 SL v NZ, Christchurch, 1982/83.
HS 74 Sri Lankans v Tasmania, Devonport, 1982/83.
BB 5–34 Sri Lanka Board President's XI v West Indians, Colombo, 1978/79.
Clubs: Nondescripts, Droylsden.

JENKINS, Huw
————LHB————

Born Swansea, S Wales, 24 Oct 1944.
Debut 1970.
GLAMORGAN (1) 1970.
HS 65 Glam v Oxford U, The Parks, 1970.

JENKINS, Roland Oliver
————RHB, LBG————

Born Worcester, 24 Nov 1918. Debut 1938. *P. Wisden* 1950.
WORCESTERSHIRE (352) 1938–58. Cap 1939. Benefit (£3411) 1953.
ENGLAND (9) 1948/49–52. WI 1950 (2); I 1952 (2). *SA 1948/49 (5).*
HST 39 E v WI, Trent Bridge, 1950. HS 109 Worcs v Notts, Trent Bridge, 1948.
BBT 5–116 E v WI, Lord's, 1950. BB 8–62 (15–122 match) Worcs v Sussex, Dudley, 1953.
1000 RUNS (4) 1356 @ 27.12 in 1948.
100 WKTS (5) 183 @ 21.19 in 1949.
DOUBLE (2) 1949, 1952.
Three hat-tricks, all against Surrey, in 1948 and twice in same match at Worcester in 1949.
Players v Gentlemen (1) 1949. Club: West Bromwich Dartmouth. Nephew P. J. Robinson (Worcs, Som).

JENNINGS, Keith Francis
————RHB, RM————

Born Wellington, Som, 5 Oct 1953.
Educ Kingsmead Sec S, Wiveliscombe.
Debut 1975.
SOMERSET (68) 1975–81. Cap 1978.
HS 49 Som v W Indians, Taunton, 1976.
BB 5–18 Som v Sussex, Hove, 1978.

JEPSON, Arthur
————RHB, RFM————

Born Selston, Notts, 12 July 1915.
Debut 1938. *P.*
NOTTINGHAMSHIRE (390) 1938–59. Cap 1939. Benefit (£2000) 1951.
Testimonial (£1511) 1959.
HS 130 Notts v Worcs, Trent Bridge, 1950.
BB 8–45 Notts v Leics, Trent Bridge, 1958.
100 WKTS (1) 115 @ 27.78 in 1947.
Fc umpire since 1960 (4 Tests, 1966–69). Clubs: Clipstone Colliery, Yeadon, Selston. Soccer: Port Vale, Stoke City, Lincoln City.

JERMAN, Lindsey Crawford Stapleton
————RHB, RFM————

Born Old Fletton, Huntingdonshire, 23 Apr 1915. Educ Rhyl GS. Debut 1950.
ESSEX (3) 1950–51.
HS 8 Essex v Surrey, Southend, 1951.
Cambridgeshire 1955–56. Clubs: Chelmsford, Romford, Essex Wanderers.

JESSUP, Anthony
————LHB, SLA————

Born Blindley Heath, Surrey, 31 Aug 1928. Educ Caterham; Jesus C, Oxford.
Debut 1950.
OXFORD UNIVERSITY (7) 1950–51.
HS 7* Oxford U v Warwicks, Stratford on Avon, 1951.
BB 5–30 Oxford U v Worcs, The Parks, 1951.

JESTY, Trevor Edward
————RHB, RM————

Born Gosport, Hants, 2 June 1948.
Educ Privet County Sec S, Gosport.
Debut 1966.
HAMPSHIRE (340) 1966–84. Cap 1971.
Benefit 1982.
S AFRICA DOMESTIC Border 1973/74, Griqualand West 1974/75–75/76, 1980/81.
N ZEALAND DOMESTIC Canterbury (6) 1979/80.
TOURS International XI to Jamaica 1982/83. England to Australasia 1982/83 (as replacement; no fc matches).
HS 248 Hants v Cambridge U, Fenner's, 1984.
BB 7–75 Hants v Worcs, Southampton, 1976.
1000 RUNS (7) 1645 @ 58.75 in 1982.
Took 32 runs of one over (666662) from R. J. Boyd-Moss, Hants v Northants,

Southampton, 1984.
Joined Surrey for 1985.

JEWELL, Guy Alonzo Frederick William
———LHB, SLA———

Born Axford, Hants, 8 Oct 1916. Died Basingstoke, Hants, 23 Dec 1965. Debut 1952.
HAMPSHIRE (1) 1952.
HS 1 Hants v Glam, Swansea, 1952.
Berkshire 1938. Club: Basingstoke (over 10,000 runs and 1800 wkts). In 1956 took all 11 wkts in 12-a-side match, Basingstoke v P.I. Bedford's XII.

JOHNS, David Frank Victor
———LHB, SLA———

Born Paddington, London, 27 June 1921. Died High Wycombe, Buckinghamshire, 20 Nov 1979. Debut 1953.
MINOR COUNTIES (1) 1953.
HS 4 Minor Counties v Australians, Stoke on Trent, 1953.
Buckinghamshire 1950–66. Clubs: Ferndale, High Wycombe.

JOHNS, Robert Leslie (Robin)
———RHB, OB———

Born Southampton, 30 June 1946. Educ St Albans S; Keele U; St Edmund's Hall, Oxford. Debut 1970.
OXFORD UNIVERSITY (8) 1970 (Blue).
NORTHAMPTONSHIRE (6) 1971.
HS 61* Oxford U v Cambridge U, Lord's, 1970.
BB 4–76 Oxford U v Notts, The Parks, 1970.
Hertfordshire 1975–. Clubs: Southampton, Deanery.

JOHNSON, Anthony *Alexander*
———RHB, RFM———

Born Loughborough, Leics, 30 Apr 1944. Educ Hartlepool GS; Carlton-le-Willows GS. Debut 1963.
NOTTINGHAMSHIRE (26) 1963–66.
MINOR COUNTIES (1) 1974.
HS 45 Notts v M'sex, Trent Bridge, 1966.
BB 4–13 Notts v Essex, Trent Bridge, 1965.
Northumberland 1968–71, 1974–77, Durham 1973. Clubs: Whitburn, Tynedale, Ashington, Gateshead Fell, Laisterdyke.

JOHNSON, Colin
———RHB, OB———

Born Pocklington, Yorks, 5 Sept 1947. Educ Pocklington S. Debut 1969.
YORKSHIRE (100) 1969–79.
HS 107 Yorks v Som, Sheffield, 1973.
BB 2–22 Yorks v Oxford U, The Parks, 1971.
Yorks 2nd XI capt 1980–. Club: Leeds.

JOHNSON, Frank Sidney Roland
———RHB———

Born Simla, India, 4 Aug 1917. Educ Trinity County Sec S, Wood Green. Debut 1942/43.
INDIA DOMESTIC Delhi and District 1942/43.
COMBINED SERVICES (1) 1947.
HS 11 Combined Services v Oxford U, The Parks, 1947.
Clubs: RAF, St Xaviers. Air Vice-Marshall. OBE.

JOHNSON, Graham William
———RHB, OB———

Born Beckenham , Kent, 8 Nov 1946. Educ Beckenham & Penge GS; Shooters Hill GS; London S of Economics; London U. Debut 1965.
KENT (365) 1965–. Cap 1970. Benefit 1983.
S AFRICA DOMESTIC Transvaal 1981/82.
TOUR D. H. Robins' XI to S Africa 1973/74.
HS 168 Kent v Surrey, Oval, 1976.
BB 7–76 Kent v Northants, Canterbury, 1983.
1000 RUNS (3) 1438 @ 31.26 in 1973 and 1438 @ 35.95 in 1975.
Brother-in-law G. R. Dilley (Kent, England).

JOHNSON, Hines Hophnine Horace
———RHB, RF———

Born Kingston, Jamaica, 17 July 1910. Debut 1934/35.
W INDIES DOMESTIC Jamaica 1934/35–50/51.
WEST INDIES (3) 1947/48–50. E 1947/48 (1). E 1950 (2).
HST 22 WI v E, Old Trafford, 1950. HS 39* Jamaica v Trinidad, Kingston, 1946/47 and 39* W Indians v Surrey, Oval, 1950.
BBT 5–41 (10–96 match) WI v E, Kingston, 1947/48 (Test debut). BB 5–33 Jamaica v Trinidad, Kingston, 1946/47 and 5–33 W Indians v Glam, Cardiff, 1950.

JOHNSON, Hubert *Laurence*
———RHB, OB, occ WK———

Born Barbados, 8 Nov 1927. Debut 1949. *P from 1955.*
DERBYSHIRE (350) 1949–66. Cap 1958. Testimonial (£2383) 1965.
HS 154 Derbys v Leics, Leicester, 1962.
BB 3–12 Derbys v Lancs, Old Trafford, 1964.
1000 RUNS (6) 1872 @ 37.44 in 1960.
Club: Swarkstone 1948.

JOHNSON, Ian William
———RHB, OB———

Born N Melbourne, Australia, 8 Dec 1918. Educ Wesley C, Melbourne. Debut 1935/36.
AUSTRALIA DOMESTIC Victoria (77) 1935/36–55/56.
AUSTRALIA (45) 1945/46–56/57. E 1946/47 (4), 1950/51 (5), 1954/55 (4); SA 1952/53 (1); WI 1951/52 (4); I 1947/48 (4). E 1948 (4), 1956 (5); SA 1949/50 (5); WI 1954/55 (5); NZ 1945/46 (1); I 1956/57 (2); P 1956/57 (1). Capt 17.
HST 77 A v E, Sydney, 1950/51. HS 132* Victoria v Queensland, Melbourne, 1948/49.
BBT 7–44 A v WI, Georgetown, 1954/55.
BB 7–42 Australians v Leics, Leicester, 1948.
Club: South Melbourne. Secretary Melbourne Cricket Club. MCC Hon. member. MBE for services to cricket. Father W. J. Johnson (Victoria); father-in-law R. L. Park (Australia).

JOHNSON, Ivan Nicholas
———LHB, SLA———

Born Nassau, Bahamas, 27 June 1953. Educ Malvern C. Debut 1972.
WORCESTERSHIRE (33) 1972–75.
HS 69 Worcs v Notts, Worcester, 1975.
BB 5–74 Worcs v Oxford U, Worcester, 1975.

JOHNSON, John Stephen
———RHB———

Born Doncaster, Yorks, 7 July 1944. Educ Ashville C. Debut 1979.
MINOR COUNTIES (1) 1979.
HS 146* Minor Counties v Indians, Wellington, Shropshire, 1979 (1st inns of only fc match).
Shropshire 1968–. Clubs: Kidderminster, Ludlow.

JOHNSON, Laurence Alan
RHB, WK

Born West Horsley, Surrey, 12 Aug 1936. Debut 1958. *P.*
NORTHAMPTONSHIRE (153) 1958–72. Cap 1960. Benefit 1973.
TOUR MCC to E Africa 1963/64.
HS 50 Northants v Worcs, Dudley, 1967.
Twice dismissed 10 batsmen in match, Northants v Sussex, Worthing, 1963 (10 ct) and Northants v Warwicks, Edgbaston, 1965 (8 ct, 2 st).

JOHNSON, Mark
RHB, RM

Born Sheffield, Yorks, 23 Apr 1958. Educ Ashleigh GS; Sheffield Polytechnic. Debut 1981.
YORKSHIRE (4) 1981.
HS 2 Yorks v Som, Dore, Sheffield, 1981.
BB 4–48 Yorks v Warwicks, Scarborough, 1981.

JOHNSON, Paul
RHB, RM

Born Newark, Notts, 24 Apr 1965. Educ Grove CS. Debut 1982.
NOTTINGHAMSHIRE (30) 1982–.
HS 133 Notts v Kent, Folkestone, 1984.

JOHNSON, Peter David
RHB, LBG

Born Nottingham, 12 Nov 1949. Educ Nottingham HS; Emmanuel C, Cambridge. Debut 1969.
D. H. ROBINS' XI (1) 1969.
CAMBRIDGE UNIVERSITY (27) 1970–72 (Blue 1970–72).
NOTTINGHAMSHIRE (58) 1970–77. Cap 1975.
MINOR COUNTIES (2) 1979–81.
HS 106* Notts v Yorks, Trent Bridge, 1977.
BB 3–34 Cambridge U v Glam, Fenner's, 1970.
1000 RUNS (1) 1063 @ 32.21 in 1975.
Lincolnshire 1978–82, 1984.

JOHNSON, Peter Lovell
RHB

Born Liverpool, 22 May 1926. Educ Liverpool C; Clare C, Cambridge. Debut 1947.
CAMBRIDGE UNIVERSITY (1) 1947.
COMBINED SERVICES (1) 1950.
HS 40 Cambridge U v M'sex, Fenner's, 1947.
Royal Navy. Regular Officer in Royal Navy.

JOHNSON, Peter Malcolm
RHB, WK

Born London, 21 Dec 1947. Educ Jesus C, Oxford. Debut 1971.
OXFORD UNIVERSITY (1) 1971.
HS 2 Oxford U v Northants, The Parks, 1971.

JOHNSTON, Andrew
RHB, OB

Born Linlithgow, Scotland, 26 Feb 1916. Educ Linlithgow Academy. Debut 1947.
SCOTLAND (2) 1947–51.
HS 50* Scotland v Yorks, Scarborough, 1951.
West Lothian County. Club: Kilmarnock.

JOHNSTON, Harry *Grant* Forsyth
LHB, SLA

Born Kirkwall, Scotland, 24 Dec 1949. Educ Northfield Sec S. Debut 1975.
SCOTLAND (2) 1975–81.
HS 12 Scotland v Ireland, Dublin, 1975.
BB 2–60 Scotland v Ireland, Clontarf, 1981.
Aberdeenshire. Club: Uddingston.

JOHNSTON, Robert *Ian*
RHB, RM

Born Belfast, N Ireland, 1 July 1948. Educ Belfast Royal Academy. Debut 1979.
IRELAND (3) 1979–83.
HS 34 Ireland v Sri Lankans, Eglinton, 1979.
Club: Woodvale.

JOHNSTON, William Arras
LHB, LFM/SLA

Born Beeac, Victoria, Australia, 26 Feb 1922. Educ Colac HS. Debut 1945/46. *Wisden* 1949.
AUSTRALIA DOMESTIC Victoria (56) 1945/46–54/55.
AUSTRALIA (40) 1947/48–54/55. E 1950/51 (5), 1954/55 (4); SA 1952/53 (5); WI 1951/52 (5); I 1947/48 (4). *E 1948 (5), 1953 (3); SA 1949/50 (5); WI 1954/55 (4).*
HST 29 A v E, Lord's, 1948. HS 38 Victoria v S Australia, Adelaide, 1948/49.
BBT 6–44 A v SA, J'burg, 1949/50. BB 8–52 Victoria v Queensland, Melbourne, 1952/53.
100 WKTS (1) 102 @ 16.42 in 1948.
Achieved a batting average of 102.00 on 1953 tour to England (17 inns, 16 not-out).
MCC Hon. member. Son D. A. Johnston (S Australia).

JOLLEY, William Turner
RHB, RFM

Born Smallthorne, Stoke on Trent, Staffordshire, 3 Aug 1923. Educ Manchester U. Debut 1947.
LANCASHIRE (2) 1947.
HS 13 Lancs v Hants, Old Trafford, 1947.
BB 4–31 same match.
Staffordshire 1949–55. President Staffordshire. Clubs: Norton, Stone.

JONES, Adrian Nicholas
LHB, RFM

Born Woking, Surrey, 22 July 1961. Educ Seaford C. Debut 1981.
SUSSEX (24) 1981–.
S AFRICA DOMESTIC Border 1981/82.
HS 35 Sussex v M'sex, Hove, 1984.
BB 5–29 Sussex v Glos, Hove, 1984.

JONES, Alan
LHB, occ ROB

Born Velindre, Swansea, S Wales, 4 Nov 1938. Educ Cwmtawe S. Debut 1957. *P. Wisden* 1978.
GLAMORGAN (610) 1957–83. Cap 1962. Benefit (£10,000) 1972. Testimonial (£35,000) 1980. Capt 1976–78.
AUSTRALIA DOMESTIC Western Australia (9) 1963/64.
S AFRICA DOMESTIC Northern Transvaal 1975/76, Natal 1976/77.
TOURS Glamorgan to W Indies 1969/70. MCC to Ceylon 1969/70.
HS 204* Glam v Hants, Basingstoke, 1980.
1000 RUNS (23) 1865 @ 34.53 in 1966.
RECORDS Most runs (34,056) and most centuries (52) for Glam. Put on 330 for 1st wkt with R. C. Fredericks, Glam v Northants, Swansea, 1972, county record for any wkt; and 238 for 2nd wkt with A. R. Lewis, Glam v Sussex, Hastings, 1962, county record. Scored more runs in fc cricket than any other player never to win an official Test cap.
England v Rest of World (1) 1970. Glam coach 1984–. Club: Clydach. MBE for services to cricket. Brother E. W. Jones (Glam).

JONES, Alan *Keith* Colin
RHB

Born Solihull, Warwicks, 20 Apr 1951. Educ Solihull S; St Edmund Hall, Oxford. Debut 1969.
WARWICKSHIRE (4) 1969–73.
OXFORD UNIVERSITY (29) 1971–73 (Blue 1971–73). Capt 1973.
HS 111 Oxford U v Notts, The Parks, 1971.

JONES, Alan Lewis
LHB

Born Alltwen, nr Swansea, S Wales, 1 June 1957. Educ Ystalyfera GS; Cardiff C of Educ. Debut 1973.
GLAMORGAN (128) 1973–. Cap 1983.
HS 132 Glam v Hants, Cardiff, 1984.
1000 RUNS (2) 1811 @ 36.96 in 1984.

JONES, Allan Arthur
RHB, RFM

Born Horley, Surrey, 9 Dec 1947. Educ St John's C, Horsham. Debut 1966.
SUSSEX (18) 1966–69.
SOMERSET (118) 1970–75. Cap 1972.
MIDDLESEX (52) 1976–79. Cap 1976.
GLAMORGAN (19) 1980–81.
S AFRICA DOMESTIC Northern Transvaal 1972/73, Orange Free State 1976/77.
HS 33 M'sex v Kent, Canterbury, 1978.
BB 9–51 Som v Sussex, Hove, 1972.
RECORD First player, since the qualification rules changed in 1873, to play fc cricket for four counties.
Appointed fc umpire for 1985.

JONES, Archibald *Trevor* Maxwell
RHB

Born Wells, Som, 9 Apr 1920. Educ Wells GS. Debut 1938.
SOMERSET (21) 1938–48.
HS 106 Som v Leics, Leicester, 1938.
Clubs: Imperial Tobacco, Bristol Optimists, XL Club.

JONES, Barry John Richardson
LHB, RM

Born Shrewsbury, Shropshire, 2 Nov 1955. Educ Wrekin C. Debut 1976.
WORCESTERSHIRE (46) 1976–80.
HS 65 Worcs v Warwicks, Edgbaston, 1977.
Shropshire 1981–82. Club: Wroxeter.

JONES, Charles Ian McMillan
RHB, RM

Born Leeds, Yorks, 11 Oct 1934. Educ Bishop's Stortford C; Cambridge U. Debut 1959.
CAMBRIDGE UNIVERSITY (2) 1959.
HS 44 Cambridge U v M'sex, Fenner's, 1959.
Hertfordshire 1959–68.

JONES, Eifion Wyn
RHB, WK

Born Velindre, S Wales, 25 June 1942. Educ Cwmtawe S. Debut 1961. *P.*
GLAMORGAN (405) 1961–83. Cap 1967.
Benefit (£17,000) 1975.
TOUR Glam to W Indies 1969/70.
HS 146* Glam v Sussex, Hove, 1968.
Made 7 dismissals in inns (6 ct, 1 st), Glam v Cambridge U, Fenner's, 1970.
Made 933 dismissals (840 ct, 93 st) in career.
Clubs: Clydach, Swansea, Llanelli.
Brother A. Jones (Glam).

JONES, Emrys Closs
RHB, OB

Born Briton Ferry, S Wales, 14 Dec 1911. Educ Cwrt Sart Central S. Debut 1934. *P from 1937.*
GLAMORGAN (100) 1934–46. Cap 1937.
Rest of England v MCC XI, Lord's 1937 (Test trial).
HS 132 Glam v Cambridge U, Swansea, 1938.
BB 7–79 Glam v Sussex, Cardiff, 1937.
Injury in Test trial reduced subsequent effectiveness. Clubs: Elba Works, Maesteg, Celtic, Swansea, Neath, Briton Ferry Steel Co, Briton Ferry Town.

JONES, Fred Alan
RHB, occ WK

Born Macclesfield, Cheshire, 23 Feb 1927. Educ King's S, Macclesfield; Oxford U. Debut 1951.
OXFORD UNIVERSITY (4) 1951–52.
SCOTLAND (8) 1954–61.
PAKISTAN DOMESTIC Hyderabad 1962/63–63/64 (capt).
HS 88 Scotland v Indians, Paisley, 1959.
Club: Grange.

JONES, Harry Ogwyn
RHB, RM

Born Llangennech, S Wales, 6 Oct 1922. Educ Llangennech S. Debut 1946.
GLAMORGAN (2) 1946.

HS 7* Glam v Worcs, Ebbw Vale, 1946.
Clubs: Llangennech, Dafen, Llanelli, Pontarddulais.

JONES, Ivor Jeffrey
RHB, LFM

Born Dafen, S Wales, 10 Dec 1941. Debut 1960. *P.*
GLAMORGAN (158) 1960–68. Cap 1965.
ENGLAND (15) 1963/64–67/68. WI 1966 (2). *A 1965/66 (4); WI 1967/68 (5); NZ 1965/66 (3); I 1963/64 (1).*
OTHER TOUR MCC to E Africa 1963/64.
HST 16 E v A, Sydney, 1965/66. HS 21 MCC v Guyana, Georgetown, 1967/68.
BBT 6–118 E v A, Adelaide, 1965/66. BB 8–11 Glam v Leics, Leicester, 1965.
100 WKTS (1) 100 @ 19.49 in 1967.
Retired 1968 through elbow injury.
Clubs: Pontarddulais, Dafen, Llanelli, Briton Ferry Steel Co.

JONES, Keith Vaughan
RHB, RM

Born Park Royal, London, 28 Mar 1942. Debut 1967.
MIDDLESEX (117) 1967–74. Cap 1971.
MINOR COUNTIES (1) 1976.
HS 57* M'sex v Surrey, Oval, 1972.
BB 7–52 M'sex v Warwicks, Coventry, 1971.
Bedfordshire 1975–. Clubs: Duport, Northampton Saints, Aston Unity, Polytechnic, Shepherds Bush.

JONES, Peter Charles Howard
RHB, LB

Born Rhodesia, 19 Aug 1948. Educ Milton HS, Rhodesia; St Edmund Hall, Oxford. Debut 1971.
OXFORD UNIVERSITY (26) 1971–72 (Blue 1971–72). Capt 1972.
HS 67 Oxford U v Warwicks, The Parks, 1971.
BB 3–51 Oxford U v Yorks, The Parks, 1971.

JONES, Peter Henry
LHB, SLA

Born Woolwich, London, 19 June 1935. Educ Erith GS. Debut 1953. *P.*
KENT (140) 1953–67. Cap 1961.
HS 132 Kent v Notts, Tunbridge Wells, 1961.
BB 6–61 Kent v Surrey, Oval, 1961.
1000 RUNS (2) 1262 @ 26.85 in 1961.
Suffolk 1971–81. Clubs: Canterbury St Laurence, Wolverhampton, Kidderminster, Duport, Barnt Green.

JONES, Prior Erskine
——————RHB, RFM——————

Born Princes Town, Trinidad, 6 June 1917. Debut 1940/41.
W INDIES DOMESTIC Trinidad 1940/41–50/51.
WEST INDIES (9) 1947/48–51/52. E 1947/48 (1). *E 1950 (2); A 1951/52 (1); I 1948/49 (5).*
HST 10* WI v E, Bridgetown, 1947/48.
HS 60* Trinidad v Barbados, Bridgetown, 1943/44.
BBT 5–85 WI v I, Bombay, 1948/49. BB 7–29 W Indians v Yorks, Bradford, 1950.

JONES, Richard Henry Cartwright
——————LHB, RM——————

Born Redditch, Worcs, 3 Nov 1916. Educ Aston Commercial S. Debut 1946.
WARWICKSHIRE (1) 1946.
HS 23 Warwicks v Som, Edgbaston, 1946.
Clubs: Kings Heath, Mitchells and Butlers, Newport (Monmouthshire), Ombersley, Worcestershire Ramblers. Now known as R. H. Cartwright-Jones.

JONES, Ronald
——————RHB——————

Born Wolverhampton, Staffordshire, 9 Sept 1938. Debut 1955.
WORCESTERSHIRE (1) 1955.
HS 23 Worcs v Cambridge U, Worcester, 1955.
Club: Stourbridge.

JONES, Watkin Edward (Watt)
——————RHB, RMF——————

Born Gwaun-cae Gurwen, W Glam, 6 July 1917. Educ Gwaun-cae Gurwen S. Debut 1946.
GLAMORGAN (5) 1946–47.
No runs.
BB 7–92 Glam v Kent, Newport, 1947.
Played as Watt Jones to distinguish him from William E. Jones (Glam). Clubs: Pontardawe, Pontarddulais, Clydach. Former police officer in Clydach.

JONES, William Edward
——————LHB, SLA——————

Born Carmarthen, S Wales, 31 Oct 1916. Debut 1937. *P from 1946.*
GLAMORGAN (340) 1937–58. Cap 1946.
Benefit (£4460) 1953.
South v North, Edgbaston, 1949 (Test trial).

HS 212* Glam v Essex, Brentwood, 1948.
BB 5–50 Glam v Kent, Gravesend, 1949.
1000 RUNS (7) 1656 @ 40.39 in 1948.
RECORDS During HS (above) added 313 for 3rd wkt with D. E. Davies; added 230 for 6th wkt with B. L. Muncer, Glam v Worcs, Worcester, 1953; added 195* for 7th wkt with W. Wooller, Glam v Lancs, Liverpool, 1947, all county records.
Club: Stroud Brewery. Former professional coach Dean Close S, Cheltenham (from 1963). Rugby: Gloucestershire, Gloucester, Wales (war-time cap).

JORDAN, John
——————RHB, WK——————

Born Cloughfield, Rossendale, Lancs, 7 Feb 1932. Debut 1955. *P.*
LANCASHIRE (62) 1955–57. Cap 1956.
HS 39 Lancs v Yorks, Headingley, 1956.

JORDEN, Anthony Mervyn
——————RHB, RFM——————

Born Radlett, Hertfordshire, 28 Jan 1947. Educ Monmouth S; Fitzwilliam C, Cambridge. Debut 1966.
ESSEX (60) 1966–70.
CAMBRIDGE UNIVERSITY (28) 1968–70 (Blue 1968–70). Capt 1969–70.
HS 67* Cambridge U v Derbys, Fenner's, 1968.
BB 5–95 Cambridge U v Sussex, Hove, 1969.
Bedfordshire 1975–77. Rugby: Blue, Blackheath, Harlequins, Bedford, England (7 caps).

JOSE, Anthony Douglas
——————RHB, RFM——————

Born Adelaide, S Australia, 17 Feb 1929. Died Los Angeles, USA, 3 Feb 1972. Educ St Peter's, Adelaide; Adelaide U; Brasenose C, Oxford. Debut 1947/48.
AUSTRALIA DOMESTIC South Australia (3) 1947/48.
OXFORD UNIVERSITY (19) 1950–51 (Blue 1950–51).
KENT (5) 1951–52.
FREE FORESTERS (2) 1952–53.
HS 39 Oxford U v Free Foresters, The Parks, 1950.
BB 6–45 Oxford U v Warwicks, Stratford on Avon, 1951.
Club: Hampstead. Doctor of Medicine.

JOSEPH, Arthur Frederick
——————RHB——————

Born Briton Ferry, Wales, 13 Mar 1919. Debut 1946.
GLAMORGAN (1) 1946.
HS 8 Glam v Derbys, Chesterfield, 1946.
Clubs: Briton Ferry Town, Neath.

JOSEPHS, John Michael
——————LHB, SLA——————

Born Hendon, M'sex, 10 Jan 1924. Educ Clifton C; Oriel C, Oxford. Debut 1946.
LEICESTERSHIRE (9) 1946–53.
HS 25* Leics v Oxford U, The Parks, 1951 and 25 v Notts, Leicester, 1951.

JOSHI, Padmanabh Govind (Nana)
——————RHB, WK——————

Born Baroda, India, 27 Oct 1926. Educ Bombay U. Debut 1946/47.
INDIA DOMESTIC Maharashtra 1946/47–64/65. Capt 1960/61–62/63.
INDIA (12) 1951/52–60/61. E 1951/52 (2); A 1959/60 (1); WI 1958/59 (1); P 1952/53 (1), 1960/61 (1). *E 1959 (3); WI 1952/53 (3).*
HST 52* I v P, Bombay, 1960/61. HS 100* Governor's XI v Commonwealth XI, Nagpur, 1949/50.
RECORD During HST (above) added 149 for 9th wkt with R. B. Desai, India Test record.

JOSHI, Udaykumar Chaganlal
——————RHB, OB——————

Born Rajkot, India, 23 Dec 1944. Debut 1965/66.
INDIA DOMESTIC Saurashtra, Railways, Gujerat, 1965/66–82/83.
SUSSEX (76) 1970–74. Cap 1971.
HS 100* Gujerat v Saurashtra, Rajkot, 1975/76.
BB 6–33 Gujerat v Saurashtra, Surat, 1972/73.
Took wkt with first ball in fc cricket, Saurashtra v Baroda, Rajkot, 1965/66.

JOSLIN, Leslie Ronald
——————LHB, OCC LM——————

Born Yarraville, Victoria, Australia, 13 Dec 1947. Debut 1966/67.
AUSTRALIA DOMESTIC Victoria (30) 1966/67–69/70.
AUSTRALIA (1) I 1967/68.
TOUR Australia to England 1968.
HST 7 A v I, Sydney, 1967/68. HS 126 Victoria v W Australia, Melbourne, 1966/67.
Club: Footscray.

JOWETT, David Colin Patrick Robert (Jumbo)
————————LHB, ROB————————

Born Bristol, 24 Jan 1931. Educ Sherborne S; St John's C, Oxford. Debut 1952.
OXFORD UNIVERSITY (46) 1952–55 (Blue 1952–55).
FREE FORESTERS (1) 1956.
MCC (2) 1956–58.
HS 57 Oxford U v Warwicks, Edgbaston, 1954.
BB 7–132 Oxford U v Surrey, Guildford, 1954.
Dorset 1952–60.

JOWETT, Richard Lund
————————RHB, OB————————

Born Rawdon, Yorks, 29 Apr 1937. Educ Bradford GS; Magdalen C, Oxford U. Debut 1957.
OXFORD UNIVERSITY (43) 1957–60 (Blue 1957–59).
HS 122 Oxford U v D. R. Jardine's XI, Eastbourne, 1957.
BB 4–67 Oxford U v Glos, The Parks, 1958.

JOYNT, Henry Walter
————————RHB, RM————————

Born St Giles, Devon, 1 July 1931. Educ Bradfield; Oxford U. Debut 1952.
OXFORD UNIVERSITY (11) 1952–53.
INDIA DOMESTIC Madras 1957/58.
HS 42* Oxford U v Free Foresters, The Parks, 1953.
BB 4–36 Madras v Ceylon, Madras, 1957/58.
Dorset 1954–59.

JUDD, Peter
————————RHB, OB (later LB)————————

Born Balham, London, 29 Apr 1938. Debut 1960.
SURREY (1) 1960.
No runs, no wkts.
Clubs: Malden Wanderers, West Surrey.

JUDGE, Peter Francis
————————RHB, RFM————————

Born Cricklewood, M'sex, 23 May 1916. Educ St Paul's S. Debut 1933. *P from 1939.*
MIDDLESEX (8) 1933–34.
GLAMORGAN (54) 1939–47. Cap 1939.
INDIA DOMESTIC Bengal 1944/45, Europeans (Bombay) 1944/45–45/46.
HS 40 Glam v Worcs, Ebbw Vale, 1946.
BB 8–75 Glam v Yorks, Bradford, 1939. Bowled by successive balls in a match, both from C. T. Sarwate, Glam v Indians, Cardiff, 1946: last man out in 1st inns and opened 2nd inns in the following-on.
Clubs: Burnley, Scarborough, Elland, Carlisle.

JULIAN, Raymond
————————RHB, WK————————

Born Cosby, Leics, 23 Aug 1936. Debut 1953. *P.*
LEICESTERSHIRE (192) 1953–71. Cap 1961.
HS 51 Leics v Worcs, Worcester, 1962.
Fc umpire 1972–.

JULIEN, Bernard Denis
————————RHB, LM/SLA————————

Born Carenage, Trinidad, 13 Mar 1950. Educ St Mary's C, Port of Spain. Debut 1967/68.
W INDIES DOMESTIC North Trinidad 1967/68, Trinidad 1968/69–81/82.
KENT (80) 1970–77. Cap 1972.
WEST INDIES (24) 1973–76/77. E 1973/74 (5); I 1975/76 (4); P 1976/77 (1). *E 1973 (3), 1976 (2); A 1975/76 (3); I 1974/75 (4); P 1974/75 (2).*
HST 121 WI v E, Lord's, 1973. HS 127 W Indians v T. N. Pearce's XI, Scarborough, 1973.
BBT 5–57 WI v E, Bridgetown, 1973/74.
BB 9–97 Trinidad v Jamaica, Port of Spain, 1981/82.
World Series Cricket (Kerry Packer) 1977/78–78/79. Barred from W Indian cricket for touring S Africa 1982/83, 1983/84 (W Indies XI).

JUMADEEN, Raphik Raziz
————————RHB, SLA————————

Born Gasparillo, Trinidad, 12 Apr 1948. Debut 1966/67.
W INDIES DOMESTIC South Trinidad, Trinidad, 1970/71–80/81.
WEST INDIES (12) 1971/72–78/79. A 1972/73 (1), 1977/78 (2); NZ 1971/72 (1); I 1975/76 (4); P 1976/77 (1). *E 1976 (1); I 1978/79 (2).*
HST 56 WI v I, Kanpur, 1978/79. HS as above.
BBT 4–72 WI v A, Port of Spain, 1977/78. BB 6–30 South Trinidad v Central Trinidad, California, 1977/78.
Brother S. Jumadeen (Trinidad).

K

KALLICHARRAN, Alvin Isaac
————LHB, ROB————

Born Paidama, British Guiana, 21 Mar 1949. Educ Fort Mourant CS. Debut 1966/67. *Wisden* 1983.
W INDIES DOMESTIC Guyana 1966/67–80/81.
WARWICKSHIRE (218) 1971–. Cap 1972. Benefit 1983.
AUSTRALIA DOMESTIC Queensland (7) 1977/78.
S AFRICA DOMESTIC Transvaal 1981/82–83/84.
WEST INDIES (66) 1971/72–80/81. E 1973/74 (5); A 1972/73 (5), 1977/78 (5); NZ 1971/72 (2); I 1975/76 (4); P 1976/77 (5). *E 1973 (3), 1976ᵉ (3), 1980 (5); A 1975/76 (6), 1979/80 (3); NZ 1979/80 (3); I 1974/75 (5), 1978/79 (6); P 1974/75 (2), 1980/81 (4).* Capt 9.
OTHER TOUR World XI to Pakistan 1973/74 (relief matches).
HST 187 WI v I, Bombay, 1978/79. HS 243* Warwicks v Glam, Edgbaston, 1983.
BBT 2–16 WI v NZ, Christchurch, 1979/80. BB 5–45 Transvaal v W Province, Cape Town, 1982/83.
1000 RUNS (10+1) 2301 @ 52.30 in 1984.
RECORDS Added 470 for 4th wkt with G. W. Humpage, Warwicks v Lancs, Southport, 1982, English record and highest for any wkt other than the 1st in English fc cricket; highest stand for any wkt for a losing side. Nine centuries for Warwicks in 1984, county record.
Scored 100* and 101 in first two Test inns, WI v NZ, Georgetown and Port of Spain, 1971/72.
Barred from W Indian cricket for playing in S Africa 1981/82 (Transvaal); subsequently toured there in 1982/83 and 1983/84 with W Indian XI. Brother D. I. Kallicharran (Trinidad).

KALUPERUMA, Lalith Wasantha
————RHB, OB————

Born Colombo, Ceylon, 25 June 1949. Educ Natlanda C. Debut 1970/71.
SRI LANKA 1970/71–81/82.

SRI LANKA (2) 1981/82. E 1981/82 (1). *P 1981/82 (1).*
OTHER TOURS Sri Lanka to India 1970/71, 1976/77. Sri Lanka to Pakistan 1973/74. Sri Lanka to England 1975, 1981. Sri Lanka to India 1975/76.
HST 11* SL v P, Faisalabad, 1981/82. HS 96 Sri Lanka v Pakistan, Colombo, 1975/76.
BB 8–43 Sri Lanka Board President's XI v Tamil Nadu, Colombo, 1975/76.
Barred from Sinhalese cricket for 25 yrs for touring S Africa 1982/83 (Arosa Sri Lanka). Club: Bloomfield.

KAMM, Anthony
————RHB, WK————

Born Hampstead, London, 2 Mar 1931. Educ Charterhouse; Worcester C, Oxford. Debut 1952.
OXFORD UNIVERSITY (6) 1952–55 (Blue 1954).
MIDDLESEX (2) 1952.
FREE FORESTERS (1) 1956.
HS 59* Oxford U v Warwicks, Edgbaston, 1954.

KANHAI, Rohan Babulal
————RHB, occ RM, occ WK————

Born Port Mourant, Berbice, British Guiana, 26 Dec 1935. Educ Port Mourant S. Debut 1954/55. *P.*
W INDIES DOMESTIC British Guiana (Guyana) 1954/55–73/74.
AUSTRALIA DOMESTIC Western Australia (8) 1961/62, Tasmania (2) 1969/70.
WARWICKSHIRE (173) 1968–77. Cap 1968. Benefit (£11,500) 1977.
WEST INDIES (79) 1957–73/74. E 1959/60 (5), 1967/68 (5), 1973/74 (5); A 1964/65 (5), 1972/73 (5); I 1961/62 (5), 1970/71 (5); P 1957/58 (5). *E 1957 (5), 1963 (5), 1966 (5), 1973 (3); A 1960/61 (5), 1968/69 (5); I 1958/59 (5), 1966/67 (3); P 1958/59 (3).* Capt 13.
OTHER TOURS Commonwealth XI to Rhodesia 1962/63. Commonwealth XI to Pakistan 1963/64. Rest of World XI to Pakistan 1970/71 (relief match). World XI to Australia 1971/72. World XI to

Pakistan 1973/74 (capt; relief matches). International XI to Pakistan 1981/82.
HST 256 WI v I, Calcutta, 1958/59. HS as above.
BB 2–5 World XI v Pakistan XI, Karachi, 1970/71.
1000 RUNS (10+2) 1894 @ 57.39 in 1970.
RECORDS Added 465* for 2nd wkt with J. A. Jameson, Warwicks v Glos, Edgbaston, 1974, world record and highest-ever unbroken partnership for any wkt in England. Scored 1073 runs @ 82.53 in 1975, best-ever season average for Warwicks. Career average 51.62 (11,615 runs) for Warwicks, only batsman to average over 50 for the county.
World Series Cricket (Kerry Packer) 1977/78–78/79. Clubs: Aberdeenshire, Blackpool, Ashington, Crompton (England), Port Mourant (W Indies), Devonport (Tasmania). Autobiographies *Blasting For Runs* (1966) and *Blashing for Runs* (1970).

KAPIL DEV, Ramlal Nikhanj
————RHB, RFM————

Born Chandigarh, India, 6 Jan 1959. Educ Punjab U. Debut 1975/76.
INDIA DOMESTIC Haryana 1975/76–.
NORTHAMPTONSHIRE (16) 1981–83.
WORCESTERSHIRE (12) 1984.
INDIA (62) 1978/79–83/84. E 1979/80 (1), 1981/82 (6); A 1979/80 (6); WI 1978/79 (6), 1983/84 (6); P 1979/80 (6), 1983/84 (3); SL 1982/83 (1). *E 1979 (4), 1982 (3); A 1980/81 (3); WI 1982/83 (5); NZ 1980/81 (3); P 1978/79 (3), 1982/83 (6).* Capt 14.
HST 126* I v WI, Delhi, 1978/79. HS 193 Haryana v Punjab, Chandigarh, 1979/80.
BBT 9–83 I v WI, Ahmedabad, 1983/84. BB as above.
RECORDS Youngest player to score 1000 Test runs (21 yrs, 27 days) and take 100 Test wkts (21 yrs, 25 days). Youngest player to take 200 Test wkts and to perform Test double of 2000 runs and 200 wkts (24 yrs, 289 days). Took 100th Test wkt in record time since Test debut (1 yr, 107 days).
Club: Nelson.

KARDAR, Abdul Hafeez
—————LHB, SLA—————

Born Lahore, India, 17 Jan 1925. Educ Islamia C; Punjab U; Oxford U. Debut 1943/44.
INDIA DOMESTIC Northern India 1943/44–45/46, Muslims 1944/45.
OXFORD UNIVERSITY (28) 1947–49 (Blue 1947–49).
WARWICKSHIRE (45) 1948–50. Cap 1949.
PAKISTAN DOMESTIC Services 1953/54–54/55.
INDIA (3) *E 1946*.
PAKISTAN (23) 1952/53–57/58. A 1956/57 (1); NZ 1955/56 (3); I 1954/55 (5). *E 1954 (4); WI 1957/58 (5); I 1952/53 (5).* Capt 23.
OTHER TOURS Pakistan Services to Ceylon 1953/54. Pakistan Services–Bahawalpur to India 1954/55.
HST 93 P v I, Karachi, 1954/55. HS 173 North Zone v Australian Services, Lahore, 1945/46.
BBT 3–35 P v NZ, Karachi, 1955/56. BB 7–25 N India v Delhi, Lahore, 1944/45.
Gentlemen v Players (1) 1949. President BCCP 1972–77. MCC Hon. member. Former Punjab Government minister. Played as Abdul Hafeez until 1947. Father-in-law C. A. F. Hastilow (Warwicks).

KASAPPILLAI, Mahendra
—————LHB, SLA—————

Born Colombo, Ceylon, 21 Sept 1927. Educ RC, Colombo; Downing C, Cambridge. Debut 1948/49.
CEYLON 1948/49–51/52.
CAMBRIDGE UNIVERSITY (9) 1956–57.
HS 62* Cambridge U v M'sex, Fenner's, 1957.
BB 2–36 Cambridge U v Sussex, Fenner's, 1957.
Cambridgeshire 1954–55.

KAYE, Michael Arthur Chadwick Porter
—————RHB, RFM—————

Born Kensington, London, 11 Jan 1916. Educ Harrow; Pembroke C, Cambridge. Debut 1937.
CAMBRIDGE UNIVERSITY (9) 1937–38 (Blue 1938).
FREE FORESTERS (6) 1937–49.
TOUR Oxford and Cambridge Universities to Jamaica 1938/39.
HS 78 Cambridge U v MCC, Lord's, 1938.
BB 5–89 same match.

KAYUM, Donald Amrul
—————RHB—————

Born La Penitence, Georgetown, British Guiana, 13 Oct 1955. Educ Selhurst GS; Lincoln C, Oxford. Debut 1977.
OXFORD UNIVERSITY (12) 1977–78 (Blue 1977–78).
HS 57 Oxford U v Yorks, The Parks, 1978.
Clubs: Thornton Heath, Broadstairs, Dover.

KEELER, John George
—————RHB, RM—————

Born South Moor, Co Durham, 2 May 1924. Debut 1953.
MINOR COUNTIES (1) 1953.
HS 10 Minor Counties v Australians, Stoke on Trent, 1953.
Durham 1947–57 (2392 runs). Clubs: South Moor, Benwell, Burnmoor, Chester-le-Street.

KEELING, Michael Edward Allis
—————RHB—————

Born London, 6 Nov 1925. Educ Eton; Christ Church C, Oxford. Debut 1948.
OXFORD UNIVERSITY (5) 1948–49.
HS 40 Oxford U v Hants, The Parks, 1948.
War-time Blue 1944. Member I Zingari.

KEETON, William *Walter*
—————RHB—————

Born Shirebrook, Derbys, 30 Apr 1905. Died Forest Town, Notts, 10 Oct 1980. Debut 1926. *P. Wisden* 1940.
NOTTINGHAMSHIRE (382) 1926–52. Cap 1931. Benefit (£3249) 1947.
ENGLAND (2) 1934–39. A 1934 (1); WI 1939 (1).
HST 25 E v A, Headingley, 1934. HS 312* Notts v M'sex, Oval, 1939.
BB 2–16 Notts v Sussex, Horsham, 1934.
1000 RUNS (12) 2258 @ 42.60 in 1933.
RECORD HS (above) highest inns for Notts.
Scored 1102 runs @ 84.76 in August 1933. Scored centuries against all fc counties except his own.
Players v Gentlemen (3) 1932–36. Clubs: Mansfield Colliery, Bingley. Soccer: Sunderland, Nottingham Forest.

KEIGHLEY, William *Geoffrey*
—————RHB—————

Born Nice, France, 10 Jan 1925. Educ Eton; Trinity C, Oxford. Debut 1947.

OXFORD UNIVERSITY (20) 1947–48 (Blue 1947–48).
YORKSHIRE (35) 1947–51. Deputy capt 1949–50, but never capped.
TOUR MCC to Canada 1951.
HS 110 Yorks v Surrey, Headingley, 1951. Last non-Yorkshire-born player to appear for the county.
Club: Eccleshill. Lately a grazier in Australia. Hon. W. G. Keighley.

KEITH, Geoffrey Leydon
—————RHB, OB—————

Born Winchester, Hants, 19 Nov 1937. Died Southampton, 26 Dec 1975. Debut 1959. *P.*
SOMERSET (15) 1959–61.
HAMPSHIRE (60) 1962–67.
S AFRICA DOMESTIC Western Province 1968/69.
HS 101* Hants v S Africans, Southampton, 1965.
BB 4–49 Hants v Glos, Bristol, 1965.
Hants coach 1971–75.

KEITH, Headley James
—————LHB, SLA—————

Born Dundee, Natal, S Africa, 25 Oct 1927. Educ Maritzburg C, Natal. Debut 1950/51.
S AFRICA DOMESTIC Natal 1950/51–57/58.
SOUTH AFRICA (8) 1952/53–56/57. *E 1956/57 (3). E 1955 (4); A 1952/53 (1).*
HST 73 SA v E, Headingley, 1955. HS 193 Natal v Transvaal, J'burg, 1951/52.
BB 5–27 Natal v Transvaal, J'burg, 1950/51.

KELLAND, Peter Alban
—————RHB, RFM—————

Born Pinner, M'sex, 20 Sept 1926. Educ Repton; St Catharine's C, Cambridge. Debut 1949.
CAMBRIDGE UNIVERSITY (12) 1949–50 (Blue 1950).
SUSSEX (3) 1951–52.
HS 25 Cambridge U v Lancs, Fenner's, 1950.
BB 3–24 Cambridge U v Warwicks, Edgbaston, 1950.
Club: Hampstead.

KELLEHER, Henry Robert Albert
—————LHB, RMF—————

Born Bermondsey, London, 3 Mar 1929. Debut 1955. *P.*
SURREY (3) 1955.
NORTHAMPTONSHIRE (52) 1956–58.

HS 25 Northants v Som, Northampton, 1957.
BB 5–23 (10–73 match) Surrey v Worcs, Oval, 1955 (fc debut).
Clubs: Southgate, Old Hill, Dudley.

KELLY, Edward Arthur
RHB, RFM

Born Bootle, Cheshire, 26 Nov 1932. Educ Christ Church S, Waterloo, Liverpool. Debut 1957. *P.*
LANCASHIRE (4) 1957.
HS 16★ Lancs v Cambridge U, Fenner's, 1957.
BB 3–77 Lancs v Glam, Old Trafford, 1957.
Clubs: Litherland, Hightown, Chorley, Army Medical Corps.

KELLY, Jack
LHB, SLA

Born Conisbrough, Yorks, 15 Sept 1930. Debut 1953. *P.*
NOTTINGHAMSHIRE (51) 1953–57.
HS 113 Notts v Sussex, Trent Bridge, 1954.
BB 4–25 Notts v Warwicks, Edgbaston, 1953.
Devon 1961. Clubs: Paignton, Torquay.

KELLY, John Martin
RHB

Born Bacup, Lancs, 19 Mar 1922. Died Rochdale, Lancs, 13 Nov 1979. Debut 1947. *P.*
LANCASHIRE (6) 1947–49.
DERBYSHIRE (253) 1950–60. Cap 1951. Benefit (£2250) 1960.
HS 131 Derbys v M'sex, Lord's, 1956.
1000 RUNS (5) 1535 @ 30.70 in 1957.
Club: Bacup.

KELSALL, Robert Stuart
RHB, OB

Born Stockport, Cheshire, 29 June 1946. Debut 1969.
NOTTINGHAMSHIRE (1) 1969.
HS 8★ Notts v Barbados, Trent Bridge, 1969.
Cheshire 1970–79. Clubs: Denton St Laurence, Elland, Werneth, Royton.

KEMBER, Owen David
LHB, WK

Born Lingfield, Surrey, 23 Jan 1943. Educ Shrewsbury; St Catharine's C, Cambridge. Debut 1962.

SURREY (4) 1962–63.
CAMBRIDGE UNIVERSITY (2) 1963.
HS 19★ Surrey v Warwicks, Coventry, 1963 and 19 v Cambridge U, Oval, 1962.

KEMP, Nicholas John
RHB, RMF

Born Bromley, Kent, 16 Dec 1956. Educ Tonbridge. Debut 1977.
KENT (13) 1977–81.
MIDDLESEX (5) 1982.
HS 46★ M'sex v Sussex, Lord's, 1982.
BB 6–119 Kent v Surrey, Oval, 1980.

KEMSLEY, Jeremy *Neil*
RHB

Born Melbourne, Australia, 28 Sept 1933. Educ Aberdeen GS. Debut 1955.
SCOTLAND (8) 1955–57.
HS 103 Scotland v MCC, Aberdeen, 1957.
Clubs: Grange, Clydesdale.

KENDALL, John Thomas
RHB, WK

Born Coventry, Warwicks, 31 Mar 1921. Educ Foxford S, Coventry. Debut 1948. *P*
WARWICKSHIRE (4) 1948–49.
HS 18★ Warwicks v Cambridge U, Fenner's, 1949.
Clubs: Daimler, GEC, Morris Motors. Soccer: Coventry City.

KENDALL, Michael Philip
RHB, LM

Born Canterbury, Kent, 10 Nov 1949. Educ Gillingham HS; Jesus C, Cambridge. Debut 1971.
CAMBRIDGE UNIVERSITY (12) 1971–72 (Blue 1972).
HS 13 Cambridge U v Glam, Swansea, 1972.
BB 6–43 Cambridge U v Oxford U, Lord's, 1972.

KENNEDY, Andrew
LHB, RM

Born Blackburn, Lancs, 4 Nov 1949. Educ Nelson GS. Debut 1970.
LANCASHIRE (149) 1970–82. Cap 1975.
TOUR D. H. Robins' XI to S Africa 1975/76.
HS 180 Lancs v Derbys, Chesterfield, 1981.
BB 3–58 Lancs v Warwicks, Liverpool, 1980.
1000 RUNS (3) 1194 @ 34.11 in 1980.

RECORD Added 249 for 5th wkt with B. Wood, Lancs v Warwicks, Edgbaston, 1975, county record.
CWC Young Cricketer of 1975. Dorset 1983–.

KENNEDY, Ian George
RHB

Born Paisley, Scotland, 29 May 1960. Debut 1983.
SCOTLAND (1) 1983.
HS 12 Scotland v Ireland, Downpatrick, 1983.
Club: Ferguslie.

KENNEDY, James Henry
RHB, LFM

Born Glasgow, Scotland, 23 Apr 1949. Educ Glasgow HS. Debut 1970.
SCOTLAND (2) 1970–71.
HS 6★ Scotland v Pakistanis, Selkirk, 1971.
Club: Clydesdale.

KENNEDY, John Maxwell
RHB

Born Manchester, 15 Dec 1931. Educ Urmston GS; Loughborough C. Debut 1960. *P.*
WARWICKSHIRE (31) 1960–62.
HS 94 Warwicks v Oxford U, Edgbaston, 1962.
BB 2–1 Warwicks v Som, Edgbaston, 1960.
Clubs: Lightcliffe, Aston Unity.

KENNY, Charles John Michael
RHB, RMF

Born Wallington, Surrey, 19 May 1929. Educ Ampleforth C; Trinity C, Cambridge. Debut 1950.
ESSEX (18) 1950–53.
FREE FORESTERS (9) 1951–62.
CAMBRIDGE UNIVERSITY (10) 1952 (Blue).
IRELAND (3) 1952–55.
HS 16 Essex v Cambridge U, Fenner's, 1952.
BB 7–45 (10–96 match) Free Foresters v Cambridge U, Fenner's, 1957.
Club: Hampstead.

KENT, Martin Francis
RHB

Born Mossman, Queensland, Australia, 23 Nov 1953. Debut 1974/75.
AUSTRALIA DOMESTIC Queensland (49) 1974/75–81/82.
AUSTRALIA (3) *E 1981.*

HST 54 A v E, Oval, 1981. HS 171 Queensland v Tasmania, Brisbane, 1980/81.
OTHER TOURS International Wanderers to S Africa 1975/76. Australia to Sri Lanka 1980/81.
Century on fc debut, 140 Queensland v NSW, Brisbane, 1974/75.
World Series Cricket (Kerry Packer) 1977/78–78/79. Club: Sandgate-Redcliffe.

KENT, Terence
——RHB, SLA——

Born Battersea, London, 21 Oct 1939. Debut 1960. P.
ESSEX (10) 1960–62.
HS 23* Essex v Som, Taunton, 1962.
BB 4–54 Essex v Northants, Wellingborough, 1961.
Clubs: Walthamstow, Addiscombe. Soccer: Southend United.

KENTISH, Esmond Seymour Maurice
——RHB, RFM——

Born Cambridge, Jamaica, 21 Nov 1916. Educ Cornwall C, Jamaica; St John's C, Oxford. Debut 1947/48.
W INDIES DOMESTIC Jamaica 1947/48–56/57.
OXFORD UNIVERSITY (14) 1956 (Blue).
WEST INDIES (2) 1947/48–53/54. E 1947/48 (1), 1953/54 (1).
HST 1* WI v E, Kingston, 1947/48. HS 15* Jamaica v British Guiana, Georgetown, 1947/48.
BBT 5–49 WI v E, Kingston, 1953/54. BB 5–36 Jamaica v Duke of Norfolk's XI, Melbourne Park, 1956/57.
RECORD Oldest player to win cricket Blue. Manager West Indies to England 1973. W Indies Test selector.

KENYON, Donald
——RHB——

Born Wordsley, Staffordshire, 15 May 1924. Educ Audnam Senior S. Debut 1946. P. Wisden 1963.
WORCESTERSHIRE (589) 1946–67. Cap 1947. Capt 1959–67. Benefit (£3840) 1957. Testimonial (£6351) 1964.
COMBINED SERVICES (5) 1946.
ROYAL AIR FORCE (1) 1946.
ENGLAND (8) 1951/52–55. A 1953 (2); SA 1955 (3). I 1951/52 (3).
OTHER TOURS Worcs to Rhodesia 1964/65 (capt). Worcs to Jamaica 1965/66 (capt).
HST 87 E v SA, Trent Bridge, 1955. HS 259 Worcs v Yorks, Kidderminster, 1956.
1000 RUNS (19) 2636 @ 51.68 in 1954.
2000 runs (7).

RECORD 34,490 runs (@ 34.04) for Worcs, county record.
Players v Gentlemen (3) 1950–55. Club: Stourbridge. England Test selector 1965–72. MBE for services to cricket.

KER, Andrew Burgher Michael
——RHB——

Born Kelso, Scotland, 16 Oct 1954. Educ Kelso HS; Jordanhill C. Debut 1981.
SCOTLAND (4) 1981–.
HS 65 Scotland v Ireland, Clontarf, 1981.
Clubs: Kelso, Heriot's Former Pupils. Rugby: Kelso, South of Scotland. Brother J. E. Ker (Scotland).

KER, John Edward
——RHB, RM——

Born Kelso, Scotland, 17 Oct 1952. Educ Kelso HS. Debut 1977.
SCOTLAND (8) 1977–.
HS 50 Scotland v N Zealanders, Broughty Ferry, Dundee, 1978.
BB 3–45 Scotland v Ireland, Downpatrick, 1983.
Clubs: Kelso, Heriot's Former Pupils. Brother A. B. M. Ker (Scotland).

KERRIGAN, Michael
——LHB, SLA——

Born Perth, Scotland, 8 Nov 1931. Educ Abbey S, Perth. Debut 1954.
SCOTLAND (12) 1954–61.
HS 18* Scotland v Ireland, Dublin, 1955.
BB 7–84 Scotland v Ireland, Paisley, 1960.
Club: Perthshire.

KERSLAKE, Roy Cosmo
——RHB, OB——

Born Paignton, Devon, 26 Dec 1942. Educ Kingswood S, Bath; St Catharine's C, Cambridge. Debut 1962.
CAMBRIDGE UNIVERSITY (30) 1962–64 (Blue 1963–64).
SOMERSET (52) 1962–68. Cap 1968. Capt 1968.
MINOR COUNTIES (1) 1976.
HS 80 Cambridge U v Surrey, Oval, 1964.
BB 6–77 Cambridge U v Worcs, Halesowen, 1964.
Chairman Som cricket committee 1981–82. Clubs: Finchley, Buccaneers.

KETTLE, Michael Keith
——RHB, LMF——

Born Stamford, Lincolnshire, 18 Mar 1944. Educ Hillside S, Bulawayo, Rhodesia. Debut 1963.

NORTHAMPTONSHIRE (88) 1963–70.
HS 88 Northants v Essex, Northampton, 1963.
BB 6–67 Northants v Sussex, Northampton, 1968.

KHALID HASSAN
——RHB, LBG——

Born Peshawar, India, 14 July 1937. Debut 1953/54.
PAKISTAN DOMESTIC Punjab, Lahore, 1953/54–58/59.
PAKISTAN (1) E 1954.
HST 10 P v E, Trent Bridge, 1954. HS 30 Pakistanis v Glam, Cardiff, 1954.
BBT 2–116 P v E, Trent Bridge, 1954. BB 3–27 Pakistanis v M'sex, Lord's, 1954.

KHALID IBADULLA (Billy)
——RHB, RM/OB——

Born Lahore, India, 20 Dec 1935. Educ Manzang HS, Lahore. Debut 1952/53 (Pakistan to India). P.
PAKISTAN DOMESTIC Punjab XI 1953/54.
WARWICKSHIRE (377) 1954–72. Cap 1957. Benefit (£7797) 1969.
N ZEALAND DOMESTIC Otago (16) 1964/65–66/67.
AUSTRALIA DOMESTIC Tasmania (4) 1970/71–71/72.
PAKISTAN (4) 1964/65–67. A 1964/65 (1). E 1967 (2); NZ 1964/65 (1).
OTHER TOURS Pakistan to India 1952/53. Commonwealth XI to Pakistan 1963/64. International XI to India, Pakistan and Ceylon 1967/68.
HST 166 P v A, Karachi, 1964/65 (Test debut). HS 171 Warwicks v Oxford U, The Parks, 1961.
BB 7–22 Warwicks v Derbys, Chesterfield, 1967.
1000 RUNS (6) 2098 @ 33.83 in 1962.
RECORDS Added 377* for 1st wkt with N. F. Horner, Warwicks v Surrey, Oval, 1960, county record and highest-ever unbroken 1st wkt stand in English cricket. Added 249 for 1st wkt with Abdul Kadir, P v A, Karachi, 1964/65, Pakistan Test record.
Fc umpire 1982–. Coach in Otago, N Zealand. Son Kaseem Ben Khalid (Otago).

KHALID WAZIR Ali
——RHB, RFM——

Born Jullundur, India, 27 Apr 1936. Debut 1952/53.
The Rest v Pakistan XI, Karachi, 1952/53. Hasan Mahmood's XI v Air Vice-Marshal Cannon's XI, Karachi, 1953/54.
PAKISTAN (2) E 1954.

HST 9* P v E, Old Trafford, 1954. HS 53 Pakistanis v Derbys, Derby, 1954.
BB 3–82 Pakistanis v Combined Services, Catterick, 1954.
Clubs: Great Chell, Sneyd Colliery, Hawarden Park, Congleton. Father S. Wazir Ali (India).

KHAN, Asad Jahangir
RHB, OB

Born Canbellpur, India, 25 Dec 1945. Educ Punjab U; Keble C, Oxford. Debut 1965/66.
PAKISTAN DOMESTIC Punjab University, Lahore, 1965/66–70/71.
OXFORD UNIVERSITY (28) 1967–69 (Blue 1968–69).
HS 92 Oxford U v D. H. Robins' XI, Eastbourne, 1969.
BB 7–84 Oxford and Cambridge Universities v Australians, Fenner's, 1968.
Father M. Jahangir Khan (Cambridge U, India); brother Majid Khan (Cambridge U, Glam, Pakistan).

KHAN MOHAMMED
RHB, RFM

Born Lahore, India, 1 Jan 1928. Educ Punjab U; Bristol U. Debut 1946/47.
INDIA DOMESTIC Northern India 1946/47.
PAKISTAN DOMESTIC Punjab University, Universities, Bahawalpur, Sind, Karachi, Lahore, 1947/48–60/61.
COMMONWEALTH XI (2) 1950–56.
SOMERSET (1) 1951.
PAKISTAN (13) 1952/53–57/58. A 1956/57 (1); NZ 1955/56 (3); I 1954/55 (4). E 1954 (2); WI 1957/58 (2); I 1952/53 (1).
OTHER TOUR Pakistan to Ceylon 1948/49.
HST 26* P v WI, Port of Spain, 1957/58.
HS 43 N India v S Punjab, Patiala, 1946/47.
BBT 6–21 P v NZ, Dacca, 1955/56. BB 7–56 Commonwealth XI v England XI, Torquay, 1951.
Clubs: Lowerhouse, Torquay, Bacup.

KHANNA, Surinder Chaman Lal
RHB, WK

Born Delhi, India, 3 June 1956. Educ Government S, Delhi; Hindu C. Debut 1976/77.
INDIA DOMESTIC Delhi 1976/77–.
TOUR India to England 1979.
HS 146 N Zone v W Zone, Cuttack, 1983/84.

KILBEE, John Richard
RHB, RM

Born Hong Kong, 24 July 1947. Educ King's S, Canterbury; St Edmund's Hall, Oxford. Debut 1968.
OXFORD UNIVERSITY (8) 1968–69.
HS 18* Oxford U v D. H. Robins' XI, Eastbourne, 1969.
BB 4–96 Oxford U v Warwicks, The Parks, 1969.
Clubs: St Laurence and Highland Court, Waverley (Sydney).

KILLICK, Edgar Thomas
RHB

Born London, 9 May 1907. Died, during a match, BR Sports Ground, Northampton, 18 May 1953. Educ St Paul's S; Jesus C, Cambridge. Debut 1926.
MIDDLESEX (47) 1926–39. Cap.
CAMBRIDGE UNIVERSITY (33) 1927–30 (Blue 1928–30).
FREE FORESTERS (6) 1931–46.
ENGLAND (2) SA 1929.
HST 31 E v SA, Edgbaston, 1929. HS 206 M'sex v Warwicks, Lord's, 1931.
1000 RUNS (2) 1384 @ 44.64 in 1929.
Club: Bishop's Stortford. Church of England Clergyman.

KIMISH, Arthur Edwards
RHB, WK

Born Southampton, 5 July 1917. Debut 1946.
HAMPSHIRE (3) 1946.
HS 12* Hants v Surrey, Kingston-upon-Thames, 1946.

KIMMINS, Simon Edward Anthony
RHB, RM

Born Belgravia, London, 26 May 1930. Educ Charterhouse. Debut 1950.
KENT (12) 1950–51.
COMBINED SERVICES (1) 1950.
FREE FORESTERS (2) 1955–59.
MCC (1) 1959.
HS 81 Free Foresters v Cambridge U, Fenner's, 1959.
BB 5–42 Kent v Minor Counties, Canterbury, 1951.
Father Anthony Kimmins (playwright and broadcaster).

KIMPTON, Roger Charles MacDonald
RHB, WK

Born Toorak, Australia, 21 Sept 1916. Educ Melbourne U; Brasenose C, Oxford. Debut 1935.

OXFORD UNIVERSITY (40) 1935–38 (Blue 1935, 1937–38).
WORCESTERSHIRE (14) 1937–49.
TOURS Oxford and Cambridge Universities to Jamaica 1938/39. E. W. Swanton's XI to W Indies 1955/56.
HS 160 Oxford U v Glos, The Parks, 1935.
BB 2–20 Worcs v Leics, Hinckley, 1937.
1000 RUNS (1) 1568 @ 34.84 in 1937.
Gentlemen v Players (2) 1936–37.
Brother S. M. Kimpton (Oxford U).

KING, Anthony Mountain
RHB

Born Laughton, Sheffield, 8 Oct 1932. Educ Bradford GS. Debut 1955. P.
YORKSHIRE (1) 1955.
HS 12 Yorks v Derbys, Bradford, 1955.
Clubs: Bradford, Salts. Rugby: Bradford. Cousin I. M. King (Warwicks, Essex).

KING, Benjamin *Philip*
RHB, occ WK

Born Leeds, Yorks, 22 Apr 1915. Died Bradford, Yorks, 31 Mar 1970. Debut 1935. P.
WORCESTERSHIRE (80) 1935–39. Cap 1938.
LANCASHIRE (37) 1946–47. Cap 1946.
HS 145 Lancs v Oxford U, The Parks, 1946.
1000 RUNS (2) 1177 @ 22.63 in 1938.
Clubs: Bingley, Leeds. Cricket and rugby correspondent of *The People*.

KING, Collis Llewellyn
RHB, RM

Born Fairview, Barbados, 11 June 1951. Educ Metropolitan HS, Bridgetown. Debut 1972/73.
W INDIES DOMESTIC Barbados 1972/73–81/82.
GLAMORGAN (16) 1977.
WORCESTERSHIRE (2) 1983.
WEST INDIES (9) 1976–80. P 1976/77 (1).
E 1976 (3), 1980 (1); A 1979/80 (1); NZ 1979/80 (3).
OTHER TOUR International XI to Pakistan 1981/82.
HST 100* WI v NZ, Christchurch, 1979/80. HS 163 W Indians v Northants, Northampton, 1976.
BB 5–91 Barbados v Jamaica, Bridgetown, 1975/76.
Scored 123 on Worcs debut, v Som, Worcester, 1983.
World Series Cricket (Kerry Packer) 1977/78–78/79. Barred from W Indian cricket for touring S Africa 1982/83, 1983/84 (W Indian XI). Clubs: Nelson, Colne, Ponthlyddyn.

KING, Horace David
————RHB, WK————

Born Brentford, M'sex, 10 Feb 1915. Died Worthing, Sussex, 7 Mar 1974. Educ Taunton S. Debut 1934/35.
MIDDLESEX (7) 1936–46.
INDIA DOMESTIC Europeans 1934/35, Services 1943/44.
HS 26 M'sex v Cambridge U, Fenner's, 1946.
Club: Richmond.

KING, Ian Metcalfe
————LHB, SLA————

Born Leeds, Yorkshire, 10 Nov 1931. Educ Hanley Castle GS, Worcester. Debut 1952. *P.*
WARWICKSHIRE (53) 1952–55.
ESSEX (28) 1957.
HS 33 Essex v Glos, Romford, 1957.
BB 5–59 Warwicks v Essex, Westcliff, 1954.
Clubs: Kidderminster, Aston Unity, Moseley. Cousin A. M. King (Yorks).

KING, James Morris Roy
————RHB, RM/LBG————

Born Bristol, 15 Sept 1942. Educ St Brendan's C, Bristol. Debut 1966.
GLOUCESTERSHIRE (3) 1966.
HS 28 Glos v Cambridge U, Lydney, 1966.
Clubs: Westbury-on-Trym, Imperial, Keynsham, Warwicks Pilgrims.

KING, Kenneth Charles William
————LHB, SLA————

Born Beddington, Surrey, 4 Dec 1915. Educ King Charles S, Wimbledon. Debut 1936. *P from 1936 (after two matches) until 1938.*
SURREY (31) 1936–38.
D. R. JARDINE'S XI (1) 1955.
HS 64 Surrey v MCC, Lord's, 1936.
BB 4–38 Surrey v Cambridge U, Oval, 1936.
Club: Westminster Bank.

KING, Lester Anthony
————RHB, RF————

Born St Catharine, Kingston, Jamaica, 27 Feb 1939. Debut 1961/62.
W INDIES DOMESTIC Jamaica 1961/62–67/68.
INDIA DOMESTIC Bengal 1962/63.
WEST INDIES XI (2) 1964.
WEST INDIES (2) 1961/62–67/68. E 1967/68 (1); I 1961/62 (1).

TOURS W Indians to England 1963. W Indies to India and Ceylon 1966/67. W Indies to Australasia 1968/69.
HST 20 WI v E, Georgetown, 1967/68.
HS 89 Jamaica v Trinidad, Port of Spain, 1963/64.
BBT 5–46 WI v E, Kingston, 1961/62 (Test debut). BB as above.
Club: Rawtenstall.

KINGSTON, Graham Charles
————RHB, RM————

Born Newport, Monmouthshire, 1 Nov 1950. Educ St Julien's HS, Newport. Debut 1967. *P.*
GLAMORGAN (9) 1967–71.
TOUR Glam to W Indies 1969/70.
HS 26 Glam v Oxford U, Llandarcy, 1971.
BB 2–18 Glam v Worcs, Neath, 1970.
Father C. Kingston (international soccer referee).

KINKEAD-WEEKES, Roderick Calder
————RHB, WK————

Born East London, S Africa, 15 Mar 1951. Educ Eton; Lincoln C, Oxford. Debut 1972.
OXFORD UNIVERSITY (4) 1972 (Blue).
MIDDLESEX (2) 1976.
HS 25★ Oxford U v Warwicks, The Parks, 1972.

KIPPAX, Peter John
————RHB, LBG————

Born Huddersfield, Yorks, 15 Oct 1940. Educ Bedford Modern S. Debut 1961. *P.*
YORKSHIRE (4) 1961–62.
HS 9 Yorks v Kent, Scarborough, 1961.
BB 5–74 Yorks v Leics, Leicester, 1961.
Northumberland 1975–77, Durham 1978–83. Clubs: Harrogate, Leeds, Idle, Hartlepool. Professional coach Woodhouse Grove S.

KIRBY, David
————RHB, OB————

Born Darlington, Co Durham, 18 Jan 1939. Educ St Peter's, York; Emmanuel C, Cambridge. Debut 1959.
CAMBRIDGE UNIVERSITY (50) 1959–61 (Blue 1959–61). Capt 1961.
LEICESTERSHIRE (63) 1959–64. Cap 1962. Capt 1962.
HS 118 Leics v Kent, Maidstone, 1962.
BB 5–76 Cambridge U v Leics, Loughborough, 1961.

1000 RUNS (3) 1158 @ 23.63 in 1961. Scored 1102 runs @ 21.60 in debut season, 1959.
Gentlemen v Players (3) 1959–62. Club: Darlington.

KIRBY, Geoffrey Norman George
————RHB, WK————

Born Reading, Berkshire, 6 Nov 1923. Debut 1947. *P.*
SOUTH (1) 1947.
SURREY/KENT (1) 1947.
SURREY (19) 1948–53.
HS 32 Surrey v W Indians, Oval, 1950.
Berkshire 1954.

KIRBY, John Edward Weston
————RHB, RM————

Born Newcastle upon Tyne, Northumberland, 4 Feb 1936. Educ Ampleforth C; Corpus Christi C, Oxford. Debut 1956.
OXFORD UNIVERSITY (3) 1956.
HS 28 Oxford U v Free Foresters, The Parks, 1956.
Clubs: Hornsey, United Banks.

KIRKMAN, Michael
————RHB, LB————

Born Bodmin, Cornwall, 11 Feb 1942. Educ Dulwich C; St Catharine's C, Cambridge. Debut 1963.
CAMBRIDGE UNIVERSITY (11) 1963 (Blue).
HS 7★ Cambridge U v Oxford U, Lord's, 1963.
BB 3–32 Cambridge U v Surrey, Fenner's, 1963.
Club: Old Alleynians.

KIRKPATRICK, Alexander Kennedy
————LHB, ROB————

Born Belfast, N Ireland, 25 July 1938. Educ Grosvenor HS, Belfast. Debut 1962.
IRELAND (1) 1962.
HS 30 Ireland v Combined Services, Belfast, 1962.
Club: Woodvale.

KIRKWOOD, Euan MacMillan
————RHB————

Born Paisley, Scotland, 7 Dec 1934. Educ Merchiston Castle S. Debut 1958.
SCOTLAND (3) 1958.
HS 10 Scotland v N Zealanders, Glasgow, 1958.
Club: Ferguslie.

KIRMANI, Syed Mujtaba Hussein
RHB, WK

Born Madras, India, 29 Dec 1949. Debut 1967/68.
INDIA DOMESTIC Mysore (Karnataka) 1967/68–.
INDIA (78) 1975/76–83/84. E 1976/77 (5), 1979/80 (1), 1981/82 (6); A 1979/80 (6); WI 1978/79 (6), 1983/84 (6); NZ 1976/77 (3); P 1979/80 (6), 1983/84 (3); SL 1982/83 (1). *E 1982 (3); A 1977/78 (5), 1980/81 (3); WI 1975/76 (4), 1982/83 (5); NZ 1975/76 (3), 1980/81 (3); P 1978/79 (3), 1982/83 (6).*
OTHER TOURS India to England 1971, 1974. A. L. Wadekar's XI to Sri Lanka 1975/76.
HST 101* I v A, Bombay, 1979/80. HS 116 Karnataka v Delhi, Delhi, 1981/82.
RECORDS Made six dismissals in inns, I v NZ, Christchurch, 1975/76, Indian Test record. 160 Test dismissals, India record. Only Indian to score 1000 Test runs and make 100 wicketkeeping dismissals.

KIRSTEN, Peter Noel
RHB, OB

Born Pietermaritzburg, S Africa, 14 May 1955. Educ S Africa College S, Cape Town; Stellenbosch U. Debut 1973/74.
S AFRICA DOMESTIC Western Province 1973/74–.
SUSSEX (1) 1975.
DERBYSHIRE (106) 1978–82. Cap 1978.
HS 228 Derbys v Som, Taunton, 1981.
BB 4–44 Derbys v M'sex, Derby, 1979.
1000 RUNS (5 + 1) 1941 @ 64.70 in 1982.
RECORDS Scored 8 centuries for Derbys in 1982, county record. Added 291 for 3rd wkt with D. S. Steele, Derbys v Som, Taunton, 1981, county record. Scored 6 centuries in 7 inns (173*, 103, 107, 165, 22, 111, 128) in 1976/77, including four in consecutive inns.
S Africa (11) 1981/82–83/84 (capt 6). Club: Creswell. Father N. Kirsten (Border).

KITCHEN, Mervyn John
LHB

Born Nailsea, Som, 1 Aug 1940. Debut 1960. *P.*
SOMERSET (352) 1960–79. Cap 1966. Testimonial (£6000) 1973.
TOUR International Wanderers to Rhodesia 1972/73.
HS 189 Som v Pakistanis, Taunton, 1967.
1000 RUNS (7) 1730 @ 36.04 in 1968.
Fc umpire 1982–. Club: Almondsbury.

KITSON, David Lees
RHB

Born Batley, Yorks, 13 Sept 1925. Debut 1952. *P.*
SOMERSET (32) 1952–54.
HS 69 Som v Leics, Leicester, 1953.
Club: Bradford.

KLINE, Lindsay Francis
LHB, SLC

Born Camberwell, Victoria, Australia, 29 Sept 1934. Debut 1955/56.
AUSTRALIA DOMESTIC Victoria (31) 1955/56–61/62.
AUSTRALIA (13) 1957/58–60/61. E 1958/59 (2); WI 1960/61 (2). *SA 1957/58 (5); I 1959/60 (3); P 1959/60 (1).*
OTHER TOURS Australia to N Zealand 1956/57. Australia to England 1961.
HST 15* A v WI, Adelaide, 1960/61. HS 37* Victoria v Queensland, Melbourne, 1961/62.
BBT 7–75 A v P, Lahore, 1959/60. BB as above.
Performed the hat-trick, A v SA, Cape Town, 1957/58. Club: Melbourne.

KNEW, George Alan
RHB

Born Leicester, 5 Mar 1954. Educ Wyggeston GS, Leicester. Debut 1972.
LEICESTERSHIRE (4) 1972–73.
HS 25 Leics v Derbys, Derby, 1973.
Father G. F. Knew (Leics).

KNIGHT, Barry Rolfe
RHB, RFM

Born Chesterfield, Derbys, 18 Feb 1938. Educ East Ham GS, London. Debut 1955. *P.*
ESSEX (239) 1955–66. Cap 1959.
LEICESTERSHIRE (46) 1967–69. Cap 1968.
ENGLAND (29) 1961/62–69. A 1968 (2); WI 1966 (1), 1969 (3); NZ 1969 (2); P 1962 (2). *A 1962/63 (1), 1965/66 (2); NZ 1962/63 (3), 1965/66 (2); I 1961/62 (4), 1963/64 (5); P 1961/62 (2).*
OTHER TOURS Cavaliers to W Indies 1964/65. Commonwealth XI to India 1964/65. Indian Board President's XI (Defence Fund match) 1963/64.
HST 127 E v I, Kanpur, 1963/64. HS 165 Essex v M'sex, Brentwood, 1962.
BBT 4–38 E v P, Trent Bridge, 1962. BB 8–69 Essex v Notts, Trent Bridge, 1963.
1000 RUNS (5) 1689 @ 34.46 in 1962.
100 WKTS (5) 140 @ 21.72 in 1963.
DOUBLE (4) 1962–65.
RECORDS During HS (above) added 206 for 6th wkt with R. A. G. Luckin, equalling county record. Added 240 for

6th wkt with P. H. Parfitt, E v NZ, Auckland, 1962/63, England Test record.
Players v Gentlemen (3) 1960–62. Club: Wanstead.

KNIGHT, John Mark
RHB, RMF

Born Oundle, Northants, 16 Mar 1958. Educ Oundle; Worcester C, Oxford. Debut 1978.
OXFORD UNIVERSITY (23) 1978–81 (Blue 1979).
HS 41* Oxford U v Yorks, The Parks, 1981.
BB 4–69 Oxford U v Cambridge U, Lord's, 1979.
Wiltshire 1977–79. Club: Lansdown.

KNIGHT, Roger David Verdon
LHB, RM

Born Streatham, London, 6 Sept 1946. Educ Dulwich C; St Catharine's C, Cambridge. Debut 1967.
CAMBRIDGE UNIVERSITY (48) 1967–70 (Blue 1967–70).
SURREY (174) 1968–70, 1978–84. Cap 1978. Capt 1978–83.
GLOUCESTERSHIRE (105) 1971–75. Cap 1971.
SUSSEX (43) 1976–77. Cap 1976.
TOURS D. H. Robins' XI to S Africa 1972/73. MCC to E Africa 1973/74. Overseas XI to India 1980/81.
HS 165* Sussex v M'sex, Hove, 1976.
BB 6–44 Glos v Northants, Northampton, 1974.
1000 RUNS (13) 1350 @ 38.57 in 1974.

KNIGHTLEY-SMITH, William
LHB

Born W Smithfield, London, 1 Aug 1932. Died, during lawn tennis match, Edinburgh, Scotland, 31 July 1962. Educ Highgate S; St John's C, Cambridge.
MIDDLESEX (26) 1952. Cap 1952.
CAMBRIDGE UNIVERSITY (26) 1953–55 (Blue 1953).
GLOUCESTERSHIRE (29) 1955–57.
MCC (2) 1958–59.
FREE FORESTERS (1) 1961.
HS 95 Cambridge U v Essex, Fenner's, 1955.
Glos assistant-secretary 1955–57. Clubs: Hornsey, Neston, Bristol Optimists, Carlton (Edinburgh). Soccer: Blue.

KNOTT, Alan Philip Eric
————RHB, WK————

Born Belvedere, Kent, 9 Apr 1946. Educ Northumberland Heath Sec S, Erith. Debut 1964. *Wisden* 1970.
KENT (330) 1964–. Cap 1965. Benefit (£27,037) 1976.
AUSTRALIA DOMESTIC Tasmania (2) 1969/70.
ENGLAND (95) 1967–81. A 1968 (5), 1972 (5), 1975 (4), 1977 (5), 1981 (2); WI 1969 (3), 1973 (3), 1976 (5), 1980 (4); NZ 1969 (3), 1973 (3), I 1971 (3), 1974 (3); P 1967 (2), 1971 (3), 1974 (3). *A 1970/71 (6), 1974/75 (6), 1976/77 (1); WI 1967/68 (2), 1973/74 (5); NZ 1970/71 (1), 1974/75 (2); I 1972/73 (5), 1976/77 (5); P 1968/69 (3), 1972/73 (3).*
TOURS Cavaliers to W Indies 1964/65. MCC Under-25 XI to Pakistan 1966/67.
HST 135 E v A, Trent Bridge, 1977. HS 156 MCC v South Zone, Bangalore, 1972/73.
1000 RUNS (2) 1209 @ 41.68 in 1971.
RECORDS 269 Test wicketkeeping dismissals, England Test record and only R. W. Marsh (A) has made more. Made 24 dismissals in series, E v A, 1970/71, English record.
Made 98 dismissals in 1967, and 1290 (1158 ct, 132 st) in career.
World Series Cricket (Kerry Packer) 1977/78–78/79. Barred from Test cricket for three yrs for touring S Africa 1981/82 (SAB England XI). Club: The Mote. Author *Stumper's View* (1972).

KNOTT, Charles James
————RHB, OB————

Born Southampton, 26 Nov 1914. Educ Taunton S, Southampton. Debut 1938.
HAMPSHIRE (166) 1938–54. Cap 1939.
THE REST v An England XI, Canterbury, 1946 (Test trial).
MCC (1) 1957.
HS 27 Hants v Sussex, Worthing, 1951.
BB 8–26 Hants v Cambridge U, Bournemouth, 1951.
100 WKTS (4) 122 @ 18.47 in 1946.
Gentlemen v Players (2) 1946–50.

KNOWLES, Joseph
————RHB, LB————

Born Nottingham, 25 Mar 1910. Debut 1935. *P.*
NOTTINGHAMSHIRE (125) 1935–46. Cap.
HS 114 Notts v Worcs, Worcester, 1938.
BB 3–56 Notts v Indians, Trent Bridge, 1936.
1000 RUNS (1) 1179 @ 25.08 in 1938.
Club: Langwith.

KNOX, Gerald Keith
————RHB, RM————

Born North Shields, Co Durham, 22 Apr 1937. Educ Newcastle upon Tyne GS. Debut 1964.
LANCASHIRE (52) 1964–67.
HS 108 Lancs v Yorks, Old Trafford, 1965.
Northumberland 1957–63. Club: Tynemouth.

KOK, Myron
————RHB, RM————

Born Johannesburg, S Africa, 7 Dec 1932. Educ Harrow; Trinity C, Cambridge. Debut 1953.
CAMBRIDGE UNIVERSITY (2) 1953.
HS 8 Cambridge U v Warwicks, Fenner's, 1953.
BB 2–38 same match.

KONIG, Peter Hans
————RHB, WK————

Born Vienna, Austria, 16 Oct 1931. Debut 1949.
LEICESTERSHIRE (1) 1949.
HS 6 Leics v Northants, Northampton, 1949.

KRIKKEN, Brian Egbert
————RHB, WK————

Born Horwich, Lancs, 26 Aug 1946. Debut 1966.
LANCASHIRE (2) 1966–67.
WORCESTERSHIRE (1) 1969.
HS 4 Lancs v Oxford U, The Parks, 1966 and 4 Worcs v Cambridge U, Halesowen, 1969.
Clubs: Horwich, Westhoughton.

KRIPAL SINGH, Amritsar Govindsingh
————RHB, RM/OB————

Born Madras, India, 6 Aug 1933. Educ Madras U. Debut 1950/51.
INDIA DOMESTIC Madras 1950/51–64/65, Hyderabad 1965/66.
INDIA (14) 1955/56–64/65. E 1961/62 (3), 1963/64 (5); A 1956/57 (2), 1964/65 (1); WI 1958/59 (1); NZ 1955/56 (4). *E 1959 (1).*
OTHER TOUR India to Ceylon 1956/57.
HST 100* I v NZ, Hyderabad, 1955/56 (Test debut). HS 208 Madras v Travancore-Cochin, Ernakulam, 1954/55.

BBT 3–43 I v A, Madras, 1964/65. BB 6–14 (12–49 match) Madras v Hyderabad, Madras, 1961/62.
Father A. G. Ram Singh (Madras); brothers A. G. Milkha Singh (India) and Satwander Singh (Madras).

KRISHNAMURTHY, Pochiah
————RHB, WK————

Born Hyderabad, Deccan, India, 12 July 1947. Educ New Science C, Hyderabad; Sind U. Debut 1966/67.
INDIA DOMESTIC Services, Hyderabad, 1966/67–78/79.
INDIA (5) *WI 1970/71.*
OTHER TOURS Hyderabad Blues to Ceylon 1966/67. India to England 1971. India to Sri Lanka 1973/74. India to N Zealand 1975/76. India to W Indies 1975/76.
HST 20 I v WI, Port of Spain, 1970/71.
HS 82 State Bank v Hyderabad, Hyderabad, 1969/70.

KUMBLEBEN, John Michael
————RHB————

Born Bloemfontein, S Africa, 26 May 1933. Educ Michaelhouse S; Cape Town U; UC, Oxford. Debut 1956.
OXFORD UNIVERSITY (13) 1956–57.
S AFRICA DOMESTIC Orange Free State 1957/58–60/61.
HS 100 Oxford U v Yorks, The Parks, 1957.
Clubs: Oxford Town, Ramblers.

KUNDERAN (formerly Kunderam) Budhisagar Krishnappa
————RHB, WK————

Born Mulki, nr Mangalore, India, 2 Oct 1939. Educ Bombay U. Debut 1958/59 (Cricket Club of India v W Indians).
INDIA DOMESTIC Railways 1959/60–64/65, Mysore 1965/66–69/70.
INDIA (18) 1959/60–67/68. E 1961/62 (1), 1963/64 (5); A 1959/60 (3); WI 1966/67 (2); NZ 1964/65 (1); P 1960/61 (2). *E 1967 (2); WI 1961/62 (2).*
OTHER TOURS State Bank to Ceylon 1966/67, 1968/69. India to E Africa 1967. International XI to Rhodesia 1975/76.
HST 192 I v E, Madras, 1963/64. HS 205 Railways v Jammu and Kashmir, Delhi, 1959/60.
BB 2–15 S Zone v N Zone, Bangalore, 1965/66.
Clubs: Penrith, Drumpellier.

L

LACY-SCOTT, David Geffrey
————RHB, RFM————

Born Calcutta, India, 18 Aug 1920. Educ Marlborough; Peterhouse C, Cambridge. Debut 1946.
CAMBRIDGE UNIVERSITY (9) 1946 (Blue).
KENT (1) 1946.
FREE FORESTERS (1) 1948.
HS 36 Cambridge U v M'sex, Fenner's, 1946.
BB 5–35 Cambridge U v Free Foresters, Fenner's, 1946.

LAIDLAW, William Kennedy
————RHB, LBG————

Born Edinburgh, Scotland, 26 Aug 1912. Educ Edinburgh Institute. Debut 1938.
SCOTLAND (15) 1938–53.
MINOR COUNTIES (2) 1950.
HS 25 Scotland v Warwicks, Edgbaston, 1948.
BB 7–70 Scotland v Yorks, Harrogate, 1938 (fc debut).
Durham 1948–52. Clubs: Melville C FP, Grange, Philadelphia, Sunderland.

LAING, James Gordon Brodie
————RHB————

Born Meigle, Scotland, 10 Jan 1938. Educ Alyth S. Debut 1964.
SCOTLAND (19) 1964–74.
HS 93 Scotland v Warwicks, Edgbaston, 1965.
Club: Perthshire. Brother J. R. Laing (Scotland).

LAING, John Ralph
————LHB————

Born Meigle, Scotland, 27 Aug 1942. Educ Alyth S. Debut 1969.
SCOTLAND (8) 1969–79.
HS 127* Scotland v Ireland, Glasgow, 1976.
Club: Perthshire. Brother J. G. B. Laing (Scotland).

LAIRD, Bruce Malcolm
————RHB————

Born Mount Lawley, W Australia, 21 Nov 1950. Debut 1972/73.
AUSTRALIA DOMESTIC Western Australia (64) 1972/73–.
AUSTRALIA (21) 1979/80–82/83. E 1979/80 (2); WI 1979/80 (3), 1981/82 (3); P 1981/82 (3). E 1980 (1); NZ 1981/82 (3); P 1979/80 (3), 1982/83 (3).
OTHER TOUR Australia to England 1975.
HST 92 A v WI, Brisbane, 1979/80 (Test debut; scored 75 in 2nd inns). HS 171 W Australia v Queensland, Brisbane, 1976/77.
World Series Cricket (Kerry Packer) 1977/78–78/79. Club: South Perth.

LAITT, David James
————RHB, RMF————

Born Oxford, 3 May 1931. Educ Northland College S. Debut 1959.
MINOR COUNTIES (2) 1959–60.
HS 10 Minor Counties v S Africans, Stoke on Trent, 1960.
BB 4–58 Minor Counties v Indians, Longton, Stoke on Trent, 1959.
Oxfordshire 1952–72. Clubs: Oxford YMCA, Cowley St John, Reading, Beddington.

LAKE, Graham Johnson
————RHB, RFM————

Born Croydon, Surrey, 13 Apr 1935. Educ Birkbeck C; London U. Debut 1956. P.
GLOUCESTERSHIRE (13) 1956–58.
HS 18 Glos v Worcs, Worcester, 1956.
BB 4–39 Glos v Lancs, Blackpool, 1956.
Hertfordshire 1953. Royal Marines. Club: Barnet.

LAKER, James Charles
————RHB, OB————

Born Frizinghall, Bradford, Yorks, 9 Feb 1922. Educ Salts HS, Saltaire. Debut 1946. P except in 1962. Wisden 1952.
SURREY (309) 1946–59. Cap 1947. Benefit (£11,086) 1956.
ESSEX (30) 1962–64. Cap 1962.
N ZEALAND DOMESTIC Auckland (4) 1951/52.
ENGLAND (46) 1947/48–58/59. A 1948 (3), 1953 (3), 1956 (5); SA 1951 (2), 1955 (1); WI 1950 (1), 1957 (4); NZ 1949 (1), 1958 (4); I 1952 (4); P 1954 (1). A 1958/59 (4); SA 1956/57 (5); WI 1947/48 (4), 1953/54 (4).
OTHER TOURS Commonwealth XI to India 1950/51. Cavaliers to Jamaica 1963/64. Cavaliers to W Indies 1964/65.
HST 63 E v A, Trent Bridge, 1948. HS 113 Surrey v Glos, Oval, 1954.
BBT 10–53 (19–90 match) E v A, Old Trafford, 1956. BB as above.
100 WKTS (11) 166 @ 15.32 in 1950.
RECORDS (above) only instance of bowler ever taking more than 17 wkts in a fc match. Also took 10–88 Surrey v Australians, Oval, 1956, only instance of one player achieving two 'all-10' analyses in same season. Returned 8–2 England v The Rest, Bradford, 1950 (Test trial), statistically best-ever inns analysis in English fc cricket. Took 46 wkts @ 9.60 in Test series, E v A, 1956, record for either country in matches between each other.
Players v Gentlemen (3) 1952–57. Clubs: Saltaire, Catford, Norton. Author Over to me (1960), which caused temporary withdrawal of MCC Hon. membership. Currently BBC Television cricket commentator.

LAKER, Peter Guy
————RHB, LB/RM————

Born Hurstpierpoint, Sussex, 5 Dec 1926. Educ Lewes County S. Debut 1948.
SUSSEX (2) 1948–49.
HS 8* Sussex v Hants, Southampton, 1949.
Clubs: Lewes Priory, Laughton Lodge. Cricket correspondent of The Mirror.

LAMB, Allan Joseph
————RHB————

Born Langebaanweg, Cape Province, S Africa, 20 June 1954. Educ Wynburg

Boys HS; Abbotts C. Debut 1972/73. *Wisden* 1981.
S AFRICA DOMESTIC Western Province 1972/73–81/82.
NORTHAMPTONSHIRE (122) 1978–. Cap 1978.
ENGLAND (27) 1982–84. WI 1984 (5); NZ 1983 (4); I 1982 (3); P 1982 (3); SL 1984 (1). *A 1982/83 (5); NZ 1983/84 (3); P 1983/84 (3).*
HST 137* E v NZ, Trent Bridge, 1983. HS 178 Northants v Leics, Leicester, 1979.
1000 RUNS (6) 2049 @ 60.26 in 1981.
RECORD Scored four Test centuries in English season in 1984 (3 v WI, 1 v SL), equalling record of H. Sutcliffe (v SA, 1929), D. G. Bradman (v E, 1930) and D. C. S. Compton (v SA, 1947).
Took 30 runs off one over (644664) from A. I. Kallicharran, Northants v Warwicks, Edgbaston, 1982.
Brother-in-law A. Bucknall (England rugby international).

LAMB, Timothy Michael
RHB, RMF

Born Hartford, Cheshire, 24 Mar 1953. Educ Shrewsbury; Queens C, Oxford. Debut 1973.
OXFORD UNIVERSITY (16) 1973–74 (Blue 1973–74).
MIDDLESEX (36) 1974–77.
NORTHAMPTONSHIRE (108) 1978–83. Cap 1978.
HS 77 M'sex v Notts, Lord's, 1976.
BB 7–56 Northants v Cambridge U, Fenner's, 1980.
M'sex secretary 1984–. Cross Arrows. Hon. T. M. Lamb.

LAMBERT, George Ernest Edward
RHB, RFM

Born Paddington, London, 11 May 1918 (not 5 May 1919). Debut 1938. *P.*
GLOUCESTERSHIRE (334) 1938–57. Cap 1939. Benefit (£2618) 1955.
SOMERSET (3) 1960 (player-coach).
HS 100* Glos v Worcs, Worcester, 1955.
BB 8–35 Glos v Yorks, Bristol, 1956.
100 WKTS (1) 113 @ 22.75 in 1952.
Somerset coach from 1959. Club: Counterslip (Bristol). Father-in-law A. J. P. Fowler (M'sex).

LAMBERT, Noel Hamilton
RHB

Born Dublin, Ireland, 5 June 1910. Educ Sandford Park S, Dublin; Rossall S. Debut 1932.
IRELAND (9) 1932–47.

HS 69* Ireland v Scotland, Belfast, 1937. Club: Leinster. Rugby: Ireland (2 caps); later international referee. Father R. J. H. Lambert; uncle S. D. Lambert (both Ireland).

LANCE, Herbert Roy (Tiger)
RHB, RFM

Born Pretoria, S Africa, 6 June 1940. Educ Pretoria HS. Debut 1958/59.
S AFRICA DOMESTIC North-Eastern Transvaal 1958/59–60/61, Transvaal 1961/62–70/71, Northern Transvaal 1971/72.
SOUTH AFRICA (13) 1961/62–69/70. A 1966/67 (5), 1969/70 (3); NZ 1961/62 (2). *E 1965 (3).*
HST 70 SA v A, J'burg, 1966/67. HS 169 Transvaal v Natal, Durban, 1967/68.
BBT 3–30 SA v NZ, J'burg, 1961/62. BB 6–55 Transvaal v Griqualand West, Pretoria, 1971/72.
RECORDS Added 174 for 10th wkt with D. Mackay-Coghill, Transvaal v Natal, J'burg, 1965/66, S African fc record; added 200 for 6th wkt with R. G. Pollock, SA v A, Durban, 1969/70, S Africa Test record.
Hit 10 sixes in inns of 122 Transvaal v E. Province, J'burg, 1966/67.
Father P. Lance and brother A. P. Lance (both N.E. Transvaal).

LANCHBURY, Robert John
RHB

Born Evesham, Worcs, 11 Feb 1950. Educ Cheltenham GS. Debut 1971.
GLOUCESTERSHIRE (5) 1971.
WORCESTERSHIRE (8) 1973–74.
HS 50* Worcs v Oxford U, The Parks, 1974.
Wiltshire 1984. Clubs: Old Hill, Dudley.

LANGDALE, George Richmond
LHB, ROB

Born Thornaby, Yorks, 11 Mar 1916. Educ Nottingham U. Debut 1936.
DERBYSHIRE (4) 1936–37.
SOMERSET (20) 1946–49. Cap 1946.
MINOR COUNTIES (1) 1953.
HS 146 Som v Leics, Wells, 1946.
BB 5–30 Som v Warwicks, Edgbaston, 1946.
Norfolk 1939. Berkshire 1952–62. Clubs: South Hampstead, Kidderminster, Camberley. Part-time cricket statistician. Former instructor RMA, Sandhurst.

LANGFORD, Brian Anthony
RHB, OB

Born Birmingham, 17 Dec 1935. Educ Dr Morgan's S, Bridgwater. Debut 1953. *P.*
SOMERSET (504) 1953–74. Cap 1957. Capt 1969–71. Testimonials (£4250) 1966 and (£2250) 1971.
HS 68* Som v Sussex, Hove, 1960 and 68 v Kent, Gillingham, 1963 and 68* v Glam, Taunton, 1972.
BB 9–26 (15–54 match) Som v Lancs, Weston-super-Mare, 1958.
100 WKTS (5) 116 @ 18.28 in 1958.
Took 26 wkts for 308 runs in first three matches (aged 17) in 1953 (all played at Bath): 1–18; 8–96 and 6–60; 6–53 and 5–81.

LANGLEY, Gilbert Roche Andrews
RHB, WK

Born Adelaide, S Australia, 14 Sept 1919. Educ Col Light Garden's S. Debut 1945/46. *Wisden* 1957.
AUSTRALIA DOMESTIC South Australia (55) 1945/46–56/57.
AUSTRALIA (26) 1951/52–56/57. E 1954/55 (2); SA 1952/53 (5); WI 1951/52 (5). *E 1953 (4), 1956 (3); WI 1954/55 (4); I 1956/57 (2); P 1956/57 (1).*
OTHER TOURS Australia to S Africa 1949/50.
HST 53 A v WI, Bridgetown, 1954/55. HS 160* S Australia v N Zealanders, Adelaide, 1953/54.
RECORDS Made nine dismissals (8 ct, 1 st) match, A v E, Lord's, 1956, Australia Test record equalled in 1982/83 by R. W. Marsh.
Speaker S Australia State Parliament. Nephew J. N. Langley (Queensland).

LANGRIDGE, James
LHB, SLA

Born Chailey, Sussex, 10 July 1906. Died Brighton, Sussex, 10 Sept 1966. Educ Newick S. Debut 1924. *P. Wisden* 1932.
SUSSEX (622) 1924–53. Cap 1927. Capt 1950–52. Benefit (£4000) 1947. Testimonial (£2600) 1956.
N ZEALAND DOMESTIC Auckland (1) 1927/28.
ENGLAND (8) 1933–46. SA 1935 (1); WI 1933 (2); I 1936 (1), 1946 (1). *I 1933/34 (3).*
OTHER TOURS MCC to Australasia 1935/36. Lord Tennyson's XI to India 1937/38. MCC to Australia 1946/47.
HST 70 E v I, Calcutta, 1933/34. HS 167 Sussex v Notts, Trent Bridge, 1936.

BBT 7–56 E v WI, Old Trafford, 1933 (Test debut). BB 9–34 Sussex v Yorks, Sheffield, 1934.
1000 RUNS (20) 2082 @ 40.82 in 1937.
100 WKTS (6) 158 @ 16.56 in 1933.
DOUBLE (6) 1930–33, 1935, 1937 (2082 runs, 101 wkts).
RECORDS Most appearances (622) for Sussex. Added 326* for 4th wkt with G. Cox, Sussex v Yorks, Headingley, 1949, county record.
Players v Gentlemen (5) 1930–37. Sussex coach 1953–59. Minor Counties umpire 1960–65. Club: Newick. Son R. J. Langridge and brother John G. Langridge (both Sussex).

LANGRIDGE, John George
————RHB————

Born Chailey, Sussex, 10 Feb 1910. Educ Newick S. Debut 1928. *P. Wisden* 1950.
SUSSEX (567) 1928–55. Cap 1933. Joint benefit (with H. W. Parks) (£1930) 1948. Testimonial (£3825) 1953.
HS 250* Sussex v Glam, Hove, 1933.
BB 3–15 Sussex v Notts, Trent Bridge, 1937.
1000 RUNS (17) 2914 @ 60.70 in 1949. 2000 runs (11).
RECORDS Added 490 for 1st wkt, with E. H. Bowley, Sussex v M'sex, Hove, 1933, county record and fourth-highest 1st wkt stand ever. Scored 2850 (@ 64.77) for Sussex in 1949 and 34,152 (@ 37.69) for Sussex in career; 12 centuries for Sussex in 1949 and 76 for Sussex in career, all county records. 779 catches for Sussex, record for any county.
Scored centuries in four successive fc inns in 1949.
Selected for MCC to India 1939/40 (cancelled owing to war). Players v Gentlemen (2) 1933–49. Fc umpire 1956–80, returning for a few matches in 1982 and 1983 (7 Tests, 1960–63). Club: Newick. MBE for services to cricket. Brother James Langridge (Sussex, England); nephew R. J. Langridge (Sussex).

LANGRIDGE, Richard James
————LHB, ROB————

Born Brighton, Sussex, 13 Apr 1939. Educ Brighton and Hove GS. Debut 1957. *P.*
SUSSEX (207) 1957–71. Cap 1961.
COMBINED SERVICES (4) 1959–60.
TOUR MCC to E Africa 1963/64.
HS 137* Sussex v Leics, Leicester, 1963.
1000 RUNS (4) 1885 @ 30.90 in 1962.
Club: Brighton and Hove. Father James Langridge (Sussex, England); uncle John G. Langridge (Sussex).

LARKHAM, William *Trevor*
————RHB, LB————

Born Kidderminster, Worcs, 10 Nov 1929. Debut 1952.
WORCESTERSHIRE (1) 1952.
HS 13 Worcs v Yorks, Worcester, 1952.
Club: Kidderminster.

LARKING, John Gordon
————RHB————

Born Maidstone, Kent, 4 Nov 1921. Educ Charterhouse. Debut 1946.
KENT (3) 1946.
HS 8 Kent v Surrey, Oval, 1946.
Clubs: The Mote, Butterflies.

LARKINS, Wayne
————RHB, RM————

Born Roxton, Bedfordshire, 22 Nov 1953. Educ Bushmead, Huntingdon. Debut 1972.
NORTHAMPTONSHIRE (227) 1972–. Cap 1976.
S AFRICA DOMESTIC Eastern Province 1982/83–.
ENGLAND (6) 1979/80–81. A 1981 (1); WI 1980 (3). *A 1979/80 (1); I 1979/80 (1).*
OTHER TOUR Overseas XI to India 1980/81.
HST 34 E v A, Oval, 1981. HS 252 Northants v Glam, Cardiff, 1983.
BB 5–59 Northants v Worcs, Worcester, 1984.
1000 RUNS (7) 1863 @ 45.43 in 1982.
RECORDS Added 322 for 2nd wkt with R. G. Williams, Northants v Leics, Leicester, 1980, county record.
Barred from Test cricket for three yrs for touring S Africa 1981/82 (SAB England XI).

LARTER, John David Frederick
————RHB, RFM————

Born Inverness, Scotland, 24 Apr 1940. Educ Framlingham C. Debut 1960. *P.*
NORTHAMPTONSHIRE (134) 1960–69.
ENGLAND (10) 1962–65. SA 1965 (2); NZ 1965 (1); P 1962 (1). *NZ 1962/63 (3); I 1963/64 (3).*
OTHER TOURS MCC to N Zealand 1960/61. International XI to Rhodesia and Pakistan 1961/62. MCC to Australasia 1962/63, 1965/66. MCC to E Africa 1963/64.
HST 10 E v SA, Trent Bridge, 1965. HS 51* Northants v Notts, Trent Bridge, 1962.
BBT 5–57 E v P, Oval, 1962. BB 8–28 Northants v Som, Northampton, 1965.

100 WKTS (2) 121 @ 16.76 in 1963.
Players v Gentlemen (1) 1961. Suffolk 1958. Club: Stourbridge. Career curtailed owing to injury.

LASHLEY, Patrick Dudley
————LHB, RM————

Born Christ Church, Barbados, 11 Feb 1937. Debut 1957/58.
W INDIES DOMESTIC Barbados 1957/58–74/75.
WEST INDIES (4) 1960/61–66. *E 1966 (2); A 1960/61 (2).*
OTHER TOURS Barbados to England 1969.
HST 49 WI v E, Trent Bridge, 1966. HS 204 Barbados v Guyana, Georgetown, 1966/67.
BB 3–15 W Indians v Glos, Bristol, 1966.
Clubs: Spartan (W Indies), Norton (England).

LATCHMAN, Amritt Harichand (Harry)
————RHB, LBG————

Born Kingston, Jamaica, 26 July 1943. Educ Christopher Wren CS, Shepherds Bush, London. Debut 1965.
MIDDLESEX (170) 1965–73. Cap 1968. Testimonial (£1486) 1974.
NOTTINGHAMSHIRE (40) 1974–76. Cap 1975.
TOUR International XI to India, Pakistan and Ceylon 1967/68.
HS 96 M'sex v Worcs, Kidderminster, 1972.
BB 7–65 Notts v Essex, Ilford, 1975.
Cambridgeshire 1977–78. Clubs: Wisbech, Cross Arrows. Played as H. C. Latchman.

LATHAM, Hubert Joseph
————RHB, RF————

Born Birmingham, 13 Nov 1932. Debut 1955.
WARWICKSHIRE (10) 1955–59.
HS 26 Warwicks v Surrey, Oval, 1958.
BB 6–49 Warwicks v Combined Services, Edgbaston, 1958.
Club: Moseley (taken over 1000 wickets).

LATHAM, Michael Edward
————RHB, RFM————

Born Birmingham, 14 Jan 1939. Debut 1961. *P.*
SOMERSET (18) 1961–62.
HS 21* Som v Hants, Frome, 1961.
BB 5–20 Som v Notts, Bath, 1962.
Northumberland 1963–70. Clubs: Clevedon, Morpeth, Tyndale.

LAVERS, Alan Braden
——————RHB, RM/OB——————

Born Melbourne, Australia, 6 Sept 1912. Educ Chigwell S. Debut 1937.
ESSEX (26) 1937–53.
HS 42* Essex v Leics, Colchester, 1953.
BB 4–68 Essex v Kent, Gravesend, 1949.
Club: Buckhurst Hill.

LAVIS, George
——————RHB, RM——————

Born Sebastopol, Monmouthshire, 17 Aug 1908. Died Pontypool, S Wales, 29 July 1956. Debut 1928. *P.*
GLAMORGAN (206) 1928–49. Cap. Testimonial 1950.
HS 154 Glam v Worcs, Cardiff, 1934 (adding 263 for 4th wkt with C. Smart, county record).
BB 4–55 Glam v Sussex, Cardiff, 1933. Glam coach 1946–56.

LAW, John Alexander Gordon Charles
——————RHB, WK——————

Born Bangalore, India, 25 Mar 1923. Educ Edinburgh Academy; St Edmund's Hall, Oxford. Debut 1940/41.
INDIA DOMESTIC Madras 1940/41–41/42, Europeans 1940/41–44/45.
OXFORD UNIVERSITY (2) 1949.
HS 35 Europeans v Indians, Madras, 1943/44.
Clubs: Army, Combined Services, Bombay Gymkhana, South Oxon Amateurs, Standard Club (Paris), Quebec.

LAWLOR, Peter John
——————RHB, OB——————

Born Gowerton, S Wales, 8 May 1960. Educ Gowerton CS. Debut 1981.
GLAMORGAN (1) 1981.
HS 8 Glam v Sri Lankans, Cardiff, 1981.
Badminton: Glam.

LAWRENCE, Arthur Alfred Kenneth
——————RHB, LB——————

Born Marlborough, Wiltshire, 3 Nov 1930. Educ Marlborough GS. Debut 1952. *P.*
SUSSEX (28) 1952–56.
HS 63* Sussex v Oxford U, Hove, 1955 and 63 v Glos, Eastbourne, 1955.
Club: Brighton and Hove.

LAWRENCE, David Valentine
——————RHB, RFM——————

Born Gloucester, 28 Jan 1964. Educ Linden S. Debut 1981.
GLOUCESTERSHIRE (29) 1981–.
HS 17 Glos v Notts, Trent Bridge, 1984.
BB 5–58 Glos v Som, Bristol, 1984.

LAWRENCE, Douglas Rosyth
——————RHB, RFM——————

Born Edinburgh, Scotland, 20 Oct 1929. Educ RHS, Edinburgh. Debut 1956.
SCOTLAND (7) 1956–58.
HS 10 Scotland v Ireland, Dublin, 1957.
BB 4–56 Scotland v MCC, Aberdeen, 1957.
Club: RHS Former Pupils.

LAWRENCE, John
——————RHB, LBG——————

Born Carlton, Yorks, 29 Mar 1914. Debut 1946. *P.*
SOMERSET (281) 1946–55. Cap 1946. Benefit (£3549) 1954.
HS 122 Som v Worcs, Worcester, 1955.
BB 8–41 Som v Worcs, Worcester, 1950.
1000 RUNS (3) 1128 @ 22.11 in 1955.
100 WKTS (2) 115 @ 18.90 in 1950.
19 runs short of double in 1950; 71 runs and seven wkts short in 1954.
Lincolnshire 1958–60. Clubs: Haslingden, East Bierley, Leeds, Wakefield, Morley, Dalton, Honley. Son J. M. Lawrence (Som).

LAWRENCE, John *Miles*
——————RHB, LB——————

Born Rothwell, Leeds, 7 Nov 1940. Educ Rothwell GS. Debut 1959. *P.*
SOMERSET (18) 1959–61.
HS 41 Som v M'sex, Taunton, 1961.
BB 3–44 Som v Notts, Taunton, 1959.
Former professional coach Leeds GS (from 1965). Clubs: Heckmondwike, Dalton, Honley. Father J. Lawrence (Som).

LAWRENCE, Mark Philip
——————LHB, SLA——————

Born Warrington, Lancs, 6 May 1962. Educ Manchester GS; Merton C, Oxford. Debut 1982.
OXFORD UNIVERSITY (13) 1982–84. (Blue 1984).
HS 18 Oxford U v M'sex, The Parks, 1982.
BB 3–79 Oxford U v Kent, The Parks, 1984.

LAWRENCE, Patrick
——————RHB, RFM——————

Born Dominica, 3 Oct 1942. Debut 1964.
MIDDLESEX (4) 1964.
HS 14* M'sex v Yorks, Leeds, 1964.
BB 3–52 M'sex v Worcs, Lord's, 1964.
No-balled for throwing, M'sex v Sussex, Lord's, 1964; did not play in fc cricket again.

LAWRENCE, Walter Nicholas Murray
——————RHB——————

Born London, 8 Feb 1935. Educ Winchester C; Trinity C, Oxford. Debut 1954.
OXFORD UNIVERSITY (3) 1954.
HS 1 Oxford U v Hants, The Parks, 1954.

LAWRY, William Justus (Jesse)
——————LHB, WK——————

Born St Just, Cornwall, 24 Apr 1940. Debut 1965.
MINOR COUNTIES (3) 1965–69.
HS 9 Minor Counties v S Africans, Jesmond, 1965.
Cornwall 1958–81. Club: Penzance.

LAWRY, William Morris
——————LHB——————

Born Thornbury, Victoria, Australia, 11 Feb 1937. Educ Preston Technical S, Melbourne. Debut 1955/56. *Wisden* 1962.
AUSTRALIA DOMESTIC Victoria (99) 1955/56–71/72. Capt 1961/62–71/72.
AUSTRALIA (67) 1961–70/71. E 1962/63 (5), 1965/66 (5), 1970/71 (5); SA 1963/64 (5); WI 1968/69 (5); I 1967/68 (4); P 1964/65 (1). *E 1961 (5), 1964 (5), 1968 (4); SA 1966/67 (5), 1969/70 (4); WI 1964/65 (5); I 1964/65 (3), 1969/70 (5); P 1964/65 (1).* Capt 25.
Rest of World v Barbados, Bridgetown, 1966/67.
HST 210 A v WI, Bridgetown, 1964/65.
HS 266 Victoria v NSW, Sydney, 1960/61.
1000 RUNS (2 + 6) 2019 @ 61.18 in 1961.
RECORDS Added 382 for 1st wkt with R. B. Simpson, A v WI, Bridgetown, 1964/65, Australia Test record.
Carried bat for 49* in total of 107, A v I, Delhi, 1969/70 and for 60* in total of 116 (one man absent) A v E, Sydney, 1970/71.
Club: Northcote. Autobiography *Run-Digger* (1966).

LAWS, Michael Lutener
————————RHB, WK————————

Born Finchley, London, 12 Aug 1926.
Educ Highgate. Debut 1946.
COMBINED SERVICES (1) 1946.
MIDDLESEX (5) 1948–50.
MCC (2) 1949–50.
HS 12 MCC v Cambridge U, Fenner's,
1949.
Club: Hornsey. Chairman Zimbabwe
Cricket Society.

LAWSON, Geoffrey Francis
————————RHB, RF————————

Born Wagga Wagga, NSW, Australia, 7
Dec 1957. Educ U of NSW. Debut
1977/78.
AUSTRALIA DOMESTIC New South Wales
(46) 1977/78–.
LANCASHIRE (1) 1979.
AUSTRALIA (23) 1980/81–83/84. E 1982/
83 (5); WI 1981/82 (1); NZ 1980/81 (1);
P 1983/84 (5). E 1981 (3); WI 1983/84
(5); P 1982/83 (3).
OTHER TOURS Australia to India 1979/80.
Australia to Pakistan 1979/80. Australia
to Sri Lanka 1980/81.
HST 57* A v P, Lahore, 1982/83. HS as
above.
BBT 7–81 A v E, Lord's, 1981. BB as
above.

LAWTON, William
————————RHB, RM————————

Born Pitses, Ashton-under-Lyne, 4
June 1920. Debut 1948. P.
LANCASHIRE (2) 1948.
HS 3 Lancs v Oxford U, The Parks,
1948.
Cumberland 1954–56. Clubs: Ashton,
St Ann's, Werneth, Oldham, Walsall,
Cleator Moor, Whitehaven. Soccer:
Oldham Athletic. Wife Dora Bryan
(stage and film actress).

LAYCOCK, David Alan
————————RHB————————

Born Woolwich, Kent, 2 Sept 1947.
Debut 1969.
KENT (10) 1969–73.
HS 58 Kent v Leics, Canterbury, 1969.
Club: Blackheath.

LEA, Antony Edward
————————RHB, LB————————

Born Wolverhampton, Staffordshire, 29
Sept 1962. Educ High Arcal S; Church-
ill C, Cambridge. Debut 1984.
CAMBRIDGE UNIVERSITY (9) 1984 (Blue).

HS 119 Cambridge U v Essex, Fenner's,
1984.
BB 2–27 Cambridge U v Notts, Trent
Bridge, 1984.
Club: Old Hill.

LEACH, Clive William
————————RHB, SLA————————

Born Bombay, India, 4 Dec 1934. Debut
1955. P.
WARWICKSHIRE (39) 1955–58.
HS 67 Warwicks v Derbys, Derby, 1957
and v Essex, Southend, 1957.
BB 3–19 Warwicks v Combined Services, Portland Road, Birmingham,
1957.
Durham 1959–65. Buckinghamshire
1966–70. Clubs: Bishop Auckland,
Amersham, High Wycombe.

LEADBEATER, Barry
————————RHB————————

Born Harehills, Leeds, Yorks, 14 Aug
1943. Educ Harehills Sec S. Debut
1966.
YORKSHIRE (144) 1966–79. Cap 1969.
Joint benefit 1980 (shared £33,846) with
G. A. Cope.
TOUR Duke of Norfolk's XI to W Indies
1969/70.
HS 140* Yorks v Hants, Portsmouth,
1976.
Fc umpire 1981–. Clubs: Hunslet Nel-
son, Leeds, Bradford.

LEADBEATER, Edric
————————RHB, LBG————————

Born Huddersfield, Yorks, 15 Aug 1927.
Debut 1949. P.
YORKSHIRE (81) 1949–56.
WARWICKSHIRE (27) 1957–58.
ENGLAND (2) I 1951/52.
HST 38 E v I, Calcutta, 1951/52. HS 116
Warwicks v Glam, Coventry, 1958.
BB 8–83 Yorks v Worcs, Worcester,
1950.
Played two Tests but never won a
county cap.
Clubs: Royton, Pudsey St Laurence,
Almondbury, Primrose Hill.

LEADBETTER, Stanley Austin
————————RHB, occ RM————————

Born Stanion, nr Kettering, Northants,
22 May 1937. Educ Kettering GS.
Debut 1956.
COMBINED SERVICES (3) 1956–57.
HS 46 Combined Services v Surrey,
Oval, 1957.

Northants 2nd XI 1953–58. Clubs:
Kettering Town, RAF, Stewarts and
Lloyds (Corby).

LEARY, Stuart Edward
————————RHB, LB————————

Born Cape Town, S Africa, 30 Apr
1933. Educ Sea Point HS, Cape Town.
Debut 1951.
KENT (381) 1951–71. Cap 1957. Benefit
(£9100) 1967.
HS 158 Kent v Northants, Kettering,
1963.
BB 5–22 Kent v Glam, Swansea, 1961.
1000 RUNS (9) 1440 @ 38.91 in 1961.
Took 6 catches in inns, Kent v Cam-
bridge U, Fenner's, 1958. Currently
coach in S Africa; manager W Province.
Soccer: Charlton Athletic, Queen's Park
Rangers.

LEDDEN, Peter Robert Varville
————————LHB, RM————————

Born Scarborough, Yorks, 12 July 1943.
Educ Wallington GS. Debut 1961. P.
SUSSEX (35) 1961–67.
HS 98 Sussex v Warwicks, Edgbaston,
1964.
BB 5–43 Sussex v Cambridge U, Hove,
1966.

LEE, Charles
————————RHB, RM————————

Born Rotherham, Yorks, 17 Mar 1924.
Debut 1952. P.
YORKSHIRE (2) 1952.
MINOR COUNTIES (1) 1953.
DERBYSHIRE (268) 1954–64. Cap 1956.
Capt 1963–64. Testimonial (£2992)
1964.
HS 150 Derbys v Glos, Chesterfield,
1958.
BB 2–9 Derbys v Surrey, Chesterfield,
1961.
1000 RUNS (8) 1503 @ 37.57 in 1962.
Clubs: Sheffield United, Rotherham
Town.

LEE, Frank Stanley
————————LHB, RM————————

Born Marylebone, London, 24 July
1905. Died London, 30 Mar 1982.
Debut 1925. P.
MIDDLESEX (2) 1925.
SOMERSET (328) 1929–47. Cap 1931.
Benefit 1947.
HS 169 Som v Notts, Trent Bridge, 1946.
BB 5–53 Som v Warwicks, Taunton,
1933.

1000 RUNS (8) 2019 @ 44.86 in 1938.
Fc umpire 1948–63 (29 Tests, 1949–62). MCC Hon. member. Author of three books, including autobiography *Cricket, Lovely Cricket* (1960). Brothers H. W. Lee (M'sex, England) and J. W. Lee (M'sex, Som).

LEE, Jack
—RHB, RM—

Born Sileby, Leics, 4 Nov 1920. Debut 1947.
LEICESTERSHIRE (1) 1947.
HS 3 Leics v Glam, Cardiff, 1947.
Took 1–13 including wkt with first ball in fc cricket (in only fc match, as above). Soccer: Leicester City, Derby County, Coventry City, England (1 cap).

LEE, Peter Granville
—RHB, RMF—

Born Arthingworth, Northants, 27 Aug 1945. Debut 1967. *Wisden* 1976.
NORTHAMPTONSHIRE (44) 1967–71.
LANCASHIRE (152) 1972–82. Cap 1972.
TOUR D. H. Robins' XI to S Africa 1973/74, 1975/76.
HS 26 Northants v Glos, Northampton, 1969.
BB 8–34 Lancs v Oxford U, The Parks, 1980.
100 WKTS (2) 112 @ 18.45 in 1975.
Durham 1983. Club: Gateshead Fell.

LEE, Richard John
—RHB, RM—

Born Ryde, NSW, Australia, 6 Mar 1950. Educ Sydney C of E GS; Sydney U; Worcester C, Oxford. Debut 1972.
OXFORD UNIVERSITY (23) 1972–74 (Blue 1972–74).
HS 130 Oxford U v Lancs, The Parks, 1973.
BB 4–56 Oxford U v Yorks, Harrogate, 1972.

LEECH, Andrew David
—RHB, RM—

Born Farnworth, Lancs, 9 Mar 1952. Educ Bolton S; Jesus C, Oxford. Debut 1972.
OXFORD UNIVERSITY (9) 1972.
HS 8* Oxford U v Derbys, The Parks, 1972.
BB 3–40 Oxford U v Warwicks, The Parks, 1972.

LEES, Geoffrey William
—RHB, LB—

Born Chorlton-cum-Hardy, Manchester, 1 July 1920. Educ King's S, Rochester; Downing C, Cambridge. Debut 1947.
CAMBRIDGE UNIVERSITY (2) 1947.
SUSSEX (1) 1951.
HS 15 Cambridge U v M'sex, Fenner's, 1947.
Club: Sevenoaks Vine.

LEES, Robin Douglas
—RHB, RM—

Born Cranleigh, Surrey, 19 May 1949. Educ Gresham's S; St Edmund's Hall, Oxford. Debut 1970.
OXFORD UNIVERSITY (3) 1970.
HS 17* Oxford U v Glam, The Parks, 1970.

LEES, Warren Kenneth
—RHB, WK—

Born Dunedin, N Zealand, 19 Mar 1952. Debut 1970/71.
N ZEALAND DOMESTIC New Zealand Under-23 XI (2) 1970/71–71/72, Otago (77) 1972/73–.
NEW ZEALAND (21) 1976/77–83. E 1977/78 (2); A 1976/77 (1); WI 1979/80 (3); P 1978/79 (3); SL 1982/83 (2). *E 1983 (2); A 1980/81 (2); I 1976/77 (3); P 1976/77 (3)*.
OTHER TOUR N Zealand to England 1979.
HST 152 NZ v P, Karachi, 1976/77 (adding 186 for 7th wkt with R. J. Hadlee, N Zealand Test record). HS as above.

LEGARD, Antony Ronald
—RHB, RM—

Born Sialkot, India, 17 Jan 1912. Educ Winchester C; Trinity C, Oxford. Debut 1932.
OXFORD UNIVERSITY (31) 1932–35 (Blue 1932, 1935).
WORCESTERSHIRE (1) 1935.
INDIA DOMESTIC Europeans (Bombay) 1943/44.
FREE FORESTERS (2) 1948–49.
MCC (1) 1952.
HS 38 Oxford U v S Americans, The Parks, 1932.
BB 7–36 Oxford U v Cambridge U, Lord's, 1935.
Secretary Delamere Golf Club.

LEGARD, Edwin
—RHB, WK—

Born Barnsley, Yorks, 23 Aug 1935. Debut 1962. *P.*

WARWICKSHIRE (20) 1962–68. Cap 1963.
HS 21 Warwicks v Scotland, Edgbaston, 1967.
Club: Barnsley.

LEIPER, John Morton
—LHB, RFM, WK—

Born Woodford Green, Essex, 17 Feb 1921. Educ Chigwell. Debut 1950.
ESSEX (2) 1950.
HS 44 Essex v Som, Bath, 1950.
Club: Woodford Wells. Son R. J. Leiper (Essex).

LEIPER, Robert James
—LHB—

Born Woodford Green, Essex, 30 Aug 1961. Educ Chigwell. Debut 1981.
ESSEX (2) 1981–82.
HS 49 Essex v Australians, Chelmsford, 1981.
Father J. M. Leiper (Essex).

LEMMY, Brian Allan
—RHB, RMF—

Born Isleworth, M'sex, 6 Jan 1937. Debut 1958. *P.*
MCC (1) 1958.
HS 7* MCC v Cambridge U, Lord's, 1958.
BB 2–92 same match.
Staffordshire 1961–62. Lord's staff 1958. Club: Stafford.

LENG, Denis
—RHB, RFM—

Born Pudsey, Yorks, 26 Nov 1934. Educ Primrose Hill Sec S, Pudsey. Debut 1966.
IRELAND (1) 1966.
HS 1 Ireland v MCC, Dublin, 1966.
Clubs: Brighouse, Idle, Farsley, Cork Wanderers.

LENHAM, Leslie John
—RHB, OB—

Born Worthing, Sussex, 24 May 1936. Educ Worthing HS. Debut 1956. *P.*
SUSSEX (300) 1956–70. Cap 1957. Joint benefit 1969 (shared £6300) with G. C. Cooper.
1000 RUNS (6) 2016 @ 32.51 in 1961.
HS 191* Sussex v Warwicks, Edgbaston, 1963.
BB 2–24 Sussex v Notts, Eastbourne, 1962.
Clubs: Brighton and Hove, Three Bridges. NCA coach. Son N. J. Lenham (Sussex).

LENHAM, Neil John
————RHB, RMF————

Born Worthing, Sussex, 17 Dec 1965.
Educ Brighton C. Debut 1984.
SUSSEX (1) 1984.
HS 31 Sussex v Sri Lankans, Hove, 1984.
Father L. J. Lenham (Sussex).

LE ROUX, Garth Sterling
————RHB, RF————

Born Kenilworth, Cape Town, S Africa,
4 Sept 1955. Educ Wynberg Boys' HS;
Stellenbosch U. Debut 1975/76.
S AFRICA DOMESTIC Western Province
1975/76–.
SUSSEX (92) 1978–. Cap 1981.
HS 83 Sussex v Surrey, Hove, 1982.
BB 8–107 Sussex v Som, Taunton, 1981.
World Series Cricket (Kerry Packer)
1978/79. South Africa (8) 1981/82–83/
84. Club: Lascelles Hall.

LESTER, Edward Ibson
————RHB, occ OB————

Born Scarborough, Yorks, 18 Feb 1923.
Educ Scarborough Boys' HS. Debut
1945. *P from 1948.*
YORKSHIRE (228) 1945–56. Cap 1948.
Testimonial (£3000) 1956.
NORTH (2) 1949–50.
HS 186 Yorks v Warwicks, Scarborough,
1949.
1000 RUNS (6) 1801 @ 37.52 in 1949.
Current Yorks scorer. Clubs: Scar-
borough, Undercliffe, Keighley, Brad-
ford.

LESTER, Gerald
————RHB, LBG————

Born Long Whatton, Leics, 27 Dec
1915. Debut 1937. *P.*
LEICESTERSHIRE (373) 1937–58. Cap
1946. Testimonial (£1500) 1953.
HS 143 Leics v Surrey, Oval, 1955.
BB 6–42 Leics v S Africans, Leicester,
1947.
1000 RUNS (5) 1599 @ 33.31 in 1949.
Leics coach 1959–66.

L'ESTRANGE, Michael Gerard
————LHB, occ RM————

Born Sydney, Australia, 12 Oct 1952.
Educ St Aloysius C, Sydney; Sydney U;
Worcester C, Oxford. Debut 1977.
OXFORD UNIVERSITY (23) 1977–79 (Blue
1977, 1979).
HS 63 Oxford U v Sussex, Pagham, 1979.

LETHBRIDGE, Christopher (Arthur)
————RHB, RM————

Born Castleford, Yorks, 23 June 1961.
Educ Normanton County Sec S. Debut
1981.
WARWICKSHIRE (47) 1981–.
HS 87* Warwicks v Som, Taunton,
1982.
BB 5–68 Warwicks v Glam, Cardiff,
1982.
Took wkt (G Boycott, of Yorks) with
first ball in fc cricket.

LEVER, Colin
————RHB, RM————

Born Todmorden, Yorks, 4 Aug 1939.
Educ Todmorden GS. Debut 1965.
MINOR COUNTIES (1) 1965.
HS 12 Minor Counties v S Africans, Jes-
mond, 1965.
Buckinghamshire 1962–78. Clubs:
Liverpool, Todmorden, Chesham,
Heywood, Northern. Brother P. Lever
(Lancs, England).

LEVER, John Kenneth
————RHB, LFM————

Born Stepney, E London, 24 Feb 1949.
Educ Dane Sec Modern, Ilford. Debut
1967. *Wisden 1978.*
ESSEX (354) 1967–. Cap 1970. Benefit
(£66,110) 1980.
S AFRICA DOMESTIC Natal 1982/83.
ENGLAND (20) 1976/77–81/82. A 1977
(3); WI 1980 (1); I 1979 (1). *A 1976/77
(1), 1978/79 (1), 1979/80 (1); NZ
1977/78 (1); I 1976/77 (5), 1979/80
(1), 1981/82 (2); P 1977/78 (3).*
OTHER TOURS D. H. Robins' XI to S
Africa 1972/73, 1973/74. D. H. Robins'
XI to Sri Lanka 1977/78. Overseas XI to
India 1980/81.
HST 53 E v I, Delhi, 1976/77. HS 91 Essex
v Glam, Cardiff, 1970.
BBT 7–46 E v I, Delhi, 1976/77. BB 8–37
Essex v Glos, Bristol, 1984.
100 WKTS (4) 116 @ 21.98 in 1984.
Barred from Test cricket for three yrs
for touring S Africa 1981/82 (SAB Eng-
land XI). Club: Ilford.

LEVER, Peter
————RHB, RFM————

Born Todmorden, Yorks, 17 Sept 1940.
Educ Todmorden GS. Debut 1960. *P.*
LANCASHIRE (268) 1960–76. Cap 1965.
Benefit (£7000) 1972.
AUSTRALIA DOMESTIC Tasmania (1) 1971/
72.

ENGLAND (17) 1970/71–75. A 1972 (1),
1975 (1); I 1971 (1); P 1971 (3). *A 1970/
71 (5), 1974/75 (2); NZ 1970/71 (2),
1974/75 (2).*
HST 88* E v I, Old Trafford, 1971. HS as
above.
BBT 6–38 E v A, Melbourne, 1974/75. BB
7–70 Lancs v Glam, Old Trafford,
1972.
Lancs coach. Clubs: Todmorden,
Kearsley. Brother C. Lever (Minor
Counties).

LEVETT, William *Howard* Vincent (Hopper)
————RHB, WK————

Born Goudhurst, Kent, 25 Jan 1908.
Educ Brighton C. Debut 1930.
KENT (142) 1930–47.
ENGLAND (1) *I 1933/34.*
HS 76 Kent v Hants, Portsmouth, 1935.
RECORD Made 9 dismissals in a match on
three occasions (1933–35), a record
equalled by Wasim Bari in 1975/76.
Gentlemen v Players (8) 1931–36. Kent
president 1975.

LEVICK, Deryck Cyril
————RHB, RM/OB————

Born Acton, London, 27 May 1929.
Educ Acton County HS. Debut 1950.
ESSEX (3) 1950–51.
HS 6 Essex v Leics, Westcliff, 1950.

LEWINGTON, Peter John
————RHB, OB————

Born Finchampstead, Berkshire, 30 Jan
1950. Debut 1970.
WARWICKSHIRE (69) 1970–82.
TOUR D. H. Robins' XI to S Africa 1972/
73.
HS 34 Warwicks v Essex, Edgbaston,
1973.
BB 7–52 Warwicks v Worcs, Worcester,
1975.
Berkshire 1967–69, 1977–81, 1983–.
Clubs: Perth (W Australia), Walsall
(England), North Taranaki (N
Zealand).

LEWIS, Anthony Charles Wilson
————RHB————

Born Stoke on Trent, Staffordshire, 29
Sept 1932. Educ Repton S; Clare C,
Cambridge. Debut 1952.
CAMBRIDGE UNIVERSITY (6) 1952–53.
HS 55 Cambridge U v Free Foresters,
Fenner's, 1952.

Club: Porthill Park. Lawn tennis: Staffordshire junior champion 1947–49; Junior Wimbledon quarter-finalist 1950.

LEWIS, Anthony Robert
——————RHB, LB——————

Born Swansea, S Wales, 6 July 1938. Educ Neath GS; Christ's C, Cambridge. Debut 1955.
GLAMORGAN (315) 1955–74. Cap 1960. Capt 1967–72. Benefit 1973.
COMBINED SERVICES (2) 1958–59.
CAMBRIDGE UNIVERSITY (44) 1960–62 (Blue 1960–62). Capt 1962.
ENGLAND (9) 1972/73–73. NZ 1973 (1). I 1972/73 (5); P 1972/73 (3). Capt 8.
OTHER TOURS Commonwealth XI to Pakistan 1967/68. Glam to W Indies 1969/70. MCC to Ceylon 1969/70.
HST 125 E v I, Kanpur, 1972/73. HS 223 Glam v Kent, Gravesend, 1966.
BB 3–18 Glam v Som, Neath, 1967.
1000 RUNS (11) 2198 @ 41.47 in 1966.
RECORD Added 238 for 2nd wkt with A. Jones, Glam v Sussex, Hastings, 1962, county record.
Gentlemen v Players (2) 1962. Club: Neath. Cricket broadcaster and writer. Rugby: Blue. Violin in Welsh Youth Orchestra.

LEWIS, Brian
——————RHB, OB——————

Born Maesteg, S Wales, 18 July 1945. Debut 1965.
GLAMORGAN (37) 1965–68.
HS 38 Glam v Notts, Swansea, 1968.
BB 7–28 Glam v Hants, Southampton, 1968.

LEWIS, Claude
——————LHB, SLA——————

Born Sittingbourne, Kent, 27 July 1908. Educ Sittingbourne GS. Debut 1933. P.
KENT (128) 1933–53. Cap 1935. Testimonial (£2082) 1952.
HS 27 Kent v Surrey, Oval, 1939.
BB 8–58 Kent v Essex, Gravesend, 1934.
Successively Kent coach and scorer until retirement in 1984.

LEWIS, David John
——————RHB——————

Born Bulawayo, Rhodesia, 27 July 1927. Educ Plumtree S; Cape Town U; Exeter C, Oxford. Debut 1949.
OXFORD UNIVERSITY (14) 1949–51 (Blue 1951).
S AFRICA DOMESTIC Rhodesia 1945/ 46–63/64.

HS 170* Rhodesia v NE Transvaal, Salisbury, 1954/55.
BB 2–19 Rhodesia v NE Transvaal, Bulawayo, 1955/56.
President Rhodesia CU 1973–75. Club: Salisbury (Rhodesia). Rugby: Blue.

LEWIS, David Wyndham
——————RHB, LB——————

Born Cardiff, S Wales, 18 Dec 1940. Educ Wycliffe C. Debut 1960. P.
GLAMORGAN (12) 1960–69.
S AFRICA DOMESTIC Transvaal 1972/73.
HS 29* Glam v Northants, Swansea, 1968.
BB 4–42 Glam v Oxford U, Colwyn Bay, 1968.
Clubs: Gowerton, Steel Co of Wales.

LEWIS, Desmond Michael
——————RHB, WK——————

Born Jamaica, 21 Feb 1946. Debut 1970.
W INDIES DOMESTIC Jamaica 1970–75/76.
WEST INDIES (3) I 1970/71.
TOUR Jamaica to England 1970.
HST 88 WI v I, Bridgetown, 1970/71. HS 96 Jamaica v Indians, Kingston, 1970/ 71.

LEWIS, Esmond Burman
——————RHB, WK——————

Born Shirley, Solihull, Warwicks, 5 Jan 1918. Died Dorridge, Solihull, 19 Oct 1983. Educ Wellesbourne House S, Birmingham. Debut 1949.
WARWICKSHIRE (43) 1949–58. Cap 1951.
HS 51 Warwicks v Combined Services, Edgbaston, 1956.
Made 9 dismissals (8 ct, 1 st) in match on fc debut, Warwicks v Oxford U, Edgbaston, 1949.
Gentlemen v Players (3) 1954–57. Warwicks committee 1958 until death. Clubs: Sparkhill, Kings Heath, Knowle and Dorridge. Chairman Knowle and Dorridge until death.

LEWIS, Euros John
——————LHB, ROB——————

Born Llanelli, S Wales, 31 Jan 1942. Debut 1961. P.
GLAMORGAN (96) 1961–66. Cap 1965.
SUSSEX (86) 1967–69. Cap 1967.
HS 80 Glam v Sussex, Cardiff, 1965.
BB 8–89 Glam v Kent, Swansea, 1965.
Clubs: Dafen, Llanelli, Pontarddulais, Steel Co of Wales, Llangennech.

LEWIS, Kenneth Humphrey
——————RHB, RFM——————

Born Penygloddfa, Llanllwchaiarn, nr Newtown, Monmouthshire, 10 Nov 1928. Debut 1950. P.
GLAMORGAN (36) 1950–56.
HS 34 Glam v Hants, Cardiff, 1956.
BB 4–25 Glam v Kent, Cardiff, 1953.
Clubs: Neath, Clydach, Ammanford.

LEWIS, Leslie Keith
——————RHB, OB——————

Born Finchley, London, 25 Sept 1929. Educ Taunton, Pembroke C, Cambridge. Debut 1952.
CAMBRIDGE UNIVERSITY (6) 1952–53.
HS 53* Cambridge U v Surrey, Guildford, 1953.
Club: Hornsey. Hockey: Blue (capt).

LEWIS, Reginald Chester Vale
——————RHB, LB——————

Born Cape Town, S Africa, 4 Oct 1927. Died S Africa, 1 Aug 1981. Educ Diocesan C, Rondesbosch; Keble C, Oxford. Debut 1949.
OXFORD UNIVERSITY (4) 1949–50.
HS 34 Oxford U v Free Foresters, The Parks, 1949.
BB 3–31 Oxford U v Warwicks, The Parks, 1950.
Oxfordshire 1949.

LEWIS, Richard Victor
——————RHB, RLB——————

Born Winchester, Hants, 6 Aug 1947. Educ Peter Symonds' S, Winchester. Debut 1967.
HAMPSHIRE (103) 1967–76.
MINOR COUNTIES (2) 1979–81.
HS 136 Hants v Glos, Bristol, 1974.
Dorset 1977–. Club: Liphook. Professional coach Charterhouse.

LEWIS, Roy Markham
——————RHB, RM——————

Born Bromley, Kent, 29 June 1948. Educ Tulse Hill CS. Debut 1968.
SURREY (38) 1968–73.
HS 87 Surrey v Kent, Blackheath, 1969.

LEWIS, William *Ian*
——————RHB——————

Born Dublin, Ireland, 29 Sept 1935. Educ St Andrew's C, Dublin. Debut 1956.
IRELAND (5) 1956–72.

HS 20 Ireland v Scotland, Edinburgh, 1956.
Clubs: Dublin YMCA, Cork, Limerick, Church of Ireland Protestants YMA.

LEYLAND, Morris (Maurice)
————LHB, SLA————

Born New Park, Harrogate, Yorks, 20 July 1900. Died Knaresborough, Yorks, 1 Jan 1967. Debut 1920. *P. Wisden* 1929.
YORKSHIRE (548) 1920–46. Cap 1922. Benefit (£3648) 1934.
INDIA DOMESTIC Maharajah of Patiala's XI 1926/27.
ENGLAND (41) 1928–38. A 1930 (3), 1934 (5), 1938 (1); SA 1929 (5), 1935 (4); WI 1928 (1), 1933 (1); I 1936 (2). *A 1928/29 (1), 1932/33 (5), 1936/37 (5); SA 1930/31 (5); WI 1934/35 (3).*
OTHER TOURS MCC to India 1926/27. Yorkshire to Jamaica 1935/36.
HST 187 E v A, Oval, 1938 (adding 382 for 2nd wkt with L. Hutton, England Test record). HS 263 Yorks v Essex, Hull, 1936.
BBT 3–91 E v SA, Cape Town, 1930/31. BB 8–63 Yorks v Hants, Huddersfield, 1938.
1000 RUNS (17) 2317 @ 50.36 in 1933. 2000 runs (3).
RECORDS Added 346 for 2nd wkt with W. Barber, Yorks v M'sex, Bramall Lane, Sheffield, 1932; 323* for 3rd wkt with H. Sutcliffe, Yorks v Glam, Huddersfield, 1928; 276 for 6th wkt with E. Robinson, Yorks v Glam, Swansea, 1926; all county records.
Scored 1013 runs (@ 84.41) in August 1932.
Players v Gentlemen (11) 1928–38. Yorks coach 1951–63. Club: Harrogate. MCC Hon. member. Father E. Leyland (groundsman Edgbaston); cousin W. Potter (Warwicks).

LIAQAT ALI Khan
————RHB, LM————

Born Karachi, Pakistan, 21 May 1955. Educ National C, Karachi. Debut 1970/71.
PAKISTAN DOMESTIC Karachi, Sind, Habib Bank, Pakistan International Airlines, 1970/71–.
PAKISTAN (5) 1974/75–78. E 1977/78 (2); WI 1974/75 (1). *E 1978 (2).*
OTHER TOUR PIA to Zimbabwe 1981/82.
HST 12 P v WI, Karachi, 1974/75. HS 51 Habib Bank v National Bank, Lahore, 1976/77.
BBT 3–80 P v E, Lord's, 1978. BB 8–44 (14–133) Sind v PIA, Lahore, 1974/75. Club: Middlesbrough.

LIDDELL, Alan William George
————RHB, RM————

Born Northampton, 8 Aug 1930. Died Duston, Northants, 9 Feb 1972. Debut 1951.
NORTHAMPTONSHIRE (18) 1951–55.
HS 38* Northants v Hants, Bournemouth, 1953.
BB 3–62 Northants v Lancs, Northampton, 1955.
Father A. G. Liddell (Northants).

LIGHTFOOT, Albert
————LHB, RM————

Born Woore, Shropshire, 8 Jan 1936. Debut 1953. *P.*
NORTHAMPTONSHIRE (290) 1953–70. Cap 1961. Benefit 1970.
HS 174* Northants v Oxford U, Northampton, 1969.
BB 7–25 Northants v Yorks, Headingley, 1966.
1000 RUNS (4) 1878 @ 41.73 in 1962.
RECORDS Added 376 for 6th wkt with R. Subba Row, Northants v Surrey, Oval, 1958, county record for any wkt.
Players v Gentlemen (1) 1962.

LILLEE, Dennis Keith
————RHB, RF————

Born Subiaco, W Australia, 18 July 1949. Educ Belmont HS, Perth. Debut 1969/70. *Wisden* 1973.
AUSTRALIA DOMESTIC W Australia (76) 1969/70–83/84.
AUSTRALIA (70) 1970/71–83/84. E 1970/71 (2), 1974/75 (6), 1976/77 (1), 1979/80 (3), 1982/83 (1); WI 1975/76 (5), 1979/80 (3), 1981/82 (3); NZ 1980/81 (3); I 1980/81 (3); P 1972/73 (3), 1976/77 (3), 1981/82 (3), 1983/84 (5). *E 1972 (5), 1975 (4), 1980 (1), 1981 (6); WI 1972/73 (1); NZ 1976/77 (2), 1981/82 (3); P 1979/80 (3); SL 1982/83 (1).*
OTHER TOURS Australia to N Zealand 1969/70. International XI to S Africa 1975/76.
HST 73* A v E, Lord's, 1975. HS as above.
BBT 7–83 A v WI, Melbourne, 1981/82.
BB 8–29 Australia v World XI, Perth, 1971/72
RECORDS Took 355 Test wkts @ 23.92, world record. Took 85 Test wkts @ 20.95 in 1981, record for a calendar yr. 10 or more wkts in a Test seven times, equalling record of S. F. Barnes (E; in 27 Tests). 163 wkts in Anglo-Australian Tests, record for either side. Took 351 wkts @ 23.02 for W Australia, state record.
World Series Cricket (Kerry Packer) 1977/78–78/79. Club: Haslingden.

LILLEY, Alan William
————RHB, RM————

Born Ilford, Essex, 8 May 1959. Educ Caterham HS, Ilford. Debut 1978.
ESSEX (31) 1978–.
HS 100* Essex v Notts, Trent Bridge, 1978 (second inns of fc debut).
BB 2–11 Essex v Surrey, Chelmsford, 1984.

LINDO, Cleveland Vincent
————RHB, RFM————

Born St Elizabeth, Jamaica, 6 June 1936. Debut 1960. *P.*
NOTTINGHAMSHIRE (1) 1960.
SOMERSET (1) 1963.
HS 24 Notts v Cambridge U, Fenner's, 1960.
BB 8–88 Som v Pakistan Eaglets, Taunton, 1963 (second and last fc match). Staffordshire 1965–66. Clubs: Sneyd, Norton, Blyth (Notts).

LINDSAY, Denis Thomson
————RHB, WK————

Born Benoni, S Africa, 4 Sept 1939. Educ Maritzburg C; Natal U. Debut 1958/59.
S AFRICA DOMESTIC North Eastern Transvaal 1958/59–70/71, Northern Transvaal 1971/72–73/74.
SOUTH AFRICA (19) 1963/64–69/70. E 1964/65 (3); A 1966/67 (5), 1969/70 (2). *E 1965 (3); A 1963/64 (3); NZ 1963/64 (3).*
OTHER TOURS S African Fezelas to England 1961. Rest of World XI in England 1967, 1968.
HST 182 SA v A, J'burg, 1966/67. HS 216 NE Transvaal v Transvaal B, J'burg, 1966/67.
1000 RUNS (0 + 1) 1014 @ 72.42 in S Africa 1966/67.
Hit W. T. Greensmith for five successive sixes (30 in one over), S African Fezelas v Essex, Chelmsford, 1961.
Father J. D. Lindsay (S Africa); grandfather N. V. Lindsay (S Africa).

LINDSAY, John Dixon
————RHB, WK————

Born Barkly East, S Africa, 8 Sept 1909. Debut 1933/34.
S AFRICA DOMESTIC Transvaal 1933/34–36/37, North Eastern Transvaal 1937/38–48/49.
SOUTH AFRICA (3) *E 1947.*
HST 9* SA v E, Old Trafford, 1947. HS 51 NE Transvaal v Rhodesia, Brakpan, 1946/47.
MCC Hon. member. Father N. V. Lindsay (S Africa); son D. T. Lindsay (S Africa).

LINDSEY, Peter John
————RHB, OB————

Born Matlock, Derbys, 29 May 1944.
Debut 1964.
ESSEX (1) 1964.
HS 7* Essex v Oxford U, The Parks,
1964.
Club: Buckhurst Hill, Wanstead.

LINDWALL, Raymond Russell
————RHB, RF————

Born Mascot, NSW, Australia, 3 Oct
1921. Educ Darlinghurst Marist
Brothers C. Debut 1941/42. *Wisden*
1949.
AUSTRALIA DOMESTIC New South Wales
(50) 1941/42–53/54, Queensland (34)
1954/55–59/60.
AUSTRALIA (61) 1945/46–59/60. E 1946/
47 (4), 1950/51 (5), 1954/55 (4), 1958/59
(2); SA 1952/53 (4); WI 1951/52 (5); I
1947/48 (5). *E 1948 (5), 1953 (5), 1956
(4); SA 1949/50 (4); WI 1954/55 (5);
NZ 1945/46 (1); I 1956/57 (3), 1959/60
(2); P 1956/57 (1), 1959/60 (2). Capt
1.*
OTHER TOURS E. W. Swanton's XI to W
Indies 1960/61. Commonwealth XI to
Rhodesia, India and Pakistan 1961/62.
Governor-General's XI v MCC, Auck-
land, 1960/61.
HST 118 A v WI, Bridgetown, 1954/55.
HS 134* NSW v Queensland, Sydney,
1945/46.
BBT 7–38 A v I, Adelaide, 1947/48. BB
7–20 Australians v Minor Counties,
Stoke on Trent, 1953.
First Australian fast bowler to take 100
Test wkts.
Clubs: St George, Northern Suburbs
(Australia), Nelson (England). MCC
Hon. member. Autobiography *Flying
Stumps* (1954).

LINEHAN, Alphonsus James
————RHB————

Born Dublin, Ireland, 20 Apr 1940.
Educ St Patrick's Christian Brothers' S,
Downpatrick. Debut 1972.
IRELAND (2) 1972–74.
HS 16 Ireland v Scotland, Greenock,
1972.
Club: Downpatrick.

LINES, Steven John
————RHB, RM————

Born Luton, Bedfordshire, 16 Mar
1963. Educ Vandyke Upper S, Leighton
Buzzard. Debut 1983.
NORTHAMPTONSHIRE (1) 1983.

HS 29 Northants v Oxford U, The Parks,
1983.
Bedfordshire 1980–. Club: Leighton
Buzzard.

LING, David John
————RHB, RM————

Born Enfield, M'sex, 2 July 1946. Debut
1966.
MIDDLESEX (14) 1966–68.
HS 40 M'sex v Oxford U, The Parks,
1966.
BB 3–24 same match.
Suffolk 1963–65.

LISTER, Derek John
————RHB————

Born Salisbury, Wiltshire, 25 Aug 1930.
Educ Cranleigh; Jesus C, Cambridge.
Debut 1954.
CAMBRIDGE UNIVERSITY (1) 1954.
HS 31 Cambridge U v M'sex, Fenner's,
1954.
Wiltshire 1951.

LISTER, John Wilton
————RHB————

Born Darlington, Co Durham, 1 Apr
1959. Debut 1978.
DERBYSHIRE (5) 1978–79.
HS 48 Derbys v Warwicks, Edgbaston,
1978.
Durham 1983–. Club: Darlington.

LISTER, Joseph
————RHB————

Born Thirsk, Yorks, 14 May 1930. Educ
Cheltenham. Debut 1951.
COMBINED SERVICES (1) 1951.
YORKSHIRE (2) 1954.
WORCESTERSHIRE (21) 1954–59.
HS 99 Worcs v Kent, Worcester, 1955.
Played for both Yorks and Worcs in fc
matches in 1954.
Worcs assistant-secretary 1954–55;
Worcs secretary 1956–71; Yorks secret-
ary 1972–. Hockey: Yorkshire. Uncle G.
G. Macaulay (Yorks, England).

LITTLEWOOD, David John
————RHB, WK————

Born Holloway, London, 28 Oct 1955.
Educ Enfield GS; St John's C, Cam-
bridge. Debut 1977.
CAMBRIDGE UNIVERSITY (10) 1977–78
(Blue 1978).
HS 51 Cambridge U v Derbys, Fenner's,
1978.
Soccer: Blue.

LIVINGSTON, Leonard (Jock)
————LHB, occ WK, occ SLA————

Born Sydney, NSW, Australia, 3 May
1920. Debut 1941/42. *P.*
AUSTRALIA DOMESTIC New South Wales
(5) 1941/42–46/47.
NORTHAMPTONSHIRE (198) 1950–57.
Cap 1950. Testimonial (£2842) 1955.
COMMONWEALTH XI (6) 1950–58.
MCC (1) 1964.
TOURS Commonwealth XI to India,
Pakistan and Ceylon 1949/50 (capt). C.
G. Howard's XI to India 1956/57
(Jubilee match).
HS 210 Northants v Som, Weston-
super-Mare, 1951.
BB 2–22 Commonwealth XI v England
XI, Hastings, 1958.
1000 RUNS (7 + 1) 2269 @ 55.34 in 1954.
2000 runs (3).
RECORD Added 320 for 3rd wkt with F.
Jakeman, Northants v S Africans,
Northampton, 1951, county record.
Clubs: North Sydney, Randwick
(Australia), Royton, Stourbridge (Eng-
land). Professional coach Rugby S 1959.
Currently cricket equipment company
executive.

LIVINGSTONE, Daintes Abbia
————LHB, occ WK————

Born St John's, Antigua, 21 Sept 1933.
Educ Antigua GS; Bathurst Heights
Collegiate S, Toronto. Debut 1959. *P.*
HAMPSHIRE (299) 1959–72. Cap 1961.
Benefit 1972.
HS 200 Hants v Surrey, Southampton,
1962.
1000 RUNS (6) 1817 @ 37.08 in 1962.
RECORDS During HS added 230
for 9th wkt with A. T. Castell and added
263 for 4th wkt with R. E. Marshall,
Hants v M'sex, Lord's, 1970, both
county records.
Club: West Bromwich Dartmouth.
Coaches in Antigua.

LIVINGSTONE, David
————RHB, OB————

Born Glasgow, Scotland, 23 Feb 1927.
Educ Shawlands Sec S. Debut 1957.
SCOTLAND (18) 1957–66.
HS 16* Scotland v Ireland, Dublin,
1957.
BB 6–33 (11–51 match), Scotland v
Ireland, Dublin, 1957.
Club: Poloc.

LIVOCK, Michael Denzil
————RHB, RFM————

Born Surbiton, Surrey, 26 July 1936.
Educ Charterhouse. Debut 1960.

FREE FORESTERS (2) 1960.
HS 12 Free Foresters v Oxford U, The Parks, 1960.
BB 4-71 Free Foresters v Cambridge U, Fenner's, 1960.
Clubs: Esher, Butterflies, Googlies, Hogs.

LLEWELLYN, Michael John
————LHB, ROB————

Born Clydach, S Wales, 27 Nov 1953. Debut 1970.
GLAMORGAN (136) 1970-82. Cap 1977.
HS 129* Glam v Oxford U, The Parks, 1977.
BB 4-35 Glam v Oxford U, The Parks, 1970.
Clubs: Clydach, Maesteg.

LLOYD, Barry John
————RHB, OB————

Born Neath, S Wales, 6 Sept 1953. Educ Llangatwg CS, Neath; Bangor Normal C. Debut 1972.
GLAMORGAN (147) 1972-83. Cap 1982.
HS 48 Glam v Sussex, Cardiff, 1982.
BB 8-70 Glam v Lancs, Cardiff, 1981.
Captained Glam for part of 1982.

LLOYD, Clive Hubert
————LHB, RM————

Born Georgetown, British Guiana, 31 Aug 1944. Educ Chatham HS, Georgetown. Debut 1963/64. *Wisden* 1971.
W INDIES DOMESTIC British Guiana (Guyana) 1963/64-82/83.
LANCASHIRE (208) 1968-. Cap 1969. Testimonial (£27,199) 1977. Capt 1981-83.
WEST INDIES (105) 1966/67-84. E 1967/68 (5), 1973/74 (5), 1980/81 (4); A 1972/73 (3), 1977/78 (2), 1983/84 (4); NZ 1971/72 (2); I 1970/71 (5), 1975/76 (4), 1982/83 (5); P 1976/77 (5). *E 1969 (3), 1973 (3), 1976 (5), 1980 (4), 1984 (5); A 1968/69 (4), 1975/76 (6), 1979/80 (2), 1981/82 (3); NZ 1968/69 (3), 1979/80 (3); I 1966/67 (3), 1974/75 (5), 1983/84 (6); P 1974/75 (2), 1980/81 (4).* Capt 69.
OTHER TOURS Rest of World XI to Pakistan 1970/71. World XI to Australia 1971/72. World XI to Pakistan 1973/74 (relief matches).
HST 242* WI v I, Bombay, 1974/75. HS as above.
BBT 2-13 WI v E, Bridgetown, 1973/74.
BB 4-48 Lancs v Leics, Old Trafford, 1970.
1000 RUNS (10 + 4) 1603 @ 47.14 in 1970.

RECORDS Capt country in Test cricket more times than any other player; and 23 times in succession undefeated (1981/82 to date), also a record. Added 335 for 5th wkt with B. F. Butcher, West Indians v Glam, Swansea, 1969 and 161 for 9th wkt with A. M. E. Roberts, WI v I, Calcutta, 1983/84, both W Indian fc records.
Scored 201* in 120 mins, W Indians v Glam, Swansea, 1976, equal fastest-ever double-century in fc cricket.
World Series Cricket (Kerry Packer) 1977/78-78/79. Club: Haslingden. Autobiography *Living for Cricket* (1980). Cousin L.R. Gibbs (Warwicks, W Indies).

LLOYD, David
————LHB, SLA————

Born Accrington, Lancs, 18 Mar 1947. Educ Accrington Technical S. Debut 1965.
LANCASHIRE (378) 1965-83. Cap 1968. Testimonial (£40,171) 1978. Capt 1973-77.
ENGLAND (9) 1974-74/75. I 1974 (2); P 1974 (3). *A 1974/75 (4).*
OTHER TOUR D. H. Robins' XI to S Africa 1975/76.
HST 214* E v I, Edgbaston, 1974. HS as above.
BB 7-38 Lancs v Glos, Lydney, 1966.
1000 RUNS (11) 1510 @ 47.18 in 1972.
Cumberland 1984. Club: Accrington.

LLOYD, Martyn Frederick Dafydd
————RHB, RM————

Born Oxford, 6 June 1954. Educ Magdalen College S; Magdalen C, Oxford. Debut 1974.
OXFORD UNIVERSITY (6) 1974-75 (Blue 1974).
HS 36 Oxford U v Yorks, The Parks, 1974.
Oxfordshire 1974-77. Dorset 1981-. Clubs: North Oxford, Brook.

LLOYD, Timothy *Andrew*
————LHB, RM/OB————

Born Oswestry, Shropshire, 5 Nov 1956. Educ Oswestry HS; Dorset C of H Educ. Debut 1977.
WARWICKSHIRE (134) 1977-. Cap 1980.
S AFRICA DOMESTIC Orange Free State 1978/79-79/80.
ENGLAND (1) WI 1984.
HST 10* (retired hurt) E v WI, Edgbaston, 1984. HS 208* Warwicks v Glos, Edgbaston, 1983.

BB 2-29 Warwicks v Indians, Edgbaston, 1982.
1000 RUNS (4) 1673 @ 45.22 in 1983.
Shropshire 1975. Clubs: Oswestry, Whittington (England); Ramblers (Bloemfontein).

LLOYDS, Jeremy William
————LHB, ROB————

Born Penang, Malaya, 17 Nov 1954. Educ Blundell's S. Debut 1979.
SOMERSET (100) 1979-. Cap 1982.
HS 132* Som v Northants, Northampton, 1982.
BB 7-88 Som v Essex, Chelmsford, 1982.
Joined Glos for 1985.

LOADER, Peter James
————RHB, RF————

Born Wallington, Surrey, 25 Oct 1929. Educ Wallington GS. Debut 1951. *P. Wisden* 1958.
SURREY (298) 1951-63. Cap 1953. Benefit 1963.
AUSTRALIA DOMESTIC W Australia (1) 1963/64.
ENGLAND (13) 1954-58/59. SA 1955 (1); WI 1957 (2); NZ 1958 (3); P 1954 (1). *A 1958/59 (2); SA 1956/57 (4).*
OTHER TOURS Commonwealth XI to India 1953/54. MCC to Australia 1954/55. Surrey to Rhodesia 1959/60. Commonwealth XI to Rhodesia 1962/63.
HST 17 E v NZ, Edgbaston, 1958. HS 81 Surrey v Yorks, Headingley, 1955.
BBT 6-36 E v WI, Headingley, 1957. BB 9-17 Surrey v Warwicks, Oval, 1958. Also returned 9-28 Surrey v Kent, Blackheath, 1953.
100 WKTS (7) 133 @ 15.47 in 1957.
Performed hat-trick, E v WI, Headingley, 1957, the last time it was done for England in a Test match.
Players v Gentlemen (1) 1954. Club: Beddington.

LOBB, Brian
————RHB, RFM————

Born Birmingham, 11 Jan 1931. Educ King Edward's S, Birmingham; St Luke's C, Exeter. Debut 1953. *P.*
WARWICKSHIRE (1) 1953.
SOMERSET (115) 1955-69. Cap 1955.
HS 42 Som v Yorks, Bath, 1958.
BB 7-43 Som v M'sex, Lord's, 1958.
100 WKTS (1) 110 @ 19.48 in 1957.
Member Som committee. Clubs: Harborne, Smethwick, Morlands.

LOBBAN, Hartley W.
—RHB, RFM—

Born Jamaica, 9 May 1922. Educ Sunderland Polytechnic (mature student). Debut 1952. *P.*
WORCESTERSHIRE (17) 1952–54.
HS 18 Worcs v Sussex, Worthing, 1953.
BB 6–51 Worcs v Glam, Cardiff, 1952.
Clubs: Kidderminster, Ashington, Sunderland, Seaham Harbour. Boxing: Professional 1948 (as Ken Lobban). Rugby: Kidderminster. Lives and teaches in United States.

LOCK, Bernard Henry
—RHB—

Born Exeter, Devon, 8 June 1915. Educ Sherborne. Debut 1952.
KENT (1) 1952.
MCC (1) 1955.
HS 57 Kent v Oxford U, The Parks, 1952.
Devon 1938–48, 1957. Club: Dover. Rugby: Exeter, Ulster.

LOCK, Graham *Anthony* Richard
—RHB, SLA—

Born Limpsfield, Surrey, 5 July 1929. Educ Limpsfield S, Surrey. Debut 1946. *P. Wisden* 1954.
SURREY (385) 1946–63. Cap 1950. Benefit (£4700) 1960.
LEICESTERSHIRE (65) 1965–67. Cap 1965. Capt 1966–67.
AUSTRALIA DOMESTIC W Australia (74) 1962/63–70/71. Capt 1963/64–70/71.
ENGLAND (49) 1952–67/68. A 1953 (2), 1956 (4), 1961 (3); SA 1955 (3); WI 1957 (3), 1963 (3); NZ 1958 (5); I 1952 (2); P 1962 (3). *A 1958/59 (4); SA 1956/57 (1); WI 1953/54 (5), 1967/68 (2); NZ 1958/59 (2); I 1961/62 (5); P 1961/62 (2).*
OTHER TOURS MCC A to Pakistan 1955/56. Surrey to Rhodesia 1959/60.
HST 89 E v WI, Georgetown, 1967/68.
HS as above.
BBT 7–35 E v NZ, Old Trafford, 1958.
BB 10–54 (16–83 match) Surrey v Kent, Blackheath, 1956. Also returned 9–57 Surrey v Oxford U, Guildford, 1960. Returned 11–65 match E v NZ, Headingley, 1958; 9–29 match E v NZ, Lord's, 1958; 11–48 match E v WI, Oval, 1957. Returned 15–182 match Surrey v Kent, Blackheath, 1958.
100 WKTS (14) 216 @ 14.39 in 1955. 200 wkts (2).
Last bowler to take 200 wkts in season: 212 @ 12.02 in 1957. Took 8 catches in match Surrey v Warwicks, Oval, 1957.

Players v Gentlemen (5) 1954–62. Club: Ramsbottom. MCC Hon. member. Autobiographies *For Surrey and England* (1957) and *Put Lock On* (1972).

LODGE, Joe Thomas
—RHB, RMF—

Born Huddersfield, Yorks, 16 Apr 1921. Debut 1948. *P.*
YORKSHIRE (2) 1948.
HS 30 Yorks v Kent, Bradford, 1948.
Clubs: Slaithwaite, Baildon, Salts, Perthshire. Former professional coach Strathallan S (from 1961). Soccer: Huddersfield Town.

LOMAX, Ian Raymond
—RHB, RFM—

Born Fulham, London, 30 July 1931. Educ Eton. Debut 1952.
FREE FORESTERS (3) 1952–60.
MINOR COUNTIES (1) 1960.
SOMERSET (6) 1962.
MCC (2) 1963–65.
HS 83 Som v Hants, Taunton, 1962 (reached 50 in 22 mins).
BB 2–45 Free Foresters v Cambridge U, Fenner's, 1958.
Buckinghamshire 1949. Wiltshire 1950–70 (capt 1968–70). Racehorse trainer in Wiltshire.

LOMAX, James *Geoffrey*
—RHB, RFM—

Born Rochdale, Lancs, 20 May 1925. Debut 1949. *P.*
LANCASHIRE (58) 1949–53. Cap 1952.
SOMERSET (211) 1954–62. Cap 1954.
HS 104* Som v Sussex, Eastbourne, 1962.
BB 6–75 Som v Surrey, Oval, 1954.
1000 RUNS (2) 1298 @ 24.96 in 1959. Devon 1966. Club: Milnrow.

LONEY, Joseph Kevin
—LHB, RM—

Born Lurgan, Co Armagh, Ireland, 30 Aug 1951. Educ Campbell C, Belfast; Emmanuel C, Cambridge. Debut 1974.
CAMBRIDGE UNIVERSITY (2) 1974.
HS 2 (in each inns) Cambridge U v Kent, Fenner's, 1974.

LONG, Arnold
—LHB, WK—

Born Cheam, Surrey, 18 Dec 1940. Educ Wallington GS. Debut 1960. *P.*

SURREY (352) 1960–75. Cap 1962. Benefit (£10,353) 1971.
SUSSEX (97) 1976–80. Cap 1976. Capt 1978–80.
TOUR D. H. Robins' XI to S Africa 1972/73.
HS 92 Surrey v Leics, Leicester, 1970.
RECORD Took 7 catches inns and 11 catches match, Surrey v Sussex, Hove, 1964, joint world record for catches in a match, with R. W. Marsh (W Australia) and D. L. Bairstow (Yorks). Made 1046 dismissals (922 ct, 124 st) in career.

LONGFIELD, Thomas Cuthbert
—RHB, RM—

Born High Halstow, Kent, 12 May 1906. Died Ealing, London, 21 Dec 1981. Educ Aldenham; Pembroke C, Cambridge. Debut 1927.
CAMBRIDGE UNIVERSITY (25) 1927–28 (Blue 1927–28).
KENT (30) 1927–39.
FREE FORESTERS (1) 1951.
INDIA DOMESTIC Europeans (Bombay) 1929/30–44/45, Viceroy's XI 1931/32–33/34, Indian XI 1933/34, Bengal 1935/36–38/39.
HS 120 Cambridge U v Leics, Fenner's, 1928.
BB 6–57 Bengal v Central India, Calcutta, 1936/37.
Gentlemen v Players (2) 1927–36. Brother G. P. Longfield (RAF); son-in-law E. R. Dexter (Sussex, England).

LONGMORE, Andrew Nigel Murray
—RHB, WK—

Born Woolwich, Kent, 24 Sept 1953. Educ Winchester; Worcester C, Oxford. Debut 1973.
OXFORD UNIVERSITY (2) 1973–75.
HS 15 Oxford U v Worcs, Worcester, 1975.
Assistant Editor of *The Cricketer International*.

LONGRIGG, Edmund Fallowfield
—LHB—

Born Bath, Som, 16 Apr 1906. Died Bath, Som, 23 July 1974. Educ Rugby S; Pembroke C, Cambridge. Debut 1925.
SOMERSET (219) 1925–47. Cap 1926. Capt 1938–46.
CAMBRIDGE UNIVERSITY (25) 1926–28 (Blue 1927–28).
HS 205 Som v Leics, Taunton, 1930.
1000 RUNS (2) 1567 @ 30.72 in 1930. Somerset president 1968/69. MCC committee 1964–69. Hockey: Somerset.

LORD, Gordon John
————————LHB, SLA————————

Born Edgbaston, Birmingham, 25 Apr 1961. Educ Warwick S; Durham U. Debut 1983.
WARWICKSHIRE (7) 1983–.
HS 61 Warwicks v Notts, Trent Bridge, 1983.

LOUDON, William *David* Grafton
————————RHB, RFM————————

Born Lanark, Scotland, 22 May 1954. Educ Edinburgh Academy. Debut 1982.
SCOTLAND (1) 1982.
HS 21 Scotland v Ireland, Edinburgh, 1982.
BB 3–4 same match.
Club: Edinburgh Academicals. Rugby: Edinburgh Academicals.

LOVE, James Derek
————————RHB————————

Born Leeds, Yorks, 22 Apr 1955. Educ Brudenell County Sec S, Leeds. Debut 1975.
YORKSHIRE (156) 1975–. Cap 1980.
HS 170* Yorks v Worcs, Worcester, 1979.
1000 RUNS (2) 1203 @ 33.41 in 1981.
Club: Leeds.

· LOWE, George
————————RHB————————

Born Mastin Moor, Derbys, 25 May 1915. Debut 1949.
DERBYSHIRE (2) 1949–53.
HS 22 Derbys v Kent, Chesterfield, 1949.

LOWE, Peter John
————————RHB, WK————————

Born Sutton Coldfield, Warwicks, 7 Jan 1935. Debut 1964.
WARWICKSHIRE (1) 1964.
Did not bat.

LOWSON, Frank Anderson
————————RHB————————

Born Bradford, Yorks, 1 July 1925. Died Pool, Wharfedale, Yorks, 8 Sept 1984. Educ Bradford GS. Debut 1949. *P.*
YORKSHIRE (252) 1949–58. Cap 1949.
Testimonial (£2500) 1959.

ENGLAND (7) 1951–55. SA 1951 (2), 1955 (1). *I 1951/52 (4).*
HST 68 E v I, Delhi, 1951/52. HS 259* Yorks v Worcs, Worcester, 1953.
1000 RUNS (8 + 1) 2152 @ 42.19 in 1950. Scored 1799 runs @ 35.98 in debut season, 1949, the second-highest total for a first season.
Players v Gentlemen (2) 1953–54. Clubs: Bowling Old Lane, Brighouse, Bradford, Bingley.

LOXTON, Samuel John Everett
————————RHB, RFM————————

Born Albert Park, Melbourne, Australia, 29 Mar 1921. Debut 1946/47.
AUSTRALIA DOMESTIC Victoria (77) 1946/47–57/58.
AUSTRALIA (12) 1947/48–50/51. E 1950/51 (3); I 1947/48 (1). *E 1948 (3); SA 1949/50 (5).*
OTHER TOURS Commonwealth XI to India 1953/54. Australia to India and Pakistan 1959/60 (manager; played one match).
HST 101 A v SA, J'burg, 1949/50. HS 232* Victoria v Queensland, Melbourne, 1946/47 (fc debut; second-highest fc debut inns).
BBT 3–55 A v E, Headingley, 1948. BB 6–49 Victoria v W Australia, Perth, 1956/57.
Appointed Test selector 1970/71. Member of Australian Parliament.

LUCAS, Frederick Charles
————————RHB, OB————————

Born Slade Green, Kent, 29 Sept 1933. Educ Erith GS. Debut 1954. *P.*
KENT (2) 1954.
HS 38 Kent v Essex, Ilford, 1954.
Soccer: Charlton Athletic, Crystal Palace.

LUCAS, John H.
————————RHB, RM/OB————————

Born Barbados, c 1923. Debut 1945/56.
W INDIES DOMESTIC Barbados 1945/46–49/50.
CANADA (3) 1951–54.
TOUR Canada to England 1954.
HS 216* Barbados v Trinidad, Bridgetown, 1948/49.
BB 4–88 Barbados v MCC, Bridgetown, 1947/48.
Club: Mount Royal, Montreal. Lives in Toronto. Brother N. S. Lucas (Barbados).

LUCKES, Walter Thomas
————————RHB, WK————————

Born London, 1 Jan 1901. Died Bridgwater, Som, 27 Oct 1982. Debut 1924. *P.*
SOMERSET (365) 1924–49. Cap 1927. Benefit 1937. Testimonial 1950.
HS 121* Som v Kent, Bath, 1937.
Kept wkt throughout totals of 574 for 7, Som v Glam, Newport, 1939, and 512, Som v Surrey, Oval, 1936, without conceding a bye. Made 827 dismissals (586 ct, 241 st) in career.

LUCKHURST, Brian William
————————RHB, SLA————————

Born Sittingbourne, Kent, 5 Feb 1939. Educ Westland Sec S. Debut 1958. *P. Wisden 1971.*
KENT (335) 1958–76. Cap 1963. Benefit (£18,231) 1973.
ENGLAND (21) 1970/71–74/75. A 1972 (4); WI 1973 (2); I 1971 (3); P 1971 (3). *A 1970/71 (5), 1974/75 (2); NZ 1970/71 (2).*
OTHER TOURS Commonwealth XI to Pakistan 1967/68. Cavaliers to W Indies 1969/70.
HST 131 E v A, Perth, 1970/71. HS 215 Kent v Derbys, Derby, 1973.
BB 4–32 Kent v Som, Gravesend, 1962.
1000 RUNS (14) 1914 @ 47.85 in 1969.
Took 391 catches in career. Kent manager 1981–.

LUCKIN, Roger Alfred Geoffrey
————————LHB————————

Born Pleshey, Essex, 25 Nov 1939. Educ Felsted S. Debut 1962.
ESSEX (29) 1962–63.
HS 82 Essex v M'sex, Brentwood, 1962.
RECORDS During HS (above) added 206 for 6th wkt with B. R. Knight, equalling county record.
Cambridgeshire 1969–70. Clubs: Hendon, Chelmsford.

LUDDINGTON, Richard Simon
————————RHB, WK————————

Born Kingston-upon-Thames, Surrey, 8 Apr 1960. Educ KCS Wimbledon; St Edmund Hall, Oxford. Debut 1982.
OXFORD UNIVERSITY (10) 1982 (Blue).
HS 65 Oxford U v Glam, Swansea, 1982.
Rugby: Blue. Hockey: Blue.

LUMB, Richard Graham
————————RHB————————

Born Doncaster, Yorks, 27 Feb 1950. Educ Mexborough GS. Debut 1970.

YORKSHIRE (239) 1970–. Cap 1974. Benefit 1983.
HS 165* Yorks v Glos, Bradford, 1984.
1000 RUNS (5) 1532 @ 41.40 in 1975.
Clubs: Leeds, Brodsworth.

LUMSDEN, Ian James Michael
————————RHB————————

Born Edinburgh, Scotland, 6 Apr 1923.
Educ George Watson's C, Edinburgh.
Debut 1946.
SCOTLAND (3) 1946–48.
COMBINED SERVICES (4) 1948–49.
HS 66 Scotland v Warwicks, Edgbaston, 1948.
Clubs: Watsonians, Bath. Rugby: Bath, Watsonians, Scotland (7).

LUMSDEN, Vincent Roy
————————RHB, OB, occ WK————————

Born Buff Bay, Jamaica, 19 July 1930.
Educ Munro C, Jamaica; Emmanuel C, Cambridge. Debut 1949/50.
W INDIES DOMESTIC Jamaica 1949/
50–59/60.
CAMBRIDGE UNIVERSITY (49) 1953–56 (Blue 1953–55).
HS 107 Cambridge U v Worcs, Worcester, 1954.
BB 4–20 Jamaica v Leeward Islands, Kingston, 1958/59.
Cambridgeshire 1955.

LYNCH, Monte Allan
————————RHB, RM————————

Born Georgetown, British Guiana, 21 May 1958. Educ Rydens S, Walton on Thames. Debut 1977.
SURREY (124) 1977–. Cap 1982.
W INDIES DOMESTIC Guyana 1982/83.
TOUR International XI to Pakistan 1981/82.

HS 144 Surrey v Leics, Oval, 1984.
BB 3–6 Surrey v Glam, Swansea, 1981.
1000 RUNS (3) 1558 @ 53.72 in 1983.
Barred from England Test cricket for 3½ yrs for touring S Africa 1983/84 (W Indies XI).

LYNCH, Ronald Victor
————————RHB, SLA————————

Born Stratford, E London, 22 May 1923. Educ St Paul's S. Debut 1954.
ESSEX (3) 1954.
HS 6* Essex v Lancs, Liverpool, 1954.
BB 4–64 Essex v Northants, Rushden, 1954.
Clubs: Ilford, Chingford.

LYNESS, George Edward *Given*
————————RHB, OB————————

Born Dunmurry, Co Antrim, N Ireland, 16 Dec 1937. Educ Wallace HS, Lisburn. Debut 1961.
IRELAND (1) 1961.
HS 9 Ireland v MCC, Dublin, 1961.
BB 6–39 (8–90 match) same match (only fc appearance).
Clubs: NICC, Lisburn.

LYON, Beverley Hamilton
————————RHB————————

Born Caterham, Surrey, 19 Jan 1902. Died Balcombe, Sussex, 22 June 1970. Educ Rugby; Queen's C, Oxford. Debut 1921.
GLOUCESTERSHIRE (238) 1921–47. Cap. Capt 1929–34.
OXFORD UNIVERSITY (16) 1922–23 (Blue 1922–23).
INDIA DOMESTIC Europeans 1924/25–45/46.
HS 189 Glos v Surrey, Cheltenham, 1934.
BB 5–72 Glos v Yorks, Bristol, 1937.
1000 RUNS (4) 1576 @ 38.43 in 1930.

RECORD Added 336 for 3rd wkt with W. R. Hammond, Glos v Leics, Leicester, 1933, county record.
Gentlemen v Players (2) 1929–30. Sir J. Cahn's XI to Ceylon 1936/37 (not fc). Wiltshire 1920. Brother M. D. Lyon (Som, Cambridge U).

LYON, John
————————RHB, WK————————

Born St Helens, Lancs, 17 May 1951. Educ Central Sec, St Helens. Debut 1973.
LANCASHIRE (84) 1973–79. Cap 1975.
TOUR D. H. Robins' XI to S Africa 1974/75.
HS 123 Lancs v Warwicks, Old Trafford, 1979 (adding 158 for 8th wkt with R. M. Ratcliffe, county record).

LYONS, Kevin James
————————RHB, RM————————

Born Cardiff, 18 Dec 1946. Educ Lady Mary's HS, Cardiff. Debut 1967.
GLAMORGAN (62) 1967–77.
TOUR Glam to W Indies 1969/70.
HS 92 Glam v Cambridge U, Fenner's, 1972.
Glam coach 1972–84. Western Province coach 1983/84–. Appointed fc umpire for 1985.

LYONS, Reginald William
————————RHB, WK————————

Born Dublin, Ireland, 12 July 1922. Died Worthing, Sussex, 12 Sept 1976. Educ Diocesan C, Dublin. Debut 1947.
IRELAND (1) 1947.
No runs but four stumpings in only match, Ireland v Scotland, Cork, 1947.
Club: YMCA Pembroke.

M

MAAZULLAH KHAN
RHB, OB

Born Peshawar, Pakistan, 1 Sept 1947.
Debut 1965/66.
PAKISTAN DOMESTIC Peshawar, Railways, 1965/66–79/80.
TOUR Pakistan to England 1974.
HS 130 Peshawar v Lahore B, Aitchison C, Lahore, 1973/74.
BB 8–97 Peshawar v Sri Lankans, Peshawar, 1973/74.

McADAM, Keith Paul William James
LHB

Born Edinburgh, Scotland, 13 Aug 1945. Educ Prince of Wales, Nairobi, Kenya; Millfield; Clare C, Cambridge. Debut 1965.
CAMBRIDGE UNIVERSITY (20) 1965–66 (Blue 1965–66).
MCC (1) 1967.
HS 63 MCC v Cambridge U, Lord's, 1967.
Buckinghamshire 1966–67. Medical practitioner living in Massachusetts.

McADAM, William James
RHB

Born Springs, S Africa, 3 Oct 1944. Educ Grey HS, Port Elizabeth; U of Cape Town. Debut 1966/67.
S AFRICA DOMESTIC Western Province 1966/67–68/69, South African Universities 1966/67, Eastern Province 1971/72.
TOUR S African Universities to England 1967 (capt).
HS 129 W Province v NE Transvaal, Cape Town, 1968/69.
Brother S. J. McAdam (E Province).

McALLISTER, Alexander Eric
RHB

Born Paisley, Scotland, 19 Dec 1920. Educ Paisley GS. Debut 1950.
SCOTLAND (1) 1950.

HS 9 Scotland v Ireland, Perth, 1950.
Club: Clydesdale.

MACAULAY, Michael John
RHB, LM/SLA

Born Durban, S Africa, 19 Apr 1939. Educ Hilton C. Debut 1957/58.
S AFRICA DOMESTIC Transvaal 1957/58–59/60, 1961/62–62/63, 1965/66, Western Province 1960/61, Orange Free State 1963/64, North-Eastern Transvaal 1966/67–68/69, Eastern Province 1977/78–78/79.
SOUTH AFRICA (1) E 1965.
HST 21 SA v E, Port Elizabeth, 1964/65.
HS 59 NE Transvaal v Natal B, Pretoria, 1966/67.
BBT 1–10 SA v E, Port Elizabeth, 1964/65. BB 7–49 (11–97 match) OFS v Rhodesia, Bloemfontein, 1963/64.
RECORDS Only player to appear for five Provinces in the Currie Cup.

McCALL, Barney Ernest Wilford
LHB

Born Bristol, 13 May 1913. Died Cambridge, 27 Nov 1982. Debut 1936.
ARMY (1) 1936.
MINOR COUNTIES (1) 1937.
COMBINED SERVICES (1) 1948.
HS 31 Army v Cambridge U, Fenner's, 1936.
Dorset 1936. Club: Grange (Edinburgh). Rugby: Welch Regiment, Newport, Wales (3).

McCALL, Hugh *Con*
RHB, SLA

Born Holywood, Co Down, Ireland, 29 Mar 1940. Educ Campbell C, Belfast. Debut 1964.
IRELAND (7) 1964–68.
HS 81 Ireland v MCC, Dublin, 1964.
Clubs: Holywood, Bangor.

McCARTHY, Cuan Neil
RHB, RF

Born Pietermaritzburg, S Africa, 24 Mar 1929. Educ Pietermaritzburg C; Pembroke C, Cambridge. Debut 1947/48.
S AFRICA DOMESTIC Natal 1947/48–50/51.
CAMBRIDGE UNIVERSITY (12) 1952 (Blue).
SOUTH AFRICA (15) 1948/49–51. E 1948/49 (5); A 1949/50 (5). *E 1951 (5)*.
HST 5 SA v E, Trent Bridge, 1951. HS 23* Cambridge U v M'sex, Fenner's, 1952.
BBT 6–43 SA v E, Durban, 1948/49. BB 8–36 S Africans v Sussex, Hove, 1951. No-balled for throwing, Cambridge U v Worcs, Worcester, 1952.
Gentlemen v Players (2) 1952. Dorset 1958–59. Boxing: Blue.

McCAY, David Laurence Cornelius
RHB, RM

Born De Aar, S Africa, 18 Nov 1943. Educ St Andrew's, Bloemfontein; Stellenbosch U, S Africa. Debut 1966/67.
S AFRICA DOMESTIC Western Province 1966/67–73/74.
TOUR S African Universities to England 1967.
HS 82 W Province v Australians, Cape Town, 1966/67.
BB 8–76 (14–154 match) W Province v Natal, Cape Town, 1967/68.

McCLOY, Thomas
RHB, RM

Born Lambeg, Co Antrim, Ireland, 31 Aug 1927. Educ Lisburn Technical C. Debut 1952.
IRELAND (12) 1952–65.
HS 53 Ireland v Combined Services, Belfast, 1962.
Club: Lisburn.

McCONNON, James Edward
————RHB, OB————

Born Burnopfield, Co Durham, 21 June
1922. Debut 1950. *P*.
GLAMORGAN (243) 1950–61. Cap 1951.
Benefit 1961.
ENGLAND (2) P 1954.
OTHER TOURS Commonwealth XI to
India 1953/54. MCC to Australia 1954/
55. (Returned home early through in-
jury each time.)
HST 11 E v P, Oval, 1954. HS 95 Glam v
M'sex, Cardiff, 1958.
BBT 3–19 E v P, Old Trafford, 1954. BB
8–36 Glam v Notts, Trent Bridge, 1953.
100 WKTS (3) 136 @ 16.07 in 1951.
Cheshire 1962–64. Clubs: Newport,
Burnley. Former professional coach
Stonyhurst S (from 1966).

McCOOL, Colin Leslie
————RHB, LBG————

Born Paddington, Sydney, NSW,
Australia, 9 Dec 1915. Debut 1939/40.
P.
AUSTRALIA DOMESTIC New South Wales
(7) 1939/40–40/41, Queensland (47)
1945/46–52/53.
SOMERSET (138) 1956–60. Cap 1956.
Testimonial (£3000) 1959.
AUSTRALIA (14) 1945/46–49/50. E 1946/
47 (5); I 1947/48 (3). *SA 1949/50 (5);
NZ 1945/46 (1)*.
OTHER TOURS Australia to England 1948.
N. D. Howard's XI to India 1956/57.
HST 104* A v E, Melbourne, 1946/47. HS
172 Queensland v S Australia, Adelaide,
1945/46.
BBT 5–41 A v E, Sydney, 1946/47. BB
8–74 Som v Notts, Trent Bridge, 1958.
1000 RUNS (5) 1966 @ 37.80 in 1956.
Clubs: Paddington, Toombul
(Australia), East Lancs, Stockport
(England). Autobiography *Cricket is a
Game* (1961). Son R. J. McCool (Som).

McCOOL, Russel John
————RHB, LB————

Born Taunton, Som, 4 Dec 1959. Educ
Woy Woy HS, NSW, Australia. Debut
1982.
SOMERSET (1) 1982.
HS 12 Som v Derbys, Derby, 1982.
Father C. L. McCool (Australia, Som).

McCORKELL, Neil Thomas
————RHB, WK————

Born Portsmouth, Hants, 23 Mar 1912.
Debut 1932. *P*.
HAMPSHIRE (383) 1932–51. Cap 1932.
Joint benefit (with four others) 1948–50.

TOUR Lord Tennyson's XI to India
1937/38.
HS 203 Hants v Glos, Gloucester, 1951.
1000 RUNS (9) 1871 @ 38.18 in 1949.
Kept wkt throughout inns of 535 for 8
dec without conceding a bye, Hants v
Leics, Leicester, 1938. Made 716 dis-
missals (532 ct, 184 st) in career.
Players v Gentlemen (2) 1932–36.
Professional coach Parktown HS,
Johannesburg from 1952.

McCORQUODALE, Alastair
————LHB, RFM————

Born Glasgow, Scotland, 5 Dec 1925.
Educ Harrow. Debut 1948.
MCC (1) 1948.
FREE FORESTERS (1) 1950.
MIDDLESEX (3) 1951.
TOUR MCC to Canada 1951 (no first-
class match).
HS 21 M'sex v Oxford U, The Parks,
1951.
BB 2–62 M'sex v Northants, Lord's,
1951.
International sprinter; finalist in Olym-
pic 100 metres, 1948. Chairman of
McCorquodale PLC, publishers of *Wis-
den Cricketers' Almanack*.

McCOSKER, Richard Bede
————RHB————

Born Inverell, NSW, Australia, 11 Dec
1946. Debut 1973/74.
AUSTRALIA DOMESTIC New South Wales
(86) 1973/74–. Capt 1979/80–.
AUSTRALIA (25) 1974/75–79/80. E 1974/
75 (3), 1976/77 (1), 1979/80 (2); WI
1975/76 (4), 1979/80 (1); P 1976/77 (3).
E 1975 (4), 1977 (5); NZ 1976/77 (2).
HST 127 A v E, Oval, 1975. HS 168 NSW
v W Australia, Sydney, 1980/81.
BB 2–28 NSW v W Australia, Perth,
1982/83.
1000 RUNS (1 + 2) 1254 @ 54.52 in 1974/
75.
World Series Cricket (Kerry Packer)
1977/78–78/79. Club: Sydney.

McCURDY, Rodney John
————RHB, RFM————

Born Melbourne, Australia, 30 Dec
1959. Debut 1979.
DERBYSHIRE (1) 1979.
AUSTRALIA DOMESTIC Tasmania (7) 1980/
81, Victoria (24) 1981/82–.
TOUR Young Australia to Zimbabwe
1982/83.
HS 55 Victoria v S Australia, Melbourne,
1983/84.
BB 7–91 Tasmania v N Zealanders,
Launceston, 1980/81.

Shropshire 1979. Clubs: Pudsey St
Laurence (England), Clarence (Tasmania), Ringwood (Melbourne).

McDERMOT, Enda Anthony
————LHB————

Born Dublin, Ireland, 1 Dec 1945.
Debut 1982.
IRELAND (1) 1982.
HS 18 Ireland v Scotland, Edinburgh,
1982.
Clubs: Clontarf, North Leinster.

McDONALD, Colin Campbell
————RHB————

Born Glen Iris, Victoria, Australia, 17
Nov 1928. Educ Scotch C, Melbourne;
Melbourne U. Debut 1947/48.
AUSTRALIA DOMESTIC Victoria (60) 1947/
48–62/63.
AUSTRALIA (47) 1951/52–61. E 1954/55
(2), 1958/59 (5); SA 1952/53 (5); WI
1951/52 (1), 1960/61 (5). *E 1956 (5),
1961 (3); SA 1957/58 (5); WI 1954/55
(5); I 1956/57 (2), 1959/60 (5); P
1956/57 (1), 1959/60 (3)*.
OTHER TOURS Australia to England 1953.
International XI to Rhodesia and Pakis-
tan 1961/62.
HST 170 A v E, Adelaide, 1958/59. HS 229
Victoria v S Australia, Adelaide, 1953/
54.
1000 RUNS (1) 1202 @ 34.34 in 1956.
RECORD Added 295 for 2nd wkt with R.
N. Harvey, A v WI, Kingston, 1954/55,
Australia Test record.
Brother I. H. McDonald (Victoria).

McDONNELL, Guy Francis
Henry
————LHB, ROB————

Born Lytham, Lancs, 24 Jan 1963. Educ
King Edward VII S, Lytham; St John's
C, Cambridge. Debut 1984.
CAMBRIDGE UNIVERSITY (2) 1984.
HS 5 Cambridge U v Essex, Fenner's,
1984.

McDOWALL, James Ian
————RHB, WK————

Born Sutton Coldfield, Warwicks, 9 May
1947. Educ Rugby S; Fitzwilliam C,
Cambridge. Debut 1969.
CAMBRIDGE UNIVERSITY (17) 1969–70
(Blue 1969).
WARWICKSHIRE (12) 1969–73.
HS 89 Warwicks v Oxford U, The Parks,
1973.

Warwicks committee since 1973. Clubs: Rugby Meteors, Knowle and Dorridge. Father J. McDowall (Warwicks Hon. treasurer 1962–79).

McENTYRE, Kenneth Brinsley
─────────RHB─────────

Born Chester, 24 Mar 1944. Debut 1965.
SURREY (3) 1965–66.
HS 15 Surrey v Cambridge U, Oval, 1966.
Cheshire 1962, 1968. Clubs: Middleton, Heywood.

McEVOY, Michael Stephen Anthony
─────────RHB, occ RM─────────

Born Jorhat, Assam, India, 25 Jan 1956. Educ Colchester RGS; Borough Road C of Educ. Debut 1976.
ESSEX (43) 1976–81.
WORCESTERSHIRE (26) 1983–.
HS 103 Worcs v Warwicks, Edgbaston, 1983.
BB 3–20 Essex v M'sex, Lord's, 1981.
Cambridgeshire 1982.

McEWAN, Kenneth Scott
─────────RHB, occ WK, OB─────────

Born Bedford, Cape Province, S Africa, 16 July 1952. Educ Queen's C, Queenstown. Debut 1972/73. *Wisden* 1978.
S AFRICA DOMESTIC Eastern Province 1972/73–77/78, Western Province 1981/82–.
ESSEX (256) 1974–. Cap 1974.
AUSTRALIA DOMESTIC Western Australia (18) 1979/80–80/81.
HS 218 Essex v Sussex, Chelmsford, 1977.
1000 RUNS (11) 2176 @ 64.00 in 1983.
RECORD Added 321 for 2nd wkt with G. A. Gooch, Essex v Northants, Ilford, 1978, county record.
Scored centuries against all fc counties except his own. Scored centuries in four successive fc inns, 1977.

McFARLANE, Leslie Leopold
─────────RHB, RFM─────────

Born Portland, Jamaica, 19 Aug 1952. Debut 1979.
NORTHAMPTONSHIRE (8) 1979.
LANCASHIRE (35) 1982–.
HS 15* Lancs v Northants, Southport, 1984.
BB 6–59 Lancs v Warwicks, Southport, 1982.
Bedfordshire 1981. Club: United Social Northampton.

McGIBBON, Anthony Roy
─────────RHB, RFM─────────

Born Christchurch, N Zealand, 28 Aug 1924. Educ Christ's C, Christchurch; Durham U. Debut 1947/48.
N ZEALAND DOMESTIC Canterbury (48) 1947/48–61/62.
NEW ZEALAND (26) 1950/51–58. E 1950/51 (2), 1954/55 (2); SA 1952/53 (1); WI 1955/56 (3). *E 1958 (5); SA 1953/54 (5); I 1955/56 (5); P 1955/56 (3).*
HST 66 NZ v E, Old Trafford, 1958. HS 94 Canterbury v Wellington, Christchurch, 1949/50.
BBT 5–64 NZ v E, Edgbaston, 1958. BB 7–56 Canterbury v Auckland, Auckland, 1954/55.
Club: Old Collegians (Christchurch).

McGIBBON, Lewis
─────────RHB, RM─────────

Born Newcastle upon Tyne, Northumberland, 8 Oct 1931. Debut 1957. *P.*
NORTHAMPTONSHIRE (13) 1957–59.
HS 4 Northants v Surrey, Northampton, 1958 and 4 v Kent, Kettering, 1959.
BB 4–46 Northants v Kent, Kettering, 1959.
Northumberland 1950–56.

MacGINTY, Raphael Joseph Anthony
─────────RHB, OB─────────

Born London, 22 Mar 1927. Educ Blackrock C; Fitzwilliam C, Cambridge. Debut 1952.
CAMBRIDGE UNIVERSITY (6) 1952.
HS 18 Cambridge U v Leics, Fenner's, 1952.
BB 4–58 Cambridge U v Worcs, Worcester, 1952.
Cambridgeshire 1951–52.

McGLEW, Derrick *John*
─────────RHB, LB─────────

Born Pietermaritzburg, S Africa, 11 Mar 1929. Educ Maritzburg C; Natal U. Debut 1947/48.
S AFRICA DOMESTIC Natal 1947/48–66/67.
SOUTH AFRICA (34) 1951–61/62. E 1956/57 (1); A 1957/58 (5); NZ 1953/54 (5), 1961/62 (5). *E 1951 (2), 1955 (5), 1960 (5); A 1952/53 (4); NZ 1952/53 (2).* Capt 14.
HST 255* SA v NZ, Wellington, 1952/53. HS as above.
BB 2–4 Natal v Transvaal, Durban, 1963/64.
1000 RUNS (3 + 1) 1871 @ 58.46 in 1955.

RECORDS During HST (above) added 246 for 7th wkt with A. R. A. Murray, S Africa Test record and at time world Test record.
During 105 SA v A, Durban, 1957/58, reached century in 545 mins, slowest fc century at time, remains second-slowest. Carried bat for 127* in total of 292, SA v NZ, Durban, 1961/62. Performed hat-trick spread over two inns, Natal v Transvaal, Durban, 1963/64.
MCC Hon. member. Selector Transvaal CU.

McHUGH, Francis Prest
─────────RHB, RFM─────────

Born Leeds, Yorks, 15 Nov 1925. Debut 1949. *P.*
YORKSHIRE (3) 1949.
GLOUCESTERSHIRE (92) 1952–56. Cap 1954.
HS 18 Glos v Essex, Clacton, 1953.
BB 7–32 Glos v Yorks, Huddersfield, 1955.
Took more wkts than scored runs. Returned 8–68 and 11–112 (Glos v Yorks, Bramall Lane, 1956) in last two fc matches.
Retired owing to illness. Club: Bristol Optimists.

McILWAINE, Richard Johnston
─────────RHB, RM─────────

Born Southsea, Hants, 16 Mar 1950. Educ Portsmouth GS. Debut 1969.
HAMPSHIRE (4) 1969–70.
HS 17 Hants v Northants, Bournemouth, 1969.
BB 2–40 Hants v Sussex, Bournemouth, 1970.

MacINDOE, David Henry
─────────RHB, RMF─────────

Born Eton, Buckinghamshire, 1 Sept 1917. Educ Eton; Christ Church C, Oxford. Debut 1937.
OXFORD UNIVERSITY (42) 1937–46 (Blue 1937–39, 1946). Capt 1946.
HS 51 Oxford U v Minor Counties, The Parks, 1939.
BB 6–61 (10–146 match) Oxford U v Lancs, The Parks 1946.
Gentlemen v Players (1) 1937. Buckinghamshire 1947.

McINERNY, James Jeremy
─────────RHB─────────

Born London, 12 Apr 1933. Educ Christ's Hospital; Hertford C, Oxford. Debut 1955.
OXFORD UNIVERSITY (2) 1955–56.
HS 22 Oxford U v MCC, Lord's, 1956.

McINTYRE, Arthur John William
————RHB, WK, LB————

Born Kennington, London, 14 May 1918. Debut 1938. *P. Wisden* 1958.
SURREY (377) 1938–63. Cap 1946.
Benefit (£8500) 1955.
ENGLAND (3) 1950–55. SA 1955 (1); WI 1950 (1). *A 1950/51 (1)*.
OTHER TOUR Surrey to Rhodesia 1959/60.
HST 7 E v A, Brisbane, 1950/51. HS 143* Surrey v Kent, Blackheath, 1949.
1000 RUNS (3) 1200 @ 24.48 in 1949.
Made 795 dismissals (639 ct, 156 st) in career. Surrey coach 1958–78.

McINTYRE, Euan James
————RHB, OB————

Born Edinburgh, Scotland, 16 Dec 1951. Educ George Heriot's. Debut 1981.
SCOTLAND (2) 1981–83.
HS 6 Scotland v Ireland, Clontarf, Dublin, 1981.
Club: Heriot's Former Pupils.

McINTYRE, John McLachlan
————LHB, SLA————

Born Auckland, N Zealand, 4 July 1944. Debut 1961/62.
N ZEALAND DOMESTIC Auckland (77) 1961/62–64/65, 1969/70–, Canterbury (21) 1965/66–68/69.
TOUR N Zealand to England 1978.
HS 87* Auckland v Otago, Dunedin, 1969/70.
BB 6–84 (11–121 match) Auckland v Wellington, Auckland, 1961/62.
Club: Grafton.

McINTYRE, Terence Frank
————RHB, WK————

Born Staines, Surrey, 2 July 1930. Debut 1959.
COMBINED SERVICES (5) 1959–64.
HS 36 Combined Services v Oxford U, Aldershot, 1964.
Bedfordshire 1957–60. Clubs: Royal Air Force, Huntingdon, Ashby (M'sex).
Flight Lt RAF.

MACK, Andrew James
————LHB, LFM————

Born Aylsham, Norfolk, 14 Jan 1956. Debut 1976.
SURREY (10) 1976–77.
GLAMORGAN (21) 1978–80.
HS 18 Glam v Indians, Swansea, 1979.

BB 4–28 Glam v Worcs, Worcester, 1978.
Retired owing to injury.

MACKAY, Kenneth Donald
————LHB, RMF————

Born Windsor, Queensland, Australia, 24 Oct 1925. Died Point Lookout, Stradbroke Island, Australia, 13 June 1982. Educ Virginia State S. Debut 1946/47.
AUSTRALIA DOMESTIC Queensland (109) 1946/47–63/64.
AUSTRALIA (37) 1956–62/63. E 1958/59 (5), 1962/63 (3); WI 1960/61 (5). *E 1956 (3), 1961 (5); SA 1957/58 (5); I 1956/57 (3), 1959/60 (5); P 1959/60 (3)*.
HST 89 A v I, Madras, 1959/60. HS 223 Queensland v Victoria, Brisbane, 1953/54.
BBT 6–42 A v P, Dacca, 1959/60. BB as above.
1000 RUNS (1) 1103 @ 52.52 in 1956.
Club: Toombul. MBE for services to cricket.

McKEE, William D.
————RHB, RFM————

Born Belfast, Ireland, 27 Aug 1923. Educ Lisburn Technical C. Debut 1946.
IRELAND (1) 1946.
HS 16 Ireland v Scotland, Greenock, 1946.
Club: Woodvale. Rugby: NIRFC, Ireland (12 caps).

McKELVEY, James Moorhead
————LHB————

Born Belfast, Ireland, 2 Apr 1933. Educ Campbell C, Belfast; Queen's U, Belfast. Debut 1954.
IRELAND (2) 1954.
HS 9 Ireland v Scotland, Paisley, 1954.
Clubs: Queen's University, NICC.
Rugby: Queen's University, Ireland (2).

McKELVEY, Patrick George
————RHB, SLA————

Born Barnet, Hertfordshire, 25 Dec 1935. Debut 1959. *P*.
SURREY (2) 1959–60.
Did not bat, one wkt.
Club: Saltaire.

McKELVIE, Robert Douglas (Roy)
————RHB, WK————

Born Blofield, Norfolk, 1 July 1912. Educ Malvern. Debut 1948.
FREE FORESTERS (1) 1948.
HS 12 Free Foresters v Cambridge U, Fenner's, 1948.
Buckinghamshire 1947. Clubs: Buccaneers, Chiswick Park, Gerrards Cross. Former writer on rackets and tennis for the *Daily Mail* and *The Times*; currently for the *Sunday Express*.

McKENNA, Robert Ogilvie
————RHB, RFM————

Born Paisley, Scotland, 21 Mar 1913. Educ Paisley GS; Glasgow U. Debut 1938.
SCOTLAND (2) 1938–46.
HS 4* Scotland v Ireland, Greenock, 1946 and 4 v Yorks, Harrogate, 1938.
Clubs: Glasgow University, Kelburne.

McKENZIE, Graham Douglas
————RHB, RF————

Born Cottesloe, Perth, W Australia, 24 June 1941. Educ John Curtis HS, Fremantle, W Australia. Debut 1959/60. *Wisden* 1965.
AUSTRALIA DOMESTIC Western Australia (81) 1959/60–73/74.
LEICESTERSHIRE (151) 1969–75. Cap 1969.
AUSTRALIA (60) 1961–70/71. E 1962/63 (5), 1965/66 (4), 1970/71 (3); SA 1963/64 (5); WI 1968/69 (5); I 1967/68 (2); P 1964/65 (1). *E 1961 (3), 1964 (5), 1968 (5); SA 1966/67 (5), 1969/70 (3); WI 1964/65 (5); I 1964/65 (3), 1969/70 (5); P 1964/65 (1)*.
OTHER TOURS Commonwealth XI to India and S Africa 1962/63. Rest of World in England 1966, 1967. Rest of World v Barbados, Bridgetown, 1966/67. International XI to Rhodesia 1972/73. International XI to S Africa 1974/75.
HST 76 A v SA, Sydney, 1963/64. HS as above.
BBT 8–71 A v WI, Melbourne, 1968/69. BB as above.
At time that reached aggregates of 100 and 200 Test wkts, youngest ever to do so. Took 246 Test wkts, third-highest aggregate for Australia.
Rest of World v England (3) 1970. Club: Claremont/Cottesloe. Father E. McKenzie (W Australia); uncle D. C. McKenzie (W Australia).

McKIDDIE, Gavin Thomson
RHB, OB

Born Forfar, Scotland, 17 May 1940.
Educ Forfar GS; Glasgow U. Debut
1977.
SCOTLAND (1) 1977.
HS 8 Scotland v Ireland, Dublin, 1977.
Club: Strathmore.

McKINNA, Gordon Hayden
RHB, RM

Born Sale, Cheshire, 2 Aug 1930. Educ
Manchester GS; Brasenose C, Oxford.
Debut 1951.
OXFORD UNIVERSITY (5) 1951–53 (Blue
1953).
COMBINED SERVICES (1) 1955.
HS 18 Oxford U v Sussex, Hove, 1953.
BB 4–39 Oxford U v Free Foresters, The
Parks, 1953.
Cheshire 1949–53. Soccer: Blue.

McKINNON, Atholl Henry
RHB, SLA

Born Port Elizabeth, S Africa, 20 Aug
1932. Died Durban, S Africa, 2 Dec
1983. Educ Grey HS, Port Elizabeth.
Debut 1952/53.
S AFRICA DOMESTIC Eastern Province
1952/53–62/63, Transvaal 1963/64–68/
69.
SOUTH AFRICA (8) 1960–66/67. E 1964/65
(2); A 1966/67 (2); NZ 1961/62 (1). E
1960 (1), 1965 (2).
HST 27 SA v E, Port Elizabeth, 1964/65.
HS 62 E Province v OFS, Port Elizabeth,
1957/58.
BBT 4–128 SA v E, J'burg, 1964/65. BB
7–37 E Province v Griqualand West,
Port Elizabeth, 1959/60.
Assistant-manager W Indies XI to S
Africa 1983/84 at time of death. Selector
Eastern Province CU. Rugby: Eastern
Province.

MACKINTOSH, David Stewart
RHB

Born Paisley, Scotland, 18 Feb 1947.
Educ Paisley GS; Glasgow U. Debut
1972.
SCOTLAND (1) 1972.
HS 57 Scotland v Ireland, Greenock,
1972.
Buckinghamshire 1971–76. Clubs: Fer-
guslie, Amersham.

MACKINTOSH, Kevin Scott
RHB, RM

Born Kingston-upon-Thames, Surrey,
30 Aug 1957. Educ Kingston GS. Debut
1978.
NOTTINGHAMSHIRE (19) 1978–80.
SURREY (14) 1981–83.
HS 31 Surrey v Som, Oval, 1982.
BB 6–61 Surrey v M'sex, Lord's, 1982.

MACLACHLAN, Andrew
RHB

Born Anglesey, N Wales, 27 Feb 1941.
Educ St Edmund Hall, Oxford; Oxford
U. Debut 1962.
OXFORD UNIVERSITY (5) 1962.
HS 28 Oxford U v Essex, The Parks,
1962.
Chairman Griqualand West CU 1982/
83.

McLACHLAN, Angus Alexander
RHB, LBG

Born Adelaide, S Australia, 11 Nov
1944. Educ St Peter's, Adelaide; Jesus
C, Cambridge. Debut 1964.
CAMBRIDGE UNIVERSITY (17) 1964–65
(Blue 1964–65).
HS 27 Cambridge U v Surrey, Oval,
1964.
BB 4–36 Cambridge U v Combined Ser-
vices, Uxbridge, 1964.
Brother I. M. McLachlan (S Australia,
Cambridge U).

McLACHLAN, Ian Murray
RHB, LB

Born Adelaide, S Australia, 2 Oct 1936.
Educ St Peter's, Adelaide; Jesus C,
Cambridge. Debut 1956.
CAMBRIDGE UNIVERSITY (35) 1956–58
(Blue 1957–58).
AUSTRALIA DOMESTIC South Australia
(31) 1960/61–63/64, Australian XI
1962/63–63/64.
TOUR E. W. Swanton's XI to W Indies
1960/61.
HS 188* S Australia v Queensland,
Adelaide, 1960/61 (Sheffield Shield
debut).
BB 2–33 Cambridge U v D. R. Jardine's
XI, Eastbourne, 1958.
Brother A. A. McLachlan (Cambridge
U).

McLAREN, Robert Stewart
RHB, WK

Born Perth, Scotland, 10 May 1919.
Educ Perth Academy. Debut 1947.

SCOTLAND (6) 1947–49.
HS 7 Scotland v Ireland, Glasgow, 1948.
Club: Carlton.

McLEAN, Roy Alastair
RHB

Born Pietermaritzburg, S Africa, 9 July
1930. Educ Hilton C, Natal, S Africa.
Debut 1949/50, Wisden 1961.
S AFRICA DOMESTIC Natal 1949/50–65/
66.
SOUTH AFRICA (40) 1951–64/65. E 1956/
57 (5), 1964/65 (2); A 1957/58 (4); NZ
1953/54 (4), 1961/62 (5). E 1951 (3),
1955 (5), 1960 (5); A 1952/53 (5); NZ
1952/53 (2).
OTHER TOURS S African Fezelas to Eng-
land 1961 (capt). Commonwealth XI to
N Zealand 1961/62.
HST 142 SA v E, Lord's, 1955. HS 207 S
Africans v Worcs, Worcester, 1960.
BB 2–22 S Africans v A. E. R. Gilligan's
XI, Hastings, 1960.
1000 RUNS (2) 1516 @ 37.90 in 1960.
MCC Hon. member. Rugby: Natal.

McLELLAN, Alan James
RHB, WK

Born Ashton-under-Lyne, Lancs, 2
Sept 1958.
Educ Williamstown HS, Melbourne,
Australia; Hartshead S, Ashton-under-
Lyne. Debut 1978.
DERBYSHIRE (26) 1978–79.
HS 41 Derbys v Hants, Basingstoke,
1979.
Club: Ashton.

McMAHON, John William Joseph
RHB, SLA

Born Balaclava, S Australia, 28 Dec
1917. Debut 1947. P.
SURREY (84) 1947–53. Cap 1948.
SOMERSET (115) 1954–57. Cap 1954.
HS 24 Som v Sussex, Frome, 1955.
BB 8–46 Surrey v Northants, Oval, 1948
and 8–46 Som v Kent, Yeovil, 1955.
100 WKTS (1) 103 @ 25.57 in 1956.
Clubs: Southgate, Milnrow, Leek,
Castleton Moor.

McMORRIS, Easton Dudley Ashton St John
RHB, OB

Born Kingston, Jamaica, 4 Apr 1935.
Debut 1955/56.
W INDIES DOMESTIC Jamaica 1955/
56–71/72.

WEST INDIES (13) 1957/58–66. E 1959/60 (4); I 1961/62 (4); P 1957/58 (1). *E 1963 (2), 1966 (2).*
OTHER TOURS Jamaica to England 1970 (capt).
HST 125 WI v I, Kingston, 1961/62. HS 218 Jamaica v Guyana, Georgetown, 1966/67.
Club: Lucas (Kingston).

McNAB, William
RHB, WK

Born Edinburgh, Scotland, 2 Oct 1916. Educ George Watson's, Edinburgh. Debut 1947.
SCOTLAND (1) 1947.
HS 10 Scotland v Ireland, Cork, 1947.
Club: Watsonians.

McNAMARA, Francis Knyvett
RHB, LMF

Born Missouri, India, 30 Apr 1912. Educ Marlborough. Debut 1952.
FREE FORESTERS (1) 1952.
HS 16 Free Foresters v Cambridge U, Fenner's, 1952.
Malaya.

McPATE, William Adamson
RHB, RM

Born Baillieston, Glasgow, Scotland, 22 July 1951. Educ Coatbridge. Debut 1983.
SCOTLAND (2) 1983–84.
HS 12* Scotland v Ireland, Glasgow, 1984.
BB 2–17 same match.
Club: Drumpellier.

McPHAIL, Angus William
RHB, WK

Born Ipswich, Suffolk, 25 May 1956. Educ Abingdon S; UC, Oxford. Debut 1977.
OXFORD UNIVERSITY (4) 1977.
HS 37 Oxford U v Notts, The Parks, 1977.

MACPHERSON, Moray Charles Livingstone
RHB, WK

Born Barton-on-Sea, Hants, 4 Nov 1959. Educ Winchester; Lincoln C, Oxford. Debut 1980.
OXFORD UNIVERSITY (5) 1980.
HS 22 Oxford U v Hants, The Parks, 1980.
Uncle H. E. Webb (Oxford U, Hants).

McPHERSON, Thomas *Ian*
RHB, SLA

Born Scone, Scotland, 14 Oct 1942. Debut 1977.
SCOTLAND (5) 1977–79.
HS 28 Scotland v Ireland, Dublin, 1977.
BB 4–74 same match.
Club: Perthshire.

McQUILKEN, Archibald Lynn
RHB, LBG

Born Muckamore, Co Londonderry, Ireland, 27 Sept 1933. Died Belfast, Ireland, 16 Oct 1983. Debut 1962.
IRELAND (2) 1962.
HS 42 Ireland v Combined Services, Belfast, 1962.
BB 5–37 same match.
Club: Muckamore. Soccer: Irish Amateurs.

MacVICAR, Angus *David* Lees
RHB, RMF

Born Sheffield, Yorks, 25 Aug 1955. Educ Rugby; Trinity C, Cambridge. Debut 1977.
CAMBRIDGE UNIVERSITY (1) 1977.
No runs.
BB 2–82 Cambridge U v Glam, Fenner's, 1977.

McVICKER, Norman Michael
RHB, RFM

Born Radcliffe, Lancs, 4 Nov 1940. Educ Stand GS, Manchester. Debut 1965.
MINOR COUNTIES (2) 1965–67.
WARWICKSHIRE (104) 1969–72. Cap 1971.
LEICESTERSHIRE (67) 1974–76. Cap 1974.
HS 83* Leics v Kent, Tunbridge Wells, 1975.
BB 7–29 Warwicks v Northants, Edgbaston, 1969.
Lincolnshire 1963–68. Club: Solihull.

MADAN LAL Sharma
RHB, RM

Born Amritsar, India, 20 Mar 1951. Educ PBN HS, Amritsar; Hindu C. Debut 1968/69.
INDIA DOMESTIC Punjab 1968/69–71/72, Delhi 1972/73–.
INDIA (37) 1974–83/84. E 1976/77 (2), 1981/82 (6); WI 1974/75 (2), 1983/84 (3); NZ 1976/77 (1); P 1983/84 (3); SL 1982/83 (1). *E 1974 (2), 1982 (3); A 1977/78 (2); WI 1975/76 (4), 1982/83 (2); NZ 1975/76 (3); P 1982/83 (3).*

TOUR India to Sri Lanka 1973/74.
HST 74 I v P, Bangalore, 1983/84. HS 223 Delhi v Rajasthan, Delhi 1977/78.
BBT 5–23 I v E, Bombay, 1981/82. BB 9–31 (13–64 match) Delhi v Haryana, Delhi, 1979/80.
Scored 140 and 100 and took 8 for 143 match, Delhi v Railways, Delhi, 1980/81.
Club: Enfield.

MADDOCKS, Leonard Victor
RHB, WK

Born Beaconsfield, Victoria, Australia, 24 May 1926. Debut 1946/47.
AUSTRALIA DOMESTIC Victoria (66) 1946/47–61/62, Tasmania (6) 1962/63–67/68.
AUSTRALIA (7) 1954/55–1956/57. E 1954/55 (3). *E 1956 (2); WI 1954/55 (1); I 1956/57 (1).*
OTHER TOURS Australia to N Zealand 1959/60. Cavaliers to S Africa 1960/61.
HST 69 A v E, Adelaide, 1954/55. HS 122* Australian XI v N Zealand XI, Auckland, 1959/60.
Manager Australia to England 1977. Victoria representative ABC. Brother R. I. Maddocks (Victoria); son I. L. Maddocks (Victoria).

MADUGALLE, Ranjan Senerath
RHB, OB

Born Kandy, Ceylon, 22 Apr 1959. Educ RC, Colombo. Debut 1979.
SRI LANKA (12) 1981/82–84. E 1981/82 (1); A 1982/83 (1); NZ 1983/84 (3). *E 1984 (1); NZ 1982/83 (2); I 1982/83 (1); P 1981/82 (3).*
OTHER TOURS Sri Lanka to England 1979, 1981. Sri Lanka to India 1980/81. Sri Lanka to Zimbabwe 1982/83.
HST 91* SL v P, Faisalabad, 1981/82. HS 142* Sri Lanka Board President's XI v England XI, Kandy, 1981/82.
Club: Nondescripts.

MAGEE, Brian Robert Boyd
LHB, LM

Born Toronto, Canada, 4 May 1918. Educ Radley; Trinity College S, Port Hope, Ontario; Toronto U. Debut 1954.
CANADA to England (1) 1954.
HS 13 Canadians v Yorks, Scarborough, 1954.

MAGUIRE, Keith Robert
RHB, RFM

Born Marston Green, Warwicks, 20 Mar 1961. Educ Sutton Coldfield Technical C. Debut 1982.

WARWICKSHIRE (3) 1982.
HS 2 Warwicks v Som, Edgbaston, 1982.
Staffordshire 1984. Clubs: Coleshill,
Moseley.

MAHER, Bernard Joseph Michael
RHB, WK

Born Hillingdon, M'sex, 11 Feb 1958.
Educ Harrow C; Loughborough U.
Debut 1981.
DERBYSHIRE (27) 1981–.
HS 66 Derbys v Essex, Chesterfield,
1984.

MAHMOOD HUSSAIN
RHB, RFM

Born Lahore, India, 2 Apr 1932. Educ
Punjab U. Debut 1949/50.
PAKISTAN DOMESTIC Universities, Pun-
jab, Karachi, East Pakistan, National
Tyre and Rubber Co, 1949/50–68/69.
PAKISTAN (27) 1952/53–62. E 1961/62
(1); WI 1958/59 (3); NZ 1955/56 (1); I
1954/55 (5). E 1954 (2), 1962 (3); WI
1957/58 (3); I 1952/53 (4), 1960/61
(5).
HST 35 P v I, Delhi, 1960/61. HS 50
Governor's XI v MCC, Lyallpur, 1961/
62.
BBT 6–67 P v I, Dacca, 1954/55. BB 8–95
Karachi Whites v Karachi Greens,
Karachi, 1956/57.
Manager Pakistan to England 1978.

MAHMOOD-UL-HASAN
RHB

Born Lucknow, India, 11 Nov 1938.
Educ Karachi U. Debut 1959/60.
PAKISTAN DOMESTIC Karachi University,
Karachi, Public Works Department,
Pakistan International Airlines, 1959/
60–73/74.
TOUR Pakistan Eaglets to England 1963.
HS 196 Karachi Whites v Quetta,
Karachi, 1963/64.

MAHONY, Noel Cameron
RHB

Born Fermoy, Co Cork, Ireland, 15 Jan
1913. Educ King's Hospital S, Dublin;
Dublin U. Debut 1948.
IRELAND (5) 1948–53.
HS 29 Ireland v MCC, Dublin, 1948.
Clubs: Cork Bohemians, Clontarf.
President ICU 1979.

MAIDLOW, William John
RHB

Born Bristol, 15 July 1949. Educ Malvern; Brasenose C, Oxford. Debut 1972.
OXFORD UNIVERSITY (2) 1972.
HS 45 Oxford U v Notts, The Parks,
1972.

MAINS, Geoffrey
RHB, RFM

Born Mangotsfield, Glos, 24 Jan 1934.
Debut 1951. P.
GLOUCESTERSHIRE (6) 1951–54.
HS 8 Glos v Northants, Northampton,
1954.
BB 2–42 Glos v Combined Services,
Bristol, 1953.
Club: Frenchay.

MAIR, Norman George Robertson
LHB, SLA

Born Edinburgh, Scotland, 7 Oct 1928.
Educ Merchiston Castle; Edinburgh U.
Debut 1952.
SCOTLAND (1) 1952.
HS 4* Scotland v Worcs, Worcester,
1952.
Edinburgh University. Rugby: Edin-
burgh University, Scotland (4).

MAJENDIE, Nicholas Lionel
RHB, WK

Born Cheltenham, Glos, 9 June 1942.
Educ Winchester C; Christ Church C,
Oxford. Debut 1961.
OXFORD UNIVERSITY (18) 1961–63 (Blue
1962–63).
SURREY (8) 1963.
HS 54 Oxford U v Glos, The Parks, 1963.

MAJID Jahangir KHAN
RHB, RMF/OB

Born Ludhiana, India, 28 Sept 1946.
Educ Aitchison C, Lahore; Punjab U;
Emmanuel C, Cambridge. Debut 1961/
62. Wisden 1970.
PAKISTAN DOMESTIC Lahore, Lahore
Board of Secondary Education, Punjab
University, Universities, Pakistan
International Airlines, Punjab, 1961/
62–82/83.
GLAMORGAN (154) 1968–76. Cap 1968.
Capt 1973–76.
CAMBRIDGE UNIVERSITY (29) 1970–72
(Blue 1970–72). Capt 1971–72.
AUSTRALIA DOMESTIC Queensland (9)
1973/74.

PAKISTAN (63) 1964/65–82/83. E 1968/
69 (3), 1972/73 (3); A 1964/65 (1), 1979/
80 (3); WI 1974/75 (2), 1980/81 (4); NZ
1964/65 (3), 1976/77 (3); I 1978/79 (3),
1982/83 (1); SL 1981/82 (1). E 1967 (3),
1971 (2), 1974 (3), 1982 (1); A 1972/
73 (3), 1976/77 (3), 1978/79 (2), 1981/
82 (3); WI 1976/77 (5); NZ 1972/73
(3), 1978/79 (2); I 1979/80 (6). Capt
3.
OTHER TOUR Pakistan Eaglets to England
1963.
HST 167 P v WI, Georgetown, 1976/77.
HS 241 Lahore Greens v Bahawalpur,
Lahore, 1965/66.
BBT 4–45 P v WI, Georgetown, 1976/77.
BB 6–67 Lahore B v Khairpur, Lahore,
1961/62 (fc debut).
1000 RUNS (8+1) 2074 @ 61.00 in
1972.
RECORD Added 217 for 6th wkt with
Hanif Mohammed, P v NZ, Lahore,
1964/65, Pakistan Test record.
On fc debut, at age of 15, scored 111*
and took 6–67, Lahore B v Khairpur,
Lahore, 1961/62. Scored 147* in 89
mins (with 13 sixes and 10 fours) before
lunch on 3rd day, taking 30 runs from
one over from R. C. Davis, Pakistanis v
Glam, Swansea, 1967. Also scored 147
before lunch, Glam v W Indians, Swansea, 1969 and 108* before lunch during
inns of 112, P v NZ, Karachi, 1976/77
(only fourth instance on first morning of
a Test).
Played until 1970 as Majid Jahangir.
Father Jahangir Khan (India); brother
Asod Jahangir Khan (Oxford U);
cousins Javed Burki and Imran Khan
(both Pakistan); uncle Baqa Jilani
(India).

MAKINSON, David John
RHB, LMF

Born Eccleston, 12 Jan 1961. Educ St
Mary's HS, Leyland. Debut 1984.
LANCASHIRE (4) 1984.
HS 9 Lancs v Glos, Bristol, 1984.
BB 2–49 Lancs v Essex, Southend,
1984.

MALALASEKERA, Vijaya Prasanna
RHB

Born Colombo, Ceylon, 8 Aug 1945.
Educ RC, Colombo; Fitzwilliam C,
Cambridge. Debut 1966.
CAMBRIDGE UNIVERSITY (27) 1966–68
(Blue 1966–67).
HS 80 Cambridge U v Essex, Fenner's,
1966.

MALCOLM, Devon Eugene
————RHB, RFM————

Born Kingston, Jamaica, 22 Feb 1963.
Educ Richmond C, Sheffield. Debut
1984.
DERBYSHIRE (7) 1984.
HS 23 Derbys v Notts, Trent Bridge,
1984.
BB 3–78 Derbys v Kent, Maidstone,
1984.
Club: Sheffield United.

MALCOLM, Henry John James
————RHB, RFM————

Born Richmond, Surrey, 4 July 1914.
Educ London U. Debut 1948.
MIDDLESEX (4) 1948.
HS 76* M'sex v Cambridge U, Fenner's,
1948.
Club: South Hampstead.

MALHOTRA, Ashok
————RHB, RM————

Born Amritsar, India, 26 Jan 1957. Educ
DAVH Sec S, Chandigarh; Punjab U.
Debut 1973/74.
INDIA DOMESTIC Haryana 1973/74–.
INDIA (6) 1981/82–83/84. E 1981/82 (2);
WI 1983/84 (3). *E 1982 (1).*
OTHER TOUR India to W Indies 1982/83.
HST 72* I v WI, Bombay, 1983/84. HS
228 Haryana v Services, Delhi, 1982/83.

MALLENDER, Neil Alan
————RHB, RFM————

Born Kirk Sandall, Yorks, 13 Aug 1961.
Educ Beverley GS. Debut 1980.
NORTHAMPTONSHIRE (89) 1980–.
N ZEALAND DOMESTIC Otago (6) 1983/84.
HS 71* Northants v Oxford U, The
Parks, 1983.
BB 7–41 Northants v Derbys, North-
ampton, 1982.

MALLETT, Anthony William
Haward
————RHB, RFM————

Born Dulwich, London, 29 Aug 1924.
Educ Dulwich; Brasenose C, Oxford.
Debut 1945.
UNDER-33 XI v Over-33 XI (1) 1945.
KENT (33) 1946–53. Cap 1949.
MCC (7) 1946–54.
OXFORD UNIVERSITY (19) 1947–48 (Blue
1947–48).
TOUR MCC to Canada 1951.
HS 97 Kent v Sussex, Tunbridge Wells,
1946.
BB 6–42 South v North, Hastings, 1948.

Gentlemen v Players (3) 1946–47. Club:
Beckenham. Son N. V. H. Mallett (Oxford U).

MALLETT, Ashley Alexander
————RHB, OB————

Born Chatswood, NSW, Australia, 13
July 1945. Debut 1967/68.
AUSTRALIA DOMESTIC South Australia
(91) 1967/68–80/81.
AUSTRALIA (38) 1968–80. E 1970/71 (2),
1974/75 (5), 1979/80 (1); WI 1968/69
(1), 1975/76 (6), 1979/80 (1); NZ 1973/
74 (3); P 1972/73 (2). *E 1968 (1), 1972
(2), 1975 (4), 1980 (1); SA 1969/70
(1); NZ 1973/74 (3); I 1969/70 (5).*
OTHER TOURS International Wanderers
to S Africa 1975/76.
HST 43* A v E, Oval, 1968. HS 92 S
Australia v W Australia, Adelaide, 1970/
71.
BBT 8–59 A v P, Adelaide, 1972/73. BB as
above.
World Series Cricket (Kerry Packer)
1977/78–78/79. Clubs: Prospect
(Australia), Ayr (Scotland). Cricket
Journalist.

MALLETT, Nicholas Vivian
Haward
————RHB, RM————

Born Haileybury, Hertfordshire, 30 Oct
1956. Educ St Andrew's C, Grahams-
town, S Africa; Brasenose C, Oxford.
Debut 1980.
OXFORD UNIVERSITY (11) 1980–81 (Blue
1981).
HS 52 Oxford U v Glam, The Parks,
1981.
BB 5–52 same match.
Father A. W. H. Mallett (Oxford U,
Kent).

MALONE, Michael Francis
————RHB, RFM————

Born Perth, W Australia, 9 Oct 1950.
Educ Scarborough HS, Perth. Debut
1974/75.
AUSTRALIA DOMESTIC Western Australia
(45) 1974/75–81/82.
LANCASHIRE (19) 1979–80.
AUSTRALIA (1) *E 1977.*
TOUR Australia to Pakistan 1979/80.
HST 46 A v E, Oval, 1977. HS as above.
BBT 5–63 A v E, Oval, 1977. BB 7–88
Lancs v Notts, Blackpool, 1979.
World Series Cricket (Kerry Packer)
1977/78–78/79. Club: Haslingden.

MALONE, Steven John
————RHB, RFM————

Born Chelmsford, Essex, 19 Oct 1953.
Educ St Edmund's, Ipswich; King's S,
Ely. Debut 1975.
ESSEX (2) 1975–78.
HAMPSHIRE (46) 1980–.
HS 23 Hants v Kent, Bournemouth,
1981.
BB 7–55 Hants v Oxford U, The Parks,
1982.

MALTBY, Norman
————LHB, RM————

Born Marske-by-the-Sea, Yorks, 16
July 1951. Debut 1972.
NORTHAMPTONSHIRE (9) 1972–74.
HS 59 Northants v Oxford U, The Parks,
1974.
BB 2–43 Northants v Som, Welling-
borough, 1972.

MANASSEH, Maurice
————RHB, OB/RM————

Born Calcutta, India, 12 Jan 1943. Educ
Epsom C; Oriel C, Oxford. Debut 1962.
OXFORD UNIVERSITY (34) 1962–64 (Blue
1964).
MIDDLESEX (7) 1964–67.
HS 129* Oxford U v Worcs, Worcester,
1964.
BB 5–51 Oxford U v Yorks, The Parks,
1964.

MANJREKAR, Vijay Lakshman
————RHB————

Born Bombay, India, 26 Sept 1931.
Died Madras, India, 17 Oct 1983. Educ
King George S, Bombay. Debut 1949/
50.
INDIA DOMESTIC Bombay, Bengal, And-
hra Pradesh, Uttar Pradesh, Rajasthan,
Maharashtra, 1949/50–67/68.
INDIA (55) 1951/52–64/65. E 1951/52
(2), 1961/62 (5), 1963/64 (4); A 1956/57
(3), 1964/65 (3); WI 1958/59 (4); NZ
1955/56 (5), 1964/65 (1); P 1952/53 (3),
1960/61 (5). *E 1952 (4), 1959 (2); WI
1952/53 (4), 1961/62 (5); P 1954/55
(5).*
OTHER TOUR India to Ceylon 1956/57.
HST 189* I v E, Delhi, 1961/62. HS 283
Vizianagram's XI v Tata Sporting Club
XI, Hyderabad, 1963/64.
BB 4–21 Bombay v Pakistan Services-
Bahawalpur, Bombay, 1954/55.
1000 RUNS (1 + 1) 1077 @ 56.68 in 1963/
64.
RECORD Added 222 for 4th wkt with V. S.
Hazare, I v E, Headingley, 1952, India
Test record.

Clubs: Ferguslie, Castleton Moor, Millom. MCC Hon. member. Uncle D. D. Hindlekar (India).

MANKAD, Ashok Vinoo
────────RHB, RM────────

Born Bombay, India, 12 Oct 1946. Educ Fellowship HS, Bombay. Debut 1963/64.
INDIA DOMESTIC Bombay 1963/64–.
INDIA (22) 1969/70–77/78. E 1976/77 (1); A 1969/70 (5); WI 1974/75 (1); NZ 1969/70 (2); NZ 1976/77 (3). *E 1971 (3), 1974 (1); A 1977/78 (3); WI 1970/71 (3).*
OTHER TOUR India to Sri Lanka 1973/74.
HST 97 I v A, Delhi, 1969/70. HS 265 Bombay v Delhi, Bombay, 1980/81.
BB 5–21 W Zone v N Zone, Ahmedabad, 1969/70.
1000 RUNS (0 + 3) 1363 @ 97.35 in 1976/77.
RECORD Scored 6619 runs (@ 76.08) in Ranji Trophy, a record, and 19 Ranji Trophy centuries, third-highest total ever.
Father M. H. Mankad (India); brother R. V. Mankad (Bombay).

MANKAD, Mulvantrai Himmatlal (Vinoo)
────────RHB, SLA────────

Born Jamnagar, India, 12 Apr 1917. Died Bombay, India, 21 Aug 1978. Educ Nawanagar HS. Debut 1935/36. *Wisden* 1947.
INDIA DOMESTIC Western India 1935/36, Bombay Hindus 1936/37–45/46, Nawanagar 1936/37–41/42, Maharashtra 1943/44, Gujerat 1944/45–50/51, Bengal 1948/49, Bombay 1951/52–55/56, Rajasthan 1956/57–61/62.
INDIA (44) 1946–58/59. E 1951/52 (5); A 1956/57 (3); WI 1948/49 (5), 1958/59 (2); NZ 1955/56 (4); P 1952/53 (4). *E 1946 (3), 1952 (3); A 1947/48 (5); WI 1952/53 (5); P 1954/55 (5).* Capt 6.
OTHER TOUR India to Ceylon 1944/45.
HST 231 I v NZ, Madras, 1955/56. HS as above.
BBT 8–52 (13–131 match) I v P, Delhi, 1952/53. BB 8–35 India v Ceylon, Colombo, 1944/45.
1000 RUNS (1) 1120 @ 28.00 in 1946.
100 WKTS (1) 129 @ 20.76 in 1946.
DOUBLE (1) 1946 (India in England; the last tourist to perform the feat).
RECORDS In 1952 became first player to complete Test double for India, in only 23 Tests, at the time a world record. Added 413 for 1st wkt with Pankaj Roy, I v NZ, Madras, 1955/56, world Test record.

Returned 8–55 (12–108 match), I v E, Madras, 1951/52. Scored 72 and 184 and bowled 97 overs for 5 wkts and 231 runs, I v E, Lord's, 1952.
Clubs: Castleton Moor, Haslingden, Stockport, Tonge. Author *How to Play Cricket* (1976). Sons A. V. Mankad (India) and R. V. Mankad (Bombay).

MANN, Francis *George*
────────RHB────────

Born Byfleet, Surrey, 6 Sept 1917. Educ Eton; Pembroke C, Cambridge. Debut 1937.
MIDDLESEX (54) 1937–54. Cap 1939. Capt 1948–49.
CAMBRIDGE UNIVERSITY (24) 1938–1939 (Blue 1938–39).
ENGLAND (7) 1948/49–49. NZ 1949 (2). *SA 1948/49 (5).* Capt 7.
HST 136* E v SA, Port Elizabeth, 1948/49. HS as above.
BB 2–16 M'sex v Sussex, Hove, 1939.
1000 RUNS (3) 1311 @ 24.73 in 1949.
Gentlemen v Players (2) 1948–49. TCCB chairman 1982. M'sex Hon. secretary 1951–65. MCC committee from 1954. Father F. T. Mann (M'sex, England); brother J. P. Mann (Cambridge U, M'sex); cousin E. J. Cunningham (Glos).

MANN, John Pelham
────────RHB, LB────────

Born Byfleet, Surrey, 13 June 1919. Educ Eton; Pembroke C, Cambridge. Debut 1939.
CAMBRIDGE UNIVERSITY (5) 1939.
MIDDLESEX (15) 1939–47. Cap 1946.
HS 77 M'sex v Warwicks, Lord's, 1946.
BB 3–71 Cambridge U v Leics, Fenner's, 1939.
Father F. T. Mann (M'sex, England); brother F. G. Mann (Cambridge U, M'sex, England); cousin E. J. Cunningham (Glos).

MANN, Norman Bertram Fleetwood (Tufty)
────────RHB, SLA────────

Born Brakpan, S Africa, 28 Dec 1920. Died Johannesburg, S Africa, 31 July 1952. Educ Michaelhouse; Caius C, Cambridge. Debut 1939/40.
S AFRICA DOMESTIC Natal 1939/40–45/46, Eastern Province 1946/47–50/51.
SOUTH AFRICA (19) 1947–51. E 1948/49 (5); A 1949/50 (5). *E 1947 (5), 1951 (4).*
HST 52 SA v A, J'burg, 1949/50. HS 97 (in 55 mins) S Africans v Glam, Cardiff, 1947.

BBT 6–59 SA v E, Durban, 1948/49. BB 8–59 E Province v W Province, Cape Town, 1947/48.
Golf: Blue; Natal amateur champion 1938.

MANNERS, John Erroll
────────RHB────────

Born Exeter, Devon, 25 Sept 1914. Educ RNC Dartmouth. Debut 1936.
HAMPSHIRE (7) 1936–48.
COMBINED SERVICES (12) 1947–53.
MCC (1) 1953.
FREE FORESTERS (1) 1953.
HS 147 Combined Services v Glos, Gloucester, 1948.
Clubs: Royal Navy, Incogniti. Royal Navy commander.

MANNING, John Stephen
────────LHB, SLA────────

Born Adelaide, S Australia, 11 June 1924. Debut 1951/52. *P.*
AUSTRALIA DOMESTIC South Australia (19) 1951/52–53/54.
NORTHAMPTONSHIRE (117) 1954–60. Cap 1956.
HS 132 Northants v Yorks, Harrogate, 1957.
BB 8–43 Northants v Glos, Peterborough, 1959.
100 WKTS (3) 116 @ 20.68 in 1956.
Club: Colne.

MANSELL, Alan William
────────RHB, WK────────

Born Redhill, Surrey, 19 May 1951. Debut 1969.
SUSSEX (58) 1969–75.
HS 72* Sussex v Yorks, Bradford, 1974.

MANSELL, Percy Neville Frank
────────RHB, LBG/RM────────

Born St George's, Shropshire, 16 Mar 1920. Educ Milton S, Bulawayo, Rhodesia, S Africa. Debut 1936/37.
S AFRICA DOMESTIC Rhodesia 1936/37–59/60. Rhodesian Invitation XI v Commonwealth XI, Salisbury, 1961/62.
SOUTH AFRICA (13) 1951–55. *E 1951 (2), 1955 (4); A 1952/53 (5); NZ 1952/53 (2).*
HST 90 SA v E, Headingley, 1951 (Test debut). HS 154 Rhodesia v Griqualand West, Kimberley, 1955.
BBT 3–58 SA v A, Melbourne, 1952/53. BB 7–43 (13–120 match) Rhodesia v Surrey, Salisbury, 1959/60.
MBE for services to cricket. Brother A. J. Mansell (Rhodesia).

MANSOOR AKHTAR
————RHB, RM————

Born Lahore, Pakistan, 25 Dec 1956.
Debut 1974/75.
PAKISTAN DOMESTIC Karachi, United
Bank, Sind, 1974/75–.
PAKISTAN (13) 1980/81–82/83. A 1982/
83 (3); WI 1980/81 (2); I 1982/83 (3); SL
1981/82 (1). *E 1982 (3); A 1981/82 (1)*.
HST 111 P v A, Faisalabad, 1982/83. HS
224* Karachi Whites v Quetta, Karachi,
1976/77.
BB 2–55 United Bank v Railways,
Lahore, 1983/84.
RECORDS During HS above added 561 for
1st wkt with Waheed Mirza, world
record.

MANTELL, David Norman
————RHB, WK————

Born Acton, London, 22 July 1934.
Educ Hastings GS. Debut 1954. *P*.
SUSSEX (25) 1954–58.
HS 34 Sussex v Kent, Tunbridge Wells,
1957.

MANTRI, Madhav Krishnaji
————RHB, WK, RM————

Born Nasik, India, 1 Sept 1921. Educ
Bombay U. Debut 1941/42.
INDIA DOMESTIC Bombay 1941/42–56/
57, Maharashtra 1942/43.
INDIA (4) 1951/52–54/55. E 1951/52 (1).
E 1952 (2); P 1954/55 (1).
HST 39 I v E, Bombay, 1951/52. HS 200
Bombay v Maharashtra, Poona, 1948/49.
BB 2–38 ACC v Chidambaram's XI,
Hyderabad, 1962/63.
Made nine dismissals (4 ct, 5 st) on fc
debut, Bombay v N India, Lahore,
1941/42.
Nephew S. M. Gavaskar (India).

MANVILLE, David Walter
————RHB, WK, occ RM————

Born Brighton, Sussex, 18 Aug 1934.
Educ Vardean GS; Cardiff C of Educ.
Debut 1956. *P*.
SUSSEX (3) 1956.
HS 8 Sussex v Kent, Tunbridge Wells,
1956.
Clubs: Haywards Heath, Ebbw Vale,
Meigle, Skipton. Chairman Sussex
League 1971.

MAQSOOD AHMED
————RHB, RM————

Born Amritsar, India, 26 Mar 1925.
Debut 1944/45.

INDIA DOMESTIC Southern Punjab 1944/
45–46/47.
PAKISTAN DOMESTIC Bahawalpur,
Karachi, Rawalpindi, 1947/48–63/64.
PAKISTAN (16) 1952/53–55/56. NZ 1955/
56 (2); I 1954/55 (5). *E 1954 (4); I 1952/
53 (5)*.
HST 99 P v I, Lahore, 1954/55. HS 144 S
Punjab v N India, Lahore, 1944/45 (fc
debut).
BBT 2–12 P v I, Lucknow, 1952/53. BB
6–45 Commander-in-Chief's XI v Ceylon XI, Rawalpindi, 1949/50.
1000 RUNS (1) 1314 @ 34.57 in 1954.
Clubs: Blythe Works, Burslem.

MARIE, Gregory Vincent
————RHB, RM————

Born Perth, W Australia, 17 Feb 1945.
Educ U of W Australia; Reading U;
Wolfson C, Oxford. Debut 1978.
OXFORD UNIVERSITY (10) 1978–79 (Blue
1978). Elected capt 1979, but injury
compelled resignation after one match.
HS 27 Oxford U v Sussex, The Parks,
1978.
BB 5–46 Oxford U v Glam, The Parks,
1979.

MARKS, Alfred *Edwin*
————RHB, WK————

Born Belfast, Ireland, 15 May 1924.
Educ Belfast Methodist C. Debut 1953.
IRELAND (3) 1953–55.
HS 17 Ireland v Scotland, Paisley, 1954.
Clubs: NICC, North Down.

MARKS, Christopher Peter
————RHB————

Born Hanley, Staffordshire, 17 July
1946. Educ Worksop C. Debut 1967.
DERBYSHIRE (14) 1967–69.
HS 39 Derbys v Northants, Derby, 1968.
Staffordshire 1970. Clubs: Longton,
Crewe LMR.

MARKS, Victor James
————RHB, OB————

Born Middle Chinnock, Som, 25 June
1955. Educ Blundell's; St John's C, Oxford. Debut 1975.
OXFORD UNIVERSITY (33) 1975–78 (Blue
1975–78). Capt 1976–77.
SOMERSET (159) 1975–. Cap 1979.
ENGLAND (6) 1982–83/84. NZ 1983 (1);
P 1982 (1). *NZ 1983/84 (1); P 1983/84
(3)*.
OTHER TOUR England to Australia 1982/
83.

HST 83 E v P, Faisalabad, 1983/84. HS
134 Som v Worcs, Weston-super-Mare,
1984.
BBT 3–78 E v NZ, Oval, 1983. BB 8–141
Som v Kent, Taunton, 1984.
1000 RUNS (1) 1262 @ 52.58 in 1984 (also
took 86 wkts @ 25.96).

MARLAR, Robin Geoffrey
————RHB, OB————

Born Eastbourne, Sussex, 2 Jan 1931.
Educ Harrow; Magdalene C, Cam-
bridge. Debut 1951.
CAMBRIDGE UNIVERSITY (39) 1951–53
(Blue 1951–53). Capt 1953.
SUSSEX (223) 1951–68. Cap 1952. Capt
1955–59.
TOUR E. W. Swanton's XI to W Indies
1955/56.
HS 64 Sussex v Australians, Hove, 1956.
BB 9–46 (15–119 match) Sussex v Lancs,
Hove, 1955.
100 WKTS (4) 139 @ 21.55 in 1955.
Gentlemen v Players (10) 1951–58.
Cricket writer for *The Daily Telegraph*
and *The Sunday Times*. Secretary
Cricket Writers' Club. Defeated Con-
servative candidate at Bolsover in the
1959 General Election.

MARLOW, Christopher *Roderick*
James
————LHB, RM————

Born Bexhill, Sussex, 30 Sept 1949.
Educ Uppingham; Magdalene C, Cam-
bridge. Debut 1973.
CAMBRIDGE UNIVERSITY (3) 1973.
HS 11 Cambridge U v Surrey, Fenner's,
1973.

MARNER, Peter Thomas
————RHB, RM————

Born Oldham, Lancs, 31 Mar 1936.
Educ Greenhill GS, Oldham. Debut
1952. *P*.
LANCASHIRE (236) 1952–64. Cap 1958.
LEICESTERSHIRE (165) 1965–70. Cap
1965.
TOUR Commonwealth XI to Pakistan
1967/68.
HS 142* Lancs v Leics, Old Trafford,
1963.
BB 7–29 Leics v Glam, Coalville, 1966.
1000 RUNS (12) 1685 @ 38.29 in 1958.
Took 378 catches in career.
Clubs: Crompton, Todmorden.

MARRIOTT, Dennis Alston
————RHB, LMF————

Born Annotto Bay, Jamaica, 29 Nov
1939. Debut 1965.

SURREY (19) 1965–67.
MIDDLESEX (11) 1972–74. Cap 1973.
HS 24* Surrey v Leics, Leicester, 1967.
BB 5–71 M'sex v Notts, Trent Bridge, 1973.
Club: Mitcham.

MARSDEN, Keith
————————RHB, RM————————

Born Carlisle, Cumberland, 24 July 1931. Educ Lancaster RGS; Caius C, Cambridge. Debut 1952.
CAMBRIDGE UNIVERSITY (1) 1952.
No runs, no wkts.
Club: Clifton. Ran half-mile for Cambridge.

MARSDEN, Robert
————————RHB, OB————————

Born Kensington, London, 2 Apr 1959. Educ Merchant Taylors', Northwood; Christ Church C, Oxford. Debut 1979.
OXFORD UNIVERSITY (13) 1979–82 (Blue 1982).
HS 60 Oxford U v Warwicks, The Parks, 1982.

MARSH, Eric
————————RHB, LB————————

Born Greenwich, London, 30 May 1940. Educ St Dunstan's C; Bristol U; St Edmund Hall, Oxford. Debut 1962.
OXFORD UNIVERSITY (10) 1962.
HS 50 Oxford U v Free Foresters, The Parks, 1962.
Shropshire 1964–76. UAU 1961 (capt). Club: Ludlow.

MARSH, Frederick *Eric*
————————LHB, SLA————————

Born Bolsover, Derbys, 17 July 1920. Debut 1946. *P.*
DERBYSHIRE (66) 1946–49. Cap 1947.
HS 86 Derbys v Indians, Chesterfield, 1946.
BB 6–37 Derbys v Northants, Rushden, 1947.
Club: Westhoughton. Professional coach Repton S from 1950. Uncle T. S. Worthington (Derbys, England).

MARSH, Paul
————————RHB, OB————————

Born Pretoria, S Africa, 5 Dec 1939. Educ St Alban's C, Pretoria; Jesus C, Cambridge. Debut 1965.
CAMBRIDGE UNIVERSITY (1) 1965.

HS 23 Cambridge U v M'sex, Fenner's, 1965.
Cambridgeshire 1965. Headmaster St Alban's C, Pretoria, S Africa.

MARSH, Rodney William
————————LHB, WK————————

Born Armadale, W Australia, 11 Nov 1947. Educ Armadale HS; U of W Australia. Debut 1968/69. *Wisden* 1982.
AUSTRALIA DOMESTIC Western Australia (97) 1968/69–83/84.
AUSTRALIA (96) 1970/71–83/84. E 1970/71 (6), 1974/75 (6), 1976/77 (1), 1979/80 (3), 1982/83 (5); WI 1975/76 (6), 1979/80 (3), 1981/82 (3); NZ 1973/74 (3), 1980/81 (3); I 1980/81 (3); P 1972/73 (3), 1976/77 (3), 1981/82 (3), 1983/84 (5). *E 1972 (5), 1975 (4), 1977 (5), 1980 (1), 1981 (6); WI 1972/73 (5); NZ 1973/74 (3), 1976/77 (2), 1981/82 (3); P 1979/80 (3), 1982/83 (3).*
HST 132 A v NZ, Adelaide, 1973/74. HS 236 W Australia v Pakistanis, Perth, 1972/73.
RECORDS Made 355 (343 ct, 12 st) dismissals in Tests, world Test record. Took 11 catches in match, W Australia v Victoria, Perth, 1975/76 equalling world record; also 10 dismissals (all ct) W Australia v S Australia, Perth, 1976/77. Made 28 dismissals (all ct) in series, A v E, 1982/83, world Test record. Scored 104 in 2nd inns of fc debut, W Australia v W Indians, Perth, 1968/69. During inns of 53, W Australia v W Indians, Perth, 1975/76, reached 50* in 11 scoring strokes, equalling world record. World Series Cricket (Kerry Packer) 1977/78–78/79.
Clubs: Nedlands, West Perth.

MARSH, Steven Andrew
————————RHB, WK————————

Born Westminster, London, 27 Jan 1961. Educ Walderslade Sec S; Mid-Kent C of H and F Educ, Maidstone. Debut 1982.
KENT (8) 1982–.
HS 48 Kent v Northants, Folkestone, 1984.
Club: Lordswood.

MARSH, William Edward
————————RHB, RM————————

Born Newbridge, S Wales, 10 Sept 1917. Died Newbridge, S Wales, 6 Feb 1978. Educ Monmouth GS. Debut 1947.
GLAMORGAN (4) 1947.
HS 13 Glam v M'sex, Lord's, 1947.

BB 3–70 Glam v Worcs, Ebbw Vale, 1947.
Club: Newbridge. Rugby: Newbridge and Cross Keys, Welsh trialist.

MARSHALL, Anthony Granville
————————RHB, RM————————

Born Isleworth, M'sex, 10 Sept 1932. Educ Chatham House S, Ramsgate. Debut 1950.
KENT (5) 1950–54.
MINOR COUNTIES (1) 1967.
HS 7 Kent v Glam, Gillingham, 1950 and 7 v Cambridge U, Folkestone, 1953.
BB 6–53 Minor Counties v Pakistanis, Swindon, 1967.
Wiltshire 1955–70. Club: Chippenham.

MARSHALL, David Alexander Cadman
————————RHB————————

Born Sheffield, Yorks, 29 Dec 1935. Educ Rugby; Brasenose C, Oxford. Debut 1957.
OXFORD UNIVERSITY (1) 1957.
HS 54* Oxford U v Free Foresters, The Parks, 1957.
Brother J. C. Marshall (Oxford U).

MARSHALL, Gordon Alex
————————RHB, RFM————————

Born Birmingham, 12 Mar 1935. Educ King's Norton GS, Birmingham. Debut 1961.
WARWICKSHIRE (4) 1961–63.
HS 18* Warwicks v Cambridge U, Portland Road, Edgbaston, 1961.
BB 5–22 same match.
Clubs: Kings Heath, Stratford on Avon.

MARSHALL, Hugh Dykes Ferguson
————————RHB, RM————————

Born Ashford, Kent, 11 Jan 1942. Educ Ashford GS; Bristol U; St Catherine's C, Oxford. Debut 1966.
OXFORD UNIVERSITY (3) 1966.
HS 48 Oxford U v Lancs, The Parks, 1966.
Clubs: St Lawrence Canterbury, Ashford. Hockey: Scotland (25 caps).

MARSHALL, John Campbell
————————RHB————————

Born Sheffield, Yorks, 30 Jan 1929. Educ Rugby; Brasenose C, Oxford. Debut 1951.

OXFORD UNIVERSITY (16) 1951–53 (Blue 1953).
HS 111 Oxford U v Free Foresters, The Parks, 1953.
Rugby: London Scottish, Scotland (5 caps). Brother D. A. C. Marshall (Oxford U).

MARSHALL, John Maurice Alex
————RHB, LB————

Born Kenilworth, Warwicks, 26 Oct 1916. Educ Warwick S. Debut 1946.
WARWICKSHIRE (28) 1946–50. Cap 1946.
MCC (1) 1956.
HS 47 Warwicks v Derbys, Derby, 1946 and 47 v Glam, Edgbaston, 1950.
BB 5–65 Warwicks v Worcs, Dudley, 1946.
Club: Leamington. Rugby: Nuneaton.

MARSHALL, Malcolm Denzil
————RHB, RF————

Born St Michael, Barbados, 18 Apr 1958. Educ Parkinson CS, Barbados. Debut 1977/78. *Wisden* 1983.
W INDIES DOMESTIC Barbados 1977/78–.
HAMPSHIRE (79) 1979–83. Cap 1981.
WEST INDIES (31) 1978/79–84. E 1980/81 (1); A 1983/84 (4); I 1982/83 (5). *E 1980 (4), 1984 (4); I 1978/79 (3), 1983/84 (6); P 1980/81 (4).*
OTHER TOURS W Indies to Australia 1979/80, 1981/82. Young W Indies to Zimbabwe 1981/82.
HST 92 WI v I, Kanpur, 1983/84. HS 116* Hants v Lancs, Southampton, 1982.
BBT 7–53 WI v E, Headingley, 1984. BB 8–71 Hants v Worcs, Southampton, 1982.
100 WKTS (1) 134 @ 15.73 in 1982.

MARSHALL, Roger Philip Twells
————RHB, LFM————

Born Horsham, Sussex, 28 Feb 1952. Educ Charterhouse. Debut 1973.
SUSSEX (24) 1973–78.
HS 37 Sussex v Notts, Trent Bridge, 1975.
BB 4–37 Sussex v Glam, Hove, 1973.
On Sussex coaching staff after retirement. Club: Horsham.

MARSHALL, Roy Edwin
————RHB, OB————

Born St Thomas, Barbados, 25 Apr 1930. Educ Lodge S, Barbados. Debut 1945/46. *P. Wisden* 1959.

W INDIES DOMESTIC Barbados 1945/46–51/52.
HAMPSHIRE (504) 1953–72. Cap 1955. Capt 1966–70. Benefit (£5865) 1961. Testimonial 1971.
WEST INDIES (4) 1951/52. *A 1951/52 (2); NZ 1951/52 (2).*
OTHER TOURS W Indies to England 1950. Commonwealth XI to India 1953/54. Duke of Norfolk's XI to Jamaica 1956/57. Commonwealth XI to S Africa 1959/60. International XI to Rhodesia, Pakistan and N Zealand 1961/62. Commonwealth XI to Rhodesia 1962/63. Cavaliers to Jamaica 1963/64. Cavaliers to W Indies 1964/65.
HST 30 WI v A, Brisbane, 1951/52. HS 228* Hants v Pakistanis, Bournemouth, 1962.
BB 6–36 Hants v Surrey, Portsmouth, 1956.
1000 RUNS (18) 2607 @ 43.45 in 1961.
RECORDS Added 249 for 1st wkt with J. R. Gray, Hants v M'sex, Portsmouth, 1960 and 263 for 4th wkt with D. A. Livingstone, Hants v M'sex, Lord's, 1970, both county records.
Players v Gentlemen (4) 1958–60. Clubs: Lowerhouse, Southampton. Autobiography *Test Outcast* (1970). Brother N. E. Marshall (W Indies).

MARSHAM, Algernon James Bullock
————RHB, LBG————

Born Chart Sutton, Kent, 14 Aug 1919. Educ Eton; Christ Church C, Oxford. Debut 1939.
OXFORD UNIVERSITY (6) 1939 (Blue).
KENT (6) 1946–47.
COMBINED SERVICES (2) 1946.
HS 74* Combined Services v Oxford U, The Parks, 1946.
BB 5–136 Oxford U v Free Foresters, The Parks, 1939.
Father C. H. B. Marsham (Oxford U, Kent); grandfather C. D. B. Marsham (Oxford U); uncle F. W. B. Marsham (MCC); great-uncles C. J. B. and R. H. B. Marsham (both Oxford U); kinsmen G. and J. Marsham (Kent).

MARSLAND, Geoffrey Peter
————RHB, OB————

Born Ashton-under-Lyne, Lancs, 17 May 1932. Educ Rossall; Lincoln C, Oxford. Debut 1953.
OXFORD UNIVERSITY (17) 1953–54 (Blue 1954).
HS 74 Oxford U v M'sex, The Parks, 1954.
BB 2–68 Oxford U v Free Foresters, The Parks, 1954.

MARTIN, Barry Robert
————RHB, RMF————

Born Hampton Court, M'sex, 18 July 1950. Educ Kingston GS; St Catharine's C, Cambridge. Debut 1971.
CAMBRIDGE UNIVERSITY (6) 1971–73.
HS 14 Cambridge U v Warwicks, Edgbaston, 1973.
BB 2–42 Cambridge U v Warwicks, Fenner's, 1973.
Hockey: Blue.

MARTIN, Eric James
————RHB————

Born Lambley, Notts, 17 Aug 1925. Debut 1949. *P.*
NOTTINGHAMSHIRE (125) 1949–59. Cap 1954.
HS 133* Notts v Leics, Trent Bridge, 1959.
Club: Steetley.

MARTIN, Herbert
————RHB————

Born Lisburn, Ireland, 4 May 1927. Educ Friends S, Lisburn; Royal Belfast Academy. Debut 1949.
IRELAND (19) 1949–68.
HS 88 Ireland v Scotland, Edinburgh, 1956.
Club: Lisburn. Brother T. Martin (Ireland).

MARTIN, John Donald
————RHB, RFM————

Born Oxford, 23 Dec 1941. Educ Magdalen College S; St Edmund Hall, Oxford. Debut 1962.
OXFORD UNIVERSITY (38) 1962–65 (Blue 1962–63, 1965).
SOMERSET (2) 1964–65.
HS 14* Oxford U v Warwicks, The Parks, 1963.
BB 7–26 Oxford U v Derbys, The Parks, 1964.
Oxfordshire 1960–61. Berkshire 1972.
Hockey: Blue.

MARTIN, John Wesley
————LHB, SLA————

Born Wingham, NSW, Australia, 28 July 1931. Debut 1956/57.
AUSTRALIA DOMESTIC New South Wales (78) 1956/57–67/68, South Australia (9) 1958/59.
AUSTRALIA (8) 1960/61–66/67. SA 1963/64 (1); WI 1960/61 (3). *SA 1966/67 (1); I 1964/65 (2); P 1964/65 (1).*

OTHER TOURS Australia to N Zealand 1956/57, 1959/60. Cavaliers to India and S Africa 1962/63. Australia to England 1964.
HST 55 A v WI, Melbourne, 1960/61. HS 101 NSW v W Australia, Perth, 1963/64.
BBT 3–56 A v WI, Melbourne, 1960/61. BB 8–97 NSW v Victoria, Sydney, 1962/63.
Clubs: Petersham-Marrickville (Australia), Colne (Lancashire).

MARTIN, John William
—————RHB, RFM—————

Born Catford, Kent, 16 Feb 1917. Educ Brockley S. Debut 1939.
KENT (33) 1939–53. Cap 1946.
ENGLAND (1) SA 1947.
HST 26 E v SA, Trent Bridge, 1947. HS 40 MCC v Cambridge U, Lord's, 1951.
BB 7–53 Kent v Leics, Folkestone, 1950.
Club: Catford Wanderers.

MARTIN, Robert Harold
—————RHB, RM—————

Born Liverpool, 7 Oct 1918. Educ Oundle S; Trinity C, Oxford. Debut 1951.
COMBINED SERVICES (1) 1951.
HS 4 Combined Services v Worcs, Worcester, 1951.
Royal Navy commander.

MARU, Rajesh Jamnadass
—————RHB, SLA—————

Born Nairobi, Kenya, 28 Oct 1962. Educ Rook's Heath HS, Harrow; Pinner Sixth Form C. Debut 1980.
MIDDLESEX (16) 1980–82.
HAMPSHIRE (17) 1984.
TOUR M'sex to Zimbabwe 1980/81.
HS 36 Hants v Sussex, Bournemouth, 1984.
BB 7–79 Hants v M'sex, Bournemouth, 1984.

MASLIN, Martin
—————RHB, RM—————

Born Grimsby, Lincolnshire, 14 Mar 1942. Educ Haileybury and ISC. Debut 1967.
MINOR COUNTIES (5) 1967–74.
HS 66* Minor Counties v Pakistanis, Swindon, 1967.
Lincolnshire 1959–80. Club: Cleethorpes.

MASON, Alan
—————RHB, SLA—————

Born Addingham, nr Ilkley, Yorks, 2 May 1921. Debut 1947. *P.*
YORKSHIRE (18) 1947–50.
HS 22 Yorks v Sussex, Hove, 1949.
BB 5–56 Yorks v Northants, Bradford, 1949.
Clubs: Morecambe, Keighley, Saltaire, Silsden.

MASON, Andrew Lindsay
—————RHB, WK—————

Born Birmingham, 22 Sept 1943. Educ Lancaster RGS; Brasenose C, Oxford. Debut 1963.
OXFORD UNIVERSITY (15) 1963–65.
HS 47 Oxford U v N Zealanders, The Parks, 1965.

MASOOD IQBAL Qureshi
—————RHB, WK—————

Born Lahore, Pakistan, 17 Apr 1952. Educ Central Model S, Lahore; Punjab U. Debut 1969/70.
PAKISTAN DOMESTIC Lahore, Punjab University, Habib Bank, Universities, Lahore City, 1969/70–.
TOURS Pakistan to Australasia 1972/73. Pakistan to England 1978.
HS 69 Habib Bank v Sargodha, Lahore, 1978/79.
Club: Borton Hall.

MASSIE, Robert Arnold Lockyer
—————LHB, RMF—————

Born Subiaco, Perth, W Australia, 14 Apr 1947. Educ Mount Lawley HS. Debut 1965/66. *Wisden* 1973.
AUSTRALIA DOMESTIC Western Australia (28) 1965/66–74/75.
AUSTRALIA (6) 1972–72/73. *P* 1972/73 (2). *E* 1972 *(4).*
OTHER TOURS Australia to W Indies 1972/73. Ranji XI to India 1972/73.
HST 42 A v P, Sydney, 1972/73. HS as above.
BBT 8–53 (16–137 match) A v E, Lord's, 1972 (Test debut). BB as above.
RECORDS Match return of 16–137 (BBT above) best-ever for a Test debut and most wkts in a Test for Australia.
Clubs: Bassendean-Bayswater (Australia), Kilmarnock (Scotland).

MASTERS, Kevin David
—————LHB, RM—————

Born Chatham, Kent, 19 May 1961. Educ Fort Luton S, Chatham. Debut 1983.

KENT (4) 1983–.
HS 1 Kent v Hants, Bournemouth, 1983.
BB 2–26 Kent v Leics, Leicester, 1983.

MATHESON, John Alexander
—————RHB, WK—————

Born Dunedin, N Zealand, 26 Oct 1950. Educ Otago Boys' HS; Otago U; Worcester C, Oxford. Debut 1977.
OXFORD UNIVERSITY (1) 1977.
Did not bat.
Rugby: Otago, New Zealand Universities. Medical practitioner.

MATHEWS, Kenneth Patrick Arthur
—————RHB, OCC RM—————

Born Worthing, Sussex, 10 May 1926. Educ Felsted; Clare C, Cambridge. Debut 1950.
SUSSEX (6) 1950–51.
CAMBRIDGE UNIVERSITY (12) 1951 (Blue).
FREE FORESTERS (2) 1954–56.
MCC (1) 1956.
HS 77 Cambridge U v Surrey, Guildford, 1951.
Golf and hockey Blues. Father J. K. Mathews (Sussex).

MATHEWS, Michael John Anderson
—————RHB, LBG—————

Born Durban, S Africa, 6 Jan 1934. Educ Diocesan C, Rondesbosch; U of Cape Town; Lincoln C, Oxford. Debut 1957.
OXFORD UNIVERSITY (2) 1957.
HS 5 Oxford U v Free Foresters, The Parks, 1957.
BB 5–58 same match.
Clubs: Western Province, Free Foresters.

MATTHEWS, Albert John
—————RHB, OB—————

Born Tain, Ross-shire, Scotland, 29 Apr 1944. Debut 1965.
LEICESTERSHIRE (16) 1965–68.
HS 32 Leics v Glos, Leicester, 1967.
BB 4–87 Leics v Cambridge U, Leicester, 1967.

MATTHEWS, Austin David George
—————RHB, RFM—————

Born Penarth, S Wales, 3 May 1904. Died Llandudno, N Wales, 29 July

1977. Educ St David's C, Lampeter. Debut 1927. *P until 1939.*
NORTHAMPTONSHIRE (224) 1927–36. Cap.
GLAMORGAN (51) 1937–47. Cap.
ENGLAND (1) NZ 1937.
HST 2* E v NZ, Oval, 1937. HS 116 Northants v Warwicks, Edgbaston, 1929.
BB 7–12 Glam v Som, Pontypridd, 1946. Returned 14–132 match, Glam v Sussex, Hastings, 1937. Scored 955 runs @ 22.73 in 1929. Took 93 wkts @ 22.19 in 1933 and 93 wkts @ 14.29 in 1946. Glam assistant-secretary 1946. Club: Undercliffe 1949. Professional coach Stowe S 1937–50. Rugby: Northampton, Penarth, East Midlands, Welsh trialist; later referee. Table tennis: Wales.

MATTHEWS, Colin
————RHB, LFM————

Born Worksop, Notts, 17 Oct 1929. Debut 1950. *P.*
NOTTINGHAMSHIRE (84) 1950–59.
HS 41 Notts v Yorks, Trent Bridge, 1954.
BB 6–65 Notts v Derbys, Ilkeston, 1955. Club: Firbeck.

MATTHEWS, John Duncan
————LHB————

Born Rainhill, Lancs, 19 Sept 1921. Educ Shrewsbury; Edinburgh U; Magdalene C, Cambridge. Debut 1951.
SCOTLAND (5) 1951–55.
HS 29 Scotland v Northants, Edinburgh, 1951.
War-time Blue 1941–42. Club: Grange.

MATTHEWS, Robin Birkby
————RHB, RM————

Born Stockton-on-Tees, Co Durham, 30 Jan 1944. Educ City S, Lincoln. Debut 1971.
LEICESTERSHIRE (25) 1971–73.
HS 16* Leics v Sussex, Hove, 1972.
BB 7–51 same match.
Oxfordshire 1964–69.

MAUDSLEY, Ronald Harling
————RHB, RM————

Born Lostock Gralam, Cheshire, 8 Apr 1918. Died San Diego, California, 29 Sept 1981. Educ Malvern; Birmingham U; Brasenose C, Oxford. Debut 1946.
OXFORD UNIVERSITY (16) 1946–47 (Blue 1946–47).

WARWICKSHIRE (45) 1946–51. Cap 1946. Joint capt (with H. E. Dollery) 1948.
HS 130 Oxford U v Sussex, Chichester, 1946.
BB 6–54 Warwicks v Surrey, Oval, 1946. Scored 992 runs @ 29.17 in 1946.
Clubs: Harborne, Free Foresters, Frogs. Golf: Blue.

MAXWELL, Cecil Reginald Napp
————RHB, WK————

Born London, 21 May 1913. Died Taunton, Som, 25 Sept 1973. Educ Brighton C. Debut 1932.
SIR J. CAHN'S XI (5) 1932–38.
NOTTINGHAMSHIRE (16) 1936–39. Cap 1937.
MCC (4) 1938–39.
MIDDLESEX (4) 1946.
WORCESTERSHIRE (7) 1948–51.
TOURS Sir J. Cahn's XI to Ceylon 1936/37. Sir J. Cahn's XI to N Zealand 1938/39.
HS 268 Sir J. Cahn's XI v Leics, W Bridgford, 1935.
Gentlemen v Players (2) 1935–37.

MAXWELL, Laurence Evan
————RHB, OB————

Born Barbados, 17 Jan 1941. Debut 1968/69.
W INDIES DOMESTIC Barbados 1968/69–78/79.
TOUR Barbados to England 1969.
HS 19 Barbados v Trinidad, Bridgetown, 1977/78.
BB 5–73 Barbados v Combined Islands, Castries, 1977/78.
Club: Police (Barbados).

MAY, Barry
————RHB————

Born Johannesburg, S Africa, 1 Nov 1944. Educ Prince Edward S, Salisbury, Rhodesia; Cape Town U; Brasenose C, Oxford. Debut 1970.
OXFORD UNIVERSITY (22) 1970–72 (Blue 1970–72). Capt 1971.
HS 103 Oxford U v Glam, The Parks, 1971.

MAY, Peter Barker Howard
————RHB————

Born Reading, Berkshire, 31 Dec 1929. Educ Charterhouse; Pembroke C, Cambridge. Debut 1948. *Wisden* 1952.
COMBINED SERVICES (7) 1948–49.
CAMBRIDGE UNIVERSITY (38) 1950–52 (Blue 1950–52).

SURREY (208) 1950–63. Cap 1950. Capt 1957–62.
ENGLAND (66) 1951–61. A 1953 (2), 1956 (5), 1961 (4); SA 1951 (2), 1955 (5); WI 1957 (5); NZ 1958 (5); I 1952 (4), 1959 (3); P 1954 (4). *A 1954/55 (5), 1958/59 (5); SA 1956/57 (5); WI 1953/54 (5), 1959/60 (3); NZ 1954/55 (2), 1958/59 (2).* Capt 41.
HST 285* E v WI, Edgbaston, 1957. HS as above.
1000 RUNS (11 + 3) 2554 @ 51.08 in 1953. 2000 runs (5).
RECORDS During HST (above) added 411 for 4th wkt with M. C. Cowdrey, world Test record. Capt in 41 Tests (including 35 consecutively 1955–59), England record.
Scored centuries in four successive fc inns in 1956/57.
Gentlemen v Players (13) 1951–61. England selector 1965–68, 1982– (chairman 1982–). Berkshire 1946. Club: Butterflies. MCC Hon. member; committee 1956–. Soccer: Blue (capt). Father-in-law A. H. H. Gilligan (Sussex, England).

MAYES, Richard
————RHB————

Born Littlebourne, Kent, 7 Oct 1921. Educ Simon Langton GS, Canterbury. Debut 1947. *P.*
KENT (80) 1947–53. Cap 1952.
HS 134 Kent v Sussex, Tunbridge Wells, 1952.
Suffolk 1957–63. Son B. Mayes (Suffolk).

MAYNARD, Christopher
————RHB, WK————

Born Haslemere, Surrey, 8 Apr 1958. Educ Bishop Vesey's GS, Sutton Coldfield. Debut 1978.
WARWICKSHIRE (23) 1978–81.
LANCASHIRE (53) 1982–.
TOUR D. H. Robins' XI to N Zealand 1979/80.
HS 85 Warwicks v Kent, Edgbaston, 1979.
Only player since 1873 to appear in competitive first-team matches for two counties in one season: Warwicks (John Player League) and Lancashire (Schweppes County Championship) in 1982.

MEAD-BRIGGS, Richard
————RHB, RFM/RM————

Born Sturry, Kent, 25 Mar 1902. Died Birmingham, 15 Jan 1956. Educ King's S, Canterbury. Debut 1946.

WARWICKSHIRE (2) 1946.
HS 44* Warwicks v Leics, Edgbaston, 1946.
Club: Harborne.

MEADS, Eric Alfred
——RHB, WK——

Born Nottingham, 17 Aug 1916. Educ Carrington S. Debut 1939. P.
NOTTINGHAMSHIRE (205) 1939–53. Cap 1939. Benefit (£1575) 1953.
HS 56* Notts v Worcs, Trent Bridge, 1948.
Club: Ellerslie House.

MEAKIN, Douglas
——RHB, RMF——

Born Swadlincote, Derbys, 28 Mar 1929. Educ Chesterfield Technical S. Debut 1959.
COMBINED SERVICES (4) 1959–62.
HS 16 Combined Services v Warwicks, Portland Road, Edgbaston, 1959.
BB 4–56 Combined Services v Som, Taunton, 1959.
Bedfordshire 1952–62. Clubs: Hitchin, Torquay, Paignton, Norwich Wanderers, Royal Air Force.

MEALE, Trevor
——LHB——

Born Auckland, N Zealand, 11 Nov 1928. Debut 1951/52.
N ZEALAND DOMESTIC Wellington (12) 1951/52–53/54.
NEW ZEALAND (2) E 1958.
HST 10 NZ v E, Edgbaston, 1958. HS 130 Wellington v Fiji, Wellington, 1953/54.

MEDHURST, Roy H.
——RHB, RFM——

Born East Chittington, Sussex, 30 Apr 1922. Debut 1948. P.
SUSSEX (3) 1948.
HS 15* Sussex v Cambridge U, Fenner's, 1948.
Cambridgeshire 1951. Club: Ditchling.

MEDLYCOTT, Keith Thomas
——RHB, SLA——

Born Whitechapel, London, 12 May 1965. Educ Parmiters GS, Wandsworth. Debut 1984.
SURREY (6) 1984.
HS 117* Surrey v Cambridge U, Banstead, 1984 (on fc debut).

RECORDS During HS (above) added 189* for 8th wkt with N. J. Falkner (101*); first instance in Britain of two fc debutants scoring hundreds in same inns.

MEE, Andrew Alexander Graham
——RHB——

Born Johannesburg, S Africa, 29 May 1963. Educ St Alban's Pretoria; Merchant Taylors' S, Northwood; Oriel C, Oxford. Debut 1984.
OXFORD UNIVERSITY (1) 1984.
HS 2 Oxford U v Glos, The Parks, 1984.

MEE, Steven Robert
——RHB, RM——

Born Nottingham, 6 Apr 1965. Educ Ellis Guilford S, Nottingham. Debut 1984.
NOTTINGHAMSHIRE (1) 1984.
Did not bat.
BB 2–44 Notts v Cambridge U, Trent Bridge, 1984.

MEESON, Martin Stewart
——LHB——

Born London, 6 Nov 1933. Educ Bedford S; Pembroke C, Cambridge. Debut 1957.
CAMBRIDGE UNIVERSITY (1) 1957.
HS 21 Cambridge U v Kent, Fenner's, 1957.

MEHTA, Praful Swantilal
——LHB, WK——

Born Dar-es-Salaam, Tanganyika, 1941. Debut 1975.
EAST AFRICA to England (1) 1975.
HS 17 E Africa v Sri Lanka, Taunton, 1975.

MELLE, Michael George
——RHB, RFM——

Born Johannesburg, S Africa, 3 June 1930. Debut 1948/49.
S AFRICA DOMESTIC Transvaal 1948/49–51/52, Western Province 1953/54.
SOUTH AFRICA (7) 1949/50–52/53. A 1949/50 (2). E 1951 (1); A 1952/53 (4).
HST 17 SA v E, Oval, 1951. HS 59 W Province v Natal, Cape Town, 1953/54.
BBT 6–71 SA v A, Brisbane, 1952/53. BB 9–22 S Africans v Tasmania, Launceston, 1952/53.
Returned analysis of 12–7–8–8, Transvaal v Griqualand West, J'burg, 1950/51.

Father B. G. von B. Melle (Transvaal, Oxford U, Hants).

MELLOR, Alan John
——RHB, SLA——

Born Horninglow, Staffordshire, 4 July 1959. Educ Dovecliffe GS, Dovecliffe. Debut 1978.
DERBYSHIRE (13) 1978–80.
HS 10* Derbys v Essex, Southend, 1978.
BB 5–52 Derbys v Kent, Maidstone, 1978 (fc debut).
Staffordshire 1981. Club: Porthill Park.

MELLOR, James Philip
——RHB, OB——

Born Oxford, 19 Jan 1953. Educ Rydal S; Emmanuel C, Cambridge. Debut 1973.
CAMBRIDGE UNIVERSITY (3) 1973.
HS 22 Cambridge U v Leics, Fenner's, 1973.

MELLUISH, Michael Edward Lovelace
——RHB, WK——

Born Westcliff, Essex, 13 June 1932. Educ Rossall; Caius C, Cambridge. Debut 1954.
CAMBRIDGE UNIVERSITY (41) 1954–56 (Blue 1954–56). Capt 1956.
MIDDLESEX (1) 1957.
D. R. JARDINE'S XI (3) 1957–58.
MCC (1) 1959.
HS 36 Cambridge U v Free Foresters, Fenner's, 1955.
Gentlemen v Players (3) 1956–57. MCC committee from 1975.

MELVILLE, Alan
——RHB, LB——

Born Carnarvon, S Africa, 19 May 1910. Died Kruger Park, Transvaal, S Africa, 18 Apr 1983. Educ Michaelhouse S, Natal; Trinity C, Oxford. Debut 1928/29. Wisden 1948.
S AFRICA DOMESTIC Natal 1928/29–29/30, Transvaal 1936/37–48/49.
OXFORD UNIVERSITY (36) 1930–33 (Blue 1930–33). Capt 1931–32.
SUSSEX (86) 1932–36. Cap. Capt 1934–35.
SOUTH AFRICA (11) 1938/39–48/49. E 1938/39 (5), 1948/49 (1). E 1947 (5). Capt 10.
HST 189 SA v E, Trent Bridge, 1947. HS 189 above.
BB 5–17 Sussex v Glos, Gloucester, 1933.

1000 RUNS (3) 1904 @ 40.51 in 1935.
RECORD Added 299 for 7th wkt with B. Mitchell, Transvaal v Griqualand West, Kimberley, 1946/47, S African fc record.
Scored four consecutive Test centuries and six consecutive Test fifties (67, 78, 103, 189, 104*, 117), SA v E, 1938/39 and 1947.
Gentlemen v Players (4) 1934–36. MCC Hon. member. Nephew C. D. McL. Melville (Oxford U).

MELVILLE, Christopher Duncan McLean
RHB, RMF

Born Pietermaritzburg, S Africa, 4 Oct 1935. Educ Michaelhouse S, Natal; Trinity C, Oxford. Debut 1956.
OXFORD UNIVERSITY (12) 1956–57 (Blue 1957).
HS 142 Oxford U v Leics, The Parks, 1957.
Uncle A. Melville (Oxford U, Sussex, S Africa).

MELVILLE, James
RHB, SLA

Born Barrow-in-Furness, Lancs, 15 Mar 1909. Died Coventry, 2 Aug 1961. Educ Barrow GS. Debut 1946.
WARWICKSHIRE (2) 1946.
HS 13 Warwicks v Kent, Edgbaston, 1946.
BB 3–34 Warwicks v Hants, Coventry, 1946.
Clubs: Millom, Courtaulds. Soccer: Blackburn Rovers, Northampton Town, Hull City. Son R. Melville (Rugby for Coventry).

MELVILLE, James Edward
RHB, RFM

Born Streatham, London, 3 Mar 1936. Educ St Aidan's C, Grahamstown, S Africa; Beaumont C. Debut 1962.
KENT (6) 1962–63.
HS 6 Kent v Som, Gillingham, 1963.
BB 4–78 Kent v Yorks, Middlesbrough, 1962.
Club: Blackheath.

MENCE, Michael David
LHB, RM

Born Newbury, Berkshire, 13 Apr 1944. Educ Bradfield. Debut 1962.
WARWICKSHIRE (31) 1962–65.
GLOUCESTERSHIRE (22) 1966–67.
HS 78 Glos v Sussex, Hove, 1967.

BB 5–26 Warwicks v Derbys, Derby, 1964.
Berkshire 1961, 1968–81. Clubs: Bradfield Waifs, Smethwick. Member of MCC committee. Father J. A. Mence (Berkshire).

MENDIS, Gehan Dixon
RHB

Born Colombo, Ceylon, 24 Apr 1955. Educ Brighton and Hove GS; Durham U. Debut 1974.
SUSSEX (176) 1974–. Cap 1980.
TOUR International XI to Pakistan 1981/82. International XI to Jamaica 1982/83.
HS 209 Sussex v Som, Hove, 1984.
1000 RUNS (5) 1627 @ 40.68 in 1983.
Club: Eastbourne.

MENDIS, Louis Rohan *Duleep*
RHB, WK

Born Moratuwa, Ceylon, 25 Aug 1952. Educ St Thomas' C, Colombo. Debut 1971/72.
SRI LANKA DOMESTIC Ceylon (Sri Lanka) 1971/72–.
SRI LANKA (10) 1981/82–84. E 1981/82 (1); A 1982/83 (1); NZ 1983/84 (3). *E 1984 (1); I 1982/83 (1); P 1981/82 (3).* Capt 5.
OTHER TOURS Sri Lanka to India 1972/73, 1974/75, 1975/76, 1976/77, 1982/83. Sri Lanka to England 1975, 1979, 1981. Sri Lanka to Australasia 1982/83. Sri Lanka to Zimbabwe 1982/83.
HST 111 SL v E, Lord's, 1984 (debut at Lord's). HS 194 Sri Lanka Board President's XI v Tamil Nadu, Madras, 1976/77.
Only Sri Lankan to score a hundred in each inns of a Test, 105 and 105, SL v I, Madras, 1982/83.

MENDL, Derek Francis
RHB, WK

Born Buenos Aires, Argentina, 1 Aug 1914. Educ Repton. Debut 1951.
FREE FORESTERS (1) 1951.
MCC (1) 1951.
HS 26 MCC v Cambridge U, Lord's, 1951.
Clubs: I Zingari, Paddington, Waverley, Gordon, Merewether (Australia), MCC. Brother J. F. Mendl (Scotland).

MENDL, Jack Francis
RHB

Born Hurlingham, Argentina, 6 Dec 1911. Educ Repton; Oxford U. Debut 1949.

MINOR COUNTIES (1) 1949.
SCOTLAND (5) 1953–55.
MCC (1) 1957.
HS 65 Scotland v Derbys, Buxton, 1954.
Oxfordshire 1946–55. Brother D. F. Mendl (MCC).

MERCER, Ian Pickford
RHB, RMF

Born Oldham, Lancs, 30 May 1930. Debut 1965.
MINOR COUNTIES (1) 1965.
HS 1 Minor Counties v S Africans, Jesmond, 1965.
Norfolk 1964–70. Clubs: Werneth, Norwich Wanderers, Cromer.

MERCER, John
RHB, RMF

Born Southwick, Sussex, 22 Apr 1895. Debut 1919. *P. Wisden 1927.*
SUSSEX (12) 1919–21.
GLAMORGAN (412) 1922–39. Cap 1924. Benefit 1936.
WALES (8) 1923–30.
NORTHAMPTONSHIRE (1) 1947.
TOURS MCC to India and Ceylon 1926/27. Sir J. Cahn's XI to Jamaica 1928/29.
HS 72 Glam v Surrey, Oval, 1934.
BB 10–51 Glam v Worcs, Worcester, 1936.
100 WKTS (9) 145 @ 20.88 in 1929.
RECORD BB (above) best-ever inns return in fc match for Glam.
Players v Gentlemen (4) 1926–34. Northants coach 1947–62; scorer 1963–81. Clubs: Southwick, Yeadon.

MERCER, William *Norman*
RHB, LBG

Born Prescot, Lancs, 30 May 1922. Debut 1942/43.
S AFRICA DOMESTIC South African Air Force 1942/43.
SUSSEX (2) 1948–56.
HS 24 Sussex v Derbys, Worthing, 1948.
BB 3–31 S African Air Force v The Rest, J'burg, 1942/43.
Club: Worthing.

MERCHANT Thackersey, Vijay Madhavji
RHB, RM

Born Bombay, India, 12 Oct 1911. Educ Sydenham C, Bombay. Debut 1929/30. *Wisden 1937.*
INDIA DOMESTIC Hindus 1929/30–45/46, Bombay 1933/34–50/51.
INDIA (10) 1933/34–51/52. E 1933/34 (3), 1951/52 (1). *E 1936 (3), 1946 (3).*

HST 154 I v E, Delhi, 1951/52. HS 359*
Bombay v Maharashtra, Bombay, 1943/
44 (adding 371 for 6th wkt with R. S.
Modi, Indian fc record).
BB 5–73 Bombay v W India, Jamnagar,
1937/38.
1000 RUNS (2 + 1) 2385 @ 74.53 in 1946.
Scored 3639 runs (@ 98.75) and 16 centuries (in 47 inns) in Ranji Trophy.
Scored century (142) and performed
hat-trick in same match, Dr Perera's XI
v Sir H. Mehta's XI, Bombay 1946/47.
Scored centuries in four successive fc
inns in 1941/42 and four double-
centuries in 1944/45.
MCC Hon. member. Chairman India
Test selectors 1963–71. Cricket writer
on Indian affairs. Brother U. M. Merchant (India).

MERRITT, William Edward
RHB, LBG

Born Sumner, N Zealand, 18 Aug 1908.
Died Christchurch, N Zealand, 9 June
1977. Debut 1926/27. *P from 1938.*
N ZEALAND DOMESTIC Canterbury (24)
1926/27–35/36.
NORTHAMPTONSHIRE (41) 1938–46. Cap
1939.
NEW ZEALAND (6) 1929/30–31. E 1929/30
(4). *E 1931 (2).*
HST 19 NZ v E, Christchurch, 1929/30.
HS 87 Northants v Sussex, Kettering,
1939.
BBT 4–104 NZ v E, Lord's, 1931. BB
8–41 (12–130 match) N Zealanders v
Essex, Leyton, 1931.
100 WKTS (1) 107 @ 23.64 in 1927
(passed 19th birthday during season).
Scored 926 runs @ 22.58 and took 87
wkts @ 28.43 in 1939.
Club: Dudley. Subsequently cricket
commentator in N Zealand.

MERRY, William Gerald
RHB, RFM

Born Newbury, Berkshire, 8 Aug 1955.
Educ Chell's Sec S. Debut 1979.
MIDDLESEX (26) 1979–82.
TOURS D. H. Robins' XI to N Zealand
1979/80. M'sex to Zimbabwe 1980/81.
HS 14* M'sex v Oxford U, The Parks,
1981.
BB 4–24 M'sex v Som, Taunton, 1980.
Hertfordshire 1976–78. Club: Stevenage.

MERSON, Ronald David
RHB

Born Stockton-on-Tees, Co Durham,
25 July 1925. Educ Merchiston Castle;
Edinburgh U. Debut 1947.
SCOTLAND (1) 1947.

HS 15 Scotland v Warwicks, Edgbaston,
1947.
Edinburgh University.

METCALFE, Ashley Anthony
RHB, OB

Born Horsforth, Yorks, 25 Dec 1963.
Educ Bradford GS. Debut 1983.
YORKSHIRE (10) 1983–.
HS 122 Yorks v Notts, Bradford, 1983
(1st inns of fc debut).
RECORD During HS (above) became third
and youngest Yorks batsman to score
century on fc debut.
Father-in-law R. Illingworth (Yorks,
Leics and England).

METCALFE, Stanley Gordon
RHB

Born Horsforth, Yorks, 20 June 1932.
Educ Leeds GS; Pembroke C, Oxford.
Debut 1954.
OXFORD UNIVERSITY (17) 1954–56 (Blue
1956).
FREE FORESTERS (8) 1958–68.
HS 133* Free Foresters v Oxford U, The
Parks, 1959.
BB 2–32 D. R. Jardine's XI v Oxford U,
Eastbourne, 1958.
Clubs: Hampstead, Arabs, I Zingari.

METSON, Colin Peter
RHB, WK

Born Cuffley, Hertfordshire, 2 July
1963. Educ Stanborough S, Welwyn;
Enfield GS. Debut 1981.
MIDDLESEX (13) 1981–.
HS 96 M'sex v Glos, Uxbridge, 1984.

MEYER, Barrie John
RHB, WK

Born Bournemouth, Hants, 21 Aug
1932. Debut 1957. *P.*
GLOUCESTERSHIRE (406) 1957–71. Cap
1958. Benefit 1971.
HS 63 Glos v Indians, Cheltenham, 1959
and 63 v Oxford U, Bristol, 1962 and 63
v Sussex, Bristol, 1964.
Made 825 dismissals (708 ct, 117 st) in
career.
Fc umpire 1973– (14 Tests, 1978–84).
Soccer: Bristol Rovers, Plymouth
Argyle, Newport County, Bristol City.
Soccer career ended by gout.

MEYER, Rollo John Oliver (Jack)
RHB, RM

Born Ampthill, Bedfordshire, 15 Mar
1905. Educ Haileybury and ISC;

Pembroke C, Cambridge. Debut 1924.
CAMBRIDGE UNIVERSITY (32) 1924–26
(Blue 1924–26).
SOMERSET (65) 1936–49. Cap. Capt 1947.
MCC (1) 1950.
INDIA DOMESTIC Bombay, Western
India, Europeans (Bombay), 1926/
27–34/35.
HS 202* Som v Lancs, Taunton, 1936.
BB 9–160 (16–188 match) Europeans v
Muslims, Bombay, 1927/28.
Gentlemen v Players (1) 1938. Bedford-
shire 1949–50. Golf: Blue. Former
headmaster Millfield S.

MIDDLETON, Tony Charles
RHB, SLA

Born Winchester, Hants, 1 Feb 1964.
Educ Montgomery of Alamein, Win-
chester; Peter Symonds C, Winchester.
Debut 1984.
HAMPSHIRE (1) 1984.
HS 10 Hants v Kent, Bournemouth,
1984.

MILBURN, Barry Douglas
RHB, WK

Born Dunedin, N Zealand, 24 Nov
1943. Debut 1963/64.
N ZEALAND DOMESTIC Otago (53) 1963/
64–82/83.
NEW ZEALAND (3) WI 1968/69.
TOURS N Zealand to England 1969. N
Zealand to India and Pakistan 1969/70.
HST 4* NZ v WI, Auckland, 1968/69 and
4* v WI, Wellington, 1968/69. HS 103
Otago v Wellington, Alexandra, 1980/
81.
Club: Albion.

MILBURN, Colin
RHB, RM

Born Burnopfield, Co Durham, 23 Oct
1941. Educ Stanley GS. Debut 1960. *P.*
Wisden 1967.
NORTHAMPTONSHIRE (196) 1960–74.
Cap 1963. Benefit 1971.
AUSTRALIA DOMESTIC Western Australia
(17) 1966/67–68/69.
ENGLAND (9) 1966–68/69. A 1968 (2);
WI 1966 (4); I 1967 (1); P 1967 (1). *P
1968/69 (1).*
OTHER TOURS MCC to E Africa 1963/64.
MCC to W Indies 1967/68.
HST 139 E v P, Karachi, 1968/69. HS 243
W Australia v Queensland, Brisbane,
1968/69 (scored 181 in two hrs between
lunch and tea).
BB 6–59 Northants v Glam, Swansea,
1962.
1000 RUNS (6 + 1) 1861 @ 48.97 in 1966.

Durham 1959, 1975–76. Clubs: Chester-le-Street, Lowerhouse, Burnopfield.
MCC Hon. member. Lost eye in car accident in May 1969. Autobiography *Largely Cricket* (1968).

MILES, Othniel
—RHB, OB—

Born Clarendon, Jamaica, 23 Sept 1939. Died Kingston, Jamaica, Feb 1982. Debut 1967/68.
JAMAICA 1967/68–75/76.
TOUR Jamaica to England 1970.
HS 43* Jamaica v Barbados, Bridgetown, 1968/69.
BB 7–71 Jamaica v Guyana, Kingston, 1968/69.
Club: Clarendon.

MILLARD, David Edward Shaxson
—RHB, OB—

Born Cape Town, S Africa, 3 Apr 1931. Died Cape Town, S Africa, 30 Jan 1978. Educ Bishop's C, W Province; Worcester C, Oxford. Debut 1951/52.
S AFRICA DOMESTIC Western Province 1951/52–54/55, Eastern Province 1952/53–53/54.
OXFORD UNIVERSITY (2) 1965.
HS 73 E Province v OFS, Port Elizabeth, 1952/53.
BB 6–68 E Province v Natal, Port Elizabeth, 1952/53.

MILLENER, David *John*
—RHB, RMF—

Born Auckland, N Zealand, 2 May 1944. Educ Auckland GS; Auckland U; St Catherine's C and Jesus C, Oxford. Debut 1964/65.
N ZEALAND DOMESTIC Auckland (13) 1964/65–67/68.
OXFORD UNIVERSITY (13) 1969–70 (Blue 1969–70).
HS 24 Oxford U v Cambridge U, Lord's, 1970.
BB 4–97 Oxford U v D. H. Robins' XI, Eastbourne, 1969.
Cornwall. Nuclear physicist.

MILLER, Andrew John Trevor
—LHB, RM—

Born Chesham, Buckinghamshire, 30 May 1963. Educ Haileybury and ISC; St Edmund Hall, Oxford. Debut 1982.
OXFORD UNIVERSITY (15) 1982–84 (Blue 1983–84).
MIDDLESEX (8) 1983–.

HS 128* Oxford U v Cambridge U, Lord's, 1984.
1000 RUNS (1) 1002 @ 43.57 in 1983.

MILLER, Frank Joseph
—RHB, WK—

Born Cork, Ireland, 2 Oct 1916. Educ Belvedere C, Dublin. Debut 1949.
IRELAND (7) 1949–54.
HS 18* Ireland v Scotland, Paisley, 1952.
Club: Railway Union.

MILLER, Geoffrey
—RHB, OB—

Born Chesterfield, Derbys, 8 Sept 1952. Educ Chesterfield GS. Debut 1973.
DERBYSHIRE (199) 1973–. Cap 1976. Capt 1979–81.
S AFRICA DOMESTIC Natal 1983/84.
ENGLAND (34) 1976–84. A 1977 (2); WI 1976 (1), 1984 (2); NZ 1978 (2); I 1979 (3), 1982 (1); P 1978 (3), 1982 (1). *A 1978/79 (6), 1979/80 (1), 1982/83 (5); WI 1980/81 (1); NZ 1977/78 (3); P 1977/78 (3).*
OTHER TOURS MCC to India, Sri Lanka and Australia 1976/77.
HST 98* E v P, Lahore, 1977/78 and 98 E v I, Old Trafford, 1982. HS 130 Derbys v Lancs, Old Trafford, 1984.
BBT 5–44 E v A, Sydney, 1978/79. BB 8–70 Derbys v Leics, Coalville, 1982.
Scored 933 runs @ 32.17 and took 87 wkts @ 25.70 in 1984.
CWC Best Young Cricketer of 1976.
Club: Chesterfield.

MILLER, George
—LHB, RFM—

Born Edinburgh, Scotland, 19 Aug 1929. Educ Heriot's; Edinburgh U. Debut 1955.
SCOTLAND (1) 1955.
HS 6* Scotland v Derbys, Edinburgh, 1955.
Club: Heriot's Former Pupils.

MILLER, Hamish David Sneddon
—RHB, RFM—

Born Blackpool, Lancs, 20 Apr 1943. Educ Rondesbosch HS; U of Cape Town; U of Wales. Debut 1962/63.
S AFRICA DOMESTIC Western Province 1962/63, Orange Free State 1969/70–70/71.
GLAMORGAN (27) 1963–66.
HS 81 Glam v Glos, Cheltenham, 1964.
BB 7–48 Glam v Notts, Trent Bridge, 1964.

S Africa Country Districts to S America 1971/72.

MILLER, Keith Ross
—RHB, RF—

Born Sunshine, Australia, 28 Nov 1919. Educ Melbourne HS. Debut 1937/38. *Wisden 1954.*
AUSTRALIA DOMESTIC Victoria (18) 1937/38–46/47, New South Wales (50) 1947/48–55/56.
NOTTINGHAMSHIRE (1) 1959.
AUSTRALIA (55) 1945/46–56/57. E 1946/47 (5), 1950/51 (5), 1954/55 (4); SA 1952/53 (4); WI 1951/52 (5); I 1947/48 (5). *E 1948 (5), 1953 (5), 1956 (5); SA 1949/50 (5); WI 1954/55 (5); NZ 1945/46 (1); P 1956/57 (1).*
OTHER TOURS Australian Services to England 1945 and to India and Ceylon 1945/46.
HST 147 A v WI, Kingston, 1954/55. HS 281* Australians v Leics, Leicester, 1956.
BBT 7–60 A v E, Brisbane, 1946/47. BB 7–12 NSW v S Australia, Sydney, 1955/56.
1000 RUNS (2 + 2) 1433 @ 51.17 in 1953.
Scored 181 on fc debut, Victoria v Tasmania, Melbourne, 1937/38, and in only match for Notts 102* v Cambridge U, Trent Bridge, 1959.
MCC Hon. member. Cricket journalist and author of several books with R. S. Whitington. MBE for services to cricket.

MILLER, Lawrence Somerville Martin
—LHB—

Born New Plymouth, N Zealand, 31 Mar 1923. Educ New Plymouth HS. Debut 1950/51.
N ZEALAND DOMESTIC Central Districts (8) 1950/51–52/53, Wellington (22) 1954/55–59/60.
NEW ZEALAND (13) 1952/53–58. SA 1952/53 (2); WI 1955/56 (3). *E 1958 (4); SA 1953/54 (4).*
HST 47 NZ v WI, Auckland, 1955/56. HS 144 Wellington v Auckland, Auckland, 1955/56.
1000 RUNS (1) 1148 @ 30.21 in 1958.

MILLER, Martin Ellis
—RHB, OB—

Born Lytham St Anne's, Lancs, 15 Dec 1940. Educ Prince Henry's GS, Hohne, West Germany; St John's C, Cambridge. Debut 1963.
CAMBRIDGE UNIVERSITY (12) 1963 (Blue).

HS 21* Cambridge U v Surrey, Fenner's, 1963.
BB 6-89 Cambridge U v M'sex, Fenner's, 1963. Club: Richmond.

MILLER, Roger Simon
RHB, RFM

Born Hailsham, Sussex, 16 Feb 1938. Educ Harrow; Trinity C, Oxford. Debut 1959.
MCC (1) 1959.
HS 1* MCC v Oxford U, Lord's, 1959.
BB 3-41 same match.
Dorset 1963-67. Sussex 2nd XI.

MILLER, Roland
RHB, SLA

Born Philadelphia, Co Durham, 6 Jan 1941. Debut 1961. P.
WARWICKSHIRE (133) 1961-68.
HS 72 Warwicks v Worcs, Edgbaston, 1965.
BB 6-28 Warwicks v Lancs, Old Trafford, 1963.
Durham 1960. Clubs: Philadelphia, Aston Unity, West Bromwich Dartmouth, Mitchells and Butlers, Milnrow.

MILLETT, Frederick William
RHB, OB

Born Macclesfield, Cheshire, 30 Mar 1928. Educ King's S, Macclesfield. Debut 1960.
MINOR COUNTIES (7) 1960-73.
HS 102* Minor Counties v W Indians, Longton, 1969.
Cheshire 1949-72 (capt 1960-70). MCC committee 1973-81.

MILLMAN, Geoffrey
RHB, WK

Born Bedford, 2 Oct 1934. Educ Bedford Modern S. Debut 1956. P.
COMBINED SERVICES (2) 1956.
NOTTINGHAMSHIRE (257) 1957-65. Cap 1957. Capt 1963-65.
ENGLAND (6) 1961/62-62. P 1962 (2). I 1961/62 (2); P 1961/62 (2).
HST 32* E v I, Madras, 1961/62. HS 131* Notts v Kent, Trent Bridge, 1960.
1000 RUNS (2) 1350 @ 22.50 in 1961.
Players v Gentlemen (2) 1961-62. Bedfordshire 1954-56, 1966-68.

MILLNER, David
RHB, OB

Born Dove Holes, Derbys, 24 July 1938. Debut 1960. P.

DERBYSHIRE (31) 1960-63.
HS 80 Derbys v Kent, Derby, 1961.
Club: Elland.

MILLS, Anthony Oliver Henry
RHB, RM/OB

Born Sherston, nr Malmesbury, Wiltshire, 12 Feb 1920. Educ Malmesbury GS. Debut 1939. P.
GLOUCESTERSHIRE (4) 1939-48.
HS 39 Glos v Combined Services, Gloucester, 1948.
BB 2-28 Glos v Cambridge U, Bristol, 1939.
Wiltshire 1954-61. Clubs: Chippenham, Banstead, Fife.

MILLS, David Cecil
RHB, RM

Born Camborne, Cornwall, 23 Apr 1937. Educ Clifton; Emmanuel C, Cambridge. Debut 1958.
GLOUCESTERSHIRE (1) 1958.
FREE FORESTERS (1) 1960.
HS 17 Glos v Cambridge U, Stroud, 1958.
Club: Old Cliftonians. Rugby: Blue, Harlequins, Cornwall.

MILLS, George Thomas
RHB, WK

Born Redditch, Worcs, 12 Sept 1923. Died Bromsgrove, Worcs, 15 Sept 1983. Educ Redditch HS; Birmingham U. Debut 1953.
WORCESTERSHIRE (2) 1953.
HS 23 Worcs v Cambridge U, Fenner's, 1953.
Clubs: Stourbridge, Redditch, Birmingham University (captained them to UAU Trophy 1950).

MILLS, John Michael
RHB, LBG

Born Birmingham, 27 July 1921. Educ Oundle; Corpus Christi C, Cambridge. Debut 1946.
CAMBRIDGE UNIVERSITY (34) 1946-48 (Blue 1946-48). Capt 1948.
WARWICKSHIRE (4) 1946.
HS 44 Cambridge U v Essex, Fenner's, 1947.
BB 7-69 Cambridge U v Yorks, Fenner's, 1946.
Club: Harborne. Son J. P. C. Mills (Northants, Cambridge U).

MILLS, John Peter Crispin
RHB, RM/OB

Born Kettering, Northants, 6 Dec 1958. Educ Oundle; Corpus Christi C, Cambridge. Debut 1979.
CAMBRIDGE UNIVERSITY (37) 1979-82 (Blue 1979-82). Capt 1982 (vice-capt to D. R. Pringle, who did not play against Oxford U).
NORTHAMPTONSHIRE (3) 1981.
HS 111 Oxford and Cambridge Universities v Sri Lankans, The Parks, 1981.
Cambridgeshire 1980. Club: Peterborough. Father J. M. Mills (Cambridge U, Warwicks).

MILNER, Joseph
RHB

Born Johannesburg, S Africa, 22 Aug 1937. Educ Athlone HS, Johannesburg, S Africa. Debut 1957. P.
ESSEX (66) 1957-61. Cap 1961.
HS 135 Essex v Leics, Leicester, 1959.
1000 RUNS (1) 1387 @ 28.89 in 1961.
Players v Gentlemen (1) 1961. Club: Walthamstow.

MILTON, Clement Arthur
RHB, RM

Born Bristol, 10 Mar 1928. Educ Cotham GS, Bristol. Debut 1948. P. Wisden 1959.
GLOUCESTERSHIRE (585) 1948-74. Cap 1949. Capt 1968. Benefit (£3235) 1961.
ENGLAND (6) 1958-59. NZ 1958 (2); I 1959 (2). A 1958/59 (2).
HST 104* E v NZ, Headingley, 1958 (Test debut; on the field throughout match). HS 170 Glos v Sussex, Cheltenham, 1965.
BB 5-64 Glos v Glam, Gloucester, 1950.
1000 RUNS (16) 2089 @ 46.42 in 1967.
Twice leading catcher (non-wicketkeeper) in season: 1954 (44 ct) and 1956 (63 ct). Took 758 catches in career. Players v Gentlemen (1) 1958. Soccer: Arsenal, Bristol City, England (1 cap).

MINNEY, John Henry
RHB

Born Finedon, Northants, 25 Apr 1939. Educ Oundle; Clare C, Cambridge. Debut 1959.
CAMBRIDGE UNIVERSITY (14) 1959-61.
NORTHAMPTONSHIRE (5) 1961-67.
HS 58 Northants v M'sex, Northampton, 1967.
Club: Oundle Rovers.

MINNS, Robert Ernest Frederick
——————RHB——————

Born Penang, Malaya, 18 Nov 1940. Educ King's S, Canterbury; Corpus Christi C, Oxford. Debut 1959.
KENT (2) 1959–63.
OXFORD UNIVERSITY (18) 1962–63 (Blue 1962–63).
HS 81 Oxford U v Sussex, Hove, 1963.

MISCHLER, Norman Martin
——————RHB, WK——————

Born Paddington, London, 9 Oct 1920. Educ St Paul's S; St Catharine's C, Cambridge. Debut 1946.
INDIA DOMESTIC Europeans 1941/42–43/44.
CAMBRIDGE UNIVERSITY (18) 1946–47 (Blue 1946–47).
FREE FORESTERS (3) 1949–51.
HS 76 Cambridge U v Som, Bath, 1947.

MISSON, Francis Michael
——————RHB, RFM——————

Born Darlinghurst, NSW, Australia, 19 Nov 1938. Debut 1958/59.
AUSTRALIA DOMESTIC New South Wales (42) 1958/59–63/64.
AUSTRALIA (5) 1960/61–61. WI 1960/61 (3). E 1961 (2).
OTHER TOUR Australia to N Zealand 1959/60.
HST 25* A v E, Lord's, 1961. HS 51* NSW v S Australia, Adelaide, 1961/62.
BBT 4–58 A v WI, Melbourne, 1960/61.
BB 6–75 Australians v Sussex, Hove, 1961.
Clubs: Glebe-South Sydney (Australia), Accrington (Lancashire).

MITCHELL, Arthur (Ticker)
——————RHB——————

Born Baildon, Yorks, 13 Sept 1902. Died Bradford, Yorks, 25 Dec 1976. Debut 1922. P.
YORKSHIRE (400) 1922–45. Cap 1928. Benefit (£2227) 1937.
ENGLAND (6) 1933/34–36. SA 1935 (2); I 1936 (1). I 1933/34 (3).
OTHER TOUR Yorkshire to Jamaica 1935/36.
HST 72 E v SA, Headingley, 1935. HS 189 Yorks v Northants, Northampton, 1926.
BB 3–49 Yorks v Jamaica, Kingston, 1935–36.
1000 RUNS (10) 2300 @ 58.97 in 1933.
Scored centuries in four successive fc inns in 1933.
Players v Gentlemen (2) 1934. Yorks coach 1945–70. Clubs: Bowling Old Lane, Hunslet.

MITCHELL, Bruce
——————RHB, OB——————

Born Johannesburg, S Africa, 8 Jan 1909. Educ St John's C, Johannesburg. Debut 1925/26. Wisden 1936.
S AFRICA DOMESTIC Transvaal 1925/26–49/50.
SOUTH AFRICA (42) 1929–48/49. E 1930/31 (5), 1938/39 (5); 1948/49 (5); A 1935/36 (5). E 1929 (5), 1935 (5), 1947 (5); A 1931/32 (5); NZ 1931/32 (2).
HST 189* SA v E, Oval, 1947. HS 195 S Africans v Surrey, Oval, 1935.
BBT 5–87 SA v A, Durban, 1935/36. BB 6–33 Transvaal v Border, E London, 1937/38.
1000 RUNS (3) 2014 @ 61.03 in 1947.
RECORDS Put on 260 for 1st wkt with I. J. Siedle, SA v E, Cape Town, 1930/31, S Africa Test record, and added 299 for 7th wkt with A. Melville, Transvaal v Griqualand West, Kimberley, 1946/47, S African fc record.

MITCHELL, Colin Gerald
——————RHB, RFM——————

Born Brislington, Som, 27 Jan 1929. Debut 1952.
SOMERSET (30) 1952–54. Cap 1953.
HS 26* Som v Worcs, Frome, 1953.
BB 6–62 same match.
Club: Brislington. Career curtailed by injury.

MITCHELL, Frank Rollason
——————RHB, RM——————

Born Goulborn, Australia, 3 June 1922. Died Myton Hamlet, Warwicks, 4 Apr 1984. Educ John Gulson S, Coventry. Debut 1946. P.
WARWICKSHIRE (17) 1946–48.
HS 43 Warwicks v Worcs, Edgbaston, 1946.
BB 4–69 Warwicks v Leics, Edgbaston, 1946.
Cornwall 1951. Professional: Dulwich C. Clubs: Kynoch, Aston Unity, Knowle and Dorridge (groundsman). Soccer: Birmingham City, Chelsea, Watford.

MITCHELL, Ian Norman
——————RHB——————

Born Bristol, 17 Apr 1925. Educ Harrow; Pembroke C, Cambridge. Debut 1949.
CAMBRIDGE UNIVERSITY (2) 1949.
GLOUCESTERSHIRE (9) 1950–52.
HS 27 Cambridge U v Warwicks, Fenner's, 1949.

MITCHELL, James Stanley Lyons
——————LHB——————

Born Londonderry, Ireland, 19 Oct 1946. Educ Foyle C, Londonderry. Debut 1974.
IRELAND (1) 1974.
HS 27 Ireland v Scotland, Ayr, 1974.
Club: Phoenix.

MITCHELL, Kenneth James
——————LHB——————

Born Old Hill, Staffordshire, 5 Dec 1924. Debut 1946.
WORCESTERSHIRE (1) 1946.
HS 10 Worcs v Notts, Worcester, 1946.
Club: Old Hill.

MITCHELL, William McFarlane
——————RHB, LBG——————

Born Lewisham, London, 15 Aug 1929. Educ Dulwich; Merton C, Oxford. Debut 1951.
OXFORD UNIVERSITY (26) 1951–53 (Blue 1951–52).
HS 48 Oxford U v Cambridge U, Lord's, 1952.
BB 5–107 Oxford U v M'sex, The Parks, 1951.
Kent 2nd XI.

MITCHELL-INNES, Norman Stewart
——————RHB, RFM——————

Born Calcutta, India, 7 Sept 1914. Educ Sedbergh; Brasenose C, Oxford. Debut 1931.
SOMERSET (69) 1931–49. Cap. Joint capt 1948.
OXFORD UNIVERSITY (43) 1934–37 (Blue 1934–37).
SCOTLAND (1) 1937.
ENGLAND (1) SA 1935.
TOUR MCC to Australasia 1935/36.
HST 5 E v SA, Trent Bridge, 1935. HS 207 Oxford U v H. D. G. Leveson Gower's XI, Reigate, 1936.
BB 4–65 Som v Sussex, Eastbourne, 1934.
1000 RUNS (3) 1438 @ 44.93 in 1936.
Gentlemen v Players (4) 1934–37. Career hindered by asthmatic allergy.

MITRA, Avijit
——————RHB, OB——————

Born Calcutta, India, 6 July 1953. Educ King Edward's S, Edgbaston, Birmingham; Keble C, Oxford. Debut 1974.
OXFORD UNIVERSITY (6) 1974–75.
HS 30 Oxford U v Som, The Parks, 1975.

MITTEN, John
—————RHB, WK—————

Born Manchester, 30 Mar 1941. Educ Beverley S. Debut 1961. *P*.
LEICESTERSHIRE (14) 1961–63.
HS 50* Leics v Pakistanis, Leicester, 1962.
Soccer: Mansfield Town, Newcastle United, Leicester City, Coventry City, Plymouth Argyle, Exeter City. Father C. Mitten (soccer for Manchester United).

MOAN, Raymond
—————RHB, OB—————

Born Sion Mills, Ireland, 12 Jan 1951. Debut 1970.
IRELAND (1) 1970.
No runs, one wkt.
Club: Sion Mills.

MOBEY, Gerald Spencer
—————RHB, WK—————

Born Surbiton, Surrey, 5 Mar 1904. Debut 1930. *P*.
SURREY (77) 1930–48. Cap 1939.
HS 75 Surrey v Cambridge U, Oval, 1939.
Selected for MCC to India 1939/40 (cancelled owing to war). Fc umpire 1948–55; Minor Counties umpire 1957. Former professional coach Tonbridge S (from 1948).

MOCATTA, John Edward Abraham
—————RHB—————

Born London, 6 May 1936. Educ Clifton; New C, Oxford. Debut 1958.
OXFORD UNIVERSITY (4) 1958.
HS 37 Oxford U v Glos, The Parks, 1958.
Clubs: Brondesbury, Hampstead. Represented England at world Jewish sports festival 1957.

MODI, Rusi Sheriyar
—————RHB, RM—————

Born Bombay, India, 11 Nov 1924. Educ Bombay U. Debut 1942/43.
INDIA DOMESTIC Parsis (Bombay) 1941/42–45/46, Bombay 1943/44–57/58 (capt 1952/53).
INDIA (10) 1946–52/53. E 1951/52 (1); WI 1948/49 (5); P 1952/53 (1). *E 1946 (3)*.
OTHER TOURS India to Ceylon 1944/45. Associated Cement Company to Pakistan 1961/62.

HST 112 I v WI, Bombay, 1948/49. HS 245* Bombay v Baroda, Baroda, 1944/45.
BB 5–25 Bombay v Nawanagar, Bombay, 1946/47.
1000 RUNS (1 + 1) 1386 @ 115.50 in 1944/45.
RECORDS Scored 1008 runs (@ 201.60) in Ranji Trophy 1944/45, record aggregate for one season. Added 410 for 4th wkt with L. Amarnath, India in England v The Rest, Calcutta, 1946/47 and 371 for 6th wkt with V. M. Merchant, Bombay v Maharashtra, Bombay, 1943/44, both Indian fc records.
Cricket writer.

MOELLER, David
—————RHB—————

Born Cardiff, S Wales, 2 Mar 1941. Educ Haileybury and ISC; Lincoln C, Oxford. Debut 1961.
OXFORD UNIVERSITY (1) 1961.
HS 24 Oxford U v Lancs, Old Trafford, 1961.

MOFFAT, Neil Thomas
—————LHB—————

Born Oxford, 10 May 1946. Educ Fitzwilliam C, Cambridge. Debut 1969.
CAMBRIDGE UNIVERSITY (1) 1969.
HS 4 Cambridge U v Warwicks, Fenner's, 1969.

MOHAMMED ASLAM
Khokhar
—————RHB, LB—————

Born Lahore, India, 5 Jan 1920. Debut 1938/39.
INDIA DOMESTIC Muslims 1938/39, North India 1941/42–46/47.
PAKISTAN DOMESTIC Railways 1953/54–64/65.
PAKISTAN (1) E 1954.
HST 18 P v E, Trent Bridge, 1954. HS 103 Railways-Quetta v Lahore, Karachi, 1960/61.
BB 6–26 N India v NWFP, Lahore, 1941/42.
Fc umpire.

MOHAMMED FAROOQ
—————RHB, RFM—————

Born Junagadh, India, 8 Apr 1938. Debut 1959/60.
PAKISTAN DOMESTIC Karachi 1959/60–65/66.
PAKISTAN (7) 1960/61–64/65. NZ 1964/65 (3). *E 1962 (2); I 1960/61 (2)*.

HST 47 P v NZ, Rawalpindi, 1964/65. HS as above.
BBT 4–70 P v E, Lord's, 1962. BB 6–87 (11–185 match) Karachi v Lahore, Karachi, 1959/60.

MOHAMMED ILYAS
—————RHB, LB—————

Born Lahore, India, 19 Mar 1946. Educ Muslim Model HS, Lahore. Debut 1961/62.
PAKISTAN DOMESTIC Lahore, Combined Education Board, Pakistan International Airlines, 1961/62–71/72.
PAKISTAN (10) 1964/65–68/69. E 1968/69 (2); NZ 1964/65 (3). *E 1967 (1); A 1964/65 (1); NZ 1964/65 (3)*.
OTHER TOURS Pakistan to Ceylon 1964/65. Pakistan to Australasia 1972/73. International XI to Rhodesia 1975/76.
HST 126 P v NZ, Karachi, 1964/65. HS 154 Pakistanis v S Australia, Adelaide, 1964/65.
BB 6–66 PIA v Bahawalpur, Bahawalpur, 1969/70.
Club: Poloc. Lives and coaches in Australia.

MOHAMMED MIAN SAEED
—————RHB—————

Born Jullundur, India, 31 Aug 1910. Died Lahore, Pakistan, 23 Aug 1979. Educ Government C, Lahore. Debut 1929/30.
INDIA DOMESTIC Muslims, Patiala, Southern Punjab, Northern India, Punjab (capt), 1929/30–46/47.
PAKISTAN DOMESTIC Punjab 1953/54–54/55.
COMMONWEALTH XI (1) 1952.
HS 170 S Punjab v Delhi, Patiala, 1945/46.
Represented Pakistan in unofficial 'Tests' v W Indies (1948/49), Ceylon (1948/49), Commonwealth XI (1949/50). Pakistan selector 1952/53 until death. Son Yawar Saeed (Som); son-in-law Fazal Mahmood (Pakistan): played with both for Punjab in 1954/55.

MOHAMMED MUNAF
—————RHB, RFM—————

Born Bombay, India, 2 Nov 1935. Debut 1953/54.
PAKISTAN DOMESTIC Sind, East Pakistan, Karachi, Pakistan International Airlines, 1953/54–70/71.
PAKISTAN (4) 1959/60–61/62. E 1961/62 (2); A 1959/60 (2).
TOURS Pakistan to W Indies 1957/58. Pakistan to India 1960/61. Pakistan Eaglets to England 1963.

HST 19 P v A, Lahore, 1959/60. HS 76 Hyderabad Commissioner's XI v Fazal Mahmood's XI, Hyderabad, 1959/60. BBT 4–42 P v E, Lahore, 1961/62. BB 8–84 Pakistan Eaglets v Kent, Dartford, 1963.

MOHAMMED NAZIR
——RHB, OB——

Born Rawalpindi, India, 8 Mar 1946. Debut 1964/65.
INDIA DOMESTIC Punjab University, Railways, 1964/65–.
PAKISTAN (14) 1969/70–83/84. E 1972/73 (1); WI 1980/81 (4); NZ 1969/70 (3). *A 1983/84 (3); I 1983/84 (3).*
TOURS Pakistan to England 1971, 1974.
HST 29* P v NZ, Karachi, 1969/70. HS 113* Railways A v Sargodha, Sargodha, 1971/72.
BBT 7–99 P v NZ, Karachi, 1969/70. BB 7–35 Railways v Karachi, Karachi, 1981/82.
Played as Nazir Junior in 1980/81.

MOHAN, Keith Frederick
——RHB——

Born Glossop, Derbys, 11 June 1935. Debut 1957. *P.*
DERBYSHIRE (10) 1957–58.
HS 49 Derbys v Worcs, Chesterfield, 1958.

MOHOL, Sadanand Namdeo
——RHB, RMF——

Born Bassein, Thana, India, 6 Oct 1938. Educ Poona C; Poona U. Debut 1959/60.
INDIA DOMESTIC Maharashtra 1959/60–70/71.
TOURS India to England 1967. India to E Africa 1967.
HS 40 Maharashtra v Bombay, Poona, 1962/63.
BB 8–42 Maharashtra v Saurashtra, Morvi, 1964/65.

MOHSIN Hasan KHAN
——RHB, RM——

Born Karachi, Pakistan, 15 Mar 1955. Debut 1970/71.
PAKISTAN DOMESTIC Railways, Karachi, Sind, Universities, Habib Bank, 1970/71–.
PAKISTAN (33) 1977/78–83/84. E 1977/78 (1), 1983/84 (3); A 1982/83 (3); I 1982/83 (6); SL 1981/82 (2). *E 1978 (3), 1982 (3); A 1978/79 (1), 1981/82 (2), 1983/84 (5); NZ 1978/79 (1); I 1983/84 (3).*

OTHER TOURS Pakistan Under-25 to Sri Lanka 1973/74. Pakistan to W Indies 1976/77. Pakistan to India 1979/80.
HST 200 P v E, Lord's, 1982. HS 246 Habib Bank v PIA, Karachi, 1976/77.
BB 2–13 Habib Bank v Railways, Lahore, 1982/83.
RECORD Added 426 for 2nd wkt with Arshad Pervez, Habib Bank v Income Tax Department, Lahore, 1977/78, Pakistan fc record.
1000 RUNS (1 + 1) 1248 @ 73.41 in 1982.
Clubs: Todmorden, Accrington.

MOIR, Alexander McKenzie
——RHB, LBG——

Born Dunedin, N Zealand, 17 July 1919. Educ King Edward Technical C, Dunedin. Debut 1949/50.
N ZEALAND DOMESTIC Otago (54) 1949/50–61/62.
NEW ZEALAND (17) 1950/51–58/59. E 1950/51 (2), 1954/55 (2), 1958/59 (2); SA 1952/53 (1); WI 1951/52 (2), 1955/56 (1). *E 1958 (2); I 1955/56 (2); P 1955/56 (3).*
HST 41* NZ v E, Oval, 1958. HS 70 N Island v S Island, Wellington, 1958/59.
BBT 6–155 NZ v E, Christchurch, 1950/51 (Test debut). BB 8–37 Otago v Northern Districts, Hamilton, 1958/59. Returned 15–203 match (7–84 and 8–119) Otago v Central Districts, New Plymouth, 1953/54; and 14–126 match (8–55 and 6–71) Otago v Canterbury, Dunedin, 1951/52.

MOIR, Dallas Gordon
——RHB, SLA——

Born Mtarfa, Malta, 13 Apr 1957. Educ Aberdeen GS, Scotland. Debut 1980.
SCOTLAND (1) 1980.
DERBYSHIRE (63) 1981–.
HS 107 Derbys v Warwicks, Chesterfield, 1984 (7 sixes, 12 fours).
BB 6–60 Derbys v Notts, Trent Bridge, 1984.
Club: Aberdeenshire.

MONEY, David Charles
——RHB, WK——

Born Oxford, 5 Oct 1918. Educ City of Oxford S; St John's C, Oxford. Debut 1947.
OXFORD UNIVERSITY (1) 1947.
HS 27* Oxford U v Combined Services, The Parks, 1947.
Oxfordshire 1946, Bedfordshire 1950–52. Clubs: North Oxford (50 yrs as player), Cryptics, Buccaneers, Incogniti, Hawkins' XI (capt).

MONKHOUSE, Graham
——RHB, RFM——

Born Langwathby, nr Penrith, Cumberland, 26 Apr 1954. Educ Queen Elizabeth GS, Penrith. Debut 1981.
SURREY (48) 1981–. Cap 1984.
HS 100* Surrey v Kent, Oval, 1984.
BB 7–51 Surrey v Notts, Oval, 1983.
Cumberland 1973–79. Clubs: Edenhall, Penrith, Carlisle, Kendal. Soccer: Carlisle United, Workington Town.

MONKS, Clifford Ian
——RHB, RM——

Born Keynsham, Bristol, 4 Mar 1912. Died Coalpit Heath, Bristol, 23 Jan 1974. Debut 1935. *P 1936–38, 1949.*
GLOUCESTERSHIRE (65) 1935–52.
HS 120 Glos v Cambridge U, Bristol, 1948.
BB 4–70 Glos v Worcs, Worcester, 1936.
Club: Frenchay.

MONKS, George Derek
——RHB, WK——

Born Sheffield, Yorks, 3 Sept 1929. Debut 1952. *P.*
YORKSHIRE (1) 1952.
HS 3 Yorks v Scotland, Glasgow, 1952.
Club: Sheffield.

MONTEITH, James *Dermott*
——RHB, SLA——

Born Lisburn, Ireland, 2 June 1943. Educ Royal Belfast Academy Institute; Queen's U, Belfast. Debut 1965.
IRELAND (19) 1965–. Capt 1982.
MIDDLESEX (9) 1981–82.
HS 95 Ireland v Scotland, Glasgow, 1984.
BB 7–38 Ireland v Scotland, Cork, 1973. Match double (26 and 78, 7–38 and 5–57), Ireland v Scotland, Cork 1973. Clubs: Queen's University, Lisburn.

MONTGOMERIE, Robert David
——RHB, LB——

Born Watford, Hertfordshire, 26 Sept 1937. Educ Merchant Taylors', Northwood; Worcester C, Oxford. Debut 1960.
FREE FORESTERS (1) 1960.
HS 15 Free Foresters v Oxford U, The Parks, 1960.
Hertfordshire 1956–61, Oxfordshire 1963–70. Clubs: Romany, Old Merchant Taylors', Cryptics, MCC.

MONTGOMERY, Stanley William
——————RHB, RM——————

Born West Ham, London, 7 July 1920. Educ Brew Road S, West Ham. Debut 1949. *P from 1950.*
GLAMORGAN (29) 1949–53.
HS 117 Glam v Hants, Bournemouth, 1949.
BB 3–29 Glam v Hants, Bournemouth, 1952.
RECORD During HS (above) added 264 for 5th wkt with M. Robinson, county record.
Clubs: Briton Ferry Steelworks, CWF, Silvertown, Torquay, Merthyr Tydfil, Hills Plymouth, Maesteg Celtic. Professional coach Bradfield S 1969. Soccer: Hull City, Southend United, Cardiff City, Newport County.

MOONEY, Francis Leonard Hugh
——————RHB, WK——————

Born Wellington, N Zealand, 26 May 1921. Educ St Patrick's C, Wellington. Debut 1941/42.
N ZEALAND DOMESTIC Wellington (35) 1941/42–54/55.
NEW ZEALAND (14) 1949–53/54. E 1950/51 (2); SA 1952/53 (2); WI 1951/52 (2).
E 1949 (3); SA 1953/54 (5).
OTHER TOUR N Zealand to Australia 1953/54.
HST 46 NZ v E, Headingley, 1949. HS 180 Wellington v Auckland, Wellington, 1943/44 (shared stands of 127 for 9th wkt and 113 for 10th wkt).

MOOR, David Child
——————LHB——————

Born Faversham, Kent, 18 Dec 1934. Educ King's S, Canterbury; Trinity C, Oxford. Debut 1956.
OXFORD UNIVERSITY (3) 1956.
HS 22 Oxford U v Hants, The Parks, 1956.

MOORE, Frederick
——————RHB, RMF——————

Born Rochdale, Lancs, 17 Jan 1931. Educ Rochdale Central Technical S. Debut 1954. *P.*
LANCASHIRE (24) 1954–58.
HS 18 Lancs v Notts, Old Trafford, 1955.
BB 6–45 Lancs v Essex, Chelmsford, 1956 (including hat-trick).
Clubs: Rochdale, Horwich, Elland, Walkden.

MOORE, Harry *Ian*
——————RHB, occ OB——————

Born Sleaford, Lincolnshire, 28 Feb 1941. Debut 1962. *P.*
NOTTINGHAMSHIRE (176) 1962–69. Cap 1965.
MINOR COUNTIES (1) 1973.
HS 206* Notts v Indians, Trent Bridge, 1967.
BB 2–37 Notts v Yorks, Trent Bridge, 1965.
1000 RUNS (3) 1188 @ 24.75 in 1965.
Lincolnshire 1959–61, 1970–77. Club: Pudsey St Laurence.

MOORE, Kenneth Francis
——————RHB, LFM——————

Born Croydon, Surrey, 4 Apr 1940. Debut 1961.
ESSEX (1) 1961.
HS 2 Essex v Cambridge U, Fenner's, 1961.
BB 4–21 same match.

MOORE, Nigel Harold
——————RHB, RMF——————

Born Norwich, Norfolk, 20 Apr 1930. Educ Norwich S; Corpus Christi C, Cambridge. Debut 1952.
CAMBRIDGE UNIVERSITY (3) 1952.
MINOR COUNTIES (1) 1960.
HS 59 Minor Counties v S Africans, Stoke on Trent, 1960.
Norfolk 1947–64. Clubs: Norwich Wanderers, Cambridge U Crusaders.

MOORES, Peter
——————RHB, WK——————

Born Macclesfield, Cheshire, 18 Dec 1962. Educ King's S, Macclesfield. Debut 1983.
WORCESTERSHIRE (11) 1983–.
HS 45 Worcs v Som, Weston-super-Mare, 1984.

MORBY-SMITH, Lynton
——————RHB, OB——————

Born Durban, S Africa, 27 May 1936. Educ Glenwood HS. Debut 1958/59.
S AFRICA DOMESTIC Natal 1958/59–60/61, Western Province 1963/64–66/67.
TOUR S Africa Fezela to England 1961.
HS 127 W Province v E Province, Port Elizabeth, 1964/65.

MORDAUNT, David John
——————RHB, RM——————

Born Chelsea, London, 24 Aug 1937. Educ Wellington C. Debut 1958.
SUSSEX (19) 1958–60.
MCC (1) 1964.
HS 96 Sussex v Oxford U, The Parks, 1958 (fc debut).
BB 5–42 Sussex v Cambridge U, Fenner's, 1960.
Berkshire 1964–70. Club: Horsham. Grandfather G. J. Mordaunt (Oxford U, Kent).

MORE, Hamish Kenneth
——————RHB, WK——————

Born Edinburgh, Scotland, 30 May 1940. Educ Heriot's. Debut 1966.
SCOTLAND (17) 1966–76.
T. N. PEARCE'S XI (1) 1976.
HS 89 Scotland v Surrey, Oval, 1969. Club: Heriot's Former Pupils.

MORGAN, Andrew Howard
——————LHB——————

Born Hastings, Sussex, 30 Nov 1945. Educ Hastings GS; St Edmund Hall, Oxford. Debut 1966.
OXFORD UNIVERSITY (11) 1966–69 (Blue 1969).
HS 59* Oxford U v Worcs, The Parks, 1969.
Club: Harlequins.

MORGAN, Charles
——————RHB, OB——————

Born Clay Cross, Derbys, 7 Feb 1917. Debut 1946. *P.*
NOTTINGHAMSHIRE (1) 1946.
HS 13 Notts v M'sex, Trent Bridge, 1946.

MORGAN, Derek Clifton
——————RHB, RMF/OB——————

Born Muswell Hill, London, 26 Feb 1929. Educ Berkhamsted S. Debut 1950. *P.*
DERBYSHIRE (540) 1950–69. Cap 1951. Capt 1965–69. Testimonial (£2500) 1961.
HS 147 Derbys v Hants, Bournemouth, 1964.
BB 7–33 Derbys v Glam, Chesterfield, 1965.
1000 RUNS (8) 1669 @ 46.36 in 1962.
Scored 937 runs @ 26.77 and took 94 wkts @ 23.04 in 1957.

RECORDS Made 563 catches for Derbys, county record for fielder. Scored 17,842 runs and took 1216 wkts for Derbys, only player to perform 10,000 runs/1000 wkts double for county.
Players v Gentlemen (2) 1958–62. Club: Ashton 1970–71.

MORGAN, Howard William
————RHB, OB————

Born Maesteg, S Wales, 29 June 1931. Debut 1958. *P*.
GLAMORGAN (2) 1958.
HS 5 Glam v Warwicks, Swansea, 1958.
Clubs: Briton Ferry Town, Neath, Maesteg Celtic.

MORGAN, Michael
————RHB, OB————

Born Ynyshir, S Wales, 21 May 1936. Debut 1957. *P*.
NOTTINGHAMSHIRE (61) 1957–61.
HS 56* Notts v Leics, Leicester, 1958.
BB 6–50 Notts v M'sex, Trent Bridge, 1959.

MORGAN, Michael Naughton
————RHB, RFM————

Born London, 15 May 1932. Educ Marlborough C; Downing C, Cambridge. Debut 1951.
CAMBRIDGE UNIVERSITY (13) 1951–54 (Blue 1954).
MCC (1) 1957.
HS 11* Cambridge U v Pakistanis, Fenner's, 1954 and 11 v Yorks, Fenner's, 1954.
BB 5–58 Cambridge U v MCC, Lord's 1954.
Berkshire 1950–59.

MORGAN, Philip Richard Llewellyn
————RHB, LB————

Born Derby, 11 Mar 1927. Educ St John's Leatherhead; Wadham C, Oxford. Debut 1946.
OXFORD UNIVERSITY (1) 1946.
HS 1 Oxford U v Indians, The Parks, 1946.
Clubs: Cryptics, Westcliff, Windsor Eclectics, Southwick. Clergyman.

MORGAN, Ross Winston
————RHB, OB————

Born Auckland, N Zealand, 12 Feb 1941. Educ Auckland GS, Debut 1957/58.

N ZEALAND DOMESTIC Auckland (90) 1957/58–76/77.
NEW ZEALAND (20) 1964/65–71/72. E 1965/66 (2), 1970/71 (2); WI 1968/69 (1); P 1964/65 (2). *E 1965 (3); WI 1971/ 72 (3); I 1964/65 (4); P 1964/65 (3)*.
OTHER TOURS N Zealand to Australia 1969/70, 1970/71.
HST 97 NZ v P, Christchurch, 1964/65.
HS 166 Auckland v Canterbury, Auckland, 1968/69.
BB 6–40 Auckland v Central Districts, New Plymouth, 1964/65.

MORGAN, Rurie Trenton
————RHB, OB————

Born Wellington, N Zealand, 30 July 1912. Died Wellington, N Zealand, 4 Jan 1980. Debut 1932/33.
N ZEALAND DOMESTIC Wellington (10) 1932/33–40/41.
TOUR New Zealand Services XI to England (1) 1945.
HS 81 Wellington v Canterbury, Wellington, 1933/34.
BB 2–34 Wellington v Canterbury, Christchurch, 1933/34.
Club: Wellington.

MORGAN, Samuel Augustus
————RHB————

Born Kingston, Jamaica, 7 Aug 1950. Debut 1969/70.
W INDIES DOMESTIC Jamaica 1969/70–73/74.
TOUR Jamaica to England 1970.
HS 126 Jamaica v Guyana, Georgetown, 1970/71.
Club: Melbourne.

MORLEY, Jeremy Dennis
————LHB————

Born Newmarket, Suffolk, 20 Oct 1950. Debut 1971.
SUSSEX (72) 1971–76. Cap 1973.
HS 127 Sussex v Warwicks, Hove, 1973.

MORRILL, Nicholas David
————RHB, OB————

Born Ryde, Isle of Wight, 9 Dec 1957. Educ Sandown GS; Millfield S; Lincoln C, Oxford. Debut 1978.
OXFORD UNIVERSITY (14) 1978–79 (Blue 1979).
HS 45 Oxford U v Worcs, The Parks, 1979.
BB 3–53 Oxford U v Sussex, Pagham, 1979.

MORRIS, Alan
————RHB, LB————

Born Staveley, Derbys, 23 Aug 1953. Debut 1974.
DERBYSHIRE (47) 1974–78.
S AFRICA DOMESTIC Griqualand West 1979/80.
HS 74 Derbys v Lancs, Old Trafford, 1976.

MORRIS, Arthur Robert
————LHB, SLC————

Born Dungog, NSW, Australia, 19 Jan 1922. Educ Newcastle HS; Canterbury HS, Sydney. Debut 1940/41. *Wisden* 1949.
AUSTRALIA DOMESTIC New South Wales (50) 1940/41–54/55 (capt 1947/48–54/ 55).
AUSTRALIA (46) 1946/47–54/55. E 1946/ 47 (5), 1950/51 (5), 1954/55 (4); SA 1952/53 (5); WI 1951/52 (4); I 1947/48 (4). *E 1948 (5), 1953 (5); SA 1949/50 (5); WI 1954/55 (4)*. Capt 2.
OTHER TOURS Cavaliers to India and S Africa 1962/63. Indian Defence Fund match 1963/64.
HST 206 A v E, Adelaide, 1950/51. HS 290 Australians v Glos, Bristol, 1948.
BB 3–36 Australian XI v Tasmania, Hobart, 1952/53.
1000 RUNS (2 + 4) 1922 @ 71.18 in 1948.
RECORDS Scored century in each inns (148 and 111) on fc debut, NSW v Queensland, Sydney, 1940/41, first batsman to do so. Also scored century on fc debut in England (1948), S Africa (1949/50) and W Indies (1954/55).
Clubs: St George, Paddington (Australia). MCC Hon. member. MBE for services to cricket.

MORRIS, Charles Anthony
————LHB, RLB————

Born Cambridge, 9 May 1939. Educ Marlborough C; King's C, Cambridge. Debut 1960.
CAMBRIDGE UNIVERSITY (4) 1960.
HS 8 Cambridge U v S Africans, Fenner's, 1960.
Cambridgeshire 1956–63. Rugby: Rosslyn Park.

MORRIS, Huw
————LHB————

Born Cardiff, S Wales, 5 Oct 1963. Educ Blundell's S. Debut 1981.
GLAMORGAN (25) 1981–.
HS 114* Glam v Yorks, Cardiff, 1984.

MORRIS, Ian
—RHB, SLA—

Born Maesteg, S Wales, 27 June 1946.
Educ Maesteg GS. Debut 1966.
GLAMORGAN (14) 1966–68.
HS 38 Glam v Hants, Cardiff, 1966.
BB 2–30 Glam v Northants, Swansea,
1968.
Club: Maesteg Celtic.

MORRIS, John Edward
—RHB, RMF—

Born Crewe, Cheshire, 1 Apr 1964.
Educ Shavington CS; Dane Bank C.
Debut 1982.
DERBYSHIRE (26) 1982–.
HS 135 Derbys v Leics, Leicester, 1984.

MORRIS, Raymond
—RHB, WK—

Born Hartlebury, Worcs, 20 June 1929.
Educ Queen Elizabeth GS, Hartlebury.
Debut 1958.
WORCESTERSHIRE (2) 1958.
HS 7 Worcs v Leics, Worcester, 1958.
Clubs: Kidderminster, Brentwood.
Hockey: Worcestershire.

MORRIS, Robert John
—RHB, OB—

Born Swansea, S Wales, 27 Nov 1926.
Educ Blundell's S; Trinity Hall, Cam-
bridge. Debut 1949.
CAMBRIDGE UNIVERSITY (20) 1949–51
(Blue 1949).
KENT (2) 1950.
HS 96 Cambridge U v Sussex, Fenner's,
1949.
Club: Beckenham. Father W. P. Morris
(Glam).

MORRIS, William Bancroft
—RHB, OB—

Born Kingston, Jamaica, 28 May 1917.
Educ Montreal HS. Debut 1946. P.
ESSEX (48) 1946–50.
HS 68 Essex v Cambridge U, Fenner's,
1949.
BB 4–90 Essex v M'sex, Westcliff, 1946.
Cambridgeshire 1951–58. Clubs: Ken-
ton, Ilford. Professional coach Berk-
hamsted S, Forest S.

MORRISON, George Charles
—RHB—

Born Downpatrick, Co Down, Ireland,
27 June 1915. Educ Methodist C, Belfast; Queen's U. Debut 1947.

IRELAND (2) 1947.
HS 16 Ireland v Derbys, Buxton, 1947.
Club: NICC.

MORTENSEN, Ole Henrek
—RHB, RFM—

Born Vejle, Jutland, Denmark, 29 Jan
1958. Educ Brondbyoster S, Copenhagen; Abedore C, Copenhagen. Debut
1983.
DERBYSHIRE (26) 1983–.
HS 40* Derbys v Glam, Derby, 1984.
BB 6–27 Derbys v Yorks, Dore, Sheffield, 1983.
Denmark (17). Instantly qualified for
Derbys under EEC regulations. The
first Dane to play fc county cricket.

MORTIMORE, John Brian
—RHB, OB—

Born Bristol, 14 May 1933. Educ
Cotham GS. Debut 1950. P.
GLOUCESTERSHIRE (594) 1950–75. Cap
1954. Capt 1965–67. Benefit (£3600)
1965.
ENGLAND (9) 1958/59–64. A 1964 (1); I
1959 (2). A 1958/59 (1); NZ 1958/59
(2); I 1963/64 (3).
OTHER TOURS F. R. Brown's XI to E
Africa 1961/62 (no fc match). MCC to E
Africa 1963/64. Commonwealth XI to
India 1964/65.
HST 73* E v I, Madras, 1963/64. HS 149
Glos v Notts, Trent Bridge, 1963.
BBT 3–36 E v I, Headingley, 1959. BB
8–59 (13–104 match) Glos v Oxford U,
The Parks, 1959.
1000 RUNS (5) 1425 @ 26.88 in 1963.
100 WKTS (3) 113 @ 18.28 in 1959.
DOUBLE (3) 1959, 1963, 1964.
Took four wkts in five balls, Glos v
Lancs, Cheltenham, 1962.

MORTON, Geoffrey Dalgleish
—RHB, RMF—

Born Acton, London, 27 July 1922.
Debut 1950. P.
MIDDLESEX (1) 1950.
MCC (1) 1952.
HS 1 M'sex v Warwicks, Lord's, 1950.
Occasional fc umpire at Lord's.
Professional coach Malvern S from
1958. Soccer: Watford, Southend
United, Exeter City.

MORTON, William
—LHB, SLA—

Born Stirling, Scotland, 21 Apr 1961.
Educ Wallace HS, Stirling. Debut 1982.
SCOTLAND (2) 1982–83.
WARWICKSHIRE (7) 1984.

HS 13* Warwicks v Surrey, Edgbaston,
1984.
BB 4–40 Scotland v Ireland, Downpatrick, 1983.
Club: Stirling County.

MOSELEY, Ezra Alphonsa
—RHB, RFM—

Born Christ Church, Barbados, 5 Jan
1958. Educ Christ Church HS, Bar-
bados. Debut 1980.
GLAMORGAN (29) 1980–81.
W INDIES DOMESTIC Barbados 1981/82.
HS 70* Glam v Kent, Canterbury, 1980.
BB 6–23 Glam v Australians, Swansea,
1981.
Barred from W Indian cricket for tour-
ing S Africa 1982/83, 1983/84 (W Indies
XI). Selected for Young W Indies to
Zimbabwe 1981/82 but withdrew
through injury.

MOSELEY, Hallam Reynold
—RHB, RFM—

Born Christ Church, Barbados, 28 May
1948. Educ The Rural Studiom, Bar-
bados. Debut 1969.
W INDIES DOMESTIC Barbados 1969–71/
72.
SOMERSET (205) 1971–82. Cap 1972.
Testimonial (£24,085) 1979.
TOUR Barbados to England 1969.
HS 67 Som v Leics, Taunton, 1972.
BB 6–34 Som v Derbys, Bath, 1975.
Club: Empire (Barbados).

MOSES, Geoffrey Haydn
—LHB, RFM—

Born Mountain Ash, Glam, 24 Sept
1952. Educ Ystalyfera GS; Emmanuel
C, Cambridge. Debut 1974.
CAMBRIDGE UNIVERSITY (3) 1974 (Blue).
HS 24* Cambridge U v Oxford U,
Lord's, 1974.
BB 5–31 same match.

MOSEY, Stuart David Houlden
—RHB, RFM—

Born Keighley, Yorks, 29 Nov 1937.
Educ Keighley GS; Fitzwilliam C,
Cambridge. Debut 1959.
CAMBRIDGE UNIVERSITY (2) 1959.
HS 13* Cambridge U v M'sex, Fenner's,
1959.

MOSS, Alan Edward
—RHB, RF—

Born Tottenham, London, 14 Nov
1930. Debut 1950. P.

MIDDLESEX (307) 1950–63. Cap 1952. Benefit (£5300) in 1962.
FREE FORESTERS (I) 1968.
ENGLAND (9) 1953/54–60. A 1956 (I); SA 1960 (2); I 1959 (3). *WI 1953/54 (I), 1959/60 (2).*
OTHER TOURS MCC A to Pakistan 1955/56. Duke of Norfolk's XI to Jamaica 1956/57. C. G. Howard's XI to India 1956/57. Commonwealth XI to S Africa and Rhodesia 1960/61.
HST 26 E v I, Lord's, 1959. HS 40 M'sex v Surrey, Oval, 1952.
BBT 4–35 E v SA, Lord's, 1960. BB 8–31 M'sex v Northants, Kettering, 1960.
100 WKTS (5) 136 @ 13.72 in 1960.
Players v Gentlemen (3) 1953–61.

MOTTRAM, Thomas James
RHB, RMF

Born Liverpool, 7 Sept 1945. Educ Quarry Bank CS; Edinburgh U; Loughborough C. Debut 1972.
HAMPSHIRE (35) 1972–76.
HS 15* Hants v Notts, Bournemouth, 1973.
BB 6–63 Hants v Warwicks, Coventry, 1973.
Club: Southport and Birkdale.

MOTZ, Richard Charles
RHB, RFM

Born Christchurch, N Zealand, 12 Jan 1940. Educ Linwood HS. Debut 1957/58. *Wisden* 1966.
N ZEALAND DOMESTIC Canterbury (61) 1957/58–68/69.
NEW ZEALAND (32) 1961/62–69. E 1962/63 (2), 1965/66 (3); SA 1963/64 (2); WI 1968/69 (3); I 1967/68 (4). *P 1964/65 (3). E 1965 (3), 1969 (3); ⬛61/62 (5); I 1964/65 (3); P 196⬛⬛).*
OTHER TOUR N Zeal⬛ o Australia 1960/61, 1967/68.
HST 60 NZ v E, Auckland, 1962/63. HS 103* Canterbury v Otago, Christchurch, 1967/68.
BBT 6–63 NZ v I, Christchurch, 1967/68. BB 8–61 Canterbury v Wellington, Christchurch, 1966/67.
HS (above) included fastest-ever fc century (53 mins) at time in N Zealand.
MCC Hon. member.

MOULDING, Roger Peter
RHB, LB

Born Enfield, M'sex, 3 Jan 1958. Educ Haberdashers' Aske's, Elstree; Christ Church C, Oxford. Debut 1977.
MIDDLESEX (I) 1977.

OXFORD UNIVERSITY (46) 1978–83 (Blue 1978–83) Capt 1981.
HS 80* Oxford U v Warwicks, Edgbaston, 1983.

MOULE, Harry George
RHB

Born Kidderminster, Worcs, 23 Dec 1921. Debut 1952.
WORCESTERSHIRE (I) 1952.
HS 57 Worcs v Cambridge U, Worcester, 1952.
Clubs: Kidderminster, Old Hill.

MOUNTFORD, Peter Neville George
RHB, RFM

Born Birmingham, 21 June 1940. Educ Bromsgrove S; Keble C, Oxford. Debut 1962.
OXFORD UNIVERSITY (18) 1962–63 (Blue 1963).
HS 22* Oxford U v Worcs, The Parks, 1963.
BB 7–47 Oxford U v W Indians, The Parks, 1963.
Club: Kidderminster.

MOXON, Howard
RHB, RMF

Born Elsecar, Yorks, 23 Mar 1940. Educ Ecclesfield GS; Downing C, Cambridge. Debut 1960.
CAMBRIDGE UNIVERSITY (I) 1960.
HS 23 Cambridge U v Sussex, Fenner's, 1960.

MOXON, Martyn Douglas
RHB, RM

Born Barnsley, Yorks, 4 May 1960. Educ Holgate GS, Barnsley. Debut 1981.
YORKSHIRE (43) 1981–. Cap 1984.
S AFRICA DOMESTIC Griqualand West 1982/83–83/84.
HS 153 Yorks v Lancs, Headingley, 1983.
BB 3–26 D. B. Close's XI v Sri Lankans, Scarborough, 1984.
RECORD First Yorkshire player to score centuries in first two home Championship matches (116 Yorks v Essex, Headingley, 1981, 2nd inns of fc debut, and 111 Yorks v Derbys, Sheffield, 1981).
Club: Barnsley.

MOYLAN, Adrian Charles David
LHB, SLA

Born Weston-super-Mare, Somerset, 26 June 1955. Educ Clifton C; Downing C, Cambridge. Debut 1976.
CAMBRIDGE UNIVERSITY (5) 1976–77 (Blue 1977).
HS 29 Cambridge U v Warwicks, Fenner's, 1976.

MOYLAN-JONES, Roger Charles
RHB, OB

Born Torquay, Devon, 18 Apr 1940. Educ King Edward VI S, Totnes. Debut 1964.
COMBINED SERVICES (I) 1964.
HS 31 Combined Services v Oxford U, Aldershot, 1964.
BB 2–36 same match.
Devon 1959–64. Clubs: Penzance, I Zingari, Royal Navy. Regular commissioned naval officer.

MUBARAK, Aziz Mohamed
RHB, RM/OB

Born Colombo, Ceylon, 4 July 1951. Educ RC, Colombo; U of Sri Lanka; Christ's C, Cambridge. Debut 1978.
CAMBRIDGE UNIVERSITY (24) 1978–80 (Blue 1978–80).
HS 105 Cambridge U v Warwicks, Fenner's, 1980.

MUCKLOW, Peter
RHB, WK

Born Warwick, 5 Nov 1949. Educ Shrewsbury; Trinity C, Oxford. Debut 1970.
OXFORD UNIVERSITY (2) 1970.
HS 32 Oxford U v Surrey, The Parks, 1970.

MUDASSAR NAZAR
RHB, RM

Born Lahore, Pakistan, 6 Apr 1956. Educ Government C, Lahore; Lahore U. Debut 1971/72.
PAKISTAN DOMESTIC Lahore, Punjab, Universities, Habib Bank, Pakistan International Airlines, United Bank, 1971/72–.
PAKISTAN (44) 1976/77–83/84. E 1977/78 (3), 1983/84 (I); A 1979/80 (3), 1982/83 (3); I 1978/79 (2), 1982/83 (3); SL 1981/82 (I). *E 1978 (3), 1982 (3); A 1976/77 (I), 1978/79 (I), 1981/82 (3), 1983/84 (5); NZ 1978/79 (I); I 1979/80 (5), 1983/84 (3).*

OTHER TOUR Pakistan to Sri Lanka 1975/76.
HST 231 P v I, Hyderabad, 1982/83. HS 241 United Bank v Rawalpindi, Lahore, 1981/82.
BBT 6–32 P v E, Lord's, 1982. BB as above.
1000 RUNS (0 + 4) 1214 @ 52.78 in 1983/84.
RECORDS During HST (above) added 451 for 3rd wkt with Javed Miandad, world Test record for 3rd wkt and equal-highest for any wkt in Tests. In scoring maiden Test century (114), P v E, Lahore, 1977/78, reached hundred in 557 mins, slowest-ever century in fc cricket. Scored 761 runs (@ 126.83) in series, P v I, 1982/83, Pakistan record. Scored 231, 152* (during which carried bat in total of 323 at Lahore) and 152 in three consecutive Test inns, P v I, 1982/83.
Cheshire 1980–. Clubs: Burnley, Horwich RMI. Father Nazar Mohammed (Pakistan).

MUDDIAH, Venatappa Musandra
—RHB, OB—

Born Bangalore, India, 8 June 1929. Educ Mysore U. Debut 1949/50.
INDIA DOMESTIC Services 1949/50–61/62 (capt 1960/61–61/62), Mysore 1951/52, India Air Force 1962/63.
INDIA (2) 1959/60–60/61. A 1959/60 (1); P 1960/61 (1).
TOUR India to England 1959.
HST 11 I v P, Kanpur, 1960/61. HS 67 Services v Delhi, Delhi, 1961/62.
BBT 2–40 I v P, Kanpur, 1960/61. BB 8–54 (12–97 match) Services v S Punjab, Patiala, 1949/50 (fc debut).
Wing Commander Indian Air Force.

MUNCER, Bernard *Leonard*
—RHB, LB/OB—

Born Hampstead, London, 23 Oct 1913. Died Camden, London, 18 Jan 1982. Debut 1933. *P*.
MIDDLESEX (82) 1933–46.
MCC (4) 1935–57.
GLAMORGAN (224) 1947–54. Cap 1947. Benefit (£3556) 1954.
HS 135 Glam v Som, Swansea, 1952.
BB 9–62 (15–151 match) Glam v Essex, Brentwood, 1948.
1000 RUNS (1) 1097 @ 24.37 in 1952.
100 WKTS (5) 159 @ 17.34 in 1948.
DOUBLE (1) 1952.
RECORD Added 230 for 6th wkt with W. E. Jones, Glam v Worcs, Worcester, 1953, county record.
Returned 15–201 match, Glam v Sussex, Swansea, 1948. Match double

(107*; 5–34 and 5–23) Glam v Derbys, Chesterfield, 1951.
Players v Gentlemen (1) 1948. Clubs: Hampstead, Crewe LMR, Reading. Lord's coach 1955–78; testimonial (£2114) from MCC 1971.

MUNDEN, Donald Francis Xavier
—RHB, LB—

Born Leicester, 17 Oct 1934. Debut 1960. *P*.
LEICESTERSHIRE (7) 1960–61.
HS 34 Leics v Derbys, Derby, 1961.
Club: Cheadle. Boxing and swimming for Leics. Brothers P. A. and V. S. Munden (both Leics).

MUNDEN, Paul Anthony
—LHB, ROB—

Born Leicester, 5 Nov 1938. Debut 1957. *P*.
LEICESTERSHIRE (47) 1957–64.
HS 77 Leics v Sussex, Eastbourne, 1963.
Brothers D. F. X. and V. S. Munden (both Leics).

MUNDEN, Victor Stanislaus
—LHB, LMF/SLA—

Born Leicester, 2 Jan 1928. Debut 1946. *P*.
LEICESTERSHIRE (228) 1946–57. Cap 1951.
HS 103 Leics v Kent, Folkestone, 1952.
BB 6–33 Leics v Som, Bath, 1953.
1000 RUNS (1) 1259 @ 29.97 in 1952.
Took 87 wkts @ 23.54 in 1955.
Players v Gentlemen (2) 1955–56.
Brothers D. F. X. and P. A. Munden (both Leics).

MUNGRUE, Alteff Ali (Alf)
—RHB, RM/OB—

Born Port of Spain, Trinidad, 25 Aug 1934. Educ QRC, Trinidad. Debut 1964.
COMBINED SERVICES (2) 1964.
HS 51 Combined Services v Cambridge U, Uxbridge, 1964.
BB 4–58 Combined Services v Oxford U, Aldershot, 1964.
Royal Air Force. Clubs: Seaham Harbour, Finchley, Streatham, BOAC 'Speed', Singapore, Malaya.

MUNIR MALIK
—RHB, RFM—

Born Leiah, India, 10 July 1934. Debut 1956/57.

PAKISTAN DOMESTIC Punjab, Rawalpindi, Services, Karachi, 1956/57–66/67.
PAKISTAN (3) 1959/60–62. A 1959/60 (1). E 1962 (2).
OTHER TOUR Pakistan Eaglets to Ceylon 1960/61.
HST 4 P v E, Headingley, 1962. HS 72 Services v Sargodha, Rawalpindi, 1962/63.
BBT 5–128 P v E, Headingley, 1962. BB 8–154 Karachi Whites v Punjab U, Lahore, 1965/66.

MUNRO, Hector Campbell
—RHB, LB—

Born Calcutta, India, 24 Oct 1920. Educ Rugby; Trinity C, Oxford. Debut 1947.
OXFORD UNIVERSITY (1) 1947.
No runs, no wkts.
Kent 2nd XI.

MURCH, Stewart *Nigel* Clifford
—RHB, RFM—

Born Warnambool, Victoria, Australia, 27 June 1944. Debut 1966/67.
AUSTRALIA DOMESTIC Victoria (9) 1966/67–69/70.
NORTHAMPTONSHIRE (1) 1968.
HS 64 Victoria v Tasmania, Melbourne, 1969/70.
BB 3–49 Victoria v Queensland, Brisbane, 1966/67.
Club: St Kilda.

MURLEY, Anthony Jonathan
—RHB, RM—

Born Radlett, Hertfordshire, 7 Aug 1957. Educ Oundle; St Catharine's C, Cambridge. Debut 1981.
CAMBRIDGE UNIVERSITY (6) 1981.
HS 48 Cambridge U v Northants, Fenner's, 1981.
Hertfordshire 1979–. Golf: Blue. Father Sir Reginald Murley (president RC of Surgeons).

MURPHY, Edward George
—RHB, RFM—

Born Sheffield, Yorks, 6 Dec 1921. Educ Guy's Hospital. Debut 1948.
COMBINED SERVICES (2) 1948.
HS 11 Combined Services v Worcs, Worcester, 1948.
British Empire XI 1945. RAF flying officer 1948. Currently medical practitioner in United States.

MURRAY, Anton Ronald Andrew
──────RHB, RM/LB──────

Born Grahamstown, S Africa, 30 Apr 1922. Educ St Andrew's C, Grahamstown; Rhodes U. Debut 1947/48.
S AFRICA DOMESTIC Eastern Province 1947/48–55/56.
SOUTH AFRICA (10) 1952/53–53/54. NZ 1953/54 (4). *A 1952/53 (4); NZ 1952/53 (2).*
OTHER TOUR S Africa to England 1955.
HST 109 SA v NZ, Wellington, 1952/53.
HS 133 E Province v W Province, Cape Town, 1947/48.
BBT 4–169 SA v A, Sydney, 1952/53. BB 7–30 E Province v OFS, Bloemfontein, 1947/48.
RECORDS Added 246 for 7th wkt with D. J. McGlew, SA v NZ, Wellington, 1952/53, S Africa Test record and at time world Test record.

MURRAY, Bruce Alexander Grenfell
──────RHB, LB──────

Born Wellington, N Zealand, 18 Sept 1940. Educ Epuni HS, Hutt Valley. Debut 1958/59.
N ZEALAND DOMESTIC Wellington (55) 1958/59–72/73.
NEW ZEALAND (13) 1967/68–70/71. E 1970/71 (1); I 1967/68 (4). *E 1969 (2); I 1969/70 (3); P 1969/70 (3).*
OTHER TOURS N Zealand to Australia 1967/68.
HST 90 NZ v P, Lahore, 1969/70. HS 213 Wellington v Otago, Dunedin, 1968/69. BB 4–43 Wellington v Auckland, Auckland, 1965/66.

MURRAY, David Anthony
──────RHB, WK──────

Born Carrington Village, Bridgetown, Barbados, 29 May 1950. Educ Modern S, Bridgetown. Debut 1970/71.
W INDIES DOMESTIC Barbados 1970/71–81/82.
WEST INDIES (19) 1977/78–81/82. E 1980/81 (4); A 1977/78 (3). *A 1981/82 (2); I 1978/79 (6); P 1980/81 (4).*
OTHER TOURS W Indies to England 1973, 1980. W Indies to India, Pakistan and Sri Lanka 1974/75. W Indies to Australia 1975/76, 1979/80.
HST 84 WI v I, Bombay, 1978/79. HS 206* W Indians v E Zone, Jamshedpur, 1978/79.
RECORDS Made 10 dismissals (all ct) in match, W Indies XI v S Africa, Port Elizabeth, 1983/84, equalling S African record.

Barred from W Indian cricket for touring S Africa 1982/83, 1983/84 (W Indies XI).

MURRAY, Deryck Lance
──────RHB, WK, LB──────

Born Port of Spain, Trinidad, 20 May 1943. Educ Queen's RC, Port of Spain; Jesus C, Cambridge; Nottingham U. Debut 1960/61.
W INDIES DOMESTIC Trinidad 1960/61–80/81 (capt 1973/74–76/77, 1979/80).
CAMBRIDGE UNIVERSITY (24) 1965–66 (Blue 1965–66). Capt 1966.
NOTTINGHAMSHIRE (97) 1966–69. Cap 1967.
WARWICKSHIRE (58) 1972–75. Cap 1972.
WEST INDIES (62) 1963–80. E 1967/68 (5), 1973/74 (5); A 1972/73 (4), 1977/78 (2); I 1975/76 (4); P 1976/77 (5). *E 1963 (5), 1973 (3), 1976 (5), 1980 (5); A 1975/76 (6), 1979/80 (3); NZ 1979/80 (3); I 1974/75 (5); P 1974/75 (2).* Capt 1.
OTHER TOUR W Indies to India and Ceylon 1966/67.
HST 91 WI v A, Bridgetown, 1972/73. HS 166* Notts v Surrey, Oval, 1966.
BB 2–50 W Indians v President's XI, Nagpur, 1966/67.
1000 RUNS (3) 1358 @ 30.17 in 1966.
RECORDS Made 24 dismissals in series, WI v E, 1963, and 189 dismissals in Test career, both W Indies Test records. Made 849 dismissals (741 ct, 108 st) in career, W Indian record.
World Series Cricket (Kerry Packer) 1977/78–78/79. Member WICB. Secretary W Indies Cricketers' Association. Father L. Murray (Trinidad); cousin C. E. Murray (Trinidad).

MURRAY, John Thomas
──────RHB, WK──────

Born Kensington, London, 1 Apr 1935. Educ St John's C of E S, London. Debut 1952. *P. Wisden 1967.*
MIDDLESEX (508) 1952–75. Cap 1956. Benefit (£8010) 1966.
ENGLAND (21) 1961–67. A 1961 (5); WI 1966 (1); I 1967 (3); P 1962 (3), 1967 (1). *A 1962/63 (1); SA 1964/65 (1); NZ 1962/63 (1), 1965/66 (1); I 1961/62 (3); P 1961/62 (1).*
OTHER TOURS MCC to N Zealand 1960/61. Cavaliers to Jamaica 1963/64. Commonwealth XI to Pakistan 1963/64, 1967/68, 1970/71. MCC to Pakistan 1968/69. D. H. Robins' XI to S Africa 1972/73, 1973/74.
HST 112 E v WI, Oval, 1966. HS 142 MCC v NE Transvaal, Pretoria, 1964/65.

BB 2–10 MCC v Bombay, Bombay, 1961/62.
1000 RUNS (6) 1160 @ 28.29 in 1965.
100 DISMISSALS (2) 104 (82 ct, 22 st) in 1957, 102 (95 ct, 7 st) in 1960.
DOUBLE (wicketkeeper's) (1) 1957.
Made 1526 dismissals in career (1268 ct, 258 st), world record until beaten by R. W. Taylor in 1982/83.
Players v Gentlemen (3) 1959–61. England selector 1977–78. MCC Hon. member. MBE for services to cricket.

MURRAY, Michael Patrick
──────RHB──────

Born Westminster, London, 14 May 1930. Debut 1949.
COMBINED SERVICES (1) 1949.
MIDDLESEX (5) 1952–53.
MCC (4) 1958–63.
HS 44 M'sex v Oxford U, The Parks, 1953.
Clubs: Beddington, Lloyds Bank.

MURRAY WILLIS, Peter Earnshaw
──────RHB──────

Born Castle Bromwich, Warwicks, 14 July 1910. Educ St George's, Harpenden. Debut 1935.
WORCESTERSHIRE (7) 1935–36.
NORTHAMPTONSHIRE (22) 1938–46. Cap 1946. Capt 1946.
HS 54 Northants v Worcs, Kidderminster, 1946.
Clubs: Walsall, Worcs Gentlemen, Warwicks Imps, Barnt Green, Richmond.

MURRAY-WOOD, William
──────RHB, LB──────

Born Dartford, Kent, 30 June 1917. Died Southwark, London, 21 Dec 1968. Educ Mill Hill; Oriel C, Oxford. Debut 1936.
OXFORD UNIVERSITY (24) 1936–38 (Blue 1936).
KENT (77) 1936–53. Cap 1951. Capt 1952–53.
MCC (3) 1955–56.
TOUR Oxford and Cambridge Universities to Jamaica 1938/39.
HS 107 Kent v Sussex, Tunbridge Wells, 1952.
BB 6–29 Oxford U v Army, The Parks, 1937.
Scored 106* Oxford U v Glos, The Parks, 1936, on fc debut.
Club: Beckenham.

MURRILLS, Timothy James
————RHB, RM, WK————

Born Sheffield, Yorks, 22 Dec 1953.
Educ The Leys; Emmanuel C, Cambridge. Debut 1973.
CAMBRIDGE UNIVERSITY (37) 1973–76
(Blue 1973–74, 1976). Capt 1976.
HS 67 Cambridge U v Surrey, Fenner's, 1976.
Dorset 1974–81.
Brothers R. J. and S. A. Murrills (Minor Counties cricketers).

MURTAGH, Andrew Joseph
————RHB, RM————

Born Dublin, Ireland, 6 May 1949.
Educ St Joseph's C, Beulah Hill, London. Debut 1973.
HAMPSHIRE (26) 1973–77.
S AFRICA DOMESTIC Eastern Province 1973/74.
HS 65 Hants v Glos, Bournemouth, 1975.
BB 2–46 Hants v Warwicks, Bournemouth, 1976.
Club: Beddington.

MUSHTAQ ALI, Syed
————RHB, SLA————

Born Indore, India, 17 Dec 1914. Educ Bengal Dol HS. Debut 1930/31 (Madras Indians).
INDIA DOMESTIC Central India 1934/35–39/40, Bombay Muslims 1934/35–44/45 (capt 1944/45), Gujerat 1940/41 (capt), Holkar 1941/42–54/55 (capt 1949/50, 1953/54–54/55), Madhya Bharat 1955/56, 1957/58, Uttar Pradesh 1956/57, 1959/60–60/61, Orissa 1958/

59. Viceroy's XI v MCC 1933/34. Bombay Chief Minister's XI 1963/64.
INDIA (11) 1933/34–51/52. E 1933/34 (2), 1951/52 (1); WI 1948/49 (3). *E 1936 (3), 1946 (2).*
OTHER TOUR India to Ceylon 1944/45.
HST 112 I v E, Old Trafford, 1936. HS 233 Holkar v United Provinces, Indore, 1947/48.
BB 7–108 Central India v United Provinces, Allahabad, 1939/40.
1000 RUNS (1) 1078 @ 25.06 in 1936.
Selected for India to Australia 1947/48 but unable to go. MCC Hon. member.
Brother S. Ishtiaq Ali (Holkar); son S. Gulraz Ali (Madhya Pradesh).

MUSHTAQ MOHAMMED
————RHB, LBG————

Born Junagadh, India, 22 Nov 1943.
Educ Christian Mission HS, Karachi.
Debut 1956/57. *Wisden* 1963.
PAKISTAN DOMESTIC Karachi, Pakistan International Airlines, 1956/57–79/80.
NORTHAMPTONSHIRE (262) 1964–77.
Cap 1967. Capt 1975–77. Benefit 1976.
D. B. CLOSE'S XI (2) 1983–84.
PAKISTAN (57) 1958/59–78/79. E 1961/62 (3), 1968/69 (3), 1972/73 (3); WI 1958/59 (1), 1974/75 (2); NZ 1969/70 (2), 1976/77 (3); I 1978/79 (3). *E 1962 (5), 1967 (3), 1971 (3), 1974 (3); A 1972/73 (3), 1976/77 (3), 1978/79 (2); WI 1976/77 (5); NZ 1972/73 (2), 1978/79 (3); I 1960/61 (5).* Capt 19.
OTHER TOURS Commonwealth XI to India 1964/65. Commonwealth XI to Pakistan 1967/68. D. H. Robins' XI to W Indies 1974/75. PIA to Zimbabwe 1981/82. Rest of World v Barbados, Bridgetown, 1966/67.
HST 201 P v NZ, Dunedin, 1972/73. HS

303* Karachi Blues v Karachi U, Karachi, 1967/68.
BBT 5–28 P v WI, Port of Spain, 1976/77. BB 7–18 Karachi Whites v Khairpur, Karachi, 1963/64.
1000 RUNS (12 + 3) 1949 @ 59.06 in 1972.
RECORDS During HST (above) added 350 for 4th wkt with Asif Iqbal, Pakistan fc record; added 291 for 2nd wkt with Zaheer Abbas, P v E, Edgbaston, 1971, Pakistan Test record.
Fc debut, Karachi Whites v Hyderabad, Hyderabad, 1956/57, at age 13 yrs 41 days; Test debut, P v WI, Lahore, 1958/59, at age 15 yrs 124 days (youngest Test cricketer). World Series Cricket (Kerry Packer) 1977/78–78/79. Northumberland 1980, Staffordshire 1982–83, Shropshire 1984. Clubs: Blackpool, Walsall. Brothers Hanif, Wazir, Sadiq Mohammed (all Pakistan) and Raees Mohammed (Karachi).

MUZZELL, Robert Kendal
————RHB, LB————

Born Stutterheim, S Africa, 23 Dec 1945. Educ Queen's C, Queenstown; Cape Town U. Debut 1964/65.
S AFRICA DOMESTIC Western Province 1964/65–67/68, South African Universities 1964/65–67, Transvaal 1968/69–73/74, 1975/76–76/77, Eastern Province 1974/75.
TOUR South African Universities to England 1967.
HS 238* Transvaal B v Natal B, J'burg, 1969/70.
BB 6–69 Transvaal B v OFS, Bloemfontein, 1970/71.
Father K. Muzzell and brother P. J. Muzzell (both Border).

N/O

NADKARNI, Rameshchandra Gangaram (Bapu)
———————LHB, SLA———————

Born Nasik, India, 4 Apr 1932. Debut 1951/52.
INDIA DOMESTIC Maharashtra 1951/52–59/60 (capt 1955/56–56/57, 1958/59–59/60), Bombay 1960/61–67/68 (capt 1963/64–65/66).
INDIA (41) 1955/56–67/68. E 1961/62 (1), 1963/64 (5); A 1959/60 (5), 1964/65 (3); WI 1958/59 (1), 1966/67 (1); NZ 1955/56 (1), 1964/65 (4); P 1960/61 (4). *E 1959 (4); A 1967/68 (3); WI 1961/62 (5); NZ 1967/68 (4)*.
OTHER TOUR India to Ceylon 1956/57. Associated Cement Company to Pakistan 1961/62.
HST 122* I v E, Kanpur, 1963/64. HS 283* Bombay v Delhi, Bombay, 1960/61.
BBT 6/43 I v NZ, Wellington, 1967/68.
BB 6–17 Maharashtra v Saurashtra, Poona, 1957/58.
1000 RUNS (1) 1190 @ 70.00 in 1962/63.
RECORDS Bowled 131 consecutive balls (and 21 six-ball overs) without conceding a run, India v England, Madras 1963/64, a fc record. Added 143 for 8th wkt with F. M. Engineer, I v NZ, Madras, 1964/65, India Test record.
Club: Ramsbottom.

NAEEM AHMED
———————RHB, SLA———————

Born Karachi, Pakistan, 20 Sept 1952. Educ Government S; Government Urdu C, Karachi. Debut 1969/70.
PAKISTAN DOMESTIC Karachi, Universities, National Bank, Pakistan International Airlines, United Bank, 1969/70–.
TOURS Pakistan Under-25 to Sri Lanka 1973/74. Pakistan to Sri Lanka 1975/76. Pakistan to England 1978. PIA to Zimbabwe 1981/82.
HS 127 PIA v Punjab B, Karachi, 1975/76.
BB 8–49 PIA v IDBP, Lahore, 1980/81.
Club: Burnley.

NAGENDA, John
———————RHB, RFM———————

Born Gahim, Rwanda, 25 Apr 1938. Educ King's C, Budo, Uganda; Makarere U, Kampala. Debut 1975.
EAST AFRICA to England (1) 1975.
HS 5* E Africa v Sri Lanka, Taunton, 1975.
BB 2–17 same match.
Clubs: Africa CC, Gymkhana, Nairobi, Stoics, Hurlingham. Editor *The Club Cricketer*.

NAIK, Sudhir Sakharam
———————RHB———————

Born Bombay, India, 22 Feb 1945. Educ Ram Mohan S, Bombay; Bombay U. Debut 1966/67.
INDIA DOMESTIC Bombay 1966/67–77/78 (capt 1970/71).
INDIA (3) 1974–74/75. WI 1974/75 (2). *E 1974 (1)*.
OTHER TOUR Cricket Club of India to Sri Lanka 1972/73.
HST 77 I v E, Edgbaston, 1974. HS 200* Bombay v Baroda, Baroda, 1973/74.

NANA, P. G.
———————RHB, SLA———————

Born N Rhodesia, 1933. Debut 1973/74.
EAST AFRICA (2) 1973/74–75.
TOUR East Africa to England 1975.
HS 16 E Africa v Sri Lanka, Taunton, 1975.
BB 3–61 same match.

NANAN, Nirmal
———————RHB, LBG———————

Born Preysal Village, Couva, Trinidad, 19 Aug 1951. Educ Alpha C, Couva. Debut 1969/70.
W INDIES DOMESTIC South Trinidad 1969/70, Central Trinidad 1972/73.
NOTTINGHAMSHIRE (32) 1971–80.
HS 72 Notts v Oxford U, The Parks, 1971.
BB 3–12 same match.

Coach in Trinidad. Nephew R. Nanan (W Indies).

NAPIER, Ronald Stuart
———————RHB, LB———————

Born Cape Town, S Africa, 23 Oct 1935. Educ Diocesan C, S Africa; Trinity C, Oxford. Debut 1956.
OXFORD UNIVERSITY (1) 1956.
No runs, no wkts.
Golf: South Transvaal. Member of board of Barclays Bank, S Africa.

NASEER MALIK
———————RHB, RMF———————

Born Lyallpur, Pakistan, 1 Feb 1950. Educ Khairpur Polytechnic Institute. Debut 1969/70.
PAKISTAN DOMESTIC Khairpur, National Bank, 1969/70–1981/82.
TOURS Pakistan Under-25 to Sri Lanka 1973/74. Pakistan to England 1974.
HS 55 Khairpur v Rawalpindi Blues, Rawalpindi, 1969/70.
BB 8–49 National Bank v Sind B, Hyderabad, 1976/77.

NASH, Malcolm Andrew
———————LHB, LM/SLA———————

Born Abergavenny, Monmouthshire, Wales, 9 May 1945. Educ Wells Cathedral S. Debut 1966.
GLAMORGAN (335) 1966–83. Cap 1969. Benefit (£18,000) 1978. Capt 1980–81.
TOUR Glamorgan to W Indies 1969/70.
HS 130 Glam v Surrey, Oval, 1976.
BB 9–56 Glam v Hants, Basingstoke, 1975.
Conceded 36 runs (six sixes) in one over to G. S. Sobers, Glam v Notts, Swansea, 1968; also 34 (five sixes, one four) in one over to F. C. Hayes, Glam v Lancs, Swansea, 1977; the two most expensive six-ball overs bowled in fc cricket.

NASIM-UL-GHANI
————LHB, SLA/LM————

Born Delhi, India, 14 May 1941. Educ
Karachi Technical HS; Karachi U;
North Staffs Polytechnic. Debut 1956/
57.
PAKISTAN DOMESTIC Karachi, Univer-
sities, Karachi University, Dacca, East
Pakistan, Public Works Department,
National Bank, 1956/57–74/75.
MINOR COUNTIES (1) 1972.
PAKISTAN (29) 1957/58–72/73. E 1961/
62 (2); A 1959/60 (2), 1964/65 (1); WI
1958/59 (3). *E 1962 (5), 1967 (2); A
1964/65 (1), 1972/73 (1); WI 1957/58
(5); NZ 1964/65 (3); I 1960/61 (4).*
HST 101 P v E, Lord's, 1962. HS 139
PWD v Khairpur, Karachi, 1971/72.
BBT 6–67 P v WI, Port of Spain, 1957/
58. BB 6–24 (12–54 match) Karachi
Whites v E Pakistan, Karachi, 1961/62.
Staffordshire 1968–76. Clubs: Whit-
burn, Longton, Great Chell, Stockton,
Lowerhouse, Darlington RA. Brother
Tehzib-ul-Ghani (Muslim Commercial
Bank).

NASIR ZAIDI, Syed Mohammed
————RHB, LB————

Born Karachi, Pakistan, 25 Mar 1961.
Debut 1983.
LANCASHIRE (19) 1983–.
HS 51 Lancs v Som, Old Trafford, 1983.
BB 3–27 Lancs v Sussex, Horsham,
1983.

NAUSHAD ALI
————RHB, WK————

Born Gowaliar, India, 1 Oct 1943. Educ
Model HS, Karachi; Sind Muslim C;
Karachi U. Debut 1960/61.
PAKISTAN DOMESTIC Karachi University,
Karachi, East Pakistan, Rawalpindi,
Peshawar, North West Frontier
Province, Punjab, Services, 1960/
61–79/80.
PAKISTAN (6) 1964/65. NZ 1964/65 (3).
NZ 1964/65 (3).
OTHER TOURS Pakistan Eaglets to Eng-
land 1963. Pakistan to England 1971.
HST 39 P v NZ, Karachi, 1964/65. HS 158
Karachi Blues v Railways, Lahore,
1962/63.

NAYAK, Surendra Vithal
————RHB, RM/LB————

Born Bombay, India, 20 Oct 1954.
Debut 1977/78.
INDIA DOMESTIC Bombay 1977/78–.
INDIA (2) *E 1982.*
HST 11 I v E, Oval, 1982. HS 100*

Bombay v Maharashtra, Bombay, 1979/
80 and 100* Bombay v Uttar Pradesh,
Kanpur, 1980/81.
BB 6–65 Bombay v Delhi, Bombay,
1980/81.
Club: Crook Town.

NAYLOR, John Edward
————LHB, SLA————

Born Thurcroft, Yorks, 11 Dec 1930.
Debut 1953. *P.*
YORKSHIRE (1) 1953.
Did not bat, no wkts.

NAYUDU, Cottari Subbanna
————RHB, LBG————

Born Nagpur, India, 18 Apr 1914.
Debut 1931/32 (Vizianagram's team v
Ghanshyamsinjhi's team, Patiala).
INDIA DOMESTIC Central Provinces and
Berar 1932/33–33/34, Bombay Hindus
1934/35–44/45, Central India 1934/
35–35/36, Baroda 1939/40–43/44,
Holkar 1944/45–49/50, Bengal 1950/
51–51/52 (capt), Andhra Pradesh 1953/
54–55/56, 1959/60 (capt 1955/56, 1959/
60), Uttar Pradesh 1956/57–58/59 (capt
1957/58–58/59), Madhya Pradesh 1960/
61 (capt).
INDIA (11) 1933/34–51/52. E 1933/34
(2), 1951/52 (1). *E 1936 (2), 1946 (2);
A 1947/48 (4).*
OTHER TOURS India to Ceylon 1944/45.
Holkar to Ceylon 1947/48.
HST 36 I v E, Calcutta, 1933/34. HS 127
Baroda v Rajputana, Baroda, 1942/43.
BB 8–93 (13–176 match) Baroda v
Nawanagar, Baroda, 1939/40.
RECORDS Bowled 917 balls and conceded
428 runs in match, Holkar v Bombay,
Bombay, 1944/45, both world records
(match analysis: 152.5 overs, 25
maidens, 428 runs, 11 wkts).
Durham 1956. Clubs: Littleborough,
Accrington, South Shields. Brothers C.
K. Nayudu (India) and C. L. Nayudu
(Central Provinces and Berar); nephew
P. Nayudu (Madhya Pradesh).

NEAL, John Howard
————RHB, WK————

Born Ditchling, Sussex, 18 Oct 1926.
Educ Hurstpierpoint C. Debut 1951.
SUSSEX (1) 1951.
HS 23 Sussex v Lancs, Old Trafford,
1951.
Clubs: Sussex Martlets, Keymer and
Hassocks, Brighton Brunswick.

NEALE, Philip Anthony
————RHB, occ RM————

Born Scunthorpe, Lincolnshire, 5 June
1954. Educ Frederick Gough GS,
Scunthorpe; Leeds U. Debut 1975.
WORCESTERSHIRE (197) 1975–. Cap 1978.
Capt 1982–.
HS 163* Worcs v Notts, Worcester,
1979.
1000 RUNS (6) 1706 @ 47.39 in 1984.
Lincolnshire 1972. Soccer: Lincoln
City.

NEALE, William Legge
————RHB, OB————

Born Berkeley, Glos, 3 Mar 1904. Died
Gloucester, 26 Oct 1955. Educ Ciren-
cester GS. Debut 1923. *P from 1929.*
GLOUCESTERSHIRE (452) 1923–48. Cap
1927. Benefit 1946.
HS 145* Glos v Hants, Southampton,
1927.
BB 6–9 Glos v Som, Bristol, 1937.
1000 RUNS (6) 1488 @ 29.76 in 1938.
RECORD Added 321 for 4th wkt with
W. R. Hammond, Glos v Leics,
Gloucester, 1937, county record.

NEAME, Arthur *Rex* Beale
————RHB, RM/OB————

Born Faversham, Kent, 14 June 1936.
Educ Harrow. Debut 1956.
KENT (4) 1956–57.
FREE FORESTERS (3) 1957–58.
MCC (1) 1957.
D. R. JARDINE'S XI (2) 1958.
HS 65 (not 69) MCC v Scotland, Aber-
deen, 1957.
BB 2–4 Free Foresters v Cambridge U,
Fenner's, 1958.

NEATE, Francis Webb
————RHB————

Born Newbury, Berkshire, 13 May
1940. Educ St Paul's S; Brasenose C,
Oxford. Debut 1960.
OXFORD UNIVERSITY (17) 1960–62 (Blue
1961–62).
HS 112 Oxford U v Hants, Portsmouth,
1961.
Berkshire 1958–79. Club: Richmond.
Brother P. W. Neate (Oxford U).

NEATE, Patrick Whistler
————LHB, RM————

Born Newbury, Berkshire, 2 May 1946.
Educ St Paul's S; Brasenose C, Oxford.
Debut 1966.

OXFORD UNIVERSITY (1) 1966.
HS 3 Oxford U v Notts, The Parks, 1966.
Berkshire 1964–. Brother F. W. Neate
(Oxford U).

NEEDHAM, Andrew
———RHB, OB———

Born Calow, Derbys, 23 Mar 1957.
Educ Ecclesbourne GS; Paisley GS;
Watford GS. Debut 1977.
SURREY (55) 1977–.
HS 134* Surrey v Lancs, Old Trafford,
1982.
BB 6–30 Surrey v Oxford U, Oval, 1983.
Clubs: Stanmore, West Ham, St
Albans.

NEEDHAM, Patrick John
Easthope
———LHB, RM———

Born Cardiff, S Wales, 6 Dec 1951.
Educ Harrow. Debut 1975.
GLAMORGAN (1) 1975.
HS 4 Glam v Cambridge U, Swansea,
1975.

NELSON, Peter John Mytton
———LHB, LM———

Born Finchley, London, 16 May 1918.
Educ St George's, Harpenden. Debut
1938.
NORTHAMPTONSHIRE (1) 1938.
KENT (1) 1946.
HS 32 Northants v Cambridge U,
Fenner's, 1938.
Club: St Lawrence Canterbury.

NEVELL, William Thomas
———RHB, RFM———

Born Balham, S London, 13 June 1916.
Died Worthing, Sussex, 25 Aug 1978.
Debut 1936. *P.*
MIDDLESEX (13) 1936–38.
SURREY (1) 1939.
NORTHAMPTONSHIRE (36) 1946–47.
HS 55* Northants v Essex, Northampton, 1946.
BB 4–11 Northants v Derbys, Derby,
1946.

NEVILLE, Patrick Augustine
———RHB———

Born Donabate, Co Dublin, Ireland, 22
June 1920. Died Dublin, Ireland, 16
Nov 1977. Educ O'Connell Christian
Brothers' S, Dublin. Debut 1956.
IRELAND (4) 1956–60.

HS 38 Ireland v Scotland, Paisley, 1960.
Club: Malahide. Hockey: Ireland.

NEVIN, Michael Robert Spencer
———RHB, RFM———

Born London, 5 Apr 1950. Educ Winchester C; Emmanuel C, Cambridge.
Debut 1969.
CAMBRIDGE UNIVERSITY (8) 1969 (Blue).
HS 14* Cambridge U v Worcs,
Halesowen, 1969.
BB 2–50 Cambridge U v Warwicks,
Fenner's, 1969.

NEWBURN, Thomas
———RHB, RFM———

Born Belfast, Ireland, 10 Aug 1918.
Debut 1949.
IRELAND (1) 1949.
HS 8 Ireland v Scotland, Belfast, 1949.
BB 3–23 same match.
Clubs: Woodvale, CPA.

NEWELL, Michael
———RHB, LB———

Born Blackburn, Lancs, 25 Feb 1965.
Educ West Bridgford S. Debut 1984.
NOTTINGHAMSHIRE (3) 1984.
HS 76 Notts v Cambridge U, Trent
Bridge, 1984.

NEWMAN, Douglas Leonard
———RHB———

Born Harringay, London, 25 June 1920.
Died UC Hospital, London, 10 Sept
1959. Debut 1948.
MIDDLESEX (11) 1948–51.
MCC (1) 1953.
HS 29 M'sex v Oxford U, The Parks,
1951.
M'sex 2nd XI 1954–58 (capt). Clubs:
Alexandra Park, Winchmore Hill.

NEWMAN, Paul Geoffrey
———RHB, RFM———

Born Leicester, 10 Jan 1959. Educ Alderman Newton's GS, Leicester. Debut
1980.
DERBYSHIRE (59) 1980–.
HS 40 Derbys v Lancs, Old Trafford,
1984.
BB 7–104 Derbys v Surrey, Oval, 1984.

NEWMAN, Roger Grant
———RHB———

Born Bristol, 23 Dec 1933. Educ Clifton;
Trinity Hall, Cambridge. Debut 1955.

CAMBRIDGE UNIVERSITY (4) 1955–57.
HS 44 Cambridge U v Hants, Bournemouth, 1957.
Club: Clifton. Rackets: Blue (capt).

NEWPORT, Philip John
———RHB, RFM———

Born High Wycombe, Buckinghamshire, 11 Oct 1962. Educ High
Wycombe RGS; Portsmouth Polytechnic. Debut 1982.
WORCESTERSHIRE (17) 1982–.
HS 41* Worcs v Warwicks, Edgbaston,
1983.
BB 5–51 Worcs v Warwicks, Worcester,
1984.
Buckinghamshire 1981–82. Club: High
Wycombe.

NEWSOM, David John
———RHB———

Born Plymouth, Devon, 5 Oct 1937.
Educ Haileybury and ISC. Debut 1960.
COMBINED SERVICES (2) 1960–61.
HS 23 Combined Services v Northants,
Northampton, 1961.
HMS Glamorgan, Royal Navy. Royal
Navy commander.

NEWTON, Harry
———RHB, RFM———

Born Little Lever, nr Bolton, Lancs, 2
May 1935. Debut 1966.
SUSSEX (2) 1966.
HS 16* Sussex v Hants, Hove, 1966 (fc
debut).
BB 5–54 same match.

NEWTON-THOMPSON, John
Oswald
———RHB———

Born Paddington, London, 2 Dec 1920.
Died, in air crash, SW Africa, 3 Mar
1974. Educ Diocesan C, Rondesbosch,
S Africa; Trinity C, Oxford (Rhodes
Scholar). Debut 1946.
OXFORD UNIVERSITY (7) 1946 (Blue).
S AFRICA DOMESTIC Western Province
1948/49.
HS 78 W Province v MCC, Cape Town,
1948/49.
Rugby: Blue, England (2 caps). MP for
S African United Party from 1961 until
death. Brother C. L. Newton-
Thompson (Cambridge U).

NIAZ AHMED
————RHB, RFM————

Born Benares, India, 11 Nov 1945. Debut 1963/64.
PAKISTAN DOMESTIC Dacca, Public Works Department, East Pakistan, Railways, 1963/64–74/75.
PAKISTAN (2) 1967–68/69. E 1968/69 (1). *E 1967 (1)*.
HST 16* P v E, Dacca, 1968/69. HS 71* PWD v Bahawalpur, Bahawalpur, 1969/70.
BB 5–86 Pakistanis v Kent, Canterbury, 1967.

NICHOL, David
————RHB, SLA————

Born Galashiels, Selkirk, Scotland, 25 Aug 1914. Educ Galashiels Academy. Debut 1952.
SCOTLAND (1) 1952.
HS 4 Scotland v Yorks, Glasgow, 1952.
BB 2–61 same match.
Club: Gala. Brothers R. J. and W. Nichol (both Scotland).

NICHOL, Robert John
————RHB, RFM————

Born Galashiels, Selkirk, Scotland, 14 Mar 1924. Educ Galashiels Academy. Debut 1951.
SCOTLAND (7) 1951–55.
HS 19 Scotland v Ireland, Belfast, 1953.
BB 5–87 Scotland v Yorks, Glasgow, 1953.
Club: Gala. Brothers D. and W. Nichol (both Scotland).

NICHOL, William
————LHB, SLA————

Born Galashiels, Selkirk, Scotland, 3 Dec 1912. Died Paisley, Scotland, 1 June 1973. Educ Galashiels Academy. Debut 1938.
SCOTLAND (26) 1938–56.
HS 139* Scotland v Warwicks, Edgbaston, 1951.
BB 7–39 Scotland v Ireland, Glasgow, 1948.
Clubs: Gala, Kelburne.

NICHOLAS, Mark Charles Jefford
————RHB, RMF————

Born London, 29 Sept 1957. Educ Bradfield C. Debut 1978.
HAMPSHIRE (119) 1978–. Cap 1982.
Appointed capt for 1985.

HS 206* Hants v Oxford U, The Parks, 1982.
BB 5–45 Hants v Worcs, Southampton, 1983.
1000 RUNS (3) 1559 @ 33.89 in 1984.
Grandfather F. W. H. Nicholas (Essex).

NICHOLLS, David
————LHB, WK, occ RLB————

Born East Dereham, Norfolk, 8 Dec 1943. Educ Gravesend GS. Debut 1960. *P*.
KENT (201) 1960–77. Cap 1969. Benefit 1980.
HS 211 Kent v Derbys, Folkestone, 1963.
1000 RUNS (1) 1000 @ 32.25 in 1971.

NICHOLLS, Ronald Bernard
————RHB, OB, occ WK————

Born Sharpness, Glos, 4 Dec 1933. Debut 1951. *P*.
GLOUCESTERSHIRE (534) 1951–75. Cap 1957. Benefit (£3750) 1966.
HS 217 Glos v Oxford U, The Parks, 1962.
BB 2–19 Glos v Glam, Neath, 1964.
1000 RUNS (15) 2059 @ 36.76 in 1962.
RECORD During HS (above) added 395 for 1st wkt with D. M. Young, county record.
Club: Cheltenham. Soccer: Bristol Rovers, Cardiff City, Bristol City.

NICHOLS, John Bowes
————RHB, SLA————

Born Latchford, Cheshire, 1 Jan 1931. Educ Wrekin; Magdalene C, Cambridge. Debut 1953.
CAMBRIDGE UNIVERSITY (5) 1953.
HS 16 Cambridge U v Sussex, Fenner's, 1953.

NICHOLSON, Anthony George
————RHB, RMF————

Born Dewsbury, Yorks, 25 June 1938. Educ Wheelwright GS, Dewsbury. Debut 1962. *P*.
YORKSHIRE (282) 1962–75. Cap 1963. Benefit (£13,214) 1973.
HS 50 Yorks v M'sex, Lord's, 1974.
BB 9–62 Yorks v Sussex, Eastbourne, 1967.
100 WKTS (2) 113 @ 15.50 in 1966.
Selected MCC to S Africa 1964/65 but could not go because of injury. Clubs: Hanging Heaton, Littleborough, Marske.

NIMBALKAR, Raosaheb Babashaheb
————RHB, WK————

Born Kolhapur, Maharashtra, India, 1 Dec 1915. Died Jalna, India, 1 June 1965. Debut 1934/35.
INDIA DOMESTIC Maharashtra 1934/35–40/41, Bombay Hindus 1938/39, Baroda 1938/39–52/53 (capt 1944/45–48/49).
TOURS India to Ceylon 1944/45. India to England 1946.
HS 132 Baroda v Bombay, Bombay, 1945/46.
Brother B. B. Nimbalkar (Baroda); nephew S. B. Nimbalkar (Maharashtra).

NIVEN, Robert Andrew
————RHB, LM————

Born Felixstowe, Suffolk, 28 Apr 1948. Educ Berkhamsted; Michigan U; New C, Oxford. Debut 1968.
OXFORD UNIVERSITY (25) 1968–73 (Blue 1968–69, 1973).
HS 24* Oxford U v Sussex, The Parks, 1968.
BB 5–60 Oxford U v Notts, The Parks, 1968.
Club: Berkhamsted.

NOBLET, Geffery
————RHB, RFM————

Born Adelaide, S Australia, 14 Sept 1916. Debut 1945/46.
AUSTRALIA DOMESTIC South Australia (49) 1945/46–52/53.
COMMONWEALTH XI (1) 1956.
AUSTRALIA (3) 1949/50–52/53. SA 1952/53 (1); WI 1951/52 (1). *SA 1949/50 (1)*.
HST 13* A v SA, Melbourne, 1952/53. HS 55* Australians v NE Transvaal, Pretoria, 1949/50.
BBT 3–21 A v SA, Port Elizabeth, 1949/50. BB 7–29 S Australia v Victoria, Adelaide, 1951/52.
Club: Nelson. President S Australian Cricket Society.

NOLAN, Geoffrey John
————RHB————

Born Colchester, Essex, 6 Oct 1937. Educ Endsleigh S. Debut 1968.
ESSEX (1) 1968.
HS 11 Essex v Derbys, Colchester, 1968.
Club: Colchester and East Essex.

NORMAN, John William
————RHB, WK————

Born Maidstone, Kent, 22 Aug 1936. Educ Downside; Queen's C,

Cambridge. Debut 1957.
CAMBRIDGE UNIVERSITY (2) 1957.
HS 9 Cambridge U v M'sex, Fenner's, 1957.
Run out in two of three fc inns.
Berkshire 1966.

NORMAN, Michael Eric John Charles
————RHB, occ RM————

Born Northampton, 19 Jan 1933. Educ Northampton GS. Debut 1952. *P.*
NORTHAMPTONSHIRE (202) 1952-65. Cap 1960.
LEICESTERSHIRE (151) 1966-75. Cap 1966. Testimonial 1975.
HS 221* Leics v Cambridge U, Fenner's, 1967.
BB 2-0 Northants v Lancs, Northampton, 1961.
1000 RUNS (8) 1964 @ 33.86 in 1960.

NORRIS, David William Worsley
————RHB, WK————

Born Hampstead, London, 1 May 1946. Educ Harrow; Selwyn C, Cambridge. Debut 1967.
CAMBRIDGE UNIVERSITY (20) 1967-68 (Blue 1967-68).
HS 43 Cambridge U v Northants, Northampton, 1967.
Member I Zingari.

NORTHCOTE-GREEN, Simon Roger
————RHB, RM————

Born Worksop, Notts, 30 Aug 1954. Educ St Edward's, Oxford; Keble C, Oxford. Debut 1974.
OXFORD UNIVERSITY (9) 1974-79.
HS 38* Oxford U v Worcs, The Parks, 1979.
Grandfather E. A. Greswell (Som); great-uncle W. T. Greswell (Som).

NORTON, Gerald *Ivor* Desmond
————RHB, SLA————

Born Earl Shilton, Leics, 19 May 1919. Educ Malvern. Debut 1958.
MCC (2) 1958-60.
HS 2* MCC v Ireland, Dublin, 1958 and 2 MCC v Ireland, Dublin, 1960.
BB 6-57 MCC v Ireland, Dublin, 1960. Returned match figures of 9-70 and 8-63 in only two fc matches.
Clubs: Free Foresters, Wimbledon.

NORTON, Ian David
————RHB————

Born Stamford, Lincolnshire, 21 Oct 1937. Educ Stamford; St Edmund Hall, Oxford. Debut 1959.
OXFORD UNIVERSITY (1) 1959.
HS 30 Oxford U v Notts, The Parks, 1959.
Club: Ilford.

NOTLEY, Bernarr
————RHB, OB————

Born Mapperley, Nottingham, 31 Aug 1918. Debut 1949.
NOTTINGHAMSHIRE (1) 1949.
No runs, one wkt.

NOURSE, Arthur *Dudley*
————RHB————

Born Durban, S Africa, 12 Nov 1910. Died Durban, S Africa, 14 Aug 1981. Educ Mansfield Road Boys' HS, Durban, S Africa. Debut 1931/32. *Wisden* 1948.
S AFRICA DOMESTIC Natal 1931/32-52/53.
SOUTH AFRICA (34) 1935-51. E 1938/39 (5), 1948/49 (5); A 1935/36 (5), 1949/50 (5). *E 1935 (4), 1947 (5), 1951 (5).* Capt 15.
HST 231 SA v A, J'burg, 1935/36. HS 260* Natal v Transvaal, J'burg, 1936/37.
1000 RUNS (2) 1681 @ 41.00 in 1935.
S Africa selector and team manager after retirement. MCC Hon. member. Father A. W. Nourse (S Africa).

NUNN, John Aynscough
————RHB————

Born Barnet, Hertfordshire, 19 Mar 1906. Educ Sherborne; New C, Oxford. Debut 1926.
OXFORD UNIVERSITY (18) 1926-28 (Blue 1926-27).
MIDDLESEX (3) 1926.
FREE FORESTERS (1) 1946.
HS 98 Oxford U v Army, The Parks, 1927.

NURSE, Seymour McDonald
————RHB, OB————

Born St Michael, Barbados, 10 Nov 1933. Educ St Stephen's S. Debut 1958/59. *Wisden* 1967.
W INDIES DOMESTIC Barbados 1958/59-71/72.
WEST INDIES (29) 1959/60-68/69. E 1959/60 (1), 1967/68 (5); A 1964/65 (4);

I 1961/62 (1). *E 1966 (5); A 1960/61 (3), 1968/69 (5); NZ 1968/69 (3); I 1966/67 (2).*
OTHER TOURS W Indies to England 1963. Commonwealth XI to Pakistan 1963/64. E. W. Swanton's XI to Commonwealth 1963/64. W Indian XI to England 1964. Rest of World XI in England 1967. Barbados to England 1969.
HST 258 WI v NZ, Christchurch, 1968/69. HS as above.
BB 3-36 W Indians v Ceylon, Colombo, 1966/67.
1000 RUNS (1) 1105 @ 44.20 in 1966.
RECORD Added 265 for 5th wkt with G. S. Sobers, WI v E, Headingley, 1966, W Indies Test record.
Club: Ramsbottom. MCC Hon. member.

NUTTER, Albert Edward
————RHB, RMF————

Born Burnley, Lancs, 28 June 1913. Debut 1935. *P.*
LANCASHIRE (70) 1935-45. Cap 1938.
NORTHAMPTONSHIRE (145) 1948-53. Cap 1948. Joint testimonial (with N. Oldfield) (£2728) 1953.
HS 109* Lancs v Notts, Old Trafford, 1939.
BB 7-52 (12-86 match) Northants v Kent, Northampton, 1948.
1000 RUNS (1) 1156 @ 32.11 in 1938.
100 WKTS (1) 105 @ 22.88 in 1948.
RECORDS Added 155 for 8th wkt with F. R. Brown, Northants v Glam, Northampton, 1952, county record.
Only nine wkts short of the double in 1938.
Clubs: Formby, Crompton, Old Hill, Mitchells and Butlers, Horton House.

NYE, John Kent
————RHB, RFM————

Born Isfield, Sussex, 23 May 1914. Debut 1934. *P.*
SUSSEX (99) 1934-47. Cap.
HS 55 Sussex v Worcs, Eastbourne, 1939.
BB 6-95 Sussex v Glos, Hove, 1947.
100 WKTS (1) 110 @ 30.60 in 1939.
Gold Coast 1949. Officials v Settlers (Nairobi) 1950.

OAKDEN, Robert *Patrick*
————RHB, RFM————

Born Kirkby-in-Ashfield, Notts, 9 May 1938. Debut 1960. *P*
NOTTINGHAMSHIRE (8) 1960-61.
HS 24 Notts v Hants, Trent Bridge, 1961.

BB 4–78 Notts v Oxford U, The Parks, 1961.

OAKES, Charles
—————RHB, LBG—————

Born Horsham, Sussex, 10 Aug 1912. Debut 1935. *P.*
SUSSEX (286) 1935–54. Cap 1937. Benefit (£4,100) 1954.
HS 160 Sussex v Glam, Chichester, 1950.
BB 8–147 Sussex v Kent, Tonbridge, 1939.
1000 RUNS (5) 1607 @ 29.21 in 1949.
Clubs: Horsham, Ayr. Former professional coach Stowe S (from 1958). Registered in 1983 as a blind person. Brother J. Y. Oakes (Sussex); father A. Oakes (groundsman at Horsham).

OAKES, Dennis Raymond
—————RHB, LB—————

Born Bedworth, Warwicks, 10 Apr 1946. Educ Nicholas Chamberlain CS, Bedworth. Debut 1965.
WARWICKSHIRE (5) 1965.
HS 33 Warwicks v Worcs, Worcester, 1965.
Coventry area coach for Warwicks. Soccer: Notts County, Peterborough United.

OAKES, John Ypres
—————RHB, OB—————

Born Horsham (cricket ground), Sussex, 29 Mar 1916. Educ Oxford Road S, Horsham. Debut 1937. *P.*
SUSSEX (128) 1937–51. Cap 1949.
HS 151 Sussex v Cambridge U, Hove, 1950.
BB 7–64 Sussex v Warwicks, Edgbaston, 1947.
1000 RUNS (1) 1157 @ 22.68 in 1950.
Northumberland County 1954–60. Clubs: Horsham, Werneth, Northumberland CC, Benwell, South Northumberland, Shottery Bridge, Chester (Boughton Hall). Former professional coach Framlingham C. Later Tyndale groundsman. Brother C. Oakes (Sussex); father A. Oakes (groundsman at Horsham).

OAKLEY, Leonard
—————LHB, SLA—————

Born Stourbridge, Worcs, 11 Jan 1916. Debut 1935. *P.*
WORCESTERSHIRE (8) 1935–48.
HS 11 Worcs v Lancs, Old Trafford, 1948.

BB 6–64 Worcs v RAF, Worcester, 1946.
Clubs: West Bromwich Dartmouth, Vono (Dudley).

OAKMAN, Alan Stanley Myles
—————RHB, OB—————

Born Hastings, Sussex, 20 Apr 1930. Educ Hastings GS. Debut 1947. *P.*
SUSSEX (497) 1947–68. Cap 1951. Benefit (£5900) 1965.
ENGLAND (2) A 1956.
TOURS E. W. Swanton's XI to W Indies 1955/56. MCC to S Africa 1956/57.
HST 10 E v A, Old Trafford, 1956. HS 229* Sussex v Notts, Worksop, 1961.
BB 7–39 Sussex v Glam, Eastbourne, 1954.
1000 RUNS (9) 2307 @ 36.61 in 1961.
Took 99 wkts @ 20.97 in 1954 and 57 catches in 1958. Made 594 catches in career.
Players v Gentlemen (1) 1956. Fc umpire 1969. Warwicks senior coach 1970–. Club: XL. Son-in-law K. D. Smith (Warwicks).

OATES, William Farrand
—————RHB, RM/OB—————

Born Aston, Sheffield, Yorks, 11 June 1929. Debut 1956. *P.*
YORKSHIRE (3) 1956.
DERBYSHIRE (121) 1959–65. Cap 1962.
HS 148* Derbys v Sussex, Worthing, 1961.
BB 6–47 Derbys v Oxford U, The Parks, 1964.
1000 RUNS (2) 1288 @ 33.02 in 1961.
Clubs: Aston Hall, Sheffield United, Paddock.

O'BRIEN, Brendan Anthony
—————RHB—————

Born Galway, Ireland, 2 Sept 1942. Educ Westland Row Christian Brothers' S. Debut 1966.
IRELAND (11) 1966–81.
HS 45* Ireland v Sri Lankans, Eglinton, 1979.
Club: Railway Union.

O'BRIEN, Gerard Peter
—————RHB—————

Born Dublin, Ireland, 12 Nov 1942. Educ O'Connell S, Dublin. Debut 1976.
IRELAND (2) 1976–77.
HS 11 Ireland v Scotland, Dublin, 1977.
Club: Malahide.

O'BRIEN, Neil Terence
—————RHB, RM—————

Born Heaton Moor, Cheshire, 9 Mar 1945. Debut 1979.
MINOR COUNTIES (2) 1979–81.
HS 14 Minor Counties v Indians, Wellington (Shropshire), 1979.
Cheshire 1970–. Clubs: Crewe, Cheadle Hulme.

O'BRIEN, Robin
—————RHB, occ OB—————

Born Shillong, Assam, India, 20 Nov 1932. Died Biddenden, Kent, 16 Aug 1959. Educ Wellington C; Corpus Christi C, Cambridge. Debut 1954.
CAMBRIDGE UNIVERSITY (35) 1954–56 (Blue 1955–56).
IRELAND (4) 1954–58.
MCC (1) 1958.
HS 146 Cambridge U v Oxford U, Lord's, 1956.
Golf: Blue.

ODENDAAL, André
—————RHB, OB—————

Born Queenstown, S Africa, 4 May 1954. Educ Queen's C, Queenstown; Stellenbosch U; St John's C, Cambridge. Debut 1980.
CAMBRIDGE UNIVERSITY (12) 1980–83 (Blue).
S AFRICA DOMESTIC Boland 1980/81–81/82.
HS 61 Cambridge U v Leics, Fenner's, 1980.
Author of *God's Forgotten Cricketers* (1976) and *Cricket in Isolation* (1977).

O'KEEFFE, Kerry James
—————RHB, LBG—————

Born Hurstville, Sydney, Australia, 25 Nov 1949. Educ Marist Brother's C, Kogarah, Australia. Debut 1968/69.
AUSTRALIA DOMESTIC New South Wales (65) 1968/69–79/80.
SOMERSET (46) 1971–72. Cap 1971.
AUSTRALIA (24) 1970/71–77. E 1970/71 (2), 1976/77 (1); NZ 1973/74 (3); P 1972/73 (2), 1976/77 (3). *E 1977 (3); WI 1972/73 (5); NZ 1973/74 (3), 1976/77 (2).*
OTHER TOUR Australia to N Zealand 1969/70.
HST 85 A v NZ, Adelaide, 1973/74. HS 99* Australians v Auckland, Auckland, 1973/74.
BBT 5–101 A v NZ, Christchurch, 1976/77. BB 7–38 (12–79 match) Som v Sussex, Taunton, 1971.

World Series Cricket (Kerry Packer) 1977/78–78/79. Clubs: St George, North Sydney, Newcastle (Australia), East Lancashire.

OLD, Alan Gerald Bernard
—RHB, RFM—

Born Middlesbrough, Yorks, 23 Sept 1945. Educ Acklam Hall GS, Middlesbrough. Debut 1969.
WARWICKSHIRE (1) 1969.
HS 34 Warwicks v Cambridge U, Edgbaston, 1969.
Durham 1968–78. Clubs: Middlesbrough, Sheffield Collegiate. Rugby: Middlesbrough, Leicester, Sheffield, England (16), British Lions to S Africa 1974. Brother C. M. Old (Yorks, Warwicks, England).

OLD, Christopher Middleton
—LHB, RFM—

Born Middlesbrough, Yorks, 22 Dec 1948. Educ Acklam Hall GS, Middlesbrough. Debut 1966. *Wisden* 1979.
YORKSHIRE (222) 1966–82. Cap 1969. Benefit (£32,916) 1979. Capt 1981.
WARWICKSHIRE (40) 1983–84. Cap 1984.
S AFRICA DOMESTIC Northern Transvaal 1981/82–82/83.
ENGLAND (46) 1972/73–81. A 1975 (3), 1977 (2), 1980 (1), 1981 (2); WI 1973 (1), 1976 (2), 1980 (1); NZ 1973 (2), 1978 (1); I 1974 (3); P 1974 (3), 1978 (3). A 1974/75 (2), 1976/77 (1), 1978/79 (1); WI 1973/74 (4), 1980/81 (1); NZ 1974/75 (1), 1977/78 (2); I 1972/73 (4), 1976/77 (4); P 1972/73 (1), 1977/78 (1).
OTHER TOURS Duke of Norfolk's XI to W Indies 1969/70. International Wanderers to Rhodesia 1975/76.
HST 65 E v P, Oval, 1974. HS 116 Yorks v Indians, Bradford, 1974.
BBT 7–50 E v P, Edgbaston, 1978. BB 7–20 Yorks v Glos, Middlesbrough, 1969.
Scored third-fastest fc century ever, in 37 mins, during inns of 107 Yorks v Warwicks, Edgbaston, 1977, when the bowling was aiming to advance a declaration. Took four wkts in five balls of one over, E v P, Edgbaston, 1978 (ww.ww, the third ball being a no-ball). Barred from Test cricket for three yrs for touring S Africa 1981/82 (SAB England XI). Club: Middlesbrough. Brother A. G. B. Old (Warwicks).

OLDFIELD, Norman (Buddy)
—RHB—

Born Dukinfield, Cheshire, 5 May 1911. Debut 1935. *P.*

LANCASHIRE (151) 1935–39. Cap 1935.
NORTHAMPTONSHIRE (159) 1948–54. Cap 1948. Testimonial (with A. E. Nutter) (£2728) 1953.
ENGLAND (1) WI 1939.
TOURS Sir J. Cahn's XI to N Zealand 1938/39. Commonwealth XI to India, Pakistan and Ceylon 1949/50.
HST 80 E v WI, Oval, 1939. HS 168 Northants v Worcs, Worcester, 1949.
1000 RUNS (11) 2192 @ 49.81 in 1949.
RECORDS Put on 361 for 1st wkt with V. Broderick, Northants v Scotland, Peterborough, 1953; added 306 for 3rd wkt with E. Paynter, Lancs v Hants, Southampton, 1938, both county records.
Scored 1066 runs @ 32.30 in debut season, 1935.
Fc umpire 1954–65. Clubs: Crompton, Birkenhead Park. Former professional coach Birkenhead S (from 1956).

OLDHAM, Stephen
—RHB, RFM—

Born High Green, Sheffield, Yorks, 26 July 1948. Educ Crossfield High Green S. Debut 1974.
YORKSHIRE (57) 1974–79, 1984.
DERBYSHIRE (70) 1980–83. Cap 1980.
HS 50 Yorks v Sussex, Hove, 1979.
BB 7–78 Derbys v Warwicks, Edgbaston, 1982.

O'LINN, Sydney
—LHB, occ WK—

Born Cape Town, S Africa, 5 May 1927. Debut 1945/46. *P.*
S AFRICA DOMESTIC Western Province 1945/46–46/47, Transvaal 1958/59–65/66.
KENT (26) 1951–54.
SOUTH AFRICA (7) 1960–61/62. NZ 1961/62 (2). E 1960 (5).
HST 98 E v SA, Trent Bridge, 1960. HS 120* S Africans v Warwicks, Edgbaston, 1960.
BB 2–14 Transvaal v W Province, Cape Town, 1960/61.
1000 RUNS (2) 1080 @ 29.18 in 1952.
Soccer: Charlton Athletic.

OLIVE, Martin
—RHB, RM—

Born Watford, Hertfordshire, 18 Apr 1958. Educ Millfield. Debut 1977.
SOMERSET (17) 1977–81.
HS 50 Som v Yorks, Weston-super-Mare, 1980.
Devon 1982–.

OLIVER, John Archibald Ralph
—RHB, RM/OB—

Born Whitwell, Hertfordshire, 25 Nov 1918. Educ Aldenham. Debut 1951.
MINOR COUNTIES (1) 1951.
HS 84* Minor Counties v Kent, Canterbury, 1951.
Bedfordshire 1946–61 (capt 1954–61). Clubs: Luton Town, MCC, XL.

OLIVER, Philip Robert
—RHB, RM/OB—

Born West Bromwich, Staffordshire, 9 May 1956. Educ Newport Sec S. Debut 1975.
WARWICKSHIRE (89) 1975–82.
HS 171* Warwicks v Northants, Northampton, 1981.
BB 2–28 Warwicks v Sussex, Edgbaston, 1978.
Shropshire 1972–74. Clubs: Newport, Penn, Old Hill.

OLLEY, Martin William Charles
—RHB, WK—

Born Romford, Essex, 27 Nov 1963. Educ Felsted. Debut 1983.
NORTHAMPTONSHIRE (1) 1983.
HS 8 Northants v Cambridge U, Fenner's, 1983.
Hertfordshire 1984.

OLLIS, Richard Leslie
—LHB, RM—

Born Clifton, Bristol, 14 Jan 1961. Educ Wellway CS, Keynsham. Debut 1981.
SOMERSET (22) 1981–.
HS 99* Som v Glos, Bristol, 1983.

OLTON, Mike Francis
—RHB, OB—

Born San Fernando, Trinidad, 20 June 1938. Educ Government S, San Fernando. Debut 1959/60. *P.*
W INDIES DOMESTIC South Trinidad 1959/60.
KENT (1) 1962.
HS 28 S Trinidad v N Trinidad, Pointe-á-Pierre, 1959/60.
BB 2–86 Kent v Pakistanis, Canterbury, 1962.
Clubs: San Fernando, Oxford, Blackheath.

O'MAILLE, Ciaran
—RHB—

Born Dublin, Ireland, 14 June 1925. Died Dublin, Ireland, 4 Mar 1977.

Educ Blackrock C, Dublin. Debut 1953.
IRELAND (2) 1953–60.
HS 5 Ireland v MCC, Dublin, 1960.
Club: Pembroke. Hockey: Ireland.

O'MEARA, Joseph Anthony
————————RHB, OB————————

Born Dublin, Ireland, 24 June, 1943.
Educ Blackrock C, Dublin. Debut 1963.
IRELAND (1) 1963.
No runs, one wkt.
Club: Railway Union. Hockey: Ireland.

O'NEILL, Norman Clifford
————————RHB, LB/RM————————

Born Carlton, Sydney, NSW, Australia,
19 Feb 1937. Educ Kogarah HS. Debut
1955/56. *Wisden* 1962.
AUSTRALIA DOMESTIC New South Wales
(70) 1955/56–66/67.
AUSTRALIA (42) 1958/59–64/65. E 1958/
59 (5), 1962/63 (5); SA 1963/64 (4); WI
1960/61 (5). *E 1961 (5), 1964 (4); WI
1964/65 (4); I 1959/60 (5), 1964/65
(2); P 1959/60 (3).*
OTHER TOURS Australia to N Zealand
1956/57, 1966/67. Cavaliers to S Africa
1960/61. Cavaliers to India and S Africa
1962/63. Prime Minister's XI v
President's XI, Bombay, 1967/68
(Koyna relief match).
HST 181 A v WI, Brisbane, 1960/61. HS
284 Australians v President's XI, Ahmedabad, 1959/60.
BBT 4–41 A v WI, Port of Spain, 1964/
65. BB 4–40 NSW v Queensland, Sydney, 1957/58.
1000 RUNS (2 + 6) 1981 @ 60.03 in 1961.
Clubs: St George, Sutherland
(Australia). MCC Hon. member.
Autobiography *Ins and Outs* (1964). Son
M. D. O'Neill (W Australia).

ONTONG, Rodney Craig
————————RHB, RMF/OB————————

Born Johannesburg, S Africa, 9 Sept
1955. Educ Selbourne C, East London,
S Africa. Debut 1972/73.
S AFRICA DOMESTIC Border 1972/73–75/
76, 1982/83–, Transvaal 1976/77–77/
78, Northern Transvaal 1978/79–81/82.
GLAMORGAN (170) 1975–. Cap 1979.
Capt for 1985.
HS 204* Glam v M'sex, Swansea, 1984.
BB 7–60 Border v N Transvaal, Pretoria,
1975/76.
1000 RUNS (4) 1320 @ 35.68 in 1984.

OPATHA, Anthony Ralph Marinon
————————RHB, RMF————————

Born Colombo, Ceylon, 5 Aug 1947.
Educ St Peter's C, Colombo. Debut
1969/70.
SRI LANKA DOMESTIC Ceylon (Sri Lanka)
1969/70–82/83.
OTHER TOURS Sri Lanka to Pakistan
1973/74. Sri Lanka to England 1975,
1979. Sri Lanka to India 1975/76.
HS 65 Sri Lankans v Universities, Ban-
galore, 1975/76.
BB 6–92 Sri Lanka v Pakistan, Lahore,
1973/74.
Barred from Sinhalese cricket for 25 yrs
for touring S Africa 1982/83 (manager of
Arosa Sri Lanka). Clubs: Denton West,
Nondescripts.

ORD, James Simpson
————————RHB————————

Born Backworth, Northumberland, 12
July 1912. Debut 1933. *P.*
WARWICKSHIRE (273) 1933–53. Cap
1935. Benefit (£4834) 1950.
HS 187* Warwicks v Cambridge U,
Fenner's, 1952.
1000 RUNS (6) 1577 @ 39.42 in 1948.
RECORD Added 250 for 7th wkt with
H. E. Dollery, Warwicks v Kent, Maid-
stone, 1953, county record.
Club: Aston Unity. Brother J. D. Ord
(Minor Counties).

ORDERS, Jonathan Oliver Darcy
————————LHB, LM————————

Born Beckenham, Kent, 12 Aug 1957.
Educ Winchester; Trinity C, Oxford.
Debut 1978.
OXFORD UNIVERSITY (26) 1978–81 (Blue
1978–81).
OXFORD AND CAMBRIDGE UNIVERSITIES (1)
1981.
HS 79 Oxford U v Worcs, Worcester,
1978.
BB 2–16 Oxford U v Glos, The Parks,
1978.
Club: Stragglers.

O'REILLY, Peter Mark
————————RHB, RFM————————

Born Dublin, Ireland, 23 July 1962.
Educ Belvedere. Debut 1982.
IRELAND (2) 1982–.
HS 1* Ireland v Scotland, Edinburgh,
1982.
BB 3–43 Ireland v Scotland, Glasgow,
1984.

Warwicks staff 1983–84. Club: Old
Belvedere.

O'RIORDAN, Alex John
————————RHB, LFM————————

Born Dublin, Ireland, 20 July 1940.
Educ Belvedere C, Dublin. Debut 1958.
IRELAND (25) 1958–77.
HS 117 Ireland v Scotland, Glasgow,
1976.
BB 6–35 Ireland v MCC, Dublin, 1966.
Clubs: Clontarf, Old Belvedere.

ORMROD, Joseph *Alan*
————————RHB, OB————————

Born Ramsbottom, Lancs, 22 Dec 1942.
Educ Kirkcaldy HS, Scotland. Debut
1962. *P.*
WORCESTERSHIRE (465) 1962–83. Cap
1966. Benefit (£19,000) 1977.
LANCASHIRE (23) 1984. Cap 1984.
TOURS Worcs to Jamaica 1965/66. MCC
Under-25 to Pakistan 1966/67.
HS 204* Worcs v Kent, Dartford, 1973.
BB 5–27 Worcs v Glos, Bristol, 1972.
1000 RUNS (13) 1535 @ 45.14 in 1978.
RECORD Added 281 for 4th wkt with
Younis Ahmed, Worcs v Notts, Trent
Bridge, 1979, county record.
Took 396 catches in career.
Clubs: Stourbridge, Dudley.

O'ROURKE, Christopher
————————RHB, WK————————

Born Widnes, Lancs, 13 Mar 1945.
Debut 1968.
WARWICKSHIRE (1) 1968.
HS 23* Warwicks v Scotland, Edgbas-
ton, 1968.

OSBORNE, Michael John
————————RHB, OB————————

Born Southend-on-Sea, Essex, 9 Apr
1932. Educ Elmwood S. Debut 1961.
COMBINED SERVICES (3) 1961–62.
HS 60 Combined Services v Cambridge
U, Fenner's, 1962.
BB 2–65 same match.
RAF. Clubs: Beddington, Cheam, West
Bromwich Dartmouth.

OSCROFT, Eric
————————RHB, LMF————————

Born Sutton-in-Ashfield, Notts, 20 Apr
1933. Debut 1950. *P*
NOTTINGHAMSHIRE (9) 1950–51.
HS 7* Notts v Kent, Trent Bridge, 1951.
BB 4–88 Notts v Surrey, Oval, 1951.

O'SHAUGHNESSY, Steven Joseph
————RHB, RM————

Born Bury, Lancs, 9 Sept 1961. Educ Harper Green Sec S, Farnworth. Debut 1980.
LANCASHIRE (68) 1980–.
HS 159* Lancs v Som, Bath, 1984.
BB 4–66 Lancs v Notts, Trent Bridge, 1982.
1000 RUNS (1) 1167 @ 34.32 in 1984.
RECORDS During inns of 105 (5 sixes, 18 fours) Lancs v Leics, Old Trafford, 1983 reached century in 35 mins, equalling world record established by P. G. H. Fender (1920), and in 25 scoring-strokes, believed to be world record; added 201 in 43 mins with G. Fowler, fastest-ever double-century stand (Leics used occasional bowlers in an attempt to get through overs rapidly and raise their over rate for the season).

OSMAN, Wayne Miles
————LHB, LM————

Born Athens, Greece, 19 Aug 1950. Debut 1970.
NORTHAMPTONSHIRE (9) 1970–71.
HS 60 Northants v Hants, Southampton, 1971.
Hertfordshire 1972–. Club: Hitchin.

O'SULLIVAN, David Robert
————RHB, SLA————

Born Palmerston North, N Zealand, 16 Nov 1944. Educ Palmerston North HS. Debut 1971.
HAMPSHIRE (26) 1971–73.
N ZEALAND DOMESTIC Central Districts (82) 1972/73–.
NEW ZEALAND (11) 1972/73–76/77. I 1975/76 (1); P 1972/73 (1). A 1973/74 (3); I 1976/77 (3); P 1976/77 (3).
OTHER TOUR N Zealand to Australia 1972/73.
HST 23* NZ v P, Lahore, 1976/77. HS

70* Central Districts v Otago, Palmerston North, 1977/78.
BBT 5–148 NZ v A, Adelaide, 1973/74.
BB 6–26 (11–41 match) Hants v Notts, Bournemouth, 1973.
Durham 1974/75. Clubs: Finchley, Horden CW, Eppleton.

OTTLEY, David George
————RHB————

Born Epsom, Surrey, 23 June 1944. Educ Tiffin S, Kingston-upon-Thames; St John's C, Exeter. Debut 1967.
MIDDLESEX (7) 1967.
HS 30 M'sex v Sussex, Hove, 1967.
Hertfordshire 1975–. Clubs: Beddington, Hertford, Loudwater.

OUTSCHOORN, Ladislau
————RHB, RM————

Born Colombo, Ceylon, 26 Sept 1918. Debut 1946. P
WORCESTERSHIRE (341) 1946–59. Cap 1948. Benefit (£3540) 1959.
HS 215* Worcs v Northants, Worcester, 1949.
BB 2–15 Worcs v Lancs, Blackpool, 1953.
1000 RUNS (9) 1761 @ 35.93 in 1951.
Former Sri Lanka national coach. Clubs: Kidderminster, Singapore.

OVENSTONE, Douglas MacPherson
————RHB, WK————

Born Cape Town, S Africa, 31 July 1921. Debut 1942/43.
S AFRICA DOMESTIC First South African Division 1942/43, Western Province 1946/47–47/48.
TOUR S Africa to England 1947.
HS 52 W Province v Transvaal, Cape Town, 1946/47.

OWEN, Joseph *Glyn*
————LHB, SLA————

Born Llanelli, S Wales, 23 Jan 1909. Died Eastbourne, Sussex, 17 Feb 1978. Debut 1930. P
SURREY (15) 1930–33.
MINOR COUNTIES (3) 1950–51.
HS 57 Minor Counties v MCC, Lord's, 1950.
BB 3–15 Surrey v MCC, Lord's, 1933.
Bedfordshire 1939–57. Club: Luton Town.

OWEN, Norman William
————RHB, RM/OB————

Born Shepherds Bush, London, 16 Mar 1915. Died Newton Aycliffe, Co Durham, 9 Sept 1977. Debut 1951.
MINOR COUNTIES (1) 1951.
HS 14 Minor Counties v Kent, Canterbury 1951.
Durham 1947–55. Clubs: Wearmouth, Sunderland, Bishop Auckland, Horden College.

OWEN-THOMAS, Dudley Richard
————RHB, OB————

Born Mombasa, Kenya, 20 Sept 1948. Educ KCS Wimbledon; Emmanuel C, Cambridge. Debut 1969.
CAMBRIDGE UNIVERSITY (37) 1969–72 (Blue 1969–72).
SURREY (73) 1970–75.
TOUR MCC to E Africa 1973/74.
HS 182* Cambridge U v M'sex, Fenner's, 1969.
BB 3–20 Cambridge U v Worcs, Halesowen, 1969.
1000 RUNS (1) 1065 @ 34.35 in 1971.
CWC Best Young Cricketer of 1972. Club: Teddington. Father P. Owen-Thomas (Kenya).

P/Q

PADGETT, Douglas Ernest Vernon
—RHB—

Born Bradford, Yorks, 20 July 1934. Debut 1951. *P*.
YORKSHIRE (487) 1951-71. Cap 1958. Benefit (£5290) 1969. Testimonial (£15,460) 1978.
ENGLAND (2) SA 1960.
TOUR MCC to N Zealand 1960/61.
HST 31 E v SA, Oval, 1960. HS 161* Yorks v Oxford U, The Parks, 1959.
1000 RUNS (12) 2181 @ 41.15 in 1959.
Players v Gentlemen (2) 1959-60. Yorks coach since retirement. Clubs: Idle, Bowling Old Lane, Marske.

PADGETT, George *Hubert*
—RHB, RMF—

Born Silkstone, Barnsley, 9 Oct 1931. Debut 1952. *P*.
YORKSHIRE (8) 1952-53.
HS 32* Yorks v Scotland, Glasgow, 1952.
BB 2-37 Yorks v Leics, Bramall Lane, Sheffield, 1952.
Clubs: Farsley, Barnsley, Porthill Park.

PADMORE, Albert Harold (Hal)
—RHB, RFM—

Born Barbados, *c* 1920. Debut 1951.
CANADA (3) 1951-54.
TOUR Canada to England 1954.
HS 15* Canadians v Essex, Clacton, 1954.
BB 5-47 same match.
Club: Montreal.

PADMORE, Albert Leroy
—RHB, OB—

Born St James, Barbados, 17 Dec 1946. Debut 1972/73.
W INDIES DOMESTIC Barbados 1972/73-81/82 (capt 1979/80-81/82).
WEST INDIES (2) 1975/76-76. I 1975/76 (1). E 1976 (1).

OTHER TOURS W Indies to India, Pakistan and Sri Lanka 1974/75. W Indies to Australia 1975/76.
HST 8* WI v E, Old Trafford, 1976. HS 79 Barbados v Australians, Bridgetown, 1977/78.
BB 6-69 W Indians v M'sex, Lord's, 1976.
World Series Cricket (Kerry Packer) 1977/78-78/79. Barred from W Indian cricket for touring S Africa 1982/83 (manager W Indies XI).

PAGE, John *Colin* Theodore
—RHB, OB/RMF—

Born Mereworth, Kent, 20 May 1930. Educ Maidstone Commercial S. Debut 1950. *P*.
KENT (198) 1950-63. Cap 1957.
HS 23 Kent v Glam, Neath, 1957.
BB 8-117 Kent v Warwicks, Edgbaston, 1957.
Kent manager 1976-80. Current Kent youth coach. Club: Westminster.

PAGE, Julian Thomas
—LHB, LM—

Born Clifton, Bristol, 1 May 1954. Educ Henbury CS, Bristol; Sidney Sussex C, Cambridge. Debut 1974.
CAMBRIDGE UNIVERSITY (2) 1974.
HS 11 Cambridge U v Notts, Fenner's, 1974.

PAGE, Michael Harry
—RHB, OB—

Born Blackpool, Lancs, 17 June 1941. Educ Francis Askew HS, Hull. Debut 1964.
DERBYSHIRE (254) 1964-75. Cap 1964. Testimonial (£3500) 1975.
HS 162 Derbys v Leics, Leicester, 1969.
1000 RUNS (6) 1344 @ 40.72 in 1970.
Clubs: Undercliffe, Hull.

PAINE, George Alfred Edward
—RHB, SLA—

Born Paddington, London, 11 June 1908. Died Solihull, W Midlands, 30 Mar 1978. Educ Droop Street S, Paddington. Debut 1926. *P. Wisden* 1935.
MIDDLESEX (5) 1926.
WARWICKSHIRE (240) 1929-47. Cap 1929. Benefit (£881) 1938.
ENGLAND (4) *WI 1934/35*.
HST 49 E v WI, Georgetown, 1934/35. HS 79 Warwicks v Glam, Edgbaston, 1933.
BBT 5-168 E v WI, Kingston, 1934/35. BB 8-43 (12-89 match) Warwicks v Worcs, Edgbaston, 1934.
100 WKTS (5) 156 @ 17.07 in 1934.
Players v Gentlemen (1) 1934. Clubs: Smethwick, Mitchells and Butlers, Walsall, Kidderminster, Moseley, Oldham, East Lancashire, Solihull. Professional coach and groundsman Solihull S until 1969.

PAIRAUDEAU, Bruce Hamilton
—RHB—

Born Georgetown, British Guiana, 14 Apr 1931. Debut 1946/47.
W INDIES DOMESTIC British Guiana 1946/47-57/58.
N ZEALAND DOMESTIC Northern Districts (45) 1958/59-66/67.
WEST INDIES (13) 1952/53-57. E 1953/54 (2); I 1952/53 (5). E 1957 (2); NZ 1955/56 (4).
HST 115 WI v I, Port of Spain, 1952/53.
HS 163 W Indians v Hants, Southampton, 1957.
Scored 130, British Guiana v Jamaica, Georgetown, 1947/48, aged 16 yrs 5 months, youngest century-scorer in fc cricket at time. Club: Burnley.

PALFREMAN, Anthony Brian
—RHB, RFM—

Born Ravenshead, Notts, 27 Aug 1946. Educ Nottingham HS; Emmanuel C, Cambridge. Debut 1966.
CAMBRIDGE UNIVERSITY (16) 1966-68 (Blue 1966).

HS 67 Cambridge U v Essex, Brentwood, 1966.
BB 5–63 same match.

PALMER, Charles Henry
——————RHB, RM——————

Born Old Hill, Staffordshire, 15 May 1919. Educ Halesowen GS; Birmingham U. Debut 1938.
WORCESTERSHIRE (66) 1938–49. Cap 1939.
LEICESTERSHIRE (231) 1950–59. Cap 1950. Capt 1950–57.
INDIA DOMESTIC Bombay Europeans 1945/46.
ENGLAND (1) *WI 1953/54.*
OTHER TOUR MCC to S Africa 1948/49.
HST 22 E v WI, Bridgetown, 1953/54. HS 201 Leics v Northants, Northampton, 1953.
BB 8–7 Leics v Surrey, Leicester, 1955.
1000 RUNS (8) 2071 @ 39.82 in 1952.
Gentlemen v Players (6) 1948–56. Player-manager MCC to W Indies 1953/54. Leics secretary 1950–57; chairman 1978/79. Club: Old Hill. MCC committee member; president 1978/79.

PALMER, Eric John
——————LHB, RFM——————

Born Romford, Essex, 16 June 1931. Educ Hylands Sec S, Hornchurch. Debut 1957.
ESSEX (4) 1957.
HS 11* Essex v Surrey, Oval, 1957.
BB 2–35 Essex v Glos, Romford, 1957.
Clubs: Romford Brewery, Romford.

PALMER, Gary Vincent
——————RHB, RFM——————

Born Taunton, Som, 1 Nov 1965. Educ Queen's C, Taunton. Debut 1982.
SOMERSET (27) 1982–.
HS 78 Som v Glos, Bristol, 1983.
BB 5–38 Som v Warwicks, Taunton, 1983.
Father K. E. Palmer (Som, England); uncle R. Palmer (Som).

PALMER, Kenneth Ernest
——————RHB, RFM——————

Born Winchester, Hants, 22 Apr 1937. Debut 1955. *P.*
SOMERSET (302) 1955–69. Cap 1958.
Testimonial (£4000) 1968.
ENGLAND (1) *SA 1964/65.*
OTHER TOURS Cavaliers to Jamaica 1963/64. Commonwealth XI to Pakistan 1963/64.

HST 10 E v SA, Port Elizabeth, 1964/65.
HS 125* Som v Northants, Northampton, 1961 (adding 265 for 6th wkt with W. E. Alley, county record).
BB 9–57 Som v Notts, Trent Bridge, 1963.
1000 RUNS (1) 1036 @ 25.90 in 1961.
100 WKTS (4) 139 @ 16.07 in 1963.
DOUBLE (1) 1961.
Played in one Test in 1964/65 while in S Africa coaching. Fc umpire 1972– (8 Tests, 1978–81). Son G. V. Palmer (Som); brother R. Palmer (Som).

PALMER, Robert William Michael
——————RHB, LM——————

Born Hong Kong, 4 June 1960. Educ Bedford· S; St Catharine's C, Cambridge. Debut 1981.
CAMBRIDGE UNIVERSITY (11) 1981–83 (Blue 1982).
HS 12 Cambridge U v Essex, Fenner's, 1982.
BB 4–96 Cambridge U v Notts, Fenner's, 1982.

PALMER, Roy
——————RHB, RFM——————

Born Devizes, Wiltshire, 12 July 1942. Debut 1965.
SOMERSET (74) 1965–70.
HS 84 Som v Leics, Taunton, 1967.
BB 6–45 Som v M'sex, Lord's, 1967.
Fc umpire 1980–. Brother K. E. Palmer (Som, England); nephew G. V. Palmer (Som).

PARFITT, Peter Howard
——————LHB, ROB——————

Born Billingford, Norfolk, 8 Dec 1936. Educ King Edward VI S, King's Lynn; Fakenham GS. Debut 1956. *P. Wisden* 1963.
MIDDLESEX (387) 1956–72. Cap 1960.
Benefit (£10,000) 1970. Capt 1968–70.
ENGLAND (37) 1961/62–72. A 1964 (4), 1972 (3); SA 1965 (2); WI 1969 (1); NZ 1965 (2); P 1962 (5). *A 1962/63 (2); SA 1964/65 (5); NZ 1962/63 (3), 1965/66 (3); I 1961/62 (2), 1963/64 (3); P 1961/62 (2).*
OTHER TOURS Board President's XI v Prime Minister's XI, Bombay, 1963/64 (defence fund match). MCC to Australia 1965/66. MCC to E Africa 1973/74 (no fc match).
HST 131* E v NZ, Auckland, 1962/63. HS 200* M'sex v Notts, Trent Bridge, 1964.
BBT 2–5 E v NZ, Christchurch, 1965/66.

BB 6–45 M'sex v Oxford U, The Parks, 1969.
1000 RUNS (14 + 1) 2121 @ 45.12 in 1962.
RECORD During HST (above) added 240 for 6th wkt with B. R. Knight, England Test record.
Took 564 catches in career.
Players v Gentlemen (1) 1962. CWC Best Young Cricketer of 1961. Norfolk 1953–55. MCC Hon. member.

PARIS, Cecil Gerard Alexander
——————RHB——————

Born Kirkee, India, 20 Aug 1911. Educ King's S, Canterbury. Debut 1933.
HAMPSHIRE (98) 1933–48. Cap. Capt 1938.
HS 134* Hants v Northants, Bournemouth, 1935.
1000 RUNS (1) 1058 @ 23.51 in 1938.
Gentlemen v Players (1) 1935. Chairman TCCB 1974–75. President MCC 1975/76. MCC committee member 1961–.

PARKAR, Ghulam Ahmed Hassan Mohamed
——————RHB——————

Born Kaluste, Ratnagiri, India, 25 Oct 1955. Debut 1978/79.
INDIA DOMESTIC Bombay 1978/79–.
INDIA (1) *E 1982.*
HST 6 I v E, Lord's, 1982. HS 156 Bombay v Bengal, Bombay, 1981/82.
During HS (above) added 421 for 1st wkt with S. M. Gavaskar.
Club: Boldon. Brother Z. A. H. M. Parkar (Bombay).

PARKER, Frederick Anthony Vivian
——————RHB, RM——————

Born London, 11 Feb 1913. Educ Winchester. Debut 1946.
HAMPSHIRE (2) 1946.
COMBINED SERVICES (3) 1946.
HS 116 Combined Services v Northants, Kettering, 1946.
Devon 1949. Clubs: I Zingari, Old Wykhamists. Father W. M. Parker (MCC).

PARKER, Grahame Wilshaw
——————RHB, RMF——————

Born Gloucester, 11 Feb 1912. Educ Crypt S, Gloucester; Selwyn C, Cambridge. Debut 1932.
GLOUCESTERSHIRE (70) 1932–51. Cap 1933.

CAMBRIDGE UNIVERSITY (18) 1934–35 (Blue 1934–35).
HS 210 Glos v Kent, Dover, 1937.
BB 5–57 Glos v Warwicks, Edgbaston, 1934.
Gentlemen v Players (1) 1933. Glos secretary 1968–76. Devon 1953–56 (capt). Author *Gloucestershire Road* (1983). Rugby: Blue, Gloucester, Blackheath, England (2).

PARKER, John Frederick
————————RHB, RM————————

Born Battersea, London, 23 Apr 1913.
Died Bromley, Kent, 26 Jan 1983.
Debut 1932. *P.*
SURREY (334) 1932–52. Cap 1937.
Benefit (£4666) 1951.
HS 255 Surrey v N Zealanders, Oval, 1949.
BB 6–34 Surrey v Derbys, Guildford, 1939.
1000 RUNS (9) 1789 @ 40.65 in 1949.
Took seven catches in match, Surrey v Kent, Blackheath, 1952, and 330 catches in career.
Selected for MCC to India 1939/40 (cancelled owing to war). Clubs: Morecambe, Dulwich.

PARKER, John Morton
————————RHB, LBG, occ WK————————

Born Dannevirke, Hawkes Bay, N Zealand, 21 Feb 1951. Educ Mahurangi C, Warkworth, N Zealand. Debut 1971.
WORCESTERSHIRE (61) 1971–75. Cap 1974.
N ZEALAND DOMESTIC Northern Districts (75) 1972/73–.
NEW ZEALAND (36) 1972/73–80/81. E 1974/75 (2), 1977/78 (3); A 1973/74 (3), 1976/77 (2); WI 1979/80 (3); I 1975/76 (3); P 1972/73 (1), 1978/79 (2). *E 1973 (3), 1978 (2); A 1973/74 (3), 1980/81 (3); I 1976/77 (3); P 1976/77 (3).*
Capt 1.
HST 121 NZ v E, Auckland, 1974/75. HS 195 Northern Districts v Canterbury, Whangarei, 1972/73.
BB 3–26 Worcs v Oxford U, Worcester, 1975.
1000 RUNS (2) 1182 @ 32.83 in 1973.
Clubs: Melville, Hamilton (N Zealand), Kidderminster (England). Brothers K. J. Parker (Auckland) and N. M. Parker (N Zealand).

PARKER, Paul William Giles
————————RHB, RM————————

Born Bulawayo, Rhodesia, 15 Jan 1956.
Educ Collyer's GS; St Catharine's C, Cambridge. Debut 1976.

CAMBRIDGE UNIVERSITY (25) 1976–78 (Blue 1976–78).
SUSSEX (163) 1976–. Cap 1979.
S AFRICA DOMESTIC Natal 1980/81.
ENGLAND (1) A 1981.
HST 13 E v A, Oval, 1981. HS 215 Cambridge U v Essex, Fenner's, 1976.
BB 2–21 Sussex v Surrey, Guildford, 1984.
1000 RUNS (6) 1692 @ 47.00 in 1984.
Hit A. I. Kallicharran for 32 runs (466664) in one over, Sussex v Warwicks, Edgbaston, 1982.
CWC Best Young Cricketer of 1979.
Father John Parker (sports journalist).

PARKER, Roland John
————————RHB————————

Born Pudsey, Yorks, 19 July 1925. Educ Uppingham. Debut 1947.
COMBINED SERVICES (2) 1947.
HS 18 Combined Services v Northants, Northampton, 1947.
Clubs: Pudsey St Laurence, Hunslet, Nelson, XL, Adastrians.

PARKES, John Leonard
————————LHB, RLB————————

Born Leamington Spa, Warwicks, 23 June 1938. Educ Warwick S; RMA Sandhurst. Debut 1960.
FREE FORESTERS (1) 1960.
No runs, one wkt.
Clubs: Leamington, Stragglers of Asia, Army, Singapore, Hong Kong. Colonel in Gurkha Rifles. Awarded OBE.

PARKHOUSE, William *Gilbert* Anthony
————————RHB————————

Born Swansea, S Wales, 12 Oct 1925.
Educ Wycliffe C. Debut 1948. *P.*
GLAMORGAN (434) 1948–64. Cap 1948.
Benefit (£3750) 1957.
ENGLAND (7) 1950–59. WI 1950 (2); I 1959 (2). *A 1950/51 (2); NZ 1950/51 (1).*
HST 78 E v I, Headingley, 1959. HS 201 Glam v Kent, Swansea, 1956.
1000 RUNS (15) 2243 @ 48.76 in 1959.
Scored centuries against all fc counties except his own.
Players v Gentlemen (2) 1950/59. Worcs coach 1966. Club: Swansea. Former professional coach Melville C, Edinburgh (from 1966). Rugby: Swansea.

PARKIN, John Maurice
————————RHB————————

Born Kimberley, Notts, 16 Oct 1944.
Debut 1966.

NOTTINGHAMSHIRE (28) 1966–68.
HS 53 Notts v Lancs, Trent Bridge, 1957.
Club: Kimberley.

PARKINS, William Richard
————————RHB————————

Born Glenfield, Leics, 20 Aug 1925.
Died Leicester, 1 Nov 1969. Educ Wyggeston GS. Debut 1950.
LEICESTERSHIRE (5) 1950.
HS 39 Leics v M'sex, Leicester, 1950.

PARKS, Henry William
————————RHB————————

Born Haywards Heath, Sussex, 18 July 1906. Died Taunton, Som, 7 May 1984.
Debut 1926. *P.*
SUSSEX (479) 1926–48. Cap 1928. Joint benefit (with J. G. Langridge) (£1,900) 1948.
TOUR Commonwealth XI to India 1949/50 (one match).
HS 200* Sussex v Essex, Chelmsford, 1931.
BB 2–37 Sussex v Cambridge U, Fenner's, 1928.
1000 RUNS (14) 2122 @ 38.58 in 1947.
RECORDS Added 297 for 5th wkt with J. H. Parks, Sussex v Hants, Portsmouth, 1937 and 178 for 9th wkt with A. F. Wensley, Sussex v Derbys, Horsham, 1930, both county records.
Players v Gentlemen (1) 1933. Fc umpire 1949. Somerset coach 1952–53.
Minor Counties umpire 1956–71.
Professional coach Taunton S 1955–69.
Brother J. H. Parks (Sussex, England); nephew J. M. Parks, (Sussex, Som, England); great-nephew R. J. Parks (Hants).

PARKS, James Horace
————————RHB, RM————————

Born Haywards Heath, Sussex, 12 May 1903. Died Cuckfield, Sussex, 21 Nov 1980. Debut 1924. *P. Wisden* 1938.
SUSSEX (434) 1924–39. Cap. Benefit (£734) 1939.
COMMONWEALTH XI (1) 1952.
N ZEALAND DOMESTIC Canterbury (3) 1946/47.
ENGLAND (1) NZ 1937.
TOURS MCC to N Zealand 1935/36.
Lord Tennyson's XI to India 1937/38.
HST 22 E v NZ, Lord's, 1937. HS 197 Sussex v Kent, Hastings, 1936.
BBT 2–26 E v NZ, Lord's, 1937. BB 7–17 Sussex v Leics, Horsham, 1924.
1000 RUNS (12) 3003 @ 50.89 in 1937.
100 WKTS (2) 103 @ 19.57 in 1935.
DOUBLE (2) 1935, 1937 (3003 runs @ 50.89, 101 wkts @ 25.83).

RECORDS Only cricketer to achieve a season's double of 3000 runs and 100 wkts, in 1937 (see DOUBLE above). Added 297 for 5th wkt with H. W. Parks, Sussex v Hants, Portsmouth, 1937, county record.
Players v Gentlemen (2) 1935–36. Notts coach 1953–57; Sussex coach 1965–68. Fc umpire 1959–64. Clubs: Haywards Heath, Accrington, Blackpool. Professional coach Rossall 1949–52. Brother H. W. Parks (Sussex); son J. M. Parks (Sussex, Som, England); grandson R. J. Parks (Hants).

PARKS, James Michael
RHB, LB, WK

Born Haywards Heath, Sussex, 21 Oct 1931. Educ Hove GS. Debut 1949. *P. Wisden* 1968.
SUSSEX (563) 1949–72. Cap 1951. Benefit (£9400) 1964. Joint Testimonial (with K. G. Suttle) (£5000) 1972. Capt 1967–68.
SOMERSET (47) 1973–76. Cap 1973.
ENGLAND (46) 1954–67/68. A 1964 (5); SA 1960 (5), 1965 (3); WI 1963 (4), 1966 (4); NZ 1965 (3); P 1954 (1). *A 1965/66 (5); SA 1964/65 (5); WI 1959/60 (1), 1967/68 (3); NZ 1965/66 (2); I 1963/64 (5).*
OTHER TOURS MCC A to Pakistan 1955/56. MCC to S Africa 1956/57 (returned home early because of illness). MCC to N Zealand 1960/61. International Wanderers to Rhodesia 1972/73.
HST 108* E v SA, Durban, 1964/65. HS 205* Sussex v Som, Hove, 1955.
BB 3–23 Sussex v Cambridge U, Hove, 1956.
1000 RUNS (20) 2314 @ 42.07 in 1955.
2000 runs (3).
RECORD Added 197 for 7th wkt with M. J. K. Smith, E v WI, Port of Spain, 1959/60, England Test record.
Dismissed 93 batsmen in 1959 and 1961 (only began keeping wicket in 1958, taking over regularly in 1959).
Players v Gentlemen (4) 1954–58. MCC Hon. member. Autobiographies *Runs in the Sun* (1961) and *Time to Hit Out* (1967). Father J. H. Parks (Sussex, England); son R. J. Parks (Hants); uncle H. W. Parks (Sussex).

PARKS, Robert James
RHB, WK

Born Cuckfield, Sussex, 15 June 1959. Educ Eastbourne GS; Southampton C of Technology. Debut 1980.
HAMPSHIRE (105) 1980–. Cap 1982.
HS 89 Hants v Cambridge U, Fenner's, 1984.
RECORD Made 10 dismissals (all ct) in

match, Hants v Derbys, Portsmouth, 1981, county record.
Father J. M. Parks (Sussex, Som, England); grandfather J. H. Parks (Sussex, England); great-uncle H. W. Parks (Sussex).

PARNABY, Alan Herring
RHB

Born Sunderland, Co Durham, 2 Sept 1916. Died Westminster, London, 25 Nov 1974. Debut 1939.
MINOR COUNTIES (1) 1939.
COMBINED SERVICES (7) 1949–53.
HS 101 Minor Counties v Oxford U, The Parks, 1939 (fc debut).
Durham 1936–39. Club: Sunderland. Brigadier RAOC. Aide-de-Camp to HM The Queen as deputy director of Ordnance Services, Southern Command HQ.

PARR, Francis David
LHB, WK

Born Wallasey, Cheshire, 1 June 1928. Educ Wallasey GS. Debut 1951. *P.*
LANCASHIRE (48) 1951–54. Cap 1953.
HS 42 Lancs v Sussex, Hove, 1952.
Clubs: Royal Air Force, Wallasey, Ravers. Professional jazz trombonist. Founder-member Merseyssippi Jazz Band; played with Mick Mulligan Band, featuring George Melly, 1956–61; manager Acker Bilk 1963–74.

PARRY, Derick Recaldo
RHB, OB

Born Cotton Grounds, Nevis, W Indies, 22 Dec 1954. Educ Charlestown Sec S. Debut 1975/76.
W INDIES DOMESTIC Leeward Islands 1975/76–81/82, Combined Islands 1976/77–80/81.
WEST INDIES (12) 1977/78–79/80. A 1977/78 (5). *NZ 1979/80 (1); I 1978/79 (6).*
OTHER TOURS W Indies to Australia 1979/80. West Indies to England 1980. West Indies to Pakistan 1980/81.
HST 65 WI v A, Port of Spain, 1977/78. HS 96 Combined Islands v Barbados, Castries, 1977/78.
BBT 5–15 WI v A, Port of Spain, 1977/78. BB 9–76 Combined Islands v Jamaica, Kingston, 1979/80.
Barred from W Indian cricket for touring S Africa 1982/83, 1983/84 (W Indies XI). Cambridgeshire 1979–. Clubs: Horden CW, Milnrow.

PARSLOW, Leonard Frederick
RHB

Born London, 11 Nov 1909. Died Rochford, Essex, 6 Aug 1963. Educ Central Foundation S, Whitechapel. Debut 1946.
ESSEX (1) 1946.
HS 5 Essex v Som, Taunton, 1946.
Club: Chingford. Top-class hockey player.

PARSONS, Arthur *Brian* Douglas
RHB, occ LB

Born Guildford, Surrey, 20 Sept 1933. Educ Brighton C; Corpus Christi C, Cambridge. Debut 1954. *P from 1958.*
CAMBRIDGE UNIVERSITY (27) 1954–55 (Blue 1954–55)
COMBINED SERVICES (5) 1956–57.
SURREY (119) 1958–63. Cap 1961.
MCC (1) 1964.
HS 125 Surrey v Glam, Ebbw Vale, 1961 and 125 v Cambridge U, Fenner's, 1962.
1000 RUNS (3) 1415 @ 32.15 in 1961.
Club: Walsall.

PARSONS, Austin Edward Werring
RHB, LB

Born Glasgow, Scotland, 9 Jan 1949. Educ Avondale C, Auckland. Debut 1971/72.
N ZEALAND DOMESTIC New Zealand Under-23 1971/72, Auckland (56) 1973/74–82/83.
SUSSEX (21) 1974–75.
HS 141 Sussex v Australians, Hove, 1975.

PARSONS, David Joseph
RHB, LMF

Born Accrington, Lancs, 28 Oct 1954. Debut 1981.
MINOR COUNTIES (1) 1981.
HS 1 Minor Counties v Sri Lankans, Reading, 1981.
Cumberland 1981–. Lancs 2nd XI. Clubs: Blackburn Northern, Netherfield.

PARSONS, Gordon James
LHB, RFM

Born Slough, Buckinghamshire, 17 Oct 1959. Educ Woodside County S, Slough. Debut 1978.
LEICESTERSHIRE (102) 1978–. Cap 1984.
S AFRICA DOMESTIC Boland 1983/84.

TOURS D. H. Robins' XI to N Zealand 1979/80 (no fc matches). Leics XI to Zimbabwe 1980/81.
HS 63 Leics v Yorks, Leicester, 1984.
BB 5–25 Leics v Essex, Leicester, 1982.
Buckinghamshire 1977. Club: Slough.

PARTRIDGE, Brian John Macpherson
——————RHB, RMF——————

Born Haddington, East Lothian, Scotland, 21 Jan 1956. Educ Loretto S, Musselburgh; Leeds U; St Edmund Hall, Oxford. Debut 1977.
OXFORD UNIVERSITY (4) 1977.
HS 4 Oxford U v Glam, The Parks, 1977.
BB 2–38 same match.
Club: Grange (Edinburgh).

PARTRIDGE, Martin David
——————LHB, RM——————

Born Birdlip, Glos, 25 Oct 1954. Educ Marling S, Stroud; Bradford U. Debut 1976.
GLOUCESTERSHIRE (46) 1976–80.
HS 90 Glos v Notts, Trent Bridge, 1979.
BB 5–29 Glos v Worcs, Worcester, 1979.
Club: Partridge XI (a family team).

PARTRIDGE, Reginald Joseph
——————RHB, RFM——————

Born Wollaston, nr Wellingborough, Northants, 11 Feb 1912. Educ Wollaston S. Debut 1929. P.
NORTHAMPTONSHIRE (277) 1929–48. Cap 1933.
ROYAL AIR FORCE (1) 1945.
HS 70 Northants v Derbys, Chesterfield, 1937.
BB 9–66 Northants v Warwicks, Kettering, 1934.
Took 94 wkts @ 25.70 in 1938 and 93 wkts @ 25.63 in 1934.
Clubs: Wollaston, British Timken.

PARVEZ Jamil MIR
——————RHB, RFM/OB——————

Born Dacca, East Pakistan, 24 Sept 1953. Debut 1970/71.
PAKISTAN DOMESTIC Rawalpindi, Punjab, Lahore, Universities, Habib Bank, National Bank, 1970/71–.
TOUR Pakistan to Sri Lanka 1975/76.
DERBYSHIRE (1) 1975.
GLAMORGAN (1) 1979.
HS 155 Punjab v Sind, Lahore, 1977/78.
BB 6–31 Lahore v Rawalpindi, Rawalpindi, 1982/83.
Norfolk 1981–. Club: Egerton. Squash professional.

PASCOE, Leonard Stephen
——————RHB, RF——————

Born Yugoslavia, 13 Feb 1950. Debut 1974/75.
AUSTRALIA DOMESTIC New South Wales (54) 1974/75–.
AUSTRALIA (14) 1977–81/82. E 1979/80 (2); WI 1979/80 (1), 1981/82 (1); NZ 1980/81 (3); I 1980/81 (3). *E 1977 (3), 1980 (1).*
OTHER TOURS Australia to N Zealand 1981/82.
HST 30* A v NZ, Perth, 1980/81. HS 51* NSW v Tasmania, Hobart, 1976/77.
BBT 5–59 A v E, Lord's, 1980. BB 8–41 NSW v Tasmania, Hobart, 1981/82.
World Series Cricket (Kerry Packer) 1977/78–78/79. Club: Bankstown-Canterbury. Changed name from Durtanovich to Pascoe.

PASQUAL, Sudath Prajeev
——————LHB, RM——————

Born Colombo, Ceylon, 15 Oct 1961. Educ RC, Colombo. Debut 1979.
SRI LANKA to England (7) 1979.
HS 101* Sri Lankans v Ireland, Eglinton, 1979.
Club: Nondescripts.

PASSEY, Michael Francis William
——————RHB, OB——————

Born Crossway Green, Worcs, 6 June 1937. Debut 1953. P.
WORCESTERSHIRE (1) 1953.
HS 1 Worcs v Glam, Worcester, 1953.

PATAUDI, NAWAB OF (Iftiqar Ali Khan)
——————RHB——————

Born Pataudi, Punjab, India, 16 Mar 1910. Died New Delhi, India, 5 Jan 1952. Educ Chief's C, Lahore; Balliol C, Oxford. Debut 1928. *Wisden 1932.*
OXFORD UNIVERSITY (35) 1928–31 (Blue 1929–31).
WORCESTERSHIRE (37) 1932–38. Cap.
INDIA DOMESTIC Patiala 1931/32, Indian States 1943/44, Southern Punjab 1945/46.
ENGLAND (3) 1932/33–34. A 1934 (1). *A 1932/33 (2).*
INDIA (3) *E 1946.* Capt 3.
HST 102 E v A, Sydney, 1932/33 (Test debut). HS 238* Oxford U v Cambridge U, Lord's, 1931.
BB 6–111 Viceroy's XI v Roshanara Club, Delhi, 1931/32.
1000 RUNS (2) 1754 @ 48.72 in 1933.
RECORDS HS (above) highest individual

inns in the Varsity match. Added 274 for 2nd wkt with H. H. I. H. Gibbons twice (Worcs v Kent, Worcester, 1933 and Worcs v Glam, Worcester, 1934), county record.
Scored centuries in four successive fc inns in 1931.
Gentlemen v Players (5) 1932–33. Son Mohammed Mansur Ali Khan, Nawab of Pataudi (Sussex, India); great-nephew Saad Bin Jung (Hyderabad).

PATAUDI, NAWAB OF (Mohammed Mansur Ali Khan)
——————RHB, RM——————

Born Bhopal, India, 5 Jan 1941. Educ Winchester; Balliol C, Oxford. Debut 1957. *Wisden 1968.*
SUSSEX (88) 1957–70. Cap 1963. Capt 1966.
OXFORD UNIVERSITY (44) 1960–63 (Blue 1960, 1963). Capt 1961 (injuries sustained in car crash – he lost an eye – prevented him playing in Varsity match) and 1963.
INDIA DOMESTIC Delhi 1960/61–64/65 (capt 1963/64–64/65), Hyderabad 1965/66–75/76.
INDIA (46) 1961/62–74/75. E 1961/62 (3), 1963/64 (5), 1972/73 (3); A 1964/65 (3), 1969/70 (5); WI 1966/67 (3), 1974/75 (4); NZ 1964/65 (4), 1969/70 (3). *E 1967 (3); A 1967/68 (3); WI 1961/62 (3); NZ 1967/68 (4).* Capt 40.
OTHER TOURS E. W. Swanton's XI to W Indies 1960/61. E. W. Swanton's XI to India 1963/64. India to E Africa 1967. Rest of World XI in England 1968.
HST 203* I v E, Delhi, 1963/64. HS as above.
1000 RUNS (4 + 3) 1416 @ 59.00 in 1964/65.
Autobiography *Tiger's Tale* (1969). MCC Hon. member. Father Iftiqar Ali Khan, Nawab of Pataudi (Worcs, England, India); nephew Saad Bin Jung (Hyderabad).

PATEL, Ashok Sitaram
——————LHB, SLA——————

Born Nairobi, Kenya, 23 Sept 1956. Educ Willesden Lane GS, London; Durham U. Debut 1978.
MIDDLESEX (2) 1978.
HS 25* M'sex v Glos, Bristol, 1978.
BB 2–55 M'sex v Sussex, Hove, 1978.
Durham 1981–82. Clubs: Gateshead Fell, Burnmoor.

PATEL, Brijesh Purshuram
——————RHB, OB——————

Born Baroda, India, 24 Nov 1952. Debut 1969/70.

INDIA DOMESTIC Mysore (Karnataka) 1969/70–.
INDIA (21) 1974–77/78. E 1976/77 (5); WI 1974/75 (3); NZ 1976/77 (3). *E 1974 (2); A 1977/78 (2); WI 1975/76 (3); NZ 1975/76 (3).*
OTHER TOURS India to Sri Lanka 1973/74. India to England 1979.
HST 115* I v WI, Port of Spain, 1975/76 (adding 204 for 5th wkt with S. M. Gavaskar, India Test record). HS 216 Karnataka v Baroda, Bangalore, 1978/79.
1000 RUNS (0 + 4) 1345 @ 53.80 in 1976/77.
Uncles B. R., K. R. and M. R. Patel (all Mysore); cousin Y. B. Patel (Mysore).

PATEL, Dipak Narshibhai
——RHB, OB——

Born Nairobi, Kenya, 25 Oct 1958. Educ George Salter CS, West Bromwich. Debut 1976.
WORCESTERSHIRE (186) 1976–. Cap 1979.
TOUR D. H. Robins' XI to N Zealand 1979/80.
HS 197 Worcs v Cambridge U, Worcester, 1984.
BB 7–46 Worcs v Lancs, Worcester, 1982.
1000 RUNS (4) 1615 @ 38.45 in 1983.
RECORDS Added 227 for 6th wkt with E. J. O. Hemsley, Worcs v Oxford U, The Parks, 1976, county record.
Clubs: West Bromwich Dartmouth, Dudley.

PATERSON, Joseph
——RHB, RM——

Born Coatbridge, Glasgow, Scotland, 27 Dec 1923. Educ Coatbridge HS. Debut 1956.
SCOTLAND (1) 1956.
HS 1 Scotland v Yorks, Hull, 1956.
Club: Drumpelier.

PATERSON, Robert Fraser Troutbeck
——RHB, RM, WK——

Born Stansted, Essex, 8 Sept 1916. Died Edinburgh, Scotland, 29 May 1980. Educ Brighton C. Debut 1946.
ESSEX (25) 1946. Cap 1946.
MIDDLESEX AND ESSEX (1) 1947.
MCC (2) 1957–58.
HS 90 MCC v Scotland, Aberdeen, 1957.
BB 4–98 Essex v Kent, Colchester, 1946.
Essex secretary 1947–50. Club: Stenhousemuir.

PATHMANATHAN, Gajanand
——RHB, occ LB——

Born Colombo, Ceylon, 23 Jan 1954. Educ RC, Colombo; U of Sri Lanka; UC, Oxford. Debut 1972/73.
SRI LANKA DOMESTIC Sri Lanka 1972/73–78/79.
OXFORD UNIVERSITY (29) 1975–78 (Blue 1975–78).
CAMBRIDGE UNIVERSITY (7) 1983 (Blue).
TOURS Sri Lanka to India 1972/73. Sri Lanka to Pakistan 1973/74.
HS 82 Oxford U v Northants, The Parks, 1976.

PATIL, Sandeep Madhusudan
——RHB, RM——

Born Bombay, India, 18 Aug 1956. Educ Balmohan. Debut 1975/76.
INDIA DOMESTIC Bombay 1975/76–.
INDIA (25) 1979/80–83/84. E 1979/80 (1), 1981/82 (4); WI 1983/84 (2); P 1979/80 (2), 1983/84 (3); SL 1982/83 (1). *E 1982 (2); A 1980/81 (3); NZ 1980/81 (3); P 1982/83 (4).*
OTHER TOUR A. L. Wadekar's XI to Sri Lanka 1975/76.
HST 174 I v A, Adelaide, 1980/81. HS 210 Bombay v Saurashtra, Bombay, 1979/80.
BBT 2–28 I v A, Melbourne, 1980/81. BB 4–58 Bombay v Gujerat, Bulsar, 1977/78.
RECORD Only batsman in a Test to hit each delivery of a six-ball over for four, off R. G. D. Willis, I v E, Old Trafford, 1982 (during inns of 129*).
Clubs: Matunga, Century Rayon, Tata Sports (India), Edmonton (England). Father Madhu Patil (Bombay).

PATTERSON, Balfour Patrick
——RHB, RFM——

Born Portland, Jamaica, 15 Sept 1961. Debut 1982/83.
W INDIES DOMESTIC Jamaica 1982/83–.
LANCASHIRE (1) 1984.
HS 10 Lancs v Northants, Southport, 1984.
BB 2–26 Jamaica v Leeward Islands, Basseterre, 1982/83.
Club: Kingston.

PATTERSON, Thomas James Taylor
——LHB, LM——

Born Downpatrick, Ireland, 26 Dec 1959. Educ Down HS. Debut 1984.
IRELAND (1) 1984.
HS 23 Ireland v Scotland, Glasgow, 1984.

BB 2–54 same match.
Club: Downpatrick.

PAUL, Nigel Aldridge
——RHB, LFM——

Born Surbiton, Surrey, 31 Mar 1933. Educ Cranleigh. Debut 1954.
WARWICKSHIRE (4) 1954–55.
FREE FORESTERS (1) 1956.
D. R. JARDINE'S XI (2) 1958.
HS 40 Warwicks v Combined Services, Edgbaston, 1955.
Clubs: Esher, Harborne.

PAULINE, Duncan Brian
——RHB——

Born Aberdeen, Scotland, 15 Dec 1960. Educ Bishop Fox S, E Molesey. Debut 1979.
SURREY (36) 1979–.
HS 115 Surrey v Sussex, Oval, 1983.
Club: East Molesey.

PAULL, Richard Kenyon
——RHB, LB——

Born Bridgwater, Som, 20 Feb 1944. Educ Millfield; Hull U; Selwyn C, Cambridge. Debut 1963.
SOMERSET (6) 1963–64.
CAMBRIDGE UNIVERSITY (7) 1967 (Blue).
HS 37 Cambridge U v Derbys, Ilkeston, 1967.
Club: Crusaders.

PAVER, Roland George Lyall
——RHB, WK——

Born Johannesburg, S Africa, 4 Apr 1950. Educ St Alban's C, Pretoria; Fort Victoria HS, Rhodesia; Rhodes U, S Africa; Pembroke C, Oxford. Debut 1972.
OXFORD UNIVERSITY (16) 1972–74 (Blue 1973–74).
HS 34 Oxford U v Cambridge U, Lord's 1974.

PAWLE, John Hanbury
——RHB——

Born Widford, Hertfordshire, 18 May 1915. Educ Harrow; Pembroke C, Cambridge. Debut 1935.
CAMBRIDGE UNIVERSITY (20) 1935–37 (Blue 1936–37).
ESSEX (6) 1935–38.
FREE FORESTERS (4) 1938–47.
MCC (1) 1946.
HS 125 Cambridge U v Hants, Basingstoke, 1937.

Clubs: Butterflies, I Zingari, Crusaders, Harrow Wanderers. Brother-in-law W. A. Anderson (Free Foresters).

PAWSON, Henry *Anthony*
————RHB————

Born Chertsey, Surrey, 22 Aug 1921. Educ Winchester; Christ Church C, Oxford. Debut 1946.
KENT (43) 1946-53. Cap 1946.
OXFORD UNIVERSITY (22) 1947-48 (Blue 1947-48). Capt 1948.
HS 150 Oxford U v Worcs, Worcester, 1950.
BB 2-26 Kent v Essex, Maidstone, 1950.
1000 RUNS (2) 1312 @ 38.58 in 1947.
Gentlemen v Players (1) 1947. Club: The Mote. Autobiography *Runs and Catches* (1980). Journalist. Soccer: Blue, Charlton Athletic, England (amateur). Father A. G. Pawson (Worcs); uncle A. C. Pawson (Oxford U).

PAYN, Leslie William
————LHB, LM/SLA————

Born Umzinto, Natal, S Africa, 6 May 1915. Educ Michaelhouse, Natal, S Africa. Debut 1936/37.
S AFRICA DOMESTIC Natal 1936/37-52/53.
TOUR S Africa to England 1947.
HS 103 Natal v Transvaal, Johannesburg, 1936/37.
BB 8-89 (11-209 match) Natal v OFS, Bloemfontein, 1936/37 (fc debut).
Clubs: Berea (Durban), Natal Technical C. President S African Country Districts CA.

PAYNE, Christopher John
————RHB, WK————

Born Hatfield, Hertfordshire, 20 Dec 1947. Debut 1968.
MIDDLESEX (5) 1968-70.
HS 22 M'sex v Derbys, Lord's, 1970.
Hertfordshire 1974. Club: Southgate.

PAYNE, Ian Roger
————RHB, RM————

Born Kennington, London, 9 May 1958. Educ Emanuel S, Wandsworth. Debut 1977.
SURREY (29) 1977-.
HS 43 Surrey v Essex, Oval, 1983.
BB 5-13 Surrey v Glos, Oval, 1983.
Club: Old Emanuel.

PAYNTER, Edward
————LHB, RM————

Born Oswaldtwistle, Lancs, 5 Nov 1901. Died Keighley, Yorks, 5 Feb 1979. Educ Clayton-le-Moors Sec S. Debut 1926. *P. Wisden* 1938.
LANCASHIRE (293) 1926-45. Cap 1931. Grant in lieu of Benefit (£1078) 1945.
ENGLAND (20) 1931-39. A 1938 (4); WI 1939 (2); NZ 1931 (1), 1937 (2); I 1932 (1). *A 1932/33 (3); SA 1938/39 (5); NZ 1932/33 (3)*.
OTHER TOUR Commonwealth XI to India 1950/51 (scorer, playing one match).
HST 243 E v SA, Durban, 1938/39. HS 322 Lancs v Sussex, Hove, 1937.
BB 3-13 Lancs v Sussex, Hove, 1933.
1000 RUNS (9 + 1) 2904 @ 53.77 in 1937. 2000 runs (4).
RECORDS Added 306 for 3rd wkt with N. Oldfield, Lancs v Hants, Southampton, 1938, county record.
HS (above) scored on first day of match, sixth-highest inns in a day's play.
Players v Gentlemen (5) 1931-39. Fc umpire 1951. Clubs: Keighley, Enfield. MCC Hon. member. Autobiography *Cricket all the Way* (1962).

PAYTON, Wilfred Ernest *Granville*
————RHB————

Born Beeston, Notts, 27 Dec 1913. Educ Nottingham HS; Emmanuel C, Cambridge. Debut 1935.
NOTTINGHAMSHIRE (1) 1935.
CAMBRIDGE UNIVERSITY (11) 1937 (Blue).
COMBINED SERVICES (13) 1947-53.
DERBYSHIRE (2) 1949.
HS 98 Combined Services v Glam, Pontypridd, 1948.
Clubs: Forest Amateurs, Royal Air Force. RAF Squadron-Leader. Ordained into Church of England; RAF chaplain, now civilian archdeacon. Father W. R. D. Payton (Notts); uncle A. I. Payton (Notts).

PEACH, Robert Arthur
————RHB, RMF————

Born Marylebone, London, 15 July 1937. Educ St Clement Danes S; London U. Debut 1960.
COMBINED SERVICES (2) 1960.
HS 6* Combined Services v Cambridge U, Fenner's, 1960.
London University 1956 (capt). Club: South Hampstead.

PEAKE, Kenneth George
————RHB, RFM————

Born Leicester, 24 July 1920. Debut 1946.
LEICESTERSHIRE (1) 1946.
HS 1* and 1 Leics v Glos, Leicester, 1946.

PEARCE, Jonathan Peter
————RHB, SLA————

Born Newcastle upon Tyne, 18 Apr 1957. Educ Ampleforth C; St Benet's Hall, Oxford. Debut 1978.
OXFORD UNIVERSITY (7) 1978-79 (Blue 1979).
HS 8 and 8* Oxford U v Sri Lankans, Guildford, 1979.
BB 4-94 same match.

PEARCE, Thomas *Alexander*
————RHB————

Born Hong Kong, 18 Dec 1910. Died Tunbridge Wells, Kent, 11 Aug 1982. Educ Charterhouse. Debut 1930.
KENT (52) 1930-46.
HS 106 Kent v Northants, Northampton, 1946.
Kent president 1978. Hong Kong 1979.

PEARCE, Thomas Neill
————RHB, RM————

Born Stoke Newington, London, 3 Nov 1905. Educ Christ's Hospital. Debut 1929.
ESSEX (231) 1929-50. Cap. Joint capt 1933-38, 1950; capt 1946-49.
HS 211* Essex v Leics, Westcliff, 1948.
BB 4-12 Essex v Worcs, Leyton, 1932.
1000 RUNS (6) 1826 @ 49.35 in 1948.
Gentlemen v Players (2) 1936-48. Test selector 1949-50. Essex president 1975-82. MCC committee 1946-66. Club: Southgate. International rugby referee. Awarded OBE.

PEARMAN, Hugh
————RHB, SLA————

Born Birmingham, 1 June 1945. Educ King Alfred's S, Golders Green; St Andrew's U; Churchill C, Cambridge. Debut 1969.
CAMBRIDGE UNIVERSITY (6) 1969 (Blue).
MIDDLESEX (5) 1969-72.
HS 61 M'sex v Glos, Cheltenham, 1972.
BB 4-56 Cambridge U v Oxford U, Lord's 1969.
Club: Hornsey. Brother R. Pearman (M'sex).

PEARMAN, Roger
—RHB, OB—

Born Lichfield, Staffordshire, 13 Feb 1943. Educ Manchester U. Debut 1962.
MIDDLESEX (8) 1962–64.
HS 72* M'sex v Notts, Lord's, 1962.
Bedfordshire 1972–73, Cheshire 1974. Clubs: Alderley Edge, Hornsey. Derbys chief executive 1981–. Brother H. Pearman (M'sex).

PEARSALL, Richard Devenish
—RHB, RM—

Born Kenilworth, Warwicks, 15 Jan 1921. Educ Oundle; King's C, Cambridge. Debut 1947.
CAMBRIDGE UNIVERSITY (15) 1947–48.
HS 80* Cambridge U v M'sex, Fenner's, 1948.
BB 4–51 Cambridge U v Free Foresters, Fenner's, 1947.
Club: Knowle and Dorridge.

PEARSON, Anthony John Grayhurst
—RHB, RFM—

Born Harrow, M'sex, 30 Dec 1941. Educ Downside; Millfield; Jesus C, Cambridge; Bristol U. Debut 1961.
CAMBRIDGE UNIVERSITY (36) 1961–63 (Blue 1961–63).
SOMERSET (6) 1961–63.
HS 30 Cambridge U v W Indians, Fenner's, 1963.
BB 10–78 Cambridge U v Leics, Loughborough, 1961.
RECORD BB (above) only instance in fc cricket of university bowler taking all 10 wkts in inns against a county.

PEARSON, Derek Brook
—RHB, RFM—

Born Stourbridge, Worcs, 29 Mar 1937. Debut 1954. P.
WORCESTERSHIRE (74) 1954–61. Cap 1959.
COMBINED SERVICES (2) 1957.
HS 49 Worcs v Glos, Stroud, 1959.
BB 6–70 Worcs v Leics, Leicester, 1959.
No-balled for throwing in 1954, 1959 and 1960. Clubs: Stourbridge, West Bromwich Dartmouth, Dudley.

PEARSON, George Timothy
—RHB, WK—

Born Kensington, London, 21 July 1921. Died Coxham, Oxfordshire, 24 July 1983. Educ Radley. Debut 1948.

FREE FORESTERS (2) 1948–59.
HS 28 Free Foresters v Oxford U, The Parks, 1948.

PEARSON, Kenneth
—RHB—

Born Bedlington, Northumberland, 30 Aug 1951. Debut 1976.
MINOR COUNTIES (1) 1976.
HS 9 Minor Counties v W Indians, Torquay, 1976.
Northumberland 1972–. Club: Northumberland County.

PEARSON, Kenneth R.
—Spin bowler—

Debut 1946. P.
MCC (1) 1946.
HS 17 MCC v Cambridge U, Lord's, 1946.
BB 2–42 same match.
Lord's groundstaff 1946.

PEARSON, Lawrence Ivor (Jack)
—LHB—

Born Darnall, Yorks, 25 Jan 1922. Debut 1946.
DERBYSHIRE (2) 1946.
HS 18 Derbys v Northants, Derby, 1946.

PECK, David Arthur
—RHB, WK—

Born Rushden, Northants, 3 May 1940. Educ Wellingborough; St John's C, Cambridge. Debut 1960.
CAMBRIDGE UNIVERSITY (1) 1960.
No runs.
Brother R. L. Peck (Combined Services).

PECK, Ian George
—RHB, WK—

Born Great Staughton, Huntingdonshire, 18 Oct 1957. Educ Bedford S; Magdalene C, Cambridge. Debut 1978.
CAMBRIDGE UNIVERSITY (26) 1978–81, 1984 (Blue 1980–81). Capt 1980–81.
NORTHAMPTONSHIRE (2) 1980–81.
HS 49* Cambridge U v Hants, Fenner's, 1984.
Returned in emergency to captain Cambridge U in four matches in 1984. Bedfordshire 1976–79, 1982. Club: Bedford Town. Rugby: Blue.

PECK, Richard Leslie
—RHB—

Born Rushden, Northants, 27 May 1937. Educ Wellingborough S. Debut 1960.
COMBINED SERVICES (2) 1960–62.
HS 19 Combined Services v Ireland, Belfast, 1962.
BB 2–1 same match.
Berkshire 1969. Member I Zingari. Officer in Royal Engineers. Brother D. A. Peck (Cambridge U).

PEDEN, David *Murray*
—RHB, RM—

Born Edinburgh, Scotland, 4 Nov 1946. Died Dunfermline, Scotland, 12 Mar 1978. Debut 1973.
SCOTLAND (3) 1973–76.
HS 45 Scotland v Ireland, Glasgow, 1976.
BB 2–53 same match.

PEEBLES, Ian Alexander Ross
—RHB, LBG/OB—

Born Aberdeen, Scotland, 20 Jan 1908. Died Speen, Buckinghamshire, 27 Feb 1980. Educ Glasgow Academy; Brasenose C, Oxford. Debut 1927 (Gentlemen v Players, Oval). *Wisden* 1931.
MIDDLESEX (165) 1928–48. Cap. Capt 1939.
OXFORD UNIVERSITY (10) 1930 (Blue).
SCOTLAND (1) 1937.
ENGLAND (13) 1927/28–31. A 1930 (2); NZ 1931 (3). *SA 1927/28 (4), 1930/31 (4)*.
OTHER TOURS Sir J. Cahn's XI to Ceylon 1936/37 (no fc match). Lord Tennyson's XI to India 1937/38.
HST 26 E v SA, J'burg, 1927/28. HS 58 M'sex v Oxford U, The Parks, 1938.
BBT 6–63 E v SA, J'burg, 1930/31. BB 8–24 (13–72 match) M'sex v Worcs, Worcester, 1930.
100 WKTS (3) 139 @ 18.51 in 1931.
Represented England in Test cricket before making fc county debut.
Gentlemen v Players (9) 1927–35. Former cricket correspondent of *The Sunday Times* and author of several books on cricket.

PELL, Godfrey Arnold
—RHB, LBG—

Born Sunderland, Co Durham, 11 Mar 1928. Educ King Edward's S, Edgbaston. Debut 1947.

WARWICKSHIRE (1) 1947.
HS 16* Warwicks v Scotland, Edgbaston, 1947.
BB 2–9 same match.
Club: Moseley.

PEMBER, John Devereaux Dubricious
—RHB, RMF—

Born Creaton, Northants, 8 June 1940.
Educ Wellingborough. Debut 1968.
LEICESTERSHIRE (24) 1968–71.
HS 53 Leics v Northants, Leicester, 1970.
BB 5–45 Leics v Som, Taunton, 1968.
Club: Horton House. Rugby: Northampton Saints.

PENN, Christopher
—LHB, RFM—

Born Dover, Kent, 19 June 1963. Educ Dover GS. Debut 1982.
KENT (21) 1982–.
HS 115 Kent v Lancs, Old Trafford, 1984.
BB 2–11 Kent v Som, Taunton, 1982 and v Glos, Canterbury, 1984.

PENNY, Thomas Simpson
—RHB, OB—

Born Bristol, 15 July 1929. Died Casterton, Cumbria, 26 July 1983. Educ Clifton; Magdalen C, Oxford. Debut 1951.
OXFORD UNIVERSITY (5) 1951–52.
HS 34 Oxford U v Notts, The Parks, 1951.
BB 4–75 Oxford U v Free Foresters, The Parks, 1951.
Club: Robertson (Bristol). Headmaster Casterton S.

PEPPER, Cecil George
—RHB, LBG—

Born Forbes, NSW, Australia, 15 Sept 1918. Debut 1938/39. P.
AUSTRALIA DOMESTIC New South Wales (16) 1938/39–40/41.
DOMINIONS XI (1) 1945.
COMMONWEALTH XI (2) 1956–57.
TOURS Australian Services to England 1945 and to India and Ceylon 1945/46. Commonwealth XI to India 1949/50.
HS 168 Australian Services v H. D. G. Leveson Gower's XI, Scarborough, 1945.
BB 6–33 Commonwealth XI v Holkar, Indore, 1949/50.
Fc umpire 1964–79. Clubs: Petersham

(Sydney), Rochdale, Burnley, Radcliffe, Oldham, Royton, Norton (England).

PEPPER, John
—RHB—

Born Wimbledon, London, 21 Oct 1922. Educ The Leys; Emmanuel C, Cambridge. Debut 1946.
CAMBRIDGE UNIVERSITY (29) 1946–48 (Blue 1946–48).
HS 185 Cambridge U v Hants, Portsmouth, 1947.
Club: Colwyn Bay.

PERCIVAL, W. Alan
—RHB, WK—

Born Canada, 1923. Debut 1951.
CANADA (5) 1951–54.
TOUR Canada to England 1954.
HS 23 Canada v Pakistan, Lord's, 1954.
Club: Toronto.

PEREIRA, Eustace Lorenz
—LHB, ROB—

Born Colombo, Ceylon, 4 July 1939. Educ RC, Colombo. Fitzwilliam C, Cambridge. Debut 1962.
CAMBRIDGE UNIVERSITY (2) 1962–63.
HS 8* Cambridge U v Notts, Fenner's, 1963.

PERKINS, George Cyril
—RHB, SLA—

Born Wollaston, Northants, 4 June 1911. Debut 1934. P.
NORTHAMPTONSHIRE (56) 1934–37.
MINOR COUNTIES (1) 1951.
HS 29 Northants v Som, Kettering, 1936.
BB 6–54 Northants v Worcs, Northampton, 1935.
Suffolk 1946–67. Club: Ipswich Greyhounds. Former coach Ipswich S (from 1946).

PERKS, Reginald Thomas David
—LHB, RFM—

Born Hereford, 4 Oct 1911. Died Worcester, 22 Nov 1977. Debut 1930. P.
WORCESTERSHIRE (561) 1930–55. Cap 1931. Capt 1955. Benefit (£3000) 1947. Testimonial (£2600) 1955.
ENGLAND (2) 1938/39–39. WI 1939 (1). SA 1938/39 (1).
HST 2* E v SA, Durban, 1938/39. HS 75 Worcs v Notts, Trent Bridge, 1938.
BBT 5–100 E v SA, Durban, 1938/39. BB 9–40 Worcs v Glam, Stourbridge, 1939.

Returned analyses of 15–106 match, Worcs v Essex, Worcester, 1937 and 14–96 match, Worcs v Glos, Cheltenham, 1946.
100 WKTS (16) 159 @ 19.22 in 1939.
RECORDS 100 wkts in season for Worcs 16 times, county record. 2143 wkts (@ 23.73) for Worcs, county record.
Players v Gentlemen (3) 1931–49. Monmouthshire 1928–29. Clubs: Yeadon, Dudley, West Bromwich Dartmouth, Kidderminster. Father T. Perks (MCC).

PERRY, Ernest Harvey
—RHB, RFM—

Born Kidderminster, Worcs, 16 Jan 1908. Debut 1933.
WORCESTERSHIRE (10) 1933–46.
HS 46 Worcs v Glam, Dudley, 1946.
BB 5–42 Worcs v Leics, Kidderminster, 1933.
Staffordshire 1946. Clubs: Royal Air Force, Kidderminster.

PERRY, Neil James
—RHB, SLA—

Born Sutton, Surrey, 27 May 1958. Debut 1979.
GLAMORGAN (13) 1979–81.
HS 6 Glam v Warwicks, Edgbaston, 1980.
BB 3–51 Glam v Indians, Swansea, 1979.

PERRYMAN, Stephen Peter
—RHB, RM—

Born Yardley, Birmingham, 22 Oct 1955. Educ Sheldon Heath CS. Debut 1974.
WARWICKSHIRE (131) 1974–81. Cap 1977.
WORCESTERSHIRE (25) 1982–83.
HS 43 Warwicks v Som, Edgbaston, 1977.
BB 7–49 Warwicks v Hants, Bournemouth, 1978.
Failed to score in first eight fc inns for Worcs, in 1982.
Clubs: Birmingham Co-op, Pickwick.

PERVEZ SAJJAD Hassan
—RHB, SLA—

Born Lahore, India, 30 Aug 1942. Debut 1961/62.
PAKISTAN DOMESTIC Lahore, Pakistan International Airlines, Karachi, 1961/62–74/75.
PAKISTAN (19) 1964/65–72/73. E 1968/69 (1), 1972/73 (2); A 1964/65 (1); NZ 1964/65 (3), 1969/70 (3). *E 1971 (3); NZ 1964/65 (3), 1972/73 (3).*

OTHER TOURS PIA Eaglets to England 1963. Pakistan to Ceylon 1964/65. Pakistan to Australia 1964/65. Pakistan to England 1967.
HST 24 P v NZ, Auckland, 1972/73. HS 56* Pakistan v Ceylon, Lahore, 1966/67. BBT 7–74 P v NZ, Lahore, 1969/70. BB 8–89 Karachi v Khairpur, Karachi, 1968/69.
Brother Waqar Hasan (Pakistan).

PESTELL, Kenneth Frederick
—RHB, RM—

Born Edmonton, London, 7 May 1931. Educ Finchley GS. Debut 1957.
D. R. JARDINE'S XI (1) 1957.
HS 21 D. R. Jardine's XI v Oxford U, Eastbourne, 1957.
Clubs: Barclays Bank, Mill Hill, United Banks.

PETCHEY, Michael David
—RHB, RM—

Born London, 16 Dec 1958. Educ Latymer Upper S; Sussex U; Christ Church C, Oxford. Debut 1983.
OXFORD UNIVERSITY (7) 1983–84 (Blue 1983).
HS 18 Oxford U v Surrey, Oval, 1983.
BB 4–65 Oxford U v M'sex, The Parks, 1984.

PETERS, Richard Charles
—RHB, RF—

Born Chew Magna, Som, 12 Sept 1911. Debut 1946.
SOMERSET (1) 1946.
HS 3 Som v Leics, Melton Mowbray, 1946.
Somerset county constabulary officer.

PETRIE, Eric Charlton
—RHB, WK—

Born Ngaruawahia, N Zealand, 22 May 1927. Debut 1950/51.
N ZEALAND DOMESTIC Auckland (14) 1950/51–54/55, Northern Districts (57) 1956/57–66/67.
NEW ZEALAND (14) 1955/56–65/66. E 1958/59 (2), 1965/66 (3). E 1958 (5); I 1955/56 (2); P 1955/56 (2).
HST 55 NZ v E, Christchurch, 1955/56.
HS 151 Auckland v Wellington, Auckland, 1953/54.
Gentlemen v Players (1) 1958.

PETTIFORD, Jack
—RHB, LBG—

Born Freshwater, Sydney, NSW, Australia, 29 Nov 1919. Died North Sydney, NSW, Australia, 11 Oct 1964. Educ North Sydney HS. Debut 1945. P.
AUSTRALIA DOMESTIC New South Wales (16) 1946/47–47/48.
KENT (153) 1954–59. Cap 1954. Benefit (£2900) 1959.
TOURS Australian Services to England 1945 and to India and Ceylon 1945/46. Commonwealth XI to India and Pakistan 1949/50.
HS 133 Kent v Essex, Blackheath, 1954. BB 6–134 Kent v Essex, Ilford, 1954.
1000 RUNS (2) 1336 @ 28.42 in 1955.
Clubs: Gord (New South Wales), Nelson, Oldham (Lancashire).

PETTIT, David William
—RHB, RMF—

Born Canterbury, Kent, 24 Mar 1937. Educ St Edmund's, Canterbury; Hertford C, Oxford. Debut 1958.
OXFORD UNIVERSITY (5) 1958–59.
HS 22 Oxford U v Yorks, The Parks, 1959.
BB 2–51 Oxford U v Notts, The Parks, 1959.

PHADKAR, Dattatraya Gajanan
—RHB, RMF—

Born Kolhapur, India, 10 Dec 1925. Died Madras, India, 17 Mar 1985. Educ Elphinstone C, Bombay; Bombay U. Debut 1942/43.
INDIA DOMESTIC Maharashtra 1942/43–43/44, Bombay 1944/45–52/53, Hindus (Bombay) 1944/45–45/46, Bengal 1954/55–57/58, Railways 1958/59–59/60.
COMMONWEALTH XI (1) 1957.
INDIA (31) 1947/48–58/59. E 1951/52 (4); A 1956/57 (1); WI 1948/49 (4), 1958/59 (1); NZ 1955/56 (4); P 1952/53 (2). E 1952 (4); A 1947/48 (4); WI 1952/53 (4); P 1954/55 (3).
OTHER TOUR Indian XI to Ceylon 1949/50.
HST 123 I v A, Adelaide, 1947/48. HS 217 Bombay v Maharashtra, Bombay, 1950/51.
BBT 7–159 I v WI, Madras, 1948/49. BB 7–26 Indians v T. N. Pearce's XI, Scarborough, 1952.
Clubs: Nelson, Rochdale, Burnley. MCC Hon. member.

PHEASANT, Steven Thomas
—RHB, LM—

Born Borough, London, 25 June 1951. Educ Thomas Bennett S, Crawley. Debut 1971.
SUSSEX (1) 1971.
HS 2* Sussex v Cambridge U, Horsham, 1971.
BB 4–88 same match.
Club: Three Bridges.

PHEBEY, Arthur Henry
—RHB—

Born Catford, Kent, 1 Oct 1924. Educ Catford GS. Debut 1946. P.
KENT (320) 1946–61. Cap 1952. Benefit (£5700) 1960.
MCC (4) 1962–64.
HS 157 Kent v Glos, Bristol, 1958.
1000 RUNS (9) 1800 @ 33.33 in 1959.

PHELAN, Patrick John
—LHB, ROB—

Born Chingford, Essex, 9 Feb 1938. Educ Newport GS. Debut 1958. P.
ESSEX (154) 1958–65. Cap 1964.
HS 63 Essex v Glos, Leyton, 1963.
BB 8–109 Essex v Kent, Blackheath, 1964.
Clubs: Bishop's Stortford, Rotherham Town, Worksop.

PHILLIP, Norbert
—RHB, RFM—

Born Bioche, Dominica, W Indies, 12 June 1948. Educ Dominica GS. Debut 1969/7.
W INDIES DOMESTIC Windward Islands 1969/70–, Combined Islands 1970/71–79/80.
ESSEX (140) 1978–. Cap 1978.
WEST INDIES (9) 1977/78–78/79. A 1977/78 (3). I 1978/79 (6).
HST 47 WI v I, Calcutta, 1978/79. HS 134 Essex v Glos, Gloucester, 1978.
BBT 4–48 WI v I, Madras, 1978/79. BB 7–33 Windward Islands v Leeward Islands, Roseau, 1981/82.
Club: Colne.

PHILLIPS, Alan Geoffrey
—RHB, LB—

Born Blackburn, Lancs, 27 Mar 1931. Educ Shrewsbury; Worcester C, Oxford. Debut 1953.
OXFORD UNIVERSITY (3) 1953–54.
HS 31 Oxford U v Worcs, The Parks, 1954.
Shropshire 1960. Club: Sussex Martlets.

PHILLIPS, Edward Frederick
——————RHB——————

Born Bridgnorth, Shropshire, 12 Jan 1932. Debut 1957. *P.*
LEICESTERSHIRE (32) 1957–59.
HS 55 Leics v Essex, Leicester, 1959.

PHILLIPS, Hugh Raymond
——————RHB——————

Born Kuala Lumpur, Malaya, 8 Apr 1929. Debut 1951.
WARWICKSHIRE (I) 1951.
HS 3 Warwicks v Scotland, Edgbaston, 1951.
Club: Harborne.

PHILLIPS, John Brydon Mills
——————RHB, RFM——————

Born Canterbury, Kent, 19 Nov 1933. Educ King's S, Canterbury; St Edmund Hall, Oxford. Debut 1955.
OXFORD UNIVERSITY (28) 1955–57 (Blue 1955).
KENT (4) 1955.
HS 25 Oxford U v Australians, The Parks, 1956.
BB 5–62 Oxford U v MCC, Lord's, 1955.
Club: Canterbury St Lawrence. Father F. Phillips (Kent 2nd XI professional).

PHILLIPS, Roy *Wycliffe*
——————RHB, LBG——————

Born St James, Barbados, 8 Apr 1941. Debut 1966/67.
W INDIES DOMESTIC Barbados 1966/67.
GLOUCESTERSHIRE (16) 1968–70.
HS 92 Barbados v Leeward Islands, Basseterre, St Kitts, 1966/67.
Club: Royton.

PHILLIPSON, Christopher *Paul*
——————RHB, RM——————

Born Vrindaban, India, 10 Feb 1952. Educ Ardingly C; Loughborough C. Debut 1970.
SUSSEX (167) 1970–83. Cap 1980.
HS 87 Sussex v Hants, Hove, 1980.
BB 6–56 Sussex v Notts, Hove, 1972.

PHILLIPSON, William *Edward*
——————RHB, RFM——————

Born N Reddish, Lancs, 3 Dec 1910. Debut 1933. *P.*

LANCASHIRE (158) 1933–48. Grant in lieu of benefit (£1750) 1948.
TOUR Sir J. Cahn's XI to N Zealand 1938/39.
HS 113 Lancs v Glam, Preston, 1939.
BB 8–100 Lancs v Kent, Dover, 1934.
100 WKTS (2) 133 @ 22.33 in 1939.
Fc umpire 1956–78 (12 Tests, 1958–65). Northumberland 1950–52. Club: Littleborough.

PHIPPS, Douglas *David*
——————RHB, RMF——————

Born Edmonton, London, 27 July 1934. Educ Mill Hill. Debut 1964.
COMBINED SERVICES (I) 1964.
HS 15 Combined Services v Cambridge U, Uxbridge, 1964.
Buckinghamshire 1952–56, Norfolk 1957. Clubs: Buckingham, Ingham, The Army. Regular army officer.

PIACHAUD, James *Daniel*
——————RHB, OB——————

Born Colombo, Ceylon, 1 Mar 1937. Educ St Thomas's C, Colombo; Keble C, Oxford. Debut 1958.
OXFORD UNIVERSITY (52) 1958–61 (Blue 1958–61).
HAMPSHIRE (12) 1960.
CEYLON (I) 1968/69.
TOUR E. W. Swanton's XI to India 1963/64.
HS 40 Oxford U v Derbys, The Parks, 1958.
BB 8–72 (13–106 match) Oxford U v Free Foresters, The Parks, 1958.
Gentlemen v Players (I) 1961. Club: Hampstead.

PICK, Robert Andrew
——————LHB, RFM——————

Born Nottingham, 19 Nov 1963. Educ Alderman Derbyshire CS, Nottingham. Debut 1983.
NOTTINGHAMSHIRE (18) 1983–.
HS 27* Notts v Oxford U, The Parks, 1984.
BB 5–25 same match.

PICKERING, Harry Gordon
——————RHB——————

Born North London, 18 Jan 1917. Died Seaford, Sussex, 4 Mar 1984. Educ Glendale County S, London. Debut 1938.
ESSEX (3) 1938.

LEICESTERSHIRE (5) 1947.
HS 79 Leics v Surrey, Oval, 1947.

PICKERING, Peter Barlow
——————RHB——————

Born York, 24 Mar 1926. Educ Archbishop Holgate S, York. Debut 1953.
NORTHAMPTONSHIRE (I) 1953.
HS 37 Northants v Lancs, Old Trafford, 1953.
Fc umpire in S Africa 1977/78–78/79. N Rhodesia 1963/64. Executive member N Rhodesia CU 1963–67. Clubs: York, Ealing Dean, British Timken, Mufulira. Soccer: York City, Chelsea, Northampton Town.

PICKETT, Christopher Arthur
——————LHB, LFM/SLA——————

Born Hedgerley Village, Buckinghamshire, 19 Aug 1926. Debut 1953.
MINOR COUNTIES (I) 1953.
HS 7* Minor Counties v Australians, Stoke on Trent, 1953.
Buckinghamshire 1949–70. Clubs: Aspro, Beaconsfield, Haslingden, Slough.

PICKLES, David
——————RHB, RFM——————

Born Halifax, Yorks, 16 Nov 1935. Debut 1957. *P.*
YORKSHIRE (41) 1957–60.
HS 12 Yorks v Essex, Middlesbrough, 1958.
BB 7–61 Yorks v Som, Taunton, 1957.
Clubs: Bowling Old Lane, Baildon Green.

PICKLES, Lewis
——————RHB, OB——————

Born Wakefield, Yorks, 17 Sept 1932. Debut 1955. *P.*
SOMERSET (47) 1955–58. Cap 1956.
HS 87 Som v Lancs, Old Trafford, 1956.
1000 RUNS (I) 1137 @ 24.71 in 1956.
Clubs: Lightcliffe, East Bierley, Pudsey St Laurence, Fife.

PICKUP, James Kenneth
——————RHB, WK——————

Born Stalybridge, Cheshire, 25 Sept 1952. Educ King's S, Macclesfield; Lincoln C, Oxford. Debut 1973.
OXFORD UNIVERSITY (3) 1973–75.

HS 14 Oxford U v Som, The Parks, 1975. Cheshire 1972–. Club: Bacup.

PIERIS, Percival Ian
RHB, RM

Born Colombo, Ceylon, 14 Mar 1933. Educ St Thomas C, Mount Lavinia; Queen's C, Cambridge. Debut 1956.
CAMBRIDGE UNIVERSITY (36) 1956–58 (Blue 1957–58).
CEYLON 1964/65–66/67.
TOUR Ceylon to India and Pakistan 1966/67.
HS 55* Cambridge U v Kent, Fenner's, 1957.
BB 6–30 Prime Minister's XI v State Bank of India, Colombo, 1965/66.

PIERPOINT, Frederick George
RHB, RMF

Born Camberwell, London, 24 Apr 1915. Debut 1936. P.
SURREY (8) 1936–46.
HS 4 Surrey v Glam, Cardiff, 1946.
BB 3–60 Surrey v Northants, Oval, 1946. Retired through ill-health after war service. Norfolk 1947–49. Former professional coach Wrekin C.

PIERRE, Lance Richard
RHB, RFM

Born Woodbrook, Port of Spain, Trinidad, 5 June 1921. Debut 1940/41.
W INDIES DOMESTIC Trinidad 1940/41–49/50.
WEST INDIES (1) E 1947/48.
TOUR W Indies to England 1950.
HS 23 Trinidad v Barbados, Bridgetown, 1948/49.
BB 8–51 W Indians v Lancs, Liverpool, 1950.

PIGOT, David Richard (jnr)
RHB

Born Dublin, Ireland, 18 July 1929. Educ Blackrock C, Dublin; Dublin U. Debut 1966.
IRELAND (11) 1966–75.
HS 88 Ireland v Scotland, Perth, 1970. Clubs: Dublin University, Phoenix. Father D. R. Pigot snr (Ireland); uncle J. P. M. Pigot (Dublin U, Madras Europeans).

PIGOTT, Anthony Charles Shackleton
RHB, RFM

Born London, 4 June 1958. Educ Harrow. Debut 1978.

SUSSEX (75) 1978–. Cap 1982.
N ZEALAND DOMESTIC Wellington (11) 1982/83–.
ENGLAND (1) NZ 1983/84.
OTHER TOUR D. H. Robins' XI to N Zealand 1979/80.
HS 63 Sussex v Notts, Hove, 1983.
BB 7–74 Sussex v Northants, Eastbourne, 1982.
Called up in emergency to play for England at Christchurch in 1983/84, having to postpone his wedding in order to do so.
Club: East Grinstead.

PILLING, Harry
RHB, OB

Born Ashton-under-Lyne, Lancs, 23 Feb 1943. Educ Ashton Technical S. Debut 1962. P.
LANCASHIRE (323) 1962–80. Cap 1965. Testimonial (£9500) 1974.
TOURS Commonwealth XI to Pakistan 1970/71. World XI to Pakistan 1973/74 (relief matches). D. H. Robins' XI to Sri Lanka 1977/78.
HS 149* Lancs v Glam, Liverpool, 1976.
1000 RUNS (8) 1606 @ 36.50 in 1967.
Clubs: Oldham, Radcliffe.

PINNOCK, Renford Augustus
RHB, WK

Born St Catherine, Jamaica, 26 Sept 1937. Debut 1963/64.
W INDIES DOMESTIC Jamaica 1963/64–74/75.
TOUR Jamaica to England 1970.
HS 176 Jamaica v Sussex, Hove, 1970.
Club: St Catherine (Jamaica).

PITHEY, Anthony John
RHB, OB

Born Umtali, Rhodesia, 17 July 1933. Educ Plumtree HS; Cape Town U. Debut 1950/51.
S AFRICA DOMESTIC Rhodesia 1950/51–68/69, Western Province 1955/56–57/58, South African Universities 1956/57.
SOUTH AFRICA (17) 1956/57–64/65. E 1956/57 (3), 1964/65 (5). E 1960 (2); A 1963/64 (4); NZ 1963/64 (3).
HST 154 SA v E, Cape Town, 1964/65.
HS 170 S Africans v Tasmania, Launceston, 1963/64.
RECORD Added 157 for 5th wkt with J. H. B. Waite, SA v E, J'burg, 1964/65, S Africa Test record.
Brother D. B. Pithey (Northants, S Africa).

PITHEY, David Bartlett
RHB, OB

Born Salisbury, Rhodesia, 4 Oct 1936. Educ Plumtree HS; Cape Town U; St Edmund Hall, Oxford. Debut 1956/57.
S AFRICA DOMESTIC Rhodesia 1956/57–66/67, Western Province 1957/58, South African Universities 1957/58, Natal 1966/67, Transvaal 1967/68.
OXFORD UNIVERSITY (37) 1960–62 (Blue 1961–62).
NORTHAMPTONSHIRE (3) 1962.
SOUTH AFRICA (8) 1963/64–66/67. A 1966/67 (2). A 1963/64 (3); NZ 1963/64 (3).
HST 55 SA vA, Cape Town, 1966/67. HS 166 Rhodesia v NE Transvaal, Pretoria, 1962/63.
BBT 6–58 SA v NZ, Dunedin, 1963/64.
BB 7–47 Oxford U v Australians, The Parks, 1961.
Gentlemen v Players (1) 1962. Brother A. J. Pithey (S Africa).

PITMAN, Raymond Walter Charles
RHB, RM

Born Bartley, Hants, 21 Feb 1933. Debut 1954. P.
HAMPSHIRE (50) 1954–59.
HS 77 Hants v Derbys, Bournemouth, 1958.

PITT, John Anthony
RHB, RM

Born Dewsbury, Yorkshire, 30 Jan 1939. Debut 1957.
COMBINED SERVICES (1) 1957.
HS 26* Combined Services v Warwicks, Edgbaston, 1957.
Army. Yorks 2nd XI 1955.

PLACE, Winston
RHB

Born Rawtenstall, Lancs, 7 Dec 1914. Debut 1937. P.
LANCASHIRE (298) 1937–55. Cap 1939. Benefit (£6297) 1952.
ENGLAND (3) WI 1947/48.
OTHER TOUR Commonwealth XI to India, Pakistan and Ceylon 1949/50.
HST 107 E v WI, Kingston, 1947/48. HS 266* Lancs v Oxford U, The Parks, 1947.
1000 RUNS (8) 2501 @ 62.52 in 1947.
Fc umpire 1957.

PLATT, Robert Kenworthy
————RHB, RM————

Born Holmfirth, Yorks, 26 Dec 1932.
Debut 1955. *P.*
YORKSHIRE (96) 1955–63. Cap 1959.
NORTHAMPTONSHIRE (2) 1964.
HS 57* Yorks v Derbys, Chesterfield,
1959.
BB 7–40 Yorks v Glos, Bristol, 1956.
Clubs: Holmfirth, Leeds, Bradford,
Halifax.

PLAYLE, William *Rodger*
————RHB————

Born Palmerston North, N Zealand, 1
Dec 1938. Debut 1956/57.
N ZEALAND DOMESTIC Auckland (36)
1956/57–63/64.
AUSTRALIA DOMESTIC Western Australia
(17) 1965/66–67/68.
NEW ZEALAND (8) 1958–62/63. E 1962/63
(3). *E 1958 (5).*
HST 65 NZ v E, Wellington, 1962/63. HS
122 W Australia v Queensland, Perth,
1965/66.

PLEASS, James Edward
————RHB————

Born Cardiff, S Wales, 21 May 1923.
Debut 1947. *P from 1948.*
GLAMORGAN (171) 1947–56. Cap 1953.
HS 102* Glam v Yorks, Harrogate, 1955.
Member Glam committee. Club: Briton
Ferry.

PLIMSOLL, John Bruce
————LHB, LM————

Born Cape Town, S Africa, 27 Oct 1917.
Debut 1939/40.
S AFRICA DOMESTIC Rest of South Africa
1942/43, Western Province 1939/
40–47/48, Natal 1948/49–49/50.
SOUTH AFRICA (1) *E 1947.*
HST 8* and 8 SA v E, Old Trafford,
1947. HS 51 W Province v E Province,
Cape Town, 1947/48.
BBT 3–128 SA v E, Old Trafford, 1947.
BB 7–35 W Province v Griqualand West,
Kimberley, 1946/47.
Manager S Africa to England 1965. Son
J. B. Plimsoll jnr (Natal).

PLUMB, Stephen George
————RHB, RM————

Born Wimbish, Essex, 17 Jan 1954.
Educ Cranleigh; Writtle Agricultural C.
Debut 1975.
ESSEX (2) 1975–77.

MINOR COUNTIES (1) 1981.
HS 37* Essex v Cambridge U, Fenner's,
1975.
BB 2–47 same match.
Norfolk 1978–. Club: Bishop's Stort-
ford. Hockey: Cambridgeshire.

PLUMMER, Peter John
————RHB, SLA————

Born Nottingham, 28 Jan 1947. Educ
Aylesbury GS. Debut 1969.
NOTTINGHAMSHIRE (33) 1969–72.
HS 46 Notts v Leics, Leicester, 1970.
BB 7–71 Notts v Oxford U, The Parks,
1972.
Buckinghamshire 1973–77. Clubs: Dar-
wen, Blackpool, Aylesbury, Burnley.

POCOCK, Howard *John*
————RHB————

Born Maidstone, Kent, 8 Apr 1921.
Debut 1947.
KENT (7) 1947–49.
HS 34 Kent v Yorks, Hull, 1947.
Present Kent chairman. Club: The
Mote (Maidstone).

POCOCK, Nicholas Edward Julian
————RHB, LMF————

Born Maracaibo, Venezuela, 15 Dec
1951. Educ Shrewsbury. Debut 1976.
HAMPSHIRE (127) 1976–84. Cap 1980.
Capt 1980–84.
HS 164 Hants v Lancs, Southampton,
1982.

POCOCK, Patrick Ian
————RHB, OB————

Born Bangor, Caernarvonshire, Wales,
24 Sept 1946. Educ Merton Sec S;
Wimbledon Technical C. Debut 1964.
SURREY (440) 1964–. Cap 1967. Benefit
(£18,500) 1977.
S AFRICA DOMESTIC Northern Transvaal
1971/72.
ENGLAND (20) 1967/68–84. A 1968 (1);
WI 1976 (2), 1984 (2); SL 1984 (1). *WI
1967/68 (2), 1973/74 (4); I 1972/73
(4); P 1968/69 (1), 1972/73 (3).*
OTHER TOURS MCC Under-25 to Pakistan 1966/67. MCC to Ceylon 1969/70.
Rest of World v Pakistan XI, Karachi,
1970/71.
HST 33 E v P, Hyderabad, 1972/73. HS
75* Surrey v Notts, Oval, 1968.
BBT 6–79 E v A, Old Trafford, 1968. BB
9–57 Surrey v Glam, Cardiff, 1979.
100 WKTS (1) 112 @ 18.22 in 1967.

RECORDS Took four wkts in four balls,
five in six, six in nine and seven in 11,
Surrey v Sussex, Eastbourne, 1972; the
last two performances are unequalled in
fc cricket, the others unsurpassed.

POLLARD, Richard
————RHB, RFM————

Born Westhoughton, Lancs, 19 June
1912. Debut 1933. *P.*
LANCASHIRE (266) 1933–50. Cap 1935.
Benefit (£8000) 1949.
COMMONWEALTH XI (1) 1952.
ENGLAND (4) 1946–48. A 1948 (2); I 1946
(1). *NZ 1946/47 (1).*
HST 10* E v I, Old Trafford, 1946. HS 63
Lancs v Derbys, Old Trafford, 1947.
BBT 5–24 E v I, Old Trafford, 1946. BB
8–33 Lancs v Northants, Old Trafford,
1947.
100 WKTS (7) 149 @ 21.58 in 1938.
Players v Gentlemen (3) 1938–47.
Clubs: Aston Unity, Preston. Accom-
plished light pianist.

POLLARD, Victor
————RHB, OB————

Born Burnley, Lancs, 7 Sept 1945. Educ
Manawatu HS, N Zealand. Debut 1964/
65.
N ZEALAND DOMESTIC Central Districts
(29) 1964/65–68/69, Canterbury (17)
1969/70–74/75.
NEW ZEALAND (32) 1964/65–73. E 1965/
66 (3), 1970/71 (1); WI 1968/69 (3); I
1967/68 (4); P 1972/73 (1). *E 1965 (3),
1969 (3), 1973 (3); I 1964/65 (4),
1969/70 (1); P 1964/65 (3), 1969/70
(3).*
OTHER TOURS N Zealand to Australia
1967/68.
HST 116 NZ v E, Trent Bridge, 1973. HS
146 Central Districts v Otago, Dunedin,
1967/68.
BBT 3–3 NZ v E, Auckland, 1965/66. BB
7–65 (11–91 match) N Zealand XI v
Australian XI, New Plymouth, 1966/67.

POLLOCK, Angus John
————RHB, RM————

Born Liversedge, Yorks, 19 Apr 1962.
Educ Shrewsbury; Trinity C, Cam-
bridge U. Debut 1982.
CAMBRIDGE UNIVERSITY (23) 1982–84
(Blue 1982–84). Capt 1984.
HS 32 Cambridge U v Essex, Fenner's,
1984.
BB 5–107 Cambridge U v Worcs, Worc-
ester, 1983.
Soccer: Blue.

POLLOCK, John *Stuart*
——RHB, OB——

Born Belfast, Ireland, 5 June 1920. Educ Campbell C, Belfast. Debut 1939.
IRELAND (20) 1939–57.
MCC (2) 1954–57.
FREE FORESTERS (I) 1958.
HS 129 Ireland v Scotland, Dublin, 1951.
Club: NICC. President ICU 1980. Squash: Ireland. Father W. Pollock (Ireland).

POLLOCK, Peter Maclean
——RHB, RF——

Born Pietermaritzburg, S Africa, 30 June 1941. Educ Grey C, Maritzburg, S Africa. Debut 1958/59.
S AFRICA DOMESTIC Eastern Province 1958/59–71/72.
SOUTH AFRICA (28) 1961/62–69/70. E 1964/65 (5); A 1966/67 (5), 1969/70 (4); NZ 1961/62 (3). *E 1965 (3); A 1963/64 (5); NZ 1963/64 (3).*
OTHER TOURS S African Fezelas to England 1961. Rest of World XI in England 1966, 1967, 1968. World XI to Australia 1971/72.
HST 75★ SA v A, Cape Town, 1966/67. HS 79 E Province v Transvaal, J'burg, 1962/63.
BBT 6–38 SA v NZ, Durban, 1961/62. BB 7–19 (10–48 match) E Province v W Province, Port Elizabeth, 1962/63.
Rest of World v England (1) 1970. Father A. M. Pollock (OFS); brother R. G. Pollock (S Africa).

POLLOCK, Robert *Graeme*
——LHB, RLB——

Born Durban, S Africa, 27 Feb 1944. Educ Grey HS, Port Elizabeth, S Africa. Debut 1960/61. *Wisden* 1966.
S AFRICA DOMESTIC Eastern Province 1960/61–77/78, Transvaal 1978/79–.
SOUTH AFRICA (23) 1963/64–69/70. E 1964/65 (5); A 1966/67 (5), 1969/70 (4). *E 1965 (3); A 1963/64 (5); NZ 1963/64 (1).*
OTHER TOURS Rest of World XI in England 1966, 1967, 1968. World XI to Australia 1971/72. International Wanderers to S Africa 1974/75.
HST 274 SA v A, Durban, 1969/70. HS as above.
BBT 2–50 SA v E, J'burg, 1964/65. BB 3–46 S Africans v Tasmania, Launceston, 1963/64.
1000 RUNS (1 + 5) 1147 @ 57.35 in 1965.
RECORDS HS (above) highest Test score for S Africa. Added 341 for 3rd wkt with E. J. Barlow, SA v A, Adelaide, 1963/64, S African fc record and S Africa Test

record for any wkt; added 200 for 6th wkt with H. R. Lance, SA v A, Durban, 1969/70, S Africa Test record. Added 338 for 5th wkt with A. L. Wilmot, E Province v Natal, Port Elizabeth, 1975/76, S African record. Scored first century at age of 16 yrs 335 days (102 E Province v Transvaal B, J'burg, 1960/61); first double-century at age of 19 yrs 20 days (209★ E Province XI v Cavaliers, Port Elizabeth, 1962/63), youngest S African to either figure. Reached century in 52 mins during 101 International Cavaliers v Barbados, Scarborough, 1969, fastest century by S African. Scored more runs in Currie Cup (11,205 @ 56.31) than any other batsman.
Rest of World v England (5) 1970. S Africa (11) 1981/82–83/84. World Series Cricket (Kerry Packer) 1977/78, but unable to play because of his nationality (and being a non-county cricketer). Autobiography *Down the Wicket* (1968); co-author, with P. M. Pollock, of *Bouncers and Boundaries* (1969). Father A. M. Pollock (OFS); brother P. M. Pollock (S Africa).

PONNIAH, Charles Edward Manoharan
——RHB, LB——

Born Colombo, Ceylon, 3 May 1943. Educ St Thomas's, Colombo; Emmanuel C, Cambridge. Debut 1963/64.
CEYLON 1963/64–64/65.
CAMBRIDGE UNIVERSITY (36) 1967–69 (Blue 1967–69).
TOUR Ceylon to India 1964/65.
HS 101★ Cambridge U v Lancs, Fenner's, 1968.
BB 5–20 Cambridge U v Glam, Colwyn Bay, 1968.
Club: Richmond.

PONT, Ian Leslie
——RHB, RM——

Born Brentwood, Essex, 28 Aug 1961. Educ Brentwood S. Debut 1982.
NOTTINGHAMSHIRE (4) 1982.
HS 16 Notts v M'sex, Lord's, 1982.
BB 2–107 Notts v Surrey, Oval, 1982.
Buckinghamshire 1983–84. Brother K. R. Pont (Essex).

PONT, Keith Rupert
——RHB, RM——

Born Wanstead, Essex, 16 Jan 1953. Educ St Martin's S, Hutton. Debut 1970.
ESSEX (181) 1970–. Cap 1976.

HS 125★ Essex v Glam, Southend, 1983.
BB 5–17 Essex v Glam, Cardiff, 1982.
Brother I. L. Pont (Notts).

POOLE, Cyril John
——LHB, occ WK——

Born Forest Town, Mansfield, Notts, 13 Mar 1921. Debut 1948. *P.*
NOTTINGHAMSHIRE (366) 1948–62. Cap 1949. Benefit (£1302) 1960.
ENGLAND (3) *I 1951/52.*
HST 69★ E v I, Calcutta, 1951/52. HS 222★ Notts v Indians, Trent Bridge, 1952.
1000 RUNS (12) 1860 @ 33.21 in 1961.
Soccer: Mansfield Town.

POOLE, Kenneth John
——RHB, RMF——

Born Thurgarton, Notts, 27 Apr 1934. Debut 1955. *P.*
NOTTINGHAMSHIRE (26) 1955–57.
HS 58 Notts v Essex, Southend, 1955.
BB 2–10 Notts v Oxford, The Parks, 1956.
Lost three fingers of right hand in accident, October 1957. Professional coach Nottingham HS in 1960s.

POPE, George Henry
——RHB, RFM——

Born Tibshelf, Derbys, 27 Jan 1911. Debut 1933. *P.*
DERBYSHIRE (169) 1933–48. Cap.
ENGLAND (1) SA 1947.
TOURS Lord Tennyson's XI to India 1937/38. Commonwealth XI to India, Pakistan and Ceylon 1949/50.
HST 8★ E v SA, Lord's, 1947. HS 207★ Derbys v Hants, Portsmouth, 1948 (adding 241★ for 7th wkt with A. E. G. Rhodes, county record).
BB 8–38 Derbys v Sussex, Burton upon Trent, 1948.
1000 RUNS (4) 1464 @ 31.82 in 1939.
100 WKTS (3) 114 @ 18.38 in 1947.
DOUBLE (2) 1938, 1948.
Players v Gentlemen (1) 1939. England v Australia (Victory matches) (3) 1945. Selected for MCC to India 1939/40 (cancelled owing to war). Fc umpire 1966–74. Clubs: Colne, Heywood, Sheffield United. Brothers A. V. and H. Pope (both Derbys).

POPE, Harold
——RHB, LB——

Born Chesterfield, Derbys, 10 May 1919. Debut 1939. *P.*
DERBYSHIRE (10) 1939–46.

HS 24* Derbys v Surrey, Oval, 1946.
BB 3–80 Derbys v Indians, Chesterfield, 1946.
Club: West Bromwich Dartmouth. Former professional coach Repton (after retirement). Brothers A. V. Pope (Derbys) and G. H. Pope (Derbys, England).

POPPLEWELL, Nigel Francis Mark
————RHB, RM————

Born Farnborough, Kent, 8 Aug 1957. Educ Radley; Selwyn C, Cambridge. Debut 1977.
CAMBRIDGE UNIVERSITY (25) 1977–79 (Blue 1977–79).
SOMERSET (100) 1979–. Cap 1983.
HS 143 Som v Glos, Bath, 1983.
BB 5–33 Som v Northants, Weston-super-Mare, 1981.
1000 RUNS (1) 1116 @ 32.82 in 1984.
RECORD During HS (above) reached century in 41 mins, fastest-ever for Som, and fifth fastest-ever in fc cricket; entire inns lasted only 62 mins (against bowlers attempting to expedite a declaration). Buckinghamshire 1975–78. Club: Amersham. Father O. B. Popplewell (Cambridge U).

POPPLEWELL, Oliver Bury
————RHB, WK————

Born Northwood, M'sex, 15 Aug 1927. Educ Charterhouse; Queen's C, Cambridge. Debut 1949.
CAMBRIDGE UNIVERSITY (34) 1949–51 (Blue 1949–51).
FREE FORESTERS (6) 1952–60.
MCC (1) 1953.
HS 74* Cambridge U v MCC, Lord's, 1951 and 74 Cambridge U v Sussex, Fenner's, 1951.
MCC committee 1971–. QC. Son N. F. M. Popplewell (Cambridge U, Som).

PORTEOUS, Thomas Wilkie
————RHB————

Born Glasgow, Scotland, 22 Jan 1948. Educ Coatbridge HS. Debut 1973.
SCOTLAND (2) 1973–74.
HS 18 Scotland v Ireland, Cork, 1973.
Club: Drumpelier.

PORTER, Arthur
————RHB, RAS————

Born Clayton-le-Moors, Lancs, 25 Mar 1914. Debut 1936.
GLAMORGAN (38) 1936–49. Cap 1946.
HS 105 Glam v Surrey, Oval, 1946.
BB 4–25 Glam v Glos, Cardiff, 1946.

PORTER, Simon Robert
————RHB, OB————

Born Oxford, 9 Aug 1950. Educ Peers S, Littlemore; St Edmund Hall, Oxford. Debut 1973.
OXFORD UNIVERSITY (7) 1973 (Blue).
HS 20 Oxford U v Derbys, The Parks, 1973.
BB 4–26 Oxford U v Warwicks, Edgbaston, 1973.
Oxfordshire 1971–. Club: Headington.

POSNETT, Charles Edward
————RHB————

Born Belfast, Ireland, 29 May 1914. Educ Connell's Institute, Belfast. Debut 1947.
IRELAND (1) 1947.
HS 26 Ireland v Derbys, Buxton, 1947.
Club: Woodvale.

POTHECARY, Arthur Ernest (Sam)
————LHB, SLA————

Born Southampton, Hants, 1 Mar 1906. Debut 1927. P.
HAMPSHIRE (271) 1927–46. Cap.
HS 130 Hants v N Zealanders, Bournemouth, 1937.
BB 4–47 Hants v Surrey, Oval, 1927 (fc debut).
1000 RUNS (4) 1357 @ 27.14 in 1938.
Fc umpire 1949–59. Uncle S. G. Pothecary (Hants).

POTHECARY, James Edward
————RHB, RMF————

Born Cape Town, S Africa, 6 Dec 1933. Educ Sea Point HS, Cape Town, S Africa. Debut 1954/55.
S AFRICA DOMESTIC Western Province 1954/55–64/65.
SOUTH AFRICA (3) E 1960.
HST 12 SA v E, Old Trafford, 1960. HS 81* W Province v E Province, Port Elizabeth, 1963/64.
BBT 4–58 SA v E, Oval, 1960. BB 5–29 W Province v Rhodesia, Cape Town, December 1959/60.
Took all 20 wkts (10 for 18 and 10 for 36) in match, Seapoint v Lansdowne, Cape Town, December 1950.

POTTER, Gordon
————RHB, LB————

Born Dormans Land, Surrey, 26 Oct 1931. Educ Skinners S. Debut 1949. P.
SUSSEX (55) 1949–57.
HS 88 Sussex v Worcs, Worcester, 1954.

BB 3–29 Sussex v Cambridge U, Fenner's, 1954.
Club: Knowle (Bristol).

POTTER, Ian Caesar
————RHB, RM————

Born Woking, Surrey, 2 Sept 1938. Educ King's S, Canterbury. Debut 1959.
KENT (3) 1959–61.
OXFORD UNIVERSITY (16) 1960–62 (Blue 1961–62).
HS 34 Oxford U v MCC, Lord's, 1961.
BB 6–74 Oxford U v Glos, The Parks, 1960.
Club: Gore Court.

POTTER, Jack
————RHB, LBG————

Born Coburg, Victoria, Australia, 13 Apr 1938. Debut 1956/57.
AUSTRALIA DOMESTIC Victoria (81) 1956/57–67/68.
TOURS Australia to N Zealand 1959/60. Australia to England 1964.
HS 221 Victoria v NSW, Melbourne, 1965/66.
BB 4–20 Victoria v Queensland, Brisbane, 1961/62.
Club: Fitzroy.

POTTER, Laurie
————RHB, LM————

Born Bexleyheath, Kent, 7 Nov 1962. Educ Kelmscott HS, Perth, W Australia. Debut 1981.
KENT (35) 1981–.
HS 118 Kent v Indians, Canterbury, 1982.
BB 2–31 Kent v Oxford U, The Parks, 1984.

POTTS, Henry James
————RHB————

Born Carlisle, Cumberland, 23 Jan 1925. Educ Stand GS, Manchester; Keble C, Oxford. Debut 1949.
OXFORD UNIVERSITY (9) 1949–50 (Blue 1950).
HS 50 Oxford U v Leics, Ashby-de-la-Zouch, 1950.
Lancs 2nd XI 1949–50. Soccer: Blue (capt), Northampton Town, England (amateur).

POULET, Roger John
————RHB————

Born Sheen, Staffordshire, 18 July 1942. Educ Christ's C, Cambridge.

227

Debut 1968.
CAMBRIDGE UNIVERSITY (1) 1968.
HS 6 Cambridge U v Leics, Fenner's, 1968.

POULTER, Stephen John
—————————RHB—————————

Born Hornsey, London, 9 Sept 1956.
Debut 1978.
MIDDLESEX (3) 1978.
HS 36 M'sex v Notts, Trent Bridge, 1978.

POUNTAIN, Francis Reginald
—————————RHB, RM—————————

Born Eastleigh, Hants, 23 Apr 1941.
Debut 1960. P.
SUSSEX (76) 1960–65.
HS 96 Sussex v Som, Glastonbury, 1964.
BB 5–91 Sussex v Surrey, Hove, 1962.
Scored 16 out of 128 for 9th wkt with G. C. Cooper, Sussex v Warwicks, Edgbaston, 1960, on fc debut.
Club: Brighton and Hove.

POWELL, Adam Gordon
—————————RHB, WK—————————

Born Boxted, Essex, 17 Aug 1912. Died Sandwich, Kent, 7 June 1982. Educ Charterhouse; Magdalene C, Cambridge. Debut 1932.
ESSEX (23) 1932–37.
CAMBRIDGE UNIVERSITY (12) 1933–34 (Blue 1934).
FREE FORESTERS (8) 1946–57.
MINOR COUNTIES (1) 1949.
TOURS MCC to N Zealand 1935/36.
HS 79 MCC v Minor Counties, Lord's, 1950.
Gentlemen v Players (1) 1945. Suffolk 1938–53. MCC to Canada 1937, 1951.

POWELL, Tyrone Lyndon
—————————RHB, OB—————————

Born Bargoed, S Wales, 17 June 1953. Educ Hereatunga C, Upper Hutt, N Zealand. Debut 1971/72.
N ZEALAND DOMESTIC New Zealand Under-23 XI (1) 1971/72.
GLAMORGAN (1) 1976.
HS 14 N Zealand Under-23 XI v Otago, Dunedin, 1971/72.
Norfolk 1982–.

PRASANNA, Erappali Anantharao Srinivasa
—————————RHB, OB—————————

Born Bangalore, India, 22 May 1940. Educ National HS, Bangalore. Debut

1961/62.
INDIA DOMESTIC Mysore/Karnataka 1961/62–78/79. Capt 1969/70–78/79.
INDIA (49) 1961/62–78/79. E 1961/62 (1), 1972/73 (3), 1976/77 (4); A 1969/70 (5); WI 1966/67 (1), 1974/75 (5); NZ 1969/70 (3). *E 1967 (3), 1974 (2); A 1967/68 (4), 1977/78 (4); WI 1961/62 (1), 1970/71 (3), 1975/76 (1); NZ 1967/68 (4), 1975/76 (3); P 1978/79 (2).*
OTHER TOURS India to E Africa 1967. India to England 1971.
HST 37 I v E, Madras, 1972/73. HS 81 Mysore v Andhra Pradesh, Bangalore, 1968/69.
BBT 8–76 (11–140 match) I v NZ, Auckland, 1975/76. BB 8–50 (12–109 match) Mysore v Andhra Pradesh, Belgaum, 1970/71.
Autobiography *One More Over* (1977).

PRATT, David
—————————RHB, SLA—————————

Born Watford, Hertfordshire, 20 July 1938. Debut 1959. P.
WORCESTERSHIRE (8) 1959.
COMBINED SERVICES (3) 1961.
NOTTINGHAMSHIRE (7) 1962.
HS 14 Combined Services v S African Fezela, Portsmouth, 1961.
BB 5–54 Worcs v Surrey, Worcester, 1959.
Hertfordshire 1957. Clubs: Beaconsfield, Stourbridge.

PRATT, Derek Edward
—————————RHB, LB—————————

Born Balham, S London, 31 Oct 1925. Debut 1954. P.
SURREY (9) 1954–57.
HS 33 Surrey v Derbys, Derby, 1956.
BB 6–119 Surrey v Combined Services, Oval, 1956.
Bedfordshire 1958–63. Club: Banstead. Brother R. C. E. Pratt (Surrey).

PRATT, Donald Montague McVeagh
—————————LHB—————————

Born Dublin, Ireland, 9 July 1935. Educ St Columbas C, Rathfarnham; Dublin U. Debut 1963.
IRELAND (6) 1963–66.
HS Ireland v N Zealanders, Ormeau, Belfast, 1965.
Clubs: Dublin University, Phoenix. Squash: Ireland. Uncle T. G. B. McVeagh (Ireland).

PRATT, Rodney Lynes
—————————RHB, RFM—————————

Born Stoney Stanton, Leics, 15 Nov 1938. Educ Hinckley GS. Debut 1955. P.
LEICESTERSHIRE (99) 1955–64.
HS 80 Leics v Essex, Leicester, 1959.
BB 7–47 Leics v Glam, Leicester, 1964.

PRATT, Ronald Charles Ernest
—————————LHB, ROB—————————

Born Balham, S London, 5 May 1928. Died Banstead, Surrey, 1 June 1977. Debut 1952. P.
SURREY (69) 1952–59.
HS 120 Surrey v Cambridge U, Guildford, 1956.
Club: Banstead. Brother D. E. Pratt (Surrey).

PRENTICE, Christopher Norman Russell
—————————RHB, RM/OB—————————

Born Borough, London, 5 Sept 1954. Educ Shrewsbury; Christ Church C, Oxford. Debut 1974.
OXFORD UNIVERSITY (1) 1974.
HS 19 Oxford U v Worcs, The Parks, 1974.

PRENTICE, Francis Thomas
—————————RHB, SRA—————————

Born Knaresborough, Yorks, 22 Apr 1912. Died Headingley, Leeds, Yorks, 10 July 1978. Debut 1934. P to 1950.
LEICESTERSHIRE (241) 1934–51. Cap 1936. Testimonial (£549) 1950.
HS 191 Leics v Notts, Loughborough, 1949.
BB 5–46 Leics v Glos, Leicester, 1946.
1000 RUNS (5) 1742 @ 38.71 in 1949.

PRESLAND, Edward Robert
—————————RHB, RM/OB—————————

Born High Beach, Essex, 27 Mar 1943. Educ Thomas Lethaby Sec S, East Ham. Debut 1962.
ESSEX (30) 1962–70.
HS 51 Essex v Northants, Northampton, 1967.
BB 2–19 Essex v Hants, Romford, 1965.
Club: Romford. Soccer: West Ham United, Crystal Palace, Colchester United.

PRESSDEE, James Stuart
————RHB, SLA————

Born Mumbles, Swansea, S Wales, 19 June 1933. Educ Oystermouth S, Swansea. Debut 1949. *P.*
GLAMORGAN (320) 1949–65. Cap 1955. Benefit 1964.
S AFRICA DOMESTIC North-Eastern Transvaal 1965/66–69/70. Capt 1965/66–69/70.
HS 150* Glam v Cambridge U, Pontypridd, 1965.
BB 9–43 Glam v Yorks, Swansea, 1965.
1000 RUNS (6) 1911 @ 34.74 in 1962.
100 WKTS (2) 106 @ 21.62 in 1963.
DOUBLE (2) 1963, 1964.
RECORD Made fc debut at 16 yrs 27 days, youngest-ever Glam cricketer.
Clubs: Swansea, Llanelli, Maesteg Celtic. Soccer: Swansea Town, Wales (schoolboy international).

PRESTON, Derek John
————RHB, SLA————

Born Leyton, Essex, 12 Jan 1936. Educ Bancroft's S. Debut 1959.
SUSSEX (12) 1959.
HS 54 Sussex v Notts, Trent Bridge, 1959.
BB 3–45 Sussex v Leics, Loughborough, 1959.
Clubs: South Woodford, Sevenoaks Vine.

PRESTON, Kenneth Charles
————RHB, RFM/RM————

Born Goodmayes, Essex, 22 Aug 1925. Educ Romford Intermediate S. Debut 1948. *P.*
ESSEX (391) 1948–64. Cap 1951. Benefit (£3650) 1959.
HS 70 Essex v Derbys, Chesterfield, 1959.
BB 7–55 Essex v Northants, Peterborough, 1956.
100 WKTS (1) 140 @ 20.35 in 1957. Also 99 wkts in 1958, 96 in 1956 and 94 in 1955.
Players v Gentlemen (1) 1951. Reduced pace after severe leg injury at soccer. Professional coach Brentwood S 1965–.

PRETLOVE, John Frederick
————LHB, SLA————

Born Camberwell, London, 23 Nov 1932. Educ Alleyn's S; Caius C, Cambridge. Debut 1954.
CAMBRIDGE UNIVERSITY (32) 1954–56 (Blue 1954–56).
KENT (85) 1955–59. Cap 1957.

MCC (4) 1961–68.
HS 137 Cambridge U v Essex, Fenner's, 1954.
BB 5–55 Cambridge U v M'sex, Fenner's, 1955.
1000 RUNS (1) 1191 @ 25.89 in 1957.
Gentlemen v Players (2) 1955–56. Kent assistant-secretary 1955–57. Club: Bromley. Soccer: Blue (capt).

PRICE, Charles Frederick Thomas
————RHB, SLA————

Born Sydney, NSW, Australia, 17 Feb 1917. Debut 1945.
AUSTRALIA DOMESTIC Australian Services (3) 1945/46.
TOUR Australian Services to England 1945 (3) and India and Ceylon (8) 1945/46.
HS 55 Australian Services v W Zone, Bombay, 1945/46.
BB 4–33 Australian Services v S Zone, Madras, 1945/46.
Sergeant in Australian Army.

PRICE, David Gregory
————RHB, OB————

Born Luton, Bedfordshire, 7 Feb 1965. Educ Haberdashers' Aske's, Homerton C, Cambridge. Debut 1984.
CAMBRIDGE UNIVERSITY (7) 1984 (Blue).
HS 49 Cambridge U v Warwicks, Fenner's, 1984.
Club: St Albans.

PRICE, David Howe
————RHB, RM————

Born Gloucester, 25 July 1955. Educ Malvern; Balliol C, Oxford. Debut 1975.
OXFORD UNIVERSITY (5) 1975–78.
HS 27 Oxford U v Yorks, The Parks, 1978.

PRICE, Eric James
————LHB, SLA————

Born Middleton, Lancs, 27 Oct 1918. Educ St Leonard's Church of England S, Middleton. Debut 1946. *P.*
LANCASHIRE (35) 1946–47. Cap 1946.
ESSEX (43) 1948–49.
HS 54 Lancs v M'sex, Old Trafford, 1946.
BB 8–125 Essex v Worcs, Worcester, 1949.
Dismissed G. Dews for king pair, Lancs v Worcs, Old Trafford, 1946.
The Rest v England, Canterbury, 1946

(Test trial). Clubs: Middleton, St Annes, Kearsley.

PRICE, John Sidney Ernest
————LHB, RF————

Born Harrow, M'sex, 22 July 1937. Educ St Marylebone GS. Debut 1961.
MIDDLESEX (242) 1961–75. Cap 1963. Benefit (£9810) 1972.
ENGLAND (15) 1963/64–72. A 1964 (2), 1972 (1); I 1971 (3); P 1971 (1). *SA 1964/65 (4); I 1963/64 (4).*
HST 32 E v I, Bombay, 1963/64. HS 53* D. H. Robins' XI v W Indians, Eastbourne, 1969.
BBT 5–73 E v I, Calcutta, 1963/64. BB 8–48 M'sex v Derbys, Lord's, 1966.
Took 94 wkts @ 18.74 in 1966.
Club: Wembley.

PRICE, Mark Richard
————RHB, SLA————

Born Liverpool, 20 Apr 1960. Educ Harper Green Sec S. Debut 1984.
GLAMORGAN (3) 1984.
HS 7 Glam v W Indies, Swansea, 1984.

PRICE, Wilfred *Frederick* Frank
————RHB, WK————

Born London, 25 Apr 1902. Died London, 13 Jan 1969. Debut 1926. *P.*
MIDDLESEX (382) 1926–47. Cap 1928. Benefit 1938.
ENGLAND (1) A 1938.
TOURS MCC to W Indies 1929/30. Sir T. E. W. Brinckman's XI to S America 1937/38.
HST 6 E v A, Headingley, 1938. HS 111 M'sex v Worcs, Dudley, 1933.
1000 RUNS (1) 1298 @ 25.96 in 1934.
Took seven catches in inns, M'sex v Yorks, Lord's, 1937, first instance by any fieldsman in fc cricket. Made 977 dismissals (665 ct, 312 st) in career.
Players v Gentlemen (2) 1938–39. Fc umpire 1949–67 (8 Tests, 1964–67). Club: Ealing.

PRICHARD, Paul John
————RHB————

Born Billericay, Essex, 7 Jan 1965. Educ Brentwood HS. Debut 1984.
ESSEX (20) 1984.
HS 100 Essex v Lancs, Old Trafford, 1984.

PRIDEAUX, Roger Malcolm
————RHB————

Born Chelsea, London, 13 July 1939. Educ Tonbridge; Sidney Sussex C, Cambridge. Debut 1958.
CAMBRIDGE UNIVERSITY (49) 1958–60 (Blue 1958–60).
KENT (33) 1960–61.
NORTHAMPTONSHIRE (234) 1962–70. Cap 1962. Capt 1967–70.
SUSSEX (65) 1971–73. Cap 1971.
S AFRICA DOMESTIC Orange Free State 1971/72–74/75.
ENGLAND (3) 1968–68/69. A 1968 (1). P 1968/69 (2).
OTHER TOURS MCC to N Zealand 1960/61. Commonwealth XI to Pakistan 1967/68.
HST 64 E v A, Headingley, 1968. HS 202* Northants v Oxford U, The Parks, 1963.
BB 2–13 Sussex v Cambridge U, Fenner's, 1972.
1000 RUNS (13) 1993 @ 41.52 in 1968. Reached century in 52 mins during inns of 118 South v North, Blackpool, 1961. Gentlemen v Players (5) 1960–62. OFS CU selector 1982/83.

PRIDGEON, Anthony *Paul*
————RHB, RMF————

Born Wall Heath, Staffordshire, 22 Feb 1954. Educ Summerhill Sec S, Kingswinford. Debut 1972.
WORCESTERSHIRE (187) 1972–. Cap 1980.
HS 67 Worcs v Warwicks, Worcester, 1984.
BB 7–35 Worcs v Oxford U, The Parks, 1976.
Club: Stourbridge.

PRIESTLEY, Neil
————LHB, WK————

Born Blyborough, Lincolnshire, 23 June 1961. Educ S Axholme CS; John Leggatt Sixth Form C, Scunthorpe. Debut 1981.
NORTHAMPTONSHIRE (1) 1981.
HS 20* Northants v Sri Lankans, Northampton, 1981.
Lincolnshire 1983–.

PRINGLE, Derek Raymond
————RHB, RMF————

Born Nairobi, Kenya, 18 Sept 1958. Educ St Mary's, Nairobi; Felsted; Fitzwilliam C, Cambridge. Debut 1978.
ESSEX (62) 1978–. Cap 1982.
CAMBRIDGE UNIVERSITY (33) 1979–82 (Blue 1979–81). Capt 1982, but did not play in Varsity match, owing to selection for England v India at Old Trafford (Second Test).

ENGLAND (10) 1982–84. WI 1984 (3); I 1982 (3); P 1982 (1). *A 1982/83 (3)*.
HST 47* E v A, Perth, 1982/83. HS 127* Cambridge U v Worcs, Fenner's, 1981.
BBT 5–108 E v WI, Edgbaston, 1984. BB 7–32 Essex v M'sex, Chelmsford, 1983.
Father D. Pringle (Kenya, E Africa).

PRIOR, Ian David
————RHB, WK————

Born London, 26 July 1930. Educ Colchester RGS. Debut 1967.
MINOR COUNTIES (1) 1967.
HS 21 Minor Counties v Pakistanis, Swindon, 1967.
Suffolk 1956–68. Clubs: Colchester, Old Ipswichians. Rugby: Suffolk.

PRIOR, John Andrew
————RHB, RM————

Born Dublin, Ireland, 14 June 1960. Educ Belvedere C. Debut 1981.
IRELAND (4) 1981–.
HS 87 Ireland v Scotland, Glasgow, 1984.
BB 2–7 same match.
Clubs: Dublin University, Old Belvedere, North Leinster.

PRITCHARD, Graham Charles
————RHB, RFM————

Born Farnborough, Kent, 14 Jan 1942. Educ King's S, Canterbury; Caius C, Cambridge. Debut 1962.
CAMBRIDGE UNIVERSITY (25) 1962–64 (Blue 1964).
ESSEX (10) 1965–66.
HS 18 Cambridge U v Leics, Fenner's, 1963.
BB 6–51 Cambridge U v Surrey, Guildford, 1963.

PRITCHARD, Thomas Leslie
————RHB, RF————

Born Kaupokonui, N Zealand, 10 Mar 1917. Educ Hawera Technical HS. Debut 1937/38. *P 1946–55.*
N ZEALAND DOMESTIC Wellington (12) 1937/38–40/41, New Zealand XI (1) 1938/39.
WARWICKSHIRE (170) 1946–55. Cap 1947. Benefit (£3816) 1952.
KENT (4) 1956.
TOUR N Zealand Services XI to England 1945.
HS 81 Warwicks v Notts, Edgbaston, 1947.
BB 8–20 Warwicks v Worcs, Dudley, 1950.

100 WKTS (4) 172 @ 18.75 in 1948.
Players v Gentlemen (2) 1948–51.
Clubs: Smethwick, West Bromwich Dartmouth, Moseley, Stourbridge.

PROCTER, Michael John
————RHB, RF/OB————

Born Durban, S Africa, 15 Sept 1946. Educ Hilton C, Natal, S Africa. Debut 1965. *Wisden* 1970.
GLOUCESTERSHIRE (259) 1965–81. Cap 1968. Benefit (£15,500) 1976. Capt 1977–81.
S AFRICA DOMESTIC Natal 1965/66–68/69, 1976/77–, Western Province 1969/70, Rhodesia 1970/71–75/76.
SOUTH AFRICA (7) 1966/67–69/70. A 1966/67 (3), 1969/70 (4).
HST 48 SA v A, Cape Town, 1969/70. HS 254 Rhodesia v W Province, Salisbury, 1970/71.
BBT 6–73 SA v A, Port Elizabeth, 1969/70. BB 9–71 Rhodesia v Transvaal, Bulawayo, 1972/73.
1000 RUNS (9) 1786 @ 45.79 in 1971.
100 WKTS (2) 109 @ 18.04 in 1977.
RECORDS Only player to score century and perform hat-trick in one match on two occasions: Glos v Essex, Westcliff, 1972 and Glos v Leics, Bristol, 1979. Scored six hundreds in consecutive fc innings (119, 129, 107, 174, 106, 254), all for Rhodesia in 1970/71, equalling world record held by C. B. Fry and D. G. Bradman. Reached 50 in 11 scoring strokes during inns of 93 Glos v Som, Taunton, 1979, equalling world record (in same inns hit six consecutive balls from D. Breakwell, spread over two overs, for six).
Scored 100 runs and took 10 wkts in same match on two occasions: 108 and 13 for 73, Glos v Worcs, Cheltenham, 1977; 73 and 35 and 14 for 76, Glos v Worcs, Cheltenham, 1980. Scored 92 in 35 mins, Glos v Warwicks, Bristol, 1979; and, during inns of 105, Glos v Northants, Bristol, 1979, reached century in 57 mins. Hit A. A. Mallett for five sixes from consecutive balls (in one over), W Province v Australians, Cape Town, 1969/70.
Selected for S Africa to England 1970 and S Africa to Australia 1971/72, both cancelled tours. Rest of World v England (5) 1970. World Series Cricket (Kerry Packer) 1977/78–78/79. S Africa (1) 1981/82 (capt). Author (with Don Nelson) of *Cricket Buccaneer* (1974) and (with Pat Murphy) *Mike Procter and Cricket* (1981). Father W. C. Procter (E Province); brother A. W. Procter (Natal).

PRODGER, John Michael
RHB

Born Forest Hill, London, 1 Sept 1935.
Educ Dartford GS. Debut 1956. *P.*
KENT (151) 1956–67. Cap 1965.
HS 170* Kent v Essex, Maidstone, 1961.
Took eight catches in match, Kent v
Glos, Cheltenham, 1961.

PROUD, Roland Barton (Bill)
RHB

Born Bishop Auckland, Co Durham, 29
Sept 1919. Died Bishop Auckland, 27
Oct 1961. Educ Winchester; Brasenose
C, Oxford. Debut 1938.
HAMPSHIRE (7) 1938–39.
OXFORD UNIVERSITY (10) 1939 (Blue).
MINOR COUNTIES (1) 1950.
HS 87 Oxford U v Cambridge U, Lord's,
1939.
Persia and Iraq 1939–45. Durham
1946–55. Club: Bishop Auckland.

PROUTON, Ralph Oliver
RHB, WK

Born Southampton, Hants, 1 Mar 1926.
Educ Central S, Southampton. Debut
1949. *P.*
HAMPSHIRE (52) 1949–54.
HS 90 Hants v Leics, Portsmouth, 1953.
Minor Counties umpire 1957–68.
Clubs: Deanery, The Ravens. Former
master-in-charge of cricket Downside.
Soccer: Swindon Town.

PRYER, Barry James Keith
RHB, LB

Born Plumstead, Kent, 1 Feb 1925.
Educ City of London S; St Catharine's
C, Cambridge. Debut 1946.
COMBINED SERVICES (5) 1946–47.
KENT (2) 1947–49.
CAMBRIDGE UNIVERSITY (19) 1948–49
(Blue 1948).
FREE FORESTERS (1) 1950.
HS 75* Cambridge U v M'sex, Fenner's,
1948.
BB 4–25 Combined Services v Surrey,
Kingston-upon-Thames, 1946.
Club: Bromley.

PUCKRIDGE, Anthony
RHB, WK

Born Bromley, Kent, 5 Apr 1943. Educ
Christ Church C, Oxford. Debut 1963.
OXFORD UNIVERSITY (1) 1963.
HS 1 Oxford U v Pakistan Eaglets, The
Parks, 1963.

PUGH, Charles *Thomas* Michael
RHB

Born London, 13 Mar 1937. Educ Eton.
Debut 1959.
GLOUCESTERSHIRE (76) 1959–62. Cap
1961. Capt 1961–62.
HS 137 Glos v Derbys, Chesterfield,
1960 (adding 256 for 2nd wkt with T. W.
Graveney, county record).
1000 RUNS (1) 1011 @ 21.51 in 1960.
Gentlemen v Players (1) 1960. Uncle
J. G. Pugh (Warwicks).

PULLAN, David Anthony
RHB, WK

Born Farsley, Yorks, 1 May 1944.
Debut 1970.
NOTTINGHAMSHIRE (95) 1970–74. Cap
1971.
HS 34 Notts v Warwicks, Trent Bridge,
1972.
Club: Farsley.

PULLAR, Geoffrey (Noddy)
LHB, RLB

Born Swinton, Lancs, 1 Aug 1935.
Debut 1954. *P from 1956. Wisden* 1960.
LANCASHIRE (312) 1954–68. Cap 1958.
Benefit (£4600) 1967.
GLOUCESTERSHIRE (25) 1969–70.
ENGLAND (28) 1959–62/63. A 1961 (5);
SA 1960 (3); I 1959 (3); P 1962 (2). *A
1962/63 (4); WI 1959/60 (5); I 1961/
62 (3); P 1961/62 (3).*
OTHER TOUR Commonwealth XI to S
Africa and Rhodesia 1960/61.
HST 175 E v SA, Oval, 1960. HS as above.
BB 3–91 Lancs v Pakistanis, Old Traf-
ford, 1962.
1000 RUNS (9 + 1) 2647 @ 55.14 in 1959.
2000 runs (2).
Players v Gentlemen (1) 1959. CWC
Best Young Cricketer of 1959. Club:
Werneth. MCC Hon. member.

PULLINGER, George Richard
RHB, RFM

Born Islington, London, 14 Mar 1920.
Educ Chadwell St Mary S. Debut 1949.
ESSEX (18) 1949–50. Cap 1949.
HS 14* Essex v Glam, Ilford, 1949.
BB 5–54 Essex v Som, Bath, 1949.
Club: Aveley.

PURVES, James Hamilton
LHB, RM

Born Hemel Hempstead, Hertfordshire,
4 Dec 1937. Educ Uppingham. Debut
1960.

ESSEX (5) 1960–61.
FREE FORESTERS (5) 1960–64.
MCC (1) 1962.
HS 74 Free Foresters v Cambridge U,
Fenner's, 1962.

PYCROFT, Andrew John
RHB, occ OB

Born Salisbury, Rhodesia, 6 June 1956.
Educ Diocesan C, Cape Town, S Africa;
Cape Town U. Debut 1975/76.
S AFRICA DOMESTIC South African
Universities 1975/76, Western Province
B 1975/76–78/79, Rhodesia 1979/80.
ZIMBABWE 1980/81–.
TOUR Zimbabwe to England 1982.
HS 133 Zimbabwe v PIA, Harare, 1981/
82.

PYEMONT, Christopher Patrick
RHB, SLA

Born Etchingham, Sussex, 17 Jan 1948.
Educ Marlborough; Magdalene C,
Cambridge. Debut 1967.
CAMBRIDGE UNIVERSITY (14) 1967 (Blue).
HS 61 Cambridge U v Leics, Fenner's,
1967.
BB 2–7 Cambridge U v Essex, Fenner's,
1967.
Clubs: Yellowhammers, Eastbourne.

QUICK, Arnold Bertram
RHB

Born Clacton-on-Sea, Essex, 10 Feb
1915. Educ Bungay S. Debut 1936.
ESSEX (19) 1936–52.
MCC (1) 1948.
HS 57 Essex v Yorks, Clacton, 1952.
Suffolk. Essex 2nd XI (capt 1956–59).

QUICK, Ian William
RHB, SLA

Born Geelong, Victoria, Australia, 5
Nov 1933. Debut 1956/57.
AUSTRALIA DOMESTIC Victoria (34) 1956/
57–61/62.
TOURS Australia to N Zealand 1959/60.
Australia to England 1961.
HS 61* Victoria v Queensland, Mel-
bourne, 1960/61.
BB 7–20 (12–98 match) Australians v
Auckland, Auckland, 1959/60.
Club: South Melbourne.

QUINN, Francis Michael
RHB, RM

Born Gort, Co Galway, Ireland, 8 Dec
1915. Educ Belvedere C, Dublin. Debut
1936.

IRELAND (7) 1936–48.
HS 140 Ireland v Scotland, Greenock, 1946.
Club: Phoenix. Brothers G. J. and K. J. Quinn (both Ireland).

QUINN, Kevin Joseph
————————RHB, SLA————————

Born Gort, Co Galway, Ireland, 14 Mar 1923. Educ Belvedere C, Dublin. Debut 1957.

IRELAND (3) 1957–59.
HS 25 Ireland v Scotland, Dublin, 1957.
Club: Phoenix. Rugby: Old Belvedere, Ireland (5). Brothers F. M. and G. J. Quinn (both Ireland).

QUINNEY, David Henry
————————RHB————————

Born Basford, Notts, 28 July 1950. Educ Nottingham HS; St John's C, Cambridge. Debut 1971.

CAMBRIDGE UNIVERSITY (1) 1971.
HS 4 Cambridge U v Surrey, Fenner's, 1971.

QUINTRELL, Robert N.
————————RHB, RM————————

Born Australia, 1932. Debut 1954.
CANADA to England (4) 1954.
HS 29 Canadians v Yorks, Scarborough, 1954.
Clubs: North Shore (Vancouver), British Columbia (capt).

R

RABONE, Geoffrey Osbourne
RHB, OB/LB/RM

Born Gore, N Zealand, 6 Nov 1921. Debut 1940/41.
N ZEALAND DOMESTIC Wellington (10) 1940/41–50/51, Auckland (22) 1951/52–59/60. Governor-General's XI v MCC, Auckland, 1960/61.
NEW ZEALAND (12) 1949–54/55. E 1954/55 (2); SA 1952/53 (1); WI 1951/52 (2). *E 1949 (4); SA 1953/54 (3).* Capt 5.
OTHER TOUR N Zealand to Australia 1953/54 (capt).
HST 107 NZ v SA, Durban, 1953/54. HS 125 Auckland v Central Districts, Auckland, 1951/52.
BBT 6–68 NZ v SA, Cape Town, 1953/54. BB 8–66 Auckland v Australians, Auckland, 1956/57.
1000 RUNS (1) 1021 @ 32.93 in 1949.

RACIONZER, Terence Beverley
RHB, OB

Born Maidenhead, Berkshire, 18 Dec 1943. Educ Queen's Park Sec S, Glasgow; Glasgow U. Debut 1965.
SCOTLAND (19) 1965–84.
SUSSEX (26) 1967–69.
HS 115 Scotland v Ireland, Downpatrick, 1983.
BB 2–11 same match.
Club: Clydesdale.

RADFORD, Neal Victor
RHB, RFM

Born Luanshya, N Rhodesia, 7 June 1957. Educ Athlone HS, Johannesburg. Debut 1978/79.
S AFRICA DOMESTIC Transvaal 1978/79–.
LANCASHIRE (24) 1980–84.
HS 76* Lancs v Derbys, Blackpool, 1981.
BB 6–41 Transvaal B v Griqualand West, Kimberley, 1980/81.
Clubs: Burnley, Bacup, Nelson. Brother W. R. Radford (OFS).

RADLEY, Clive Thornton
RHB, LB

Born Hertford, 13 May 1944. Educ King Edward VI GS, Norwich. Debut 1964. *Wisden 1979.*
MIDDLESEX (458) 1964–. Cap 1967. Benefit (£26,000) 1977.
ENGLAND (8) 1977/78–78. NZ 1978 (3); P 1978 (3). *NZ 1977/78 (2).*
OTHER TOURS D. H. Robins' XI to S Africa 1972/73, 1974/75. England to Australia 1978/79. M'sex to Zimbabwe 1980/81.
HST 158 E v NZ, Auckland, 1977/78 (in 648 mins). HS 171 M'sex v Cambridge U, Fenner's, 1976.
1000 RUNS (15) 1491 @ 57.34 in 1980.
RECORD Added 227 for 6th wkt with F. J. Titmus, M'sex v S Africans, Lord's, 1965, county record.
485 catches in career. Norfolk 1961.

RAE, Allan Fitzroy
LHB

Born Kingston, Jamaica, 30 Sept 1922. Educ Wolmer's S, Kingston. Debut 1946/47.
W INDIES DOMESTIC Jamaica 1946/47–59/60.
WEST INDIES (15) 1948/49–52/53. I 1952/53 (2). *E 1950 (4); A 1951/52 (3); NZ 1951/52 (1); I 1948/49 (5).*
HST 109 WI v I, Madras, 1948/49 and 109 v E, Oval, 1950. HS 179 W Indians v Sussex, Hove, 1950.
1000 RUNS (1 + 1) 1330 @ 39.11 in 1950.
President WICB. W Indies Test selector since 1971. Club: Winchmore Hill. Father E. A. Rae (Jamaica, W Indies to England 1928).

RAE, Robert Burns
RHB, RFM

Born Littleborough, Lancs, 4 July 1912. Believed dead, but unconfirmed. Debut 1945. *P.*
LANCASHIRE (1) 1945.
HS 74 Lancs v Yorks, Bradford, 1945.
Clubs: Bingley, Stockport, Huddersfield, Rishton.

RAIKES, Douglas Charles Gordon
RHB, WK

Born Bristol, Glos, 26 Jan 1910. Educ Shrewsbury; Queen's C, Oxford. Debut 1931.
OXFORD UNIVERSITY (5) 1931 (Blue).
GLOUCESTERSHIRE (5) 1932.
KENT (2) 1948.
HS 37 Oxford U v MCC, Lord's, 1931.
Club: Sevenoaks Vine.

RALPH, Louis Henry *Roy*
RHB, RM

Born East Ham, London, 22 May 1920. Educ Clark's C, Ilford. Debut 1953. *P from 1958.*
ESSEX (174) 1953–61. Cap 1957. Testimonial 1961.
HS 73 Essex v Northants, Leyton, 1960.
BB 7–42 Essex v Glos, Romford, 1956.
100 WKTS (1) 102 @ 22.00 in 1957.
Took wkt of E. D. Weekes (W Indians) with fourth ball in fc cricket.
Clubs: Hale End, Ilford, Longton. Former professional coach Bancroft's S (from 1964).

RAMADHIN, Sonny
RHB, OB/LB

Born Esperance Village, Trinidad, 1 May 1929. Educ Canadian Mission S, Duncan Village, Trinidad. Debut 1949/50. *Wisden 1951.*
W INDIES DOMESTIC Trinidad 1949/50–52/53.
LANCASHIRE (33) 1964–65. Cap 1964.
WEST INDIES (43) 1950–60/61. E 1953/54 (5), 1959/60 (4); A 1954/55 (4); I 1952/53 (4). *E 1950 (4), 1957 (5); A 1951/52 (5), 1960/61 (2); NZ 1951/52 (2), 1955/56 (4); I 1958/59 (2); P 1958/59 (2).*
OTHER TOURS Commonwealth XI to India and Ceylon 1950/51. Commonwealth XI to India 1953/54. International XI to Rhodesia, N Zealand, India and Pakistan 1961/62. E. W. Swanton's XI to India 1963/64.

HST 44 WI v NZ, Dunedin, 1955/56. HS as above.
BBT 7–49 WI v E, Edgbaston, 1957. BB 8–15 (13–51 match) W Indians v Glos, Cheltenham, 1950.
100 WKTS (2) 135 @ 14.88 in 1950.
RECORDS Delivered 588 balls in inns (returned 2–179), WI v E, Edgbaston, 1957, a fc record; delivered 774 balls in same match (9–228), a Test record.
Lincolnshire 1968–70. Clubs: Crompton, Ashcombe Park, Radcliffe, Liversedge, Wakefield, Mansfield, Delph, Nantwich, Little Lever, Daisy Hill. MCC Hon. member. Son-in-law W. Hogg (Lancs, Warwicks).

RAMAGE, Alan
——LHB, RFM——

Born Guisborough, Yorks, 29 Nov 1957. Educ Warsett CS, Brotton. Debut 1979.
YORKSHIRE (23) 1979–83.
HS 52 Yorks v Glos, Bristol, 1981.
BB 5–65 Yorks v Surrey, Harrogate, 1981.
Club: Marske. Soccer: Middlesbrough, Derby County.

RAMAGE, Paul Frederick
——LHB, SLA——

Born Leamington Spa, Warwicks, 13 Mar 1940. Educ Warwick S; Fitzwilliam C, Cambridge. Debut 1962.
CAMBRIDGE UNIVERSITY (13) 1962–63.
HS 50 Cambridge U v Free Foresters, Fenner's, 1962.
BB 4–65 Cambridge U v Combined Services, Fenner's, 1962.
Buckinghamshire 1970. Headmaster at St John's, Northwood.

RAMCHAND Gulabrai Sipahahimalai
——RHB, RM——

Born Karachi, India, 26 July 1927. Educ Bombay U. Debut 1945/46.
INDIA DOMESTIC Sind 1945/46–46/47, Bombay 1948/49–55/56, 1957/58–62/63, Rajasthan 1956/57, Dungarpur XI 1967/68.
COMMONWEALTH XI (2) 1953–57.
INDIA (33) 1952–59/60. A 1956/57 (3), 1959/60 (5); WI 1958/59 (3); NZ 1955/56 (5); P 1952/53 (3). E 1952 (4); WI 1952/53 (5); P 1954/55 (5). Capt 5.
OTHER TOUR India to Ceylon 1956/57.
HST 109 I v A, Bombay, 1956/57. HS 230* Bombay v Maharashtra, Bombay, 1950/51.

BBT 6–49 I v P, Karachi, 1954/55. BB 8–12 Bombay v Saurashtra, Bombay, 1959/60.
Clubs: Furness, Nantwich, Crewe LMR, Norton. MCC Hon. member.

RAMNARACE, Randolph
——RHB, RM——

Born British Guiana, 25 July 1941. Debut 1965/66.
W INDIES DOMESTIC Berbice 1960/61–73/74, British Guiana (Guyana) 1965/66–72/73.
TOUR Rest of World XI in England 1968.
HS 71 Guyana v Jamaica, Kingston, 1968–69.
BB 6–101 Berbice v Demerara, Georgetown, 1971/72.
Clubs: Colne, Great Chell.

RAMSAMOOJ, Donald
——RHB, OB——

Born San Fernando, Trinidad, 5 July 1932. Debut 1952/53.
W INDIES DOMESTIC Trinidad 1952/53–56/57.
NORTHAMPTONSHIRE (71) 1958–64.
HS 132 Northants v Derbys, Northampton, 1963.
Scored 123 Northants v Derbys, Northampton, 1960, in maiden Championship match.

RANASINGHE, Anura Nandana
——RHB, LM/SLA——

Born Diyatalawa, Ceylon, 13 Oct 1956. Educ Nalanda C. Debut 1974/75.
SRI LANKA DOMESTIC Sri Lanka 1974/75–82/83.
SRI LANKA (2) 1981/82–82/83. I 1982/83 (1); P 1981/82 (1).
OTHER TOURS Sri Lanka to India 1974/75, 1975/76, 1980/81. Sri Lanka to England 1975 (no fc match), 1981.
HST 77 SL v I, Madras, 1982/83. HS as above.
BB 5–65 Sri Lankans v Oxford and Cambridge Universities, The Parks, 1981.
Barred from Sinhalese cricket for 25 yrs for touring S Africa 1982/83 (Arosa Sri Lanka). Clubs: Bloomfield (Sri Lanka), Hyde (England).

RANDALL, Derek William
——RHB——

Born Retford, Notts, 24 Feb 1951. Educ Sir Frederick Milner Sec S, Retford. Debut 1972. *Wisden* 1980.

NOTTINGHAMSHIRE (235) 1972–.
ENGLAND (47) 1976/77–84. A 1977 (5); WI 1984 (1); NZ 1983 (3); I 1979 (3), 1982 (3); P 1982 (3). A 1976/77 (1), 1978/79 (6), 1979/80 (2), 1982/83 (4); NZ 1977/78 (3), 1983/84 (3); I 1976/77 (4); P 1977/78 (3), 1983/84 (3).
OTHER TOUR D. H. Robins' XI to S Africa 1975/76.
HST 174 E v A, Melbourne, 1976/77. HS 209 Notts v M'sex, Trent Bridge, 1979 (scored 146 in 2nd inns of same match).
BB 3–15 Notts v MCC, Lord's, 1982.
1000 RUNS (9) 1546 @ 42.94 in 1976.
Club: Retford.

RANDHIR SINGH Baldeosingh
——RHB, RMF——

Born Delhi, India, 16 Aug 1957. Debut 1980/81.
INDIA DOMESTIC Orissa 1978/79–79/80, Bihar 1980/81–.
TOUR India to England 1982.
HS 40 Bihar v Bengal, Dhanbad, 1983/84.
BB 6–141 Bihar v Saurashtra, Jamshedpur, 1981/82.

RANSOM, Victor Joseph
——RHB, RFM——

Born New Malden, Surrey, 17 May 1917. Debut 1947.
HAMPSHIRE (34) 1947–50. Cap 1949.
MCC (2) 1950–51.
SURREY (2) 1951–55.
HS 58 Hants v Glos, Portsmouth, 1949.
BB 5–50 Hants v Northants, Northampton, 1947.
Club: Malden Wanderers.

RAPER, James Rhodes Stanley
——RHB, RM——

Born Bradford, Yorks, 9 Aug 1909. Educ The Leys. Debut 1936.
YORKSHIRE (3) 1936–47.
HS 15 Yorks v Derbys, Chesterfield, 1936.
Yorks 2nd XI (capt). Club: Yeadon.

RASPIN, Peter Hugh
——LHB, SLA——

Born Bolton Lancs, 26 Nov 1951. Educ Birkenhead S; St Edmund Hall, Oxford. Debut 1973.
OXFORD UNIVERSITY (2) 1973.
HS 10 Oxford U v Warwicks, The Parks, 1973.
BB 2–69 same match.

RATCLIFFE, Alan
RHB

Born Dulwich, London, 31 Mar 1909.
Died Toronto, Canada, 21 Aug 1967.
Educ Rydal; Trinity Hall, Cambridge.
Debut 1928.
WALES (4) 1928–30.
CAMBRIDGE UNIVERSITY (33) 1930–32
(Blue 1930–32).
MCC (4) 1931–39.
SURREY (7) 1932–33.
OVER-33 XI (1) 1945.
HS 201 Cambridge U v Oxford U,
Lord's, 1931.
HS (above) at time highest-ever inns in
Varsity match but beaten next day by
the Nawab of Pataudi (238*). Also
scored century (124) in 1932 University
match.
Denbighshire 1930–31, Buckingham-
shire 1937–39. Club: Canterbury St
Lawrence.

RATCLIFFE, David Philip
RHB

Born Hall Green, Birmingham, 11 May
1939. Debut 1957. P.
WARWICKSHIRE (20) 1957–68.
HS 79 Warwicks v Scotland, Edgbaston,
1961.
Clubs: Pickwick, Moseley, West Bromwich Dartmouth, Mitchells and Butlers.

RATCLIFFE, Robert Malcolm
RHB, RM

Born Accrington, Lancs, 29 Nov 1951.
Educ Hollins County S. Debut 1972.
LANCASHIRE (82) 1972–80. Cap 1976.
HS 101* Lancs v Warwicks, Old Traf-
ford, 1979.
BB 7–58 Lancs v Hants, Bournemouth,
1978.
RECORD During HS (above) added 158 for
8th wkt with J. Lyon, county record.
Cumberland 1981–. Club: Perth.

RATNAYEKE, Joseph *Ravindran*
LHB, RMF

Born Colombo, Ceylon, 2 May 1960.
Educ Trinity C, Colombo. Debut 1980/
81.
SRI LANKA DOMESTIC Sri Lanka 1980/
81–84.
SRI LANKA (8) 1981/82–84. NZ 1983/84
(2). *E 1984 (1); NZ 1982/83 (2); I
1982/83 (1); P 1981/82 (2).*
OTHER TOURS Sri Lanka to England
1981. Sri Lanka to Zimbabwe 1982/83.
HST 29* SL v NZ, Wellington, 1982/83.
HS 66 Sri Lankans v Sussex, Hove, 1984.

BBT 5–42 SL v NZ, Colombo, 1983/84.
BB as above.

RAW, George *David*
RHB

Born Leeds, Yorks, 14 Nov 1944. Educ
Tiffin S, Kingston-upon-Thames; St
Catharine's C, Cambridge. Debut 1967.
CAMBRIDGE UNIVERSITY (6) 1967–68.
HS 21 Cambridge U v S African Univer-
sities, Fenner's, 1967.
Cambridgeshire 1968. Clubs: East
Molesey, Redcar, Great Broughton.

RAWLENCE, John Rooke
RHB

Born Lymington, Hants, 23 Sept 1915.
Died Ascot, Berkshire, 17 Jan 1983.
Debut 1934.
HAMPSHIRE (2) 1934.
ARMY (2) 1938.
COMBINED SERVICES (1) 1950.
HS 38 Hants v Notts, Southampton,
1934.

RAWLINSON, Henry Thomas
RHB, RM

Born Edgware, M'sex, 21 Jan 1963.
Educ Eton; Christ Church C, Oxford.
Debut 1982.
OXFORD UNIVERSITY (16) 1982–84 (Blue
1983–84).
HS 24 Oxford U v Worcs, The Parks,
1983.
BB 5–123 same match.
Brother J. L. Rawlinson (Oxford U).

RAWLINSON, John *Lawrence*
RHB

Born Edgware, M'sex, 4 Aug 1959.
Educ Eton; UC, Oxford. Debut 1979.
OXFORD UNIVERSITY (9) 1979–80.
HS 19 Oxford U v Hants, The Parks,
1980.

RAWSON, Peter Walter Edward
RHB, RFM

Born Salisbury, Rhodesia, 25 May 1957.
Debut 1982.
ZIMBABWE 1982–.
TOUR Zimbabwe to England 1982.
HS 63* Zimbabwe v Sri Lanka, Harare,
1982/83.
BB 7–49 Zimbabwe v Young Indians,
Harare, 1983/84.
Returned 13–143 match Zimbabwe v
Young Australians, Harare, 1983/84.
Suffolk 1984. Hockey: Zimbabwe.

RAYBOULD, John Griffith
LHB, LBG

Born Middlesbrough, Yorks, 26 July
1934. Educ Leeds GS; New C, Oxford.
Debut 1957.
OXFORD UNIVERSITY (17) 1957–59 (Blue
1959).
FREE FORESTERS (1) 1962.
HS 81* Oxford U v Derbys, The Parks,
1958.
BB 4–31 Oxford U v Leics, The Parks,
1959.

RAYMENT, Alan William Harrington
RHB, RM/LBG

Born Finchley, M'sex, 29 May 1928.
Educ Finchley GS; West Hill C, Selly
Oak, Birmingham; Sussex U (mature
student). Debut 1947. P.
COMBINED SERVICES (1) 1947.
HAMPSHIRE (198) 1949–58. Cap 1952.
HS 126 Hants v Glos, Bristol, 1953.
BB 4–75 Hants v Cambridge U,
Bournemouth, 1957.
1000 RUNS (2) 1056 @ 23.46 in 1952.
Clubs: Finchley, Deanery, Eastbourne,
Rottingdean, Royal Air Force. After
retirement from county cricket ran a
dancing school. Obtained degree in
Social Work at age of 50.

RAZZALL, Edward Timothy
RHB, RM/OB

Born London, 12 June 1943. Educ St
Paul's; Worcester C, Oxford. Debut
1964.
OXFORD UNIVERSITY (6) 1964.
HS 25* Oxford U v Essex, The Parks,
1964.
BB 3–44 Oxford U v Free Foresters, The
Parks, 1964.

READ, Holcombe Douglas (Hopper)
RHB, RF

Born Woodford Green, Essex, 28 Jan
1910. Educ Winchester. Debut 1933.
SURREY (2) 1933.
ESSEX (32) 1933–35. Cap.
MCC (4) 1935–48.
ENGLAND (1) SA 1935.
TOUR MCC to Australasia 1935/36.
HS 25* MCC v Canterbury,
Christchurch, 1935/36.
BBT 4–136 E v SA, Oval, 1935. BB 7–35
Essex v Surrey, Brentwood, 1934.
Took 97 wkts @ 22.16 in 1935.
Gentlemen v Players (2) 1934–35.
Clubs: Heathfield, Butterflies. Father
A. H. Read (Essex).

REDDICK, Tom Bockenham
——————RHB, LB——————

Born Shanghai, China, 17 Feb 1912.
Died Cape Town, S Africa, 1 June 1982.
Educ KCS Wimbledon. Debut 1931. *P 1946–47.*
MIDDLESEX (2) 1931.
SIR J. CAHN'S XI (5) 1932–38.
NOTTINGHAMSHIRE (50) 1946–47. Cap 1946.
S AFRICA DOMESTIC Western Province 1950/51.
TOUR Sir J. Cahn's XI to Ceylon 1936/37.
HS 139 Notts v Kent, Trent Bridge, 1947.
1000 RUNS (1) 1231 @ 35.17 in 1947.
Notts coach 1946–47; Lancs coach 1963–64. Coach and selector S African Universities CA up to death. Club: Wimbledon. Autobiography *Never Cross a Bat* (1979).

REDDY, Bharat
——————RHB, WK——————

Born Madras, India, 12 Nov 1954.
Debut 1973/74.
INDIA DOMESTIC Tamil Nadu 1973/74–.
INDIA (4) *E 1979.*
OTHER TOURS India to Sri Lanka 1973/74. India to Australia 1977/78. India to Pakistan 1978/79. India to Australasia 1980/81.
HST 21 I v E, Edgbaston, 1979. HS 88 Tamil Nadu v Kerala, Madras, 1981/82.

REDDY, Nayini Santosh Kumar
——————LHB, SLA——————

Born Madras, India, 22 Oct 1938. Educ Dehra Dun S; St John's C, Cambridge. Debut 1959.
CAMBRIDGE UNIVERSITY (42) 1959–61 (Blue 1959–61).
INDIA DOMESTIC Hyderabad 1966/67–70/71.
HS 113* Cambridge U v Som, Taunton, 1961.
BB 3–26 same match.

REDMAN, James
——————RHB, RMF——————

Born Bath, Som, 1 Mar 1926. Died Salisbury, Wiltshire, 24 Sept 1981.
Debut 1948. *P from 1949.*
SOMERSET (65) 1948–53. Cap 1951.
HS 45 Som v Essex, Brentwood, 1951.
BB 7–23 Som v Derbys, Frome, 1951.
Wiltshire 1958–64. Club: South Wiltshire.

REDMOND, Rodney Ernest
——————LHB, SLA——————

Born Whangarei, N Zealand, 29 Dec 1944. Debut 1963/64.
N ZEALAND DOMESTIC New Zealand Under-23 1963/64–65/66, Wellington (7) 1966/67–67/68, Auckland (29) 1969/70–75/76.
NEW ZEALAND (1) P 1972/73.
TOURS N Zealand B to Australia 1972/73. N Zealand to England 1973.
HST 107 NZ v P, Auckland, 1972/73 (scored 107 and 56 in only Test). HS 141* Auckland v Wellington, Wellington, 1970/71.
BB 6–56 (10–110 match) N Zealand Under-23 v Wellington, Wellington, 1965/66.
Troubled by indifferent eye-sight.

REDPATH, Ian Ritchie
——————RHB, RM——————

Born Geelong, Victoria, Australia, 11 May 1941. Educ Geelong C, Victoria. Debut 1961/62.
AUSTRALIA DOMESTIC Victoria (92) 1961/62–75/76.
AUSTRALIA (66) 1963/64–75/76. E 1965/66 (1), 1970/71 (6), 1974/75 (6); SA 1963/64 (1); WI 1968/69 (5), 1975/76 (6); I 1967/68 (3); P 1972/73 (3). *E 1964 (5), 1968 (5); SA 1966/67 (5), 1969/70 (4); WI 1972/73 (5); NZ 1973/74 (3); I 1964/65 (2), 1969/70 (5); P 1964/65 (1).*
HST 171 A v E, Perth, 1970/71. HS 261 Victoria v Queensland, Melbourne, 1962/63.
BB 3–24 Victoria v Queensland, Melbourne, 1964/65.
1000 RUNS (2 + 5) 1474 @ 43.35 in 1968. Carried bat for 159* in total of 346, A v NZ, Auckland, 1973/74. No-balled for throwing, Australians v Glam, Cardiff, 1964. Hit N. Rosendorff for 32 runs (666644) in one over, Australians v OFS, Bloemfontein, 1969/70.
World Series Cricket (Kerry Packer) 1977/78. Awarded MBE for services to cricket.

REED, Barry Lindsay
——————RHB, RM——————

Born Southsea, Hants, 17 Sept 1937. Educ Winchester. Debut 1958.
HAMPSHIRE (122) 1958–70. Cap 1967.
HS 138 Hants v Oxford U, The Parks, 1970.
1000 RUNS (3) 1136 @ 24.17 in 1967.

REES, Alan
——————RHB, RM——————

Born Port Talbot, S Wales, 17 Feb 1938.
Debut 1955. *P.*
GLAMORGAN (216) 1955–68. Cap 1963.
HS 111* Glam v Lancs, Cardiff, 1964.
BB 3–68 Glam v Kent, Cardiff, 1960.
1000 RUNS (4) 1206 @ 30.15 in 1964.
Dismissed 'handled the ball', Glam v M'sex, Lord's, 1965.
Clubs: Briton Ferry Town, Maesteg, Port Talbot, Ammanford, Steel Co of Wales, Dafen. Rugby: Maesteg, Wales (3 caps); turned professional with Leeds RLFC.

REEVE, Dermot Alexander
——————RHB, RMF——————

Born Kowloon, Hong Kong, 2 Apr 1963. Educ King George V S, Kowloon, Hong Kong. Debut 1983.
SUSSEX (38) 1983–.
HS 119 Sussex v Surrey, Guildford, 1984.
BB 5–22 Sussex v Cambridge U, Fenner's, 1984.
Hong Kong 1982 (ICC Trophy).

REID, John Richard
——————RHB, RMF, WK——————

Born Auckland, N Zealand, 3 June 1928. Educ Hutt Valley HS. Debut 1947/48. *Wisden 1959.*
N ZEALAND DOMESTIC Wellington (57) 1947/48–64/65, Otago (11) 1956/57–57/58.
NEW ZEALAND (58) 1949–65. E 1950/51 (2), 1954/55 (2), 1958/59 (2), 1962/63 (3); SA 1952/53 (2), 1963/64 (3); WI 1951/52 (2), 1955/56 (4); P 1964/65 (3). *E 1949 (2), 1958 (5), 1965 (3); SA 1953/54 (5), 1961/62 (5); I 1955/56 (5), 1964/65 (4); P 1955/56 (3), 1964/65 (3).* Capt 34.
OTHER TOURS N Zealand to Australia 1953/54, 1961/62. Cavaliers to S Africa 1962/63. Rest of World XI in England 1965.
HST 142 NZ v SA, J'burg, 1961/62. HS 296 Wellington v N Districts, Wellington, 1962/63.
BBT 6–60 NZ v SA, Dunedin, 1963/64.
BB 7–20 Otago v C Districts, Dunedin, 1956/57.
1000 RUNS (2 + 3) 2188 @ 57.58 in 1961/62.
RECORDS HS (above) included 15 sixes, a world record; went from 0* to 174* at lunch on 2nd morning, and added remaining 122 before tea. Scored 1012 runs @ 37.48 and took 51 wkts @ 19.33 N Zealand to S Africa 1953/54, first double of 1000 runs and 50 wkts in a

S African season. Scored 1915 runs @ 68.39 N Zealand to S Africa 1961/62, highest aggregate for a S African season (2188 @ 57.58 in entire 1961/62 non-English season, a record at the time). Added 324 for 4th wkt with W. M. Wallace, N Zealanders v Cambridge U, Fenner's, 1949, N Zealand fc record; added 222* for 3rd wkt with B. Sutcliffe, NZ v I, Delhi, 1955/56, N Zealand Test record.
Awarded OBE for services to cricket. Club: Heywood. MCC Hon. member. Autobiography *Sword of Willow* (1963). Now lives and coaches in N Transvaal. Son R. B. Reid (Wellington, Transvaal).

REID, Keith Patrick
————RHB, RM————

Born Port Elizabeth, S Africa, 24 July 1951. Educ Grey HS, Port Elizabeth, S Africa. Debut 1970/71.
S AFRICA DOMESTIC Eastern Province (56) 1970/71–80/81.
NORTHAMPTONSHIRE (1) 1973.
HS 109 E Province B v W Province B, Port Elizabeth, 1979/80.
BB 7–50 E Province v Rhodesia, Port Elizabeth, 1972/73.
Brother T. B. Reid (E Province).

REIDY, Bernard Wilfrid
————LHB, LM/SLA————

Born Bramley Meade, Whalley, Lancs, 18 Sept 1953. Educ St Mary's C, Blackburn. Debut 1973.
LANCASHIRE (107) 1973–82. Cap 1980.
HS 131* Lancs v Derbys, Chesterfield, 1979.
BB 5–61 Lancs v Worcs, Worcester, 1979.
Cumberland 1983–. Clubs: St Anne's, Blackpool, Kearsley.

REIFER, Elvis Leroy
————LHB, LMF————

Born St Michael, Barbados, 21 Mar 1961. Educ St George's, Barbados. Debut 1984.
HAMPSHIRE (20) 1984.
HS 47 Hants v Som, Southampton, 1984.
BB 4–43 Hants v Cambridge U, Fenner's, 1984.
Brothers L. N. Reifer and G. N. Reifer (his twin) (both Barbados).

REITH, Michael Stevens
————LHB, RM————

Born Lurgan, Co Armagh, Ireland, 2 May 1948. Educ Lurgan C. Debut 1970.

IRELAND (9) 1970–80.
HS 82 Ireland v Scotland, Perth, 1970.
Clubs: Waringstown, North Down.

RENNEBERG, David Alexander
————RHB, RF————

Born Balmain, Sydney, NSW, Australia, 23 Sept 1942. Debut 1964/65.
AUSTRALIA DOMESTIC New South Wales (54) 1964/65–70/71.
AUSTRALIA (8) 1966/67–67/68. I 1967/68 (3). *SA 1966/67 (5).*
OTHER TOURS Australia to England 1968. Australia to N Zealand 1969/70.
HST 9 A v SA, J'burg, 1966/67. HS 26 NSW v S Australia, Sydney, 1969/70.
BBT 5–39 A v I, Adelaide, 1967/68. BB 8–72 Australians v Essex, Southend, 1968.
Clubs: Balmain (Sydney), Rawtenstall (Lancashire).

REOCH, Earl Clark
————RHB, SLA————

Born Monifieth, Angus, Scotland, 5 Mar 1942. Educ Dundee HS; St Andrew's U. Debut 1973.
SCOTLAND (1) 1973.
HS 7 Scotland v Ireland, Cork, 1973.
Club: Forfarshire.

REVILL, Alan Chambers
————RHB, OB————

Born Sheffield, Yorks, 27 Mar 1923. Debut 1946. *P.*
DERBYSHIRE (321) 1946–57. Cap 1947. Testimonial (£1701) 1955.
LEICESTERSHIRE (64) 1958–60. Cap 1958.
HS 156* Derbys v Leics, Ashby-de-la-Zouch, 1949.
BB 3–12 Derbys v Ireland, Buxton, 1947.
1000 RUNS (9) 1643 @ 35.71 in 1950. 396 catches in career.
Berkshire 1962–68. Clubs: Reading, Cricket Society. Father T. F. Revill (Derbys).

REYNOLDS, Brian Leonard
————RHB, occ OB, occ WK————

Born Kettering, Northants, 10 June 1932. Debut 1950. *P.*
NORTHAMPTONSHIRE (426) 1950–70. Cap 1956. Benefit (£3886) 1965.
HS 169 Northants v Essex, Westcliff, 1957.
1000 RUNS (10) 1843 @ 35.44 in 1962. Players v Gentlemen (2) 1957–58. Northants coach 1971–.

REYNOLDS, Graham Edward Arthur
————LHB, RM————

Born Newport, Monmouthshire, Wales, 23 Sept 1937. Educ St Julian's HS, Newport. Debut 1970.
GLAMORGAN (2) 1970–71.
HS 23* Glam v Northants, Northampton, 1971.
BB 2–24 Glam v Jamaica, Swansea, 1970.
Soccer: Newport County.

RHIND, Peter Alan
————RHB, RFM————

Born Dundee, Scotland, 20 June 1945. Educ Morgan Academy, Dundee. Debut 1968.
SCOTLAND (6) 1968–82.
HS 10 Scotland v Ireland, Dublin, 1969.
BB 3–62 Scotland v Ireland, Edinburgh, 1982.
Clubs: Forfarshire, Heriot's FP.

RHODES, Albert Ennion Groucott (Dusty)
————RHB, LBG/RMF————

Born Tintwhistle, Cheshire, 10 Oct 1916. Died Barlow, Derbys, 17 Oct 1983. Debut 1937. *P.*
DERBYSHIRE (267) 1937–54. Cap 1938. Testimonial (£2000) 1952.
TOUR MCC to India 1951/52 (returned home early owing to injury).
HS 127 Derbys v Som, Taunton, 1949.
BB 8–162 Derbys v Yorks, Scarborough, 1947.
1000 RUNS (1) 1156 @ 25.68 in 1949.
100 WKTS (1) 130 @ 22.19 in 1950.
RECORD Added 241* for 7th wkt with G. H. Pope, Derbys v Hants, Portsmouth, 1948, county record.
Fc umpire 1959–79 (8 Tests, 1963–73). Clubs: Milnrow, Blythe Works, Glossop, Dunfermline. Professional coach Stowe S 1954–57. Table-tennis: Derbys. Correct birth name A. E. Grouchtt-Rhodes. Son H. J. Rhodes (Derbys, England).

RHODES, Harold James
————RHB, OB/RF————

Born Glossop, Derbys, 22 July 1936. Debut 1953. *P.*
DERBYSHIRE (288) 1953–75. Cap 1958. Testimonial (£8495) 1968.
ENGLAND (2) I 1959.
TOURS Commonwealth XI to S Africa 1959/60. E. W. Swanton's XI to W Indies 1960/61. International XI to

Rhodesia, N Zealand, India and Pakistan 1961/62. International XI to India, Pakistan and Ceylon 1967/68.
HS 48 Derbys v M'sex, Chesterfield, 1958.
BBT 4–50 E v I, Headingley, 1959. BB 7–38 Derbys v Warwicks, Edgbaston, 1965.
100 WKTS (3) 119 @ 11.04 in 1965.
No-balled for throwing in 1960, 1961 (also reported for doubtful action during a truce in 1961) and 1965; taken off from bowling at request of umpire, Derbys v Som, Burton upon Trent, 1966. Delivery action officially cleared in 1968.
Players v Gentlemen (2) 1959–60. Nottinghamshire (limited-overs matches) 1970. Clubs: Frickley, Burnley. Father A. E. G. Rhodes (Derbys).

RHODES, Steven John
────────RHB, WK────────

Born Bradford, Yorks, 17 June 1964. Educ Carlton-Bolling S, Bradford. Debut 1981.
YORKSHIRE (3) 1981–84.
HS 35 Yorks v Som, Middlesbrough, 1984.
Joined Worcs for 1985. Father W. E. Rhodes (Notts).

RHODES, William Ernest
────────RHB, WK────────

Born Bradford, Yorks, 5 Aug 1936. Debut 1961. P.
NOTTINGHAMSHIRE (36) 1961–64.
HS 132 Notts v Cambridge U, Trent Bridge, 1962.
Clubs: Eccleshill, Spen Victoria. Son S. J. Rhodes (Yorks).

RIAZ-UR-REHMAN
────────RHB, WK────────

Born India, 1940. Died, in road-traffic accident, nr Loughborough, Leics, 10 July 1966. Debut 1958/59.
PAKISTAN DOMESTIC Lahore, Rawalpindi-Peshawar, Karachi, 1958/59–61/62.
LEICESTERSHIRE (1) 1966.
HS 70 Rawalpindi-Peshawar v Lahore, Lahore, 1960/61.

RICE, Alan Sedgwick
────────LHB, RFM────────

Born Leicester, 29 Aug 1929. Educ Wyggeston GS. Debut 1954.
LEICESTERSHIRE (3) 1954.
HS 13 Leics v M'sex, Lord's, 1954.
BB 3–34 Leics v Som, Leicester, 1954.

RICE, Clive Edward Butler
────────RHB, RFM────────

Born Johannesburg, S Africa, 23 July 1949. Educ St John's C; Damelin C; Natal U. Debut 1969/70. Wisden 1981.
S AFRICA DOMESTIC Transvaal 1969/70–.
D. H. ROBINS' XI (2) 1973–74.
NOTTINGHAMSHIRE (220) 1975–. Cap 1975. Capt 1979–.
HS 246 Notts v Sussex, Hove, 1976.
BB 7–62 Transvaal v W Province, J'burg, 1975/76.
1000 RUNS (10) 1871 @ 66.82 in 1978.
RECORD Scored 105* in inns total of 143, Notts v Hants, Bournemouth, 1981, lowest fc inns total to contain individual century.
Match double: 90 and 11 and 11–112, Transvaal v W Province, J'burg, 1975/76.
Appointed Notts captain in 1978, but dismissed without playing a match when signing for World Series Cricket announced. World Series Cricket (Kerry Packer) 1978/79. S Africa (11) 1981/82–83/84 (capt 2). Selected for S Africa to Australia 1971/72 (cancelled). Clubs: Bedfordview (Johannesburg), Ramsbottom (Lancashire). Grandfather P. S. S. Bower (Oxford U).

RICE, David
────────RHB, RM────────

Born Low Hellesdon, Norwich, Norfolk, 8 Apr 1914. Educ Lancing; Cambridge U. Debut 1960.
L. C. STEVENS' XI (2) 1960–61. Capt 2.
HS 23 L. C. Stevens' XI v Cambridge U, Eastbourne, 1961.
Sussex chairman 1982. Norfolk 1946. Clubs: MCC, United Hospitals, Sussex Martlets, Royal Navy. RN Surgeon-Commander; medical practitioner.

RICE, John Michael
────────RHB, RM────────

Born Chandler's Ford, Hants, 23 Oct 1949. Educ Brockley County GS. Debut 1971.
HAMPSHIRE (168) 1971–82. Cap 1975.
HS 161* Hants v Warwicks, Edgbaston, 1981.
BB 7–48 Hants v Worcs, Worcester, 1977.
Wiltshire 1983–.

RICHARDS, Barry Anderson
────────RHB, OB────────

Born Durban, S Africa, 21 July 1945. Educ Durban HS. Debut 1964/65. Wisden 1969.

S AFRICA DOMESTIC Natal 1964/65–82/83 (capt 1973/74–75/76), Transvaal XI 1970/71.
GLOUCESTERSHIRE (1) 1965.
HAMPSHIRE (204) 1968–78. Cap 1968. Benefit 1977.
AUSTRALIA DOMESTIC South Australia (10) 1970/71.
SOUTH AFRICA (4) A 1969/70.
HST 140 SA v A, Durban, 1969/70. HS 356 S Australia v W Australia, Perth, 1970/71.
BB 7–63 Hants v Rest of World XI, Bournemouth, 1968.
1000 RUNS (9 + 6) 2395 @ 47.90 in 1968.
RECORDS During HS (above) scored 325* on 1st day of match, highest-ever individual score in a day's play by a S African and fifth-highest ever. Exceeded 1000 runs in a S African season 5 times, a record; this includes the three highest aggregates: 1285 runs @ 80.31 in 1973/74; 1247 @ 69.27 in 1972/73; and 1172 @ 73.25 in 1969/70. Only batsman to score 1000 runs in a Currie Cup season (1089 runs @ 77.78 in 1971/72 and 1064 @ 70.93 in 1972/73).
Scored 2395 runs @ 47.90 in first full season in England, in 1968, and 1538 runs @ 109.85 in only season in Australia, in 1970/71. Scored century before lunch 9 times. Took 366 catches in career.
Rest of World v England (5) 1970. World Series Cricket (Kerry Packer) 1977/78–78/79. S Africa 1981/82–82/83 (6). Autobiography The Barry Richards Story (1978).

RICHARDS, Clifton James (Jack)
────────RHB, WK────────

Born Penzance, Cornwall, 10 Aug 1958. Educ Humphry Davy GS, Penzance. Debut 1976.
SURREY (175) 1976–. Cap 1978.
S AFRICA DOMESTIC Orange Free State 1983/84.
TOURS D. H. Robins' XI to Australasia 1979/80. England to India and Sri Lanka 1981/82. International XI to Jamaica 1982/83.
HS 117* Surrey v Notts, Oval, 1982.

RICHARDS, Gwyn
────────RHB, OB────────

Born Maesteg, S Wales, 29 Nov 1951. Debut 1971.
GLAMORGAN (107) 1971–79. Cap 1976.
HS 102* Glam v Yorks, Middlesbrough, 1976.
BB 5–55 Glam v Som, Taunton, 1978.
Club: Maesteg Town.

RICHARDS, Ian Michael
————LHB, RM————

Born Stockton-on-Tees, Co Durham, 9 Dec 1957. Educ Grangefield GS, Stockton-on-Tees; Stockton Sixth Form C. Debut 1976.
NORTHAMPTONSHIRE (23) 1976–79.
HS 50 Northants v Notts, Northampton, 1976.
BB 4–57 Northants v Warwicks, Edgbaston, 1978.
Durham County 1981–. Clubs: Stockton-on-Tees, Middlesbrough.

RICHARDS, Isaac *Vivian* Alexander
————RHB, OB————

Born St John's, Antigua, 7 Mar 1952. Educ Antigua GS. Debut 1971/72. *Wisden* 1977.
W INDIES DOMESTIC Leeward Islands 1971/72–, Combined Islands 1971/72–80/81.
SOMERSET (154) 1974–. Cap 1974. Benefit 1982.
AUSTRALIA DOMESTIC Queensland (5) 1976/77.
WEST INDIES (68) 1974/75–84. E 1980/81 (4); A 1977/78 (2), 1983/84 (5); I 1975/76 (4), 1982/83 (5); P 1976/77 (5). *E 1976 (4), 1980 (5), 1984 (5); A 1975/76 (6), 1979/80 (3), 1981/82 (3); I 1974/75 (5), 1983/84 (6); P 1974/75 (2), 1980/81 (4)*. Capt 1.
HST 291 WI v E, Oval, 1976. HS as above.
BBT 2–20 WI v P, Lahore, 1980/81. BB 5–88 W Indians v Queensland, Brisbane, 1981/82.
1000 RUNS (10 + 3) 2161 @ 65.48 in 1977.
RECORDS Scored 1710 runs (in 11 Tests, @ 95.00) in 1976, a record for a calendar yr of Test cricket by one batsman. Scored 829 runs @ 118.42 in series (playing in only 4 Tests), WI v E, 1976, fourth-highest aggregate ever, highest for WI and highest for batsman playing in less than 5 Tests. Scored centuries against all 17 fc counties, equalling feat of G. M. Turner. Added 124 for 8th wkt with K. D. Boyce, WI v I, Delhi, 1974/75, W Indies Test record; added 172 for 8th wkt with I. T. Botham, Som v Leics, Leicester, 1983, county record. World Series Cricket (Kerry Packer) 1977/78–78/79. Soccer: Antigua. Brothers D. and M. Richards (both Leeward Islands); father M. Richards (Antigua).

RICHARDS, Robert John
————RHB, WK————

Born Winchester, Hants, 5 June 1934. Educ Crayland's S, Basildon. Debut 1970.

ESSEX (1) 1970.
Did not bat.

RICHARDSON, Alan
————RHB, RFM————

Born Woodborough, Notts, 28 Oct 1926. Debut 1949. *P.*
NOTTINGHAMSHIRE (28) 1949–51.
HS 7* Notts v Sussex, Horsham, 1951.
BB 4–73 Notts v Yorks, Bramall Lane, Sheffield, 1951.

RICHARDSON, Bertram Harold
————LHB, SLA————

Born Ashton-under-Lyne, Lancs, 12 Mar 1932. Debut 1950. *P.*
DERBYSHIRE (27) 1950–53.
HS 29 Derbys v Sussex, Derby, 1953.
BB 4–39 Derbys v Hants, Derby, 1950.

RICHARDSON, Bryan Anthony
————LHB, RLB————

Born Kenilworth, Warwicks, 24 Feb 1944. Educ Malvern. Debut 1963.
WARWICKSHIRE (40) 1963–67.
HS 126 Warwicks v Cambridge U, Edgbaston, 1967 (scored 105 in 2nd inns; only centuries of fc career).
Club: Smethwick. Brothers D. W. Richardson (Worcs, England) and P. E. Richardson (Worcs, Kent, England).

RICHARDSON, Derek Walter (Dick)
————LHB, LM————

Born Hereford, 3 Nov 1934. Educ Hereford Cathedral S. Debut 1952. *P from 1956.*
WORCESTERSHIRE (371) 1952–67. Cap 1956. Benefit 1967.
ENGLAND (1) WI 1957.
TOURS Worcs to Rhodesia 1964/65. Worcs to Jamaica 1965/66.
HST 33 E v WI, Trent Bridge, 1957. HS 169 Worcs v Derbys, Dudley, 1957.
BB 2–11 Worcs v Lancs, Old Trafford, 1963.
1000 RUNS (9) 1830 @ 32.67 in 1957.
Took 65 catches in 1961.
Players v Gentlemen (3) 1957–58. Clubs: Stourbridge, Old Hill. Brothers B. A. Richardson (Warwicks) and P. E. Richardson (Worcs, Kent, England).

RICHARDSON, George *William*
————RHB, LFM————

Born Marylebone, London, 26 Apr 1938. Educ Winchester. Debut 1959.

DERBYSHIRE (62) 1959–65. Cap 1963.
MCC (3) 1959–61.
HS 91 Derbys v Glam, Swansea, 1959.
BB 8–54 Derbys v Kent, Chesterfield, 1959.
Gentlemen v Players (4) 1959–62. Father A. W. Richardson (Derbys).

RICHARDSON, John *Alan*
————RHB, RM————

Born Sleights, Yorks, 4 Aug 1908. Died Scarborough, Yorkshire, April 1985. Debut 1934.
YORKSHIRE (7) 1936–47.
HS 61 Yorks v MCC, Scarborough, 1947.
BB 2–23 Yorks v RAF, Scarborough, 1945.
Gentlemen v Players (1) 1934. Club: Scarborough.

RICHARDSON, John Charles
————RHB, RM————

Born Carron-on-Spey, Moray, Scotland, 5 Dec 1912. Debut 1953.
SCOTLAND (2) 1953.
HS 24 Scotland v Northants, Peterborough, 1953.
Club: Aberdeenshire.

RICHARDSON, Peter Edward
————LBH————

Born Hereford, 4 July 1931. Educ Hereford Cathedral S. Debut 1949. *P from 1960. Wisden* 1957.
WORCESTERSHIRE (161) 1949–58. Cap 1952. Capt 1956–58.
COMBINED SERVICES 1954–55.
KENT (162) 1959–65. Cap 1960.
ENGLAND (34) 1956–63. A 1956 (5); WI 1957 (5), 1963 (1); NZ 1958 (4). *A 1958/59 (4); SA 1956/57 (5); NZ 1958/59 (2); I 1961/62 (5); P 1961/62 (3)*.
OTHER TOURS MCC A to Pakistan 1955/56. MCC to E Africa 1957/58 (not fc). Cavaliers to Jamaica 1963/64. Commonwealth XI to Pakistan 1963/64. Cavaliers to W Indies 1964/65. Commonwealth XI to India 1964/65.
HST 126 E v WI, Trent Bridge, 1957. HS 185 Worcs v Som, Kidderminster, 1954.
BBT 2–10 E v I, Bombay, 1961/62. BB as above.
1000 RUNS (11 + 1) 2294 @ 39.55 in 1953. 2000 runs (4).
Worcs joint-secretary 1956–57. Kent committee 1979–. Club: Stourbridge. MCC Hon. member. Brothers B. A. Richardson (Warwicks) and D. W. Richardson (Worcs, England).

RICHARDSON, Philip Charles
————RHB, OB————

Born Paddington, London, 12 June 1965. Educ Humphry Davy GS, London; Magdalene C, Cambridge. Debut 1984.
CAMBRIDGE UNIVERSITY (1) 1984.
HS 7 Cambridge U v Essex, Fenner's, 1984.

RICHARDSON, Richard Benjamin
————RHB, OB————

Born Antigua, 12 Jan 1962. Debut 1981/82.
W INDIES DOMESTIC Leeward Islands 1981/82–.
WEST INDIES (6) 1983/84. A 1983/84 (5). I 1983/84 (1).
OTHER TOUR W Indies to England 1984.
HST 154 WI v A, St John's, Antigua, 1983/84. HS 162 Leeward Islands v Trinidad, St John's, Antigua, 1983/84.

RICHES, John Dansey Hurry
————RHB, SLA————

Born Cardiff, S Wales, 30 Dec 1920. Educ Repton. Debut 1947.
GLAMORGAN (1) 1947.
HS 4 Glam v Yorks, Bramall Lane, Sheffield, 1947.
Glamorgan 2nd XI 1947–54 (capt). Clubs: Cardiff, MCC, XL, S Wales Hunts. Father N. V. H. Riches (Glam).

RICKARDS, Kenneth Roy
————RHB————

Born Kingston, Jamaica, 23 Aug 1923. Debut 1945/46.
W INDIES DOMESTIC Jamaica 1945/46–58/59.
COMMONWEALTH XI (1) 1952.
ESSEX (1) 1953.
WEST INDIES (2) 1947/48–51/52. E 1947/48 (1). A 1951/52 (1).
OTHER TOUR W Indies to India 1948/49.
HST 67 WI v E, Kingston, 1947/48. HS 195 Jamaica v British Guiana, Kingston, 1950/51.
Club: Darwen.

RICKETTS, Michael Rodney
————RHB————

Born Birmingham, 29 Sept 1923. Educ Sherborne; Trinity C, Oxford. Debut 1948.
FREE FORESTERS (1) 1948.
HS 1 Free Foresters v Oxford U, The Parks, 1948.

Suffolk 1947–54. Clubs: I Zingari, Free Foresters, MCC. Manager MCC Schools to S Africa 1965/66. Former headmaster Sutton Valence S.

RIDDELL, Neil Anthony
————LHB, RM————

Born Staindrop, Co Durham, 16 July 1947. Educ Barnard Castle. Debut 1976.
MINOR COUNTIES (1) 1976.
HS 20 Minor Counties v W Indians, Torquay, 1976.
Durham County 1972–. Club: Darlington.

RIDDINGTON, Anthony
————LHB, SLA/LM————

Born Countesthorpe, Leics, 22 Dec 1911. Debut 1931. P.
LEICESTERSHIRE (128) 1931–50. Cap.
HS 104* Leics v Northants, Northampton, 1946.
BB 5–34 Leics v Yorks, Leicester, 1946.
Clubs: Stourbridge, Kilmarnock, Aberdeen, Stenhousemuir. Professional Uppingham S 1951.

RIDGE, Stuart Peter
————RHB, RM————

Born Beaconsfield, Buckinghamshire, 23 Nov 1961. Educ Dr Challenor's S, Amersham; Worcester C, Oxford. Debut 1981.
OXFORD UNIVERSITY (11) 1981–82 (Blue 1982).
HS 22 Oxford U v Hants, The Parks, 1982.
BB 4–128 Oxford U v Glos, The Parks, 1982.
Buckinghamshire 1980–82. Soccer: Blue.

RIDGWAY, Frederick
————RHB, RFM————

Born Stockport, Cheshire, 10 Aug 1923. Educ Dialstone Central, Rochdale. Debut 1946. P.
KENT (298) 1946–61. Cap 1947. Benefit (£4644) 1958.
ENGLAND (5) I 1951/52.
OTHER TOUR Commonwealth XI to India and Ceylon 1950/51.
HST 24 E v I, Calcutta, 1951/52. HS 94 Kent v Cambridge U, Folkestone, 1953.
BBT 4–83 E v I, Calcutta, 1951/52. BB 8–39 Kent v Notts, Dover, 1950.
100 WKTS (1) 105 @ 23.32 in 1949.
RECORD Added 161 for 9th wkt with B. R. Edrich, Kent v Sussex, Tunbridge Wells, 1949, county record.

Took four wkts in four balls, Kent v Derbys, Folkestone, 1951.
Club: Stockport.

RIDLAND, James David
————RHB, occ WK————

Born New Plymouth, N Zealand, 17 Jan 1923. Died New Plymouth, N Zealand, 4 Feb 1978. Debut 1945.
NEW ZEALAND SERVICES XI to England (1) 1945.
HS 44 N Zealand Services XI v H. D. G. Leveson Gower's XI, Scarborough, 1945 (only match).

RIDLEY, Christopher Jonathan Ben
————RHB, RMF————

Born Bulawayo, Rhodesia, 17 June 1946. Educ Milton HS, Bulawayo; Keble C, Oxford. Debut 1971.
OXFORD UNIVERSITY (6) 1971.
HS 23 Oxford U v Yorks, The Parks, 1971.
BB 2–70 Oxford U v Northants, The Parks, 1971.
Brother G. N. S. Ridley (Oxford U, Kent).

RIDLEY, Giles Nicholas Spencer
————RHB, SLA————

Born Bulawayo, Rhodesia, 27 Nov 1944. Educ Milton HS, Bulawayo; Pembroke C, Oxford. Debut 1965.
OXFORD UNIVERSITY (41) 1965–68 (Blue 1965–68). Capt 1967.
KENT (1) 1965.
MCC (1) 1968.
MINOR COUNTIES (2) 1971–72.
HS 50* Oxford U v W Indians, The Parks, 1966.
BB 7–110 Oxford U v Glos, The Parks, 1965 (fc debut).
Oxfordshire 1969–72. Brother C. J. B. Ridley (Oxford U).

RIDLEY, Robert Michael
————RHB————

Born Pago Pago, SE Tutuila, Samoa, 8 Jan 1947. Educ Clifton C; St Edmund Hall, Oxford. Debut 1967.
OXFORD UNIVERSITY (22) 1967–70 (Blue 1968–70).
IRELAND (1) 1968.
HS 79 Oxford U v Leics, The Parks, 1968.
Berkshire 1972.

RILEY, Jack
————RHB, SLA————

Born Accrington, Lancs, 27 Apr 1927. Educ All Saint's S, Clayton-le-Moors. Debut 1953. *P.*
WORCESTERSHIRE (1) 1953.
HS 1 Worcs v Cambridge U, Fenner's, 1953.
BB 3–25 same match.
Clubs: Enfield, Great Harwood. Runs steel company in Blackburn.

RILEY, John
Christopher William
————RHB, WK————

Born Esher, Surrey, 6 Apr 1934. Educ Uppingham; St Catharine's C, Cambridge. Debut 1955.
CAMBRIDGE UNIVERSITY (2) 1955–56.
No runs.

RILEY, Terence Michael Noel
————RHB, occ LB————

Born Birmingham, 25 Dec 1939. Educ Wellesbourne S, Birmingham. Debut 1961. *P.*
WARWICKSHIRE (12) 1961–64.
GLOUCESTERSHIRE (11) 1964.
HS 84 Warwicks v Derbys, Derby, 1961 (fc debut).
Played for Warwicks and Glos in 1964.
Clubs: Pickwick, Aston Unity, Knowle and Dorridge.

RILSTONE, Thomas *Melville*
————LHB, RLB————

Born Wallaroo Mines, S Australia, 12 Jan 1918. Educ S Australian S of Mines and Industry; Adelaide U. Debut 1951.
CANADA (3) 1951–54.
TOUR Canada to England 1954.
HS 38 Canada v MCC, Toronto, 1951.
Canada to Bermuda 1958. Clubs: Kadina, Adelaide University, Port Adelaide (Australia), St Catharine's Ontario, Canada Adastrians, Quebec, Montreal (Canada).

RIMELL, Anthony Geoffrey
Jordan
————LHB, ROB————

Born Kasauli, India, 29 Aug 1928. Educ Charterhouse; Magdalene C, Cambridge. Debut 1946.
HAMPSHIRE (2) 1946–50.
CAMBRIDGE UNIVERSITY (21) 1949–50 (Blue 1949–50).

HS 160 Cambridge U v Worcs, Worcester, 1949.
BB 6–100 Cambridge U v Glos, Bristol, 1950.

RIMMER, Joseph
————RHB, RFM————

Born Langwith, Derbys, 26 Jan 1925. Debut 1949. *P.*
DERBYSHIRE (3) 1949.
HS 1* Derbys v N Zealanders, Derby, 1949.
BB 2–71 Derbys v Notts, Ilkeston, 1949.

RING, Douglas Thomas
————RHB, LBG————

Born Hobart, Tasmania, Australia, 14 Oct 1918. Debut 1938/39.
AUSTRALIA DOMESTIC Victoria (67) 1938/39–52/53.
AUSTRALIA (13) 1947/48–53. SA 1952/53 (5); WI 1951/52 (5); I 1947/48 (1). *E 1948 (1), 1953 (1).*
OTHER TOUR Australia B to N Zealand 1949/50.
HST 67 A v WI, Adelaide, 1951/52. HS 145 Victoria v Queensland, Melbourne, 1946/47.
BBT 6–72 A v SA, Brisbane, 1952/53. BB 7–88 Australia B v N Zealand XI, Dunedin, 1949/50.
Club: Richmond (Melbourne).

RIPLEY, David
————RHB, WK————

Born Farsley, Yorks, 13 Sept 1966. Educ Royds S, Leeds. Debut 1984.
NORTHAMPTONSHIRE (14) 1984.
HS 61 Northants v Surrey, Northampton, 1984.

RIPPON, Thomas *John*
————RHB, WK————

Born Swansea, S Wales, 6 July 1918. Educ Brynmill S, Swansea. Debut 1947.
GLAMORGAN (3) 1947–48.
HS 30 Glam v Northants, Kettering, 1947.
Club: Swansea. Worked in National Fire Service.

RIST, Frank Henry
————RHB, WK, RM————

Born Wandsworth, London, 30 Mar 1914. Educ Farmer Road S, Leyton. Debut 1934. *P.*
ESSEX (65) 1934–53. Cap 1949.
Testimonial (£1274) 1954.

HS 62 Essex v Kent, Blackheath, 1953.
Former Essex coach (from 1949). Club: Walthamstow. Soccer: Charlton Athletic.

RIX, David William
————RHB, LMF————

Born Bulawayo, Rhodesia, 7 Dec 1939. Educ Milton C, Bulawayo; Oxford U. Debut 1964.
OXFORD UNIVERSITY (1) 1964.
No runs.
BB 3–90 Oxford U v Australians, The Parks, 1964.
Only three wkts in fc cricket all Test players, R. M. Cowper, B. C. Booth and B. N. Jarman.
University lecturer and spare-time poet.

RIXON, Stephen John
————RHB, WK————

Born Albury, NSW, Australia, 25 Feb 1954. Debut 1974/75.
AUSTRALIA DOMESTIC New South Wales (95) 1974/75–.
AUSTRALIA (10) 1977/78. I 1977/78 (5). *WI 1977/78 (5).*
OTHER TOURS Australia to Sri Lanka 1980/81. Australia to England 1981.
HST 54 A v WI, Georgetown, 1977/78. HS 128 NSW v Victoria, Melbourne, 1976/77.
Clubs: Waverley, Western Suburbs, Sutherland (all Sydney Grade).

ROBERTS, Alan C.
————RHB, RM————

Born N Zealand. Educ Mount Albert GS. Debut 1945.
N ZEALAND DOMESTIC Auckland (1) 1947/48.
TOUR N Zealand Services XI to England (1) 1945.
HS 12 N Zealand Services XI v H. D. G. Leveson Gower's XI, Scarborough, 1945.
BB 3–83 same match.
Club: Parnell.

ROBERTS, Anderson
Montgomery Everton
————RHB, RF————

Born Urlings Village, Antigua, 29 Jan 1951. Educ Princess Margaret S, Antigua. Debut 1969/70. *Wisden 1975.*
W INDIES DOMESTIC Leeward Islands 1969/70–83/84, Combined Islands 1970/71–80/81.
HAMPSHIRE (58) 1973–78. Cap 1974.
LEICESTERSHIRE (36) 1981–.

AUSTRALIA DOMESTIC New South Wales (2) 1976/77.
WEST INDIES (47) 1973/74–83/84. E 1973/74 (1), 1980/81 (3); A 1977/78 (2); I 1975/76 (2), 1982/83 (5); P 1976/77 (5). *E 1976 (5), 1980 (3); A 1975/76 (5), 1979/80 (3), 1981/82 (2); NZ 1979/80 (2); I 1974/75 (5), 1983/84 (2); P 1974/75 (2).*
HST 68 WI v I, Calcutta, 1983/84. HS 89 Leics v Glam, Swansea, 1984.
BBT 7–54 WI v A, Perth, 1975/76. BB 8–47 Hants v Glam, Cardiff, 1974.
100 WKTS (1) 119 @ 13.62 in 1974.
RECORD During HST (above) added 161 for 9th wkt with C. H. Lloyd, W Indies fc record.
Reached 100 Test wkts in 2 yrs 142 days, a world record at time (1976).
World Series Cricket (Kerry Packer) 1977/78–78/79.

ROBERTS, Bruce
——RHB, RM——

Born Lusaka, Zambia, 30 May 1962. Educ Prince Edward S, Salisbury. Debut 1982/83.
S AFRICA DOMESTIC Transvaal B 1982/83–.
DERBYSHIRE (17) 1984.
HS 89 Transvaal B v OFS, J'burg, 1983/84 and 89 v Boland, Stellenbosch, 1983/84.
BB 4–32 Transvaal B v OFS, J'burg, 1982/83.

ROBERTS, Christopher *Paul*
——RHB, RM——

Born Cleethorpes, Lincolnshire, 12 Oct 1951. Died in climbing accident, Coombe Ghyl, Borrowdale, Cumberland, 9 June 1977. Educ Humberston Foundation S, Cleethorpes; Borough Road C of Educ, Isleworth. Debut 1974.
WORCESTERSHIRE (1) 1974.
No runs, one wkt.
Lincolnshire 1971–72.

ROBERTS, David John
——LHB, RFM——

Born Harpenden, Hertfordshire, 1 Oct 1942. Educ Manland Sec, Harpenden. Debut 1963.
MCC (1) 1963.
HS 6 MCC v Scotland, Glasgow, 1963.
Hertfordshire 1964. M'sex 2nd XI. Clubs: Harpenden, MCC (groundstaff), Cross Arrows.

ROBERTS, Harry Edmund
——LHB——

Born Earlsdon, Coventry, Warwicks, 5 June 1924. Educ Bablake S. Debut 1949. P.
WARWICKSHIRE (5) 1949–50.
HS 30 Warwicks v Cambridge U, Fenner's, 1949.
Clubs: Courtaulds (Coventry), GEC Coventry, Coventry and North Warwicks.

ROBERTS, James Brown
——RHB, RFM——

Born Dundee, Scotland, 11 Oct 1933. Educ RHS Dundee. Debut 1956.
SCOTLAND (10) 1956–59.
HS 31* Scotland v MCC, Edinburgh, 1959.
BB 3–70 Scotland v Yorks, Hull, 1956.
Clubs: RHS Dundee FP, Clydesdale.

ROBERTS, John Francis Esdale
——RHB, RMF——

Born Kearsley, Lancs, 4 Mar 1933. Educ Loweburn S, Manchester. Debut 1957. P.
LANCASHIRE (2) 1957.
HS 5 Lancs v Cambridge U, Liverpool, 1957.
Clubs: Kearsley, Radcliffe, Preston, Lascelles Hall, Kidderminster, Padiham, Bradshaw.

ROBERTS, John Frederick
——LHB——

Born Pontardawe, S Wales, 24 Feb 1913. Educ Pontardawe GS. Debut 1934.
GLAMORGAN (5) 1934–36.
COMBINED SERVICES (3) 1946–49.
HS 52 Combined Services v S Africans, Portsmouth, 1947.
Clubs: Pontardawe, Watford, Cheltenham, MCC, Royal Air Force. Air Vice-Marshal (retired). Awarded CB, CBE and OBE.

ROBERTS, John Kelvin
——RHB, LM——

Born Liverpool, Lancs, 9 Oct 1949. Educ Aireborough GS. Debut 1969.
SOMERSET (8) 1969–70.
HS 2* Som v Yorks, Headingley, 1969.
BB 4–38 same match.
Club: Keighley.

ROBERTS, Pascall
——RHB, LM/SLA——

Born Trinidad, 15 Dec 1937. Debut 1960/61.
W INDIES DOMESTIC Trinidad 1960/61–71/72, North Trinidad 1966/67–78/79.
TOUR W Indians to England 1969.
HS 105* North Trinidad v South Trinidad, Dubissoon Park, 1976/77.
BB 6–17 (10–34 match) North Trinidad v Tobago, Port of Spain, 1978/79.
No-balled for throwing (three times), Trinidad v Jamaica, Kingston, 1966/67.
Club: Paragon (Trinidad), Lowerhouse (Lancashire).

ROBERTS, Simon Nicholas
——RHB, LB——

Born Durban, S Africa, 11 Sept 1926. Educ Michaelhouse, Natal; Caius C, Cambridge. Debut 1947.
CAMBRIDGE UNIVERSITY (6) 1947–49.
HS 49* Cambridge U v Worcs, Fenner's, 1947.
Cambridgeshire 1947. Former president Natal Law Society.

ROBERTS, William Braithwaite
——RHB, SLA——

Born Kirkham, Lancs, 27 Sept 1914. Died Caernarvon and Anglesey Hospital, Bangor, N Wales, 24 Aug 1951. Debut 1939. P.
LANCASHIRE (114) 1939–49. Cap 1939. Testimonial (£2623) 1950.
HS 51 Lancs v Glam, Old Trafford, 1948.
BB 8–50 Lancs v Oxford U, The Parks, 1949.
100 WKTS (1) 123 @ 19.34 in 1946. Took 99 wkts @ 20.05 in 1948.
England v Australia (Victory matches) (3) 1945. Club: West Bromwich Dartmouth.

ROBERTSON, Frank
——RHB, RFM——

Born Aberdeen, Scotland, 25 Feb 1944. Educ Robert Gordon's C. Debut 1971.
SCOTLAND (12) 1971–81.
HS 51 Scotland v Ireland, Dublin, 1979.
BB 6–58 Scotland v Ireland, Belfast, 1971.
Club: Aberdeenshire.

ROBERTSON, George André
——————RHB, RM——————

Born St-Jean-de-Luz, France, 3 Sept 1929. Educ Ampleforth; Peterhouse C, Cambridge. Debut 1950.
CAMBRIDGE UNIVERSITY (1) 1950.
FREE FORESTERS (1) 1950.
HS 7* Free Foresters v Cambridge U, Fenner's, 1950.
BB 2–53 Cambridge U v Hants, Fenner's, 1950.

ROBERTSON, John David Benbow
——————RHB, OB——————

Born Chiswick, London, 22 Feb 1917. Educ Arlington Park C, London. Debut 1937. P. Wisden 1948.
MIDDLESEX (423) 1937–59. Cap 1938. Benefit (£4500) 1951. Second benefit (£3610) 1959.
ENGLAND (11) 1947–1951/52. SA 1947 (1); NZ 1949 (1). WI 1947/48 (4); I 1951/52 (5).
HST 133 E v WI, Port of Spain, 1947/48.
HS 331* M'sex v Worcs, Worcester, 1949.
BBT 2–17 E v I, Kanpur, 1951/52. BB 4–37 M'sex v Leics, Leicester, 1955.
1000 RUNS (14 + 1) 2917 @ 56.09 in 1951. 2000 runs (9), including 1946–52 consecutively.
RECORDS HS (above) highest-ever inns for M'sex and fourth-highest score by a batsman in one day's play.
Scored centuries against every fc county except his own.
Players v Gentlemen (5) 1957–62. M'sex coach from 1960. Club: Turnham Green. MCC Hon. member.

ROBERTSON, L. G.
——————RMF——————

Debut 1955.
D. R. JARDINE'S XI (1) 1955.
HS 2* D. R. Jardine's XI v Oxford U, Eastbourne, 1955.
BB 4–44 same match.

ROBINS, Derrick Harold
——————RHB, WK——————

Born Bexleyheath, Kent, 27 June 1914. Educ Champion Hill House S, Dulwich. Debut 1947.
WARWICKSHIRE (2) 1947.
D. H. ROBINS' XI (3) 1969–71.
HS 29* Warwicks v M'sex, Edgbaston, 1947.
Organiser of an XI which, until 1980, played against Oxford and Cambridge Universities and against touring sides,
initially in fc fixtures (1969–74). From 1972/73 until 1979/80 organised fc tours overseas, usually to S Africa, where he now lives.
Clubs: Coventry and North Warwicks, Leamington. Soccer: former chairman Coventry City.

ROBINS, Glen Lello
——————SLA——————

Born Kingston-upon-Thames, Surrey, 23 Oct 1922. Educ Merchant Taylors' S, Northwood; St Catharine's C, Cambridge. Debut 1947.
CAMBRIDGE UNIVERSITY (1) 1947.
No runs.
BB 2–60 Cambridge U v M'sex, Fenner's, 1947.
War-time Blue.

ROBINS, Robert Victor Charles
——————RHB, LBG——————

Born Burnham, Buckinghamshire, 13 Mar 1935. Educ Eton. Debut 1953.
MIDDLESEX (44) 1953–60.
MCC (3) 1954–59.
FREE FORESTERS (9) 1955–62.
D. R. JARDINE'S XI (1) 1957.
HS 49 M'sex v Lancs, Liverpool, 1959.
BB 7–78 M'sex v Cambridge U, Fenner's, 1954.
Gentlemen v Players (1) 1959. Buckinghamshire, 1951. Club: Brondesbury. MCC committee 1974–. Father R. W. V. Robins (M'sex, England).

ROBINS, Robert Walter Vivian
——————RHB, LBG——————

Born Stafford, 3 June 1906. Died London, 12 Dec 1968. Educ Highgate; Queen's C, Cambridge. Debut 1925. Wisden 1930.
MIDDLESEX (258) 1925–51. Cap Capt 1935–38, 1946–47, 1950.
CAMBRIDGE UNIVERSITY (35) 1926–28 (Blue 1926–28).
ENGLAND (19) 1929–37. A 1930 (2); SA 1929 (1), 1935 (3); WI 1933 (2); NZ 1931 (1), 1937 (3); I 1932 (1), 1936 (2). A 1936/37 (4). Capt 3.
OTHER TOURS Sir J. Cahn's XI to Argentina 1929/30. MCC to Canada 1951 (capt).
HST 108 E v SA, Old Trafford, 1935. HS 140 M'sex v Cambridge U, Fenner's, 1930.
BBT 6–32 E v WI, Lord's, 1933. BB 8–69 M'sex v Glos, Lord's, 1929.
1000 RUNS (4) 1397 @ 31.04 in 1946.
100 WKTS (1) 162 @ 21.53 in 1929. Took 99 wkts @ 20.00 in 1937.
DOUBLE (1) 1929.
Gentlemen v Players (8) 1928–52. England Test selector 1946–48, 1962–64 (chairman 1962–64). Manager MCC to W Indies 1959/60. M'sex Hon. secretary 1935–49. MCC committee 1950–64. Soccer: Corinthians, Blue, Nottingham Forest. Son R. V. C. Robins (M'sex); brother W. V. H. Robins (Army).

ROBINSON, Albert George
——————RHB, RFM——————

Born Leicester, 22 Mar 1917. Educ Wyggeston GS. Debut 1937. P.
NORTHAMPTONSHIRE (24) 1937–46.
HS 32 Northants v Combined Services, Kettering, 1946.
BB 5–37 Northants v Derbys, Northampton, 1938.
Cambridgeshire 1948–49, Berkshire 1951–55. Clubs: Wisbech, Radley Rangers, Royal Air Force. Professional coach Radley 1949–83.

ROBINSON, Arthur Leslie (Rocker)
——————LHB, LFM——————

Born Brompton, nr Northallerton, Yorks, 17 Aug 1946. Debut 1971.
YORKSHIRE (84) 1971–77. Cap 1976.
HS 30* Yorks v Glam, Cardiff, 1977.
BB 6–61 Yorks v Surrey, Oval, 1974.
Clubs: Leeds, Northallerton.

ROBINSON, Ellis Pembroke
——————LHB, ROB——————

Born Denaby Main, Yorks, 10 Aug 1911. Debut 1934. P.
YORKSHIRE (207) 1934–49. Cap. Grant (£1500) 1949.
SOMERSET (90) 1950–52. Cap 1950.
TOUR Yorks to Jamaica 1935/36.
HS 75* Yorks v Glos, Bristol, 1937.
BB 8–35 (13–115 match) Yorks v Lancs, Headingley, 1939.
Returned 15–78 match, Som v Sussex, Weston-super-Mare, 1952.
100 WKTS (5) 167 @ 14.95 in 1946.
Players v Gentlemen (1) 1946. Uncle G. L. Robinson (Notts).

ROBINSON, Geoffrey
——————LHB, WK, occ SLA——————

Born Bridlington, Yorks, 13 Jan 1944. Debut 1971.
MINOR COUNTIES (2) 1971–72.
HS 36 Minor Counties v Australians, Longton, 1972.
Lincolnshire 1965–. Club: Ross Group.

ROBINSON, George Adrian
—————LHB, WK—————

Born Preston, Lancs, 3 Nov 1949. Educ Preston Cathedral C; Pembroke C, Oxford. Debut 1970.
OXFORD UNIVERSITY (14) 1970–71 (Blue 1971).
HS 62 Oxford U v Notts, The Parks, 1971.

ROBINSON, Henry Basil Oswin
—————RHB, OB—————

Born Eastbourne, Sussex, 3 Mar 1919. Educ North Shore C, Vancouver; Oriel C, Oxford. Debut 1947.
OXFORD UNIVERSITY (19) 1947–48 (Blue 1947–48).
CANADA (5) 1951–54. Capt.
TOUR Canada to England 1954 (capt).
HS 51 Oxford U v Lancs, The Parks, 1947.
BB 6–55 Oxford U v Worcs, Worcester, 1947.
Clubs: New Edinburgh (Ottawa), Hampstead (England).

ROBINSON, Keith
—————RHB, OB—————

Born Thirsk, Yorks, 17 Dec 1933. Educ Enfield GS. Debut 1961.
COMBINED SERVICES (1) 1961.
HS 18 Combined Services v Northants, Northampton, 1961.
Clubs: Enfield, Marlow, Incogniti.

ROBINSON, Maurice
—————RHB, RMF—————

Born Lisburn, Ireland, 16 July 1921. Debut 1942/43.
INDIA DOMESTIC Madras Europeans 1942/43–44/45, Bombay Europeans 1943/44, Hyderabad 1943/44, Madras 1944/45.
GLAMORGAN (66) 1946–50. Cap 1950.
COMBINED SERVICES (1) 1946.
WARWICKSHIRE (8) 1951–52.
HS 190 Glam v Hants, Bournemouth, 1949 (adding 264 for 5th wkt with S. W. Montgomery, county record).
BB 7–51 Europeans v Indians, Madras, 1944/45.
Club: Moseley.

ROBINSON, Miles Trevor
—————LHB, RFM—————

Born Eastbourne, Sussex, 13 Dec 1929. Educ Shrewsbury. Debut 1947.

SUSSEX (2) 1947.
HS 4 Sussex v Glos, Hove, 1947.
Club: Eastbourne.

ROBINSON, Paul Andrew
—————RHB, RFM—————

Born Boksburg, S Africa, 16 July 1956. Educ Brakpan HS. Debut 1977/78.
S AFRICA DOMESTIC Northern Transvaal 1977/78–.
LANCASHIRE (1) 1979.
HS 49 N Transvaal v E Province, Port Elizabeth, 1983/84.
BB 6–46 N Transvaal v Natal, Durban, 1983/84.
Cheshire 1978. Club: Cleckheaton. 6 ft 8 in tall.

ROBINSON, Peter James
—————LHB, SLA—————

Born Worcester, 9 Feb 1943. Debut 1963.
WORCESTERSHIRE (5) 1963–64.
SOMERSET (180) 1965–77. Cap 1966.
HS 140 Som v Northants, Northampton, 1970.
BB 7–10 Som v Notts, Trent Bridge, 1966.
1000 RUNS (1) 1158 @ 26.93 in 1970.
Somerset groundsman-coach. Clubs: Kidderminster, Stourbridge. Uncle R. O. Jenkins (Worcs, England).

ROBINSON, Peter Michael Heasty
—————RHB, OB—————

Born Port of Spain, Trinidad, 14 Oct 1929. Educ Lancing; Magdalene C, Cambridge. Debut 1961.
L. C. STEVENS' XI (1) 1961.
HS 12 L. C. Stevens' XI v Cambridge U, Eastbourne, 1961.
Clubs: Middleton-on-Sea, Esher, Free Foresters, MCC, Sussex Martlets. Squash: England.

ROBINSON, Philip Edward
—————RHB, LM—————

Born Keighley, Yorks, 3 Aug 1963. Educ Greenhead GS, Keighley. Debut 1984.
YORKSHIRE (15) 1984.
HS 92 Yorks v Glam, Bradford, 1984.
Club: Keighley.

ROBINSON, Raymond Thomas
—————RHB—————

Born Charmouth, Dorset, 15 Sept 1940. Debut 1964.

SOMERSET (1) 1964.
No runs, no wkts.
Rugby: Somerset, Royal Navy.

ROBINSON, Richard Daryl
—————RHB, WK—————

Born East Melbourne, Victoria, Australia, 8 June 1946. Debut 1971/72.
AUSTRALIA DOMESTIC Victoria (76) 1971/72–81/82.
AUSTRALIA (3) E 1977.
OTHER TOUR Australia to England 1975.
HST 34 A v E, Trent Bridge, 1977. HS 185 Victoria v S Australia, Adelaide, 1976/77.
Club: Northcote.

ROBINSON, Robert Geoffrey
—————RHB, SLA—————

Born Wellingborough, Northants, 23 Sept 1924. Died Wellingborough, Northants, 21 Dec 1973. Educ Park Street S, Wellingborough. Debut 1946. P.
NORTHAMPTONSHIRE (4) 1946.
HS 53 Northants v Combined Services, Kettering, 1946.
Club: Wellingborough Priory.

ROBINSON, Robert *Timothy*
—————RHB, RM—————

Born Sutton-in-Ashfield, Notts, 21 Nov 1958. Educ Dunstable GS; Sheffield U. Debut 1978.
NOTTINGHAMSHIRE (109) 1978–. Cap 1983.
HS 207 Notts v Warwicks, Trent Bridge, 1983.
1000 RUNS (2) 2032 @ 50.80 in 1984.
Club: Teversal.

ROBINSON, Thomas *Lloyd*
—————RHB, RMF—————

Born Swansea, S Wales, 21 Dec 1912. Educ Wycliffe C. Debut 1946.
WARWICKSHIRE (4) 1946.
HS 13* Warwicks v Indians, Edgbaston, 1946.
BB 2–74 Warwicks v Essex, Southend, 1946.
Glos president 1980. Clubs: Moseley Ashfield, Warwicks Imps, Clifton. Rugby: Moseley, North Midlands. Wife's uncle F. R. Foster (Warwicks, England).

ROBOTHAM, Reginald
————RHB, occ WK————

Born Bidford-on-Avon, Warwicks, 14 July 1911. Died Hastings, Sussex, 31 Jan 1978. Educ Hastings GS. Debut 1946.
SUSSEX (1) 1946.
HS 21 Sussex v MCC, Hastings, 1946.
Clubs: Hastings Priory, Attleborough, Nuneaton.

ROCHFORD, Peter
————RHB, WK————

Born Halifax, Yorks, 27 Aug 1928. Debut 1952. *P.*
GLOUCESTERSHIRE (80) 1952–57. Cap 1955.
HS 31* Glos v Oxford U, The Parks, 1956.
Fc umpire 1975–77. Yorkshire 2nd XI 1950–51. Club: Scarborough.

ROCK, David John
————RHB, RM————

Born Southsea, Hants, 20 Apr 1957. Educ Portsmouth GS. Debut 1976.
HAMPSHIRE (37) 1976–79.
HS 114 Hants v Leics, Leicester, 1977.

RODGER, Richard Gordon
————RHB, SLA————

Born Norwich, Norfolk, 1 Oct 1947. Educ Heriot's; Edinburgh U; Liverpool U. Debut 1975.
SCOTLAND (1) 1975.
HS 2 Scotland v Ireland, Dublin, 1975.
Cheshire 1972–. Clubs: Westhoughton, Sefton, Nantwich, Newcastle under Lyme.

RODRIGUEZ, William Vincente
————RHB, LBG————

Born Port of Spain, Trinidad, 25 June 1934. Debut 1953/54.
W INDIES DOMESTIC Trinidad 1953/54–69/70.
WEST INDIES (5) 1961/62–67/68. E 1967/68 (1); A 1964/65 (1); I 1961/62 (2). *E 1963 (1).*
OTHER TOUR W Indies to India and Pakistan 1958/59.
HST 50 WI v I, Port of Spain, 1961/62.
HS 105 Trinidad v Pakistanis, Port of Spain, 1957/58.
BBT 3–51 WI v I, Port of Spain, 1961/62.
BB 7–90 W Indians v Indian Universities, Nagpur, 1958/59.
Manager W Indians to Australasia 1979/80.

ROE, Brian
————RHB————

Born Cleethorpes, Lincolnshire, 27 Jan 1939. Debut 1957. *P.*
SOMERSET (131) 1957–66. Cap 1962.
COMBINED SERVICES (5) 1959–60.
HS 128 Som v Essex, Brentwood, 1962.
1000 RUNS (3) 1552 @ 26.30 in 1962.
Devon 1972–74. Clubs: Barnstaple, Nondescripts, North Devon.

ROEBUCK, Paul Gerrard Peter
————LHB, RMF————

Born Bath, Som, 13 Oct 1963. Educ Millfield; Emmanuel C, Cambridge. Debut 1983.
CAMBRIDGE UNIVERSITY (10) 1983– (Blue 1984).
GLOUCESTERSHIRE (1) 1984.
HS 62 Cambridge U v Notts, Trent Bridge, 1984.
BB 2–44 Cambridge U v Kent, Fenner's, 1983.
Brother P. M. Roebuck (Som).

ROEBUCK, Peter Michael
————RHB, LB————

Born Oxford, 6 Mar 1956. Educ Millfield; Emmanuel C, Cambridge. Debut 1974.
SOMERSET (177) 1974–. Cap 1978.
CAMBRIDGE UNIVERSITY (26) 1975–77 (Blue 1975–77).
HS 159 Som v Northants, Northampton, 1984.
BB 6–50 Cambridge U v Kent, Canterbury, 1977.
1000 RUNS (4) 1702 @ 47.28 in 1984.
RECORD Added 319 for 3rd wkt with M. D. Crowe, Som v Leics, Taunton, 1984, county record.
Played for Somerset 2nd XI at age of 13. Author of *Slices of Cricket* (1984) and *It Never Rains . . . A Cricketer's Lot* (1985). Brother P. G. P. Roebuck (Cambridge U).

ROGERS, James Julian
————RHB————

Born Kendal, Westmorland, 20 Aug 1958. Educ Sedbergh; UC, Oxford. Debut 1979.
OXFORD UNIVERSITY (26) 1979–81 (Blue 1979–81).
HS 54 Oxford U v Cambridge U, Lord's, 1981.
Cumberland 1979. Club: Kendal.

ROGERS, Neville Hamilton
————RHB————

Born Oxford, 9 Mar 1918. Debut 1946. *P.*
HAMPSHIRE (285) 1946–55. Cap 1947. Testimonial (£1676) 1956.
HS 186 Hants v Glos, Portsmouth, 1951.
1000 RUNS (9) 2244 @ 40.80 in 1952.
Twelfth man, E v SA, Oval, 1951. Test trial 1953 (The Rest v England XI, Edgbaston). Carried bat through completed inns four times in 1954.
Clubs: Southampton, XL.

ROGERS, Peter James
————RHB, LB/OB————

Born Swansea, S Wales, 28 Dec 1928. Educ Harrow GS. Debut 1967.
MCC (1) 1967.
HS 24* MCC v Scotland, Glasgow, 1967.
Clubs: Kenton, Wanstead, MCC, Army, REME.

ROGERS, Stuart Scott
————RHB————

Born Muswell Hill, London, 18 Mar 1923. Died Chartridge, Buckinghamshire, 6 Nov 1969. Educ Highgate; Pembroke C, Cambridge. Debut 1946/47.
INDIA DOMESTIC Madras Europeans 1946/47.
SOMERSET (118) 1948–53. Cap 1949. Capt 1950–52.
HS 107* Som v S Africans, Taunton, 1951.
BB 2–13 Som v Notts, Trent Bridge, 1950.
1000 RUNS (1) 1127 @ 25.61 in 1950.
War-time Blue. Club: Hornsey. Soccer: War-time Blue.

ROLL, Lawson Macgregor
————RHB, OB————

Born Thornbury, Bristol, Glos, 8 Mar 1965. Educ Colstons S, Bristol. Debut 1984.
GLOUCESTERSHIRE (1) 1984.
No runs, no wkts.
Grandfather H. Roll (Warwicks).

ROMAINES, Paul William
————RHB————

Born Bishop Auckland, Co Durham, 25 Dec 1955. Educ Leeholme S, Bishop Auckland. Debut 1975.
NORTHAMPTONSHIRE (6) 1975–76.
GLOUCESTERSHIRE (63) 1982–. Cap 1983.

HS 186 Glos v Warwicks, Nuneaton, 1982.
1000 RUNS (2) 1844 @ 35.46 in 1984.
Durham County 1977–81. Clubs: Darlington, Synthonia, Alnwick.

ROOPE, Graham Richard James
————RHB, RM————

Born Fareham, Hants, 12 July 1946.
Educ Bradfield. Debut 1964.
SURREY (342) 1964–82. Cap 1969.
Benefit 1980.
S AFRICA DOMESTIC Griqualand West 1973/74.
ENGLAND (21) 1972/73–78. A 1975 (1), 1977 (2); WI 1973 (1); NZ 1973 (3), 1978 (1); P 1978 (3). *NZ 1977/78 (3); I 1972/ 73 (2); P 1972/73 (2), 1977/78 (3).*
OTHER TOURS MCC to Ceylon 1969/70.
D. H. Robins' XI to S Africa 1973/74.
International Wanderers to S Africa 1974/75. International Wanderers to Rhodesia 1975/76.
HST 77 E v A, Oval, 1975. HS 171 Surrey v Yorks, Oval, 1971.
BB 5–14 Surrey v W Indians, Oval, 1969.
1000 RUNS (8) 1641 @ 44.35 in 1971.
Took 59 catches in 1971 and 599 catches in career.
Berkshire 1963, 1983–. Club: Nelson.

ROOPNARAINE, Rupert
————RHB, OB————

Born Georgetown, British Guiana, 31 Jan 1943. Educ Berbice HS; Queen's C, British Guiana; St John's C, Cambridge. Debut 1964.
CAMBRIDGE UNIVERSITY (29) 1964–66 (Blue 1965–66).
HS 50* Cambridge U v Scotland, Fenner's, 1966.
BB 8–88 Cambridge U v Essex, Fenner's, 1965.
Cambridgeshire 1967.

ROPER, Arthur William
————RHB, RFM————

Born Petersham, NSW, Australia, 20 Feb 1917. Died Woy Woy, NSW, Australia, 4 Sept 1972. Debut 1939/40.
AUSTRALIA DOMESTIC New South Wales (2) 1939/40, Australian Services (1) 1945/46.
TOUR Australian Services to England (1) 1945 and India and Ceylon (7) 1945/46.
HS 28 Australian Services v East Zone, Calcutta, 1945/46.
BB 2–9 Australian Services v Ceylon, Colombo, 1945/46.
Club: Petersham.

ROPER, Colin
————RHB, WK————

Born Dorchester, Dorset, 25 July 1936.
Debut 1957. *P.*
HAMPSHIRE (1) 1957.
HS 7 Hants v Oxford U, The Parks, 1957.
Dorset 1959–69. Club: Dorchester.

ROPER, Donald George Beaumont
————RHB————

Born Botley, South Stoneham, Southampton, Hants, 14 Dec 1922.
Debut 1947.
HAMPSHIRE (1) 1947.
HS 30 Hants v Cambridge U, Portsmouth, 1947.
Club: Southgate. Soccer: Southampton, Arsenal.

ROSE, Brian Charles
————LHB, LM————

Born Dartford, Kent, 4 June 1950. Educ Weston-super-Mare GS; Borough Road C of Educ, Isleworth. Debut 1969.
Wisden 1980.
SOMERSET (209) 1969–. Cap 1975. Capt 1978–. Benefit 1983.
ENGLAND (9) 1977/78–80/81. WI 1980 (3). *WI 1980/81 (1); NZ 1977/78 (2); P 1977/78 (3).*
HST 70 E v WI, Old Trafford, 1980. HS 205 Som v Northants, Weston-super-Mare, 1977.
BB 3–9 Som v Glos, Taunton, 1975.
1000 RUNS (8) 1624 @ 46.40 in 1976.
Returned home early from tour to W Indies 1980/81 because of eye trouble.

ROSE, Edward McQueen
————LHB————

Born Oxted, Surrey, 2 Sept 1936. Educ Rugby; Sidney Sussex C, Cambridge.
Debut 1958.
CAMBRIDGE UNIVERSITY (24) 1958–60.
HS 57 Cambridge U v Kent, Gillingham, 1959.
Club: Limpsfield.

ROSE, Michael Harrison
————RHB————

Born Hereford, 8 Apr 1942. Educ Pocklington S; Christ's C, Cambridge.
Debut 1962.
CAMBRIDGE UNIVERSITY (26) 1962–64 (Blue 1963–64).
LEICESTERSHIRE (4) 1963–64.
HS 86 Cambridge U v Essex, Fenner's, 1963.

ROSS, Christopher *Jonathan*
————RHB, RM————

Born Warri, Nigeria, 24 June 1954.
Educ Wanganui C; Wellington U; Magdalen C, Oxford. Debut 1975/76.
N ZEALAND DOMESTIC Wellington (7) 1975/76.
OXFORD UNIVERSITY (24) 1978–80 (Blue 1978–80). Capt 1980.
HS 23* Oxford U v Cambridge U, Lord's, 1980.
BB 4–34 Oxford U v Worcs, Worcester, 1978.

ROSS, Nicholas Peter Gilbert
————LHB, RLBG————

Born Edinburgh, Scotland, 2 Oct 1947.
Educ Marlborough; Selwyn C, Cambridge. Debut 1969.
CAMBRIDGE UNIVERSITY (8) 1969–70 (Blue 1969).
HS 68 Cambridge U v Essex, Fenner's, 1969.
BB 2–22 Cambridge U v Oxford U, Lord's, 1969.
Cambridgeshire 1979–. Club: Camden.

ROSS, Nigel Patrick Dorai
————RHB, WK————

Born Chelsea, London, 5 Apr 1953.
Debut 1973.
MIDDLESEX (25) 1973–77.
HS 53 M'sex v Essex, Lord's, 1977.
Retired in 1977 because of back injury.

ROUGHT-ROUGHT, Desmond Charles
————RHB, RFM————

Born Brandon, Norfolk, 3 May 1912.
Died, in road accident, Cambridge, 7 Jan 1970. Educ privately; Emmanuel C, Cambridge. Debut 1934.
CAMBRIDGE UNIVERSITY (19) 1934–37 (Blue 1937).
FREE FORESTERS (3) 1934–47.
MINOR COUNTIES (2) 1935–39.
HS 92 Cambridge U v Sussex, Fenner's, 1937.
BB 7–100 (10–201 match) Cambridge U v Notts, Fenner's, 1935.
Norfolk 1931–47. Brothers B. W. Rought-Rought (Minor Counties) and R. C. Rought-Rought (Cambridge U).

ROUNDELL, James
————LHB, RMF————

Born Nantwich, Cheshire, 23 Oct 1951.
Educ Winchester; Magdalene C, Cambridge. Debut 1973.

CAMBRIDGE UNIVERSITY (10) 1973 (Blue).
HS 10* Cambridge U v Leics, Fenner's, 1973.
BB 3–12 Cambridge U v Oxford U, Lord's, 1973.
Clubs: I Zingari, Old Wykehamists. 6 ft 7 in tall.

ROUSE, Stephen John
——LHB, LMF——

Born Merthyr Tydfil, S Wales, 20 Jan 1949. Educ Moseley S. Debut 1970.
WARWICKSHIRE (124) 1970–81. Cap 1974.
TOUR D. H. Robins' XI to S Africa 1974/75.
HS 93 Warwicks v Hants, Bournemouth, 1976.
BB 6–34 Warwicks v Leics, Leicester, 1976.
Coaching assistant at Edgbaston. Clubs: Moseley, Mitchells and Butlers. Suffered many injuries during career.

ROUTLEDGE, Reginald
——RHB, RM——

Born Kensington, London, 7 July 1920. Debut 1946. *P.*
MIDDLESEX (64) 1946–54. Cap 1951.
HS 121 M'sex v Worcs, Worcester, 1953.
BB 4–29 M'sex v Oxford U, The Parks, 1953.
Devon 1947. Player/coach Paignton 1947. Club: Aberdeenshire.

ROWAN, Athol Matthew Burchell
——RHB, OB——

Born Johannesburg, S Africa, 7 Feb 1921. Educ Jeppe HS, Johannesburg. Debut 1939/40.
S AFRICA DOMESTIC Transvaal 1939/40–50/51.
SOUTH AFRICA (15) 1947–51. E 1948/49 (5). *E 1947 (5), 1951 (5).*
HST 41 SA v E, Oval, 1951. HS 100* S Africans v Glam, Cardiff, 1947.
BBT 5–68 SA v E, Trent Bridge, 1951. BB 9–19 (15–68 match) Transvaal v Australians, J'burg, 1949/50.
100 WKTS (1) 102 @ 24.97 in 1947.
Retired in 1951 because of knee injury sustained during war service in Western Desert. Brother E. A. B. Rowan (S Africa).

ROWAN, Eric Alfred Burchell
——RHB——

Born Johannesburg, S Africa, 20 July 1909. Educ Jeppe HS, Johannesburg. Debut 1929/30. *Wisden* 1952.
S AFRICA DOMESTIC Transvaal 1929/30–1953/54, Eastern Province 1945/46 (capt).
SOUTH AFRICA (26) 1935–51. E 1938/39 (4), 1948/49 (4); A 1935/36 (3), 1949/50 (5). *E 1935 (5), 1951 (5).*
HST 236 SA v E, Headingley, 1951 (adding 198 for 2nd wkt with C. B. van Ryneveld, S Africa Test record). HS 306* Transvaal v Natal, J'burg, 1939/40.
BB 3–11 E Province v OFS, Bloemfontein, 1945/46.
RECORD HS (above) highest-ever inns in fc cricket in S Africa. Added 342 for 4th wkt with P. J. M. Gibb, Transvaal v NE Transvaal, J'burg, 1952/53, S African fc record.
1000 RUNS (2) 1948 @ 44.27 in 1935.
Director Transvaal Cricket Council 1982/83. Brother A. M. B. Rowan (S Africa).

ROWE, Charles James Castell
——RHB, OB——

Born Hong Kong, 27 Nov 1951. Educ King's S, Canterbury. Debut 1974.
KENT (122) 1974–81. Cap 1977.
GLAMORGAN (53) 1982–. Cap 1983.
HS 147* Kent v Sussex, Canterbury, 1979.
BB 6–46 Kent v Derbys, Dover, 1976.
1000 RUNS (2) 1071 @ 32.45 in 1982.

ROWE, Edmund John
——RHB, WK——

Born Netherfield, Notts, 21 July 1920. Debut 1949. *P.*
NOTTINGHAMSHIRE (103) 1949–57. Cap 1954.
HS 16 Notts v Kent, Blackheath, 1955.
Fc umpire 1971. Professional coach Ellesmere C 1969.

ROWE, Lawrence George
——RHB——

Born Kingston, Jamaica, 8 Jan 1949. Educ Jamaica Commercial Institute. Debut 1968/69.
W INDIES DOMESTIC Jamaica 1968/69–81/82. Capt 1980/81–81/82.
DERBYSHIRE (17) 1974.
WEST INDIES (30) 1971/72–1979/80. E 1973/74 (5); A 1972/73 (3); NZ 1971/72 (4); I 1975/76 (4). *E 1976 (2); A 1975/76 (6), 1979/80 (3); NZ 1979/80 (3).*

OTHER TOURS Jamaica to England 1970. W Indies to England 1973, 1980 (both curtailed because of injury). W Indies to India 1974/75 (curtailed through eye trouble).
HST 302 WI v E, Bridgetown, 1973/74. HS as above.
1000 RUNS (1 + 1) 1117 @ 79.78 in 1973/74.
RECORDS Scored 214 and 100*, WI v NZ, Kingston, 1971/72, only instance of batsman reaching hundred in each inns of Test debut; aggregate of 314 runs most for a first Test appearance; one of only four players to score double-century and century in same Test. Aggregate of 1117 runs, in 1973/74, record for a W Indian in W Indies fc season.
Scored centuries in four successive fc inns, in 1971/72.
World Series Cricket (Kerry Packer) 1977/78–78/79. Barred from W Indian cricket for touring S Africa 1982/83, 1983/84 (W Indies XI, capt).

ROWE, Leonard Charles
——RHB——

Born Northampton, 23 Jan 1938. Educ Northampton GS; Lincoln C, Oxford. Debut 1958.
OXFORD UNIVERSITY (5) 1958.
HS 35 Oxford U v Derbys, The Parks, 1958.
Durham County 1963–66. Clubs: Northampton GSOB, Durham City. Rugby: Northampton.

ROY, Pankaj Khirod
——RHB——

Born Calcutta, India, 31 May 1928. Educ Sarada Charan Aryan Institution, Calcutta; Vidhyasagar C; Calcutta U. Debut 1946/47.
INDIA DOMESTIC Bengal 1946/47–67/68.
INDIA (43) 1951/52–60/61. E 1951/52 (5); A 1956/57 (3), 1959/60 (5); WI 1958/59 (5); NZ 1955/56 (3); P 1952/53 (3), 1960/61 (1). *E 1952 (4), 1959 (5); WI 1952/53 (4); P 1954/55 (5).* Capt 1.
OTHER TOUR India to Ceylon 1956/57.
HST 173 I v NZ, Madras, 1955/56. HS 202* Bengal v Orissa, Cuttack, 1963/64.
BB 5–53 Indians v Som, Taunton, 1952.
1000 RUNS (1) 1207 @ 28.73 in 1959.
RECORD During HST (above) added 413 for 1st wkt with M. H. Mankad, world Test record.
Scored century (112* Bengal v United Provinces, Calcutta, 1946/47) on fc debut, as his son, P. P. Roy, was to do in

1978/79. Scored centuries in four successive fc inns, in 1962/63.
Club: Blackpool. Son P. P. Roy (India), nephew A. Roy (India).

ROY, Pranab Pankaj
————————RHB, RM————————

Born Calcutta, India, 10 Feb 1957. Debut 1978/79.
INDIA DOMESTIC Bengal 1978/79–.
INDIA (2) E 1981/82.
TOUR India to England 1982.
HST 60* I v E, Madras, 1981/82. HS 206* Bengal v Assam, Calcutta, 1983/84.
Scored century (105, Bengal v Assam, Dibrugarh, 1978/79) on fc debut, as his father, P. K. Roy, had done in 1946/47.
Father P. K. Roy (India); cousin A. Roy (India).

ROYNON, Gavin Devonald
————————RHB, LB————————

Born Sutton, Surrey, 26 Apr 1936. Educ Charterhouse; Worcester C, Oxford. Debut 1958.
OXFORD UNIVERSITY (9) 1958.
HS 58 Oxford U v M'sex, The Parks, 1958.
Oxfordshire 1954–58. Squash: Blue (capt).

RUDD, Clifford Robin David
————————RHB————————

Born Kenilworth, Cape Province, S Africa, 25 Mar 1929. Educ Eton; Trinity C, Oxford. Debut 1949.
OXFORD UNIVERSITY (15) 1949–50 (Blue 1949).
FREE FORESTERS (4) 1950–52.
MCC (2) 1950–60.
TOUR MCC to Canada 1951.
HS 70 MCC v Ireland, Dublin, 1950.
M'sex 2nd XI. Son P. S. B. Rudd (Griqualand West).

RUDGE, Lloyd Maurice
————————RHB, RFM————————

Born Walsall, Staffordshire, 11 Feb 1934. Debut 1952.
WORCESTERSHIRE (1) 1952.
HS 1 Worcs v Combined Services, Worcester, 1952.

RUMBOLD, Jack Seddon
————————RHB————————

Born N Zealand, 5 Mar 1920.
Educ St Andrew's C, N Zealand; Brasenose C, Oxford. Debut 1946.

OXFORD UNIVERSITY (7) 1946–47 (Blue 1946).
HS 25 Oxford U v M'sex, The Parks, 1946.

RUMSEY, Frederick Edward
————————RHB, LFM————————

Born Stepney, London, 4 Dec 1935. Educ Coopers' Co S, London. Debut 1960. *P.*
WORCESTERSHIRE (13) 1960–62.
SOMERSET (153) 1963–68. Cap 1963.
DERBYSHIRE (1) 1970. Cap 1973.
ENGLAND (5) 1964–65. A 1964 (1); SA 1965 (1); NZ 1965 (3).
HST 21* E v NZ, Edgbaston, 1965. HS 45 Som v Sussex, Weston-super-Mare, 1967.
BBT 4–25 E v NZ, Lord's, 1965. BB 8–26 Som v Hants, Bath, 1965.
100 WKTS (3) 119 @ 16.18 in 1965.
Played largely limited-overs matches for Derbys. Former Derbys PRO (from 1969). Clubs: Wanstead, Kidderminster.

RUSHMERE, Colin George
————————RHB, RFM————————

Born Port Elizabeth, S Africa, 16 Apr 1937. Educ Grey HS, Port Elizabeth; Stellenbosch U; Rhodes U. Debut 1956/57.
S AFRICA DOMESTIC Eastern Province 1956/57–65/66, Western Province 1957/58.
TOUR S African Fezelas to England 1961.
HS 153 E Province v W Province, Cape Town, 1962/63.
BB 4–29 S African Fezelas v Essex, Chelmsford, 1961.

RUSHWORTH, William Robert
————————FM————————

Born Dulwich, London, 4 Nov 1914. Died Bedford, 19 Jan 1966. Educ Alleyn's. Debut 1946.
SURREY (1) 1946.
No runs.

RUSSELL, David Francis
————————RHB, OB————————

Born Ashtead, Surrey, 29 Oct 1936. Educ St John's, Leatherhead; St Peter's Hall, Oxford. Debut 1959.
OXFORD UNIVERSITY (5) 1959.
HS 22 Oxford U v Essex, The Parks, 1959.
BB 3–53 Oxford U v Free Foresters, The Parks, 1959.

RUSSELL, David Paul
————————RHB, RM————————

Born St Helens, Lancs, 4 June 1951.
Educ West Park GS; St John's C, Cambridge. Debut 1974.
CAMBRIDGE UNIVERSITY (16) 1974–75 (Blue 1974–75).
HS 56* Cambridge U v Kent, Fenner's, 1974.
BB 3–60 Cambridge U v Warwicks, Fenner's, 1975.
Cambridgeshire 1976. Club: Camden.

RUSSELL, Philip Edgar
————————RHB, RM/OB————————

Born Ilkeston, Derbys, 9 May 1944. Educ Ilkeston GS. Debut 1965.
DERBYSHIRE (167) 1965–79. Cap 1975.
HS 72 Derbys v Glam, Swansea, 1970.
BB 7–46 Derbys v Yorks, Dore, Sheffield, 1976.
Derbys coach 1977–.

RUSSELL, Robert Charles
————————LHB, WK————————

Born Stroud, Glos, 15 Aug 1963. Educ Archway CS; Bristol Polytechnic. Debut 1981.
GLOUCESTERSHIRE (50) 1981–.
HS 64* Glos v Worcs, Bristol, 1983.

RUSSELL, Sidney Edward James
————————RHB, RM————————

Born Feltham, M'sex, 4 Oct 1937. Educ Ashford GS. Debut 1960. *P.*
MIDDLESEX (61) 1960–64.
GLOUCESTERSHIRE (80) 1965–68. Cap 1965.
HS 130 M'sex v Glos, Lord's, 1962.
1000 RUNS (2) 1256 @ 25.12 in 1965.
Scored 1119 runs @ 31.08 in debut season, 1960.
Clubs: East Molesey, Almondsbury.
Soccer: Brentford.

RUSSELL, Stephen George
————————RHB, RFM————————

Born Sutton, Surrey, 13 Mar 1945. Educ Tiffin S, Kingston-upon-Thames; Trinity Hall, Cambridge. Debut 1965.
CAMBRIDGE UNIVERSITY (34) 1965–67 (Blue 1965–67). Capt 1967.
SURREY (1) 1967.
HS 21* Cambridge U v MCC, Lord's, 1966.
BB 5–41 Cambridge U v Scotland, Fenner's, 1966.
Club: Sutton (Surrey).

RUSSELL, William *Eric*
————RHB, RM————

Born Dumbarton, Scotland, 3 July 1936. Educ Atholl House S, Pinner, M'sex. Debut 1956. *P.*
MIDDLESEX (400) 1956–72. Cap 1959. Benefit (£8005) 1969.
ENGLAND (10) 1961/62–67. SA 1965 (1); WI 1966 (2); P 1967 (1). *A 1965/66 (1); NZ 1965/66 (3); I 1961/62 (1); P 1961/62 (1).*
OTHER TOUR MCC to N Zealand 1960/61.
HST 70 E v SA, Oval, 1965. HS 193 M'sex v Hants, Bournemouth, 1964.
BB 3–20 MCC v President's XI, Wellington, N Zealand, 1965/66.
1000 RUNS (13) 2342 @ 45.92 in 1964. 2000 runs (3).
Players v Gentlemen (3) 1960–61. Berkshire 1976–77.

RUSSOM, Neil
————RHB, RMF————

Born Finchley, London, 3 Dec 1958. Educ Huish's GS, Taunton; St Catharine's C, Cambridge. Debut 1979.
CAMBRIDGE UNIVERSITY (20) 1979–81 (Blue 1980–81).
SOMERSET (4) 1980–83.
HS 79* Cambridge U v Northants, Fenner's, 1980.
BB 4–84 Cambridge U v Leics, Fenner's, 1980.

RUTHERFORD, Ian Alexander
————RHB, RM/OB————

Born Dunedin, N Zealand, 30 June 1957. Educ King's HS, Dunedin. Debut 1974/75.
N ZEALAND DOMESTIC Otago (63) 1974/75–.
WORCESTERSHIRE (2) 1976.
HS 222 Otago v Central Districts, New Plymouth, 1978/79.

RUTHERFORD, John Robert Fulton
————RHB, RM————

Born Hawkhurst, Kent, 9 Aug 1935. Educ Nottingham HS; Queen's C, Cambridge. Debut 1957.
CAMBRIDGE UNIVERSITY (11) 1957–58.
HS 37* Cambridge U v Sussex, Fenner's, 1958.
BB 3–53 Cambridge U v Worcs, Fenner's, 1957.

RUTHERFORD, John Walter
————RHB, RM————

Born Bungulluping, W Australia, 24 Sept 1929. Debut 1952/53.
AUSTRALIA DOMESTIC Western Australia (38) 1952/53–60/61.
AUSTRALIA (1) *I 1956/57.*
OTHER TOUR Australia to England 1956.
HST 30 A v I, Bombay, 1956/57. HS 167 W Australia v S Australia, Adelaide, 1954/55.

BB 3–12 W Australia v MCC, Perth, 1958/59.
Career curtailed after he suffered a stroke while captaining W Australia v W Indians, Perth, 1960/61.

RUTTER, Allen Edward Henry (Claude)
————RHB————

Born Bromley, Kent, 24 Dec 1928. Educ Monkton Combe S, Bath; Dauntsey's S, Devizes; Queen's C, Cambridge. Debut 1953.
CAMBRIDGE UNIVERSITY (2) 1953.
FREE FORESTERS (1) 1955.
HS 45 Free Foresters v Cambridge U, Fenner's, 1955.
Wiltshire 1948–55, Norfolk 1962–65. Clubs: MCC, Free Foresters, The Mote, Bath, Dereham, Compton House (Dorset). Ordained clergyman.

RYAN, Melville
————RHB, RFM————

Born Huddersfield, Yorks, 23 June 1933. Debut 1954. *P.*
YORKSHIRE (150) 1954–65. Cap 1962.
HS 26* Yorks v Worcs, Worcester, 1963 and 26 v Essex, Clacton, 1963.
BB 7–45 Yorks v Warwicks, Edgbaston, 1958.
Member Yorks committee. Clubs: Bradford, Baildon Green, David Brown Tractors.

S

SABINE, Peter Noel Barrington
LHB, LBG

Born Cookham Dean, Berkshire, 29 Sept 1941. Educ Marlborough; Hertford C, Oxford. Debut 1962.
OXFORD UNIVERSITY (12) 1962–63 (Blue 1963).
HS 56 Oxford U v Surrey, Oval, 1963.
BB 4–51 Oxford U v MCC, Lord's, 1963.

SADIQ MOHAMMED
LHB, RLBG

Born Junagadh, India, 5 May 1945. Educ Karachi U. Debut 1959/60 (Fazal Mahmood's XI; at age of 14 yrs 9 months).
PAKISTAN DOMESTIC Karachi Schools, Karachi, Pakistan International Airlines, United Bank, 1959/60–.
D. H. ROBINS' XI (1) 1969.
ESSEX (1) 1970.
GLOUCESTERSHIRE (193) 1972–82. Cap 1973. Benefit 1982.
D. B. CLOSE'S XI (1) 1983.
AUSTRALIA DOMESTIC Tasmania (2) 1974/75.
PAKISTAN (41) 1969/70–80/81. E 1972/73 (3), 1977/78 (2); WI 1974/75 (1); 1980/81 (3); NZ 1969/70 (3), 1976/77 (3); I 1978/79 (1). *E 1971 (3), 1974 (3), 1978 (3); A 1972/73 (3), 1976/77 (2); WI 1976/77 (5); NZ 1972/73 (3); I 1979/80 (3).*
OTHER TOURS Pakistan Eaglets to England 1963. PIA to E Africa 1964/65.
HST 166 P v NZ, Wellington, 1972/73.
HS 203 Glos v Sri Lankans, Bristol, 1981.
BB 7–34 United Bank v Universities, Peshawar, 1978/79.
1000 RUNS (7 + 2) 1759 @ 47.54 in 1976.
Scored centuries in four successive fc inns in 1976, all for Glos.
Brothers Hanif, Mushtaq, Wazir (all Pakistan) and Raees Mohammed (Karachi); nephews Shoaib (Pakistan), Shahid and Asif Mohammed (both PIA).

SAEED AHMED
RHB, OB

Born Jullundur, India, 1 Oct 1937. Educ Moslem HS, Lahore; Punjab U. Debut 1954/55.
PAKISTAN DOMESTIC Punjab, Railways, Universities, Punjab University, Lahore, Pakistan International Airlines, Karachi, Public Works Department, Sind, 1954/55–71/72.
MCC (1) 1966.
PAKISTAN (41) 1957/58–72/73. E 1961/62 (3), 1968/69 (3); A 1959/60 (3), 1964/65 (1); WI 1958/59 (3); NZ 1964/65 (3). *E 1962 (5), 1967 (3), 1971 (1); A 1964/65 (1), 1972/73 (2); WI 1957/58 (5); NZ 1964/65 (3); I 1960/61 (5). Capt 3.*
OTHER TOURS International XI to Rhodesia 1961/62. Rest of World in England 1968.
HST 172 P v NZ, Karachi, 1964/65. HS 203* Karachi Blues v PWD, Karachi, 1970/71.
BBT 4–64 P v E, Lahore, 1968/69. BB 8–41 PWD v Kalat, Karachi, 1969/70.
1000 RUNS (1 + 2) 1294 @ 34.97 in 1962.
Scored centuries in four successive fc inns in 1961/62. Returned home early from tour to Australasia 1972/73 because of dispute with the team management.
Club: Nelson. Half-brother Younis Ahmed (Surrey, Worcs, Pakistan).

SAGGERS, Ronald Arthur
RHB, WK

Born Sydenham, NSW, Australia, 15 May 1917. Debut 1939/40.
AUSTRALIA DOMESTIC New South Wales (40) 1939/40–50/51.
AUSTRALIA (6) 1948–49/50. E 1948 (1); *SA 1949/50 (5).*
HST 14 A v SA, J'burg, 1949/50. HS 104* Australians v Essex, Southend, 1948.
Made 7 dismissals in inns (7 ct) and 10 in match (9 ct, 1 st), NSW v Combined XI, Brisbane, 1940/41.
Club: Marrickville.

SAINSBURY, Gary Edward
RHB, LFM

Born Wanstead, East London, 17 Jan 1958. Educ Beal GS; Bath U. Debut 1979.

ESSEX (3) 1979–80.
GLOUCESTERSHIRE (45) 1983–.
HS 13 Glos v Glam, Cheltenham, 1983.
BB 6–66 Glos v Worcs, Worcester, 1983.

SAINSBURY, John Popham
RHB, LM

Born Axbridge, Som, 8 Jan 1927. Educ Clifton. Debut 1951.
SOMERSET (2) 1951.
HS 16 Som v Sussex, Weston-super-Mare, 1951.
Dismissed for a duck in each of first three fc inns.
Club: Clifton. Rugby: Weston-super-Mare and Somerset.

SAINSBURY, Peter James
RHB, SLA

Born Chandler's Ford, Hants, 13 June 1934. Educ Bitterne Sec S. Debut 1954. *P. Wisden* 1974.
HAMPSHIRE (593) 1954–76. Cap 1955. Benefit (£6035) 1965.
TOURS MCC A to Pakistan 1955/56. International XI to Rhodesia 1974/75.
HS 163 Hants v Oxford U, The Parks, 1962.
BB 8–76 Hants v Glos, Portsmouth, 1971.
1000 RUNS (6) 1533 @ 30.05 in 1961.
100 WKTS (2) 107 @ 17.51 in 1971.
Took 102 wkts @ 18.50 in 1955, first full season. Missed double by 41 runs in 1971. Took 56 catches in 1957 and 617 catches in career.
Players v Gentlemen (3) 1958–60. D. H. Robins' XI to W Indies 1974/75.

SALAH-UD-DIN Mulla
RHB, OB

Born Aligarh, India, 14 Feb 1947. Debut 1964/65.
PAKISTAN DOMESTIC Karachi, Pakistan International Airlines, 1964/65–79/80.
PAKISTAN (5) 1964/65–69/70. E 1968/69 (1); NZ 1964/65 (3), 1969/70 (1).
OTHER TOURS Pakistan Eaglets to England 1963. Pakistan to England 1967.
HST 34* P v NZ, Rawalpindi, 1964/65.

HS 256 Karachi v E Pakistan, Karachi, 1968/69 (scored 102* in 2nd inns of same match).
BBT 2–36 P v NZ, Rawalpindi, 1964/65.
BB 6–76 PIA v Karachi A, Karachi, 1977/78.
RECORD During HS (above) added 353 for 6th wkt with Zaheer Abbas, Pakistan fc record.
Club: Ayr.

SALE, Richard
————LHB————

Born Shrewsbury, Shropshire, 4 Oct 1919. Educ Repton; Oriel C, Oxford. Debut 1939.
OXFORD UNIVERSITY (21) 1939, 1946 (Blue 1939, 1946).
WARWICKSHIRE (19) 1939–46. Cap 1946.
DERBYSHIRE (24) 1949–54. Cap 1951.
HS 157 Warwicks v Indians, Edgbaston, 1946.
1000 RUNS (1) 1047 @ 34.90 in 1946.
Soccer: Blue. Former headmaster at Repton. Father R. Sale snr (Derbys).

SALEEM ALTAF Bokhari
————RHB, RFM————

Born Lahore, India, 19 Apr 1944. Educ St Anthony's C, Lahore; Punjab U. Debut 1963/64.
PAKISTAN DOMESTIC Lahore, Punjab University, Pakistan International Airlines, 1963/64–78/79.
PAKISTAN (21) 1967–78/79. E 1972/73 (3); NZ 1969/70 (2); I 1978/79 (1). E 1967 (2), 1971 (2); A 1972/73 (3), 1976/77 (3); WI 1976/77 (3); NZ 1972/73 (3).
HST 53* P v NZ, Auckland, 1972/73. HS 111 PIA v Sind, Karachi, 1976/77.
BBT 4–11 P v E, Headingley, 1971. BB 7–69 (11–155 match) Punjab U v Lahore Greens, Lahore, 1965/66.
Now cricket commentator in Pakistan.

SALEEM MALIK
————RHB, OB/RM————

Born Lahore, Pakistan, 16 Apr 1963. Debut 1978/79.
PAKISTAN DOMESTIC Lahore, Habib Bank, 1978/79–.
PAKISTAN (16) 1981/82–83/84. E 1983/84 (3); I 1982/83 (6); SL 1981/82 (2). A 1983/84 (3); I 1983/84 (2).
TOURS Pakistan to Australia 1981/82. Pakistan to England 1982.
HST 107 P v I, Faisalabad, 1982/83. HS 132 Habib Bank v HBFC, Lahore, 1983/84.
BB 5–36 same match.
RECORD Scored 100* in 2nd inns of first

Test, P v SL, Karachi, 1981/82, at age of 18 yrs 328 days, youngest-ever player to score century on Test debut.

SALEEM YOUSUF
————RHB, WK————

Born Karachi, Pakistan, 7 Dec 1959. Debut 1978/79.
PAKISTAN DOMESTIC Sind, Karachi, Industrial Development Bank of Pakistan, Allied Bank, 1978/79–.
PAKISTAN (1) SL 1981/82.
TOUR Pakistan to England 1982.
HST 4 P v SL, Karachi, 1981/82. HS 145* Allied Bank v Rawalpindi, Rawalpindi, 1982/83.

SALIM-UD-DIN
————RHB————

Born Ajmer, India, 28 Aug 1938. Debut 1954/55.
PAKISTAN DOMESTIC Combined Schools, Karachi, 1954/55–62/63.
TOUR Pakistan Eaglets to England 1963.
HS 137 Karachi C v Sind A, Karachi, 1957/58.
Brother Alim-ud-Din (Pakistan).

SAMARANAYAKE, Alutge Don Anusha
————RHB, RFM————

Born Colombo, Ceylon, 25 Feb 1962. Debut 1984.
SRI LANKA to England (5) 1984.
HS 9* Sri Lankans v Sussex, Hove, 1984.
BB 4–142 Sri Lankans v Kent, Canterbury, 1984.

SANDERS, Ian Edward Wakefield
————RHB, RMF————

Born Edinburgh, Scotland, 26 Feb 1961. Educ Cheltenham C, Bristol U; St John's C, Cambridge. Debut 1984.
CAMBRIDGE UNIVERSITY (1) 1984.
HS 9 Cambridge U v Leics, Fenner's, 1984.
BB 2–78 same match.

SANDERSON, John Frederick Waley
————RHB, RM————

Born Highgate, London, 10 Sept 1954. Educ Westminster S; New C, Oxford. Debut 1979.
OXFORD UNIVERSITY (6) 1979–80 (Blue 1980).

HS 9 Oxford U v Lancs, The Parks, 1980.
BB 6–67 Oxford U v M'sex, The Parks, 1980.

SANDS, Jeremy Nigel
————RHB————

Born Carshalton, Surrey, 9 Jan 1944. Educ Edinburgh Academy; Edinburgh U. Debut 1965.
SCOTLAND (2) 1965.
MCC (2) 1965–67.
HS 17 Scotland v N Zealanders, Glasgow, 1965.
Club: Edinburgh Academicals.

SARDESAI, Dilip Naryan
————RHB————

Born Margao, Goa, India, 8 Aug 1939. Educ Bombay U. Debut 1960/61.
INDIA DOMESTIC Universities 1960/61, Bombay 1960/61–72/73.
INDIA (30) 1961/62–72/73. E 1961/62 (1), 1963/64 (5), 1972/73 (1); A 1964/65 (3), 1969/70 (1); WI 1966/67 (2); NZ 1964/65 (3). E 1967 (1), 1971 (3); A 1967/68 (2); WI 1961/62 (3), 1970/71 (5).
OTHER TOUR Associated Cement Company to Pakistan 1961/62.
HST 212 I v WI, Kingston, 1970/71. HS 222 ACC XI v Indian Starlets XI, Hyderabad, 1964/65.
BB 2–15 Bombay v Rajasthan, Bombay, 1966/67.
1000 RUNS (0 + 4) 1428 @ 62.08 in 1964/65.
RECORDS Added 193* for 6th wkt with Hanumant Singh, I v NZ, Bombay, 1964/65 and 186 for 7th wkt with E. D. Solkar, I v WI, Bridgetown, 1970/71, both India Test records.

SARFRAZ NAWAZ, Malik
————RHB, RFM————

Born Lahore, Pakistan, 1 Dec 1948. Educ Government C, Lahore; Punjab U. Debut 1967/68.
PAKISTAN DOMESTIC Lahore, Punjab University, Punjab, Railways, United Bank, Lahore City, 1967/68–.
NORTHAMPTONSHIRE (151) 1969–82. Cap 1975.
PAKISTAN (55) 1968/69–83/84. E 1968/69 (1), 1972/73 (2), 1977/78 (2), 1983/84 (3); A 1979/80 (3); WI 1974/75 (2), 1980/81 (2); NZ 1976/77 (3); I 1978/79 (3), 1982/83 (6). E 1974 (3), 1978 (2), 1982 (1); A 1972/73 (2), 1976/77 (2), 1978/79 (2), 1981/82 (3), 1983/84 (3); WI 1976/77 (4); NZ 1972/73 (3), 1978/79 (3).

OTHER TOURS Pakistan to England 1971 (co-opted for 3 matches). Pakistan to Sri Lanka 1975/76.
HST 90 P v E, Lahore, 1983/84. HS as above and 90 Northants v Sri Lankans, Northampton, 1981.
BBT 9–86 (11–125 match) P v A, Melbourne, 1978/79. BB as above.
100 WKTS (1) 101 @ 20.30 in 1975.
RECORD BB (above) best inns return in a Test for Pakistan and during it took seven wkts for one run in 33 balls.
Club: Nelson.

SARGENT, Murray Alfred James
──────────RHB, LB──────────

Born Adelaide, S Australia, 23 Aug 1928. Debut 1951. *P.*
LEICESTERSHIRE (13) 1951–52.
AUSTRALIA DOMESTIC South Australia (9) 1960/61.
HS 164 S Australia v Queensland, Brisbane, 1960/61.
BB 2–18 S Australia v Queensland, Adelaide, 1960/61.

SARWATE, Chandrasekhar Trimbak Rao (Chandu)
──────────RHB, LB/OB──────────

Born Saugor, Vidarbha, India, 22 June 1920. Educ City C, Nagpur; Nagpur U. Debut 1936/37.
INDIA DOMESTIC Central Provinces and Berar 1936/37, Maharashtra 1940/41–42/43, Bombay Hindus 1941/42–44/45, Bombay 1943/44, Holkar 1944/45–54/55, Madhya Bharat 1955/56–56/57 (capt), Madhya Pradesh 1958/59–67/68 (capt), Vidarbha 1968/69.
INDIA (9) 1946–51/52. E 1951/52 (1); WI 1948/49 (2). *E 1946 (1); A 1947/48 (5).*
OTHER TOURS Indians to Ceylon 1944/45. Holkar to Ceylon 1947/48. India to England 1952.
HST 37 I v WI, Delhi, 1948/49. HS 246 Holkar v Bengal, Calcutta, 1950/51.
BB 9–61 Holkar v Mysore, Indore, 1945/46 (also scored 101 in only inns).
RECORDS Added 236 for 8th wkt with R. P. Singh, Holkar v Delhi and District, Delhi, 1949/50, Indian fc record; added 249 for 10th wkt with S. N. Banerjee, Indians v Surrey, Oval, 1946, Indian fc record and record for fc cricket in England; only instance of numbers 10 and 11 both making centuries in same inns.

SAUNDERS, Christopher Joseph
──────────RHB, WK──────────

Born Worthing, Sussex, 7 May 1940. Educ Lancing; Cambridge U; Wadham C, Oxford. Debut 1962.

CAMBRIDGE UNIVERSITY (8) 1962–63.
OXFORD UNIVERSITY (4) 1964 (Blue 1964).
HS 21 Cambridge U v Essex, Fenner's, 1963.

SAUNDERS, John Graham
──────────RHB, OB──────────

Born S Africa, 30 Nov 1936. Educ Worcester C, Oxford. Debut 1966.
OXFORD UNIVERSITY (2) 1966.
HS 47* Oxford U v Lancs, The Parks, 1966.
BB 5–50 (10–102 match) Oxford U v Lancs, The Parks, 1966 (fc debut).

SAUNDERS, Martyn
──────────RHB, RFM──────────

Born Worcester, 16 May 1958. Educ Worcester Technical C. Debut 1980.
WORCESTERSHIRE (3) 1980.
HS 12 Worcs v Notts, Worcester, 1980.
BB 3–47 Worcs v Kent, Worcester, 1980.

SAUNDERS, Philip Frederick
──────────RHB, LB──────────

Born Adelaide, S Australia, 28 Apr 1929. Debut 1951. *P.*
LEICESTERSHIRE (9) 1951–52.
HS 30 Leics v Kent, Folkestone, 1952.
BB 3–57 Leics v Glam, Neath, 1952.

SAVAGE, John Scholes
──────────RHB, OB──────────

Born Ramsbottom, Lancs, 3 Mar 1929. Debut 1953. *P.*
LEICESTERSHIRE (281) 1953–66. Cap 1958. Testimonial (£2500) 1966.
LANCASHIRE (58) 1967–69. Cap 1967.
HS 33 Leics v Yorks, Leicester, 1957.
BB 8–50 Leics v Glos, Gloucester, 1957. Returned 8–62 (14–99 match) Leics v Northants, Northampton, 1958.
100 WKTS (3) 122 @ 18.93 in 1961.
Players v Gentlemen (2) 1958–61. Lancs coach 1970–82; joint-coach 1983–. Club: Ramsbottom.

SAVAGE, Richard Le Quesne
──────────RHB, RM/OB──────────

Born Waterloo, London, 10 Dec 1955. Educ Marlborough; Pembroke C, Oxford. Debut 1976.
OXFORD UNIVERSITY (20) 1976–78 (Blue 1976–78).
WARWICKSHIRE (23) 1976–79.

HS 22* Oxford U v Worcs, The Parks, 1977.
BB 7–50 Warwicks v Glam, Nuneaton, 1977.

SAVILL, Leslie Austin
──────────RHB──────────

Born Brentwood, Essex, 30 June 1935. Educ Norlington Sec S, Leyton. Debut 1953. *P.*
ESSEX (125) 1953–61. Cap 1959.
HS 115 Essex v Northants, Northampton, 1959.
1000 RUNS (1) 1197 @ 32.35 in 1959.
Devon 1964. Club: Barclays Bank.

SAVILLE, Graham John
──────────RHB, LBG──────────

Born Leytonstone, London, 5 Feb 1944. Educ George Monoux GS, Walthamstow. Debut 1963.
ESSEX (124) 1963–74. Cap 1970.
HS 126* Essex v Glam, Swansea, 1972.
BB 2–30 Essex v Kent, Chelmsford, 1971.
1000 RUNS (1) 1133 @ 29.81 in 1970.
Retired 1973 to become Essex assistant-secretary. Norfolk 1967–69. Cousin G. A. Gooch (Essex, England).

SAXELBY, Kevin
──────────RHB, RMF──────────

Born Worksop, Notts, 23 Feb 1959. Educ Magnus GS, Newark. Debut 1978.
NOTTINGHAMSHIRE (63) 1978–. Cap 1984.
HS 59* Notts v Derbys, Chesterfield, 1982.
BB 5–43 Notts v M'sex, Lord's, 1984.
Club: Worksop.

SAXENA, Ramesh Chand
──────────RHB, LB──────────

Born Delhi, India, 20 Sept 1944. Debut 1960/61.
INDIA DOMESTIC Delhi 1960/61–65/66, Bihar 1966/67–81/82 (capt 1970/71, 1972/73, 1979/80–80/81).
INDIA (1) *E 1967.*
OTHER TOURS State Bank to Ceylon 1966/67. India to E Africa 1967. India to Australasia 1967/68.
HST 16 I v E, Lord's, 1967. HS 202* Bihar v Assam, Dhanbad, 1969/70.
BB 4–24 Indian Starlets v ACC XI, Hyderabad, 1964/65.
Scored century in 1st inns (2nd match) in fc cricket, 113* Delhi v S Punjab, Delhi, 1960/61.

SAYER, David Michael
——RHB, RFM——

Born Romford, Essex, 19 Sept 1936.
Educ Maidstone GS; Brasenose C, Oxford. Debut 1955.
KENT (154) 1955–76. Cap 1962. Joint benefit (with A. Brown) 1971.
OXFORD UNIVERSITY (39) 1958–60 (Blue 1958–60).
TOUR MCC to N Zealand 1960/61.
HS 62 Oxford U v Notts, The Parks, 1959.
BB 7–37 Kent v Leics, Leicester, 1958.
Gentlemen v Players (2) 1959–60. Club: The Mote.

SAYER, John Druce
——RHB, SLA——

Born Hong Kong, 29 Oct 1920. Educ Shrewsbury. Debut 1950.
COMBINED SERVICES (4) 1950–52.
HS 49 Combined Services v Worcs, Worcester, 1951.
BB 4–38 Combined Services v Worcs, Worcester, 1950.
Royal Navy. RN Lt-Commander.

SAYERS, Denis
——RHB, RM——

Born St Pancras, London, 17 Mar 1934.
Educ Haverstock Hill GS. Debut 1967.
ESSEX (1) 1967.
No runs, one wkt.
Clubs: Walthamstow, Sutton.

SCHEPENS, Martin
——RHB, LB——

Born Barrow-upon-Soar, Leics, 12 Aug 1955. Educ Rawlins GS, Quorn. Debut 1973.
LEICESTERSHIRE (19) 1973–80.
HS 57 Leics v Glam, Leicester, 1979.
Club: West Bromwich Dartmouth.

SCHOFIELD, Dennis
——RHB, RM——

Born Holmfirth, Yorks, 9 Oct 1947.
Debut 1970.
YORKSHIRE (3) 1970–74.
HS 6* Yorks v Notts, Worksop, 1974.
BB 5–42 same match.
Clubs: Castleton Moor, Lightcliffe, Holmfirth, Broad Oak.

SCHOLEY, John *Colin*
——RHB, WK——

Born Leeds, Yorks, 28 Sept 1930. Debut 1952. *P.*

WORCESTERSHIRE (10) 1952–53.
HS 16 Worcs v Kent, Worcester, 1952.
Club: Leeds.

SCOTLAND, Kenneth James Forbes
——RHB——

Born Edinburgh, Scotland, 29 Aug 1936. Educ Heriot's; Trinity C, Cambridge. Debut 1958.
SCOTLAND (1) 1958.
No runs; did not bowl.
Club: Heriot's FP. Rugby: Cambridge U, Heriot's FP, Leicester, Scotland (27 caps).

SCOTT, Andrew Archibald Steele
——RHB——

Born Liberton, Midlothian, Scotland, 26 Jan 1918. Educ Sedbergh. Debut 1947.
SCOTLAND (1) 1947.
HS 12 Scotland v Ireland, Cork, 1947.
Club: Grange.

SCOTT, Christopher John
——LHB, WK——

Born Swinton, Lancs, 16 Sept 1959.
Educ Eccles GS. Debut 1977.
LANCASHIRE (46) 1977–82.
HS 27* Lancs v Notts, Trent Bridge, 1981.
Club: Egerton.

SCOTT, Christopher Wilmot
——RHB, WK——

Born Thorpe-on-the-Hill, Lincolnshire, 23 Jan 1964. Educ Robert Pattinson CS. Debut 1981.
NOTTINGHAMSHIRE (7) 1981–.
HS 78 Notts v Cambridge U, The Parks, 1983.

SCOTT, Colin James
——RHB, RMF/OB——

Born Syston Common, Glos, 1 May 1919. Debut 1938. *P.*
GLOUCESTERSHIRE (235) 1938–54. Cap 1939. Testimonial (£1140) 1956.
HS 90 Glos v Surrey, Oval, 1947.
BB 8–90 Glos v Surrey, Oval, 1953.
100 WKTS (2) 121 @ 22.89 in 1939.
Club: Downend.

SCOTT, Edward Keith
——RHB, LB——

Born Truro, Cornwall, 14 June 1918.
Educ Clifton C; Lincoln C, Oxford. Debut 1937.
GLOUCESTERSHIRE (2) 1937.
OXFORD UNIVERSITY (5) 1938.
MINOR COUNTIES (1) 1949.
TOUR MCC to Canada 1951.
HS 31 Oxford U v Leics, The Parks, 1938.
BB 2–21 Oxford U v Minor Counties, The Parks, 1938.
Cornwall 1946–54 (capt 1952). Rugby: Oxford U, Redruth, St Mary's Hospital, Harlequins, England (5 caps). Medical practitioner.

SCOTT, Gary Michael
——RHB——

Born Bulawayo, Rhodesia, 8 Mar 1960.
Educ Cranborne HS, Bulawayo. Debut 1979/80.
S AFRICA DOMESTIC Rhodesia B 1979/80.
TOUR Zimbabwe to England 1982.
HS 21 Rhodesia B v Border, Triangle, 1979/80.

SCOTT, Hugh *Wilson*
——RHB, RM——

Born Belfast, Ireland, 18 Dec 1927.
Educ Belfast Technical HS. Debut 1958.
IRELAND (1) 1958.
Did not bat, no wkts.
Club: Cliftonville.

SCOTT, Malcolm Ernest
——RHB, SLA——

Born South Shields, Co Durham, 8 May 1936. Debut 1958. *P.*
COMBINED SERVICES (2) 1958.
NORTHAMPTONSHIRE (183) 1959–69. Cap 1964.
HS 62 Northants v M'sex, Lord's, 1967.
BB 7–32 (13–68 match) Northants v Sussex, Hastings, 1964.
100 WKTS (1) 113 @ 19.27 in 1964.
Bowled 14 consecutive maiden overs, Northants v Cambridge U, Fenner's, 1964. Doubts about bowling action led to three-match ban at end of 1967 season.
Durham 1953–56. Clubs: South Shields, Walsall. Soccer: Newcastle United, Darlington, York City.

SCOTT, Mark Stephen
—RHB—

Born Muswell Hill, London, 10 Mar 1959. Educ Creighton CS, Muswell Hill. Debut 1981.
WORCESTERSHIRE (32) 1981–83.
HS 109 Worcs v Glos, Bristol, 1981.
Scored 968 runs @ 26.88 in first season.
Club: Stourbridge.

SCOTT, Michael David
—RHB, WK—

Born London, 14 Nov 1933. Educ Winchester; Worcester C, Oxford. Debut 1956.
OXFORD UNIVERSITY (20) 1956–57 (Blue 1957).
MCC (1) 1963.
HS 52 Oxford U v Surrey, Guildford, 1957.
Wiltshire 1959–69.

SCOTT, Verdun John
—RHB—

Born Devonport, Auckland, N Zealand, 31 July 1916. Died Devonport, Auckland, N Zealand, 2 Aug 1980. Educ Stanley Bay S. Debut 1937/38.
N ZEALAND DOMESTIC Auckland (43) 1937/38–52/53.
NEW ZEALAND (10) 1945/46–51/52. E 1946/47 (1), 1950/51 (2); A 1945/46 (1); WI 1951/52 (2). E 1949 (4).
HST 84 NZ v WI, Auckland, 1951/52. HS 204 Auckland v Otago, Dunedin, 1947/48.
BB 3–22 Auckland v Otago, Auckland, 1948/49.
1000 RUNS (1) 1572 @ 40.30 in 1949.
Scored 122 Auckland v Canterbury, Auckland, 1937/38, on fc debut.
Rugby League: Auckland, New Zealand.

SEAGER, Christopher Paul
—RHB—

Born Salisbury, Rhodesia, 5 Apr 1951. Educ Peterhouse; Jesus C, Cambridge. Debut 1971.
CAMBRIDGE UNIVERSITY (8) 1971 (Blue).
HS 23 Cambridge U v Oxford U, Lord's 1971.
Berkshire 1970.

SEAMER, John Wemyss (Jake)
—RHB—

Born Shapwick, Som, 23 June 1913. Educ Marlborough; Brasenose C, Oxford. Debut 1932.

SOMERSET (59) 1932–48. Cap. Joint capt 1948.
OXFORD UNIVERSITY (21) 1933–36 (Blue 1934–36).
FREE FORESTERS (1) 1949.
HS 194 Oxford U v Minor Counties, The Parks, 1934.
BB 2–6 Oxford U v Leics, The Parks, 1936.
Wiltshire 1956. Hockey: Blue.

SEARLE, Cyril John
—RHB, WK—

Born Battersea, London, 12 May 1921. Debut 1947.
ESSEX (1) 1947.
HS 5* Essex v Cambridge U, Fenner's, 1947.

SEATON, Geoffrey Stuart
—RHB, SLA—

Born Brighton, Sussex, 6 Mar 1926. Educ Denstone; Peterhouse C, Cambridge; Merton C, Oxford. Debut 1946.
CAMBRIDGE UNIVERSITY (5) 1946–47.
OXFORD UNIVERSITY (3) 1957.
HS 51 Cambridge U v Sussex, Fenner's, 1947.
First player to appear for both Cambridge and Oxford Universities.

SEDGLEY, John Brian
—RHB—

Born West Bromwich, Staffordshire, 17 Feb 1939. Debut 1959. P.
WORCESTERSHIRE (15) 1959–61.
HS 95 Worcs v Derbys, Derby, 1960.
Clubs: Dudley, Stourbridge, Old Hill.

SELLERS, Arthur *Brian*
—RHB—

Born Keighley, Yorks, 5 Mar 1907. Died Eldwich, nr Bingley, Yorks, 20 Feb 1981. Educ St Peter's, York. Debut 1932. *Wisden* 1940.
YORKSHIRE (334) 1932–48. Cap 1932. Capt 1933–47.
HS 204 Yorks v Cambridge U, Fenner's, 1936.
BB 2–10 Yorks v M'sex, Bradford, 1933.
1000 RUNS (3) 1143 @ 27.21 in 1938.
Led Yorks to six County Championships as official capt. Took seven catches in match, Yorks v Essex, Leyton, 1933, all on same day.
Gentlemen v Players (3) 1934–38. England Test selector 1938–46, 1949–50, 1955. Yorks committee to 1972. Club: Keighley. MCC committee 1960–70.

MCC Hon. member. Awarded MBE for services to cricket. Father A. Sellers (Yorks).

SELLERS, Reginald Hugh Durning (Rex)
—RHB, LBG—

Born Bulsar, India, 20 Aug 1940. Debut 1959/60.
AUSTRALIA DOMESTIC South Australia (39) 1959/60–66/67.
AUSTRALIA (1) *I 1964/65.*
OTHER TOUR Australia to England 1964.
HS 87 S Australia v W Australia, Perth, 1966/67.
BB 5–36 Australians v Yorkshire, Bramall Lane, Sheffield, 1964.
No runs and no wkts in only Test.

SELLS, Hugh Michael
—LHB, WK—

Born Rochford, Southend-on-Sea, 23 Mar 1922. Died Chelsea, London, 17 Jan 1978. Educ Malvern. Debut 1946.
ROYAL AIR FORCE (1) 1946.
HS 26 RAF v Worcs, Worcester, 1946.
Gold Coast 1949. Clubs: Adastrians, Free Foresters.

SELVEY, Michael Walter William
—RHB, RFM—

Born Chiswick, London, 24 Apr 1948. Educ Battersea GS; Manchester U; Emmanuel C, Cambridge. Debut 1968.
SURREY (6) 1968–71.
CAMBRIDGE UNIVERSITY (6) 1971 (Blue).
MIDDLESEX (213) 1972–82. Cap 1973. Benefit 1982.
GLAMORGAN (39) 1983–84. Cap 1983. Capt 1983–84.
S AFRICA DOMESTIC Orange Free State 1973/74.
ENGLAND (3) 1976–76/77. WI 1976 (2). *I 1976/77 (1).*
OTHER TOURS M'sex to Zimbabwe 1980/81. International XI to Pakistan 1981/82.
HST 5* E v I, Bombay, 1976/77. HS 67 M'sex XI v Zimbabwe, Bulawayo, 1980/81.
BBT 4–41 E v WI, Old Trafford, 1976.
BB 7–20 M'sex v Glos, Gloucester, 1976.
100 WKTS (1) 101 @ 19.09 in 1978.

SELWOOD, Timothy
—RHB, RM—

Born Prestatyn, N Wales, 1 Sept 1944. Educ William Ellis S, Highgate; St Luke's C, Exeter. Debut 1966.

MIDDLESEX (18) 1966–69, 1972–73.
N ZEALAND DOMESTIC Central Districts
(2) 1972/73.
HS 89 Central Districts v Pakistanis,
Wanganui, 1972/73.
Durham County, 1974. Clubs: Finchley, Darlington.

SEMMENCE, Derek John
————RHB, RM————

Born Worthing, Sussex, 20 Apr 1938.
Educ Shoreham GS. Debut 1956. *P.*
SUSSEX (35) 1956–59, 1967–68.
COMBINED SERVICES (3) 1957–58.
ESSEX (1) 1962.
HS 108 Sussex v Notts, Trent Bridge,
1956.
Devon 1963–66, Northumberland
1973–74, Cambridgeshire 1976. Clubs:
Worthing, Paignton, Torquay, Brechin.

SEN, Prabir (Khokan)
————RHB, WK, SRA————

Born Comilla, India, 31 May 1926. Died
Calcutta, India, 27 Jan 1970. Educ La
Martinere, Comilla; Calcutta U. Debut
1943/44.
INDIA DOMESTIC Bengal 1943/44–57/58.
Capt 1952/53–57/58.
INDIA (14) 1947/48–52/53. E 1951/52
(2); WI 1948/49 (5); P 1952/53 (2). *E
1952 (2); A 1947/48 (3).*
HST 25 I v P, Delhi, 1952/53. HS 168
Bengal v Bihar, Jamshedpur, 1950/51.
BB 3–4 (including hat-trick; 5–11 in 14.4
overs in match), Bengal v Orissa, Cuttack, 1954/55.

SENGHERA, Ravindra
————RHB, OB————

Born Delhi, India, 25 Jan 1947. Debut
1974.
WORCESTERSHIRE (23) 1974–76.
D. H. ROBINS' XI (1) 1974.
HS 36* Worcs v Glos, Cheltenham,
1975.
BB 5–81 Worcs v Oxford U, The Parks,
1974.
Club: Smethwick.

SENIOR, Eric Malcolm
————RHB————

Born Shaftesbury, Dorset, 6 Oct 1920.
Died Oxford, 24 Apr 1970. Debut 1961.
COMBINED SERVICES (1) 1961.
HS 1 Combined Services v Notts, Trent
Bridge, 1961.
Oxfordshire 1946, Lincolnshire
1957–58. Clubs: High Wycombe, RAF
Cranwell, Lincoln Lindum. RAF
Squadron-Leader.

SERJEANT, Craig Stanton
————RHB————

Born Nedlands, Perth, W Australia, 1
Nov 1951. Debut 1976/77.
AUSTRALIA DOMESTIC Western Australia
(51) 1976/77–82/83.
AUSTRALIA (12) 1977–77/78. I 1977/78
(4). *E 1977 (3); WI 1977/78 (5).*
HST 124 A v WI, Port of Spain, 1977/78.
HS 159 Australians v Notts, Trent
Bridge, 1977.

SETHI, Ramesh Kumar
————RHB————

Born Kenya, 4 Sept 1941. Debut 1975.
EAST AFRICA to England (1) 1975.
HS 12 E Africa v Sri Lanka, Taunton,
1975.
Shropshire 1976–81. Club: Oswestry.

SETH-SMITH, Derek John
————RHB, RFM————

Born Hartley, Kent, 11 Aug 1920. Died
Chelsea, London, 24 June 1964. Educ
Charterhouse; Clare C, Cambridge.
Debut 1950.
FREE FORESTERS (1) 1950.
HS 3 Free Foresters v Oxford U, The
Parks, 1950.
Club: I Zingari.

SHACKLETON, Derek
————RHB, RFM/RM————

Born Todmorden, Yorks, 12 Aug 1924.
Educ Roomfield S, Todmorden. Debut
1948. *P. Wisden* 1959.
HAMPSHIRE (583) 1948–69. Cap 1949.
Benefit (£5000) 1958. Testimonial
(£5000) 1967.
ENGLAND (7) 1950–63. SA 1951 (1); WI
1950 (1), 1963 (4). *I 1951/52 (1).*
OTHER TOUR Commonwealth XI to India
and Ceylon 1950/51.
HST 42 E v WI, Trent Bridge, 1950. HS
87* Hants v Essex, Bournemouth, 1949.
BBT 4–72 E v WI, Lord's, 1963. BB 9–30
(12–85 match) Hants v Warwicks,
Portsmouth, 1960.
100 WKTS (20) 172 @ 20.15 in 1962.
RECORDS Took 100 or more wkts in
season 20 consecutive times (1949–68),
a record; only W. Rhodes (23) has taken
100 or more wkts in a season more often.
Took 2669 wkts @ 18.23 for Hants, a
county record.
Also returned inns analyses of 9–59
Hants v Glos, Bristol, 1958; 9–77 Hants
v Glam, Newport, 1953; 9–81 Hants v
Glos, Bristol, 1959. Returned inns
analysis of 11.1–7–4–8 (14–29 match)
Hants v Som, Weston-super-Mare,
1955.

Players v Gentlemen (3) 1950–62. Fc
umpire 1979–81. Dorset 1971–74. Club:
Todmorden. Professional coach Canford 1969. Son J. H. Shackleton (Glos).

SHACKLETON, Julian Howard
————RHB, RM————

Born Todmorden, Yorks, 29 Jan 1952.
Educ Millfield. Debut 1971.
GLOUCESTERSHIRE (48) 1971–78.
HS 41* Glos v Surrey, Cheltenham,
1977.
BB 4–38 Glos v Surrey, Bristol, 1971.
Father D. Shackleton (Hants, England).

SHADDICK, Rowland Allen
————RHB, OB————

Born Hackney, London, 26 Mar 1920.
Educ City of London S. Debut 1946.
MIDDLESEX (7) 1946–47.
MCC (5) 1947–52.
FREE FORESTERS (8) 1947–55.
HS 12* MCC v Surrey, Lord's, 1947.
BB 5–34 Free Foresters v Oxford U, The
Parks, 1952.
Clubs: Southgate, London Hospital.
Medical practitioner.

SHAFIQ AHMED
————RHB, RM————

Born Lahore, Pakistan, 28 Mar 1949.
Educ Punjab U. Debut 1967/68.
PAKISTAN DOMESTIC Punjab University,
Lahore, Punjab, National Bank, United
Bank, Lahore City, 1967/68–.
PAKISTAN (6) 1974–80/81. E 1977/78 (3);
WI 1980/81 (2). *E 1974 (1).*
OTHER TOURS Pakistan Under-25 to Sri
Lanka 1973/74. Pakistan to Sri Lanka
1975/76.
HST 27* P v E, Hyderabad, 1977/78. HS
217* National Bank v Muslim Commercial Bank, Karachi, 1978/79 (scored 129
in 1st inns of same match).
BB 4–27 National Bank v Lahore,
Lahore, 1980/81.
1000 RUNS (0 + 5) 1409 @ 82.88 in 1978/
79.
Club: Church.

SHAFQAT RANA
————RHB, OB————

Born Simla, India, 10 Aug 1943. Educ
Government C, Lahore. Debut 1959/
60.
PAKISTAN DOMESTIC Lahore, Lahore
Education Board, Pakistan International Airlines, 1959/60–75/76.

PAKISTAN (5) 1964/65–69/70. E. 1968/69 (2); A 1964/65 (1); NZ 1969/70 (2).
TOURS Pakistan Eaglets to Ceylon 1960/61. Pakistan Eaglets to England 1963. Pakistan to Ceylon 1964/65. Pakistan to Australasia 1964/65. PIA to E Africa 1964/65. Pakistan to England 1971.
HST 95 P v NZ, Lahore, 1969/70. HS 174 Lahore v Sargodha, Lahore, 1964/65.
BB 2–8 BCCP XI v MCC, Bahawalpur, 1968/69.
Current BCCP assistant-secretary. Assistant manager Pakistan to Australia 1981/82. Cricket writer. Brothers Azmat Rana (Pakistan) and Sultan Rana (Habib Bank).

SHAHID MAHMOOD
——————LHB, LM——————

Born Lucknow, India, 17 Mar 1939. Educ Karachi U. Debut 1956/57.
PAKISTAN DOMESTIC Karachi, Karachi University, Universities, Public Works Department, 1956/57–69/70.
PAKISTAN (1) E 1962.
HST 16 P v E, Trent Bridge, 1962. HS 220 Karachi U v Peshawar U, Karachi, 1958/59.
BB 10–58 Karachi Whites v Khairpur, Karachi, 1969/70.
RECORD BB (above) only all-ten analysis to be returned in fc cricket in Pakistan.

SHAKOOR AHMED
——————RHB, WK——————

Born Kampala, Uganda, 15 Sept 1928. Educ Punjab U. Debut 1947/48.
PAKISTAN DOMESTIC Punjab University, Punjab, Multan, Montgomery, Lahore, 1951/52–67/68.
TOURS Pakistan to England 1954. Pakistan Eaglets to Ceylon 1960/61.
HS 280 Lahore Greens v Railways, Lahore, 1964/65.

SHANTRY, Brian Keith
——————LHB, LFM——————

Born Bristol, Glos, 26 May 1955. Educ Whitefield CS, Fishponds, Bristol. Debut 1978.
GLOUCESTERSHIRE (3) 1978–79.
Did not bat.
BB 2–63 Glos v Som, Bristol, 1978.
Retired from fc cricket after serious illness in 1979. Dorset 1983–. Club: Stapleton.

SHARDLOW, Bertie
——————LHB, SLA——————

Born Stone, Staffordshire, 15 Dec 1909. Died Stoke on Trent, Staffordshire, 30 Apr 1976. Debut 1949. P.
MINOR COUNTIES (2) 1949–50.
HS 24* Minor Counties v Yorks, Lord's, 1949.
BB 5–25 Minor Counties v MCC, Lord's, 1950.
Offered contract by Warwicks c 1936, but preferred trade of canal-boat builder.
Staffordshire 1936–57. Clubs: Stone, Leek, West Bromwich Dartmouth, Crewe LMR. Son P. Shardlow (soccer for Stoke City).

SHARMAN, Graham John
——————RHB, LBG——————

Born London, 30 May 1938. Educ Lancing; Lincoln C, Oxford. Debut 1958.
OXFORD UNIVERSITY (2) 1958.
HS 6 Oxford U v Yorks, The Parks, 1958.
Squash: Oxford U.

SHARP, George
——————RHB, WK, SLA——————

Born Hartlepool, Co Durham, 12 Mar 1950. Educ Elwick Road Sec S, Hartlepool. Debut 1968.
NORTHAMPTONSHIRE (294) 1968–. Cap 1973. Benefit 1982.
HS 98 Northants v Yorks, Northampton, 1983.
Made 635 dismissals (548 ct, 87 st) in career.

SHARP, Harry Philip Hugh
——————RHB, RMF/OB——————

Born Kentish Town, London, 6 Oct 1917. Debut 1946. P.
MIDDLESEX (162) 1946–55. Cap 1948. Joint benefit (with A. W. Thompson) (£7437) 1955.
MCC (4) 1947–57.
HS 165 M'sex v Northants, Northampton, 1951.
BB 5–52 M'sex v Oxford U, The Parks, 1949.
1000 RUNS (3) 1564 @ 32.58 in 1953.
Former MCC coach; testimonial from MCC (£2114) 1971. Current M'sex scorer.

SHARP, John Aubrey Taylor
——————RHB——————

Born Blaby, Leics, 6 Sept 1917. Died Oslo, Norway, 15 Jan 1977. Educ Repton; Jesus C, Cambridge. Debut 1937.
LEICESTERSHIRE (4) 1937–46.
CAMBRIDGE UNIVERSITY (1) 1939.
HS 36 Cambridge U v Essex, Brentwood, 1939.
BB 4–63 Leics v Cambridge U, Fenner's, 1939.
Club: Sandhurst Wanderers. Army General. Knighted. Father A. T. Sharp (Leics).

SHARP, Kevin
——————LHB, ROB——————

Born Leeds, Yorks, 6 Apr 1959. Educ Abbey Grange HS, Leeds. Debut 1976.
YORKSHIRE (104) 1976–. Cap 1982.
S AFRICA DOMESTIC Griqualand West 1981/82–.
TOUR D. H. Robins' XI to N Zealand 1979/80.
HS 173 Yorks v Derbys, Chesterfield, 1984.
BB 2–13 Yorks v Glam, Bradford, 1984.
1000 RUNS (1) 1445 @ 39.05 in 1984.
Missed latter stages of 1980 season through nervous trouble.

SHARP, Thomas *Murray*
——————RHB, LB——————

Born Gisborne, N Zealand, 23 Jan 1916. Educ Gisborne HS. Debut 1934/35.
N ZEALAND North Island (1) 1934/35, Canterbury (2) 1936/37–45/46.
TOUR New Zealand Services XI to England 1945.
HS 28 Canterbury v Otago, Dunedin, 1936/37.
BB 3–65 same match.
Northern Districts selector 1968–73. Poverty Bay 1933–58. Clubs: Gisborne HS Old Boys, West Christchurch Rugby Old Boys. Poverty Bay CA executive member.

SHARPE, Philip John
——————RHB——————

Born Shipley, Yorks, 27 Dec 1936. Educ Bradford GS; Worksop C. Debut 1956. P.
COMBINED SERVICES (4) 1956–57.
YORKSHIRE (411) 1958–74. Cap 1960. Benefit (£6668) 1971.
DERBYSHIRE (40) 1975–76.
ENGLAND (12) 1963–69. A 1964 (2); WI 1963 (3), 1969 (3); NZ 1969 (3). I 1963/64 (1).

OTHER TOURS Cavaliers to S Africa 1969/
70. Duke of Norfolk's XI to W Indies
1969/70.
HST 111 E v NZ, Trent Bridge, 1969. HS
228 Derbys v Oxford U, The Parks,
1976.
1000 RUNS (12) 2252 @ 40.94 in 1962.
Took 71 catches in 1962 and 616 catches
in career.
Players v Gentlemen (1) 1962. Norfolk
1977–81. Club: Manningham Mills.

SHASTRI, Ravishankar Jayadith
————————RHB, SLA————————

Born Bombay, India, 27 May 1962.
Educ Dom Bosco HS, Vadala; Podar C.
Debut 1979/80.
INDIA DOMESTIC Bombay 1979/80–.
INDIA (27) 1980/81–83/84. E 1981/82
(6); WI 1983/84 (6); P 1983/84 (2). *E
1982 (3); WI 1982/83 (5); NZ 1980/81
(3); P 1982/83 (2).*
HST 128 I v P, Karachi, 1982/83. HS 134
West Zone v East Zone, Bombay, 1981/
82.
BBT 5–75 I v P, Nagpur, 1983/84. BB
9–101 Bombay v The Rest, Indore,
1981/82.

SHAW, Christopher
————————RHB, RFM————————

Born Hemsworth, Yorks, 17 Feb 1964.
Educ Crofton HS. Debut 1984.
YORKSHIRE (3) 1984.
HS 17 Yorks v Worcs, Scarborough,
1984.
BB 4–68 Yorks v M'sex, Lord's, 1984.
Club: Heckmondwike.

SHAW, Dennis George
————————RHB, LBG————————

Born Salford, Lancs, 16 Feb 1931. Educ
Queen Mary's GS, Walsall. Debut
1949. P.
WARWICKSHIRE (1) 1949.
HS 17 Warwicks v Combined Services,
Edgbaston, 1949.
BB 2–60 same match.
Clubs: Streetley, Walsall.

SHAW, George Bernard
————————RHB, OB————————

Born Treharris, S Wales, 24 Oct 1931.
Died, in road traffic accident, Port Pirie,
S Australia, Sept 1984. Debut 1951. P.
GLAMORGAN (16) 1951–55.
HS 11 Glam v Combined Services, Car-
diff, 1952.
BB 5–38 same match.
Club: Ebbw Vale.

SHEA, William *Dennis*
————————RHB, LB————————

Born Briton Ferry, Wales, 7 Feb 1924.
Died Ormskirk Hospital, Lancs, 22 Sept
1982. Educ Neath Boys' S. Debut 1947.
GLAMORGAN (3) 1947–48.
HS 18* Glam v Combined Services,
Pontypridd, 1948.
BB 4–68 same match.
Clubs: Briton Ferry Steelworks, South-
port, Neath, Hightown. Father A. J.
Shea (Glam).

SHEAHAN, Andrew *Paul*
————————RHB————————

Born Werribee, Victoria, Australia, 30
Sept 1946. Educ Melbourne U. Debut
1965/66.
AUSTRALIA DOMESTIC Victoria (47) 1965/
66–73/74.
AUSTRALIA (31) 1967/68–73/74. E 1970/
71 (2); WI 1968/69 (5); NZ 1973/74 (2);
I 1967/68 (4); P 1972/73 (2). *E 1968 (5),
1972 (2); SA 1969/70 (4); I 1969/70
(5).*
OTHER TOUR Australia to N Zealand
1973/74.
HST 127 A v P, Melbourne, 1972/73. HS
202 Victoria v S Australia, Melbourne,
1966/67.
1000 RUNS (0 + 1) 1002 @ 83.50 in 1972/
73.
Clubs: North Melbourne, Melbourne
University. Great-grandfather W. H.
Cooper (Australia).

SHEARER, Edgar *Donald* Reid
————————RHB————————

Born Harrow, M'sex, 6 June 1909. Educ
Aldenham. Debut 1933.
IRELAND (13) 1933–52.
MCC (1) 1947.
HS 72 Ireland v Scotland, Belfast, 1937.
President ICU 1966. Clubs: City of
Derry, NICC, North Down, Free
Foresters. Soccer: England (amateur).
Former chairman Northern Ireland
Sports Council. Awarded OBE for ser-
vices to sport.

SHEARWOOD, Kenneth Arthur
————————RHB, WK————————

Born Derby, 5 Sept 1921. Educ Shrews-
bury; Brasenose C, Oxford. Debut 1949.
OXFORD UNIVERSITY (4) 1949–51.
DERBYSHIRE (1) 1949.
HS 28 Oxford U v Glos, The Parks, 1949.
Cornwall 1947. Soccer: Blue.

SHELMERDINE, Neville
————————RHB, RM/OB————————

Born Manchester, 23 Dec 1909. Educ
Chorlton GS. Debut 1945.
ROYAL AIR FORCE (1) 1945.
Did not bat or bowl (suffered injury and
footwear trouble in only fc match).
Clubs: Urmston, Little Hulton.

SHENTON, Peter Anthony
————————RHB, OB————————

Born Redcar, Yorks, 5 May 1936. Debut
1958. P.
NORTHAMPTONSHIRE (1) 1958.
KENT (7) 1960.
HS 33 Northants v Glam, Northampton,
1958.
BB 5–68 Kent v Som, Maidstone, 1960.
Clubs: Redcar, Saltburn, Blackhall,
Guisborough.

SHEPHERD, David Robert
————————RHB————————

Born Bideford, Devon, 27 Dec 1940.
Educ Barnstaple GS; St Luke's C,
Exeter. Debut 1965.
GLOUCESTERSHIRE (282) 1965–79. Cap
1969. Joint benefit (with J. Davey) 1978.
HS 153 Glos v M'sex, Bristol, 1968.
1000 RUNS (2) 1079 @ 26.97 in 1970.
Scored 108 on fc debut, Glos v Oxford
U, The Parks, 1965.
Fc umpire 1981–. Devon 1959–64.
Club: Bideford. Rugby: Bideford.

SHEPHERD, Donald John
————————RHB, RFM/OB————————

Born Port-Eynon, Glam, 12 Aug 1927.
Educ Gowerton County GS. Debut
1950. P. *Wisden* 1970.
GLAMORGAN (647) 1950–72. Cap 1952.
Benefit (£3200) 1960. Testimonial
(£5000) 1968.
TOURS F. R. Brown's XI to E Africa
1961/62 (not fc). Commonwealth XI to
Pakistan 1967/68, 1970/71. Glam to W
Indies 1969/70. MCC to Ceylon 1969/
70.
HS 73 Glam v Derbys, Cardiff, 1961.
BB 9–47 Glam v Northants, Cardiff,
1954. Also returned 9–48 Glam v Yorks,
Swansea, 1965.
100 WKTS (12) 177 @ 15.36 in 1956.
RECORDS 2174 wkts @ 20.95 and 647
matches for Glam, both county records.
Leading wkt-taker among bowlers not
to play in Tests. Reached 50 in 15 mins,
with 11 scoring-strokes (equalling world
record) during 51* Glam v Australians,
Swansea, 1961, fastest-ever fifty for
Glam.
Players v Gentlemen (5) 1952–57.

SHEPHERD, John Neil
——RHB, RFM/RM——

Born St Andrew, Barbados, 9 Nov 1943.
Educ Alleyn's S, Barbados. Debut 1964/
65. *Wisden* 1979.
W INDIES DOMESTIC Barbados 1964/
65–70/71.
KENT (303) 1966–81. Cap 1967. Benefit
(£58,537) 1979.
GLOUCESTERSHIRE (69) 1982–. Cap 1983.
S AFRICA DOMESTIC Rhodesia 1975/76.
WEST INDIES (5) 1969–70/71. I 1970/71
(2). E 1969 (3).
OTHER TOURS D. H. Robins' XI to S
Africa 1973/74, 1974/75. International
Wanderers to S Africa 1974/75, 1975/
76.
HST 32 WI v E, Lord's, 1969. HS 170
Kent v Northants, Folkestone, 1968.
BBT 5–104 WI v E, Old Trafford, 1969.
BB 8–40 W Indians v Glos, Bristol, 1969.
1000 RUNS (2) 1157 @ 29.66 in 1968 (also
took 96 wkts @ 18.72).
First black cricketer to play in Currie
Cup in S Africa, in 1975/76.

SHEPPARD, David Stuart
——RHB, SLA——

Born Reigate, Surrey, 6 Mar 1929. Educ
Sherborne; Trinity Hall, Cambridge.
Debut 1947. *Wisden* 1953.
SUSSEX (141) 1947–62. Cap 1949. Capt
1953.
CAMBRIDGE UNIVERSITY (36) 1950–52
(Blue 1950–52). Capt 1952.
ENGLAND (22) 1950–62/63. A 1956 (2);
WI 1950 (1), 1957 (2); I 1952 (2); P 1954
(2), 1962 (2). A 1950/51 (2), 1962/63
(5); NZ 1950/51 (1), 1962/63 (3).
Capt 2.
HST 119 E v I, Oval, 1952. HS 239* Cam-
bridge U v Worcs, Worcester, 1952.
1000 RUNS (6) 2270 @ 45.40 in 1953.
2000 runs (3).
RECORDS Scored 1581 runs @ 79.05 for
Cambridge U in 1952, a record for either
fc university; seven centuries during
season (1952) and 14 centuries in
university career, also records. Shared
in two first-wkt stands of over 300 with
J. G. Dewes in 1950 (349 Cambridge U
v Sussex, Hove and 343 Cambridge U v
West Indians, Fenner's).
Gentlemen v Players (6) 1951–62. Club:
Slinford. MCC committee 1957–59.
Autobiography *Parson's Pitch* (1964).
Ordained as Church of England priest
1955; current Bishop of Liverpool (only
parson to play Test cricket).

SHEPPARD, Harold Frederick
——RHB——

Born Glasgow, Scotland, 11 Sept 1917.
Educ Glasgow HS; Glasgow U. Debut
1938.

SCOTLAND (13) 1938–52.
HS 72 Scotland v Ireland, Paisley, 1952.
Glasgow University. Club: Poloc.
Father H. H. Sheppard (Scotland).

SHEPPERD, John
——RHB, RMF——

Born Willesden, London, 8 May 1937.
Debut 1959. *P.*
MIDDLESEX (3) 1959–60.
L. C. STEVENS' XI (1) 1960.
HS 13 M'sex v Indians, Lord's, 1959.
BB 3–35 M'sex v Essex, Westcliff, 1960.
Minor Counties umpire 1971–74. Nor-
folk 1963–68. Norfolk scorer 1983.
Clubs: Ayr, Norwich Union, Carrow.

SHERMAN, Howard Richard
——RHB, OB——

Born Seven Kings, Essex, 15 June 1943.
Educ Chigwell. Debut 1967.
ESSEX (13) 1967–69.
HS 66 Essex v Notts, Leyton, 1967.
Club: Ilford.

SHILLINGFORD, Grayson Cleophas
——LHB, RFM——

Born Dublanc, Dominica, 25 Sept 1944.
Educ Dominica GS. Debut 1967/68.
W INDIES DOMESTIC Windward Islands
1967/68–78/79, Combined Islands
1968/69–78/79.
WEST INDIES (7) 1969–71/72. NZ 1971/
72 (2); I 1970/71 (3). E 1969 (2).
OTHER TOUR W Indies to England 1973.
HST 25 WI v I, Port of Spain, 1970/71.
HS 42 Combined Islands v Barbados,
Roseau, 1971/72.
BBT 3–63 WI v NZ, Kingston, 1971/72.
BB 6–49 Combined Islands v Trinidad,
Basseterre, 1971/72.
Club: Thornaby. Cousin I. T. Shilling-
ford (W Indies).

SHINDE, Sadashiv Ganpatrao
——RHB, LBG——

Born Bombay, India, 18 Aug 1923. Died
Bombay, India, 22 June 1955. Educ
Bombay U. Debut 1940/41.
INDIA DOMESTIC Maharashtra 1940/
41–46/47, 1949/50, Bombay Hindus
1945/46, Baroda 1947/48–48/49, Bom-
bay 1950/51–54/55.
INDIA (7) 1946–52. E 1951/52 (3); WI
1948/49 (1). E 1946 (1), 1952 (2).
HST 14 I v E, Kanpur, 1951/52. HS 50* V.
M. Merchant's XI v Maharaja of
Patiala's XI, Delhi, 1946/47.

BBT 6–91 I v E, Delhi, 1951/52. BB
8–162 Bombay v Gujerat, Ahmedabad,
1950/51.

SHIPPEY, Peter *Anthony*
——LHB, ROB——

Born Newton, Wisbech, Cambridge-
shire, 31 Aug 1939. Debut 1967.
MCC (1) 1967.
MINOR COUNTIES (3) 1969–71.
HS 94* Minor Counties v W Indians,
Longton, Stoke on Trent, 1969.
Cambridgeshire 1957–81. Club: Wis-
bech.

SHIRREFF, Alexander Campbell
——RHB, RM——

Born Ealing, London, 12 Feb 1919.
Educ Dulwich; Pembroke C, Cam-
bridge. Debut 1939.
CAMBRIDGE UNIVERSITY (12) 1939 (Blue).
HAMPSHIRE (12) 1946–47.
COMBINED SERVICES (40) 1946–57.
ROYAL AIR FORCE (1) 1946.
MCC (4) 1946–55.
FREE FORESTERS (2) 1949–50.
KENT (46) 1950–56. Cap 1952.
SOMERSET (2) 1958.
HS 115* Combined Services v Essex,
Chelmsford, 1950.
BB 8–111 Kent v Leics, Leicester, 1956.
Som coach/assistant-secretary 1957–58.
Club: Dulwich. RAF Squadron-Leader
(retired).

SHIVLAL YADAV, Nandlal
——RHB, OB——

Born Hyderabad, Deccan, India, 26 Jan
1957. Debut 1977/78.
INDIA DOMESTIC Hyderabad 1977/78–.
INDIA (18) 1979/80–83/84. E 1979/80
(1), 1981/82 (1); A 1979/80 (5); WI
1983/84 (3); P 1979/80 (5). A 1980/81
(2); NZ 1980/81 (1).
OTHER TOUR India to England 1982.
HST 43 I v NZ, Auckland, 1980/81. HS 50
Hyderabad v Kerala, Cochin, 1983/84.
BBT 5–131 I v WI, Bombay, 1983/84. BB
6–64 President's XI v W Indians, Bombay, 1978/79.

SHORE, Richard Graham
——RHB, RM——

Born Bournemouth, Hants, 9 Mar 1941.
Educ Blundell's S; Brasenose C, Oxford. Debut 1962.

OXFORD UNIVERSITY (4) 1962.
HS 24 Oxford U v M'sex, The Parks, 1962.
BB 3-57 Oxford U v Free Foresters, The Parks, 1962.

SHORT, Arthur Martin
RHB

Born Graaff-Reinet, Cape Province, S Africa, 27 Sept 1947. Educ St Andrew's C, Grahamstown; Natal U. Debut 1966/67.
S AFRICA DOMESTIC Eastern Province 1966/67-68/69, 1973/74-74/75, South African Universities 1966/67-67, Natal 1969/70-72/73.
TOUR S African Universities to England 1967.
HS 118 E Province v Transvaal, Port Elizabeth, 1973/74.
BB 2-2 E Province v Transvaal, J'burg, 1968/69.
Selected for cancelled S Africa tours to England 1970 and Australia 1971/72. S African Country Districts XI 1981/82 (capt).

SHORT, John David
RHB, OB

Born Chesterfield, Derbys, 13 June 1934. Educ Denstone. Debut 1957. P 1960.
DERBYSHIRE (11) 1957-60.
HS 86 Derbys v Warwicks, Chesterfield, 1960.
Royal Air Force.

SHORT, John Francis
RHB

Born Cork, Ireland, 12 Apr 1951. Educ Presentation Brothers' C, Cork. Debut 1974.
IRELAND (10) 1974-83.
HS 114 Ireland v Scotland, Dublin, 1975.
Clubs: Cork Bohemians, Leinster.

SHORT, Robert Leslie
RHB

Born Chesterfield, Derbys, 24 Sept 1948. Educ Denstone; Emmanuel C, Cambridge. Debut 1969.
CAMBRIDGE UNIVERSITY (11) 1969-70 (Blue 1969).
HS 58 Cambridge U v Essex, Fenner's, 1969.

SHORTLAND, Norman Arthur
RHB, RM

Born Coventry, Warwicks, 6 July 1916.
Died Finham, Coventry, 14 Mar 1973.
Educ Stoke S, Coventry. Debut 1938. P 1938-39.
WARWICKSHIRE (23) 1938-50. Cap 1946.
HS 70 Warwicks v Sussex, Edgbaston, 1946.
Clubs: Coventry and North Warwicks.
Rugby: England Schoolboys, Nuneaton. Uncle W. Duckham (Suffolk).

SHUJA-UD-DIN Butt
RHB, SLA

Born Lahore, India, 10 Apr 1930. Debut 1946/47.
INDIA DOMESTIC Northern India 1946/47.
PAKISTAN DOMESTIC Punjab University, Services, Bahawalpur, Rawalpindi, 1947/48-69/70.
PAKISTAN (19) 1954-61/62. E 1961/62 (2); A 1959/60 (3); WI 1958/59 (3); NZ 1955/56 (3); I 1954/55 (5). E 1954 (3).
OTHER TOUR Pakistan to India 1960/61.
HST 47 P v NZ, Karachi, 1955/56. HS 147 Services v MCC, Sargodha, 1955/56.
BBT 3-18 P v WI, Karachi, 1958/59. BB 8-53 (12-61 match) Services v Lahore, Lahore, 1961/62.
Colonel Pakistan Army (retired).

SHUJA-UD-DIN Butt
RHB

Debut 1953/54.
PAKISTAN DOMESTIC Punjab, Railways, Lahore, 1953/54-59/60.
TOUR Pakistan to England 1962 (1 match in emergency).
HS 77 Railways v Peshawar, Peshawar, 1957/58.
BB 2-49 Railways v Karachi, Karachi, 1954/55.

SHUTT, Albert
RHB, RM

Born Stockton-on-Tees, Co Durham, 21 Sept 1952. Educ Stockton GS. Debut 1972.
WORCESTERSHIRE (2) 1972.
Did not bat.
Durham 1977. Clubs: Thornaby, Stockton, Stourbridge.

SHUTTLEWORTH, Guy Mitchell
RHB

Born Blackburn, Lancs, 6 Nov 1926.
Educ Queen Elizabeth GS, Blackburn; King's C, Cambridge. Debut 1946.
CAMBRIDGE UNIVERSITY (25) 1946-48 (Blue 1946-48).
HS 96 Cambridge U v Sussex, Hove, 1946.
Lancashire 2nd XI 1946-48. Clubs: East Lancs, Hampstead. Soccer: Blue.

SHUTTLEWORTH, Kenneth
RHB, RFM

Born St Helens, Lancs, 13 Nov 1944.
Debut 1964.
LANCASHIRE (177) 1964-75. Cap 1968.
Joint testimonial (with J. Sullivan) (£12,500) 1975.
LEICESTERSHIRE (41) 1977-80. Cap 1977.
ENGLAND (5) 1970/71-71. P 1971 (1). A 1970/71 (2); NZ 1970/71 (2).
OTHER TOUR Commonwealth XI to Pakistan 1967/68.
HST 21 E v P, Edgbaston, 1971. HS 71 Lancs v Glos, Cheltenham, 1967.
BBT 5-47 E v A, Brisbane, 1970/71.
BB 7-41 Lancs v Essex, Leyton, 1968.

SIDDIQI, Shaw Naweed
RHB, RM

Born London, 13 Sept 1959. Educ City of London S; Bart's Medical C; Hughes Hall, Cambridge. Debut 1984.
CAMBRIDGE UNIVERSITY (6) 1984.
HS 52 Cambridge U v Sussex, Fenner's, 1984.
BB 5-90 Cambridge U v Warwicks, Fenner's, 1984.

SIDDONS, Anthony
RHB, OB

Born Nottingham, 29 Dec 1941. Debut 1959. P 1960.
NOTTINGHAMSHIRE (5) 1959-60.
HS 8 Notts v Kent, Folkestone, 1959 and 8 v Hants, Portsmouth, 1960.
BB 4-37 Notts v Hants, Portsmouth, 1960.

SIDEBOTTOM, Arnold
RHB, RFM

Born Barnsley, Yorks, 1 Apr 1954. Educ Barnsley Broadway GS. Debut 1973.
YORKSHIRE (137) 1973-. Cap 1980.
S AFRICA DOMESTIC Orange Free State 1981/82-.
HS 124 Yorks v Glam, Cardiff, 1977.

BB 7–18 Yorks v Oxford U, The Parks, 1980.
Barred from Test cricket for three yrs for touring S Africa 1981/82 (SAB England XI). Soccer: Manchester United, Huddersfield Town, Halifax Town.

SIKANDER BAKHT
————RHB, RFM————

Born Karachi, Pakistan, 25 Aug 1957. Debut 1974/75.
PAKISTAN DOMESTIC Public Works Department, Pakistan International Airlines, Sind, Karachi, United Bank, 1974/75–.
PAKISTAN (26) 1976/77–82/83. E 1977/78 (2); WI 1980/81 (1); NZ 1976/77 (1); I 1978/79 (2), 1982/83 (1). *E 1978 (3), 1982 (2); A 1978/79 (2), 1981/82 (3); WI 1976/77 (1); NZ 1978/79 (3); I 1979/80 (5).*
HST 22★ P v I, Karachi, 1978/79. HS 67 United Bank v PIA, Lahore, 1982/83.
BBT 8–69 P v I, Delhi, 1979/80. BB as above.

SILK, Dennis Raoul Whitehall
————RHB, LB————

Born Eureka, California, United States, 8 Oct 1931. Educ Christ's Hospital; Sidney Sussex C, Cambridge. Debut 1952.
CAMBRIDGE UNIVERSITY (40) 1952–55 (Blue 1953–55). Capt 1955.
SOMERSET (33) 1956–60. Cap 1957.
TOUR MCC to N Zealand 1960/61 (capt).
HS 126 Cambridge U v MCC, Fenner's, 1953.
Scored centuries v Oxford U in both 1953 and 1954 Varsity matches.
Gentlemen v Players (2) 1958–60. MCC committee 1967–81. Rugby: Blue.

SILVESTER, Stephen
————RHB, RFM————

Born Hull, Yorks, 12 Mar 1951. Educ Kelvin Hall S, Hull; St John's C of Educ, York. Debut 1976.
YORKSHIRE (6) 1976–77.
HS 14 Yorks v Worcs, Worcester, 1977.
BB 4–86 Yorks v Hants, Headingley, 1977.
Northumberland 1979. Club: Bowling Old Lane.

SIM, Archibald Millar Robertson
————RHB————

Born Johannesburg, S Africa, 8 Jan 1942. Educ Dale C, Johannesburg. Debut 1962/63.

S AFRICA DOMESTIC North-Eastern Transvaal 1962/63.
NORTHAMPTONSHIRE (4) 1964–66.
HS 66★ Northants v Oxford U, The Parks, 1965.

SIME, William Arnold
————RHB, SLA————

Born Wepener, OFS, S Africa, 8 Feb 1909. Died Wymeswold, Leics, 5 May 1983. Educ Bedford S; Balliol C, Oxford. Debut 1929.
MINOR COUNTIES (2) 1929–34.
OXFORD UNIVERSITY (1) 1931.
NOTTINGHAMSHIRE (91) 1935–50. Cap 1947. Capt 1947–50.
NORTH (1) 1948.
S AFRICAN AIR FORCE XI v Rest of S Africa, J'burg, 1942/43.
HS 176★ Notts v Sussex, Hove, 1948.
BB 4–51 Notts v M'sex, Lord's, 1949.
Notts president 1976; Notts committee. Bedfordshire 1927–34. Club: Notts Amateurs. MCC committee 1958–60. Rugby: Bedford, East Midlands. Barrister; became QC and Judge. Awarded OBE.

SIMMONS, Jack
————RHB, OB————

Born Clayton-le-Moors, Lancs, 28 Mar 1941. Educ Accrington Technical S; Blackburn Technical C. Debut 1968. *Wisden 1985.*
LANCASHIRE (344) 1968–. Cap 1971. Benefit (£128,000) 1980.
AUSTRALIA DOMESTIC Tasmania (20) 1972/73–78/79.
TOUR Overseas XI to India 1980/81.
HS 112 Lancs v Sussex, Hove, 1970.
BB 7–59 Tasmania v Queensland, Brisbane, 1978/79.
Club: Enfield.

SIMONS, Robert George
————RHB, WK————

Born Watford, Hertfordshire, 23 Mar 1922. Educ Berkhamsted S. Debut 1959.
MINOR COUNTIES (1) 1959.
No runs.
Hertfordshire 1948–69. Clubs: MCC, Abbots Langley, Stoics, Hedgehogs.

SIMPKINS, David Paul
————RHB, OB————

Born Chippenham, Wiltshire, 28 Mar 1962. Educ Sheldon S, Chippenham. Debut 1982.

GLOUCESTERSHIRE (1) 1982.
HS 1★ Glos v M'sex, Cheltenham, 1982.
Wiltshire 1981–82. Club: Chippenham.

SIMPKINS, Peter Antony
————RHB, SLA————

Born Dover, Kent, 27 Nov 1928. Debut 1962.
FREE FORESTERS (1) 1962.
Did not bat.
BB 3–69 Free Foresters v Oxford U, The Parks, 1962.
Berkshire 1958–76. Club: Maidenhead and Bray.

SIMPSON, David John
————RHB————

Born Irvine, Ayrshire, Scotland, 23 Feb 1961. Debut 1984.
SCOTLAND (1) 1984.
HS 9 Scotland v Ireland, Glasgow, 1984.

SIMPSON, Frank William
————RHB, RM————

Born Blything, Suffolk, 27 Mar 1909. Educ Merchant Taylors', Crosby. Debut 1931.
ARMY (1) 1931.
COMBINED SERVICES (1) 1948.
HS 40 Combined Services v Glam, Pontypridd, 1948.
Lt-Colonel Royal Engineers (retired).

SIMPSON, Jack
————RHB, RFM————

Born Lisburn, Ireland, 1 Dec 1920. Educ Lisburn Technical C. Debut 1954.
IRELAND (1) 1954.
HS 26 Ireland v Scotland, Paisley, 1954.
Club: Lisburn.

SIMPSON, Reginald Thomas
————RHB, OB————

Born Sherwood Rise, Notts, 27 Feb 1920. Educ Nottingham HS. Debut 1944/45. *Wisden 1950.*
INDIA DOMESTIC Sind 1944/45–45/46, Bombay Europeans 1944/45–45/46.
NOTTINGHAMSHIRE (366) 1946–63. Cap 1946. Capt 1951–60.
ENGLAND (27) 1948/49–54/55. A 1953 (3); SA 1951 (3); WI 1950 (3); NZ 1949 (2); I 1952 (2); P 1954 (3). *A 1950/51 (5), 1954/55 (1); SA 1948/49 (1); NZ 1950/51 (2), 1954/55 (2).*
OTHER TOURS Commonwealth XI to India 1953/54. C. G. Howard's XI to India 1956/57.
HST 156★ E v A, Melbourne, 1950/51. HS 259 MCC v NSW, Sydney, 1950/51.

BBT 2–4 E v NZ, Christchurch, 1950/51.
BB 3–22 Notts v Warwicks, Edgbaston, 1949.
1000 RUNS (13 + 1) 2576 @ 62.82 in 1950. 2000 runs (5).
Scored centuries against all fc counties except his own.
Gentlemen v Players (13) 1947–56. Notts committee. MCC Hon. member.

SIMPSON, Robert Baddeley
RHB, LBG

Born Marrickville, NSW, Australia, 3 Feb 1936. Educ Marrickville. Debut 1952/53. *Wisden* 1965.
AUSTRALIA DOMESTIC New South Wales (67) 1952/53–77/78, Western Australia (24) 1956/57–60/61.
AUSTRALIA (62) 1957/58–77/78. E 1958/59 (1), 1962/63 (5), 1965/66 (3); SA 1963/64 (5); WI 1960/61 (5); I 1967/68 (3), 1977/78 (5); P 1964/65 (1). *E 1961 (5), 1964 (5); SA 1957/58 (5), 1966/67 (5); WI 1964/65 (5), 1977/78 (5); I 1964/65 (3); P 1964/65 (1).* Capt 39.
OTHER TOURS Australia to N Zealand 1956/57, 1959/60. Commonwealth XI to S Africa 1959/60. Rest of World XI to England 1960. Cavaliers to S Africa 1960/61. Commonwealth XI to N Zealand, India and Pakistan 1961/62.
HST 311 A v E, Old Trafford, 1964. HS 359 NSW v Queensland, Brisbane, 1963/64.
BBT 5–57 A v E, Sydney, 1962/63. BB 5–33 Australians v Glamorgan, Swansea, 1964.
1000 RUNS (2 + 9) 2063 @ 68.76 in 1964/65.
RECORDS HST (above) second-highest inns for A in Tests; took 762 mins, longest Test inns for A; 646 runs added while at wkt, most in a Test for A and fourth-highest in all Tests. HS (above) highest inns in Australia since 1939–45 war. Scored 12 double-centuries in career, most in post-1945 era by any player. Added 382 for 1st wkt with W. M. Lawry, A v WI, Bridgetown, 1964/65, Australia Test record.
Took 110 catches in 62 Tests. Retired in 1968/69 but returned in 1977/78, during Packer period, to capt NSW and Australia.
Clubs: Petersham, Marrickville, Western Suburbs (Australia); Accrington (Lancashire). MCC Hon. member. Son-in-law A. M. J. Hilditch (Australia).

SIMS, James Morton
RHB, LBG

Born Leyton, London, 13 May 1903. Died Canterbury, Kent, 27 Apr 1973. Debut 1929. *P.*

MIDDLESEX (381) 1929–52. Cap 1932. Benefits 1946 (£3000) and 1950 (£2960).
MCC (36) 1930–53.
SOUTH (5) 1947–52.
ENGLAND (4) 1935–36/37. SA 1935 (1); I 1936 (1). *A 1936/37 (2).*
OTHER TOURS MCC to N Zealand 1935/36. Sir T. E. W. Brinckman's XI to S America 1937/38.
HST 12 E v SA, Headingley, 1935. HS 123 MCC v Kent, Lord's, 1931.
BBT 5–73 E v I, Oval, 1936. BB 10–90 East v West, Kingston-upon-Thames, 1948. Also returned 9–92 M'sex v Lancs, Old Trafford, 1934.
100 WKTS (8) 159 @ 20.30 in 1939.
Players v Gentlemen (1) 1935. M'sex scorer to 1973; died while scoring county match. Outstanding raconteur and leg-puller.

SINCLAIR, Barry Whitley
RHB

Born Wellington, N Zealand, 23 Oct 1936. Educ Rongotai C. Debut 1955/56.
N ZEALAND DOMESTIC Wellington (68) 1955/56–70/71.
NEW ZEALAND (21) 1962/63–67/68. E 1962/63 (3), 1965/66 (3); SA 1963/64 (3); I 1967/68 (2); P 1964/65 (2). *E 1965 (3); I 1964/65 (2); P 1964/65 (3).* Capt 3.
OTHER TOUR N Zealand to Australia 1967/68.
HST 138 NZ v SA, Auckland, 1963/64. HS 148 Wellington v Australians, Dunedin, 1966/67.
BBT 2–32 NZ v P, Lahore, 1964/65. BB as above.
Clubs: Kilbirnie (N Zealand); Mitchells and Butlers (England).

SINGLETON, Alexander Parkinson
RHB

Born Repton, Derbys, 5 Aug 1914. Educ Shrewsbury; Brasenose C, Oxford. Debut 1934.
WORCESTERSHIRE (58) 1934–46. Cap. Capt 1946.
OXFORD UNIVERSITY (42) 1934–37 (Blue 1934–37). Capt 1937.
S AFRICA DOMESTIC Rhodesia 1946/47–49/50. Capt 6.
HS 164 Worcs v Warwicks, Edgbaston, 1946.
BB 6–44 (10–161 match) Oxford U v H. D. G. Leveson Gower's XI, Reigate, 1934.
1000 RUNS (1) 1773 @ 34.09 in 1946.
Gentlemen v Players (2) 1936–46. Tobacco grower. Brother G. M. Singleton (Worcs).

SINGLETON, George Michael
RHB, SLA

Born Repton, Derbys, 12 May 1913. Educ Uppingham; Pembroke C, Cambridge. Debut 1946.
WORCESTERSHIRE (2) 1946.
FREE FORESTERS (1) 1946.
HS 23 Worcs v Combined Services, Worcester, 1946.
Brother A. P. Singleton (Worcs, Rhodesia).

SINKER, Nigel Dalcour
LHB, SLA

Born Writtle, Chelmsford, Essex, 19 Apr 1946. Educ Winchester; Jesus C, Cambridge. Debut 1966.
CAMBRIDGE UNIVERSITY (13) 1966/67 (Blue 1966).
HS 31* Cambridge U v Northants, Fenner's, 1966.
BB 4–10 Cambridge U v Scotland, Fenner's, 1966.
Member I Zingari.

SISMEY, Stanley George
RHB, WK

Born Junee, NSW, Australia, 15 July 1916. Debut 1938/39.
AUSTRALIA DOMESTIC New South Wales (20) 1938/39–50/51, Australian Services 1945/46.
SCOTLAND (1) 1952.
TOUR Australian Services to England (6) 1945 and India and Ceylon (3) 1945/46. Australia to N Zealand 1949/50 (no fc matches).
HS 78 Australian Services v H. D. G. Leveson Gower's XI, Scarborough, 1945.
Australia v England (Victory matches) (5) 1945. Clubs: Western Suburbs (Sydney), Clydesdale (Scotland).

SIVITER, Kenneth
RHB, RMF

Born Southport, Lancs, 10 Dec 1953. Educ Liverpool C; Keble C, Oxford. Debut 1974.
OXFORD UNIVERSITY (16) 1974–77 (Blue 1976).
HS 26 Oxford U v Warwicks, The Parks, 1974.
BB 4–67 Oxford U v Warwicks, The Parks, 1976.
6 ft 5 in tall.

SKALA, Steven Michael
——RHB, WK——

Born Brisbane, Australia, 6 Oct 1955.
Educ Brisbane GS; Queensland U;
Wadham C, Oxford. Debut 1979.
OXFORD UNIVERSITY (2) 1979.
HS 11 Oxford U v Hants, The Parks,
1979.
Club: Toombul. Represented Australia
in 1973 and 1977 Maccabean Games in
Israel.

SKINNER, Alan Frank
——RHB——

Born Brighton, Sussex, 22 Apr 1913.
Died Bury St Edmunds, Suffolk, 28 Feb
1982. Educ The Leys S; Trinity C,
Cambridge. Debut 1931.
DERBYSHIRE (83) 1931–38. Cap.
CAMBRIDGE UNIVERSITY (2) 1934.
NORTHAMPTONSHIRE (1) 1949. Capt on
only appearance.
HS 102 Derbys v Glos, Gloucester, 1934.
BB 2–12 Derbys v Northants, Chester-
field, 1933.
1000 RUNS (1) 1019 @ 27.54 in 1934.
Suffolk 1954–55. Brother D. A. Skinner
(Derbys).

SKINNER, David Anthony
——RHB, LB/OB——

Born Duffield, Derbys, 22 Mar 1920.
Educ The Leys S. Debut 1947.
DERBYSHIRE (23) 1947–49. Cap 1949.
Capt 1949.
HS 63 Derbys v Sussex, Worthing, 1949.
Clubs: MCC, Cryptics, Gents of Suf-
folk, Gents of Essex, Derbys Friars.
Brother A. F. Skinner (Derbys, North-
ants).

SKINNER, Ivor John
——RHB, RFM——

Born Walthamstow, London, 1 Apr
1928. Educ William Morris S, Wal-
thamstow. Debut 1950. P.
ESSEX (13) 1950.
HS 7* Essex v Yorks, Bramall Lane,
Sheffield, 1950.
BB 4–56 Essex v Warwicks, Edgbaston,
1950.
Cornwall 1956–59.

SKINNER, Lonsdale Ernest
——RHB, WK——

Born Plaisance, British Guiana, 7 Sept
1950. Educ Hillcroft CS, Tooting, London. Debut 1971.
SURREY (71) 1971–77. Cap 1975.

W INDIES DOMESTIC Guyana 1973/74–76/
77.
HS 93 Surrey v Yorks, Oval, 1976.
Club: Demerara.

SLACK, John Kenneth Edward
——RHB——

Born Wembley, London, 23 Dec 1930.
Educ UCS, Oxford; St John's C, Cam-
bridge. Debut 1954.
CAMBRIDGE UNIVERSITY (7) 1954 (Blue).
HS 135 Cambridge U v M'sex, Fenner's,
1954 (on fc debut).
Buckinghamshire 1966–69 (capt
1968–69). Club: UCS Old Boys. Rugby:
Middlesex. Currently a Judge. Awarded
TD.

SLACK, Wilfred Norris
——LHB, RM——

Born Troumaca, St Vincent, W Indies,
12 Dec 1954. Educ Wellesbourne S,
High Wycombe. Debut 1977.
MIDDLESEX (118) 1977–. Cap 1981.
W INDIES DOMESTIC Windward Islands
1981/82–82/83.
TOURS M'sex XI to Zimbabwe 1980/81.
International XI to Pakistan 1981/82.
HS 248* M'sex v Worcs, Lord's, 1981.
BB 3–17 M'sex v Leics, Uxbridge, 1982.
1000 RUNS (4) 1631 @ 42.92 in 1984.
RECORD Put on 367* for 1st wkt with
G. D. Barlow, M'sex v Kent, Lord's,
1981, county record.
Buckinghamshire 1976. Club: High
Wycombe.

SLADE, Douglas Norman Frank
——RHB, SLA——

Born Feckenham, Worcs, 24 Aug 1940.
Debut 1958. P.
WORCESTERSHIRE (266) 1958–71. Cap
1960. Benefit 1971.
HS 125 Worcs v Leics, Leicester, 1969.
BB 7–47 Worcs v M'sex, Lord's, 1960.
TOURS Commonwealth XI to Pakistan
1963/64, 1970/71. Worcs to Rhodesia
1964/65. Worcs to Jamaica 1965/66.
Took 97 wkts @ 19.83 in 1960.
Shropshire 1973–78. Clubs: Worcester
City, West Bromwich Dartmouth,
Dudley.

SLADE, William Douglas
——RHB, RM——

Born Briton Ferry, S Wales, 27 Sept
1941. Debut 1961. P.
GLAMORGAN (67) 1961–67.
HS 73* Glam v Derbys, Swansea, 1963.

BB 4–144 Glam v M'sex, Lord's, 1962.
Clubs: Briton Ferry Town, Pontard-
dulais, Swansea. Professional coach
Marlborough 1969.

SLAVEN, Francis Ferguson
——RHB——

Born Bulawayo, Rhodesia, 3 Mar 1931.
Educ St George's C, Salisbury,
Rhodesia; Rhodes U, Grahamstown;
Lincoln C, Oxford. Debut 1955.
OXFORD UNIVERSITY (2) 1955.
HS 13 Oxford U v Glos, The Parks, 1955.
Brother M. D. Slaven (Rhodesia).

SLINGER, Edward
——RHB, LB——

Born Accrington, Lancs, 2 Feb 1938.
Educ Accrington GS; Balliol C, Oxford.
Debut 1967.
MCC (1) 1967.
HS 12* MCC v Oxford U, The Parks,
1967.
Lancashire 2nd XI. Clubs: Enfield,
Blackpool, Guildford, Northern
Nomads.

SLOCOMBE, Philip Anthony
——RHB, RM——

Born Weston-super-Mare, Som, 6 Sept
1954. Educ Weston GS; Millfield.
Debut 1975.
SOMERSET (135) 1975–83. Cap 1978.
TOUR D. H. Robins' XI to S Africa 1975/
76.
HS 132 Som v Notts, Taunton, 1975.
1000 RUNS (2) 1221 @ 38.15 in 1978.
Scored 1125 @ 35.15 in debut season,
1975.

SLY, Gerald Brian
——RHB, RF——

Born Ealing, London, 21 Oct 1932.
Educ Manor Sec S, London. Debut
1953. P.
SUSSEX (1) 1953.
Did not bat; one wkt.
Lord's groundstaff 1950. Clubs:
Eastcote (M'sex), Kilmarnock, Ayr,
Cupar, Fife (Scotland).

SMAIL, Alastair Harold Kurt
——RHB, LM——

Born Kingston-upon-Thames, Surrey,
3 July 1964. Educ Bilborough Sixth
Form C; Exeter C, Oxford. Debut 1983.
OXFORD UNIVERSITY (6) 1983.
HS 13* Oxford U v Surrey, Oval, 1983.
BB 3–49 Oxford U v Sussex, The Parks,
1983.

SMAILES, Thomas *Francis*
——LHB, RFM/RM/OB——

Born Ripley, Yorks, 27 Mar 1910. Died Harrogate, Yorks, 1 Dec 1970. Educ Pocklington S. Debut 1932. *P.*
YORKSHIRE (262) 1932–48. Cap 1934. Benefit (£5104) 1948.
ENGLAND (1) I 1946.
TOUR Yorks to Jamaica 1935/36.
HST 25 E v I, Lord's, 1946.
HS 117 Yorks v Glam, Cardiff, 1938.
BBT 3–44 E v I, Lord's, 1946. BB 10–47 Yorks v Derbys, Bramall Lane, Sheffield, 1939.
1000 RUNS (1) 1002 @ 25.05 in 1938.
100 WKTS (4) 130 @ 17.54 in 1936.
DOUBLE (1) 1938.
Players v Gentlemen (2) 1938. Club: Walsall.

SMALES, Kenneth
——RHB, OB——

Born Horsforth, Leeds, Yorks, 15 Sept 1927. Educ Aireborough GS. Debut 1948. *P.*
YORKSHIRE (13) 1948–50.
NOTTINGHAMSHIRE (148) 1951–58. Cap 1955.
HS 64 Notts v Glam, Trent Bridge, 1958.
BB 10–66 Notts v Glos, Stroud, 1956.
100 WKTS (1) 117 @ 24.12 in 1955.
RECORD BB (above) best inns bowling figures returned for Notts.
Clubs: Keighley, Bradford. Retired to become secretary of Nottingham Forest FC.

SMALL, Gladstone Cleophas
——RHB, RF——

Born St George, Barbados, 18 Oct 1961. Educ Moseley S; Hall Green Technical C. Debut 1979/80.
WARWICKSHIRE (90) 1980–. Cap 1982.
TOURS D. H. Robins' XI to N Zealand 1979/80. International XI to Pakistan 1981/82.
HS 57* Warwicks v Oxford U, The Parks, 1982.
BB 7–68 Warwicks v Yorks, Edgbaston, 1982.

SMART, Cyril Cecil
——RHB, LB——

Born Lacock, Wiltshire, 23 July 1898. Died Abertillery, S Wales, 21 May 1975. Educ Westbury Church of England S. Debut 1920. *P.*
WARWICKSHIRE (45) 1920–22. Cap 1922.
GLAMORGAN (191) 1927–46. Cap 1934.
HS 151* Glam v Sussex, Hastings, 1935.

BB 5–39 Glam v Som, Weston-super-Mare, 1939.
1000 RUNS (5) 1560 @ 36.28 in 1935.
RECORD Added 263 for 4th wkt with G. Lavis, Glam v Worcs, Cardiff, 1934, county record.
Hit G. Hill for 32 runs (664664) in one over, Glam v Hants, Cardiff, 1935, at time most runs from a six-ball over not containing a no-ball.
Brother J. A. Smart (Warwicks).

SMEDLEY, Michael John
——RHB——

Born Maltby, Yorks, 28 Oct 1941. Educ Woodhouse GS, Sheffield. Debut 1964.
NOTTINGHAMSHIRE (357) 1964–79. Cap 1966. Benefit (£8500) 1975. Capt 1975–79.
HS 149 Notts v Glam, Cardiff, 1970.
1000 RUNS (9) 1718 @ 38.17 in 1971.
RECORD Added 204 for 7th wkt with R. A. White, Notts v Surrey, Oval, 1967, county record.

SMETHERS, Michael Charles
——RHB, WK——

Born Enfield, London, 18 Aug 1947. Educ Highgate; St John's C, Cambridge. Debut 1967.
CAMBRIDGE UNIVERSITY (2) 1967.
HS 14 Cambridge U v Sussex, Fenner's, 1967.
Clubs: Southgate, Incogniti.

SMITH, Alan Christopher
——RHB, WK, RMF——

Born Hall Green, Birmingham, 25 Oct 1936. Educ King Edward's S, Edgbaston; Brasenose C, Oxford. Debut 1958.
OXFORD UNIVERSITY (45) 1958–60 (Blue 1958–60). Capt 1959–60.
WARWICKSHIRE (358) 1958–74. Cap 1961. Capt 1968–74.
ENGLAND (6) 1962/63. *A 1962/63 (4); NZ 1962/63 (2).*
OTHER TOURS E. W. Swanton's XI to W Indies 1960/61. MCC to Australia 1974/75 (1 match in emergency).
HST 69* E v NZ, Wellington, 1962/63. HS 145 Oxford U v Hants, Bournemouth, 1959 (scored 124 in second innings).
BB 5–32 (9–77 match) Oxford U v Free Foresters, The Parks, 1960.
1000 RUNS (1) 1201 @ 31.60 in 1962.
RECORDS During HST (above) added 163 unbroken for 9th wkt with M. C. Cowdrey, world Test record at time and remains England Test record. Performed hat-trick, Warwicks v Essex, Clacton, 1965, after earlier in the inns keeping wicket, a unique achievement in fc cricket.

After 1971 gave up wicketkeeping to concentrate on bowling and batting. Gentlemen v Players (4) 1960–62. Warwicks secretary since 1976. Manager MCC to Ceylon 1969/70; MCC to Australia and N Zealand 1974/75; England to W Indies 1980/81; England to N Zealand and Pakistan 1983/84. England Test selector 1969–73, 1982–. Soccer: Blue; former director of Aston Villa.

SMITH, Alexander Victor
——LHB——

Born Dublin, Ireland, 11 May 1945. Educ St Brendan's Christian Brothers' S, Bray. Debut 1978.
IRELAND (2) 1978–79.
HS 11* Ireland v Sri Lankans, Eglinton, 1979.
Club: Pembroke.

SMITH, Anthony John Shaw
——RHB, WK——

Born Johannesburg, S Africa, 8 Feb 1951. Educ St Stithian's C, Johannesburg; King Edward VII S, Johannesburg; Natal U. Debut 1971/72.
S AFRICA DOMESTIC South African Universities 1971/72, Natal 1972/73–.
D. H. ROBINS' XI (1) 1974.
HS 150* Natal v Transvaal, J'burg, 1975/76.
Rugby: Natal.

SMITH, Anthony Mervyn
——LHB, SLA——

Born Castle Combe, Wiltshire, 26 Feb 1930. Debut 1965.
MINOR COUNTIES (1) 1965.
HS 12 Minor Counties v S Africans, Jesmond, 1965.
Wiltshire 1955–65. Clubs: Chippenham, Grittleton.

SMITH, Cameron Wilberforce
——RHB, WK——

Born Christ Church, Barbados, 29 July 1933. Debut 1951/52.
W INDIES DOMESTIC Barbados 1951/52–64/65.
WEST INDIAN XI (3) 1964.
WEST INDIES (5) 1960/61–61/62. I 1961/62 (1). *A 1960/61 (4).*
OTHER TOUR Commonwealth XI to India 1964/65.
HST 55 WI v I, Sydney, 1960/61. HS 140 Barbados v Trinidad, Bridgetown, 1962/63.
Club: Blackpool. Involved with youth cricket in W Indies.

SMITH, Christopher Lyall
————RHB, OB————

Born Durban, S Africa, 15 Oct 1958.
Educ Northlands HS, Durban. Debut
1977/78.
S AFRICA DOMESTIC Natal 1977/78–82/
83.
GLAMORGAN (1) 1979.
HAMPSHIRE (75) 1980–.
ENGLAND (7) 1983–83/84. NZ 1983 (2),
1983/84 (2); P 1983/84 (3).
HST 91 E v NZ, Auckland, 1983/84. HS
193 Hants v Derbys, Derby, 1983.
BBT 2–31 E v NZ, Trent Bridge, 1983.
BB 3–35 Hants v Glam, Southampton,
1983.
1000 RUNS (4) 1923 @ 53.41 in 1983.
Grandfather V. L. Shearer (Natal);
brother R. A. Smith (Natal, Hants).

SMITH, Colin Milner
————RHB, WK————

Born Mottingham, Kent, 2 Nov 1936.
Educ Tonbridge; Brasenose C, Oxford.
Debut 1958.
OXFORD UNIVERSITY (1) 1958.
HS 12 Oxford U v Sussex, The Parks,
1958.

SMITH, Colin Stansfield
————RHB, RFM————

Born Didsbury, Manchester, 1 Oct
1932. Educ William Hulme's GS, Man-
chester; Christ's C, Cambridge. Debut
1951.
LANCASHIRE (45) 1951–57. Cap 1956.
COMBINED SERVICES (4) 1952–53.
CAMBRIDGE UNIVERSITY (53) 1954–57
(Blue 1954–57).
FREE FORESTERS (1) 1958.
D. R. JARDINE'S XI (1) 1958.
MCC (1) 1958.
HS 103* Cambridge U v Warwicks, Edg-
baston, 1957.
BB 6–35 Cambridge U v Free Foresters,
Fenner's, 1955.
Took 91 wkts @ 19.91 in 1957.
Gentlemen v Players (1) 1957. Cheshire
1949–50. Clubs: Stockport, Dulwich,
Esher. MCC committee 1977–81.
Lacrosse: Cambridge. Well-known
architect. Changed name to Colin
Stansfield-Smith subsequent to fc
career.

SMITH, David Henry Kilner
————LHB, occ WK————

Born Shipley, Yorks, 29 June 1940.
Educ Bingley GS. Debut 1965.
DERBYSHIRE (112) 1965–70. Cap 1968.

S AFRICA DOMESTIC Orange Free State
1976/77–77/78.
HS 136 Derbys v Lancs, Derby, 1970.
1000 RUNS (3) 1397 @ 28.61 in 1968.
Club: Undercliffe.

SMITH, David James
————LHB, WK————

Born Brighton, Sussex, 28 Apr 1962.
Educ Hove GS. Debut 1981.
SUSSEX (14) 1981–.
HS 13 Sussex v Som, Hove, 1983.

SMITH, David Mark
————LHB, RM————

Born Balham, London, 9 Jan 1956.
Educ Battersea GS. Debut 1973.
SURREY (141) 1973–83. Cap 1980.
WORCESTERSHIRE (17) 1984.
HS 189* Worcs v Kent, Worcester, 1984.
BB 3–40 Surrey v Sussex, Oval, 1976.
1000 RUNS (2) 1093 @ 42.04 in 1984.

SMITH, David Martin
————LHB, SLA————

Born Coventry, Warwicks, 21 Jan 1962.
Educ Caludon Castle S, Coventry.
Debut 1981.
WARWICKSHIRE (4) 1981–83.
HS 100* Warwicks v Oxford U, Edgbas-
ton, 1983.
Clubs: GEC Coventry, Leamington.

SMITH, David Robert
————RHB, RMF————

Born Bristol, Glos, 5 Oct 1934. Debut
1956. P.
GLOUCESTERSHIRE (357) 1956–70. Cap
1957. Benefit (£3800) 1968.
ENGLAND (5) I 1961/62.
OTHER TOUR MCC to N Zealand 1960/
61.
HST 34 E v I, Madras, 1961/62. HS 74
Glos v MCC, Lord's, 1961.
BBT 2–60 E v I, Calcutta, 1961/62. BB
7–20 Glos v Sussex, Stroud, 1962.
100 WKTS (5) 143 @ 20.30 in 1960.
Club: Gloucester City. Soccer: Bristol
City, Millwall.

SMITH, Denis
————LHB, occ WK, occ RM————

Born Somercotes, Derbys, 24 Jan 1907.
Died Derby, 12 Sept 1979. Educ Clay
Cross Sec S. Debut 1927. P. Wisden
1936.
DERBYSHIRE (420) 1927–52. Cap.
Testimonial (£1950) 1947.

ENGLAND (2) SA 1935.
TOUR MCC to Australasia 1935/36.
HST 57 E v SA, Headingley, 1935. HS 225
Derbys v Hants, Chesterfield, 1935.
BB 5–37 Derbys v Notts, Trent Bridge,
1948.
1000 RUNS (12) 2175 @ 39.54 in 1935.
RECORDS Added 328 for 4th wkt with P.
Vaulkhard, Derbys v Notts, Trent
Bridge, 1946, county record. Most runs
(20,516 @ 31.41) and most centuries
(30) for Derbys.
Derbys coach for 1951–71. Club: Lidget
Green.

SMITH, Donald James
————RHB, LFM————

Born Accrington, Lancs, 1 May 1929.
Debut 1951. P.
LANCASHIRE (3) 1951–52.
HS 14 Lancs v Hants, Portsmouth, 1951.
Club: David Brown Tractors.

SMITH, Donald Joseph
————LHB, RFM————

Born Stockport, Cheshire, 19 Oct 1933.
Educ Stockport GS; St John's C, Cam-
bridge. Debut 1955.
CAMBRIDGE UNIVERSITY (28) 1955–57
(Blue 1955–56).
HS 18* Cambridge U v Surrey,
Fenner's, 1955.
BB 7–55 Cambridge U v Glos, Bristol,
1955.
Cheshire 1949–70. Clubs: Stockport,
Royal Air Force.

SMITH, Donald Victor
————LHB, LM————

Born Broadwater, Sussex, 14 June 1923.
Debut 1946. P.
SUSSEX (360) 1946–62. Cap 1950. Benefit
(£3078) 1959.
ENGLAND (3) WI 1957.
TOUR Duke of Norfolk's XI to Jamaica
1956/57.
HST 16* E v WI, Trent Bridge, 1957. HS
206* Sussex v Notts, Trent Bridge,
1950.
BB 7–40 MCC v Oxford U, Lord's,
1956.
1000 RUNS (8) 2088 @ 42.61 in 1957.
Players v Gentlemen (2) 1957–58.
Professional coach Lancing 1963–.

SMITH, Douglas Maxwell
————RHB, RFM————

Born Haywards Heath, Sussex, 14 Sept
1915. Educ Weston Road S, Lewes.
Debut 1938. P.

SUSSEX (6) 1938–46.
HS 34 Sussex v Oxford U, Eastbourne, 1939.
BB 5–25 Sussex v Hants, Horsham, 1938.
During HS (above), batting at number 11, added 71 for 10th wkt with J. Duffield, going in with 128 runs needed for victory.
Club: Lewes Priory.

SMITH, Edwin
—RHB, OB—

Born Grassmoor, Chesterfield, Derbys, 2 Jan 1934. Debut 1951. *P.*
DERBYSHIRE (497) 1951–71. Cap 1954.
Testimonial (£2810) 1966.
HS 90 Derbys v Notts, Ilkeston, 1962.
BB 9–46 (14–112 match) Derbys v Scotland, Edinburgh, 1955.
100 WKTS (1) 105 @ 17.65 in 1955.
Took 8–21 in second fc match, Derbys v Worcs, Chesterfield, 1951.
Former Derbys coach (after retirement). Clubs: Chesterfield, Norton Oakes, Rotherham Phoenix, Grassmoor.

SMITH, Frank Brunton
—RHB—

Born Rangiroa, N Zealand, 13 Mar 1922. Debut 1942/43.
N ZEALAND DOMESTIC South Island Army (1) 1942/43, Canterbury (19) 1946/47–52/53.
NEW ZEALAND (4) 1946/47–51/52. E 1946/47 (1); WI 1951/52 (1). *E 1949 (2).*
HST 96 NZ v E, Headingley, 1949. HS 153 Canterbury v Otago, Christchurch, 1948/49.
1000 RUNS (1) 1008 @ 28.00 in 1949.
Son G. B. Smith (Canterbury).

SMITH, Geoffrey
—RHB, RMF—

Born Huddersfield, Yorks, 30 Nov 1925. Educ Christ's Hospital. Debut 1951.
KENT (42) 1951–58. Cap 1953.
HS 60 Kent v Worcs, Gravesend, 1953.
BB 8–110 Kent v Sussex, Tunbridge Wells, 1957.
Clubs: Canterbury St Lawrence, Bromley.

SMITH, Geoffrey John
—RHB, OB—

Born Braintree, Essex, 2 Apr 1935. Educ Braintree County HS. Debut 1955. *P.*
ESSEX (239) 1955–66. Cap 1960.

HS 148 Essex v Derbys, Chesterfield, 1961.
BB 5–39 Essex v Derbys, Derby, 1965.
1000 RUNS (4) 1908 @ 32.89 in 1961.
Hertfordshire 1967–69.

SMITH, Graham Stuart
—RHB—

Born Leicester, 4 July 1923. Educ Bedford S. Debut 1949.
LEICESTERSHIRE (1) 1949.
HS 22 Leics v Northants, Northampton, 1949.

SMITH, Ian David Stockley
—RHB, WK—

Born Nelson, N Zealand, 28 Feb 1957. Debut 1977/78.
N ZEALAND DOMESTIC New Zealand Under-23 1977/78–79/80, Central Districts (40) 1977/78–.
NEW ZEALAND (9) 1980/81–83. A 1981/82 (3); I 1980/81 (3). *E 1983 (2); A 1980/ 81 (1).*
HST 113* NZ v E, Auckland, 1983/84. HS 145 C Districts v Auckland, Napier, 1982/83.

SMITH, Jack
—RHB, OB—

Born Stotfold, Bedfordshire, 7 Mar 1936. Educ Bedford S. Debut 1965.
MINOR COUNTIES (1) 1965.
HS 17 Minor Counties v S Africans, Jesmond, 1965.
BB 2–47 same match.
Bedfordshire 1959–75. Club: Letchworth.

SMITH, John Westwood Rowley
—RHB, WK—

Born Leicester, 28 July 1924. Educ Repton. Debut 1950.
LEICESTERSHIRE (3) 1950–55.
HS 4 Leics v Notts, Leicester, 1950.

SMITH, Kenneth *David*
—RHB—

Born Jesmond, Newcastle upon Tyne, 9 July 1956. Educ Heaton GS, Newcastle upon Tyne. Debut 1973.
WARWICKSHIRE (191) 1973–. Cap 1978.
HS 140 Warwicks v Worcs, Worcester, 1980.
1000 RUNS (4) 1582 @ 36.79 in 1980.
Father K. D. Smith (Leics); brother P. A. Smith (Warwicks); father-in-law A. S. M. Oakman (Sussex, England).

SMITH, Kenneth Desmond
—RHB—

Born Bishop Auckland, Co Durham, 30 Apr 1922. Debut 1950. *P.*
LEICESTERSHIRE (26) 1950–51.
HS 70* Leics v Northants, Northampton, 1950.
BB 2–37 Leics v Glos, Bristol, 1951.
Northumberland 1949, 1953–61. Club: Ashington. Sons K. D. and P. A. Smith (both Warwicks).

SMITH, Kevin Brian
—LHB, SLA—

Born Lewes, Sussex, 28 Aug 1957. Debut 1978.
SUSSEX (4) 1978.
HS 43 Sussex v Kent, Hove, 1978.

SMITH, Lewis Alfred
—RHB, RFM—

Born Brentford, M'sex, 12 July 1913. Died N London, 10 Sept 1978. Debut 1934.
MIDDLESEX (3) 1934–37.
NORTHAMPTONSHIRE (2) 1947.
HS 55 Northants v S Africans, Northampton, 1947.
BB 4–55 same match.
Club: Mill Hill Park.

SMITH, Martin Graham Milner
—RHB, WK—

Born Otford, Kent, 28 Sept 1941. Educ Tonbridge; St John's C, Cambridge. Debut 1961.
CAMBRIDGE UNIVERSITY (1) 1961.
HS 18* Cambridge U v Worcs, Fenner's, 1961.
Club: Stragglers.

SMITH, Michael John
—RHB, SLA—

Born Enfield, M'sex, 4 Jan 1942. Educ Enfield GS. Debut 1959. *P.*
MIDDLESEX (399) 1959–80. Cap 1967.
Benefit (£20,000) 1976.
TOURS D. H. Robins' XI to S Africa 1972/73, 1973/74. D. H. Robins' XI to Sri Lanka 1977/78.
HS 181 M'sex v Lancs, Old Trafford, 1967.
BB 4–13 M'sex v Glos, Lord's, 1961.
1000 RUNS (11) 1705 @ 39.65 in 1970.
Club: Enfield.

SMITH, Michael John Knight
—RHB—

Born Broughton Astley, Leics, 30 June 1933. Educ Stamford S; St Edmund

Hall, Oxford. Debut 1951. *Wisden* 1960.
LEICESTERSHIRE (28) 1951–55. Cap 1955.
OXFORD UNIVERSITY (43) 1954–56 (Blue 1954–56). Capt 1956.
WARWICKSHIRE (430) 1956–75. Cap 1957. Capt 1957–67.
ENGLAND (50) 1958–72. A 1961 (1), 1972 (3); SA 1960 (4), 1965 (3); WI 1966 (1); NZ 1958 (3), 1965 (3); I 1959 (2). *A 1965/66 (5); SA 1964/65 (5); WI 1959/60 (5); NZ 1965/66 (3); I 1961/62 (4), 1963/64 (5); P 1961/62 (3).* Capt 25.
OTHER TOURS MCC to E Africa 1957/58. Cavaliers to S Africa 1960/61. MCC to E Africa (capt) 1963/64.
HST 121 E v SA, Cape Town, 1964/65.
HS 204 Cavaliers v Natal, Durban, 1960/61.
1000 RUNS (19 + 1) 3245 @ 57.94 in 1959. 2000 runs (6), 1957–62 consecutively.
RECORDS Scored three centuries for Oxford U v Cambridge U at Lord's, first batsman to do so (201* in 1954, 104 in 1955 and 117 in 1956). Scored 1540 runs @ 39.48 in first full season, 1954, after three matches in 1951. Scored 1209 runs @ 93.00 in July 1959, a record aggregate for that month. Reached 3000 runs for season by 21 August in 1959, third behind T. W. Hayward (1906) and W.R. Hammond (1937), who both reached the total on August 20. Scored 2417 runs @ 60.42 in season for Warwicks, in 1959, a county record. Added 197 for 7th wkt with J.M. Parks, E v WI, Port of Spain, 1959/60, England Test record.
Scored centuries against all fc counties except Warwicks.
Gentlemen v Players (13) 1955–62. Club: King's Heath. MCC committee 1973–75; MCC Hon. member. Rugby: Leicester, Blue, England (1). OBE for services for cricket.

SMITH, Neil
RHB, WK

Born Dewsbury, Yorks, 1 Apr 1949. Educ Ossett GS. Debut 1970.
YORKSHIRE (8) 1970–71.
MINOR COUNTIES (1) 1972.
ESSEX (178) 1973–81. Cap 1975.
HS 126 Essex v Som, Leyton, 1976.
Club: Bradford.

SMITH, O'Neil Gordon (Collie)
RHB, OB

Born Kingston, Jamaica, 5 May 1933. Died, in road-traffic accident, Stoke on Trent, Staffordshire, 9 Sept 1959. Educ Kingston C, Jamaica. Debut 1954/55. *Wisden* 1958.

W INDIES DOMESTIC Jamaica 1954/55–57/58.
WEST INDIES (26) 1954/55–58/59. A 1954/55 (4); P 1957/58 (5). *E 1957 (5); NZ 1955/56 (4); I 1958/59 (5); P 1958/59 (3).*
HST 168 WI v E, Trent Bridge, 1957. HS 169 Jamaica v Australians, Kingston, 1954/55.
BBT 5–90 WI v I, Delhi, 1958/59. BB 5–63 W Indians v Board President's XI, Ahmedabad, 1958/59.
1000 RUNS (1) 1483 @ 41.19 in 1957.
Scored 104 in 2nd inns of Test debut, WI v A, Kingston, 1954/55.
Clubs: Boys' Town (Jamaica); Burnley (England). Half-brother L. N. G. Wright (Jamaica).

SMITH, Paul Andrew
RHB, RFM

Born Jesmond, Newcastle upon Tyne, 15 Apr 1964. Educ Heaton GS. Debut 1982.
WARWICKSHIRE (46) 1982–.
HS 114 Warwicks v Oxford U, Edgbaston, 1983.
BB 4–41 Warwicks v Worcs, Edgbaston, 1984.
1000 runs (1) 1040 @ 28.10 in 1984.
Father K. D. Smith snr (Leics); brother K. D. Smith jnr (Warwicks).

SMITH, Peter Bruce
RHB, RM

Born Oxford, 18 Mar 1944. Educ Magdalen College S, Oxford; Lincoln C, Oxford. Debut 1967.
OXFORD UNIVERSITY (5) 1967.
HS 18 Oxford U v Glam, The Parks, 1967.
BB 4–92 Oxford U v M'sex, The Parks, 1967.
Oxfordshire 1963–77. Club: Leamington.

SMITH, Peter Thomas
RHB

Born Leicester, 5 Oct 1934. Debut 1956. *P.*
LEICESTERSHIRE (15) 1956–57.
HS 40 Leics v Surrey, Leicester, 1956.

SMITH, R.
MF

Debut 1947.
COMBINED SERVICES (1) 1947.
HS 22 Combined Services v Glos, Bristol, 1947.
RAF corporal.

SMITH, Raymond
RHB, RMF/OB

Born Boreham, Essex, 10 Aug 1914. Educ King Edward VI S, Chelmsford. Debut 1934. *P.*
ESSEX (419) 1934–56. Cap 1938. Benefit (£3600) 1951. Testimonial (£1288) 1955.
TOUR Commonwealth XI to India, Pakistan and Ceylon 1949/50.
HS 147 Essex v S Africans, Ilford, 1951.
BB 8–63 Essex v Glam, Pontypridd, 1955.
1000 RUNS (4) 1386 @ 28.87 in 1947.
100 WKTS (7) 136 @ 28.87 in 1952.
DOUBLE (3) 1947, 1950, 1952.
Took 125 wkts @ 37.26 in 1947, most expensive 100-wkt haul in an English season.
Former professional coach Felsted (from 1963). Lately a restauranteur in Warwicks. Cousin T. P. B. Smith (Essex, England).

SMITH, Raymond Charles
RHB, SLA

Born Duddington, Northants, 3 Aug 1935. Educ Stamford S. Debut 1956. *P.*
LEICESTERSHIRE (104) 1956–64.
HS 36 Leics v Som, Leicester, 1958 and 36 v Warwicks, Edgbaston, 1964.
BB 7–54 Leics v Notts, Trent Bridge, 1957.

SMITH, Robin Arnold
RHB, LB

Born Durban, S Africa, 13 Sept 1963. Educ Northlands HS, Durban. Debut 1980/81.
S AFRICA DOMESTIC Natal 1980/81–.
HAMPSHIRE (15) 1982–.
HS 132 Hants v Sri Lankans, Southampton, 1984.
Brother C. L. Smith (Natal, Glam, Hants, England).

SMITH, Rodney
RHB, SLA

Born Batley, Yorks, 6 Apr 1944. Debut 1969.
YORKSHIRE (5) 1969–70.
HS 37* Yorks v Glos, Gloucester, 1969.
Club: Heckmondwike.

SMITH, Ronald
RHB, RFM

Born Dudley, Worcs, 16 Feb 1926. Debut 1954. *P.*
NORTHAMPTONSHIRE (1) 1954.
HS 19* Northants v Surrey, Oval, 1954.

SMITH, Roy
RHB

Born Stoke on Trent, Staffordshire, 20 Jan 1910. Died Great Chell, Staffordshire, 19 Oct 1971. Debut 1949.
MINOR COUNTIES (1) 1949.
HS 29 Minor Counties v Yorks, Lord's, 1949.
Staffordshire 1946–54. Clubs: Great Chell, Norton, Caverswall, Stoke.

SMITH, Roy
RHB, SLA

Born Taunton, Som, 14 Apr 1930. Debut 1949. P.
SOMERSET (96) 1949–55. Cap 1953.
HS 100 Som v Worcs, Frome, 1953.
BB 4–91 Som v Leics, Leicester, 1952.
1000 RUNS (1) 1176 @ 26.13 in 1953.
Devon 1957–60.

SMITH, Stanley
RHB

Born Heywood, Lancs, 14 Jan 1929. Debut 1950. P.
COMBINED SERVICES (6) 1950–51.
LANCASHIRE (38) 1952–56.
HS 101* Combined Services v Essex, Chelmsford, 1950.
Clubs: Rochdale, Kendal, Idle.

SMITH, Thomas *Peter* Bromley
RHB, LBG

Born Ipswich, Suffolk, 30 Oct 1908. Died Hyeres, France, 4 Aug 1967. Educ Highfield C, Leigh-on-Sea, Essex; King Edward VI S, Chelmsford. Debut 1929. *P. Wisden* 1947.
ESSEX (434) 1929–51. Cap 1930. Benefit (£3000) 1947.
ENGLAND (4) 1946–46/47. I 1946 (1). A 1946/47 (2); NZ 1946/47 (1).
OTHER TOURS Lord Tennyson's XI to India 1937/38. Sir J. Cahn's XI to N Zealand 1938/39.
HST 24 E v A, Sydney, 1946/47. HS 163 Essex v Derbys, Chesterfield, 1947.
BBT 2–172 E v A, Sydney, 1946/47. BB 9–77 (16–215 match) Essex v M'sex, Colchester, 1947.
1000 RUNS (1) 1065 @ 23.66 in 1947.
100 WKTS (6) 172 @ 27.13 in 1947.
DOUBLE (1) 1947.
RECORDS During HS (above) added 218 for 10th wkt with F. H. Vigar, county record; 163 highest-ever inns by a number 11 batsman. Return of 9–121 MCC v NSW, Sydney, 1946/47, best for English tourist in Australia.

Returned inns analyses of 9–108 Essex v Kent, Maidstone, 1948 and 9–117 Essex v Notts, Southend, 1948. Match double (1 and 101, 2–69 and 8–99) Essex v M'sex, Chelmsford, 1938.
Selected for MCC to India 1939/40 (cancelled owing to war). Club: West Bromwich Dartmouth. Cousin Raymond Smith (Essex).

SMITH, Vivian *Ian*
RHB, LB

Born Durban, S Africa, 23 Feb 1925. Educ Hilton C, Durban; Natal U. Debut 1945/46.
S AFRICA DOMESTIC Natal 1945/46–57/58.
SOUTH AFRICA (9) 1947–57/58. A 1949/50 (3), 1957/58 (1). E 1947 (4), 1955 (1).
HST 11* SA v A, J'burg, 1949/50 and 11 v E, Lord's, 1947. HS 37 Natal v E Province, Port Elizabeth, 1952/53.
BBT 4–143 SA v E, Trent Bridge, 1947. BB 9–88 Natal v Border, Pietermaritzburg, 1946/47.
Returned inns analysis of 4.5–3–1–6, S Africans v Derbys, Derby, 1947.

SMITH, Walter Alfred
RHB, SLA

Born Leicester, 23 Feb 1913. Educ Wyggeston GS; Birmingham U. Debut 1930.
LEICESTERSHIRE (27) 1930–46.
HS 125* Leics v Hants, Portsmouth, 1935.

SMITH, William Albert
LHB, RM

Born Salisbury, Wiltshire, 15 Sept 1937. Debut 1961. P.
SURREY (144) 1961–70. Cap 1968.
HS 103 Surrey v Glos, Oval, 1963.
1000 RUNS (1) 1002 @ 24.43 in 1968.
Wiltshire 1971–76. Club: Sutton (Surrey).

SMITHSON, Gerald Arthur
LHB

Born Spofforth, Yorks, 1 Nov 1926. Died Abingdon, Berkshire, 6 Sept 1970. Debut 1946. P.
YORKSHIRE (39) 1946–50. Cap 1947.
LEICESTERSHIRE (154) 1951–56. Cap 1951.
ENGLAND (2) WI 1947/48.
HST 35 E v WI, Port of Spain, 1947/48.
HS 169 Yorks v Leics, Leicester, 1947.
1000 RUNS (1) 1351 @ 27.57 in 1952.

As a Bevin Boy was granted Government permission to tour W Indies 1947/48. Hertfordshire 1957–62. Clubs: Askern, Queensbury. Former professional coach Caterham S and Abingdon S.

SMITHURST, Isaiah
LHB, SLA

Born Hill Top, Eastwood, Notts, 6 Nov 1920. Debut 1946. P.
NOTTINGHAMSHIRE (1) 1946.
HS 1 Notts v Glos, Trent Bridge, 1946.

SMITHYMAN, Michael James
RHB, RM

Born Pietermaritzburg, S Africa, 17 Nov 1945. Educ Michaelhouse; Natal U. Debut 1965/66.
S AFRICA DOMESTIC Natal 1965/66–74/75.
TOUR S African Universities to England 1967.
HS 73 S African Universities v Oxford U, The Parks, 1967.
BB 4–25 Natal B v W Province, Durban, 1968/69.
Golf: S Africa.

SMYTH, Richard Ian
RHB, LB

Born Sunderland, Co Durham, 19 Nov 1951. Educ Sedbergh; Emmanuel C, Cambridge. Debut 1973.
CAMBRIDGE UNIVERSITY (21) 1973–75 (Blue 1973–75).
HS 61 Cambridge U v Yorks, Fenner's, 1974.
Durham County 1974. Clubs: Whitburn, Darlington.

SMYTH, Richard Nicholas Paul
RHB

Born Chichester, Sussex, 27 June 1950. Educ Brighton C. Debut 1970.
SUSSEX (3) 1970.
HS 25 Sussex v Jamaica, Hove, 1970.

SNAPE, Maurice *Desmond*
RHB

Born Creswell, Derbys, 7 July 1923. Debut 1949. P.
DERBYSHIRE (2) 1949.
No runs.

SNEDDEN, Martin Colin
——————LHB, RM——————

Born Auckland, N Zealand, 23 Nov 1958. Educ Rosmini C, Auckland. Debut 1977/78.
N ZEALAND DOMESTIC New Zealand Under-23 1977/78–79/80, Auckland (25) 1977/78–.
NEW ZEALAND (10) 1980/81–83/84. E 1983/84 (1); A 1981/82 (3); I 1980/81 (3); SL 1982/83 (2). *E 1983 (1)*.
OTHER TOURS N Zealand to Australia 1980/81, 1982/83.
HST 32 NZ v A, Christchurch, 1981/82.
HS 69 N Zealand Under-23 v D. H. Robins' XI, Auckland, 1979/80.
BBT 3–21 NZ v SL, Wellington, 1982/83. BB 7–49 Auckland v Canterbury, Auckland, 1982/83.
Grandfather A. N. C. Snedden (Auckland); uncle C. A. Snedden (Auckland, N Zealand).

SNELLGROVE, Kenneth Leslie
——————RHB——————

Born Shepton Mallet, Som, 12 Nov 1941. Educ Bootle GS. Debut 1965.
LANCASHIRE (105) 1965–74. Cap 1971.
HS 138 Lancs v M'sex, Old Trafford, 1970.
Scored 991 runs @ 31.96 in 1971.
Club: Whalley.

SNODGRASS, David Lang
——————RHB, RFM——————

Born Cross Row, Glasgow, Scotland, 21 Nov 1958. Educ Hyndland Sec S; Strathclyde U. Debut 1982.
SCOTLAND (1) 1982.
HS 6 Scotland v Ireland, Edinburgh, 1982.
BB 2–30 same match.
Club: West of Scotland.

SNOW, John Augustine
——————RHB, RF——————

Born Peopleton, Worcs, 13 Oct 1941. Educ Christ's Hospital, Horsham; Chichester HS; Culham Teacher Training C. Debut 1961. *P. Wisden 1973*.
SUSSEX (267) 1961–77. Cap 1964. Benefit (£18,000) 1974.
ENGLAND (49) 1965–76. A 1968 (5); 1972 (5); 1975 (4); SA 1965 (1); WI 1966 (3); 1969 (3), 1973 (1), 1976 (3); NZ 1965 (1), 1969 (2), 1973 (3); I 1967 (3), 1971 (2); P 1967 (1). *A 1970/71 (6); WI 1967/68 (4); P 1968/69 (2)*.
OTHER TOURS Cavaliers to W Indies 1969/70. D. H. Robins' XI to S Africa 1972/73, 1973/74. International XI to Rhodesia 1975/76.

HST 73 E v I, Lord's, 1971. HS as above and 73* Sussex v Worcs, Worcester, 1977.
BBT 7–40 E v A, Sydney, 1970/71. BB 8–87 Sussex v M'sex, Lord's, 1975.
100 WKTS (2) 126 @ 19.09 in 1966.
Added 128 for 10th wkt with K. Higgs, E v WI, Oval, 1966.
World Series Cricket (Kerry Packer) 1977/78. Played for Warwicks in limited-overs matches 1980. Club: Pudsey St Laurence. Autobiography *Cricket Rebel* (1976). Author of two volumes of poems: *Contrasts* (1971) and *Moments and Thoughts* (1973).

SNOWDEN, William
——————RHB, RM——————

Born Prescot, Lancs, 27 Sept 1952. Educ Merchant Taylors', Crosby; Emmanuel C, Cambridge. Debut 1972.
CAMBRIDGE UNIVERSITY (36) 1972–75 (Blue 1972–75). Capt 1974.
HS 108* Cambridge U v Kent, Fenner's, 1973.

SOBERS, Garfield St Aubrun
——————LHB, versatile LA bowler——————

Born Bridgetown, Barbados, 28 July 1936. Educ Bay Street S, Barbados. Debut 1952/53. *Wisden 1964*.
W INDIES DOMESTIC Barbados 1952/53–73/74. Capt 1964/65–70/71.
AUSTRALIA DOMESTIC South Australia (26) 1961/62–63/64.
NOTTINGHAMSHIRE (107) 1968–74. Cap 1968. Capt 1968–71, 1973. Benefit 1972.
WEST INDIES (93) 1953/54–73/74. E 1953/54 (1); 1959/60 (5); 1967/68 (5); 1973/74 (4); A 1954/55 (4), 1964/65 (5); NZ 1971/72 (5); I 1961/62 (5), 1970/71 (5); P 1957/58 (5). *E 1957 (5), 1963 (5), 1966 (5), 1969 (3), 1973 (3); A 1960/61 (5), 1968/69 (5); NZ 1955/56 (4), 1968/69 (3); I 1958/59 (5), 1966/67 (3); P 1958/59 (3). Capt 39*.
OTHER TOURS E. W. Swanton's XI to India 1963/64. Commonwealth XI to India 1964/65. Rest of World XI to Pakistan 1970/71. World XI to Australia 1971/72 (capt).
HST 365* WI v P, Kingston, 1957/58. HS as above.
BBT 6–73 WI v A, Brisbane, 1968/69. BB 9–49 W Indians v Kent, Canterbury, 1966.
1000 RUNS (9 + 6) 1742 @ 75.73 in 1970.
RECORDS HST (above) highest-ever inns in Test cricket and highest-ever in fc cricket by a W Indian. Scored 8032 runs @ 57.78 in Tests, a W Indies record; first of three batsmen to score 8000 runs in Tests. Played 85 consecutive Tests, 1954/55–71/72, a W Indies record. During HST (above) added 446 for 2nd

wkt with C. C. Hunte; added 399 for 4th wkt with F. M. M. Worrell (in 570 mins over four days, Sobers scoring 226 in 647 mins), WI v E, Bridgetown, 1959/60; added 265 for 5th wkt with S. M. Nurse, WI v E, Headingley, 1966; added 274* for 6th wkt with D. A. J. Holford, WI v E, Lord's, 1966; the first is a W Indian Test record, all are W Indies Test records. 109 catches in Tests, a W Indies record. Hit six sixes off one six-ball over, from M. A. Nash, Notts v Glam, Swansea, 1968, only batsman to do so. Scored 1000 runs and took 50 wkts twice in an Australian season (for S Australia in 1962/63 and 1963/64), a unique achievement. First player to score 4000 or more Test runs and take 200 or more Test wkts (235 @ 34.03). Match double (17 and 105*, 7–69 and 7–87), Notts v Kent, Dover, 1968, including century in 77 mins, fastest of the season.
Rest of World v England (5) 1970 (capt). Clubs: Police (Barbados), Radcliffe, Norton, Littleborough (England). MCC Hon. member. Knighted for services to cricket.

SOHONI, Sriranga Wasudeo
——————RHB, RMF/OB——————

Born Nimbora, Maharashtra, India, 5 Mar 1918. Educ Bombay U. Debut 1935/36.
INDIA DOMESTIC Maharashtra 1935/36–47/48, 1949/50–50/51, 1957/58–59/60 (capt 1957/58–58/59), Bombay Hindus 1941/42–45/46, Baroda 1948/49, Bombay 1951/52–54/55 (capt 1952/53, 1954/55).
INDIA (4) 1946–51/52. E 1951/52 (1). *E 1946 (2); A 1947/48 (1)*.
HST 29* I v E, Oval, 1946. HS 218* Maharastra v W India, Rajkot, 1940/41.
BB 7–20 (11–103 match) Maharashtra v W India, Jamnagar, 1937/38.
Clubs: Rishton, Lowerhouse.

SOLANKY, John William
——————RHB, OB——————

Born Dar-es-Salaam, Tanganyika, 30 June 1942. Debut 1963/64.
EAST AFRICA (2) 1963/64–64/65.
GLAMORGAN (82) 1972–76. Cap 1973.
HS 73 Glam v Cambridge U, Swansea, 1975.
BB 6–63 Glam v Derbys, Buxton, 1975.
Devon 1967–69.

SOLKAR, Eknath Dhondu
——————LHB, LM/SLA——————

Born Bombay, India, 18 Mar 1948. Educ Maratha S, Bombay. Debut 1965/66.

INDIA DOMESTIC Bombay 1966/67–80/81.
SUSSEX (1) 1969.
INDIA (27) 1969/70–76/77. E 1972/73 (5), 1976/77 (1); A 1969/70 (4); WI 1974/75 (4); NZ 1969/70 (1). *E 1971 (3), 1974 (3); WI 1970/71 (5), 1975/76 (1).*
OTHER TOURS India to Sri Lanka 1973/74. India to N Zealand 1975/76.
HST 102 I v WI, Bombay, 1974/75. HS 145* W Zone v N Zone, Bombay, 1968/69 and 145 Bombay v Maharashtra, Nasik, 1974/75.
BBT 3–28 I v E, Oval, 1971. BB 6–38 Bombay v Saurashtra, Jamnagar, 1966/67.
RECORDS Took 12 catches in Test series, I v E, 1972/73, India Test record. Added 186 for 7th wkt with D. N. Sardesai, I v WI, Bridgetown, 1970/71, India Test record.

SOLOMON, Joseph Stanislaus
—————RHB, RM/LB—————

Born Corentyne, Berbice, British Guiana, 26 Aug 1930. Debut 1956/57.
W INDIES DOMESTIC British Guiana (Guyana) 1956/57–68/69.
WEST INDIES (27) 1958/59–64/65. E 1959/60 (2); A 1964/65 (4); I 1961/62 (4). *E 1963 (5); A 1960/61 (5); I 1958/59 (4); P 1958/59 (3).*
OTHER TOUR W Indies to England 1966.
HST 100* WI v I, Delhi, 1958/59. HS 201* Berbice v MCC, Blairmont, 1959/60.
BB 4–28 British Guiana v Barbados, Bridgetown, 1965/66.
RECORD Only batsman to score centuries in first three fc inns (114* v Jamaica, Georgetown, 1956/57; 108 v Barbados, Georgetown, 1956/57; 121 v Pakistanis, Georgetown, 1957/58; all for British Guiana).
W Indies Test selector since 1971.
MCC Hon. member.

SOMERVILLE, Reginald James
—————RHB—————

Born Camberwell, London, 9 Oct 1918. Died London, 13 Aug 1979. Debut 1955.
D. R. JARDINE'S XI (1) 1955.
HS 3 D. R. Jardine's XI v Oxford U, Eastbourne, 1955.
Club: Bank of England.

SOUNESS, James McGill
—————RHB, RFM—————

Born Leith, Scotland, 9 Nov 1928. Educ Heriot's. Debut 1954.

SCOTLAND (3) 1954–55.
HS 7 Scotland v Worcs, Glasgow, 1955.
BB 2–63 Scotland v Warwicks, Coventry, 1954.
Club: Heriot's FP.

SOUTER, James Stewart
—————RHB—————

Born Kanpur, India, 9 Feb 1924. Educ Haileybury and ISC; Brasenose C, Oxford. Debut 1948.
OXFORD UNIVERSITY (3) 1948.
HS 30 Oxford U v Free Foresters, The Parks, 1948.

SOUTHERN, John William
—————RHB, SLA—————

Born King's Cross, London, 2 Sept 1952. Educ Wm Ellis S, London; Southampton U. Debut 1975.
HAMPSHIRE (164) 1975–83. Cap 1978.
HS 61* Hants v Yorks, Bradford, 1979.
BB 6–46 Hants v Glos, Bournemouth, 1975.

SPANSWICK, John George
—————RHB, RFM—————

Born Folkestone, Kent, 30 Sept 1933. Debut 1955. *P.*
KENT (16) 1955–56.
HS 24 Kent v Worcs, Worcester, 1955.
BB 4–64 Kent v Lancs, Maidstone, 1955.
Club: Folkestone.

SPARLING, John Trevor
—————RHB, OB—————

Born Auckland, N Zealand, 24 July 1938. Educ Auckland U. Debut 1956/57.
N ZEALAND DOMESTIC Auckland (83) 1956/57–70/71 (capt 1962/63–70/71).
NEW ZEALAND (11) 1958–63/64. E 1958/59 (2), 1962/63 (1); SA 1963/64 (2). *E 1958 (3); SA 1961/62 (3).*
HST 50 NZ v E, Old Trafford, 1958. HS 105 Auckland v Canterbury, Christchurch, 1959/60.
BB 7–49 Auckland v Otago, Auckland, 1964/65.

SPEAK, Gary John
—————RHB, RMF—————

Born Chorley, Lancs, 26 Apr 1962. Educ Rivington and Blackrod HS. Debut 1981.
LANCASHIRE (5) 1981–82.
HS 15* Lancs v Cambridge U, Fenner's, 1982.

SPELMAN, Guy Denis
—————LHB, RM—————

Born Westminster, London, 18 Oct 1958. Educ Sevenoaks S; Nottingham U. Debut 1980.
KENT (7) 1980–82.
HS 4 Kent v Notts, Trent Bridge, 1980.
BB 2–27 Kent v Sussex, Tunbridge Wells, 1980.
Career curtailed by back injury; received through his county, in 1983, £25,000 in compensation.

SPENCE, Lawrence Arthur
—————RHB, LB—————

Born Blaby, Leics, 14 Jan 1932. Debut 1952. *P.*
LEICESTERSHIRE (20) 1952–54.
HS 44 Leics v Glos, Leicester, 1952.

SPENCER, Alan Horace
—————RHB, OB—————

Born Lee Green, Kent, 4 July 1936. Debut 1957. *P.*
WORCESTERSHIRE (27) 1957–61.
HS 85 Worcs v Northants, Dudley, 1960.
Club: Dudley.

SPENCER, Charles *Terry*
—————RHB, RFM—————

Born Leicester, 18 Aug 1931. Debut 1952. *P.*
LEICESTERSHIRE (496) 1952–74. Cap 1952. Benefit (£3500) 1964.
HS 90 Leics v Essex, Leicester, 1964.
BB 9–63 Leics v Yorks, Huddersfield, 1954.
100 WKTS (1) 123 @ 19.56 in 1961.
RECORD During HS (above) added 164 for 8th wkt with M. R. Hallam, county record.
Test Trial 1953. Fc umpire 1979–83.
Uncle Haydn Smith (Leics).

SPENCER, John
—————RHB, RMF—————

Born Brighton, Sussex, 6 Oct 1949. Educ Brighton, Hove and Sussex GS; Queen's C, Cambridge. Debut 1969.
SUSSEX (186) 1969–80. Cap 1973. Benefit 1981.
CAMBRIDGE UNIVERSITY (28) 1970–72 (Blue 1970–72).
HS 79 Sussex v Hants, Southampton, 1975.
BB 6–19 Sussex v Glos, Gloucester, 1974.

SPENCER, Thomas William
RHB, RM

Born Deptford, London, 22 Mar 1914. Debut 1935. *P*.
KENT (76) 1935–46. Cap.
HS 96 Kent v Sussex, Tunbridge Wells, 1946.
Fc umpire 1950–80 (17 Tests, 1954–78). Professional coach Wrekin S 1947–49.

SPENCER, Walter Gordon
RHB, SLA

Born Chingford, Essex, 2 Aug 1912. Died Chelmsford, Essex, 20 July 1971. Educ Bancroft's S. Debut 1938.
ESSEX (3) 1938–48.
HS 25 Essex v M'sex, Brentwood, 1948. Club: Chingford.

SPERRY, James
LHB, LFM

Born Thornton, Leics, 19 Mar 1910. Debut 1937. *P*.
LEICESTERSHIRE (187) 1937–52. Cap 1939. Testimonial (£1414) 1952.
HS 35 Leics v Warwicks, Leicester, 1951.
BB 7–19 Leics v Hants, Leicester, 1939.

SPICER, Peter Alfred
LHB, SLA

Born Ilford, Essex, 11 May 1939. Died, in road-traffic accident, Hainault, Essex, 15 Aug 1969. Educ Fairlop Sec S, Ilford. Debut 1962. *P*.
ESSEX (17) 1962–63.
HS 86 Essex v Pakistanis, Leyton, 1962.
BB 2–1 Essex v M'sex, Lord's, 1962.
Scored 80 on fc debut, Essex v Som, Taunton, 1962, his first scoring-stroke being a six.
Clubs: Ilford, Clayhill, Wanstead. Coached in Holland 1969.

SPILSBURY, John William Edward
RHB, RFM

Born Worcester, 27 Oct 1933. Debut 1952.
WORCESTERSHIRE (1) 1952.
HS 16 Worcs v Combined Services, Worcester, 1952.
Grandfather G. F. Wheldon (Worcs).

SPOONER, Richard Thomas
LHB, WK

Born Stockton-on-Tees, Co Durham, 30 Dec 1919. Debut 1948. *P*.

WARWICKSHIRE (312) 1948–59. Cap 1948. Benefit (£3784) 1957.
ENGLAND (7) 1951/52–55. SA 1955 (1). *I 1951/52 (5); WI 1953/54 (1)*.
OTHER TOUR Commonwealth XI to India 1950/51.
HST 92 E v I, Calcutta, 1951/52. HS 168* MCC v Pakistan, Lahore, 1951/52 and 168 Warwicks v Lancs, Old Trafford, 1953.
1000 RUNS (6) 1767 @ 43.09 in 1951.
Durham County 1946–47. Club: Norton-on-Tees.

SPRAY, Philip Henry
RHB

Born Bedford, 28 Sept 1945. Educ Bedford S; St Edmund Hall, Oxford. Debut 1967.
OXFORD UNIVERSITY (9) 1967–68.
HS 54 Oxford U v Som, The Parks, 1967.
Bedfordshire 1964–67. Club: Buccaneers.

SPRINGALL, John Dennis
RHB, RM

Born S London, 19 Sept 1932. Debut 1955. *P*.
NOTTINGHAMSHIRE (119) 1955–63. Cap 1960.
HS 107* Notts v Leics, Coalville, 1959.
BB 6–43 Notts v Surrey, Oval, 1959.
1000 RUNS (2) 1488 @ 35.42 in 1959.
Club: Walsden.

SQUIRES, Harry *Stanley*
RHB, LB/OB

Born Kingston-upon-Thames, Surrey, 22 Feb 1909. Died Richmond, Surrey, 24 Jan 1950. Debut 1928. *P from 1930*.
SURREY (402) 1928–49. Cap 1931. Benefit (£2900) 1948.
HS 236 Surrey v Lancs, Oval, 1933.
BB 8–52 Surrey v Hants, Kingston-upon-Thames, 1946.
1000 RUNS (11) 1847 @ 36.94 in 1947.
Scored centuries against all fc counties except his own.
Club: Richmond.

SQUIRES, Peter John
RHB

Born Ripon, Yorks, 4 Aug 1951. Educ Ripon GS; St John's C, York. Debut 1972.
YORKSHIRE (49) 1972–76.
HS 70 Yorks v Notts, Bradford, 1976.
Clubs: Ripon, Billingham Synthonia. Rugby: Harrogate, Yorkshire, England (29).

STACKPOLE, Keith Raymond
RHB, LB

Born Collingwood, Melbourne, Australia, 10 July 1940. Educ Christian Brothers' C, Clifton Hill, Melbourne. Debut 1959/60. *Wisden* 1973.
AUSTRALIA DOMESTIC Victoria (75) 1959/60–73/74.
AUSTRALIA (43) 1965/66–73/74. E 1965/66 (2), 1970/71 (6); WI 1968/69 (5); NZ 1973/74 (3); P 1972/73 (1). *E 1972 (5); SA 1966/67 (5), 1969/70 (4); WI 1972/73 (4); NZ 1973/74 (3); I 1969/70 (5)*.
HST 207 A v E, Brisbane, 1970/71. HS as above.
BBT 2–33 A v E, Adelaide, 1965/66. BB 5–38 Victoria v Queensland, Melbourne, 1965/66.
1000 RUNS (1 + 3) 1309 @ 43.63 in 1972.
Clubs: Collingwood (Melbourne), Ramsbottom (Lancashire).
Awarded MBE for services to cricket.
Father K. W. Stackpole (Victoria).

STAINTON, Robert George
RHB

Born Blean, Kent, 23 May 1910. Educ Malvern; Brasenose C, Oxford. Debut 1932.
OXFORD UNIVERSITY (16) 1932–34 (Blue 1933).
SUSSEX (45) 1936–47. Cap 1938.
HS 89 Oxford U v W Indians, The Parks, 1933.
Clubs: Sussex Martlets, Corinthians, Free Foresters.

STALLIBRASS, Michael James Dahl
LHB, ROB

Born Exeter, Devon, 28 June 1951. Educ Lancing; Magdalen C, Oxford. Debut 1972.
OXFORD UNIVERSITY (20) 1972–74 (Blue 1974).
HS 24 Oxford U v Worcs, The Parks, 1974.
BB 5–80 Oxford U v Lancs, The Parks, 1972.

STANDEN, James Alfred
RHB, LB/RM

Born Edmonton, London, 30 May 1935. Debut 1959.
WORCESTERSHIRE (133) 1959–70. Cap 1962.
HS 92* Worcs v Oxford U, The Parks, 1970.
BB 7–30 Worcs v Oxford U, Halesowen, 1964.

Hertfordshire 1956–57. Club: Camberley. Soccer: Arsenal, Luton Town, West Ham United, Portsmouth, Millwall (England), Detroit Cougars (US).

STANDING, David Kevin
——————RHB, OB——————

Born Brighton, Sussex, 21 Oct 1963. Educ Tideway S, Newhaven; Brighton and Hove GS. Debut 1983.
SUSSEX (6) 1983–.
HS 60 Sussex v Worcs, Worcester, 1983.

STANDRING, Kenneth Brooks
——————LHB, RM——————

Born Clitheroe, Lancs, 17 Feb 1935. Educ Clitheroe GS; Leeds U. Debut 1955.
LANCASHIRE (8) 1955–59.
COMBINED SERVICES (5) 1957–58.
HS 41 Lancs v Leics, Leicester, 1959.
BB 4–61 Combined Services v Warwicks, Edgbaston, 1958.
Dismissed L. Hutton for first wkt in fc cricket. Clubs: Ribblesdale Wanderers, Bingley, Southport, Birkdale.

STANFORD, Ross Milton

Born Fulham, S Australia, 25 Sept 1917. Debut 1935/36.
AUSTRALIA DOMESTIC S Australia (10) 1935/36–47/48, Australian Services (4) 1945/46.
TOUR Australian Services to England (4) 1945 and India and Ceylon (5) 1945/46.
HS 153 Australian Services v Tasmania, Launceston, 1945/46.
Australia v England (Victory matches) (3) 1945.

STANLEY, Ernest Arthur William
——————RHB, OB——————

Born Leyton, London, 27 Sept 1926. Debut 1950. P.
ESSEX (13) 1950–52.
HS 35 Essex v Yorks, Bradford, 1951.

STANNING, John
——————RHB——————

Born London, 24 June 1919. Educ Winchester; Christ Church C, Oxford. Debut 1939.
OXFORD UNIVERSITY (7) 1939 (Blue).
WORCESTERSHIRE (9) 1939–46.
HS 56* Worcs v Northants, Rushden, 1939.

STANWORTH, John
——————RHB, WK——————

Born Oldham, Lancs, 30 Sept 1960. Educ Chadderton GS; Padgate C. Debut 1983.
LANCASHIRE (13) 1983–.
HS 31* Lancs v Essex, Old Trafford, 1983.

STANYARD, Anthony Roy
——————RHB, RM——————

Born Plaistow, Essex, 5 Apr 1938. Debut 1960. P.
ESSEX (2) 1960.
HS 26 Essex v Kent, Ilford, 1960.

STARKIE, Sydney
——————RHB, OB——————

Born Burnley, Lancs, 4 Apr 1926. Debut 1951. P.
NORTHAMPTONSHIRE (95) 1951–56. Cap 1954.
HS 60 Northants v Lancs, Northampton, 1955 (adding 156 for 9th wkt with R. Subba Row, county record).
BB 6–33 Northants v Warwicks, Edgbaston, 1954.

STATHAM, John *Brian* (George)
——————LHB, RF——————

Born Manchester, 17 June 1930. Educ Manchester Central GS. Debut 1950. P. *Wisden* 1955.
LANCASHIRE (430) 1950–68. Cap 1950. Benefit (£13,047) 1961. Testimonial (£1850) 1969. Capt 1965–67.
ENGLAND (70) 1950/51–65. A 1953 (1), 1956 (3), 1961 (4); SA 1951 (2), 1955 (4), 1960 (5), 1965 (1); WI 1957 (3), 1963 (2); NZ 1958 (2); I 1959 (3); P 1954 (4), 1962 (3). *A 1954/55 (5), 1958/59 (4), 1962/63 (5); SA 1956/57 (4); WI 1953/54 (4), 1959/60 (3); NZ 1950/51 (1), 1954/55 (2); I 1951/52 (5).*
OTHER TOURS MCC to Australasia 1950/51 (replacement). Cavaliers to S Africa and Rhodesia 1960/61. President's XI v Prime Minister's XI, Bombay, 1967/68.
HST 38 E v I, Lord's, 1959. HS 62 Lancs v Leics, Old Trafford, 1955.
BBT 7–39 E v SA, Lord's, 1955. BB 8–34 (15–89 match) Lancs v Warwicks, Coventry, 1957.
Returned 8–37 inns (15–108 match) Lancs v Leics, Leicester, 1964; and 11–97 match E v SA, Lord's, 1960.
100 WKTS (13) 139 @ 15.01 in 1959.
RECORD Took 1816 wkts (@ 15.12) for Lancs, a county record.
In 1965 became second bowler after F. S. Trueman to reach 250 Test wkts.

Players v Gentlemen (4) 1951–60. MCC Hon. member. Awarded CBE for services to cricket.

STAZIKER, Michael William
——————RHB, RMF——————

Born Croston, Lancs, 7 Nov 1947. Educ Hutton GS, nr Preston, Lancs. Debut 1970.
LANCASHIRE (2) 1970.
HS 1* Lancs v Hants, Southampton, 1970.
Cumberland 1976. Clubs: Lancaster, Morecambe, Preston, Leyland Motors.

STEAD, Barry
——————LHB, LFM——————

Born Leeds, Yorks, 21 June 1939. Died Drighlington, Leeds, 15 Apr 1980. Educ Green Lane Sec S, Leeds. Debut 1959. P.
YORKSHIRE (2) 1959.
COMBINED SERVICES (5) 1960–61.
ESSEX (1) 1962 (did not take the field).
NOTTINGHAMSHIRE (215) 1962–76. Cap 1969. Benefit 1966.
S AFRICA DOMESTIC Northern Transvaal 1975/76.
HS 58 Notts v Glos, Bristol, 1972.
BB 8–44 Notts v Som, Trent Bridge, 1972.
Took 98 wkts @ 20.38 in 1972. Returned 7–76 inns on fc debut, Yorks v Indians, Bradford, 1959.
Clubs: Salts, Undercliffe.

STEAD, Peter
——————RHB, RFM——————

Born West Yorkshire, c 1931. Debut 1954.
CANADA to England (3) 1954.
HS 4* Canada v Pakistan, Lord's, 1954.
BB 4–52 Canadians v Yorks, Scarborough, 1954.

STEELE, Alexander
——————RHB, WK——————

Born Salisbury, Rhodesia, 25 Feb 1941. Educ Morgan Academy. Debut 1967.
SCOTLAND (14) 1967–80.
HS 97 Scotland v Ireland, Glasgow, 1968.
Club: Forfarshire.

STEELE, David Stanley
——————RHB, SLA——————

Born Bradeley, N Staffordshire, 29 Sept 1941. Educ Enden Sec S, Stoke on Trent. Debut 1963. *Wisden* 1976.

NORTHAMPTONSHIRE (416) 1963–78, 1982–84. Cap 1965. Benefit (£25,000) 1975.
DERBYSHIRE (64) 1979–81. Capt 1979 (resigned during season). Cap 1979.
ENGLAND (8) 1975–76. A 1975 (3); WI 1976 (5).
TOURS D. H. Robins' XI to S Africa 1975/76. Leics XI to Zimbabwe 1980/81.
HST 106 E v WI, Trent Bridge, 1976. HS 140* Northants v Worcs, Worcester, 1971.
BB 8–29 Northants v Lancs, Northampton, 1966.
1000 RUNS (10) 1756 @ 48.77 in 1975.
RECORD Added 291 for 3rd wkt with P. N. Kirsten, Derbys v Somerset, Taunton, 1981, county record.
Staffordshire 1958–62. Clubs: Sneyd Colliery, Hartshill. Autobiography (with John Morris) *Come in Number 3* (1977). Brother J. F. Steele (Leics); cousin B. S. Crump (Northants); uncle F. Steele (soccer for Stoke City and England).

STEELE, Howard Keith
————RHB, RM————

Born Auckland, N Zealand, 6 Apr 1951. Educ King's C, Auckland; Corpus Christi C, Cambridge. Debut 1970.
CAMBRIDGE UNIVERSITY (21) 1970–72 (Blue 1971–72).
N ZEALAND DOMESTIC Auckland (5) 1974/75.
HS 103* Cambridge U v Sussex, Fenner's, 1972.
BB 4–71 Auckland v Canterbury, Auckland, 1974/75.

STEELE, John Frederick
————RHB, SLA————

Born Brown Edge, N Staffordshire, 23 July 1946. Educ Endon Sec S, Stoke on Trent. Debut 1970.
LEICESTERSHIRE (312) 1970–83. Cap 1971.
GLAMORGAN (26) 1984. Cap 1984.
S AFRICA DOMESTIC Natal 1973/74, 1975/76, 1977/78.
TOURS D. H. Robins' XI to S Africa 1974/75.
HS 195 Leics v Derbys, Leicester, 1971.
BB 7–29 Natal B v Griqualand West, Umzinto, 1973/74 and 7–29 Leics v Glos, Leicester, 1980.
1000 RUNS (6) 1347 @ 31.32 in 1972.
RECORD Added 390 for 1st wkt with B. Dudleston, Leics v Derbys, Leicester, 1979, county record.
Staffordshire 1965–69. Clubs: Sneyd Colliery, Leek. Brother D. S. Steele (Northants, Derbys, England); cousin

B. S. Crump (Northants); uncle F. Steele (soccer for Stoke City and England).

STENTON, John Derek
————RHB, SLA————

Born Sheffield, Yorks, 26 Oct 1924. Debut 1953.
SOMERSET (1) 1953.
HS 18 Som v Surrey, Taunton, 1953.
After only fc match was found not to be qualified.

STEPHENS, John Patrick
Rhodes *Felix*
————RHB, LM————

Born Cheltenham, Glos, 6 Aug 1942. Educ Ampleforth C; St Benet's Hall, Oxford. Debut 1966.
OXFORD UNIVERSITY (3) 1966–67.
HS 27 Oxford U v Essex, The Parks, 1966.
Clubs: Saints (Yorks), Free Foresters. A monk (Order of St Benedict) and cricket master at Ampleforth C.

STEPHENSON, Franklyn
Dacosta
————RHB, RFM————

Born St James, Barbados, 8 Apr 1959. Educ Samuel Jackman Prescod Polytechnic, Barbados. Debut 1981/82.
AUSTRALIA DOMESTIC Tasmania (7) 1981/82.
W INDIES DOMESTIC Barbados 1981/82.
GLOUCESTERSHIRE (7) 1982–83.
HS 165 Barbados v Leeward Islands, Basseterre, 1981/82.
BB 6–19 Tasmania v Victoria, Melbourne, 1981/82.
Barred from W Indian cricket for touring S Africa 1982/83, 1983/84 (W Indies XI). Staffordshire 1980. Clubs: Littleborough, Royton, Rawtenstall.

STEPHENSON, George *Robert*
————RHB, WK————

Born Derby, 19 Nov 1942. Educ Derby S. Debut 1967.
DERBYSHIRE (9) 1967–68.
HAMPSHIRE (263) 1969–80. Cap 1969. Capt 1979. Benefit (£24,204) 1979.
HS 100* Hants v Som, Taunton, 1976.
Soccer: Derby County, Shrewsbury Town, Rochdale. Father George Stephenson (soccer for England).

STEPHENSON, Harold William
————RHB, WK————

Born Haverton Hill, Co Durham, 18 July 1920. Debut 1948. *P.*

SOMERSET (428) 1948–64. Cap 1949. Capt 1960–64. Benefit (£4030) 1957. Testimonial 1964.
TOURS Commonwealth XI to India and Ceylon 1950/51. MCC to Pakistan 1955/56. International XI to Rhodesia, India and Pakistan 1961/62.
HS 147* Som v Notts, Bath, 1962.
1000 RUNS (5) 1143 @ 21.56 in 1953.
RECORDS Added 183 for 9th wkt with C. M. H. Greetham, Som v Leics, Weston-super-Mare, 1963, county record. Made 1007 dismissals for Som, county record; 1082 dismissals (748 ct, 334st) in career. Durham 1947, Dorset 1965–68. Clubs: Stockton-on-Tees, Billingham Synthonia.

STEPHENSON, John William
Arthur
————RHB, RFM————

Born Hong Kong, 1 Aug 1907. Died Pulborough, Sussex, 20 May 1982. Educ Claysmore S; RMC Sandhurst. Debut 1928/29.
INDIA DOMESTIC Bombay Europeans 1928/29–29/30, Madras Europeans 1928/29–30/31.
ARMY (10) 1931–38.
ESSEX (61) 1934–39. Cap. Joint capt 1939.
MCC (3) 1936–39.
WORCESTERSHIRE (1) 1947.
HS 135 Europeans v Parsees, Bombay, 1928/29.
BB 9–46 Gentlemen v Players, Lord's, 1936.
RECORD BB (above) best-ever return for Gentlemen against Players. Gentlemen v Players (4) 1936–39. England v Australia (Victory match) (1) 1945. Buckinghamshire 1931–32. Club: Kidderminster.

STEVENS, James Norman
————RHB, RMF————

Born Bexhill-on-Sea, Sussex, 4 June 1910. Educ Northampton GS; Pembroke C, Oxford. Debut 1937.
NORTHAMPTONSHIRE (5) 1937
FREE FORESTERS (2) 1953.
HS 19 Northants v Derbys, Chesterfield, 1937.
BB 3–85 Northants v Worcs, Northampton, 1937.
Suffolk 1949–55. Clubs: St Andrew's Hospital, Chippenham, Moseley, Pudsey St Laurence, Felixstowe, Deban Valley, Free Foresters, RAF Swindon.

STEVENS, Keith Brian Havelock
————RHB, OB————

Born Bombay, India, 22 Aug 1942. Educ Bradfield C; Worcester C, Oxford. Debut 1962.

OXFORD UNIVERSITY (5) 1962.
HS 52 Oxford U v Lancs, The Parks, 1962.
Berkshire 1960–62.

STEVENS, Roy Gilbert
————LHB, WK————

Born Walney, Kent, 6 Feb 1933. Debut 1962.
COMBINED SERVICES (1) 1962.
HS 29 Combined Services v Ireland, Belfast, 1962.
Som secretary 1975–79. Sussex chief executive 1980–83. Club: Royal Navy.

STEVENSON, Graham Barry
————RHB, RFM————

Born Hemsworth, Yorks, 16 Dec 1955.
Educ Minsthorpe GS. Debut 1973.
YORKSHIRE (171) 1973–. Cap 1978.
ENGLAND (2) 1979/80–80/81. WI 1980/81 (1); I 1979/80 (1).
HST 27* E v I, Bombay, 1979/80. HS 115* Yorks v Warwicks, Edgbaston, 1982.
BBT 3–111 E v WI, St John's, Antigua, 1980/81. BB 8–57 Yorks v Northants, Headingley, 1980.
RECORDS During HS (above) added 149 for 10th wkt with G. Boycott, county record; and became one of only eight batsmen to score a fc century at number 11.
Club: Ackworth.

STEVENSON, James Alexander
————RHB, RM————

Born Edinburgh, Scotland, 24 June 1915. Educ Edinburgh Academy.
Debut 1937.
SCOTLAND (4) 1937–51.
HS 45* Scotland v Yorks, Scarborough, 1951.
Club: Edinburgh Academicals.

STEVENSON, Keith
————RHB, RFM————

Born Derby, 6 Oct 1950. Educ Bemrose GS, Derby. Debut 1974.
DERBYSHIRE (47) 1974–77.
HAMPSHIRE (99) 1978–83. Cap 1979.
HS 33 Derbys v Northants, Chesterfield, 1974.
BB 7–22 Hants v Oxford U, The Parks, 1979.

STEVENSON, Michael Hamilton
————RHB, SLA————

Born Chinley, Derbys, 13 June 1927. Educ Rydal S; Christ's C, Cambridge.
Debut 1949.

CAMBRIDGE UNIVERSITY (48) 1949–52 (Blue 1949–52).
DERBYSHIRE (3) 1950–52.
IRELAND (5) 1952–64.
MCC (10) 1955–67.
HS 122 MCC v Cambridge U, Lord's, 1959.
BB 5–36 Cambridge U v Free Foresters, Fenner's, 1950.
Staffordshire 1947. Clubs: Great Chell, Colwyn Bay, Leinster, Clontarf, Pocklington Pixies. Cricket and rugby correspondent for *The Daily Telegraph* until 1982.

STEVENSON, Ronald Leckie
————RHB, OB————

Born Ayr, Scotland, 26 Nov 1938. Educ Bedford Modern. Debut 1962.
COMBINED SERVICES (2) 1962.
HS 17* Combined Services v Ireland, Belfast, 1962.
BB 3–86 Combined Services v Cambridge U, Fenner's, 1962.
Bedfordshire 1962. Clubs: Bedford Town, Kimbolton.

STEWARD, Exley *Anthony* Whitefoord
————RHB, LB, occ WK————

Born Durban, S Africa, 27 June 1941.
Educ Stanger HS, S Africa; Maritzburg C, S Africa. Debut 1964.
ESSEX (15) 1964–65.
S AFRICA DOMESTIC Natal B 1967/68.
HS 47 Essex v M'sex, Westcliff, 1964.
Clubs: Durban Collegians, Buckhurst Hill.

STEWART, Alec James
————RHB, WK————

Born Wimbledon, London, 8 Apr 1963.
Educ Tiffin GS. Debut 1981.
SURREY (27) 1981–.
HS 118* Surrey v Oxford U, Oval, 1983.
Father M. J. Stewart (Surrey, England).

STEWART, David
————RHB, RM————

Born Perth, Scotland, 21 May 1924.
Educ Perth Academy. Debut 1950.
SCOTLAND (1) 1950.
HS 5* Scotland v Ireland, Perth, 1950.
BB 2–12 same match.
Club: Perthshire.

STEWART, David Ernest Robertson
————RHB, OB————

Born Bombay, India, 22 May 1948.
Educ Robert Gordon's C; Cathedral HS, Bombay. Debut 1969.
SCOTLAND (9) 1969–79.
WORCESTERSHIRE (23) 1970–73.
HS 69 Worcs v N Zealanders, Worcester, 1973.
Clubs: Stourbridge, Old Hill, Ferguslie, Dunbartonshire, Selkirk.

STEWART, Michael James
————RHB————

Born Herne Hill, London, 16 Sept 1932.
Educ Alleyn's S. Debut 1954. *P. Wisden* 1958.
SURREY (499) 1954–72. Cap 1955. Capt 1963–72. Benefit (£7028) 1965.
Testimonial 1972.
ENGLAND (8) 1962–63/64. WI 1963 (4); P 1962 (2). *I 1963/64 (2)*.
OTHER TOURS E. W. Swanton's XI to W Indies 1955/56. Surrey to Rhodesia 1959/60. Cavaliers to India and S Africa 1962/63. MCC to E Africa 1963/64. International XI to India, Pakistan and Ceylon 1967/68 (capt). Commonwealth XI to Pakistan 1970/71 (capt).
HST 87 E v WI, Old Trafford, 1963. HS 227* Surrey v M'sex, Oval, 1964.
1000 RUNS (15) 2045 @ 44.45 in 1962.
RECORDS Took seven catches in inns, Surrey v Northants, Northampton, 1957, equalling world record for non-wicketkeeper. Took 77 catches (all for Surrey) in 1957, a county record and second-highest for non-wicketkeeper in season (W. R. Hammond 78 in 1928).
604 catches for Surrey in career, a county record.
Players v Gentlemen (2) 1960–62.
Cricket manager Surrey since 1979.
Club: West Surrey. Soccer: Charlton Athletic, England (amateur international). Son A. J. Stewart (Surrey).

STEWART, Richard William (Wes)
————RHB, RFM————

Born Portland, Jamaica, 28 Feb 1945.
Debut 1966.
GLOUCESTERSHIRE (1) 1966.
MIDDLESEX (51) 1966–68.
HS 19 M'sex v Glos, Bristol, 1967.
BB 6–65 M'sex v Glam, Lord's, 1966 (on M'sex debut).

STEWART, William *James* Perver
————RHB————

Born Llanelli, S Wales, 31 Aug 1934. Debut 1955. *P.*
WARWICKSHIRE (279) 1955–69. Cap 1957. Benefit (£8346) 1967.
NORTHAMPTONSHIRE (1) 1971.
TOUR MCC to N Zealand 1960/61.
HS 182* Warwicks v Leics, Hinckley, 1962.
BB 2–4 Warwicks v Sussex, Hove, 1959.
1000 RUNS (6) 2318 @ 43.73 in 1962.
RECORDS Hit 17 sixes in match, Warwicks v Lancs, Blackpool, 1959 (10 in first inns of 155, seven in second inns of 125), a world record. Also hit 11 sixes in match, Warwicks v Som, Street, 1961. Scored 131* (during inns of 151) before lunch on first day of match, Warwicks v Combined Services, Portland Road, Edgbaston, 1959.
Professional coach Rugby S 1970.
Rugby: Coventry, Warwickshire, Welsh trialist. Suffered amputation of one big toe in winter of 1962/63.

STILL, Stuart John
————RHB, RMF————

Born Hove, Sussex, 14 Dec 1957. Educ Knoll S, Hove. Debut 1975.
SUSSEX (1) 1975.
HS 6 Sussex v Notts, Trent Bridge, 1975.

STIMPSON, Peter John
————RHB, RM————

Born Aberfan, S Wales, 25 May 1947. Educ Cathay's HS, Cardiff. Debut 1971.
WORCESTERSHIRE (30) 1971–72.
HS 103 Worcs v Glam, Worcester, 1971. Twice shared century opening stands in each inns of match with R. G. A. Headley in 1971, the first four occasions on which they had opened the inns together.
Club: West Bromwich Dartmouth.

STINCHCOMBE, Frederick William
————RHB, LB————

Born Barnby Moor, Notts, 12 Mar 1930. Died Worksop, Notts, 19 Sept 1984. Debut 1950. *P.*
NOTTINGHAMSHIRE (6) 1950–51.
HS 48 Notts v Kent, Trent Bridge, 1951. Former professional coach Worksop C (from 1959). Club: Worksop Town.

STOCKLEY, Anthony John
————RHB, OB————

Born Kingston-upon-Thames, Surrey, 4 Apr 1940. Debut 1968.
SURREY (3) 1968.
HS 5 Surrey v Australians, Oval, 1968.
BB 4–74 same match.
6 ft 7½ in tall. Club: Epsom.

STOCKS, Frederick Wilfred
————LHB, RM————

Born Carcroft, Yorks, 6 Nov 1918. Debut 1946. *P.*
NOTTINGHAMSHIRE (283) 1946–57. Cap 1946. Benefit (£2000) 1956.
HS 171 Notts v Australians, Trent Bridge, 1956.
BB 6–37 Notts v Essex, Trent Bridge, 1950.
1000 RUNS (5) 1396 @ 34.04 in 1951.
RECORD Scored 114 on fc debut, Notts v Kent, Trent Bridge, 1946; subsequently took wkt with first ball in fc cricket, Notts v Lancs, Old Trafford, 1946, a unique double.
Father F. Stocks (Northants).

STODDART, Peter Laurence Bowring
————RHB, RM————

Born Regents Park, London, 24 June 1934. Educ Eton; Trinity C, Oxford. Debut 1958.
MCC (1) 1958.
HS 11 MCC v Ireland, Dublin, 1958.
Buckinghamshire 1955–67. Clubs: I Zingari, Free Foresters, Butterflies.

STOLLMEYER, Jeffrey Baxter
————RHB, LB————

Born Santa Cruz, Trinidad, 11 Apr 1921. Educ Queen's C, Trinidad. Debut 1938/39.
W INDIES DOMESTIC Trinidad 1938/39–56/57.
WEST INDIES (32) 1939–54/55. E 1947/48 (2), 1953/54 (5); A 1954/55 (2); I 1952/53 (5). *E 1939 (3), 1950 (4); A 1951/52 (5); NZ 1951/52 (2); I 1948/49 (4).* Capt 13.
HST 160 WI v I, Madras, 1948/49. HS 324 Trinidad v British Guiana, Port of Spain, 1946/47.
BBT 3–32 WI v E, Kingston, 1947/48. BB as above and 3–32 Trinidad v Barbados, Bridgetown, 1938/39.
1000 RUNS (1 + 1) 1334 @ 37.05 in 1950.
RECORDS HS (above) highest fc score in W Indian inter-island cricket; during inns added 434 for 3rd wkt with G. E. Gomez, W Indian fc record.

President WICB. W Indies Test selector. Club: Queens Park. MCC Hon. member. Senator Trinidad legislature. Brother V. H. Stollmeyer (W Indies).

STONE, Donald Harry
————LHB, RFM————

Born Clayton, Manchester, 9 Jan 1927. Educ Droylsden S. Debut 1949. *P.*
LANCASHIRE (6) 1949–50.
HS 46 Lancs v Kent, Folkestone, 1949.
BB 4–30 Lancs v Oxford U, The Parks, 1950.
Clubs: Barton Hall, Flixton.

STORER, Richard Elliott Daniel
————RHB, WK————

Born Nottingham, 9 May 1948. Educ Nottingham HS; Brasenose C, Oxford. Debut 1972.
OXFORD UNIVERSITY (4) 1972.
HS 9 Oxford U v Hants, The Parks, 1972.

STOREY, Stewart James
————RHB, RM————

Born Worthing, Sussex, 6 Jan 1941. Educ Purley GS. Debut 1960. *P.*
SURREY (315) 1960–74. Cap 1964. Benefit (£9500) 1973.
SUSSEX (16) 1978.
HS 164 Surrey v Derbys, Oval, 1971.
BB 8–22 Surrey v Glam, Swansea, 1965.
1000 RUNS (5) 1184 @ 35.87 in 1971.
100 WKTS (1) 104 @ 18.39 in 1966.
DOUBLE (1) 1966.
Sussex coach 1979–.

STOTT, William *Brian*
————LHB, ROB————

Born Yeadon, Yorks, 18 July 1934. Educ Aireborough GS. Debut 1952. *P.*
YORKSHIRE (187) 1952–63. Cap 1957.
COMBINED SERVICES (3) 1955–56.
HS 186 Yorks v Warwicks, Edgbaston, 1960.
BB 4–34 Yorks v Surrey, Bramall Lane, Sheffield, 1962.
1000 RUNS (5) 2034 @ 37.66 in 1959.
Clubs: Salts, Harrogate.

STOVOLD, Andrew Willis
————RHB, occ WK————

Born Bristol, Glos, 19 Mar 1953. Educ Filton HS; Loughborough C. Debut 1973.
GLOUCESTERSHIRE (241) 1973–. Cap 1976.

S AFRICA DOMESTIC Orange Free State 1974/75–75/76.
HS 212* Glos v Northants, Northampton, 1982.
1000 RUNS (6) 1671 @ 42.85 in 1983.
Correct birth name A. Willis-Stovold, though plays as the above. Brother M. W. Stovold (Glos).

STOVOLD, Martin Willis
————LHB————

Born Almondsbury, Bristol, Glos, 28 Dec 1955. Educ Thornbury GS; Marlwood S; Loughborough C. Debut 1979.
GLOUCESTERSHIRE (25) 1979–82.
HS 75* Glos v Oxford U, The Parks, 1980.
Club: Almondsbury. Correct birth name M. Willis-Stovold, though plays as the above. Brother A. W. Stovold (Glos).

STRACHAN, George Robson
————RHB, RM————

Born Blackridge, W Lothian, Scotland, 29 Aug 1932. Educ Lindsay HS. Debut 1965.
SCOTLAND (2) 1965.
HS 17* Scotland v Ireland, Dublin, 1965.
Club: West Lothian County.

STRATTON, Robert Arthur
————RHB, WK————

Born Birmingham, 10 Oct 1924. Educ St Peter's York; Emmanuel C, Cambridge. Debut 1946.
CAMBRIDGE UNIVERSITY (3) 1946.
HS 12* Cambridge U v M'sex, Fenner's, 1946.
War-time Blue 1944–45.

STRAW, David Sorby
————LHB, WK————

Born Croydon, Surrey, 28 May 1935. Educ Whitgift. Debut 1964.
MCC (1) 1964.
HS 10 MCC v Ireland, Dublin, 1964.
Surrey 2nd XI 1958–61. Clubs: Limpsfield, Old Whitgiftians. Rugby: London Counties, Surrey, Old Whitgiftians. Works for ACAS.

STREET, Lawrence Charles
————RHB, RFM————

Born Birmingham, 4 Feb 1920. Educ Moseley GS. Debut 1946. P.
WARWICKSHIRE (4) 1946.

HS 8* Warwicks v Som, Edgbaston, 1946.
BB 2–15 same match.
Clubs: Harborne Somerville, Harborne, City Officials (Birmingham).

STRETTON, Terry Kevin
————RHB, RM————

Born Cosby, Leics, 23 May 1953. Debut 1972.
LEICESTERSHIRE (6) 1972–75.
HS 6* Leics v M'sex, Lord's, 1974.
BB 2–71 Leics v Pakistanis, Leicester, 1974.
Club: Lightcliffe.

STRINGER, Peter Michael
————LHB, RFM————

Born Leeds, Yorks, 23 Feb 1943. Debut 1967.
YORKSHIRE (19) 1967–69.
LEICESTERSHIRE (37) 1970–72.
HS 22 Leics v Sussex, Leicester, 1971.
BB 5–43 Leics v Yorks, Bramall Lane, Sheffield, 1970.
Clubs: East Bierley, Bradford, Pudsey St Laurence.

STRIPP, David Arthur
————RHB, RM————

Born Crawley Down, Sussex, 4 Apr 1935. Educ Crawley Down Sec S; Plumpton Agricultural C. Debut 1956. P.
SUSSEX (12) 1956–57.
HS 32* Sussex v Hants, Portsmouth, 1957.
BB 2–12 Sussex v Kent, Tunbridge Wells, 1957.
Club: Crawley Down.

STUCHBURY, Stephen
————LHB, LFM————

Born Sheffield, Yorks, 22 June 1954. Educ Ecclesfield GS. Debut 1978.
YORKSHIRE (3) 1978–81.
HS 4* Yorks v Lancs, Headingley, 1981.
BB 3–82 same match.
Club: Holmfirth.

STURT, Michael Ormond Cleasby
————RHB, WK————

Born Wembley, London, 12 Sept 1940. Educ Mora S, Gladstone Park. Debut 1961.
MIDDLESEX (33) 1961–78. Cap 1967.
HS 26 M'sex v Oxford U, The Parks, 1961.
Club: Brondesbury.

SUBBA ROW, Raman
————LHB, LBG————

Born Streatham, Surrey, 29 Jan 1932. Educ Whitgift; Trinity C, Cambridge. Debut 1951.
CAMBRIDGE UNIVERSITY (40) 1951–53 (Blue 1951–53).
SURREY (41) 1953–54. Cap 1953.
NORTHAMPTONSHIRE (113) 1955–61. Cap 1955. Capt 1958–61.
COMBINED SERVICES (2) 1956–57.
MCC (6) 1954–64.
ENGLAND (13) 1958–61. A 1961 (5); SA 1960 (4); NZ 1958 (1); I 1959 (1). WI 1959/60 (2).
OTHER TOURS Commonwealth XI to India 1953/54. MCC to Australasia 1958/59. International XI to India and Pakistan 1961/62.
HST 137 E v A, Oval, 1961. HS 300 Northants v Surrey, Oval, 1958.
BB 5–21 Cambridge U v Oxford U, Lord's, 1951.
1000 RUNS (6) 1917 @ 46.75 in 1959.
RECORDS HS (above) highest-ever score for Northants; during inns added 376 for 6th wkt with A. Lightfoot, and added 156 for 9th wkt with S. Starkie, Northants v Lancs, Northampton, 1955, both county records.
Gentlemen v Players (3) 1958–60. Manager England to India and Sri Lanka 1981/82. Chairman Surrey 1978–80. MCC committee 1968–71. MCC Hon. member.

SUBRAMANYAM, Venkatraman
————RHB, LBG————

Born Bangalore, India, 16 July 1936. Educ Central C, Bangalore; Mysore U. Debut 1959/60.
INDIA DOMESTIC Mysore 1959/60–69/70. Capt 1963/64–69/70.
INDIA (9) 1964/65–67/68. WI 1966/67 (2); NZ 1964/65 (1). E 1967 (2); A 1967/68 (2); NZ 1967/68 (2).
OTHER TOURS India to E Africa 1967. State Bank of India to Ceylon 1968/69.
HST 75 I v A, Adelaide, 1967/68. HS 213* Mysore v Madras, Madras, 1966/67.
BBT 2–32 I v NZ, Delhi, 1964/65. BB 7–78 Mysore v Kerala, Bangalore, 1959/60.

SUCH, Peter Mark
————RHB, OB————

Born Helensburgh, Dunbartonshire, Scotland, 12 June 1964. Educ Harry Carlton CS, Notts. Debut 1982.
NOTTINGHAMSHIRE (33) 1982–.
HS 16 Notts v M'sex, Lord's, 1984.
BB 6–123 Notts v Kent, Trent Bridge, 1983.

SULLIVAN, John
—RHB, RM—

Born Ashton-under-Lyne, Lancs, 5 Feb 1945. Debut 1963.
LANCASHIRE (154) 1963–76. Cap 1969.
HS 81* Lancs v Hants, Bournemouth, 1972.
BB 4–19 Lancs v Yorks, Bramall Lane, Sheffield, 1973.
Club: Holmfirth. Boxing: former ABA title-holder.

SULLIVAN, John Patrick
—RHB, occ WK—

Born Bristol, Glos, 11 Mar 1948. Educ Withywood CS. Debut 1968.
GLOUCESTERSHIRE (23) 1968–77.
HS 53 Glos v Notts, Trent Bridge, 1970.
BB 2–50 Glos v Glam, Bristol, 1977.
Club: Long Ashton.

SULLY, Haydn
—LHB, ROB—

Born Sampford Brett, Som, 1 Nov 1939. Debut 1959. *P*.
SOMERSET (12) 1959–63.
NORTHAMPTONSHIRE (110) 1964–69. Cap 1966.
HS 48 Northants v Worcs, Northampton, 1966.
BB 7–29 Northants v Sussex, Hove, 1966.
100 WKTS (1) 101 @ 21.23 in 1966.
Devon 1970. Club: Sidmouth.

SUMAR, Shiraz
—RHB—

Born Tanganyika, 1950. Debut 1975.
EAST AFRICA to England (1) 1975.
HS 15 E Africa v Sri Lanka, Taunton, 1975.

SUNNUCKS, Peter Regan
—RHB—

Born Boughton Monchelsea, Maidstone, Kent, 22 June 1916. Educ Maidstone GS. Debut 1934. *P*.
KENT (68) 1934–46. Cap.
HS 162 Kent v Notts, Trent Bridge, 1937.
RECORD Put on 283 for 1st wkt with A. E. Fagg, Kent v Essex, Colchester, 1938, county record.
Club: Marden.

SURENDRANATH
—RHB, RFM—

Born Meerut, Delhi District, India, 4 Jan 1937. Educ National Defence Academy. Debut 1955/56.
INDIA DOMESTIC Services 1955/56–68/69.
INDIA (11) 1958/59–60/61. A 1959/60 (2); WI 1958/59 (2); P 1960/61 (2). E 1959 (5).
HST 27 I v E, Oval, 1959. HS 119 Services v S Punjab, Patiala, 1961/62.
BBT 5–75 I v E, Oval, 1959. BB 7–14 (13–76 match) Services v Railways, Delhi, 1958/59.
Regular Army officer.

SURRIDGE, David
—RHB, RFM—

Born Bishop's Stortford, Hertfordshire, 6 Jan 1956. Educ Richard Hale S, Hertford; Southampton U; Hughes Hall, Cambridge. Debut 1979.
CAMBRIDGE UNIVERSITY (9) 1979 (Blue).
GLOUCESTERSHIRE (25) 1980–82.
HS 14* Cambridge U v Yorks, Fenner's, 1979.
BB 5–78 Glos v Worcs, Bristol, 1982.
Hertfordshire 1977–79. Club: Bishop's Stortford.

SURRIDGE, John Giles Clive
—RHB, RFM—

Born Sutton, Surrey, 10 Aug 1935. Educ Marlborough; St John's C, Oxford. Debut 1956.
OXFORD UNIVERSITY (1) 1956.
HS 1 Oxford U v Yorks, The Parks, 1956.
Berkshire 1955–58.

SURRIDGE, Stuart Spicer
—RHB, WK—

Born Westminster, London, 28 Oct 1951. Educ Westminster. Debut 1978.
SURREY (1) 1978.
HS 2* Surrey v Pakistanis, Oval, 1978.
Father W. S. Surridge (Surrey).

SURRIDGE, Walter *Stuart*
—RHB, RFM—

Born Herne Hill, Surrey, 3 Sept 1917. Educ Emanuel S, Wandsworth. Debut 1939. *Wisden* 1953.
MINOR COUNTIES (1) 1939.
SURREY (254) 1947–59/60. Cap 1948.
Capt 1952–56 (county champions every season).
TOUR Surrey to Rhodesia 1959/60 (capt).

HS 87 Surrey v Glam, Oval, 1951.
BB 7–49 Surrey v Lancs, Oval, 1951.
Gentlemen v Players (3) 1953–55. President Surrey 1981. Son S. S. Surridge (Surrey).

SURTI, Rusi Framroz
—LHB, LM/SLA—

Born Surat, India, 25 May 1936. Debut 1956/57.
INDIA DOMESTIC Gujerat 1956/57–67/68 (capt 1962/63–67/68), Rajasthan 1959/60–60/61.
AUSTRALIA DOMESTIC Queensland (35) 1968/69–72/73.
INDIA (26) 1960/61–69/70. E 1963/64 (1); A 1964/65 (2), 1969/70 (1); WI 1966/67 (2); NZ 1964/65 (1), 1969/70 (2); P 1960/61 (2). *E 1967 (2); A 1967/68 (4), WI 1961/62 (5); NZ 1967/68 (4)*.
HST 99 I v NZ, Auckland, 1967/68. HS 246* Rajasthan v Uttar Pradesh, Udaipur, 1959/60.
BBT 5–74 I v A, Adelaide, 1967/68. BB 5–42 Rajasthan v Vidarbha, Udaipur, 1959/60.
Club: Haslingden.

SUTCLIFFE, Bert
—LHB, SLA—

Born Ponsonby, Auckland, N Zealand, 17 Nov 1923. Educ Takapuna GS, N Zealand. Debut 1941/42. *Wisden* 1950.
N ZEALAND DOMESTIC Auckland (12) 1941/42–48/49, Otago (60) 1946/47–61/62, Northern Districts (22) 1962/63–65/66 (capt 1965/66).
NEW ZEALAND (42) 1946/47–65. E 1946/47 (1), 1950/51 (2), 1954/55 (2), 1958/59 (2); SA 1952/53 (2); WI 1951/52 (2), 1955/56 (2). *E 1949 (4), 1958 (4), 1965 (1); SA 1953/54 (5); I 1955/56 (5), 1964/65 (4); P 1955/56 (3), 1964/65 (3)*. Capt 4.
OTHER TOURS N Zealand to Australia 1953/54. Commonwealth XI to S Africa 1959/60.
HST 230* NZ v I, Delhi, 1955/56. HS 385 Otago v Canterbury, Christchurch, 1952/53.
BBT 2–38 NZ v P, Lahore, 1964/65. BB 5–19 Otago v C Districts, Palmerston North, 1957/58.
1000 RUNS (2 + 2) 2627 @ 59.70 in 1949.
RECORDS HS (above) highest inns by a N Zealander, in N Zealand, and by a left-hander. During inns of 355, Otago v Auckland, Dunedin, 1949/50, added 266 for 5th wkt with W. S. Haig, a N Zealand fc record. Added 220 and 286 for 1st wkt with D. D. Taylor, Auckland v Canterbury, Auckland, 1948/49, only instance in fc cricket of double-century 1st-wkt stands in each inns of same

match. Added 222* for 3rd wkt with J. R. Reid, NZ v I, Delhi, 1955/56, N Zealand Test record.
MCC Hon. member.

SUTCLIFFE, Herbert
──────RHB──────

Born Summer Bridge, Yorks, 24 Nov 1894. Died Crosshills, Yorks, 22 Jan 1978. Educ Pudsey S. Debut 1919. P. Wisden 1920.
YORKSHIRE (602) 1919–45. Cap 1919. Benefits (£3056) 1929 and (£701) 1935.
ENGLAND (54) 1924–35. A 1926 (5), 1930 (4), 1934 (4); SA 1924 (5), 1929 (5), 1935 (2); WI 1928 (3), 1933 (2); NZ 1931 (2); I 1932 (1). A 1924/25 (5), 1928/29 (4), 1932/33 (5); SA 1927/28 (5); NZ 1932/33 (2).
OTHER TOURS Maharaj of Vizianagram's XI to India and Ceylon 1930/31 (not fc). Yorks to Jamaica 1935/36.
HST 194 E v A, Sydney, 1932/33. HS 313 Yorks v Essex, Leyton, 1932.
BB 2–16 Yorks v Surrey, Oval, 1937.
1000 RUNS (21 + 3) 3336 @ 74.14 in 1932. 2000 runs (15), including 1922–35 consecutively. Scored 3006 runs @ 96.96 in 1931 and 3002 @ 76.97 in 1928.
RECORDS During HS (above) added 555 for 1st wkt with P. Holmes, record for any wkt in fc cricket in England, an English record for any wkt and second-highest ever for 1st wkt. Shared in six 1st-wkt stands of 300 or more runs, a record. Added 323* for 3rd wkt with M. Leyland, Yorks v Glam, Huddersfield, 1928, county record. Scored 2883 runs @ 80.08 and 12 centuries for Yorks in 1932; 38,561 runs @ 50.21 and 112 centuries for Yorks in career; all county records. Scored 1839 runs @ 44.85 in debut season (1919), a record aggregate for first season. Scored 1193 runs @ 108.45 in June 1932 (at time a record aggregate for June) and 1006 @ 83.83 in August 1932, one of only four batsmen to score 1000 runs in two months of same season. Test average of 60.73 (for 4555 runs), an England record (qualification: 15 inns). Scored four centuries in Test series, in 1929 (v SA), equalling record for series in England. Shared in 69 century stands for Yorks 1st wkt with P. Holmes, a record for any county; shared in 11 century stands for England 1st wkt with J. B. Hobbs, a Test record. Scored centuries against all fc counties except his own. Scored centuries in four consecutive fc inns twice, in 1931 and 1939. Scored 1000 or more runs in every season from 1919 to 1939 (21). During inns of 113, Yorks v Northants, Kettering, 1933, hit 10 sixes.
Players v Gentlemen (18) 1923–38. England Test selector 1959–61. Club: Pudsey Britannia. MCC Hon. member.

Autobiography *For England and Yorkshire* (1935). Son W. H. H. Sutcliffe (Yorks).

SUTCLIFFE, Richard John
──────RHB, RMF──────

Born Rochdale, Lancs, 18 Sept 1954. Educ King Edward VII S, Lytham St Anne's. Debut 1978.
LANCASHIRE (1) 1978.
HS 10* Lancs v Essex, Southport, 1978.
Club: Milnrow.

SUTCLIFFE, Simon Paul
──────RHB, OB──────

Born Watford, Hertfordshire, 22 May 1960. Educ Bedford Modern; King George V GS, Southport; Lincoln C, Oxford; Loughborough C. Debut 1980.
OXFORD UNIVERSITY (17) 1980–81 (Blue 1980–81).
WARWICKSHIRE (18) 1981–.
HS 20 Warwicks v Glos, Nuneaton, 1982.
BB 6–19 Oxford U v Warwicks, The Parks, 1980.
Club: Mitchells and Butlers. Father Peter W. Sutcliffe (former national coach).

SUTCLIFFE, William Herbert Hobbs
──────RHB, RM──────

Born Pudsey, Yorks, 10 Oct 1926. Educ Rydal. Debut 1948.
YORKSHIRE (177) 1948–57. Cap 1952. Capt 1956–57.
MCC (7) 1950–59.
TOURS Commonwealth XI to India and Ceylon 1950/51. MCC to Pakistan 1955/56.
HS 181 Yorks v Kent, Canterbury, 1952.
BB 2–12 Commonwealth XI v Madras Governor's XI, Madras, 1950/51.
1000 RUNS (1) 1261 @ 33.18 in 1955. Gentlemen v Players (6) 1951–57. England Test selector 1969–70. Club: Leeds. Father H. Sutcliffe (Yorks, England).

SUTHERLAND, Ian
──────RHB, LBG──────

Born Leicester, 7 July 1926. Educ Wyggeston GS, Leicester; Sidney Sussex C, Cambridge. Debut 1949.
CAMBRIDGE UNIVERSITY (1) 1949.
HS 9 Cambridge U v Warwicks, Fenner's, 1949.

SUTTLE, Kenneth George
──────LHB, SLA──────

Born Brook Green, London, 25 Aug 1928. Educ Worthing HS. Debut 1949. P.
SUSSEX (601) 1949–71. Cap 1952. Benefit (£5500) 1966.
TOURS MCC to W Indies 1953/54. International XI to India, Pakistan and Ceylon 1967/68.
HS 204* Sussex v Kent, Tunbridge Wells, 1962.
BB 6–64 Sussex v Worcs, Worcester, 1970.
1000 RUNS (17) 2326 @ 39.42 in 1962.
RECORD Played 423 consecutive county championship matches (1954–69), a record for all counties.
Scored centuries against all fc counties except his own.
Soccer: Brighton and Hove Albion.

SUTTON, John *Arthur*
──────LHB, ROB──────

Born Manchester, 26 June 1939. Debut 1969.
MINOR COUNTIES (4) 1969–72.
HS 57 Minor Counties v N Zealanders, Lincoln, 1969.
BB 2–44 Minor Counties v Australians, Longton, 1972.
Cheshire 1959– (scored 10,122 runs for Cheshire in Minor Counties competition, a county record). Clubs: Kendal, Edgley, Newcastle and Hartshill, Little Lever, Westhoughton.

SUTTON, Michael Antony
──────RHB, OB──────

Born Weymouth, Dorset, 29 Mar 1921. Educ Ampleforth; Worcester C, Oxford. Debut 1946.
OXFORD UNIVERSITY (18) 1946–47 (Blue 1946).
SOMERSET (1) 1948.
HS 13* Som v Oxford U, Bath, 1948 and 13 Oxford U v Combined Services, The Parks, 1947.
BB 5–63 Oxford U v Leics, The Parks, 1946.
Devon 1954. Club: East Somerset Nomads.

SUTTON-MATTOCKS, Christopher John
──────LHB──────

Born Hammersmith, London, 10 July 1951. Educ Winchester; St Edmund Hall, Oxford. Debut 1972.
OXFORD UNIVERSITY (6) 1972–73.
HS 37 Oxford U v Lancs, The Parks, 1972.
Clubs: I Zingari, Harlequins.

SWALLOW, Ian Geoffrey
------RHB, OB------

Born Barnsley, Yorks, 18 Dec 1962.
Educ Hoyland S. Debut 1983.
YORKSHIRE (13) 1983–.
HS 34* Yorks v Som, Middlesbrough,
1984.
BB 4–52 Yorks v Kent, Tunbridge
Wells, 1984.

SWALLOW, Raymond
------RHB------

Born Southwark, London, 15 June
1935. Debut 1957. P.
MCC (1) 1957.
DERBYSHIRE (37) 1959–63.
HS 115 Derbys v Oxford U, The Parks,
1962.
Soccer: Arsenal, Derby County.

SWAN, Richard Gilroy
------RHB------

Born Duns, Berwickshire, Scotland, 6
Dec 1951. Educ Merchiston Academy;
Durham U. Debut 1980.
SCOTLAND (5) 1980–84.
HS 66 Scotland v Ireland, Edinburgh,
1982.
Clubs: Manderston, Carlton.

SWANN, John Lassam
------LHB, LB------

Born Ealing, London, 8 Oct 1926.
Debut 1949.
MIDDLESEX (4) 1949–51.
HS 29* M'sex v Cambridge U, Fenner's,
1951.
BB 3–39 M'sex v Oxford U, The Parks,
1951.
Club: Brentham.

SWARANJIT SINGH
------LHB, RM------

Born Amritsar, N Punjab, India, 18 July
1932. Educ Khalsa C; Punjab U;
Christ's C, Cambridge. Debut 1950/51.
INDIA DOMESTIC East Punjab 1950/
51–52/53, 1958/59 (capt 1951/52, 1958/
59), Bengal 1959/60–61/62.
CAMBRIDGE UNIVERSITY (38) 1954–56
(Blue 1955–56).
WARWICKSHIRE (27) 1956–58.
TOURS E. W. Swanton's XI to W Indies
1955/56. Madras to Ceylon 1958/59.
HS 145 E Punjab v Delhi, Delhi, 1951/
52.
BB 6–20 (10–63 match) Cambridge U v
Worcs, Worcester, 1955.
Club: Moseley.

SWARBROOK, Frederick William
------LHB, SLA------

Born Derby, 17 Dec 1950. Debut 1967.
DERBYSHIRE (199) 1967–79. Cap 1975.
S AFRICA DOMESTIC Griqualand West
1972/73–76/77, 1981/82–, Orange Free
State 1979/80.
HS 90 Derbys v Essex, Leyton, 1970.
BB 9–20 (13–62 match) Derbys v
Sussex, Hove, 1975.
RECORD Made fc debut for Derbys aged
16 yrs 6 months, youngest-ever to play
for the county.

SWART, Peter Douglas
------RHB, RFM/RM------

Born Bulawayo, Rhodesia, 27 Apr 1946.
Educ Jameson HS, Gatooma. Debut
1965/66.
S AFRICA DOMESTIC Rhodesia 1965/66,
Western Province 1967/68–80/81,
1983/84, Boland 1981/82–82/83.
D. H. ROBINS' XI (1) 1974.
GLAMORGAN (44) 1978–79. Cap 1979.
TOUR International Cavaliers to England
1969.
HS 122 Glam v Worcs, Swansea, 1979.
BB 6–85 (11–109 match) W Province v
Natal, Pietermaritzburg, 1971/72.
1000 RUNS (1) 1078 @ 31.70 in 1978.
Cambridgeshire 1974–76. Clubs:
Accrington, Haslingden, East Lan-
cashire.

SWETMAN, Roy
------RHB, WK------

Born Westminster, London, 25 Oct
1933. Debut 1953. P.
COMBINED SERVICES (2) 1953.
SURREY (129) 1954–61. Cap 1958.
NOTTINGHAMSHIRE (56) 1966–67. Cap
1966.
GLOUCESTERSHIRE (45) 1972–74. Cap
1972.
ENGLAND (11) 1958/59–59/60. I 1959
(3). A 1958/59 (2); WI 1959/60 (4);
NZ 1958/59 (2).
OTHER TOURS MCC to Pakistan 1955/
56. Surrey to Rhodesia 1959/60. Com-
monwealth XI to India, S Africa and
Rhodesia 1962/63. Cavaliers to S Africa
1962/63.
HST 65 E v I, Oval, 1959. HS 115 Notts v
Essex, Trent Bridge, 1966.
Players v Gentlemen (1) 1960. Clubs:
Addiscombe, Banstead, Bristol Optim-
ists.

SWIFT, Brian Tennant
------RHB, WK------

Born Adelaide, S Australia, 9 Sept 1937.
Died, in road-traffic accident, Higham,
Suffolk, 8 Mar 1958. Educ St Peter's,
Adelaide; Caius C, Cambridge. Debut
1957.
CAMBRIDGE UNIVERSITY (17) 1957 (Blue).
HS 25 Cambridge U v Notts, Trent
Bridge, 1957.

SWINBURNE, John Warwick
------RHB, OB------

Born Wath-on-Dearne, Yorks, 4 Dec
1939. Educ Wath-on-Dearne GS;
Leeds U. Debut 1970.
NORTHAMPTONSHIRE (29) 1970–74.
HS 25 Northants v Lancs, Southport,
1971.
BB 6–57 Northants v Warwicks, North-
ampton, 1971.
Devon 1963–69, Shropshire 1975–77.
Clubs: Old Hill, Kidderminster,
Plymouth, Middleton.

SWINDELL, Robert Stephen
------RHB, OB------

Born Derby, 22 Jan 1950. Educ Hall-
croft Sec S. Debut 1972.
DERBYSHIRE (23) 1972–77.
HS 38 Derbys v Som, Chesterfield, 1972.
BB 6–79 Derbys v Oxford U, Burton
upon Trent, 1975.
Club: Pudsey St Laurence.

SYDENHAM, David Alfred Donald
------RHB, LFM------

Born Surbiton, Surrey, 6 Apr 1934.
Educ London U. Debut 1957. P.
SURREY (142) 1957–65, 1972. Cap
1962.
HS 24* Surrey v Glos, Lydney, 1963.
BB 9–70 (12–101 match) Surrey v Glos,
Oval, 1964.
100 WKTS (2) 115 @ 17.65 in 1962.

SYKES, James Frederick
------RHB, OB------

Born Shoreditch, London, 30 Dec
1965. Educ Bow S. Debut 1983.
MIDDLESEX (1) 1983.
HS 4 M'sex v Lancs, Old Trafford,
1983.

SYME, Ian Alexander Hastie
————RHB, RFM————

Born Stirling, Scotland, 29 Dec 1929.
Educ Edinburgh Academy; Glasgow U.
Debut 1950.
SCOTLAND (1) 1950.
HS 12 Scotland v Ireland, Perth, 1950.
Club: Stirling County.

SYMINGTON, Stuart Johnston
————RHB, RMF————

Born Bexhill-on-Sea, Sussex, 16 Sept
1926. Educ Canford. Debut 1948.
LEICESTERSHIRE (23) 1948–49. Cap 1949.
Capt 1949.
HS 65 Leics v Essex, Leicester, 1949.

BB 5–45 Leics v Derbys, Ashby-de-la-Zouch, 1949.
RECORDS Youngest post-war county capt
and youngest-ever Leics capt.
Regular Army officer (now retired); in
1952 appointed ADC to Governor of
Bahamas.

T

TABER, Hedley *Brian*
RHB, WK

Born Wagga Wagga, NSW, Australia, 29 Apr 1940. Debut 1964/65.
AUSTRALIA DOMESTIC New South Wales (73) 1964/65–73/74.
AUSTRALIA (16) 1966/67–69/70. WI 1968/69 (1). *E 1968 (1); SA 1966/67 (5), 1969/70 (4); I 1969/70 (5).*
OTHER TOUR Australia to England 1972.
HST 48 A v WI, Sydney, 1968/69. HS 109 NSW v S Australia, Adelaide, 1968/69.
RECORD Dismissed 12 batsmen (9 ct, 3 st) in one match (including 7 in an inns), NSW v S Australia, Adelaide, 1968/69, equalling world record.
ACB coach. Club: Gordon.

TAHIR NAQQASH
RHB, OB/RMF

Born Lahore, Pakistan, 28 June 1959. Debut 1975/76.
PAKISTAN DOMESTIC Punjab, Lahore, Servis Industries, Muslim Commercial Bank, 1975/76–.
PAKISTAN (14) 1981/82–83/84. A 1982/83 (3); I 1982/83 (2); SL 1981/82 (3). *E 1982 (2); I 1983/84 (3); A 1983/84 (1).*
OTHER TOUR Pakistan to Australia 1981/82.
HST 57 P v SL, Karachi, 1981/82. HS 60 Lahore A v Sargodha, Lahore, 1975/76.
BBT 5–40 P v E, Edgbaston, 1982. BB 9–45 MCB v Karachi, Karachi, 1980/81.
Brother Arif Naqqash (Lahore).

TAIT, Alan
LHB, ROB

Born Washington, Co Durham, 27 Dec 1953. Debut 1971.
NORTHAMPTONSHIRE (52) 1971–75.
GLOUCESTERSHIRE (11) 1978.
HS 99 Northants v Lancs, Blackpool, 1974.
Cambridgeshire 1976–77. Club: Peterborough.

TALAT ALI, Malik
RHB, RM

Born Lahore, Pakistan, 29 May 1950. Educ St Anthony's S, Lahore; Punjab U. Debut 1967/68.
PAKISTAN DOMESTIC Lahore, Punjab University, Pakistan International Airlines, United Bank, 1967/68–78/79.
PAKISTAN (10) 1972/73–78/79. E 1972/73 (3). *E 1978 (2); A 1972/73 (1); NZ 1972/73 (1), 1978/79 (3).*
OTHER TOURS Pakistan to England 1971. Pakistan Under-25 to Sri Lanka 1973/74.
HST 61 P v NZ, Christchurch, 1978/79.
HS 258 PIA v Rawalpindi, Rawalpindi, 1975/76.
1000 RUNS (0 + 1) 1124 @ 34.06 in 1973/74.

TALBOT, Basil Lynch
RHB, WK

Born Southsea, Hants, 23 Feb 1903. Died Wareham, Dorset, 18 Feb 1962. Debut 1947.
SUSSEX (1) 1947.
HS 25 Sussex v Oxford U, Chichester, 1947.
Club: Sussex Martlets.

TALLON, Donald
RHB, WK, LB

Born Bundaberg, Queensland, Australia, 17 Feb 1916. Died Bundaberg, Queensland, Australia, 7 Sept 1984. Educ N Bundaberg S. Debut 1933/34. *Wisden* 1949.
AUSTRALIA DOMESTIC Queensland (86) 1933/34–53/54.
AUSTRALIA (21) 1945/46–53. E 1946/47 (5), 1950/51 (5); I 1947/48 (5). *E 1948 (4), 1953 (1); NZ 1945/46 (1).*
OTHER TOUR Australia to N Zealand 1949/50.
HST 92 A v E, Melbourne, 1946/47. HS 193 Queensland v Victoria, Brisbane, 1935/36.
RECORD Dismissed 12 batsmen (9 ct, 3 st) in match, Queensland v NSW, Sydney, 1938/39, equalling world record.

Made 7 dismissals (3 ct, 4 st) in inns, Queensland v Victoria, Brisbane 1938/39.
Clubs: Eastern Suburbs, South Brisbane, Valley (Brisbane). Brother L. W. T. Tallon (Queensland).

TAMHANE, Narendra Shankar
RHB, WK

Born Bombay, India, 4 Aug 1931. Educ Bombay U. Debut 1951/52.
INDIA DOMESTIC Universities 1951/52, Bombay 1953/54–63/64.
INDIA (21) 1954/55–60/61. A 1956/57 (3), 1959/60 (1); WI 1958/59 (4); NZ 1955/56 (4); P 1960/61 (2). *E 1959 (2); P 1954/55 (5).*
OTHER TOUR India to Ceylon 1956/57.
HST 54* I v P, Bahawalpur, 1954/55. HS 109* Bombay v Baroda, Bombay, 1958/59.
BB 2–43 Present v Past, Delhi, 1957/58.
RECORD First wicketkeeper to make 100 dismissals in Ranji Trophy.

TAMPLIN, Clifford
RHB, WK

Born Cardiff, S Wales, 27 May 1921. Debut 1942/43.
INDIA DOMESTIC Bengal 1942/43.
GLAMORGAN (3) 1947.
HS 40* Glam v Kent, Newport, 1947.
Club: Cardiff YMCA.

TANNER, John Denys Parkin
LHB, WK

Born Harrogate, Yorks, 2 July 1921. Educ Charterhouse; Brasenose C, Oxford. Debut 1947.
OXFORD UNIVERSITY (6) 1947–49.
MCC (1) 1955.
HS 25* Oxford U v Som, Bath, 1948.
Did not concede a bye in inns of 512 on fc debut, Oxford U v Lancs, The Parks, 1947.
Oxfordshire 1951. Soccer: Blue, Huddersfield Town.

TASKER, Alfred George Ernest
——————RHB, WK——————

Born Southwark, London, 16 June 1934. Educ William Ellis GS, London. Debut 1956. *P*.
WORCESTERSHIRE (1) 1956.
Did not bat or bowl.
Lord's staff 1955–56. Clubs: Wembley, Turnham Green.

TATTERSALL, Keith
——————LHB, SLA——————

Born Tunbridge Wells, Kent, 6 Mar 1946. Educ Prince Edward S, Salisbury, Rhodesia; Cape Town U. Debut 1965/66.
S AFRICA DOMESTIC South African Universities 1965/66–69/70, Western Province 1965/66–69/70, Rhodesia 1973/74–75/76.
TOUR S African Universities to England 1967.
HS 112 W Province v E Province, Kimberley, 1967/68.
Selected for Rhodesian Ridgebacks to England 1976 (vetoed by British Sports Minister on political grounds).

TATTERSALL, Roger Hartley
——————LHB, LM——————

Born Nelson, Lancs, 12 Mar 1952. Educ The Leys. Debut 1971.
LANCASHIRE (2) 1971.
No runs; one wkt.

TATTERSALL, Roy
——————LHB, RMF/OB——————

Born Bolton, Lancs, 17 Aug 1922. Debut 1948. *P*.
LANCASHIRE (277) 1948–60. Cap 1950. Joint benefit (with M. J. Hilton) (£11,655) 1960.
MCC (1) 1964.
ENGLAND (16) 1950/51–54. A 1953 (1); SA 1951 (5); P 1954 (1). *A 1950/51 (2); NZ 1950/51 (2); I 1951/52 (5).*
HST 10* E v I, Bombay, 1951/52 and 10 E v A, Melbourne, 1950/51. HS 58 Lancs v Leics, Old Trafford, 1958.
BBT 7–52 (12–101 match) E v SA, Lord's, 1951. BB 9–40 (including hattrick) Lancs v Notts, Old Trafford, 1953.
100 WKTS (8) 193 @ 13.59 in 1950.
Took 7 wkts in 19 balls, Lancs v Notts, Old Trafford, 1953.
Players v Gentlemen (5) 1950–53. Club: Kidderminster.

TAVARÉ, Christopher James
——————RHB——————

Born Orpington, Kent, 27 Oct 1954. Educ Sevenoaks S; St John's C, Oxford. Debut 1974.
KENT (162) 1974–. Cap 1978. Capt 1983–84.
OXFORD UNIVERSITY (19) 1975–77 (Blue 1975–77).
ENGLAND (30) 1980–84. A 1981 (2); WI 1980 (2), 1984 (2); NZ 1983 (4); I 1982 (3); P 1982 (3); SL 1984 (1). *A 1982/83 (5); NZ 1983/84 (2); I 1981/82 (6); SL 1981/82 (1).*
HST 149 E v I, Delhi, 1981/82. HS 168* Kent v Essex, Chelmsford, 1982.
1000 RUNS (8) 1770 @ 53.63 in 1981.
Batted 710 mins in match, E v A, Old Trafford, 1981, 287 mins (for 69) in 1st inns and 423 mins (for 78) in 2nd.

TAYFIELD, Hugh Joseph
(Toey)
——————RHB, OB——————

Born Durban, S Africa, 31 Jan 1929. Educ Durban HS. Debut 1945/46. *Wisden 1956.*
S AFRICA DOMESTIC Natal 1945/46–46/47, 1949/50–55/56, Rhodesia 1947/48–48/49, Transvaal 1956/57–62/63.
SOUTH AFRICA (37) 1949/50–60. E 1956/57 (5); A 1949/50 (5), 1957/58 (5); NZ 1953/54 (5). *E 1955 (5), 1960 (5); A 1952/53 (5); NZ 1952/53 (2).*
OTHER TOUR S Africa to England 1951.
HST 75 SA v A, Cape Town, 1949/50. HS 77 Transvaal v E Province, Port Elizabeth, 1962/63.
BBT 9–113 (13–192 match) SA v E, J'burg, 1956/57. BB as above.
Returned 14–126 match, S Africans v Hants, Southampton, 1955, and 13–165 match, SA v A, Melbourne, 1952/53.
100 WKTS (2) 143 @ 15.75 in 1955.
RECORD Took 170 wkts @ 25.91 in Tests, the leading wkt-taker for S Africa.
Club: East Lancs. MCC Hon. member. Brothers C. Tayfield (Transvaal, Griqualand West) and A. Tayfield (Transvaal); uncle S. H. Martin (Worcs, Natal, Rhodesia).

TAYLOR, Brian (Tonker)
——————LHB, WK——————

Born West Ham, London, 19 June 1932. Educ Central Park S, East Ham. Debut 1949. *P. Wisden 1972.*
ESSEX (539) 1949–73. Cap 1956. Testimonials (£2500) 1966 and (£6500) 1972. Capt 1967–73.
TOUR MCC to S Africa 1956/57.
HS 135 Essex v M'sex, Lord's, 1959.

1000 RUNS (8) 1837 @ 30.61 in 1959.
RECORDS 539 matches for Essex, a county record. Made 89 dismissals for Essex in 1962 and 1205 dismissals in career, both county records.
1294 dismissals (1081 ct, 213 st) in career. Played 301 successive County Championship matches (1961–72).
Players v Gentlemen (1) 1957. Test selector 1973–74.

TAYLOR, Bruce Richard
——————LHB, RFM——————

Born Timaru, N Zealand, 12 July 1943. Educ Timaru HS. Debut 1963/64.
N ZEALAND DOMESTIC New Zealand Under-23 (1) 1963/64, Canterbury (20) 1964/65–69/70, Wellington (36) 1970/71–79/80 (capt 1972/73–73/74).
NEW ZEALAND (30) 1964/65–73. E 1965/66 (1); WI 1968/69 (3); I 1967/68 (3); P 1972/73 (3). *E 1965 (2), 1969 (2), 1973 (3); WI 1971/72 (4); I 1964/65 (3), 1969/70 (2); P 1964/65 (3), 1969/70 (1).*
OTHER TOURS N Zealand to Australia 1967/68, 1970/71.
HST 124 NZ v WI, Auckland, 1968/69. HS 173 Wellington v Otago, Dunedin, 1972/73.
BBT 7–74 NZ v WI, Bridgetown, 1971/72. BB as above.
RECORD Scored 105* and took 5 for 86 NZ v I, Calcutta, 1964/65, only player to score century and take 5 wkts in inns on Test debut.

TAYLOR, Chilton Richard Vernon
——————RHB, WK——————

Born Birkenhead, Cheshire, 3 Oct 1951. Educ Birkenhead S; Trinity C, Cambridge. Debut 1970.
WARWICKSHIRE (1) 1970.
CAMBRIDGE UNIVERSITY (28) 1971–73 (Blue 1971–73).
OXFORD AND CAMBRIDGE UNIVERSITIES (2) 1972–73.
MIDDLESEX (2) 1981.
HS 25 Cambridge U v Warwicks, Fenner's, 1972.
Played for M'sex (v Essex, Ilford, 1981) while unregistered; county penalised by deduction of seven bonus points.
Cheshire 1969–70. Club: Oxton.

TAYLOR, Derek John Somerset
——————RHB, WK——————

Born Amersham, Buckinghamshire, 12 Nov 1942. Educ Amersham C. Debut 1966.

SURREY (10) 1966–69. Cap 1969.
SOMERSET (280) 1970–82. Cap 1971.
Testimonial (£20,764) 1978.
S AFRICA DOMESTIC Griqualand West
1970/71–71/72.
HS 179 Som v Glam, Swansea, 1974.
1000 RUNS (1) 1121 @ 28.02 in 1975.
Buckinghamshire 1962. Twin brother
M. N. S. Taylor (Notts, Hants).

TAYLOR, Derief David Samuel
LHB, SLA

Born Kingston, Jamaica, 17 Sept 1916.
Debut 1948. P.
WARWICKSHIRE (16) 1948–50.
HS 121 Warwicks v Leics, Edgbaston,
1949.
BB 3–41 Warwicks v Hants, Edgbaston,
1948.
Warwicks coach 1951–81. Club: West
Bromwich Dartmouth. Returned to
Jamaica 1983.

TAYLOR, Donald Dougald
RHB, OB

Born Auckland, N Zealand, 2 Mar 1923.
Died Auckland, N Zealand, 5 Dec 1980.
Educ Mount Albert GS. Debut 1946/
47. P.
N ZEALAND DOMESTIC Auckland (41)
1946/47–60/61.
WARWICKSHIRE (45) 1949–53.
NEW ZEALAND (3) 1946/47–55/56. E
1946/47 (1); WI 1955/56 (2).
HST 77 NZ v WI, Wellington, 1955/56.
HS 143 Auckland v Canterbury, Auckland, 1948/49 (out for 99 in 1st inns).
BB 4–24 Warwicks v Combined Services, Edgbaston, 1949.
RECORDS Added 220 and 286 for 1st wkt
with B. Sutcliffe, Auckland v Canterbury, Auckland, 1948/49, only instance
in fc cricket of 1st wkt pair producing
double-century stands in each inns of
match.
Club: Old Hill.

TAYLOR, Frederick
RHB, RFM

Born Leek, Staffordshire, 29 Apr 1916.
Educ Leek Council S. Debut 1939. P.
WARWICKSHIRE (1) 1939.
MINOR COUNTIES (1) 1953.
HS 8 Minor Counties v Australians,
Stoke on Trent, 1953.
BB 5–71 same match.
Staffordshire 1937–38, 1946–51. Clubs:
Leek, Burslem, Knypersley, Stone,
Porthill Park. Father C. J. Taylor (War-
wicks).

TAYLOR, Henry John Corbett
RHB, OB

Born Solihull, Warwicks, 16 Apr 1949.
Educ Solihull S; Jesus C, Cambridge.
Debut 1968.
CAMBRIDGE UNIVERSITY (13) 1968–69.
HS 50 Cambridge U v Leics, Fenner's,
1968.
Club: Solihull.

TAYLOR, James Alexander Simpson
RHB, OB

Born Weston-super-Mare, Som, 19
June 1917. Educ Oakham S; St John's
C, Cambridge. Debut 1937.
LEICESTERSHIRE (3) 1937.
SCOTLAND (6) 1952–54.
HS 78 Scotland v Yorks, Glasgow, 1952.
Club: Grange.

TAYLOR, James Robert Niven
RHB

Born Calcutta, India, 11 Aug 1929.
Educ Edinburgh U. Debut 1949.
SCOTLAND (1) 1949.
INDIA DOMESTIC Bengal 1952/53.
HS 41 Bengal v Bihar, Calcutta, 1952/53.
Edinburgh University.

TAYLOR, John Dennis
RHB, RMF

Born Ipswich, Suffolk, 18 Dec 1923.
Debut 1947. P.
HAMPSHIRE (4) 1947–49.
HS 27* Hants v Yorks, Bournemouth,
1947.

TAYLOR, John Frederick
RHB, WK

Born West Ham, London, 9 June 1937.
Debut 1960. P.
ESSEX (14) 1960–61.
MCC (1) 1967.
HS 86 Essex v Som, Westcliff, 1961.
Clubs: Wanstead, Moseley.

TAYLOR, Jonathan Paul
LHB, LFM

Born Ashby-de-la-Zouch, Leics, 8 Aug
1964. Educ Pingle S, Swadlincote.
Debut 1984.
DERBYSHIRE (3) 1984.
HS 11 Derbys v M'sex, Derby, 1984.
BB 2–92 Derbys v Som, Taunton, 1984.

TAYLOR, Kenneth
RHB, RM

Born Huddersfield, Yorks, 21 Aug 1935.
Educ Huddersfield S of Art; Slade S of
Fine Art, London. Debut 1953. P.
YORKSHIRE (303) 1953–68. Cap 1957.
Benefit (£6301) 1968.
N ZEALAND DOMESTIC Auckland (5) 1963/
64.
ENGLAND (3) 1959–64. A 1964 (1); I 1959
(2).
TOUR E. W. Swanton's XI to India 1963/
64.
HST 24 E v I, Trent Bridge, 1959. HS
203* Yorks v Warwicks, Edgbaston,
1961.
BB 6–75 Yorks v Lancs, Old Trafford,
1961.
1000 RUNS (6) 1494 @ 34.74 in 1961.
Norfolk 1972. Clubs: Primrose Hill,
Brighouse. Soccer: Huddersfield Town,
Bradford City. Son N. S. Taylor (Yorks,
Surrey); brother Jeff Taylor (soccer for
Huddersfield Town, Fulham, Brent-
ford; professional pop guitarist).

TAYLOR, Kenneth Alexander
RHB, RM

Born Muswell Hill, London, 29 Sept
1916. Educ Tollington S, London.
Debut 1946. P.
WARWICKSHIRE (87) 1946–49. Cap 1946.
HS 102 Warwicks v Glos, Edgbaston,
1947.
1000 RUNS (1) 1259 @ 26.22 in 1947.
Notts cricket manager 1979–; Notts
committee 1963–78. Clubs: North
Middlesex, Nottingham Forest.

TAYLOR, Leslie Brian
RHB, RFM

Born Earl Shilton, Leics, 25 Oct 1953.
Educ Heathfield S, Earl Shilton. Debut
1977.
LEICESTERSHIRE (118) 1977–. Cap 1981.
S AFRICA DOMESTIC Natal 1981/82–.
TOUR Leics XI to Zimbabwe 1980/81.
HS 47 Leics v Derbys, Derby, 1983.
BB 7–28 Leics v Derbys, Leicester,
1981.
Barred from Test cricket for three yrs
for touring S Africa 1981/82 (SAB Eng-
land XI). Club: West Bromwich Dart-
mouth. Related to Sam Coe (Leics).

TAYLOR, Michael Norman Somerset
RHB, RM

Born Amersham, Buckinghamshire, 12
Nov 1942. Educ Amersham C. Debut
1964.

NOTTINGHAMSHIRE (230) 1964–72. Cap 1967.
HAMPSHIRE (145) 1973–80. Cap 1973.
HS 105 Notts v Lancs, Trent Bridge, 1967.
BB 7–23 Hants v Notts, Basingstoke, 1977.
Took 99 wkts @ 21.00 in 1968.
Buckinghamshire 1961–62. Twin brother D. J. S. Taylor (Surrey, Som).

TAYLOR, Neil Royston
RHB, OB

Born Farnborough, Kent, 21 July 1959. Educ Cray Valley Technical HS. Debut 1979.
KENT (89) 1979–.
HS 155* Kent v Glam, Cardiff, 1983.
BB 2–58 Kent v Som, Taunton, 1982.
1000 RUNS (3) 1340 @ 34.35 in 1982.
Scored 110 Kent v Sri Lankans, Canterbury, 1979, on fc debut.

TAYLOR, Nicholas Simon
RHB, RFM

Born Holmfirth, Yorks, 2 June 1963. Educ Gresham's S, Holt. Debut 1982.
YORKSHIRE (8) 1982–83.
SURREY (3) 1984.
HS 6* Surrey v Som, Oval, 1984.
BB 5–49 Yorks v Sussex, Headingley, 1983.
Father K. Taylor (Yorks, Auckland, England).

TAYLOR, Paul Adrian
LHB, LFM

Born E Kirkby, Notts, 9 Mar 1939. Debut 1958. P.
NOTTINGHAMSHIRE (6) 1958.
HS 13 Notts v Glam, Trent Bridge, 1958.
BB 2–82 Notts v Essex, Trent Bridge, 1958.

TAYLOR, Reginald Minshall
RHB, SLA

Born Southend, Essex, 30 Nov 1909. Educ Southend HS. Debut 1931. P to 1939.
ESSEX (206) 1931–46. Cap 1932.
HS 193 Essex v Sussex, Colchester, 1938.
BB 7–99 Essex v Som, Taunton, 1946.
1000 RUNS (2) 1181 @ 24.10 in 1933.
RECORD Added 263 for 8th wkt with D. R. Wilcox, Essex v Warwicks, Southend, 1946, county record.

TAYLOR, Robert William
RHB, WK

Born Stoke on Trent, Staffordshire, 17 July 1941. Educ St Peter's Sec S, Stoke on Trent. Debut 1960. P.

MINOR COUNTIES (1) 1960.
DERBYSHIRE (514) 1961–84. Cap 1962. Testimonials (£6672) 1973 and (£54,000) 1981. Capt 1975–76.
ENGLAND (57) 1970/71–83/84. A 1981 (3); NZ 1978 (3), 1983 (4); I 1979 (3), 1982 (3); P 1978 (3), 1982 (3). A 1978/79 (6), 1979/80 (3), 1982/83 (5); NZ 1970/71 (1), 1977/78 (3), 1983/84 (3); I 1979/80 (1), 1981/82 (6); P 1977/78 (3), 1983/84 (3); SL 1981/82 (1).
OTHER TOURS MCC to Ceylon 1969/70. MCC to Australia 1970/71. World XI to Australia 1971/72. MCC to W Indies 1973/74. MCC to Australia 1974/75. International Wanderers to S Africa 1975/76.
HST 97 E v A, Adelaide, 1978/79. HS 100 Derbys v Yorks, Dore, Sheffield, 1981.
RECORDS Made 7 dismissals in inns three times, a record (Derbys v Glam, Derby, 1966; Derbys v Yorks, Chesterfield, 1975; E v I, Bombay, 1979/80 – joint world Test record). Made 10 dismissals match, E v I, Bombay, 1979/80, world Test record. Made 1646 dismissals (1471 ct, 175 st) in career, a world record; surpassed the total of 1527 by J. T. Murray, the previous record holder, in 1982/83. 1471 catches also a world record. Made 1303 dismissals for Derbys, a county record.
Made 10 dismissals match, Derbys v Hants, Chesterfield, 1963.
Staffordshire 1958–60. Club: Bignall End. Autobiography *Standing Up, Standing Back* (with Pat Murphy) (1985). MBE for services to cricket.

TAYLOR, Timothy John
RHB, SLA

Born Romiley, Cheshire, 28 Mar 1961. Educ Stockport GS; Magdalen C, Oxford. Debut 1981.
LANCASHIRE (4) 1981–82.
OXFORD UNIVERSITY (8) 1981–82 (Blue 1981–82).
OXFORD AND CAMBRIDGE UNIVERSITIES (1) 1981.
MINOR COUNTIES (1) 1981.
HS 28* Oxford U v Kent, The Parks, 1981.
BB 5–81 Oxford U v M'sex, The Parks, 1981.
Cheshire 1980–. Club: Romiley.

TAYLOR, William
RHB, RFM

Born Manchester, 24 Jan 1947. Debut 1971.
NOTTINGHAMSHIRE (95) 1971–77. Cap 1975.
HS 26* Notts v Leics, Trent Bridge, 1972.

BB 6–42 Notts v Warwicks, Trent Bridge, 1972.
Lancs 2nd XI 1964–67. Club: Leek.

TEBAY, Kevan
RHB

Born Bolton, Lancs, 2 Feb 1936. Educ Thornleigh C, Bolton. Debut 1961. P.
LANCASHIRE (15) 1961–63.
HS 106 Lancs v Hants, Old Trafford, 1962.
Club: Egerton.

TEDDER, Ernest Cranfield
RHB

Born Woodford Green, Essex, 5 Sept 1915. Died Ipswich, Suffolk, 9 Sept 1972. Educ Chigwell. Debut 1946.
ESSEX (8) 1946.
HS 55 Essex v Sussex, Ilford, 1946.
Club: Woodford Wells.

TEDSTONE, Geoffrey Alan
RHB, WK

Born Southport, Lancs, 19 Jan 1961. Educ Warwick S; St Paul's C, Cheltenham. Debut 1982.
WARWICKSHIRE (17) 1982–84.
HS 67* Warwicks v Cambridge U, Fenner's, 1983.
Club: Leamington. Sister Janet Tedstone (England Women).

TENNANT, Peter Norie
RHB, WK

Born Sutton Coldfield, Warwicks, 17 Apr 1942. Educ Solihull S. Debut 1964.
WARWICKSHIRE (1) 1964.
Did not bat.
Club: Aston Unity.

TENNEKOON, Annura Punchi Banda
RHB, SLA

Born Anuradhapura, Ceylon, 29 Oct 1946. Educ St Thomas' C, Colombo. Debut 1965/66.
CEYLON (Sri Lanka) 1965/66–79.
TOURS Ceylon (Sri Lanka) to Pakistan 1966/67, 1973/74. Sri Lanka to England 1975 (capt), 1979. Ceylon (Sri Lanka) to India 1966/67, 1968/69, 1970/71, 1975/76.

HS 169* Sri Lanka v India, Colombo, 1973/74.
BB 2–23 Ceylon v Madras, Colombo, 1965/66.

TERRY, Vivian *Paul*
————————RHB, RM————————

Born Osnabruck, W Germany, 14 Jan 1959. Educ Millfield. Debut 1978.
HAMPSHIRE (53) 1978–. Cap 1983.
ENGLAND (2) WI 1984.
HST 8 E v WI, Headingley, 1984. HS 175* Hants v Glos, Bristol, 1984.
1000 RUNS (2) 1208 @ 48.32 in 1984.

THACKARA, Anthony Leonard Samuel Salter
————————RHB————————

Born Portsmouth, Hants, 4 Mar 1917. Educ RNC Dartmouth. Debut 1949.
COMBINED SERVICES (3) 1949–55.
D. R. JARDINE'S XI (1) 1955.
HS 42 Combined Services v Worcs, Worcester, 1949.
Cornwall 1950–52. Royal Navy. Clubs: Free Foresters, I Zingari, Incogniti. Commander Royal Navy (retired).

THACKERAY, Peter Robert
————————RHB, RM————————

Born Nairobi, Kenya, 26 Sept 1950. Educ St Edward's, Oxford; Exeter U; Keble C, Oxford. Debut 1974.
OXFORD UNIVERSITY (8) 1974 (Blue).
HS 65* Oxford U v Worcs, The Parks, 1974.
Devon 1971. Kent 2nd XI. Club: Exeter.

THEWLIS, Joseph
————————RHB————————

Born Percy Main, Northumberland, 14 Apr 1939. Debut 1962.
COMBINED SERVICES (1) 1962.
HS 17 Combined Services v Cambridge U, Fenner's, 1962.
Northumberland 1963–81. Club: Northumberland County.

THOMAS, Alan
————————RHB, OB————————

Born Bolton, Lancs, 7 Jan 1947. Educ Canon Slade Sec S, Bolton. Debut 1966.
LANCASHIRE (1) 1966.

HS 4 Lancs v Oxford U, The Parks, 1966.
Clubs: Farnworth, Farnworth Social Circle, Clifton, Horwich RMI.

THOMAS, David James
————————LHB, LFM————————

Born Solihull, Warwicks, 30 June 1959. Educ Licensed Victuallers S, Slough. Debut 1977.
SURREY (98) 1977–. Cap 1983.
S AFRICA DOMESTIC Northern Transvaal 1980/81, Natal 1983/84.
HS 119 Surrey v Notts, Oval, 1983.
BB 6–36 Surrey v Som, Oval, 1984.

THOMAS, Frederick Oswald
————————RHB, RFM————————

Born Corstorphine, Midlothian, Scotland, 19 Nov 1917. Educ RHS, Glasgow. Debut 1951.
SCOTLAND (1) 1951.
HS 21 Scotland v Worcs, Dundee, 1951.
Club: RHS Glasgow FP.

THOMAS, Gary Philip
————————RHB————————

Born Birmingham, 8 Nov 1958. Educ George Dixon GS, Birmingham. Debut 1978.
WARWICKSHIRE (8) 1978–81.
HS 52 Warwicks v Yorks, Scarborough, 1981.
Club: Mitchells and Butlers.

THOMAS, Grahame
————————RHB————————

Born Croydon Park, NSW, Australia, 21 Mar 1938. Debut 1957/58.
AUSTRALIA DOMESTIC New South Wales (68) 1957/58–65/66.
REST OF WORLD XI v England XI, Scarborough, 1966.
AUSTRALIA (8) 1964/65–65/66. E 1965/66 (3). WI 1964/65 (5).
OTHER TOURS Australia to N Zealand 1959/60. Australia to S Africa 1966/67.
HST 61 A v WI, Port of Spain, 1964/65.
HS 229 NSW v Victoria, Melbourne, 1965/66.
1000 RUNS (0 + 1) 1171 @ 58.55 in 1965/66.
Club: Bankstown-Canterbury (Australia).

THOMAS, John Gregory
————————RHB, RFM————————

Born Trebannws, S Wales, 12 Aug 1960. Educ Cwmtawe CS; S Glam Institute of H Educ. Debut 1979.
GLAMORGAN (44) 1979–.
S AFRICA DOMESTIC Border 1983/84.
HS 84 Glam v Surrey, Guildford, 1982.
BB 5–56 Glam v Som, Cardiff, 1984.

THOMAS, Neil Peter
————————LHB, SLA————————

Born Tenterden, Kent, 26 May 1964. Educ Sevenoaks S; Downing C, Cambridge. Debut 1984.
CAMBRIDGE UNIVERSITY (1) 1984.
Made a pair in his only match.

THOMAS, Rhodri James Alban
————————RHB————————

Born St Dogmaels, Pembrokeshire, Wales, 13 Mar 1942. Educ Radley; Corpus Christi C, Oxford. Debut 1963.
OXFORD UNIVERSITY (15) 1963–65 (Blue 1965).
HS 135* Oxford U v Northants, The Parks, 1963.

THOMAS, Richard James
————————RHB, RM————————

Born Griffithstown, Monmouthshire, Wales, 18 June 1944. Educ W Monmouth GS, Pontypool. Debut 1974.
GLAMORGAN (1) 1974.
HS 8* Glam v Lancs, Liverpool, 1974.

THOMAS, William Owen
————————LHB, SLA————————

Born Middlesbrough, Yorks, 27 Apr 1921. Educ Dulwich C; Pembroke C, Cambridge. Debut 1948.
CAMBRIDGE UNIVERSITY (3) 1948.
MCC (1) 1954.
HS 19* MCC v Cambridge U, Lord's, 1954.
Norfolk 1952–59.

THOMAS, William Richard Keay
————————RHB, RM————————

Born Redditch, Worcs, 22 July 1960. Educ Dean Close S, Cheltenham. Debut 1981.
WORCESTERSHIRE (1) 1981.
HS 44 Worcs v Sri Lankans, Worcester, 1981.

THOMPSON, Alexander William
RHB

Born Liverpool, 17 Apr 1916. Educ Highbury County S, London. Debut 1939. *P.*
MIDDLESEX (195) 1939–55. Cap 1946. Joint benefit (with H. P. H. Sharp) (£7427) 1955.
HS 158 M'sex v Worcs, Dudley, 1952.
BB 2–35 M'sex v Oxford U, The Parks, 1953.
1000 RUNS (3) 1245 @ 31.92 in 1953.

THOMPSON, Eric Richard
RHB, RFM

Born Kirkwall, Orkney, Scotland, 6 Oct 1938. Educ Melville C. Debut 1965.
SCOTLAND (16) 1965–74.
HS 29* Scotland v Warwicks, Edgbaston, 1969.
BB 5–11 Scotland v Ireland, Dublin, 1965 (fc debut).
Clubs: Melville FP, Stewart's-Melville.

THOMPSON, Hugh Reginald *Patrick*
RHB, OB

Born Scunthorpe, Lincolnshire, 11 Apr 1934. Educ Cheltenham. Debut 1953.
HAMPSHIRE (2) 1953–54.
HS 16 Hants v Oxford U, The Parks, 1953.
BB 2–106 Hants v Oxford U, The Parks, 1954.

THOMPSON, John Ross
RHB, OB

Born Berkhamsted, Hertfordshire, 10 May 1918. Educ Tonbridge; St John's C, Cambridge. Debut 1938.
CAMBRIDGE UNIVERSITY (22) 1938–39. (Blue 1938–39).
WARWICKSHIRE (44) 1938–54. Cap 1947.
UNDER-33 (1) 1945.
TOUR MCC to Canada 1951.
HS 191 Cambridge U v Free Foresters, Fenner's, 1938.
Wiltshire 1955–63. Club: Solihull. Squash: British amateur champion 1954–59; British Open champion 1959.

THOMPSON, Leslie Baines
RHB, OB

Born Brentford, M'sex, 12 Nov 1908. Debut 1946.
MIDDLESEX (6) 1946–49.
HS 13 M'sex v Oxford U, The Parks, 1949.

BB 3–50 M'sex v Northants, Lord's, 1946.
Club: Ealing.

THOMPSON, Neil Powney
LHB, LFM

Born Colombo, Ceylon, 10 Oct 1938. Educ Christ's Hospital; Worcester C, Oxford. Debut 1961.
OXFORD UNIVERSITY (7) 1961.
HS 4* Oxford U v Surrey, Oval, 1961 and 4 v Glam, The Parks, 1961 and 4 v Notts, The Parks, 1961.
BB 4–72 Oxford U v Derbys, Buxton, 1961.

THOMPSON, Roland George
RHB, RFM

Born Binley Village, Coventry, Warwicks, 26 Sept 1932. Educ Binley S. Debut 1949. *P.*
WARWICKSHIRE (158) 1949–62. Cap 1955.
COMBINED SERVICES (1) 1952.
HS 25* Warwicks v Notts, Trent Bridge, 1956 and 25* v Glos, Coventry, 1961.
BB 9–65 Warwicks v Notts, Edgbaston, 1952.
Took 97 wkts @ 17.96 in 1959 and 92 wkts @ 21.38 in 1955.
Clubs: Coventry and North Warwicks, Moseley, Kidderminster, Lockheed.

THOMPSON, Thomas
RHB, OB

Born Workington, Cumberland, 24 Feb 1934. Educ Workington GS; Manchester U. Debut 1963.
LEICESTERSHIRE (9) 1963–64.
HS 12 Leics v Northants, Leicester, 1964.
BB 3–53 Leics v Essex, Leicester, 1964.
Cumberland 1955–61, 1967–74. Club: Whitehaven.

THOMPSON, Graeme Bruce
LHB, LMF

Born Invercargill, N Zealand, 31 July 1951. Debut 1973/74.
N ZEALAND DOMESTIC Otago (39) 1973/74–80/81.
TOUR N Zealand to England 1978.
HS 34* Otago v C Districts, Wanganui, 1975/76.
BB 6–41 (10–80 match) Otago v Wellington, Alexandra, 1980/81.

THOMSON, James
RHB, SLA

Born Kilmarnock, Ayrshire, Scotland, 13 Feb 1940. Debut 1962.
SCOTLAND (2) 1962–84.
HS 1* Scotland v Ireland, Greenock, 1962.
BB 4–116 Scotland v Ireland, Glasgow, 1984.
Interval of 22 yrs between his two fc appearances. Club: Kilmarnock.

THOMSON, Jeffrey Robert
RHB, RF

Born Greenacre, Sydney, NSW, Australia, 16 Aug 1950. Educ Punchbowl HS, Sydney. Debut 1972/73.
AUSTRALIA DOMESTIC New South Wales (7) 1972/73–73/74, Queensland (62) 1974/75–.
MIDDLESEX (8) 1981.
AUSTRALIA (49) 1972/73–82/83. E 1974/75 (5), 1979/80 (1), 1982/83 (4); WI 1975/76 (6), 1979/80 (1), 1981/82 (2); I 1977/78 (5); P 1972/73 (1), 1976/77 (1), 1981/82 (3). *E 1975 (4), 1977 (5); WI 1977/78 (5); NZ 1981/82 (3); P 1982/83 (3).*
OTHER TOUR Australia to England 1980.
HST 49 A v E, Edgbaston, 1975. HS 61 Queensland v Victoria, Brisbane, 1974/75.
BBT 6–46 A v E, Brisbane, 1974/75. BB 7–33 (12–122 match) Queensland v NSW, Brisbane, 1976/77.
World Series Cricket (Kerry Packer) 1978/79. Clubs: Toombul, Eastern Suburbs (Sydney), Bankstown-Canterbury.

THOMSON, Norman *Ian*
RHB, RMF

Born Walsall, Staffordshire, 23 Jan 1929. Educ Forest S. Debut 1952. *P from 1953.*
SUSSEX (403) 1952–65, 1972. Cap 1953. Benefit (£6089) 1963.
ENGLAND (5) *SA 1964/65.*
OTHER TOUR MCC A to Pakistan 1955/56.
HST 39 E v SA, Port Elizabeth, 1964/65. HS 77 Sussex v Leics, Leicester, 1959.
BBT 2–55 E v SA, Port Elizabeth, 1964/65. BB 10–49 (15–75 match) Sussex v Warwicks, Worthing, 1964.
100 WKTS (12) 134 @ 20.98 in 1961.
BB (above) most recent instance in fc cricket in England of bowler taking all 10 wkts in an inns.
Club: Ilford.

THOMSON, Richard Harry
—LHB—

Born Bexhill, Sussex, 19 Oct 1938. Educ Bexhill GS; Christ's C, Cambridge. Debut 1961.
CAMBRIDGE UNIVERSITY (23) 1961–62 (Blue 1961–62).
SUSSEX (2) 1961.
HS 84 Cambridge U v MCC, Lord's, 1962.

THOMSON, Samuel Johnstone
—RHB, LBG—

Born Johnstone, Renfrewshire, Scotland, 27 May 1911. Educ Camphill Sec S; Glasgow U. Debut 1938.
SCOTLAND (4) 1938–51.
HS 21* Scotland v Ireland, Glasgow, 1938.
BB 5–54 same match.
Club: Ferguslie.

THORN, Philip Leslie
—RHB, SLA—

Born Bristol, Glos, 17 Nov 1951. Educ Cotham GS; Manchester U. Debut 1974.
GLOUCESTERSHIRE (4) 1974.
HS 25 Glos v Worcs, Cheltenham, 1974.
BB 2–53 same match.
Wiltshire 1980–. Club: Westbury on Trym. Writer on Western club cricket.

THORNE, David Anthony
—RHB, LM—

Born Coventry, Warwicks, 12 Dec 1964. Educ Bablake S, Coventry; Keble C, Oxford. Debut 1983.
WARWICKSHIRE (6) 1983–84.
OXFORD UNIVERSITY (8) 1984 (Blue).
HS 69* Oxford U v Kent, The Parks, 1984.
BB 5–39 Oxford U v Cambridge U, Lord's, 1984.

THORNE, David Calthorpe
—RHB, SLA—

Born Hertford, 13 Dec 1933. Educ St Edward's, Oxford. Debut 1964.
COMBINED SERVICES (2) 1964.
HS 59 Combined Services v Oxford U, Aldershot, 1964.
BB 2–74 Combined Services v Cambridge U, Uxbridge, 1964.
Norfolk 1954–62. Army. Club: West Norfolk; Regular Army; Army Major-General. Knighted. Twin brother M. E. Thorne (Norfolk).

THORNTON, Thomas
—RHB—

Born Elland, Yorks, 29 May 1922. Educ Elland GS. Debut 1946.
ROYAL AIR FORCE (1) 1946.
HS 23 RAF v Worcs, Worcester, 1946.
Mashonaland (Rhodesia). Clubs: Elland, Undercliffe.

THORNYCROFT, Guy Mytton
—RHB—

Born Ulverston, Lancs, 1 Apr 1917. Educ Shrewsbury. Debut 1947.
WORCESTERSHIRE (1) 1947.
HS 3 Worcs v Combined Services, Worcester, 1947.

THOY, Reginald Ernest
—RHB—

Born Singapore, 12 May 1921. Educ Singapore. Debut 1955.
D. R. JARDINE'S XI (2) 1955–57.
HS 13 D. R. Jardine's XI v Oxford U, Eastbourne, 1957.
Clubs: Coutts' Bank, Private Banks, United Banks.

THRESHER, Ronald Stanley
—RHB, RF—

Born Tonbridge, Kent, 31 Dec 1930. Educ Maidstone GS. Debut 1957.
KENT (2) 1957.
D. R. JARDINE'S XI (2) 1957–58.
HS 19 Kent v Yorks, Tunbridge Wells, 1957.
BB 4–29 D. R. Jardine's XI v Oxford U, Eastbourne, 1957.
Clubs: Coutts' Bank, United Banks.

THURSTING, Lawrence Denis
—RHB, SLA—

Born Lambeth, London, 9 Sept 1915. Debut 1938.
LEICESTERSHIRE (29) 1938–47.
HS 94 Leics v Warwicks, Edgbaston, 1938.
BB 3–34 Leics v Glam, Ashby-de-la-Zouch, 1938.
Club: Baildon Green.

THWAITES, Ian Guy
—RHB—

Born Brighton, Sussex, 4 Mar 1943. Educ Eastbourne; Caius C, Cambridge. Debut 1963.
CAMBRIDGE UNIVERSITY (22) 1963–64.
HS 60 Cambridge U v Essex, Fenner's, 1964.

TIDY, Warwick Nigel
—RHB, LBG—

Born Birmingham, 10 Feb 1953. Educ John Wilmott GS, Sutton Coldfield. Debut 1970.
WARWICKSHIRE (36) 1970–74.
HS 12* Warwicks v Cambridge U, Fenner's, 1972.
BB 5–24 Warwicks v Leics, Nuneaton, 1970.
Clubs: Stratford on Avon, Walmley, Old Hill.

TILLARD, John Robert
—RHB—

Born Kensington, London, 26 May 1924. Educ Winchester; Trinity C, Oxford. Debut 1949.
SUSSEX (1) 1949.
HS 3 Sussex v Oxford U, The Parks, 1949.
Club: I Zingari. Regular Army officer.

TILLEY, Eric Warrington
—RHB, RMF/OB—

Born Whatstandwell, Derbys, 22 Sept 1914. Died Leicester, 1 Dec 1977. Debut 1946.
LEICESTERSHIRE (4) 1946.
HS 2 Leics v Derbys, Derby, 1946.
BB 3–33 Leics v Indians, Leicester, 1946.
Clubs: Sparkenhoe Rovers, Windhill.

TILLY, Henry William
—RHB, RFM—

Born Edmonton, London, 25 May 1932. Debut 1954. P.
MIDDLESEX (59) 1954–61.
MINOR COUNTIES (1) 1967.
HS 49* M'sex v Oxford U, Lord's, 1955.
BB 6–33 M'sex v Essex, Southend, 1958.
Hertfordshire 1963–70.

TIMMIS, Peter John
—RHB, RFM—

Born Stoke on Trent, Staffordshire, 30 July 1942. Debut 1971.
MINOR COUNTIES (1) 1971.
Did not bat; no wkts.
Staffordshire 1962–76. Club: Porthill Park.

TIMMS, Bryan Stanley Valentine
—RHB, WK—

Born Ropley, Hants, 17 Dec 1940. Debut 1959. P.

HAMPSHIRE (208) 1959–68. Cap 1963.
WARWICKSHIRE (24) 1969–71. Cap 1971.
HS 120 Hants v Oxford U, The Parks, 1966.

TIMMS, John Edward
—RHB, OB/RM—

Born Silverstone, Northants, 3 Nov 1906. Died Buckingham, 18 May 1980. Educ Wellingborough. Debut 1925. *P from 1927.*
NORTHAMPTONSHIRE (468) 1925–49. Cap. Testimonial (£1650) 1940.
HS 213 Northants v Worcs, Stourbridge, 1934.
BB 6–18 Northants v Worcs, Worcester, 1938.
1000 RUNS (11) 1632 @ 34.72 in 1934.
Professional coach Bloxham S 1950–62. Golf: Buckingham Club professional and greenkeeper after retirement from cricket.

TIMUR MOHAMED
—LHB, RLB—

Born Georgetown, British Guiana, 7 June 1957. Debut 1975/76.
W INDIES DOMESTIC Guyana 1975/76–.
TOURS West Indies to England 1980 (one match as replacement). Young West Indies to Zimbabwe 1981/82, 1983/84 (capt).
HS 193 Guyana v Combined Islands, Rose Hall, 1978/79.
Suffolk 1979–80.

TINDALL, Robert Michael
—LHB, SLA—

Born Harrow, M'sex, 16 June 1959. Educ Harrow. Debut 1980.
NORTHAMPTONSHIRE (14) 1980–81.
HS 60* Northants v Cambridge U, Fenner's, 1980.
BB 2–1 Northants v Warwicks, Edgbaston, 1981.
Father M. Tindall (M'sex).

TINDALL, Ronald Albert Ernest
—RHB, OB—

Born Streatham, London, 23 Sept 1935. Debut 1956. *P.*
SURREY (172) 1956–66.
HS 109* Surrey v Notts, Oval, 1963.
BB 5–41 Surrey v Cambridge U, Oval, 1962.
1000 RUNS (1) 1126 @ 28.15 in 1963.
Soccer: Chelsea, West Ham United, Reading, Portsmouth; manager Portsmouth.

TINKLER, Edgar
—RHB, RM—

Born Burnley, Lancs, 11 Mar 1921. Educ Worcester RGS. Debut 1953.
WORCESTERSHIRE (1) 1953.
MCC (2) 1960–61.
HS 7 Worcs v Northants, Worcester, 1953.
Clubs: Worcester City, Dudley.

TISSERA, Michael Hugh
—RHB, LB—

Born Colombo, Ceylon, 23 Mar 1939. Debut 1958/59.
CEYLON (Sri Lanka) 1958/59–75.
TOURS Ceylon to India 1959/60, 1961/62, 1964/65. Ceylon to Pakistan 1966/67. Sri Lanka to England 1975.
HS 122 Ceylon v India, Hyderabad, 1964/65.
BB 5–95 Sri Lanka v East Africa, Taunton, 1975.
Club: Nondescripts.

TITMUS, Frederick John
—RHB, OB—

Born St Pancras, London, 24 Nov 1932. Educ Wm Ellis S, Highgate. Debut 1949. *P. Wisden* 1963.
MIDDLESEX (642) 1949–82. Cap 1953. Benefits (£6833) 1963 and (£6196) 1973. Capt 1965–68.
SURREY (1) 1978.
S AFRICA DOMESTIC Orange Free State 1975/76.
ENGLAND (53) 1955–74/75. A 1964 (5); SA 1955 (2), 1965 (3); WI 1963 (4), 1966 (3); NZ 1965 (3); P 1962 (2), 1967 (2). *A 1962/63 (5), 1965/66 (5), 1974/75 (4); SA 1964/65 (5); WI 1967/68 (2); NZ 1962/63 (3); I 1963/64 (5).*
OTHER TOURS MCC A to Pakistan 1955/56. D. H. Robins' XI to S Africa 1975/76.
HST 84* E v I, Bombay, 1963/64. HS 137* MCC v S Australia, Adelaide, 1962/63.
BBT 7–79 E v A, Sydney, 1962/63. BB 9–52 M'sex v Cambridge U, Fenner's, 1962.
1000 RUNS (8) 1703 @ 37.02 in 1961.
100 WKTS (16) 191 @ 16.31 in 1955.
DOUBLE (8) 1955–57, 1959–62, 1967.
RECORDS Took 158 wkts @ 14.63 for M'sex in 1955, and 2361 @ 21.27 for M'sex in career, both county records. Added 227 for 6th wkt with C. T. Radley, M'sex v S Africans, Lord's, 1965, county record. 642 matches for M'sex, also a county record. Scored more than 20,000 runs and took over 2500 wkts, one of only five players to do so in fc cricket.

Returned 9–57 inns M'sex v Lancs, Lord's, 1964 and 15–95 match M'sex v Som, Bath, 1955.
Players v Gentlemen (2) 1955–62. Surrey coach 1977–78. Club: Enfield. MCC Hon. member. Lost four toes in boating accident in W Indies 1967/68. Awarded MBE for services to cricket.

TODD, Leslie John
—LHB, SLA/LM—

Born Catford, Kent, 19 June 1907. Died Dover, Kent, 20 Aug 1967. Debut 1927. *P.*
KENT (426) 1927–50. Cap 1930. Benefit 1947.
HS 174 Kent v Leics, Maidstone, 1949.
BB 6–26 (11–64 match) Kent v Notts, Tonbridge, 1936.
1000 RUNS (10) 2312 @ 46.24 in 1947.
100 WKTS (1) 103 @ 21.93 in 1936.
DOUBLE (1) 1936. Missed double by 9 wkts in 1937.
Players v Gentlemen (1) 1936. Fc umpire 1951 (did not stand), 1963–64. Club: Catford. Table tennis: England.

TODD, Paul Adrian
—RHB—

Born Morton, Southwell, Notts, 12 Mar 1953. Educ Edward Cludd S, Southwell. Debut 1972.
NOTTINGHAMSHIRE (156) 1972–82. Cap 1977.
HS 178 Notts v Glos, Trent Bridge, 1975.
1000 RUNS (3) 1181 @ 29.52 in 1978.

TOFT, David Penn
—RHB—

Born Tunbridge Wells, Kent, 1 Mar 1945. Educ Tonbridge; UC, Oxford. Debut 1965.
OXFORD UNIVERSITY (27) 1965–67 (Blue 1966–67).
HS 145 Oxford U v Cambridge U, Lord's, 1967.
Club: Old Tonbridgeians.

TOLCHARD, Jeffrey Graham
—RHB, RM/WK—

Born Torquay, Devon, 17 Mar 1944. Educ Malvern; Loughborough C. Debut 1970.
LEICESTERSHIRE (77) 1970–77.
MINOR COUNTIES (1) 1981.
HS 78 Leics v Derbys, Burton upon Trent, 1977.

Devon 1963–69, 1979–. Soccer: Torquay United, Exeter City. Brothers R. W. Tolchard (Leics, England) and R. C. Tolchard (Devon).

TOLCHARD, Roger William
————————RHB, WK————————

Born Torquay, Devon, 15 June 1946. Educ Malvern. Debut 1965.
LEICESTERSHIRE (428) 1965–83. Cap 1966. Benefit (£40,000) 1979. Capt 1981–83.
ENGLAND (4) I 1976/77.
OTHER TOURS International XI to India, Pakistan and Ceylon 1967/68. MCC to India, Pakistan and Sri Lanka 1972/73. D. H. Robins' XI to S Africa 1974/75, 1975/76. International XI to S Africa 1974/75. International XI to Rhodesia 1975/76. D. H. Robins' XI to Sri Lanka 1977/78. England to Australia 1978/79. Leics XI to Zimbabwe 1980/81. Overseas XI to India 1980/81.
HST 67 E v I, Calcutta, 1976/77. HS 126* Leics v Cambridge U, Fenner's, 1970. Scored 998 runs @ 30.24 in 1970.
RECORDS 896 dismissals (787 ct, 109 st) for Leics, county record. Added 233 for 5th wkt with N. E. Briers, Leics v Som, Leicester, 1979, county record.
Devon 1963–64. Brothers J. G. Tolchard (Leics) and R. C. Tolchard (Devon).

TOMLINS, Keith Patrick
————————RHB, RM————————

Born Kingston-upon-Thames, Surrey, 23 Oct 1957. Educ St Benedict's S, Ealing; St Hilda's and St Bede's C, Durham U. Debut 1977.
MIDDLESEX (75) 1977–. Cap 1983.
TOUR M'sex to Zimbabwe 1980/81.
HS 146 M'sex v Oxford U, The Parks, 1982.
BB 2–28 M'sex v Kent, Lord's, 1982.
Club: Ealing.

TOMLINSON, John Derek Williams
————————RHB————————

Born S Normanton, Yorks, 26 Mar 1926. Debut 1946.
DERBYSHIRE (1) 1946.
HS 2 Derbys v Som, Frome, 1946.
Club: Hornsey.

TOMPKIN, Maurice
————————RHB————————

Born Countesthorpe, Leics, 17 Feb 1919. Died Leicester, 27 Sept 1956. Debut 1938. P.

LEICESTERSHIRE (349) 1938–56. Cap 1946. Benefit (£3157) 1954.
TOUR MCC A to Pakistan 1955/56.
HS 186 Leics v Pakistanis, Leicester, 1954.
1000 RUNS (10) 2190 @ 37.11 in 1955. Players v Gentlemen (4) 1951–55. Soccer: Leicester City, Bury, Huddersfield Town.

TONGUE, Christopher Hugh
————————RHB, spin bowler————————

Born Uppingham, Rutland, 2 Apr 1943. Educ Kingswood S, Bath; Jesus C, Cambridge. Debut 1963.
CAMBRIDGE UNIVERSITY (1) 1963.
HS 13 Cambridge U v Leics, Fenner's, 1963.
Somerset 2nd XI 1962.

TOOGOOD, Giles John
————————RHB, OB/RM————————

Born W Bromwich, Staffordshire, 19 Nov 1961. Educ N Bromsgrove HS; Lincoln C, Oxford. Debut 1982.
OXFORD UNIVERSITY (22) 1982–84 (Blue 1982–84). Capt 1983.
HS 109 Oxford U v Cambridge U, Lord's, 1984.
Club: Stourbridge.

TOOLE, Charles Laurence
————————RHB, RFM————————

Born Paddington, London, 9 Jan 1939. Educ Finchley Catholic GS. Debut 1967.
MCC (1) 1967.
HS 54 MCC v Scotland, Glasgow, 1967. M'sex 2nd XI 1961. Club Cricket Conference to Australia 1970. Clubs: Finchley, Pinner, Chepstow, Westbury-on-Trym, Sussex Martlets, Stoics, Glos Gypsies.

TOON, James Henry Cecil
————————RHB, RFM————————

Born Oundle, Northants, 17 Jan 1916. Educ Oundle. Debut 1946.
NORTHAMPTONSHIRE (1) 1946.
HS 1 Northants v Combined Services, Kettering, 1946.
BB 3–79 same match.
London Counties 1945. Club: Oundle.

TOPHAM, Robert Denham Nigel
————————RHB————————

Born Trowbridge, Wiltshire, 17 July 1952. Educ Shrewsbury; Australian

National U, Canberra; St Edmund Hall, Oxford. Debut 1976.
OXFORD UNIVERSITY (4) 1976 (Blue).
HS 31 Oxford U v Sussex, Pagham, 1976.

TOPLEY, Peter Aland
————————RHB, SLA————————

Born Canterbury, Kent, 29 Aug 1950. Educ Simon Langton S, Canterbury. Debut 1972.
KENT (18) 1972–75.
HS 38* Kent v Notts, Dover, 1975.
BB 2–28 Kent v Oxford U, The Parks, 1975.

TORDOFF, Gerald George
————————LHB, RM————————

Born Whitwood, Yorks, 6 Dec 1929. Educ Normanton GS; Manchester U; St John's C, Cambridge. Debut 1950.
SOMERSET (54) 1950–55. Cap 1952. Capt 1955.
CAMBRIDGE UNIVERSITY (12) 1952 (Blue).
COMBINED SERVICES (18) 1952–62.
HS 156* Combined Services v Pakistanis, Catterick, 1954.
BB 4–43 Som v Northants, Glastonbury, 1952.
1000 RUNS (2) 1196 @ 22.56 in 1955. Gentlemen v Players (1) 1955. Berkshire 1962. UAU 1950. Clubs: Britannic, RNC Dartmouth.

TORKINGTON, Harold Fleming
————————RHB————————

Born Poynton, Cheshire, 4 Dec 1959. Educ Stockport GS; Fitzwilliam C, Cambridge. Debut 1981.
CAMBRIDGE UNIVERSITY (1) 1981.
HS 9 Cambridge U v Notts, Fenner's, 1981.

TORRENS, Robert
————————RHB, RFM————————

Born Londonderry, Ireland, 17 May 1948. Educ Londonderry Technical C. Debut 1966.
IRELAND (6) 1966–82.
HS 17 Ireland v Scotland, Edinburgh, 1982.
BB 7–40 Ireland v Scotland, Ayr, 1974.
Club: Brigade.

TOSHACK, Ernest Raymond Herbert
──────RHB, LM──────

Born Cobar, NSW, Australia, 15 Dec 1914. Debut 1945/46.
AUSTRALIA DOMESTIC New South Wales (21) 1945/46–49/50.
AUSTRALIA (12) 1945/46–48. E 1946/47 (5); I 1947/48 (2). *E 1948 (4); NZ 1945/46 (1)*.
HST 20* A v E, Lord's, 1948. HS 20* as above.
BBT 6–29 (11–31 match) A v I, Brisbane, 1947/48. BB 7–81 Australians v Yorks, Bramall Lane, Sheffield, 1948.
Clubs: Marrickville, Randwick.

TOWNSEND, Alan
──────RHB, RM──────

Born Stockton-on-Tees, Co Durham, 26 Aug 1921. Debut 1948. *P.*
WARWICKSHIRE (340) 1948–60. Cap 1948. Benefit (£4143) 1960.
HS 154 Warwicks v Worcs, Dudley, 1957.
BB 7–84 Warwicks v Essex, Brentwood, 1949.
1000 RUNS (5) 1227 @ 29.92 in 1953.
Took 409 catches for Warwicks, second-best for county.
Current Warwicks assistant coach. Durham 1947. Clubs: Thornaby, Eppleton, Mitchells and Butlers.

TOWNSEND, Arnold Frederick
──────RHB──────

Born Long Eaton, Derbys, 29 Mar 1912. Debut 1934. *P.*
DERBYSHIRE (116) 1934–50. Cap.
S AFRICA DOMESTIC South African Air Force XI 1942/43.
HS 142* Derbys v Som, Taunton, 1939.
1000 RUNS (2) 1348 @ 30.63 in 1947.
Club: Long Eaton. Brother L. F. Townsend (Derbys, England).

TOWNSEND, David Charles Humphery
──────RHB, RM──────

Born Norton-on-Tees, Co Durham, 20 Apr 1912. Educ Winchester; New C, Oxford. Debut 1933.
OXFORD UNIVERSITY (19) 1933–34 (Blue 1933–34).
MINOR COUNTIES (3) 1935–37.
MCC (1) 1946.
FREE FORESTERS (2) 1947–48.
ENGLAND (3) *WI 1934/35.*
HST 36 E v WI, Trinidad, 1934/35. HS 195 Oxford U v Free Foresters, The Parks, 1933.

BB 2–31 Oxford U v Surrey, Oval, 1933. Durham County 1935–50. Club: Norton. MCC committee 1966. Grandfather F. Townsend (Glos); uncles A. F. M. Townsend (Glos, Essex) and F. N. Townsend (Glos); father C. L. Townsend (Glos, England); son J. R. A. Townsend (Oxford U); brother P. N. Townsend (Oxford U).

TOWNSEND, Jonathan Richard Arthur
──────RHB──────

Born Filkins, Glos, 30 Nov 1942. Educ Winchester; Corpus Christi C, Oxford. Debut 1964.
OXFORD UNIVERSITY (10) 1964–65.
HS 64 Oxford U v Australians, The Parks, 1964.
Durham County 1964. Wiltshire 1967–68. Suffolk 1973. Clubs: Norton, Clifton. Father D. C. H. Townsend (England, Oxford U); grandfather C. L. Townsend (Glos, England); great-grandfather F. Townsend (Glos); great-uncles A. F. M. Townsend (Glos, Essex) and F. N. Townsend (Glos).

TOWNSLEY, Richard Andrew John
──────LHB, RM──────

Born Castleford, Yorks, 24 June 1952. Educ Rothwell GS. Debut 1974.
YORKSHIRE (2) 1974–75.
HS 12 Yorks v Sussex, Hove, 1975.
Clubs: Birstall, Lidgett Green, Billingham Synthonia.

TRACY, Sean Robert
──────RHB, RMF──────

Born Auckland, N Zealand, 7 June 1963. Educ Penrose HS, Auckland. Debut 1982/83.
N ZEALAND DOMESTIC Auckland (11) 1982/83–83/84.
GLOUCESTERSHIRE (1) 1983.
TOUR N Zealand to England 1983 (co-opted for 2 matches).
HS 9* Auckland v Canterbury, 1983/84. BB 5–29 N Zealanders v D. B. Close's XI, Scarborough, 1983.
Club: Westbury-on-Trym.

TRAICOS, Athanasios *John*
──────RHB, OB──────

Born Zagazig, Egypt, 17 May 1947. Educ Fort Victoria HS; Thornhill HS; Natal U. Debut 1967.
S AFRICA DOMESTIC Rhodesia 1967/68–79/80.
ZIMBABWE 1979/80–. Capt 1983/84.

SOUTH AFRICA (3) A 1969/70.
TOURS S African Universities to England 1967. Zimbabwe to England 1982.
HST 5* SA v A, Durban, 1969/70. HS 43 Rhodesia B v Natal B, Bulawayo, 1977/78.
BBT 2–70 SA v A, Durban, 1969/70. BB 6–66 Rhodesia v NE Transvaal, Pretoria, 1968/69.
Selected for S Africa to England 1970 (cancelled).

TRAPNELL, Barry Maurice Waller
──────RHB, RM──────

Born London, 18 May 1924. Educ UCS, Oxford; St John's C, Cambridge. Debut 1946.
CAMBRIDGE UNIVERSITY (9) 1946 (Blue).
MIDDLESEX (1) 1946.
HS 41 Cambridge U v Oxford U, Lord's, 1946.
BB 5–73 Cambridge U v MCC, Lord's, 1946.
Gentlemen v Players (1) 1946. War-time Blue 1944–45. Club: UCS Old Boys. Headmaster at Denstone until 1967, Oundle from 1968.

TRAVERS, Basil Holmes (Jaika)
────── RHB, RMF──────

Born Sydney, NSW, Australia, 7 July 1919. Educ Sydney U; New C, Oxford. Debut 1946.
OXFORD UNIVERSITY (23) 1946–48 (Blue 1946, 1948).
FREE FORESTERS (1) 1948.
HS 65* Oxford U v Surrey, Guildford, 1946.
BB 4–65 Oxford U v Leics, The Parks, 1946.
Oxfordshire 1946–47. Rugby: Oxford U, Harlequins, England (6). Headmaster Shaw S, Sydney.

TRAVERS, Timothy James
──────RHB, OB──────

Born Wimbledon, 28 Dec 1962. Educ Wimbledon C; Churchill C, Cambridge. Debut 1984.
CAMBRIDGE UNIVERSITY (1) 1984.
HS 15 Cambridge U v Warwicks, Fenner's, 1984.

TREMBATH, Christopher Richard
──────RHB, RM──────

Born London, 27 Oct 1961. Educ Dulwich C; Clifton C; UC, Cardiff. Debut 1982.

GLOUCESTERSHIRE (4) 1982–84.
HS 17* Glos v M'sex, Uxbridge, 1984.
BB 5–91 Glos v Oxford U, The Parks, 1982.

TREMLETT, Maurice Fletcher
————RHB, RFM————

Born Stockport, Cheshire, 5 July 1923.
Died Southampton, Hants, 30 Sept 1984. Educ Taunton Priory. Debut 1947. *P.*
SOMERSET (353) 1947–60. Cap 1947.
Benefit (£3559) 1956. Capt 1956–59.
N ZEALAND DOMESTIC Central Districts (2) 1951/52.
ENGLAND (3) *WI 1947/48.*
OTHER TOUR MCC to S Africa 1948/49.
HST 18*E v WI, Georgetown, 1947/48.
HS 185 Som v Northants, Northampton, 1951.
BBT 2–98 E v WI, Kingston, 1947/48. BB 8–31 Som v Glam, Weston-super-Mare, 1948.
1000 RUNS (10) 2101 @ 35.61 in 1951.
Scored 1056 runs and took 86 wkts in 1949.
Club: Darlington RA. Son T. M. Tremlett (Hants).

TREMLETT, Timothy Maurice
————RHB, RMF————

Born Wellington, Som, 26 July 1956.
Educ Bellemoor Sec S, Taunton. Debut 1976.
HAMPSHIRE (110) 1976–. Cap 1983.
HS 88 Hants v Lancs, Old Trafford, 1981.
BB 6–82 Hants v Derbys, Portsmouth, 1983.
Club: Deanery. Father M. F. Tremlett (Som, England).

TRESTRAIL, Kenneth Basil
————RHB, LB————

Born Port of Spain, Trinidad, 26 Nov 1927. Educ Queen's RC, Trinidad. Debut 1943/44.
W INDIES DOMESTIC Trinidad 1943/44–49/50.
TOURS W Indies to England 1950.
Canada to England 1954.
HS 161* Trinidad v Jamaica, Port of Spain, 1949/50.
BB 3–20 same match.
Clubs: Queen's Park (Trinidad), Gracechurch (Toronto). Brother A. L. Trestrail (Trinidad).

TREVETT, John Charles Pullman
————RHB, SLA————

Born Woking, Surrey, 30 July 1942.
Educ Steyning GS, W Sussex; Wadham C, Oxford. Debut 1962.
OXFORD UNIVERSITY (2) 1962.
HS 1 Oxford U v Lancs, The Parks, 1962.
Sussex 2nd XI 1961. Clubs: Brighton and Hove, Preston Nomads, Ardingley.

TRIBE, George Edward
————LHB, SLA————

Born Yarraville, Victoria, Australia, 4 Oct 1920. Educ St Augustine's S, Yarraville. Debut 1945/46. *P. Wisden* 1955.
AUSTRALIA DOMESTIC Victoria (13) 1945/46–46/47.
NORTHAMPTONSHIRE (233) 1951–59.
Cap 1952. Testimonial (£2659) 1956.
AUSTRALIA (3) E 1946/47.
TOURS Commonwealth XI to India, Pakistan and Ceylon 1949/50. Commonwealth XI to India and Ceylon 1950/51. Duke of Norfolk's XI to Jamaica 1956/57. C. G. Howard's XI to India 1956/57.
HST 25* A v E, Melbourne, 1946/47. HS 136* Northants v Cambridge U, Northampton, 1954.
BBT 2–48 A v E, Brisbane, 1946/47. BB 9–43 (13–99 match) Northants v Worcs, Northampton, 1958.
1000 RUNS (7) 1260 @ 36.00 in 1953.
100 WKTS (8) 176 @ 19.12 in 1955. Took 99 wkts @ 17.23 in India 1949/50 (Commonwealth XI).
DOUBLE (7) 1952–57, 1959.
RECORDS Took 175 wkts @ 18.70 for Northants in 1955, and returned 15–31 match, Northants v Yorks, Northampton, 1958, both county records.
Returned 9–45 inns Victoria v Queensland, Brisbane, 1945/46; 9–45 (15–75 match) Northants v Yorks, Bradford, 1955; and 9–50 (13–101 match) Commonwealth XI v Governor's XI, Calcutta, 1949/50.
Players v Gentlemen (1) 1958. Clubs: North Melbourne (Australia), Milnrow, Rawtenstall (Lancashire).

TRICK, William Mervyn *Stanley*
————RHB, SLA————

Born Neath, S Wales, 31 Oct 1916. Educ Court Shart, Briton Ferry. Debut 1946.
GLAMORGAN (19) 1946–50.
HS 15 Glam v Leics, Swansea, 1949.
BB 6–29 (12–106 match) Glam v Som, Swansea, 1948.
Clubs: Briton Ferry Steelworks, Neath.

TRIM, Geoffrey Edward
————RHB, LB————

Born Openshaw, Manchester, 6 Apr 1956. Debut 1976.
LANCASHIRE (15) 1976–80.
HS 91 Lancs v Derbys, Chesterfield, 1979.

TRIMBORN, Patrick Henry Joseph
————RHB, RFM————

Born Durban, S Africa, 18 May 1940.
Educ Marist Brothers, Durban; Natal U. Debut 1961/62.
S AFRICA DOMESTIC Natal 1961/62–75/76.
INTERNATIONAL CAVALIERS v Barbados, Scarborough, 1969.
SOUTH AFRICA (4) 1966/67–69/70. A 1966/67 (3), 1969/70 (1).
HST 11* SA v A, J'burg, 1966/67. HS 52 Natal v S African Universities, Pietermaritzburg, 1969/70.
BBT 3–12 SA v A, Port Elizabeth, 1966/67. BB 6–36 Natal v S African Universities, Pietermaritzburg, 1969/70.
Selected for S Africa to England 1970 and S Africa to Australia 1971/72 (both cancelled). Club: East Lancashire.

TRIPP, Graham Malcolm
————RHB————

Born Clevedon, Som, 29 June 1932.
Debut 1955. *P.*
SOMERSET (34) 1955–59.
HS 62 Som v Essex, Colchester, 1957.
Devon 1960–64. Club: Clevedon.

TROUP, Gary Bertram
————RHB, LFM————

Born Taumarunui, N Zealand, 3 Oct 1952. Debut 1974/75.
N ZEALAND DOMESTIC Auckland (54) 1974/75–.
NEW ZEALAND (12) 1976/77–81/82. A 1981/82 (2); WI 1979/80 (3); I 1980/81 (2); P 1978/79 (2). *A 1980/81 (2); I 1976/77 (1).*
OTHER TOURS D. H. Robins' XI to S Africa 1975/76. N Zealand to England 1978. N Zealand to Australia 1982/83.
HST 13* NZ v WI, Christchurch, 1979/80. HS 58* Auckland v C Districts, Nelson, 1974/75.
BBT 6–95 (10–169 match) NZ v WI, Auckland, 1979/80. BB 6–48 Auckland v Canterbury, Auckland, 1979/80.

TRUBSHAW, Ernest *Brian*
————RHB————

Born Liverpool, 29 Jan 1924. Educ Winchester. Debut 1946.
ROYAL AIR FORCE (1) 1946.
HS 1 RAF v Worcs, Worcester, 1946.
Clubs: I Zingari, Adastrians, Free Foresters, Butterflies. Gained fame as chief test pilot of Concorde. Awarded CBE and OBE for services to flying.

TRUEMAN, Frederick Sewards
————RHB, RF————

Born Scotch Springs, Stainton, nr Maltby, Yorks, 6 Feb 1931. Educ Maltby Hall Sec S. Debut 1949. *P. Wisden* 1953.
YORKSHIRE (459) 1949–68. Cap 1951. Benefit (£9331) 1962.
ENGLAND (67) 1952–65. A 1953 (1), 1956 (2), 1961 (4), 1964 (4); SA 1955 (1), 1960 (5); WI 1957 (5), 1963 (5); NZ 1958 (5), 1965 (2); I 1952 (4), 1959 (5); P 1962 (4). *A 1958/59 (3), 1962/63 (5); WI 1953/ 54 (3), 1959/60 (5); NZ 1958/59 (2), 1962/63 (2).*
OTHER TOURS C. G. Howard's XI to India 1956/57. Cavaliers to Rhodesia and S Africa 1960/61. Cavaliers to Jamaica 1963/64. Cavaliers to W Indies 1964/65.
HST 39* E v NZ, Oval, 1958. HS 104 Yorks v Northants, Northampton, 1963.
BBT 8–31 E v I, Old Trafford, 1952. BB 8–28 Yorks v Kent, Dover, 1954 (all wkts taken before lunch on first day).
100 WKTS (12) 175 @ 13.98 in 1960.
RECORDS First bowler to take 300 Test wkts (E v A, Oval, 1964); with 307 wkts @ 21.57 remained leading Test wkt-taker for any country until 1975/76 and for England until 1983/84.
Performed four hat-tricks.
Players v Gentlemen (11) 1955–62. Played for Derbys in limited-overs matches (John Player League) 1972. Club: Leeds. MCC Hon. member. Cricket commentator and writer.

TUCKETT, Lindsay
————RHB, RFM————

Born Durban, S Africa, 6 Feb 1919. Debut 1934/35.
S AFRICA DOMESTIC Orange Free State 1934/35–54/55.
SOUTH AFRICA (9) 1947–48/49. E 1948/49 (4). *E 1947 (5).*
HST 40* SA v E, Oval, 1947. HS 101 OFS v NE Transvaal, Pretoria, 1939/40.
BBT 5–68 SA v E, Trent Bridge, 1947. BB 8–32 (13–66 match) OFS v Griqualand West, Kimberley, 1951/52.
Father L. R. Tuckett (S Africa).

TUDOR, Richard Thornhill
————RHB, RM————

Born Shrewsbury, 27 Sept 1948. Educ Shrewsbury. Debut 1976.
WARWICKSHIRE (1) 1976.
HS 6 Warwicks v Cambridge U, Fenner's, 1976.
Shropshire 1975–77. Club: Shrewsbury.

TULK, Derek Thomas
————RHB, RM————

Born Southampton, Hants, 21 Apr 1934. Educ Taunton's S, Southampton. Debut 1956. *P.*
HAMPSHIRE (2) 1956–57.
HS 8* Hants v Cambridge U, Bournemouth, 1957.

TUNNICLIFFE, Colin John
————RHB, LMF————

Born Derby, 11 Aug 1951. Debut 1973.
DERBYSHIRE (150) 1973–83. Cap 1977.
HS 91 Derbys v Hants, Portsmouth, 1983.
BB 7–36 Derbys v Essex, Chelmsford, 1980.

TUNNICLIFFE, Howard *Trevor*
————RHB, RM————

Born Derby, 4 Mar 1950. Educ Malvern C; Loughborough C. Debut 1973.
NOTTINGHAMSHIRE (65) 1973–80.
HS 100* Notts v M'sex, Trent Bridge, 1980.
BB 4–30 Notts v Sri Lankans, Trent Bridge, 1979.
Clubs: Creswell, Old Malvernians.

TURNBULL, Jonathan Richard
————RHB, RM————

Born Northwood, M'sex, 13 Nov 1962. Educ Merchant Taylors' S, Northwood; Jesus C, Oxford. Debut 1983.
OXFORD UNIVERSITY (12) 1983–.
HS 6 Oxford U v Kent, The Parks, 1984.
BB 4–51 Oxford U v Sussex, The Parks, 1983.

TURNER, Alan
————LHB————

Born Camperdown, NSW, Australia, 23 July 1950. Debut 1968/69.
AUSTRALIA DOMESTIC New South Wales (76) 1968/69–77/78.
AUSTRALIA (14) 1975–76/77. WI 1975/76 (6); P 1976/77 (3). *E 1975 (3); NZ 1976/ 77 (2).*
OTHER TOUR Australia to N Zealand 1969/70.
HST 136 A v WI, Adelaide, 1975/76. HS 156 Australians v Kent, Canterbury, 1975.
Club: Randwick (Sydney).

TURNER, Brian
————LHB, RMF————

Born Sheffield, Yorks, 25 July 1938. Debut 1960. *P.*
YORKSHIRE (2) 1960–61.
HS 3* Yorks v Glos, Bristol, 1961.
BB 2–9 Yorks v S Africans, Bramall Lane, Sheffield, 1960.
Club: Sheffield United. Father C. Turner (Yorks).

TURNER, Cyril
————LHB, RM————

Born Wombwell, Yorks, 11 Jan 1902. Died Wath-on-Dearne, Yorks, 19 Nov 1968. Debut 1925. *P.*
YORKSHIRE (200) 1925–46. Cap. Testimonial (£2439) 1946.
HS 130 Yorks v Som, Bramall Lane, Sheffield, 1936.
BB 7–54 Yorks v Glos, Gloucester, 1935.
1000 RUNS (1) 1153 @ 28.82 in 1934.
Club: Sheffield United. Yorks scorer 1952–60. Son B. Turner (Yorks).

TURNER, David Roy
————LHB, RM————

Born Corsham, nr Chippenham, Wiltshire, 5 Feb 1949. Educ Chippenham HS. Debut 1966.
HAMPSHIRE (342) 1966–. Cap 1970. Benefit (£23,011) 1981.
S AFRICA DOMESTIC Western Province 1977/78.
TOUR D. H. Robins' XI to S Africa 1972/ 73.
HS 181* Hants v Surrey, Oval, 1969.
BB 2–7 Hants v Glam, Bournemouth, 1981.
1000 RUNS (7) 1365 @ 41.36 in 1984.
Wiltshire 1965. Club: Chippenham.

TURNER, Francis *Michael*
————RHB, LB————

Born Leicester, 8 Aug 1934. Debut 1954. *P.*
LEICESTERSHIRE (10) 1954–59.
HS 28* Leics v Warwicks, Edgbaston, 1959 and 28 v Essex, Colchester, 1959.

BB 3–56 Leics v Cambridge U, Fenner's, 1956.
Leics secretary 1960–78; secretary-manager 1979–.

TURNER, Glenn Maitland
────────RHB, OB────────

Born Dunedin, N Zealand, 26 May 1947. Educ Otago HS. Debut 1964/65. *Wisden* 1971.
N ZEALAND DOMESTIC Otago (59) 1964/65–79/80, 1982/83, Northern Districts (7) 1976/77.
WORCESTERSHIRE (284) 1967–82. Cap 1968. Benefit (£21,103) 1978. Capt 1981.
NEW ZEALAND (41) 1968/69–82/83. E 1970/71 (2), 1974/75 (2); A 1973/74 (3), 1976/77 (2); WI 1968/69 (3); I 1975/76 (3); P 1972/73 (3); SL 1982/83 (2). *E 1969 (2), 1973 (3); A 1973/74 (2); WI 1971/72 (5); I 1969/70 (3), 1976/77 (3); P 1969/70 (1), 1976/77 (2)*. Capt 10.
OTHER TOURS New Zealand to Australia 1969/70. International Wanderers to Rhodesia 1972/73. International Wanderers to S Africa and Rhodesia 1975/76.
HST 259 NZ v WI, Georgetown, 1971/72. HS 311* Worcs v Warwicks, Worcester, 1982.
BB 3–18 Worcs v Pakistanis, Worcester, 1967.
1000 RUNS (15 + 3). 2416 @ 67.11 in 1973. 2000 runs (3).
RECORDS Only N Zealander to score 100 fc centuries. HS (above) highest inns by batsman scoring his 100th century and only instance of it being reached before lunch on 1st day of match (entire inns took place on 1st day). Also highest-ever inns for Worcs. Scored 72 centuries for Worcs in career and 10 for Worcs in 1970, both county records. HST (above) highest-ever score for N Zealand and longest fc inns by a N Zealander (704 mins); during inns added 387 for 1st wkt with T. W. Jarvis, N Zealand Test record for any wkt. Added 220 for 6th wkt with K. J. Wadsworth, NZ v WI, Kingston, 1971/72, N Zealand Test record, during which inns carried bat for 223* in total of 386, highest score by batsman carrying bat in Test cricket. Carried bat for 43* in total of 131, NZ v E, Lord's, 1969, youngest batsman (22 yrs 63 days) to do so in Tests. Scored 672 runs @ 96.00 in series, NZ v WI, 1971/72, a N Zealand record. Scored 7 Test centuries, equalling the N Zealand Test record. Reached 1000 runs for season before June, in 1973, one of only seven batsmen to do so. Scored 1244 runs @ 77.75 in N Zealand season, in 1975/76, a record aggregate. Scored 141* out of inns total of 169, Worcs v Glam, Swansea, 1977, a world-record proportion (83.4%) of a completed inns. In 1979 became first batsman to score centuries against all 17 fc counties. Scored four double-centuries for N Zealanders in W Indies in 1971/72, equalling record for a non-English season.
Turned down by Warwicks before joining Worcs. Club: Stourbridge. Hockey: Worcs.

TURNER, John Bernard
────────RHB, SLA────────

Born Princes Risborough, Buckinghamshire, 2 Jan 1949. Debut 1974.
MINOR COUNTIES (1) 1974.
HS 106 Minor Counties v Pakistanis, Jesmond, 1974 (in only fc match).
Buckinghamshire 1968–. Clubs: Ernest Turner's, Eastcote, Princes Risborough.

TURNER, Murray Stewart
────────RHB, RMF────────

Born Shaftesbury, Dorset, 27 Jan 1964. Educ Huish GS, Taunton. Debut 1984.
SOMERSET (1) 1984.
HS 1 Som v Lancs, Bath, 1984.

TURNER, Richard Vinson
────────RHB────────

Born Torquay, Devon, 6 Apr 1932. Educ Clifton; Corpus Christi C, Cambridge. Debut 1953.
CAMBRIDGE UNIVERSITY (10) 1953–54.
HS 113* Cambridge U v MCC, Fenner's, 1953.
Devon 1953–55.

TURNER, Simon Jonathan
────────LHB, WK────────

Born Cuckfield, Sussex, 28 Apr 1960. Educ Broadoak S. Debut 1984.
SOMERSET (5) 1984.
HS 27* Som v Glam, Taunton, 1984.

TURNER, Stuart
────────RHB, RM────────

Born Chester, 18 July 1943. Educ St John's Sec S, Epping. Debut 1965.
ESSEX (347) 1965–. Cap 1970. Benefit (£37,288) 1979.
S AFRICA DOMESTIC Natal 1976/77–77/78.
TOUR D. H. Robins' XI to S Africa 1974/75.
HS 121 Essex v Som, Taunton, 1970.
BB 6–26 Essex v Northants, Northampton, 1977.
Club: Buckhurst Hill.

TYRWHITT-DRAKE, Thomas William
────────RHB, WK────────

Born London, 5 Nov 1926. Educ Haileybury and ISC; Trinity C, Cambridge. Debut 1946.
CAMBRIDGE UNIVERSITY (3) 1946–48.
FREE FORESTERS (1) 1957.
HS 38 Free Foresters v Oxford U, The Parks, 1957.
Hertfordshire 1946–58. Clubs: Bishop's Stortford, Knowle and Dorridge, Crusaders.

TYSON, Frank Holmes
────────RHB, RF────────

Born Farnworth, Lancs, 6 June 1930. Educ Queen Elizabeth GS, Middleton; Durham U. Debut 1952. *P. Wisden* 1956.
NORTHAMPTONSHIRE (170) 1952–60. Cap 1954. Testimonial (£2380) 1960.
ENGLAND (17) 1954–58/59. A 1956 (1); SA 1955 (2); P 1954 (1). *A 1954/55 (5), 1958/59 (2); SA 1956/57 (2); NZ 1954/55 (2), 1958/59 (2)*.
OTHER TOURS E. W. Swanton's XI to W Indies 1955/56. Commonwealth XI to S Africa 1959/60.
HST 37* E v A, Brisbane, 1954/55. HS 82 Northants v Sussex, Hove, 1960.
BBT 7–27 E v A, Melbourne, 1954/55. BB 8–60 (13–112 match) Northants v Surrey, Oval, 1957.
100 WKTS (1) 101 @ 21.47 in 1957. Took 99 wkts @ 18.04 in 1958.
Players v Gentlemen (5) 1955–57. Victoria CA cricket organiser. Clubs: Middleton, Knypersley, Todmorden, MCC Hon. member. Autobiography *A Typhoon Called Tyson* (1961). Cricket commentator in Australia.

U/V

UDAL, Geoffrey Francis Uvedale
————————RHB, RF————————

Born Holborn, London, 23 Feb 1908.
Died Frimley, Surrey, 5 Dec 1980.
Debut 1932.
MIDDLESEX (1) 1932.
ROYAL AIR FORCE (1) 1932.
LEICESTERSHIRE (2) 1946.
HS 2* Leics v Som, Melton Mowbray,
1946.
BB 2–105 RAF v Army, Oval, 1932.
Grandfather Hon. J. S. Udal (MCC).

UFTON, Derek Gilbert
————————LHB, WK————————

Born Crayford, Kent, 31 May 1928.
Educ Dartford GS. Debut 1949. P.
KENT (148) 1949–62. Cap 1956.
HS 119* Kent v Sussex, Hastings, 1952.
Clubs: Dartford, The Mote, Maidstone.
Soccer: Charlton Athletic, England (1).

UMRIGAR, Pehlon Ratanji
(Polly)
————————RHB, RM————————

Born Bombay, India, 28 Mar 1926.
Educ St Xavier's C, Bombay; Bombay
U. Debut 1944/45.
INDIA DOMESTIC Parsees 1944/45–45/46,
Bombay 1946/47–49/50, 1953/54–62/63
(capt 1957/58–62/63), Gujerat 1950/
51–51/52, Dungarpur XI 1966/67–67/
68.
INDIA (59) 1948/49–61/62. E 1951/52
(5), 1961/62 (4); A 1956/57 (3), 1959/60
(3); WI 1948/49 (1), 1958/59 (5); NZ
1955/56 (5); P 1952/53 (5), 1960/61 (5).
*E 1952 (4), 1959 (4); WI 1952/53 (5),
1961/62 (5); P 1954/55 (5).* Capt 8.
OTHER TOUR India to Ceylon 1956/57
(capt).
HST 223 I v NZ, Hyderabad, 1955/56. HS
252* Indians v Cambridge U, Fenner's,
1959.
BBT 6–74 I v P, Bahawalpur, 1954/55. BB
7–32 (12–90 match) ACC XI v Imtiaz
Ahmed's XI, Rawalpindi, 1961/62.
1000 RUNS (2 + 2) 1826 @ 55.33 in
1959.

RECORDS Added 238 for 3rd wkt with V.
L. Manjrekar, I v NZ, Hyderabad,
1955/56, India Test record.
Indian Test selector and manager.
MCC Hon. member. Clubs: Werneth,
Church, Oldham.

UNDERWOOD, Arthur Joseph
————————RHB, LM————————

Born Wiseton, Notts, 21 Sept 1927.
Debut 1949. P.
NOTTINGHAMSHIRE (14) 1949–54.
COMBINED SERVICES (2) 1950–51.
HS 39 Notts v Kent, Trent Bridge, 1951.
BB 2–72 Notts v Sussex, Trent Bridge,
1951.

UNDERWOOD, Derek Leslie
————————RHB, SLA/LM————————

Born Bromley, Kent, 8 June 1945. Educ
Beckenham; Penge GS. Debut 1963.
Wisden 1969.
KENT (449) 1963–. Cap 1964. Benefit
(£24,114) 1975.
ENGLAND (86) 1966–81/82. A 1968 (4),
1972 (2), 1975 (4), 1977 (5); WI 1966 (2),
1969 (2), 1973 (3), 1976 (5), 1980 (1); NZ
1969 (3), 1973 (1); I 1971 (1), 1974 (3);
P 1967 (2), 1971 (1), 1974 (3). *A 1970/71
(5), 1974/75 (5), 1976/77 (1), 1979/80
(3); WI 1973/74 (4); NZ 1970/71 (2),
1974/75 (2); I 1972/73 (4), 1976/77
(5), 1979/80 (1), 1981/82 (6); P 1968/
69 (3), 1972/73 (2); SL 1981/82 (1).*
OTHER TOURS MCC Under-25 to Pakistan 1966/67. International XI to India,
Pakistan and Ceylon 1967/68. Duke of
Norfolk's XI to W Indies 1969/70.
International XI to S Africa 1975/76.
HST 45* E v A, Headingley, 1968. HS 111
Kent v Sussex, Hastings, 1984.
BBT 8–51 (13–71 match) E v P, Lord's,
1974. BB 9–28 Kent v Sussex, Hastings,
1964.
100 WKTS (10) 157 @ 13.80 in 1966.
RECORDS Took 101 wkts in debut season,
in 1963, youngest bowler to do so. Took
1000th wkt, in 1970/71, aged 25 yrs 264
days, third-youngest to do so, after G.
A. Lohmann (1890) and W. Rhodes
(1902).

Took 10 wkts in a Test match on six
occasions, a total beaten only by S. F.
Barnes, C. V. Grimmett and D. K.
Lillee (seven each). Returned 9–32 inns
Kent v Surrey, Oval, 1978; 9–37 Kent v
Essex, Westcliff, 1966; 8–9 Kent v
Sussex, Hastings, 1973; 8–10 (15–43
match) International XI v President's
XI, Colombo, 1967/68; and 14–158
match Kent v Worcs, Canterbury, 1983.
World Series Cricket (Kerry Packer)
1977/78–78/79. Barred from Test
cricket for three yrs for touring S Africa
in 1981/82 (SAB England XI). Club:
Beckenham. Awarded MBE for services
to cricket.

UNWIN, Frederick St George
————————RHB, RM————————

Born Halstead, Essex, 23 Apr 1911.
Educ Haileybury and ISC; Wye C.
Debut 1932.
ESSEX (52) 1932–50. Cap 1939. Joint capt
1939.
FREE FORESTERS (1) 1951.
HS 60 Essex v Kent, Colchester, 1946.
Brother E. J. Unwin (Essex).

UPTON, Mark
————————RHB, SLA————————

Born Poole, Dorset, 30 June 1950.
Debut 1971.
SUSSEX (1) 1971.
HS 2* Sussex v Cambridge U, Horsham,
1971.
Clubs: Horsham, Brighton Brunswick.

URQUHART, John Rankin
————————RHB, RFM————————

Born Chelmsford, Essex, 29 May 1921.
Educ King Edward VI S, Chelmsford;
Emmanuel C, Cambridge. Debut 1948.
CAMBRIDGE UNIVERSITY (4) 1948 (Blue).
HS 6* Cambridge U v Glos, Bristol,
1948.
BB 4–21 Cambridge U v M'sex,
Fenner's, 1948.

VALENTINE, Alfred Lewis
————————RHB, SLA————————

Born Kingston, Jamaica, 29 Apr 1930.
Educ St Catharine's S, Spanish Town.
Debut 1949/50. *Wisden* 1951.
W INDIES DOMESTIC Jamaica 1949/
50–64/65.
WEST INDIES (36) 1950–61/62. E 1953/54
(3); A 1954/55 (3); I 1952/53 (5), 1961/
62 (2); P 1957/58 (1). E 1950 (4), 1957
(2); A 1951/52 (5), 1960/61 (5); NZ
1951/52 (2), 1955/56 (4).
OTHER TOUR W Indies to England 1963.
HST 14 WI v A, Melbourne, 1951/52. HS
24 Jamaica v Cavaliers, Kingston, 1963/
64.
BBT 8–104 WI v E, Old Trafford, 1950.
BB 8–26 (13–67 match) W Indians v
Lancs, Old Trafford, 1950.
100 WKTS (1) 123 @ 17.94 in 1950.
RECORD Took 33 wkts @ 20.42 in series,
WI v E, 1950, which equals the W
Indies Test record.
Clubs: Walsall, Rishton. MCC Hon.
member.

VALENTINE, Bryan Herbert
————————RHB, RM————————

Born Blackheath, Kent, 17 Jan 1908.
Died Otford, 2 Feb 1983. Educ Repton;
Pembroke C, Cambridge. Debut 1927.
KENT (308) 1927–48. Cap. Joint capt
1936–37; capt 1946–48.
CAMBRIDGE UNIVERSITY (13) 1928–29
(Blue 1929).
ENGLAND (7) 1933/34–38/39. SA 1938/
39 (5); I 1933/34 (2).
OTHER TOUR Lord Tennyson's XI to
Jamaica 1931/32.
HST 136 E v I, Bombay, 1933/34. HS 242
Kent v Leics, Oakham, 1938.
BB 3–58 Free Foresters v Cambridge U,
Fenner's, 1933.
1000 RUNS (9) 1738 @ 33.42 in 1933.
Gentlemen v Players (7) 1932–46. Kent
president 1967. Soccer: Blue. Cousin J.
C. Christopherson (Kent); kinsmen S.
Christopherson (Kent, England) and P.
Christopherson (Kent).

VAN DER BIJL, Vintcent Adriaan Pieter
————————RHB, RFM————————

Born Cape Town, S Africa, 19 Mar
1948. Educ Diocesan C, Cape Town;
Natal U. Debut 1967/68. *Wisden* 1981.
S AFRICA DOMESTIC South African
Universities 1967/68, Natal (109) 1968/
69–81/82 (capt 33), Transvaal 1982/83.
MIDDLESEX (21) 1980–81.
HS 87 Natal v Zimbabwe-Rhodesia,
Durban, 1979/80.

BB 8–35 (13–53 match) Natal v W
Province, Pietermaritzburg, 1971/72.
RECORDS Took 75 wkts @ 14.92 in
season, in 1981/82, record for a S
African in S Africa. Took 572 wkts @
16.42 in Currie Cup, a record.
Returned 14–111 match Natal v N
Transvaal, Pretoria, 1981/82. Topped fc
bowling averages in only full English
season, in 1980.
S Africa (6) 1981/82–82/83. Father P.
G. V. van der Bijl (Oxford U, S Africa);
great-uncle V. A. W. van der Bijl (W
Province, G. J. V. Weigall's XI); grand-
father V. P. van der Bijl (W Province).

VAN DER KNAPP, David Saunders
————————RHB, OB————————

Born Johannesburg, S Africa, 7 Sept
1948. Educ Parktown HS, Transvaal, S
Africa. Debut 1967.
LANCASHIRE (1) 1967.
S AFRICA DOMESTIC Transvaal 1967/
68–78/79.
HS 44 Transvaal v E Province, Port
Elizabeth, 1974/75.
BB 6–61 Transvaal v Rhodesia,
Bulawayo, 1974/75.

VAN DER MERWE, Peter Laurence
————————RHB, SLA————————

Born Paarl, Cape Province, S Africa, 14
Mar 1937. Educ St Andrew's C,
Grahamstown; Cape Town U. Debut
1956/57.
S AFRICA DOMESTIC South African
Universities 1956/57–57/58, Western
Province 1958/59–65/66 (capt 1962/
63–65/66), Eastern Province 1966/
67–68/69 (capt 1966/67–67/68).
SOUTH AFRICA (15) 1963/64–66/67. E
1964/65 (2); A 1966/67 (5). E 1965 (3);
A 1963/64 (3); NZ 1963/64 (2). Capt 8.
OTHER TOUR S African Fezelas to Eng-
land 1961.
HST 76 SA v A, J'burg, 1966/67. HS 128
E Province v Transvaal, J'burg, 1966/
67.
BB 6–40 W Province v Natal, Durban,
1959/60.
Hockey: Western Province.

VAN GELOVEN, Jack
————————RHB, RM————————

Born Guiseley, Leeds, Yorks, 4 Jan
1934. Debut 1955. *P.*
YORKSHIRE (3) 1955.
LEICESTERSHIRE (244) 1956–65. Cap
1959.

HS 157* Leics v Som, Leicester, 1960.
BB 7–56 Leics v Hants, Leicester, 1959.
1000 RUNS (3) 1324 @ 23.22 in 1959.
100 WKTS (1) 100 @ 28.11 in 1962.
DOUBLE (1) 1962.
Fc umpire 1977–. Northumberland
1966–73. Clubs: Lidget Green,
Ashington, Morpeth, Northumberland
County.

VAN RYNEVELD, Anthony John
————————RHB, RFM————————

Born Plumstead, Cape Town, S Africa,
17 Nov 1925. Educ Diocesan C, Cape
Town; Trinity College, Oxford. Debut
1947.
OXFORD UNIVERSITY (1) 1947.
HS 50 Oxford U v Free Foresters, The
Parks, 1947.
Brother C. B. van Ryneveld (S Africa);
uncle J. M. Blankenberg (S Africa).

VAN RYNEVELD, Clive Berrange
————————RHB, LBG————————

Born Cape Town, S Africa, 19 Mar
1928. Educ Diocesan C, Cape Town;
UC, Oxford. Debut 1946/47.
S AFRICA DOMESTIC Western Province
1946/47–62/63. Capt 1953/54–57/58.
OXFORD UNIVERSITY (28) 1948–50 (Blue
1948–50). Capt 1949.
SOUTH AFRICA (19) 1951–57/58. E 1956/
57 (5); A 1957/58 (4); NZ 1953/54 (5). E
1951 (5). Capt 8.
HST 83 SA v E, Headingley, 1951 (ad-
ding 198 for 2nd wkt with E. A. B.
Rowan, S Africa Test record). HS 150 S
Africans v Yorks, Bramall Lane, Shef-
field, 1951.
BBT 4–57 SA v NZ, Port Elizabeth,
1953/54. BB 8–48 W Province v OFS,
Cape Town, 1954/55.
Gentlemen v Players (1) 1949. Rugby:
Blue, England (4). Former member S
African Parliament (East London for
Progressive Party). Brother A. J. van
Ryneveld (Oxford U); uncle J. M. Blan-
kenburg (S Africa).

VAREY, David William
————————RHB————————

Born Darlington, Co Durham, 15 Oct
1961. Educ Birkenhead S; Pembroke C,
Cambridge. Debut 1981.
CAMBRIDGE UNIVERSITY (22) 1981–83
(Blue 1982–83).
LANCASHIRE (8) 1984.
HS 156* Cambridge U v Northants,
Fenner's, 1982.

Played opposite twin brother, Jonathan, in the 1982 and 1983 Varsity matches. Cheshire 1982–83. Club: Oxton. Twin brother J. G. Varey (Oxford U).

VAREY, Jonathan Guy
————————RHB, RM————————

Born Darlington, Co Durham, 15 Oct 1961. Educ Birkenhead S; St Edmund Hall, Oxford. Debut 1982.
OXFORD UNIVERSITY (16) 1982–83 (Blue 1982–83).
HS 69* Oxford U v Northants, The Parks, 1983.
BB 3–69 Oxford U v Worcs, The Parks, 1983.
Played opposite twin brother, David, in the 1982 and 1983 Varsity matches. Cheshire 1982. Club: Oxton. Twin brother D. W. Varey (Cambridge U).

VAULKHARD, Patrick
————————RHB, occ WK————————

Born Nottingham, 15 Sept 1911. Educ Oakham S. Debut 1934.
NOTTINGHAMSHIRE (9) 1934.
SIR J. CAHN'S XI (2) 1935.
OVER-33 XI (1) 1945.
DERBYSHIRE (65) 1946–52. Cap 1946. Capt 1950.
HS 264 Derbys v Notts, Trent Bridge, 1946 (his only fc century; adding 328 for 4th wkt with D. Smith, county record). Northumberland 1939. Club: Notts Amateurs. Brother D. H. Vaulkhard (Sir J. Cahn's XI).

VAVASOUR, Geoffrey William
————————RHB————————

Born Queenstown, Ireland, 5 Sept 1914. Educ RNC Dartmouth. Debut 1947.
COMBINED SERVICES (1) 1947.
HS 8 Combined Services v Northants, Northampton, 1947.
Royal Navy (capt 1947). Clubs: Free Foresters, Incogniti. Knighted.

VEIVERS, Thomas Robert
————————LHB, ROB————————

Born Beenleigh, Queensland, Australia, 6 Apr 1937. Debut 1958/59.
AUSTRALIA DOMESTIC Queensland (55) 1958/59–67/68.
AUSTRALIA (21) 1963/64–66/67. E 1965/66 (2), SA 1963/64 (3); P 1964/65 (1). E 1964 (5); SA 1966/67 (4); I 1964/65 (3); P 1964/65 (1).
HST 88 A v P, Melbourne, 1964/65. HS 137 Queensland v S Australia, Brisbane, 1962/63.

BBT 4–68 A v I, Bombay, 1964/65. BB 5–63 Queensland v Victoria, Melbourne, 1963/64.
Returned analysis of 95.1–36–155–3 (571 balls) A v E, Old Trafford, 1964. Club: University (Brisbane).

VENGSARKAR, Dilip Balwant
————————RHB————————

Born Bombay, India, 6 Apr 1956. Educ King George HS, Dadar, India; Bombay U. Debut 1975/76.
INDIA DOMESTIC Bombay 1975/76–.
INDIA (69) 1975/76–83/84. E 1976/77 (1), 1979/80 (1), 1981/82 (6); A 1979/80 (6); WI 1978/79 (6), 1983/84 (5); P 1979/80 (5), 1983/84 (1); SL 1982/83 (1). E 1979 (4), 1982 (3); A 1977/78 (5), 1980/81 (3); WI 1975/76 (2), 1982/83 (5); NZ 1975/76 (3), 1980/81 (3); P 1978/79 (3), 1982/83 (6).
HST 159 I v WI, Delhi, 1983/84. HS 210 Bombay v Baroda, Baroda, 1979/80.
1000 RUNS (0 + 4) 1495 @ 57.50 in 1979/80.
RECORDS Added 344* for 2nd wkt with S. M. Gavaskar, I v WI, Calcutta, 1978/79, India Test record and highest unbroken stand in Test cricket for any wkt.

VENKATARAGHAVAN, Srinivasaraghavan
————————RHB, OB————————

Born Madras, India, 21 Apr 1945. Educ Madras Engineering C; Madras U. Debut 1963/64.
INDIA DOMESTIC Madras (Tamil Nadu) 1963/64–.
DERBYSHIRE (46) 1973–75. Cap 1973.
INDIA (57) 1964/65–83/84. E 1972/73 (2), 1976/77 (1); A 1969/70 (5), 1979/80 (3); WI 1966/67 (2), 1974/75 (2), 1978/79 (6); NZ 1964/65 (4), 1969/70 (2), 1976/77 (3), 1983/84 (2). E 1967 (1), 1971 (3), 1974 (2), 1979 (4); A 1977/78 (1); WI 1970/71 (5), 1975/76 (3), 1982/83 (5); NZ 1975/76 (1). Capt 5.
OTHER TOURS Madras to Ceylon 1965/66, 1967/68, 1969/70, 1971/72. India to E Africa 1967. India to Sri Lanka 1973/74. India to Pakistan 1978/79.
HST 64 I v NZ, Madras, 1976/77. HS 137 Tamil Nadu v Kerala, Tellicherry, 1970/71.
BBT 8–72 I v NZ, Delhi, 1964/65. BB 9–93 Indians v Hants, Bournemouth, 1971.
Took 500 wkts @ 18.04 in Ranji Trophy, second-highest aggregate, after R. Goel.

VERITY, Stuart Anthony
————————RHB, RM————————

Born Bradford, Yorks, 11 Nov 1948. Educ Bradford GS; Corpus Christi C, Oxford. Debut 1969.
OXFORD UNIVERSITY (4) 1969–70.
HS 15 Oxford U v Worcs, The Parks, 1969.
BB 3–42 Oxford U v Glam, The Parks, 1969.
Clubs: Bankfoot, Oxford University Authentics.

VERNON, John *Michael*
————————RHB, RM————————

Born Port Said, Egypt, 27 July 1922. Educ Tonbridge. Debut 1949.
COMBINED SERVICES (8) 1949–52.
HS 83 Combined Services v Warwicks, Edgbaston, 1951.
Royal Navy. Royal Navy regular officer.

VERNON, Martin Jeffrey
————————RHB, RMF————————

Born Marylebone, London, 9 July 1951. Debut 1974.
MIDDLESEX (16) 1974–76.
GLOUCESTERSHIRE (5) 1977.
HS 27 M'sex v Sussex, Hove, 1974.
BB 6–58 M'sex v Som, Taunton, 1974.
MCC groundstaff 1966–72. Club: Cross Arrows.

VERRINDER, Alan Otto Charles
————————RHB, RFM————————

Born Henley-on-Thames, Oxfordshire, 28 July 1955. Educ Windsor GS. Debut 1974.
SURREY (3) 1974–76.
KENT (1) 1977.
HS 23 Kent v Cambridge U, Canterbury, 1977.
BB 2–42 Surrey v Cambridge U, Fenner's, 1976.

VICKERY, Anthony
————————RHB————————

Born Taunton, Som, 26 Aug 1925. Debut 1947.
SOMERSET (6) 1947–48.
HS 21 Som v Worcs, Worcester, 1947.
Cheshire 1949–59. Club: Neston.

VIGAR, Frank Henry
————————RHB, LBG————————

Born Bruton, Som, 14 July 1917. Educ Clacton Sec S. Debut 1938. P.

ESSEX (256) 1938–54. Cap 1946. Benefit
(£2307) 1953.
HS 145 M'sex/Essex v Surrey/Kent,
Kingston-upon-Thames, 1947.
BB 8–128 Essex v Leics, Clacton, 1946.
1000 RUNS (3) 1735 @ 35.40 in 1947.
RECORD Added 218 for 10th wkt with T.
P. B. Smith, Essex v Derbys, Chester-
field, 1947, county record.
Club: West of Scotland.

VILJOEN, Kenneth George
——RHB——

Born Kimberley, Cape Province, S
Africa, 14 May 1910. Died Johannesburg, S Africa, 21 Jan 1974. Debut
1926/27.
S AFRICA DOMESTIC Griqualand West
1926/27–30/31, Orange Free State
1933/34–35/36, Transvaal 1936/37–48/
49 (capt 1936/37).
SOUTH AFRICA (27) 1930/31–48/49. E
1930/31 (3), 1938/39 (4), 1948/49 (2); A
1935/36 (4). *E 1935 (4), 1947 (5); A
1931/32 (4); NZ 1931/32 (1).*
HST 124 SA v E, Old Trafford, 1935. HS
215 Griqualand West v W Province,
Kimberley, 1929/30.
BB 4–23 Griqualand West v E Province,
Kimberley, 1929/30.
1000 RUNS (2) 1454 @ 46.90 in 1935.
Manager S Africa to Australasia 1952/
53, 1963/64, and S Africa to England
1955. S Africa CA president 1962/63,
1964/65. MCC Hon. member.

VIRGIN, Roy Thomas
——RHB, occ LB, occ WK——

Born Taunton, Som, 26 Aug 1939. Educ
Huish's GS, Taunton. Debut 1957. *P.
Wisden* 1971.
SOMERSET (321) 1957–72. Cap 1960.
Testimonial (£4000) 1969.
NORTHAMPTONSHIRE (103) 1973–77.
Cap 1974. Capt 1975 (resigned in
August).
S AFRICA DOMESTIC Western Province
1972/73.
TOUR Commonwealth XI to Pakistan
1970/71.
HS 179* Som v Lancs, Old Trafford,
1971.
1000 RUNS (12) 2223 @ 47.29 in 1970.
RECORD Added 370 for 4th wkt with P.
Willey, Northants v Som, Northamp-
ton, 1976, county record.
Club: Walsall.

VISVANATH, Gundappa
Ranganath
——RHB, LB——

Born Bhadrawadi, India, 12 Feb 1949.
Educ Fort HS; Bangalore U. Debut
1967/68.
INDIA DOMESTIC Mysore (Karnataka)
1967/68–.
INDIA (91) 1969/70–82/83. E 1972/73
(5), 1976/77 (5), 1979/80 (1), 1981/82
(6); A 1969/70 (4), 1979/80 (6); WI
1974/75 (5), 1978/79 (6); NZ 1976/77
(3); P 1979/80 (6); SL 1982/83 (1). *E
1971 (3), 1974 (3), 1979 (4), 1982 (3);
A 1977/78 (5), 1980/81 (3); WI 1970/
71 (3), 1975/76 (4); NZ 1975/76 (3),
1980/81 (3); P 1978/79 (3), 1982/83
(6).* Capt 2.
OTHER TOUR India to Sri Lanka 1973/74.
HST 222 I v E, Madras, 1981/82. HS 247
Karnataka v Uttar Pradesh, Mohan
Nagar, 1977/78.
BB 2–21 Karnataka v Bombay, Bangalore, 1981/82.
1000 RUNS (0 + 7) 1538 @ 53.03 in 1974/
75.
RECORDS Played 87 consecutive Tests,
from 1970/71 to 1982/83, a world
record. During HST (above) added 316
for 3rd wkt with Yashpal Sharma, India
Test record. Scored century (137) on
Test debut, I v A, Kanpur, 1969/70, and
century (230) on fc debut, Mysore v
Andhra, Vijayawada, 1967/68, a feat
equalled only by D. M. Wellham.
Scored 1388 runs @ 60.35 in calendar
year of 1979.
Brother-in-law   S.   M.   Gavaskar
(India).

VIVIAN, Graham Ellery
——LHB, RLB——

Born Auckland, N Zealand, 28 Feb
1946. Debut 1964/65.
N ZEALAND DOMESTIC Auckland (58)
1966/67–78/79.
NEW ZEALAND (5) 1964/65–71/72. *WI
1971/72 (4); I 1964/65 (1).*
OTHER TOURS N Zealand to England
1965. N Zealand to Australia 1969/70,
1972/73.
HST 43 NZ v I, Calcutta, 1964/65. HS
137* N Zealanders v Victoria, Melbourne, 1969/70.
BB 5–59 Auckland v C Districts, Auckland, 1967/68.

Only post–1945 cricketer to make fc
debut in a Test match, NZ v I, Calcutta,
1964/65.
Father H. G. Vivian (N Zealand).

VOCE, William
——RHB, LF/SMLA——

Born Annesley Woodhouse, Notts, 8
Aug 1909. Died Nottingham, 6 June
1984. Debut 1927. *P. Wisden* 1933.
NOTTINGHAMSHIRE (345) 1927–52. Cap.
Benefit (£980) 1939.
ENGLAND (27) 1929/30–46/47. NZ 1931
(1), 1937 (1); I 1932 (1), 1936 (1), 1946
(1). *A 1932/33 (4), 1936/37 (5), 1946/
47 (2); SA 1930/31 (5); WI 1929/30
(4); NZ 1932/33 (2).*
HST 66 E v NZ, Christchurch, 1932/33.
HS 129 Notts v Glam, Trent Bridge,
1931.
BBT 7–70 (11–149 match) E v WI, Port of
Spain, 1929/30. BB 8–30 Notts v Som,
Weston-super-Mare, 1939.
1000 RUNS (1) 1020 @ 35.17 in 1933.
100 WKTS (6) 139 @ 21.58 in 1935.
Also took 98 wkts in 1938 and 97 in
1939.
RECORD HS (above) completed in 75
mins, including his century in 45 mins.
Returned 10–57 match, E v A, Brisbane,
1936/37.
Players v Gentlemen (1) 1932. Notts
coach 1947–52. MCC Hon. member.

VON HAGHT, Marlon Dudley
——RHB, RM——

Born Kalutara, Ceylon, 31 Mar 1965.
Debut 1983/84.
SRI LANKA DOMESTIC Sri Lanka 1983/
84–.
TOUR Sri Lanka to England 1984.
HS 75 Sri Lankans v Warwicks, Edgbas-
ton, 1984.

VOWLES, Roger Charles
——RHB, RM——

Born Grimsby, Lincolnshire, 5 Apr
1932. Educ Brentwood S. Debut 1957.
NOTTINGHAMSHIRE (16) 1957–61.
HS 54 Notts v Derbys, Ilkeston, 1957.
BB 4–106 Notts v Essex, Westcliff,
1961.

W/X/Y/Z

WADE, Thomas Henry
LHB, WK, ROB

Born Maldon, Essex, 24 Nov 1910. Educ Maldon GS. Debut 1929. *P.*
ESSEX (318) 1929–50. Cap. Benefit (£3900) 1948.
TOUR MCC to Australia 1936/37 (in emergency, because of injuries, but awarded tour colours).
HS 96 Essex v Oxford U, Leyton, 1932.
BB 5–64 Essex v Som, Chelmsford, 1929.
Originally bowler; took over as regular wicketkeeper in 1934. Soccer: Southend United.

WADEKAR, Ajit Laxman
LHB, SLA

Born Bombay, India, 1 Apr 1941. Educ Elphinstone C, Bombay; Bombay U. Debut 1958/59.
INDIA DOMESTIC Bombay 1958/59–74/75 (capt 1969/70–74/75).
INDIA (37) 1966/67–74. E 1972/73 (5); A 1969/70 (5); WI 1966/67 (2); NZ 1969/70 (3). *E 1967 (3), 1971 (3), 1974 (3); A 1967/68 (4); WI 1970/71 (5); NZ 1967/68 (4).* Capt 16.
OTHER TOURS State Bank to Ceylon 1966/67, 1968/69. India to E Africa 1967. India to Sri Lanka 1973/74.
HST 143 I v NZ, Wellington, 1967/68. HS 323 Bombay v Mysore, Bombay, 1966/67.
BB 2–0 State Bank of India v Dungapur XI, Hyderabad, 1966/67.
1000 RUNS (1 + 4) 1321 @ 60.04 in 1966/67.
Autobiography *My Cricketing Years* (with K. N. Prabhu) (1973).

WADEY, Alan Nigel Charles
RHB, RM

Born Billingshurst, Sussex, 12 Sept 1950. Educ Seaford C. Debut 1975.
SUSSEX (1) 1975.
No runs, one wkt.

WADSWORTH, Kenneth John
RHB, WK

Born Nelson, N Zealand, 30 Nov 1946. Died Nelson, N Zealand, 19 Aug 1976. Debut 1968/69.
N ZEALAND DOMESTIC Central Districts (15) 1968/69–71/72, Canterbury (19) 1972/73–75/76.
NEW ZEALAND (33) 1969–75/76. E 1970/71 (2), 1974/75 (2); A 1973/74 (3); I 1975/76 (3); P 1972/73 (3). *E 1969 (3), 1973 (3); A 1973/74 (3); WI 1971/72 (5); I 1969/70 (3); P 1969/70 (3).*
OTHER TOURS N Zealand to Australia 1969/70, 1970/71.
HST 80 NZ v A, Melbourne, 1973/74. HS 117 Canterbury v Otago, Christchurch, 1975/76 (last fc inns).
RECORD Added 220 for 6th wkt with G. M. Turner, NZ v WI, Kingston, 1971/72, N Zealand Test record.

WAGSTAFFE, Michael Christopher
LHB, SLA

Born Kohat, India, 26 Sept 1945. Educ Rossall; Exeter U; St Edmund Hall, Oxford. Debut 1972.
OXFORD UNIVERSITY (13) 1972 (Blue).
HS 42 Oxford U v Worcs, The Parks, 1972.
BB 4–96 Oxford U v Essex, The Parks, 1972.
Devon 1972–80, Dorset 1981–. Clubs: Bristol Optimists, Blandford. Master-in-charge of cricket Bryanston.

WAINWRIGHT, Thomas Dodsworth
RHB

Born Bombay, India, 12 Nov 1940. Educ Eastbourne; Emmanuel C, Cambridge. Debut 1961.
L. C. STEVENS' XI (1) 1961.
HS 28 L. C. Stevens' XI v Cambridge U, Eastbourne, 1961.
Sussex 2nd XI 1961. Clubs: Eastbourne, Crusaders, Free Foresters, Sussex Martlets. Headmaster Eastbourne Preparatory S.

WAIT, Owen *John*
RHB, RMF

Born Dulwich, London, 2 Aug 1926. Died Bromley, Kent, 26 Apr 1981. Educ Dulwich C; King's C, Cambridge. Debut 1949.
CAMBRIDGE UNIVERSITY (34) 1949–52 (Blue 1949, 1951).
D. R. JARDINE'S XI (2) 1957–58.
MCC (3) 1959–61.
HS 19 D. R. Jardine's XI v Oxford U, Eastbourne, 1957.
BB 6–18 Cambridge U v Sussex, Worthing, 1951.
Clubs: Beckenham, Hampstead. MCC committee 1977–80. Master-in-charge cricket Mill Hill.

WAITE, Anthony Charles
RHB, RFM

Born Pinner, M'sex, 29 May 1943. Debut 1962. *P.*
MIDDLESEX (11) 1962–64.
HS 29 M'sex v Worcs, Kidderminster, 1964.
BB 4–25 M'sex v Surrey, Oval, 1964.
Buckinghamshire 1965–74.

WAITE, John Henry Bickford
RHB, WK

Born Johannesburg, S Africa, 19 Jan 1930. Educ Hilton C, Natal; Rhodes U. Debut 1948/49.
S AFRICA DOMESTIC Eastern Province 1948/49–51/52, Transvaal 1953/54–65/66.
SOUTH AFRICA (50) 1951–64/65. E 1956/57 (5), 1964/65 (2); A 1957/58 (5); NZ 1953/54 (5), 1961/62 (5). *E 1951 (4), 1955 (5), 1960 (5); A 1952/53 (5), 1963/64 (4); NZ 1952/53 (2), 1963/64 (3).*
HST 134 SA v A, Durban, 1957/58. HS 219 E Province v Griqualand West, Kimberley, 1950/51.
1000 RUNS (1) 1011 @ 33.70 in 1951.
RECORD Added 157 for 5th wkt with A. J. Pithey, SA v E, J'burg, 1964/65, S Africa Test record.

Made 26 dismissals (23 ct, 3 st) in series, SA v NZ, 1961/62, record at time for a five-Test series.
Director of Transvaal Cricket Council.

WALCOTT, Clyde Leopold
——————RHB, WK, RM——————

Born Bridgetown, Barbados, 17 Jan 1926. Educ Harrison C, Barbados. Debut 1941/42. *Wisden* 1958.
W INDIES DOMESTIC Barbados 1941/42–55/56, British Guiana 1954/55–63/64.
WEST INDIES (44) 1947/48–59/60. E 1947/48 (4), 1953/54 (5), 1959/60 (2); A 1954/55 (5); I 1952/53 (5); P 1957/58 (4). E 1950 (4), 1957 (5); A 1951/52 (3); NZ 1951/52 (2); I 1948/49 (5).
HST 220 WI v E, Bridgetown, 1953/54.
HS 314* Barbados v Trinidad, Port of Spain, 1945/46.
BBT 3–50 WI v A, Kingston, 1954/55. BB 5–41 F. M. M. Worrell's XI v C. C. Hunte's XI, Kingston, 1963/64.
1000 RUNS (2 + 2) 1674 @ 55.80 in 1950.
RECORDS HS (above) highest-ever score for Barbados; during inns added 574* for 4th wkt with F. M. M. Worrell, at time world record for any wkt in fc cricket and remains best unbroken stand in fc cricket and W Indian fc record. Scored five centuries (and 827 runs) in Test series, WI v A, in W Indies in 1954/55, a world record.
Player/coach British Guiana from 1954/55. Manager of several W Indies touring teams. Clubs: Spartan (Barbados), Enfield (England). Awarded OBE for services to cricket. Son M. A. C. Walcott (Barbados).

WALDRON, Alan Noel Edwin
——————RHB, RMF——————

Born Portsmouth, Hants, 23 Dec 1920. Educ St Edward's, Oxford, Debut 1948.
HAMPSHIRE (2) 1948.
COMBINED SERVICES (2) 1948.
HS 52 Hants v Combined Services, Aldershot, 1948.
BB 2–66 Hants v Cambridge U, Aldershot, 1948.
Regular Army officer.

WALDRON, Patrick Henry Pearse
——————RHB——————

Born Limerick, Ireland, 5 Feb 1917. Educ Catholic US, Dublin. Debut 1946.
IRELAND (4) 1946–47.
HS 32 Ireland v Scotland, Greenock, 1946.
Club: Merrion.

WALES, Peter John
——————RHB, RM——————

Born Hove, Sussex, 30 Oct 1928. Educ Hove GS. Debut 1951.
SUSSEX (1) 1951.
HS 29 Sussex v Hants, Worthing, 1951.
BB 3–12 same match.
Returned match analysis of 13–9–13–5 on only fc appearance.
Club: Brighton and Hove.

WALFORD, Michael Moore
——————RHB, SLA——————

Born Stockton-on-Tees, Co Durham, 27 Nov 1915. Educ Rugby; Trinity C, Oxford. Debut 1935.
OXFORD UNIVERSITY (38) 1935–38 (Blue 1936, 1938).
SOMERSET (52) 1946–53. Cap 1946.
TOURS Oxford and Cambridge Universities to Jamaica 1938/39. MCC to Canada 1951.
HS 264 Som v Hants, Weston-super-Mare, 1947.
BB 6–49 Oxford and Cambridge Universities v Jamaica, Kingston, 1938/39.
Durham 1935–37, Dorset 1954–62. Clubs: Norton, Sherborne. Hockey: England (capt), 1948 Olympics. Rugby: Blue.

WALKER, Alan
——————LHB, RFM——————

Born Emley, Yorks, 7 July 1962. Educ Shelley HS. Debut 1983.
NORTHAMPTONSHIRE (19) 1983–.
HS 19 Northants v Sussex, Horsham, 1984.
BB 4–50 Northants v M'sex, Lord's, 1984.

WALKER, Alan Keith
——————RHB, LFM——————

Born Manly, Sydney, NSW, Australia, 4 Oct 1925. Debut 1948/49. *P.*
AUSTRALIA DOMESTIC New South Wales (26) 1948/49–52/53.
NOTTINGHAMSHIRE (49) 1954–58. Cap 1956.
TOUR Australia to S Africa 1949/50.
HS 73 Notts v Glam, Trent Bridge, 1957.
BB 7–56 Notts v M'sex, Lord's, 1957.
Took four wkts with consecutive balls, Notts v Leics, Leicester, 1956 (wkts with the first three balls of 2nd inns, having taken wkt with last ball of 1st inns).
Clubs: Manly (Sydney), Rawtenstall, Norton (England). Rugby League: Australia to England 1947/48.

WALKER, Clifford
——————RHB, RM——————

Born Huddersfield, Yorks, 27 June 1919. Debut 1947. *P.*
YORKSHIRE (5) 1947–48.
HAMPSHIRE (126) 1949–54. Cap 1949.
HS 150* Hants v Glos, Bristol, 1953.
BB 5–40 Hants v Combined Services, Portsmouth, 1949.
1000 RUNS (4) 1302 @ 36.16 in 1953.
Clubs: Brighouse, Windhill, David Brown Tractors, Salts.

WALKER, Harold
——————RHB——————

Born Desborough, Northants, 12 June 1918. Debut 1947.
NORTHAMPTONSHIRE (1) 1947.
HS 7 Northants v Essex, Ilford, 1947.

WALKER, Jack
——————RHB, WK——————

Born Cobham, Kent, 2 Mar 1914. Died Cobham, Kent, 29 May 1968. Debut 1949.
KENT (1) 1949.
HS 19* Kent v Essex, Gravesend, 1949.
Club: Gravesend.

WALKER, Keith Gordon Eldridge
——————LHB, RLB——————

Born Wimbledon, London, 30 Nov 1922. Educ Rutlish S. Debut 1955.
D. R. JARDINE'S XI (2) 1955–57.
HS 26 D. R. Jardine's XI v Oxford U, Eastbourne, 1957.
Clubs: Malden Wanderers, Barclays Bank. Father Jimmy Walker (noted personality in London club cricket).

WALKER, Malcolm
——————RHB, OB——————

Born Mexborough, Yorks, 14 Oct 1933. Debut 1952. *P.*
SOMERSET (29) 1952–58.
HS 100 Som v Essex, Romford, 1955.
BB 5–45 Som v Glos, Bristol, 1955.
Yorks 2nd XI 1950. Clubs: Wombwell, Salts, Doncaster Town.

WALKER, Maxwell Henry Norman
——————RHB, RFM——————

Born West Hobart, Tasmania, Australia, 12 Sept 1948. Debut 1968/69.

AUSTRALIA DOMESTIC Victoria (70) 1968/69–81/82.
AUSTRALIA (34) 1972/73–77. E 1974/75 (6), 1976/77 (1); WI 1975/76 (3); NZ 1973/74 (1); P 1972/73 (2), 1976/77 (2). *E 1975 (4), 1977 (5); WI 1972/73 (5); NZ 1973/74 (3), 1976/77 (2).*
OTHER TOURS D. H. Robins' XI to S Africa 1974/75. International Wanderers to S Africa 1975/76.
HST 78* A v E, Oval, 1977. HS as above.
BBT 8–143 A v E, Melbourne, 1974/75. BB as above.
World Series Cricket (Kerry Packer) 1977/78–78/79. Club: Melbourne. Three autobiographies (each with 'ghosts'), *Tangles* (1976), *Cricketer at the Cross Roads* (1978) and *Back to Bay 13* (1981).

WALKER, Peter Michael
———RHB, LM/SLA———

Born Clifton, Bristol, 17 Feb 1936. Educ Highlands North S, Johannesburg, S Africa. Debut 1956. *P.*
GLAMORGAN (437) 1956–72. Cap 1958. Benefit (£4500) 1966.
S AFRICA DOMESTIC Transvaal 1956/57–57/58, Western Province 1962/63.
ENGLAND (3) SA 1960.
TOUR Glam to W Indies 1969/70.
HST 52 E v SA, Lord's, 1960. HS 152* Glam v M'sex, Lord's, 1962.
BB 7–58 Glam v M'sex, Lord's, 1962.
1000 RUNS (11) 1564 @ 34.00 in 1959.
100 WKTS (1) 101 @ 24.04 in 1961.
DOUBLE (1) 1961.
RECORDS Took 656 catches for Glam in career, 67 catches for Glam in 1961 (season's record for any county) and eight catches in match, Glam v Derbys, Swansea, 1970, all Glam records for a non-wicketkeeper.
Players v Gentlemen (1) 1962. Club: Neath. Author and broadcaster on cricket and other topics.

WALL, Stephen
———RHB, RMF———

Born Ulverston, Lancs, 10 Dec 1959. Educ Dondales S. Debut 1984.
WARWICKSHIRE (7) 1984.
HS 19 Warwicks v Hants, Edgbaston, 1984.
BB 2–65 same match.
Cumberland 1983. Club: Vickers.

WALLACE, Gary Charles
———LHB, SLA———

Born Salisbury, Rhodesia, 8 Feb 1958. Educ St George's C, Rhodesia. Debut 1978/79.

S AFRICA DOMESTIC Rhodesia B 1978/79–79/80.
ZIMBABWE 1980/81–82/83.
TOUR Zimbabwe to England 1982.
HS 111 Rhodesia B v OFS, Bloemfontein, 1979/80.
BB 3–61 Rhodesia B v Transvaal B, J'burg, 1978/79.

WALLACE, Kenneth William
———RHB, RM———

Born Romford, Essex, 27 Aug 1936. Educ St Edward's C of E S, Romford. Debut 1967.
ESSEX (10) 1967–72.
HS 55 Essex v Hants, Ilford, 1967.
Club: Romford.

WALLACE, Walter *Mervyn*
———RHB———

Born Auckland, N Zealand, 19 Dec 1916. Debut 1933/34.
N ZEALAND DOMESTIC Auckland (46) 1933/34–56/57. Governor-General's XI v MCC, Auckland, 1960/61.
NEW ZEALAND (13) 1937–52/53. E 1946/47 (1), 1950/51 (2); A 1945/46 (1); SA 1952/53 (2). *E 1937 (3), 1949 (4).* Capt 2.
OTHER TOUR N Zealand to Australia 1937/38.
HST 66 NZ v E, Christchurch, 1950/51.
HS 211 Auckland v Canterbury, Auckland, 1939/40.
1000 RUNS (2) 1722 @ 49.03 in 1949.
RECORD Added 324 for 4th wkt with J. R. Reid, N Zealanders v Cambridge U, Fenner's, 1949, N Zealand fc record.
MCC Hon. member.

WALLER, Christopher Edward
———RHB, SLA———

Born Guildford, Surrey, 3 Oct 1948. Educ St Bede's C of E S, Send. Debut 1967.
SURREY (40) 1967–73. Cap 1972.
SUSSEX (211) 1974–. Cap 1976.
HS 51* Sussex v Cambridge U, Fenner's, 1981.
BB 7–64 Surrey v Sussex, Oval, 1971.

WALLER, Guy de Warrenne
———RHB———

Born Ham, Wiltshire, 10 Feb 1950. Educ Hurstpierpoint C; Worcester C, Oxford. Debut 1973.
OXFORD UNIVERSITY (13) 1973–74 (Blue 1974).
HS 29 Oxford U v Leics, The Parks, 1974.
Hockey: Blue.

WALLIS MATHIAS
———RHB, RM———

Born Karachi, India, 4 Feb 1935. Debut 1953/54.
PAKISTAN DOMESTIC Sind, Karachi, National Bank, 1953/54–77/78.
PAKISTAN (21) 1955/56–62. E 1961/62 (1); A 1956/57 (1), 1959/60 (2); WI 1958/59 (3); NZ 1955/56 (1). *E 1962 (3); WI 1957/58 (5); I 1960/61 (5).*
HST 77 P v WI, Kingston, 1977/78. HS 278* Karachi Blues v Railway Greens, Karachi, 1965/66.
BB 2–4 Karachi v Karachi University, Karachi, 1964/65.

WALLWORK, Mark Andrew
———RHB, WK———

Born Urmston, Lancs, 14 Dec 1960. Educ Eccles GS; Newcastle upon Tyne U. Debut 1982.
LANCASHIRE (1) 1982.
Did not bat.

WALMSLEY, Walter Thomas
———RHB, LBG———

Born Homebush, NSW, Australia, 16 Mar 1916. Died Hamilton, N Zealand, 25 Feb 1978. Debut 1945/46.
AUSTRALIA DOMESTIC New South Wales (1) 1945/46, Tasmania (3) 1947/48, Queensland (28) 1954/55–58/59.
COMMONWEALTH XI (1) 1953.
N ZEALAND DOMESTIC Combined Districts XI (1) 1958/59, Northern Districts (3) 1959/60.
HS 180* Tasmania v Indians, Launceston, 1947/48.
BB 6–56 Queensland v S Australia, Brisbane, 1958/59.
Clubs: Western Suburbs (Sydney), South Launceston (Tasmania), Eastern Suburbs (Brisbane), Hamilton Star, Waikato (N Zealand), Stockport, Oldham, Hawker Athletic (England).

WALSH, Courtney Andrew
———RHB, RFM———

Born Kingston, Jamaica, 30 Oct 1962. Educ Excelsior HS, Kingston. Debut 1981/82.
W INDIES DOMESTIC Jamaica 1981/82–.
GLOUCESTERSHIRE (6) 1984.
TOURS Young W Indies to Zimbabwe 1983/84. W Indies to England 1984.
HS 30 Glos v Lancs, Bristol, 1984.
BB 6–35 Jamaica v Guyana, Kingston, 1983/84.

WALSH, David Robert
———RHB, RM———

Born Bombay, India, 17 Dec 1946. Educ Marlborough; Brasenose C, Oxford. Debut 1966.
OXFORD UNIVERSITY (39) 1966–69 (Blue 1967–69).
HS 207 Oxford U v Warwicks, The Parks, 1969.
BB 3–34 Oxford U v Yorks, The Parks, 1969.
Clubs: Yellowhammers, Harlequins.

WALSH, John Edward
———LHB, SLA———

Born Sydney, NSW, Australia, 4 Dec 1912. Died Wallsend, NSW, Australia, 20 May 1980. Debut 1936/37. *P.*
LEICESTERSHIRE (279) 1937–56. Cap 1946. Benefit (£3021) 1955.
SIR J. CAHN'S XI (1) 1938.
AUSTRALIA DOMESTIC New South Wales (2) 1939/40.
TOURS Sir J. Cahn's XI to Ceylon 1936/37. Sir J. Cahn's XI to N Zealand 1938/39.
HS 106 Leics v Essex, Loughborough, 1949.
BB 9–101 Sir J. Cahn's XI v Glam, Newport, 1938.
Returned 16–225 match, Leics v Oxford U, The Parks, 1953; 15–100 match, Leics v Sussex, Hove, 1948; and 15–164 match, Leics v Notts, Loughborough, 1949.
1000 RUNS (1) 1106 @ 24.04 in 1952.
100 WKTS (7) 174 @ 19.56 in 1948.
DOUBLE (1) 1952.
Leics coach after retirement. Club: Petersham (Sydney).

WALSHE, Aubrey *Peter*
———RHB, WK———

Born Salisbury, Rhodesia, 1 Jan 1934. Educ Milton S, Rhodesia; Wadham C, Oxford. Debut 1953.
OXFORD UNIVERSITY (46) 1953–56 (Blue 1953, 1955–56).
HS 77 Oxford U v M'sex, The Parks, 1955.
Club: Salisbury Sports Club.

WALTERS, John
———LHB, RMF———

Born Brampton, Yorks, 7 Aug 1949. Debut 1977.
DERBYSHIRE (58) 1977–80.
HS 90 Derbys v Yorks, Chesterfield, 1978.
BB 4–100 Derbys v Worcs, Derby, 1979.
Clubs: Cortonwood, Lascelles Hall.

WALTERS, Joseph Arthur
———RHB, LB———

Born Bolsover, Derbys, 12 Feb 1940. Debut 1958. *P.*
NOTTINGHAMSHIRE (5) 1958–59.
HS 21* Notts v Northants, Northampton, 1959.
BB 6–139 Notts v Oxford U, The Parks, 1959.

WALTERS, Kevin *Douglas*
———RHB, RM———

Born Dungog, NSW, Australia, 21 Dec 1945. Debut 1962/63.
AUSTRALIA DOMESTIC New South Wales (103) 1962/63–80/81.
AUSTRALIA (74) 1965/66–80/81. E 1965/66 (5), 1970/71 (6), 1974/75 (6), 1976/77 (1); WI 1968/69 (4); NZ 1973/74 (3), 1980/81 (3); I 1967/68 (2), 1980/81 (3); P 1972/73 (1), 1976/77 (3). *E 1968 (5), 1972 (4), 1975 (4), 1977 (5); SA 1969/70 (4); WI 1972/73 (5); NZ 1973/74 (3), 1976/77 (2); I 1969/70 (5).*
HST 250 A v NZ, Christchurch, 1976/77 (adding 217 for 7th wkt with G. J. Gilmour, Australia Test record). HS 253 NSW v S Australia, Adelaide, 1964/65.
BBT 5–66 A v WI, Georgetown, 1972/73. BB 7–63 NSW v S Australia, Adelaide, 1964/65.
1000 RUNS (0 + 3) 1332 @ 70.10 in 1965/66.
Scored 155 A v E, Brisbane, 1965/66 on Test debut and 22 and 115 in his second Test. Scored 242 and 103 match, A v WI, Sydney, 1968/69, first batsman to score century and double-century in same Test and part of run of six consecutive Test fifties: 76, 118, 110, 50, 242, 103.
World Series Cricket (Kerry Packer) 1977/78–78/79. Club: Central Cumberland (Sydney). Autobiographies *Looking for Runs* (1971) and *Doug Walters Story* (with Ken Laws) (1981).

WALTON, Arthur *Christopher*
———RHB———

Born Georgetown, British Guiana, 26 Sept 1933. Educ Radley; Lincoln C, Oxford. Debut 1953.
COMBINED SERVICES (1) 1953.
OXFORD UNIVERSITY (42) 1955–57 (Blue 1955–57). Capt 1957.
MCC (2) 1956–57.
MIDDLESEX (35) 1957–59. Cap 1957.
FREE FORESTERS (2) 1958–59.
D. R. JARDINE'S XI (1) 1958.
HS 152 Oxford U v Warwicks, Edgbaston, 1956.
1000 RUNS (1) 1200 @ 38.70 in 1956.
Gentlemen v Players (2) 1956–57. Bedfordshire 1952–56.

WALUSIMBI, Samuel
———RHB, LM———

Born Uganda, 1948. Debut 1973/74.
EAST AFRICA (2) 1973/74–75.
TOUR East Africa to England 1975.
HS 54 E Africa v Sri Lanka, Taunton, 1975.

WAQAR AHMED
———RHB———

Born Lahore, India, 19 Dec 1946. Educ Punjab U. Debut 1964/65.
PAKISTAN DOMESTIC Punjab University, Lahore, Punjab, 1964/65–72/73.
TOUR Pakistan to England 1967.
HS 199 (run out) Lahore v Sargodha, Lahore, 1968/69.
Scored 195, Punjab U v Lahore Reds, Lahore, 1964/65 (on fc debut).
Father Dilawar Hussain (India).

WAQAR HASAN
———RHB———

Born Amritsar, India, 12 Sept 1932. Educ Punjab U. Debut 1948/49.
PAKISTAN DOMESTIC Punjab University, Universities, Punjab, Combined Services, Karachi, 1948/49–65/66.
PAKISTAN (21) 1952/53–59/60. A 1956/57 (1), 1959/60 (1); WI 1958/59 (1); NZ 1955/56 (3); I 1954/55 (5). *E 1954 (4); WI 1957/58 (1); I 1952/53 (5).*
TOUR Pakistan Services to Ceylon 1953/54.
HST 189 P v NZ, Lahore, 1955/56. HS 201* Air Vice-Marshal Cannon's XI v Hasan Mahmood's XI, Karachi, 1953/54.
1000 RUNS (1) 1263 @ 32.38 in 1954.
RECORDS During HST (above) 308 for 7th wkt with Imtiaz Ahmed, Pakistan fc record.
Brother Pervez Sajjad (Pakistan).

WARD, Alan
———RHB, RF———

Born Dronfield, Derbys, 10 Aug 1947. Debut 1966.
DERBYSHIRE (115) 1966–76. Cap 1969.
S AFRICA DOMESTIC Border 1971/72.
LEICESTERSHIRE (22) 1977–78. Cap 1977.
ENGLAND (5) 1969–76. WI 1976 (1); NZ 1969 (3); P 1971 (1).
TOURS Duke of Norfolk's XI to W Indies 1969/70. MCC to Australia 1970/71.
HST 2 E v NZ, Oval, 1969. HS 44 Derbys v Notts, Ilkeston, 1969.
BBT 4–61 E v NZ, Trent Bridge, 1969.
BB 7–42 Derbys v Glam, Burton upon Trent, 1974.

Sent off field for refusing to bowl, Derbys v Yorks, Chesterfield, 1973. CWC Best Young Cricketer of 1969.

WARD, Brian
RHB, RM

Born Chelmsford, Essex, 28 Feb 1944. Educ Chelmsford Technical HS. Debut 1967.
ESSEX (128) 1967–72. Cap 1970.
HS 164* Essex v Notts, Trent Bridge, 1970.
Derbyshire 2nd XI 1965–66. MCC groundstaff 1961–66. Argentine 1979 (ICC Trophy).

WARD, Donald
RHB, OB

Born Tonypandy, S Wales, 30 Aug 1934. Debut 1954. P.
GLAMORGAN (135) 1954–62. Cap 1961.
HS 86 Glam v Som, Cardiff, 1956.
BB 7–60 Glam v Lancs, Blackpool, 1962.
Clubs: Pontardawe, Neath, Gowerton, Briton Ferry Town, Pontardulais, Gorseinon, Maesteg Celtic.

WARD, Geoffrey Hubert
RHB, WK

Born Rainham, Kent, 22 Nov 1926. Educ King's S, Rochester; Sutton Valence S. Debut 1949. P.
KENT (2) 1949.
ESSEX (1) 1950.
HS 6* Kent v Lancs, Old Trafford, 1949.

WARD, John Daniel
RHB, RMF

Born S Africa, 25 May 1931. Educ Trinity Hall, Cambridge. Debut 1954.
CAMBRIDGE UNIVERSITY (1) 1954.
HS 5* Cambridge U v M'sex, Fenner's, 1954.

WARD, John Michael
RHB

Born Sandon, Staffordshire, 14 Sept 1948. Educ Newcastle under Lyme HS; Mansfield C, Oxford. Debut 1970.
OXFORD UNIVERSITY (28) 1970–73 (Blue 1971–73).
DERBYSHIRE (20) 1973–75.
HS 104 Derbys v Hants, Southampton, 1975.
Staffordshire 1969–70. Rugby: Staffordshire.

WARD, John Thomas
RHB, WK

Born Timaru, N Zealand, 11 Mar 1937. Educ Timaru C. Debut 1957/58.
N ZEALAND DOMESTIC South Island (Trial match) 1957/58, Canterbury (54) 1959/60–70/71.
NEW ZEALAND (8) 1963/64–67/68. SA 1963/64 (1); I 1967/68 (1); P 1964/65 (1). E 1965 (1); I 1964/65 (4).
OTHER TOURS N Zealand to England 1958. N Zealand to Australia and S Africa 1961/62.
HST 35* NZ v I, Madras, 1964/65. HS 54* Canterbury v Wellington, Wellington, 1969/70.
RECORD Made 153 dismissals for Canterbury, a record for any N Zealand Association.

WARDLE, John Henry
LHB, SLA

Born Ardsley, Yorks, 8 Jan 1923. Educ Wath-on-Dearne GS. Debut 1946. P. Wisden 1954.
YORKSHIRE (330) 1946–58. Cap 1947. Benefit (£8129) 1957.
ENGLAND (28) 1947/48–57. A 1953 (3), 1956 (1); SA 1951 (2), 1955 (3); WI 1950 (1), 1957 (1); P 1954 (4). A 1954/55 (4); SA 1956/57 (4); WI 1947/48 (1), 1953/54 (2); NZ 1954/55 (2).
President's XI v Prime Minister's XI, Bombay, 1967/68 (relief match).
HST 66 E v WI, Kingston, 1953/54. HS 79 Yorks v Lancs, Old Trafford, 1951.
BBT 7–36 (12–89 match) E v SA, Cape Town, 1956/57. BB 9–25 Yorks v Lancs, Old Trafford, 1954.
Returned 9–48 (16–112 in match) Yorks v Sussex, Hull, 1954.
100 WKTS (10) 195 @ 16.14 in 1955. Took 90 wkts (12.25) in S Africa 1956/57.
Selected for MCC to Australia 1958/59, but invitation withdrawn following non-retention, then dismissal, by Yorks, after contentious newspaper articles under his name.
Players v Gentlemen (9) 1948–58. Cambridgeshire 1963–69. Clubs: Eccleshill, Nelson, Rishton, Barnby Dun, Hickleton, Brampton, Denaby. MCC Hon. member. Autobiography *Happy go Johnny* (with A. A. Thomson) (1954).

WARING, John Shaw
RHB, RFM

Born Ripon, Yorks, 1 Oct 1942. Debut 1963.
YORKSHIRE (28) 1963–66.
WARWICKSHIRE (1) 1967.
HS 26 Yorks v M'sex, Lord's, 1966.

BB 7–40 Yorks v Lancs, Headingley, 1966.
Cumberland 1970–73. Clubs: Leeds, Bingley, Kendal.

WARKE, Laurance
RHB, RM

Born Belfast, N Ireland, 6 May 1927. Educ Royal Belfast Academical Institute; Dublin U. Debut 1950.
IRELAND (17) 1950–61.
HS 120 Ireland v Scotland, Paisley, 1954.
Clubs: Leinster, Woodvale. Son S. J. S. Warke (Ireland).

WARKE, Stephen John Simon
RHB

Born Belfast, N Ireland, 11 July 1959. Educ Belfast Royal Academy. Debut 1981.
IRELAND (3) 1981–84.
HS 63 Ireland v Scotland, Downpatrick, 1983.
Clubs: Woodvale, Ulster. Father L. Warke (Ireland).

WARNAPURA, Bandula
RHB, RM

Born Rambukkana, Ceylon, 1 Mar 1953. Educ Nalanda C. Debut 1970/71.
SRI LANKA DOMESTIC Sri Lanka 1970/71–82/83.
SRI LANKA (4) 1981/82–82/83. E 1981/82 (1). I 1982/83 (1); P 1981/82 (2). Capt 4.
OTHER TOURS Sri Lanka to India 1972/73, 1975/76, 1976/77. Sri Lanka to Pakistan 1973/74. Sri Lanka to England 1975, 1979, 1981.
HST 38 SL v E, Colombo, 1981/82. HS 154 Sri Lanka Under-25 v Pakistan Under-25, Colombo, 1973/74.
BB 2–33 Sri Lankans v Warwicks, Edgbaston, 1981.
Barred from Sinhalese cricket for 25 yrs for touring S Africa 1982/83 (Arosa Sri Lanka; capt).

WARNER, Alan Esmond
RHB, RFM

Born Birmingham, 12 May 1957. Educ Tabernacle S, St Kitts, W Indies. Debut 1982.
WORCESTERSHIRE (28) 1982–.
HS 67 Worcs v Warwicks, Edgbaston, 1982.
BB 5–27 Worcs v Glam, Worcester, 1984.
Club: Mitchells and Butlers.

WARNER, Charles Simon
————LHB————

Born Liverpool, 19 Nov 1938. Educ
Repton; Keble C, Oxford. Debut 1962.
OXFORD UNIVERSITY (7) 1962.
HS 77 Oxford U v Sussex, The Parks,
1962.
Lancashire 2nd XI.

WARNER, Christopher John
————LHB————

Born Bloemfontein, S Africa, 15 Jan
1945. Debut 1978.
SCOTLAND (8) 1978–84.
HS 70 Scotland v Ireland, Downpatrick,
1983.
Club: Grange (Edinburgh). Father E.
W. Warner (Orange Free State).

WARNER, Graham Sydney
————RHB, OB————

Born Darlaston, Staffordshire, 27 Nov
1945. Educ Darlaston GS. Debut 1966.
WARWICKSHIRE (30) 1966–71.
HS 118* Warwicks v Scotland, Edgbaston, 1968.
Staffordshire 1976–. Clubs: Mitchells
and Butlers, Smethwick.

WARR, Antony Lawley
————RHB, WK————

Born Selly Oak, Birmingham, 15 May
1913. Educ Bromsgrove S; Brasenose C,
Oxford. Debut 1933.
OXFORD UNIVERSITY (4) 1933–34.
MCC (1) 1950.
HS 24 Oxford U v Lancs, The Parks, 1933.
Rugby: Blue, Moseley, Harlequins,
Wakefield, Gloucester, Richmond,
England (1).

WARR, John James
————RHB, RFM————

Born Ealing, London, 16 July 1927.
Educ Ealing GS; Emmanuel C, Cambridge. Debut 1949.
CAMBRIDGE UNIVERSITY (43) 1949–52
(Blue 1949–52). Capt 1951.
MIDDLESEX (260) 1949–60. Cap 1949.
Capt 1958–60.
ENGLAND (2) A 1950/51.
OTHER TOURS MCC to Canada 1951. E.
W. Swanton's XI to W Indies 1955/56.
Duke of Norfolk's XI to Jamaica 1956/
57. MCC to E Africa 1957/58 (non fc
tour).
HST 4 E v A, Sydney, 1950/51. HS 54* T.
N. Pearce's XI v Pakistanis, Scarborough, 1954.

BB 9–65 (14–92 match) M'sex v Kent,
Lord's, 1956.
100 WKTS (2) 116 @ 18.17 in 1956.
Took 169 wkts @ 21.07 for Cambridge
U.
Gentlemen v Players (14) 1950–60.
Club: Ealing.

WARRINGTON, Anthony George
————RHB————

Born Ipswich, Suffolk, 28 Mar 1947.
Debut 1973.
MINOR COUNTIES (2) 1973–74.
HS 92 Minor Counties v W Indians,
Torquay, 1973 (fc debut).
Suffolk 1965–83. Club: Brown's.

WARRINGTON, John Michael
————RHB, RM————

Born Northampton, 3 July 1924. Educ
Ashby-de-la-Zouch S. Debut 1951.
NORTHAMPTONSHIRE (2) 1951.
HS 18 Northants v Glos, Bristol, 1951.
Club: Northampton Saints.

WASHBROOK, Cyril
————RHB————

Born Barrow, nr Blackburn, Lancs, 6
Dec 1914. Educ Clitheroe GS. Debut
1933. P.
LANCASHIRE (500) 1933–59. Cap 1933.
Benefit (£14,000) 1948. Testimonial
(£1520) 1959. Capt 1954–59.
ENGLAND (37) 1937–56. A 1948 (4), 1956
(3); SA 1947 (5); WI 1950 (2); NZ 1937
(1), 1949 (2); I 1946 (3). A 1946/47 (5),
1950/51 (5); SA 1948/49 (5); NZ
1946/47 (1), 1950/51 (1).
HST 195 E v SA, J'burg, 1948/49. HS
251* Lancs v Surrey, Old Trafford,
1947.
BB 2–8 MCC v Victoria, Melbourne,
1950/51.
1000 RUNS (17 + 3) 2662 @ 68.25 in
1947.
RECORD During HST (above) added 359
for 1st wkt with L. Hutton, England
Test record.
Players v Gentlemen (7) 1946–56. Test
selector 1956–57, 1971–72. MCC Hon.
member.

WASIM BARI
————RHB, WK————

Born Karachi, Pakistan, 23 Mar 1948.
Educ St Patrick's C, Karachi. Debut
1964/65.

PAKISTAN DOMESTIC Karachi, Pakistan
International Airlines, Sind, 1964/
65–82/83.
PAKISTAN (81) 1967–83/84. E 1968/69
(3), 1972/73 (3), 1977/78 (3); A 1982/83
(3); WI 1974/75 (2), 1980/81 (2); NZ
1969/70 (3), 1976/77 (2); I 1978/79 (3),
1982/83 (6). E 1967 (3), 1971 (3), 1974
(3), 1978 (3), 1982 (3); A 1972/73 (3),
1976/77 (3), 1978/79 (2), 1981/82 (3),
1983/84 (5); WI 1976/77 (5); NZ
1972/73 (3), 1978/79 (3); I 1979/80
(6), 1983/84 (3). Capt 6.
OTHER TOURS Pakistan to Sri Lanka
1972/73, 1975/76.
HST 85 P v I, Lahore, 1978/79. HS 177
PIA v Sind, Karachi, 1976/77.
RECORDS Made seven dismissals in inns, P
v NZ, Auckland, 1978/79, which equals
world Test record. Made 228 dismissals
(201 ct, 27 st) in Tests, a Pakistan Test
record. Added 133 for 10th wkt with
Wasim Raja, P v WI, Bridgetown, 1976/
77, Pakistan Test record.
Made 822 dismissals (676 ct, 146 st) in
career.

WASIM Hasan RAJA
————LHB, RLBG————

Born Multan, Pakistan, 3 July 1952.
Educ Model HS, Lahore; Punjab U.
Debut 1967/68.
PAKISTAN DOMESTIC Lahore, Sargodha,
Punjab University, Universities, Pakistan International Airlines, Punjab, National Bank, 1967/68–82/83.
D. B. CLOSE'S XI (1) 1984.
PAKISTAN (53) 1972–83/84. E 1972/
73 (1), 1977/78 (3), 1983/84 (3); A 1979/
80 (3); WI 1974/75 (2), 1980/81 (4); NZ
1976/77 (1); I 1982/83 (1); SL 1981/82
(3). E 1974 (2), 1978 (3), 1982 (1); A
1978/79 (1), 1981/82 (3), 1983/84 (2);
WI 1976/77 (5); NZ 1972/73 (3), 1978/
79 (3); I 1979/80 (6), 1983/84 (3).
OTHER TOURS Pakistan Under-25 to Sri
Lanka 1973/74. Pakistan to Sri Lanka
1975/76.
HST 117* P v WI, Bridgetown, 1976/77
(adding 133 for 10th wkt with Wasim
Bari, Pakistan Test record). HS 165 Punjab v Universities, Lahore, 1973/74.
BBT 4–50 P v I, Jullundur, 1983/84.
8–65 Pakistan Under-25 v Sri Lanka
Under-25, Colombo, 1973/74.
Scored 117 and took 5–77 and 5–23,
Universities v PWD, Lahore, 1972/73;
and scored 85 and 50 and took 6–118 and
8–65, Pakistan Under-25 v Sri Lanka
Under-25, Colombo, 1973/74. Scored
1010 runs @ 32.58 and took 99 wkts @
22.41 in 1973/74.
Durham 1978–82, Northumberland
1983. Clubs: Chester-le-Street, Whitburn, Durham City. Brothers Rameez
Raja (Pakistan) and Zaeem Raja (National Bank).

WASSELL, Alan Robert
——LHB, SLA——

Born Brighton, Sussex, 15 Apr 1940. Debut 1957. *P.*
HAMPSHIRE (121) 1957–66. Cap 1963.
HS 61 Hants v Lancs, Southampton, 1962.
BB 7–87 Hants v Surrey, Bournemouth, 1961.

WATERMAN, Peter Andrew
——RHB, RMF——

Born Hendon, M'sex, 26 Mar 1961. Educ Rooks Heath HS; Pinner Sixth Form C. Debut 1983.
SURREY (5) 1983–.
HS 6* Surrey v Sussex, Oval, 1983.
BB 2–16 Surrey v Leics, Oval, 1984.

WATERS, Robin Hugh Clough
——RHB, WK——

Born Calcutta, India, 6 Dec 1937. Educ Shrewsbury; St Edmund Hall, Oxford. Debut 1960.
L. C. STEVENS' XI (1) 1960.
OXFORD UNIVERSITY (24) 1961–62. Car accident prevented winning Blue in 1961.
SUSSEX (8) 1961–65.
IRELAND (3) 1968–69.
INDIA DOMESTIC Bengal 1962/63.
HS 70 Ireland v Scotland, Glasgow, 1968.
Clubs: Clontarf, Old Belvedere.

WATERTON, Stuart Nicholas Varney
——RHB, WK——

Born Dartford, Kent, 6 Dec 1960. Educ Gravesend S; London S of Economics. Debut 1980.
KENT (21) 1980–.
HS 50 Kent v Lancs, Old Trafford, 1984.

WATKINS, Albert John (Alan)
——LHB, LMF——

Born Usk, Monmouthshire, Wales, 21 Apr 1922. Debut 1939. *P.*
GLAMORGAN (408) 1939–61. Cap 1947. Benefit (£4750) 1955.
MCC (1) 1963.
ENGLAND (15) 1948–52. A 1948 (1); NZ 1949 (1); I 1952 (3). *SA 1948/49 (5); I 1951/52 (5).*
OTHER TOURS Commonwealth XI to India 1953/54. MCC A to Pakistan 1955/56.
HST 137* E v I, Delhi, 1951/52. HS 170* Glam v Leics, Swansea, 1954.

BBT 3–20 E v I, Bombay, 1951/52. BB 7–28 Glam v Derbys, Chesterfield, 1954.
1000 RUNS (13) 1640 @ 34.89 in 1954.
100 WKTS (2) 114 @ 20.49 in 1955.
DOUBLE (2) 1954, 1955.
Players v Gentlemen (1) 1952. Former professional coach Christ's C, Brecon (1964); Framlingham (from 1965). Soccer: Plymouth Argyle.

WATKINS, David
——RHB, RM——

Born St Albans, Hertfordshire, 18 Aug 1928. Educ Westcliff HS. Debut 1949.
ESSEX (12) 1949–54.
HS 32 Essex v Notts, Southend, 1953.
BB 2–45 Essex v Northants, Westcliff, 1949.
Club: Southend.

WATKINS, Stephen George
——RHB——

Born Hereford, 23 Mar 1959. Educ Lady Hankin's S, Kington. Debut 1983.
WORCESTERSHIRE (1) 1983.
HS 77 Worcs v Oxford U, The Parks, 1983.
Club: Hereford Town.

WATKINS, William Martin
——RHB, LBG——

Born Swansea, S Wales, 18 Jan 1923. Educ Dynevor GS, Swansea. Debut 1950.
GLAMORGAN (1) 1950.
HS 3 Glam v Hants, Swansea, 1950.
Royal Air Force. Club: Swansea.

WATKINS, William Richard
——RHB, OB——

Born Ealing, London, 22 June 1904. Debut 1930. *P.*
MIDDLESEX (27) 1930–37.
MCC (5) 1936–47.
HS 115 MCC v Kent, Folkestone, 1936.
BB 5–31 MCC v Cambridge U, Lord's, 1939.
Club: Ealing Dean. Coached in Uganda; MCC groundstaff coach until 1969. Baggageman MCC to E Africa 1957/58.

WATKINSON, Michael
——RHB, RM——

Born Westhoughton, Lancs, 1 Aug 1961. Educ Rivington and Blackrod HS, Horwich. Debut 1982.
LANCASHIRE (32) 1982–.

HS 77 Lancs v M'sex, Liverpool, 1984.
BB 6–39 Lancs v Leics, Leicester, 1984.
Cheshire 1982. Clubs: Westhoughton, British Aerospace.

WATSON, Alexander Garth MacLaren
——LHB, RFM——

Born Lucknow, India, 27 Dec 1945. Educ St Lawrence S, Ramsgate; Corpus Christi C, Oxford. Debut 1965.
OXFORD UNIVERSITY (42) 1965–68 (Blue 1965–66, 1968).
HS 65* Oxford U v Essex, The Parks, 1966.
BB 5–44 Oxford U v Cambridge U, Lord's, 1965.
Dorset 1973–79. Club: Wimborne.

WATSON, George Sutton
——RHB, LM——

Born Milton Regis, Kent, 10 Apr 1907. Died Guildford, Surrey, 1 Apr 1974. Educ Shrewsbury. Debut 1928. *P from 1934.*
KENT (8) 1928–29.
LEICESTERSHIRE (225) 1934–50. Cap. Testimonial 1950.
HS 145 Leics v Glam, Leicester, 1939.
1000 RUNS (3) 1314 @ 25.76 in 1947.
Chief coach Shropshire 1952. Club: Catford. Former professional coach Cranleigh (from 1956). Soccer: Charlton Athletic, Crystal Palace, England (amateur).

WATSON, Graeme Donald
——RHB, RM——

Born Kew, Melbourne, Australia, 8 Mar 1945. Debut 1964/65.
AUSTRALIA DOMESTIC Victoria (40) 1964/65–70/71, Western Australia (25) 1971/72–74/75, New South Wales (5) 1976/77.
AUSTRALIA (5) 1966/67–72. E 1972 (2); SA 1966/67 (3).
OTHER TOUR Australia to N Zealand 1969/70.
HST 50 A v SA, Cape Town, 1966/67. HS 176 Australians v Hants, Southampton, 1972.
BBT 2–67 A v SA, J'burg, 1966/67. BB 6–61 Victoria v S Australia, Melbourne, 1965/66.
Seriously injured when hit on nose while playing for Australian XI v World XI, Melbourne, 1971/72.
Clubs: Melbourne, Gordon (Sydney), Subiaco (Perth), East Lancashire.

WATSON, Gregory George
——————RHB, RFM——————

Born Mudgee, NSW, Australia, 29 Jan 1955. Educ Mudgee HS; U of NSW. Debut 1977/78.
AUSTRALIA DOMESTIC New South Wales (14) 1977/78–78/79, Western Australia (1) 1979/80.
WORCESTERSHIRE (30) 1978–79.
HS 38 Worcs v Som, Taunton, 1978.
BB 6–45 Worcs v Sussex, Eastbourne, 1978.
Clubs: Smethwick, Stourbridge (England), Claremont-Cottesloe (Perth).

WATSON, Ian Ronald
——————RHB——————

Born Staines, M'sex, 9 June 1947. Debut 1969.
MIDDLESEX (1) 1969.
NORTHAMPTONSHIRE (1) 1971.
HAMPSHIRE (1) 1973.
HS 16 Northants v Oxford U, The Parks, 1971.
Unique career of three fc matches each for a different county.

WATSON, James Mackman
——————RHB——————

Born Rotherham, Yorks, 17 June 1936. Educ Uppingham; Caius C, Cambridge U. Debut 1957.
CAMBRIDGE UNIVERSITY (5) 1957–59.
HS 31 Cambridge U v Sussex, Fenner's, 1958.

WATSON, Richard Martin
——————LHB, RLB——————

Born Bakewell, Derbys, 31 Dec 1921. Educ Trent C. Debut 1947.
DERBYSHIRE (6) 1947.
HS 25* Derbys v S Africans, Derby, 1947.

WATSON, Roger Graeme
——————LHB, ROB——————

Born Rawtenstall, Lancs, 14 Jan 1964. Educ Fearns Sec S, Bacup. Debut 1982.
LANCASHIRE (1) 1982.
HS 11 Lancs v Som, Taunton, 1982.

WATSON, William
——————LHB——————

Born Bolton-on-Dearne, Yorks, 7 Mar 1920. Educ Paddock Council S, Huddersfield. Debut 1939. P. Wisden 1954.

YORKSHIRE (283) 1939–57. Cap 1947. Benefit (£5357) 1956.
LEICESTERSHIRE (117) 1958–64. Cap 1958. Capt 1958–61.
ENGLAND (23) 1951–58/59. A 1953 (3), 1956 (2); SA 1951 (5), 1955 (1); NZ 1958 (2); I 1952 (1). *A 1958/59 (2); WI 1953/54 (5); NZ 1958/59 (2).*
OTHER TOURS Duke of Norfolk's XI to Jamaica 1956/57. C. G. Howard's XI to India 1956/57. MCC to N Zealand 1960/61. Commonwealth XI to Rhodesia 1962/63 (capt). MCC to E Africa 1963/64 (no fc match).
HST 116 E v WI, Kingston, 1953/54. HS 257 MCC v British Guiana, Georgetown, 1953/54.
1000 RUNS (14) 2212 @ 55.30 in 1959.
RECORDS During HS (above) added 402 for 4th wkt with T. W. Graveney, a record for an MCC touring team. Added 316* with A. Wharton, Leics v Som, Taunton, 1961, county record.
Players v Gentlemen (10) 1951–61. Test selector 1962–64. Leics assistant-secretary 1958–61. Club: Paddock. Coach/administrator Wanderers CC, J'burg from 1968. Soccer: Huddersfield Town, Sunderland, Halifax Town, England; manager Halifax Town, Bradford City. Father W. Watson snr (soccer for England).

WATSON, William *Kenneth*
——————RHB, RFM——————

Born Port Elizabeth, S Africa, 21 May 1955. Educ Dale C, Kingwilliamstown. Debut 1974/75.
S AFRICA DOMESTIC Border 1974/75, Northern Transvaal 1975/76, Eastern Province 1976/77–.
NOTTINGHAMSHIRE (22) 1976–80.
HS 99* E Province v N Transvaal, Port Elizabeth, 1982/83.
BB 7–50 E Province v Natal, Durban, 1982/83.
S Africa (3) 1981/82–83/84. Clubs: Walsden, Retford.

WATT, Alan Edward
——————RHB, RFM——————

Born Limpsfield Chart, Westerham, Kent, 19 June 1907. Died Pembury, Kent, 3 Feb 1974. Educ Westerham S. Debut 1929. P.
KENT (226) 1929–39. Cap.
M. LEYLAND'S XI (1) 1947.
HS 96 (in 65 mins) Kent v MCC, Lord's, 1932.
BB 8–100 Kent v Leics, Tunbridge Wells, 1937.
100 WKTS (1) 108 @ 27.09 in 1937.
Returned 14–90 match, Kent v M'sex, Maidstone, 1938.

Players v Gentlemen (1) 1933. Wife second female scorer at Lord's (see W. S. Ashmore).

WATT, Jonathan
——————RHB, OB——————

Born Eastbourne, Sussex, 11 Sept 1937. Educ Eastbourne C; Worcester C, Oxford. Debut 1960.
L. C. STEVENS' XI (2) 1960–61.
HS 34 L. C. Stevens' XI v Cambridge U, Eastbourne, 1960.
Sussex 2nd XI. Clubs: Free Foresters, Sussex Martlets, MCC.

WATTS, Andrew
——————LHB, RFM——————

Born Chapeltown, Sheffield, Yorks, 4 Oct 1960. Educ Penistone GS. Debut 1982.
DERBYSHIRE (3) 1982–83.
HS 33* Derbys v Northants, Derby, 1983.

WATTS, Edward Alfred
——————RHB, RFM——————

Born Peckham, London, 1 Aug 1911. Died Cheam, Surrey, 2 May 1982. Debut 1933. P.
SURREY (240) 1933–49. Cap 1934. Benefit (£5000) 1949.
TOURS Sir T. E. W. Brinckman's XI to S America 1937/38. Sir J. Cahn's XI to N Zealand 1938/39.
HS 123 Surrey v Yorks, Bradford, 1934.
BB 10–67 Surrey v Warwicks, Edgbaston, 1939.
100 WKTS (2) 129 @ 18.47 in 1938.
Scored 928 runs and took 91 wkts in 1934.
Club: Mitchells and Butlers. Professional coach Whitgift S from 1951. Brother-in-law A. R. Gover (Surrey, England).

WATTS, Hugh Edmund
——————LHB, RLB——————

Born Stratton-on-the-Fosse, Som, 4 Mar 1922. Educ Downside; Peterhouse C, Cambridge. Debut 1939.
SOMERSET (61) 1939–52. Cap 1947.
CAMBRIDGE UNIVERSITY (11) 1947 (Blue).
HS 110 Som v Glam, Weston-super-Mare, 1949.

WATTS, Laurence Dursley
———RHB———

Born Bristol, Glos, 2 May 1935. Educ
Bristol GS; Wadham C, Oxford. Debut
1957.
OXFORD UNIVERSITY (10) 1957–58.
GLOUCESTERSHIRE (1) 1958.
HS 69 Oxford U v Sussex, The Parks,
1958.
Rugby: Blue, Gloucester, Bristol.

WATTS, Patrick James
———LHB, RM———

Born Henlow, Bedfordshire, 16 June
1940. Educ Stratton GS, Biggleswade;
Nene C, Northampton. Debut 1959. P.
NORTHAMPTONSHIRE (372) 1959–80.
Cap 1962. Benefit (£6351) 1974. Capt
1971–74, 1978–80.
HS 145 Northants v Hants, Bournemouth, 1962.
BB 6–18 Northants v Som, Taunton,
1965.
1000 RUNS (7) 1798 @ 43.85 in 1962.
Scored 1118 runs @ 28.66 in debut
season, 1959. Left Northants staff after
1966 season, returned in 1970; left again
after 1974 season to train as teacher.
Played occasionally in 1975, and returned as captain in 1978.
Bedfordshire 1976. Club: Old Hill.
Brother P. D. Watts (Northants, Notts).

WATTS, Peter David
———LHB, RLBG———

Born Henlow, Bedfordshire, 31 Mar
1938. Educ Bedford Modern S. Debut
1958. P.
NORTHAMPTONSHIRE (158) 1958–66.
Cap 1962.
NOTTINGHAMSHIRE (23) 1967.
HS 91 Northants v Worcs, Worcester,
1964.
BB 7–77 (13–140 match) Northants v
Hants, Bournemouth, 1962.
Bedfordshire 1955. Clubs: King's
Heath, West Bromwich Dartmouth.
Brother P. J. Watts (Northants).

WAZIR MOHAMMED
———RHB———

Born Junagadh, India, 22 Dec 1929.
Debut 1949/50.
PAKISTAN DOMESTIC Bahawalpur,
Karachi, 1949/50–63/64.
PAKISTAN (20) 1952/53–59/60. A 1956/
57 (1), 1959/60 (1); WI 1958/59 (3); NZ
1955/56 (2); I 1954/55 (5). E 1954 (2);
WI 1957/58 (5); I 1952/53 (1).
OTHER TOUR Pakistan Eaglets to England
1963.

HST 189 P v WI, Port of Spain, 1957/58.
HS as above.
Club: Olton and West Warwickshire.
Brothers Hanif, Mushtaq, Sadiq
Mohammed (all Pakistan) and Raees
Mohammed (Karachi); nephews Shoaib
Mohammed (Pakistan), Asif and Shahid
Mohammed (PIA).

WEBB, Hubert Eustace
———RHB, LBG———

Born Tonk, Rajputna, India, 30 May
1927. Educ Winchester; New C, Ox-
ford. Debut 1946.
OXFORD UNIVERSITY (14) 1946–48 (Blue
1948).
HAMPSHIRE (1) 1954.
HS 145* Oxford U v Cambridge U,
Lord's, 1948.
Clubs: Authentics, Butterflies, Free
Foresters, Harlequins, I Zingari, MCC,
Army. Doctor; FRCP. Nephew M. C.
L. McPherson (Oxford U).

WEBB, Peter Mitchell
———RHB, RM———

Born Dublin, Ireland, 5 Feb 1932. Educ
Avoca S, Dublin; Portora RS, Ennis-
killen. Debut 1953.
IRELAND (2) 1953.
HS 3* Ireland v Glam, Port Talbot,
1953.
BB 2–11 same match.
Clubs: Dublin University, Pembroke.

WEBB, Rupert Thomas
———RHB, WK———

Born Harrow, M'sex, 11 July 1922.
Debut 1948. P.
SUSSEX (255) 1948–60. Cap 1950. Benefit
(£4100) 1960.
MCC (1) 1959.
HS 49* Sussex v Lancs, Hove, 1955.
Member Sussex committee.

WEBSTER, Andrew John
———LHB, RMF———

Born Burton upon Trent, Staffordshire,
5 Mar 1959. Educ Forest of Needwood
HS. Debut 1981.
WORCESTERSHIRE (9) 1981–82.
HS 25 Worcs v Warwicks, Edgbaston,
1982.
BB 5–87 Worcs v Hants, Southampton,
1982.
Staffordshire 1980–81. Club: Burton
upon Trent.

WEBSTER, David
———LHB, RM———

Born Sheffield, Yorks, 22 May 1944.
Debut 1975.
DERBYSHIRE (1) 1975.
HS 26 Derbys v Oxford U, Burton upon
Trent, 1975.
Club: Chesterfield.

WEBSTER, Jack
———RHB, RMF———

Born Bradford, Yorks, 28 Oct 1917.
Educ Bradford GS; St Catharine's C,
Cambridge. Debut 1938.
CAMBRIDGE UNIVERSITY (9) 1938–39
(Blue 1939).
NORTHAMPTONSHIRE (60) 1946–55. Cap
1947.
MCC (1) 1954.
HS 65 Northants v Surrey, Oval, 1948.
BB 7–78 Cambridge U v Essex, Brent-
wood, 1939.

WEBSTER, Rudi Valentine
———RHB, RFM———

Born St Philip, Barbados, 10 June 1939.
Educ Edinburgh U. Debut 1961.
SCOTLAND (3) 1961–64.
WARWICKSHIRE (60) 1962–66. Cap 1963.
N ZEALAND DOMESTIC Otago (7) 1966/
67–67/68.
HS 47 Warwicks v Glam, Edgbaston,
1966.
BB 8–19 Warwicks v Cambridge U,
Fenner's, 1966.
Returned 7–6 (12–58 match) Warwicks
v Yorks, Edgbaston, 1964. Took wkts
with first balls of each inns of fc debut,
Scotland v MCC, Greenock, 1961.
Edinburgh U; Otago U. Medical Prac-
titioner specialising in children's
diseases.

WEBSTER, William Hugh
———RHB, SLA———

Born Hackney, East London, 22 Feb
1910. Educ Highgate; Pembroke C,
Cambridge. Debut 1930.
CAMBRIDGE UNIVERSITY (14) 1930–33
(Blue 1932).
MIDDLESEX (45) 1930–47. Cap.
HS 111 M'sex v Glos, Bristol, 1936.
BB 3–12 Cambridge U v M'sex,
Fenner's, 1933.
M'sex president 1980. MCC president
1977; MCC committee 1968–71; MCC
Hon. member. Club: Hampstead.
Awarded CBE.

WEEDON, Mark John Hayley
————RHB, RM————

Born Singapore, Malaya, 24 Oct 1940.
Educ Harrow; Magdalene C, Cambridge. Debut 1961.
CAMBRIDGE UNIVERSITY (17) 1961–62 (Blue 1962).
HS 35 Cambridge U v Notts, Trent Bridge, 1962.
BB 5–67 Cambridge U v Surrey, Fenner's, 1962.
Took 17–264 in first two fc matches.

WEEKES, Donald James
————RHB, RMF————

Born Horsham, Sussex, 8 May 1930.
Educ Oxford Senior S, Horsham.
Debut 1952.
SUSSEX (1) 1952.
No runs, no wkts.
Royal Air Force. Clubs: Horsham, Horsham Leatherhunters, Beckenham.
Father-in-law L. T. A. Bates (Warwicks).

WEEKES, Everton de Courcy
————RHB, LBG————

Born Bridgetown, Barbados, 26 Feb 1925. Educ St Leonard's S, Bridgetown. Debut 1944/45. Wisden 1951.
W INDIES DOMESTIC Barbados 1944/45–63/64.
WEST INDIES (48) 1947/48–57/58. E 1947/48 (4), 1953/54 (4); A 1954/55 (5); I 1952/53 (5); P 1957/58 (5). E 1950 (4), 1957 (5); A 1951/52 (5); NZ 1951/52 (2), 1955/56 (4); I 1948/49 (5).
OTHER TOURS E. W. Swanton's XI to W Indies 1960/61. International XI to Rhodesia, Pakistan, New Zealand and India 1961/62.
HST 207 WI v I, Port of Spain, 1952/53.
HS 304* W Indians v Cambridge U, Fenner's, 1950.
BB 4–38 Barbados v MCC, Bridgetown, 1959/60.
1000 RUNS (2 + 1) 2310 @ 79.65 in 1950.
RECORDS HS (above) highest inns by a W Indian on tour. Added 338 for 3rd wkt with F. M. M. Worrell, WI v E, Port of Spain, 1953/54, W Indies Test record. Scored five consecutive Test centuries (141 v E, 1947/48; 128, 194, 162 and 101 v I, 1948/49), a world record; scored 90 and 56 in next two inns, to complete seven consecutive Test fifties, also a world record. Scored 246*, 200* and 129 in consecutive inns in 1950, for 575 runs before being dismissed, a record in English fc cricket.
Made five double-centuries for W Indies in England in 1950. Scored five centuries in consecutive fc inns in New Zealand in 1955/56 (156, 148, 123, 119* and 103).
Club: Bacup. Awarded MBE for services to cricket. International bridge player.

WEEKS, Raymond Thomas
————LHB, SLA————

Born Camborne, Cornwall, 30 Apr 1930. Debut 1950. P.
WARWICKSHIRE (105) 1950–57. Cap 1951.
HS 51 Warwicks v Combined Services, Edgbaston, 1951.
BB 7–70 Warwicks v Notts, Trent Bridge, 1951.
Took 94 wkts @ 21.75 in 1951.
Cornwall 1947–48, 1960–65. Clubs: West Bromwich Dartmouth, Camborne.

WEIGHTMAN, Neil Ivan
————LHB, ROB————

Born Normanton-on-Trent, Notts, 5 Oct 1960. Educ Magnus GS, Newark. Debut 1981.
NOTTINGHAMSHIRE (4) 1981–82.
HS 105 Notts v Leics, Hinckley, 1981.

WEIR, Robert Scott
————RHB————

Born Glasgow, Scotland, 1 May 1953.
Educ Glasgow HS; Jordanhill C. Debut 1975.
SCOTLAND (4) 1975–82.
HS 65 Scotland v Ireland, Edinburgh, 1982.
Club: Clydesdale.

WELLARD, Arthur William
————RHB, RFM/OB————

Born Southfleet, Kent, 8 Apr 1902.
Died Eastbourne, Sussex, 31 Dec 1980. Debut 1927. P. Wisden 1936.
SOMERSET (391) 1927–50. Cap 1929.
Testimonial (£2345) 1951.
ENGLAND (2) 1937–38. A 1938 (1); NZ 1937 (1).
TOURS Lord Tennyson's XI to India 1937/38.
HST 38 E v A, Lord's, 1938. HS 112 Som v Surrey, Oval, 1934 and 112 v Lancs, Old Trafford, 1935.
BBT 4–81 E v NZ, Old Trafford, 1937.
BB 8–52 (15–101 match) Som v Worcs, Bath, 1947.
1000 RUNS (4) 1347 @ 31.32 in 1935.
100 WKTS (8) 172 @ 20.29 in 1938.
DOUBLE (3) 1933, 1935, 1937.
RECORDS Hit 72 sixes in a season (1935), and over 500 sixes in career, both fc records. Twice hit five sixes from consecutive balls: off T. R. Armstrong (in one over), Som v Derbys, Wells, 1936; off F. E. Woolley (31 runs in over), Som v Kent, Wells, 1938.
Players v Gentlemen (6) 1931–38.
Selected for MCC to India 1939/40 (cancelled owing to war). Clubs: Bexley, Lancaster, Sutton, Kidderminster. Professional coach Epsom C from 1960.

WELLHAM, Dirk MacDonald
————RHB————

Born Summer Hill, NSW, Australia, 13 Mar 1959. Debut 1980/81.
AUSTRALIA DOMESTIC New South Wales (32) 1980/81–.
AUSTRALIA (4) 1981–81/82. WI 1981/82 (1); P 1981/82 (2). E 1981 (1).
OTHER TOUR Young Australia to Zimbabwe 1982/83 (capt).
HST 103 A v E, Oval, 1981 (2nd inns of Test debut). HS 136 NSW v W Australia, Perth, 1982/83.
RECORDS Scored centuries on fc debut, 100 NSW v Victoria, Melbourne, 1980/81, and on Test debut (see HST above), equalling feat of G. R. Visvanath.
Club: Western Suburbs (Sydney).
Uncle W. A. Wellham (NSW).

WELLINGS, Evelyn Maitland
————RHB, OB/RM————

Born Alexandria, Egypt, 6 Apr 1909.
Educ Cheltenham; Christ Church C, Oxford. Debut 1928.
OXFORD UNIVERSITY (29) 1928–31 (Blue 1929, 1931).
SURREY (4) 1931.
H. D. G. LEVESON GOWER'S XI (2) 1933.
MCC (1) 1946.
HS 125 H. D. G. Leveson Gower's XI v Cambridge U, Eastbourne, 1933.
BB 6–75 Oxford U v Leics, The Parks, 1931.
Cricket journalist for Evening News and other newspapers. Author of several books, including Vintage Cricketers (1983).

WELLINGTON, Livern
————RHB, RFM————

Born Kingston, Jamaica, 5 Jan 1950.
Debut 1969/70.
W INDIES DOMESTIC Jamaica 1969/70–70/71.
TOUR Jamaica to England 1970.
HS 49 Jamaica v Trinidad, Port of Spain, 1969/70.
BB 3–29 Jamaica v Barbados, Kingston, 1969/70.
Club: St Catherine (Jamaica).

WELLS, Alan Peter
————RHB, RM————

Born Newhaven, Sussex, 2 Oct 1961.
Educ Tideway CS, Newhaven. Debut
1981.
SUSSEX (47) 1981–.
HS 127 Sussex v Northants, Northampton, 1984.
1000 RUNS (1) 1045 @ 32.66 in 1984.
Brother C. M. Wells (Sussex).

WELLS, Arthur Luty
————RHB, RM————

Born Leeds, Yorks, 23 Nov 1909. Debut
1954.
NORTHAMPTONSHIRE (5) 1954–55.
HS 18 Northants v Glam, Cardiff, 1954.
BB 4–67 same match.

WELLS, Bryan Douglas
(Bomber)
————RHB, OB————

Born Gloucester, 27 July 1930. Debut
1951. *P.*
GLOUCESTERSHIRE (141) 1951–59. Cap
1954.
NORTHAMPTONSHIRE (151) 1960–65.
Cap 1960.
TOURS E. W. Swanton's XI to W Indies
1960/61.
HS 55 Notts v Glam, Swansea, 1962.
BB 8–31 Glos v Som, Bristol, 1953.
100 WKTS (3) 123 @ 18.60 in 1956. Also
took 99 wkts in 1961, 97 in 1963 and 95
in 1954.
Club: Gloucester City. Semi-
autobiography ('ghosted') *Well, well,
Wells* (1982).

WELLS, Colin Mark
————RHB, RM————

Born Newhaven, Sussex, 3 Mar 1960.
Educ Tideway CS, Newhaven. Debut
1979.
SUSSEX (111) 1979–. Cap 1982.
S AFRICA DOMESTIC Border 1980/81.
HS 203 Sussex v Hants, Hove, 1984.
BB 5–25 Sussex v Kent, Hastings, 1984.
1000 RUNS (3) 1389 @ 43.41 in 1984.
Brother A. P. Wells (Sussex).

WELLS, Richard Raymond
Collingwood
————RHB————

Born Salisbury, Rhodesia, 19 Jan 1956.
Educ Cranleigh; Christ Church C, Oxford. Debut 1977.

OXFORD UNIVERSITY (11) 1977–78.
HS 85 Oxford U v Leics, The Parks,
1977.

WELLS, Thomas Umphrey
————LHB————

Born Panmure, N Zealand, 6 Feb 1927.
Educ King's C, Auckland; Auckland U;
King's C, Cambridge. Debut 1950.
CAMBRIDGE UNIVERSITY (20) 1950–51
(Blue 1950).
WORCESTERSHIRE (1) 1950.
HS 77* Cambridge U v Leics, Fenner's,
1950.
BB 2–25 Cambridge U v Hants,
Fenner's, 1950.
Club: Clifton. Rugby: Blue, England
trialist.

WENLOCK, David Alan
————RHB, RM————

Born Leicester, 16 Apr 1959. Educ Lutterworth GS. Debut 1980.
LEICESTERSHIRE (10) 1980–82.
TOUR Leics XI to Zimbabwe 1980/81.
HS 62 Leics v Sri Lankans, Leicester,
1981.
BB 3–50 Leics v Cambridge U,
Fenner's, 1982.

WESLEY, Colin
————LHB, OCC SLA————

Born Durban, S Africa, 5 Sept 1937.
Educ Durban HS, Natal U. Debut
1956/57.
S AFRICA DOMESTIC South African
Universities 1956/57–57/58, Natal/
Natal B 1957/58–65/66 (capt Natal B
1965/66).
SOUTH AFRICA (3) *E 1960.*
HST 35 SA v E, Lord's, 1960. HS 131
Natal v N Zealanders, Durban, 1961/62.
BB 4–51 S Africans v T. N. Pearce's XI,
Scarborough, 1960.
Director Transvaal Cricket Council
1983.

WESSELS, Kepler Christoffel
————LHB, ROB————

Born Bloemfontein, S Africa, 14 Sept
1957. Educ Grey C, Bloemfontein.
Debut 1973/74.
S AFRICA DOMESTIC Orange Free State
1973/74–75/76, Western Province
1976/77, Northern Transvaal 1977/78.
SUSSEX (53) 1976–80. Cap 1977.
AUSTRALIA DOMESTIC Queensland (43)
1979/80–.

AUSTRALIA (12) 1982/83–83/84. E 1982/
83 (4); P 1983/84 (5). *SL 1982/83 (1);
WI 1983/84 (2).*
HST 179 A v P, Adelaide, 1983/84. HS 254
Sussex v M'sex, Hove, 1980.
1000 RUNS (2 + 2) 1800 @ 52.94 in 1979.
Scored 162 A v E, Brisbane, 1982/83, on
Test debut.
World Series Cricket (Kerry Packer)
1978/79. Father N. Wessels (OFS).

WEST, Gordon Harry Sinclair
————RHB————

Born Upton Park, E London, 7 Aug
1923. Educ Southend HS. Debut 1949.
P.
ESSEX (2) 1949–53.
HS 55 Essex v Cambridge U, Fenner's,
1949.
Club: Southend.

WESTERMAN, Peter
————RHB, RFM————

Born E Sheen, Surrey, 12 Aug 1920.
Educ Hampton GS. Debut 1949.
SURREY (9) 1949–51.
HS 10* Surrey v Yorks, Bradford, 1949.
BB 5–49 Surrey v Cambridge U, Oval,
1950.
Club: Hounslow.

WESTLEY, Roger Bancroft
————RHB, OB————

Born Preston, Lancs, 21 Mar 1947. Died
Haileybury, Herts, 12 May 1982. Educ
Lancaster RGS; Durham U; Corpus
Christi C, Oxford. Debut 1969.
OXFORD UNIVERSITY (5) 1969.
HS 14 Oxford U v Surrey, The Parks,
1969.
BB 2–65 Oxford U v Yorks, The Parks,
1969.
Lancashire 2nd XI 1965–66. Club:
Hoddesdon. Master-in-charge of
cricket Haileybury and ISC until his
death. Twin brother S. A. Westley (Oxford U, Glos); last twins to play together
for same side (four matches for Oxford
U in 1969) in fc cricket.

WESTLEY, Stuart Alkar
————RHB, WK————

Born Preston, Lancs, 21 Mar 1947.
Educ Lancaster RGS; Queen's C, Oxford. Debut 1968.
OXFORD UNIVERSITY (22) 1968–69 (Blue
1968–69).
OXFORD AND CAMBRIDGE UNIVERSITIES (1)
1968.
GLOUCESTERSHIRE (10) 1969–71.

MINOR COUNTIES (I) 1976.
HS 93* Oxford U v Warwicks, The Parks, 1969.
Suffolk 1973–. Clubs: Quilibets, Ransomes. Rugby: Fylde and Oxford U. Twin brother R. B. Westley (Oxford U); last twins to play together for same side (four matches for Oxford U in 1969) in fc cricket.

WESTON, Martin John
RHB, RM

Born Worcester, 8 Apr 1959. Educ Samuel Southall Sec S. Debut 1979.
WORCESTERSHIRE (70) 1979–.
HS 145* Worcs v Northants, Worcester, 1984.
BB 4–44 Worcs v Northants, Wellingborough, 1984.
1000 RUNS (I) 1061 @ 27.92 in 1984.
Clubs: Worcester City, Old Hill.

WETTIMUNY, Sidath
RHB, RM

Born Colombo, Ceylon, 12 Aug 1956.
Educ Ananda C, Colombo. Debut 1975/76. *Wisden* 1985.
SRI LANKA DOMESTIC Sri Lanka 1975/76–.
SRI LANKA (II) 1981/82–84. E 1981/82 (I); A 1982/83 (I); NZ 1983/84 (3). *E 1984 (I); NZ 1982/83 (2); P 1981/82 (3).*
OTHER TOURS Sri Lanka to England 1981. Sri Lanka to Zimbabwe 1982/83.
HST 190 SL v E, Lord's, 1984. HS as above.
RECORDS During HST (above) batted 642 mins, longest-ever Test inns at Lord's, and his 190 is highest inns by any batsman in his first Test in England.
Carried bat for 63* in total of 144, SL v NZ, Christchurch, 1982/83.
Club: Sinhalese Sports Club (Colombo). Brothers S. R. de S. Wettimuny (Sri Lanka in non-Tests) and M. D. Wettimuny (Sri Lanka).

WETTIMUNY, Sunil Ramsay de Silva
RHB, RM, occ WK

Born Colombo, Ceylon, 2 Feb 1949.
Educ Ananda C, Ceylon. Debut 1969/70.
SRI LANKA DOMESTIC Ceylon (Sri Lanka) 1969/70–81/82.
TOURS Ceylon (Sri Lanka) to India 1970/71, 1972/73, 1975/76. Sri Lanka to Pakistan 1973/74. Sri Lanka to England 1975, 1979.
HS 121 Sri Lankans v Punjab, Lyallpur, 1973/74.

Club: Sinhalese Sports Club (Colombo). Brothers M. D. and S. Wettimuny (both Sri Lanka).

WHARTON, Alan
LHB, RMF

Born Heywood, Lancs, 30 Apr 1923.
Debut 1946. *P.*
LANCASHIRE (392) 1946–60. Cap 1946.
Benefit (£4352) in 1958.
LEICESTERSHIRE (79) 1961–63. Cap 1961.
ENGLAND (I) NZ 1949.
TOUR C. G. Howard's XI to India 1956/57.
HST 13 E v NZ, Headingley, 1949. HS 199 Lancs v Sussex, Hove, 1959.
BB 7–33 Lancs v Sussex, Old Trafford, 1951.
1000 RUNS (II) 2157 @ 40.69 in 1959.
RECORDS Added 316* for 3rd wkt with W. Watson, Leics v Som, Taunton, 1961, county record. Scored 87* and 33*, sharing 1st-wkt stands of 166 and 66, both unbroken, with J. Dyson, when Lancs beat Leics by 10 wkts, at Old Trafford, 1956, the only instance in English fc cricket of a side winning a match without losing a wkt.
Players v Gentlemen (I) 1956. Cumberland 1964. Rugby League: Salford.

WHEATLEY, Garth Angus
RHB, WK

Born Twickenham, M'sex, 28 May 1923. Educ Uppingham; Balliol C, Oxford. Debut 1946.
OXFORD UNIVERSITY (II) 1946 (Blue).
SURREY (5) 1947.
FREE FORESTERS (2) 1947–50.
HS 66 Oxford U v Sussex, Chichester, 1946.

WHEATLEY, Keith James
RHB, OB

Born Guildford, Surrey, 20 Jan 1946.
Educ Lord Wandsworth C, Long Sutton, Debut 1965.
HAMPSHIRE (79) 1965–70.
HS 79* Hants v Kent, Maidstone, 1969.
BB 4–1 Hants v Glam, Southampton, 1968.
Club: Basingstoke and North Hampshire.

WHEATLEY, Oswald Stephen
RHB, RMF

Born Low Fell, Gateshead, Durham, 28 May 1935. Educ King Edward's S, Birmingham; Caius C, Cambridge. Debut 1956. *Wisden* 1969.

FREE FORESTERS (I) 1956.
CAMBRIDGE UNIVERSITY (35) 1957–58 (Blue 1957–58).
WARWICKSHIRE (63) 1957–60. Cap 1959.
GLAMORGAN (206) 1961–69/70. Cap 1961. Capt 1961–66.
TOURS E. W. Swanton's XI to W Indies 1960/61. Glam to W Indies 1969/70.
HS 34* Gentlemen v Players, Scarborough, 1961.
BB 9–60 Glam v Sussex, Ebbw Vale, 1968.
100 WKTS (5) 136 @ 19.32 in 1962.
RECORD 80 wkts (@ 17.63) for Cambridge U in 1958, a season's record for either fc university.
Test selector 1973–74. Gentlemen v Players (6) 1958–62. Glam chairman 1977–. Club: Harborne.

WHEELER, James *Anthony*
RHB

Born Lacock, nr Chippenham, Wiltshire, 10 Apr 1913. Died Horwood, nr Bideford, Devon, 30 Aug 1977. Debut 1949.
MINOR COUNTIES (I) 1949.
HS 54 Minor Counties v Yorks, Lord's, 1949.
Wiltshire 1947–55.

WHEELHOUSE, Alan
LHB, RMF

Born Nottingham, 4 Mar 1934. Educ Nottingham HS; Emmanuel C, Cambridge. Debut 1958.
CAMBRIDGE UNIVERSITY (16) 1958–59 (Blue 1959).
NOTTINGHAMSHIRE (I) 1961.
HS 17 Cambridge U v Lancs, Fenner's, 1959.
BB 4–69 Cambridge U v Derbys, Fenner's, 1959.

WHILEY, Richard Kingscote
RHB

Born Gloucester, 10 Oct 1935. Educ Malvern; Brasenose C, Oxford. Debut 1954.
GLOUCESTERSHIRE (I) 1954.
OXFORD UNIVERSITY (I) 1958.
HS 7* Glos v Pakistanis, Cheltenham, 1954.
Dorset 1964–67.

WHITAKER, John *James*
RHB, OB

Born Skipton, Yorks, 5 May 1962. Educ Uppingham. Debut 1983.

LEICESTERSHIRE (29) 1983–.
HS 160 Leics v Som, Leicester, 1984.
1000 RUNS (1) 1097 @ 36.57 in 1984.

WHITAKER, Mark Robin
————RHB, RFM————

Born Walton-on-Thames, Surrey, 20 Sept 1946. Educ Bryanston; Peterhouse C, Cambridge. Debut 1965.
CAMBRIDGE UNIVERSITY (12) 1965–67.
HS 4* Cambridge U v Essex, Fenner's, 1965.
BB 5–62 Cambridge U v M'sex, Fenner's, 1965.

WHITBY, Robert Lionel
————RHB, RMF————

Born Calcutta, India, 29 Oct 1928. Educ Charterhouse; Caius C, Cambridge. Debut 1950.
CAMBRIDGE UNIVERSITY (1) 1950.
MCC (1) 1957.
HS 12 Cambridge U v Essex, Fenner's, 1950.

WHITCOMBE, Philip Arthur
————RHB, RFM————

Born Kensington, London, 23 Apr 1923. Educ Winchester; Christ Church C, Oxford. Debut 1947.
OXFORD UNIVERSITY (24) 1947–49 (Blue 1947–49).
MIDDLESEX (3) 1948.
FREE FORESTERS (8) 1954–60.
MCC (1) 1956.
HS 68 Oxford U v Glos, The Parks, 1949.
BB 7–51 Oxford U v Cambridge U, Lord's, 1948.
Gentlemen v Players (1) 1948. Wiltshire 1947, 1962. Father P. S. Whitcombe (Essex).

WHITCOMBE, Philip John
————RHB, WK————

Born Worcester, 11 Nov 1928. Educ Worcester RGS; Hertford C, Oxford. Debut 1949.
WORCESTERSHIRE (8) 1949–52.
OXFORD UNIVERSITY (26) 1950–52 (Blue 1951–52).
HS 104 Oxford U v Hants, Basingstoke, 1951.
Club: Brentwood.

WHITE, Allan Frederick Tinsdale
————RHB————

Born Coventry, Warwicks, 5 Sept 1915. Educ Uppingham; Pembroke C, Cambridge. Debut 1936.
CAMBRIDGE UNIVERSITY (22) 1936–37 (Blue 1936).
WARWICKSHIRE (9) 1936–37.
WORCESTERSHIRE (110) 1939–49. Cap 1946. Capt 1947–48; joint capt 1949.
FREE FORESTERS (1) 1947.
HS 95 Worcs v Combined Services, Worcester, 1946.
1000 RUNS (2) 1179 @ 26.80 in 1946.
Club: Moseley.

WHITE, Colin Derek
————LHB————

Born Chiswick, London, 4 Apr 1937. Educ Cranleigh; Cambridge. Debut 1958.
CAMBRIDGE UNIVERSITY (22) 1958–60.
FREE FORESTERS (1) 1961.
HS 64 Cambridge U v Notts, Fenner's, 1960.
Surrey 2nd XI 1958.

WHITE, David William (Butch)
————LHB, RF————

Born Sutton Coldfield, Warwicks, 14 Dec 1935. Debut 1957. *P*.
HAMPSHIRE (315) 1957–71. Cap 1960. Benefit (£4547) 1969.
GLAMORGAN (1) 1972.
ENGLAND (2) *P 1961/62*.
OTHER TOUR Cavaliers to W Indies 1964/65.
HS 58* Hants v Essex, Portsmouth, 1963.
BBT 3–65 E v P, Lahore, 1961/62. BB 9–44 Hants v Leics, Portsmouth, 1966.
100 WKTS (4) 124 @ 19.10 in 1960.
Club: Aston Unity.

WHITE, Edmund
————RHB, WK————

Born Putney, London, 29 Jan 1928. Educ Wellingborough. Debut 1946.
NORTHAMPTONSHIRE (3) 1946–48.
HS 16 Northants v Combined Services, Northampton, 1947.

WHITE, Luke Robert
————RHB————

Born London, 15 Mar 1927. Educ Eton; Trinity C, Cambridge. Debut 1945.
MIDDLESEX (3) 1946–47.
ROYAL AIR FORCE (1) 1946.

MCC (1) 1950.
HS 46 RAF v Worcs, Worcester, 1946.
England v Australia (1) 1945 (Victory match); his fc debut. Now the fifth Baron Annaly.

WHITE, Malcolm Frank
————RHB, WK————

Born Walsall, Staffordshire, 15 May 1924. Educ Queen Mary's GS, Walsall; Magdalene C, Cambridge. Debut 1946.
WARWICKSHIRE (1) 1946.
No runs.
Staffordshire 1954. War-time Blue 1944. Club: Walsall.

WHITE, Raymond Christopher
————RHB, RM————

Born Johannesburg, S Africa, 29 Jan 1941. Educ Hilton C, Natal; Jesus C, Cambridge. Debut 1960/61.
S AFRICA DOMESTIC South African Universities 1960/61, Transvaal 1965/66–72/73.
CAMBRIDGE UNIVERSITY (52) 1962–65 (Blue 1962–65). Capt 1965.
GLOUCESTERSHIRE (40) 1962–64.
HS 205 Transvaal B v Griqualand West, J'burg, 1965/66.
BB 3–17 Cambridge U v Essex, Fenner's, 1963.
1000 RUNS (2) 1696 @ 29.24 in 1962.
Gentlemen v Players (1) 1962. Director Transvaal CU 1972–83. Club: Hampstead.

WHITE, Robert Arthur
————LHB, ROB————

Born Fulham, London, 6 Oct 1936. Educ Chiswick GS. Debut 1958. *P*.
MIDDLESEX (114) 1958–65. Cap 1963.
NOTTINGHAMSHIRE (298) 1966–80. Cap 1966. Benefit (£11,000) 1974.
HS 116* Notts v Surrey, Oval, 1967.
BB 7–41 Notts v Derbys, Ilkeston, 1971.
1000 RUNS (1) 1355 @ 33.87 in 1963.
RECORD Added 204 for 7th wkt with M. J. Smedley, Notts v Surrey, Oval, 1967, county record.
Notts coaching staff since retirement. Fc umpire 1983–.

WHITE, Roger Frank
————RHB, SLA————

Born Perivale, M'sex, 22 Nov 1943. Debut 1964.
MIDDLESEX (13) 1964–66.
HS 7* M'sex v Oxford U, The Parks, 1966.
BB 4–79 M'sex v Kent, Canterbury, 1965.

WHITE, William *Michael* Eastwood
————RHB, RFM————

Born Barnes, Surrey, 22 May 1913. Educ Dover C; Trinity Hall, Cambridge. Debut 1937.
CAMBRIDGE UNIVERSITY (8) 1937.
ARMY (1) 1939.
COMBINED SERVICES (7) 1947–48.
NORTHAMPTONSHIRE (5) 1947–49.
HS 48 Combined Services v Hants, Aldershot, 1948.
BB 4–67 Cambridge U v Army, Fenner's, 1937.
Club: Incogniti.

WHITE, William *Neil*
————RHB, SLA————

Born Troon, Ayrshire, Scotland, 2 May 1920. Educ The Leys S; Trinity Hall, Cambridge. Debut 1948.
CAMBRIDGE UNIVERSITY (2) 1948.
HS 19 Cambridge U v Free Foresters, Fenner's, 1948.
BB 4–16 same match.
Cambridgeshire 1947–49. Clubs: Sou'westers, Camden.

WHITE, Winston *Anthony* Wilbur
————RHB, RM/OB————

Born Bridgetown, Barbados, 20 Nov 1938. Debut 1958/59.
W INDIES DOMESTIC Barbados 1958/59–65/66.
WEST INDIES (2) A 1964/65.
TOUR W Indies to England 1963.
HST 57* WI v A, Kingston, 1964/65. HS 75 Barbados v British Guiana, Bridgetown, 1961/62.
BBT 2–34 WI v A, Kingston, 1964/65. BB 6–80 Barbados v Trinidad, Port of Spain, 1960/61.
Club: Pickwick (Barbados).

WHITEHEAD, Alan Geoffrey Thomas
————LHB, SLA————

Born Butleigh, Som, 28 Oct 1940. Debut 1957. *P*.
SOMERSET (38) 1957–61.
HS 15 Som v Hants, Southampton, 1959.
BB 6–74 Som v Sussex, Eastbourne, 1959.
Minor Counties umpire 1969. Fc umpire 1970– (1 Test, 1982). Professional coach Wells Cathedral S 1969.

WHITEHEAD, John Parkin
————RHB, RFM————

Born Saddleworth, Yorks, 3 Sept 1925. Educ Oldham GS; London U. Debut 1946. *P*.
YORKSHIRE (37) 1946–51.
COMBINED SERVICES (4) 1947.
WORCESTERSHIRE (33) 1953–55.
HS 71 Combined Services v Northants, Northampton, 1947 and 71 Worcs v Derbys, Worcester, 1954.
BB 5–10 Combined Services v Worcs, Hereford, 1947.
Suspended by Bradford League in 1952 for five yrs for breaking contract with Pudsey St Laurence by signing for Worcs.
London University. Clubs: Oldham, Littleborough, Dulwich, Pudsey St Laurence, Cheltenham, Downend.

WHITEHILL, William
————RHB, WK————

Born Newport, Monmouthshire, 13 June 1934. Debut 1960. *P*.
GLAMORGAN (7) 1960.
HS 16 Glam v Glos, Bristol, 1960.

WHITEHOUSE, John
————RHB, ROB/SLA————

Born Nuneaton, Warwicks, 8 Apr 1949. Educ King Edward VI S, Nuneaton; Bristol U. Debut 1971.
WARWICKSHIRE (179) 1971–80. Cap 1973. Capt 1978–79.
MCC (1) 1978.
HS 197 Warwicks v Glam, Edgbaston, 1980.
BB 2–55 Warwicks v Yorks, Edgbaston, 1977.
1000 RUNS (3) 1543 @ 42.86 in 1977.
Scored 173 (with 35 fours; went from 20* to 150* on 2nd morning) Warwicks v Oxford U, The Parks, 1971 on fc debut.
Warwicks committee 1984–. Club: Nuneaton.

WHITELEY, John Peter
————RHB, OB————

Born Otley, Yorks, 22 Feb 1955. Educ Ashville C, Harrogate; Bristol U. Debut 1978.
YORKSHIRE (45) 1978–82.
HS 20 Yorks v Northants, Northampton, 1979.
BB 4–14 Yorks v Notts, Scarborough, 1978.

WHITELEY, Peter
————RHB, SLA————

Born Rochdale, Lancs, 12 Aug 1935. Debut 1957. *P*.
LANCASHIRE (5) 1957–58.
HS 32 Lancs v Hants, Old Trafford, 1957.
BB 3–70 Lancs v W Indies, Old Trafford, 1957.
Clubs: Crompton, Milnrow, Harrogate.

WHITESIDE, Peter Geary
————RHB, WK————

Born New Malden, Surrey, 21 Feb 1930. Educ Denstone; St Catharine's C, Cambridge. Debut 1955.
CAMBRIDGE UNIVERSITY (2) 1955.
HS 1 Cambridge U v Surrey, Fenner's, 1955.
Club: Hornsey.

WHITFIELD, Edward Walter
————RHB, RM————

Born Clapham, London, 31 May 1911. Debut 1930. *P*
SURREY (106) 1930–39. Cap 1939.
NORTHAMPTONSHIRE (19) 1946.
HS 198 Surrey v Cambridge U, Oval, 1938.
BB 4–63 Surrey v Som, Oval, 1935.
1000 RUNS (1) 1005 @ 35.89 in 1938.
Clubs: Morecambe, Greenock, Ebbw Vale.

WHITING, Norman Harry
————RHB, OB————

Born Wollaston, Worcs, 2 Oct 1920. Debut 1947. *P*.
WORCESTERSHIRE (59) 1947–52. Cap 1950.
HS 118 Worcs v Essex, Romford, 1950.
BB 2–27 Worcs v Yorks, Scarborough, 1951.
Club: Stourbridge.

WHITTINGTON, Richard Smallpeice
————RHB————

Born Unley Park, Adelaide, S Australia, 30 June 1912. Died Sydney, NSW, Australia, 13 Mar 1984. Educ Scotch C, Adelaide; Adelaide U. Debut 1932/33.
AUSTRALIA DOMESTIC South Australia (36) 1932/33–39/40, Australian Services (5) 1945/46.
TOUR Australian Services to England 1945 (6) and India (7) 1945/46.

HS 155 Australian Services v Indian XI, Calcutta, 1945/46.
Cricket writer from 1946, author of 24 books.

WHITNEY, Michael Roy
————RHB, LFM————

Born Sydney, NSW, Australia, 24 Feb 1959. Educ South Sydney HS; Sydney Technical C. Debut 1980/81.
AUSTRALIA DOMESTIC New South Wales (25) 1980/81–.
GLOUCESTERSHIRE (3) 1981.
D. B. CLOSE'S XI (1) 1983.
AUSTRALIA (2) E 1981.
OTHER TOUR Young Australians to Zimbabwe 1982/83.
HST 4 A v E, Oval, 1981. HS 28* NSW v W Australia, Sydney, 1982/83.
BBT 2–50 A v E, Old Trafford, 1981. BB 5–29 Young Australians v Zimbabwe, Harare, 1982/83.
Co-opted into Australian team in England 1981 for three matches. Clubs: Randwick (Australia), Fleetwood (England).

WHITTAKER, Geoffrey James
————RHB————

Born Peckham, London, 29 May 1916. Debut 1937. P.
SURREY (124) 1937–53. Cap 1949.
HS 185* Surrey v Kent, Oval, 1951.
1000 RUNS (2) 1439 @ 39.97 in 1951.
Professional coach Victoria C, Jersey 1954 until retirement.

WHITTICASE, Philip
————RHB, WK————

Born Marston Green, Solihull, 15 Mar 1965. Educ Crestwood S, Kingswinford. Debut 1984.
LEICESTERSHIRE (8) 1984.
HS 14 Leics v Lancs, Leicester, 1984.
Club: Stourbridge.

WHITTINGHAM, Norman *Barrie*
————LHB, ROB————

Born Silsden, Yorks, 22 Oct 1940. Debut 1962. P.
NOTTINGHAMSHIRE (77) 1962–66. Cap 1963.
HS 133 Notts v Hants, Trent Bridge, 1966.
1000 RUNS (1) 1249 @ 25.48 in 1963.
Cumberland 1969–72. Clubs: Bingley, Queensbury, Saltaire.

WHITTLE, Charles James Richardson
————RHB, LB————

Born Birkenhead, Cheshire, 26 Sept 1921. Educ Sedbergh; Christ Church C, Oxford. Debut 1947.
OXFORD UNIVERSITY (2) 1947.
HS 10 Oxford U v Glos, The Parks, 1947.
Oxfordshire 1947.

WHYATT, Christopher
————RHB, WK————

Born Old Whittington, Chesterfield, Derbys, 12 June 1954. Educ Chesterfield S; W Midlands C of Educ. Debut 1976.
DERBYSHIRE (1) 1976.
HS 6 Derbys v Cambridge U, Burton upon Trent, 1976.

WIGGS, Robert James
————RHB, SLA————

Born Woodford Green, Essex, 6 Sept 1950. Educ Chigwell S; Pembroke C, Cambridge. Debut 1970.
CAMBRIDGE UNIVERSITY (1) 1970.
HS 6 Cambridge U v Leics, Fenner's, 1970.
Essex 2nd XI. Clubs: South Woodford, Sou'westers, Essex Clergy. Church of England clergyman.

WIGHT, Peter Bernard
————RHB, OB————

Born Georgetown, British Guiana, 25 June 1930. Debut 1950/51. P.
W INDIES DOMESTIC British Guiana 1950/51.
SOMERSET (321) 1953–65. Cap 1954. Benefit (£5000) 1963.
N ZEALAND DOMESTIC Canterbury (4) 1963/64.
HS 222* Som v Kent, Taunton, 1959.
BB 6–29 Som v Derbys, Chesterfield, 1957.
1000 RUNS (10) 2375 @ 41.66 in 1960.
Fc umpire 1966–. Club: Burnley. Brothers G. L. Wight (W Indies) and H. A. and N. Wight (both British Guiana).

WIGNALL, Eric William Edward
————RHB, LB————

Born Harrow, M'sex, 25 Dec 1932. Debut 1952. P.
GLOUCESTERSHIRE (3) 1952–53.
HS 14 Glos v Combined Services, Bristol, 1953.

BB 2–50 same match.
Lord's groundstaff 1948–51. Father W. H. Wignall (M'sex).

WIJESURIYA, Roger Gerald Christopher Ediriweera
————RHB, SLA————

Born Moratuwa, Ceylon, 18 Feb 1960. Educ St Sebastian's C, Ceylon. Debut 1978/79.
SRI LANKA DOMESTIC Sri Lanka 1978/79–82/83.
SRI LANKA (1) P 1981/82.
OTHER TOURS Sri Lanka to England 1979, 1981. Sri Lanka to Zimbabwe 1982/83. Sri Lanka to Australia 1982/83.
HST 3 SL v P, Lahore, 1981/82. HS 25 Sri Lankans v Scotland, Glasgow, 1981.
BB 5–35 Sri Lankans v Oxford and Cambridge Universities, The Parks, 1981.
Club: Sebastianites.

WILCOCK, Howard *Gordon*
————RHB, WK————

Born New Malden, Surrey, 26 Feb 1950. Educ Giggleswick S, Settle, Yorks. Debut 1971.
WORCESTERSHIRE (99) 1971–78.
HS 74 Worcs v Yorks, Worcester, 1977.
Club: Stourbridge.

WILCOX, Alfred George Sidney
————LHB————

Born Cheltenham, Glos, 10 July 1920. Debut 1939.
GLOUCESTERSHIRE (39) 1939–49.
HS 73 Glos v Hants, Bournemouth, 1948.

WILCOX, Denys Robert
————RHB————

Born Westcliff, Essex, 4 June 1910. Died Westcliff, Essex, 6 Feb 1953. Educ Dulwich; Pembroke C, Cambridge. Debut 1928.
ESSEX (118) 1928–47. Cap. Joint capt 1933–39.
CAMBRIDGE UNIVERSITY (38) 1931–33 (Blue 1931–33).
FREE FORESTERS (8) 1934–51.
MCC (6) 1938–47.
HS 157 Cambridge U v Oxford U, Lord's, 1932.
1000 RUNS (4) 1390 @ 44.83 in 1937.
RECORD Added 263 for 8th wkt with R. M. Taylor, Essex v Warwicks, Southend, 1946, county record.

Gentlemen v Players (3) 1933–47. Joint author (with T. E. Bailey) first edition *Cricketers in the Making* (1950). Son J. W. T. Wilcox (Essex).

WILCOX, John Warren Theodore
────RHB, OB────

Born Newton Abbot, Devon, 16 Aug 1940. Educ Malvern; Pembroke C, Cambridge. Debut 1961.
CAMBRIDGE UNIVERSITY (12) 1961–62.
ESSEX (19) 1964–67.
HS 87 Essex v Worcs, Brentwood, 1965.
Club: Old Malvernians. Father D. R. Wilcox (Essex).

WILD, Duncan James
────LHB, RM────

Born Northampton, 28 Nov 1962. Educ Northampton Boys' S. Debut 1980.
NORTHAMPTONSHIRE (34) 1980–.
HS 144 Northants v Lancs, Southport, 1984.
BB 3–15 Northants v Hants, Southampton, 1984.
Father J. Wild (Northants).

WILD, John
────RHB, OB────

Born Northampton, 24 Feb 1935. Debut 1953. *P.*
NORTHAMPTONSHIRE (39) 1953–61.
COMBINED SERVICES (2) 1956.
HS 95 Northants v Warwicks, Northampton, 1960.
BB 4–44 Northants v Essex, Wellingborough, 1961.
Club: Kidsgrove. Son D. J. Wild (Northants).

WILDE, David
────LHB, LFM────

Born Glossop, Derbys, 3 July 1950. Debut 1971.
DERBYSHIRE (13) 1971–72.
HS 12 Derbys v Northants, Chesterfield, 1972.
BB 3–27 Derbys v Essex, Burton upon Trent, 1972.

WILENKIN, Boris Charles George
────RHB────

Born London, 20 June 1933. Educ Harrow; Trinity C, Cambridge. Debut 1955.

FREE FORESTERS (5) 1955–59.
CAMBRIDGE UNIVERSITY (10) 1956 (Blue).
D. R. JARDINE'S XI (1) 1958.
HS 103 Cambridge U v Leics, Fenner's, 1956.
Oxfordshire 1951–56.

WILEY, John Walter Eddington
────RHB────

Born Cape Town, S Africa, 7 Feb 1927. Educ Diocesan C, Cape Town; Cape Town U; Lincoln C, Oxford. Debut 1947/48.
S AFRICA DOMESTIC Western Province 1947/48–48/49, South African Universities 1948/49.
OXFORD UNIVERSITY (9) 1949–51.
HS 70 W Province v Rhodesia, Salisbury, 1947/48.
Member of Parliament for Simonstown, S Africa. Brother W. G. A. Wiley (Oxford U; W Province).

WILEY, William Gordon Anthony
────RHB, LBG────

Born Cape Town, S Africa, 7 Nov 1931. Educ Diocesan C, Cape Town; Lincoln C, Oxford. Debut 1952.
OXFORD UNIVERSITY (12) 1952 (Blue).
S AFRICA DOMESTIC Western Province 1952/53–53/54.
HS 100 Oxford U v Sussex, Worthing, 1952.
Oxfordshire 1952. Brother J. W. E. Wiley (W Province, Oxford U).

WILKIN, Charles Lucien Arthur
────RHB, SLA────

Born St Kitts, W Indies, 1 Jan 1949. Educ St Kitts GS; Pembroke C, Cambridge. Debut 1969.
CAMBRIDGE UNIVERSITY (11) 1969–70 (Blue 1970).
W INDIES DOMESTIC Leeward Islands 1973/74–76/77, Combined Islands 1976/77.
HS 26 Leeward Islands v Windward Islands, Basseterre, 1976/77.
BB 3–74 Cambridge U v M'sex, Fenner's, 1970.
Club: St Kitts. Father Calvin Wilkin (Leeward Islands).

WILKINS, Alan Haydn
────RHB, LFM────

Born Cardiff, S Wales, 22 Aug 1953. Educ Whitchurch GS; Loughborough C. Debut 1976.
GLAMORGAN (65) 1976–79, 1983.

GLOUCESTERSHIRE (40) 1980–81.
S AFRICA DOMESTIC Northern Transvaal 1981/82.
TOUR Overseas XI to India 1980/81.
HS 70 Glos v Notts, Worksop, 1970.
BB 8–57 Glos v Lancs, Old Trafford, 1981.
Rugby: Cardiff, Glamorgan Wanderers, Bristol.

WILKINS, Christopher Peter
────RHB, RM, occ WK────

Born Kingwilliamstown, S Africa, 31 July 1944. Educ Selborne C, East London. Debut 1962/63.
S AFRICA DOMESTIC Border 1962/63–70/71, Eastern Province 1972/73–77/78 (capt 16), Natal 1978/79–82/83.
DERBYSHIRE (71) 1970/72. Cap 1970.
HS 156 Derbys v Lancs, Old Trafford, 1971.
BB 4–19 E Province v Rhodesia, Port Elizabeth, 1972/73.
1000 RUNS (3) 1638 @ 39.95 in 1970.
RECORD Added 203 for 5th wkt with I. R. Buxton, Derbys v Lancs, Old Trafford, 1971, a county record.
Brother A. D. Wilkins (Border).

WILKINSON, Donald John
────LHB, RLB────

Born Irvine, Ayrshire, Scotland, 14 Feb 1955. Educ Lancaster RGS; Keble C, Oxford. Debut 1975.
OXFORD UNIVERSITY (4) 1975–76.
HS 5 Oxford U v Derbys, Burton upon Trent, 1975.
BB 4–89 Oxford U v Warwicks, The Parks, 1975.

WILKINSON, Keith William
────LHB, LM────

Born Fenton, Stoke on Trent, Staffordshire, 15 Jan 1950. Debut 1969.
WORCESTERSHIRE (49) 1969–75.
HS 141 Worcs v Oxford U, The Parks, 1974.
BB 5–60 Worcs v Sussex, Worcester, 1971.
Clubs: Stourbridge, Old Hill.

WILKINSON, Leonard Litton
────RHB, LB────

Born Northwich, Cheshire, 5 Nov 1916. Debut 1937. *P.*
LANCASHIRE (63) 1937–47. Cap 1938.
ENGLAND (3) *SA 1938/39*.
HST 2 E v SA, J'burg, 1938/39. HS 48 Lancs v Worcs, Old Trafford, 1938.

BBT 2–12 E v SA, Durban, 1938/39. BB 8–53 Lancs v Hants, Old Trafford, 1939.
100 WKTS (1) 151 @ 23.38 in 1938.
Clubs: Burnley, Barrow.

WILKINSON, Philip Alan
————RHB, RM————

Born Hucknall, Notts, 23 Aug 1951. Debut 1971.
NOTTINGHAMSHIRE (92) 1971–77. Cap 1974.
HS 77 Notts v M'sex, Trent Bridge, 1975.
BB 6–81 Notts v M'sex, Trent Bridge, 1977.
Club: Elland.

WILKINSON, Robert William
————RHB, RM————

Born Rotherhithe, London, 23 Dec 1939. Debut 1959. *P.*
KENT (23) 1959–63.
HS 63 Kent v Leics, Maidstone, 1959.
BB 2–31 Kent v Essex, Westcliff, 1959.
Club: Honor Oak. Great-uncle R. Abel (Surrey, England).

WILKINSON, Stephen George
————RHB, SLA————

Born Hounslow, M'sex, 12 Jan 1949. Educ Isleworth GS. Debut 1972.
SOMERSET (18) 1972–74.
HS 69 Som v Surrey, Oval, 1972.
Cousin P. Bainbridge (Glos).

WILLARD, Michael James Lewis
————LHB, RM————

Born Hawkhurst, Kent, 24 Mar 1938. Educ Judd S, Tonbridge; Corpus Christi C, Cambridge. Debut 1959.
CAMBRIDGE UNIVERSITY (41) 1959–61 (Blue 1959–61).
HS 101* Cambridge U v Som, Taunton, 1960.
BB 7–62 Cambridge U v Surrey, Fenner's, 1961.
Kent 2nd XI. Clubs: Tunbridge Wells, Leamington.

WILLATT, Guy Longfield
————LHB————

Born Nottinghamshire, 7 May 1918. Educ Repton; St Catharine's C, Cambridge. Debut 1938.
CAMBRIDGE UNIVERSITY (28) 1938–47 (Blue 1946–47). Capt 1947.
NOTTINGHAMSHIRE (22) 1939–48.

SCOTLAND (5) 1948–50.
DERBYSHIRE (125) 1950–56. Cap 1950. Capt 1951–54.
MCC (3) 1953–61.
HS 146 Derbys v Worcs, Chesterfield, 1952.
BB 2–18 Cambridge U v Hants, Portsmouth, 1947.
1000 RUNS (4) 1624 @ 35.30 in 1952.
Gentlemen v Players (2) 1947–52.
Clubs: Grange, Kendal. Soccer: Blue. Headmaster at Heversham GS, then at Pocklington.

WILLETT, Elquemedo Tonito
————LHB, SLA————

Born Nevis, Leeward Islands, 1 May 1953. Debut 1970/71.
W INDIES DOMESTIC Leeward Islands 1970/71–, Combined Islands 1970/71–79/80.
WEST INDIES (5) 1972/73–74/75. A 1972/73 (3). I 1974/75 (2).
OTHER TOUR W Indies to England 1973.
HST 26 WI v I, Delhi, 1974/75. HS 56 W Indians v Yorks, Scarborough, 1973.
BBT 3–33 WI v A, Port of Spain, 1972/73. BB 8–73 W Indians v Glam, Swansea, 1973.
Club: Nevis.

WILLETT, Michael David
————RHB, RM————

Born W Norwood, Surrey, 21 Apr 1933. Educ Thornton's GS, Clapham. Debut 1955. *P.*
SURREY (172) 1955–67. Cap 1962. Testimonial 1969.
HS 126 Surrey v Kent, Oval, 1961 and 126 v Hants, Bournemouth, 1964.
BB 3–36 Surrey v Cambridge U, Oval, 1966.
1000 RUNS (3) 1789 @ 45.87 in 1964.
Club: Beddington.

WILLETTS, Frank Terence
————LHB————

Born Birmingham, 20 Nov 1939. Debut 1964.
SOMERSET (16) 1964–67.
HS 38 Som v Glam, Weston-super-Mare, 1965.
Shropshire 1968, Cornwall 1977–83.
Clubs: Wolverhampton, St Austell, Truro. Professional coach Wolverhampton RGS 1968.

WILLEY, Peter
————RHB, RMF/OB————

Born Sedgefield, Co Durham, 6 Dec 1949. Educ Seaham Sec S. Debut 1966.

NORTHAMPTONSHIRE (319) 1966–83. Cap 1971. Benefit (£31,400) 1981.
LEICESTERSHIRE (26) 1984. Cap 1984.
S AFRICA DOMESTIC Eastern Province 1982/83–.
ENGLAND (20) 1976–81. A 1980 (1), 1981 (4); WI 1976 (2), 1980 (5); I 1979 (1). A 1979/80 (3); WI 1980/81 (4).
OTHER TOURS D. H. Robins' XI to S Africa 1972/73. D. H. Robins' XI to Sri Lanka 1977/78.
HST 102* E v WI, St John's, Antigua, 1980/81. HS 227 Northants v Som, Northampton, 1976.
BBT 2–73 E v WI, Lord's, 1980. BB 7–37 Northants v Oxford U, The Parks, 1975.
1000 RUNS (5) 1783 @ 50.94 in 1982.
RECORDS Added 342 for 2nd wkt with W. Larkins, Northants v Lancs, Northampton, 1983; during HS (above) added 370 for 4th wkt with R. T. Virgin; added 290* for 4th wkt with T. J. Boon, Leics v Warwicks, Leicester, 1984, all county records.
Added 117* for 10th wkt with R. G. D. Willis, E v WI, Oval, 1980.
Barred from Test cricket for three yrs for touring S Africa 1981/82 (SAB England XI).

WILLIAMS, Cecil Beaumont (Boogles)
————RHB, LBG————

Born Bridgetown, Barbados, 8 Mar 1926. Educ Harrison C; Durham U. Debut 1947/48.
W INDIES DOMESTIC Barbados 1947/48–56/57.
TOUR W Indies to England 1950.
HS 133 Barbados v E. W. Swanton's XI, Bridgetown, 1955/56.
BB 7–55 W Indians v MCC, Lord's, 1950.
Club: Carlton (Barbados). Appointed Barbados High Commissioner to Britain 1976. Awarded OBE for diplomatic services.

WILLIAMS, Charles Cuthbert Powell
————RHB————

Born Oxford, 9 Feb 1933. Educ Westminster; Christ Church C, Oxford. Debut 1952.
OXFORD UNIVERSITY (42) 1952–55 (Blue 1953–55). Capt 1955.
ESSEX (40) 1954–59.
HS 139* Oxford U v Hants, The Parks, 1954.
1000 RUNS (2) 1219 @ 31.25 in 1955.
Gentlemen v Players (1) 1956. Oxfordshire 1952. Appointed chairman of The Price Commission 1977. Labour Parliamentary candidate. Made life peer in 1985.

WILLIAMS, Charles *Derek*
RHB, RM

Born Cardiff, S Wales, 24 Nov 1924.
Educ Cardiff S; Merton C, Oxford.
Debut 1946.
OXFORD UNIVERSITY (1) 1946.
HS 3 Oxford U v Glos, The Parks, 1946.
Berkshire 1949.

WILLIAMS, Christopher *Mark* Bebb
RHB, RM

Born Stamford Hill, N London, 11 Jan
1955. Educ Highgate; Trinity C, Cambridge. Debut 1976.
CAMBRIDGE UNIVERSITY (1) 1976.
HS 29 Cambridge U v Warwicks,
Fenner's, 1976.
Eton Fives: Half-Blue. Mother Gwen
Watford (actress).

WILLIAMS, David
RHB, SLA

Born Barnsley, Yorks, 25 May 1948.
Educ Penistone GS; Queen's C, Oxford.
Debut 1968.
OXFORD UNIVERSITY (20) 1968–73.
HS 52 Oxford U v Warwicks, The Parks,
1972.
BB 5–19 Oxford U v Surrey, The Parks,
1968.

WILLIAMS, David *Lawrence*
LHB, RFM

Born Tonna, Neath, S Wales, 20 Nov
1946. Educ Neath County GS. Debut
1969.
GLAMORGAN (150) 1969–76. Cap 1971.
TOUR Glam to W Indies 1969/70.
HS 37* Glam v Essex, Chelmsford, 1969.
BB 7–60 Glam v Lancs, Blackpool, 1970.
Club: Ynysygerwn.

WILLIAMS, Dennis Stanley
RHB, LM

Born Sutton, Surrey, 15 Nov 1936.
Debut 1959.
COMBINED SERVICES (8) 1959–64.
HS 82 Combined Services v Cambridge
U, Fenner's, 1960.
Buckinghamshire 1958.

WILLIAMS, Edward Lovell
RHB, LFM

Born Shaftesbury, Dorset, 15 Sept
1926. Educ Charterhouse. Debut 1949.
LEICESTERSHIRE (1) 1949.

HS 14 Leics v Glos, Leicester, 1949.
BB 2–33 same match.

WILLIAMS, Gwynfor Lloyd
RHB

Born Kidwelly, Carmarthenshire, S
Wales, 30 May 1925. Educ Christ C,
Brecon; Oxford U. Debut 1955.
SOMERSET (3) 1955.
HS 24 Som v Glam, Weston-super-
Mare, 1955.
Club: Bath. Table tennis: Oxford U.

WILLIAMS, Neil FitzGerald
RHB, RFM

Born Hopewell, St Vincent, 12 July
1962. Educ Acland Burghley S. Debut
1982.
MIDDLESEX (55) 1982–.
W INDIES DOMESTIC Windward Islands
1982/83.
HS 63 M'sex v Worcs, Worcester, 1983.
BB 5–77 M'sex v Yorks, Headingley,
1983.

WILLIAMS, Norman Roy
RHB, RFM

Born March, Cambridgeshire, 4 Jan
1931. Debut 1961.
COMBINED SERVICES (1) 1961.
HS 5 Combined Services v Notts, Trent
Bridge, 1961.
BB 4–67 same match.
Notts 2nd XI. A late substitute in only
fc match; not a serviceman.

WILLIAMS, Owen Leslie
RHB, SLA

Born Cape Town, S Africa, 8 Apr 1938.
Debut 1967.
WARWICKSHIRE (1) 1967.
HS 6* Warwicks v Scotland, Edgbaston,
1967.
Club: Ratcliffe.

WILLIAMS, Richard Grenville
RHB, OB

Born Bangor, Caernarvonshire, N
Wales, 10 Aug 1957. Educ Ellesmere
Port GS. Debut 1974.
NORTHAMPTONSHIRE (179) 1974–. Cap
1979.
TOUR D. H. Robins' XI to N Zealand
1979/80.
HS 175* Northants v Leics, Leicester,
1980.
BB 7–73 Northants v Cambridge U,
Fenner's, 1980.

1000 RUNS (6) 1262 @ 34.10 in 1980.
RECORD During HS (above) added 322 for
2nd wkt with W. Larkins, a county
record.
Club: Walsall.

WILLIAMS, Robert Graham
RHB, RFM

Born Australia, 4 Apr 1911. Died
Adelaide, S Australia, 31 Aug 1978.
Debut 1932/33.
AUSTRALIA DOMESTIC South Australia
(18) 1932/33–37/38, Australian Services
(3) 1945/46.
TOUR Australian Services to England (6)
1945.
HS 75* S Australia v Queensland, Brisbane, 1937/38.
BB 6–21 S Australia v Queensland,
Adelaide, 1937/38.
Club: East Torrens. Awarded MBE for
work in teaching war-blinded prisoners
touch-typing and braille.

WILLIAMS, Stephen
RHB, LB

Born Swindon, Wiltshire, 11 Mar 1954.
Educ Herod Burna S, Swindon. Debut
1978.
GLOUCESTERSHIRE (1) 1978.
No runs; did not bowl.
Wiltshire 1975–77, 1979–83. Club:
Swindon.

WILLIAMSON, John Gordon
RHB, RMF

Born Stockton-on-Tees, Co Durham, 4
Apr 1936. Debut 1958. *P.*
COMBINED SERVICES (1) 1958.
NORTHAMPTONSHIRE (55) 1959–62.
HS 106* Northants v Cambridge U,
Northampton, 1960.
BB 6–47 Northants v Kent, Kettering,
1959.
Durham 1954–56, 1963–69, Cheshire
1974. Clubs: Bishop Auckland, Norton,
Macclesfield, Solihull. Changed name
to Barkass-Williamson in 1965.

WILLIS, Robert George Dylan
RHB, RF

Born Sunderland, Co Durham, 30 May
1949. Educ Guildford RGS. Debut
1969. *Wisden* 1978.
SURREY (34) 1969–71.
WARWICKSHIRE (136) 1972–84. Cap
1972. Benefit (£44,951) 1981. Capt
1980–84.
S AFRICA DOMESTIC Northern Transvaal
1972/73.

ENGLAND (90) 1970/71–84. A 1977 (5), 1981 (6); WI 1973 (1), 1976 (2), 1980 (4), 1984 (3); NZ 1978 (3), 1983 (4); I 1974 (1), 1979 (3), 1982 (3); P 1974 (1), 1978 (3), 1982 (2). *A 1970/71 (4), 1974/75 (5), 1976/77 (1), 1978/79 (6), 1979/80 (3), 1982/83 (5); WI 1973/74 (3); NZ 1970/71 (1), 1977/78 (3), 1983/84 (3); I 1976/77 (5), 1981/82 (5); P 1977/78 (3), 1983/84 (1); SL 1981/82 (1).* Capt 18.

OTHER TOURS D. H. Robins' XI to S Africa 1972/73. England to W Indies 1980/81 (no fc matches).

HST 28* E v P, Edgbaston, 1982 and 28 E v I, Lord's, 1982. HS 72 Warwicks v Indians, Edgbaston, 1982.

BBT 8–43 E v A, Headingley, 1981. BB 8–32 Warwicks v Glos, Bristol, 1977.

RECORDS Took 325 wkts @ 25.20 in Tests, an England record and second only to D. K. Lillee's 355. Took 128 Test wkts @ 26.14 against Australia, an England record.

Added 117* for 10th wkt with P. Willey, E v WI, Oval, 1980.

Added forename Dylan in adulthood. Awarded MBE for services to cricket.

WILLOWS, Alan
——RHB, SLA——

Born Portslade, Sussex, 24 Apr 1961. Educ Portslade Community C. Debut 1980.

SUSSEX (5) 1980–83.

HS 4 Sussex v Notts, Hove, 1982.

BB 4–33 Sussex v Hants, Southampton, 1980.

WILLS, Robert Thomas
——RHB——

Born Belfast, N Ireland, 19 July 1950. Debut 1981.

IRELAND (4) 1981–84.

HS 48 Ireland v Scotland, Clontarf, Dublin, 1981.

Clubs: Woodvale, Ulster Town.

WILLS, Roy
——RHB——

Born Northampton, 5 Dec 1944. Debut 1963.

NORTHAMPTONSHIRE (33) 1963–69.

HS 151* Northants v Cambridge U, Fenner's, 1966.

WILLSON, Bernard John (Tug)
——RHB, LM——

Born Strood, Kent, 20 June 1935. Debut 1964.

COMBINED SERVICES (2) 1964.

HS 53 Combined Services v Oxford U, Aldershot, 1964.

BB 4–87 Combined Services v Oxford U, Aldershot, 1964.

Royal Air Force. Kent 2nd XI. Hong Kong. Clubs: Little Sai Wan, Kai Tak. Retired Squadron Leader. Cathay Pacific Airways pilot. Lives in Hong Kong.

WILLSON, Ronald Henry
——LHB, SLA——

Born Seaford, Sussex, 14 July 1933. Educ Burgess Hill S, Sussex. Debut 1955. *P.*

SUSSEX 1955–57.

S AFRICA DOMESTIC Rhodesia 1961/62.

HS 113* Sussex v Som, Hove, 1957. Devon 1959. Club: Torquay. Former groundsman/coach Falcon C, Essexvale, Bulawayo, Rhodesia (from 1960).

WILSON, Arthur Edward (Andy)
——LHB, WK——

Born Paddington, London, 18 May 1910. Debut 1932. *P.*

MIDDLESEX (7) 1932–33.

GLOUCESTERSHIRE (318) 1936–55. Cap 1938. Benefit (£3444) 1953.

HS 188 Glos v Sussex, Chichester, 1949.

1000 RUNS (6) 1327 @ 31.59 in 1947.

RECORD Added 239 for 8th wkt with W. R. Hammond, Glos v Lancs, Bristol, 1938, county record.

Took ten catches match Glos v Hants, Portsmouth, 1953, at time record for wicketkeeper.

Glos coach from 1950 until retirement. Cricket journalist.

WILSON, Ben Ambler
——LHB, SLA——

Born Harrogate, Yorks, 22 Sept 1921. Educ Harrogate GS. Debut 1951. *P.*

WARWICKSHIRE (1) 1951.

No runs; no wkt.

Suffolk 1955–59. Clubs: Spen Victoria, Cupar. Former professional coach Blundell's S (from 1963). Father B. B. Wilson (Yorks).

WILSON, Donald
——LHB, SLA——

Born Settle, Yorks, 7 Aug 1937. Debut 1957. *P.*

YORKSHIRE (392) 1957–74. Cap 1960. Benefit (£7621) 1972.

ENGLAND (6) 1963/64–70/71. *NZ 1970/71 (1); I 1963/64 (5).*

OTHER TOURS MCC to N Zealand 1960/61. MCC to Ceylon 1969/70. MCC to Australia 1970/71.

HST 42 E v I, Madras, 1963/64. HS 112 MCC v South Zone, Hyderabad, 1963/64.

BBT 2–17 E v I, Calcutta, 1963/64. BB 8–36 (14–71 match) MCC v Ceylon, Colombo, 1969/70.

100 WKTS (5) 109 @ 13.95 in 1968.

Hit R. N. S. Hobbs for 30 runs (466266) in one over, Yorks v MCC, Scarborough, 1966.

Lincolnshire 1975–77. Clubs: Guisborough, Saltburn, Manningham Mills, Holmfirth. Head coach Lord's Cricket S.

WILSON, Alan (Ranji)
——RHB, WK——

Born Newton-le-Willows, Lancs, 24 Apr 1921. Debut 1948. *P.*

LANCASHIRE (171) 1948–62. Cap 1951. Testimonial (£4023) 1962.

HS 37* Lancs v Leics, Old Trafford, 1958.

WILSON, George
——RHB, OB——

Born Belfast, N Ireland, 30 June 1916. Educ Belfast Technical C. Debut 1948.

IRELAND (3) 1948–51.

HS 39 Ireland v Scotland, Glasgow, 1948.

BB 2–12 Ireland v Scotland, Belfast, 1949.

Club: Woodvale.

WILSON, Gerald Charles
——RHB, RMF——

Born Hayes, M'sex, 25 Dec 1936. Educ Townfield CS, London. Debut 1957. *P.*

MCC (2) 1957.

HS 7* MCC v Scotland, Aberdeen, 1957.

BB 2–85 same match.

Somerset 2nd XI. Minor Counties umpire 1970–78. Clubs: Hayes, Street, Morlands. Professional coach Millfield since 1959.

WILSON, Thomas *Grenville* Owen
——LHB, LFM——

Born Elmley Lovett, Worcs, 9 Apr 1932. Debut 1951. *P.*

WORCESTERSHIRE (13) 1951–53.

HS 4* Worcs v Surrey, Kidderminster, 1952.

BB 3–42 Worcs v M'sex, Lord's, 1952.

Clubs: Kidderminster, Old Hill.

WILSON, Ian Barclay Justly
LHB, SLA

Born Clonmel, Co Tipperary, Ireland, 13 Oct 1932. Educ Wrekin C. Debut 1956.
IRELAND (3) 1956–61.
HS 18 Ireland v MCC, Dublin, 1956.
BB 3–10 Ireland v Scotland, Dublin, 1957.
Clubs: Cahir Park, Phoenix Park.

WILSON, John Deva Kumar
LHB, RLB

Born Jaffua, Ceylon, 4 Sept 1944. Educ RC, Colombo; Princeton Theological Seminary US; Mansfield C, Oxford. Debut 1977.
OXFORD UNIVERSITY (1) 1977.
HS 18 Oxford U v Notts, The Parks, 1977.
Club: Colts (Colombo).

WILSON, John Stuart
RHB, RFM

Born Middleton, Manchester, 22 Jan 1932. Educ Brechin HS. Debut 1957.
SCOTLAND (16) 1957–64.
HS 22 Scotland v Warwicks, Edgbaston, 1964.
BB 5–51 Scotland v MCC, Edinburgh, 1959.
Clubs: Brechin, Forfarshire.

WILSON, John *Victor*
LHB, RM

Born Scampston, Malton, Yorks, 17 Jan 1921. Educ Malton GS. Debut 1946. *P. Wisden* 1961.
YORKSHIRE (480) 1946–62. Cap 1948. Benefit (£5758) 1958. Capt 1960–62.
MCC (1) 1963.
TOUR MCC to Australasia 1954/55.
HS 230 Yorks v Derbys, Bramall Lane, Sheffield, 1960.
BB 2–1 MCC v NSW, Sydney, 1954/55.
1000 RUNS (14) 2027 @ 48.26 in 1951.
Players v Gentlemen (5) 1951–58.
Lincolnshire 1964–66. Clubs: Bingley, Saltaire, Wakefield, Malton, York, Scarborough, Undercliffe, Pudsey St Laurence.

WILSON, John William
RHB, SLA

Born Albert Park, Melbourne, Australia, 20 Aug 1921 (not 1922). Debut 1949/50.
AUSTRALIA DOMESTIC Victoria (1) 1949/50, South Australia (55) 1950/51–57/58.
AUSTRALIA (1) *I* 1956/57.
OTHER TOUR Australia to England 1956.
HS 19* S Australia v W Australia, Adelaide, 1950/51.
BB 7–11 (12–61 match) Australians v Glos, Bristol, 1956.
Club: South Melbourne.

WILSON, Peter *Hugh* L'Estrange
RHB, RFM

Born Guildford, Surrey, 17 Aug 1958. Educ Wellington C. Debut 1978.
SURREY (37) 1978–82.
SOMERSET (14) 1983–.
S AFRICA DOMESTIC Northern Transvaal 1979/80.
HS 29 N Transvaal v Transvaal, Pretoria, 1979/80.
BB 5–36 N Transvaal v E Province, Pretoria, 1979/80.

WILSON, Peter James
LHB

Born Weston-super-Mare, Som, 9 Aug 1942. Educ Worcester C, Oxford. Debut 1964.
OXFORD UNIVERSITY (2) 1964.
HS 30 Oxford U v Derbys, The Parks, 1964.

WILSON, Peter Robert Bain
RHB, LB

Born Bulawayo, Rhodesia, 31 Oct 1944. Educ Milton HS, Bulawayo; St Edmund Hall, Oxford. Debut 1968.
OXFORD UNIVERSITY (23) 1968–70 (Blue 1968, 1970).
HS 94 Oxford U v Notts, The Parks, 1968.
BB 4–60 Oxford U v Glam, The Parks, 1970.

WILSON, Robert
RHB, RFM

Born Edinburgh, Scotland, 8 Apr 1916. Educ N District S, Edinburgh. Debut 1952.
SCOTLAND (3) 1952.
HS 4 Scotland v Yorks, Glasgow, 1952.
BB 2–16 Scotland v Ireland, Paisley, 1952.
Club: Perthshire.

WILSON, Robert
LHB, SLA

Born Paisley, Scotland, 12 Feb 1935. Educ Paisley GS. Debut 1955.
SCOTLAND (3) 1955–56.
HS 29 Scotland v Derbys, Edinburgh, 1955.
Club: Kelburne.

WILSON, Robert Colin
LHB

Born Bapchild, Kent, 18 Feb 1928. Debut 1952. *P.*
KENT (365) 1952–67. Cap 1954. Benefit (£6679) 1964.
HS 159 Kent v Glam, Blackheath, 1960 and 159* v Northants, Kettering, 1963.
BB 3–38 Kent v Glam, Pontypridd, 1962.
1000 RUNS (13) 2038 @ 46.31 in 1964.
Club: Gore Court.

WILSON, Robert Greenwood
RHB, RFM

Born Arnside, Westmorland, 20 Dec 1922. Died Swindon, Wiltshire, 7 Mar 1980. Educ Bradfield C. Debut 1948.
COMBINED SERVICES (13) 1948–52.
FREE FORESTERS (1) 1951.
HS 100 Combined Services v Hants, Portsmouth, 1949.
BB 5–41 Combined Services v Worcs, Worcester, 1949.
Notts secretary 1972–77. Royal Air Force. Group-captain RAF.

WILSON, Robert Warley
RHB, OB

Born Warley, Worcs, 15 July 1934. Educ Warwick S; Brasenose C, Oxford. Debut 1956.
OXFORD UNIVERSITY (13) 1956–57 (Blue 1957).
HS 36* Oxford U v Free Foresters, The Parks, 1956.
BB 4–42 Oxford U v D. R. Jardine's XI, Eastbourne, 1957.
British Columbia. Club: Wellesbourne. Rugby: Blue.

WILSON, Roger Graham
RHB, SLA

Born Maidstone, Kent, 13 Jan 1943. Educ Churchill C, Cambridge. Debut 1964.
CAMBRIDGE UNIVERSITY (1) 1964.
HS 3* Cambridge U v Warwicks, Fenner's, 1964.
BB 2–35 same match.

WILSON, Thomas *Crichton*
————RHB, RMF————

Born Eastbourne, Sussex, 18 Nov 1936.
Educ Eastbourne; Clare C, Cambridge.
Debut 1960.
L. C. STEVENS' XI (1) 1960.
No runs; one wkt.
Clubs: Eastbourne, Crusaders, Old
Eastbournians.

WILTSHIRE, Graham George
Morley
————RHB, RMF————

Born Chipping Sodbury, Glos, 16 Apr
1931. Debut 1953. *P.*
GLOUCESTERSHIRE (19) 1953–60.
HS 39 Glos v Derbys, Bristol, 1958.
BB 7–52 Glos v Yorks, Headingley,
1958.
Current Glos coach.

WINCER, Robert Colin
————LHB, RFM————

Born Portsmouth, Hants, 2 Apr 1952.
Educ Hemsworth GS. Debut 1978.
DERBYSHIRE (23) 1978–80.
HS 26 Derbys v Kent, Chesterfield,
1979.
BB 4–42 Derbys v Leics, Derby, 1978.

WINDAYBANK, Stephen James
————RHB————

Born Pinner, M'sex, 10 Oct 1956. Educ
Cotham GS; Bristol Polytechnic. Debut
1979.
GLOUCESTERSHIRE (15) 1979–82.
HS 53 Glos v Cambridge U, Fenner's,
1979.

WINDOWS, Anthony Robin
————RHB, RM————

Born Bristol, Glos, 25 Sept 1942. Educ
Clifton; Jesus C, Cambridge. Debut
1960.
GLOUCESTERSHIRE (98) 1960–68. Cap
1965.
CAMBRIDGE UNIVERSITY (47) 1962–64
(Blue 1962–64).
TOUR MCC Under-25 to Pakistan 1966/
67.
HS 82 Cambridge U v Combined Ser-
vices, Fenner's, 1962.
BB 8–78 Glos v W Indies, Bristol, 1966.
1000 RUNS (1) 1003 @ 20.90 in 1962.
Club: Clifton.

WINDSOR, Raymond Thomas
Albert
————RHB————

Born Wellington, Som, 9 Feb 1943.
Debut 1969.
SOMERSET (1) 1969.
No runs; no wkts.

WINFIELD, Hugh *Mervyn*
————RHB————

Born Gainsborough, Lincolnshire, 13
June 1933. Debut 1954. *P.*
NOTTINGHAMSHIRE (172) 1954–66. Cap
1962.
HS 134 Notts v Glam, Swansea, 1962.
1000 RUNS (4) 1552 @ 30.43 in 1959.
Shropshire 1967–69, Lincolnshire
1970–71.

WING, Derek Charles
————RHB, RFM————

Born Wisbech, Cambridgeshire, 11 Feb
1943. Educ Kimbolton S. Debut 1967.
MCC (2) 1967–68.
MINOR COUNTIES (3) 1969–76.
HS 42 Minor Counties v W Indians,
Torquay, 1976.
BB 3–20 MCC v Cambridge U, Lord's,
1967.
Cambridgeshire 1964–. Club: Wisbech.

WINGFIELD DIGBY, Andrew
Richard
————LHB, RMF————

Born Sherborne, Dorset, 25 July 1950.
Educ Sherborne; Keble C, Oxford;
Wycliffe Hall, Oxford. Debut 1971.
OXFORD UNIVERSITY (38) 1971–77 (Blue
1971, 1975–77).
HS 69 Oxford U v Sussex, The Parks,
1975.
BB 5–79 Oxford U v Warwicks, The
Parks, 1971.
Dorset 1972–. Ordained into Church of
England 1977.

WINN, Christopher Elliott
————LHB————

Born Beckenham, Kent, 13 Nov 1926.
Educ KCS Wimbledon; Exeter C, Ox-
ford. Debut 1948.
OXFORD UNIVERSITY (38) 1948–51 (Blue
1948–51).
SUSSEX (15) 1948–52.
FREE FORESTERS (2) 1958.
D. R. JARDINE'S XI (2) 1957–58.
MCC (2) 1959–61.
HS 146* Oxford U v Free Foresters, The
Parks, 1950.

Clubs: Horsham, Hampstead, Richmond. Rugby: Blue, Rosslyn Park, England (8). Wife Valerie, née Ball (Olympic athlete).

WINROW, Frederick *Henry*
————LHB, SLA————

Born Manton, Notts, 17 Jan 1916. Died
East London, S Africa, 19 Aug 1973.
Debut 1938. *P.*
NOTTINGHAMSHIRE (113) 1938–51. Cap
1947. Testimonial (£300) 1952.
HS 204* Notts v Derbys, Trent Bridge,
1947.
BB 6–56 Notts v Surrey, Oval, 1947.
1000 RUNS (2) 1459 @ 37.41 in 1950.
RECORD During HS (above) added 303*
for 6th wkt with P. F. Harvey, county
record.
Executive member Border CU. Club:
Worksop. Professional coach Selborne
C, East London, S Africa 1952–60.
President Border Umpires' Association.
Brother R. Winrow (Notts, Scotland).

WINROW, Robert
————LHB, SLA————

Born Manton, Notts, 30 Dec 1910.
Debut 1932. *P.*
NOTTINGHAMSHIRE (5) 1932–35.
SCOTLAND (2) 1949.
HS 137 Notts v Som, Trent Bridge, 1935.
RECORD During HS (above) added 220 for
8th wkt with G. F. H. Heane, county
record.
Clubs: Manton, Drumpellier. Brother
F. H. Winrow (Notts).

WINSLOW, Paul Lyndhurst
————RHB————

Born Johannesburg, S Africa, 21 May
1929. Educ King Edward VII S, Johannesburg. Debut 1949.
SUSSEX (1) 1949.
S AFRICA DOMESTIC Transvaal 1949/
50–55/56, Rhodesia 1956/57–59/60,
Rhodesia XI 1961/62.
SOUTH AFRICA (5) 1949/50–55. A 1949/
50 (2). *E 1955 (3).*
HS 108 SA v E, Old Trafford, 1955. HS
139 Rhodesia v Australians, Salisbury,
1957/58.
Hit J. T. Ikin for 30 runs (446646) in one
over, S Africans v Lancs, Old Trafford,
1955.
Johannesburg Old Edwardians. Related
to several Winslows who played for
Sussex and Warwicks in 19th Century.

WISDOM, Nicholas
——RHB, RM——

Born Barnet, Hertfordshire, 18 Mar 1953. Educ Charterhouse. Debut 1974.
SUSSEX (2) 1974.
HS 31* Sussex v Oxford U, Horsham, 1974.
Club: Bognor. Father Norman Wisdom (comedian).

WISSON, Philip Wesley
——RHB——

Born Everton, Bedfordshire, 26 Apr 1935. Educ Enfield GS; Jesus C, Cambridge. Debut 1958.
CAMBRIDGE UNIVERSITY (2) 1958.
HS 14 Cambridge U v Lancs, Fenner's, 1958.
M'sex 2nd XI 1958. Club: Enfield.

WITHERDEN, Edwin George
——RHB, OB——

Born Goudhurst, Kent, 1 May 1922. Educ Rolvenden GS. Debut 1951. P.
KENT (40) 1951–55.
HS 125* Kent v Surrey, Blackheath, 1953.
BB 5–32 Kent v Minor Counties, Canterbury, 1951.
Norfolk 1956–62. Professional coach Bishop's Stortford C from 1963.

WOLFE-MURRAY, James Archibald
——RHB, RMF——

Born Edinburgh, Scotland, 25 Apr 1936. Educ Eton; Worcester C, Oxford. Debut 1957.
OXFORD UNIVERSITY (3) 1957.
HS 25 Oxford U v Leics, The Parks, 1957.
Clubs: Free Foresters, Grange, St Boswells.

WOLLOCOMBE, Richard Henry
——RHB, LB——

Born Panchmarhi, India, 12 Jan 1926. Educ Wellington C; Worcester C, Oxford. Debut 1951.
OXFORD UNIVERSITY (9) 1951–52.
HS 119 Oxford U v Worcs, The Parks, 1952.
BB 2–33 Oxford U v Sussex, Worthing, 1952.
Berkshire 1950.

WOLTON, Albert Victor George
——RHB, OB——

Born Maidenhead, Berkshire, 12 June 1919. Educ Holyport, Berkshire. Debut 1947. P.
WARWICKSHIRE (296) 1947–60. Cap 1949. Benefit (£3543) 1959.
HS 165 Warwicks v Worcs, Dudley, 1954.
BB 4–15 Warwicks v M'sex, Edgbaston, 1953.
1000 RUNS (7) 1809 @ 34.13 in 1955.
Berkshire 1937–39. Clubs: Bray, Aston Unity, Mitchells and Butlers, West Bromwich Dartmouth, Kings Heath, Berkshire Gentlemen.

WOOD, Arthur
——RHB, WK——

Born Fagley, Bradford, Yorks, 25 Aug 1898. Died Middleton, Ilkley, Yorks, 1 Apr 1973. Debut 1927. P. Wisden 1939.
YORKSHIRE (408) 1927–46. Cap 1929. Benefit (£2563) 1939.
ENGLAND XI (1) 1948.
ENGLAND (4) 1938–39. A 1938 (1); WI 1939 (3).
TOURS Yorks to Jamaica 1935/36. Sir T. E. W. Brinckman's XI to S America 1937/38.
HST 53 E v A, Oval, 1938. HS 123* Yorks v Worcs, Bramall Lane, Sheffield, 1935.
1000 RUNS (1) 1249 @ 30.46 in 1935.
Players v Gentlemen (1) 1938. Clubs: Bradford, Undercliffe.

WOOD, Barry
——RHB, RM——

Born Ossett, Yorks, 26 Dec 1942. Debut 1964.
YORKSHIRE (5) 1964.
LANCASHIRE (260) 1966–79. Cap 1968. Benefit (£62,429) 1979.
DERBYSHIRE (63) 1980–83. Cap 1980. Capt 1981–82.
S AFRICA DOMESTIC Eastern Province 1971/72–73/74.
ENGLAND (12) 1972–78. A 1972 (1), 1975 (3); WI 1976 (1); P 1978 (1). NZ 1974/75 (2); I 1972/73 (3); P 1972/73 (1).
OTHER TOUR International Wanderers to Rhodesia 1975/76.
HST 90 E v A, Oval, 1972. HS 198 Lancs v Glam, Liverpool, 1976.
BB 7–52 Lancs v M'sex, Old Trafford, 1968.
1000 RUNS (8) 1492 @ 38.25 in 1971.
RECORD Added 249 for 5th wkt with A. Kennedy, Lancs v Warwicks, Edgbaston, 1975, county record.
Club: Mirfield. Brother R. Wood (Yorks).

WOOD, Christopher Harland
——RHB, RFM——

Born Bradford, Yorks, 23 July 1934. Debut 1959. P.
YORKSHIRE (4) 1959.
HS 10 Yorks v Derbys, Chesterfield, 1959.
BB 4–39 Yorks v Essex, Colchester, 1959.
Clubs: Saltaire, Pudsey St Laurence.

WOOD, David John
——LHB, SLA——

Born Cuckfield, Sussex, 10 Jan 1965. Educ Oathan S. Debut 1984.
SUSSEX (2) 1984.
HS 15 Sussex v Surrey, Oval, 1984.

WOOD, Douglas *James*
——RHB, LFM——

Born Horsted Keynes, Sussex, 19 May 1914. Debut 1936. P.
SUSSEX (213) 1936–55. Cap 1938. Benefit (£4450) 1955.
HS 42 Sussex v Notts, Trent Bridge, 1951.
BB 7–24 Sussex v M'sex, Hove, 1949.
100 WKTS (1) 103 @ 24.56 in 1952.
Fc umpire 1957–62. Former professional coach Ardingly (from 1968).

WOOD, Graeme Malcolm
——LHB, RM——

Born E Fremantle, Perth, W Australia, 6 Nov 1956. Debut 1976/77.
AUSTRALIA DOMESTIC Western Australia (54) 1976/77–.
AUSTRALIA (43) 1977/78–83/84. E 1978/79 (6), 1982/83 (1); WI 1981/82 (3); NZ 1980/81 (3); I 1977/78 (1), 1980/81 (3); P 1978/79 (1), 1981/82 (3). E 1980 (1), 1981 (6); WI 1977/78 (5), 1983/84 (1); NZ 1981/82 (3); I 1979/80 (2); P 1982/83 (3); SL 1982/83 (1).
OTHER TOUR Australia to Sri Lanka 1980/81.
HST 126 A v WI, Georgetown, 1977/78.
HS 173* W Australia v NSW, Sydney, 1983/84.
BB 3–18 Australians v W Zone, Ahmedabad , 1979/80.
Club: Melville.

WOOD, James
——RHB, LB——

Born Burnley, Lancs, 26 June 1933. Died Blackpool, Lancs, 30 June 1977. Debut 1956. P.

LANCASHIRE (1) 1956.
Did not bat.
BB 3–56 Lancs v Oxford U, The Parks, 1956.
Royal Air Force 1952. Clubs: Castleton Moor, Royton, Burnley, Brackley. Brother John Wood (soccer for Aldershot); father James Wood (soccer for West Ham United).

WOOD, Lindsay Jonathan
LHB, SLA

Born Ruislip, M'sex, 12 May 1961. Educ Simon Langton GS; King Alfred's C, Winchester. Debut 1981.
KENT (2) 1981–82.
HS 5 Kent v Essex, Chelmsford, 1981.
BB 4–124 same match.

WOOD, Maurice
RHB, RFM

Born Nottingham, 6 July 1933. Died Nottingham, 18 Mar 1978. Debut 1955. P.
NOTTINGHAMSHIRE (4) 1955.
HS 4 Notts v Lancs, Trent Bridge, 1955.
BB 2–68 Notts v Surrey, Trent Bridge, 1955.
Officer in Nottingham Police.

WOOD, Ronald
RHB, SLA

Born Ossett, Yorks, 3 June 1929. Debut 1952. P.
YORKSHIRE (22) 1952–56.
HS 17 Yorks v Leics, Bramall Lane, Sheffield, 1952.
BB 8–45 Yorks v Scotland, Glasgow, 1952.
Clubs: Walsden, Baildon Green, Lidget Green, Bingley, Windhill. Brother B. Wood (Yorks, Lancs, Derbys, England).

WOOD, Russell Brown
RHB, WK

Born Staple Hill, Bristol, 15 Dec 1929. Educ Cotham GS, Bristol. Debut 1950.
GLOUCESTERSHIRE (8) 1950–51.
HS 48 Glos v Cambridge U, Bristol, 1950.
Club: Bristol Imperial.

WOODCOCK, Roy Gordon
RHB, SLA

Born Burnley, Lancs, 26 Nov 1934. Educ Worcester RGS. Debut 1956.

OXFORD UNIVERSITY (29) 1956–58 (Blue 1957–58).
HS 57 Oxford U v Leics, The Parks, 1957 and 57 v New Zealanders, The Parks, 1958.
BB 4–54 Oxford U v M'sex, The Parks, 1957.

WOODFORD, John Douglas
RHB, RM

Born Bradford, Yorks, 9 Sept 1943. Educ Carlton GS, Bradford. Debut 1968.
YORKSHIRE (38) 1968–72.
HS 101 Yorks v Warwicks, Middlesbrough, 1971.
BB 2–20 Yorks v Worcs, Dudley, 1971.
Northumberland 1975–79. Clubs: Marske, Spen Victoria, Bankfoot, Guisborough, Middlesbrough.

WOODHEAD, David Leonard
RHB, LB

Born Birmingham, 17 Mar 1940. Educ Fitzwilliam C, Cambridge. Debut 1968.
CAMBRIDGE UNIVERSITY (8) 1968.
HS 68 Cambridge U v Sussex, Fenner's, 1968.

WOODHEAD, Francis Gerald
RHB, RFM

Born Edwinstowe, Notts, 30 Oct 1912. Debut 1934. P.
NOTTINGHAMSHIRE (141) 1934–50. Cap 1937. Testimonial 1979.
HS 52★ Notts v Hants, Trent Bridge, 1936.
BB 7–24 Notts v Worcs, Trent Bridge, 1938.
Notts coach 1970–79. Clubs: South Hampstead, Great Horton, Todmorden. Professional coach Nottingham HS 1951–65.

WOODHOUSE, Arthur James Powys
RHB, RM

Born Bromley, Kent, 20 Oct 1933. Educ Oundle. Debut 1957.
FREE FORESTERS (1) 1957.
HS 17 Free Foresters v Oxford U, The Parks, 1957.
Kent 2nd XI 1953–58.

WOODHOUSE, George Edward Sealey
RHB

Born Blandford, Dorset, 15 Feb 1924. Educ Marlborough; Trinity C, Cambridge. Debut 1946.
SOMERSET (58) 1946–53. Cap 1947. Capt 1949.
COMBINED SERVICES (4) 1947.
FREE FORESTERS (2) 1948–50.
MCC (1) 1949.
HS 109 Som v Leics, Leicester, 1947.
Dorset 1954–64. War-time Blue 1943.

WOODROFFE, Alfred
LHB

Born Birmingham, 1 Sept 1918. Died Sutton Coldfield, Warwicks, 23 July 1964. Debut 1947. P.
WARWICKSHIRE (4) 1947–48.
HS 41 Warwicks v Glos, Edgbaston, 1947.
Club: Aston Unity.

WOODS, Basil Joseph Pontifex
RHB, LBG

Born S Africa, 28 Aug 1922. Educ Pembroke C, Cambridge. Debut 1951.
CAMBRIDGE UNIVERSITY (2) 1951.
HS 1 Cambridge U v Yorks, Fenner's, 1951.
BB 2–61 same match.

WOOKEY, Stephen Mark
RHB, RM

Born Upavon, Wiltshire, 2 Sept 1954. Educ Malvern; Emmanuel C, Cambridge; Wycliffe Hall, Oxford. Debut 1975.
CAMBRIDGE UNIVERSITY (9) 1975–76 (Blue 1975–76).
OXFORD UNIVERSITY (10) 1978–80 (Blue 1978).
HS 48 Cambridge U v Oxford U, Lord's, 1976.
BB 3–61 Oxford U v Sussex, The Parks, 1978.
Wiltshire 1974–78. Club: Malvern. Ordained into Church of England 1978.

WOOLER, Charles Robert Dudley
RHB, RFM

Born Bulawayo, Rhodesia, 30 June 1930. Educ Plumtree S, Rhodesia. Debut 1949. P.
LEICESTERSHIRE (51) 1949–51.
S AFRICA DOMESTIC Rhodesia 1951/52–56/57.
HS 49★ Leics v Derbys, Leicester, 1950.
BB 5–47 Leics v Kent, Leicester, 1951.

WOOLFRIES, Simon Andrew
RHB, OB

Born Moreton-in-Marsh, Glos, 10 Jan 1953. Educ Ipswich S; Sidney Sussex C, Cambridge. Debut 1972.
CAMBRIDGE UNIVERSITY (1) 1972.
HS 3 Cambridge U v Warwicks, Fenner's, 1972.

WOOLLER, Wilfred
RHB, RMF

Born Rhos-on-Sea, Denbighshire, N Wales, 20 Nov 1912. Educ Rydal; Christ's C, Cambridge. Debut 1935.
CAMBRIDGE UNIVERSITY (18) 1935–36 (Blue 1935–36).
GLAMORGAN (400) 1938–62. Cap 1939. Capt 1947–60.
HS 128 Glam v Warwicks, Neath, 1955.
BB 8–45 Glam v Warwicks, Ebbw Vale, 1953.
1000 RUNS (5) 1270 @ 27.02 in 1947.
100 WKTS (2) 120 @ 24.55 in 1949.
DOUBLE (1) 1954.
RECORD Added 195* for 7th wkt with W. E. Jones, Glam v Lancs, Liverpool, 1947, county record.
Gentlemen v Players (3) 1947–53. England Test selector 1955–61. Glam secretary until 1977. Denbighshire 1933–34. Rugby: Blue, Sale, Cardiff, Wales (18).

WOOLLETT, Anthony Frank
LHB

Born Lambeth, London, 20 Sept 1927. Debut 1950. P.
KENT (44) 1950–54.
HS 96 Kent v Yorks, Dover, 1953.
Berkshire 1958.

WOOLLEY, Kenneth McDowell
RHB, RFM

Born Cape Town, S Africa, 9 Dec 1924. Educ Diocesan C, Cape Town; Peterhouse C, Cambridge. Debut 1947.
CAMBRIDGE UNIVERSITY (1) 1947.
HS 4 Cambridge U v M'sex, Fenner's, 1947.

WOOLMER, Robert Andrew
RHB, RM

Born Kanpur, India, 14 May 1948. Educ Skinner's S. Debut 1968. Wisden 1976.
KENT (279) 1968–84. Cap 1970. Benefit 1984.
S AFRICA DOMESTIC Natal 1973/74–75/76, Western Province 1980/81.

ENGLAND (19) 1975–81. A 1975 (2), 1977 (5), 1981 (2); WI 1976 (5), 1980 (2). A 1976/77 (1); I 1976/77 (2).
OTHER TOUR D. H. Robins' XI to S Africa 1973/74.
HST 149 E v A, Oval, 1975. HS 203 Kent v Sussex, Tunbridge Wells, 1982.
BB 7–47 Kent v Sussex, Canterbury, 1969.
1000 RUNS (5) 1749 @ 47.27 in 1976. World Series Cricket (Kerry Packer) 1977/78–78/79. Barred from Test cricket for three yrs for touring S Africa in 1981/82 (SAB England XI). Autobiography Pirate and Rebel? (1984). Father C. Woolmer (Uttar Pradesh).

WOOTTON, Simon Howard
LHB, LM

Born Perivale, M'sex, 24 Feb 1959. Educ Arthur Terry S, Sutton Coldfield. Debut 1981.
WARWICKSHIRE (11) 1981–83.
GLOUCESTERSHIRE (4) 1984.
HS 104 Warwicks v Cambridge U, Fenner's, 1983.
Club: Lichfield. Badminton: Warwickshire, England Under-18, England B squad. Father B. A. Wootton (outstanding wicketkeeper in London club cricket 1940s and 1950s); brother-in-law Alan Lee (cricket writer).

WORKMAN, James Allen
RHB

Born Australia, 17 Mar 1917. Died Westminster, London, 23 Dec 1970. Debut 1945.
AUSTRALIA DOMESTIC Australian Services (5) 1945/46.
TOUR Australian Services to England (4) 1945 and to India and Ceylon (8) 1945/46.
HS 76 Australian Services v Indian XI, Bombay, 1945/46 and 76 v S Zone, Madras, 1945/46.

WORRELL, Frank Mortimer Maglinne
RHB, LM/SLA

Born St Michael, Barbados, 1 Aug 1924. Died Kingston, Jamaica, 13 Mar 1967. Educ Combermere S; Manchester U. Debut 1941/42. Wisden 1951.
W INDIES DOMESTIC Barbados 1941/42–46/47, Jamaica 1947/48–63/64.
WEST INDIES (51) 1947/48–63. E 1947/48 (3), 1953/54 (4), 1959/60 (4); A 1954/55 (4); I 1952/53 (5), 1961/62 (5). E 1950 (4), 1957 (5), 1963 (5); A 1951/52 (5), 1960/61 (5); NZ 1951/52 (2). Capt 15.

OTHER TOURS Commonwealth XI to India, Pakistan and Ceylon 1949/50. Commonwealth XI to India and Ceylon 1950/51. Commonwealth XI to India 1953/54. West Indian XI in England 1964 (capt).
HST 261 WI v E, Trent Bridge, 1950. HS 308* Barbados v Trinidad, Bridgetown, 1943/44.
BBT 7–70 WI v E, Headingley, 1957. BB as above.
1000 RUNS (2 + 2) 1900 @ 63.33 in 1950/51.
RECORDS Added 574* for 4th wkt with C. L. Walcott, Barbados v Trinidad, Port of Spain, 1945/46, at time world record for any wkt (still second-highest), remains W Indian 4th-wkt record and highest unbroken fc stand. During HS (above) added 502* for 4th wkt with J. D. C. Goddard, at time world record for any wkt; only batsman to share in two fc stands of over 500 runs. Added 338 for 3rd wkt with E. D. Weekes, WI v E, Port of Spain, 1953/54; 399 for 4th wkt with G. S. Sobers, WI v E, Bridgetown, 1959/60 (in 570 mins over four days); and added 98* for 10th wkt with W. W. Hall, WI v I, Port of Spain, 1961/62, all W Indies Test records; in 1959/60 match batted 682 mins for 197*, longest Test inns for W Indies.
Carried bat for 191* in total of 372, WI v E, Trent Bridge, 1957.
Clubs: Radcliffe, Norton. MCC Hon. member. Knighted for services to cricket. Senator in Jamaican Parliament. Second cousin L. R. Worrell (Hants).

WORRELL, Lawrence Roosevelt
RHB, OB

Born St Thomas, Barbados, 28 Aug 1943. Educ Combermere S, Barbados. Debut 1969.
HAMPSHIRE (32) 1969–72.
HS 50 Hants v Kent, Canterbury, 1971.
BB 5–67 Hants v Lancs, Southampton, 1971.
Dorset 1969. Second cousin Sir F. M. M. Worrell (W Indies).

WORSLEY, Duncan Robert
LHB, RM

Born Bolton, Lancs, 18 July 1941. Educ Bolton S; St Edmund Hall, Oxford. Debut 1960.
LANCASHIRE (62) 1960–67. Cap 1966.
OXFORD UNIVERSITY (50) 1961–64 (Blue 1961–64).
HS 139 Oxford U v M'sex, The Parks, 1961.
BB 4–21 Lancs v Leics, Leicester, 1966.
1000 RUNS (1) 1498 @ 31.87 in 1964.
Club: Bradshaw.

WORTHINGTON, Thomas Stanley
————RHB, RFM————

Born Bolsover, Derbys, 21 Aug 1905. Died King's Lynn, Norfolk, 31 Aug 1973. Educ Netherthorpe GS. Debut 1924. *P. Wisden* 1937.
DERBYSHIRE (406) 1924–47. Cap.
ENGLAND (9) 1929/30–36/37. I 1936 (2). *A 1936/37 (3); NZ 1929/30 (4).*
OTHER TOUR Lord Tennyson's XI to India 1937/38.
HST 128 E v I, Oval, 1936. HS 238* Derbys v Sussex, Derby, 1937.
BBT 2–19 E v NZ, Christchurch, 1929/30. BB 8–29 (10–68 match) Derbys v Sussex, Derby, 1929.
1000 RUNS (10) 1774 @ 41.25 in 1937.
RECORD Added 212 for 6th wkt with G. M. Lee, Derbys v Essex, Chesterfield, 1932, county record.
Players v Gentlemen (2) 1928–32. Chief coach Lancs 1952–62. Northumberland 1949. Clubs: Bolsover Colliery, Todmorden. Nephew F. E. Marsh (Derbys).

WREGHITT, Peter Hadfield
————RHB, RM————

Born Sheffield, Yorks, 11 May 1929. Educ King Edward VII S, Sheffield; Keble C, Oxford. Debut 1951.
OXFORD UNIVERSITY (1) 1951.
HS 1 Oxford U v Free Foresters, The Parks, 1951.
BB 3–64 same match.
Club: Hampstead.

WRIGHT, Albert
————RHB, RM————

Born Arley, nr Nuneaton, Warwicks, 25 Aug 1941. Debut 1960. *P.*
WARWICKSHIRE (76) 1960–64. Cap 1962.
HS 27 Warwicks v Glam, Edgbaston, 1961.
BB 6–58 Warwicks v Surrey, Edgbaston, 1962.
100 WKTS (1) 116 @ 21.31 in 1962.
Clubs: Mitchells and Butlers, Gorseinon.

WRIGHT, Douglas Vivian Parson
————RHB, LBG————

Born Sidcup, Kent, 21 Aug 1914. Debut 1932. *P. Wisden* 1940.
KENT (397) 1932–57. Cap 1936. Benefit (£5254) 1950 and (£3602) 1957. Capt 1954–56.
ENGLAND (34) 1938–50/51. A 1938 (3), 1948 (1); SA 1947 (4); WI 1939 (3), 1950 (1); NZ 1949 (1); I 1946 (2). *A 1946/47*

(5), 1950/51 (5); SA 1938/39 (3), 1948/49 (3); NZ 1946/47 (1), 1950/51 (2).
OTHER TOUR Duke of Norfolk's XI to Jamaica 1956/57.
HST 45 E v NZ, Christchurch, 1950/51.
HS 84* Kent v Hants, Southampton, 1939.
BBT 7–105 E v A, Sydney, 1946/47. BB 9–47 Kent v Glos, Bristol, 1939.
100 WKTS (10) 177 @ 21.12 in 1947.
RECORD Performed the hat-trick on seven occasions, a world record. Returned 9–51 inns (15–163 match) Kent v Leics, Maidstone, 1949; 16–80 match, Kent v Som, Bath, 1939; and 15–173 match, Kent v Sussex, Hastings, 1947.
Players v Gentlemen (3) 1939–50. Former professional coach Charterhouse (from 1958). MCC Hon. member.

WRIGHT, John Geoffrey
————LHB, RM————

Born Darfield, N Zealand, 5 July 1954. Educ Christ's C, Christchurch, N Zealand; Otago U. Debut 1975/76.
N ZEALAND DOMESTIC Northern Districts (43) 1975/76–.
DERBYSHIRE (122) 1977–. Cap 1977.
NEW ZEALAND (31) 1977/78–83/84. E 1977/78 (3), 1983/84 (3); A 1981/82 (3); WI 1979/80 (3); I 1980/81 (3); P 1978/79 (3); SL 1982/83 (2). *E 1978 (2), 1983 (3); A 1980/81 (3); SL 1983/84 (3).*
OTHER TOURS D. H. Robins' XI to Sri Lanka 1977/78. International XI to Jamaica 1982/83.
HST 141 NZ v A, Christchurch, 1981/82.
HS 190 Derbys v Yorks, Derby, 1982.
1000 RUNS (6) 1830 @ 55.45 in 1982.
RECORD Added 195 for 2nd wkt with G. P. Howarth, NZ v P, Napier, 1978/79, N Zealand Test record.

WRIGHT, John Vaughan
————RHB————

Born Colchester, Essex, 31 Dec 1935. Educ Colchester RGS. Debut 1962.
ESSEX (4) 1962–67.
HS 40 Essex v Northants, Colchester, 1962.

WRIGHT, Lynden Norman Gordon
————RHB, LB/RM————

Born Kingston, Jamaica, 18 Apr 1950. Debut 1968/69.
W INDIES DOMESTIC Jamaica 1968/69–78/79.
TOUR Jamaica to England 1970.

HS 33 Jamaica v Combined Islands, Castries, 1969/70.
BB 5–36 Jamaica v Barbados, Mobay, 1974/75.
Club: Boy's Town. Half-brother O. G. Smith (W Indies).

WRIGHT, Malcolm Graeme
————LHB————

Born Kandy, Ceylon, 2 June 1926. Educ Oxford U (St Catharine's Society). Debut 1950.
OXFORD UNIVERSITY (2) 1950.
HS 17 Oxford U v Warwicks, The Parks, 1950.

WRIGHT, Stephen
————RHB————

Born Muswell Hill, N London, 4 Feb 1952. Educ Mill Hill; Emmanuel C, Cambridge. Debut 1973.
CAMBRIDGE UNIVERSITY (10) 1973 (Blue).
HS 41 Cambridge U v Notts, Trent Bridge, 1973.
Soccer: Blue.

WRIGHTSON, Roger Wilfred
————LHB, occ WK————

Born Elsecar, Yorks, 29 Oct 1939. Educ Palmer's S, Grays; Loughborough C. Debut 1965.
ESSEX (12) 1965–67.
HS 84 Essex v Warwicks, Clacton, 1965.
Cumberland 1970–71. Clubs: Interknit, Undercliffe.

WRIGLEY, Michael Harold
————RHB, RFM————

Born Knutsford, Cheshire, 30 July 1924. Educ Harrow; Worcester C, Oxford. Debut 1946.
COMBINED SERVICES (1) 1946.
OXFORD UNIVERSITY (14) 1948–50 (Blue 1949).
MCC (1) 1948.
HS 17 Oxford U v Yorks, The Parks, 1949.
BB 6–57 Oxford U v Surrey, Oval, 1949.
Lancashire 2nd XI.

WYATT, Gerald
————RHB, WK————

Born New Mills, Derbys, 4 June 1933. Debut 1954. *P.*
DERBYSHIRE (11) 1954–60.
HS 59 Derbys v Oxford U, The Parks, 1958.
Club: David Brown.

WYATT, Julian George
——————RHB——————

Born Paulton, Som, 19 June 1963. Educ Wells Cathedral S. Debut 1983.
SOMERSET (22) 1983–.
HS 103 Som v Oxford U, The Parks, 1984.

WYATT, Robert Elliott Storey
——————RHB, RMF——————

Born Milford, Surrey, 2 May 1901. Educ King Henry VIII S, Coventry. Debut 1923. *Wisden* 1930.
WARWICKSHIRE (404) 1923–39. Cap 1923. Capt 1930–37.
WORCESTERSHIRE (86) 1946–51. Cap 1946. Joint capt 1949; capt 1950–51.
FREE FORESTERS (4) 1952–57.
ENGLAND (40) 1927/28–36/37. A 1930 (1), 1934 (4); SA 1929 (2), 1935 (5); WI 1933 (2); I 1936 (1). *A 1932/33 (5), 1936/37 (2); SA 1927/28 (5), 1930/31 (5); WI 1929/30 (2), 1934/35 (4); NZ 1932/33 (2).* Capt 16.
OTHER TOURS MCC to India and Ceylon 1926/27. Sir T. E. W. Brinckman's XI to S America 1937/38.
HST 149 E v SA, Trent Bridge, 1935. HS 232 Warwicks v Derbys, Edgbaston, 1937.
BBT 3–4 E v SA, Durban, 1927/28. BB 7–43 Warwicks v M'sex, Lord's, 1926.
1000 runs (17 + 1) 2630 @ 53.67 in 1929. 2000 runs (5).
Scored 1485 runs and took 92 wkts in 1926.
RECORD Added 228 for 8th wkt with A. J. W. Croom, Warwicks v Worcs, Dudley, 1925, county record.
Final fc match, in 1957, at age of 56. Gentlemen v Players (23) 1926–47. Selected for MCC to India 1939/40 (cancelled owing to war). Test selector 1949–53 (chairman 1950). Clubs: Meriden, Moseley. MCC committee 1951–53. MCC Hon. member. Author of *The Ins and Outs of Cricket* (1936), an instructional book, and autobiography *Three Straight Sticks* (1951).

WYKES, James Cochrane
——————RHB, WK——————

Born Leigh-on-Sea, Essex, 19 Oct 1913. Educ Oundle; Cambridge U. Debut 1946.
SCOTLAND (1) 1946.
HS 23 Scotland v Ireland, Greenock, 1946.
Club: Grange.

YAJURVINDRASINH, Jaswantsinh
——————RHB, RM——————

Born Rajkot, India, 1 Aug 1952. Educ Rajkumar C; Wadia C; Poona U. Debut 1971/72.
INDIA DOMESTIC Maharashtra 1971/72–78/79 (capt 1976/77–78/79), Saurashtra 1979/80–81/82 (capt 1979/80–81/82).
INDIA (4) 1976/77–79/80. E 1976/77 (2); A 1979/80 (1). *E 1979 (1).*
HST 43* I v E, Oval, 1979. HS 214 Saurashtra v Maharashtra, Satara, 1979/80.
BB 7–20 (10–87 match) Maharashtra v Saurashtra, Pune, 1977/78.
RECORDS Took five catches in inns and seven in match, I v E, Bangalore, 1976/77 (his Test debut), both equalling the Test record for a non-wicketkeeper.

YALLOP, Graham Neil
——————LHB——————

Born Balwyn, Victoria, Australia, 7 Oct 1952. Debut 1972/73.
AUSTRALIA DOMESTIC Victoria (81) 1972/73–.
AUSTRALIA (38) 1975/76–83/84. E 1978/79 (6); WI 1975/76 (3); I 1977/78 (1); P 1978/79 (1), 1981/82 (1), 1983/84 (5). *E 1980 (1), 1981 (6); WI 1977/78 (4); I 1979/80 (6); P 1979/80 (3); SL 1982/83 (1).* Capt 7.
OTHER TOUR Australia to Sri Lanka 1980/81.
HST 268 A v P, Melbourne, 1983/84 (batting for 716 mins). HS as above.
BB 4–63 Australians v Essex, Chelmsford, 1981.
RECORD Scored 1254 runs @ 69.66 in Sheffield Shield season, in 1982/83, a record.
1000 RUNS (0 + 2) 1418 @ 67.52 in 1982/83.
Clubs: Richmond (Melbourne), Walsall (England).

YARDLEY, Norman Walter Dransfield
——————RHB, RM——————

Born Barnsley, Yorks, 19 Mar 1915. Educ St Peter's, York; St John's C, Cambridge. Debut 1935. *Wisden* 1948.
CAMBRIDGE UNIVERSITY (45) 1935–38 (Blue 1935–38). Capt 1938.
YORKSHIRE (302) 1936–55. Cap. Capt 1948–55.
ENGLAND (20) 1938/39–50. A 1948 (5); SA 1947 (5); WI 1950 (3). *A 1946/47 (5); SA 1938/39 (1); NZ 1946/47 (1).* Capt 14.

OTHER TOURS Lord Tennyson's XI to India 1937/38.
HST 99 E v SA, Trent Bridge, 1947. HS 183* Yorks v Hants, Headingley, 1951.
BBT 3–67 E v A, Melbourne, 1946/47. BB 6–29 MCC v Cambridge U, Lord's, 1946.
1000 RUNS (8) 1906 @ 44.32 in 1947. Gentlemen v Players (16) 1937–55. England Test selector 1951–54 (chairman 1951–52). President Yorks 1981–84; Yorks committee to 1984. Club: Harrogate. Cricket writer and journalist. Hockey: Blue. Squash: six times North of England champion.

YARDLEY, Thomas *James*
——————LHB, RM, occ WK——————

Born Chaddesley Corbett, Worcs, 27 Oct 1946. Educ King Charles I GS. Debut 1967.
WORCESTERSHIRE (153) 1967–75. Cap 1972.
NORTHAMPTONSHIRE (107) 1976–82. Cap 1978.
HS 135 Worcs v Notts, Worcester, 1973.
1000 RUNS (1) 1066 @ 30.45 in 1971.
Club: Kidderminster.

YARNOLD, Henry (Hugo)
——————RHB, WK——————

Born Worcester, 6 July 1917. Died, after road-traffic accident, Leamington Spa, Warwicks, 13 Aug 1974. Debut 1938. P.
WORCESTERSHIRE (283) 1938–55. Cap 1947. Benefit (£2700) 1954.
HS 68 North v South, Kingston, 1947.
RECORD Made six stumpings (seven dismissals) in inns, Worcs v Scotland, Broughty Ferry, 1951, a world record. Dismissed 110 batsmen (63 ct, 47 st) in 1949, third-highest season's total for a wicketkeeper.
Fc umpire 1959–74.

Mulkraj YASHPAL SHARMA
——————RHB, RM——————

Born Ludhiana, India, 11 Aug 1954. Educ Arya HS, Ludhiana; Punjab U. Debut 1973/74.
INDIA DOMESTIC Punjab 1973/74–.
INDIA (37) 1979–83/84. E 1979/80 (1), 1981/82 (2); A 1979/80 (6); WI 1983/84 (1); P 1979/80 (6), 1983/84 (3); SL 1982/83 (1). *E 1979 (3), 1982 (3); A 1980/81 (3); WI 1982/83 (5); NZ 1980/81 (1); P 1982/83 (2).*
OTHER TOUR India to Pakistan 1978/79.
HST 140 I v E, Madras, 1981/82. HS 173 N Zone v S Zone, Bangalore, 1977/78.
BB 3–98 Punjab v Karnataka, Bangalore, 1981/82.

RECORD During HST (above) added 316 for 3rd wkt with G. R. Visvanath, an India Test record.

YATES, Kenneth Clement
RHB, WK

Born Keetmanshoop, SW Africa, 4 Aug 1938. Educ Natal U; Christ's C, Cambridge. Debut 1961.
CAMBRIDGE UNIVERSITY (1) 1961.
No runs.

YAWAR SAEED
RHB, RM

Born Lahore, India, 22 Jan 1935. Debut 1953. *P.*
SOMERSET (50) 1953–55. Cap 1954.
INDIA DOMESTIC Punjab 1953/54–1958/59.
HS 64 Som v Northants, Northampton, 1954 and 64 v M'sex, Bath, 1955.
BB 5–32 President's XI v Chief Commissioner's XI, Karachi, 1958/59.
Manager Pakistan to N Zealand 1984/85. Club: Richmond. Father Mohammed Mian Saeed (Pakistan); brother-in-law Fazal Mahmood (Pakistan).

YEABSLEY, Douglas Ian
LHB, LMF

Born Exeter, Devon, 3 Jan 1942. Educ Exeter S. Debut 1974.
MINOR COUNTIES (4) 1974–79.
HS 14* Minor Counties v W Indians, Torquay, 1976.
BB 3–45 Minor Counties v Pakistanis, Jesmond, 1974.
Devon 1959–. Club: Radlett.

YEATMAN, Rex Herbert
RHB, RM

Born Kew, London, 4 Oct 1919. Educ St Paul's. Debut 1946.
SURREY (5) 1946–47.
COMBINED SERVICES (1) 1946.
HS 21 Surrey v Combined Services, Kingston, 1946.

YOULL, Michael
LHB, SLA

Born Newcastle upon Tyne, 26 Apr 1939. Educ Heanor GS. Debut 1956. *P.*
WARWICKSHIRE (4) 1956–57.
HS 9 Warwicks v Combined Services, Portland Road, Edgbaston, 1957.
BB 5–99 Warwicks v Scotland, Edgbaston, 1956.

Northumberland 1962–81. Club: Northumberland County.

YOUNG, Douglas *Martin*
RHB

Born Coalville, Leics, 15 Apr 1924. Debut 1946. *P.*
WORCESTERSHIRE (31) 1946–48.
GLOUCESTERSHIRE (435) 1949–64. Cap 1950. Benefit (£4600) 1963.
TOUR Commonwealth XI to Rhodesia 1962/63.
HS 198 Glos v Oxford U, The Parks, 1962.
BB 2–35 Glos v Surrey, Oval, 1964.
1000 RUNS (13) 2179 @ 41.11 in 1959.
RECORD During HS (above) added 395 for 1st wkt with R. B. Nicholls, county record.
Sports reporter BBC West after retirement; now cricket commentator in S Africa.

YOUNG, John Albert
RHB, SLA

Born Paddington, London, 14 Oct 1912. Debut 1933. *P.*
MIDDLESEX (292) 1933–56. Cap 1946.
Benefit (£5000) 1952.
ENGLAND (8) 1947–49. A 1948 (3); SA 1947 (1); NZ 1949 (2). *SA 1948/49 (2).*
HST 10* E v SA, J'burg, 1948/49. HS 62 M'sex v Yorks, Bramall Lane, Sheffield, 1949.
BBT 3–65 E v NZ, Lord's, 1949. BB 9–55 England XI v Commonwealth XI, Hastings, 1951.
100 WKTS (8) 163 @ 19.88 in 1952.
Club: Highgate.

YOUNG, Robert William
RHB

Born Perth, Scotland, 2 Jan 1933. Educ Perth Academy. Debut 1962.
SCOTLAND (6) 1962–64.
HS 96 Scotland v Ireland, Greenock, 1962.
Club: Perthshire.

YOUNG, Stuart Harrison
LHB, RMF

Born Blackhall, Co Durham, 6 July 1938. Debut 1959.
MINOR COUNTIES (3) 1959–69.
HS 14 Minor Counties v W Indians, Longton, Stoke on Trent, 1969.
BB 4–44 same match.
Durham 1956–72. Clubs: Blackhall, Hordern CW, Chester-le-Street, Darlington, South Shields, Philadelphia, Bishop Auckland.

YOUNGSON, George William
RHB, RFM

Born Aberdeen, Scotland, 12 Dec 1919. Died Aberdeen, Scotland, 8 Dec 1982. Educ Robert Gordon's C, Aberdeen; Aberdeen U. Debut 1947.
SCOTLAND (19) 1947–55.
HS 18 Scotland v Ireland, Glasgow, 1948.
BB 7–42 (11–119 match) Scotland v Ireland, Perth, 1950.
Club: Aberdeenshire.

YOUNIS AHMED, Mohammed
LHB, LM

Born Jullundur, India, 20 Oct 1947. Educ Moslem HS, Lahore; Government C, Lahore. Debut 1961/62.
PAKISTAN DOMESTIC Combined Education Boards, Lahore Education Board, Lahore, Karachi, Pakistan International Airlines, 1961/62–69/70.
SURREY (262) 1965–78. Cap 1969.
WORCESTERSHIRE (85) 1979–83. Cap 1979.
GLAMORGAN (21) 1984.
AUSTRALIA DOMESTIC South Australia (6) 1972/73.
PAKISTAN (2) NZ 1969/70.
TOURS Cavaliers to Jamaica 1969/70. Commonwealth XI to Pakistan 1970/71. D. H. Robins' XI to S Africa 1973/74, 1974/75. International Wanderers to S Africa 1974/75, 1975/76.
HST 62 P v NZ, Karachi, 1969/70. HS 221* Worcs v Notts, Trent Bridge, 1979.
BB 4–10 Surrey v Cambridge U, Fenner's, 1975.
1000 RUNS (11) 1760 @ 47.56 in 1969.
RECORD During HS (above) added 281 for 4th wkt with J. A. Ormrod, county record.
Barred from Pakistani cricket because of S African connections. Dismissed by Worcs in 1983 for disciplinary reasons. Half-brother Saeed Ahmed (Pakistan).

YOUNUS BADAT
RHB

Born Northern Rhodesia, 1943. Debut 1975.
EAST AFRICA to England (1) 1975.
HS 3 E Africa v Sri Lanka, Taunton, 1975.

YUILE, Bryan William
RHB, SLA

Born Palmerston North, N Zealand, 29 Oct 1941. Educ Palmerston North HS. Debut 1959/60.

N ZEALAND DOMESTIC Central Districts (61) 1959/60–71/72.
NEW ZEALAND (17) 1962/63–69/70. E 1962/63 (2); WI 1968/69 (3); I 1967/68 (1); P 1964/65 (3). *E 1965 (1); I 1964/65 (3), 1969/70 (1); P 1964/65 (1), 1969/70 (2)*.
OTHER TOURS N Zealand to Australia and S Africa 1961/62. N Zealand to Australia 1967/68. N Zealand to England 1969.
HST 64 NZ v E, Auckland, 1962/63. HS 146 C Districts v Canterbury, Napier, 1967/68.
BBT 4–43 NZ v P, Auckland, 1964/65. BB 9–100 C Districts v Canterbury, New Plymouth, 1965/66.

YUSUF, Mumtaz Mohammed
——————RHB, OB——————

Born Colombo, Ceylon, 1 June 1950. Debut 1983/84.
SRI LANKA DOMESTIC Sri Lankan Board President's XI (1) 1983/84.
TOUR Sri Lanka to England 1984.
HS 2* Sri Lankans v Notts, Trent Bridge, 1984.

ZAHEER ABBAS, Syed
——————RHB, OB——————

Born Sialkot, India, 24 July 1947. Educ Government S, Karachi; Islamia C; Karachi U. Debut 1965/66. *Wisden* 1972.
PAKISTAN DOMESTIC Karachi, Public Works Department, Dawood Industries, Sind, Pakistan International Airlines, 1965/66–.
GLOUCESTERSHIRE (205) 1972–. Cap 1975. Benefit 1983.
PAKISTAN (69) 1969/70–83/84. E 1972/73 (2), 1983/84 (3); A 1979/80 (2), 1982/83 (3); WI 1974/75 (2), 1980/81 (3); NZ 1969/70 (1), 1976/77 (3); I 1978/79 (3), 1982/83 (6); SL 1981/82 (1). *E 1971 (3), 1974 (3), 1982 (3); A 1972/73 (3), 1976/77 (3), 1978/79 (2), 1981/82 (2), 1983/84 (5); WI 1976/77 (3); NZ 1972/73 (3), 1978/79 (2); I 1979/80 (5), 1983/84 (3)*. Capt 9.
OTHER TOURS World XI to Australia 1971/72. Pakistan to Sri Lanka 1975/76.
HST 274 P v E, Edgbaston, 1971. HS as above.
BB 5–15 Dawood Industries v Railways, Lahore, 1975/76.
1000 RUNS (11 + 6). 2554 @ 75.11 in 1976.
RECORDS Scored 100 fc centuries, the first Asian to do so, reaching the target in a Test match (215 P v I, Lahore, 1982/83), the second batsman to achieve this, after G. Boycott. Scored a century in each inns of a match on eight occasions, a world record, including a century and a double-century on four occasions, also world record (216* and 156* Glos v Surrey, Oval, 1976; 230* and 104* Glos v Kent, Canterbury, 1976; 205* and 108* Glos v Sussex, Cheltenham, 1977; and 215* and 150* Glos v Som, Bath, 1981). Match aggregate of 372 runs without being dismissed, in above match at the Oval in 1976, a record for English fc cricket. Scored 4747 runs @ 46.53 in Tests, a Pakistan record. Aggregate of 583 runs @ 194.33, P v I, 1978/79, a record for a three-match series. Added 291 for 2nd wkt with Mushtaq Mohammed, P v E, Edgbaston, 1971, a Pakistan Test record; added 353 for 6th wkt with Salah-ud-Din, Karachi v East Pakistan, Karachi, 1968/69, Pakistan fc record.
Hit D. Breakwell for 30 runs (466626) in one over, Glos v Som, Taunton, 1979. Scored centuries in four consecutive fc inns twice, in 1970/71 and 1982/83.

ZUILL, Andrew Morison
——————RHB——————

Born Falkirk, Scotland, 22 Apr 1937. Educ Merchiston Castle S. Debut 1962.
SCOTLAND (9) 1962–79.
HS 62 Scotland v Ireland, Glasgow, 1968.
Club: Stenhousemuir.

ZULFIQAR AHMED
——————RHB, OB——————

Born Lahore, India, 22 Nov 1926. Debut 1946/47.
INDIA DOMESTIC North Zone 1946/47.
PAKISTAN DOMESTIC Bahawalpur, Pakistan International Airlines, 1953/54–65/66.
PAKISTAN (9) 1952/53–56/57. A 1956/57 (1); NZ 1955/56 (3). *E 1954 (2); I 1952/53 (3)*.
OTHER TOUR Pakistan to W Indies 1957/58 (covered tour as journalist, but played in one match).
HST 63* P v I, Madras, 1952/53. HS 73 Bahawalpur v Punjab A, Bahawalpur, 1957/58.
BBT 6–42 (11–79 match) P v NZ, Karachi, 1955/56. BB 7–69 (12–114 match) Pakistanis v Kent, Canterbury, 1954.

ZULFIQAR ALI
——————RHB, RM——————

Born Mombassa, Kenya, 1947. Debut 1973/74.
EAST AFRICA (2) 1973/74–75.
TOUR E Africa to England 1975.
HS 20 East Africa v Sri Lanka, Taunton, 1975.
BB 3–43 East Africa v MCC, Nairobi, 1973/74.

FIRST-CLASS AND
TEST CAREER RECORDS

	Career span	M	I	NO	Runs	HS	Avge	100	Runs	Wkts	Avge
			BATTING						BOWLING		
Aamer Hameed	1972/73–79	53	69	10	872	103	14.77	2	4138	110	37.61
Abberley, R.N.	1954–79	261	439	27	10082	117*	24.47	3	294	5	58.80
Abbey, D.R.	1967	2	2	0	14	12	7.00	–	23	0	–
Abbott, A.W.	1946	1	2	0	5	5	2.50	–	8	0	–
Abdul Qadir	1975/76–	126	153	30	2425	112	19.72	1	13165	620	21.23
T		27	34	4	454	50	15.13	–	3380	96	35.21
Abell, J.N.	1952–53	3	5	0	56	25	11.20	–	–	–	–
Abell, R.B.	1967	1	–	–	–	–	–	–	112	4	28.00
Abell, T.G.	1954	1	2	1	4	4*	–	–	1	0	–
Abid Ali, S.	1959/60–78/79	213	334	35	8741	173*	29.23	13	11336	397	28.55
T		29	53	3	1018	81	20.36	–	1980	47	42.12
Ablack, R.K.	1946–49	3	4	2	24	16	12.00	–	220	6	36.67
Abrahams, J.	1973–	191	294	40	7293	201*	28.71	9	2472	47	52.60
Acfield, D.L.	1966–	376	377	191	1545	42	8.31	–	24214	876	27.64
Ackerman, H.M.	1963/64–81/82	234	409	33	12219	208	32.49	20	1400	32	43.75
A'Court, D.G.	1960–63	49	68	31	420	47*	11.35	–	3890	145	26.82
Adams, K.	1954	1	2	0	34	34	–	–	–	–	–
Adcock, N.A.T.	1952/53–62/63	99	117	35	451	41	5.50	–	6989	405	17.25
T		26	39	12	146	24	5.40	–	2195	104	21.10
Adderley, C.H.	1946	5	8	2	27	12	4.50	–	255	4	63.75
Addison, J.P.	1983	1	2	0	67	51	33.50	–	–	–	–
Adhikari, H.R.	1936/37–59/60	151	234	28	8628	230*	41.88	17	1820	49	37.14
T		21	36	8	872	114*	31.14	1	82	3	27.33
Aers, D.R.	1966–68	15	26	2	288	48	12.00	–	882	18	49.00
Afaq Hussain	1957/58–73/74	67	83	24	1448	122*	24.54	1	4156	214	19.42
T		2	4	4	66	35*	–	–	106	1	–
Afford, J.A.	1984	3	–	–	–	–	–	–	256	7	36.57
Aftab Baloch	1969/70–	163	249	41	8717	428	41.91	20	6579	213	30.89
T		2	3	1	97	60*	48.50	–	17	0	–
Aftab Gul	1964/65–77/78	100	173	7	6131	140	36.92	11	465	14	33.21
T		6	8	0	182	33	22.75	–	4	0	–
Agnew, J.P.	1978–	81	79	14	600	56	9.23	–	6446	209	30.84
T		2	3	2	8	5	–	–	274	4	68.50
Ainsworth, M.L.Y.	1946–64	49	86	2	2034	137	24.22	3	126	2	63.00
Aitchison, J.	1946–63	50	87	2	2786	190*	32.78	5	3	0	–
Aitchison, J.E.	1949–50	3	3	0	6	4	2.00	–	88	3	29.33
Aizazuddin, F.S.	1957–68/69	44	81	6	1875	187	25.00	3	815	22	37.04
Alabaster, J.C.	1955/56–71/72	143	212	30	2427	82	13.34	–	12688	500	25.38
T		21	34	6	272	34	9.71	–	1863	49	38.02
Alderman, A.E.	1928–48	318	529	52	12376	175	25.95	12	171	4	42.75
Alderman, T.M.	1974/75–	110	121	61	537	52*	8.95	–	10006	414	24.17
T		18	27	14	79	21*	6.08	–	2258	70	32.26
Alderson, R.	1948–49	2	2	0	55	55	27.50	–	–	–	–
Aldridge, K.J.	1956–63/64	79	112	35	511	24*	6.63	–	6033	256	23.56
Alexander, F.C.M.	1952–60/61	92	141	30	3238	108	29.17	1	7	0	–
T		25	38	6	961	108	30.03	1	–	–	–
Alexander, F.R.	1951	2	3	0	15	8	5.00	–	–	–	–
Alim-ud-Din	1942/43–67/68	140	238	16	7276	142	32.77	14	959	40	23.97
T		25	45	2	1091	109	25.37	2	75	1	–
Allan, D.W.	1955/56–66	54	64	12	764	56	14.69	–	–	–	–
T		5	7	1	75	40*	12.50	–	–	–	–
Allan, J.	1951	1	2	0	2	2	1.00	–	78	3	26.00
Allan, J.M.	1953–72	179	268	45	4988	153	22.37	5	11179	435	25.70
Allan, W.R.	1950	3	6	0	73	30	12.17	–	–	–	–
Allbrook, M.E.	1975–80	47	56	19	320	39	8.64	–	3504	76	46.10
Alldis, J.S.	1970	2	4	1	7	4*	2.33	–	37	1	–

	Career span	M	I	NO	Runs	HS	Avge	100	Runs	Wkts	Avge
			BATTING						BOWLING		
Allen, A.W.	1932–47	35	64	1	1928	144	30.60	4	–	–	–
Allen, B.O.	1932–51	307	512	20	14195	220	28.85	14	429	3	143.00
Allen, D.A.	1953–72	457	641	147	9291	121*	18.81	1	28585	1209	23.64
T	39	51	15	918	88	25.50	–	3779	122	30.97	
Allen, G.O.B.	1921–54	265	376	54	9232	180	28.67	11	17518	778	21.22
T	25	33	2	750	122	24.19	1	2379	81	29.37	
Allen, J.W.	1948	1	1	0	0	0	–	–	–	–	–
Allen, M.H.J.	1956–66	193	231	56	1723	59	9.85	–	11219	500	22.44
Allerton, J.W.O.	1967–69	15	26	1	605	67	24.20	–	7	0	–
Alley, W.E.	1945/46–68	400	682	67	19612	221*	31.88	31	17421	768	22.68
Alleyne, H.L.	1978/79–	54	60	12	549	72	11.44	–	4546	177	25.68
Allin, A.W.	1976	13	16	8	108	32	13.50	–	1011	44	22.97
Allison, D.F.	1970	6	9	2	48	21	6.86	–	–	–	–
Allom, A.T.C.	1960	5	8	3	94	34*	18.80	–	439	15	29.27
Allott, P.J.W.	1978–	112	111	29	1135	52*	13.84	–	8018	303	26.46
T	9	13	2	186	52*	16.91	–	787	21	37.48	
Altham, R.J.L.	1947–48	2	3	0	14	14	4.67	–	–	–	–
Alwyn, N.	1961	5	10	0	141	41	14.10	–	–	–	–
Amarnath, M.	1966/67–	191	300	49	10425	207	41.53	22	8386	261	32.13
T	42	72	5	2660	120	39.70	7	1525	27	56.48	
Amarnath, Lala	1929/30–60/61	183	281	33	10323	262	41.62	31	10481	457	22.93
T	24	40	4	878	118	24.38	1	1481	45	32.91	
Ames, L.E.G.	1926–51	592	951	95	37248	295	43.51	102	721	22	32.27
T	47	72	12	2434	149	40.56	8	–	–	–	
Amiss, D.L.	1960–	581	1004	112	39118	262*	43.85	91	718	18	39.89
T	50	88	10	3612	262*	46.30	11	–	–	–	
Anderson, E.W.	1961–62	12	15	5	38	13*	3.80	–	727	18	40.39
Anderson, I.J.	1966–82	19	33	8	947	147	37.88	3	249	17	14.65
Anderson, I.M.	1951–53	5	8	0	114	40	14.25	–	–	–	–
Anderson, I.S.	1978–	93	146	21	2994	112	23.95	2	1281	20	64.05
Anderson, J.D.	1955	2	3	2	4	4*	–	–	118	4	29.50
Anderson, R.M.B.	1946	1	1	0	0	0	–	–	60	0	–
Anderson, R.W.	1967/68–81/82	111	197	14	5609	155	30.65	8	154	5	30.80
T	9	18	0	423	92	23.50	–	–	–	–	
Anderson, W.A.	1946	1	1	0	14	14	–	–	–	–	–
Anderton, F.M.	1953	3	5	1	64	38	16.00	–	11	0	–
Andrew, C.R.	1984–	9	18	1	405	101*	23.82	1	568	6	94.67
Andrew, F.J.	1959–63	21	26	7	53	6	2.79	–	1366	57	23.96
Andrew, K.V.	1952–66	390	476	160	4230	76	13.38	–	31	2	15.50
T	2	4	1	29	15	9.67	–	–	–	–	
Andrew, S.J.W.	1984–	7	6	4	12	6*	6.00	–	530	11	48.18
Andrews, C.J.	1938–48	7	10	1	127	29	14.11	–	–	–	–
Andrews, W.H.R.	1930–47	231	371	54	5000	80	15.78	–	18033	770	23.42
Angell, F.L.	1947–56	132	251	11	4596	114	19.15	1	31	0	–
Angus, T.	1956–57	7	11	5	49	18*	8.17	–	353	23	15.34
Anson, G.F.	1947	10	18	0	460	106	25.55	1	–	–	–
Anton, J.H.H.	1949–50	14	24	1	361	45	15.68	–	–	–	–
Antrobus, E.P.	1963	2	4	0	53	31	13.25	–	20	0	–
Anurasiri, S.D.	1984–	4	3	1	5	5	2.50	–	336	–	–
Appleyard, F.	1939–50	18	25	14	74	15*	6.72	–	1210	30	40.33
Appleyard, R.	1950–58	152	145	54	776	63	8.52	–	10965	708	15.48
T	9	9	6	51	19*	17.00	–	554	31	17.87	
Apte, A.L.	1955/56–70/71	58	91	8	2782	165	33.51	6	76	2	38.00
T	1	2	0	15	8	7.50	–	–	–	–	
Archer, K.A.	1946/47–56/57	82	139	13	3774	134	29.95	3	698	13	53.69
T	5	9	0	234	48	26.00	–	–	–	–	

	Career span	M		I	NO	Runs	HS	Avge	100		Runs	Wkts	Avge
							BATTING					BOWLING	
Archer, R.G.	1951/52–58/59	98		137	19	3768	148	31.93	4		5958	255	23.36
	T	19		30	1	713	128	24.58	1		1318	48	27.45
Ardington, A.J.	1965	3		5	0	29	11	5.80	–		–	–	–
Arenhold, J.A.	1953–59/60	33		47	7	403	45	10.07	–		2226	82	27.14
Arif Butt	1960/61–77/78	97		154	16	4017	180	29.10	4		5386	201	26.79
	T	3		5	0	59	20	11.80	–		288	14	20.57
Arkell, R.H.M.	1953–55	3		5	1	18	10	4.50	–		125	6	20.83
Armitage, A.K.	1950–51	7		12	2	348	115	34.80	1		–	–	–
Armstrong, G. de L.	1973/74–77/78	40		54	12	642	93	15.28	–		3199	91	35.15
Armstrong, P.A.N.	1982	1		2	0	34	34	17.00	–		–	–	–
Armstrong, R.L.G.	1948–53	5		10	1	118	29*	13.11	–		129	6	21.50
Armstrong, T.R.	1929–50	58		83	33	314	28*	6.28	–		3239	133	24.35
Arnold, G.G.	1963–82	365		379	90	3952	73	13.67	–		24761	1130	21.91
	T	34		46	11	421	59	12.02	–		3254	115	28.29
Arnold, J.	1929–50	402		710	45	21831	227	32.82	37		1182	17	69.52
	T	1		2	0	34	34	17.00	–		–	–	–
Arnold, P.	1951–60	174		306	15	8013	122	27.53	7		85	3	28.33
Arrowsmith, R.	1976–79	43		40	12	286	39	10.21	–		2796	99	28.24
Arshad Pervez	1969/70–	127		214	18	8104	251*	41.35	23		658	17	38.71
Asgarali, N.	1940/41–62/63	50		89	5	2761	141*	32.87	7		980	23	42.61
	T	2		4	0	62	29	15.50	–		–	–	–
Ash, D.L.	1965	3		3	0	22	12	7.33	–		22	0	–
Ashdown, W.H.	1914–47	488		812	77	22589	332	30.73	39		19551	602	32.47
Ashenden, M.	1959–65	34		41	12	70	15	2.41	–		2095	64	32.73
Ashman, J.R.	1951–54	34		41	15	149	24	5.73	–		2546	61	41.73
Ashmore, W.S.	1946–48	3		5	3	24	15*	12.00	–		129	3	43.00
Ashworth, D.A.	1966–67	7		13	0	173	67	13.31	–		–	–	–
Asif Ahmad	1959/60–71/72	60		94	13	2140	148	26.41	4		97	0	–
Asif Din, M.	1981–	65		101	11	2243	102	24.92	1		1845	33	55.91
Asif Iqbal	1959/60–82	441		703	76	23375	196	37.28	45		8776	291	30.15
	T	58		99	7	3575	175	38.85	11		1502	53	28.33
Asif Masood	1963/64–76/77	121		119	46	635	34	8.69	–		8854	305	29.02
	T	16		19	10	93	30*	10.33	–		1568	38	41.26
Aslett, D.G.	1981–	64		113	11	3910	221*	38.33	9		653	10	65.30
Aspinall, R.	1946–50	37		48	8	763	75*	19.75	–		2670	131	20.38
Asquith, J.P.K.	1953–54	5		8	1	46	12	6.56	–		–	–	–
Athey, C.W.J.	1976–	189		320	25	8615	134	29.20	15		1114	21	53.05
	T	3		6	0	17	9	2.83	–		–	–	–
Atkins, G.	1958–61	20		36	3	394	49	11.94	–		96	2	48.00
Atkinson, C.R.M.	1959–67	164		240	41	3796	97	19.08	–		5982	192	31.26
Atkinson, D.st.E.	1946/47–60/61	78		115	16	2812	219	28.40	5		5290	201	26.32
	T	22		35	6	922	219	31.79	1		1647	47	35.04
Atkinson, G.	1954–69	347		608	41	17654	190	31.13	27		260	5	52.00
Atkinson, T.	1957–60	64		104	19	1127	48	13.26	–		5157	116	44.46
August, G.L.B.	1950–53	2		4	0	41	27	10.25	–		–	–	–
Avery, A.V.	1935–54	269		455	35	14137	224	33.66	25		627	9	69.66
Aworth, C.J.	1973–76	56		104	6	2552	135	26.04	3		476	7	68.00
Axford, W.I.	1960	2		2	0	13	7	6.50	–		–	–	–
Azad, Kirti	1977/78–	63		89	7	2733	186	33.33	7		3041	103	29.52
	T	7		12	0	135	24	11.25	–		373	4	93.25
Azmat Rana	1969/70–	95		143	18	6060	206*	48.48	16		85	0	–
	T	1		1	0	2	2	–	–		–	–	–

FIRST-CLASS AND TEST CAREER RECORDS

	Career span	M	I	NO	Runs	HS	Avge	100	Runs	Wkts	Avge
					BATTING				BOWLING		
Bacchus, S.F.A.F.	1971/72–	95	153	13	5126	250	36.61	7	27	0	–
	T	19	30	0	782	250	26.06	1	3	0	–
Bacher, A.	1959/60-73/74	120	212	10	7894	235	39.07	18	87	2	43.50
	T	12	22	1	679	73	32.33	–	–	–	–
Badcock, F.T.	1924/25-45	53	96	3	2383	155	25.62	4	5211	221	23.57
	T	7	9	2	137	64	19.57	–	610	16	38.12
Baig, Abbas Ali	1954/55-75/76	235	391	29	12367	224*	34.16	21	432	9	48.00
	T	10	18	0	428	112	23.77	1	15	0	–
Baig, M.A.	1958/59-70/71	46	81	12	1898	103	27.51	1	299	6	49.83
Bailey, D.	1968-81	32	46	2	1265	136	28.75	1	139	3	46.33
Bailey, Sir D.T.L.	1949-52	60	95	12	2029	111	24.44	2	398	12	33.17
Bailey, F.R.	1950-60	3	5	1	118	79	29.50	–	–	–	–
Bailey, H.J.	1967-69	3	4	0	50	25	12.50	–	68	3	22.67
Bailey, J.	1927-52	248	418	37	9500	133	24.94	5	12886	473	27.24
Bailey, J.A.	1953-68	112	148	38	641	29*	5.83	–	7503	347	21.63
Bailey, M.J.	1979-82	20	29	9	228	24	11.40	–	996	18	55.33
Bailey, R.A.	1948	3	5	1	0	0*	0.00	–	250	2	125.00
Bailey, R.J.	1982–	30	53	9	1515	114	34.43	3	80	4	20.00
Bailey, R.R.	1964-72	49	48	21	253	25	9.37	–	2906	108	26.91
Bailey, T.E.	1946-67	681	1072	215	28642	205	33.42	28	48170	2082	23.14
	T	61	91	14	2290	134*	29.74	1	3856	132	29.21
Bainbridge, A.B.	1961-63	5	10	0	93	24	9.30	–	358	20	17.90
Bainbridge, P.	1977–	122	213	34	5453	146	30.46	7	4885	122	40.04
Bairamian, R.	1957	2	3	1	45	24	22.50	–	6	1	–
Bairstow, D.L.	1970–	357	508	97	10285	145	25.02	4	247	6	41.17
	T	4	7	1	125	59	20.83	–	–	–	–
Baker, D.W.	1961-65	34	37	13	101	15	4.21	–	2856	78	36.63
Baker, J.	1952-56	15	24	6	338	91*	18.78	–	424	9	47.11
Baker, R.K.	1972-74	20	34	3	505	59*	16.29	–	–	–	–
Baker, R.P.	1973-78	54	56	30	563	91	21.65	–	2942	104	28.29
Balderstone, J.C.	1961–	351	556	55	17353	181*	34.64	29	7949	307	25.89
	T	2	4	0	39	35	9.75	–	80	1	–
Baldry, D.O.	1953-62	139	242	19	4661	151	20.90	3	3076	83	37.06
Bamber, M.J.	1982–	13	26	2	638	77	26.58	–	3	0	–
Banerjee, S.S.	1931/32-59/60	137	207	28	3671	138	20.51	5	10141	381	26.62
	T	1	2	0	13	8	6.50	–	127	5	25.40
Banks, D.A.	1983–	13	22	1	495	100	23.57	1	17	0	–
Bannister, C.S.	1975-77	17	30	2	383	50	13.68	–	813	19	42.78
Bannister, J.D.	1950-68	374	456	123	3140	71	9.42	–	26258	1198	21.92
Baptiste, E.A.E.	1981–	71	99	18	2240	136*	27.65	2	4788	174	27.52
	T	9	10	1	224	87*	24.89	–	485	15	32.33
Barber, R.W.	1954-69	386	651	52	17631	185	29.43	17	16176	549	29.46
	T	28	45	3	1495	185	35.59	1	1806	42	43.00
Barber, T.D.	1960	2	3	1	5	3	2.50	–	–	–	–
Barber, Wilfred	1926-47	374	526	49	16402	255	34.39	29	419	16	26.19
	T	2	4	0	83	44	20.75	–	0	1	–
Barber, William	1946	1	2	1	4	4	–	–	–	–	–
Barclay, J.R.T.	1970–	250	414	38	9384	119	24.96	9	8958	293	30.57
Barcroft, P.	1956	3	3	0	40	29	13.33	–	–	–	–
Barford, M.T.	1970-71	15	27	4	606	95	26.39	–	–	–	–
Baring, A.E.G.	1930-39	70	103	27	664	46	8.73	–	5607	197	28.46
Barker, A.H.	1964-67	44	67	8	864	94	14.65	–	2906	70	41.51
Barker, A.R.P.	1967-69	27	43	3	544	67	13.60	–	–	–	–
Barker, G.	1954-71	451	809	46	22288	181*	29.21	30	200	5	40.00
Barker, M.P.	1946	5	9	2	55	17	7.86	–	378	16	23.62
Barker, P.D.	1974	1	2	0	15	14	7.50	–	–	–	–

	Career span	M	I	NO	Runs	HS	Avge	100	Runs	Wkts	Avge
Barkham, F.	1948–49	2	4	1	7	3*	2.33	–	–	–	–
Barling, H.T.	1927–48	391	609	54	19209	269	34.61	34	550	7	78.57
Barlow, A.	1947–51	85	101	26	863	44	11.51	–	0	0	–
Barlow, E.J.	1959/60–82/83	283	493	28	18212	217	39.17	43	13786	571	24.14
T		30	57	2	2516	201	45.74	6	1362	40	34.05
Barlow, G.D.	1969–	226	366	54	10850	177	34.78	19	54	3	18.00
T		3	5	1	17	7*	4.25	–	–	–	–
Barnard, H.M.	1952–66	276	463	41	9314	128*	22.07	6	563	16	35.18
Barnes, F.B.	1948	2	2	0	61	39	30.50	–	–	–	–
Barnes, R.J.	1930–47	8	15	1	199	48	14.21	–	99	9	11.00
Barnes, S.G.	1936/37–52/53	110	164	10	8333	234	54.11	26	1836	57	32.21
T		13	19	2	1072	234	63.05	3	218	4	54.40
Barnes, T.P.	1956	1	1	0	7	7	–	–	–	–	–
Barnett, B.A.	1929/30–61	173	243	42	5531	131	27.51	3	20	1	–
T		4	8	1	195	57	27.85	–	–	–	–
Barnett, C.J.	1927–52	497	821	45	25389	259	32.72	48	12207	394	30.98
T		20	35	4	1098	129	35.41	2	93	0	–
Barnett, K.J.	1979–	130	199	22	5888	144	33.27	11	1527	18	84.83
Barnwell, C.J.P.	1935–48	69	111	6	1592	83	15.16	–	40	0	–
Barnwell, L.M.L.	1965–70/71	19	33	2	612	74	19.74	–	194	3	64.67
Barr, D.	1954–70	41	70	9	1199	86	19.66	–	2747	88	31.22
Barraclough, E.S.	1949–50	2	4	2	43	24*	21.50	–	136	4	34.00
Barratt, R.J.	1961–70	70	88	16	604	39	8.39	–	4007	141	28.42
Barrett, A.G.	1966/67–80/81	57	75	13	1086	102*	17.52	1	5276	169	31.22
T		6	7	1	40	19	6.67	–	603	13	46.38
Barrett, P.	1975–76	6	11	0	138	26	12.54	–	4	0	–
Barrick, D.W.	1949–60	301	490	62	13970	211	32.64	20	3575	79	45.25
Barrington, K.F.	1953–68	533	831	136	31714	256	45.63	76	8905	273	32.62
T		82	131	15	6806	256	58.67	20	1300	29	44.82
Barrington, W.E.J.	1982	4	6	1	174	59	34.80	–	–	–	–
Barron, W.	1945–51	119	200	13	4772	161*	25.52	6	200	5	40.00
Bartels, C.W.	1952/53–57/58	5	8	1	215	88	30.71	–	317	14	22.64
Bartlett, H.T.	1933–51	217	350	34	10098	183	31.96	16	269	10	26.90
Bartlett, J.N.	1946–53	49	70	32	351	28	9.24	–	3443	107	32.18
Barton, M.R.	1935–55	147	247	16	5965	192	25.82	7	–	–	–
Barwell, T.I.	1959–73	44	77	8	1344	84*	19.70	–	–	–	–
Barwick, S.R.	1981–	47	48	23	282	25	11.28	–	2945	100	29.45
Baskervylle-Glegg, J.	1962	1	2	0	43	35	21.50	–	–	–	–
Bates, D.L.	1950–71	315	358	157	1525	37*	7.58	–	22776	880	25.88
Baxter, A.G.	1952–53	13	22	1	314	98	14.95	–	–	–	–
Bayley, M.G.	1969	2	2	1	2	1*	–	–	125	3	41.67
Baylis, K.R.	1966–67	6	7	1	89	26	14.83	–	495	14	35.36
Bear, M.J.	1954–68	322	562	44	12564	137	24.25	9	53	0	–
Beard, G.R.	1975/76–81/82	54	71	10	1441	75	23.62	–	3524	125	28.19
T		3	5	0	114	49	22.80	–	109	1	–
Beaumont, D.J.	1977–78	11	16	1	258	44	17.20	–	–	–	–
Beaumont, H.	1946–47	28	46	6	716	60	17.90	–	236	9	26.22
Beck, G.E.	1946	3	6	0	72	50	12.00	–	–	–	–
Beddow, A.M.	1962–66	32	54	3	775	112*	15.20	1	473	15	31.53
Bedford, P.I.	1947–66	77	84	24	979	75*	16.32	–	4208	128	32.88
Bedi, B.S.	1961/62–80/81	370	426	11	3584	61	11.37	–	33843	1560	21.69
T		67	101	28	656	50*	8.98	–	7637	266	28.71
Bedser, A.V.	1939–60	484	576	181	5735	126	14.52	1	39281	1924	20.42
T		51	71	15	714	79	12.75	–	5876	236	24.89
Bedser, E.A.	1939–61	458	692	79	14716	163	24.01	10	20784	833	24.95
Beet, G.A.	1956–61	6	7	2	36	17	7.20	–	100	2	50.00

	Career span	M		I	NO	Runs	HS	Avge	100		Runs	Wkts	Avge
						BATTING					BOWLING		
Begbie, D.W.	1933/34–49/50	58		85	9	2727	207*	35.88	6		2085	88	23.69
	T	5		7	0	138	48	19.70	–		130	1	–
Bell, D.L.	1971–81	7		13	3	234	60	23.40	–		–	–	–
Bell, R.V.	1952–64	189		233	54	1558	53*	8.70	–		11111	392	28.34
Belle, B.H.	1934–50	43		72	5	1235	70	18.43	–		33	1	–
Benaud, R.	1948/49–67/68	259		365	44	11719	187	36.50	23		23370	945	24.73
	T	63		97	7	2201	122	24.45	3		6704	248	27.03
Benham, F.C.	1949	1		2	1	9	9	–	–		–	–	–
Benke, A.F.	1962	19		29	4	240	26	9.60	–		1964	50	39.28
Bennett, A.C.L.	1947–49	16		29	0	586	68	20.21	–		–	–	–
Bennett, D.	1950–68	404		612	125	10656	117*	21.88	4		20598	784	26.27
Bennett, B.W.P.	1979	2		2	0	4	4	2.00	–		–	–	–
Bennett, M.	1946	1		2	0	10	8	5.00	–		–	–	–
Bennett, N.H.	1946	31		45	2	688	79	16.00	–		25	1	–
Bennett, R.	1962–66	49		82	3	1814	112	22.96	2		0	0	–
Benson, G.L.	1959–61	3		5	2	102	46	34.00	–		32	2	16.00
Benson, M.R.	1980–	83		142	15	4840	152*	38.11	12		72	0	–
Bentley, M.	1957	1		2	0	12	10	–	–		–	–	–
Bergin, S.F.	1949–65	27		52	5	1610	137	34.25	2		–	–	–
Bernard, J.R.	1956–64	56		100	17	1891	119*	22.78	1		1705	35	48.71
Bernstein, R.E.	1960–62	6		10	0	89	18	8.90	–		406	16	25.36
Berry, G.L.	1924–51	610		1056	57	30225	232	30.26	45		606	10	60.60
Berry, R.	1948–62	273		305	112	1463	40	7.58	–		17389	703	24.74
	T	2		4	2	6	4*	3.00	–		228	9	25.33
Bethell, J.A.L.	1963/64–69/70	16		25	6	496	84*	26.10	–		391	10	39.10
Betts, G.F.	1951	1		2	0	1	1	0.50	–		95	5	19.00
Bevan, D.G.	1964–73/74	36		57	4	706	80	13.32	–		30	3	10.00
Bhatia, A.N.	1966/67–69	13		21	2	277	43	14.57	–		866	30	28.57
Bick, D.A.	1954–67	147		190	31	2221	85	13.97	–		6482	234	27.70
Biddulph, K.D.	1955–61	91		119	50	468	41	6.78	–		7457	270	27.59
Bielby, S.R.	1967–71	43		58	12	837	62	18.19	–		161	3	53.67
Biggs, A.Ll.	1964/65–80/81	62		112	8	3409	156	32.77	8		2811	82	34.28
Bilbie, A.R.	1960–63	14		27	1	291	39	11.19	–		–	–	–
Binks, J.G.	1955–	502		598	129	6910	95	14.73	–		82	0	–
	T	2		4	0	91	55	22.75	–		–	–	–
Birch, J.D.	1973–	168		252	38	5856	125	27.37	5		1856	38	48.84
Bird, H.D.	1956–64	93		170	10	3314	181*	20.71	2		22	0	–
Bird, R.E.	1946–58	195		327	32	7700	158*	26.10	7		1121	23	48.74
Birkenshaw, J.	1958–81	490		665	123	12780	131	23.57	4		29276	1073	27.28
	T	5		7	0	148	64	21.14	–		469	13	36.07
Birks, D.T.M.	1949	1		1	0	3	3	–	–		–	–	–
Birrell, H.B.	1947/48–59/60	54		95	3	2446	134	26.58	3		1939	55	35.25
Birtle, T.W.	1952	7		7	2	12	4*	2.40	–		593	8	74.12
Bishop, M.M.	1976–78	3		4	1	4	3	1.33	–		165	2	82.50
Bissex, M.	1961–72	212		354	35	6492	104*	20.35	2		6783	237	28.62
Black, C.J.M.	1970–73	17		26	1	400	71	16.00	–		649	13	49.92
Black, T.McM.	1979	1		2	0	88	57	44.00	–		–	–	–
Blackburn, J.D.H.	1956	1		2	0	18	15	9.00	–		–	–	–
Blackburn, P.H.	1954	1		2	0	7	5	3.50	–		30	0	–
Blackledge, J.F.	1962	26		41	4	569	68	15.37	–		10	0	–
Blackmore, G.P.M.	1944/45–48	3		3	0	12	8	4.00	–		127	2	63.50
Blades, C.F.	1963/64–69/70	12		22	0	406	75	18.45	–		21	0	–
Blagg, E.A.	1948	1		–	–	–	–	–	–		20	0	–
Blair, P.D.	1967/68–70/71	21		21	9	71	20*	5.91	–		1631	54	30.20
Blair, R.W.	1951/52–64/65	119		172	36	1672	79	12.29	–		9961	537	18.54
	T	19		34	6	189	64*	6.75	–		1515	43	35.23

	Career span	M		I	NO	Runs	HS	Avge	100		Runs	Wkts	Avge
Blake, D.E.	1949–61	73		129	9	2909	100	24.24	1		–	–	–
Blake, P.D.S.	1946–53	58		99	6	2067	130	22.23	3		52	0	–
Bland, K.C.	1956/57–73/74	131		219	28	7249	197	37.95	13		1512	43	35.16
	T	21		39	5	1669	144*	49.08	3		125	2	62.50
Blatcher, R.B.	1955	2		3	1	16	5	8.00	–		120	4	30.00
Blaxland, L.B.	1925–47	19		31	1	483	64	16.10	–		18	0	–
Blenkiron, W.	1964–74	118		139	30	1467	62	13.46	–		8149	287	28.39
Block, S.A.	1928–48	58		93	4	2488	117	27.96	2		40	2	20.00
Blofeld, H.C.	1958–60	17		32	1	758	138	24.45	1		15	0	–
Bloom, G.R.	1964	1		1	0	2	2	–	–		–	–	–
Bloy, N.C.F.	1946–58	31		53	9	964	77	21.91	–		613	8	76.62
Bluett, J.D.J.	1950	2		2	0	16	10	8.00	–		–	–	–
Blunt, L.	1942/43–46	15		20	5	109	18	7.27	–		966	37	26.11
Boddington, M.A.	1946	1		2	0	23	23	11.50	–		13	0	–
Bodell, E.H.	1954–59	5		8	4	25	11*	6.25	–		461	11	41.91
Bodkin, P.E.	1946	9		17	0	328	48	19.29	–		330	8	41.25
Bolton, A.	1957–61	40		71	6	1223	96	18.81	–		80	2	40.00
Bolus, J.B.	1956–75	469		833	81	25598	202*	34.04	39		886	24	36.92
	T	7		12	0	496	88	41.33	–		16	0	–
Bond, J.D.	1955–74	362		548	80	12125	157	25.90	14		69	0	–
Bond, R.E.	1973	1		–	–	–	–	–	–		107	2	53.50
Boobbyer, B.	1949–52	40		75	2	1970	126	26.98	2		19	0	–
Booden, C.D.	1980–81	4		3	2	10	6*	–	–		258	3	86.00
Boock, S.L.	1973/74–	105		128	47	699	35*	8.63	–		8562	405	21.14
	T	16		24	7	87	35	5.12	–		1103	37	29.81
Boon, T.J.	1980–	59		100	12	2383	144	27.08	4		57	0	–
Booth, A. (Yorks)	1931–47	38		40	15	137	29	5.48	–		1931	131	14.74
Booth, A. (Lancs)	1950–51	4		5	0	81	49	16.20	–		–	–	–
Booth, B.C.	1954/55–68/69	183		283	35	11265	214*	45.42	26		956	16	59.75
	T	29		48	6	1773	169	42.21	5		146	3	48.67
Booth, B.J.	1956–73	350		600	52	15298	183*	27.92	18		4677	146	32.03
Booth, P.	1972–81	90		80	21	767	58*	13.00	–		4549	162	28.08
Booth, P.A.	1982–	12		16	4	78	26	6.50	–		821	17	48.29
Booth, R.	1951–70	468		671	134	10138	113*	18.89	2		3	0	–
Booth, S.C.	1983–	22		26	12	124	42	8.86	–		2021	59	34.25
Booth-Jones, T.D.	1980–81	26		44	1	1034	95	24.04	–		–	–	–
Booton, W.T.	1970	1		1	0	12	12	–	–		72	2	36.00
Borde, C.G.	1952/53–73/74	250		370	57	12821	207*	40.96	30		9044	331	27.32
	T	55		97	11	3061	177*	35.59	5		2417	52	46.48
Border, A.R.	1976/77–	134		227	36	9821	200	51.42	24		1727	49	35.25
	T	61		107	20	4489	196	51.60	9		539	15	35.93
Bore, M.K.	1969–	152		151	51	856	37*	8.56	–		10858	359	30.25
Borrett, N.F.	1937–46	3		4	2	33	15*	16.50	–		43	0	–
Borrill, P.D.	1971	2		–	–	–	–	–	–		61	5	12.20
Borrington, A.J.	1971–80	122		203	24	4230	137	23.63	3		19	0	–
Bose, G.	1968/69–78/79	77		126	5	3741	170	30.92	8		1905	71	26.83
Boshier, B.S.	1953–64	170		226	92	579	30	4.32	–		11742	510	23.02
Boston, G.F.	1946	3		6	0	38	19	6.33	–		–	–	–
Botham, I.T.	1974–	250		387	26	11907	228	32.98	24		21581	852	25.33
	T	73		117	3	4159	208	36.48	13		8191	312	26.25
Botten, J.T.	1957/58–71/72	98		143	31	1775	90	15.84	–		8125	399	20.36
	T	3		6	0	65	33	10.83	–		337	8	42.13
Botton, N.D.	1974–75	15		30	6	286	38*	11.92	–		714	11	64.91
Boucher, J.C.	1930–54	28		51	5	625	85	13.58	–		2359	168	14.04
Bourne, W.A.	1970/71–77	60		78	15	1325	107	21.03	1		4164	128	32.53

	Career span	M	I	NO	Runs	HS	Avge	100	Runs	Wkts	Avge
					BATTING				BOWLING		
Bowden, J.	1946–55	6	9	0	52	34	5.78	–	369	19	19.42
Bowes, J.B.	1938–48	10	13	1	106	39	8.83	–	602	21	28.66
Bowes, W.E.	1928–47	372	326	148	11530	43*	8.60	–	27470	1639	16.76
T		15	11	5	28	10*	4.67	–	1519	68	22.33
Bowles, R.A.	1957	3	6	0	92	43	15.33	–	–	–	–
Bowling, K.	1954	1	2	1	7	4*	–	–	–	–	–
Bowman, R.	1955–64	26	37	9	454	75	16.21	–	1902	51	37.30
Boxill, D.	1964/65–71/72	15	19	1	149	38	8.27	–	–	–	–
Boyce, K.D.	1964/65–77	285	420	27	8800	147*	22.39	4	21324	852	25.03
T		21	30	3	657	95*	24.33	–	1801	60	30.02
Boycott, G.	1962–	575	960	149	45777	261*	56.45	143	1430	45	31.78
T		108	193	23	8114	246*	47.72	22	382	7	54.57
Boyd-Moss, R.J.	1980–	98	171	13	4892	139	30.96	9	1499	33	45.42
Boyers, M.J.H.	1969	1	2	0	2	2	–	–	–	–	–
Boyns, C.D.	1976–79	37	54	7	871	95	18.53	–	1668	36	46.33
Boys, F.C.	1947–51	7	13	0	273	84	21.00	–	–	–	–
Bracewell, B.P.	1977/78–	49	67	16	484	36*	9.49	–	3099	112	27.67
T		5	10	2	17	8	2.12	–	456	10	45.60
Bracewell, J.G.	1978/79–	62	97	14	1781	104*	21.46	1	5539	236	23.47
T		10	16	2	108	28	7.72	–	810	25	32.40
Bradbury, L.	1971	1	–	–	–	–	–	–	53	1	–
Bradfield, G.W.	1970	1	1	0	50	50	–	–	–	–	–
Bradley, M.E.	1951–52	9	9	7	9	6*	4.50	–	867	23	37.69
Bradley, P.	1973–74	2	3	2	11	9*	–	–	249	9	27.66
Bradman, Sir D.G.	1927/28–48/49	234	338	43	28067	452*	95.14	117	1367	36	37.97
T		52	80	10	6996	334	99.94	29	72	2	36.00
Brailsford, F.C.	1958	3	5	0	41	14	8.20	–	2	1	–
Brain, B.M.	1959–81	259	271	68	1704	57	8.39	–	20194	824	24.50
Brancker, R.C.	1955/56–69/70	47	68	7	1666	135*	27.32	5	2895	106	27.32
Branston, J.R.M.	1956	5	6	2	32	19	8.00	–	235	9	26.11
Brassington, A.J.	1974–	124	153	44	878	35	8.06	–	10	0	–
Brayshay, P.B.	1945/46–52	3	5	1	23	13	5.75	–	223	4	55.75
Brazier, A.F.	1948–56	58	94	14	1366	92	17.07	–	158	4	39.50
Breakwell, D.	1969–83	231	306	64	4792	100*	19.80	1	13008	422	30.83
Brearley, H.	1937–49	5	10	0	134	37	13.40	–	–	–	–
Brearley, J.M.	1961–83	455	768	102	25185	312*	37.82	45	192	3	64.00
T		39	66	3	1442	91	22.88	–	–	–	–
Breddy, M.N.	1984	10	20	1	339	61	17.84	–	–	–	–
Bremner, C.D.	1945–45/46	7	9	6	8	4*	2.67	–	–	–	–
Brennan, D.V.	1947–53	232	258	74	1937	67*	10.53	–	–	–	–
T		2	2	0	16	16	8.00	–	–	–	–
Brettell, D.N.	1975–78	13	19	4	175	39	11.67	–	549	18	30.50
Brettell, J.G.	1984	1	2	1	0	0*	–	–	74	1	–
Brewster, V.C.	1965	2	4	1	58	35*	19.33	–	175	10	17.50
Brice, G.H.J.	1949–52	25	35	5	412	82*	13.73	–	2426	72	33.69
Bridge, D.J.W.	1947	4	7	1	55	25*	9.17	–	261	5	52.20
Bridge, W.B.	1955–68	99	133	33	1058	56*	10.58	–	7438	283	26.28
Bridger, J.R.	1945–54	40	69	4	1883	142	28.96	2	56	0	–
Brierley, T.L.	1931–54	232	362	33	6244	116*	18.98	4	45	0	–
Briers, N.	1967	1	1	0	1	1	–	–	31	0	–
Briers, N.E.	1971–	165	265	26	6672	201*	27.92	9	607	22	27.59
Briggs, K.R.	1961	1	2	1	29	17*	–	–	44	1	–
Briggs, P.D.	1963–64	21	35	2	533	91	16.15	–	7	0	–
Bright, R.J.	1972/73–	136	185	39	3088	108	21.15	1	10978	352	31.19
T		16	27	5	303	33	13.77	–	1343	37	36.29

	Career span	M	I	NO	Runs	HS	Avge	100	Runs	Wkts	Avge
									BATTING				BOWLING		
Brindle, R.G.	1949	1	2	0	74	42	37.00	–	–	–	–
Bristowe, W.R.	1984	5	8	3	104	30*	20.80	–	–	–	–
Broad, C.B.	1979–	112	199	14	6353	145	34.34	9	787	13	60.53
_T_		5	9	0	281	86	31.22	–	–	–	–
Broadbent, R.G.	1950–63	307	520	56	12800	155	27.58	13	382	4	95.50
Brocklebank, J.M.	1936–49	21	26	14	112	23	9.33	–	1998	68	29.38
Brocklehurst, B.G.	1952–54	64	116	9	1671	89	15.62	–	36	1	36.00
Broderick, V.	1939–57	253	384	44	7530	190	22.15	6	15007	548	27.40
Brodhurst, A.H.	1937–46	20	33	2	658	111	21.23	2	321	6	53.50
Brodie, J.B.	1959–63/64	22	36	11	305	37	12.20	–	1743	48	36.31
Brodrick, P.D.	1959–61	22	34	11	321	49	13.96	–	1927	44	43.79
Bromfield, H.D.	1956/57–68/69	62	91	32	374	44	6.33	–	5256	205	25.63
_T_		9	12	7	59	21	11.80	–	599	17	35.23
Bromley, P.H.	1947–56	49	66	11	1183	121*	21.52	1	1264	35	36.12
Bromley, R.C.	1970	5	9	0	78	18	8.67	–	–	–	–
Brooke, B.	1950	2	4	0	16	14	4.00	–	191	2	95.50
Brooker, M.E.W.	1974–76	15	28	15	43	9	3.31	–	1149	25	45.96
Brookes, D.	1934–59	525	925	70	30874	257	36.10	71	128	3	42.67
_T_		1	2	0	17	10	8.50	–	–	–	–
Brooke-Taylor, D.K.	1947–49	15	26	1	375	61*	15.00	–	–	–	–
Brooks, K.G.	1980	1	2	0	11	8	5.50	–	–	–	–
Brooks, R.A.	1967–68	35	45	16	317	44	10.93	–	–	–	–
Brooks, V.C.G.	1970–71	3	5	0	53	22	10.60	–	–	–	–
Broome, I.	1984	2	4	3	35	26*	–	–	82	2	41.00
Broughton, P.N.	1956–62	30	33	17	162	17*	10.13	–	2430	85	28.59
Brown, Alan (Kent)	1957–70	251	312	87	2189	81	9.72	–	18326	743	24.67
_T_		2	1	1	3	3*	–	–	150	3	50.00
Brown, Alan (Worcs)	1979	1	–	–	–	–	–	–	–	–	–
Brown, Alexander	1977–	6	9	0	110	30	12.22	–	–	–	–
Brown, A.J.T.	1960	2	4	1	41	40*	13.67	–	–	–	–
Brown, A.S.	1953–76	496	808	99	12851	116	18.13	3	31546	1230	25.65
Brown, D.B.S.	1973–76	3	6	0	115	58	19.17	–	–	–	–
Brown, D.J.	1961–82	390	446	111	4110	79	12.26	–	28961	1165	24.85
_T_		26	34	5	342	44*	11.79	–	2237	79	28.31
Brown, D.W.J.	1964–67	89	153	11	2863	142	20.16	1	84	3	28.00
Brown, F.R.	1930–61	355	536	49	13327	212	27.37	22	32007	1221	26.21
_T_		22	30	1	734	79	25.31	–	1398	45	31.06
Brown, J.	1953–73	59	85	18	1306	90	19.49	–	–	–	–
Brown, K.R.	1984	1	1	0	6	6	6.00	–	–	–	–
Brown, R.D.	1976–77	36	69	2	1643	200*	24.52	3	–	–	–
Brown, S.M.	1937–55	329	580	40	15756	232*	29.18	22	80	3	26.67
Brown, W.A.	1932/33–49/50	189	284	15	13840	265*	51.44	39	110	6	18.33
_T_		22	35	1	1592	206*	46.82	4	–	–	–
Bruyns, A.	1965/66–76/77	90	160	9	5050	197	33.44	11	25	1	25.00
Bryant, D.J.	1970–71	6	10	7	19	6*	6.33	–	423	8	52.88
Bryant, L.E.	1958–60	22	29	14	133	17	8.87	–	943	34	27.73
Bryant, M.	1982	2	2	0	6	6	3.00	–	158	2	79.00
Buck, W.D.	1969	2	2	0	11	6	5.50	–	135	2	67.50
Buckingham, A.D.	1955–60	10	20	1	349	61	18.37	–	43	0	–
Buckland, J.E.	1948	1	2	2	17	17*	–	–	55	3	18.33
Budd, W.L.	1934–46	60	98	16	941	77*	11.47	–	2506	64	39.15
Bugge, D.A.B.	1977	1	–	–	–	–	–	–	22	0	–
Bulcock, L.	1946	1	1	0	1	1	–	–	90	2	45.00
Bullen, C.K.	1982	1	–	–	–	–	–	–	29	0	–
Buller, J.S.	1930–46	112	171	44	1746	64	12.75	–	–	–	–
Bunyard, G.S.	1959/60–62/63	14	17	3	192	35	13.72	–	1082	48	22.54

	Career span	M		I	NO	Runs	HS	Avge	100		Runs	Wkts	Avge
						BATTING						BOWLING	
Burch, G.W.	1958–64	46		79	10	1067	64*	15.46	–		3	0	–
Burchnall, R.L.	1968–71	32		57	2	874	85	15.89	–		–	–	–
Burden, M.D.	1953–63	174		191	59	901	51	6.83	–		12559	481	26.11
Burge, P.J.P.	1952/53–67/68	233		354	46	14640	283	47.53	38		129	1	–
	T	42		68	8	2290	181	38.17	4		–	–	–
Burger, C.G.de V.	1955–65/66	48		74	5	2073	131	30.04	2		17	1	–
	T	2		4	1	62	37*	20.67	–		–	–	–
Burgess, A.T.	1940/41–51/52	14		23	2	466	61*	22.19	–		491	16	30.69
Burgess, G.I.	1966–79	252		414	37	7129	129	18.91	2		13543	474	28.57
Burgess, M.G.	1963/64–80/81	192		322	35	10281	146	35.82	20		1148	30	38.27
	T	50		92	6	2684	119*	31.21	5		212	6	35.33
Burgin, E.	1952–53	12		10	3	92	32	13.14	–		795	31	25.65
Burke, C.	1937/38–53/54	58		70	17	935	51	17.64	–		5047	194	26.02
	T	1		2	0	4	3	2.00	–		30	2	15.00
Burke, J.P.	1953–58	4		4	1	36	19*	12.00	–		105	3	35.00
Burke, J.W.	1948/49–58/59	130		204	36	7563	220	45.02	21		2941	101	29.12
	T	24		44	7	1280	189	34.60	3		230	8	28.75
Burn, E.H.M.	1954	2		4	0	31	12	7.75	–		–	–	–
Burnell, P.J.	1967	6		10	3	71	28	10.14	–		–	–	–
Burnet, J.R.	1958–59	55		77	6	897	54	12.63	–		26	1	–
Burnett, A.C.	1949–58	27		40	6	790	79*	23.24	–		16	–	–
Burnley, I.D.	1984	3		6	0	232	86	38.67	–		–	–	–
Burridge, A.J.	1973	1		2	0	42	37	21.00	–		–	–	–
Burrough, H.D.	1927–47	171		272	18	5316	135	20.93	4		14	0	–
Burrows, D.A.	1984	1		1	0	0	0	–	–		76	0	–
Burton, C.	1956	2		1	0	0	0	–	–		80	0	–
Burton, M St J.W.	1964/65–71	37		59	5	821	84	15.20	–		3317	77	43.08
Burtt, T.B.	1943/44–54/55	84		124	29	1644	68*	17.31	–		9054	408	22.19
	T	10		15	3	252	42	21.00	–		1170	33	35.45
Bury, T.E.O.	1979–80	4		4	1	32	22	10.67	–		–	–	–
Buse, H.F.T.	1929–53	304		523	54	10623	132	22.65	7		18908	657	28.78
Bush, J.E.	1950–52	8		15	1	417	67	29.77	–		–	–	–
Bushby, M.H.	1952–66	46		78	1	1919	113	24.92	3		11	1	–
Bushe, E.A.	1979–80	2		2	1	14	14	–	–		–	–	–
Buss, A.	1958–74	310		412	76	4415	83	13.13	–		23989	958	25.04
Buss, M.A.	1961–78	316		547	47	11996	159	23.99	11		15349	547	28.06
Butchart, I.P.	1980/81–	13		21	3	278	54	15.44	–		325	9	36.11
Butcher, A.R.	1972–	248		419	40	12693	216*	33.49	26		4054	103	39.36
	T	1		2	0	34	20	17.00	–		9	0	–
Butcher, B.F.	1954/55–71/72	169		262	29	11628	209*	49.90	31		1217	40	30.43
	T	44		78	6	3104	209*	43.11	7		90	5	18.00
Butcher, I.P.	1980–	49		83	5	2560	139	32.82	8		15	1	–
Butcher, M.S.	1982	1		–	–	–	–	–	–		2	0	–
Butcher, R.O.	1974–	176		278	25	7817	197	30.90	12		76	0	–
	T	3		5	0	71	32	14.20	–		–	–	–
Butler, H.J.	1933–54	329		381	100	2962	62	10.54	–		23276	952	24.45
	T	2		2	1	15	15*	–	–		215	12	17.92
Buxton, I.R.	1959–73	350		579	86	11803	118*	23.94	5		12742	483	26.38
Bynoe, M.R.	1957/58–71/72	56		97	10	3572	190	41.05	6		246	9	27.33
	T	4		6	0	111	48	18.50	–		5	1	–
Caesar, W.C.	1922–46	4		4	1	14	7	4.67	–		252	10	25.20
Cairns, B.L.	1971/72–	131		206	22	3734	110	20.29	1		11140	429	25.97
	T	37		58	7	852	64	16.71	–		3550	115	30.87
Cairns, J. D.	1946–49	7		14	0	179	36	12.78	–		–	–	–

	Career span	M	I	NO	Runs	HS	Avge	100	Runs	Wkts	Avge
Camacho, S.G.	1964/65–78/79	76	125	8	4079	166	34.86	7	216	8	27.00
T		11	22	0	640	87	29.09	–	12	0	–
Came, K.C.	1957	1	2	0	12	6	6.00	–	46	0	–
Cameron, F.J. (Can)	1945/46–58/59	21	27	5	551	75*	25.04	–	1411	29	48.65
T		5	7	1	151	75*	25.16	–	278	3	92.67
Cameron, F.J. (NZ)	1952/53–66/67	119	176	92	993	43	11.82	–	9658	447	21.60
T		19	30	20	116	27*	11.60	–	1849	62	29.82
Cameron, J.H.	1932–47	105	164	12	2772	113	18.23	4	5662	184	30.77
T		2	3	0	6	5	2.00	–	88	3	29.33
Cammish, J.W.	1950/51–54	7	10	3	31	7*	4.43	–	781	25	31.24
Campbell, A.N.	1968–70	15	27	1	530	73	20.38	–	–	–	–
Campbell, A.U.	1969/70–79/80	22	35	3	509	48*	15.90	–	–	–	–
Campbell, I.P.	1946–54	22	36	4	482	60*	15.06	–	–	–	–
Candler, D.C.	1950–51	5	7	0	115	54	16.42	–	–	–	–
Cangley, B.G.M.	1947	8	14	1	295	76	22.69	–	–	–	–
Cannings, V.H.D.	1947–59	285	373	128	2660	61	10.85	–	21077	927	22.73
Cantlay, C.P.T.	1975	6	9	5	19	9	4.75	–	419	11	38.09
Cantwell, N.E.C.	1956	1	2	1	48	31	–	–	13	0	–
Capel, D.J.	1981–	49	76	15	1820	109*	29.84	1	1343	25	53.72
Caplan, J.J.N.	1962	2	3	0	38	26	12.67	–	97	3	32.33
Caple, R.G.	1958–67	68	103	17	1581	64*	18.38	–	1235	34	36.33
Capon, S.	1950	1	1	0	4	4	–	–	98	0	–
Caprani, J.D.	1948–60	5	10	0	95	44	9.50	–	–	–	–
Card, A.J.	1955–58	2	4	2	51	19*	25.50	–	87	7	12.43
Carew, M.C.	1955/56–73/74	129	221	18	7810	182	38.47	13	3215	108	29.77
T		19	36	3	1127	109	34.15	1	437	8	54.62
Carless, E.F.	1934–46	3	3	0	35	25	11.67	–	–	–	–
Carling, P.G.	1967–70	30	55	3	1160	104	22.31	1	25	0	–
Carlstein, P.R.	1954/55–79/80	148	255	16	7554	229	31.60	9	480	9	53.33
T		8	14	1	190	42	14.62	–	–	–	–
Carmichael, I.R.	1983/84–	18	17	6	17	4*	1.54	–	2107	58	36.33
Carmody, D.K.	1939/40–55/56	65	123	2	3496	198	28.89	2	187	3	62.33
Carnill, D.J.	1950	1	1	0	8	8	–	–	33	1	–
Carpenter, D.	1954–63	117	210	6	3741	95	18.34	–	36	0	–
Carr, D.B.	1945–64	447	745	72	19257	170	28.61	24	11396	328	34.74
T		2	4	0	135	76	33.75	–	140	2	70.00
Carr, J.D.	1983–	18	24	4	535	123	26.75	2	1361	31	43.99
Carr, M.L.	1953	1	2	1	1	1*	–	–	–	–	–
Carr, R.B.	1960–64/65	2	3	2	35	28*	–	–	107	0	–
Carrick, P.	1970–	263	333	64	5826	131*	21.66	3	19307	656	29.43
Carroll, P.R.	1969–71	14	27	2	403	60*	16.12	–	64	0	–
Carse, J.A.	1977/78–	44	57	24	380	44	11.51	–	3421	103	33.21
Carter, C.E.P.	1968–69	26	35	10	73	16	2.92	–	–	–	–
Carter, H.S.	1946	3	4	0	8	7	2.00	–	46	2	23.00
Carter, J.W.	1959	7	14	0	209	41	14.92	–	–	–	–
Carter, R.	1953–55	17	22	4	130	25	7.22	–	752	30	25.07
Carter, R.G.	1951–61	89	109	20	635	37	7.13	–	6759	243	27.81
Carter, R.G.M.	1961–73	178	165	95	324	23	4.63	–	13714	523	26.22
Carter, R.M.	1978–82/83	58	81	16	1042	79	16.03	–	1566	39	40.15
Carter-Shaw, R.	1962	1	1	0	2	2	–	–	78	1	–
Cartridge, D.C.	1953	3	6	0	6	4	1.00	–	–	–	–
Cartwright, H.	1973–79	82	128	16	2384	141*	21.28	1	11	0	–
Cartwright, T.W.	1952–77	479	737	94	13710	210	21.32	7	29357	1536	19.11
T		5	7	2	26	9	5.20	–	544	15	36.26
Carty, R.A.	1949–54	55	79	25	798	53	14.77	–	4164	138	30.17
Cass, G.R.	1964–75	155	231	34	4304	172*	21.84	2	–	–	–

	Career span	M		I	NO	Runs	HS	Avge	100		Runs	Wkts	Avge
						BATTING						BOWLING	
Cassidy, J.J.	1982	1		1	0	0	0	–	–		12	0	–
Castell, A.T.	1961–71	112		141	39	1622	76	15.90	–		7094	229	30.97
Castle, F.	1946–49	23		36	3	686	60*	20.78	–		43	1	–
Catt, A.W.	1954–67/68	138		218	37	3123	162	17.25	1		2	0	–
Cave, H.B.	1945/46–58/59	117		175	39	2187	118	16.08	2		8664	362	23.93
	T	19		31	5	229	22*	8.80	–		1467	34	43.14
Cawthray, G.	1939–52	4		6	0	114	30	19.00	–		304	4	76.00
Chadd, J.E.	1955–56	2		1	0	4	4	–	–		98	2	49.00
Chadwick, J.P.G.	1960–65	6		9	3	106	59	17.67	67		–	2	33.50
Chadwick, M.R.	1983–	8		16	0	295	61	18.44	–		–	–	–
Chamberlain, W.R.F.	1946	6		9	0	67	14	7.44	–		–	–	–
Chambers, R.E.J.	1966	12		22	0	386	58	17.54	–		4	0	–
Chanmugan, D.R.	1972/73–75/76	14		18	3	180	35	12.00	–		780	19	41.08
Chandrasekhar, B.S.	1963/64–79/80	246		244	114	600	25	4.62	–		25547	1063	24.43
	T	58		80	39	167	22	4.07	–		7199	242	29.74
Chapman, T.A.	1946–52/53	58		95	5	1413	124*	15.70	1		23	0	–
Chappell, G.S.	1966/67–83/84	321		542	72	24535	247*	52.20	74		8717	291	29.96
	T	87		151	19	7110	247*	53.86	24		1913	47	40.70
Chappell, I.M.	1961/62–79/80	262		448	41	19680	209	48.35	59		6614	176	37.57
	T	75		136	10	5345	196	42.42	14		1316	20	65.80
Chappell, T.M.	1972/73–	85		145	13	3934	150	29.80	5		1391	56	24.84
	T	3		6	1	79	27	15.80	–		–	–	–
Chatfield, E.J.	1973/74–	93		86	42	407	24*	9.25	–		8138	408	19.94
	T	15		20	11	80	13*	8.89	–		1464	45	32.53
Chauhan, C.P.S.	1967/68–82/83	170		283	20	10514	207	39.98	20		1660	50	33.20
	T	40		68	2	2084	97	31.57	–		106	2	53.00
Cheatle, R.G.L.	1974–83	60		44	18	338	49	13.00	–		3303	104	31.76
Checksfield, M.F.J.	1960–61	2		4	0	59	42	14.75	–		–	–	–
Cheetham, A.G.	1936/37–45/46	24		46	3	899	85	20.90	–		1517	42	36.12
Cheetham, J.E.	1939/40–55	108		170	35	5697	271*	42.20	8		375	8	46.88
	T	24		43	6	883	89	23.86	–		2	0	–
Cheetham, J.L.	1947	1		2	0	9	6	4.50	–		–	–	–
Chessher, J.R.	1982–83	4		6	1	78	47	15.60	–		–	–	–
Chesterton, G.H.	1948–66	72		102	34	598	43	8.79	–		5993	263	22.79
Chidgey, G.J.	1962–64	3		6	0	164	113	27.33	1		–	–	–
Childs, J.H.	1975–	165		151	72	535	34*	6.77	–		13464	421	31.98
Childs-Clark, A.W.	1923–48	66		107	9	1674	68	17.08	–		1098	25	43.92
Chisholm, J.R.	1947	1		2	0	14	12	7.00	–		33	1	–
Chisholm, R.H.E.	1948–71	61		106	6	2354	105	23.54	1		839	26	32.27
Chowdhury, N.R.	1941/42–58/59	59		87	27	424	30*	7.06	–		5030	200	25.15
	T	2		2	1	3	3*	–	–		205	1	–
Christen, B.	1951–54	5		7	3	29	9*	7.25	–		384	17	22.59
Christiani, R.J.	1938/39–53/54	88		142	16	5103	181	40.50	12		1088	18	60.44
	T	22		37	3	896	107	26.35	1		108	3	36.00
Christie, R.D.	1964	4		6	2	47	21	11.75	–		315	8	39.37
Chubb, G.W.A.	1931/32–51	49		61	15	835	71*	18.15	–		3826	160	23.91
	T	5		9	3	63	15*	10.50	–		577	21	27.47
Church, L.G.	1957	1		2	0	1	1	0.50	–		16	0	–
Clapp, R.J.	1972–77	15		16	5	49	32	4.45	–		734	25	29.36
Clark, A.R.	1981	1		2	0	13	12	6.50	–		–	–	–
Clark, D.G.	1946–51	75		133	9	1959	78	15.80	–		44	1	–
Clark, E.A.	1959–76	200		339	39	8733	149	29.11	6		1883	58	32.47
Clark, E.W.	1922–47	338		510	195	1971	30	6.25	–		25967	1208	21.49
	T	8		9	5	36	10	9.00	–		899	32	28.09
Clark, J.	1969–82	13		16	3	104	29	8.00	–		800	43	18.60
Clark, L.S.	1946–47	24		44	3	745	64	18.17	–		15	0	–

	Career span	M		I	NO	Runs	HS	Avge	100		Runs	Wkts	Avge
Clark, T.H.	1947–59/60	263		426	35	11490	191	29.39	12		2314	75	30.85
Clark, W.	1946	1		2	0	13	9	6.50	–		–	–	–
Clarke, C. B.	1937/38–61	97		145	40	1292	86	12.31	–		8782	333	26.37
	T	3		4	1	3	2	1.00	–		261	6	43.50
Clarke, C.C.	1929–47	28		43	3	472	35*	11.80	–		–	–	–
Clarke, D.H.	1946	2		4	0	32	27	8.00	–		–	–	–
Clarke, F.	1956–60	31		41	15	98	31	3.77	–		1868	50	37.36
Clarke, J.M.	1969	1		2	0	0	0	0.00	–		–	–	–
Clarke, R.W.	1947–57	212		263	84	2745	56	15.33	–		16749	484	34.61
Clarke, S.J.S.	1958–62	8		14	0	99	19	7.07	–		–	–	–
Clarke, S.T.	1977/78–	166		186	30	2397	100*	15.37	1		13236	634	20.88
	T	11		16	5	172	35*	15.63	–		1170	42	27.85
Clarkson, A.	1963–71	110		189	12	4458	131	25.19	2		367	13	28.23
Claughton, J.A.	1976–80	55		96	7	1910	130	21.46	4		4	0	–
Clay, J.C.	1921–49	374		555	90	7186	115*	15.45	2		26028	1317	19.76
	T	1		–	–	–	–	–	–		75	0	–
Clay, J.D.	1948–61	236		400	17	9991	192	26.08	11		133	0	–
Clayton, G.	1957–67	274		415	66	6154	106	17.63	1		–	–	–
Cleaton, H.	1971	1		1	0	1	1	–	–		23	0	–
Clements, S.C.	1976–79	29		47	5	860	91	20.47	–		205	3	68.33
Cleveley, A.B.	1955	1		2	1	4	4*	–	–		107	3	35.67
Clifford, C.C.	1972–80	47		45	16	210	26	7.24	–		4740	126	37.61
Clift, Patrick B.	1971/72–	251		360	80	6652	100*	23.76	1		17170	699	24.56
Clift, Phil. B.	1937–55	183		306	21	6055	125*	21.24	7		675	11	61.36
Clifton, E.G.	1962–66	25		29	16	128	25	9.85	–		–	–	–
Clinton, G.S.	1974–	150		252	29	6802	192	30.50	11		127	4	31.75
Close, D.B.	1949–84	784		1221	171	34926	198	33.26	52		30843	1168	26.41
	T	22		37	2	887	70	25.34	–		532	18	29.55
Close, P.A.	1964–65	15		27	2	344	54	13.76	–		44	1	–
Clube, S.V.M.	1956–59	17		25	3	132	25	6.00	–		1514	47	32.22
Clugston, D.L.	1928–46	6		9	0	64	17	7.11	–		475	4	118.75
Cobb, R.A.	1980–	44		68	1	1335	64	19.93	–		5	0	–
Cobham, M.D.	1953	1		2	0	0	0	0.00	–		54	2	27.00
Cock, D.F.	1939–46	14		20	2	355	98	19.72	–		–	–	–
Cockbain, I.	1979–83	46		78	9	1456	98	21.10	–		14	0	–
Cockett, J.A.	1951–53	8		15	2	311	121	23.92	1		6	0	–
Coe, G.	1963	1		–	–	–	–	–	–		77	2	38.50
Cogger, G.L.	1954–57	8		8	1	12	5	1.72	–		286	7	40.86
Coghlan, T.B.L.	1958–61	20		33	8	257	24	10.28	–		1622	30	54.06
Cohen, M.F.	1980–84	2		2	0	0	0	0.00	–		–	–	–
Cohen, R.A.	1963/64–66/67	37		42	20	160	32*	7.27	–		2576	81†	31.80
Coldwell, L.J.	1955–69	310		347	99	1474	37	5.94	–		22791	1076	21.18
	T	7		7	5	9	6*	4.50	–		610	22	27.72
Coldwell, W.R.	1954–55	2		4	0	15	8	3.75	–		–	–	–
Cole, D.H.	1959–67	3		4	0	86	36	21.50	–		82	2	41.00
Coles, W.N.	1949	2		3	0	26	14	8.67	–		–	–	–
Colhoun, O.D.	1959–79	28		35	19	74	9*	4.62	–		–	–	–
Colledge, F.	1949–52	4		4	2	21	12*	10.50	–		267	6	44.50
Colley, D.J.	1969/70–77/78	87		123	23	2374	101	23.74	1		7459	236	31.60
	T	3		4	0	84	54	21.00	–		312	6	52.00
Collinge, J.G.	1964	2		3	0	18	9	6.00	–		–	–	–
Collinge, R.A.	1962	2		4	0	101	41	25.25	–		186	11	16.90
Collinge, R.O.	1963/64–78	163		178	50	1848	68*	14.43	–		12793	524	24.41
	T	35		50	13	533	68*	14.40	–		3393	116	29.25
Collingwood, B.E.	1948–53	2		3	0	21	15	7.00	–		–	–	–

† + 1 wkt for which no analysis

	Career span	M	I	NO	Runs	HS	Avge	100	Runs	Wkts	Avge
					BATTING				BOWLING		
Collins, B.G.	1979	I	–	–	–	–	–	–	110	3	26.67
Collins, R.	1954–62	120	183	18	3436	107*	20.82	2	4831	159	30.40
Collins, R.P.	1967/68–75/76	23	43	3	1061	88*	26.52	–	910	31	29.35
Collinson, J.	1939–46	3	6	0	109	34	18.17	–	–	–	–
Collyer, F.E.	1967–79	5	8	I	96	46	13.71	–	–	–	–
Comber, J.T.H.	1931–48	57	78	18	833	62	13.88	–	–	–	–
Compton, D.C.S.	1936–64	516	839	88	38942	300	51.85	123	20074	622	32.27
	T	78	131	15	5807	278	50.06	17	1410	25	56.40
Compton, L.H.	1938–56	274	393	46	5814	107	16.76	I	569	12	47.42
Compton-Burnett, R.J.	1981	I	2	0	23	18	11.50	–	–	–	–
Coney, J.V.	1970/71–	117	199	34	5368	174*	32.53	5	2495	85	29.35
	T	30	51	9	1567	174*	37.31	I	520	15	34.67
Congdon, B.E.	1960/61–78	241	416	40	13101	202*	34.84	23	6125	204	30.02
	T	61	114	7	3448	176	32.22	7	2154	59	36.50
Conibere, W.J.	1950	4	5	0	16	8	3.20	–	220	7	31.42
Connolly, A.N.	1959/60–70/71	201	215	93	1073	40	8.79	–	17974	676	26.58
	T	29	45	20	260	37	10.40	–	2981	102	29.22
Connor, C.A.	1984	21	23	9	65	13*	4.64	–	1949	62	31.44
Conradi, E.R.	1946	7	13	3	164	50*	16.40	–	–	–	–
Constable, B.	1939–64	446	701	82	18849	205*	30.45	27	3017	64	47.14
Constable, D.	1949	2	2	0	20	12	10.00	–	–	–	–
Constant, D.J.	1961–68	61	93	14	1517	80	19.20	–	36	I	–
Constantine, L.N.	1921/22–45	119	197	11	4475	133	24.06	5	8991	439	20.48
	T	18	33	0	635	90	19.24	–	1746	58	30.10
Contractor, N.J.	1952/53–70/71	138	234	18	8611	176	39.86	22	1040	26	40.00
	T	31	52	I	1611	108	31.58	I	80	I	–
Cook, C.	1946–64	506	612	248	1965	35*	5.40	–	36578	1782	20.53
	T	I	2	0	4	4	2.00	–	127	0	–
Cook, C.J.	1974–75	2	2	I	I	I	–	–	105	I	–
Cook, C.R.	1981–84	11	18	2	393	79	24.56	–	–	–	–
Cook, D.R.	1962–68	9	13	5	108	28*	13.50	–	534	23	23.21
Cook, G.	1971–	342	606	43	17618	172	31.29	26	669	14	47.79
	T	7	13	0	203	66	15.61	–	27	0	–
Cook, G.W.	1956–61	47	77	11	1858	140	28.15	3	2309	64	36.08
Cook, J.	1961–63	2	4	0	52	35	13.00	–	103	7	14.72
Cook, M.S.	1961–62	2	4	0	110	52	27.50	–	–	–	–
Cook, N.G.B.	1978–	152	156	47	1293	75	11.86	–	12109	427	28.36
	T	9	15	I	101	26	7.21	–	1212	40	30.30
Cooke, N.H.	1958–59	12	16	0	242	33	15.12	–	93	3	31.00
Cooke, R.M.O.	1972–76	42	70	5	1450	139	22.30	2	184	4	46.00
Coomb, A.G.	1948–53	5	10	4	55	16	9.17	–	321	8	40.13
Coomaraswamy, I.	1971–72	2	4	0	7	4	1.75	–	–	–	–
Coope, M.	1947–49	71	136	4	2789	113	21.13	2	479	8	59.88
Cooper, A.W.M.	1954	I	2	0	50	31	25.00	–	38	2	19.00
Cooper, E.	1936–51	250	444	28	13304	216*	31.98	18	44	0	–
Cooper, F.	1946–50	44	84	13	1369	113*	19.28	I	30	0	–
Cooper, G.C.	1955–69	252	407	56	8134	142	23.17	2	3677	100	36.77
Cooper, H.P.	1971–80	101	113	30	1191	56	14.34	–	6529	233	28.02
Cooper, K.E.	1976–	159	157	36	1113	38*	9.20	–	10301	371	27.77
Cooper, N.H.C.	1975–79	24	39	2	825	106	22.29	I	277	7	39.57
Cooper, R.C.	1972	I	2	0	4	4	2.00	–	–	–	–
Cooper, R.S.	1941/42–51	22	29	6	1205	127*	52.39	3	61	0	–
Coote, D.E.	1977	I	I	0	20	20	–	–	–	–	–
Cope, G.A.	1966–80	246	261	93	2383	78	14.18	–	16948	686	24.70
	T	3	3	0	40	22	13.33	–	277	8	34.63
Copson, W.H.	1932–50	279	359	108	1711	43	6.80	–	20752	1094	18.97
	T	3	I	0	6	6	–	–	297	15	19.80

	Career span	M		I	NO	Runs	HS	Avge	100		Runs	Wkts	Avge
Cordaroy, T.M.	1968	2		3	0	104	81	34.67	–		–	–	–
Cordle, A.E.	1963–80	312		433	76	5239	81	14.67	–		19281	701	27.50
Cordner, J.P.	1951/52–52	4		4	2	13	8*	6.50	–		236	3	78.67
Corke, M.D.	1953–58	5		10	0	116	53	11.60	–		–	–	–
Corlett, S.C.	1970–	30		42	7	534	60	15.26	–		2126	70	30.37
Corling, G.E.	1963/64–68/69	65		78	32	484	42*	10.52	–		5546	173	32.05
	T	5		4	1	5	3	1.67	–		447	12	37.25
Cornelius, B.W.	1947	1		2	1	9	9*	–	–		–	–	–
Cornford, J.H.	1931–52	334		399	144	1357	34	5.40	–		26999	1019	26.49
Cornford, W.L.	1921–47	496		649	211	6554	82	14.96	–		65	0	–
	T	4		4	0	36	18	9.00	–		–	–	–
Cornock, W.B.	1948	26		43	2	801	60	19.53	–		1007	15	67.13
Cornwell, A.E.	1949	1		2	0	0	0	0.00	–		60	3	20.00
Corrall, P.	1930–51	288		422	126	2846	64	9.61	–		–	–	–
Corran, A.J.	1958–65	132		207	55	2476	75	16.28	–		10556	410	25.73
Corry, C.V.	1959–66	4		7	1	40	17	6.83	–		–	–	–
Cosh, N.J.	1966–69	36		64	6	1731	138	29.84	2		34	1	–
Cosh, S.H.	1950–59	36		57	3	873	99	16.17	–		7	0	–
Cosier, G.J.	1971/72–80/81	91		161	9	5005	168	32.93	7		2301	75	30.68
	T	18		32	1	897	168	28.94	2		341	5	68.20
Cottam, R.M.H.	1963–76	289		280	97	1278	62*	6.98	–		21125	1010	20.91
	T	4		5	1	27	13	6.75	–		327	14	23.26
Cotterell, T.A.	1983–	20		28	4	328	52	13.67	–		1832	30	61.67
Cotton, J.	1958–69	239		298	107	1631	58	8.54	–		16674	652	25.57
Cotton, R.H.	1947	2		3	1	0	0*	–	–		128	2	64.00
Cottrell, G.A.	1966–68	39		70	4	1108	81	16.78	–		2121	60	35.35
Cottrell, P.R.	1979	10		9	1	119	34	14.87	–		–	–	–
Courtenay, G.W.L.	1947–57	8		14	0	168	69	12.00	–		–	–	–
Cousens, P.	1950–55	39		50	26	72	13	3.00	–		1707	44	38.80
Coutts, I.D.F.	1951–52	15		25	5	108	16*	5.40	0		1180	33	35.75
Coverdale, S.P.	1973–80	45		75	6	1245	85	18.04	–		0	1	–
Cowan, J.F.	1960–62	3		5	0	52	18	10.40	–		–	–	–
Cowan, M.J.	1953–62	99		94	51	233	22	5.42	–		6783	276	24.58
Cowan, R.S.	1980–83	28		52	5	1406	143*	29.92	3		798	9	88.67
Cowans, N.G.	1980–	67		73	11	509	66	8.21	–		4715	190	24.82
	T	13		23	5	143	36	7.94	–		1248	35	35.66
Cowdrey, C.S.	1977–	160		234	37	6163	125*	31.28	8		2775	73	38.01
Cowdrey, G.R.	1984–	1		1	0	7	7	–	–		22	1	–
Cowdrey, M.C.	1950–76	692		1130	134	42719	307	42.89	107		3329	65	51.21
	T	114		188	15	7624	182	44.06	22		104	0	–
Cowie, J.	1932/33–49/50	86		104	29	762	54	10.16	–		8001	359	22.29
	T	9		13	4	90	45	10.00	–		969	45	21.53
Cowley, N.G.	1974–	208		302	42	5767	109*	22.18	2		11092	327	33.92
Cownley, J.M.	1952–62	4		6	1	64	25	12.80	–		155	3	51.67
Cowper, R.M.	1959/60–69/70	147		228	31	10595	307	53.78	26		5709	183	31.19
	T	27		46	2	2061	307	46.84	5		1139	36	31.63
Cox, A.L.	1926–47	230		410	31	6631	104	17.50	1		7926	199	39.83
Cox, D.F.	1949–57	42		52	17	660	57	18.86	–		2316	68	34.06
Cox, D.W.	1969	1		2	0	8	8	4.00	–		77	1	–
Cox, G.	1931–61	455		754	57	22949	234*	33.06	50		5935	192	30.92
Cox, H.R.	1930–54	30		42	9	419	64	12.70	–		1556	47	33.11
Cox, R.	1971	1		2	1	24	24	–	–		–	–	–
Coxon, A.	1945–50	146		188	33	2814	83	18.16	–		9893	473	20.92
	T	1		2	0	19	19	9.50	–		172	3	57.33
Coxon, A.J.	1951–58	18		26	14	144	43*	12.00	–		1350	28	48.21
Crabtree, H.P.	1931–47	24		41	1	1281	146	32.02	4		63	0	–

	Career span	M	I	NO	Runs	HS	Avge	100	Runs	Wkts	Avge
					BATTING				BOWLING		
Cragg, J.R.A.	1970	7	13	0	149	55	11.46	–	–	–	–
Craig, E.J.	1961–63	50	93	7	3103	208*	36.08	7	16	0	–
Craig, H.S.	1945	1	2	0	88	56	44.00	–	–	–	–
Craig, I.D.	1951/52–61/62	144	208	15	7328	213*	37.96	15	127	1	–
T		11	18	0	358	53	19.88	–	–	–	–
Craig, I.T.	1959	1	1	0	1	1	–	–	85	2	42.50
Craig, V.A.	1948	1	1	0	12	12	–	–	–	–	–
Cranfield, L.M.	1934–51	162	228	55	2466	90	14.25	–	7670	233	32.92
Cranmer, P.	1934–54	175	284	13	5853	113	21.60	4	1208	29	41.65
Cranston, K.	1947–50	78	104	15	3099	156*	34.82	3	4985	178	28.00
T		8	14	0	209	45	14.92	–	461	18	25.61
Crapp, J.F.	1936–56	451	754	80	23615	175	35.04	38	306	6	51.00
T		7	13	2	319	56	29.00	–	–	–	–
Crawford, I.C.	1975–78	5	7	0	104	73	14.85	–	174	3	58.00
Crawford, M.G.	1951	1	2	0	22	13	11.00	–	–	–	–
Crawford, N.C.	1978–80	22	22	2	262	46*	13.10	–	1030	32	32.19
Crawford, T.A.	1930–51	13	16	1	150	32	10.00	–	13	0	–
Crawford, W.P.A.	1954/55–57/58	37	42	20	424	86	19.27	–	2313	110	21.02
T		4	5	2	53	34	17.67	–	107	7	15.29
Crawley, A.M.	1927–49	87	141	6	5061	204	37.49	11	565	15	37.66
Cray, S.J.	1938–50	102	177	6	4218	163	24.67	7	40	1	–
Creese, W.L.C.	1928–46	281	455	42	9938	241	29.06	6	11246	410	27.42
Crerar, G.G.	1947–48	2	4	0	76	36	19.00	–	–	–	–
Cresswell, G.F.	1948/49–54/55	33	36	19	89	12*	5.23	–	2794	124	22.53
T		3	5	3	14	12*	7.00	–	292	13	22.46
Crichton, I.G.	1963	1	1	0	4	4	–	–	61	0	–
Crick, H.	1937–49	11	15	2	124	22	9.54	–	–	–	–
Crisp, J.G.	1951	1	2	1	12	12	–	–	26	0	–
Cristofani, D.R.	1941/42–46/47	18	30	2	749	110*	26.75	1	1581	48	32.93
Croft, C.E.H.	1971/72–83/84	121	136	54	865	46*	10.55	–	10527	428	24.60
T		27	37	22	158	33	10.53	–	2915	125	23.32
Croft, P.D.	1955–57	18	29	2	402	47*	14.89	–	29	0	–
Cromack, B.	1959–68	34	55	2	626	55	11.80	–	1006	38	26.47
Crookes, D.V.	1953–54	11	16	3	227	33	17.46	–	125	3	41.67
Crookes, N.S.	1962/63–69/70	50	64	5	1123	68	19.03	–	4489	153	29.33
Croom, L.C.B.	1949	4	8	0	72	26	9.13	–	–	–	–
Cross, A.J.	1966–69	6	10	1	151	39*	16.77	–	19	0	–
Cross, G.F.	1961–76	83	128	15	2079	78	18.40	–	2756	92	29.96
Crosskey, T.R.	1949–50	4	8	0	236	81	29.50	–	26	0	–
Crothers, G.M.	1931–47	10	19	1	174	41	9.67	–	–	–	–
Crothers, J.G.	1972	1	2	0	10	10	5.00	–	–	–	–
Crouch, H.R.	1935–46	3	3	0	11	7	3.67	–	101	2	50.50
Crouch, M.A.	1950–52	4	7	0	205	81	29.29	–	–	–	–
Crowe, J.J.	1977/78–	62	109	10	3353	157	33.87	7	19	1	–
T		10	16	0	424	128	26.50	1	0	0	–
Crowe, M.D.	1979/80–	85	139	21	5359	190	45.42	17	2604	84	31.00
T		13	21	1	429	100	21.45	1	225	3	75.00
Crowe, P.J.	1982	1	2	0	11	11	5.50	–	121	1	–
Crowther, P.G.	1977–78	9	14	0	185	99	13.21	–	22	1	–
Crump, B.S.	1960–72	321	479	111	8789	133*	23.88	5	20163	814	24.77
Crush, E.	1946–49	45	72	5	1078	78	16.09	–	3163	83	38.11
Crutchley, E.	1947	2	4	0	28	14	7.00	–	–	–	–
Cullinan, M.R.	1979/80–	16	21	2	215	59	11.32	–	4	1	–
Cumbes, J.	1963–82	161	133	67	499	43	7.56	–	11447	379	30.20
Cunis, R.S.	1960/61–76/77	132	157	45	1849	111	16.50	1	10287	386	26.65
T		20	31	8	295	51	12.82	–	1887	51	37.00

	Career span	M	I	NO	Runs	HS	Avge	100	Runs	Wkts	Avge
					BATTING				BOWLING		
Cunningham, E.J.	1982–	14	23	6	271	61	15.94	–	264	4	66.00
Curley, S.A.	1948–51	5	10	1	175	43	19.44	–	–	–	–
Curran, K.M.	1980/81–	18	29	5	601	96	25.04	–	973	42	23.17
Currie, J.D.	1953–57	10	20	1	283	38	14.89	–	–	–	–
Curtis, A.D.	1966	1	1	0	15	15	–	–	–	–	–
Curtis, I.J.	1980–84	31	30	14	77	20*	4.81	–	2109	51	41.35
Curtis, T.S.	1979–	60	104	14	2809	129	31.21	3	194	4	48.50
Curzon, C.C.	1978–81	18	23	5	307	45	17.05	–	–	–	–
Curzon, J.T.	1978	1	1	0	0	0	–	–	22	0	–
Cushing, V.G.B.	1971–73	14	25	5	565	77*	28.25	–	–	–	–
Cuthbertson, J.L.	1962–63	28	51	7	1294	94	29.41	–	1646	34	48.41
Cutler, R.W.	1965–66	6	12	1	79	18	7.18	–	341	9	37.89
Dale, C.S.	1984	8	8	2	100	49	16.67	–	467	7	66.72
Dale, J.R.	1958	1	1	0	0	0	–	–	31	1	–
Dalrymple, J.J.H.	1978	3	4	2	27	15	13.50	–	260	7	37.14
Dalton, A.J.	1969–72	21	31	2	710	128	24.48	3	–	–	–
Daniel, A.R.H.	1975–77	4	5	0	96	75	19.20	–	–	–	–
Daniel, W.W.	1975/76	205	189	85	1304	53*	12.54	–	14222	670	21.23
	T	10	11	4	46	11	6.57	–	910	36	25.28
Daniels, D.M.	1964–65	18	32	0	562	82	17.56	–	7	0	–
Daniels, J.G.U.	1964	2	4	0	51	22	12.75	–	–	–	–
Daniels, R.C.	1965–66	7	14	1	97	26	7.47	–	148	1	–
Daniels, S.A.B.	1981–82	16	23	10	227	73	17.46	–	1162	28	41.50
D'Arcy, J.W.	1955/56–61/62	53	90	3	2009	89	23.09	–	12	1	–
	T	5	10	0	136	33	13.60	–	–	–	–
Dare, R.	1949–54	109	169	32	1679	109*	12.25	1	6479	185	35.02
Dargan, M.J.	1954	1	2	0	10	7	5.00	–	–	–	–
Darks, G.C.	1946–50	7	8	3	89	39	17.80	–	452	13	34.77
Darvell, B.S.	1952	1	1	0	5	5	–	–	2	0	–
Darwall-Smith, R.F.H.D.	1935–46	46	69	16	649	54	12.25	–	4153	151	27.50
Datta, P.B.	1942/43–55/56	34	52	3	1459	143	29.77	4	1520	41	37.07
Dauncey, J.G.	1957	2	4	0	54	34	13.50	–	–	–	–
Davey, C.F.	1953–55	13	25	4	261	46	12.42	–	–	–	–
Davey, J.	1966–78	175	208	90	918	53*	7.77	–	11720	411	28.51
Davidson, A.K.	1949/50–62/63	193	246	39	6804	129	32.86	9	14048	672	20.90
	T	44	61	7	1328	80	24.59	–	3819	186	20.53
Davidson, J.N.G.	1951	4	7	1	86	40	14.33	–	–	–	–
Davidson, W.W.	1947–56	22	23	6	118	31	6.94	–	–	–	–
Davies, A.G.	1982–	12	18	5	325	69	25.00	–	–	–	–
Davies, D.E.	1924–54	621	1033	79	26566	287*	27.85	32	26458	903	29.30
Davies, G.	1947–48	2	2	0	9	7	4.50	–	–	–	–
Davies, H.D.	1955–60	52	70	26	247	28	5.61	–	3659	115	31.82
Davies, H.G.	1935–58	427	601	96	6613	80	13.06	–	20	1	–
Davies, J.A.	1952	1	2	0	11	11	5.50	–	–	–	–
Davies, J.G.W.	1931–61	153	262	12	5982	168	23.93	4	7847	258	30.42
Davies, J.T.	1956–58	8	15	0	94	29	6.26	–	–	–	–
Davies, M.K.	1975–76	2	2	1	14	12	–	–	–	–	–
Davies, M.N.	1982	2	1	0	0	0	–	–	–	–	–
Davies, R.D.	1950	1	1	0	7	7	–	–	–	–	–
Davies, R.J.	1976	1	2	0	18	18	9.00	–	–	–	–
Davies, T.	1979–	50	68	15	956	69*	18.04	–	–	–	–
Davies, T.C.	1971–72	7	6	4	9	5	4.50	–	625	18	34.72
Davies, T.E.	1955–61	20	30	5	481	76	19.24	–	169	6	28.17
Davies, W.G.	1954–60	32	58	0	674	64	11.62	–	646	16	40.36

	Career span	M	I	NO	Runs	HS	Avge	100	Runs	Wkts	Avge
Davis, A.T.	1967	2	3	0	57	37	19.00	–	–	–	–
Davis, B.A.	1959/60–70/71	112	193	14	6231	188*	34.81	5	434	9	48.22
	T	4	8	0	245	68	30.62	–	–	–	–
Davis, C.A.	1960/61–75/76	90	152	18	5538	183	41.32	14	2480	63	39.36
	T	15	29	5	1301	183	54.20	4	330	2	165.00
Davis, C.P.	1935–52	170	303	22	6363	237	22.63	10	491	6	81.83
Davis, E.	1947–56	104	159	14	4126	171	28.46	3	8	1	–
Davis, F.J.	1959–67	28	47	13	552	63	16.24	–	1694	52	32.96
Davis, I.C.	1973/74–82/83	88	147	9	4609	156	33.40	1	7	0	–
	T	15	27	1	692	105	26.61	1	–	–	–
Davis, M.J.	1963	1	–	–	–	–	–	–	58	2	29.00
Davis, M.R.	1982–	42	43	13	368	60*	12.27	–	2923	103	28.38
Davis, P.V.	1946	9	17	0	276	136	16.23	1	–	–	–
Davis, R.C.	1964–76	214	371	30	7367	134	21.60	5	7793	241	32.33
Davis, W.W.	1979/80–	82	99	38	906	77	14.85	–	7637	273	27.97
	T	9	10	4	141	77	23.50	–	894	22	40.64
Davison, B.F.	1967/68–	426	700	68	25644	189	40.58	52	2635	82	32.13
Davison, I.J.	1959–66	178	246	65	1641	60*	9.07	–	15588	541	28.81
Dawkes, G.O.	1937–61	482	736	105	11411	143	18.08	1	20	0	–
Dawson, G.W.	1947–49	60	107	7	2643	158*	26.43	4	7	0	–
Dawson, H.	1947–48	10	19	1	236	37	13.11	–	8	0	–
Dawson, O.C.	1938/39–61/62	75	119	9	3804	182	34.58	6	3429	123	27.87
	T	9	15	1	293	55	20.92	–	578	10	57.80
Day, A.R.	1968	1	1	0	5	5	–	–	–	–	–
Day, A.S.	1953	1	2	0	3	2	1.50	–	–	–	–
Day, F.G.K.	1950–56	7	13	2	201	56*	18.27	–	–	–	–
Day, K.B.	1958–59	3	–	–	–	–	–	–	–	–	–
Deakin, M.J.	1981	4	6	0	45	15	7.50	–	–	–	–
De Alwis, R.G.	1982/83–	14	19	0	281	74	14.79	–	–	–	–
Dean, P.J.	1978	2	4	0	75	39	18.75	–	–	–	–
Dean, T.A.	1939–56/57	29	46	13	285	26	8.63	–	1706	54	31.59
Dean, W.H.	1952	1	2	1	21	21	–	–	17	0	–
Dearlove, J.A.	1954	1	1	0	1	1	–	–	74	0	–
Deas, K.R.	1947/48–60/61	18	34	4	522	73	17.40	–	313	9	34.77
Debnam, A.F.H.	1948–51	21	33	6	327	64	12.11	–	862	20	43.10
De Courcy, J.H.	1947/48–57/58	79	113	11	3778	204	37.03	6	67	0	–
	T	3	6	1	81	41	16.20	–	–	–	–
Deighton, J.H.G.	1947–62	35	63	13	994	62*	19.88	–	3081	127	24.27
Delisle, G.P.S.	1954–58	91	163	16	3283	130	22.33	3	–	–	–
Deller, R.P.	1951–53	3	3	3	4	3*	–	–	127	2	63.50
De Mel, A.L.F.	1980/81–	29	40	7	747	100*	22.64	1	2963	72	37.40
	T	7	14	3	188	34	17.09	–	1015	29	35.00
Dempster, C.S.	1921/22–47/48	185	306	36	12145	212	44.98	35	300	8	37.50
	T	10	15	4	723	136	65.72	2	10	0	–
Denman, H.W.	1950–52	7	5	4	4	3	–	–	–	–	–
Denman, J.	1970–73	49	65	20	713	50*	15.84	–	3065	70	43.78
Denness, M.H.	1959–80	501	838	65	25886	195	33.48	33	62	2	31.00
	T	28	45	3	1667	188	39.69	4	–	–	–
Denning, P.W.	1969–84	269	447	44	11559	184	28.68	8	96	1	–
Dennis, S.J.	1980–	47	51	20	313	53*	10.10	–	4152	136	30.53
Dennison, D.G.	1983	1	2	0	17	16	8.50	–	–	–	–
Dermont, R.W.A.	1967	1	1	0	0	0	–	–	31	2	15.50
Derrick, J.	1983–	15	20	10	403	69*	40.30	–	472	8	59.00
Desai, A.H.	1947/48–63/64	41	51	12	1700	147*	43.58	5	1378	55	25.05
Desai, R.B.	1958/59–71/72	150	179	48	2384	107	18.19	1	11282	468	24.10
	T	28	44	13	418	85	13.48	–	2761	74	37.31

	Career span	M		I	NO	Runs	HS	Avge	100		Runs	Wkts	Avge
Deshon, D.P.T.	1947–53	4		8	1	82	21	11.72	–		–	–	–
De Silva, D.L.S.	1979	4		3	1	11	7	5.50	–		199	6	33.16
De Silva, D.S.	1966/67–	64		95	16	1733	97	21.94	–		6714	238	28.21
	T	12		22	3	406	61	21.37	–		1347	37	36.41
De Silva, G.R.A.	1973/74–82/83	53		68	27	317	75	7.73	–		4418	161	27.44
	T	4		7	2	41	14	8.20	–		385	7	55.00
De Silva, P.A.	1983/84	9		10	1	259	75	28.77	–		19	0	–
	T	1		2	0	19	16	9.50	–		–	–	–
Devapriya, H.H.	1980/81–82/83	10		20	0	522	95	26.10	–		–	–	–
Devereux, L.N.	1949–60	192		327	47	5560	108*	19.86	1		6286	178	35.32
Devereux, R.J.	1963	11		16	3	216	55*	16.61	–		581	13	44.69
De Ville, R.T.	1963–64	3		5	2	26	17	8.67	–		146	2	73.00
De Villiers, J.O.	1951–53/54	11		20	4	347	81	21.69	–		38	0	–
Dew, D.G.du B.	1959	2		2	0	4	4	2.00	–		–	–	–
Dew, J.A.	1947–61	3		5	0	60	29	12.00	–		–	–	–
Dewar, A.	1960–62	5		7	4	15	4*	5.00	–		366	11	33.27
Dewdney, D.T.	1954/55–61	40		49	19	171	37*	5.70	–		2828	92	30.74
	T	9		12	5	17	5*	2.42	–		807	21	38.42
Dewes, A.R.	1978–79	14		21	1	368	84	18.40	–		146	1	–
Dewes, J.G.	1945–57	137		229	24	8564	212	41.78	18		71	2	35.50
	T	5		10	0	121	67	12.10	–		–	–	–
Dews, G.	1946–61	376		642	53	16803	145	28.52	20		202	2	101.00
Dexter, E.R.	1956–68	324		567	48	21150	205	40.75	51		12539	419	29.93
	T	62		102	8	4502	205	47.89	9		2306	66	34.93
Dexter, R.E.	1975–81	22		36	6	464	57	15.46	–		–	–	–
Dias, R.L.	1974/75–	64		105	11	2978	127	31.68	3		24	1	–
	T	9		17	0	747	109	43.94	2		–	–	–
Dick, A.E.	1956/57–68/69	78		126	12	2315	127	20.31	1		20	0	–
	T	17		30	4	370	50*	14.23	–		–	–	–
Dickinson, D.C.	1953–57	13		18	7	111	36*	10.09	–		653	24	27.21
Dickinson, T.E.	1950–57	9		12	6	21	9	3.50	–		419	20	20.95
Dilley, G.R.	1977–	114		119	42	1205	81	15.65	–		7491	269	28.59
	T	18		28	8	330	56	16.50	–		1564	49	31.92
Dilley, M.R.	1957–63	33		38	16	232	31*	10.55	–		2471	80	30.89
Diment, R.A.	1952–58	60		102	5	1595	71	16.44	–		4	0	–
Dindar, A.	1962–63	7		10	2	100	55	12.50	–		70	3	23.33
Dineen, P.J.	1962–71	7		12	2	179	84	17.90	–		–	–	–
Dines, W.J.	1947–49	20		30	7	431	69*	18.74	–		980	15	65.33
Dinsdale, S.C.	1969/70–75/76	15		26	2	581	88	24.21	–		160	8	20.00
Disbury, B.E.	1954–57	14		21	3	288	74*	16.00	–		204	5	40.80
Divecha, R.V.	1946/47–62/63	61		88	18	1423	92	20.32	–		5401	217	24.88
	T	5		5	0	60	26	12.00	–		361	11	32.82
Dixon, A.L.	1950–1973/74	381		580	71	9589	125*	18.84	3		24060	935	25.73
Dixon, A.S.	1971	1		2	0	12	12	6.00	–		–	–	–
Dixon, J.H.	1973–81	16		20	8	77	13*	6.42	–		1136	21	54.09
Dobree-Carey, P.A.H.	1942/43–48	53		82	16	869	96	13.17	–		4448	136	32.71
Docwra, E.D.	1974	1		2	0	26	20	13.00	–		–	–	–
Dodds, T.C.	1943/44–61	395		693	18	19405	157	28.75	17		1126	36	31.27
Doggart, A.P.	1947–51	9		16	3	228	43	17.54	–		41	2	20.50
Doggart, G.H.G.	1948–61	210		347	28	10054	219*	31.51	20		2056	60	34.25
	T	2		4	0	76	29	19.00	–		–	–	–
Doggart, S.J.G.	1980–83	35		50	11	878	70	22.52	–		2223	34	65.39
Dolding, D.L.	1950–51	3		3	1	11	8	5.50	–		103	3	34.33
D'Oliveira, B.L.	1961/62–80	362		566	88	18919	227	39.57	43		15021	548	27.41
	T	44		70	8	2484	158	40.06	5		1859	47	39.55
D'Oliveira, D.B.	1982–	49		80	6	1833	102	24.77	1		603	14	43.07

	Career span	M	I	NO	Runs	HS	Avge	100	Runs	Wkts	Avge
			←——————BATTING——————→						←——BOWLING——→		
D'Oliveira, I.	1967	1	1	0	0	0	–	–	–	–	–
Dollery, H.E.	1933–55	436	717	66	24413	212	37.50	32	0	–	
T		4	7	0	72	37	10.29	–	–	–	–
Dollery, K.R.	1947/48–56	80	107	27	958	41	11.97	–	6018	227	26.51
Donald, P.C.G.	1978	1	1	0	1	1	–	–	–	–	–
Donald, W.A.	1978–	6	10	1	157	45	17.44	–	64	1	–
Donellan, R.O.	1963	5	10	0	173	47	17.30	–	–	–	–
Donnelly, M.P.	1936/37–60/61	131	221	26	9250	208*	47.44	23	1683	43	39.14
T		7	12	1	582	206	52.90	1	20	0	–
Dooland, B.	1945/46–57/58	214	326	33	7141	115*	24.37	4	22332	1016	21.98
T		3	5	1	76	29	19.00	–	419	9	46.55
Dorrell, P.G.	1946	1	1	0	1	1	–	–	–	–	–
Doshi, D.R.	1968/69–	228	242	68	1396	44	8.02	–	22856	872	26.21
T		33	38	10	129	20	4.61	–	3502	114	30.72
Doughty, D.G.	1963–64	17	20	5	104	22	6.93	–	710	35	20.28
Doughty, R.J.	1981–	14	19	7	214	32*	17.83	–	939	23	40.83
Douglas-Home, A.	1970	4	6	1	33	23	6.60	–	273	9	30.33
Douglas-Pennant, S.	1959–61	35	53	31	101	14*	4.59	–	3031	83	36.52
Dovey, R.R.	1938–54	263	404	74	3841	65*	11.64	–	21391	777	27.53
Dowe, W.D.F.	1956–67	13	16	4	107	18	8.92	–	1015	38	26.71
Dowding, A.L.	1951–56	43	73	5	1950	105	28.68	2	116	1	–
Dowell, A.McQ.	1951–55	3	4	1	6	5	2.00	–	136	2	68.00
Dowling, G.T.	1958/59–71/72	158	282	13	9399	239	34.94	16	378	9	42.00
T		39	77	3	2306	239	31.16	3	19	1	–
Downend, R.H.	1972	1	2	0	6	5	3.00	–	71	1	–
Downer, H.R.	1946	2	4	0	8	4	2.00	–	–	–	–
Downton, G.C.	1948–59	10	15	5	88	20	8.80	–	–	–	–
Downton, P.R.	1977–	163	193	37	3055	90*	19.58	–	–	–	–
T		10	18	2	279	56	17.44	–	–	–	–
Draffan, N.G.H.	1971–72	4	7	1	35	29	5.83	–	–	–	–
Dredge, C.H.	1976–	159	184	58	1749	56*	13.88	–	11033	380	29.03
Dring, C.F.	1955	1	2	0	8	8	4.00	–	–	–	–
Drummond, D.W.	1951–61	17	22	1	263	33	12.52	–	771	20	38.55
Drybrough, C.D.	1958–67	133	161	41	1848	88	15.40	–	9270	319	29.06
D'Souza, Antao	1956/57–66/67	61	72	29	815	45	18.95	–	4946	190	26.03
T		6	10	8	76	23*	38.00	–	745	17	43.82
Duckworth, C.A.R.	1952/53–62/63	77	124	12	2572	158	22.96	3	–	–	–
T		2	4	0	28	13	7.00	–	–	–	–
Duckworth, G.	1923–47	504	545	196	4945	75	14.17	–	73	0	–
T		24	28	12	234	39*	14.62	–	–	–	–
Dudhia, M.H.E.M.	1980/81–82	2	1	0	0	0	–	–	71	5	14.20
Dudleston, B.	1966–83	295	501	47	14747	202	32.48	32	1365	47	29.04
Dudley-Jones, R.D.L.	1972–73	5	7	2	15	5	3.00	–	351	13	27.00
Dudman, L.C.	1955–68	35	61	3	1286	161	22.17	1	–	–	–
Duff, A.R.	1959–68	36	57	16	676	55*	16.49	–	1396	54	25.85
Duffield, J.	1938–47	16	23	6	263	60*	15.47	–	1043	29	35.96
Duffy, G.A.A.	1953–73	16	27	6	317	55*	15.10	–	426	15	28.40
Dujon, J.	1974/75	82	119	17	4340	135*	42.55	11	1	0	–
Dumbrill, R.	1960/61–67/68	51	82	7	1761	94	23.48	–	2909	132	22.03
T		5	10	0	153	36	15.30	–	336	9	37.33
Dunham, N.L.	1949	1	2	1	15	12*	–	–	60	0	–
Dunkels, P.R.	1971–72	3	2	1	3	3*	–	–	253	3	84.33
Dunning, M.L.	1962–64	2	4	0	134	85	33.50	–	22	0	–
Dunstan, M.S.T.	1971–74	12	20	3	283	52	16.64	–	–	–	–
Durack, J.P.	1980	7	13	0	136	45	10.46	–	32	0	–
Durden-Smith, N.	1961–67	4	6	1	111	50	22.20	–	–	–	–

					BATTING					BOWLING	
	Career span	M	I	NO	Runs	HS	Avge	100	Runs	Wkts	Avge
Durley, A.W.	1957	5	8	0	38	16	4.75	–	–	–	–
Durose, A.J.	1964–69	70	71	23	447	30	9.31	–	4035	150	26.90
Duthie, P.G.	1984	1	2	0	64	34	32.00	–	73	1	–
Dutton, R.S.	1981–82	6	6	4	7	7*	3.50	–	261	1	–
Dye, J.C.J.	1962–77	266	247	125	778	29*	6.37	–	17272	725	23.82
Dyer, A.W.	1965–66	25	41	9	765	67	23.91	–	–	–	–
Dyer, D.D.	1965/66–81/82	109	191	18	5651	196*	32.66	8	46	0	–
Dyer, D.V.	1939/40–48/49	34	53	7	1725	185	37.50	3	16	0	–
T		3	6	0	96	62	16.00	–	–	–	–
Dyer, R.I.H.B.	1981–	34	60	6	1510	106*	27.96	1	41	0	–
Dymock, G.	1971/72–81/82	126	159	54	1518	101*	14.46	1	11438	425	26.91
T		21	32	7	236	31*	9.44	–	2116	78	27.13
Dyson, A.H.	1926–48	413	697	37	17922	208	27.15	24	160	1	–
Dyson, E.M.	1958–68	27	48	3	819	68*	18.20	–	8	0	–
Dyson, Jack	1954–64	150	242	35	4433	118*	21.42	1	4447	161	27.62
Dyson, John	1975/76–	111	197	22	7040	241	40.23	14	43	1	–
T		27	52	7	1282	127*	28.48	2	–	–	–
Eagar, E.D.R.	1935–57	363	599	42	12178	158*	21.86	10	1481	31	47.77
Eagar, M.A.	1956–66	58	105	8	2465	125	25.41	1	4	0	–
Eaglestone, J.T.	1947–49	60	97	7	1420	77	15.78	–	–	–	–
Ealham, A.G.E.	1966–82	305	466	68	10996	153	27.62	7	189	3	63.00
Eames, D.G.R.	1958	1	2	0	21	14	10.50	–	9	0	–
Earl, K.J.	1950	2	4	0	4	4	1.00	–	162	9	18.00
Earls-Davies, M.R.G.	1947–50	6	7	1	14	4	2.33	–	361	12	30.08
Earnshaw, R.O.	1960–61	2	3	1	11	9	5.50	–	211	0	–
East, D.E.	1981–	90	118	17	1814	91	17.96	–	11	0	–
East, R.E.	1965–84	410	517	112	7178	113	17.72	1	26210	1019	25.72
Easter, J.N.C.	1966–68	28	36	13	90	14	3.91	–	1940	58	33.45
Eato, A.	1950–55	25	28	5	220	44	9.57	–	1429	50	28.58
Eaton, V.J.	1926–46	36	52	8	465	44	10.57	–	5	0	–
Eckersley, R.	1945	1	1	1	9	9*	–	–	62	0	–
Edbrooke, R.M.	1982–	11	20	2	591	84*	32.83	–	–	–	–
Eddington, R.I.	1975–76	8	14	4	130	24	13.00	–	329	8	41.13
Edgar, B.A.	1975/76–	104	188	15	6615	161	38.24	13	29	1	–
Edge, G.D.	1957	2	4	0	55	33	13.75	–	2	0	–
T		27	48	3	1521	161	33.80	3	3	0	–
Edmeades, B.E.A.	1961–76	335	555	69	12593	163	25.91	14	9688	374	25.90
Edmonds, J.W.	1975	1	–	–	–	–	–	–	82	3	27.33
Edmonds, P.H.	1971–	307	401	68	6566	142	19.72	3	25248	1021	24.73
T		23	28	6	430	64	19.55	–	1733	59	29.37
Edmonds, R.B.	1962–67	78	100	31	1006	102*	14.59	1	3994	146	27.35
Edrich. B.R.	1947–67	181	302	25	5529	193*	19.96	4	4546	137	33.18
Edrich, E.H.	1938–48	35	46	5	949	121	23.15	2	–	–	–
Edrich, G.A.	1946–58	339	508	60	15600	167*	34.82	26	399	5	79.80
Edrich, J.H.	1956–78	564	979	104	39790	310*	45.47	103	53	0	–
T		77	127	9	5138	310*	43.54	12	23	0	–
Edrich, W.J.	1934–58	571	964	92	36965	267*	42.39	86	15956	479	33.31
T		39	63	2	2440	219	40.00	6	1693	41	41.29
Edward, W.A.	1947–55	28	43	5	898	99	23.63	–	1475	38	38.82
Edwards, A.M.E.	1947	1	1	0	0	0	–	–	71	3	23.67
Edwards, G.	1973	9	16	4	191	46*	15.92	–	224	12	18.67
Edwards, G.N.	1973/74–81/82	91	163	8	4585	177*	29.58	5	32	0	–
T		8	15	0	377	55	25.13	–	–	–	–
Edwards, H.C.	1946	1	2	0	11	10	5.50	–	–	–	–

	Career span	M	I	NO	Runs	HS	Avge	100	Runs	Wkts	Avge
					BATTING				BOWLING		
Edwards, M.J.	1960–74	255	452	26	11378	137	26.71	12	179	2	89.50
Edwards, R.	1964/65–79/80	126	212	25	7345	170*	39.28	14	75	1	–
T	20	32	3	1171	170*	40.37	2		20	0	–
Edwards, R.M.	1961/62–69/70	35	43	10	389	34	11.78	–	2831	78	36.29
T	5	8	1	65	22	9.28	–		626	18	34.77
Edwards, T.D.W.	1979–81	12	21	2	393	57	20.68	–	58	1	–
Eele, P.J.	1958–65	54	70	20	612	103*	12.24	1	–	–	–
Eggar, J.D.	1938–54	41	64	6	1847	219	31.85	4	193	1	–
Ehtesham-ud-Din	1969/70–	206	138	47	1048	83	11.52	–	9782	472	20.73
T	5	3	1	2	2	1.00	–		375	16	23.43
Elder, J.W.G.	1973–80	8	8	2	25	7	4.17	–	310	12	25.83
Elgie, M.K.	1957/58–61/62	32	55	5	1834	162*	36.68	3	405	10	40.50
T	3	6	0	75	56	12.50	–		46	0	–
Elgood, B.C.	1948	14	21	2	631	127*	33.21	2	–	–	–
Eliot, R.F.	1961	2	4	2	55	30	27.50	–	140	1	–
Ellcock, RMcD	1982–	25	33	8	337	45*	13.48	–	1919	63	30.46
Elliott, C.S.	1932–53	275	468	29	11965	215	27.26	9	526	11	47.82
Elliott, H.	1920–47	532	764	220	7580	94	13.93	–	5	0	–
T	4	5	1	61	37*	15.25	–		–	–	–
Elliott, J.W.	1959–65	10	11	3	66	18*	8.25	–	–	–	–
Ellis, G.P.	1970–76	75	139	10	2673	116	20.72	1	1418	24	59.08
Ellis, P.M.	1953	1	–	–	–	–	–	–	120	0	–
Ellis, R.	1963–74	10	13	3	133	35	13.30	–	379	6	63.17
Ellis, R.G.P.	1981–	39	71	3	1997	105*	29.37	2	264	4	66.00
Ellis, R.S.	1945–45/46	21	28	12	47	10*	2.94	–	2070	78	26.54
Ellis, W.	1948	2	1	0	29	29	–	–	77	1	–
Ellis, W.A.	1954	1	1	0	6	6	–	–	–	–	–
Ellison, C.C.	1982–83	11	13	6	105	21	15.00	–	469	12	39.08
Ellison, R.M.	1981–	57	75	23	1379	108	26.52	1	3391	130	26.09
T	2	3	1	74	41	37.00	–		200	6	33.33
Elms, R.B.	1970–78	72	73	23	558	48	11.16	–	4606	116	39.70
Elsdon, H.	1949	1	2	1	12	12*	–	–	100	3	33.33
Elson, G.	1947	1	2	1	7	4	–	–	116	1	–
Elviss, R.W.	1966–67	19	26	9	114	16	6.72	–	1718	65	26.44
Emburey, J.E.	1973–	246	296	66	4703	133	20.45	2	19634	834	23.54
T	22	33	6	326	57	12.07	–		1696	56	30.28
Emery, K.st.J.D.	1982–83	25	27	15	45	18*	3.75	–	2231	88	25.35
Emmett, G.M.	1936–59	509	865	50	25602	188	31.41	37	2641	60	44.02
T	1	2	0	10	10	5.00	–		–	–	–
Endean, W.R.	1945/46–64	134	230	25	7757	247	37.83	15	73	2	36.50
T	28	52	4	1630	162*	33.95	3		–	–	–
Engineer, F.M.	1958/59–76	335	510	55	13436	192	29.52	13	117	1	–
T	46	87	3	2611	121	31.08	2		–	–	–
English, W.	1966/67–69/70	12	16	5	479	112	43.54	1	916	27	33.92
Enthoven, H.J.	1923–48	194	301	30	7362	139	27.17	9	8099	252	32.14
Entwistle, R.	1962–76	49	81	4	1612	85	20.94	–	–	–	–
Estcourt, N.S.D.	1953–54	21	34	7	513	56*	19.00	–	1262	23	54.87
Etheridge, R.J.	1955–66	39	64	14	796	48	15.92	–	–	–	–
Etherington, M.W.	1946–48	5	9	2	64	27	9.14	–	292	8	36.50
Evans, D.G.Ll.	1956–69	270	364	91	2875	46*	10.53	–	2458	72	34.14
Evans, G.	1938–49	33	56	6	824	65*	16.48	–	22	0	–
Evans, G.H.D.	1953	8	14	0	180	42	12.85	–	–	–	–
Evans, J.B.	1958–69	88	131	19	1535	62*	13.71	–	6789	251	27.05
Evans, K.P.	1984	3	4	0	48	42	12.00	–	173	2	86.50
Evans, M.	1946	3	4	1	26	14*	8.67	–	130	6	21.67
Evans, N.J.	1976	1	1	0	0	0	–	–	62	0	–

	Career span	M	I	NO	Runs	HS	Avge	100	Runs	Wkts	Avge
					BATTING					BOWLING	
Evans, R.E.	1950–57	17	29	0	482	79	16.62	–	–	–	–
Evans, T.G.	1939–69	465	753	52	14882	144	21.22	7	261	2	130.50
T		91	133	14	2439	104	20.49	2	–	–	–
Eve, S.C.	1949–57	32	51	4	1041	120	22.15	1	–	–	–
Exton, R.N.	1946	4	5	1	39	24*	9.75	–	40	0	–
Eyre, J.R.	1963–67	48	84	4	1194	106	14.93	1	248	1	–
Eyre, T.J.P.	1959–72	197	264	49	3436	102	15.98	1	10305	359	28.70
Ezekowitz, R.A.B.	1980–81	18	32	1	635	93	20.48	–	–	–	–
Faber, M.J.J.	1970–76	78	144	8	3009	176	22.13	3	66	1	–
Fagg, A.E.	1932–57	435	803	46	27291	269*	36.05	58	47	0	–
T		5	8	0	150	39	18.75	–	–	–	–
Fairbairn, A.	1947–51	21	34	4	776	110*	25.87	2	2	0	–
Fairbrother, N.H.	1982–	40	65	6	1960	102	33.22	1	21	1	–
Fairweather, J.H.W.	1971	2	4	0	23	9	5.75	–	–	–	–
Falkner, N.J.	1984	1	1	1	101	101*	–	1	–	–	–
Fallows, J.A.	1946	25	22	1	171	35	8.14	–	–	–	–
Fantham, W.E.	1935–48	63	103	12	1168	51	12.83	–	2907	64	45.42
Faragher, H.A.	1949–50	6	9	2	274	85*	39.14	–	–	–	–
Farmer, J.J.S.	1958	2	4	0	10	6	2.50	–	–	–	–
Farooq Hamid	1961/62–68/69	43	54	12	546	38	13.00	–	2799	111	25.22
T		1	2	0	3	3	1.50	–	107	1	–
Farr, B.H.	1949–52	7	12	2	143	37	14.30	–	538	10	53.80
Farrar, H.	1955	1	–	–	–	–	–	–	25	0	–
Farrimond, W.	1924–45	153	169	45	2921	174	23.56	1	16	0	–
T		4	7	0	116	35	16.57	–	–	–	–
Fasken, D.K.	1953–62	36	53	8	559	61	12.42	–	2862	73	39.21
Fasihuddin, Rashid	1957/58–74/75	51	83	5	2286	237	29.30	6	–	–	–
Faulkner, W.G.	1946	1	2	0	23	18	11.50	–	56	0	–
Fawcett, G.W.	1956–59	6	9	2	56	21	8.00	–	–	–	–
Fawkes, J.	1959–60	4	6	0	117	41	19.50	–	–	–	–
Fazal Mahmood	1943/44–63/64	111	146	33	2602	100*	23.02	1	8823	460	19.18
T		34	50	6	620	60	14.09	–	3434	139	24.70
Fearnley, C.D.	1962–68	97	174	14	3294	112	20.59	1	37	1	–
Fearnley, M.C.	1962–64	3	4	2	19	11*	9.50	–	133	6	22.17
Featherstone, N.G.	1967/68–81/82	329	528	54	13922	147	29.37	10	4986	181	27.54
Fee, F.	1956–59	5	9	2	57	15*	8.14	–	356	37	9.62
Fell, D.R.	1931/32–49/50	39	64	2	1958	161	31.58	5	1	0	–
Fell, M.A.	1982–83	15	27	0	408	108	15.11	1	157	1	–
Fellows-Smith, J.P.	1953–64	94	157	21	3999	109*	29.40	5	4414	149	29.62
T		4	8	2	166	35	27.66	–	61	0	–
Feltham, M.A.	1983–	13	15	5	206	44	20.60	–	1056	34	31.06
Felton, N.A.	1982–	29	48	2	1221	173*	26.54	2	4	0	–
Fenner, D.A.	1954	1	1	0	21	21	–	–	63	2	31.50
Fenner, M.D.	1949–64	33	54	6	708	77	14.75	–	1	1	–
Ferguson, W.H.N.	1951–64	5	9	1	122	37	15.25	–	375	19	19.74
Fernando, E.R.	1964/65–83/84	41	70	4	1436	81	21.76	–	–	–	–
T		5	10	0	112	46	11.20	–	–	–	–
Fernando, P.L.J.	1980/81–82/83	8	7	1	65	21	10.83	–	430	5	86.00
Ferreira, A.M.	1974/75	151	230	43	5016	112*	26.82	2	12469	414	30.12
Ferris, G.J.F.	1982/83–	20	22	10	85	26	7.08	–	1657	67	24.73
Ferris, S.W.	1956	2	3	2	10	4*	–	–	144	4	36.00
Fetherstonhaugh, C.B.R.	1956–64	4	8	2	59	20*	9.83	–	–	–	–
Fiddling, K.	1938–53	160	191	73	1380	68	11.69	–	–	–	–
Field, M.N.	1974–75	11	15	5	122	39*	12.20	–	896	24	37.33

	Career span	M		I	NO	Runs	HS	Avge	100		Runs	Wkts	Avge
						BATTING						BOWLING	
Filglas, F.M.	1948	1		2	0	3	3	1.50	–		–	–	–
Fillery, E.W.J.	1963–66	45		83	11	1371	75	19.04	–		2163	82	26.38
Finan, N.H.	1975–79	8		4	2	26	18	13.00	–		313	4	78.25
Fincham, A.L.R.	1976	1		1	1	3	3*	–	–		64	5	12.80
Findlay, F.	1948	2		3	0	9	6	3.00	–		–	–	–
Findlay, T.A.	1947	1		2	0	19	19	9.50	–		–	–	–
Findlay, T.M.	1964/65–78/79	110		170	25	2927	90	20.18	–		–	–	–
	T	10		16	3	212	44*	16.30	–		–	–	–
Finlay, A.J.	1957–65	9		16	1	170	30	11.33	–		–	–	–
Finlay, I.W.	1965–75/76	43		69	5	1640	150	25.63	2		691	18	38.39
Finney, R.J.	1982–	45		73	7	1296	78	16.94	–		2780	93	29.89
Firth, J.	1949–58	235		340	94	3588	90*	14.59	–		–	–	–
Fisher, P.B.	1974–81	57		85	14	654	42	9.21	–		–	–	–
Fishlock, L.B.	1931–52	417		699	54	25376	253	39.34	56		504	11	45.82
	T	4		5	1	47	19*	11.75	–		–	–	–
Fisk, E.	1950–51	3		5	0	37	16	7.40	–		123	2	61.50
Fitzgerald, J.F.	1966–68	15		24	11	147	27*	11.31	–		894	29	30.83
Fitzmaurice, D.M.J.	1947/48–50	17		18	2	272	45	17.00	–		798	28	28.50
Flaherty, K.F.	1969	1		–	–	–	–	–	–		107	4	26.75
Flanagan, J.P.D.	1965/66–77/78	57		91	15	1835	98	24.14	–		3191	116	27.50
Flavell, J.A.	1949–67	401		453	141	2032	54	6.51	–		32847	1529	21.48
	T	4		6	2	31	14	7.75	–		367	7	52.43
Fleming, R.C.J.	1974	9		15	7	60	13*	7.50	–		522	7	74.57
Fletcher, B.E.	1956–61	49		79	13	1511	102*	22.89	1		13	0	–
Fletcher, C.D.B.	1979	1		–	–	–	–	–	–		51	1	–
Fletcher, D.A.G.	1969/70–	106		189	23	3867	89	23.30	–		5845	213	27.44
Fletcher, D.G.W.	1946–61	316		519	41	14461	194	30.25	22		0	0	–
Fletcher, K.W.R.	1962–	651		1062	151	35013	228*	38.52	62		2252	50	45.04
	T	59		96	14	3272	216	39.90	7		193	2	96.50
Fletcher, S.D.	1983–	11		9	3	49	28*	8.17	–		657	22	29.86
Flick, B.J.	1969–73	16		14	8	46	18	7.67	–		–	–	–
Flint, D.	1948–49	10		10	3	33	11	4.72	–		465	12	38.75
Flockton, R.G.	1951/52–62/63	35		50	9	1695	264*	41.34	2		1027	27	38.03
Flood, R.D.	1956–60	24		43	5	885	138*	23.28	1		9	0	–
Flower, R.W.	1978	9		8	4	23	10*	5.75	–		554	10	55.40
Flynn, V.A.P.	1976–78	3		2	1	21	15	–	–		–	–	–
Foat, J.C.	1972–79	91		150	15	2512	126	18.60	5		40	0	–
Folkes, C.	1967/68–70/71	13		9	1	36	9	4.50	–		745	25	29.80
Folley, I.	1982–	46		52	17	450	36	12.86	–		2295	68	33.75
Foord, C.W.	1947–53	52		36	16	125	35	6.25	–		3469	128	27.10
Forbes, C.	1959–73	245		319	69	3597	86	14.39	–		17993	707	25.45
Ford, J.K.	1951	1		1	0	0	0	–	–		44	1	–
Ford, J.M.C.	1960–66	10		17	4	235	50	18.08	–		–	–	–
Ford, W.R.	1946–49	4		7	0	69	36	9.86	–		–	–	–
Foreman, D.J.	1951/52–67	130		203	23	3277	104	18.20	1		273	9	30.33
Forman, P.R.	1959–62	16		25	8	180	26	10.59	–		1291	40	32.28
Forster, G.	1980–82	5		4	2	45	22*	22.50	–		275	4	68.75
Fortin, R.C.G.	1963	2		4	0	52	25	13.00	–		–	–	–
Fosh, M.K.	1976–78	30		48	2	1069	109	23.23	1		–	–	–
Foster, D.C.G.	1980	4		6	1	124	67	24.80	–		–	–	–
Foster, M.L.C.	1963/64–77/78	112		175	26	6731	234	45.17	17		4056	132	30.72
	T	14		24	5	580	125	30.52	1		600	9	66.67
Foster, N.A.	1980–	48		55	16	725	54*	18.59	–		4523	175	25.85
	T	6		8	2	62	18*	10.33	–		614	12	51.17
Foster, P.G.	1936–46	30		50	2	882	107	18.38	1		7	0	–
Foster, W.J.	1964	2		4	0	79	36	19.75	–		13	0	–

	Career span	M	I	NO	Runs	HS	Avge	100	Runs	Wkts	Avge
					BATTING				BOWLING		
Foulds, F.G.	1952–56	2	4	0	1	1	0.75	–	–	–	–
Fowler, G.	1979–	109	183	9	6548	226	37.63	18	94	2	47.00
	T	16	29	0	869	106	29.97	2	11	0	–
Fowler, W.P.	1979/80–	49	82	13	1823	116	26.42	2	1059	14	75.64
Fox, J.G.	1959–61	43	54	6	515	52	10.73	–	0	0	–
Francis, B.C.	1968/69–74/75	109	192	10	6183	210	33.97	13	15	1	–
	T	3	5	0	52	27	10.40	–	–	–	–
Francis, D.A.	1973–84	138	237	36	4938	142*	24.57	3	31	0	–
Franklin, T.J.	1980/81–	43	80	8	2346	136	32.58	4	10	0	–
	T	1	2	0	9	7	4.50	–	–	–	–
Franks, J.G.	1983–84	13	20	2	268	42*	14.89	–	–	–	–
Frasat Ali	1975	1	2	0	42	30	21.00	–	82	2	41.00
Fraser, A.R.C.	1984	1	–	–	–	–	–	–	124	1	–
Fraser, D.D.	1967–69	4	2	2	0	0*	–	–	363	8	45.38
Fraser, T.W.	1936–48	23	37	11	249	61*	9.58	–	1834	58	31.62
Fraser-Darling, C.D.	1984	1	–	–	–	–	–	–	55	3	18.33
Frederick, M.C.	1944/45–53/54	6	10	0	294	84	29.40	–	–	–	–
	T	1	2	0	30	30	15.00	–	–	–	–
Fredericks, R.C.	1963/64–82/83	223	391	34	16384	250	45.89	40	2846	75	37.94
	T	59	109	7	4334	169	42.49	8	548	7	78.28
Freeman, E.W.	1964/65–73/74	83	123	6	2244	116	18.92	1	6690	241	27.76
	T	11	18	0	345	76	19.16	–	1128	34	33.17
Freeman, T.	1954	1	1	0	4	4	–	–	90	1	–
French, B.N.	1976–	170	221	44	3303	98	18.66	–	–	–	–
Frost, G.	1967–73	104	169	17	3439	107	22.43	2	680	15	45.33
Frost, P.D.	1961	1	–	–	–	–	–	–	–	–	–
Fry, C.A.	1959–68	50	85	7	1952	103*	25.02	2	13	0	–
Fuller, E.R.H.	1950/51–58	59	86	16	1062	69	15.17	–	5026	190	26.45
	T	7	9	1	64	17	8.00	–	668	22	30.36
Fullerton, G.M.	1942/43–51	63	97	8	2768	167	31.10	3	107	3	35.66
	T	7	13	0	325	88	25.00	–	–	–	–
Fullerton, I.R.	1958/59–65/66	31	56	2	1853	145	34.31	5	8	0	–
Fullwood, W.	1946	6	10	1	41	13	4.56	–	–	–	–
Furniss, J.B.	1955–56	4	5	1	9	6	2.25	–	259	7	37.00
Fursdon, E.D.	1973–75	17	29	6	484	112*	21.04	1	1428	43	33.20
Fussell, P.H.	1953–56	2	4	0	10	5	2.50	–	71	1	–
Gaekwad, A.D.	1969/70–	159	258	27	9333	225	40.40	25	3420	105	32.57
	T	35	62	4	1776	201	30.62	2	107	0	–
Gaekwad, D.K.	1943/44–63/64	109	171	13	5783	249*	36.60	17	979	24	40.79
	T	11	20	1	350	52	18.42	–	12	0	–
Gaekwad, H.G.	1941/42–63/64	100	146	18	2484	164	19.40	2	8827	374	23.60
	T	1	2	0	22	14	11.00	–	47	0	–
Gale, R.A.	1955–68	242	439	13	12505	200	29.35	15	1748	47	3719
Gallagher, T.N.	1965–66	4	5	0	126	73	25.20	–	–	–	–
Gallaugher, R.G.	1945	1	1	0	2	2	–	–	27	0	–
Galley, J.	1969	3	6	1	27	17	4.50	–	–	–	–
Gamble, N.W.	1967	13	17	5	87	24	7.25	–	786	19	41.36
Gamsy, D.	1958/59–72/73	93	145	14	3106	137*	23.70	2	13	0	–
	T	2	3	1	39	30*	19.50	–	–	–	–
Gandon, N.J.C.	1979	8	13	1	170	38	14.16	–	–	–	–
Ganteaume, A.G.	1940/41–62/63	50	85	5	2785	159	34.81	5	51	0	–
	T	1	1	0	112	112	–	1	–	–	–
Gard, T.	1976–	64	73	15	827	51*	14.26	–	8	0	–
Gardiner, S.J.	1967/68–78	34	49	16	556	40*	16.84	–	2772	111	24.97

	Career span	M		I	NO	Runs	HS	Avge	100		Runs	Wkts	Avge
Gardiner-Hill, P.F.	1949	2		2	0	78	50	39.00	–		–	–	–
Gardner, F.C.	1947–61	340		597	66	17905	215*	33.71	29		99	0	–
Gardner, L.R.	1954–62	126		227	19	4119	102*	19.80	2		199	5	39.80
Gardom, B.K.	1973–74	17		25	2	427	79*	18.57	–		700	17	41.18
Garlick, P.L.	1984	10		15	6	13	6*	1.44	–		1092	12	91.00
Garlick, R.G.	1938–50	121		152	32	1664	62*	13.87	–		8670	332	26.11
Garner, J.	1975/76–	147		164	39	2176	104	17.41	1		11801	665	17.75
	T	42		51	9	519	60	12.36	–		3924	191	20.55
Garnham, M.A.	1979–	52		78	14	1541	84	24.08	–		–	–	–
Garofall, A.R.	1966–68	27		47	0	874	99	18.59	–		8	0	–
Gatehouse, P.W.	1957–62	19		23	8	85	20	5.66	–		1551	53	29.27
Gatting, M.W.	1975–	224		347	56	12833	258	44.10	30		2642	103	25.65
	T	30		52	4	1144	81	23.83	–		115	2	57.50
Gaunt, R.A.	1955/56–63/64	85		92	33	616	32*	10.44	–		7143	266	26.85
	T	3		4	2	6	3	3.00	–		310	7	44.28
Gauntlett, G.B.	1957	1		–	–	–	–	–	–		–	–	–
Gavaskar, S.M.	1966/67–	302		495	54	22853	340	51.82	73		1185	22	53.86
	T	99		174	14	8394	221	52.46	30		177	1	–
Gavin, N.L.	1946	1		2	1	52	29	–	–		102	3	34.00
Gay, D.W.M.	1949	4		6	1	16	11	3.20	–		288	9	32.00
Genders, W.R.	1946–49	10		19	4	245	55*	16.33	–		98	3	32.67
Ghavri, K.D.	1969/70–	154		195	48	4265	102	29.01	1		12930	448	28.86
	T	39		57	14	913	86	21.23	–		3656	109	33.54
Ghazali, M.E.Z.	1942/43–54/55	46		68	7	1569	160	25.72	2		2053	62	33.11
	T	2		4	0	32	18	8.00	–		18	0	–
Ghorpade, J.M.	1948/49–65/66	82		116	13	2631	123	25.54	2		3524	114	30.91
	T	8		15	0	229	41	15.26	–		131	0	–
Ghulam Abbas	1962/63–81/82	100		162	18	5242	276	36.40	9		229	7	32.72
	T	1		2	0	12	12	6.00	–		–	–	–
Ghulam Ahmed	1939/40–58/59	98		126	30	1341	90	13.97	–		9189	407	22.57
	T	22		31	9	192	50	8.72	–		2052	68	30.17
Gibaut, R.P.	1983	2		2	0	7	7	3.50	–		–	–	–
Gibb, P.A.	1934–56	287		479	33	12520	204	28.07	19		161	5	32.20
	T	8		13	0	581	120	44.69	2		–	–	–
Gibbons, H.H.I.	1927–46	383		671	57	21087	212*	34.34	44		737	7	105.28
Gibbs, L.R.	1953/54–75/76	330		352	150	1729	43	8.55	–		27878	1024	27.22
	T	79		109	39	488	25	6.97	–		8989	309	29.09
Gibbs, P.J.K.	1964–72	178		319	14	8885	138*	29.13	11		321	4	80.25
Gibson, A.L.	1946	2		3	0	17	11	5.67	–		–	–	–
Gibson, D.	1957–69	185		211	45	3143	98	18.93	–		12266	552	22.22
Gibson, I.	1955–61	51		92	7	1697	100*	19.96	1		1959	51	38.41
Gidney, B.B.	1963	1		2	0	16	9	8.00	–		–	–	–
Gifford, N.	1960–	617		715	226	6649	89	13.60	–		43556	1889	23.06
	T	15		20	9	179	25*	16.27	–		1026	33	31.09
Gilchrist, R.	1956/57–62/63	42		43	10	255	43*	7.72	–		4342	167	26.00
	T	13		14	3	60	12	5.45	–		1521	57	26.68
Giles, R.J.	1937–59	195		310	19	7639	142	26.25	9		1318	23	57.30
Gilfillan, A.D.	1982	3		4	1	40	31	13.33	–		218	2	109.00
Gill, A.	1960–65	53		98	7	1756	67	19.30	–		481	10	48.10
Gill, J.R.	1948	1		2	0	106	106	53.00	1		–	–	–
Gill, P.N.	1976–79	2		4	0	64	20	16.00	–		–	–	–
Gill, R.I.	1947–50	3		6	1	72	37	14.40	–		130	3	43.33
Gillhouley, K.	1961–66	108		166	28	2051	75*	14.86	–		6922	255	27.14
Gilliat, R.M.C.	1964–78	269		441	46	11589	223*	29.33	18		157	3	52.33
Gillott, E.K.	1971/72–78/79	31		37	17	172	22	8.60	–		2493	81	30.77
Gilmour, G.J.	1971/72–78/79	75		120	18	3126	122	30.64	5		7345	233	31.52
	T	15		22	1	483	101	23.00	1		1406	54	26.03

	Career span	M	I	NO	Runs	HS	Avge	100	Runs	Wkts	Avge
					BATTING				BOWLING		
Gimblett, H.	1935–54	368	673	37	23007	310	36.17	50	2124	41	51.81
T		3	5	1	129	67*	32.25	–	–	–	–
Gladwin, Christopher	1981–	36	60	3	1919	162	33.67	1	59	0	–
Gladwin, Clifford	1939–58	374	510	148	6283	124*	17.36	1	30265	1653	18.31
T		8	11	5	170	51*	28.33	–	571	15	38.06
Glassford, J.	1969	2	1	0	0	0	–	–	161	5	32.20
Gleeson, J.W.	1966/67–74/75	116	137	38	1095	59	11.06	–	10729	430	24.95
T		29	46	8	395	45	10.39	–	3367	93	36.20
Glenn, M.	1975–76	7	7	4	23	11*	7.67	–	398	6	66.33
Glennie, M.S.	1939–47	3	5	0	19	1	3.80	–	–	–	–
Glerum, H.W.	1957	1	2	0	1	1	0.50	–	32	3	10.67
Glover, T.R.	1973–75	22	42	1	769	117	18.75	–	12	0	–
Glynn, B.T.	1959–61	2	3	1	13	7	6.50	–	–	–	–
Gobey, S.C.	1946	2	3	0	2	2	0.67	–	9	0	–
Goddard, G.F.	1960–80	22	33	5	371	39	13.25	–	1112	41	27.12
Goddard, J.D.C.	1936/37–57/58	110	145	32	3769	218*	33.35	5	3845	146	26.32
T		27	39	11	859	83*	30.67	–	1050	33	31.81
Goddard, T.L.	1952/53–69/70	179	297	19	11279	222	40.57	26	11563	534	21.65
T		41	78	5	2516	112	34.46	1	3226	123	26.22
Goddard, T.W.J.	1922–52	593	775	218	5234	71	9.40	–	59116	2979	19.84
T		8	5	3	13	8	6.50	–	588	22	26.72
Godfrey, J.F.	1939–47	12	19	5	61	25*	4.35	–	753	15	50.20
Goldie, C.F.E.	1981–	22	24	3	302	77	14.38	–	–	–	–
Goldring, S.	1964	1	2	2	23	14*	–	–	43	0	–
Gomes, H.A.	1971/72–	191	310	44	11139	200*	41.88	28	3866	98	39.45
T		40	60	8	2232	143	42.92	7	793	11	72.09
Gomez, G.E.	1937/38–55/56	126	182	27	6764	216*	43.63	14	5052	200	25.26
T		29	46	5	1243	101	30.31	1	1590	58	27.41
Golding, A.K.	1983	9	15	2	197	44	15.15	–	919	8	114.88
Goldstein, F.S.	1966–77/78	89	163	4	4810	155	30.25	2	53	1	–
Gooch, G.A.	1973–	292	493	43	18963	227	42.14	47	4549	140	32.49
T		42	75	4	2540	153	35.77	4	348	8	43.50
Gooch, P.A.	1970	4	3	1	0	0*	0.00	–	252	6	42.00
Good, A.J.	1973–76	8	8	2	10	6	1.67	–	482	17	28.35
Good, D.C.	1946–47	4	7	3	54	21	13.50	–	300	8	37.50
Goodfellow, A.	1960–62	21	42	1	941	81	22.95	–	4	0	–
Goodreds, W.A.	1952	1	1	1	4	4*	–	–	48	0	–
Goodson, D.	1950–53	9	13	4	36	22*	4.00	–	394	7	56.28
Goodway, C.C.	1937–47	40	66	12	434	37*	8.04	–	–	–	–
Goodwin, D.E.	1965–73	11	16	2	188	39	13.43	–	583	20	29.15
Goodwin, F.	1955–56	11	10	4	47	21*	7.83	–	715	27	26.48
Goodwin, K.	1960–74	124	153	43	636	23	5.78	–	–	–	–
Goodwin, T.J.	1950–59	136	167	80	474	23*	5.45	–	10108	335	30.17
Goonesena, G.	1947/48–68	194	304	37	5751	211	21.53	3	16430	674	24.37
Goonatillake, F.R.M.	1973/74–79	11	12	4	130	60*	16.25	–	688	16	43.00
Goonatillake, H.M.	1975/76–82/83	26	39	7	430	56	13.43	–	–	–	–
T		5	10	2	177	56	22.13	–	–	–	–
Gopinath, C.D.	1949/50–62/63	83	119	18	4260	234	42.18	9	389	14	27.78
T		8	12	1	242	50*	22.00	–	11	1	–
Gordon, A.	1966–71	34	59	4	891	65	16.20	–	1	0	–
Gordon-Walker, R.A.	1981	3	5	1	19	12	4.75	–	–	–	–
Gore, H.E.I.	1972/73–80	32	41	12	382	67	13.17	–	1917	57	33.63
Gothard, E.J.	1947–48	45	63	19	543	50	12.34	–	730	18	40.56
Gould, A.V.E.	1964–66	13	24	0	241	38	10.04	–	16	1	–
Gould, I.J.	1975–	183	245	34	4782	128	22.66	1	35	0	–
Gover, A.R.	1928–48	361	414	167	2312	41*	9.36	–	36753	1555	23.64
T		4	1	1	2	2*	–	–	359	8	44.87

	Career span	M	I	NO	Runs	HS	Avge	100	Runs	Wkts	Avge
					BATTING				**BOWLING**		
Govindraj, D.	1964/65–74/75	93	107	18	1202	72	13.50	–	5256	190	27.66
Gower, D.I.	1975–	236	378	35	13631	200*	39.74	28	180	4	45.00
	T	65	113	10	4486	200*	43.55	9	2	1	–
Gracey, P.B.K.	1945/46–48	5	9	1	176	61	22.00	–	54	2	27.00
Graf, S.F.	1979/80–	54	75	15	1510	100*	25.17	1	4115	120	34.29
Graham, D.	1948	1	2	0	13	7	6.50	–	20	1	–
Graham, G.R.	1954	1	1	1	1	1*	–	–	100	2	50.00
Graham, J.N.	1964–77	189	178	73	404	23	3.84	–	13722	614	22.34
Graham, P.A.O.	1948	6	11	2	82	33	9.11	–	316	7	45.14
Graham-Brown, J.H.M.	1974–78	30	37	7	368	43	12.27	–	696	12	58.00
Grainge, C.M.	1950–52	14	15	6	47	14*	5.22	–	1090	25	43.60
Grant, C.R.W.	1968	3	6	0	125	48	20.83	–	–	–	–
Grant, T.J.D.	1946	1	2	0	6	6	3.00	–	–	–	–
Graveney, D.A.	1972–	265	365	95	5087	119	18.84	2	17150	594	28.87
Graveney, J.K.R.	1947–64	111	167	26	2034	62	14.43	–	4819	173	27.86
Graveney, T.W.	1948–71/72	735	1223	159	47793	258	44.92	122	3037	80	37.96
	T	79	123	13	4882	258	44.38	11	167	1	–
Graves, P.J.	1965–80	292	502	51	12076	145*	26.77	14	797	15	53.13
Gray, D.A.A.	1947	3	5	0	22	8	4.40	–	182	3	60.67
Gray, J.D.	1968–69	7	6	3	34	18	11.33	–	534	21	25.43
Gray, J.R.	1948–66	458	818	81	22650	213*	30.73	30	13719	457	30.01
Gray, E.J.	1975/76–	76	122	24	2760	126	28.16	3	5055	194	26.06
	T	2	4	0	38	17	9.50	–	128	4	32.00
Gray, L.H.	1934–51	219	252	130	901	35*	7.38	–	16014	637	25.14
Gray, R.I.	1947	1	2	0	11	11	5.50	–	57	0	–
Greasley, D.G.	1950–55	58	85	11	1659	104*	22.42	1	573	16	35.81
Green, A.M.	1980–	58	102	5	2441	99	25.12	–	563	13	43.31
Green, D.J.	1953–61	87	152	7	2929	134	20.20	1	99	1	–
Green, D.M.	1959–72/73	266	479	15	13381	233	28.84	14	4460	116	38.45
Green, R.C.	1984–	2	1	1	3	3*	–	–	92	2	46.00
Greene, R.M.	1949–50/51	2	4	3	59	26*	–	–	79	1	–
Greenhough, T.	1951–66	261	313	86	1913	76*	8.42	–	16802	751	22.37
	T	4	4	1	4	2	1.33	–	357	16	22.31
Greenidge, C.G.	1970–	374	641	55	26492	273*	45.21	62	449	17	26.41
	T	57	96	11	4338	223	51.04	11	4	0	–
Greenidge, G.A.	1966/67–75/76	182	332	22	9112	205	29.39	16	948	13	72.92
	T	5	9	2	209	50	29.86	–	75	0	–
Greensmith, W.T.	1947–63	379	566	152	8248	138*	19.92	1	21196	733	28.91
Greensword, S.	1963–81	41	71	8	1025	84*	16.26	–	917	28	32.75
Greenwood, H.W.	1933–46	79	133	4	2590	115	20.08	1	37	0	–
Greenwood, P.	1948–52	75	92	15	1270	113	16.49	1	5080	208	24.42
Greetham, C.M.H.	1957–66	205	332	26	6723	151*	21.97	5	5525	195	28.35
Gregory, H.V.	1960	1	2	0	18	14	9.00	–	66	0	–
Gregory, R.J.	1925–47	432	646	78	19495	243	34.32	39	14122	437	32.32
Greig, A.W.	1965/66–78	350	579	45	16660	226	31.29	26	24702	856	28.85
	T	58	93	4	3599	148	40.43	8	4541	141	32.20
Greig, I.A.	1974/75–	123	166	19	3739	147*	25.44	4	7812	276	28.30
	T	2	4	0	26	14	6.50	–	114	4	28.50
Grieves, K.J.	1945/46–64	490	746	79	22454	224	33.66	29	7209	242	29.78
Griffin, G.M.	1957/58–62/63	42	58	8	895	73	17.90	–	2324	108	21.51
	T	2	4	0	25	14	6.25	–	192	8	24.00
Griffin, N.F.	1963	1	2	1	90	83*	–	–	45	0	–
Griffith, C.C.	1959/60–68/69	96	119	32	1502	98	17.26	–	7172	332	21.60
	T	28	42	10	530	54	16.56	–	2683	94	28.54
Griffith, G.H.C.	1949–51	5	6	0	62	33	10.33	–	177	2	88.50
Griffith, K.	1967–72	44	61	8	795	58	15.00	–	1753	50	35.06

	Career span	M	I	NO	Runs	HS	Avge	100	Runs	Wkts	Avge
					BATTING				BOWLING		
Griffith, M.G.	1962–74	276	455	90	8890	158	24.35	5	28	1	–
Griffith, S.C.	1934–54	215	336	41	4846	140	16.43	3	23	0	–
	T	3	5	0	157	140	31.40	1	–	–	–
Griffiths, A.	1981	1	1	0	26	26	–	–	–	–	–
Griffiths, B.J.	1974–	154	123	44	255	16	3.23	–	11240	391	28.75
Griffiths, C.	1951–53	27	41	3	625	105	16.18	1	22	0	–
Griffiths, J.V.C.	1952–57	34	53	10	396	32	9.21	–	1167	48	24.31
Griffiths, P.D.	1982	1	2	0	1	1	0.50	–	39	0	–
Griffiths, S.	1956–58	27	26	12	76	17★	5.42	–	1827	74	24.69
Griffiths, W.H.	1946–49	38	48	13	147	19	4.20	–	3210	102	31.47
Grimes, A.D.H.	1984	7	11	2	58	13	6.44	–	427	3	142.33
Gripper, R.A.	1957/58–71/72	83	154	11	4353	279★	30.44	7	120	3	40.00
Groome, J.J.	1974–78	40	74	3	1120	86	15.78	–	0	0	–
Grout, A.T.W.	1946/47–65/66	183	253	24	5168	119	22.56	4	115	3	38.33
	T	51	67	8	890	74	15.08	–	–	–	–
Grove, C.W.	1938–54	217	310	37	3161	104★	11.58	1	16866	744	22.67
Groves, M.G.M.	1960/61–68	55	97	10	2541	86	29.20	–	374	7	53.43
Guard, D.R.	1946–49	16	29	1	430	89	15.35	–	–	–	–
Guest, M.R.J.	1964–66	23	37	3	576	77	16.88	–	882	22	40.09
Guha, S.	1965/66–76/77	85	102	18	1067	75	12.70	–	6068	299	20.29
	T	4	7	2	17	6	3.40	–	311	3	103.67
Gul Mahomed	1938/39–58/59	117	186	21	5600	319	33.93	12	2909	107	27.13
	T	9	17	1	205	34	12.81	–	24	2	12.00
Gunasekera, Y.	1980/81–82/83	11	16	2	429	79★	30.64	–	38	1	–
	T	2	4	0	48	23	12.00	–	–	–	–
Gunn, B.G.H.	1946	4	7	0	105	39	15.00	–	–	–	–
Gunn, G.V.	1928–50	266	395	43	10337	184	29.37	11	10026	281	35.68
Gunn, L.J.H.	1951–54	2	2	0	47	46	23.50	–	–	–	–
Gunn, T.	1961–67	41	54	19	179	19★	5.12	–	–	–	–
Gupte, S.P.	1948/49–63/64	115	125	32	761	47	8.18	–	12567	530	23.71
	T	36	42	13	183	21	6.31	–	4403	149	29.55
Gurr, D.R.	1976–79	41	48	23	410	46★	16.40	–	3079	110	27.99
Guthrie, J.S.	1953	1	2	0	1	1	0.50	–	30	0	–
Guy, J.B.	1938–50	9	16	0	130	45	8.12	–	–	–	–
Guy, J.W.	1953/54–72/73	90	165	13	3923	115	25.80	3	82	1	–
	T	12	23	2	440	102	20.95	1	–	–	–
Hacker, P.J.	1974–82	71	77	30	449	35	9.55	–	4792	153	31.32
Hacking, J.K.	1946	1	2	0	17	14	8.50	–	–	–	–
Hadlee, D.R.	1966/67–	111	152	39	2113	109★	18.70	1	8853	351	25.22
	T	26	42	5	530	56	14.32	–	2389	71	33.64
Hadlee, R.J.	1971/72	231	320	54	7787	210★	29.27	9	18339	980	18.71
	T	50	85	11	1820	103	24.60	1	5626	235	23.94
Hadlee, W.A.	1933/34–51/52	116	202	17	7421	198	40.11	17	293	6	48.83
	T	11	19	1	543	116	30.16	1	–	–	–
Hadley, R.J.	1971–73	28	36	16	65	17	3.25	–	1647	56	29.41
Haggett, N.L.	1962–64	4	8	0	204	71	25.50	–	–	–	–
Haggo, D.J.	1983	1	2	0	9	9	4.50	–	–	–	–
Hake, G.J.G.	1948	1	1	0	2	2	–	–	84	1	–
Hale, I.E.	1946–48	16	28	3	314	61	12.56	–	65	2	32.50
Hale, T.S.	1965	1	2	0	8	8	4.00	–	–	–	–
Hales, L.A.	1947	2	4	0	76	62	19.00	–	38	0	–
Halfyard, D.J.	1956–70	264	348	51	3242	79	10.91	–	24822	963	25.78
Hall, B.	1952	1	2	0	14	10	7.00	–	55	1	–
Hall, B.C.	1956–57	3	4	1	34	21	11.33	–	97	3	32.33

			BATTING						BOWLING		
	Career span	M	I	NO	Runs	HS	Avge	100	Runs	Wkts	Avge
Hall, D.	1955–58	20	29	16	43	10*	3.31	–	1386	48	28.87
Hall, G.H.	1961–65	48	51	26	90	12*	3.60	–	3425	111	30.86
Hall, I.W.	1959–72	270	483	32	11666	136*	25.87	9	23	0	–
Hall, J.B.	1935–46	7	13	1	114	24	9.50	–	516	21	24.57
Hall, J.E.	1969–70	14	26	0	385	69	14.80	–	–	–	–
Hall, J.K.	1958–62	21	22	6	57	22	3.56	–	1532	54	28.37
Hall, M.J.	1958–59	17	30	1	430	72	14.83	–	–	–	–
Hall, P.J.	1948–55/56	12	14	3	235	49	21.36	–	1045	28	37.32
Hall, T.A.	1949–58	66	103	23	892	69*	11.13	–	5108	183	27.91
Hall, W.W.	1955/56–70/71	170	215	38	2673	102*	15.10	1	14273	546	26.14
T		48	66	14	818	50*	15.73	–	5066	192	26.38
Hallam, M.R.	1950–70	504	905	56	24488	210*	28.84	32	142	4	35.50
Halliday, H.	1938–53	187	287	18	8556	144	31.82	12	3201	107	29.91
Halliday, M.	1970–83	10	9	4	75	30	15.00	–	594	27	22.00
Halliday, S.J.	1980–82	9	14	2	348	113*	29.00	1	–	–	–
Hamblin, C.B.	1971–73	29	45	10	693	123*	19.80	1	1696	38	44.63
Hamence, R.A.	1935/36–50/51	99	155	15	5285	173	37.73	11	239	8	29.87
T		3	4	1	81	30*	27.00	–			
Hamer, A.	1938–60	295	515	19	15465	227	31.18	19	2363	71	33.28
Hamilton, A.C.	1975–76	12	24	0	308	45	12.82	–	6	0	–
Hammond, H.E.	1928–46	196	267	40	4251	103*	18.64	1	12290	428	28.72
Hammond, J.R.	1969/70–80/81	69	87	31	922	53	16.46	–	5315	184	28.89
T		5	5	2	28	19	9.33	–	488	15	32.53
Hammond, R.J.L.	1948–51	6	11	0	199	46	18.09	–	–	–	–
Hammond, W.R.	1920–51	634	1005	104	50551	336*	56.11	167	22391	732	30.59
T		85	140	16	7249	336*	58.45	22	3138	83	37.80
Hampshire, A.W.	1975	1	2	0	18	17	9.00	–	–	–	–
Hampshire, J.H.	1961–84	576	924	112	28059	183*	34.56	43	1637	30	54.57
T		8	16	1	403	107	28.86	1	–	–	–
Hands, B.O.	1946–47	3	2	0	13	9	6.50	–	137	4	34.25
Hanif Mohammed	1951/52–75/76	238	370	44	17059	499	52.32	55	1515	53	28.58
T		55	97	8	3915	337	43.98	12	95	1	–
Hanley, R.W.	1970/71–	109	96	43	314	33*	5.93	–	8326	398	20.92
Hanna, M.	1951–54	2	3	1	5	4*	2.50	–	–	–	–
Hansell, T.M.G.	1975–77	14	26	5	319	54	15.19	–	0	0	–
Hanson, R.L.	1973	1	1	1	1	1*	–	–	–	–	–
Hanumant Singh	1956/57–78/79	206	331	50	12338	213*	43.91	29	2292	56	40.92
T		14	24	2	686	105	31.18	1	51	0	–
Harbin, L.	1935/36–51	12	18	1	337	89	19.82	–	633	25	25.32
Harcourt, A.B.	1947	4	8	2	76	25*	12.67	–	–	–	–
Hardie, B.R.	1970–	261	421	51	12579	162	34.00	14	80	2	40.00
Hardie, K.M.	1966–76	10	11	4	158	65*	22.57	–	626	35	17.89
Harding, N.W.	1937–47	84	123	22	966	71	9.57	–	6531	229	28.51
Hardstaff, J. (Notts)	1930–55	517	812	94	31847	266	44.36	83	2142	36	59.50
T		23	38	3	1636	205*	46.74	4	–	–	–
Hardstaff, J. (F.F.)	1961–62	2	4	0	57	36	14.25	–	32	1	–
Hardy, D.W.	1965	1	2	0	29	29	14.50	–	–	–	–
Hardy, E.M.P.	1959	1	2	0	15	15	7.50	–	–	–	–
Hardy, J.J.E.	1984	13	20	6	513	95	36.64	–	3	0	–
Hardy, M.J.	1958	1	2	0	15	15	7.50	–	35	1	–
Hare, P.M.C.	1947	1	1	0	39	39	–	–	–	–	–
Hare, T.	1953–54	10	17	1	218	47	13.62	–	754	19	39.68
Hare, W.H.	1971–77	10	18	4	171	36	12.21	–	0	0	–
Harford, N.S.	1953/54–66/67	74	122	8	3149	158	27.62	3	478	18	26.58
T		8	15	0	229	93	15.26	–	–	–	–
Harilal Shah	1975	1	2	0	92	59	46.00	–	7	0	–

	Career span	M	I	NO	Runs	HS	Avge	100	Runs	Wkts	Avge
					BATTING				BOWLING		
Harkness, D.	1954	13	19	0	488	163	25.68	1	274	6	56.67
Harman, R.	1961–68	144	147	52	947	34	9.97	–	8977	378	23.75
Haroon Rashid	1971/72–	146	230	27	7426	153	36.58	15	255	8	31.88
T		23	36	1	1217	153	34.77	3	3	0	–
Harper, N.J.	1961	1	1	0	1	1	–	–	39	1	–
Harper, R.A.	1979/80–	48	60	3	1068	86	18.74	–	3822	157	24.23
T		11	12	1	152	39*	13.81	–	703	24	29.29
Harpur, T.	1980–81	2	2	0	10	6	5.00	–	5	0	–
Harrington, W.J.R.	1946–51	12	19	2	143	45	8.41	–	376	16	23.50
Harris, A.	1960–64	49	91	3	1698	110	19.29	2	0	0	–
Harris, C.B.	1928–51	362	601	64	18823	239*	35.05	30	8395	196	42.83
Harris, C.R.	1964–65	12	16	6	48	14	4.80	–	896	17	52.70
Harris, D.F.	1946	1	1	0	2	2	–	–	–	–	–
Harris, E.J.	1975	4	5	2	26	16	8.67	–	295	9	32.78
Harris, J.H.	1952–59	15	18	4	154	41	11.00	–	619	19	32.57
Harris, L.J.	1947	3	4	2	7	5	3.50	–	183	5	36.60
Harris, M.J.	1964–82	344	581	58	19196	201*	36.70	41	3459	79	43.78
Harris, T.A.	1933/34–48/49	55	80	7	3028	191*	41.47	6	33	0	–
T		3	5	1	100	60	25.00	–	–	–	–
Harris, W.E.	1938–47	5	8	0	59	25	7.36	–	43	0	–
Harrison, B.R.S.	1957–62	14	24	2	519	110	23.59	1	65	1	–
Harrison, D.S.	1983	1	2	0	9	8	4.50	–	–	–	–
Harrison, D.W.	1978–79	2	1	0	0	0	–	–	–	–	–
Harrison, E.E.	1946–47	10	17	5	120	23	10.00	–	498	17	29.30
Harrison, G.D.	1983–	2	3	1	139	86	69.50	–	54	2	27.00
Harrison, J.	1969–77	8	15	1	309	100*	22.07	1	–	–	–
Harrison, L.	1939–66	396	606	100	8854	153	17.49	6	166	0	–
Harrison, R.	1968	1	2	0	16	12	8.00	–	–	–	–
Harrison, S.C.	1971–77	5	6	0	32	15	5.33	–	314	7	44.85
Harron, D.G.	1951	10	14	2	186	53	15.50	–	–	–	–
Harrop, D.J.	1972	1	2	1	11	11*	–	–	–	–	–
Hart, M.de.L.	1951	4	5	0	8	4	1.60	–	330	6	55.00
Hart, P.R.	1981	3	5	0	23	11	4.60	–	140	2	70.00
Harte, C.C.J.	1973–81	2	3	0	82	40	27.33	–	–	–	–
Hartley, F.	1924–45	2	1	0	2	2	–	–	44	1	–
Hartley, G.E.	1946	1	2	0	6	3	3.00	–	–	–	–
Hartley, P.J.	1982	3	4	1	31	16	10.33	–	215	2	107.50
Hartley, S.N.	1978–	92	144	21	2970	114	24.15	3	1552	33	47.03
Harvey, J.F.	1961–72	206	344	32	7538	168	24.16	4	21	1	–
Harvey, J.R.W.	1963–65	6	8	2	5	3	0.83	–	431	17	25.35
Harvey, P.F.	1947–58	175	244	46	3645	150	18.40	2	11908	335	35.54
Harvey, P.V.	1949	1	1	0	9	9	–	–	–	–	–
Harvey, R.C.	1952	1	2	2	12	12*	–	–	88	3	29.33
Harvey, R.N.	1946/47–62/63	306	461	35	21699	231*	50.93	67	1106	30	36.86
T		79	137	10	6149	205	48.41	21	120	3	40.00
Harvey-Walker, A.J.	1971–78	81	143	10	3186	117	23.95	3	1150	34	33.82
Hasan Jamil	1969/70–	115	168	31	4049	172	29.56	4	6038	196	30.81
Haseeb Ahsan	1956/57–63	49	50	16	242	36	5.62	–	3931	142	27.70
T		12	16	7	61	14	6.77	–	1330	27	49.25
Haslop, P.	1962	1	1	1	2	2*	–	–	82	2	41.00
Hassan, F.A.	1959/60–63	11	14	6	44	17	5.50	–	664	15	44.27
Hassan, S.B.	1963/64–	329	544	53	14285	182*	29.09	14	407	6	67.83
Hassett, A.L.	1932/33–53	216	322	32	16890	232	58.24	59	703	18	39.05
T		43	69	3	3073	198*	46.56	10	78	0	–
Hastie, J.H.	1951	1	2	0	37	22	18.50	–	–	–	–
Hastings, B.F.	1957/58–76/77	163	273	32	7686	226	31.89	15	239	4	59.75
T		31	56	6	1510	117*	30.20	4	9	0	–

	Career span	M		I	NO	Runs	HS	Avge	100		Runs	Wkts	Avge
Hatch, P.G.	1960–61	5		7	0	60	15	8.56	–		–	–	–
Hatteea, S.A.	1969/70–70/71	8		5	0	1	1	0.20	–		764	27	28.29
Hatton, A.G.	1960–61	3		1	1	4	4*	–	–		202	6	33.67
Haughton, W.E.	1953	1		2	0	0	0	0.00	–		–	–	–
Hawke, C.R.J.	1953	1		2	1	31	23*	–	–		–	–	–
Hawke, N.J.N.	1959/60–70/71	145		198	57	3383	141*	23.99	1		12088	458	26.39
	T	27		37	15	365	45*	16.59	–		2677	91	29.41
Hawkey, R.B.	1948–49	3		6	0	42	13	7.00	–		139	1	–
Hawkins, C.G.	1957	4		5	2	16	11*	5.33	–		–	–	–
Hawkins, D.G.	1952–62	134		220	14	3755	106	18.23	3		1153	38	30.34
Haye, W.	1970–71/72	7		8	0	198	60	24.75	–		287	6	47.83
Hayes, F.C.	1970–84	272		421	58	13018	187	35.86	23		15	0	–
	T	9		17	1	244	106*	15.25	1		–	–	–
Hayes, J.A.	1946/47–60/61	78		100	36	611	36	9.54	–		6758	292	23.14
	T	15		22	7	73	19	4.86	–		1217	30	40.56
Hayes, K.A.	1980–	38		63	4	1268	152	21.49	1		537	17	31.59
Hayes, P.J.	1974–77	27		44	11	343	56*	10.39	–		1832	51	35.92
Hayles, B.R.M.	1938–49	7		10	1	69	40	7.67	–		–	–	–
Haynes, D.L.	1976/77–	117		190	16	7269	184	41.78	12		27	2	13.50
	T	45		71	5	2643	184	40.05	7		8	1	–
Haynes, D.M.	1956	1		2	0	8	8	4.00	–		–	–	–
Haynes, J.P.	1946	1		2	0	0	0	0.00	–		34	0	–
Haynes, M.W.	1959–61	9		16	1	119	23	7.93	–		–	–	–
Hays, D.L.	1965–80	25		47	1	751	72	16.33	–		5	0	–
Haysman, M.D.	1982/83–	24		44	7	1520	153	41.08	4		219	0	–
Hayward, J.G.R.	1951	1		–	–	–	–	–	–		78	2	39.00
Hayward, R.E.	1981–83/84	26		42	7	852	102	24.34	2		42	0	–
Hayward, W.I.D.	1950–54	27		33	4	309	57	10.67	–		1948	68	28.35
Haywood, D.C.	1968	9		15	0	284	62	18.93	–		–	–	–
Haywood, P.R.	1969–73	54		82	8	1570	100*	21.22	1		324	9	36.00
Haywood, R.O.	1949	1		2	0	12	12	6.00	–		–	–	–
Hazare, V.S.	1934/35–66/67	238		367	45	18635	309	57.87	60		14501	592	24.49
	T	30		52	6	2192	164*	47.65	7		1220	20	61.00
Hazell, H.L.	1929–52	350		507	228	2280	43	8.17	–		22941	957	23.97
Head, T.J.	1976–81	22		26	6	335	52*	16.75	–		–	–	–
Headley, G.A.	1927/28–54	103		164	22	9921	344*	69.86	33		1842	51	36.11
	T	22		40	4	2190	270*	60.83	10		230	0	–
Headley, R.G.A.	1958–74	423		758	61	21695	187	31.12	32		588	12	49.00
	T	2		4	0	62	42	15.50	–		–	–	–
Heal, M.G.	1969–72	22		41	1	637	124*	15.93	1		–	–	–
Healey, R.D.	1964	2		4	0	14	7	3.50	–		146	0	–
Heane, G.F.H.	1927–51	189		268	24	6183	138	25.62	9		7307	222	33.05
Heard, H.	1967–70	30		45	14	273	31	8.81	–		2048	49	41.90
Hearn, P.	1947–56	200		351	32	8138	172	25.52	7		1245	22	56.59
Heath, D.M.W.	1949–53	19		28	1	580	149	21.48	1		–	–	–
Heath, G.E.M.	1937–49	132		188	83	586	34*	5.58	–		11359	404	28.11
Heath, J.R.P.	1980–83	17		33	4	611	101*	21.07	1		58	0	–
Heath, M.	1954–62	143		163	66	569	33	5.86	–		13237	527	25.11
Hebden, G.G.L.	1937–51	6		11	3	69	22*	8.62	–		172	3	57.33
Hector, P.A.	1977	3		5	1	75	40	18.75	–		190	7	27.14
Hedges, B.	1950–67	422		744	41	17733	182	25.22	21		260	3	86.67
Heggie, W.R.	1937–47	5		10	0	123	44	12.30	–		–	–	–
Heighes, B.	1967	1		1	1	6	6*	–	–		61	2	30.50
Heine, P.S.	1951/52–64/65	61		97	14	1255	67	15.12	–		5924	277	21.38
	T	14		24	3	209	31	9.95	–		1455	58	25.08
Hellawell, M.S.	1962	1		2	2	59	30*	–	–		114	6	19.00

	Career span	M		I	NO	Runs	HS	Avge	100		Runs	Wkts	Avge
Hellmuth, L.	1951–52	7		13	1	34	11	2.83	–		383	8	47.88
Hemming, L.E.G.	1951	1		2	0	28	14	14.00	–		60	1	–
Hemmings, E.E.	1966–	322		436	95	6848	127	20.08	1		26635	932	28.58
	T	5		10	1	198	95	22.00	–		558	12	46.50
Hemsley, E.J.O.	1963–82	243		389	57	9740	176★	29.33	8		2497	70	35.67
Hemsley, P.D.	1980–81	3		5	2	26	12★	8.67	–		143	1	–
Henderson, A.A.	1972	1		2	0	11	9	5.50	–		132	5	26.40
Henderson, A.W.	1953	1		1	0	2	2	–	–		10	0	–
Henderson, D.	1949–54	16		20	8	131	21★	10.92	–		1039	34	30.56
Henderson, J.D.	1946–56	14		22	3	429	121	22.58	1		650	29	22.41
Henderson, S.P.	1977–	63		104	13	2305	209★	25.33	3		185	3	61.67
Hendrick, M.	1969–84	267		267	109	1601	46	10.13	–		15785	770	20.50
	T	30		35	15	128	15	6.40	–		2248	87	25.83
Hendriks, J.L.	1953/54–69	83		113	23	1568	82	17.42	–		61	0	–
	T	20		32	8	447	64	18.62	–		–	–	–
Hendy, A.S.	1951–54	4		6	0	46	22	7.67	–		222	10	22.20
Henley-Welch, D.F.	1946–48	17		30	4	558	58	21.46	–		931	23	40.48
Henry, D.P.	1948	1		1	0	1	1	–	–		16	0	–
Henwood, P.P.	1965/66–79/80	79		102	22	769	46	9.62	–		5877	212	27.72
Herbert, R.	1976–80	6		9	1	62	14★	7.75	–		148	3	49.33
Herkes, R.	1978–79	3		5	3	0	0	0.00	–		93	6	15.50
Herman, O.W.	1929–48	322		496	105	4336	92	11.08	–		28222	1045	27.00
Herman, R.S.	1965–77	189		189	49	1426	56	10.18	–		13348	506	26.37
Hermiston, W.	1949	2		4	0	35	21	8.75	–		84	2	42.00
Heron, J.G.	1967/68–82/83	60		113	5	2830	175	26.20	5		17	0	–
Heroys, N.	1960	1		2	0	10	10	5.00	–		35	0	–
Herting, F.J.	1960	5		7	2	44	16★	8.80	–		506	7	72.28
Heseltine, P.J.	1983	6		10	1	176	40	19.56	–		–	–	–
Hettiaratchy, N.D.P.	1970/71–82/83	20		32	1	686	80	22.12	–		–	–	–
Hever, N.G.	1947–53	145		177	81	897	40	9.35	–		7901	333	23.73
Hewitt, E.J.	1954–57	2		3	0	55	40	18.33	–		60	1	–
Hewitt, F.S.A.	1966	1		2	0	53	36	26.50	–		44	0	–
Hewitt, S.G.P.	1983–	9		12	6	29	14★	4.83	–		–	–	–
Hewitt, S.M.	1984	4		6	1	60	22	12.00	–		232	4	58.00
Heys, W.	1957	5		7	0	74	46	10.56	–		–	–	–
Hichens, A.L.	1957–59	3		2	0	4	4	2.00	–		270	6	45.00
Hick, G.A.	1983/84	7		12	3	272	82★	30.22	–		196	3	65.33
Hickinbottom, G.A.	1959	5		7	5	6	4★	3.00	–		–	–	–
Hickman, M.F.	1954–57	12		22	2	232	40	11.60	–		–	–	–
Higginson, T.W.	1960	4		4	2	50	20	25.00	–		24	1	–
Higgs, J.D.	1970/71–82/83	122		131	60	384	21	5.41	–		11838	399	29.67
	T	22		36	16	111	16	5.55	–		2057	66	31.16
Higgs, K.	1958–82	509		528	206	3637	98	11.29	–		36196	1531	23.64
	T	15		19	3	185	63	11.56	–		1473	71	20.74
Highton, E.F.W.	1950–51	2		3	0	34	26	11.33	–		162	7	23.14
Hignell, A.F.	1947	1		1	0	7	7	–	–		48	0	–
Hignell, A.J.	1974–83	170		289	36	7459	149★	29.48	11		230	3	76.67
Higson, T.A.	1932–46	26		32	1	326	51	10.52	–		302	6	50.33
Hill, A.	1972–	224		393	38	10585	160★	29.82	14		343	8	42.88
Hill, E.	1947–51	72		138	5	2118	85	15.93	–		55	1	–
Hill, G.	1932–54	371		595	94	9089	161	18.14	4		18464	617	29.92
Hill, G.H.	1957–60	42		48	6	247	23	5.88	–		3195	108	29.59
Hill, J.C.	1945/46–55/56	69		78	24	867	51★	16.05	–		5040	218	23.11
	T	3		6	3	21	8★	7.00	–		273	8	34.12
Hill, J.W.	1946–51	7		12	7	82	18★	16.40	–		367	17	21.59
Hill, L.W.	1964–76	76		130	20	2690	96★	24.45	–		44	0	–

	Career span	M	I	NO	Runs	HS	Avge	100	Runs	Wkts	Avge
					BATTING					BOWLING	
Hill, M.	1953–71	272	484	39	10722	137*	24.09	7	311	5	62.20
Hill, M.J.	1973–76	6	8	4	68	27*	17.00	–	–	–	–
Hill, N.W.	1953–68	283	518	32	14303	201*	29.43	23	261	2	130.50
Hill, R.G.	1963–69	6	9	0	105	50	11.67	–	–	–	–
Hill, R.K.	1975	1	–	–	–	–	–	–	58	1	–
Hill, W.A.	1929–48	169	279	22	6423	147*	25.00	6	27	1	–
Hillary, A.A.	1951	1	1	0	49	49	–	–	–	–	–
Hiller, R.	1966	8	11	1	87	64	8.70	–	494	17	29.06
Hills, R.W.	1973–80	85	95	25	995	45	14.21	–	4494	161	27.91
Hill-Wood, P.D.	1960	1	1	0	30	30	–	–	20	1	–
Hilton, C.	1957–64	115	133	43	665	36	7.38	–	9041	321	28.16
Hilton, J.	1952–57	79	129	29	1093	61*	10.93	–	3675	135	27.21
Hilton, M.J.	1946–61	270	324	42	3416	100*	12.11	1	19536	1006	19.41
T	4	6	1	37	15	7.40	–	477	14	34.07
Hindlekar, D.D.	1934/35–46/47	93	147	8	2411	135	17.34	1	–	–	–
T	4	7	2	71	26	14.20	–	–	–	–
Hinks, S.G.	1982–	16	28	1	450	87	16.67	–	58	2	29.00
Hirst, C.H.	1967	1	2	1	8	6*	–	–	–	–	–
Hitchcock, R.E.	1947/48–64	322	517	71	12442	153*	27.90	13	5749	194	29.63
Hoadley, S.J.	1975–76	7	13	2	202	58	18.36	–	22	0	–
Hoadley, S.P.	1978–79	12	19	0	329	112	17.31	1	–	–	–
Hobbs, J.A.D.	1956–58	18	36	1	614	95	17.54	–	–	–	–
Hobbs, R.N.S.	1961–81	440	546	138	4940	100	12.10	2	29776	1099	27.09
T	7	8	3	34	15*	6.80	–	481	12	40.08
Hobson, B.S.	1946	7	14	3	50	16*	4.54	–	460	10	46.00
Hodge, R.S.	1938–51	10	16	0	178	38	11.13	–	817	30	27.23
Hodgkins, J.S.	1938–51	3	5	0	106	44	21.20	–	238	3	79.33
Hodgkinson, G.F.	1935–46	19	32	0	472	44	14.75	–	–	–	–
Hodgson, A.	1970–79	99	118	24	909	41*	9.67	–	5964	206	28.95
Hodgson, C.A.T.	1979/80–82/83	7	12	1	248	87	22.55	–	3	0	–
Hodgson, G.	1964–65	2	2	0	5	4	2.50	–	–	–	–
Hodgson, K.I.	1981–83	27	34	9	633	50	25.32	–	2093	55	38.06
Hodgson, P.	1954–57	17	11	4	65	26	9.28	–	946	39	24.26
Hodson, R.P.	1971–73	19	36	3	687	111	20.81	1	766	29	26.41
Hofmeyr, M.B.	1949–53/54	44	81	10	3178	161	44.76	7	12	1	–
Hogan, C.R.	1962–64	6	6	0	25	7	4.17	–	415	24	17.29
Hogan, R.P.	1954–55	3	4	0	18	8	4.50	–	218	3	72.67
Hogg, R.M.	1975/76	89	121	22	1037	52	10.48	–	7596	320	23.74
T	34	51	10	385	52	9.39	–	3025	112	27.01
Hogg, V.R.	1971/72–83/84	43	54	21	181	30	5.48	–	3235	123	26.30
Hogg, W.	1976–83	95	90	25	394	31	6.06	–	6437	222	29.00
Holder, J.W.	1968–72	47	49	14	374	33	10.68	–	3415	139	24.56
Holder, V.A.	1966/67–80	311	354	81	3559	122	13.03	1	23183	947	24.48
T	40	59	11	682	42	14.20	–	3627	109	33.27
Holding, M.A.	1972/73–	123	152	25	1884	69	14.84	–	10586	448	23.63
T	49	64	10	763	69	14.13	–	4945	209	23.66
Holdsworth, W.E.N.	1952–53	27	26	12	111	22*	7.93	–	1598	53	30.01
Hole, G.B.	1949/50–57/58	98	166	12	5647	226	36.67	11	2686	61	44.03
T	18	33	2	789	66	25.45	–	126	3	42.00
Holford, D.A.J.	1960/61–78/79	99	149	27	3821	111	31.31	3	8096	253	32.00
T	24	39	5	768	105*	22.58	1	2009	51	39.39
Hollick, A.P.	1957	1	2	0	0	0	0.00	–	–	–	–
Holliday, D.C.	1979–81	29	37	8	522	76*	18.00	–	400	6	66.67
Hollies, W.E.	1932–57	515	616	282	1673	47	5.01	–	48656	2323	20.94
T	13	15	8	37	18*	5.28	–	1332	44	30.27
Hollington, H.B.	1972	1	2	0	21	15	10.50	–	–	–	–

	Career span	M	I	NO	Runs	HS	Avge	100	Runs	Wkts	Avge
Hollinshead, C.	1946	1	–	–	–	–	–	–	7	0	–
Holman, J.C.	1962–64	2	4	1	39	17	13.00	–	–	–	–
Holmes, E.R.T.	1924–55	301	465	51	13598	236	32.85	24	9531	283	33.68
	T	5	9	2	114	85*	16.28	–	76	2	38.00
Holmes, G.C.	1978–	75	122	24	2435	100*	24.85	1	1288	29	44.41
Holmes, J.R.R.	1949–51	3	4	0	41	24	10.25	–	–	–	–
Holmes, J.T.	1969	1	2	0	8	8	4.00	–	–	–	–
Holt, A.G.	1935–48	79	140	13	2853	116	22.46	2	47	1	–
Holt, R.A.A.	1938–47	6	9	1	60	30	7.50	–	–	–	–
Hone, D.J.	1970	3	5	0	26	13	5.20	–	284	1	–
Hood, J.A.	1977	2	3	0	9	7	3.00	–	–	–	–
Hook, J.S.	1975	1	2	1	7	4*	–	–	29	0	–
Hooker, R.W.	1956–69	300	442	71	8222	137	22.16	5	13457	490	27.46
Hookes, D.W.	1975/76–	90	152	9	6276	193	43.89	15	1072	19	56.42
	T	19	34	2	1171	143*	36.59	1	35	0	–
Hool, N.B.	1947–61	9	16	8	132	27	16.50	–	601	18	33.39
Hooper, A.J.M.	1966–69	13	13	4	70	35	7.77	–	493	16	30.81
Hooper, J.M.McK.	1967–71	21	36	10	406	41*	15.62	–	10	1	–
Hope, K.W.	1958–66	9	14	3	75	21	6.82	–	339	12	28.25
Hopkins, D.C.	1977–81	36	44	12	332	34*	10.38	–	2021	53	38.13
Hopkins, J.A.	1970–	239	426	27	11305	230	28.33	16	68	0	–
Hopkins, J.D.	1969–72	4	5	0	8	4	1.60	–	–	–	–
Hopkins, V.	1934–48	139	210	34	2608	83*	14.82	–	–	–	–
Hopwood, J.A.	1951	1	2	0	9	8	4.50	–	–	–	–
Horner, N.F.	1950–65	362	656	34	18533	203*	29.80	25	78	0	–
Horrex, G.W.	1956–57	7	13	0	141	41	10.85	–	–	–	–
Horsfall, R.	1947–56	214	361	25	9777	206	29.09	17	41	1	–
Horsley, N.	1947	3	1	0	0	0	–	–	249	6	41.50
Horton, H.	1946–67	417	744	84	21669	160*	32.83	32	194	3	64.67
Horton, M.J.	1952–70/71	410	724	49	19945	233	29.55	23	22226	825	26.94
	T	2	2	0	60	58	30.00	–	59	2	29.50
Hosen, R.W.	1965	1	2	0	2	2	1.00	–	73	1	–
Hoskyns, Sir J.C.	1949	2	4	1	63	42*	21.00	–	–	–	–
Hossell, J.J.	1939–47	35	62	5	1217	83	21.35	–	370	7	52.86
Hotchkin, N.S.	1934–48	23	37	2	736	74	21.03	–	–	–	–
Hough, E.J.	1981/82–82/83	4	3	1	13	9	6.50	–	287	12	23.92
Houghton, D.L.	1978/79–83/84	36	66	3	1608	87	25.52	–	0	0	–
Houghton, W.E.	1946–47	7	11	0	165	41	15.00	–	–	–	–
Houlton, G.	1961–63	20	33	2	688	86	22.19	–	6	0	–
Howard, A.S.	1961	3	2	0	0	0	0.00	–	352	8	44.00
Howard, B.J.	1947–51	34	50	3	1232	114	26.21	3	–	–	–
Howard, J.	1946–48	41	66	14	589	38*	11.33	–	5	0	–
Howard, K.	1960–66	61	82	35	395	23	8.40	–	3175	104	30.53
Howard, N.D.	1946–54	198	279	30	6152	145	24.71	3	52	1	–
	T	4	6	1	86	23	17.20	–	–	–	–
Howarth, G.P.	1968/69–	315	544	41	16615	183	33.03	32	3543	112	31.63
	T	40	71	5	2270	147	34.39	6	254	3	84.67
Howarth, H.J.	1962/63–78/79	145	179	58	1668	61	13.79	–	13674	541	25.28
	T	30	42	18	291	61	12.13	–	3178	86	36.95
Howarth, J.S.	1966–67	13	7	3	0	0*	0.00	–	642	19	33.79
Howat, M.G.	1977–80	26	22	3	194	32	10.21	–	1560	26	60.00
Howgego, J.A.	1977	1	2	0	91	52	45.50	–	–	–	–
Howick, N.K.	1974	5	10	0	51	14	5.10	–	–	–	–
Howland, C.B.	1956–68	64	104	8	1629	124*	16.97	1	11	0	–
Howland, P.C.	1969	6	11	1	104	21	10.40	–	7	0	–
Howorth, R.	1933–51	372	611	56	11479	114	20.68	4	29427	1345	21.87
	T	5	10	2	145	45*	18.12	–	635	19	33.42

	Career span	M	I	NO	Runs	HS	Avge	100	Runs	Wkts	Avge
					—BATTING—				—BOWLING—		
Hoyer-Millar, G.C.	1952	2	3	1	17	10	8.50	–	–	–	–
Hudson, G.D.	1964	1	2	0	6	6	3.00	–	–	–	–
Huey, S.S.J.	1951–66	20	30	4	135	23★	5.19	–	1203	66	18.23
Hughes, D.G.	1955	1	1	0	2	2	–	–	–	–	–
Hughes, D.P.	1967–	344	447	82	8201	153	22.47	8	18228	609	29.93
Hughes, G.	1962–65	27	41	4	457	92	12.35	–	1368	31	44.13
Hughes, K.J.	1975/76–	165	279	13	10273	213	38.62	22	59	2	29.50
	T	66	116	6	4334	213	39.40	9	28	0	–
Hughes, L.P.	1965–72	5	8	3	55	35	11.00	–	439	9	48.78
Hughes, M.G.	1981/82	14	15	5	76	17	7.60	–	1739	40	43.48
Hughes, N.	1953–54	21	32	6	651	95	25.04	–	317	10	31.70
Hughes, R.C.	1950–51	11	10	2	47	21	5.88	–	694	15	46.27
Hughes, S.P.	1980–	65	64	29	274	41★	7.83	–	4989	184	27.11
Hughes, W.L.	1947	1	1	0	3	3	–	–	28	0	–
Hugo, S.G.	1966/67–77/78	22	29	6	584	68★	25.39	–	951	48	19.81
Humpage, G.W.	1974–	223	367	45	11878	254	36.89	23	444	10	44.40
Humphrey, R.G.	1964–70	2	2	1	63	58	–	–	–	–	–
Humphries, D.J.	1974–	174	251	45	5054	133★	24.53	4	–	–	–
Humphries, N.H.	1946	7	11	1	137	22	13.70	–	52	0	–
Hunt, R.G.	1935–47	26	46	4	831	117	19.79	1	959	32	29.97
Hunte, C.C.	1950/51–66/67	132	222	19	8916	263	43.92	16	644	17	37.88
	T	44	78	6	3245	260	45.06	8	110	2	55.00
Hunter, C.M.G.	1971	1	2	1	50	41	–	–	52	0	–
Hunter, W.R.	1958–65	11	18	0	202	39	11.22	–	445	19	23.42
Hurd, A.	1958–60	90	106	36	376	21	5.37	–	7671	249	30.81
Hurst, A.G.	1972/73–80/81	77	88	30	504	27★	8.68	–	7360	280	26.28
	T	12	20	3	102	26	6.00	–	1200	43	27.90
Hurst, G.C.	1962	1	2	1	0	0★	–	–	–	–	–
Hurst, G.T.	1947–49	9	13	4	27	9	3.00	–	760	28	27.14
Hurst, R.J.	1954–61	105	128	56	721	62	10.01	–	6189	255	24.27
Huskinson, G.M.C.	1959	1	2	0	10	7	5.00	–	–	–	–
Hutson, A.M.	1972	1	1	1	0	0★	–	–	54	0	–
Hutton, G.	1966–67	2	2	1	0	0★	–	–	56	2	28.00
Hutton, L.	1934–60	513	814	91	40140	364	55.51	129	5090	173	29.42
	T	79	138	15	6971	364	56.67	19	232	3	77.33
Hutton, R.A.	1962–75/76	281	410	58	7561	189	21.48	5	15008	625	24.01
	T	5	8	2	219	81	36.50	–	257	9	28.55
Huxford, P.N.	1980–81	7	9	4	27	10	5.40	–	–	–	–
Huxter, R.J.A.	1981	4	5	0	34	20	6.80	–	224	5	44.80
Iddon, J.	1924–45	504	712	95	22681	222	36.76	46	14803	550	26.93
	T	5	7	1	170	73	28.33	–	27	0	–
Iftiqar A.Bokhari	1957–65/66	18	30	6	938	203★	39.08	3	25	0	–
Ijaz Butt	1955/56–67/68	67	120	8	3842	161	34.30	7	146	3	48.67
	T	8	16	2	279	58	19.92	–	–	–	–
Ijaz Hussain	1956/57–73/74	82	141	6	4580	173	33.92	8	400	16	25.00
Ikin, J.T.	1938–64	365	554	66	17968	192	36.81	27	10214	340	30.04
	T	18	31	2	606	60	20.89	–	354	3	118.00
Ikin, M.J.	1972–79	2	3	0	40	31	13.33	–	112	0	–
Ikram Elahi	1952/53–69/70	47	59	5	1076	73	19.92	–	2403	106	22.66
Illingworth, N.J.B.	1981–83	15	20	5	207	49	13.80	–	694	16	43.38
Illingworth, R.	1951–83	787	1073	213	24134	162	28.06	22	42023	2072	20.28
	T	61	90	11	1836	113	23.24	2	3807	122	31.20
Illingworth, R.K.	1982–	57	71	17	810	55	15.00	–	4513	123	36.69
Ilsley, S.T.	1956	2	2	0	8	8	4.00	–	137	5	27.40

	Career span	M	I	NO	Runs	HS	Avge	100	Runs	Wkts	Avge
					BATTING				BOWLING		
Imran Khan	1969/70–	289	451	70	13307	170	34.93	22	21999	995	22.11
T		51	77	12	2023	123	31.12	2	5318	232	22.92
Imtiaz Ahmed	1944/45–73/74	180	311	32	10383	300*	37.21	22	167	4	41.75
T		41	72	1	2079	209	29.28	3	0	0	–
Inchmore, J.D.	1973–	192	229	49	2982	113	16.57	1	13371	464	28.82
Indrajitsinhji, K.S.	1954/55–71/72	90	146	8	3694	124	26.77	5	61	0	–
T		4	7	1	51	23	8.50	–	–	–	–
Ingham, P.G.	1979–81	8	14	0	290	64	20.71	–	–	–	–
Ingleby-Mackenzie, A.C.D.	1951–	343	574	64	12421	132*	24.35	11	35	0	–
Inglis, R.	1965–69	3	6	1	91	43	18.20	–	24	2	12.00
Ingram, E.	1928–53	31	55	4	766	64	15.02	–	1896	79	24.00
Inman, C.C.	1956/57–71	255	422	42	13112	178	34.51	21	89	1	–
Inshan Ali	1965/66–79/80	90	118	21	1341	63	13.82	–	9491	328	28.93
T		12	18	2	172	25	10.75	–	1621	34	47.67
Insole, D.J.	1947–63	450	743	72	25237	219*	37.61	54	4680	138	33.91
T		9	17	2	408	110*	27.20	1	–	–	–
Intikhab Alam	1957/58–82	489	725	78	14331	182	22.14	9	43472	1571	27.67
T		47	77	10	1493	138	22.28	1	4494	125	35.95
Inverarity, R.J.	1962/63–	213	361	47	11414	187	36.35	26	5764	178	32.38
T		6	11	1	174	56	17.40	–	93	4	23.25
Iqbal Qasim	1971/72–	143	144	36	1464	61	13.56	–	12382	563	21.99
T		37	42	12	278	56	9.27	–	3473	115	30.20
Irish, A.F.	1950	16	29	4	629	76	25.16	–	206	3	68.67
Irvine, B.L.	1962/63–76/77	157	271	26	9919	193	40.48	21	142	1	–
T		4	7	0	353	102	50.42	1	–	–	–
Isles, D.	1967	1	2	2	21	17*	–	–	–	–	–
Ivey, A.M.	1949–51	7	12	0	220	40	18.33	–	160	2	80.00
Jackman, R.D.	1966–82/83	399	478	157	5681	92*	17.69	–	31978	1402	22.80
T		4	6	0	42	17	7.00	–	445	14	31.78
Jackson, A.B.	1963–68	149	160	83	647	27	8.40	–	8656	457	18.94
Jackson, E.J.W.	1974–76	28	51	6	762	63	16.93	–	2215	43	51.51
Jackson, H.L.	1947–63	418	489	153	2083	39*	6.20	–	30101	1733	17.37
T		2	2	1	15	8	–	–	155	7	22.15
Jackson, P.B.	1981–	4	5	1	106	46	26.50	–	–	–	–
Jackson, P.F.	1929–50	385	549	208	2052	40*	6.02	–	30521	1159	26.33
Jackson, R.F.	1962	2	3	2	8	5*	–	–	126	0	–
Jackson, V.E.	1936/37–58	354	605	53	15698	170	28.44	21	23874	965	24.74
Jacobs, J.	1927/28–45	12	21	1	464	69	23.20	–	–	–	–
Jacobson, L.C.	1948–52	4	7	2	153	101*	30.60	1	–	–	–
Jaffey, I.M.	1953	1	–	–	–	–	–	–	–	–	–
Jaisimha, M.L.	1954/55–76/77	245	387	27	13515	259	37.54	33	12873	431	29.86
T		39	71	4	2056	129	30.68	3	829	9	92.11
Jakeman, F.	1946–54	134	205	19	5952	258*	32.00	11	162	5	32.40
Jakeman, R.S.	1962–63	3	4	0	31	20	7.75	–	–	–	–
Jakobson, T.R.	1960–61	14	19	7	112	20	9.33	–	1184	37	32.00
Jalal-ud-din	1975/76–	53	66	18	687	60*	14.31	–	4663	212	22.00
T		3	2	2	1	1*	–	–	244	7	34.85
James, A.E.	1948–60	299	414	135	3411	63*	12.22	–	22841	843	27.16
James, B.	1954	4	5	3	22	11*	11.00	–	228	8	28.50
James, D.H.	1948	1	1	0	17	17	–	–	59	–	–
James, D.J.G.	1961	1	2	0	40	29	20.00	–	–	–	–
James, E.Ll	1946–47	9	12	4	232	62*	29.00	–	45	1	–
James, K.C.	1923/24–46/47	204	330	41	6413	109*	22.19	7	17	0	–
T		11	13	2	52	14	4.72	–	–	–	–

	Career span	M	I	NO	Runs	HS	Avge	100	Runs	Wkts	Avge
			—BATTING—						—BOWLING—		
James, K.D.	1980–	15	16	6	220	34	22.00	–	494	25	19.76
James, R.M.	1956–64/65	51	90	10	2208	168	27.60	4	1356	38	35.68
Jameson, J.A.	1960–76	361	611	43	18941	240*	33.34	33	3782	89	42.49
	T	4	8	0	214	82	26.75	–	17	1	–
Jameson, T.E.N.	1970	10	17	2	181	32	12.07	–	531	10	53.10
Jaques, P.H.	1949	1	2	0	69	55	34.50	–	–	–	–
Jardine, D.R.	1920–48	262	378	61	14848	214	46.84	35	1493	48	31.10
	T	22	33	6	1296	127	48.00	1	10	0	–
Jarman, B.N.	1955/56–68/69	191	284	37	5615	196	22.73	5	98	3	32.67
	T	19	30	3	400	78	14.81	–	–	–	–
Jarman, H.J.	1961–71	45	74	18	1041	67*	18.59	–	131	0	–
Jarrett, D.W.	1974–76	21	41	0	678	62	16.53	–	7	0	–
Jarrett, G.M.	1971–74	3	4	2	32	24*	16.00	–	260	2	130.00
Jarrett, K.S.	1967	2	3	1	27	18*	13.50	–	76	0	–
Jarvis, K.B.S.	1975–	205	150	65	275	19	3.24	–	15718	543	28.95
Jarvis, P.W.	1981–	21	22	9	186	37	14.31	–	1778	43	41.35
Jarvis, T.W.	1964/65–76/77	97	167	8	4666	182	29.34	6	89	0	–
	T	13	22	1	625	182	29.76	1	3	0	–
Javed Akhtar	1959/60–75/76	51	63	10	835	88	15.75	–	3396	187	18.16
	T	1	2	1	4	2*	–	–	52	0	–
Javed Burki	1955/56–74/75	177	290	31	9426	127	36.39	22	1554	35	44.40
	T	25	48	4	1341	140	30.47	3	23	0	–
Javed Miandad	1973/74–	284	460	74	20416	311	52.89	56	6192	187	33.11
	T	60	95	14	4519	280*	55.79	11	661	17	38.88
Jawahir Shah	1967/68–75	3	6	0	141	50	23.50	–	13	0	–
Jayantilal, H.K.	1967/68–78/79	91	154	25	4685	197	36.31	8	311	6	51.83
	T	1	1	0	5	5	–	–	–	–	–
Jayasekhera, R.S.A.	1979–81/82	8	13	1	356	79*	29.67	–	8	0	–
	T	1	2	0	2	1	1.00	–	–	–	–
Jayasinghe, S.	1949/50–66/67	144	254	10	6811	135	27.91	6	1189	34	34.97
Jayasinghe, S.A.	1979	6	7	1	183	64	30.50	–	–	–	–
Jefferies, S.T.	1978/79–	73	97	19	2016	75*	25.85	–	6788	251	27.04
Jefferson, R.I.	1961–69	94	137	31	2094	136	19.75	2	7250	263	27.57
Jeffery, H.W.J.	1964	2	3	1	6	6	3.00	–	103	2	51.50
Jeganathan, S.	1973/74–82/83	27	36	4	432	74	13.50	–	1425	47	30.31
	T	2	4	0	19	8	4.75	–	12	0	–
Jenkins, H.	1970	1	2	1	81	65	–	–	–	–	–
Jenkins, R.O.	1938–58	386	573	120	10073	109	22.23	1	30925	1309	23.62
	T	9	12	1	198	39	18.00	–	1098	32	34.31
Jennings, K.F.	1975–81	68	73	24	521	49	10.63	–	3403	96	35.44
Jepson, A.	1938–59	392	534	89	6369	130	14.31	1	30567	1051	29.08
Jerman, L.C.S.	1950–51	3	2	0	8	8	4.00	–	222	1	–
Jessup, J.A.	1950–51	7	10	7	18	7*	6.00	–	432	19	22.73
Jesty, T.E.	1966–	366	584	75	15970	248	31.38	27	15065	555	27.14
Jewel, G.A.F.W.	1952	1	2	0	1	1	0.50	–	–	–	–
John, V.B.	1981/82–	18	20	8	70	27*	5.83	–	1681	67	25.09
	T	6	10	5	53	27*	10.60	–	614	28	21.93
Johns, D.F.V.	1953	1	2	0	4	4	2.00	–	55	1	–
Johns, R.L.	1970–71	14	22	2	335	61*	16.75	–	730	17	42.94
Johnson, A.A.	1963–74	27	37	4	289	45	8.76	–	1717	49	35.04
Johnson, C.	1969–79	100	152	14	2960	107	21.44	2	265	4	66.25
Johnson, F.S.R.	1942/43–47	2	4	0	14	11	3.50	–	–	–	–
Johnson, G.W.	1965–	374	582	73	12549	168	24.65	11	17058	555	30.74
Johnson, H.H.H.	1934/35–50/51	28	30	12	316	39*	17.56	–	1589	68	23.67
	T	3	4	0	38	22	9.50	–	238	13	18.30
Johnson, H.L.	1949–66	351	606	65	14286	154	26.41	16	822	21	39.14

	Career span	M	I	NO	Runs	HS	Avge	100	Runs	Wkts	Avge
					—BATTING—				—BOWLING—		
Johnson, I.N.	1972–75	33	43	10	716	69	21.69	–	1533	37	41.43
Johnson, I.W.	1935/36–56/57	189	243	29	4905	132*	22.92	1	14433	619	23.31
T		45	66	12	1000	77	18.51	–	3182	109	29.19
Johnson, J.S.	1979	1	2	1	170	146*	–	1	–	–	–
Johnson, L.A.	1958–72	156	189	40	1573	50	10.55	–	61	1	–
Johnson, M.	1981	4	4	2	2	2	1.00	–	301	7	43.00
Johnson, P.	1982–	30	49	4	1349	133	29.98	3	23	2	11.50
Johnson, P.D.	1969–81	89	149	14	3363	106*	24.91	2	972	11	88.36
Johnson, P.L.	1947–50	2	3	0	61	40	20.33	–	–	–	–
Johnson, P.M.	1971	1	2	0	2	2	1.00	–	–	–	–
Johnston, A.	1947–51	2	4	1	82	50*	27.33	–	47	1	–
Johnston, H.G.F.	1975–81	2	3	0	24	12	8.00	–	86	3	28.67
Johnston, R.I.	1979–83	3	5	2	86	34	28.67	–	3	0	–
Johnston, W.A.	1945/46–54/55	142	162	73	1129	38	12.68	–	12936	554	23.35
T		40	49	25	273	29	11.37	–	3826	160	23.91
Jolley, W.T.	1947	2	2	1	21	13	–	–	132	5	26.40
Jones, A.	1957–83	645	1168	72	36049	204*	32.89	56	333	3	111.00
Jones, A.A.	1966–81	214	216	68	799	33	5.40	–	15414	549	28.07
Jones, A.K.C.	1969–73	35	65	1	1403	111	21.92	1	7	0	–
Jones, A.L.	1973–	128	230	18	5483	132	25.86	5	128	1	–
Jones, A.N.	1981–	26	27	12	146	35	9.73	–	1485	54	27.50
Jones, A.T.M.	1938–48	21	35	0	399	106	11.40	1	132	3	44.00
Jones, B.J.R.	1976–80	46	81	3	1076	65	13.79	–	–	–	–
Jones, C.I.McM	1959	2	3	0	44	44	14.67	–	–	–	–
Jones, E.C.	1934–46	101	142	30	2016	132	18.00	2	3345	103	32.48
Jones, E.W.	1961–83	405	591	119	8341	146*	17.67	3	5	0	–
Jones, F.A.	1951–63/64	16	31	0	618	88	19.94	–	1	0	–
Jones, H.O.	1946	2	3	3	10	7*	–	–	53	0	–
Jones, I.J.	1960–68	198	213	84	513	21	3.97	–	13278	511	25.98
T		15	17	9	38	16	4.75	–	1769	44	40.20
Jones, K.V.	1967–76	118	157	37	2064	57*	17.20	–	6603	242	27.28
Jones, P.C.H.	1971–72	26	45	8	521	67	14.08	–	525	13	40.38
Jones, P.E.	1940/41–51/52	61	71	16	775	60*	14.09	–	4531	169	26.81
T		9	11	2	47	10*	5.22	–	751	25	30.04
Jones, P.H.	1953–67	141	232	32	4196	132	20.98	2	6549	231	28.35
Jones, R.	1955	1	2	0	25	23	12.50	–	–	–	–
Jones, R.H.	1946	1	2	0	32	23	16.00	–	27	0	–
Jones, Watkin E.	1946–47	5	1	0	0	0	–	–	342	13	26.31
Jones, William E.	1937–58	345	563	64	13535	212*	27.12	11	5782	192	30.10
Jordan, J.	1955–57	62	75	7	754	39	11.09	–	–	–	–
Jorden, A.M.	1966–70	89	130	31	1112	67*	11.23	–	5347	176	30.38
Jose, A.D.	1947/48–53	29	44	8	269	39	7.47	–	2293	75	30.57
Joseph, A.F.	1946	1	2	0	8	8	4.00	–	–	–	–
Josephs, J.M.	1946–53	9	14	2	116	25*	9.67	–	86	1	–
Joshi, P.G.	1946/47–64/65	78	111	10	1724	100*	17.06	1	13	0	–
T		12	20	1	207	52*	10.89	–	–	–	–
Joshi, U.C.	1965/66–82/83	186	238	55	2347	100*	12.82	1	16192	557	29.07
Joslin, L.R.	1966/67–69/70	44	67	6	1816	126	29.77	2	73	1	–
T		1	2	0	9	7	4.50	–	–	–	–
Jowett, D.C.P.R.	1952–58	50	73	25	578	57	12.04	–	4074	125	32.59
Jowett, R.L.	1957–60	43	78	5	1499	122	20.53	2	802	20	40.10
Joynt, H.W.	1952–57/58	12	23	4	280	42*	14.74	–	879	18	48.83
Judd, P.	1960	1	–	–	–	–	–	–	14	0	–
Judge, P.F.	1933–47	68	90	31	454	40	7.69	–	4676	173	27.03
Julian, R.	1953–71	192	288	23	2581	51	9.74	–	–	–	–
Julien, B.D.	1967/68–83/84	195	273	36	5792	127	24.44	3	13871	483	28.72
T		24	34	6	866	121	30.92	2	1868	50	37.36

	Career span	M	I	NO	Runs	HS	Avge	100	Runs	Wkts	Avge
					BATTING				*BOWLING*		
Jumadeen, R.R.	1966/67–80/81	99	119	48	604	56	8.50	–	9686	347	27.91
	T	12	14	10	84	56	21.00	–	1141	29	39.34
Kallicharran, A.I.	1966/67–	421	693	73	28096	243*	45.32	75	3280	74	44.32
	T	66	109	10	4399	187	44.43	12	158	4	39.50
Kaluperuma, L.W.	1970/71–82/83	57	81	22	1023	96	17.33	–	3931	129	30.47
	T	2	4	1	12	11*	4.00	–	93	0	–
Kamm, A.	1952–56	9	11	4	154	59*	22.00	–	–	–	–
Kanhai, R.B.	1954/55–81/82	416	669	82	28774	256	49.01	83	1008	18	56.00
	T	79	137	6	6227	256	47.53	15	85	0	–
Kapil Dev	1975/76–	154	218	22	5762	193	29.40	8	13322	499	26.70
	T	62	92	8	2483	126*	29.56	3	6844	247	27.71
Kardar, A.H.	1943/44–65/66	174	262	33	6814	173	29.75	8	8447	344	24.55
	T	26	42	3	927	93	23.76	–	954	21	45.42
Kasipillai, M.	1948/49–57	11	21	2	276	62*	14.52	–	130	3	43.33
Kaye, M.A.C.P.	1937–49	17	28	6	395	78	17.95	–	1244	31	40.13
Kayum, D.A.	1977–78	12	18	1	423	57	24.88	–	–	–	–
Keeler, J.G.	1953	1	2	0	11	10	5.50	–	–	–	–
Keeling, M.E.A.	1948–49	5	6	0	75	40	12.50	–	–	–	–
Keeton, W.W.	1926–52	397	657	43	24276	312*	39.54	54	103	2	51.50
	T	2	4	0	57	25	14.25	–	–	–	–
Keighley, W.G.	1947–51	65	102	8	2539	110	27.01	2	79	0	–
Keith, G.L.	1959–68/69	77	124	14	2108	101*	19.16	1	561	13	43.15
Keith, H.J.	1950/51–57/58	74	113	8	3203	193	30.50	8	2174	79	27.51
	T	8	16	1	318	73	21.20	–	63	0	–
Kelland, P.A.	1949–52	15	15	7	72	25	9.00	–	1053	27	39.00
Kelleher, H.R.A.	1955–58	55	51	17	256	25	7.53	–	3097	112	27.65
Kelly, E.A.	1957	4	6	2	38	16*	9.50	–	248	4	62.00
Kelly, J.	1953–57	51	72	11	1303	113	21.36	1	1844	38	48.52
Kelly, J.M.	1947–60	259	437	29	9614	131	23.56	9	103	1	–
Kelsall, R.S.	1969	1	1	1	8	8*	–	–	6	1	–
Kember, O.D.	1962–63	6	9	2	61	19*	8.72	–	–	–	–
Kemp, N.J.	1977–82	18	19	4	210	46*	14.00	–	801	16	50.06
Kemsley, J.N.	1955–57	8	14	0	285	103	20.36	1	–	–	–
Kendall, J.T.	1948–49	4	4	1	26	18*	8.67	–	–	–	–
Kendall, M.P.	1971–72	12	16	4	60	13	5.00	–	852	23	37.04
Kennedy, A.	1970–82	150	243	20	6298	180	28.24	6	398	10	39.80
Kennedy, I.G.	1983	1	2	0	15	12	7.50	–	–	–	–
Kennedy, J.H.	1970–71	2	2	1	7	6*	–	–	99	1	–
Kennedy, J.M.	1960–62	31	55	9	1188	94	25.82	–	1	2	0.50
Kenny, C.J.M.	1950–62	40	38	16	75	16	3.41	–	3348	117	28.62
Kent, M.F.	1974/75–81/82	64	110	11	3567	171	36.03	7	3	0	–
	T	3	6	0	171	54	28.50	–	–	–	–
Kent, T.	1960–62	10	10	4	74	23*	12.33	–	561	15	37.40
Kentish, E.S.M.	1947/48–56/57	27	29	21	109	15*	13.63	–	2084	78	26.72
	T	2	2	1	1	1*	–	–	178	8	22.25
Kenyon, D.	1946–67	643	1159	59	37002	259	33.63	74	187	1	–
	T	8	15	0	192	87	12.80	–	–	–	–
Ker, A.B.M.	1981–	4	7	1	178	65	29.67	–	–	–	–
Ker, J.E.	1977–	8	12	5	147	50	21.00	–	313	11	28.45
Kerrigan, M.	1954–61	12	18	4	84	18*	6.00	–	892	39	22.87
Kerslake, R.C.	1962–76	85	132	14	1939	80	16.43	–	2617	114	22.96
Kettle, M.K.	1963–70	88	105	20	1117	88	13.14	–	4800	179	26.81
Khalid Hasan	1953/54–58/59	17	16	6	113	30	11.30	–	1071	28	38.25
	T	1	2	1	17	10	–	–	116	2	58.00

	Career span	M		I	NO	Runs	HS	Avge	100		Runs	Wkts	Avge
Khalid Ibadulla	1952/53–71/72	416		702	78	17039	171	27.30	22		14264	462	30.87
	T	4		8	0	253	166	31.62	1		99	1	–
Khalid Wazir	1952/53–54	18		23	5	271	53	15.05	–		746	14	53.28
	T	2		3	1	14	9*	7.00	–		–	–	–
Khan, Asad J.	1965/66–70/71	40		64	5	1154	92	19.55	–		2030	53	38.30
Khan Mohammed	1946/47–60/61	53		64	18	524	93	11.39	–		4939	212	23.30
	T	13		17	7	100	26*	10.00	–		1292	54	23.92
Khanna, S.C.L.	1976/77–	70		96	16	3506	146	43.83	11		21	0	–
Kilbee, J.R.	1968–69	8		12	4	70	18*	8.75	–		270	8	33.75
Killick, E.T.	1926–46	92		153	11	5730	206	40.35	15		229	3	76.33
	T	2		4	0	81	31	20.25	–		–	–	–
Kimish, A.E.	1946	3		4	1	18	12*	6.00	–		–	–	–
Kimmins, S.E.A.	1950–59	16		29	3	563	81	21.65	–		996	24	41.50
Kimpton, R.C.M.	1935–55/56	62		109	8	3562	160	35.27	8		1336	28	47.71
King, A.M.	1955	1		1	0	12	12	–	–		–	–	–
King, B.P.	1935–47	117		196	9	4124	145	22.05	6		4	0	–
King, H.D.	1934/35–46	9		13	4	104	26	11.56	–		–	–	–
King, I.M.	1952–57	81		96	39	476	33	8.35	–		3706	128	28.96
King, J.M.R.	1966	3		5	0	47	28	9.40	–		–	–	–
King, C.L.	1972/73–83/84	106		173	24	5836	163	39.17	13		3812	119	32.03
	T	9		16	3	418	100*	32.15	1		282	3	94.00
King, K.C.W.	1936–55	32		40	8	361	64	11.28	–		1201	34	35.32
King, L.A.	1961/62–67/68	62		87	19	1404	89	20.64	–		4463	142	31.42
	T	2		4	0	41	20	10.25	–		154	9	17.11
Kingston, G.C.	1967–71	9		15	2	161	26	12.38	–		210	4	52.50
Kinkead-Weekes, R.C.	1972–76	6		9	2	76	25*	10.86	–		–	–	–
Kippax, P.J.	1961–62	4		7	2	37	9	7.40	–		279	8	34.88
Kirby, D.	1959–64	117		218	9	4105	118	19.64	3		4251	113	37.62
Kirby, G.N.G.	1947–53	23		21	8	168	32	12.92	–		–	–	–
Kirby, J.E.W.	1956	3		6	0	78	28	13.00	–		–	–	–
Kirkman, M.	1963	11		15	11	28	7*	7.00	–		741	14	52.92
Kirkpatrick, A.K.	1962	1		2	1	31	30	–	–		46	0	–
Kirkwood, E.McM.	1958	3		5	0	17	10	3.40	–		–	–	–
Kirmani, S.M.H.	1967/68–	209		294	58	6285	116	26.63	3		68	1	–
	T	78		113	20	2418	101*	26.00	1		13	1	–
Kirsten, P.N.	1973/74–83/84	209		361	41	14876	228	46.49	39		2571	68	37.81
Kitchen, M.J.	1960–79	354		612	32	15230	189	26.25	17		109	2	54.50
Kitson, D.L.	1952–54	32		60	3	886	69	15.54	–		–	–	–
Kline, L.F.	1955/56–61/62	88		96	31	559	37*	8.60	–		7562	276	27.39
	T	13		16	9	58	15*	8.28	–		776	34	22.82
Knew, G.A.	1972–73	4		6	1	59	25	11.80	–		–	–	–
Knight, B.R.	1955–69	379		602	83	13336	165	25.70	12		26203	1089	24.06
	T	29		38	7	812	127	26.19	2		2223	70	31.75
Knight, J.M.	1978–81	23		35	3	318	41*	9.93	–		1413	33	43.36
Knight, R.D.V.	1967–84	384		668	59	19518	165*	32.05	31		13252	369	35.91
Knightley-Smith, W.	1952–61	87		155	10	2530	95	17.45	–		72	0	–
Knott, A.P.E.	1964–	492		721	129	17726	156	29.94	17		87	2	43.50
	T	95		149	15	4389	135	32.75	5		–	–	–
Knott, C.J.	1938–57	173		245	98	1023	27	6.95	–		15771	676	23.32
Knowles, J.	1935–46	125		188	18	4194	114	24.67	2		1441	34	42.38
Knox, G.K.	1964–67	52		92	3	1698	108	19.08	3		161	2	80.50
Kok, M.	1953	2		2	0	14	8	7.00	–		68	2	34.00
Konig, P.H.	1949	1		1	0	6	6	–	–		–	–	–
Krikken, B.E.	1966–69	3		3	0	8	4	2.67	–		–	–	–
Kripal Singh, A.G.	1950/51–65/66	96		143	22	4947	208	40.88	10		5031	177	28.42
	T	14		20	5	422	100*	28.13	1		584	10	58.40

	Career span	M		I	NO	Runs	HS	Avge	100		Runs	Wkts	Avge
Krishnamurthy, P.	1966/67–78/79	98		121	22	1481	82	14.95	–		32	0	–
	T	5		6	0	33	20	5.50	–		–	–	–
Kumbleben, J.M.	1956–60/61	29		50	2	955	100	19.89	1		–	–	–
Kunderan, B.K.	1958/59–75/76	129		217	20	5708	205	28.47	12		160	3	53.33
	T	18		34	4	981	192	32.70	2		13	0	–
Kuruppu, D.S.B.P.	1981/82	9		15	0	249	55	16.60	–		–	–	–
Lacy-Scott, D.G.	1946–48	11		21	0	294	36	14.00	–		268	9	29.77
Laidlaw, W.K.	1938–53	17		27	9	132	25	7.33	–		1225	42	29.17
Laing, J.G.B.	1964–74	19		32	4	655	93	23.39	–		–	–	–
Laing, J.R.	1969–79	8		15	1	301	127*	21.50	1		–	–	–
Laird, B.M.	1972/73–	103		186	14	6085	171	35.38	8		69	0	–
	T	21		40	2	1341	92	35.28	–		12	0	–
Laitt, D.J.	1959–60	2		3	1	25	10	12.50	–		186	6	31.00
Lake, G.J.	1956–58	13		18	4	106	18	7.56	–		464	17	27.30
Laker, J.C.	1946–64/65	450		548	108	7304	113	16.60	2		35791	1944	18.41
	T	46		63	15	676	63	14.08	–		4101	193	21.24
Laker, P.G.	1948–49	2		2	1	14	8*	14.00	–		70	0	–
Lamb, A.J.	1972/73–	217		374	64	15058	178	48.57	39		98	4	24.50
	T	27		49	4	1714	137*	38.09	7		6	0	–
Lamb, T.M.	1973–83	160		163	61	1274	77	12.49	–		10459	361	28.97
Lambert, G.E.E.	1938–60	339		489	61	6375	100*	14.89	1		26189	917	28.56
Lambert, N.H.	1932–47	9		17	2	213	69*	14.20	–		–	–	–
Lance, H.R.	1958/59–71/72	103		171	18	5336	169	34.87	11		4284	167	25.65
	T	13		22	1	591	70	28.14	–		479	12	39.92
Lanchbury, R.J.	1971–74	13		22	3	357	50*	18.79	–		–	–	–
Langdale, G.R.	1936–53	25		42	3	709	146	18.18	1		939	23	40.83
Langford, B.A.	1953–74	510		720	162	7588	68*	13.59	–		34964	1410	24.79
Langley, G.R.A.	1945/46–56/57	122		165	39	3236	160*	25.68	4		2	0	–
	T	26		37	12	374	53	14.96	–				
Langridge, J.	1924–53	692		1058	157	31716	167	35.20	42		34524	1530	22.56
	T	8		9	0	242	70	26.88	–		413	19	21.73
Langridge, J.G.	1928–55	574		984	66	34380	250*	37.45	76		1848	44	42.00
Langridge, R.J.	1957–71	212		391	28	8310	137*	22.89	5		91	0	–
Larkham, T.W.	1952	1		2	0	13	13	6.50	–		64	1	–
Larking, J.G.	1946	3		6	1	15	8	3.00	–		–	–	–
Larkins, W.	1972–	261		452	27	14665	252	34.51	34		1360	38	35.79
	T	6		11	0	176	34	16.00	–		–	–	–
Larter, J.D.F.	1960–69	182		162	57	639	51*	6.08	–		13013	666	19.53
	T	10		7	2	16	10	3.20	–		941	37	25.43
Lashley, P.D.	1957/58–74/75	85		132	13	4932	204	41.44	8		958	27	35.48
	T	4		7	0	159	49	22.71	–		1	1	–
Latchman, A.H.	1965–76	213		240	64	2333	96	13.25	–		13588	487	27.90
Latham, H.J.	1955–59	10		13	2	129	26	11.72	–		751	27	27.82
Latham, M.E.	1961–62	18		21	12	133	21*	14.77	–		888	29	30.62
Lavers, A.B.	1937–53	26		46	3	734	42*	17.07	–		497	13	38.23
Lavis, G.	1928–49	207		312	43	4957	154	18.43	3		7768	155	50.12
Law, J.A.G.C.	1940/41–49	9		17	0	194	35	11.41	–		–	–	–
Lawlor, P.J.	1981	1		2	0	8	8	4.00	–		50	1	–
Lawrence, A.A.K.	1952–56	28		44	7	632	63*	17.08	–		40	1	–
Lawrence, D.R.	1956–58	7		12	4	32	10	4.00	–		491	12	40.92
Lawrence, D.V.	1981–	29		34	8	157	17	6.04	–		2304	50	46.08
Lawrence, J.	1946–55	283		500	52	9183	122	20.49	3		19927	798	24.97
Lawrence, J.M.	1959–61	18		33	9	372	41	15.50	–		363	9	40.33
Lawrence, M.P.	1982–	13		16	5	69	18	6.27	–		1271	15	84.73

	Career span	M	I	NO	Runs	HS	Avge	100	Runs	Wkts	Avge
					BATTING					BOWLING	
Lawrence, P.	1964	4	4	1	19	14*	6.33	–	186	6	31.00
Lawrence, W.N.M.	1954	3	3	0	2	1	0.67	–	–	–	–
Lawry, W.J.	1965–69	3	4	3	13	9	–	–	–	–	–
Lawry, W.M.	1955/56–71/72	249	417	49	18734	266	50.90	50	188	5	37.60
T	67	123	12	5234	210	47.15	13	6	0	–	
Laws, M.L.	1946–50	8	8	3	19	12	3.80	–	–	–	–
Lawson, G.F.	1977/78–	83	105	24	1121	57*	13.84	–	7689	310	24.80
T	23	37	7	446	57*	14.87	–	2621	95	27.59	
Lawton, W.	1948	2	2	0	3	3	1.50	–	64	1	–
Laycock, D.A.	1969–73	10	16	2	266	58	19.00	–	–	–	–
Lea, A.E.	1984	9	18	0	395	119	21.94	1	92	2	46.00
Leach, C.W.	1955–58	39	64	6	1025	67	17.66	–	657	26	25.27
Leadbeater, B.	1966–79	147	241	29	5373	140*	25.34	1	5	1	–
Leadbeater, E.	1949–58	118	138	36	1548	116	15.18	1	7947	289	27.50
T	2	2	0	40	38	20.00	–	218	2	109.00	
Leadbetter, S.A.	1956–57	3	6	1	112	46	22.40	–	15	0	–
Leary, S.E.	1951–71	387	627	96	16517	158	31.10	18	4935	146	33.80
Ledden, P.R.V.	1961–67	35	56	6	756	98	15.12	–	338	8	42.25
Lee, C.	1952–64	271	472	16	12129	150	26.60	8	721	21	34.33
Lee, F.S.	1925–47	332	586	38	15310	169	27.93	23	862	25	34.48
Lee, J.	1947	1	2	0	3	3	1.50	–	13	1	–
Lee, P.G.	1967–82	202	164	68	779	26	8.11	–	15339	599	25.60
Lee, R.J.	1972–74	24	45	1	951	130	21.61	1	1081	29	37.27
Leech, A.D.	1972	9	11	4	24	8*	3.42	–	521	12	43.41
Lees, G.W.	1947–51	3	5	0	28	15	5.60	–	–	–	–
Lees, R.D.	1970	3	6	2	29	17*	7.25	–	144	1	–
Lees, W.K.	1970/71–	115	196	33	3966	152	24.33	4	103	2	51.50
T	21	37	4	778	152	23.58	1	4	0	–	
Legard, A.R.	1932–52	36	52	10	234	38	5.57	–	2793	93	30.03
Legard, E.	1962–68	20	24	11	144	21	11.08	–	–	–	–
Leiper, J.M.	1950	2	4	0	50	44	12.50	–	79	1	–
Leiper, R.J.	1981–82	2	4	0	53	49	13.25	–	–	–	–
Lemmy, B.A.	1958	1	2	2	12	7*	–	–	117	3	39.00
Leng, D.	1966	1	2	1	1	1	–	–	36	1	–
Lenham, L.J.	1956–70	300	539	50	12796	191*	26.16	7	306	6	51.00
Lenham, N.J.	1984–	1	1	0	31	31	–	–	–	–	–
Le Roux, G.S.	1975/76–	157	191	53	3364	83	24.38	–	11892	587	20.26
Lester, E.I.	1945–56	232	347	28	10912	186	34.21	25	170	3	56.67
Lester, G.	1937–58	373	649	54	12857	143	21.61	9	10882	307	35.45
L'Estrange, M.G.	1977–79	23	37	3	521	63	15.32	–	–	–	–
Lethbridge, C.	1981–	47	55	12	949	87*	22.07	–	2733	72	37.96
Lever, C.	1965	1	2	0	20	12	10.00	–	23	2	11.50
Lever, J.K.	1967–	442	453	171	3067	91	10.88	–	34400	1458	23.59
T	20	29	4	306	53	12.24	–	1785	67	26.64	
Lever, P.	1960–76	301	314	66	3534	88*	14.25	–	20377	796	25.59
T	17	18	2	350	88*	21.87	–	1509	41	36.80	
Levett, W.H.V.	1930–47	175	264	58	2524	76	12.25	–	6	0	–
T	1	2	1	7	5	–	–	–	–	–	
Levick, D.C.	1950–51	3	6	0	14	6	2.33	–	–	–	–
Lewington, P.J.	1970–82	72	73	21	383	34	7.36	–	5705	191	29.86
Lewis, A.C.W.	1952–53	6	9	0	83	55	9.22	–	–	–	–
Lewis, A.R.	1955–74	409	708	76	20495	223	32.42	30	432	6	72.00
T	9	16	2	457	125	32.64	1	–	–	–	
Lewis, B.	1965–68	37	45	5	333	38	8.32	–	2001	82	24.40
Lewis, C.	1933–53	128	187	72	738	27	6.42	–	8198	301	27.23
Lewis, D.J.	1945/46–63/64	88	146	16	3686	170*	28.35	8	457	11	41.54

	Career span	M		I	NO	Runs	HS	Avge	100		Runs	Wkts	Avge
Lewis, D.M.	1970–75/76	36		56	5	1623	96	31.82	–		–	–	–
	T	3		5	2	259	88	86.33	–		–	–	–
Lewis, D.W.	1960–72/73	14		20	7	122	29★	9.38	–		958	21	45.61
Lewis, E.B.	1949–58	47		56	12	553	51	12.57	–		–	–	–
Lewis, E.J.	1961–69	182		276	28	3487	80	14.06	–		9286	341	27.23
Lewis, K.H.	1950–56	36		48	14	312	34	9.18	–		2044	55	37.17
Lewis, L.K.	1952–53	6		11	1	155	53★	15.50	–		–	–	–
Lewis, R.C.V.	1949–50	4		6	2	65	34	16.25	–		222	8	27.75
Lewis, R.M.	1968–73	38		68	9	1746	87	29.59	–		7	0	–
Lewis, R.V.	1967–81	105		190	14	3471	136	19.72	2		104	1	–
Lewis, W.I.	1956–72	5		10	0	67	20	6.70	–		–	–	–
Leyland, M.	1920–47	685		932	101	33659	263	40.50	80		13651	466	29.29
	T	41		65	5	2764	187	46.06	9		585	6	97.50
Liaqat Ali	1970/71–	144		143	58	665	51	7.82	–		10451	438	23.86
	T	5		7	3	28	12	7.00	–		359	6	59.83
Liddell, A.W.G.	1951–55	18		20	6	201	38★	14.36	–		1399	24	58.28
Lightfoot, A.	1953–69	294		495	61	12000	174★	27.64	12		6192	172	36.00
Lillee, D.K.	1969/70–83/84	184		223	65	2220	73★	14.05	–		19317	845	22.86
	T	70		90	24	905	73★	13.71	–		8493	355	23.92
Lilley, A.W.	1978–	31		48	2	1175	100★	25.54	1		21	2	10.50
Lindo, C.V.	1960–63	2		3	1	65	24	32.50	–		162	8	20.25
Lindsay, D.T.	1958/59–73/74	124		214	15	7074	216	35.54	12		14	0	–
	T	19		31	1	1130	182	37.67	3		–	–	–
Lindsay, J.D.	1933/34–48/49	30		45	14	346	51	11.16	–		–	–	–
	T	3		5	1	21	9★	7.00	–		–	–	–
Lindsey, P.J.	1964	1		1	1	7	7★	–	–		50	1	–
Lindwall, R.R.	1941/42–61/62	228		270	39	5042	134★	21.82	5		16956	794	21.35
	T	61		84	13	1502	118	21.15	2		5251	228	23.03
Linehan, A.J.	1972–74	2		4	0	29	16	7.25	–		–	–	–
Lines, S.J.	1983	1		1	0	29	29	–	–		–	–	–
Ling, D.J.	1966–68	14		15	3	174	40	14.50	–		386	7	55.14
Lister, D.J.	1954	1		2	0	35	31	17.50	–		–	–	–
Lister, J.	1951–59	24		43	4	796	99	20.41	–		–	–	–
Lister, J.W.	1978–79	5		10	0	205	48	20.50	–		–	–	–
Littlewood, D.J.	1977–78	10		10	3	95	51	13.57	–		–	–	–
Livingston, L.	1941/42–58	236		384	45	15260	210	45.01	34		50	4	12.50
Livingstone, D.	1957–66	18		26	10	102	16★	6.38	–		1255	50	25.10
Livingstone, D.A.	1959–72	301		519	63	12722	200	27.89	16		93	1	–
Livock, M.D.	1960	2		2	0	21	12	10.50	–		235	8	29.37
Llewellyn, M.J.	1970–82	136		215	30	4288	129★	23.17	3		615	23	26.73
Lloyd, B.J.	1972–83	147		184	47	1631	48	11.91	–		10133	247	41.02
Lloyd, C.H.	1963/64–	469		699	92	29865	242★	49.20	76		4104	114	36.00
	T	105		167	13	7159	242★	46.49	18		622	10	62.20
Lloyd, D.	1965–83	408		652	74	19269	214★	33.34	38		7172	237	30.26
	T	9		15	2	552	214★	42.46	1		17	0	–
Lloyd, M.F.D.	1974–75	6		11	0	74	36	6.73	–		–	–	–
Lloyd, T.A.	1977–	146		258	30	8365	208★	36.69	15		740	9	82.22
	T	1		1	1	10	10★	–	–		–	–	–
Lloyds, J.W.	1979–	101		163	21	4050	132★	28.52	5		4667	135	34.57
Loader, P.J.	1951–63/64	371		382	110	2314	81	8.51	–		25260	1326	19.05
	T	13		19	6	76	17	5.84	–		878	39	22.51
Lobb, B.	1953–69	117		170	50	624	42	5.20	–		8760	370	23.68
Lobban, H.W.	1952–54	17		23	11	81	18	6.75	–		1452	47	30.89
Lock, B.H.	1952–55	2		4	0	69	57	17.25	–		–	–	–
Lock, G.A.R.	1946–70/71	654		812	161	10342	89	15.89	–		54710	2844	19.24
	T	49		63	9	742	89	13.74	–		4451	174	25.58

	Career span	M	I	NO	Runs	HS	Avge	100	Runs	Wkts	Avge
Lodge, J.T.	1948	2	3	0	48	30	16.00	–	17	0	–
Logie, A.L.	1977/78–	58	88	9	2894	171	36.63	8	99	2	49.50
	T	9	11	0	327	130	29.72	1	4	0	–
Lomax, I.R.	1952–65	12	21	1	370	83	18.50	–	229	4	57.25
Lomax, J.G.	1949–62	269	463	23	8672	104*	19.71	2	10773	316	34.09
Loney, J.K.	1974	2	2	0	4	2	2.00	–	–	–	–
Long, A.	1960–80	452	537	131	6801	92	16.75	–	2	0	–
Longfield, T.C.	1927–51	82	127	18	2446	120	22.44	2	6416	195	32.90
Longmore, A.N.M.	1973–75	2	4	1	28	15	9.33	–	–	–	–
Longrigg, E.F.	1925–47	248	407	25	9411	205	24.64	10	100	1	–
Lord, G.J.	1983–	7	9	0	174	61	19.33	–	12	0	–
Loudon, W.D.G.	1982	1	1	0	21	21	–	–	11	3	3.67
Love, J.D.	1975–	158	259	38	6869	170*	31.08	11	233	1	–
Lowe, G.	1949–53	2	3	0	43	22	14.33	–	–	–	–
Lowe, P.J.	1964	1	–	–	–	–	–	–	–	–	–
Lowson, F.A.	1949–58	277	449	37	15321	259*	37.18	31	31	0	–
	T	7	13	0	245	68	18.84	–	–	–	–
Loxton, S.J.E.	1946/47–59/60	140	192	23	6249	232*	36.97	13	5971	232	25.73
	T	12	15	0	554	101	36.93	1	349	8	43.62
Lucas, F.C.	1954	2	4	0	62	38	15.50	–	17	0	–
Lucas, J.H.	1945/46–54	15	25	5	1074	216*	53.70	2	484	15	32.26
Luckes, W.T.	1924–49	365	564	212	5640	121*	16.02	1	–	–	–
Luckhurst, B.W.	1958–76	388	660	76	22293	215	38.17	48	2744	64	42.87
	T	21	41	5	1298	131	36.05	4	32	1	–
Luckin, R.A.G.	1962–63	29	46	3	735	82	17.10	–	–	–	–
Luddington, R.S.	1982	10	14	1	290	65	22.30	–	–	–	–
Lumb, R.G.	1970–84	245	406	30	11723	165*	31.18	22	5	0	–
Lumsden, I.J.M.	1946–49	7	14	0	379	66	27.07	–	–	–	–
Lumsden, V.R.	1949/50–59/60	57	102	5	2699	107	27.83	1	355	11	32.27
Lynch, M.A.	1977–	140	239	25	6889	144	32.19	14	663	15	44.20
Lynch, R.V.	1954	3	3	2	7	6*	7.00	–	107	4	26.75
Lyness, G.E.G.	1961	1	2	0	12	9	6.00	–	91	8	11.37
Lyon, B.H.	1921–48	267	448	20	10694	189	24.99	16	2341	52	45.02
Lyon, J.	1973–79	86	91	18	1016	123	13.91	1	–	–	–
Lyons, K.J.	1967–77	62	99	14	1673	92	19.68	–	252	2	126.00
Lyons, R.W.	1947	1	1	1	0	0*	–	–	–	–	–
Maazullah Khan	1965/66–79/80	45	70	7	1300	130	20.63	2	2734	119	22.97
McAdam, K.P.W.J.	1965–67	21	39	0	815	63	20.88	–	2	0	–
McAdam, W.J.	1966/67–71/72	19	30	1	668	129	23.03	1	3	0	–
McAllister, A.E.	1950	1	2	0	13	9	6.50	–	–	–	–
Macaulay, M.J.	1957/58–78/79	69	91	23	888	59	13.05	–	5357	234	22.89
	T	1	2	0	33	21	16.50	–	73	2	36.50
McCall, B.E.W.	1936–48	3	6	0	56	31	9.33	–	35	1	–
McCall, H.C.	1964–68	7	14	1	308	81	23.69	–	1	0	–
McCarthy, C.N.	1947/48–52	59	67	35	141	23*	4.40	–	4551	176	25.85
	T	15	24	15	28	5	3.11	–	1510	36	41.94
McCay, D.L.C.	1966/67–73/74	17	25	3	345	82	15.68	–	1071	49	21.85
McCloy, T.	1952–65	12	24	0	374	53	15.58	–	15	0	–
McConnon, J.E.	1950–61	255	366	42	4661	95	14.39	–	16285	819	19.88
	T	2	3	1	18	11	9.00	–	74	4	18.50
McCool, C.L.	1939/40–60	251	412	34	12420	172	32.85	18	16542	602	27.47
	T	14	17	4	459	104*	35.30	1	958	36	26.61
McCool, R.J.	1982	1	2	0	19	12	9.50	–	63	0	–
McCorkell, N.T.	1932–51	396	696	67	16107	203	25.60	17	117	1	–

FIRST-CLASS AND TEST CAREER RECORDS

	Career span	M	I	NO	Runs	HS	Avge	100	Runs	Wkts	Avge
					BATTING				**BOWLING**		
McCorquodale, A.	1948–51	5	6	2	34	21	8.50	–	399	4	99.75
McCosker, R.B.	1973/74–83/84	127	228	24	8983	168	44.03	27	177	2	88.50
T		25	46	5	1622	127	39.56	4	–	–	–
McCurdy, R.J.	1979–	34	44	10	327	55	9.62	–	3887	117	33.22
McDermott, E.A.	1982	1	2	0	18	18	9.00	–	–	–	–
MacDonald, C.C.	1947/48–62/63	192	307	26	11375	229	40.48	24	192	3	64.00
T		47	83	4	3107	170	39.32	5	3	0	–
McDonnell, G.F.H.	1984	2	4	0	7	5	1.75	–	–	–	–
McDowall, J.I.	1969–73	29	53	5	811	89	16.89	–	–	–	–
McEntyre, K.B.	1965–66	3	3	0	33	15	11.00	–	–	–	–
McEvoy, M.S.A.	1976–84	69	113	2	2128	103	19.17	1	103	3	34.33
McEwan, K.S.	1972/73–	356	589	52	21842	218	40.67	58	309	4	77.25
McFarlane, L.L.	1979–	43	36	18	115	15*	6.39	–	3132	86	36.42
MacGibbon, A.R.	1947/48–61/62	123	204	20	3611	94	19.62	–	9228	352	26.21
T		26	46	5	814	66	19.85	–	2160	70	30.85
McGibbon, L.	1957–59	13	11	5	17	4	2.83	–	858	33	26.00
MacGinty, R.J.A.	1952	6	8	1	32	18	4.57	–	504	17	29.64
McGlew, D.J.	1947/48–66/67	190	299	34	12170	255*	42.92	27	932	35	26.62
T		34	64	6	2440	255*	42.06	7	23	0	–
McHugh, F.P.	1949–56	95	111	43	179	18	2.64	–	6857	276	24.84
McIlwaine, R.J.	1969–70	4	3	1	29	17	14.50	–	273	4	68.25
Macindoe, D.H.	1937–46	42	64	12	747	51	14.36	–	4339	152	28.54
McInerney, J.J.	1955–56	2	3	0	25	22	8.33	–	–	–	–
McIntyre, A.J.W.	1938–63	391	567	79	11145	143*	22.84	7	180	4	45.00
T		3	6	0	19	7	3.16	–	–	–	–
McIntyre, E.J.	1981–83	2	3	1	7	6	3.50	–	39	0	–
McIntyre, J.McL.	1961/62–82/83	113	148	55	1668	87*	17.93	–	7917	336	23.56
McIntyre, T.F.	1959–64	5	9	0	87	36	9.67	–	–	–	–
Mack, A.J.	1976–80	31	32	10	102	18	4.63	–	1889	44	42.93
MacKay, K.D.	1946/47–63/64	201	294	46	10823	223	43.64	23	8363	251	33.31
T		37	52	7	1507	89	33.48	–	1721	50	34.42
McKee, W.D.	1946	1	1	0	16	16	–	–	57	0	–
McKelvey, J.M.	1954	2	4	0	25	9	6.25	–	–	–	–
McKelvey, P.G.	1959–60	2	–	–	–	–	–	–	19	1	–
McKelvie, R.D.	1948	1	2	0	22	12	11.00	–	–	–	–
McKenna, R.O.	1938–46	2	4	1	8	4*	2.67	–	129	2	64.50
McKenzie, G.D.	1959/60–75	383	471	109	5662	76	15.64	–	32868	1219	26.96
T		60	89	12	945	76	12.27	–	7328	246	29.78
McKiddie, G.T.	1977	1	2	0	10	8	5.00	–	41	2	20.50
McKinna, G.H.	1951–55	6	8	2	40	18	6.67	–	391	17	23.00
McKinnon, A.H.	1952/53–68/69	111	152	39	1687	62	14.92	–	9937	470	21.14
T		8	13	7	107	27	17.83	–	925	26	35.57
Mackintosh, D.S.	1972	1	2	0	66	57	33.00	–	–	–	–
Mackintosh, K.S.	1978–83	31	33	17	303	31	18.94	–	2092	59	35.46
Maclachlan, A.	1962	5	10	3	99	28	14.14	–	239	3	79.67
McLachlan, A.A.	1964–65	17	28	3	232	27	9.28	–	1198	32	37.44
McLachlan, I.M.	1956–63/64	72	128	10	3743	188*	31.72	9	382	6	63.67
McLaren, R.S.	1947–49	6	10	2	23	7	2.88	–	–	–	–
McLean, R.A.	1949/50–65/66	200	318	19	10969	207	36.68	22	122	2	61.00
T		40	73	3	2120	142	30.28	5	1	0	–
McLellan, A.J.	1978–79	26	24	8	99	41	6.18	–	–	–	–
McMahon, J.W.	1947–57	201	285	125	989	24	6.18	–	16289	590	27.61
McMorris, E.D.A.st.J.	1956/57–71/72	95	158	18	5906	218	42.18	18	107	0	–
T		13	21	0	564	125	26.85	1	–	–	–
McNab, W.	1947	1	2	0	10	10	5.00	–	–	–	–

	Career span	M	I	NO	Runs	HS	Avge	100	Runs	Wkts	Avge
McNamara, F.K.	1952	1	2	0	18	16	9.00	–	–	–	–
McPate, W.A.	1983–	2	3	2	17	12*	–	–	115	3	38.33
MacPhail, A.W.	1977	4	8	1	63	37	9.00	–	–	–	–
Macpherson, M.C.L.	1980	5	10	1	52	22	5.77	–	–	–	–
McPherson, T.I.	1977–79	5	7	3	83	28	20.75	–	230	10	23.00
McQuilken, A.L.	1962	2	4	0	140	42	35.00	–	60	5	12.00
MacVicar, A.D.L.	1977	1	–	–	–	–	–	–	141	2	70.50
McVicker, N.M.	1965–76	173	210	53	3108	83*	19.80	–	11567	453	25.53
Madan Lal	1968/69–	187	277	80	8836	223	44.85	20	13013	504	25.82
	T	37	59	16	1000	74	23.26	–	2704	67	40.36
Maddocks, L.V.	1946/47–67/68	112	158	33	4106	122*	32.84	6	4	1	–
	T	7	12	2	177	69	17.70	–	–	–	–
Madugalle, R.S.	1979–	47	70	8	1972	142*	31.81	1	107	2	53.50
	T	12	24	3	681	91*	32.43	–	4	0	–
Magee, B.R.B.	1954	1	2	0	16	13	8.00	–	40	1	–
Maguire, K.R.	1982	3	3	0	3	2	1.00	–	123	1	–
Maher, B.J.M.	1981–	27	37	10	351	66	13.00	–	–	–	–
Mahmood Hussain	1949/50–68/69	95	115	12	1107	50	9.06	–	8074	322	25.13
	T	27	39	6	336	35	10.18	–	2628	68	38.64
Mahmood-ul-Hasan	1959/60–73/74	63	95	7	3199	196	36.35	6	337	4	84.25
Mahoney, N.C.	1948–53	5	10	0	116	29	11.60	–	–	–	–
Maidlow, W.J.	1972	2	4	0	53	45	13.25	–	–	–	–
Mains, G.	1951–54	6	10	1	19	8	2.11	–	305	6	50.83
Mair, N.G.R.	1952	1	1	1	4	4*	–	–	–	–	–
Majendie, N.L.	1961–63	26	33	6	313	54	11.59	–	–	–	–
Majid J. Khan	1961/62–82/83	407	697	60	27328	241	42.90	73	7197	224	32.12
	T	63	106	5	3931	167	38.92	8	1456	27	53.92
Malalesekera, V.P.	1966–68	27	50	1	699	80	14.26	–	9	0	–
Makinson, D.J.	1984–	4	5	2	18	9	6.00	–	313	7	44.72
Malcolm, D.E.	1984–	7	8	1	40	23	5.72	–	674	16	42.13
Malcolm, H.J.J.	1948	4	6	1	139	76*	27.80	–	6	0	–
Malhotra, A.	1973/74–	84	133	21	5176	228	46.21	12	79	1	–
	T	6	9	1	199	72*	24.88	–	0	0	–
Mallender, N.A.	1980–	96	109	34	887	71*	11.83	–	7115	234	30.41
Mallett, A.A.	1967/68–80/81	183	230	59	2326	92	13.60	–	18208	693	26.27
	T	38	50	13	430	43*	11.62	–	3940	132	29.84
Mallett, A.W.H.	1945–54	73	108	14	1764	97	18.77	–	5748	213	26.99
Mallett, N.V.H.	1980–81	11	20	2	237	52	13.16	–	841	19	44.26
Malone, M.F.	1974/75–81/82	73	79	22	914	46	16.03	–	6441	260	24.77
	T	1	1	0	46	46	–	–	77	6	12.83
Malone, S.J.	1975–84	48	40	14	178	23	6.85	–	3582	105	34.11
Maltby, N.	1972–74	9	14	4	185	59	18.50	–	97	2	48.50
Manasseh, M.	1962–67	42	73	11	1607	129*	25.92	2	2557	61	41.92
Manjrekar, V.L.	1949/50–67/68	198	295	38	12832	283	49.92	38	657	20	32.85
	T	55	92	10	3208	189*	39.12	7	44	1	–
Mankad, A.V.	1963/64–82/83	218	326	71	12980	265	50.92	31	3276	72	45.50
	T	22	42	3	991	97	25.41	–	43	0	–
Mankad, M.H.	1935/36–61/62	231	358	27	11558	231	34.91	26	19098	776	24.61
	T	44	72	5	2109	231	31.47	5	5236	162	32.32
Mann, F.G.	1938–58	166	262	17	6350	136*	25.92	7	389	3	129.67
	T	7	12	2	376	136*	37.60	1	–	–	–
Mann, J.P.	1939–47	21	32	3	608	77	20.97	–	366	6	61.00
Mann, N.B.F.	1939/40–51	73	99	16	1446	97	17.42	–	5952	251	23.71
	T	19	31	1	400	52	13.33	–	1920	58	33.10
Manners, J.E.	1936–53	21	37	0	1162	147	31.40	4	16	0	–
Manning, J.S.	1951/52–60	146	207	31	2766	132	15.71	1	11662	513	22.73

	Career span	M	I	NO	Runs	HS	Avge	100	Runs	Wkts	Avge
					BATTING				BOWLING		
Mansell, A.W.	1969–75	58	93	21	1098	72*	15.25	–	–	–	–
Mansell, P.N.F.	1936/37–61/62	113	172	17	4598	154	29.66	5	7798	299	26.08
T		13	22	2	355	90	17.75	–	736	11	66.90
Mansoor Akhtar	1974/75–	77	129	12	4470	224*	38.21	6	345	6	57.50
T		13	22	3	484	111	25.47	1	–	–	–
Mantell, D.N.	1954–58	26	31	6	150	34	6.00	–	–	–	–
Manville, D.W.	1956	3	5	0	13	8	2.60	–	–	–	–
Mantri, M.K.	1941/42–67/68	95	141	11	4403	200	33.86	7	121	3	40.33
T		4	8	1	67	39	9.57	–	–	–	–
Maqsood Ahmed	1944/45–63/64	81	125	9	3716	144	32.03	6	3412	120	28.43
T		16	27	1	507	99	19.50	–	191	3	63.66
Marie, G.V.	1978–79	10	13	2	104	27	9.45	–	666	20	33.30
Marks, A.E.	1953–55	3	6	0	35	17	5.83	–	–	–	–
Marks, C.P.	1967–69	14	21	2	216	39	11.37	–	–	–	–
Marks, V.J.	1975–	209	318	50	7789	134	29.06	4	16152	498	32.43
T		6	10	1	249	83	27.67	–	484	11	44.00
Marlar, R.G.	1951–68	289	379	67	3032	64	9.71	–	24469	970	25.22
Marlow, C.R.J.	1973	3	6	1	29	11	5.80	–	7	1	–
Marner, P.T.	1952–70	414	680	62	17513	142*	28.34	18	11385	360	31.63
Marriott, D.A.	1965–74	30	26	13	139	24*	10.69	–	1990	67	29.70
Marsden, K.	1952	1	–	–	–	–	–	–	56	0	–
Marsden, R.	1979–82	13	23	1	507	60	23.04	–	–	–	–
Marsh, E.	1962	10	20	3	419	50	24.64	–	–	–	–
Marsh, F.E.	1946–49	66	109	20	1627	86	18.28	–	1698	44	38.59
Marsh, P.	1965	1	2	0	25	23	12.50	–	22	0	–
Marsh, R.W.	1968/69–83/84	257	396	41	11067	236	31.18	12	84	1	–
T		96	150	13	3633	132	26.52	3	54	0	–
Marsh, S.A.	1982–	8	10	2	121	48	15.13	–	–	–	–
Marsh, W.E.	1947	4	6	1	39	13	7.80	–	290	8	36.25
Marshall, A.G.	1950–67	6	11	1	37	7	3.70	–	399	13	30.69
Marshall, D.A.C.	1957	1	2	2	68	54*	–	–	–	–	–
Marshall, G.A.	1961–63	4	5	3	24	18*	12.00	–	221	9	24.55
Marshall, H.D.F.	1966	3	5	0	86	48	17.20	–	–	–	–
Marshall, J.C.	1951–53	16	27	0	710	111	26.30	1	–	–	–
Marshall, J.M.A.	1946–56	29	51	4	812	47	17.26	–	1604	47	34.12
Marshall, M.D.	1977/78–	164	207	24	4005	116*	21.89	4	12966	709	18.29
T		31	38	2	536	92	14.89	–	3117	133	23.44
Marshall, R.E.	1945/46–72	602	1053	59	35725	228*	35.94	68	5092	176	28.93
T		4	7	0	143	30	20.42	–	15	0	–
Marshall, R.P.T.	1973–78	24	37	15	315	37	14.31	–	1927	49	39.32
Marsham, A.J.B.	1939–47	17	26	4	362	74*	16.45	–	1381	35	39.46
Marsland, G.P.	1953–54	17	31	3	448	74	16.00	–	138	2	69.00
Martin, B.R.	1971–73	6	10	1	36	14	4.00	–	400	9	44.44
Martin, E.J.	1949–59	125	199	20	4086	133*	22.82	3	–	–	–
Martin, H.	1949–68	19	38	3	671	88	19.17	–	–	–	–
Martin, J.D.	1962–65	40	52	14	148	14*	3.89	–	2701	93	29.04
Martin, J.W.(Aust)	1956/57–67/68	135	193	26	3970	101	23.77	1	13872	445	31.17
T		8	13	1	214	55	17.83	–	832	17	48.94
Martin, J.W.(Kt)	1939–53	44	69	15	623	40	11.54	–	3888	162	24.00
T		1	2	0	26	26	–	–	129	1	–
Martin, R.H.	1951	1	2	0	4	4	2.00	–	91	1	–
Maru, R.J.	1980–	33	36	7	393	36	13.55	–	2430	70	34.71
Maslin, M.	1967–74	5	10	1	274	66*	30.44	–	44	0	–
Mason, A.	1947–50	18	19	3	105	22	6.56	–	1473	51	28.88
Mason, A.L.	1963–65	15	23	4	213	47	11.21	–	–	–	–
Masood Iqbal	1969/70–	121	185	28	2327	69	14.82	–	134	3	44.67

	Career span	M	I	NO	Runs	HS	Avge	100	Runs	Wkts	Avge
Massie, R.A.L.	1965/66–74/75	52	54	14	385	42	9.62	–	4446	179	24.83
	T	6	8	1	78	42	11.14	–	647	31	20.87
Masters, K.D.	1983–	4	7	1	1	1	0.17	–	294	6	49.00
Matheson, J.A.	1977	1	–	–	–	–	–	–	–	–	–
Mathews, K.P.A.	1950–56	21	30	1	796	77	27.45	–	19	0	–
Mathews, M.J.A.	1957	2	4	0	9	5	2.25	–	77	6	12.83
Matthews, A.D.G.	1927–47	281	437	70	5909	116	16.10	2	19099	816	23.41
	T	1	1	1	2	2*	–	–	65	2	32.50
Matthews, A.J.	1965–68	16	20	3	167	32	9.82	–	786	24	32.75
Matthews, C.	1950–59	85	103	36	493	41	7.36	–	5433	147	36.95
Matthews, J.D.	1951–55	5	7	0	81	29	11.56	–	–	–	–
Matthews, R.B.	1971–73	25	18	8	89	16*	8.90	–	1338	48	27.88
Maudsley, R.H.	1946–51	67	116	5	2676	130	24.11	4	1470	52	28.27
Maxwell, C.R.N.	1932–51	44	67	7	1564	268	26.07	1	–	–	–
Maxwell, L.E.	1968/69–78/79	16	23	11	90	19	7.50	–	1261	34	37.08
May, B.	1970–72	22	40	1	703	103	18.03	1	–	–	–
May, P.B.H.	1948–63	388	618	77	27592	285*	51.00	85	49	0	–
	T	66	106	9	4537	285*	46.77	13	–	–	–
Mayes, R.	1947–53	80	144	7	2689	134	19.63	4	46	0	–
Maynard, C.	1978–	79	97	17	1613	85	20.16	–	8	0	–
Mead-Briggs, R.	1946	2	2	1	46	44*	–	–	96	1	–
Meads, E.A.	1939–53	205	240	90	1475	56*	9.83	–	5	0	–
Meakin, D.	1959–62	4	6	3	55	16	18.33	–	206	10	20.60
Meale, T.	1951/52–58	32	54	5	1352	100	27.59	1	3	0	–
	T	2	4	0	21	10	5.25	–	–	–	–
Medhurst, R.H.	1948	3	3	2	17	15*	–	–	233	3	77.67
Medlycott, K.T.	1984–	6	6	5	128	117*	–	1	186	7	26.57
Mee, A.A.G.	1984–	1	1	0	2	2	–	–	–	–	–
Mee, S.R.	1984–	1	–	–	–	–	–	–	63	2	31.50
Meeson, M.S.	1957	1	2	0	25	21	12.50	–	–	–	–
Mehta, P.S.	1975	1	2	0	29	17	14.50	–	–	–	–
Melle, M.G.	1948/49–53/54	53	69	20	544	59	11.10	–	3990	160	24.93
	T	7	12	4	68	17	8.50	–	851	26	32.73
Mellor, A.J.	1978–80	13	15	6	26	10*	2.88	–	653	17	38.41
Mellor, J.P.	1973	3	5	0	27	22	5.40	–	–	–	–
Melluish, M.E.L.	1954–59	49	67	17	524	36	10.28	–	–	–	–
Melville, A.	1928/29–48/49	190	295	15	10598	189	37.85	25	3959	132	29.99
	T	11	19	2	894	189	52.58	4	–	–	–
Melville, C.D.McL.	1956–57	12	22	3	758	142	39.90	2	368	6	61.33
Melville, J.	1946	2	3	0	14	13	4.67	–	84	5	16.80
Melville, J.E.	1962–63	6	8	4	20	6	5.00	–	404	14	28.86
Mence, M.D.	1962–67	54	78	15	949	78	15.06	–	3050	86	35.47
Mendis, G.D.	1974–	181	320	27	9865	209*	33.67	17	11	0	–
Mendis, L.R.D.	1971/72–	82	138	13	4569	194	36.55	9	32	1	–
	T	10	20	0	726	111	36.30	3	–	–	–
Mendl, D.F.	1951	2	4	0	59	26	14.75	–	–	–	–
Mendl, J.F.	1949–55	7	13	2	269	65	24.45	–	–	–	–
Mercer, I.P.	1965	1	2	0	1	1	0.50	–	–	–	–
Mercer, J.	1919–47	458	629	12	6159	72	11.91	–	37302	1593	23.41
Mercer, W.N.	1942/43–56	3	4	1	40	24	13.33	–	103	6	17.16
Merchant, V.M.	1929/30–51/52	146	229	43	13248	359*	71.11	44	2072	65	31.87
	T	10	18	0	859	154	47.72	3	40	0	–
Merritt, W.E.	1926/27–46	125	191	33	3147	87	19.91	–	13669	536	25.50
	T	6	8	1	73	19	10.43	–	617	12	51.41
Merry, W.G.	1979–82	27	17	11	42	14*	7.00	–	1554	49	31.71
Merson, R.D.	1947	1	2	0	16	15	8.00	–	–	–	–

	Career span	M	I	NO	Runs	HS	Avge	100	Runs	Wkts	Avge
					BATTING				BOWLING		
Metcalfe, A.A.	1983–	10	15	0	345	122	23.00	1	6	0	–
Metcalfe, S.G.	1954–68	27	50	3	1200	133*	25.53	2	352	9	39.11
Metson, C.P.	1981–	13	18	6	338	96	28.17	–	–	–	–
Meyer, B.J.	1957–71	406	569	190	5367	63	14.16	–	28	0	–
Meyer, R.J.O.	1924–50	128	212	15	4709	202*	23.90	2	10426	412	25.30
Middleton, T.C.	1984–	1	2	0	15	10	7.50	–	–	–	–
Milburn, B.D.	1963/64–82/83	75	97	33	737	103	11.51	1	–	–	–
	T	3	3	2	8	4*	–	–	–	–	–
Milburn, C.	1960–74	255	435	34	13262	243	33.07	23	3171	99	32.03
	T	9	16	2	654	139	46.71	2	–	–	–
Miles, O.	1967/68–75/76	21	22	6	214	43*	13.37	–	1588	58	27.37
Millard, D.E.S.	1951/52–65	14	26	2	497	73	20.70	–	448	15	29.86
Millener, D.J.	1964/65–70	26	30	12	176	24	9.77	–	1958	57	34.35
Miller, A.J.T.	1982–	24	43	4	1275	128*	32.69	2	4	1	–
Miller, F.J.	1949–54	7	11	6	44	18*	8.80	–	–	–	–
Miller, Geoffrey	1973–	276	411	67	9444	130	27.45	1	18300	711	25.74
	T	34	51	4	1213	98*	25.81	–	1859	60	30.98
Miller, George	1955	1	2	1	8	6*	–	–	50	0	–
Miller, H.D.S.	1962/63–70/71	38	58	7	589	81	11.54	–	2200	76	28.94
Miller, K.R.	1937/38–59	226	326	36	14183	281*	48.90	41	11087	497	22.30
	T	55	87	7	2958	147	36.97	7	3906	170	22.97
Miller, L.S.M.	1950/51–59/60	82	142	15	4777	144	37.61	5	75	3	25.00
	T	13	25	0	346	47	13.84	–	1	0	–
Miller, M.E.	1963	12	15	5	48	21*	4.80	–	770	33	23.33
Miller, R.	1961–68	133	166	34	1658	72	12.56	–	7289	241	30.24
Miller, R.S.	1959	1	2	2	1	1*	–	–	91	5	18.20
Millett, F.W.	1960–73	7	13	3	312	102*	31.20	1	106	2	53.00
Millman, G.	1956–65	282	471	59	7770	131*	18.85	3	32	0	–
	T	6	7	2	60	32*	12.00	–	–	–	–
Millner, D.	1960–63	31	56	1	701	80	12.75	–	27	0	–
Mills, A.O.H.	1939–48	4	5	0	81	39	16.20	–	62	3	20.67
Mills, D.C.	1958–60	2	2	0	19	17	9.50	–	25	0	–
Mills, G.T.	1953	2	4	0	46	23	11.50	–	–	–	–
Mills, J.M.	1946–48	38	60	10	743	44	14.86	–	2743	95	28.87
Mills, J.P.C.	1979–82	41	68	2	1585	111	24.01	1	5	0	–
Milner, J.	1957–61	67	119	12	2767	135	25.86	3	14	0	–
Milton, C.A.	1948–74	620	1078	125	32150	170	33.74	56	3630	79	45.95
	T	6	9	1	204	104*	25.50	1	12	0	–
Minney, J.H.	1959–67	19	33	3	572	58	19.07	–	7	0	–
Minns, R.E.F.	1959–63	20	38	3	947	81	27.06	–	–	–	–
Mischler, N.M.	1941/42–51	24	38	1	568	76	15.35	–	–	–	–
Misson, F.M.	1958/59–63/64	71	77	17	1052	51*	17.53	–	5511	177	31.13
	T	5	5	3	38	25*	19.00	–	616	16	38.50
Mitchell, A.	1922–45	425	593	72	19523	189	37.47	44	327	7	46.72
	T	6	10	0	298	72	29.80	–	4	0	–
Mitchell, B.	1925/26–49/50	173	281	30	11395	195	45.39	30	6382	249	25.63
	T	42	80	9	3471	189*	38.88	8	1380	27	51.11
Mitchell, C.G.	1952–54	30	45	20	186	26*	7.44	–	2035	53	38.40
Mitchell, F.R.	1946–48	17	29	2	224	43	8.30	–	856	22	28.90
Mitchell, I.N.	1949–52	11	17	0	156	27	9.18	–	–	–	–
Mitchell, J.S.L.	1974	1	2	0	29	27	14.50	–	–	–	–
Mitchell, K.J.	1946	1	2	0	10	10	5.00	–	–	–	–
Mitchell, W.McF.	1951–53	26	40	8	480	48	15.00	–	1998	35	57.09
Mitchell-Innes, N.S.	1931–49	132	239	18	6944	207	31.42	13	2844	82	34.68
	T	1	1	0	5	5	–	–	–	–	–
Mitra, A.	1974–75	6	12	0	157	30	13.08	–	–	–	–

	Career span	M		I	NO	Runs	HS	Avge	100		Runs	Wkts	Avge
Mitten, J.	1961–63	14		23	2	259	50*	12.33	–		–	–	–
Moan, R.	1970	1		1	1	0	0*	–	–		58	1	–
Mobey, G.S.	1930–48	81		112	19	1684	75	18.11	–		–	–	–
Mocatta, J.E.A.	1958	4		8	0	106	37	13.25	–		–	–	–
Modi, R.S.	1941/42–59/60	104		153	12	7492	245*	53.13	20		1225	32	38.28
	T	10		17	1	736	112	46.00	1		14	0	–
Moeller, D.	1961	1		2	0	25	24	12.50	–		–	–	–
Moffat, N.T.	1969	1		2	0	6	4	3.00	–		–	–	–
Mohammed Aslam	1938/39–64/65	45		73	8	1700	103	26.15	1		630	21	30.00
	T	1		2	0	34	18	17.00	–		–	–	–
Mohammed Farooq	1959/60–65/66	33		31	17	173	47	12.35	–		3319	123	26.98
	T	7		9	4	85	47	17.00	–		682	21	32.47
Mohammed Ilyas	1961/62–75/76	82		139	10	4607	154	35.71	12		1643	53	31.00
	T	10		19	0	441	126	23.21	1		63	0	–
Mohammed Mian Saeed	1929/30–54/55	51		81	2	2338	170	29.59	3		268	5	53.60
Mohammed Munaf	1953/54–70/71	71		90	13	1356	76	17.61	–		4360	180	24.22
	T	4		7	2	63	19	12.60	–		341	11	31.00
Mohammed Nazir	1964/65–	148		206	53	3624	113*	23.68	2		13086	629	20.72
	T	14		18	10	144	29*	18.00	–		1123	34	33.03
Mohan, K.F.	1957–58	10		17	2	163	49	11.87	–		23	0	–
Mohol, S.N.	1959/60–70/71	48		55	12	554	40	12.88	–		3659	174	21.02
Mohsin Khan	1970/71–	171		286	29	10425	246	40.56	30		522	14	37.29
	T	33		54	5	2165	200	44.18	7		30	0	–
Moir, A.McK.	1949/50–61/62	97		150	22	2102	70	16.42	–		9040	368	24.56
	T	17		30	8	327	41*	14.86	–		1418	28	50.64
Moir, D.G.	1980–	64		77	11	990	107	15.00	1		6161	187	32.95
Money, D.C.	1947	1		1	1	27	27*	–	–		–	–	–
Monkhouse, G.	1981–	48		59	21	793	100*	20.87	1		2932	116	25.28
Monks, C.I.	1935–52	65		101	17	1589	120	18.92	1		1629	36	45.25
Monks, G.D.	1952	1		1	0	3	3	–	–		–	–	–
Monteith, J.D.	1965–	28		39	5	530	95	15.59	–		1921	94	20.44
Montgomerie, R.D.	1960	1		2	0	16	15	8.00	–		–	–	–
Montgomery, S.W.	1949–53	29		43	2	763	117	18.62	1		99	6	16.50
Mooney, F.L.H.	1941/42–54/55	90		148	14	3134	180	23.39	2		0	0	–
	T	14		22	2	343	46	17.15	–		0	0	–
Moor, D.C.	1956	3		6	1	42	22	8.40	–		–	–	–
Moore, F.	1954–58	24		26	7	151	18	7.95	–		1516	54	29.08
Moore, H.I.	1962–73	177		299	29	6765	206*	25.05	7		144	5	28.80
Moore, K.F.	1961	1		1	0	2	2	–	–		43	4	10.75
Moore, N.H.	1952–60	4		6	0	139	59	23.17	–		–	–	–
Moores, P.	1983–84	11		15	3	215	45	17.92	–		–	–	–
Morby-Smith, L.	1958/59–66/67	35		55	4	1743	127	34.17	2		33	2	16.50
Mordaunt, D.J.	1958–64	20		29	3	599	96	23.04	–		601	24	25.04
More, H.K.	1966–76	18		36	2	639	89	18.79	–		–	–	–
Morgan, A.H.	1966–69	11		20	4	381	59*	23.81	–		–	–	–
Morgan, C.	1946	1		2	0	13	13	6.50	–		94	0	–
Morgan, D.C.	1950–69	556		882	146	18356	147	24.94	9		31302	1248	25.08
Morgan, H.W.	1958	2		3	1	11	5	5.50	–		58	2	29.00
Morgan, M.	1957–61	61		86	16	488	56*	6.97	–		5287	146	36.21
Morgan, M.N.	1951–57	14		14	9	49	11*	9.80	–		1062	30	35.40
Morgan, P.R.Ll.	1946	1		1	0	1	1	–	–		38	0	–
Morgan, R.T.	1932/33–45	11		20	2	374	81	20.77	–		384	12	32.00
Morgan, R.W.	1957/58–76/77	136		229	13	5940	166	27.50	3		3558	108	32.94
	T	20		34	1	734	97	22.24	–		609	5	121.80
Morgan, S.A.	1969/70–73/74	22		35	3	998	126	31.18	1		82	1	–

	Career span	M	I	NO	Runs	HS	Avge	100	Runs	Wkts	Avge
									BOWLING		
					BATTING						
Morley, J.D.	1971–76	72	131	12	2752	127	23.12	2	2	0	–
Morrill, N.D.	1978–79	14	21	3	241	45	13.38	–	741	12	61.75
Morris, A.	1974–79/80	49	81	5	1188	74	15.63	–	118	0	–
Morris, A.R.	1940/41–63/64	162	250	15	12614	290	53.67	46	592	12	49.33
T		46	79	3	3533	206	46.48	12	50	2	25.00
Morris, C.A.	1960	4	6	1	23	8	4.60	–	47	0	–
Morris, H.	1981–	25	42	10	1004	114*	31.38	1	68	1	–
Morris, I.	1966–68	14	25	2	253	38	11.00	–	141	4	35.35
Morris, J.E.	1982–	26	50	2	1327	135	27.65	3	73	1	–
Morris, R.	1958	2	3	0	7	7	2.33	–	–	–	–
Morris, R.J.	1949–51	22	36	2	778	96	22.89	–	192	2	96.00
Morris, W.B.	1946–50	48	78	10	1219	68	17.93	–	1985	43	46.16
Morrison, G.C.	1947	2	4	0	48	16	12.00	–	32	0	–
Mortensen, O.H.	1983–	26	31	19	139	40*	11.58	–	2175	84	25.89
Mortimore, J.B.	1950–75	636	989	122	15891	149	18.33	4	41904	1807	23.19
T		9	12	2	243	73*	24.30	–	733	13	56.38
Morton, G.D.	1950–52	3	3	2	1	1	–	–	146	0	–
Morton, W.	1983–	10	10	2	47	13*	5.88	–	765	23	33.26
Moseley, E.A.	1980–83/84	41	51	11	877	70*	21.93	–	3467	149	23.27
Moseley, H.R.	1969–82	213	217	94	1533	67	12.46	–	13668	557	24.53
Moses, G.H.	1974	3	4	2	37	24*	18.50	–	176	9	19.55
Mosey, S.D.H.	1959	2	2	1	17	13*	–	–	203	1	–
Moss, A.E.	1950–68	382	410	171	1667	40	6.97	–	27035	1301	20.78
T		9	7	1	61	26	10.16	–	626	21	29.80
Mottram, T.J.	1972–76	35	35	18	95	15*	5.58	–	2677	111	24.11
Motz, R.C.	1957/58–69	142	225	21	3494	103*	17.12	1	11767	518	22.71
T		32	56	3	612	60	11.54	–	3148	100	31.48
Moulding, R.P.	1977–83	47	79	9	1344	80*	19.20	–	22	0	–
Moule, H.G.	1952	1	2	0	102	57	51.00	–	–	–	–
Mountford, P.N.G.	1962–63	18	27	11	111	22*	6.94	–	1606	40	40.15
Moxon, H.	1960	1	2	0	24	23	12.00	–	–	–	–
Moxon, M.D.	1981–	53	96	4	3135	153	34.08	6	659	10	65.90
Moylan, A.C.D.	1976–77	5	9	0	176	29	19.55	–	3	0	–
Moylan-Jones, R.C.	1964	1	2	0	34	31	17.00	–	36	2	18.00
Mubarak, A.M.	1978–80	24	38	2	765	105	21.25	1	6	0	–
Mucklow, P.	1970	2	4	0	48	32	12.00	–	–	–	–
Mudassar Nazar	1971/72–	158	262	26	11333	241	48.02	36	3357	99	33.91
T		44	68	5	2542	231	40.35	6	1352	33	40.97
Muddiah, V.M.	1949/50–62/63	61	71	13	885	67	13.87	–	4160	175	24.42
T		2	3	1	11	11	5.50	–	134	3	44.67
Muncer, B.L.	1933–57	317	478	64	8646	135	20.88	4	15784	755	20.91
Munden, D.F.X.	1960–61	7	13	0	98	34	7.54	–	13	0	–
Munden, P.A.	1957–64	47	85	6	1193	77	15.09	–	–	–	–
Munden, V.S.	1946–57	232	376	43	5786	103	17.38	–	10603	371	28.58
Mungrue, A.A.	1964	2	4	0	102	51	25.50	–	129	8	16.13
Munir Malik	1956/57–66/67	49	71	10	675	72	11.06	–	4285	197	21.75
T		3	4	1	7	4	2.33	–	358	9	39.78
Munro, H.C.	1947	1	2	0	0	0	0.00	–	–	–	–
Murch, S.N.C.	1966/67–69/70	10	15	3	215	64	17.91	–	868	17	51.05
Murley, A.J.	1981	6	11	0	152	48	13.81	–	1	0	–
Murphy, E.G.	1948	2	4	0	24	11	6.00	–	–	–	–
Murray, A.R.A.	1947/48–55/56	64	100	10	2685	133	29.33	4	4683	188	24.90
T		10	14	1	289	109	22.23	1	710	18	39.44
Murray, B.A.G.	1958/59–72/73	102	187	11	6257	213	35.55	6	868	30	28.93
T		13	26	1	598	90	23.92	–	0	1	–
Murray, D.A.	1970/71–	114	176	30	4503	206*	30.84	7	11	0	–
T		19	31	3	601	84	21.46	–	–	–	–

377

	Career span	M	I	NO	Runs	HS	Avge	100	Runs	Wkts	Avge
					BATTING				BOWLING		
Murray, D.L.	1960/61–80/81	367	554	85	13289	166*	28.34	10	376	5	75.20
	T	62	96	9	1993	91	22.90	–	–	–	–
Murray, J.T.	1952–75	635	936	136	18872	142	23.59	16	243	6	40.50
	T	21	28	5	506	112	22.00	1	–	–	–
Murray, M.P.	1949–63	10	19	2	216	44	12.71	–	3	0	–
Murray-Willis, P.E.	1935–46	29	47	2	467	54	10.38	–	–	–	–
Murray-Wood, W.	1936–56	106	177	15	2262	107	13.96	3	3850	100	38.50
Murrills, T.J.	1973–76	37	69	4	996	67	15.32	–	4	0	–
Murtagh, A.J.	1973–77	27	47	5	640	65	15.23	–	489	6	81.50
Mushtaq Ali, S.	1930/31–63/64	222	380	16	13009	233	35.74	30	4569	155	29.47
	T	11	20	1	612	112	32.21	2	202	3	67.33
Mushtaq Mohammed	1956/57–84	501	841	104	31066	303*	42.15	72	22785	936	24.34
Muzzell, R.K.	1964/65–76/77	75	128	12	4052	238*	34.93	7	2028	61	33.24
Nadkarni, R.G.	1951/52–71/72	191	266	46	8880	283*	40.36	14	10686	500	21.37
	T	41	67	12	1414	122*	25.70	1	2559	88	29.07
Naeem Ahmed	1969/70–	120	156	39	3439	127	29.39	3	9674	356	27.17
Nagenda, J.	1975	1	2	2	5	5*	–	–	91	3	30.33
Naik, S.S.	1966/67–77/78	82	141	16	4398	200*	35.18	7	165	5	33.00
	T	3	6	0	141	77	23.50	–	–	–	–
Nana, P.G.	1973/74–75	2	4	0	21	16	5.25	–	170	4	42.50
Nanan, N.	1969/70–80	34	62	5	900	72	15.78	–	322	9	35.78
Napier, R.S.	1956	1	1	0	0	0	–	–	18	0	–
Naseer Malik	1969/70–81/82	71	81	12	765	55	11.08	–	5034	201	25.04
Nash, M.A.	1966–83	336	469	67	7129	130	17.73	2	25698	993	25.88
Nasim-ul-Ghani	1956/57–74/75	117	175	17	4490	139	28.41	7	8630	343	25.16
	T	29	50	5	747	101	16.60	1	1959	52	37.67
Nasir Zaidi, M.	1983–84	19	22	9	313	51	24.08	–	827	19	43.53
Naushad Ali	1960/61–79/80	85	135	16	4406	158	37.06	9	5	0	–
	T	6	11	0	156	39	14.18	–	–	–	–
Nayak, S.V.	1977/78–	50	65	17	1488	100*	31.00	2	3022	89	33.96
	T	2	3	1	19	11	9.50	–	132	1	–
Naylor, J.E.	1953	1	–	–	–	–	–	–	88	0	–
Nayudu, C.S.	1931/32–60/61	172	264	25	5666	127	23.71	3	16957	639	26.53
	T	11	19	3	147	36	9.18	–	359	2	179.50
Neal, J.H.	1951	1	2	0	28	23	14.00	–	–	–	–
Neale, P.A.	1975–	198	341	41	10514	163*	35.05	16	201	1	–
Neale, W.L.	1923–48	452	700	79	14752	145*	23.76	14	3970	100	39.70
Neame, A.R.B.	1956–58	10	18	0	230	65	12.78	–	170	4	42.50
Neate, F.W.	1960–62	17	30	6	914	112	38.08	1	–	–	–
Neate, P.W.	1966	1	1	0	3	3	3	–	53	0	–
Needham, A.	1977–	55	78	10	1141	134*	16.78	1	3185	80	39.81
Needham, P.J.E.	1975	1	1	0	4	4	–	–	105	2	52.50
Nelson, P.J.M.	1938–46	2	4	1	55	32	18.33	–	51	2	25.50
Nevell, W.T.	1936–47	51	81	9	671	55*	9.32	–	3488	105	33.22
Neville, P.A.	1956–60	4	8	0	143	38	17.88	–	–	–	–
Nevin, M.R.S.	1969	8	12	8	34	14*	8.50	–	407	5	81.40
Newell, M.	1984–	4	7	1	109	76	18.17	–	14	0	–
Newburn, T.	1949	1	2	0	12	8	6.00	–	31	3	10.33
Newman, D.L.	1948–53	12	19	1	256	29	14.22	–	–	–	–
Newman, P.G.	1980–	61	67	13	640	40	11.85	–	5046	151	33.42
Newman, R.G.	1955–57	4	7	0	133	44	19.00	–	–	–	–
Newport, P.J.	1982–	18	20	7	297	41*	22.85	–	1045	30	34.83
Newsom, D.J.	1960–61	2	2	0	33	23	16.50	–	–	–	–
Newton, H.	1966	2	4	2	16	16*	8.00	–	141	6	23.50

	Career span	M	I	NO	Runs	HS	Avge	100	Runs	Wkts	Avge
Newton-Thompson, J.O.	1946–48/49	9	18	1	281	78	16.52	–	125	0	–
Niaz Ahmed	1963/64–74/75	39	48	16	466	71*	14.56	–	2384	62	38.45
T		2	3	3	17	16*	–	–	94	3	31.33
Nichol, D.	1952	1	2	0	6	4	3.00	–	61	2	30.50
Nichol, R.J.	1951–55	7	10	2	67	19	8.38	–	505	12	42.08
Nichol, W.	1938–56	26	43	3	931	139*	23.28	2	1395	55	25.36
Nicholas, M.C.J.	1978–	120	208	25	6003	206*	32.80	13	1297	36	36.03
Nicholls, D.	1960–77	202	342	24	7072	211	22.23	2	23	2	11.50
Nicholls, R.B.	1951–75	534	954	52	23607	217	26.17	18	719	11	65.36
Nichols, J.B.	1953	5	5	0	33	16	6.60	–	81	0	–
Nicholson, A.G.	1962–75	283	268	126	1669	50	11.75	–	17371	879	19.76
Nimbalkar, R.B.	1934/35–52/53	62	93	5	2645	132	30.05	4	179	3	59.67
Niven, R.A.	1968–73	25	31	14	182	24*	10.70	–	1806	53	34.07
Noblet, G.	1945/46–56	71	99	29	975	55*	13.92	–	5432	282	19.26
T		3	4	1	22	13*	7.33	–	183	7	26.14
Nolan, G.J.	1968	1	2	0	14	11	7.00	–	–	–	–
Norman, J.W.	1957	2	3	0	12	9	4.00	–	–	–	–
Norman, M.E.J.C.	1952–75	363	640	44	17441	221*	29.26	24	164	2	82.00
Norris, D.W.W.	1967–68	20	33	2	307	43	9.91	–	–	–	–
Northcote-Green, S.R.	1974–79	9	16	2	138	38*	9.86	–	–	–	–
Norton, G.I.D.	1958–60	2	3	2	4	2*	–	–	133	17	7.83
Norton, I.D.	1959	1	1	0	30	30	–	–	–	–	–
Notley, B.	1949	1	1	0	0	0	–	–	90	1	–
Nourse, A.D.	1931/32–52/53	175	269	27	12472	260*	51.54	41	124	0	–
T		34	62	7	2960	231	53.81	9	9	0	–
Nunn, J.A.	1926–46	22	36	2	641	98	18.85	–	–	–	–
Nurse, S.McD.	1958/59–71/72	141	235	19	9489	258	43.93	26	389	12	32.41
T		29	54	1	2523	258	47.60	6	7	0	–
Nutter, A.E.	1935–53	224	294	47	4828	109*	19.55	1	15739	600	26.23
Nye, J.K.	1934–47	99	136	33	885	55	8.60	–	10407	304	34.23
Oakden, R.P.	1960–61	8	10	3	68	24	9.71	–	728	17	42.82
Oakes, C.	1935–54	290	474	40	10893	160	25.10	14	14326	458	31.28
Oakes, D.R.	1965	5	8	1	81	33	11.56	–	1	0	–
Oakes, J.Y.	1937–51	127	218	19	4410	151	22.16	2	6508	166	39.21
Oakley, L.	1935–48	8	13	4	43	11	4.77	–	403	12	33.58
Oakman, A.S.M.	1947–68	538	912	79	21800	229*	26.17	22	20343	736	27.63
T		2	2	0	14	10	7.00	–	21	0	–
Oates, W.F.	1956–65	124	214	14	4588	148*	22.94	2	577	13	44.38
O'Brien, B.A.	1966–81	11	17	1	319	45*	19.94	–	–	–	–
O'Brien, G.P.	1976–77	2	4	0	22	11	5.50	–	–	–	–
O'Brien, N.T.	1979–81	2	2	0	27	14	13.50	–	101	1	–
O'Brien, R.	1954–58	40	74	3	1609	146	22.67	2	4	0	–
Odendaal, A.	1980–83	22	37	3	659	61	19.38	–	–	–	–
O'Keeffe, K.J.	1968/69–79/80	169	233	73	4169	99*	26.05	–	13382	476	28.11
T		24	34	9	644	85	25.76	–	2018	53	38.07
Old, A.G.B.	1969	1	1	0	34	34	–	–	93	1	–
Old, C.M.	1966–	371	455	89	7634	116	20.86	6	24615	1058	23.27
T		46	66	9	845	65	14.82	–	4020	143	28.11
Oldfield, N.	1935–54	332	521	51	17811	168	37.89	38	121	2	60.50
T		1	2	0	99	80	49.50	–	–	–	–
Oldham, S.	1974–	126	96	40	640	50	11.43	–	8817	269	32.78
O'Linn, S.	1945/46–65/66	92	156	29	4525	120*	35.63	4	119	2	59.50
T		7	12	1	297	98	27.00	–	–	–	–

					BATTING				BOWLING		
	Career span	M	I	NO	Runs	HS	Avge	100	Runs	Wkts	Avge
Olive, M.	1977–81	17	32	2	467	50	15.56	–	–	–	–
Oliver, J.A.R.	1951	1	2	1	93	84*	93.00	–	–	–	–
Oliver, P.R.	1975–82	89	128	20	2679	171*	24.81	2	2115	27	78.33
Olley, M.W.C.	1983	1	1	0	8	8	8	–	–	–	–
Ollis, R.L.	1981–	22	40	3	691	99*	18.68	–	2	0	–
Olton, M.F.	1959/60–62	3	6	1	98	28	19.60	–	199	2	99.50
O'Maille, C.	1953–60	2	3	1	10	5	5.00	–	–	–	–
O'Meara, J.A.	1963	1	2	0	0	0	0.00	–	14	1	–
O'Neill, N.C.	1955/56–66/67	188	306	34	13859	284	50.95	45	4060	99	41.01
	T	42	69	8	2779	181	45.55	6	667	17	39.23
Ontong, R.C.	1972/73–	241	414	46	10477	204*	28.47	16	16530	555	29.78
Opatha, A.R.M.	1969/70–82/83	39	53	7	790	65	17.17	–	3413	111	30.74
Ord, J.S.	1933–53	273	459	35	11788	187*	27.80	16	244	2	122.00
Orders, J.O.D.	1978–81	27	49	3	1072	79	23.30	–	656	11	59.63
O'Reilly, P.M.	1982–	2	3	2	1	1*	–	–	81	5	16.20
O'Riordan, A.J.	1958–77	25	44	5	614	117	15.74	1	1604	75	21.39
Ormrod, J.A.	1962–	496	839	95	23151	204*	31.12	32	1094	25	43.76
O'Rourke, C.	1968	1	1	1	23	23*	–	–	–	–	–
Osborne, M.J.	1961–62	3	6	0	155	60	25.83	–	81	2	40.50
Oscroft, E.	1950–51	9	8	3	8	7*	1.60	–	707	13	54.38
O'Shaughnessy, S.J.	1980–	68	108	18	2726	159*	30.29	5	2708	83	32.63
Osman, W.M.	1970–71	9	16	0	287	60	17.94	–	–	–	–
O'Sullivan, D.R.	1971–	128	179	44	2093	70*	15.50	–	12505	485	25.78
	T	11	21	4	158	23*	9.29	–	1221	18	67.83
Ottley, D.G.	1967	7	9	1	109	30	13.63	–	–	–	–
Outschoorn, L.	1946–59	346	595	53	15496	215*	28.59	25	2030	33	61.52
Overstone, D.MacP.	1942/43–47/48	20	32	2	437	52	14.56	–	–	–	–
Owen, J.G.	1930–51	18	19	3	361	57	22.56	–	837	16	52.32
Owen, N.W.	1951	1	2	0	26	14	13.00	–	33	1	–
Owen-Thomas, D.R.	1969–75	112	188	20	4891	182*	29.11	8	798	20	39.90
Padgett, D.E.V.	1951–71	506	806	67	21124	161*	28.58	32	216	6	36.00
	T	2	4	0	51	31	12.75	–	8	0	–
Padgett, G.H.	1952	6	7	4	56	32*	18.67	–	336	4	84.00
Padmore, A.H.	1951–54	3	5	1	34	15*	8.50	–	312	14	22.29
Padmore, A.L.	1972/73–81/82	65	63	21	544	79	12.95	–	5503	188	29.27
	T	2	2	1	8	8*	–	–	135	1	–
Page, J.C.T.	1950–63	198	273	124	818	23	5.49	–	14967	521	28.72
Page, J.T.	1974	2	4	0	31	11	7.75	–	95	1	–
Page, M.H.	1964–75	254	451	47	11538	162	28.56	9	527	7	75.29
Paine, G.A.E.	1926–47	258	349	62	3430	79	11.95	–	23334	1021	22.85
	T	4	7	1	97	49	16.17	–	467	17	27.47
Pairaudeau, B.H.	1946/47–66/67	89	159	5	4930	163	32.01	11	82	0	–
	T	13	21	0	454	115	21.61	1	3	0	–
Palfreman, A.B.	1966–68	16	31	3	432	67	15.43	–	1158	31	37.35
Palmer, C.H.	1938–59	336	588	38	17458	201	31.74	33	9183	365	25.16
	T	1	2	0	22	22	11.00	–	15	0	–
Palmer, E.J.	1957	4	6	5	39	11*	–	–	225	7	32.14
Palmer, G.V.	1982–	27	35	4	451	78	14.55	–	1918	50	38.36
Palmer, K.E.	1955–69	314	481	105	7761	125*	20.64	2	18485	866	21.35
	T	1	1	0	10	10	–	–	189	1	–
Palmer, R.	1965–70	74	110	32	1037	84	13.29	–	5439	172	31.62
Palmer, R.W.M.	1981–83	11	9	5	20	12	5.00	–	954	16	59.63
Parfitt, P.H.	1956–72	498	845	104	26924	200*	36.33	58	8381	277	30.26
	T	37	52	6	1882	131*	40.91	7	574	12	47.83
Paris, C.G.A.	1933–48	100	172	9	3730	134*	22.88	2	216	4	54.00

	Career span	M	I	NO	Runs	HS	Avge	100	Runs	Wkts	Avge
			┌─────────────BATTING─────────────┐						┌──────BOWLING──────┐		
Parkar, G.A.H.M.	1978/79–	54	87	7	3196	156	39.95	10	118	2	59.00
	T	1	2	0	7	6	3.50	–	–	–	–
Parker, F.A.V.	1946	5	9	0	147	116	16.33	1	–	–	–
Parker, G.W.	1932–51	90	147	12	2956	210	21.90	5	2291	57	40.19
Parker, J.F.	1932–52	340	523	71	14272	255	31.58	20	15677	543	28.87
Parker, J.M.	1971–	207	362	39	11254	195	34.84	21	681	14	48.64
	T	36	63	2	1498	121	24.55	3	24	1	–
Parker, P.W.G.	1976–	204	343	48	10251	215	34.75	24	541	10	54.10
	T	1	2	0	13	13	6.50	–	–	–	–
Parker, R.J.	1947	2	3	0	36	18	12.00	–	–	–	–
Parkes, J.L.	1960	1	2	0	0	0	0.00	–	61	1	–
Parkhouse, W.G.A.	1948–64	455	791	49	23508	201	31.68	32	125	2	62.50
	T	7	13	0	373	78	28.69	–	–	–	–
Parkin, J.M.	1966–68	28	39	8	349	53	11.25	–	–	–	–
Parkins, W.R.	1950	5	10	0	125	39	12.50	–	–	–	–
Parks, H.W.	1926–49/50	482	745	98	21725	200*	33.57	42	705	13	54.23
Parks, J.H.	1924–52	468	758	63	21369	197	30.75	41	22789	852	26.75
	T	1	2	0	29	22	14.50	–	36	3	12.00
Parks, J.M.	1949–76	739	1227	172	36673	205*	34.76	51	2235	51	43.82
	T	46	68	7	1962	108*	32.16	2	51	1	–
Parks, R.J.	1980–	105	121	27	1537	89	16.35	–	0	0	–
Parnaby, A.H.	1939–53	8	16	0	433	101	27.06	1	10	0	–
Parr, F.D.	1951–54	49	53	11	507	42	12.07	–	–	–	–
Parry, D.R.	1975/76–	77	119	23	2552	96	26.58	–	7268	251	28.96
	T	12	20	3	381	65	22.41	–	936	23	40.69
Parslow, L.F.	1946	1	2	0	9	5	4.50	–	–	–	–
Parsons, A.B.D.	1954–63	152	263	22	6376	125	26.46	3	23	0	–
Parsons, A.E.W.	1971/72–82/83	82	156	10	3847	141	26.34	4	183	2	91.50
Parsons, D.J.	1981	1	1	0	1	1	–	–	53	1	–
Parsons, G.J.	1978–	110	142	33	2077	63	19.06	–	7913	252	31.40
Partridge, B.J.M.	1977	4	6	4	5	4	2.50	–	170	4	42.50
Partridge, M.D.	1976–80	46	66	21	1202	90	26.71	–	2076	41	50.63
Partridge, R.J.	1929–48	280	462	122	3922	70	11.53	–	19947	638	31.26
Parvez Mir	1970/71–82/83	71	120	13	3338	155	31.19	5	4161	162	25.68
Pascoe, L.S.	1974/75–	80	81	25	502	51*	8.96	–	7913	309	25.61
	T	14	19	9	106	30*	10.60	–	1668	64	26.06
Pasqual, S.P.	1979	7	9	2	250	101*	35.71	1	144	2	72.00
Passey, M.F.W.	1953	1	1	0	1	1	–	–	57	1	–
Pataudi, Nawab of (1)	1928–46	127	204	24	8750	238*	48.61	29	529	15	35.27
	T	6	10	0	199	102	19.90	1	–	–	–
Pataudi, Nawab of (2)	1957-75/76	310	499	41	15425	203*	33.67	33	776	10	77.60
	T	46	83	3	2793	203*	34.91	6	88	1	–
Patel, A.S.	1978	2	3	1	56	25*	28.00	–	55	2	27.50
Patel, B.P.	1969/70–	179	273	39	10068	216	43.03	30	215	7	30.72
	T	21	38	5	972	115*	29.45	1	–	–	–
Patel, D.N.	1976–	188	295	19	7863	197	28.49	14	10767	300	35.89
Paterson, J.	1956	1	2	0	1	1	0.50	–	–	–	–
Paterson, R.F.T.	1946–58	28	45	5	884	88	22.10	–	464	13	35.69
Pathmanathan, G.	1972/73–83	44	77	3	1553	82	20.98	–	26	0	–
Patil, S.M.	1975/76–	78	122	8	4685	210	41.10	13	1365	34	40.15
	T	25	41	4	1363	174	36.84	3	240	9	26.67
Patterson, B.P.	1982/83	3	5	0	16	10	3.20	–	180	4	45.00
Patterson, T.J.T.	1984	1	1	0	23	23	–	–	96	3	32.00
Paul, N.A.	1954–58	7	10	0	157	40	15.70	–	196	3	65.33
Pauline, D.B.	1979–	36	58	4	1411	115	26.13	1	28	0	–
Paull, R.K.	1963–67	13	20	1	257	37	13.53	–	104	1	–

			BATTING							BOWLING		
	Career span	M	I	NO	Runs	HS	Avge	100	Runs	Wkts	Avge
Paver, R.G.L.	1972–74	16	26	2	290	34	12.08	–	–	–	–
Pawle, J.H.	1935–47	34	59	4	1544	125	28.08	3	13	0	–
Pawson, H.A.	1946–53	70	113	11	3807	150	37.32	7	280	7	40.00
Payn, L.W.	1936/37–52/53	51	51	5	657	103	14.28	–	3893	151	25.78
Payne, C.J.	1968–70	5	8	0	40	22	5.00	–	–	–	–
Payne, I.R.	1977–84	29	37	5	338	43	10.56	–	1127	26	43.35
Payne, T.R.O.	1977/78–	34	53	8	1829	140	40.64	4	–	–	–
Paynter, E.	1926–50/51	348	533	58	20075	322	42.26	45	1317	30	43.90
T		20	31	5	1540	243	59.23	4	–	–	–
Payton, W.E.G.	1935–53	27	52	4	995	98	20.73	–	–	–	–
Peach, R.A.	1960	2	1	1	6	6*	–	–	13	0	–
Peake, K.G.	1946	1	2	1	2	1*	–	–	52	0	–
Pearce, J.P.	1978–79	7	11	5	22	8*	3.67	–	501	11	45.54
Pearce, T.A.	1930–46	55	82	8	1213	106	16.39	1	22	1	–
Pearce, T.N.	1929–52	250	406	54	12061	211*	34.26	22	927	15	61.80
Pearman, H.	1969–72	12	17	1	294	61	18.38	–	578	16	36.13
Pearman, R.	1962–64	8	13	3	264	72*	26.40	–	–	–	–
Pearsall, R.D.	1947–48	15	19	4	230	80*	15.33	–	982	27	36.37
Pearson, A.J.G.	1961–63	42	51	11	355	30	8.87	–	3918	139	28.18
Pearson, D.B.	1954–61	76	107	21	734	49	8.53	–	5540	210	26.38
Pearson, G.T.	1948–59	2	3	2	54	28	–	–	–	–	–
Pearson, K.	1976	1	2	0	13	9	6.50	–	–	–	–
Pearson, K.R.	1946	1	2	0	26	17	13.00	–	74	2	37.00
Pearson, L.I.	1946	2	4	0	24	18	6.00	–	–	–	–
Peck, D.A.	1960	1	1	0	0	0	–	–	–	–	–
Peck, I.G.	1978–	29	43	5	507	49*	13.34	–	–	–	–
Peck, R.L.	1960–62	2	2	0	24	19	12.00	–	1	2	0.50
Peden, D.M.	1973–76	3	5	0	108	45	21.60	–	74	2	37.00
Peebles, I.A.R.	1927–48	251	330	101	2213	58	9.67	–	19738	923	21.38
T		13	17	8	98	26	10.88	–	1391	45	30.91
Pell, G.A.	1947	1	2	1	24	16*	–	–	31	4	7.75
Pember, J.D.D.	1968–71	24	25	10	271	53	18.07	–	1370	43	31.86
Penn, C.	1982–	21	24	6	395	115	21.94	1	934	17	54.94
Penny, T.S.	1951–52	5	5	2	73	34	24.33	–	400	11	36.36
Pepper, C.G.	1938/39–56/57	44	72	7	1927	168	29.64	1	5019	171	29.35
Pepper, J.	1946–48	29	49	1	1108	185	23.08	1	–	–	–
Percival, W.A.	1951–54	5	7	0	61	23	8.72	–	–	–	–
Pereira, E.L.	1962–63	2	2	1	11	8*	–	–	–	–	–
Perkins, G.C.	1934–51	57	95	23	589	29	8.18	–	3359	93	36.12
Perks, R.T.D.	1930–55	592	884	150	8956	75	12.20	–	53777	2233	24.08
T		2	2	2	3	2*	–	–	355	11	32.27
Perry, E.H.	1933–46	10	16	0	148	46	9.25	–	732	22	33.27
Perry, N.J.	1979–81	13	12	4	19	6	2.38	–	920	21	43.81
Perryman, S.P.	1974–83	156	162	68	872	43	9.28	–	11337	358	31.67
Pervez Sajjad	1961/62–74/75	133	128	53	786	56*	10.48	–	10750	493	21.81
T		19	20	11	123	24	13.67	–	1410	59	23.89
Pestell, K.F.	1957	1	2	0	37	21	18.50	–	17	0	–
Petchey, M.D.	1983–	7	6	0	21	18	3.50	–	886	16	55.38
Peters, R.C.	1946	1	2	1	5	3	–	–	18	0	–
Petrie, E.C.	1950/51–66/67	115	189	34	2788	151	17.98	2	16	0	–
T		14	25	5	258	55	12.90	–	–	–	–
Pettiford, J.	1945–59	201	324	48	7077	133	25.64	4	9259	295	31.38
Pettit, D.W.	1958–59	5	7	4	33	22	11.00	—	432	6	72.00
Phadkar, D.G.	1942/43–59/60	133	178	29	5377	217	36.08	8	10271	464	22.14
T		31	45	7	1229	123	32.34	2	2285	62	36.85
Pheasant, S.T.	1971	1	2	1	2	2*	–	–	121	4	30.25

	Career span	M	I	NO	Runs	HS	Avge	100	Runs	Wkts	Avge
					—BATTING—				—BOWLING—		
Phebey, A.H.	1946–61	327	599	34	14643	157	25.91	13	4	0	–
Phelan, P.J.	1958–65	160	199	71	1693	63	13.23	–	9006	314	28.70
Phillip, N.	1969/70	221	321	37	6694	134	23.57	1	16395	668	25.54
T		9	15	5	297	47	29.70	–	1041	28	37.17
Phillips, A.G.	1953–54	3	5	0	71	31	14.20	–	–	–	–
Phillips, E.F.	1957–59	32	54	7	629	55	13.38	–	–	–	–
Phillips, H.R.	1951	1	1	0	3	3	–	–	–	–	–
Phillips, J.B.M.	1955–57	32	43	15	151	25	5.39	–	2567	72	35.56
Phillips, R.W.	1966/67–70	18	28	0	529	92	18.89	–	6	0	–
Phillipson, C.P.	1970–83	167	225	61	3046	87	18.57	–	5213	153	34.07
Phillipson, W.E.	1933–48	162	208	49	4096	113	25.76	2	13722	555	24.72
Phipps, D.D.	1964	1	2	0	15	15	7.50	–	53	1	–
Piachaud, J.D.	1958–68/69	71	103	18	1037	40	12.20	–	5070	205	24.73
Pick, R.A.	1983–	18	18	7	180	27*	16.36	–	1273	32	39.78
Pickering, H.G.	1938–47	8	16	0	297	79	18.56	–	–	–	–
Pickering, P.B.	1953	1	2	0	59	37	29.50	–	–	–	–
Pickett, C.A.	1953	1	2	1	10	7*	–	–	54	0	–
Pickles, D.	1957–60	41	40	10	74	12	2.47	–	2062	96	21.48
Pickles, L.	1955–58	47	88	5	1703	87	20.53	–	65	1	–
Pickup, J.K.	1973–75	3	6	0	19	14	3.17	–	–	–	–
Pieris, P.I.	1956–66/67	44	66	13	917	55*	17.30	–	3530	101	34.95
Pierpoint, F.G.	1936–46	8	11	7	15	4	3.75	–	592	13	45.54
Pierre, L.R.	1940/41–50	35	35	14	131	23	6.23	–	2522	102	24.76
T		1	–	–	–	–	–	–	28	0	–
Pigot, D.R.jnr.	1966–75	11	21	0	406	88	19.33	–	–	–	–
Pigott, A.C.S.	1978–	89	103	21	1228	63	14.98	–	6363	230	27.67
T		1	2	1	12	8*	–	–	75	2	37.50
Pilling, H.	1962–80	333	542	68	15279	149*	32.23	25	195	1	–
Pinnock, R.A.	1963/64–74/75	44	71	5	2662	176	40.33	6	52	1	–
Pithey, A.J.	1950/51–68/69	124	213	16	7073	170	35.90	13	17	0	–
T		17	27	1	819	154	31.50	1	5	0	–
Pithey, D.B.	1956/57–67/68	99	160	13	3420	166	23.26	3	7388	240	30.78
T		8	12	1	138	55	12.54	–	577	12	48.08
Pitman, R.W.C.	1954–59	50	76	8	926	77	13.61	–	68	1	–
Pitt, J.A.	1957	1	2	1	36	26*	–	–	4	0	–
Place, W.	1937–55	324	487	49	15609	266*	35.63	36	42	1	–
T		3	6	1	144	107	28.80	1	–	–	–
Platt, R.K.	1955–64	101	107	49	424	57*	7.31	–	6799	301	22.58
Playle, W.R.	1956/57–67/68	85	145	13	2888	122	21.87	4	94	1	–
T		8	15	0	151	65	10.07	–	–	–	–
Pleass, J.E.	1947–56	171	253	31	4293	102*	19.34	1	15	0	–
Plimsoll, J.B.snr.	1939/40–49/50	39	47	13	386	51	11.35	–	3581	155	23.10
T		1	2	1	16	8*	–	–	143	3	47.67
Plumb, S.G.	1975–81	3	5	1	97	37*	24.25	–	60	2	30.00
Plummer, P.J.	1969–72	33	37	7	386	46	12.86	–	2016	63	32.00
Pocock, H.J.	1947–49	7	11	1	118	34	11.80	–	70	1	–
Pocock, N.E.J.	1976–84	127	186	22	3790	164	23.11	2	396	4	99.00
Pocock, P.I.	1964–	501	538	138	4543	75*	11.36	–	38989	1506	25.89
T		20	32	2	167	33	5.57	–	2321	54	42.98
Pollard, R.	1933–52	296	328	63	3522	63	13.29	–	25314	1122	22.56
T		4	3	2	13	10*	–	–	378	15	25.20
Pollard, V.	1964/65–74/75	130	207	33	5314	146	30.54	6	6931	224	30.94
T		32	59	7	1266	116	24.34	2	1853	40	46.32
Pollock, A.J.	1982–	23	26	4	198	32	9.00	–	1853	49	37.82
Pollock, J.S.	1939–58	23	43	2	1036	129	25.27	1	2	0	–
Pollock, P.MacL.	1958/59–71/72	127	177	44	3028	79	22.76	–	10620	485	21.89
T		28	41	13	607	75*	21.67	–	2806	116	24.18

	Career span	M	I	NO	Runs	HS	Avge	100	Runs	Wkts	Avge
					BATTING				BOWLING		
Pollock, R.G.	1961/62–	237	399	51	19246	274	55.31	59	2062	43	47.95
	T	23	41	4	2256	274	60.97	7	204	4	51.00
Ponniah, C.E.M.	1963/64–69	45	87	8	1978	101*	25.03	1	82	6	13.67
Pont, I.L.	1982	4	7	1	32	16	5.33	–	302	3	100.67
Pont, K.R.	1970–	181	277	40	6122	125*	25.83	7	2689	83	32.40
Poole, C.J.	1948–62	383	637	42	19364	222*	32.54	24	347	4	86.75
	T	3	5	1	161	69*	40.25	–	9	0	–
Poole, K.J.	1955–57	26	44	5	612	58	15.69	–	1361	21	64.81
Pope, G.H.	1933–49/50	205	312	44	7518	207*	28.05	8	13488	677	19.92
	T	1	1	1	8	8*	–	–	85	1	–
Pope, H.	1939–46	10	16	3	81	24*	6.23	–	599	15	39.93
Popplewell, N.F.M.	1977–	125	184	25	4006	143	25.20	3	4284	103	41.59
Popplewell, O.B.	1949–60	41	56	13	881	74*	20.49	–	10	0	–
Porteous, T.W.	1973–74	2	4	0	18	18	4.50	–	–	–	–
Porter, A.	1936–49	38	64	7	1292	105	22.67	2	480	16	30.00
Porter, S.R.	1973	7	12	2	76	20	7.60	–	600	18	33.33
Posnet, C.E.	1947	1	2	0	46	26	23.00	–	–	–	–
Pothecary, A.E.	1927–46	271	445	39	9477	130	23.34	9	2140	52	41.15
Pothecary, J.E.	1954/55–64/65	54	77	11	1039	81*	15.74	–	4054	143	23.34
	T	3	4	0	26	12	6.50	–	354	9	39.33
Potter, G.	1949–57	55	84	11	1313	88	17.99	–	863	19	45.42
Potter, I.C.	1959–62	19	24	10	123	34	8.78	–	1300	45	28.89
Potter, J.	1956/57–67/68	104	169	20	6142	221	41.22	14	1287	31	41.51
Potter, L.	1981–	35	63	4	1706	118	28.92	3	243	7	34.72
Potts, H.J.	1949–50	9	14	1	290	50	22.31	–	–	–	–
Poulet, R.J.	1968	1	2	0	6	6	3.00	–	–	–	–
Poulter, S.J.	1978	3	3	0	47	36	15.67	–	–	–	–
Pountain, F.R.	1960–65	76	119	17	1920	96	18.83	–	3054	86	35.51
Powell, A.G.	1932–57	53	82	13	1149	79	16.65	–	–	–	–
Powell, T.L.	1971/72–76	2	4	0	24	14	6.00	–	–	–	–
Prasanna, E.A.S.	1961/62–78/79	235	275	67	2476	81	11.90	–	22442	957	23.45
	T	49	84	20	735	37	11.48	–	5742	189	30.38
Pratt, D.	1959–62	18	23	7	50	14	3.12	–	1141	23	49.61
Pratt, D.E.	1954–57	9	12	4	171	33	21.38	–	392	13	30.15
Pratt, D.M.McV	1963–66	6	12	0	171	58	14.25	–	–	–	–
Pratt, R.C.E.	1952–59	69	102	14	1900	120	21.59	1	138	3	46.00
Pratt, R.L.	1955–64	102	158	22	1824	80	13.41	–	6726	259	25.97
Prentice, C.N.R.	1974	1	2	0	23	19	11.50	–	–	–	–
Prentice, F.T.	1934–51	241	421	24	10997	191	27.70	17	5847	117	49.97
Presland, E.R.	1962–70	30	41	4	625	51	16.89	–	761	13	58.54
Pressdee, J.S.	1949–69/70	347	583	88	14267	150*	28.82	13	10666	481	22.18
Preston, D.J.	1959	12	15	2	154	54	11.84	–	562	13	43.23
Preston, K.C.	1948–64	397	468	168	3053	70	10.18	–	30543	1160	26.33
Pretlove, J.F.	1954–68	124	212	21	5115	137	26.79	10	1319	43	30.68
Price, C.F.T.	1945–45/46	15	22	3	385	55	20.26	–	728	24	30.33
Price, D.G.	1984	7	11	0	239	49	21.72	–	–	–	–
Price, D.H.	1975–78	5	10	0	104	27	10.40	–	174	2	87.00
Price, E.J.	1946–49	79	95	31	558	54	8.72	–	5720	215	26.60
Price, J.S.E.	1961–75	279	224	92	1108	53*	8.39	–	19221	817	23.55
	T	15	15	6	66	32	7.33	–	1401	40	35.02
Price, M.R.	1984	3	2	0	8	7	4.00	–	109	5	54.50
Price, W.F.F.	1926–47	402	590	97	9035	111	18.33	3	–	–	–
	T	1	2	0	6	6	3.00	–	–	–	–
Prideaux, R.M.	1958–74/75	446	808	75	25136	202*	34.29	41	176	3	58.67
	T	3	6	1	102	64	20.40	–	0	0	–
Pridgeon, A.P.	1972–	187	185	75	1032	67	9.38	–	14226	417	34.12

	Career span	M	I	NO	Runs	HS	Avge	100	Runs	Wkts	Avge
						BATTING				BOWLING	
Priestley, N.	1981	1	1	1	20	20*	–	–	–	–	–
Pringle, D.R.	1978–	114	168	35	3965	127*	29.81	6	7312	260	28.12
	T	10	17	3	247	47*	17.64	–	752	16	47.00
Prior, I.D.	1967	1	2	0	21	21	10.50	–	–	–	–
Prior, J.A.	1981–	4	6	0	186	87	31.00	–	111	3	37.00
Pritchard, G.C.	1962–66	35	42	15	111	18	4.11	–	2058	56	36.75
Pritchard, T.L.	1937/38–56	200	293	41	3363	81	13.35	–	19062	818	23.30
Procter, M.J.	1965–	398	663	57	21904	254	36.15	48	27249	1407	19.37
	T	7	10	1	226	48	25.11	–	616	41	15.02
Prodger, J.M.	1956–67	151	259	22	4831	170*	20.38	3	14	1	–
Proud, R.B.	1938–50	18	33	1	681	87	21.28	–	–	–	–
Prouton, R.O.	1949–54	52	79	11	982	90	14.44	–	–	–	–
Pryer, B.J.K.	1946–50	27	37	10	252	75*	9.33	–	1888	48	39.33
Puckridge, A.	1963	1	1	0	1	1	–	–	–	–	–
Pugh, C.T.M.	1959–62	80	142	9	2469	137	18.56	1	30	1	–
Pullan, D.A.	1970–74	95	106	36	613	34	8.75	–	–	–	–
Pullar, G.	1954–70	400	672	63	21528	175	35.35	41	387	10	38.70
	T	28	49	4	1974	175	43.86	4	37	1	–
Pullinger, G.R.	1949–50	18	20	11	53	14*	5.89	–	1557	41	37.98
Purves, J.H.	1960–64	11	19	0	474	74	24.95	–	–	–	–
Pycroft, A.J.	1975/76–	39	72	9	2545	133	40.40	3	47	1	–
Pyemont, C.P.	1967	14	25	2	516	61	22.43	–	83	3	27.67
Quick, A.B.	1936–52	20	33	1	439	57	13.69	–	10	0	–
Quick, I.W.	1956/57–61/62	63	71	13	816	61*	14.06	–	5922	195	30.36
Quinn, F.M.	1936–48	7	14	0	227	140	16.21	1	22	0	–
Quinn, K.J.	1957–59	3	5	0	49	25	9.80	–	14	0	–
Quinney, D.H.	1971	1	2	0	4	4	2.00	–	–	–	–
Quintrell, R.N.	1954	4	6	0	76	29	12.67	–	43	0	–
Rabone, G.O.	1940/41–60/61	82	135	14	3425	125	28.30	3	4835	173	27.94
	T	12	20	2	562	107	31.22	1	635	16	39.68
Racionzer, T.B.	1965–	45	80	9	1552	115	21.86	1	71	2	35.50
Radford, N.V.	1978/79–	64	75	16	1148	76*	19.46	–	5366	175	30.66
Radley, C.T.	1964–	498	796	113	23901	171	34.99	41	117	6	19.50
	T	8	10	0	481	158	48.10	2	–	–	–
Rae, A.F.	1946/47–59/60	80	128	7	4798	179	39.65	17	26	0	–
	T	15	24	2	1016	109	46.18	4	–	–	–
Rae, R.B.	1945	1	1	0	74	74	–	–	29	0	–
Raikes, D.C.G.	1931–48	12	12	2	76	37	7.60	–	–	–	–
Ralph, L.H.R.	1953–61	174	262	39	3763	73	16.87	–	11053	460	24.02
Ramadhin, S.	1949/50–65	184	191	65	1092	44	8.67	–	15345	758	20.24
	T	43	58	14	361	44	8.20	–	4579	158	28.98
Ramage, A.	1979–83	23	22	9	219	52	16.85	–	1649	44	37.48
Ramage, P.F.	1962–63	13	22	7	252	50	16.80	–	613	17	36.06
Ramchand, G.S.	1945/46–67/68	145	202	36	6027	230*	36.30	16	7518	255	29.48
	T	33	53	5	1180	109	24.58	2	1899	41	46.31
Ramnarace, R.	1960/61–73/74	28	46	3	972	71	22.60	–	2336	75	31.14
Ramsamooj, D.	1952/53–64	79	143	9	2755	132	20.56	4	178	3	59.33
Ranasinghe, A.N.	1974/75–82/83	33	58	6	1253	77	24.09	–	1656	39	42.46
	T	2	4	0	88	77	22.00	–	69	1	–
Ranatunga, A.	1981/82	24	39	3	1186	118*	32.94	1	560	15	37.33
	T	9	18	0	521	90	28.94	–	173	5	34.60
Randall, D.W.	1972–	324	549	48	18448	209	36.82	32	185	6	30.83
	T	47	79	5	2470	174	33.38	7	3	0	–

	Career span	M	I	NO	Runs	HS	Avge	100	Runs	Wkts	Avge
									BATTING		BOWLING
Randhir Singh	1978/79–	32	36	14	207	40	9.41	–	2940	80	36.75
Ransom, V.J.	1947–55	40	58	11	455	58	9.68	–	3469	98	35.40
Raper, J.R.S.	1936–47	3	4	0	24	15	6.00	–	–	–	–
Raspin, P.H.	1973	2	2	1	15	10	–	–	117	3	39.00
Ratcliffe, A.	1928–45	49	82	7	1969	201	26.25	5	22	0	–
Ratcliffe, D.P.	1957–68	20	33	2	603	79	19.45	–	–	–	–
Ratcliffe, R.M.	1972–80	82	84	22	1022	101*	16.48	1	5411	205	26.39
Ratnayeke, J.R.	1980/81–	'31	44	14	551	66	18.37	–	2221	59	37.64
	T	8	16	4	150	29*	12.50	–	687	17	40.41
Raw, G.D.	1967–68	6	10	0	82	21	8.20	–	–	–	–
Rawlence, J.R.	1934–50	5	6	0	87	38	14.50	–	–	–	–
Rawlinson, H.T.	1982–	16	21	3	156	24	8.67	–	1407	23	61.17
Rawlinson, J.L.	1979–80	9	16	2	112	19	8.00	–	–	–	–
Rawson, P.W.E.	1982–	12	18	5	182	63*	14.00	–	1186	71	16.70
Raybould, J.G.	1957–62	18	32	10	281	81*	12.77	–	1302	34	38.29
Rayment, A.W.H.	1947–58	199	340	28	6338	126	20.31	4	772	19	40.63
Razzall, E.T.	1964	6	9	4	57	25*	11.40	–	396	13	30.46
Read, H.D.	1933–48	54	70	27	158	25*	3.67	–	5022	219	22.94
	T	1	–	–	–	–	–	–	200	6	33.33
Reddick, T.B.	1931–50/51	62	99	11	2688	139	30.55	2	468	6	78.00
Reddy, B.	1973/74–	85	101	18	1484	88	17.88	–	–	–	–
	T	4	5	1	38	21	9.50	–	–	–	–
Reddy, N.S.K.	1959–70/71	60	102	8	2284	113*	24.29	2	306	5	61.20
Redman, J.	1948–53	65	105	23	1012	45	12.34	–	4169	117	35.63
Redmond, R.E.	1963/64–75/76	53	100	7	3134	141*	33.69	5	481	17	28.29
	T	1	2	0	163	107	81.50	1	–	–	–
Redpath, I.R.	1961/62–75/76	226	391	34	14993	261	41.99	32	466	13	45.84
	T	66	120	11	4737	171	43.45	8	41	0	–
Reed, B.L.	1958–70	123	215	11	4962	138	24.32	2	0	0	–
Rees, A.	1955–68	216	372	53	7681	111*	24.07	2	398	6	66.33
Reeve, D.A.	1983–	38	42	9	678	119	20.55	1	2653	97	27.35
Reid, J.R.	1947/48–65	246	418	28	16128	296	41.35	39	10535	466	22.60
	T	58	108	5	3428	142	33.28	6	2835	85	33.35
Reid, K.P.	1970/71–80/81	57	97	20	1518	109	19.71	1	2335	78	29.93
Reidy, B.W.	1973–82	107	162	26	3641	131*	26.77	2	2508	60	41.80
Reifer, E.L.	1984	20	26	8	357	47	19.83	–	1761	49	35.94
Reith, M.S.	1970–80	9	16	0	346	82	21.63	–	56	1	–
Renneberg, D.A.	1964/65–70/71	90	109	43	466	26	7.06	–	8527	291	29.30
	T	8	13	7	22	9	3.67	–	830	23	36.08
Reoch, E.C.	1973	1	2	0	7	7	3.50	–	–	–	–
Revill, A.C.	1946–60	387	654	53	15917	156*	26.48	16	1924	49	39.27
Reynolds, B.L.	1950–70	429	737	65	18824	169	28.01	21	284	4	71.00
Reynolds, G.E.A.	1970–71	2	3	2	37	23*	–	–	75	2	37.50
Rhind, P.A.	1968–82	6	7	4	23	10	7.67	–	332	6	55.33
Rhodes, A.E.G.	1937–54	275	422	34	7363	127	18.98	4	18660	661	28.23
Rhodes, H.J.	1953–75	322	399	143	2427	48	9.48	–	21145	1073	19.71
	T	2	1	1	0	0*	–	–	244	9	27.11
Rhodes, S.J.	1981–	3	2	1	41	35	–	–	–	–	–
Rhodes, W.E.	1961–64	36	66	6	1207	132	20.11	1	0	0	–
Riaz-ur-Rehman	1958/59–66	7	12	0	354	70	29.50	–	10	0	–
Rice, A.S.	1954	3	2	0	15	13	7.50	–	269	8	33.63
Rice, C.E.B.	1969/70–	347	559	84	19099	246	40.21	30	15645	712	21.97
Rice, D.	1960–61	2	3	1	32	23	16.00	–	84	1	–
Rice, J.M.	1971–82	168	271	22	5091	161*	20.44	2	7707	230	33.50
Richards, B.A.	1964/65–82/83	339	576	58	28358	356	54.75	80	2886	77	37.48
	T	4	7	0	508	140	72.57	2	26	1	–

	Career span	M		I	NO	Runs	HS	Avge	100		Runs	Wkts	Avge
						BATTING					BOWLING		
Richards, C.J.	1976–	190		242	54	4364	117*	23.21	3		44	0	–
Richards, G.	1971–79	107		173	25	3370	102*	22.77	1		2257	48	47.02
Richards, I.M.	1976–79	23		25	4	467	50	22.23	–		201	7	28.72
Richards, I.V.A.	1971/72–	326		525	36	24089	291	49.26	74		6161	146	42.20
	T	68		101	5	5237	291	54.55	17		904	17	53.18
Richards, R.J.	1970	1		–	–	–	–	–	–		–	–	–
Richardson, A.	1949–51	28		31	16	73	7*	4.87	–		1819	40	45.47
Richardson, B.A.	1963–67	40		72	4	1323	126	19.46	2		153	1	–
Richardson, B.H.	1950–53	27		36	11	279	29	11.16	–		1003	33	30.39
Richardson, D.W.	1952–67	383		660	65	16303	169	27.40	16		354	8	44.25
	T	1		1	0	33	33	–	–		–	–	–
Richardson, G.W.	1959–65	69		107	15	1460	91	15.87	–		4072	147	27.70
Richardson, J.A.	1934–47	8		14	3	343	61	31.18	–		108	2	54.00
Richardson, J.C.	1953	2		3	0	32	24	10.67	–		–	–	–
Richardson, P.C.	1984–1	1		1	0	7	7	–	–		122	1	–
Richardson, P.E.	1949–65	456		794	41	26055	185	34.60	44		499	11	45.36
	T	34		56	1	2061	126	37.47	5		48	3	16.00
Richardson, R.B.	1981/82–	30		46	1	1739	162	38.64	6		2	0	–
	T	6		7	1	353	154	58.83	2		–	–	–
Riches, J.D.H.	1947	1		2	0	5	4	2.50	–		–	–	–
Rickards, K.R.	1945/46–58/59	38		60	7	2065	195	38.96	2		128	1	–
	T	2		3	0	104	67	34.66	–		–	–	–
Ricketts, M.R.	1948	1		1	0	1	1	–	–		–	–	–
Riddell, N.A.	1976	1		2	0	34	30	17.00	–		–	–	–
Riddington, A.	1931–50	128		214	17	3650	104*	18.53	1		3232	83	38.94
Ridge, S.P.	1981–82	11		15	6	71	22	7.88	–		894	14	63.86
Ridgway, F.	1946–61	341		486	115	4081	94	11.00	–		25381	1069	23.74
	T	5		6	0	49	24	8.17	–		379	7	54.14
Ridland, J.D.	1945	1		2	0	62	44	31.00	–		–	–	–
Ridley, C.J.B.	1971	6		10	2	88	23	11.00	–		356	3	118.67
Ridley, G.N.S.	1965–72	45		68	8	889	50*	14.81	–		3051	123	24.80
Ridley, R.M.	1967–70	23		42	1	994	79	24.24	–		0	0	–
Riley, J.	1953	1		1	0	1	1	–	–		48	3	16.00
Riley, J.C.W.	1955–56	2		3	1	0	0*	–	–		–	–	–
Riley, T.M.N.	1961–64	23		43	2	678	84	16.54	–		15	0	–
Rilstone, T.M.	1951–54	3		3	0	54	38	18.00	–		150	0	–
Rimell, A.G.J.	1946–50	23		35	5	854	160	28.46	1		1445	40	36.12
Rimmer, J.	1949	3		3	2	1	1*	–	–		264	5	52.80
Ring, D.T.	1938/39–53	129		169	22	3418	145	23.25	1		12847	451	28.48
	T	13		21	2	426	67	22.42	–		1305	35	37.28
Ripley, D.	1984–	14		21	3	281	61	15.61	–		–	–	–
Rippon, T.J.	1947–48	3		4	2	45	30	22.50	–		–	–	–
Rist, F.H.	1934–53	65		108	9	1496	62	15.11	–		8	1	–
Rix, D.W.	1964	1		2	0	0	0	0.00	–		90	3	30.00
Rixon, S.J.	1974/75–	119		174	30	3351	128	23.27	5		20	0	–
	T	10		19	3	341	54	21.31	–		–	–	–
Roberts, A.C.	1945–47/48	2		3	1	26	12	13.00	–		182	4	45.50
Roberts, A.M.E.	1969/70–	228		291	67	3516	89	15.70	–		18679	889	21.01
	T	47		62	11	762	68	14.94	–		5174	202	25.61
Roberts, B.	1982/83–	29		48	7	1167	89	28.46	–		1613	48	33.60
Roberts, C.P.	1974	1		1	1	0	0*	–	–		40	1	–
Roberts, D.J.	1963	1		1	0	6	6	–	–		–	–	–
Roberts, H.E.	1949–50	5		8	0	52	30	6.50	–		–	–	–
Roberts, J.B.	1956–59	10		17	5	154	31*	12.83	–		434	13	33.38
Roberts, J.F.	1934–49	8		11	1	204	52	20.40	–		–	–	–
Roberts, J.F.E.	1957	2		4	2	5	5	2.50	–		90	0	–

	Career span	M		I	NO	Runs	HS	Avge	100		Runs	Wkts	Avge
Roberts, J.K.	1969–70	8		9	6	3	2*	1.00	–		485	15	32.33
Roberts, P.	1960/61–78/79	67		83	20	871	105*	13.82	–		5286	211	25.05
Roberts, S.N.	1947–49	6		11	1	158	49*	15.80	–		21	0	–
Roberts, W.B.	1939–49	119		120	39	865	51	10.68	–		8296	392	21.17
Robertson, F.	1971–81	12		17	1	163	51	10.18	–		743	36	20.63
Robertson, G.A.	1950	2		2	1	7	7*	–	–		106	3	35.33
Robertson, J.D.B.	1937–59	509		897	46	31914	331*	37.50	67		2536	73	34.74
	T	11		21	2	881	133	46.36	2		58	2	29.00
Robertson, L.G.	1955	1		1	1	2	2*	–	–		60	5	12.00
Robins, D.H.	1947–71	5		7	3	70	29*	17.50	–		–	–	–
Robins, G.L.	1947	1		2	1	0	0*	–	–		104	2	52.00
Robins, R.V.C.	1953–62	61		92	9	1055	49	12.71	–		3597	107	33.62
Robins, R.W.V.	1925–58	379		565	39	13884	140	26.40	11		22580	969	23.30
	T	19		27	4	612	108	26.60	1		1758	64	27.46
Robinson, A.G.	1937–46	24		37	12	167	32	6.68	–		1464	35	41.83
Robinson, A.L.	1971–77	84		69	31	365	30*	9.60	–		4927	196	25.13
Robinson, E.P.	1934–52	301		388	71	3492	75*	11.02	–		22784	1009	22.58
Robinson, G.	1971–72	2		4	0	100	36	25.00	–		–	–	–
Robinson, G.A.	1970–71	14		25	0	573	62	22.92	–		–	–	–
Robinson, H.B.O.	1947–54	24		31	7	325	51	13.54	–		1442	53	27.21
Robinson, K.	1961	1		1	0	18	18	–	–		–	–	–
Robinson, M.	1942/43–52	82		134	11	2719	190	22.11	2		870	34	25.59
Robinson, M.T.	1947	2		2	0	4	4	2.00	–		157	0	–
Robinson, P.A.	1977/78–	25		37	9	398	49	14.21	–		1927	64	30.11
Robinson, P.E.	1984–	15		24	5	756	92	39.79	–		12	0	–
Robinson, P.J.	1963–77	185		287	55	4936	140	21.27	3		8101	297	27.27
Robinson, P.M.H.	1961	1		2	0	19	12	9.50	–		41	0	–
Robinson, R.D.	1971/72–81/82	97		153	33	4776	185	39.80	7		6	0	–
	T	3		6	0	100	34	16.67	–		–	–	–
Robinson, R.G.	1946	4		8	1	85	53	12.14	–		90	0	–
Robinson, Ray, T.	1964	1		2	0	0	0	0.00	–		–	–	–
Robinson, R.Tim.	1978–	109		189	24	6117	207	37.07	9		94	2	47.00
Robinson, T.Ll.	1946	4		7	1	27	13*	4.50	–		277	6	46.17
Robotham, R.	1946	1		2	0	31	21	15.50	–		–	–	–
Rochford, P.	1952–57	80		113	22	479	31*	5.26	–		–	–	–
Rock, D.J.	1976–79	37		65	1	1227	114	19.17	3		0	0	–
Rodger, R.G.	1975	1		2	0	2	2	1.00	–		38	0	–
Rodriquez, W.V.	1953/54–69/70	64		98	15	2061	105	24.83	1		3342	119	28.08
	T	5		7	0	96	50	13.71	–		374	7	53.42
Roe, B.	1957–66	136		234	9	5010	128	22.27	4		104	2	52.00
Roebuck, P.G.P.	1983–	11		19	5	368	62	26.29	–		269	6	44.83
Roebuck, P.M.	1974–	206		342	49	9990	159	34.10	13		2022	42	48.14
Rogers, J.J.	1979–81	26		45	3	693	54	16.50	–		39	1	–
Rogers, N.H.	1946–55	298		529	28	16056	186	32.05	28		37	0	–
Rogers, P.J.	1967	1		2	1	24	24*	–	–		95	0	–
Rogers, S.S.	1946/47–53	119		202	11	3608	107*	18.89	3		145	2	72.50
Roll, L.M.	1984–	1		–	–	–	–	–	–		49	–	–
Romaines, P.W.	1975–	69		126	7	3795	186	31.89	8		17	0	–
Roope, G.R.J.	1964–82	401		644	129	19037	171	36.96	26		8395	225	37.31
	T	21		32	4	860	77	30.71	–		76	0	–
Roopnaraine, R.	1964–66	29		52	14	302	50*	7.95	–		2119	58	36.54
Roper, A.W.	1939/40–45/46	11		15	0	102	28	6.80	–		503	13	38.69
Roper, C.	1957	1		1	0	7	7	–	–		–	–	–
Roper, D.G.B.	1947	1		2	0	30	30	15.00	–		–	–	–
Rose, B.C.	1969–	248		412	44	12196	205	33.14	23		224	6	37.33
	T	9		16	2	358	70	25.57	–		–	–	–

	Career span	M	I	NO	Runs	HS	Avge	100	Runs	Wkts	Avge
					BATTING				BOWLING		
Rose, E.McQ.	1958–60	24	47	2	700	57	15.56	–	19	1	–
Rose, M.H.	1962–64	31	52	4	808	86	16.83	–	–	–	–
Ross, C.J.	1975/76–80	31	41	13	132	23*	4.71	–	1938	55	35.24
Ross, N.P.D.	1973–77	25	36	3	506	53	15.33	–	13	0	–
Ross, N.P.G.	1969–70	8	14	6	224	68	28.00	–	261	9	29.00
Rought-Rought, D.C.	1934–47	24	39	5	739	92	21.74	–	2129	74	28.77
Roundell, J.	1973	10	14	9	36	10*	7.20	–	509	9	56.56
Rouse, S.J.	1970–81	127	156	34	1924	93	15.77	–	8312	270	30.78
Routledge, R.	1946–54	65	98	18	1331	121	16.64	2	1604	38	42.21
Rowan, A.M.B.	1939/40–51	58	82	20	1492	100*	24.06	1	6408	273	23.47
T		15	23	6	290	41	17.05	–	2084	54	38.59
Rowan, E.A.B.	1929/30–53/54	157	258	17	11710	306*	48.58	30	168	4	42.00
T		26	50	5	1965	236	43.66	3	7	0	–
Rowe, C.J.C.	1974–84	175	277	43	6173	147*	26.38	6	5127	128	40.06
Rowe, E.J.	1949–57	103	122	68	295	16	5.46	–	–	–	–
Rowe, L.C.	1958	5	10	2	61	35	7.63	–	–	–	–
Rowe, L.G.	1968/69–	149	245	12	8755	302	37.58	18	224	2	112.00
T		30	49	2	2047	302	43.55	7	44	0	–
Roy, P.K.	1946/47–67/68	185	298	18	11868	202*	42.38	33	648	21	30.85
T		43	79	4	2442	173	32.56	5	66	1	–
Roy, P.P.	1978/79–	40	67	7	2273	206*	37.88	7	49	1	–
T		2	3	1	71	60*	35.50	–	–	–	–
Roynon, G.D.	1958	9	15	2	188	58	14.46	–	6	0	–
Rudd, C.R.D.	1949–60	21	40	4	604	70	16.78	–	–	–	–
Rudge, L.M.	1952	1	1	0	1	1	–	–	36	0	–
Rumbold, J.S.	1946–47	7	14	0	175	25	12.50	–	–	–	–
Rumsey, F.E.	1960–68	180	204	84	1015	45	8.46	–	11773	580	20.30
T		5	5	3	30	21*	15.00	–	461	17	27.11
Rushmere, C.G.	1956/57–65/66	33	58	4	1245	153	23.06	2	576	20	28.80
Rushworth, W.R.	1946	1	1	0	0	0	–	–	86	2	43.00
Russell, D.F.	1959	5	6	2	57	22	14.25	–	344	11	31.27
Russell, D.P.	1974–75	16	30	4	514	56*	19.76	–	952	16	59.50
Russell, P.E.	1965–79	167	207	44	2015	72	12.36	–	10108	335	30.17
Russell, R.C.	1981–	50	66	17	1102	64*	22.49	–	–	–	–
Russell, S.E.J.	1960–68	142	248	19	5464	130	23.86	4	121	2	60.50
Russell, S.G.	1965–67	35	58	21	203	21*	5.49	–	2480	76	32.63
Russell, W.E.	1956–72	448	796	64	25525	193	34.87	41	993	22	45.14
T		10	18	1	362	70	21.29	–	44	0	–
Russom, N.	1979–83	25	34	14	641	79*	32.05	–	1744	42	41.52
Rutherford, I.A.	1974/75–	79	144	4	3794	222	27.10	5	56	2	28.00
Rutherford, J.R.F.	1957–58	11	21	5	105	37*	6.56	–	555	10	55.50
Rutherford, J.W.	1952/53–60/61	67	115	9	3367	167	31.76	5	1313	29	45.28
T		1	1	0	30	30	–	–	15	1	–
Rutter, A.E.H.	1953–55	3	4	0	49	45	12.25	–	–	–	–
Ryan, M.	1954–65	150	149	58	683	26*	7.51	–	9466	413	22.92
Sabine, P.N.B.	1962–63	12	23	3	420	56	21.00	–	553	15	36.87
Sadiq Mohammed	1959/60–	380	671	40	23775	203	37.68	50	7444	234	31.81
T		41	74	2	2579	166	35.81	5	98	0	–
Saeed Ahmed	1954/55–77/78	213	346	25	12847	203*	40.02	34	8216	332	24.74
T		41	78	4	2991	172	40.41	5	802	22	36.45
Saggers, R.A.	1939/40–50/51	77	93	14	1888	104*	23.89	1	–	–	–
T		6	5	2	30	14	10.00	–	–	–	–
Sainsbury, G.E.	1979–	48	45	25	112	13	5.60	–	3801	114	33.34
Sainsbury, J.P.	1951	2	4	0	16	16	4.00	–	–	–	–

	Career span	M	I	NO	Runs	HS	Avge	100	Runs	Wkts	Avge
					BATTING				BOWLING		
Sainsbury, P.J.	1954–76	618	948	197	20176	163	26.86	7	31777	1316	24.14
Salah-uddin	1964/65–79/80	111	168	31	5729	256	41.81	14	4431	155	28.59
T		5	8	2	117	34*	19.50	–	187	7	26.72
Sale, R.	1939–54	66	115	8	2923	157	27.32	3	4	1	–
Saleem Altaf	1963/64–78/79	143	184	50	3067	111	22.89	1	9479	334	28.38
T		21	31	12	276	53*	14.52	–	1710	46	37.17
Saleem Malik	1978/79–	58	92	8	3474	132	41.36	12	489	17	28.76
T		16	22	2	775	116	38.75	3	20	2	10.00
Saleem Yousouf	1978/79–	57	95	7	2715	145*	30.85	6	16	1	–
T		1	1	0	4	4	–	–	–	–	–
Salim-ud-Din	1954/55–63	9	13	0	467	137	35.92	1	40	1	–
Samaranayeke, A.D.A.	1984–	6	2	1	14	9*	–	–	499	9	55.44
Sanders, I.E.W.	1984–	1	2	0	9	9	4.50	–	93	3	31.00
Sanderson, J.F.W.	1979–80	6	6	2	18	9	4.50	–	282	10	28.20
Sands, J.N.	1965–67	4	5	0	37	17	7.40	–	–	–	–
Sardesai, D.N.	1960/61–72/73	179	271	26	10231	222	41.75	25	552	8	69.00
T		30	55	4	2001	212	39.23	5	45	0	–
Sarfraz Nawaz	1967/68–	297	366	72	5705	90	19.41	–	24661	1003	24.59
T		55	72	13	1045	90	17.71	–	5798	177	32.76
Sargent, M.A.J.	1951–60/61	22	38	4	804	164	23.65	1	204	3	68.00
Sarwate, C.T.	1936/37–68/69	171	257	30	7430	246	32.73	14	11574	494	23.42
T		9	17	1	208	37	13.00	–	374	3	124.67
Saunders, C.J.	1962–64	12	14	8	69	21	11.50	–	–	–	–
Saunders, J.G.	1966	2	4	1	48	47*	16.00	–	163	10	16.30
Saunders, M.	1980	3	2	0	12	12	6.00	–	212	6	35.33
Saunders, P.F.	1951–52	9	11	4	93	30	13.28	–	190	6	31.67
Savage, J.S.	1953–69	347	460	161	2154	33	7.20	–	23777	965	24.64
Savage, R.le Q.	1976–79	44	52	25	196	22*	7.25	–	3787	127	29.81
Savill, L.A.	1953–61	125	200	16	3919	115	21.30	4	26	1	–
Saville, G.J.	1963–74	126	218	29	4474	126*	23.67	3	76	3	25.33
Saxelby, K.	1978–	63	71	19	671	59*	12.90	–	4223	148	28.53
Saxena, R.C.	1960/61–81/82	148	231	29	8155	202*	40.37	17	933	33	28.27
T		1	2	0	25	16	12.50	–	11	0	–
Sayer, D.M.	1955–76	204	237	86	1252	62	8.29	–	14397	613	23.48
Sayer, J.D.	1950–52	4	7	0	81	49	11.56	–	274	7	39.14
Sayers, D.	1967	1	1	1	0	0*	–	–	64	1	–
Schepens, M.	1973–80	19	28	5	407	57	17.69	–	13	0	–
Schofield, D.	1970–74	3	4	4	13	6*	–	–	112	5	22.40
Scholey, J.C.	1952–53	10	7	2	32	16	6.40	–	–	–	–
Scotland, K.J.F.	1958	1	1	0	0	0	–	–	–	–	–
Scott, A.A.S.	1947	1	2	0	12	12	6.00	–	–	–	–
Scott, Chris J.	1977–82	46	51	13	262	27*	6.89	–	–	–	–
Scott, Colin J.	1938–54	235	326	43	3375	90	11.93	–	16766	531	31.57
Scott, C.W.	1981–	7	8	2	151	78	25.17	–	–	–	–
Scott, E.K.	1937–51	9	15	1	136	31	9.71	–	444	12	37.00
Scott, G.M.	1979/80–82	2	2	0	31	21	15.50	–	–	–	–
Scott, H.W.	1958	1	–	–	–	–	–	–	9	0	–
Scott, M.D.	1956–63	21	38	5	499	52	15.12	–	–	–	–
Scott, M.E.	1958–69	185	253	63	2445	62	12.86	–	11397	461	24.72
Scott, M.S.	1981–83	32	60	3	1383	109	24.26	1	37	0	–
Scott, V.J.	1937/38–52/53	79	128	16	5575	204	49.78	16	205	5	41.00
T		10	17	1	458	84	28.62	–	14	0	–
Seager, C.P.	1971	8	11	1	104	23	10.40	–	–	–	–
Seamer, J.W.	1932–49	81	134	12	2483	194	20.35	4	171	4	42.75
Searle, C.J.	1947	1	1	1	5	5*	–	–	–	–	–
Seaton, G.S.	1946–57	8	15	2	196	51	15.08	–	–	–	–

	Career span	M	I	NO	Runs	HS	Avge	100	Runs	Wkts	Avge
					BATTING				BOWLING		
Sedgley, J.B.	1959–61	15	27	2	389	95	15.56	–	–	–	–
Sellers, A.B.	1932–48	344	455	53	9273	204	23.07	4	663	9	73.67
Sellers, R.H.D.	1959/60–66/67	53	80	20	1089	87	18.15	–	4653	121	38.45
T		1	1	0	0	0	–	–	17	0	–
Sells, H.M.	1946	1	2	0	46	26	23.00	–	–	–	–
Selvey, M.W.W.	1968–84	278	278	88	2405	67	12.66	–	20582	772	26.66
T		3	5	3	15	5*	7.50	–	343	6	57.17
Selwood, T.	1966–73	20	35	4	603	89	19.45	–	1	0	–
Semmence, D.J.	1956–68	39	63	2	890	108	14.60	1	123	1	–
Sen, P.	1943/44–57/58	82	118	7	2580	168	23.24	3	106	7	15.15
T		14	18	4	165	25	11.78	–	–	–	–
Senghera, R.	1974–76	24	25	7	281	36*	15.61	–	2303	59	39.03
Senior, E.M.	1961	1	2	0	1	1	0.50	–	–	–	–
Serjeant, C.S.	1976/77–82/83	80	134	19	4030	159	35.04	9	4	0	–
T		12	23	1	522	124	23.72	1	–	–	–
Sethi, R.K.	1975	1	2	0	12	12	6.00	–	27	0	–
Seth-Smith, D.J.	1950	1	2	0	3	3	1.50	–	23	0	–
Shackleton, D.	1948–69	647	852	197	9574	87*	14.61	–	53303	2857	18.65
T		7	13	7	113	42	18.83	–	768	18	42.67
Shackleton, J.H.	1971–78	48	64	20	596	41*	13.55	–	2242	49	45.76
Shaddick, R.A.	1946–55	20	25	13	62	12*	5.17	–	1418	49	28.94
Shafiq Ahmed	1967/68–	174	299	37	13637	217*	52.05	41	2818	86	32.77
T		6	10	1	99	27*	11.00	–	1	–	–
Shafqat Rana	1959/50–75/76	107	158	18	4947	174	35.33	9	560	16	35.00
T		5	7	0	221	95	31.57	–	9	1	–
Shahid Mahmood	1956/57–69/70	66	107	9	3117	220	31.80	5	1931	89	21.70
T		1	2	0	25	16	12.50	–	23	0	–
Shakoor Ahmed	1947/48–67/68	53	84	4	2958	280	36.96	8	8	0	–
Shantry, B.K.	1978–79	3	–	–	–	–	–	–	167	3	55.67
Shardlow, B.	1949–50	2	4	1	45	24*	15.00	–	89	6	14.83
Sharman, G.J.	1958	2	4	0	9	6	2.25	–	–	–	–
Sharp, G.	1968–	295	383	80	6143	98	20.27	–	68	1	–
Sharp, H.P.H.	1946–57	167	276	30	6422	165	26.11	10	1670	52	32.12
Sharp, J.A.T.	1937–46	5	10	0	64	36	6.40	–	172	7	24.57
Sharp, K.	1976–	126	211	15	6245	173	31.86	11	321	7	45.86
Sharp, T.M.	1934/35–45/46	4	7	2	74	28	14.80	–	222	6	37.00
Sharpe, P.J.	1956–76	493	811	78	22530	228	30.74	29	197	3	65.67
T		12	21	4	786	111	46.23	1	–	–	–
Shastri, R.J.	1979/80–	69	101	17	2844	161*	33.86	5	5590	187	29.89
T		27	41	6	1083	128	30.94	2	2368	62	38.19
Shaw, C.	1984–	3	5	2	32	17	10.67	–	177	5	35.40
Shaw, D.G.	1949	1	1	0	17	17	–	–	106	2	53.00
Shaw, G.B.	1951–55	16	20	13	30	11	4.28	–	706	26	27.15
Shea, W.D.	1947–48	3	3	1	27	18*	13.50	–	180	5	36.00
Sheahan, A.P.	1965/66–73/74	133	206	33	7987	202	46.16	19	66	1	–
T		31	53	6	1594	127	33.91	2	–	–	–
Shearer, E.D.R.	1933–52	14	27	1	628	72	24.15	–	–	–	–
Shearwood, K.A.	1949–51	5	6	1	45	28	9.00	–	–	–	–
Shelmerdine, N.	1945	1	–	–	–	–	–	–	–	–	–
Shenton, P.A.	1958–60	8	8	3	68	33	13.60	–	442	17	26.00
Shepherd, D.J.	1950–72	668	837	248	5696	73	9.67	–	47298	2218	21.32
Shepherd, D.R.	1965–79	282	476	40	10672	153	24.47	12	106	2	53.00
Shepherd, J.N.	1964/65–	421	611	106	13354	170	26.44	10	31933	1155	27.65
T		5	8	0	77	32	9.62	–	479	19	25.21
Sheppard, D.S.	1947–62/63	231	395	31	15838	239*	43.51	45	88	2	44.00
T		22	33	2	1172	119	37.80	3	–	–	–

	Career span	M	I	NO	Runs	HS	Avge	100	Runs	Wkts	Avge
					BATTING				BOWLING		
Sheppard, H.F.	1938–52	13	24	1	509	72	22.13	–	7	0	–
Shepperd, J.	1959–60	4	6	2	32	13	8.00	–	253	4	63.25
Sherman, H.R.	1967–69	13	21	3	448	66	24.89	–	23	0	–
Shillingford, G.C.	1967/68–78/79	81	106	28	791	42	10.14	–	5760	217	26.54
	T	7	8	1	57	25	8.14	–	537	15	35.80
Shinde, S.G.	1940/41–54/55	79	95	33	871	50*	14.04	–	7496	230	32.59
	T	7	11	5	85	14	14.17	–	717	12	59.75
Shippey, P.A.	1967–71	4	7	1	187	94*	31.17	–	–	–	–
Shirreff, A.C.	1939–58	119	203	24	3887	115*	21.71	1	9575	304	31.49
Shivlal, Yadav, N.	1977/78–	60	63	15	829	50	17.27	–	5467	157	34.82
	T	18	23	6	236	43	13.88	–	1778	50	35.56
Shore, R.G.	1962	4	8	2	46	24	7.67	–	395	10	39.50
Short, A.M.	1966/67–74/75	66	123	4	3318	118	27.88	2	62	3	20.67
Short, J.D.	1957–60	11	19	0	271	86	14.26	–	11	0	–
Short, J.F.	1974–	11	18	2	533	114	33.31	1	–	–	–
Short, R.L.	1969–70	11	20	1	355	58	18.68	–	–	–	–
Shortland, N.A.	1938–50	23	40	5	487	70	13.91	–	50	0	–
Shuja-ud-Din Butt	1946/47–69/70	98	156	21	3342	147	24.75	6	6714	298	22.53
	T	19	32	6	395	47	15.19	–	801	20	40.05
Shuja-ud-Din Butt	(1962) 1953/54–62	18	32	6	633	77	24.35	–	440	9	48.89
Shutt, A.	1972	2	–	–	–	–	–	–	181	2	90.50
Shuttleworth, G.M.	1946–48	25	39	5	786	96	23.12	–	–	–	–
Shuttleworth, K.	1964–80	239	241	85	2589	71	16.60	–	15270	623	24.51
	T	5	6	0	46	21	7.67	–	427	12	35.58
Siddiqi, S.N.	1984–	6	12	0	219	52	18.25	–	90	5	18.00
Siddons, A.	1959–60	5	8	3	36	8	7.20	–	266	8	33.25
Sidebottom, A.	1973–	147	167	40	2987	124	23.52	1	8544	364	23.47
Sikander Bakht	1974/75–	127	130	42	1292	67	14.68	–	10273	392	26.21
	T	26	35	12	146	22*	6.34	–	2412	67	36.00
Silk, D.R.W.	1952–60/61	83	140	11	3845	126	29.81	7	240	1	–
Silva, S.A.R.	1981/82–	11	19	3	655	161*	40.94	2	–	–	–
	T	2	4	1	118	102*	39.33	1	–	–	–
Silvester, S.	1976–77	6	7	4	30	14	10.00	–	313	12	26.08
Sim, A.M.R.	1962/63–66	7	12	1	196	66*	17.81	–	12	1	–
Sime, W.A.	1929–50	97	138	17	2473	176*	20.44	1	2300	49	46.94
Simmons, J.	1968–	365	454	117	7953	112	23.60	5	22482	822	27.35
Simons, R.G.	1959	1	1	0	0	0	–	–	–	–	–
Simpkins, D.P.	1982	1	2	1	1	1*	–	–	15	0	–
Simpkins, P.A.	1962	1	–	–	–	–	–	–	114	3	38.00
Simpson, D.J.	1984–	1	2	0	12	9	6.00	–	–	–	–
Simpson, F.W.	1931–48	2	4	0	92	40	23.00	–	–	–	–
Simpson, J.	1954	1	1	0	26	26	–	–	50	0	–
Simpson, R.B.	1952/53–77/78	257	436	62	21029	359	56.22	60	13287	349	38.07
	T	62	111	7	4869	311	46.82	10	3001	71	42.27
Simpson, R.T.	1944/45–63	495	852	55	30546	259	38.32	64	2227	59	37.74
	T	27	45	3	1401	156*	33.35	4	22	2	11.00
Sims, J.M.	1929–53	462	635	116	8984	123	17.31	4	39401	1581	24.92
	T	4	4	0	16	12	4.00	–	480	11	43.64
Sinclair, B.W.	1955/56–70/71	118	204	18	6114	148	32.87	6	86	2	43.00
	T	21	40	1	1148	138	29.44	3	32	2	16.00
Singleton, A.P.	1934–49/50	114	191	21	4700	164	27.65	4	7317	240	30.49
Singleton, G.M.	1946	3	5	1	34	23	8.50	–	146	5	29.20
Sinker, N.D.	1966–67	13	23	4	188	31*	9.89	–	705	22	32.05
Sismey, S.G.	1938/39–52	35	52	11	725	78	17.68	–	–	–	–
Siviter, K.	1974–77	16	28	9	138	26	7.26	–	964	25	38.56

	Career span	M	I	NO	Runs	HS	Avge	100	Runs	Wkts	Avge
Skala, S.M.	1979	2	3	0	18	11	6.00	–	–	–	–
Skinner, A.F.	1931–49	86	142	7	3537	102	26.20	1	250	6	41.67
Skinner, D.A.	1947–49	23	36	1	475	63	13.10	–	182	2	91.00
Skinner, I.J.	1950	13	21	7	28	7*	2.00	–	808	21	38.48
Skinner, L.E.	1971–77	79	127	17	2503	93	22.75	–	–	–	–
Slack, J.K.E.	1954	7	14	0	434	135	31.00	1	–	–	–
Slack, W.N.	1977–	129	219	23	7213	248*	36.80	12	462	18	25.67
Slade, D.N.F.	1958–71	280	395	103	5275	125	18.06	1	11785	502	23.47
Slade, W.D.	1961–67	67	116	11	1482	73*	14.11	–	1493	32	46.66
Slaven, F.F.	1955	2	2	0	13	13	6.50	–	–	–	–
Slinger, E.	1967	1	1	1	12	12*	–	–	–	–	–
Slocombe, P.A.	1975–83	139	233	29	5640	132	27.65	7	54	3	18.00
Sly, G.B.	1953	1	–	–	–	–	–	–	29	1	–
Smail, A.H.K.	1983	6	6	1	24	13*	4.80	–	222	5	44.40
Smailes, T.F.	1932–48	269	349	43	5892	117	19.26	3	17034	823	20.70
	T	1	1	0	25	25	–	–	62	3	20.67
Smales, K.	1948–58	161	229	55	2512	64	14.44	–	11946	389	30.71
Small, G.C.	1979/80–	92	112	26	1087	57*	12.64	–	6966	214	32.55
Small, M.A.	1983/84–	11	10	5	17	3*	3.40	–	866	33	26.24
	T	2	1	1	3	3*	–	–	153	4	38.25
Smart, C.C.	1920–46	235	383	46	8992	151*	26.68	9	7505	180	41.70
Smedley, M.J.	1964–79	360	604	76	16482	149	31.22	28	4	0	–
Smethers, M.C.	1967	2	3	0	19	14	6.33	–	–	–	–
Smith, A.C.	1958–74/75	428	612	85	11027	145	20.92	3	3074	131	23.47
	T	6	7	3	118	69*	29.50	–	–	–	–
Smith, A.J.S.	1971/72–	103	168	25	3909	150*	27.34	2	35	1	–
Smith, A.M.	1965	1	2	0	20	12	10.00	–	–	–	–
Smith, A.V.	1978–79	2	1	1	11	11*	–	–	–	–	–
Smith, C.L.	1977/78–	115	205	21	6924	193	37.63	18	1661	31	53.58
	T	7	12	1	358	91	32.55	–	39	3	13.00
Smith, C.W.	1951/52–64/65	37	64	3	2277	140	37.32	5	97	3	32.33
	T	5	10	1	222	55	24.67	–	–	–	–
Smith, C.M.	1958	1	2	0	16	12	8.00	–	–	–	–
Smith, C.S.	1951–58	106	153	28	2339	103*	18.71	1	7183	293	24.52
Smith, D.	1927–52	443	753	63	21843	225	31.66	32	734	20	36.70
	T	2	4	0	128	57	32.00	–	–	–	–
Smith, D.H.K.	1965–77/78	114	202	14	4995	136	26.57	4	23	1	–
Smith, David J.	1981–	14	14	2	29	13	2.42	–	–	–	–
Smith, Donald Jas.	1951–52	3	4	0	26	14	6.50	–	205	4	51.25
Smith, Donald Jos.	1955–57	28	37	21	128	18*	8.00	–	2297	73	31.47
Smith, David Mark	1973–	158	246	53	6313	189*	32.71	10	1485	28	53.04
Smith, Dav. Martin	1981–83	4	5	2	148	100*	49.33	1	201	2	100.50
Smith, Douglas M.	1938–46	6	10	2	55	34	6.88	–	401	20	20.55
Smith, D.R.	1956–70	386	520	116	4970	74	12.30	–	29655	1250	23.72
	T	5	5	1	38	34	9.50	–	359	6	59.83
Smith, D.V.	1946–62	377	625	66	16960	206*	30.34	19	9670	339	28.53
	T	3	4	1	25	16*	8.33	–	97	1	–
Smith, E.	1951–71	503	674	144	6998	90	13.02	–	31448	1217	25.84
Smith, F.B.	1942/43–52/53	48	83	5	2588	153	33.17	4	48	1	–
	T	4	6	1	237	96	47.40	–	–	–	–
Smith, G.	1951–58	42	71	72	728	60	12.34	–	3766	165	22.82
Smith, G.J.	1955–66	243	419	30	8797	148	22.61	5	951	33	28.82
Smith, G.S.	1949	1	2	0	29	22	14.50	–	–	–	–
Smith, J.	1965	1	2	0	17	17	8.50	–	99	4	24.75
Smith, I.D.S.	1977/78–	69	105	12	2288	145	24.60	4	6	0	–
	T	15	21	6	416	113*	27.73	1	–	–	–

	Career span	M	I	NO	Runs	HS	Avge	100	Runs	Wkts	Avge
Smith, J.W.R.	1950–55	3	3	0	5	4	1.67	–	–	–	–
Smith, K.B.	1978	4	8	1	90	43	12.86	–	–	–	–
Smith, Kenneth David	1973–	192	337	28	8614	140	27.88	9	3	0	–
Smith, Ken. Desm'd	1950–51	26	43	7	621	70*	17.25	–	103	3	34.33
Smith, L.A.	1934–47	5	8	2	92	55	15.33	–	397	11	36.09
Smith, M.G.M.	1961	1	2	1	24	18*	–	–	–	–	–
Smith, M.J.	1959–80	422	704	78	19814	181	31.65	40	1866	57	32.74
Smith, M.J.K.	1951–75	637	1091	139	39832	204	41.84	·69	305	5	61.00
T		50	78	6	2278	121	31.64	3	128	1	–
Smith, N.	1970–81	187	239	53	3336	126	17.94	2	–	–	–
Smith, O'N.G.	1954/55–58/59	70	112	12	4031	169	40.31	10	3754	121	31.02
T		26	42	0	1331	168	31.69	4	1625	48	33.85
Smith, P.A.	1982–	46	74	8	1881	114	28.50	1	2219	51	43.51
Smith, P.B.	1967	5	6	1	36	18	7.20	–	291	7	41.57
Smith, P.T.	1956–57	15	24	2	152	40	6.91	–	–	–	–
Smith, R.	1947	1	2	0	23	22	11.50	–	50	0	–
Smith, Raymond	1934–56	445	682	88	12042	147	20.27	8	41265	1350	30.57
Smith, Rodney	1969–70	5	8	3	99	37*	19.80	–	–	–	–
Smith, Ronald	1954	1	2	1	19	19*	–	–	38	1	–
Smith, Roy (St)	1949–55	96	173	21	2600	100	17.11	1	1083	19	57.00
Smith, Roy (M.C.)	1949	1	2	0	29	29	14.50	–	–	–	–
Smith, R.A.	1980/81–	36	64	11	2058	132	38.83	5	30	0	–
Smith, R.C.	1956–64	104	156	37	115	36	9.37	–	5514	203	27.16
Smith, S.	1950–56	44	66	5	1117	101*	18.31	1	–	–	–
Smith, T.P.B.	1929–51	467	690	125	10161	163	17.98	8	45059	1697	26.55
T		4	5	0	33	24	6.60	–	319	3	106.33
Smith, V.I.	1945/46–57/58	97	114	61	547	37	10.32	–	8233	365	22.56
T		9	16	6	39	11*	3.90	–	769	12	64.08
Smith, Walter A.	1930–46	27	44	4	754	125*	18.85	1	122	3	40.67
Smith, William A.	1961–70	144	242	18	5024	103	22.43	2	1	0	–
Smithson, G.A.	1946–56	200	333	27	6940	169	22.68	8	117	1	–
T		2	3	0	70	35	23.33	–	–	–	–
Smithurst, I.	1946	1	2	0	1	1	0.50	–	48	0	–
Smithyman, M.J.	1965/66–74/75	40	59	10	1162	73	23.71	–	2027	79	25.66
Smyth, R.I.	1973–75	21	41	2	711	61	18.23	–	–	–	–
Smyth, R.N.P.	1970	3	5	0	42	25	8.40	–	–	–	–
Snape, M.D.	1949	2	3	1	0	0*	0.00	–	–	–	–
Snedden, M.C.	1977/78–	55	64	15	1034	69	21.10	–	4531	179	25.31
T		10	12	2	147	32	14.70	–	819	23	35.61
Snellgrove, K.L.	1965–74	106	172	16	3948	138	25.31	2	27	3	9.00
Snodgrass, D.L.	1982	1	1	0	6	6	–	–	80	3	26.67
Snow, J.A.	1961–77	346	451	110	4832	73*	14.17	–	26675	1174	22.72
T		49	71	14	772	73	13.54	–	5387	202	26.66
Snowden, W.	1972–75	37	69	3	1413	108*	21.41	3	13	0	–
Sobers, G.st.A.	1952/53–74	383	609	93	28315	365*	54.87	86	28941	1043	27.74
T		93	160	21	8032	365*	57.78	26	7999	235	34.04
Sohoni, S.W.	1935/36–59/60	107	162	14	4245	218*	28.68	8	7505	232	32.34
T		4	7	2	83	29*	16.60	–	202	2	101.00
Solanky, J.W.	1963/64–76	84	138	22	2374	73	20.47	–	4639	183	25.35
Solkar, E.D.	1965/66–80/81	189	270	36	6851	145*	29.28	8	8283	276	30.01
T		27	48	6	1068	102	25.42	1	1070	18	59.44
Solomon, J.S.	1956/57–68/69	104	156	28	5318	201*	41.55	12	1950	51	38.23
T		27	46	7	1326	100*	34.00	1	268	4	67.00
Somerville, R.J.	1955	1	1	0	3	3	–	–	–	–	–
Souness, J.McG.	1954–55	3	5	0	11	7	2.20	–	301	4	75.25
Souter, J.S.	1948	3	2	0	47	30	23.50	–	–	–	–

	Career span	M		I	NO	Runs	HS	Avge	100		Runs	Wkts	Avge
						BATTING						BOWLING	
Southern, J.W.	1975–83	164		179	71	1653	61*	15.31	–		12283	412	29.81
Spanswick, J.G.	1955–56	16		22	1	135	24	6.43	–		1175	36	32.64
Sparling, J.T.	1956/57–70/71	127		215	26	4606	105	24.37	2		7223	318	22.71
	T	11		20	2	229	50	12.72	–		327	5	65.40
Speak, G.J.	1981–82	5		6	4	27	15*	13.50	–		230	1	–
Spelman, G.D.	1980–82	7		7	1	9	4	1.50	–		357	10	35.70
Spence, L.A.	1952–54	20		34	6	326	44	11.64	–		9	0	–
Spencer, A.H.	1957–61	27		52	1	934	85	18.32	–		23	0	–
Spencer, C.T.	1952–74	506		687	142	5871	90	10.77	–		36486	1367	26.69
Spencer, J.	1969–80	215		286	80	2787	79	13.53	–		14622	554	26.39
Spencer, T.W.	1935–46	75		120	13	2152	96	20.11	–		19	1	–
Spencer, W.G.	1938–48	3		5	1	52	25	13.00	–		8	1	–
Sperry, J.	1937–52	188		265	99	1193	35	7.19	–		13958	492	28.37
Spicer, P.A.	1962–63	17		29	2	526	86	19.47	–		55	2	27.50
Spilsbury, J.W.E.	1952	1		1	0	16	16	–	–		86	0	–
Spooner, R.T.	1948–59	359		580	72	13851	168*	27.27	12		46	0	–
	T	7		14	1	354	92	27.23	–		–	–	–
Spray, P.H.	1967–68	9		132	2	135	54	12.27	–		–	–	–
Springall, J.D.	1955–63	121		224	24	5176	107*	25.88	2		3312	80	41.40
Squires, H.S.	1928–49	410		658	44	19186	236	31.25	37		10817	306	35.35
Squires, P.J.	1972–76	49		84	8	1271	70	16.72	–		32	0	–
Stackpole, K.R.	1959/60–73/74	167		279	22	10100	207	39.29	22		5814	148	39.28
	T	43		80	5	2807	207	37.42	7		1001	15	66.73
Stainton, R.G.	1932–47	61		104	8	2330	89	24.27	–		25	1	–
Stallibrass, M.J.D.	1972–74	21		31	7	194	24	8.08	–		993	22	45.14
Standen, J.A.	1959–70	133		174	28	2092	92*	14.33	–		7934	313	25.35
Standing, D.K.	1983–	6		10	4	252	60	42.00	–		32	0	–
Standring, K.B.	1955–59	13		22	5	255	41	15.00	–		867	25	34.68
Stanford, R.M.	1935/36–47/48	23		35	3	832	153	26.00	1		25	0	–
Stanley, E.A.W.	1950–52	13		21	3	226	35	12.56	–		8	0	–
Stanning, J.	1939–46	16		22	3	403	56*	21.21	–		–	–	–
Stanyard, A.R.	1960	2		3	0	47	26	15.67	–		–	–	–
Stanworth, J.	1983–	13		16	5	108	31*	9.82	–		–	–	–
Starkie, S.	1951–56	95		110	30	857	60	10.71	–		5685	166	34.25
Statham, J.B.	1950–68	559		647	145	5424	62	10.80	–		36995	2260	16.37
	T	70		87	28	675	38	11.44	–		6261	252	24.85
Staziker, M.	1970	2		2	2	1	1*	–	–		269	1	–
Stead, B.	1959–76	232		253	77	2166	58	12.30	–		18318	653	28.05
Stead, P.	1954	3		4	3	6	4*	–	–		177	9	19.67
Steele, A.	1967–80	14		25	0	621	97	24.84	–		–	–	–
Steele, D.S.	1963–84	500		812	124	22346	140*	32.48	30		15511	623	24.90
	T	8		16	0	673	106	42.06	1		39	2	19.50
Steele, H.K.	1970–74/75	26		40	4	711	103*	19.75	1		1276	30	42.53
Steele, J.F.	1970–	356		576	77	14489	195	29.04	20		14629	564	25.94
Stenton, J.D.	1953	1		2	0	19	18	9.50	–		44	1	–
Stephens, J.P.R.F.	1966–67	3		6	0	73	27	12.17	–		–	–	–
Stephenson, F.D.	1981/82–	29		43	4	877	165	22.49	1		2434	108	22.54
Stephenson, G.R.	1967–80	272		357	66	4781	100*	16.42	1		39	0	–
Stephenson, H.W.	1948–64	463		747	91	13195	147*	20.11	7		135	1	–
Stephenson, J.W.A.	1928/29–48	102		158	37	2582	135	21.34	2		7455	311	23.99
Stevens, J.N.	1937–53	7		12	1	76	19	6.91	–		571	9	63.44
Stevens, KB.H.	1962	5		10	0	102	52	10.20	–		–	–	–
Stevens, R.G.	1962	1		2	0	38	29	19.00	–		47	2	23.50
Stevenson, G.B.	1973–	181		220	31	3806	115*	20.14	2		13681	478	28.62
	T	2		2	1	28	27*	–	–		183	5	36.60
Stevenson, J.A.	1937–51	4		8	2	127	45*	21.17	–		–	–	–
Stevenson, K.	1974–83	146		167	58	1046	33	9.60	–		10536	355	29.68

| | Career span | M | | BATTING | | | | | | | BOWLING | | |
			I	NO	Runs	HS	Avge	100		Runs	Wkts	Avge
Stevenson, M.H.	1949–67	66	106	7	2467	122	24.92	4		1882	50	37.64
Stevenson, R.L.	1962	2	4	1	33	17*	11.00	–		230	3	76.67
Steward, E.A.W.	1964–67/68	18	27	3	310	47	12.91	–		–	–	–
Stewart, A.J.	1981–	27	42	7	1130	118*	32.29	1		–	–	–
Stewart, D.	1950	1	2	1	7	5*	–	–		21	2	10.50
Stewart, D.E.R.	1969–79	32	51	3	854	69	17.79	–		72	0	–
Stewart, M.J.	1954–72	531	898	93	26492	227*	32.91	49		99	1	–
	T	8	12	1	385	87	35.00	–		–	–	–
Stewart, R.W.	1966–68	52	36	11	107	19	4.28	–		3133	131	23.92
Stewart, W.J.P.	1955–71	290	491	56	14826	182*	34.08	25		15	2	17.50
Still, S.J.	1975	1	2	0	6	6	3.00	–		42	1	–
Stimpson, P.J.	1971–72	30	54	3	1327	103	26.01	1		19	0	–
Stinchcombe, F.W.	1950–51	6	8	2	87	48	14.50	–		539	4	134.75
Stockley, A.J.	1968	3	2	0	5	5	2.50	–		194	10	19.40
Stocks, F.W.	1946–57	284	430	45	11397	171	29.60	13		9794	223	43.92
Stoddart, P.L.B.	1958	1	2	0	22	11	11.00	–		–	–	–
Stollmeyer, J.B.	1938/39–56/57	117	194	16	7942	324	44.61	14		2482	55	45.12
	T	32	56	5	2159	160	42.33	4		507	13	39.00
Stone, D.H.	1949–50	6	8	2	86	46	14.33	–		472	9	52.44
Storer, R.E.D.	1972	4	6	3	13	9	4.33	–		–	–	–
Storey, S.J.	1960–78	332	492	62	10776	164	25.06	12		13175	496	26.56
Stott, W.B.	1952–63	190	314	20	9248	186	31.46	17		112	7	16.00
Stovold, A.W.	1973–	249	450	24	13292	212*	31.20	15		86	2	43.00
Stovold, M.W.	1979–82	25	37	6	518	75*	16.71	–		19	0	–
Strachan, G.R.	1965	2	1	1	17	17*	–	–		34	2	17.00
Stratton, R.A.	1946	3	4	3	23	12	–	–		–	–	–
Straw, D.S.	1964	1	1	0	10	10	–	–		–	–	–
Street, L.C.	1946	4	7	2	17	8*	3.40	–		146	3	48.67
Stretton, T.K.	1972–75	6	7	3	20	6*	5.00	–		338	4	84.50
Stringer, P.M.	1967–72	56	63	21	333	22	7.93	–		2772	88	31.50
Stripp, D.A.	1956–57	12	20	3	183	32*	10.77	–		297	6	49.50
Stuchbury, S.	1978–81	3	3	2	7	4*	–	–		236	8	29.50
Sturt, M.O.C.	1961–78	33	35	9	202	26	12.44	–		–	–	–
Subba Row, R.	1951–67/68	260	407	65	14182	300	41.47	30		3363	87	38.66
	T	13	22	1	984	137	46.85	3		2	0	–
Subramaynam, V.	1959/60–69/70	101	150	17	4219	213*	31.72	8		3093	70	44.18
	T	9	15	1	263	75	18.79	–		201	3	67.00
Such, P.M.	1982–	33	34	12	45	16	2.05	–		2441	87	28.06
Sullivan, J.	1963–76	154	241	32	4286	81*	20.51	–		2216	76	29.16
Sullivan, J.P.	1968–77	23	40	1	480	53	12.31	–		50	2	25.00
Sully, H.	1959–69	122	134	50	722	48	8.60	–		8686	314	27.66
Sumar, S.	1975	1	2	0	25	15	12.50	–		–	–	–
Sunnucks, P.R.	1934–46	68	121	8	2016	162	17.84	1		–	–	–
Surendra Nath	1955/56–68/69	88	115	29	1351	119	15.70	1		7055	278	25.37
	T	11	20	7	136	27	10.46	–		1053	26	40.50
Surridge, D.	1979–82	34	28	16	103	14*	8.58	–		2599	87	29.87
Surridge, J.G.C.	1956	1	2	0	1	1	0.50	–		3	0	–
Surridge, S.S.	1978	1	1	1	2	2*	–	–		–	–	–
Surridge, W.S.	1939–59/60	267	333	33	3882	87	12.94	–		14623	506	28.90
Surti, R.F.	1956/57–72/73	160	278	17	8066	246*	30.90	6		10528	284	37.07
	T	26	48	4	1263	99	28.70	–		1962	42	46.71
Sutcliffe, B.	1941/42–65/66	232	405	39	17283	385	47.22	44		3264	86	37.95
	T	42	76	8	2727	230*	40.10	5		344	4	86.00
Sutcliffe, H.	1919–45	748	1088	123	50138	313	51.96	149		527	10	52.70
	T	54	84	9	4555	194	60.73	16		–	–	–
Sutcliffe, R.J.	1978	1	2	2	10	10*	–	–		37	1	–
Sutcliffe, S.P.	1980–83	38	47	11	141	20	3.92	–		4020	96	41.88

FIRST-CLASS AND TEST CAREER RECORDS

	Career span	M	I	NO	Runs	HS	Avge	100	Runs	Wkts	Avge
					BATTING				BOWLING		
Sutcliffe, W.H.H.	1948–59	211	326	41	7530	181	26.42	6	332	15	22.13
Sutherland, I.	1949	1	1	0	9	9	–	–	23	0	–
Suttle, K.G.	1949–71	612	1064	92	30225	204*	31.10	49	8727	266	32.81
Sutton, J.A.	1969–72	4	8	0	164	57	20.50	–	197	4	49.25
Sutton, M.A.	1946–48	19	26	8	144	13*	8.00	–	1218	47	25.92
Sutton-Mattocks, C.J.	1972–73	6	12	0	107	37	8.92	–	–	–	–
Swallow, I.G.	1983–	13	12	5	155	34*	22.14	–	702	17	41.29
Swallow, R.	1957–63	38	68	2	1323	115	20.05	1	8	0	–
Swan, R.G.	1980–	5	10	1	203	66	22.26	–	0	0	–
Swann, J.L.	1949–51	4	6	3	69	29*	23.00	–	220	6	36.67
Swaranjit Singh	1950/51–61/62	88	153	17	3684	145	27.09	4	5427	183	29.66
Swarbrook, F.W.	1967–	231	340	89	5300	90	21.12	–	13998	467	29.97
Swart, P.D.	1965/66	158	250	27	5652	122	25.35	6	9070	358	25.34
Swetman, R.	1953–74	284	411	73	6495	115	19.22	2	69	1	–
T	11	17	2	254	65	16.93	–	–	–	–	
Swift, B.T.	1957	17	23	7	160	25	10.00	–	–	–	–
Swinbourne, J.W.	1970–74	29	36	8	160	25	5.72	–	2281	83	27.48
Swindell, R.S.	1972–77	23	32	11	242	38	11.52	–	1665	50	33.30
Sydenham, D.A.D.	1957–72	145	133	65	487	24*	7.16	–	9732	487	19.98
Sykes, J.F.	1983	1	1	0	4	4	–	–	54	1	–
Syme, I.A.H.	1950	1	2	0	12	12	6.00	–	7	0	–
Symington, S.J.	1948–49	23	40	6	744	65	21.88	–	1448	36	40.22
Taber, H.B.	1964/65–73/74	129	182	35	2648	109	18.01	1	6	0	–
T	16	27	5	353	48	16.04	–	–	–	–	
Tahir Naqqash	1975/76–	47	51	9	863	60	20.55	–	3657	108	33.86
T	14	17	5	299	57	24.92	–	1317	31	42.48	
Tait, A.	1971–78	63	104	1	1897	99	18.42	–	0	0	–
Talat Ali	1967/68–78/79	115	205	13	7296	258	38.00	14	247	2	123.50
T	10	18	2	370	61	23.13	–	7	0	–	
Talbot, B.L.	1947	1	2	0	35	25	17.50	–	–	–	–
Tallon, D.	1933/34–53/54	150	228	21	6034	193	29.14	9	202	0	–
T	21	26	3	394	92	17.13	–	–	–	–	
Tamhane, N.S.	1951/52–68/69	93	96	16	1460	109*	18.25	1	43	2	21.50
T	21	27	5	225	54*	10.23	–	–	–	–	
Tamplin, C.	1942/43–47	4	5	2	56	40*	18.67	–	–	–	–
Tanner, J.D.P.	1947–55	7	13	4	112	25*	12.44	–	–	–	–
Tasker, A.G.E.	1956	1	–	–	–	–	–	–	–	–	–
Tattersall, K.	1965/66–75/76	33	58	2	1275	112	22.77	1	101	1	–
Tattersall, R.	1948–64	327	369	151	2040	58	9.36	–	24704	1369	18.05
T	16	17	7	50	10*	5.00	–	1513	58	26.09	
Tattersall, R.H.	1971	2	–	–	–	–	–	–	219	1	–
Tavare, C.J.	1974–	231	392	40	13460	168*	38.23	25	293	2	146.50
T	30	55	2	1753	149	33.08	2	11	0	–	
Tayfield, H.J.	1945/46–62/63	187	259	47	3668	77	17.30	–	18890	864	21.86
T	37	60	9	862	75	16.90	–	4405	170	25.92	
Taylor, B.	1949–73	572	949	73	19091	135	21.79	9	30	1	–
Taylor, B.R.	1963/64–79/80	141	210	25	4579	173	24.75	4	10605	422	25.13
T	30	50	6	898	124	20.41	2	2953	111	26.60	
Taylor, C.R.V.	1970–81	33	45	5	276	25	6.90	–	–	–	–
Taylor, D.D.	1946/47–60/61	93	164	6	3734	143	23.63	1	1019	30	33.97
T	3	5	0	159	77	31.80	–	–	–	–	
Taylor, D.D.S.	1948–50	17	23	7	519	121	32.44	1	607	15	40.47
Taylor, D.J.S.	1966–82	302	420	95	7404	179	22.78	4	16	0	–
Taylor, F.	1939–53	2	3	0	8	8	2.67	–	142	8	17.75

	Career span	M		I	NO	Runs	HS	Avge	100		Runs	Wkts	Avge
Taylor, H.J.C.	1968–69	13		25	1	246	50	10.25	–		5	0	–
Taylor, J.A.S.	1937–54	9		10	0	198	78	19.80	–		58	1	–
Taylor, J.D.	1947–49	4		8	3	76	27*	15.20	–		24	0	–
Taylor, J.F.	1960–67	15		24	7	461	86	27.12	–		–	–	–
Taylor, J.P.	1984–	3		2	0	11	11	5.50	–		188	2	94.00
Taylor, J.R.N.	1949–52/53	4		8	1	129	41	18.43	–		–	–	–
Taylor, K.	1953–68	313		524	36	13053	203*	26.75	16		3763	131	28.73
	T	3		5	0	57	24	11.40	–		6	0	–
Taylor, K.A.	1946–49	87		155	10	3145	102	21.69	1		33	1	–
Taylor, L.B.	1977–	138		117	51	673	47	10.20	–		9787	401	24.41
Taylor, M.N.S.	1964–80	375		518	116	8031	105	19.97	3		22016	830	26.52
Taylor, N.R.	1979–	90		159	21	4615	155*	33.44	11		288	5	57.60
Taylor, N.S.	1982–	11		7	2	16	6*	3.20	–		974	32	30.44
Taylor, P.A.	1958	6		10	5	34	13	6.80	–		335	7	47.86
Taylor, R.M.	1931–46	206		349	21	6755	193	20.60	5		2933	92	31.88
Taylor, R.W.	1960–84	637		878	167	12040	100	16.93	1		75	1	–
	T	57		83	12	1156	97	16.28	–		–	–	–
Taylor, T.J.	1981–82	14		17	7	115	28*	11.50	–		1272	37	34.38
Taylor, W.	1971–77	95		97	39	374	26*	6.44	–		6291	211	29.81
Tebay, K.	1961–63	15		27	2	509	106	20.36	1		–	–	–
Tedder, E.C.	1946	8		14	0	208	55	14.86	–		–	–	–
Tedstone, G.A.	1982–	17		22	6	288	67*	18.00	–		–	–	–
Tennant, P.N.	1964	1		–	–	–	–	–	–		–	–	–
Tennekoon, A.P.B.	1965/66–	61		107	11	3481	169*	36.26	5		60	2	30.00
Terry, V.P.	1978–	55		90	13	2673	175*	34.71	8		39	0	–
	T	2		3	0	16	8	5.33	–		–	–	–
Thackara, A.L.S.S.	1949–55	4		6	0	112	42	18.67	–		–	–	–
Thackeray, P.R.	1974	8		15	4	315	65*	28.64	–		1	0	–
Thewlis, J.	1962	1		2	0	18	17	9.00	–		–	–	–
Thomas. A.	1966	1		2	0	4	4	2.00	–		7	0	–
Thomas, D.J.	1977–	109		148	29	2386	119	20.05	2		8237	252	32.69
Thomas, F.O.	1951	1		2	0	21	21	10.50	–		–	–	–
Thomas, G.	1957/58–66/67	100		154	12	5726	229	40.32	17		30	0	–
	T	8		12	1	325	61	29.54	–		–	–	–
Thomas, G.P.	1978–81	8		15	1	277	52	19.79	–		–	–	–
Thomas, J.G.	1979–	51		68	9	865	84	14.66	–		3778	128	29.52
Thomas, N.P.	1984–	1		2	0	0	0	0.00	–		–	–	–
Thomas, R.J.	1974	1		1	1	8	8*	–	–		40	1	–
Thomas, R.J.A.	1963–65	15		28	2	622	135*	23.92	1		5	1	–
Thomas, W.O.	1948–54	4		5	4	44	19*	–	–		145	3	48.33
Thomas, W.R.K.	1981	1		2	1	57	44	–	–		54	0	–
Thompson, A.W.	1939–55	202		329	30	7915	158	26.47	4		831	12	69.25
Thompson, E.R.	1965–74	16		20	7	135	29*	10.38	–		1118	35	31.94
Thompson, H.R.P.	1953–54	2		1	0	16	16	–	–		259	2	129.50
Thompson, J.R.	1938–54	68		116	5	3455	191	31.13	6		13	0	–
Thompson, L.B.	1946–49	6		4	2	16	13	8.00	–		248	5	49.60
Thompson, N.P.	1961	7		7	3	16	4*	4.00	–		637	17	37.47
Thompson, R.G.	1949–62	159		187	71	657	25*	5.66	–		10901	479	22.77
Thompson, T.	1963–64	9		14	5	43	12	4.77	–		497	17	29.24
Thomson, G.B.	1973/74–80/81	47		59	22	340	34*	9.19	–		3180	110	28.91
Thomson, J.	1962–84	2		2	1	1	1*	–	–		154	4	38.50
Thomson, J.R.	1972/73–	152		183	48	1818	61	13.47	–		14356	566	25.36
	T	49		69	16	641	49	12.09	–		5326	197	27.04
Thomson, N.I.	1952–72	425		583	100	7120	77	14.74	–		32866	1597	20.58
	T	5		4	1	69	39	23.00	–		568	9	63.11
Thomson, R.H.	1961–62	25		48	5	883	84	20.54	–		13	0	–

	Career span	M		I	NO	Runs	HS	Avge	100		Runs	Wkts	Avge
						BATTING					BOWLING		
Thomson, S.J.	1938–51	4		7	2	75	21*	15.00	–		246	17	14.47
Thorn, P.L.	1974	4		6	2	45	25	11.25	–		227	4	56.75
Thorne, D.A.	1983–	14		23	6	368	69*	21.65	–		754	17	44.35
Thorne, D.C.	1964	2		4	1	98	59	32.67	–		133	2	66.50
Thorneycroft, G.M.	1947	1		2	0	3	3	1.50	–		–	–	–
Thornton, T.	1946	1		2	0	29	23	14.50	–		–	–	–
Thoy, R.E.	1955–57	2		3	0	24	13	8.00	–		–	–	–
Thresher, R.S.	1957–58	5		9	4	51	19	10.20	–		407	14	29.07
Thursting, L.D.	1938–47	29		45	10	882	94	25.20	–		660	13	50.77
Thwaites, I.G.	1963–64	22		38	4	769	60	22.62	–		127	4	31.75
Tidy, W.N.	1970–74	36		34	14	70	12*	3.50	–		2775	81	34.26
Tillard, J.R.	1949	1		2	0	3	3	1.50	–		–	–	–
Tilley, E.W.	1946	4		3	0	3	2	1.00	–		256	10	25.60
Tilly, H.W.	1954–67	64		88	13	814	49	10.85	–		3502	134	26.13
Timmis, P.J.	1971	1		–	–	–	–	–	–		36	0	–
Timms, B.S.V.	1959–71	232		306	74	3657	120	15.76	1		–	–	–
Timms, J.E.	1925–49	470		847	30	20457	213	25.04	31		6626	149	44.47
Timur Mohamed	1975/76–	31		51	5	1596	193	34.70	4		99	2	49.50
Tindall, R.A.E.	1956–66	173		257	38	5446	109*	24.87	2		4857	150	32.38
Tindall, R.M.	1980–81	14		22	4	330	60*	18.33	–		331	4	82.75
Tinkler, E.	1953–61	3		5	0	15	7	3.00	–		14	0	–
Tissera, M.H.	1958/59–75	30		54	5	1394	122	28.44	2		856	27	31.70
Titmus, F.J.	1949–82	792		1142	208	21588	137*	23.11	6		63313	2830	22.37
	T	53		76	11	1449	84*	22.29	–		4931	153	32.23
Todd, L.J.	1927–50	437		727	93	20087	174	31.68	38		15883	572	27.79
Todd, P.A.	1972–82	156		276	16	7168	178	27.56	8		3	0	–
Toft, D.P.	1965–67	27		48	4	1222	145	27.77	1		–	–	–
Tolchard, J.G.	1970–81	78		109	17	1865	78	20.27	–		5	0	–
Tolchard, R.W.	1965–83	483		680	189	15288	126*	31.14	12		34	1	–
	T	4		7	2	129	67	25.80	–		–	–	–
Tomlins, K.P.	1977–	75		108	13	2529	146	26.62	4		317	4	79.25
Tomlinson, J.D.W.	1946	1		1	0	2	2	–	–		–	–	–
Tompkin, M.	1938–56	378		655	29	19927	186	31.83	31		106	1	–
Tongue, C.H.	1963	1		2	0	20	13	10.00	–		23	0	–
Toogood, G.J.	1982–	22		39	5	865	109	25.44	1		221	3	73.67
Toole, C.L.	1967	1		2	0	78	54	39.00	–		56	1	–
Toon, J.H.C.	1946	1		2	0	1	1	0.50	–		126	4	31.50
Topham, R.D.N.	1976	4		7	1	91	31	15.17	–		–	–	–
Topley, P.A.	1972–75	19		19	4	184	38*	12.26	–		741	15	49.40
Tordoff, G.G.	1950–62	85		155	13	3975	156*	27.99	5		1985	40	49.63
Torkington, H.F.	1981	1		2	0	9	9	4.50	–		–	–	–
Torrens, R.	1966–82	6		8	1	42	17	6.00	–		402	26	15.46
Toshack, E.R.H.	1945/46–49/50	48		45	13	185	20*	5.78	–		3973	195	20.37
	T	12		11	6	73	20*	14.60	–		989	47	21.04
Townsend, A.	1948–60	342		553	70	12054	154	24.96	6		9374	325	28.84
Townsend, A.F.	1934–50	117		200	13	4327	142*	23.14	5		39	0	–
Townsend, D.C.H.	1933–48	37		64	2	1801	195	29.05	4		513	6	85.50
	T	3		6	0	77	36	12.83	–		9	0	–
Townsend, J.R.A.	1964–65	10		18	0	245	64	13.61	–		–	–	–
Townsley, R.A.J.	1974–75	2		4	0	22	12	5.50	–		0	0	–
Tracy, S.R.	1982/83–	14		14	4	34	9*	3.40	–		1103	40	27.58
Traicos, A.J.	1967–	77.		111	49	824	43	13.29	–		6166	198	31.14
	T	3		4	2	8	5*	4.00	–		207	4	51.75
Trapnell, B.M.W.	1946	11		20	3	283	41	16.65	–		621	16	38.81
Travers, B.H.	1946–48	24		37	9	718	65*	25.64	–		1450	48	30.21
Travers, T.J.	1984–	1		2	0	20	15	10.00	–		–	–	–

	Career span	M		I	NO	Runs	HS	Avge	100		Runs	Wkts	Avge
						BATTING					BOWLING		
Trembath, C.R.	1982–	4		4	3	33	17*	–	–		444	11	40.36
Tremlett, M.F.	1947–60	388		681	49	16038	185	25.37	16		10752	351	30.63
		T	3	5	2	20	18*	6.67	–		226	4	56.50
Tremlett, T.M.	1976–	110		151	25	2516	88	19.97	–		5031	214	23.51
Trestrail, K.B.	1943/44–54	41		65	8	2183	161*	38.29	5		114	4	28.50
Trevett, J.C.P.	1962	2		3	1	1	1	0.50	–		139	0	–
Tribe, G.E.	1945/46–59	308		454	82	10177	136*	27.34	7		28321	1378	20.55
		T	3	3	1	35	25*	17.50	–		330	2	165.00
Trick, W.M.S.	1946–50	19		22	11	52	15	4.72	–		1087	56	19.41
Trim, G.E.	1976–80	15		25	0	399	91	15.96	–		13	0	–
Trimborn, P.H.J.	1961/62–75/76	94		111	37	880	52	11.89	–		7102	314	22.62
		T	4	4	2	13	11*	6.50	–		257	11	23.36
Tripp, G.M.	1955–59	34		62	7	700	62	12.72	–		10	0	–
Troup, G.B.	1974/75–	77		88	31	627	58*	11.00	–		5951	210	28.34
		T	12	15	6	43	13*	4.78	–		1114	34	32.76
Trubshaw, E.B.	1946	1		2	0	2	1	1.00	–		–	–	–
Trueman, F.S.	1949–68	604		711	120	9231	104	15.57	3		42154	2304	18.30
		T	67	85	14	981	39*	13.82	–		6625	307	21.58
Tuckett, L.	1934/35–54/55	60		101	16	1496	101	17.60	1		5191	225	23.07
		T	9	14	3	131	40*	11.91	–		980	19	51.58
Tudor, R.T.	1976	1		1	0	6	6	–	–		42	0	–
Tulk, D.T.	1956–57	2		2	2	8	8*	–	–		70	0	–
Tunnicliffe, C.J.	1973–83	150		176	30	2092	91	14.33	–		10265	319	32.18
Tunnicliffe, H.T.	1973–80	65		110	27	2116	100*	25.49	1		1601	42	38.12
Turnbull, J.R.	1983–	12		16	7	17	6	1.89	–		778	15	51.87
Turner, A.	1968/69–77/78	105		196	10	5744	156	30.88	7		10	1	–
		T	14	27	1	768	136	29.54	1		–	–	–
Turner, B.	1960–61	2		4	2	7	3*	3.50	–		47	4	11.75
Turner, C.	1925–46	201		266	32	6132	130	26.21	2		5354	173	30.95
Turner, D.R.	1966–	352		581	53	15435	181*	29.23	24		332	9	36.89
Turner, F.M.	1954–59	10		16	5	196	28*	17.82	–		223	3	74.33
Turner, G.M.	1964/65–82/83	455		792	101	34346	311*	49.71	103		189	5	37.80
		T	41	73	6	2991	259	44.64	7		5	0	–
Turner, M.S.	1984–	1		2	0	1	1	0.50	–		85	0	–
Turner, J.B.	1974	1		2	0	127	106	63.50	1		–	–	–
Turner, R.V.	1953–54	10		16	4	213	113*	17.75	1		–	–	–
Turner, S.	1965–	354		502	100	9261	121	23.04	4		20892	808	25.86
Turner, S.J.	1984–	5		6	3	75	27*	25.00	–		–	–	–
Tyrwhitt-Drake, T.W.	1946–57	4		8	0	122	38	15.25	–		–	–	–
Tyson, F.H.	1952–60	244		316	76	4103	82	17.10	–		16030	767	20.89
		T	17	24	3	230	37*	10.95	–		1411	76	18.57
Udal, G.F.U.	1932–46	4		8	3	4	2*	0.80	–		216	3	72.00
Ufton, D.G.	1949–62	149		244	48	3919	219*	20.00	1		–	–	–
Umrigar, P.R.	1944/45–67/68	243		350	41	16154	252*	52.28	49		3849	325	25.69
		T	59	94	8	3631	223	42.22	12		1473	35	42.09
Underwood, A.J.	1949–54	16		15	4	109	39	9.91	–		907	10	90.70
Underwood, D.L.	1963–	604		639	177	4630	111	10.02	1		45525	2301	19.79
		T	86	116	35	937	45*	11.57	–		7674	297	25.84
Unwin, FstG.	1932–51	53		87	8	1138	60	14.41	–		41	0	–
Upton, M.	1971	1		1	1	2	2*	–	–		120	1	–
Urquhart, J.R.	1948	4		6	2	13	6*	3.25	–		231	15	15.40

	Career span	M	I	NO	Runs	HS	Avge	100	Runs	Wkts	Avge
			BATTING						BOWLING		
Valentine, A.L.	1949/50–64/65	125	142	48	470	24*	5.00	–	12452	475	26.22
T		36	51	21	141	14	4.70	–	4215	139	30.32
Valentine, B.H.	1927–50	399	645	38	18306	242	30.16	35	1125	27	41.67
T		7	9	2	454	136	64.86	2	–	–	–
Van der Bijl, V.A.P.	1967/68–82/83	156	188	48	2269	87	16.21	–	12692	767	16.55
Van der Knaap, D.S.	1967–78/79	43	43	16	289	44	10.70	–	3389	121	28.01
Van der Merwe, P.L.	1956/57–68/69	94	152	12	4086	128	29.19	4	2108	82	25.71
T		15	23	2	533	76	25.38	–	22	1	–
Van Geloven, J.	1955–65	247	431	44	7522	157*	19.44	5	13912	486	28.63
Van Ryneveld, A.J.	1947	1	2	0	69	50	34.50	–	2	0	–
Van Ryneveld, C.B.	1946/47–62/63	101	171	12	4803	150	30.21	4	6230	206	30.24
T		19	33	6	724	83	26.82	–	671	17	39.47
Varey, D.W.	1981–	30	56	6	1206	83	24.12	1	4	0	–
Varey, J.G.	1982–83	13	22	8	426	69*	30.43	–	866	6	144.33
Vaulkhard, P.	1934–52	77	122	7	2460	264	21.39	1	124	1	–
Vavasour, G.W.	1947	1	2	0	14	8	7.00	–	–	–	–
Veivers, T.R.	1958/59–67/68	106	162	24	5100	137	36.95	4	7393	191	38.70
T		21	30	4	813	88	31.27	–	1375	33	41.67
Vengsarkar, D.B.	1975/76–	159	248	27	10609	210	48.00	29	88	0	–
T		69	113	10	3970	159	38.54	8	36	0	–
Venkataraghavan, S.	1963/64–	335	449	80	6561	137	17.78	1	32956	1360	24.23
T		57	76	12	748	64	11.69	–	5634	156	36.12
Verity, S.A.	1969–70	4	7	2	55	15	11.00	–	260	4	65.00
Vernon, J.M.	1949–52	8	13	0	290	83	22.31	–	100	2	50.00
Vernon, M.J.	1974–77	22	27	5	146	27	6.64	–	1198	31	38.65
Verrinder, A.O.C.	1974–77	4	4	1	24	23	8.00	–	144	4	36.00
Vickery, A.	1947–48	6	12	1	89	21	8.09	–	–	–	–
Vigar, F.H.	1938–54	257	399	62	8859	145	26.29	12	9135	241	37.91
Viljoen, K.G.	1926/27–48/49	133	209	25	7964	215	43.28	23	722	29	24.90
T		27	50	2	1365	124	28.44	2	23	0	–
Virgin, R.T.	1957–77	437	773	39	21930	179*	29.88	37	340	4	85.00
Viswanath, G.R.	1967/68–	286	451	41	16732	247	40.81	41	716	15	47.73
T		91	155	10	6080	222	41.93	14	46	1	0
Vivian, G.E.	1964/65–78/79	88	140	25	3259	137*	28.33	3	2128	56	38.00
T		5	6	0	110	43	18.33	–	107	1	–
Voce, W.	1927–52	426	525	130	7583	129	19.19	4	35961	1558	23.08
T		27	38	15	308	66	13.39	–	2733	98	27.89
Von Hagt, D.M.	1983/84–	6	11	1	269	75	26.90	–	–	–	–
Vowles, R.C.	1957–61	16	28	3	292	54	11.68	–	920	23	40.00
Wade, T.H.	1929–50	321	476	134	5024	96	14.69	–	1412	48	29.42
Wadekar, A.L.	1958/59–74/75	237	360	33	15380	323	47.03	36	908	21	43.24
T		37	71	3	2113	143	31.07	1	55	0	–
Wadey, A.N.C.	1975	1	2	2	0	0*	–	–	44	1	–
Wadsworth, K.J.	1968/69–75/76	118	166	23	3664	117	25.62	2	10	0	–
T		33	51	4	1010	80	21.49	–	–	–	–
Wagstaffe, M.G.	1972	13	23	7	233	42	14.56	–	870	28	31.07
Wainwright, T.D.	1961	1	2	0	37	28	18.50	–	–	–	–
Wait, O.J.	1949–61	45	40	17	132	19	5.74	–	3280	125	26.24
Waite, A.C.	1962–64	12	14	8	58	29	9.67	–	691	18	38.39
Waite, J.H.B.	1948/49–65/66	199	314	34	9812	219	35.04	23	8	0	–
T		50	86	7	2405	134	30.44	4	–	–	–
Walcott, C.L.	1941/42–63/64	146	238	29	11820	314*	56.56	40	1269	35	36.25
T		44	74	7	3798	220	56.69	15	408	11	37.09
Waldron, A.N.E.	1948	4	7	0	91	52	13.00	–	204	3	68.00

	Career span	M	I	NO	Runs	HS	Avge	100	Runs	Wkts	Avge
					BATTING				BOWLING		
Waldron, P.H.P.	1946–47	4	8	0	99	32	12.28	–	–	–	–
Wales, P.J.	1951	1	2	1	38	29	–	–	13	5	2.60
Walford, M.M.	1935–53	97	169	11	5327	264	33.72	9	249	8	31.13
Walker, A.	1983–	19	19	7	82	19	6.83	–	1696	49	34.61
Walker, A.K.	1948/49–58	94	118	26	1603	73	17.42	–	6072	221	27.48
Walker, C.	1947–54	131	224	34	5258	150*	27.67	8	2615	53	49.33
Walker, H.	1947	1	2	0	8	7	4.00	–	–	–	–
Walker, J.	1949	1	2	1	19	19*	–	–	–	–	–
Walker, K.G.E.	1955–57	2	3	0	54	26	18.00	–	82	0	–
Walker, M.	1952–58	29	52	3	574	100	11.72	1	976	28	34.86
Walker, M.H.N.	1968/69–81/82	135	170	40	2014	78*	15.49	–	13209	499	26.47
T		34	43	13	586	78*	19.53	–	3792	138	27.48
Walker, P.M.	1956–72	469	788	110	17650	152*	26.03	13	23881	834	28.63
T		3	4	0	128	52	32.00	–	34	0	–
Wall, S.	1984–	7	9	4	47	19	9.40	–	545	9	60.55
Wallace, G.C.	1978/79–82/83	16	30	2	757	111	27.04	1	238	5	47.60
Wallace, K.W.	1967–72	10	16	0	219	55	13.69	–	–	–	–
Wallace, W.M.	1933/34–60/61	120	190	17	7609	211	43.98	16	18	0	–
T		13	21	0	439	66	20.90	–	5	0	–
Waller, C.E.	1967–	251	257	108	1444	51*	6.69	–	17430	610	28.57
Waller, G.de W.	1973–74	13	25	1	203	29	8.46	–	4	0	–
Wallis Mathias	1953/54–77/78	146	206	37	7520	278*	44.50	16	555	13	42.69
T		21	36	3	783	77	23.72	–	20	0	–
Wallwork, M.A.	1982	1	–	–	–	–	–	–	–	–	–
Walmsley, W.T.	1945/46–59/60	37	50	11	1064	180*	27.28	2	3861	122	31.64
Walsh, C.A.	1981/82–	30	41	7	259	30	7.62	–	2826	100	28.26
Walsh, D.R.	1966–69	39	69	10	1508	207	25.56	2	129	6	21.50
Walsh, J.E.	1936/37–56	296	460	52	7247	106	17.76	2	29226	1190	24.56
Walshe, A.P.	1953–56	46	69	8	900	77	14.75	–	–	–	–
Walters, J.	1977–80	58	80	15	1296	90	19.94	–	1935	47	41.17
Walters, J.A.	1958–59	5	9	8	64	21*	–	–	464	10	46.40
Walters, K.D.	1962/63–80/81	258	426	57	16180	253	43.85	45	6782	190	35.69
T		74	125	14	5357	250	48.26	15	1425	49	29.08
Walton, A.C.	1953–59	85	155	2	3797	152	24.82	3	8	0	–
Walusimbi, S.	1973/74–75	2	4	0	78	54	19.50				
Waqar Ahmed	1964/65–72/73	33	51	6	1705	199	37.89	3	67	1	–
Waqar Hasan	1948/49–65/66	97	141	11	4620	201*	35.54	8	173	2	86.50
T		21	35	1	1071	189	31.50	1	10	0	–
Ward, A.	1966–78	163	157	47	928	44	8.44	–	10495	460	22.82
T		5	6	1	40	21	8.00	–	453	14	32.86
Ward, B.	1967–72	128	222	19	4799	164*	23.64	4	68	5	13.60
Ward, D.	1954–62	135	206	33	2496	86	14.43	–	4974	187	26.60
Ward, G.H.	1949–50	3	6	2	23	6*	5.75	–	–	–	–
Ward, J.D.	1954	1	1	1	5	5*	–	–	79	1	–
Ward, J.M.	1970–75	49	87	4	1743	104	21.00	1	–	–	–
Ward, J.T.	1957/58–70/71	95	129	39	1117	54*	12.41	–	7	0	–
T		8	12	6	75	35*	12.50	–	–	–	–
Wardle, J.H.	1946–67/68	412	527	71	7333	79	16.08	–	35027	1846	18.98
T		28	41	8	653	66	19.78	–	2080	102	20.39
Waring, J.S.	1963–67	29	29	15	152	26	10.86	–	1251	55	22.75
Warke, L.	1950–61	17	29	0	405	120	13.97	1	326	7	46.57
Warke, S.J.S.	1981–	3	4	0	166	63	41.50	–	–	–	–
Warnapura, B.	1970/71–82/83	57	99	8	2280	154	25.06	2	628	13	48.30
T		4	8	0	96	38	12.00	–	46	0	–
Warner, A.E.	1982–	28	39	9	480	67	16.00	–	1947	61	31.92
Warner, C.J.	1978–	8	14	1	391	70	30.03	–	–	–	–

	Career span	M		I	NO	Runs	HS	Avge	100		Runs	Wkts	Avge
						BATTING						BOWLING	
Warner, C.S.	1962	7		14	0	365	77	26.07	–		–	–	–
Warner, G.S.	1966–71	30		48	7	965	118*	23.54	2		14	0	–
Warr, A.L.	1933–50	5		7	1	54	24	9.00	–		–	–	–
Warr, J.J.	1949–60	344		454	119	3838	54*	11.46	–		21796	956	22.80
	T	2		4	0	4	4	1.00	–		281	1	–
Warrington, A.G.	1973–74	2		4	0	152	92	38.00	–		–	–	–
Warrington, J.M.	1951	2		1	0	18	18	–	–		164	3	54.67
Washbrook, C.	1933–59	591		906	107	34101	251*	42.68	76		309	7	44.14
	T	37		66	6	2569	195	42.82	6		33	1	–
Wasim Bari	1964/65–	286		357	92	5749	177	21.69	2		30	1	–
	T	81		112	26	1366	85	15.88	–		2	0	–
Wasim Raja	1967/68–	235		358	51	10897	165	35.50	16		15306	529	28.93
	T	53		86	13	2678	125	36.69	4		1660	48	34.58
Wassell, A.R.	1957–66	122		160	25	1209	61	8.95	–		8667	320	27.08
Waterman, P.A.	1983–	5		4	2	6	6*	3.00	–		345	6	57.50
Waters, R.H.C.	1960–69	38		62	11	929	70	18.22	–		–	–	–
Waterton, S.N.V.	1980–	21		26	3	364	50	15.83	–		–	–	–
Watkins, A.J.	1939–63	484		753	87	20362	170*	30.57	32		20393	833	24.48
	T	15		24	4	810	137*	40.50	2		554	11	50.36
Watkins, D.	1949–54	12		17	4	210	32	16.15	–		421	8	52.63
Watkins, S.G.	1983	1		2	0	105	77	52.50	–		–	–	–
Watkins, W.M.	1950	1		1	0	3	3	–	–		–	–	–
Watkins, W.R.	1930–47	32		53	7	867	115	18.85	1		376	18	20.89
Watkinson, M.	1982–	33		49	10	836	77	21.44	–		2203	65	33.89
Watson, A.G.McL.	1965–68	42		67	16	666	65*	13.06	–		2708	68	39.82
Watson, G.D.	1964/65–76/77	107		162	19	4674	176	32.68	7		4709	186	25.31
	T	5		9	0	97	50	10.78	–		254	6	42.33
Watson, G.G.	1977/78–79/80	45		58	15	552	38	12.83	–		3832	102	37.56
Watson, G.S.	1928–50	236		393	20	8566	145	22.97	5		51	1	–
Watson, I.R.	1969–73	3		5	1	37	16	9.25	–		–	–	–
Watson, J.M.	1957–59	5		9	0	74	31	8.22	–		1	1	–
Watson, R.G.	1982	1		2	0	15	11	7.50	–		–	–	–
Watson, R.M.	1947	6		11	3	68	25*	8.50	–		–	–	–
Watson, W.	1939–64	468		753	109	25670	257	39.86	55		127	0	–
	T	23		37	3	879	116	25.85	2				
Watson, W.K.	1974/75–	96		126	40	1152	99*	13.40	–		7943	321	24.75
Watt, A.E.	1929–47	230		330	37	4098	96	13.99	–		17586	610	28.82
Watt, J.	1960–61	2		3	0	69	34	23.00	–		–	–	–
Watts, A.	1982–83	3		3	1	39	33*	19.50	–		118	1	–
Watts, E.A.	1933–49	243		357	69	6158	123	21.29	2		19004	729	26.07
Watts, H.E.	1939–52	72		124	8	2958	110	25.50	1		117	1	–
Watts, L.D.	1957–58	11		20	0	361	69	18.05	–		–	–	–
Watts, P.D.	1958–67	182		277	60	4567	91	21.05	–		10067	307	32.79
Watts, P.J.	1959–80	375		607	90	14449	145	27.95	10		8710	333	26.16
Webb, H.E.	1946–54	15		23	1	461	145*	20.95	1		15	1	–
Webb, P.M.	1953	2		2	1	3	3*	–	–		52	4	13.00
Webb, R.T.	1948–60	256		333	104	2685	49*	11.73	–		43	1	–
Wazir Mohammed	1949/50–63/64	105		149	26	4952	189	40.26	11		41	0	–
	T	20		33	4	801	189	27.62	2		15	0	–
Webster, A.J.	1981–82	9		11	5	81	25	13.50	–		734	15	48.93
Webster, D.	1975	1		1	0	26	26	–	–		28	1	–
Webster, J.	1938–55	70		95	15	617	65	7.71	–		4649	145	32.06
Webster, R.V.	1961–67/68	70		82	19	867	47	13.76	–		5290	272	19.45
Webster, W.H.	1930–47	65		103	9	1870	111	19.89	1		478	21	22.76
Weedon, M.J.H.	1961–62	17		24	11	164	35	12.62	–		1604	45	35.64
Weekes, D.J.	1952	1		1	0	0	0	–	–		34	0	–

	Career span	M	I	NO	Runs	HS	Avge	100	Runs	Wkts	Avge
					BATTING				BOWLING		
Weekes, E.De C.	1944/45–63/64	152	241	24	12010	304*	55.35	36	731	17	43.00
	T	48	81	5	4455	207	58.62	15	77	1	–
Weeks, R.T.	1950–57	107	141	36	1051	51	10.01	–	6198	236	26.26
Weightman, N.I.	1981–82	4	6	0	175	105	29.17	–	4	0	–
Weir, R.S.	1975–82	4	8	2	187	65	31.17	–	–	–	–
Wellard, A.W.	1927–50	417	679	45	12515	112	19.74	2	39302	1614	24.35
	T	2	4	0	47	38	11.75	–	237	7	33.86
Wellham, DMcD	1980/81–	46	73	13	2773	136*	46.22	7	11	1	–
	T	4	7	0	221	103	31.57	1	–	–	–
Wellings, E.M.	1928–46	36	47	6	836	125	20.39	1	3256	108	30.15
Wellington, L.	1969/70–70/71	11	14	6	208	49	26.00	–	483	12	40.25
Wells, A.L.	1954–55	5	6	1	28	18	5.60	–	333	8	41.63
Wells, A.P.	1981–	48	79	14	2021	127	31.09	2	42	0	–
Wells, B.D.	1951–65	301	423	100	2413	55	7.47	–	24219	998	24.26
Wells, C.M.	1979–	114	180	26	5115	203	33.21	10	3980	126	31.59
Wells, R.R.C.	1977–78	11	17	1	212	85	13.25	–	–	–	–
Wells, T.U.	1950–51	21	28	1	446	77*	16.52	–	119	5	23.80
Wenlock, D.A.	1980–82	10	13	4	148	62	16.44	–	268	7	38.29
Wesley, C.	1956/57–65/66	51	79	9	1892	131	27.02	3	354	15	23.60
	T	3	5	0	49	35	9.80	–	–	–	–
Wessels, K.C.	1973/74–	139	244	22	11208	254	50.49	29	137	4	34.25
	T	12	20	1	815	179	42.90	3	2	0	–
West, G.H.S.	1949–53	2	4	0	79	55	19.75	–	–	–	–
Westerman, P.	1949–51	9	12	5	25	10*	3.57	–	596	21	28.38
Westley, R.B.	1969	5	7	0	32	14	4.57	–	270	4	67.50
Westley, S.A.	1968–76	34	55	18	577	93*	15.59	–	–	–	–
Weston, M.J.	1979–	70	120	6	2764	145*	24.25	2	760	22	34.55
Wettimuny, S.	1975/76–	38	63	4	1933	190	32.76	4	46	2	23.00
	T	11	22	1	819	190	39.00	2	21	0	–
Wettimuny, S.R.de S.	1969/70–81/82	39	70	1	1693	121	24.54	2	49	1	–
Wharton, A.	1946–63	482	745	69	21796	199	32.24	31	7488	237	31.59
	T	1	2	0	20	13	10.00	–	–	–	–
Wheatley, G.A.	1946–50	18	30	2	478	66	17.07	–	–	–	–
Wheatley, K.J.	1965–70	79	110	14	1781	79*	18.55	–	1954	69	28.31
Wheatley, O.S.	1956–69/70	316	362	145	1251	34*	5.77	–	22910	1099	20.85
Wheeler, J.A.	1949	1	2	0	75	54	37.50	–	–	–	–
Wheelhouse, A.	1958–61	17	26	7	133	17	7.00	–	1705	48	35.52
Whiley, R.K.	1954–58	2	4	2	17	7*	8.50	–	–	–	–
Whitaker, J.J.	1983–	29	48	6	1402	160	33.38	2	–	–	–
Whitaker, M.R.	1965–67	12	20	7	16	4*	1.23	–	700	20	35.00
Whitby, R.L.	1950–57	2	2	0	23	12	11.50	–	140	0	–
Whitcombe, P.A.	1947–60	38	56	5	956	68	18.75	–	2489	112	22.22
Whitcombe, P.J.	1949–52	34	53	6	1156	104	24.60	1	10	1	–
White, A.F.T.	1936–49	142	247	17	5035	95	21.89	–	26	0	–
White, C.D.	1958–61	23	41	2	606	64	15.54	–	24	0	–
White, D.W.	1957–72	337	395	104	3080	58*	10.58	–	26913	1143	23.54
	T	2	2	0	0	0	0.00	–	119	4	29.75
White, E.	1946–48	3	4	0	44	16	11.00	–	–	–	–
White, L.R.	1945–50	6	10	1	134	46	14.89	–	–	–	–
White, M.F.	1946	1	2	0	0	0	0.00	–	–	–	–
White, R.A.	1958–80	413	642	105	12452	116*	23.19	5	21138	693	30.50
White, R.C.	1960/61–72/73	141	248	4	6824	205	27.97	10	589	17	34.65
White, R.F.	1964–66	13	11	6	18	7*	3.60	–	518	17	30.47
White, W.A.W.	1958/59–65/66	31	46	7	996	75	25.54	–	2665	95	28.05
	T	2	4	1	71	57*	23.67	–	152	3	50.67

	Career span	M	I	NO	Runs	HS	Avge	100	Runs	Wkts	Avge
					BATTING				BOWLING		
White, W.M.E.	1937–49	21	35	6	398	48	13.73	–	1524	42	36.28
White, W.N.	1948	2	3	0	19	19	6.33	–	106	4	26.50
Whitehead, A.G.T.	1957–61	38	49	25	137	15	5.71	–	2306	67	34.42
Whitehead, J.P.	1946–55	73	91	26	1246	71	19.17	–	4297	147	29.23
Whitehill, W.	1960	7	11	3	60	16	7.50	–	–	–	–
Whitehouse, J.	1971–80	180	309	38	8693	197	32.08	15	471	6	78.50
Whiteley, J.P.	1978–82	45	38	17	231	20	11.00	–	2410	70	34.43
Whiteley, P.	1957–58	5	8	2	86	32	14.33	–	266	9	29.56
Whiteside, P.G.	1955	2	2	0	1	1	0.50	–	–	–	–
Whitfield, E.W.	1930–46	125	189	21	3995	198	23.78	6	1562	35	44.63
Whiting, N.H.	1947–52	59	96	11	1583	118	18.62	2	657	13	50.54
Whitington, R.S.	1932/33–45/46	54	90	4	2782	155	32.35	4	91	1	–
Whitney, M.R.	1980/81–	34	32	8	90	28*	3.75	–	3354	108	31.06
	T	2	4	0	4	4	1.00	–	246	5	49.20
Whittaker, G.J.	1937–53	129	191	20	4988	185*	29.17	8	47	1	–
Whitticase, P.	1984–	8	9	2	35	14	5.00	–	–	–	–
Whittingham, N.B.	1962–66	77	141	7	2964	133	22.12	2	122	1	–
Whittle, C.J.R.	1947	2	4	0	23	10	5.75	–	–	–	–
Whyatt, C.	1976	1	1	0	6	6	–	–	–	–	–
Wiggs, R.J.	1970	1	2	1	6	6	–	–	44	1	–
Wight, P.B.	1950/51–65	333	590	53	17773	222*	33.10	28	2262	68	33.26
Wignall, E.W.E.	1952–53	3	4	1	24	14	8.00	–	63	2	31.50
Wijesuriya, R.G.C.E.	1978/79–	14	12	4	69	25	8.63	–	1157	31	37.32
	T	1	2	0	3	3	1.50	–	105	0	–
Wilcock, H.G.	1971–78	99	137	31	1697	74	16.01	–	3	0	–
Wilcox, A.G.S.	1939–49	39	58	5	835	73	15.75	–	–	–	–
Wilcox, D.R.	1928–51	178	297	11	8354	157	29.21	15	154	3	51.33
Wilcox, J.W.T.	1961–67	31	54	7	903	87	19.21	–	–	–	–
Wild, D.J.	1980–	34	55	7	1258	144	26.21	1	945	19	49.74
Wild, J.	1953–61	41	51	4	664	95	14.13	–	2588	57	45.40
Wilde, D.	1971–72	13	15	5	31	12	3.10	–	860	23	36.09
Wilenken, B.C.G.	1955–59	16	28	1	661	103	24.48	1	4	0	–
Wiley, J.W.E.	1947/48–51	12	23	1	410	70	18.64	–	–	–	–
Wiley, W.G.A.	1952–53/54	16	29	0	666	100	22.97	1	5	0	–
Wilkin, C.L.A.	1969–76/77	19	30	10	302	26	15.10	–	1440	30	48.00
Wilkins, A.H.	1976–83	107	124	29	902	70	9.50	–	7511	243	30.91
Wilkins, C.P.	1962/63–82/83	198	357	21	10966	156	32.64	18	5013	142	35.30
Wilkinson, D.J.	1975–76	4	8	2	11	5	1.83	–	350	7	50.00
Wilkinson, K.W.	1969–75	49	77	11	1657	141	25.10	2	1651	48	39.40
Wilkinson, L.L.	1937–47	77	69	27	321	48	7.64	–	7121	282	25.25
	T	3	2	1	3	2	–	–	271	7	38.71
Wilkinson, P.A.	1971–77	92	117	38	949	77	12.01	–	6335	175	36.20
Wilkinson, R.W.	1959–63	23	39	7	635	63	19.84	–	626	10	62.60
Wilkinson, S.G.	1972–74	18	27	5	452	69	20.55	–	9	0	–
Willard, M.J.L.	1959–61	41	75	1	1866	101*	25.22	1	2326	72	32.31
Willatt, G.L.	1938–61	185	303	17	8325	146	29.11	13	135	3	45.00
Willett, E.T.	1970/71–83/84	84	112	37	933	56	12.44	–	7147	252	28.36
	T	5	8	3	74	26	14.80	–	482	11	43.82
Willett, M.D.	1955–67	172	273	45	6535	126	28.66	8	1105	23	48.04
Willetts, F.T.	1964–67	16	30	0	333	38	11.10	–	–	–	–
Willey, P.	1966–	397	656	95	16960	227	30.23	31	17506	593	29.52
	T	20	38	5	923	102*	27.97	2	441	6	73.50
Williams, C.B.	1947/48–56/57	37	39	5	987	133	29.03	2	2182	75	29.09
Williams, C.C.P.	1952–59	87	153	8	4090	139*	28.21	6	61	1	–
Williams, C.D.	1946	1	2	0	3	3	1.50	–	9	0	–
Williams, C.M.B.	1976	1	2	0	31	29	15.50	–	–	–	–

	Career span	M	I	NO	Runs	HS	Avge	100	Runs	Wkts	Avge
Williams, D.	1968–73	29	50	10	497	52	12.43	–	847	24	35.29
Williams, D.L.	1969–76	151	146	73	403	37*	5.52	–	9883	364	27.15
Williams, D.S.	1959–64	8	15	1	225	82	16.07	–	–	–	–
Williams, E.L.	1949	1	2	0	17	14	8.50	–	33	2	16.50
Williams, T.G.O.	1955	3	6	0	30	24	5.00	–	–	–	–
Williams, N.F.	1982–	67	75	17	1069	63	18.43	–	5339	174	30.68
Williams, O.L.	1967	1	2	1	6	6*	–	–	60	1	–
Williams, N.R.	1961	1	1	0	5	5	–	–	101	5	20.20
Williams, Rich. G.	1974–	182	296	36	7990	175*	30.73	13	8225	246	33.44
Williams, Robt. G.	1932/33–45/46	26	41	8	531	75*	16.09	–	1957	67	29.21
Williams, S.	1978	1	1	0	0	0	–	–	–	–	–
Williamson, J.G.	1958–62	56	67	19	820	106*	17.08	1	3921	120	32.68
Willis, R.G.D.	1969–84	308	333	145	2690	72	14.31	–	22468	899	24.99
	T	90	128	55	840	28*	11.51	–	8190	325	25.20
Willows, A.	1980–83	5	3	1	5	4	2.50	–	253	8	31.63
Wills, R.	1963–69	33	54	6	824	151*	17.17	1	–	–	–
Wills, R.T.	1981–	4	6	0	112	48	18.67	–	–	–	–
Willson, B.J.	1964	2	4	0	87	53	21.75	–	197	7	28.14
Willson, R.H.	1955–61/62	22	34	5	411	113*	14.17	1	390	4	97.50
Wilson, A.	1948–62	171	186	59	760	37*	5.98	–	–	–	–
Wilson, A.E.	1932–55	328	502	77	10744	188	25.28	7	1	0	–
Wilson, B.A.	1951	1	1	0	0	0	–	–	75	1	–
Wilson, D.	1957–74	422	533	91	6230	112	14.10	1	24977	1189	21.01
	T	6	7	1	75	42	12.50	–	466	11	42.36
Wilson, G.	1948–51	3	6	0	116	39	19.33	–	12	2	6.00
Wilson, G.C.	1957	2	2	2	10	7*	–	–	211	3	70.33
Wilson, I.B.J.	1956–61	3	5	0	49	18	9.80	–	120	7	17.14
Wilson, J.D.K.	1977	1	2	0	19	18	9.50	–	6	0	–
Wilson, J.S.	1957–64	16	19	6	66	22	5.08	–	1109	44	25.20
Wilson, J.V.	1946–63	503	770	79	21650	230	31.33	30	435	9	48.33
Wilson, J.W.	1949/50–57/58	78	97	47	287	19*	5.74	–	7019	230	30.52
	T	1	–	–	–	–	–	–	64	1	–
Wilson, P.H.L.	1978–84	61	50	25	261	29	10.44	–	3394	110	30.85
Wilson, P.J.	1964	2	3	0	56	30	18.67	–	–	–	–
Wilson, P.R.B.	1968–70	23	39	1	664	94	17.47	–	233	7	33.29
Wilson, R.	1952	3	3	2	5	4	–	–	167	8	20.88
Wilson, R.	1955–56	3	5	0	64	29	12.80	–	–	–	–
Wilson, R.C.	1952–67	367	647	39	19515	159*	32.10	30	90	4	22.50
Wilson, Robt. G.	1948–52	14	25	2	662	100	28.78	1	655	24	27.29
Wilson, Roger G.	1964	1	1	1	3	3*	–	–	65	2	32.50
Wilson, R.W.	1956–57	13	24	6	169	36*	9.39	–	1265	34	37.21
Wilson, T.C.	1960	1	1	1	0	0*	–	–	42	1	–
Wilson, T.G.O.	1951–53	13	16	7	10	4*	1.11	–	1000	18	55.56
Wiltshire, G.G.M.	1953–60	19	30	4	218	39	8.38	–	835	25	33.40
Wincer, R.C.	1978–80	23	21	8	131	26	10.08	–	1653	46	35.93
Windaybank, S.J.	1979–82	15	19	4	385	53	25.67	–	–	–	–
Windows, A.R.	1960–68	149	241	34	3537	82	17.09	–	8308	286	29.05
Windsor, R.T.A.	1969	1	1	0	0	0	–	–	–	–	–
Winfield, H.M.	1954–66	172	311	16	6799	134	23.04	7	5	0	–
Wing, D.C.	1967–76	5	5	1	59	42	14.75	–	375	7	53.57
Wingfield-Digby, A.R.	1971–77	39	62	4	720	69	12.41	–	3152	96	33.88
Winn, C.E.	1948–61	59	100	2	2449	146*	24.99	2	34	1	–
Winrow, F.H.	1938–51	113	180	20	4769	204*	29.81	6	4009	95	42.20
Winrow, R.	1932–49	7	10	1	237	137	26.33	1	76	1	–
Winslow, P.L.	1949–61/62	75	124	6	2755	139	23.35	2	61	1	–
	T	5	9	0	186	108	20.67	1	–	–	–
Wisdom, N.	1974	2	2	1	35	31*	–	–	33	2	16.50

	Career span	M		I	NO	Runs	HS	Avge	100		Runs	Wkts	Avge
						BATTING						BOWLING	
Wisson, P.W.	1958	2		4	0	24	14	6.00	–		–	–	–
Witherden, E.G.	1951–55	40		71	9	1380	125*	22.26	2		371	9	41.22
Wolfe-Murray, J.A.	1957	3		5	2	43	25	14.33	–		155	3	51.67
Wollocombe, R.H.	1951–52	9		16	2	314	119	22.43	1		623	10	62.30
Wolton, A.V.G.	1947–60	297		478	61	12930	165	31.01	12		1226	37	33.14
Wood, A.	1927–48	419		500	83	8842	123*	21.20	–		33	1	–
	T	4		5	1	80	53	20.00	–		–	–	–
Wood, B.	1964–83	357		591	75	17453	198	33.82	30		9160	298	30.74
	T	12		21	0	454	90	21.62	–		50	0	–
Wood, C.H.	1959	4		4	1	22	10	7.33	–		319	11	29.00
Wood, David J.	1984	3		3	0	32	15	10.67	–		–	–	–
Wood, D.J.	1936–55	213		251	72	1305	42	7.29	–		18140	589	30.80
Wood, G.M.	1976/77–	126		218	15	7431	151	36.61	17		132	5	26.40
	T	48		83	5	2642	126	33.87	7		–	–	–
Wood, J.	1956	1		–	–	–	–	–	–		103	4	25.75
Wood, L.J.	1981–82	2		2	0	5	5	2.50	–		182	4	45.50
Wood, M.	1955	4		5	2	5	4	1.67	–		231	4	57.75
Wood, R.	1952–56	22		18	4	60	17	4.29	–		1346	51	26.39
Wood, R.B.	1950–51	8		12	3	110	48	12.22	–		–	–	–
Woodcock, R.G.	1956–58	29		52	9	779	57	18.11	–		1793	53	33.83
Woodford, J.D.	1968–72	38		61	2	1204	101	20.41	1		185	4	46.25
Woodhead, D.L.	1968	8		15	1	190	68	13.57	–		190	0	–
Woodhead, F.G.	1934–50	141		174	44	1100	52*	8.46	–		10550	320	32.97
Woodhouse, A.J.P.	1957	1		2	0	29	17	14.50	–		20	1	–
Woodhouse, G.E.S.	1946–53	65		118	14	2048	109	19.69	1		8	1	–
Woodroffe, A.	1947–48	4		7	0	77	41	11.00	–		–	–	–
Woods, B.J.P.	1951	2		2	0	1	1	0.50	–		108	3	36.00
Wookey, S.M.	1975–80	19		27	6	260	48	12.38	–		1158	28	41.36
Wooler, C.R.D.	1949–56/57	60		93	16	835	49*	10.84	–		4030	130	31.00
Woolfries, S.A.	1972	1		1	0	3	3	3.00	–		–	–	–
Wooller, W.	1935–62	430		679	77	13593	128	22.55	5		25830	958	26.96
Woollett, A.F.	1950–54	44		81	4	1445	96	18.77	–		–	–	–
Woolley, K.McD,	1947	1		2	0	4	4	2.00	–		56	0	–
Woolmer, R.A.	1968–84	350		545	75	15771	203	33.56	34		10868	420	25.88
	T	19		34	2	1059	149	33.09	3		299	4	74.75
Wootton, S.H.	1981–	15		24	3	558	104	26.57	1		7	0	–
Workman, J.A.	1945–45/46	17		31	2	588	76	20.28	–		6	1	–
Worrell, F.M.M.	1941/42–64	208		326	49	15025	308*	54.24	39		10114	349	28.98
	T	51		87	9	3860	261	49.49	9		2672	69	38.73
Worrell, L.R.	1969–72	32		42	17	289	50	11.56	–		2116	65	32.55
Worsley, D.R.	1960–67	113		205	11	5062	139	26.09	4		1520	37	41.08
Worthington, T.S.	1924–47	453		720	59	19221	238*	29.08	31		19939	682	29.84
	T	9		11	0	321	128	29.18	1		316	8	39.50
Wreghitt, P.H.	1951	1		1	0	1	1	–	–		105	3	35.00
Wright, A.	1960–64	76		76	27	315	27	6.43	–		5953	236	25.23
Wright, A.J.	1982–	42		75	7	1750	139	25.74	1		3	0	–
Wright, D.V.P.	1932–57	497		703	225	5903	84*	12.35	–		49307	2056	23.98
	T	34		39	13	289	45	11.12	–		4224	108	39.11
Wright, J.G.	1975/76–	222		386	27	14582	190	40.62	34		181	1	90.50
	T	31		54	2	1586	141	30.50	3		2	0	–
Wright, J.V.	1962–67	4		6	0	60	40	10.00	–		–	–	–
Wright, L.N.G.	1968/69–78/79	24		30	11	316	33	16.63	–		1073	40	26.83
Wright, M.G.	1950	2		4	0	35	17	8.75	–		–	–	–
Wright, S.	1973	10		19	0	277	41	14.57	–		–	–	–
Wrightson, R.W.	1965–67	12		20	4	332	84	20.75	–		–	–	–
Wrigley, M.H.	1946–50	16		17	5	71	17	5.92	–		1076	48	22.42

	Career span	M		BATTING							BOWLING		
			I	NO	Runs	HS	Avge	100		Runs	Wkts	Avge
Wyatt, G.	1954–60	11	20	4	184	59	11.50	–		2	0	–
Wyatt, J.G.	1983–	22	40	2	1018	103	26.79	1		4	1	–
Wyatt, R.E.S.	1923–57	739	1141	157	39405	232	40.05	85		29597	901	32.85
T		40	64	6	1839	149	31.71	2		642	18	35.67
Wykes, J.C.	1946	1	2	0	38	23	19.00	–		–	–	–
Yajurvindrasinh, J.	1971/72–81/82	78	115	26	3785	214	42.30	9		1552	50	31.04
T		4	7	1	109	43*	18.17	–		50	0	–
Yallop, G.N.	1972/73–	142	247	26	10319	268	46.69	27		747	11	67.91
T		38	68	3	2753	268	42.35	8		116	1	–
Yardley, N.W.D.	1935–55	445	658	75	18173	183*	31.17	27		8506	279	30.49
T		20	34	2	812	99	25.38	–		707	21	33.67
Yardley, T.J.	1967–82	260	390	69	8287	135	25.82	5		38	0	–
Yarnold, H.	1938–55	286	417	69	3741	68	10.75	–		–	–	–
Yashpal Sharma	1973/74–	122	193	40	6909	201*	45.16	14		923	27	34.19
T		37	59	11	1606	140	33.46	2		17	1	–
Yates, K.C.	1961	1	1	1	0	0*	–	–		–	–	–
Yawar Saeed	1953–58/59	59	106	6	1545	64	15.45	–		2610	107	24.39
Yeabsley, D.I.	1974–79	4	6	3	27	14*	9.00	–		389	13	29.92
Yeatman, R.H.	1946–47	6	9	1	53	21	6.63	–		18	0	–
Youll, M.	1956–57	4	2	0	15	9	7.50	–		303	14	21.64
Young, D.M.	1946–64	474	842	42	24555	198	30.69	40		172	4	43.00
Young, J.A.	1933–56	341	392	114	2485	62	8.94	–		26795	1361	19.69
T		8	10	5	28	10*	5.60	–		757	17	44.53
Young, R.W.	1962–64	6	9	0	358	96	39.78	–		–	–	–
Young, S.H.	1959–69	3	4	2	16	14	8.00	–		289	12	24.08
Youngson, G.W.	1947–55	19	31	14	64	18	3.76	–		1861	75	24.81
Younis Ahmed	1961/62–	413	693	104	23122	221*	39.26	38		1639	39	42.03
T		2	4	0	89	62	22.25	–		–	–	–
Younus Badat	1975	1	2	0	3	3	1.50	–		–	–	–
Yuile, B.W.	1959/60–71/72	123	187	31	3850	146	24.68	1		8209	375	21.89
T		17	33	6	481	64	17.82	–		1213	34	35.68
Yusuf, M.M.	1983/84–	5	1	1	2	2*	–	–		282	1	–
Zaheer Abbas	1965/66–	436	733	88	33844	274	52.47	106		1020	26	39.23
T		69	112	10	4747	274	46.54	11		93	1	–
Zuill, A.M.	1962–79	9	17	2	231	62	15.40	–		–	–	–
Zulfiqar Ahmed	1946/47–65/66	60	70	19	971	73	19.04	–		3529	163	21.65
T		9	10	4	200	63*	33.33	–		366	20	18.30
Zulfiqar Ali	1973/74–75	2	4	0	30	20	7.50	–		290	8	36.25

Addendum

DE ALWIS, Ronal *Guy*
————RHB, WK————

Born Colombo, Ceylon, 15 Feb 1960.
Debut 1981/82 (Sri Lanka, in Zimbabwe).
SRI LANKA (5) 1982/83–83/84. A 1982/83 (1); NZ 1983/84 (3). *NZ 1982/83 (1)*.
OTHER TOURS Sri Lankans to Zimbabwe 1981/82. Sri Lankans to England 1984.
HST 28 SL v NZ, Colombo, 1983/84. HS 74 Sri Lankans v Notts, Cleethorpes, 1984.
Club: Sinhalese Sporting.

DUJON, Peter *Jeffrey*
————RHB, WK————

Born Kingston, Jamaica, 28 May 1956.
Debut 1974/75.
WEST INDIES DOMESTIC Jamaica 1974/75–. Capt 1982/83.
WEST INDIES (24) 1981/82–84. A 1983/84 (5); I 1982/83 (5). *E 1984 (5); A 1981/82 (3); I 1983/84 (6)*.
HST 130 WI v A, Port of Spain, 1983/84.
HS 135* Jamaica v Barbados, Chedwin Park, 1980/81.

JEYARAJASINGHAM,
Vinodhan John Bede
(known as V. B. John)
————RHB, RMF————

Born Colombo, Ceylon, 27 June 1960.
Debut 1981/82.
SRI LANKA DOMESTIC Sri Lanka 1981/82–.
SRI LANKA (6) 1982/83–84. NZ 1983/84 (3). *E 1984 (1); NZ 1982/83 (2)*.
HST 27* SL v NZ, Kandy, 1983/84. HS as above.
BBT 5–60 SL v NZ, Wellington, 1982/83. BB 6–58 Sri Lankans v Glos, Cheltenham, 1984.
Club: Bloomfield CC.

KURUPPU, Don Sardha *Brendon*
Priyantha
————RHB, WK————

Born Colombo, Ceylon, 5 Jan 1962.
Debut 1982/83.

SRI LANKA DOMESTIC Sri Lanka 1982/83–.
TOURS Sri Lanka Under-23 to Pakistan 1983/84. Sri Lanka to England 1984.
HS 55 Sri Lanka Under-23 v Pakistan Under-23, Lahore, 1983/84.
Club: Leyland (England).

LOGIE, Augustine Lawrence
————RHB, OB————

Born Sobo, Trinidad, 28 Sept 1960.
Educ La Brea School, Trinidad. Debut 1978/79.
WEST INDIES DOMESTIC South Trinidad 1978/79–, Trinidad 1978/79–.
WEST INDIES (9) 1982/83–83/84. A 1983/84 (1); I 1982/83 (5). *I 1983/84 (3)*.
OTHER TOURS West Indies to Australia 1981/82. West Indies to England 1984. West Indies Under-26 to Zimbabwe 1981/82.
HST 130 WI v I, Bridgetown, 1982/83.
HS 171 Trinidad v Jamaica, Port of Spain, 1981/82.
Club: Texaco-Brighton.

PAYNE,
Thelston Rodeny O'Neale
————LHB, WK, occ OB————

Born Foul Bay, St Philip, Barbados, 13 Feb 1957. Educ Princess Margaret S, St Philip. Debut 1977/78.
WEST INDIES DOMESTIC Barbados 1977/78–.
TOURS Young West Indies to Zimbabwe 1983/84. West Indies to England 1984.
HS 140 Barbados v Combined Islands, Bridgetown, 1979/80.
Club: Victoria (Barbados).

RANATUNGE, Arjuna
————LHB————

Born Colombo, Ceylon, 1 Jan 1963.
Educ Ananda C, Colombo. Debut 1981/82.
SRI LANKA DOMESTIC Sri Lanka 1981/82–.

SRI LANKA (9) 1981/82–84. E 1981/82 (1); A 1982/83 (1); NZ 1983/84 (1). *E 1984 (1); I 1982/83 (1); P 1981/82 (2)*.
HST 90 SL v A, Kandy, 1982/83. HS 118 Sri Lankans v Kent, Canterbury, 1984.
BBT 2–17 SL v NZ, Kandy, 1983/84. BB as above.
Club: Sinhalese Sporting.

SILVA, Sampathage *Amal* Rohita
————RHB, WK————

Born Moratuwa, Ceylon, 12 Dec 1960.
Debut 1982/83 (Sri Lanka XI v New Zealand).
SRI LANKA (2) 1982/83–84. *E 1984 (1); NZ 1982/83 (1)*.
OTHER TOURS Sri Lanka to Zimbabwe 1982/83 (no fc matches).
HST 102* SL v E, Lord's, 1984. HS 161* Sri Lankans v Warwicks, Edgbaston, 1984.
Club: Nondescripts CC.

SMALL, Milton Aster
————RHB, RFM————

Born Bridgetown, Barbados, 12 Feb 1964. Debut 1983/84.
WEST INDIES DOMESTIC Barbados 1983/84–.
WEST INDIES (2) 1983/84–84. A 1983/84 (1). *E 1984 (1)*.
HST 3* WI v E, Lord's, 1984. HS 6 Barbados v Australians, Bridgetown, 1983/84.
BBT 3–40 WI v E, Lord's, 1984. BB 5–57 Barbados v Trinidad, Bridgetown, 1983/84.
Club: Wanderers (Barbados).

WRIGHT, Anthony John
————RHB, RM————

Born Stevenage, Herts, 27 July 1962.
Educ Alleyn's School, Stevenage.
Debut 1982.
GLOUCESTERSHIRE (42) 1982–.
HS 139 Glos v Surrey, Cheltenham, 1984.

Bibliography

WISDEN CRICKETERS' ALMANACK, 1919–84
PLAYFAIR CRICKET ANNUAL, 1948–85
THE CRICKETERS' WHO'S WHO, 1980–84
THE CRICKETER, 1921–85
PLAYFAIR CRICKET MONTHLY, 1960–73
DAILY WORKER CRICKET HANDBOOK, 1948–50
SPORTS ARGUS CRICKET ANNUAL, 1949–68
AUSTRALIAN CRICKET YEARBOOK/ANNUAL, 1970–83
SOUTH AFRICAN CRICKET ALMANACK, 1949/50
SOUTH AFRICAN CRICKET ANNUAL, 1951–84
WEST INDIES CRICKET ANNUAL, 1970–84
CRICKET ALMANACK OF NEW ZEALAND, 1948–84

INDIAN CRICKET, 1946/47–84
INDIAN CRICKET FIELD ANNUAL, 1957/58–64/65
BCCP ANNUAL, 1964/65–74
THE CRICKETER (PAKISTAN)
THE CRICKET STATISTICIAN, 1973–85
MINOR COUNTIES CRICKET ANNUAL, 1976–85
CRICKET NEWS, 1977–79
THE CRICKET QUARTERLY, 1963–70
THE CRICKETER QUARTERLY, 1973–85
WISDEN CRICKET MONTHLY, 1979–85

The above items were the ones most regularly consulted. A list of *all* books looked at would comprise a large part of cricket literature for the past fifty years.